Advising the Family Owned Business

Advising the Family Owned Business

Nicholas Smith
Consultant, The Family Business Consultancy

LexisNexis®

Published by LexisNexis

LexisNexis
Regus
Terrace Floor
Castlemead
Lower Castle Street
Bristol BS1 3AG

Whilst the publishers and the author have taken every care in preparing the material included in this work, any statements made as to the legal, tax, commercial or other implications of any particular course of action or transaction are made in good faith purely for general guidance and cannot be regarded as a substitute for professional advice in the circumstances concerned. Consequently, no liability can be accepted for loss or expense incurred as a result of relying in particular circumstances on statements made in this work.

© RELX (UK) Limited, trading as LexisNexis 2017

All rights reserved. No part of this publication may be reproduced, stored in a retrieval system, or transmitted in any way or by any means, including photocopying or recording, without the written permission of the copyright holder, application for which should be addressed to the publisher.

Crown Copyright material is reproduced with kind permission of the Controller of Her Majesty's Stationery Office.

British Library Cataloguing-in-Publication Data

A catalogue record for this book is available from the British Library.

ISBN 978 1 84661 557 3

Typeset by Letterpart Limited, Caterham on the Hill, Surrey CR3 5XL

Printed in Great Britain by Hobbs the Printers Limited, Totton, Hampshire SO40 3WX

FOREWORD

There is something unique about family businesses – from the local shopkeeper to the international corporation. The ethos of a family business is special. Because the business and the product it sells is attached so intimately to a person and their relations, I believe that family businesses look at the world differently than other businesses.

Family businesses see themselves in terms of their legacy. They take a much longer-term approach to investment often making sustainable investment that leaves them better able to weather inevitable storms.

And this ethos and good practice is passed down from family member to family member, but also to the staff who are employed in the business. Working for a family business means working for a family, and staff turnover is often much lower than in other businesses.

But these strengths can also be weaknesses. A refusal to change or a lack of outside objectivity can stop a family business from achieving its true potential. A good family businesses knows that there are times to look for outside help.

That is why I am very pleased this book is available to help family business and their advisors deal with the particular issues they face. Succession, ownership, and disputes are taken to a whole new level when family is involved!

I am an enthusiastic supporter of the family business model. It is a business model as old as business itself. It is strong today, and I have no doubt that it will continue to thrive in the future as long as family businesses continue to evolve and adapt to the changing world. This book will help them do just that.

John Stevenson
November 2016

John Stevenson is MP for Carlisle, Chair of The All-Party Parliamentary Group for Family Business, and is a practicing solicitor and partner at Bendles LLP solicitors

PREFACE

This book would not have come into being without the help of a great number of people.

The support and encouragement of friends and family has been invaluable, especially my wife Susan, without whose long term amnesty on decorating projects the book may never have been written.

Most of the thinking included in the book is the result of countless hours of discussions with family business clients and colleagues from across the family business movement. In terms of both the frequency and depth of discussion, the time spent with my former colleague Emma Rudge stands out, closely followed by other members of the Veale Wasbrough Vizards family business team and colleagues from the International Centre for Families in Business (ICFIB) network. To the greatest extent possible sources have been acknowledged in the body of the book. However it would not be possible to identify, much less list, all of the source and influences that have helped me to arrive at the current stage of my family business journey.

More precisely a considerable number of colleagues have made direct and extremely valuable contributions to the book itself, for example by producing first drafts the legal or technical content forming part of the chapters, reviewing drafts of other chapters or in some cases both. Unless otherwise stated these are past or present colleagues from Veale Wasbrough Vizards. In detail these are:

Part A – The Family Owned Business and its Dynamics

David Pierce of D R Pierce Consultancy Limited and John Tucker of the Family Business Consultancy for the contributions they have each made to these chapters including reviewing and commentating on various drafts.

Part B – Business Matters

David Pierce who wrote chapter 4 on Tax Basics and the Family Business Structure and did so whilst struggling with serious health issues, together with his former partner Ruth Dooley of Hazlewoods accountants and Emma Bradley tax partner of Veale Wasbrough Vizards, who reviewed this chapter.

Various members of the employment team at Veale Wasbrough Vizards contributed text for chapters 5 and 6 (Employing Family Members and Non-family Employees, respectively) and/or reviewed later drafts of these chapters, including, Victoria McMeel, Paul Esmiley, Matthew Welch, Michael Halsey, Sarah Want and Jessica Ryan.

Thanks are due to Professor Andrew Keay of Leeds University for his review of and helpful comments in relation to chapter 8 (Director's Duties) also to Emma Rudge and Richard Hiscoke for their work on this.

Paula Williams and Steve McGuigan wrote the legal content for chapters 9 and 10 (The Name above the Door and Property and the Family Firm Respectively). David Pierce also provided tax and commercial comments on aspects of the latter chapter.

Part C – Ownership

So far as the section on ownership is concerned, once again David Pierce contributed comments on commercial and valuation points for chapter 12 (Selling the Family Business) which David Emanuel kindly reviewed. Jos Moule provided comments on chapter 13 (Family Partnerships).

Natalie Payne produced an early draft of chapter 14 (Family Business Trusts) and Edward Cumming of XXIV, Old Buildings Lincoln's Inn provided many detailed comments and insights, which have been incorporated into the final draft.

So far as chapter 16 (Tax and Family Ownership) is concerned, once again thanks are due to David Pierce, who wrote this chapter and to his former partners Ruth Dooley and Peter Griffiths of Hazlewoods, together with Emma Bradley tax partner of Veale Wasbrough Vizards, who each reviewed parts of this chapter.

Part D – Family Matters

I am grateful to Irene Pedder, Chair of the Clark's Shareholder Council for reviewing and commenting on the case study on the Clark's governance system contained in chapter 17.

The chapter on the family business and marriage (chapter 18) was a truly collaborative effort with original content provided by Oliver Early, with Samantha Hickman of Veale Wasbrough Vizards and Andrew Commins of St John's Chambers in Bristol both contributing many helpful thoughts and suggestions which have been included in the final draft.

Julia Hardy can be thanked for her contribution in preparing the first draft and reviewing final drafts of chapter 19 (Inheritance Disputes) and for her enthusiasm and commitment to this project generally.

Part E – Family Business Disputes

Huge thanks are due to Andrew Marsden of Commercial Chambers Bristol for his sterling contribution in reviewing all five chapters dealing with the legal aspects of disputes in family companies contained in this part.

Part F – The Family Business Advisor

John Tucker of the Family Business Consultancy shared his wisdom and experience, which added significantly to the chapter on process consulting and the role of the family business consultant (chapter 25). Similarly chapter 26 (Advising the Family Business Client) was tempered and hardened by robust discussions with Claire Ainley the Veale Wasbrough Vizards compliance partner.

Kate Hather, Mary Kenny and their colleagues at Jordan Publishing, now part of LexisNexis, together with my editor Tracy Robinson provided huge support and valuable guidance, without which as a first time author, I would have struggled to take the concept of this book through to the finished article. The practical assistance of Katie Hanson in keeping track of innumerable drafts of the various chapters has been invaluable.

But the final vote of thanks must go to my friend and colleague John Tucker, who not only introduced me to the particular challenges of advising family owned businesses over 15 years ago, but who has been a constant guide and companion on that fascinating and rewarding journey ever since.

Nicholas Smith
Bath
November 2016

BIOGRAPHICAL NOTES

Nicholas Smith

Family Business Consultant – The Family Business Consultancy

www.thefbc.co.uk

Nick has over 30 years experience as a corporate lawyer, specialising in advising family owned businesses for the second half of this period on matters such as family business re-organisations, governance projects, dispute resolution and sales. He set up and led one of the first dedicated family business teams in the UK at Veale Wasbrough Vizards. He no longer practices as a lawyer and now concentrates on consultancy work for family businesses together with writing, teaching and speaking about family business issues.

Nick is a fellow of and chairman of the International Centre for Families in Business, a member of the editorial board of an academic family business journal and has worked extensively on training and education programmes for family businesses and their advisors.

CONTENTS

Foreword	v
Preface	vii
Biographical Notes	xi
Table of Cases	xxv
Table of Statutes	xxxiii
Table of Statutory Instruments	xxxvii
Table of Abbreviations	xxxix
Introduction	xli

Part A
The Family Owned Business and its Dynamics

Chapter 1
An Introduction to the Family Business — 3

1.1	In praise of family business: the importance of family businesses to the economy	3
1.2	Family business – a definition?	13
1.3	A definition of family?	20
1.4	Family business challenges	23
1.5	Five family business stories	27
1.6	Conclusion	33

Chapter 2
Themes — 35

2.1	Introduction	35
2.2	The founder	36
2.3	Ambivalence	41
2.4	Communication and taboos	43
2.5	Conflict	45
2.6	Fairness and equality	52
2.7	Insiders and outsiders	53
2.8	Father and son relationships	54
2.9	Father and daughter relationships	54
2.10	Psychological status of the family business	55
2.11	Sibling rivalry	56
2.12	Professionalisation	62
2.13	Myths	68
2.14	Scripts	68

2.15	Conclusion	69

Chapter 3
Tools, Models and Theories — 71

3.1	Introduction	71
3.2	Genograms	71
3.3	Systems theory	79
3.4	Family business life-cycle theory	88
3.5	Individual life-cycle theory	94
3.6	Communication theory	101
3.7	Family firm typology	104
3.8	Saul D Harrison – revisited	106
3.9	Conclusion	112
3.10	Further reading for Part A	113

Part B
Business Matters

Chapter 4
Tax Basics and the Family Business Structure — 117

4.1	Introduction	117
4.2	Choice of family business structure	117
4.3	Overview of basic tax issues	119
4.4	Limited company or sole trader / partnership?	123
4.5	Family LLPs	124
4.6	Tax efficient extraction of profits from a company	128
4.8	Overview of basic accounting and financial management issues	130
4.9	Wealth planning	134
4.10	Liquidation and the family business	138
4.11	Employing family members – tax and alternative methods of reward	141
4.12	Employee ownership and tax	143

Chapter 5
Employing Family Members — 153

5.1	Overview	153
5.2	Family employment terms and the family business system	155
5.3	Family employment	156
5.4	Governance and family employment policies	157
5.5	Family remuneration	159
5.6	Letting go and compulsory retirement ages	162
5.7	Employment law and employment claims	163
5.8	Unfair dismissal	163
5.9	The law on discrimination	168
5.10	Informality and family business employment practice	172
5.11	Family members and employment status	172
5.12	Contract of employment	175
5.13	Employing young family members	177

5.14	National minimum wage/national living wage	178
5.15	Working Time Regulations (WTR 1998)	180
5.16	Disciplinary and grievance procedures	181
5.17	Capability and performance	185
5.18	Ill health	188
5.19	Family dynamics; behaviour and boundaries	189
5.20	Protected and without prejudice conversations and settlement agreements	193
5.21	ACAS and early conciliation	196
5.22	Conclusion	196

Chapter 6
Non-family Employees — 197

6.1	Overview	197
6.2	Introducing non-family managers	198
6.3	Non-family managers and professionalisation	200
6.4	The family business culture clash	202
6.5	Motivating non-family managers	203
6.6	Employee ownership	205
6.7	Family employee and share ownership	209
6.8	Non-family managers and governance	209
6.9	Discrimination and nepotism	210
6.10	Non-family managers and the family business glass ceiling	215
6.11	Conclusion	216

Chapter 7
Management Succession — 217

7.1	Introduction	217
7.2	Succession dissected	218
7.3	Family business life stage and succession	220
7.4	Barriers to succession	222
7.5	Succession and the senior generation	224
7.6	Family management succession and the next generation	231
7.7	Co-leadership	235
7.8	Non-family leadership	237
7.9	Family leadership	240
7.10	The succession process	240
7.11	The management succession process: Stage 1 – opening the door	241
7.12	Stage 2: Finding their feet	244
7.13	Stage 3: Passing the baton	248
7.14	Formal succession plans	252
7.15	Management succession: conclusion	253

Chapter 8
Directors' Duties — 257

8.1	Introduction	257
8.2	Overview	261

8.3	Directors' duties – an overview	264
8.4	Ratification	269
8.5	Claims and consequences	274
8.6	The 'family director'	277
8.7	Conflicts of interest	288
8.8	Remuneration	300
8.9	Balancing interests – CA, s 172 and the duty to promote the success of the company	303
8.10	The sinking ship – insolvency and the family company	307
8.11	Directors' duties – conclusion	316

Chapter 9
The Family Business Name — 319
9.1	Introduction	319
9.2	The family business as a brand	319
9.3	Protecting the family name	321
9.4	Whose name is it anyway?	323
9.5	Family name for sale?	328
9.6	Conclusion	329

Chapter 10
Property and the Family Firm — 331
10.1	Overview	331
10.2	Property inside or outside the family business	332
10.3	Property and hybrid ownership solutions	334
10.4	Parallel interests	335
10.5	Informality and family business property issues	336
10.6	Types of interest	338
10.7	Licences and family businesses	340
10.8	Commercial Leases and Part II of the Landlord and Tenant Act 1954	341
10.9	Agricultural holdings	342
10.10	Residential leases	342
10.11	Estate management (or property governance)	344
10.12	Occupation by and sharing with third parties	344
10.13	Joint ownership within the family business	345
10.14	Joint ownership case study	348
10.15	Family businesses and property ownership: conclusion	350
10.16	Further reading for Part B	351

Part C
Ownership

Chapter 11
Ownership Overview — 355
11.1	The importance of ownership	355
11.2	Basic shareholder rights	356
11.3	Legal control	357

11.4	Ownership and control	359
11.5	Ownership structures	360
11.6	Employees and ownership policy	360
11.7	Dividend policies	360
11.8	Owner controls	362
11.9	Weighted voting rights	364
11.10	Sale of the family company	366
11.11	Share transfer provisions	367
11.12	The ownership tree	371
11.13	Pruning the ownership tree: the case for pruning	372
11.14	Pruning and tree surgery	374
11.15	Compulsory divestment provisions	375
11.16	Pre-emption provisions	377
11.17	Exit arrangements	382
11.18	Company buy-backs	384
11.19	Re-organisations	388
11.20	Other methods of adjusting the balance of ownership	390
11.21	Conclusion	391

Chapter 12
Selling the Family Owned Business — 393

12.1	Introduction	393
12.2	Family dynamics and sale	393
12.3	Sale process – overview	396
12.4	Maximising the value on sale	400
12.5	Valuing the family business for sale	402
12.6	Price and transaction structure	403
12.7	Choice of buyer	405
12.8	FBO's and MBO's	406
12.9	Minority interests	407
12.10	Family employees	412
12.11	Family owned property	417
12.12	Capacity issues	418
12.13	Procedural issues	419
12.14	Seller due diligence	424
12.15	Warranties and indemnities	425
12.16	Post sale restrictions and the family name	431
12.17	Family business trusts and the position of trustees	432

Chapter 13
Family Business Partnerships — 437

13.1	Introduction	437
13.2	The Ham family	438
13.3	The Ham family and family business theory	439
13.4	Key legal features of partnerships	440
13.5	The Hams in court	445
13.6	Conclusion	453

Chapter 14
Family Business Trusts — 455
- 14.1 Overview — 455
- 14.2 Family business trusts and tax — 456
- 14.3 Discretionary trusts — 457
- 14.4 Family business trusts and the three-circle model — 459
- 14.5 Uses of family business trusts — 461
- 14.6 Family business trusts and bivalency — 463
- 14.7 Family business trusts and hybrid ownership approaches — 464
- 14.8 Choice of beneficiaries — 465
- 14.9 Trusts and matrimonial claims — 467
- 14.10 Choice of trustees — 471
- 14.11 The *Bartlett* case and ownership vacuum — 473
- 14.12 Protectors — 475
- 14.13 Settlor's and reserved powers — 478
- 14.14 Removal of trustees — 478
- 14.15 Letter of wishes — 484
- 14.16 Sham trusts, letting go and bivalency — 485
- 14.17 Trusts and governance — 486
- 14.18 Employment policies and remuneration — 489
- 14.19 Information — 489
- 14.20 Selling the family silver — 491
- 14.21 The trust deed and modification of trustees' duties — 497
- 14.22 Other types of trust and similar arrangements found in family businesses — 501
- 14.23 Alternatives to family business trusts — 504
- 14.24 Family business trusts: conclusion — 505

Chapter 15
Ownership Succession — 507
- 15.1 Introduction — 507
- 15.2 Fairness and equality revisited — 508
- 15.3 Ownership succession — 508
- 15.4 Ownership succession typologies — 509
- 15.5 Succession decisions now and for future generations — 511
- 15.6 Family ownership succession and planning — 511
- 15.7 A shared dream? — 512
- 15.8 Ownership philosophy — 513
- 15.9 Factors influencing ownership approach — 515
- 15.10 Gifts ... with strings attached? — 520
- 15.11 Strings and red tape — 521
- 15.12 Value and ownership — 522
- 15.13 Ownership structures — 523
- 15.14 Carried outsider interests — 532
- 15.15 Sale to family members or family buy-out (FBO) — 532
- 15.16 FBO/MBO hybrids — 536
- 15.17 Third party sales — 536
- 15.18 Barriers to ownership succession — 536

15.19	Fair process	537
15.20	Parallel planning	539
15.21	Conclusion	543

Chapter 16
Tax and Family Business Ownership 545

16.1	Overview	545
16.2	Inheritance tax – business property relief	545
16.3	Inheritance tax – excepted assets	549
16.4	Agricultural property relief	550
16.5	Inheritance tax and family business trusts	552
16.6	Capital gains tax	555
16.7	Entrepreneur's relief	557
16.8	Valuing a business for tax and other non-sale reasons	561
16.9	Tax and buy-backs	562
16.10	Property and tax	565
16.11	Some tax planning ideas for ownership succession	575
16.12	Conclusion	579
16.13	Further reading for Part C	580

Part D
Family Matters

Chapter 17
Governance and the Family Owned Business 585

17.1	Governance overview	585
17.2	The case for governance in the family owned business	588
17.3	A definition of governance?	590
17.4	Sources of governance	591
17.5	Case study – C & J Clark	592
17.6	The IOD Code	596
17.7	Stages in family business governance	600
17.8	Governance and the later stage family business: bridging the divide	605
17.9	The family business board	606
17.10	Board composition	611
17.11	Family governance systems	617
17.12	Family assemblies	619
17.13	Family council	622
17.14	Family charters	627
17.15	Contents of family charters	632
17.16	Philanthropy	638
17.17	Family venturing	638
17.18	Legal documents	639
17.19	Contents of legal governance documents	642
17.20	Sale of the company	645
17.21	Drag and tag	646
17.22	Dispute resolution	648

17.23	Other family business governance documents	652
17.24	Governance conclusion	654

Chapter 18
The Family Business and Marriage — 655

18.1	Introduction	655
18.2	Copreneurs and the early stage family business	657
18.3	Martin and Pamela White	659
18.4	Making it work: governance and copreneurship	659
18.5	Early warning signs	662
18.6	Governance	663
18.7	Divorce: the end of the road?	665
18.8	Divorce: the legal starting point MCA 1973, s 25	666
18.9	The family business, needs and the golden goose	668
18.10	Clean break liquidity, risk and reward	669
18.11	Equal contributions and special contributions	671
18.12	The yardstick of equality: *White v White*	673
18.13	The family business: matrimonial or non-matrimonial property?	674
18.14	The family business and the corporate veil	681
18.15	In-laws and the later stage family business	682
18.16	Blood and water: the competing claims of family members	683
18.17	Interveners	684
18.18	Ante and post nuptial agreements	686
18.19	Governance documents	690
18.20	Conclusion	694

Chapter 19
Inheritance Disputes — 695

19.1	Overview: 'one day all this will be yours'	695
19.2	Case study: an emerging dispute	697
19.3	*Davies v Davies*: the case of the cowshed Cinderella	703
19.4	Family business themes	705
19.5	Legal complexity	710
19.6	Proprietary estoppel: the key elements	710
19.7	Assurance	711
19.8	Reliance	712
19.9	Detriment	713
19.10	Equity and conscience	714
19.11	Remedy: all this?	714
19.12	Volatility and governance	719
19.13	Uncertainty and the legal position	721
19.14	Constructive trust	722
19.15	Failed cases	722
19.16	Equitable claims: practicalities	726
19.17	Inheritance and I(PFD)A 1975 claims	727
19.18	The I(PFD)A 1975 and the next generation; the maintenance standard	728

19.19	Spouses and the I(PFD)A 1975	733
19.20	Practical considerations and checklist for inheritance claims	738
19.21	Inheritance disputes: conclusion	739
19.22	Further reading for Part D	741

Part E
Family Business Disputes

Chapter 20
Family Business Shareholder Disputes – Overview and Key Issues 745

20.1	Introduction	745
20.2	Overview	746
20.3	Reasonable offers and costs	750
20.4	'Quasi-partnerships'	750
20.5	Family owned businesses – 'something more'?	763
20.6	Family business factors	767
20.7	Remedies and governance structure	777
20.8	Bad faith	781
20.9	Mismanagement	788
20.10	Conclusion – *Saul D Harrison* – governance application points?	790

Chapter 21
Unfair Prejudice and the Family Company 793

21.1	Overview	793
21.2	*O'Neill v Phillips*	801
21.3	Unfair prejudice and succession	805
21.4	Sibling partnerships – exclusion cases	811
21.5	Cousin consortia – unfair prejudice and the later stage family owned business	815
21.6	Breach of duty	818
21.7	Unfair prejudice – remedies, reasonable offers and costs	835

Chapter 22
Just and Equitable Winding Up 837

22.1	Overview	837
22.2	The legislation	838
22.3	Alternative remedy	838
22.4	Equitable principles: fairness and rules based approach	838
22.5	Equitable bars	839
22.6	Dual claims	840
22.7	The Harding family	841
22.8	Circumstances justifying just and equitable winding up	842
22.9	Exclusion	843
22.10	Breakdown of trust and confidence	843
22.11	Deadlock	844
22.12	Loss of substratum	845
22.13	Oppression	845

22.14	Appropriation	846
22.15	Refusal of just and equitable winding up	847
22.16	Alternative remedy	847
22.17	Just and equitable winding-up – conclusion	850

Chapter 23
Derivative Claims and the Disgruntled Family Member — 851

23.1	Overview	851
23.2	The rule in *Foss v Harbottle*	852
23.3	Fraud on the minority	852
23.4	CA, ss 260–264	853
23.5	A derivative claim in practice – *Singh v Singh*	857
23.6	Substantive failure	860
23.7	Derivative claims – successful categories	862
23.8	Fraud on the minority	863
23.9	Conclusion	865

Chapter 24
Shareholder Disputes – Remedies, Reasonable Offers and Costs — 867

24.1	Introduction	867
24.2	Unfair prejudice remedies – overview – CA, s 996	868
24.3	Share purchase orders	868
24.4	Valuation – basic principles	871
24.5	Minority discounts?	871
24.6	Other valuation issues	877
24.7	Other unfair prejudice remedies	880
24.8	Offers to purchase	882
24.9	Costs	889
24.10	Conclusion	893
24.11	Further reading for Part E	894

Part F
The Family Business Advisor

Chapter 25
Process Consulting and the Role of the Family Business Consultant — 897

25.1	Introduction	897
25.2	The three-circle model and the family business advisor	897
25.3	Family business consultancy	899
25.4	Process and content consulting	902
25.5	Process, content and context	905
25.6	Defining the issues	906
25.7	Family business clients and roles	907
25.8	The family business advisor and conflict resolution	907
25.9	Alternative family dispute resolution	910
25.10	The family business movement	918
25.11	Conclusion	919

Chapter 26
Advising the Family Business Client 921
26.1 Introduction 921
26.2 The trusted advisor 921
26.3 Collaborative practice 922
26.4 Collegiate practice: internal family business teams 928
26.5 Defining the family business client 934
26.6 One client many roles? 937
26.7 The lawyers' role in *Cadman Developments* 938
26.8 Conflicts of interest 939
26.9 Conflicts and outcomes focused regulation 941
26.10 Confidentiality 944
26.11 Fit for family business purpose? 946
26.12 Conclusion 953
26.13 Further reading for Part F 955

Appendix 1
Glossary 957

Appendix 2
The Family Business Movement 961

Index 965

TABLE OF CASES

References are to paragraph numbers.

AB v CB (Financial Remedy; Variation of Trust [2014] EWHC 2998 (Fam)	18.19.2
Aberdeen Railway Co v Blaikie Bros (1854) 1 Macq 461	8.7.13
Ackerman v Ackerman Estates Gazette (2012) July 1	26.6
AE v BE [2014] EWHC 4868 (Fam)	18.10
AG (Manchester) Ltd, Re [2008] EWHC 64 (Ch)	8.6.3
Allders International Ltd v Parkins [1981] IRLR 68, EAT	5.8.2
Allen v Gold Reefs of West Africa Ltd [1900] Ch 656	21.6.14
American Pioneer Leather Company Co, Re [1918] 1 Ch 556	20.7.3
Anheuser-Busch Inc v Budejovicky Budvar Narodni Poidnik (C-245-02) [2005] ETMR 27	9.4.2
AR v AR (Treatment of Inherited Wealth) [2011] EWHC 2717 (Fam), [2012] 2 FLR 1, [2011] All ER (D) 241 (Oct), FD	18.13.1, 18.13.7, 18.13.8
Arbuthnott v Bonnyman and others. [2015] EWCA Civ 536	21.6.14
Armitage v Nurse [1998] Ch 241, [1997] 2 All ER 705, [1997] 3 WLR 1046, 74 P & CR D13, [1997] PLR 51	14.21.4
Arnander (Executors of McKenna Deceased) v HMRC (2006) STC (SCD) 800	16.4
ASIC v Healey [2011] FCA 717	8.6.3
Asprey & Garrard Limited v WRA (Guns) Limited and Asprey [2002] ETMR 47	9.4.3, 9.5
Astec (BSR) plc [1988] 2 BCLC 556	20.5
Atlas Wright (Europe) Limited v Wright and another [1999] EWCA Civ 669	8.4.5
Attwood v Maidment [2011] EWHC 3180	24.5.4
Aveling Barford Ltd v Perion Ltd (1989) 5 BCC 677, [1989] BCLC 626, 1989 PCC 370, (1989) *Financial Times*, April 28, ChD	8.4.2
Bahouse v Negus [2008] WTLR 97	19.18
Bamford v Bamford [1970] Ch 212, [1969] 1 All ER 969, [1969] 2 WLR 1107, 113 SJ 123, CA; affirming [1968] 2 All ER 655, [1968] 3 WLR 317, 112 SJ 416, [1968] CLY 441	8.4.1, 8.4.2, 23.6.3
Barclays Bank Trust Co Ltd v IRC (1998) STC (SCD) 125	16.3.1
Barings plc (no 5), Re [1999] 1 BCLC 433	8.10.4
Barrett v Duckett [1995] 1 BCLC 243, [1995] BCC 362, CA	20.8, 20.8.2, 23.5.5
Bartlett v Barclays Bank Trust Company [1980] 1 All ER 139	7.8.1, 11.12.1, 14.10.1, 14.11, 14.12.4, 14.14.1, 14.20.2, 14.21.2, 14.21.3
BDG Roof Bond Ltd v Douglas [2000] BCC 770, [2000] BCLC 401	8.4.5, 12.13.4
Bell Bros Ltd, Re (1891) 65 LT 245	11.11.1
Bermuda Cablevision Ltd v Colica Trust Co Ltd [1998] AC 198	21.1.7
Bhullar Brothers Ltd, Re [2003] EWCA Civ 424, [2003] 2 BCLC 241, [2003] BCC 711, [2003] NPC 45, 147 Sol Jo LB 421	8.5.2, 8.7.2, 8.7.12, 8.7.13, 8.7.14, 8.11, 10.11
Bird Precision Bellows Ltd, Re [1986] Ch 658, [1985] 3 All ER 523, [1986] 2 WLR 158, CA; affirming [1984] Ch 419, [1984] 3 All ER 444, [1984] BCLC 395	20.4, 20.7.1, 24.5.1, 24.5.2, 24.5.3, 24.6.2
Blair Open Hearth Furnace Co Ltd v Reigart (1913) 108 LT 665, 29 TLR 449	17.19.5
BMW v Deenik [1999] ECR I-905	9.4.3
Bonham-Carter and another v Situ Ventures Ltd [2012] EWHC 230 (Ch)	8.4.5
Boswell and Co (Steels) Ltd, Re [1988] 5 BCC 145	24.8.4
Bovey Hotel Ventures, Re (unreported) 31 July 1981	21.1.3
Bowthorpe Ltd v Hills [2002] EWHC 2331 (Ch)	8.4.2
Branch v Bagley [2004] EWHC 426 (Ch)	24.9.3

Breakspear and others v Ackland and others [2008] EWHC 220 (Ch) 14.19.3
Brooke v Purton [2014] EWHC 547 (Ch) 26.11.7
Brooks v Brooks [1996] 1 AC 375 18.19.2
Browne v Browne [1989] 1 FLR 291, [1989] Fam Law 147, CA 14.9.4
Brownlow v GH Marshall Ltd [2001] BCC 152, [2000] 2 BCLC 655, (2000) *The Independent*, March 20, ChD   20.4.4, 20.6.2, 20.7.2, 21.1.10, 21.1.11, 21.4.1, 21.4.2, 21.4.3, 21.4.4, 21.4.5
Bunning (Susan) v GT Bunning & Sons Ltd [2005] EWCA Civ 983 5.8.2
Burry & Knight Ltd [2014] EWCA Civ 604, [2015] 1 All ER 37, [2014] 1 WLR 4046, [2015] 1 BCLC 61   2.5.3, 20.8.1, 24.9.2
Bushell v Faith [1970] AC 1099, [1970] 2 WLR 272, 114 Sol Jo 54 11.9, 15.13.3
Butt v Kelson [1952] Ch 197, *sub nom* Re Butt, Butt v Kelson [1952] 1 All ER 167, [1952] 1 TLR 214, [1962] WN 34, CA 14.19.3
Byrne Brothers (Formwork) Ltd v Baird and others [2002] IRLR 96 5.11.2

C v C [2003] EWHC 1222 (Fam), [2003] 2 FLR 493 14.9.3, 18.7, 18.10
C v C [2007] EWHC 2033 (Fam), [2009] 1 FLR 8, FD 18.13.8
Calderbank v Calderbank [1976] Fam 93, [1975] 3 WLR 586, (1975) FLR Rep 113, [1975] 3 All ER 333, CA 24.9.2
Callaghan (Deceased), Estate of, Re [1985] Fam 1, [1984] 3 WLR 1076, [1984] 3 All ER 790, FD 19.18.3
Carlen v Drury (1812) 1 Ves & B154 2.5.4
Charman v Charman [2007] EWCA Civ 503, [2007] 2 FCR 217, [2007] 1 FLR 1246   14.9.3, 18.11, 18.12
Chez Nico Restaurants Ltd [1992] BCLC 192 12.9.2
Christie (Deceased), Re; Christie v Keeble [1979] Ch 168, [1979] 2 WLR 105, [1979] 1 All ER 546, ChD 19.18
City Fire Insurance Co, Re [1925] Ch 407 8.6.1, 8.6.3
Clark v Cutland [2003] EWHC 810 24.9.3
Clearsprings (Management) Ltd, Re [2003] EWHC 2516 (Ch) 24.3.3
Clemens v Clemens Bros Ltd [1976] 2 All ER 268   20.4.4, 20.6.11, 21.5.2, 21.5.3, 24.7.2
Cohen v Selby [2002] BCC 82, [2001] 1 BCLC 176, CA; *sub nom* Simmon Box (Diamonds) Ltd, Re [2000] BCC 275, ChD 8.2.4
Coker and Osamor v The Lord Chancellor and the Lord Chancellor's Department [2001] EWCA Civ 1756 6.9.1
Company (No 001363 of 1988), Re [1989] BCLC 57 24.8.4
Company (No 00370 of 1987), Re, ex parte Glossup [1988] 1 WLR 1068   21.1.6, 21.1.9, 21.6.4
Company (No 004377 of 1986), Re [1987] WLR 102 20.7.1
Company (No 004502 of 1988), Re [1988] BCLC 701 24.9.3
Company (No 005134 of 1986), Re, ex parte Harries [1989] BCLC 383 20.6.9
Company (No 00836 of 1995), Re (Gippeswyck Case) [1996] BCC 432   20.8.3, 21.1.2, 21.3.9, 24.3.2, 24.8.1, 24.8.3, 24.8.4, 24.8.5, 24.8.6
Company ex parte Burr, Re [1992] BCLC 724 21.6.3
Conegrade Ltd, Re [2002] EWHC 2411 (Ch), [2003] BPIR 358, ChD 8.4.5
Cook v Deeks [1916] AC 554, 85 LJPC 161, [1916-17] All ER Rep 285, PC 8.4.2, 8.7.1
Cook v Thomas [2010] EWCA Civ 227 19.15
Copeland v Craddock Ltd, Re [1997] BCC 294 24.3.2
Cornick v Cornick [1994] 2 FLR 530 18.10
Cotton and another v Brudenell-Bruce and others [2014] EWCA Civ 1312 14.5.2
Cottrell v King [2004] 2 BCLC 413 12.13.2
Coventry (Deceased), Re; Coventry v Coventry [1980] Ch 461, [1979] 3 WLR 802, (1979) FLR Rep 142, [1979] 3 All ER 815, CA 19.18
Cowan v Cowan [2001] EWCA Civ 679, [2002] Fam 97, [2001] 3 WLR 684, [2001] 2 FCR 331, [2001] 2 FLR 192   7.12.4, 18.11, 18.13.2, 18.16
Crown Dilmun v Sutton [2004] EWHC 52 (Ch), [2004] 1 BCLC 468, ChD 8.4.2
Cruikshank v Sutherland [1922] 92 LJ CH 136 (HL) 13.4.8
Cumana Ltd, Re [1986] BCLC 430, CA   21.6.3, 21.6.6, 21.6.13, 24.6.4, 24.6.5
Cunliffe v Fielden, [2006] Ch 361 19.19.2
Cuthbert Cooper and Sons Ltd, Re [1937] Ch 392 20.6.4

D'Jan of London Ltd, Re [1993] 1 BCC 646 8.4.5, 8.5.3

Daniel v Daniels [1978] Ch 406   10.11, 23.8.3
Dann v Spurrier [1802] 7 Ves 231   19.7.4
Dashfield and another v Davidson and others [2008] EWHC 486 (Ch)   8.4.5
Davies and Anor v Davies [2015] EWHC 015 (Ch); [2014] EWCA Civ 568, [2014] Fam
    Law 1252, [2016] WTLR 1175   14.6, 19.1, 19.3, 19.4, 19.4.1, 19.4.3, 19.4.4, 19.4.6,
           19.4.7, 19.5, 19.7.1, 19.8, 19.9
Davies v Davies [2015] EWHC 1384 (Ch)   1.5.2, 2.4, 15.4, 19.4.1, 19.4.3, 19.4.4, 19.4.5,
           19.4.6, 19.4.7, 19.5, 19.9
Dennis (deceased), Re [1981] 2 All ER 140 [1981] 2 All ER 140   19.18
Devlin v Slough Estates [1983] BCLC 497, (1982) 126 SJ 623   23.7.3
DKG Contractors, Re [1990] BCC 903   8.10.4, 8.10.6, 8.11
Dorechester Finance Co Ltd v Stebbing [1989] BCLC 498   8.6.3
DR Chemicals Ltd [1989] 5 BCC 39   20.6.13
Duomatic Ltd, Re [1969] 2 Ch 365, [1969] 1 All ER 161, [1969] 2 WLR 114   8.4.5,
           12.13.4, 26.11.3

Ebrahimi v Westbourne Galleries Ltd [1973] AC 360, [1972] 2 All ER 492, [1972] 2
    WLR 1289, 116 SJ 412, HL; reversing *sub nom* Westbourne Galleries Ltd, Re [1971]
    Ch 799, [1971] 1 All ER 56, [1971] 2 WLR 618, (1970) 115 SJ 74, CA; reversing
    [1970] 3 All ER 374, [1970] 1 WLR 1378, 114 SJ 785   20.4, 20.4.1, 20.4.2, 20.4.3,
           20.4.5, 20.4.6, 20.4.7, 20.4.8, 20.4.9, 20.5, 20.6.4, 20.6.11, 20.6.12,
           21.3.6, 21.4.5, 21.5.2, 21.6.6, 22.5.1, 22.8, 22.9, 24.5.2, 24.5.3, 24.8.3
Elgindata Ltd (No 2), Re [1993] 1 All ER 232, [1992] 1 WLR 1207, [1993] BCLC 119,
    (1992) 136 SJ (LB) 190, [1992] Gazette 15 July, 33, (1992) *The Times*, June 18, CA;
    reversing *sub nom* Elgindata Ltd, Re [1991] BCLC 959, ChD   20.9.1
Ely v Positive Government Security Life Assurance Co Ltd (1876) 2 Ex D 88 (HL)   17.18.2
Equitable Life Assurance Society v Bowley [2003] EWHC 2263 (Comm), [2003] BCC 829,
    [2004] 1 BCLC 180, [2003] All ER (D) 308, Comm Ct   8.6.1
Espinosa v Burke [1999] 3 FCR 76   19.18.5

F v F [2012] EWHC 438 (Fam)   18.7, 18.16, 18.19.1, 26.11.5
F&C Alternative Investments Holdings Ltd v Barthelemy [2012] Ch 613   20.6.11
Facchini v Bryson [1952] 1 TLR 1386 (CA)   10.7
Farmer (Executors of Farmer Deceased) v IRC (1999) STC 321   16.2.3
Fields v Fields [2015] EWHC 1670 (Fam)   18.10
Fisher Meredith LLP v JH & PH [2002] EWHC 408 (Fam)   18.17
Fisher v Cadman [2005] EWHC 377 (Ch), [2006] 2 BCLC 499, [2005] All ER (D) 213   1.5.3,
           2.2.1, 2.11.3, 3.2.3, 8.1.1, 8.8.3, 10.1, 14.14.4, 14.15.2, 20.4.7, 20.6.3,
           20.6.5, 20.9.1, 21.4.1, 21.1.11, 21.4.7, 21.5.3, 21.6.3, 21.6.7, 21.6.10,
           21.6.11, 22.5.2, 23.8.3, 24.5.2, 24.8.3, 26.7, 26.11.7
Fiske Nominees Ltd v Dwyka Diamond Ltd [2002] BCLC 123   12.9.2
Foss v Harbottle [1843] 2 Hare 461   8.1.1, 20.6.10, 23.2, 23.6.3, 23.7, 23.8
Fulham Football Club v Richards and another [2011] EWCA Civ 855   20.7.3, 25.8.2,
           25.9.10
FZ v SZ and Others (Ancillary Relief: Conduct: Valuations) [2010] EWHC 1630 (Fam),
    [2011] 1 FLR 64, FD   18.10

G v G (Financial Provision: Equal Division) [2002] EWHC 1339 (Fam), [2002] 2 FLR
    1143, [2002] Fam Law 792, FD   18.7, 18.10
G v W [2015] EWHC 834 (Fam)   18.11
Gamlestaden Fastigheter AB v Baltic Partners Ltd [2007] UKPC 26   21.1.10
Gemma Ltd v Davies [2008] EWHC 546 (Ch), [2009] Bus LR D4, [2008] 2 BCLC 281,
    [2008] BCC 812   8.6.2, 8.6.3, 8.7.8, 8.7.9, 8.11, 17.7.2, 18.4.3, 18.6
Gerolsteiner Brunnen v Putsch [2004] RPC 39   9.4.3
Gillett v Holt [2001] Ch 210, [2000] 2 FLR 266, [1998] 3 All ER 917, CA   19.11.2
Gillette v La-Laboratories C-228/03 [2005] ETMR 67   9.4.3
Gold v Curtis [2005] WTLR 637   19.18.5
Goodchild, Re [1996] IWLR 694   19.18.5
Gourisaria v Gourisaria [2010] EWCA Civ 1019   18.17
Grace v Biagioli [2005] EWCA Civ 1222   24.7, 24.7.1

Granatino v Radmacher (formerly Granatino) [2010] UKSC 42, [2011] 1 AC 534, [2010]
3 WLR 1367, *sub nom* Radmacher (formerly Granatino) v Granatino [2010] 2 FLR
1900, [2011] 1 All ER 373, SC   18.18.1, 18.18.2, 18.18.3, 18.18.4, 18.18.7, 18.18.8,
18.18.9
Guinness v Saunders [1990] 2 AC 663, [1990] 1 All ER 652, [1990] 2 WLR 324, [1990]
BCC 205, [1990] BCLC 402, [1990] LS Gaz March 7, 42, (1990) 134 SJ 457, HL;
affirming *sub nom* Guinness v Ward [1988] 2 All ER 940, [1988] 1 WLR 863,
(1988) 4 BCC 377, [1988] BCLC 607, (1988) 138 NLJ 142, 1988 PCC 270, (1988)
132 SJ 820; affirming [1988] BCLC 43   8.8.1, 8.8.2
GW v RW (Financial Provision: Departure from Equality [2003] EWHC 611 (Fam)   18.13.3

Halsey v Milton Keynes General NHS Trust; Steel v Joy [2004] EWCA Civ 576, [2004] 4
All ER 920, [2004] 1 WLR 3002, 81 BMLR 108, [2004] 22 LS Gaz R 31, [2004]
NLJR 769, *Times*, 27 May, 148 Sol Jo LB 629, [2004] All ER (D) 125, May   19.2.8,
19.16.3
Halt Garage, Re (1964) Ltd [1982] 2 All ER 1016   8.4.2, 8.8.4
Ham v Ham [2013] EWCA Civ 1301   10.1, 13.1, 13.4.5, 13.5.1, 13.6, 16.10.12, 26.8,
26.11.10
Hancock (dec'd), Re [1993] 1 FCR 500   19.18.5
Harding Limited, Re [2014] EWHC 247 (Ch)   2.11.3, 20.4.5, 20.6.2, 20.6.3, 21.4.6, 22.5.1,
22.6, 22.7.1, 22.7.2, 22.7.3, 22.7.4, 22.7.5, 22.16.1, 22.16.2, 24.8.3
Harmer Ltd, Re [1959] 1 WLR 62   5.6, 21.1.3, 21.3.5, 21.3.6, 21.3.7, 21.3.8, 21.4.5, 22.13,
22.16.1, 24.3.2, 24.7.1
Harrison (Saul D) & Sons plc, Re [1994] BCC 475, [1995] 1 BCLC 14   1.5.4, 2.5.4, 8.8.1,
8.8.4, 10.1, 10.11, 11.1, 13.3, 14.1.1, 14.4, 14.21.2, 14.23.1, 15.9.9,
15.13.3, 15.20, 20.2.1, 20.4.9, 20.5, 20.6.5, 20.6.8, 20.6.9, 20.6.12,
20.6.13, 20.7.2, 20.9, 20.10, 21.1.9, 21.2.4, 21.5, 21.5.1, 21.5.2, 21.5.3,
21.6.3, 21.6.4, 21.6.5, 21.6.11, 22.12, 24.6.1, 24.9.2, 26.8, 26.11.4
Hawks v Cuddy [2008] BCC 390   24.3.1
Henry v Henry [2010] UKPC 3   19.6
Hewett v First National Group plc [2010] EWCA Civ 312   18.18.7
Hodge v Hodge [2008] Fam LR 51   18.10
Holder v Holder [1968] Ch 353, [1968] 1 All ER 665, [1968] 2 WLR 237, (1967) 1122
SJ 17, CA   14.20.5
Hölterhoff v Freiesleben (Case C-2/00) [2002] ECR I-4187, ECJ   18.19.1, 26.11.5
Hooper v Patterson (unreported), judgment of 9 February 2008, High Court Case No
11688 of 2008   6.2.1, 8.10.2, 8.10.7
Hotel Cipriani SRL v Cipriani (Grosvenor Street) Limited [2010] EWCA Civ 110, [2010]
RPC 16   9.4.2, 9.4.4
Hydrodan (Corby) Ltd (in Liquidation), Re [1994] BCC 161, [1994] 2 BCLC 180, (1994)
The Times, February 19, ChD   8.6.2

I N Newman Limited v Richard T Adlem [2005] EWCA Civ 741   9.4.1, 9.5
Iceland Frozen Foods Ltd v Jones [1983] ICR 17, [1982] IRLR 439, (1982) 79 LS Gaz
1257, EAT   5.8.4
Ilott v Mitson [2015] EWCA Civ 797   19.18.1, 19.18.2
Industrial Development Consultants v Cooley [1972] 2 All ER 162, [1972] 1 WLR 443,
(1971) 116 SJ 255   8.7.1
Irvine v Irvine (No 1) [2006] EWHC 406 (Ch), [2007] 1 BCLC 349   8.8.2, 20.2.4, 20.4.8,
20.6.5, 20.6.6, 20.6.12, 21.1.5, 21.6.3, 21.6.4, 21.6.10, 24.8.1
Irvine v Irvine (No 2) [2006] EWHC 583 (Ch), [2006] 4 All ER 102, [2007] 1 BCLC
445   8.8.7, 20.4, 20.4.8, 24.4, 24.5.3, 24.6.3
Irvine v Irvine (No 3) [2006] EWHC 1875 (Ch), [2006] All ER (D) 329 (Jul)   24.4, 24.5.3,
24.6.3
Issacs v Belfield Furnishings [2006] 2 BCLC 705   20.7.1
Ivory v Palmer [1975] ICR 340, 119 SJ 405, CA   10.10.4

J v J (Financial Orders: Wife's long tem needs) [2011] EWHC 1010 (Fam)   18.13.1
J&W Sanderson Ltd v Fenox Ltd [2014] EWHC 4322 (Ch)   20.7.3
JE Cade and Sons Ltd [1992] BCLC 213, [1991] BCC 360   20.5, 20.7.2, 21.1.10
Jennings v Rice [2003] 1 P&CR 8   19.11.1

JJ Harrison (Properties) Ltd v Harrison [2001] EWCA Civ 1467, [2002] 1 BCLC 162,
   [2002] BCC 729   8.1.1, 8.3.8, 8.5.2, 8.5.3, 8.7.2, 8.7.9, 8.7.10, 8.7.11, 10.1, 10.11,
                                                                                                   26.4.5
JL v SL (No 2) (Financial Remedies: Rehearing: Non-Matrimonial Property) [2015]
   EWHC 360   18.13.6
Jones v Garnett (Inspector of Taqxes) [2007] UKHL 35, [2007] 1 WLR 2030, [2007] 4 All
   ER 857, HL   4.6
Jones v Jones [2011] EWCA Civ 41, [2012] Fam 1, [2011] 3 WLR 582, [2011] 1 FLR
   1723   18.13.3, 19.19.2
Joseph Rodgers & Sons Limited v W N Rodgers & Co (1924) 41 RPC 277   9.4.1
Jowell v O'Neill and Brennan Construction Limited (1998) STC 482   4.3.6

K v L (Non-Matrimonial Property: Special Contribution) [2011] EWCA Civ 550, [2012] 1
   WLR 306, [2011] 2 FLR 980, [2011] 3 All ER 733, CA   18.13.7
Kaytech International plc, Re [1999] 2 BCLC 351, [1999] BCC 390, (1998) *The*
   Independent, 7 December, CA   8.6.2
Keech v Sandford (1776) Sel Cas t King 61   8.7.12
Kenyon Swansea Ltd, Re [1987] BCLC 514   24.9.3
Kershaw v Mickelthwaite and others [2010] EWHC 506 (Ch)   14.14, 14.14.2
Kinlan v Crimmin [2006] EWHC 779 (Ch)   8.4.5
Kleanthous v Paphitis [2011] EWHC 2287 (Ch)   23.4.2
Kremen v Agrest (Financial Remedy: Non-Disclosure: Postnuptial Agreement) [2012]
   EWHC 45 (Fam), [2012] 2 FLR 414, FD   26.5
Kremen v Agrest [2012] EWHC 45 (Fam), [2012] 2 FLR 414, FD   18.18.5

Langley v Appleby (Inspector of Taxes) [1976] 3 All ER 391   10.10.4
Letterstedt v Broers [1884] 9 App Cas 371   14.14, 14.14.2
Lexi Holdings plc v Luqman [2009] EWCA Civ 117   8.6.4, 8.6.5, 8.11
Lifecare International plc, Re [1990] BCLC 222   12.9.2
Lilleyman v Lilleyman [2012] EWHC 821 (Ch), [2013] 1 FLR 47, ChD   18.13.5, 19.18.1,
                                    19.19, 19.19.1, 19.19.2, 19.19.3, 19.19.4, 19.19.5
Little Olympian Each-Ways Ltd (No 3), Re [1995] 1 BCLC 636, ChD   21.6.8
Lloyd v Casey [2002] 1 BCLC 454   8.8.3
Lloyds TSB as personal representatives of R Antrobus Deceased v CIR (2002) STC (SCD)
   468   16.4
Lo-Line Electric Motors Ltd and Others, Re [1988] Ch 477, [1988] 3 WLR 26, [1998]
   BCLC 698, [1988] 2 All ER 692, ChD   8.5.4
Loch v John Blackwood Ltd [1924] AC 783, 93 LJPC 257, [1924] All ER Rep 200, PC   20.4,
                                                                  21.6.9, 21.6.11, 22.14, 22.15.3
London School of Electronics Ltd, Re [1986] Ch 211, [1985] 3 WLR 474, [1985] BCLC
   273   12.9.3, 20.4, 21.1.11, 21.6.6, 21.6.13
Londonderry's Settlement, Re [1964] 3 All ER 855   14.19.3
Luckwell v Limata [2014] EWHC 502 (Fam)   18.18.2

Macdonald v Frost [2009] EWHC 2276 (Ch)   19.15
MacDougal v Gardiner (1875) 1 Ch 13   23.6.4
Macro (Ipswich) Ltd & another, Re [1994] BCC 781   20.9.1, 21.3.9
Mann Aviation Group (Engineering) Ltd (In Administration) v Longmint Aviation Ltd
   [2011] EWHC 2238 (Ch)   10.7
Marini Ltd, Re [2003] EWHC 334 (Ch)   8.5.3
McAlpine Limited (Sir Robert) v Alfred McAlpine plc [2004] EWHC 630 (Ch)   9.4.1
McCall and Keenan (as personal representatives of McClean Dec'd) v HMRC (2009) STC
   990   16.3
McCarthy Surfacing Ltd, Re [2008] EWHC 2279 (Ch), [2009] 1 BCLC 622, [2009] BCC
   464   20.6.7, 21.6.3, 21.6.4, 24.6.3
Mea Copr Ltd, Re [2007] BCC 288   8.6.2
Mercury Communications Limited v Mercury Interactive (UK) Limited [1995] FSR 850   9.4.2
Meyer v Scottish Co-operative Wholesale Society (1957) SC 381   21.1.3, 21.3.5, 22.16.1
Midland Bank Trust Co v Hett Stubbs & Kemp [1979] Ch 384   26.4.2
Midland Bank v Wyatt [1995] 1 FLR 696   14.16
Milgate Developments Ltd, Re [1993] BCLC 291   24.9.3

Millen v Karen Millen Fashions Limited and Mosaic Fashions US Limited [2016] EWHC 2104 (Ch)	9.6
Miller v Miller; McFarlane v McFarlane [2006] UKHL 24, [2006] 2 AC 618, [2006] 2 WLR 1283, [2006] 1 FLR 1186, [2006] 3 All ER 1, HL	18.8, 18.12, 18.13, 19.19.2
Mosely v Koffyfontein Mines Ltd (No 1) [1904] 2 Ch 108, 73 LJ Ch 569, 53 WR 140, CA	23.7.3
Mumtaz Properties Ltd, Re [2011] EWCA Civ 610	8.6.2
Myers v Myers [2004] EWHC 1944 (Fam), (unreported) 3 August 2004, FD	19.18.5
N v F (Financial Orders: Pre-Acquired Wealth [2011] EWHC 586 (Fam)	18.13.6, 18.13.8
N v N (Financial Provision: Sale of a Company) [2001] 2 FLR 69	18.9
NA v MA [2006] EWHC 2900 (Fam), [2007] 1 FLR 1760, FD	18.9, 18.18.6
Neptune Vehicle Washing Equipment) Ltd v Fitzgerald [1995] 1 BCLC 352	8.7.7
Ng Eng Hiam v Ng Kee Wei [1964] 31 MLJ	22.11
Nicholls v Registrar of Trade Marks [2005] RPC 12	9.3.1
Nisbet v Shepherd [1994] BCLC 300	12.13.3
Nordenfelt v Maxim Nordenfelt Guns and Ammunition Co Ltd [1894] AC 635	9.5, 12.16
Norris v Checksfield [1989] 1 WLR 1241	10.10.4
Norton Tool v Tewson [1972] ICT 501	5.8.6
Nuneaton Borough AFC Ltd ex parte Shooter and Broadhurst [1990] BCLC 384	24.3.2
Nurcombe v Nurcombe [1985] 1 WLR 370	20.8.2
O'Neill v Phillips [1999] 1 WLR 1092, [1999] 2 BCLC 1, [1999] BCC 600, HL reversing [1997] 2 BCLC 739, CA	20.2.1, 20.4, 20.4.6, 20.4.9, 20.5, 20.6.8, 20.6.9, 20.7.2, 21.1.2, 21.1.3, 21.1.10, 21.2.1, 21.2.2, 21.2.3, 21.2.4, 21.2.6, 21.3.2, 21.3.6, 21.4.4, 21.4.7, 24.5.1, 24.5.3, 24.8.2, 24.8.4, 24.8.5, 24.8.7
Oak Investment Partners XII Ltd Partnership v Broughtwood [2010] EWCA Civ 23	24.3.3
P v P (Financial Relief: Illiquid Assests) [2004] EWHC 2277 (Fam), [2005] 1 FLR 548, [2005] Fam Law 207	18.7, 18.10
P v P (Inherited Property) [2004] EWHC 1364 (Fam)	18.9, 18.13.7
P v P [2015] EWCA Civ 447	14.9.4
Palvides v Jensen [1956] Ch 565, [1956] 2 All ER 518, [1956] 3 WLR 224	20.9.2, 23.4.1, 23.8.3
Papier v (1) Formara Print Ltd (2) Phoenix Offset Ltd (3) Steven Ball (Case 3202018/2003) (unreported) 27 August 2004	5.8.2, 5.19.1, 6.9.1
Park House Properties Ltd, Re [1998] BCC 847	1.5.1, 6.2.1, 8.5.4, 8.6.5, 8.6.7, 8.7.2, 8.7.8, 8.11, 17.7.2
Parker-Knoll Limited v Knoll International Limited [1962] RPC 265	9.4.1
Pearce, Re [1998] 2 FLR 705	19.18.5
Pelling v Families Need Fathers Ltd [2001] EWCA Civ 1280	20.8.1
Petrodell Resources Ltd v Prest [2013] UKSC 34	18.14
Pettitt v Pettitt [1970] AC 777, [1969] 2 WLR 966, (1969) FLR Rep 555, [1969] 2 All ER 385, HL	10.13.4
Peverill Gold Mines Ltd, Re [1989] 1 Ch 122	20.7.3
Phillips and Others (Phillips' Executors) v HMRC (2006) STC SCD 639	16.2.3
Plimmer v Wellington Corporation (1883–84) LR 9 App Cas 699	19.11.1
Polkey v AE Dayton Services Ltd [1987] IRLR 503, HL	5.8.5
Polly Peck International plc (No 2), Re [1994] 1 BCLC 574	8.6.5
Popely v Planarrive Ltd [1997] 1 BCLC 8, (1996) *The Times*, 28 March, ChD	11.11.1
Prudential Assurance v Newman Industries (No 2) [1982] Ch 204, [1982] 2 WLR 31, [1982] 1 All ER 354, CA	23.4.2
Purves (Inspector of Taxes) v Harrison (2001) STC 267	16.10.5, 16.10.12
Quin and Axtens Ltd v Salmon [1909] AC 442 HL	23.7.2
R A Noble & Sons (Clothing) Ltd [1983] BCLC 273	21.1.3, 21.1.6
R v CIR, ex p Newfields Developments Ltd (2001) STC 901	4.3.4
R v R [2005] 2 FLR 365	18.10
Rahman v Malik (Gate of India (Tynemouth) Ltd) [2008] EWHC 959 (Ch), [2008] 2 BCLC 403, [2008] All ER (D) 392 (Feb)	20.2.1, 20.4, 20.4.6, 20.4.9, 20.5, 20.6.2,

Rahman v Malik (Gate of India (Tynemouth) Ltd) [2008] EWHC 959 (Ch), [2008] 2 BCLC 403, [2008] All ER (D) 392 (Feb)—*continued*
        20.6.4, 20.6.8, 20.6.9, 20.7.2, 21.1.2, 21.1.3, 21.1.10, 21.1.11, 21.2.1, 21.2.2, 21.2.3, 21.2.4, 21.2.6, 21.3.2, 21.3.6, 21.4.4, 21.4.7, 21.4.8, 21.6.2, 21.6.4, 21.6.9, 22.5.2, 24.5.1, 24.5.3, 24.6.3, 24.8.2, 24.8.4, 24.8.5, 24.8.7, 25.9.6

Ramsay v Inland Revenue Commissioners [1982] AC 300   14.16
RDF Media Group plc v Clements [2007] EWHC 2892 (QB)   9.5, 12.16
Ready Mix Concrete (South East) Limited v the Minister of Pensions and National Insurance [1968] 2 QB 497, [1968] 2 WLR 775, [1968] 1 All ER 433   5.11.1
Reckitt & Colman Products Limited v Borden Inc. [1990] RPC 341   9.3.2
Reed Executive plc v Reed Business Information Limited [2004] EWCA Civ 159   9.4.1, 9.4.3
Regal Hastings v Gulliver [1967] 2 AC 134   8.4.3
Revenue and Customs Commissioners v Holland [2010] UKSC 51   8.2.4
Rica Gold Washing Co, Re [1879] 11 ChD 36   21.6.1, 22.15.4
Ringtower Holdings plc [1989] 5 BCC 82   24.3.2
Robertson v RM Supplies (Inverkeithing) Ltd [2009] CSOH 23   20.9.1, 24.3.2, 24.5.4, 24.6.3
Robertson v Robertson [2016] EWHC 613 (Fam)   18.11, 18.13.8
Robson v Robson [2010] EWCA Civ 1171   18.13.7
Rossi v Rossi [2006] EWHC 1482 (Fam), [2007] 1 FLR 790, FD   18.13.6
Royal Brunei Airlines Snd Bhd v Tan [1995] 2 AC 378   8.5.3
RW Peak (King's Lynn) Ltd [1998] BCC 596   8.4.5

S v S [2014] EWHC 4732 (Fam)   18.13.8
SA v PA [2014] EWHC 392 (Eam)   18.18.5
Schmidt v Rosewood Trust Ltd [2003] UKPC 26   14.19.3
Schofield v Schofield and others [2011] EWCA Civ 154   8.4.5
Secretary of State for Trade and Industry v Van Hengel and Another [1995] BCC 173   8.8.7, 21.6.3
Seldon v Clarkson Wright and Jakes [2012] UKEAT 0434   5.6
Sevenoaks Stationers (Retail) Ltd, Re [1991] Ch 164, [1990] 3 WLR 1165, [1991] 3 All ER 578, [1991] BCLC 325, CA   8.5.4
Shah v Shah [2010] EWHC 313 (Ch)   20.4.4, 20.6.2, 21.1.11, 21.4.6, 22.5.1, 24.5.2
Shaw v Shaw SLT (Notes 94)   13.4.8
Shield v Shield [2014] EWHC 23 (Fam)   18.17
Shirt v Shirt [2010] EWHC 3820 (Ch)   19.7.3, 19.15, 19.15.1, 19.15.2, 19.16, 19.16.1
Shuttleworth v Cox Brothers & Co (Maidenhead) Ltd [1927] 2 KB 9, 96 LJKB 104, 136 LT 337, CA   21.6.14
Sidebottom v Kershaw Leese and Co Ltd [1920] 1 Ch 154   21.6.14
Sikorski v Sikorski [2012] EWHC 1613 (Ch)   24.7.1
Simmons Box (Diamonds) Ltd, Re; Cohen v Selby [2002] BCC 82, [2001] 1 BCLC 176, CA   8.5.2, 8.5.3, 8.5.4, 8.6.6, 8.6.7, 8.11
Simpsons Motor Sales London Ltd v Hendon Corporation [1964] AC 1088   20.6
Singh (Sukhpaul) v Singh (Satpaul), Singh Brothers Contractors (North West) Limited [2013] EWHC 2138 (Ch)   24.9.3
Singh v Singh [1971] P 226, [1971] 2 WLR 963, [1971] 2 All ER 828, CA   2.11.3, 20.8.2, 23.4.2, 23.5.1, 23.5.4
SK v TK [2013] EWHC 834 (Fam)   18.10
Smith v Croft [1986] 1 WLR 580, [1986] 2 All ER 551, (1986) 130 SJ 314   21.6.3
Soloman v A Soloman & Co [1897] AC 22   18.14
Sorrell v Sorrell [2005] EWHC 1717 (Fam), [2006] 1 FLR 497, FD   18.11, 18.13.3
Stedman's Executors v IRC (2002) STI issue 33   16.2.3
Strachan v Wilcock [2006] EWCA Civ 13   24.5.2, 24.5.3, 24.5.4
Street v Mountford [1985] AC 809, [1985] 2 WLR 877, [1985] 2 All ER 289, HL   10.7
Suggitt v Suggitt [2012] EWCA Civ 1140   19.11.2
Sunrise Radio Limited, Re; Kohli v Lit and others [2009] EWHC 2893 (Ch), [2010] 1 BCLC 367   11.20.2, 20.2.4, 20.6.9, 21.6.13, 22.16.1, 24.5.4, 24.8.3
Sussex Brick Co Ltd, Re [1961] Ch 289   12.9.2
Swain Mason v Mills & Reeve [2012] EWCA Civ 498, [2012] STC 1760   26.4.2
Swaledale Cleaners Ltd, Re [1968] 3 All ER 619   11.11.1
Sykes (Butchers) Ltd, Re [1998] 1 BCLC 110   8.2.7
Symington v Symington Quarries Ltd [1905] 8 F 121   11.11.3, 20.6.8, 22.9, 22.11, 22.12, 22.14

Systems Reliability Plc v Smith [1990] IRLR 377   12.16

Tett v Phoenix Property and Investment Co Ltd [1986] BCLC 149, 1986 PCC 210, (1985)
    129 SJ 869, CA; [1984] BCLC 599, ChD   11.16.4
Theakston v London Trust plc [1984] BCLC 390, ChD   11.11.2
Thomas and Agnes Carvel Foundation v Carvel [2007] EWHC 1314 (Ch), [2008] Ch 395,
    ChD   14.14.2, 14.14.3
Thorner v Major [2009] UKHL 18, [2009] 1 WLR 776, [2009] 2 FLR 405, [2009] 3 All
    ER 945, HL   13.5.10, 19.4.3, 19.6, 19.7.1, 19.7.2, 19.7.3, 19.8, 19.9, 19.11.1, 19.13,
    19.14, 19.15, 19.16, 19.18.3
TL v ML (Ancillary Relief: Claim against Assets of Extended Family) [2005] EWHC 2860
    (Fam)   18.17
Tobian Properties Ltd & Maidment v Attwood, Re [2013] BCC 98   8.8.3
Tower Hamlets London Borough Council v Sherwood [2002] EWCA Civ 229   10.7
Turquand v Marshall [1869] 4 Ch App 376   8.6.1

Unisoft Group Ltd (No 2), Re [1994] BCC 766, [1994] 1 BCLC 609, ChD   21.1.5

V v V (Financial Relief) [2005] 2 FLR 697   18.10
Vento v Chief Constable of West Yorkshire Police (No 2) [2003] IRLR 102   5.8.6
Vestey's Case [1979] WLR 915   14.12.3
Vinton v Fladgate Fielder [2010] EWHC 904 (Ch), [2010] STC 1868   26.4.2, 26.9
Virdi v Abbey Leisure Ltd [1990] BCC 60   20.7.1, 22.16.1, 22.17

Wallersteiner v Moir (No 2) [1975] QB 373, [1975] 2 WLR 389, [1975] 1 All ER 849,
    CA   24.9.3
Ward v Warnke [1990] 22 HLR 496   10.7, 10.12
Weller (Sam) and Sons [1990] Ch 682, [1989] 5 BCC 810   8.1.2, 8.9.3, 20.9.1, 21.1.3,
    21.1.6, 21.1.9, 21.6.4
Wells v Wells [2002] EWCA Civ 476, [2002] 2 FLR 97   18.10
West v Blatchet [2000] 1 BCLC 795   24.8.3
Westdeutsche Landesbank v Islington [1996] AC 669   14.22.4
Westmid Packing Services Ltd, Re [1998] 2 All ER 124, [1998] BCC 836   8.5.4, 8.6.3, 8.6.5
WF v HF [2012] EWHC 438 (Fam)   18.10
White (Dennis), Decd, Re; White v Minnis and Another [2000] 3 WLR 885, CA   13.4.6,
    13.4.9
White v White [2001] 1 AC 596, [2000] 3 WLR 1571, [2000] 2 FLR 981, [2001] 1 All
    ER 1, HL   18.3, 18.8, 18.12, 19.19.2
Willow Oak Developments Ltd v Silverwood [2006] IRLR 607   5.8.3
Wright, Layman & Umney v Wright (1946) RPC 149   9.4.1
WW v HW [2015] EWHC 1844 (Fam)   18.18.2, 18.18.5
Wyatt v Frank Wyatt & Son Ltd [2003] EWHC 520 (Ch)   21.6.11, 24.8.3, 24.8.6

Y v Y [2014] EWHC 1844 (Fam)   18.18.5
Yenidje Tobacco Co Ltd, Re [1916] 2 Ch 426, [1916–17] All ER Rep 1050   22.10
Young v Pearce (1996) STC 743   4.6

Zivnovstenska Banka National Corporation v Frankman [1950] AC 57, [1949] 2 All ER
    671, HL   18.13.6

TABLE OF STATUTES

References are to paragraph numbers.

Administration of Justice Act 1985	
s 50	14.14
Agricultural Tenancies Act 1995	16.4
Capital Allowances Act 2001	
s 33A	16.10.9
s 266	4.3.1, 4.4
s 267	4.3.1, 4.4
Children Act 1989	
Sch 1	18.1
Civil Partnership Act 2004	18.1
Companies Act 1948	
s 184	11.9
s 210	20.4.1, 21.1.3, 21.3.5, 22.16.1, 24.7.1
Companies Act 1980	21.1.3
s 75	22.16.1
Companies Act 2006	8.2.5, 8.7.15, 11.2.4, 16.11.4, 17.19.4, 20.4.9, 21.2.5
s 17	17.18.2
s 20	17.18.2
s 21	11.3, 17.18.2
s 22	21.6.14
ss 22–24	17.18.2
s 25	21.6.14
s 26	17.18.2
s 29	17.18.4
s 30	17.18.4
s 33(1)	17.18.2
s 78	11.3
s 84	11.3
s 94	20.8.1
s 116	20.8.1
s 117	20.8.1
s 117(3)	20.8.1
s 125	12.13.2, 12.13.4
s 125(2)	24.8.1
s 127	12.13.4
s 128	12.13.2, 12.13.4
s 162	8.1.1
s 168	11.1, 11.3, 11.9, 17.19.5, 20.4.1
s 168(1)	17.19.5
s 169(3)	11.2.6
ss 170–179	8.1
s 170((5)	8.2.4
s 170(1)	8.4.1
s 170(3)	8.3.1
s 170(4)	8.3.1
s 171	8.3.2

Companies Act 2006—*continued*	
s 172	2.12.6, 8.1.2, 8.1.3, 8.3.3, 8.3.4, 8.4.4, 8.7.6, 8.8.5, 8.9, 8.9.1, 8.9.3, 8.9.4, 8.9.5, 23.4.2, 23.5.2
s 172(1)	8.3.3, 8.9.1
s 172(1)(a)	8.9.3
s 172(1)(b)	21.5.1
s 172(1)(f)	8.9.2
s 172(10)(f)	21.6.11
s 173	8.3.4
s 173(1)	8.3.4
s 173(2)	8.3.4
s 173(2)(a)	8.3.4
s 173(2)(b)	8.3.4
s 174	8.3.5, 8.5.2, 8.5.3, 8.6.1, 8.6.3, 8.10.3, 20.9.2, 23.4.1
s 174(2)	8.3.5, 8.6.3
s 174(2)(a)	8.6.3
s 175	8.3.6, 8.3.7, 8.7.3, 8.8.1
s 175(1)	8.3.6
s 175(2)	8.3.6, 8.7.1, 8.7.12
s 175(3)	8.3.6, 8.7.3, 8.8.1
s 175(4)(a)	8.3.6, 8.7.13
s 175(4)(b)	8.7.4
s 175(5)(a)	8.3.6, 8.7.4
s 175(6)	8.3.6, 8.7.4
s 176	8.3.7
s 176(4)	8.3.7
s 177	8.3.6, 8.3.8, 8.7.3, 8.7.5, 8.8.1, 8.8.2
s 178	8.5.2
s 178(2)	8.5.2
s 179	8.7.6
s 180	8.3.6
s 182	8.3.8, 8.7.5
s 183	8.3.8
s 186	8.7.7
s 188	8.7.15, 8.8.2
ss 188–189	8.8.1
s 188(1)	8.7.15
s 189	8.7.15
s 190	8.4.1, 8.4.5, 8.7.15
ss 190–196	8.7.15
s 191	8.7.15
s 195(2)	8.7.15
s 196	8.7.15
s 197	8.7.15
ss 197–214	8.7.15
s 204	8.7.15
s 206	8.7.15
s 207(1)	8.7.15

Companies Act 2006—*continued*

s 214	8.7.15, 8.10.1
s 215	8.7.15
ss 215–222	8.7.15
s 217	8.7.15, 8.8.2
s 218	8.7.15
s 219	8.7.15
s 220(1)(c)	8.7.15
s 222(1)(a)	8.7.15
s 222(1)(b)	8.7.15
s 223(2)	8.7.15
s 223(3)	8.7.15
ss 227–230	8.8.1
s 231	8.7.7
s 231(3)	8.7.7
s 232	24.9.3
s 233	24.9.3
s 234(1)	24.9.3
s 239	8.4.4
s 239(1)	8.4.4
s 239(2)	8.4.4
s 239(3)	8.4.4
s 239(4)	8.4.4
s 239(6)(a)	8.4.4
s 239(6)(b)	8.4.4
s 239(7)	8.4.4, 23.4.2
s 250	8.2.1, 8.2.7
s 251(1)	8.2.4
s 252	8.4.4, 11.4
s 253	1.3.2, 1.3.4, 1.3.6, 8.4.4, 8.8.2, 11.4
s 253(2)	1.3.2
s 254	8.8.2
s 255	11.4
s 260	8.9.5, 20.2.3, 20.8.2, 20.9.2, 21.7, 22.16.2, 23.1, 23.4.3, 23.6.5, 23.8.1, 23.8.2, 23.8.3, 23.9, 24.1
ss 260–264	23.4.1
s 260(2)	23.4.1
s 260(3)	23.8.3
s 261	20.8.2, 23.4.2
s 261(2)	23.4.2
s 262	23.4.2
s 263(2)	23.4.2, 23.5.3
s 263(2)(a)	23.4.2
s 263(2)(b)	23.4.2
s 263(2)(c)(i)	23.4.2
s 263(2)(c)(ii)	23.4.2
s 263(3)	23.4.2, 23.5.3
s 263(3)(a)	20.8.2, 23.4.2
s 263(3)(b)	23.4.2, 23.5.2
s 263(3)(c)	23.4.2
s 263(3)(d)	23.4.2
s 263(3)(e)	23.4.2
s 263(3)(f)	21.7, 23.4.2, 24.1
s 263(4)	23.4.2, 23.5.6
ss 265–269	23.4.1
s 282	11.3
s 283	11.3
s 292	11.3
s 293(3)	8.4.4
s 293(4)	8.4.4
s 303	11.3

Companies Act 2006—*continued*

s 307	11.3
s 314	11.3, 20.8.1
s 317	20.8.1
s 319	8.4.5
s 321	11.3
s 423	11.2.5, 17.15.8
s 459	20.4.6
s 476	11.3
s 488	11.3
s 563	12.13.2
s 568	12.13.2
s 569	11.3
ss 690–700	12.13.1
ss 690–708	11.17.5, 11.18.2, 11.18.5
s 690(1)	12.13.1
s 690(1)(b)	11.18.2
s 691(1)	11.18.2
s 691(2)	11.17.5, 11.18.2, 11.18.4, 12.13.1
s 692	11.18.2
s 692(2)(1)(a)	11.18.3
s 692(2)(1)(b)	11.18.3
s 692(2)(a)(i)	11.18.3, 12.13.1
s 693A	11.18.2
s 694	8.4.5, 11.3, 11.18.2
s 695	11.18.5, 12.13.1
s 696(2)(a)	11.18.5, 12.13.1
s 696(2)(b)	12.13.1
s 696(2)(b)(i)	11.18.5
s 696(5)	12.13.4
s 707	8.5.1
s 707(7)	11.18.5, 12.13.1
ss 709–723	11.18.3
ss 711–177	8.3.1
s 719(2)(b)	11.18.3
s 899	12.13.4
s 974	12.9.2
ss 974–991	12.9.2, 17.21
s 975(2)	12.9.2
s 979	11.3
s 980(2)	12.9.2
s 982	12.9.2
s 983	12.9.2, 17.21
ss 983–985	17.21
s 984	12.9.2
s 986	12.9.2
s 986(5)	12.9.2
s 994	8.1.1, 8.7.5, 11.2.8, 11.17.5, 12.9.3, 20.2.1, 20.5, 20.6.9, 21.1.9, 21.1.10, 21.1.11, 21.3.2, 21.3.5, 21.4.2, 21.4.5, 21.5.1, 21.5.2, 21.7, 22.4, 22.9, 22.16.1, 23.5.5, 23.8.1, 23.8.3, 24.1, 24.8.1, 25.6
s 994(1)	21.1.2
s 994(2)	21.1.7
s 996	20.2.1, 21.1.3, 21.3.2, 22.1, 22.16.1, 23.8.3, 24.1, 24.2.1, 24.3.1, 24.4, 24.7, 25.9.12
s 996(1)	24.2.1
s 996(2)	24.2.2
s 996(2)(a)	20.7.3, 24.7.1
s 996(2)(b)	24.7.2

Companies Act 2006—*continued*		Income Tax Act 2007—*continued*	
s 996(2)(c)	23.4.2, 24.7.3	s 836	4.6
s 996(2)(d)	24.7.4	Income Tax (Earnings and Pensions)	
s 996(2)(e)	20.6.8, 21.7, 24.1, 24.3.4	Act 2003	
s 1157	8.5.3, 8.6.6, 8.7.6, 8.10.8	s 206	16.10.10
s 1157(1)	8.5.3	s 431	4.12.10, 4.12.12
s 1159	16.2	Income Tax (Trading and Other	
Sch 6	16.2	Income) Act 2005	
Company Directors Disqualification		s 620	4.6
Act 1986		ss 620–628	4.6
s 7(2A)	8.5.4	s 629	4.6
s 8(2A)	8.5.4	s 648	4.6
Corporation Tax Act 2010		Inheritance (Provision for Family and	
s 18	4.3.4	Dependents) Act 1975	18.1,
s 27	4.3.6	19.17, 19.18.4, 19.18.5, 19.18.6,	
s 439	4.3.4		19.19.2, 19.20
s 448	4.3.4	s 1	19.18
s 450	4.3.4	s 1(1)(e)	19.18.3
s 451	4.3.4	s 1(2)	19.18
s 455	4.3.5, 4.12.4, 16.10.10	s 2	19.18
s 748	16.11.4	s 3	19.18.1, 19.18.2, 19.19.3, 19.19.4
ss 1033–1048	16.9.2	s 3(1)	19.19
s 1042	16.9.5	s 3(1)(c)	19.18.3
s 1044	16.9.6	s 3(1)(d)	19.19.4
s 1064	4.3.4	s 3(1)(e)	19.18.3
s 1065	4.3.4	s 3(1)(g)	19.18.3
		s 3(2)	19.19
Employment Rights Act 1996		s 3(2A)	19.19
s 1	5.10, 5.12.1	Inheritance Tax Act 1984	
s 4	5.12.1	s 3(3)	16.10.14
s 23(4A)	5.14.4	s 15	4.6
s 23(4B)	5.14.4	s 103(1)	16.2
s 98	5.16.6, 5.17.3	s 103(2)	16.2
s 98(1)	5.8.1, 5.8.3, 5.8.4	s 104	16.2
s 98(2)	5.8.1, 5.8.3	s 105(3)	16.2.3
s 98(2)(a)	5.17.3	s 105(4)	16.2.3
s 98(3)	5.17.3	s 111	16.10.13
s 98(4)	5.8.1, 5.8.4	s 111(b)	16.2.3
s 118	5.8.6	s 112	16.3
s 123	5.8.6	s 161	16.10.2
s 139	5.8.3	s 269	16.10.2
s 227	5.8.6	Insolvency Act 1986	
s 230	5.11.1, 5.11.2	s 84(1)(b)	22.1
Equality Act 2010	5.9.4, 5.9.5, 5.9.6,	s 110	4.9.1
	6.9.1	s 122(1(g)	12.9.3
s 4	5.9, 6.9	s 122(1)	22.2.1
s 13(1)	5.9.1	s 122(1)(g)	20.2.2, 21.1.3, 21.7,
s 15(1)	5.9.7		22.2.1, 22.4, 22.17, 24.1
s 26	5.9.3	s 122(2)	22.3
		s 122(2)(a)	22.2.1
Family Law (Scotland) Act 1985		s 122(10(g)	24.8.1
s 10	18.12	s 125(2)	21.7, 22.2.1, 22.16, 24.1
Finance Act 2013	4.3.1, 4.12.12	s 125(2)(a)	22.16.1
		s 125(2)(b)	22.16.1
		s 212	8.6.6, 8.10.4, 8.10.5, 8.10.8
Housing Act 1988	10.10.2, 10.10.3	s 214	8.10.3, 8.10.8, 21.6.3
s 20	10.10.3	s 214(2)(b)	8.10.3
Housing Act 1996	10.10.3	s 214(3)	8.10.3
		s 214(4)	8.10.3
		s 238	8.10.5
Income Tax Act 2007		s 238(3)	8.10.5
s 72	4.4	s 238(5)	8.10.5
s 132	4.10.3	s 239	8.6.2, 8.10.6
s 392	4.3.4		

Insolvency Act 1986—*continued*
s 239(5)	8.10.6
s 239(6)	8.10.6
s 240	8.10.6
s 240)1)(a)	8.10.5

Land Registration Act 2002
s 33(a)(i)	10.13.7
s 42(1)(b)	10.13.7
s 44(1)	10.13.7

Landlord and Tenant Act 1954   10.8.1
s 38A	10.7, 10.8.2

Landlord and Tenant Act 1985
s 11	10.10.5

Law of Property Act 1925
s 2	10.13.7
s 27	10.13.7
s 34	10.13.5
s 34(2)	10.13.3

Limitation Act 1980
s 21(1)(b)	8.7.10

Matrimonial Causes Act 1973   18.1
s 23	18.8
s 24	18.8, 18.14, 18.15, 18.19.1, 18.19.2
s 24(1)(c)	14.9.4, 18.19.1
s 25	18.8, 18.12, 18.13.8, 18.17, 18.19.2
s 25(1)	18.8
s 25(1)(b)	18.16
s 25(2)	18.8
s 25(2)(c)	18.13.1
s 25(2)(d)	18.13.6
s 25A	18.10
s 34	18.19.1

National Minimum Wage Act 1998   5.14

Partnership Act 1890   13.4.2, 13.5.1, 26.11.6
s 1	4.2.2, 13.4.1, 26.11.6
s 24	13.4.5
s 26	13.5.10
s 26(1)	13.4.3
s 32(c)	13.4.3

Protection from Eviction Act 1977
s 5(1)(b)	10.10.5

Rent Act 1977   10.10.1

Settled Land Act 1925
s 64	14.21.7

Stamp Act 1891
s 17	12.13.3

Taxation of Chargeable Gains Act 1992
s 24(2)	4.10.3
ss 126–136	16.2.9
s 127	11.19.2, 16.11.4, 16.11.5
s 132	4.10.3
s 138	16.11.4
s 155	16.10.6
s 162	4.3.1, 4.4
s 165	4.3.1, 4.4, 4.5.3, 4.12.10, 16.6, 16.6.1, 16.6.2, 16.6.3, 16.6.4, 16.7.4, 16.7.5, 16.10.14, 16.11.2, 16.11.3
s 165A	16.7.5
s 168	16.6.4
s 253(3)	4.10.3
s 253(4)	4.10.3
s 260	16.6, 16.6.3, 16.6.4, 16.10.14, 16.11.3
s 272	4.12.12
s 273	4.12.12
Sch 5B	16.10.7

Trade Marks Act 1994
s 1(1)	9.3.1
s 3(1)(b)	9.3.1
s 3(1)(c)	9.3.1
s 3(1)(d)	9.3.1
s 10	9.4.2
s 11(2)	9.4.2
s 21	9.4.2

Trustee Act 1925   14.21.1
s 34(3)	10.13.3
s 41	14.14
s 57	14.21.7

Trustee Act 2000
s 1	14.11

Trustees of Land and Appointment of Trustees Act 1996
s 6(1)	10.13.5
s 14	10.13.6, 10.14
s 15	10.13.6, 10.14

Variation of Trusts Act 1958   14.21.7

TABLE OF STATUTORY INSTRUMENTS

References are to paragraph numbers.

Civil Procedure Rules 1998,
SI 1998/3132
r 1.1(2)(c)(i)	24.9.2
Pt 8	19.18.6
r 19.9E	24.9.3
Pt 36	24.9.2
Pt 57	19.18.6

Companies (Model Articles) Regulations 2008, SI 2008/3229
	8.3.2, 8.8.2, 17.18.2, 17.19.4
Sch 1, Art 17(1)	17.19.5
Sch 1, Art 19	21.6.3
Sch 1, Art 19(2)(a)	8.8.1
Sch 1, Art 20	17.19.6
Sch 1, Art 26(5)	11.11.1
Sch 1, Art 42	11.2.4
Sch 1, Art 63(5)	26.11.2

Companies (Unfair Prejudice Applications) Proceedings Rules 2009, SI 2009/2469   24.9.3

Family Proceedings Rules 2010, SI 2010/2955
r 9.26B(1)	18.17

Limited Liability Partnerships (Application of Companies Act 2006) Regulations 2009 (SI 2009/1804)   21.1.2

Limited Liability Partnerships (Application of Companies Act 2006) Regulations, SI 2009/1804
reg 48	20.7.3

National Minimum Wage Regulations 2015, SI 2015/621   5.14

Regulatory Reform (Business Tenancies) (England and Wales) Order 2003, SI 2003/3096
Sch 2	10.7, 10.8.2

Working Time Regulations 1998, SI 1998/1833   5.8.1, 5.13, 5.15

TABLE OF ABBREVIATIONS

ADR	alternative dispute resolution
APR	agricultural property relief
BPR	business property relief
CA	Companies Act 2006
CAA 2001	Capital Allowances Act 2001
CDDA 1986	Company Directors Disqualification Act 1986
CGT	capital gains tax
CPR	Civil Procedure Rules
CSOP	company share option plan
CTA 2010	Corporation Tax Act 2010
EA 2010	Equality Act 2010
EHRC	Equality and Human Rights Commission
EMI	enterprise management scheme
ER	entrepreneur's relief
ERA 1996	Employment Rights Act 1996
ESOT	employee share ownership trust
FFI	Family Firm Institute
FIM	family involvement in management
FIO	family involvement in ownership
FPR	Family Procedure Rules
IA	Insolvency Act 1986
IFB	Institute of Family Business
IHT	inheritance tax
IHTA 1984	Inheritance Tax Act 1984
IOD	Institute of Directors
I(PFD)A 1975	Inheritance (Provision for Family and Dependents) Act 1975
ITA 2007	Income Tax Act 2007
ITEPA 2003	Income Tax (Earnings and Pensions) Act 2003
ITTOIA 2005	Income Tax (Trading and Other Income) Act 2005
KPI	key performance indicator
LLP	limited liability partnership
MCA	Matrimonial Causes Act 1973
MCFO	multi-client family office
MFO	multi-family office
NMW	national minimum wage
NMWA	National Minimum Wage Act 1998

PA 1890	Partnership Act 1890
SAYE	save as you earn
SFO	single family office
SIP	share incentive plan
SRA	Solicitors Regulation Authority
TCGA 1992	Taxation of Chargeable Gains Act 1992
TLATA	Trustees of Land and Appointment of Trustees Act 1996
USP	unique selling point
WTR 1998	Working Time Regulations 1998, SI 1998/1833

INTRODUCTION

Why this book?

The family business is the oldest and most common form of economic organisation on the planet. A selection of the evidence supporting this claim is contained in chapter 1 (Introducing the Family Owned Business).

Even so neither the management and behavioral professions nor the academic world had, until recently, paid much attention to family businesses as a distinct category. This has changed significantly over the last thirty years or so. During this period a whole raft of writing, theorising and thinking has taken place about family business issues. Various organisations have been formed to help family owned businesses and their advisors access this body of new knowledge. Most significantly a new breed of professional, family business consultants, has evolved and have developed new approaches and methods based on this thinking to help business-owning families with the particular challenges they face.

But awareness of this new family business movement amongst the traditional financial professions, including law, accountancy, banking and financial advisors, is, at best, fairly patchy.

Although the traditional professions have been dealing with family businesses, in some cases for millennia, they have been slow to recognise family owned businesses as a separate category from other non-family businesses. To illustrate the point feel free to try this simple test. Pick a professional textbook at random, turn to the index and look for 'family business' or similar terms. Of the sample we have tried we have yet to make a hit.

Of course it is possible to reverse engineer the process. With experience and knowledge of where family business issues are likely to be encountered, the technical professional will be able to unearth relevant content: for example a tax accountant may open the index of a tax manual to look under close companies for relevant legislation and commentary to advise a smaller family company. So the technical issues relevant to the business owning family can be found within the vast sea of knowledge available to the financial advisor. But this is likely to be in general terms rather than specific to particular family business situations. It is even less likely that works covering general technical advisory issues will take any account of the thinking generated by the family business movement.

A further challenge faced by technical advisory professionals is increased specialisation, not only between but also, within professions. But one of the key messages in family business thinking is that the advice needed to support a family business client undertaking a complex process, such as succession, cannot be neatly confined to a single profession such as organisational development, accountancy, or family business consultancy. Such advice most certainly cannot be provided from within individual silos of specialisation, for example the private client or corporate restructuring teams of a law firm.

Working on the basis that family business advisors, individual professions and specialist teams within those separate professions inhabit separate worlds, the hope is that this book can help to provide a bridge, or rather a number of bridges, between those worlds. So that, for example, a lawyer dealing with the early stages of conflict in a family owned company, will find some useful background on family dynamics which has been developed within the family business world, as well as some application of that thinking to the technical legal issues that they are dealing with.

Who is the book for?

In short the book has been written for family business champions. By which we mean anyone with an interest in and involvement with family owned businesses. Certainly family business champions can be found within the ranks of every family business client. They should also be present in any professional organisation with family business clients. That is not a moral judgment or a plea for fellow professionals to share an interest in the complex form of entity that is the family business. It is simply common sense. On the basis that family owned businesses make up a significant proportion of the client base of most professional firms, as will usually be the case, it must be in the commercial interests of those firms to take sensible steps to understand the dynamics and issues facing those family business clients and to consider how the service offering of the professional can be modified to best meet those client needs.

Inevitably a book commissioned by legal publishers, and written by a legally trained lead author, supported by various other lawyers as contributors or collaborators, has been written primarily with a legal audience in mind. But the aim has been to produce something that will also have direct relevance to family business members facing particular issues and challenges within their own family business, such as the introduction of family charters or other family business governance mechanisms and to members of other professions, for example accountants or family business consultants whose own family business clients might be facing a divorce or a family shareholder dispute and who wish to gain an overview of the legal background so as to be able to support their client through that process.

On the basis that readers may potentially come from different worlds, separate glossaries have been included. For ease of reference a list of concepts and terms forming the language of the family business world. Also, for non-lawyers, a glossary of basic legal expressions and terminology used in the book has been added.

The approach taken

The law applicable to family owned businesses is the law. There is clearly a huge amount of law out there. Although much of it has arisen in the context of the family owned business this is almost never categorised or indexed as such. But it is not our intention to restate topics that are well covered elsewhere. Neither is it our intention to comprehensively cover all topics that affect family businesses.

Instead we have attempted to select topics of particular relevance to the family owned business situation and to provide a broad overview of those topics. That overview is intended to help orientate the non-specialist, be they a family business owner, a non-legal professional or a lawyer needing a broad understanding of an area of law that they do not routinely work in. In many cases we have signposted further and general works or reading on the subject matter concerned.

Alongside that overview we have attempted to apply some of the family business theory referred to above to particular legal situations. The hope is that this will be relevant to specialist and non-specialist alike.

Finally, in a number of areas we have delved deeper into technical legal issues, for example in relation to shareholder remedies, to consider a number of legal issues in the context of family business situations. The aim here is to provide a specialist practitioner with an alternative and family business centric perspective of some particular technical legal issues.

Compared with a standard legal text this book cites fewer cases but looks at these in much more detail than would usually be the case. This is for various reasons. First, for the ease of reference of non-lawyer readers who might not have ready access to law reports. Secondly much family business writing and teaching is based on case studies of real life family business situations. By applying an extended treatment to a selected number of legal cases we aim to use these to illustrate various issues of family business dynamics as well as to explain legal principles. It follows that some of the cases have been chosen on the basis that they illustrate issues of family business dynamics and whilst they are relevant to legal issues are by no means leading or landmark cases on the subject concerned. As such the cases cited in the book should be read for their value as much or more as family business stories or case studies rather than as legal precedents.

Of course the information to be obtained from case reports is limited to the facts reported in the transcript or judgment concerned. Examples based on personal practice and information in the public domain relating to well-known family businesses have also been used to supplement the reported legal cases largely relied on for practical real life examples.

Maintaining perspective

The purpose of this book is neither to praise nor to bury the family business as an ownership model. Rather it is to explain it.

Inevitably much of this book (and of course the legal disputes used as case studies) highlights the negative aspects of family business life. It is important to maintain a sense of balance and perspective. The danger is that good aspects of the family business model become obscured by the bad and the downright ugly. Equally there is a danger of over-compensating and swinging too far in the direction of romanticising family firms as paragons of business virtue. Succession, longevity and continued family ownership become prized as goals in their own right, even when the interests of individual family members might be best served by separation from the family business or that of the wider business owning family by an outright sale.

One of the key objectives of the process consulting methodology used by family business consultants and explained in chapter 25, is that the role of the family business advisor is to help their client identify the best course of action for them. This must be done in a way that is free from the pre-conceptions and bias of their advisors.

Succession

The working assumption of anyone picking up a book about family business is that it will be about succession. This book is no exception. The topic of succession is one of two key threads running throughout this book. Whilst the subject of succession forms the express subject matter of only two relatively short chapters, its presence can be felt on almost every page. Every mention of the next generation carries with it the implicit assumption of succession plans.

Although succession is often seen and treated as a generic issue we have separated the specific treatment of the topic into two separate parts, management and ownership succession (dealt with in chapters 7 and 15 respectively). Partly this is to help illustrate that succession is a multi-faceted topic. Partly this is because the issue of management succession fits most logically into Part B dealing with business issues and that of ownership succession into Part C – Ownership

Governance

The second core thread running through this book is governance. In many ways the whole book can be read as an advertisement of the benefits to business owning families of investing in governance process. No apology is made for this.

Whereas the question of succession can be seen as a background presence the treatment of governance (broadly interpreted) is much more explicit. There is a lengthy chapter (chapter 17) dealing with specific family business governance mechanisms.

The very fact that the families featured in the law reports used as case studies points to a catastrophic breakdown of family relationships. The question becomes could that have been avoided, at any stage, by the intervention of some form of governance? Potential interventions, labelled as a **governance application points** or **GAP** are flagged at various points in the book.

It will be seen that in most of those cases the governance application point identified does not involve formal documents or procedures such as family councils or family charters. The 'application' suggested might be much more simple and straightforward, such as detailed thought and discussion on the basic wisdom of families deciding to go into business together, or to admit a family member to ownership. This reflects a very broad working definition (attributed to a leading family business academic John Davies) that family business governance involves 'getting the right people in the right place to discuss the right things at the right time'. It will be seen that this definition goes way beyond formal meetings and paper.

Obviously these governance application points are raised with the benefit of hindsight and based solely on the reports or transcripts of the relevant case. So the points are framed as tentative questions, such as 'was this tried?' or 'would this have made a difference?' rather than absolute and definitive statements of recommended best practice.

Tax

This is not a tax book. Often the subject of family business succession is discussed in the context of tax. So much so that tax and succession are sometimes seen as two sides of the same coin. Although there are short chapters dealing with the basics of family business tax issues, tax is not covered in any detail. Clearly the taxation implications of any ownership or disposal decision are a significant factor for the family business member concerned. But one of the arguments made in this book is that more significant difficulties can be caused for the business owning family if tax treatment is allowed to dominate the succession and ownership debate. Partly for this reason, and also because tax issues and estate planning are well catered for in many technical publications, the subject receives a comparatively light touch treatment here.

The scheme of the book

One of the points that will quickly emerge is the complexity of the family business situation and with that, how family business issues are often intertwined. For example succession can raise issues relating to employment, personal and corporate tax, company structures, property and pensions. That is to say nothing of the organisational, family dynamic and operational issues raised.

It therefore follows that any attempt to place family business issues into rigid categories is doomed to failure. But some structure is necessary. The scheme chosen has been to divide the book into separate parts. These are briefly outlined below. But, as will be apparent from the degree of cross-referencing within the body of the book itself that categorisation is, in many cases, inevitably arbitrary. For example a case could be made to fit chapter 10 dealing with family business property into the sections dealing with ownership or family matters just as much as the section on business issues actually chosen.

The book is structured in parts as follows:

Part A – The Family Owned Business and its Dynamics

These three chapters are intended to provide an introduction to family business concepts. They are almost entirely free from legal or other technical content

Chapter 1, introducing the family owned business, is intended to orientate the reader by positioning the importance of the family owned business within both the UK and the world economy. It also looks in some detail at the definition of a family business and introduces the main case studies or family business stories discussed at various stages in the book

The next chapter, Themes, introduces some of the key issues identified with family business life, such as sibling rivalry and the character and psychology of the founding entrepreneur.

As the first two chapters raise questions about the complexity of family businesses, chapter 3 is intended to introduce some key tools, models and theories to help advisors and business families understand and deal with that complexity.

These include the foundation stone of family business thinking, the three-circle model. As with the best of business models, the three-circle model is sufficiently simple so as to appear blindingly obvious once encountered and also useful enough to be used time and again.

Once introduced these tools and models, and especially the three-circle model, are referred to extensively throughout the rest of the book in an attempt to provide the bridge between technical content issues and family business thinking.

Part B – Business Matters

There then follows a series of chapters covering topics primarily positioned within the business system of the three-circle model. But it will readily be seen that in all of these cases there is an inescapable link between the topics discussed and the other two systems.

Taking employment issues as an example, the overlap between business and family issues will be entirely obvious in the case of family employees, discussed in chapter 5. Perhaps less obvious will be the influence of the family system on the position of non-family employees covered in the following chapter. For example where do the employment practices of an individual family business sit on a spectrum with equal opportunities at one end, actionable discrimination at the other and nepotism sitting somewhere between those points?

Chapter 7 – Management succession, deals with the logical endgame of family business employment issues. Will it be the family member or non-family management that take over the leadership of a family firm?

Part C – Ownership

The book then moves into the circle of the ownership system.

Chapter 11 – Ownership Overview, looks at some of the technical advisory issues relating to family business ownership including the application of share buy-back arrangements to 'prune the family tree' where the business owning family decide that some narrowing of ownership is appropriate.

The narrow or wider ownership question is especially acute where the family business comprises the lion's share of the family wealth. Family farming businesses are a prime example. Chapter 13 examines the technical legal difficulties of translating ownership approach into workable partnership arrangements.

Chapter 12 – Selling the family business looks at some of the particular features that apply when the target in a corporate transaction is a family company.

Part D – Family Matters

The chapters in this section, deal with family business governance, matrimonial issues and inheritance disputes in relation to a family business. They can be seen to both illustrate the power of the three-circle model and the virtual impossibility of categorising family business issues into neat boxes. Those last two chapters show how irretrievably interconnected family, business and ownership issues are within a family firm. The governance chapter explains how the family business movement has generated mechanisms to balance and deal with that complexity.

Part E – Family Business Disputes

This group of chapters provides a fairly detailed overview of the remedies available to shareholders in family companies, including the primary remedy of an unfair prejudice petition. In practice these chapters provide the best advertisement for family business governance. If the situations of the families featured in those chapters do not convince business families and their advisors of the benefits of governance as a preventative process nothing will.

As will appear from the detail of the chapters the remedies are based in either equity or discretion conferred on judges by statute and, as such, are largely within the discretion of individual judges. The remedies can therefore be of uncertain application.

Partly this might be seen as a clash in the courts between the business and family systems. There is a long tradition of the law seeking to provide certainty in business dealings, dating back to Lord Mansfield, credited as being the effective founder of modern commercial law and his view that 'Nothing is more mischievous than uncertainty in mercantile law'.[1] It will inevitably be difficult to reconcile this desire for certainty with the ambiguities and contradictions of family life. The theme of the struggle of the courts to do so with family businesses is explored in detail, in particular in chapter 20 (Family shareholder disputes – an overview). The remaining chapters in this part introduce the individual remedies available to shareholders in family companies and explore how the courts have applied these to particular family business situations.

Part F – The family Business Advisor

The final part of the book concentrates on the process and practicalities of advising family businesses. Chapter 25 – Introduces the concept of process consulting, a different approach to advising business families, based on the practice of therapy and organisational development professions and examines the differences between this approach and that typically taken by the technical and expert or 'content' professionals in the legal, accountancy and similar fields.

The chapter also explains the role of the specialist family business consultant, as a relatively new citizen of the family business world as well as providing a very brief overview of what we have termed the family business movement.

---

[1] *Metcalfe v Hall* [1782] Mss. Rep. Vol. 18. Fol 16 MS. Room S. 1 BR Durnf 168, 408 (VC), discussed in *Lord Mansfield – Justice in the Age of Reason* by Norman S Poser McGill-Queens (University Press, 2013).

Chapter 26 – Advising the family business client, attempts to apply the lessons learned from the rest of the book to the day to day practice of the legal and other financial advisory professional and asks the question is the advice that is being delivered 'fit for family business purpose'?

Linked to these chapters is a separate appendix with a brief overview and contact details of the main organisations comprising the family business movement and of most relevance to family businesses and their advisors in the UK.

Contributors and collaborators

Finally, before turning to the detailed content, a short explanation of how this book has been put together. Although the vast majority of the book has been written by the main author, Nicholas Smith, the book has immeasurably benefited from review and comments by other colleagues and collaborators mentioned in the preface.

More generally the views and thoughts expressed in this book have been formed and shaped as a result of a huge volume of conversations, reading, discussions, learning, teaching and above all working with family business clients over many years.

On this basis, whilst taking responsibility for the views expressed (subject, of course to the usual legal disclaimer) it would be entirely inappropriate for the lead author to claim sole ownership of these views and ideas. Accordingly the second person pronoun 'we' has been used throughout the book.

PART A

THE FAMILY OWNED BUSINESS AND ITS DYNAMICS

CHAPTER 1

AN INTRODUCTION TO THE FAMILY BUSINESS

1.1 IN PRAISE OF FAMILY BUSINESS: THE IMPORTANCE OF FAMILY BUSINESSES TO THE ECONOMY

1.1.1 Introduction

Family businesses are often associated with continuity, stewardship and a commitment to core business values, including the quality of the goods and services produced by the family business concerned. For example the imagery and advertising of the Gallo Family wine making business from California tells us that 'for four generations the Gallo Family has passed on a love of making quality wine' and leans heavily on family tradition and culture. Similar messages can be found closer to home. In the UK, Wharburtons brand themselves as 'family bakers'. Family owned branding is to be found across all industries and sizes of business across the UK.

But the popular image of family business is much less than wholly positive. Asked to picture a typical family business, the image evoked will often be that of a small, staid parochial concern. When challenged to identify the characteristics of family business life negative factors will often emerge, such as lack of professionalism, nepotism and vulnerability to family disputes. A perception of a high failure rate may also be mentioned. There is a danger that this book may be seen to reinforce these negative stereotypes. Inevitably much of the content concerns what can go wrong in family business life. To a large extent the book deals with various aspects of family business failure. But this should not obscure the fact that many business families work together to create successful enterprises, sometimes delivering world-beating products and services and that they have managed to do so in relative family harmony. Those business-owning families have been able to leverage the positive features of being in business together.

The Gallo business also appears in *Family Wars*,[1] a collection of stories about disputes involving well-known family businesses. The reality is that the family business model should neither be demonised nor lionised. It has many strengths. It also has its flaws.

Our main aim in focusing on some of the more negative aspects of family business life is to highlight potential traps in the hope that some business families and their advisors can avoid a few of these in the future. Before doing so, and to avoid these being lost amidst the negative seas of family dynamics, it is appropriate to highlight some of the benefits of involvement in family businesses.

---

[1] Grant Gordon and Nigel Nicholson *Family Wars* (Kogan Page, 2008).

1.1.2 Family business positives

Various advantages of the family business model have been identified by a number of commentators.[2] It is also fair to say that for most of the advantages potentially enjoyed by the family businesses model which have been identified below there is a corresponding disadvantage. This core theme of the ambiguity of the family business model is explored in chapter 2 below. For now we intend to focus on the positive. The advantages of the family business format include:

Loyalty

A key concern in the modern business world generally is the transient nature of the modern employment world. Young people are told to expect that they will need to move freely between jobs and careers over their working life. The average tenure of senior executives in listed companies is now measured in years rather than decades. The converse is true for senior family management in family owned concerns.[3] Inevitably long term loyalty and commitment to individual businesses will diminish as a result of this transience. Of course family owned businesses are not immune from these demographic trends. But the presence of key members of the business owning family, who have a long-term allegiance to the business, arising from family ties, can provide core structural stability to a family company. In short 'the name above the door' factor.

Long-term perspective

Quoted companies are frequently criticised for their short-term approach and the need to respond to investors' demands for increased returns on a quarterly basis. Often the USA and UK markets are unfavourably compared with Germany and other continental European economies in this regard. Venture capital and private equity backed companies will typically require a return on their investment via an exit within a 3 to 5-year time frame. The owners of other non-family businesses will typically look to build and sell their businesses during the remainder of their working life.

Family owned businesses on the other hand often have what leading family business commentator John Ward describes as 'infinite time horizons' so far as ownership of their family firm is concerned.[4] Against this background family businesses are better able to take long-term investment decisions rather than concentrating on short-term performance.[5]

Financial strength

The effects of this long-term perspective are often seen on the balance sheets of family businesses. The expression 'patient capital' is sometimes used. With less pressure on management to produce dividends family firm managers can conserve cash for future investment. Anecdotally most advisors can point to family business clients with

---

[2] See, for example, D Miller and I Le Bretton-Miller *Managing for the long run: lessons in competitive advantage from great family businesses* (Harvard Business School Press, 2005).
[3] Herbert Simon in 'Hidden Champions' (2004) *Business Week* suggested that the average tenure of chief executives in family companies was 35 years.
[4] *Perpetuating the Family Business* (Palgrave, 2004) at pp 110–111.
[5] See *European Commission Final Report of The Expert Group on Family Business Relevant Issues* – European Commission (2009).

significant cash reserves sitting in their bank accounts. Our impression is that family firms are more likely than others to own their own operation premises and often further investment property as well. A survey from 2011 by the Institute for Family Business[6] supports this proposition, showing that over a 3-year period family firms retained a higher percentage of their profits than their non-family counterparts. This held true right across firm size, with the largest family firms retaining the highest percentage of their profits (at about 25%) compared with approximately 11% for non-family companies. Although family companies may be less highly leveraged than other businesses they have the least difficulty in obtaining external funding when they need it. The IFB Survey showed that 76% of family firms that applied for external finance in 2010 were successful compared to 68% of non-family firms.

A similar position emerged in relation to insolvency and business failure. Both family and non-family businesses suffered in the post-2007 recession. But, again, irrespective of size, family firms a smaller percentage of family firms became insolvent over the period covered by this survey, 2007–2009.

Agency costs

Economic theory has it that the directors and managers of a company are the agents of its shareholder owners. The interests of the two groups are logically in conflict. The extreme expression of agency theory is that managers will be interested in extracting the highest wage for the minimum of effort. They will be pretty much indifferent to profit for shareholders. Shareholders will have the opposite view.

Agency costs are the price that the business has to pay to secure the commitment of the director agents to their owner principals. This can be the cost of both sticks, such as governance mechanisms and reporting structures, or carrots, for example share incentive schemes or bonus payments. For publicly quoted companies these costs can be huge. Just follow the on-going story about the levels of executive remuneration featuring regularly in the business pages.[7]

The countervailing logic is that, for family companies, the interests of family management and family owners will naturally be more aligned, so that agency costs for a family business will be negligible. The same argument will of course apply to other non-family owner managed businesses. Whether the wider family factor sitting in the background means that the reduced agency costs argument will be stronger for family firms depends largely on how well the family functions. Will the loyalty of those controlling a family firm to the wider family owners be greater than that between unrelated colleagues? In strong families this may well be so.

Market knowledge

Family members will usually have been immersed in their family's business from a very early age. *Brick by Brick*[8] tells the story of LEGO, one of the most successful family businesses on the planet. Godtfred Kirk Kristiansen, the son of the founder, worked for

---

[6] *The UK Family Business Sector: Working to grow the UK economy* (The Institute for Family Business with Oxford Economics, November 2011).

[7] See for example 'Few people doubt that chief executive pay is out of control. Employers would not appoint people who needed to be "bribed" to do their job' (www.ft.com accessed 30 May 2016).

[8] David Robertson *Brick by Brick* (Random House, 2013).

LEGO from the age of 12. Whilst further education at a leading business school and an apprenticeship at another major business might be a more typical preparation nowadays, the younger generation will still usually have developed a keen awareness of their family business, its ethos, culture and challenges. This awareness might be as a result of formal next generation training programmes.[9] More likely it will be through a process of osmosis. The family business would have been being an ever-present topic of conversation from their parents for the next generation whilst growing up. They are likely to have listened to parents and other relatives talk about business issues at a series of 'kitchen table board meetings'. Perhaps they will have worked in the family business themselves from an early age outside of school hours.

Behaviouralists would describe this as the process of the 'socialisation' of the next generation in the family firm. Either way the net result is likely to be that, in the next generation, the family business possesses a pool of highly knowledgeable potential family managers, well aware of the capabilities and weaknesses of their own family business and the market in which it operates. This knowledge, combined with other factors mentioned here, should equip family businesses to make better, safer and quicker investment decisions.

A comparative survey by the Credit Suisse Research Institute in July 2015[10] suggested that whilst the absolute level of R&D investment by quoted family businesses was lower than that of their non-family counterparts, the return generated by family businesses on their investment was greater. Similarly the report found that whilst family businesses engaged in fewer mergers and acquisitions, those that were undertaken tended to be more successful.

Speed of decision-making

Family members who have grown up together will be have developed a deep understanding of their family business and instinctive teamwork. This, when combined with entrepreneurial zeal and the absence of bureaucratic management structures found in more corporate businesses, can provide family businesses with a competitive advantage in being able to make quicker and better business decisions.

Shortly after leaving a subsidiary of a large quoted engineering group to join a large family owned firm in the same industry, a production director we know walked into the office of the third generation family managing director and suggested that the business could usefully acquire a new machine costing over £100,000. Used to having to prepare and present detailed business cases to main board committees for capital expenditure of this level, the production director was both surprised and energised to leave the managing director's office a few minutes later with permission to place an order. The managing director both saw the point of the new machine and was able to authorise its purchase without more ado.

Commitment to quality

All businesses profess a commitment to the quality of their goods and services. One consequence of the name above the door factor is that if quality is compromised for a family business both business goodwill and family reputation will suffer. Accordingly it

---

[9] Discussed in more detail in chapter 17 (Governance).
[10] *The Family Business Model* (Credit Suisse, 2015).

is argued that family businesses tend to have a greater commitment to the quality of their goods and services than their non-family counterparts.[11] *Brick by Brick*[12] includes an anecdote from the early days of the LEGO business when the company, still under the control of its founder Ole Kirk Kristiansen, produced wooden toys.[13] His son, Godtfred Kirk had boasted about saving the company money by applying two coats of varnish to a batch of toy ducks, instead of LEGO's customary three, only to be dispatched to the railway station by Ole Kirk to retrieve the batch in question as failing to meet the family company maxim of 'only the best is good enough'.

Stakeholder engagement

Just as business owning families can be seen to take a long term view of their own engagement with their family business they are also often said to have a natural affinity for building relations with other stakeholders in the family business. For example employee turnover is often lower and employee loyalty stronger in family businesses than non-family run concerns.[14] Relationships with suppliers and customers tend to be deeper and more long-standing. Similarly family businesses can often be both large employers and a key part of the local community in which they are based, supporting a wide range of charities and local sports clubs, for example.

Lifestyle

Working for one's family business can often be perceived by the outside world as an easy option and frequently one taken by family members who could not 'cut it in the real world'. There are clear, reasons, both for the health of the business and also the validation of the family member concerned, why family businesses should take steps to address these concerns. These issues are discussed in detail in chapter 7 (Management Succession).

From the perspective of the family member a career with their family business can have many legitimate lifestyle benefits, including avoiding the bureaucracy and ultra-competitiveness of the corporate world, the satisfaction of working with family members and of making a contribution for the benefit of the wider family. Statistics[15] suggest that proportionally family businesses are much more likely to have female CEO's than their non-family counterparts (especially listed companies) suggesting that the family business environment is more family friendly than more corporate businesses.

---

[11] Of course this is a generalisation. Family owned businesses too have their share of high profile quality scandals. For example the phone tapping scandal at family controlled News Group. In 2016 the Volkswagen group, controlled by the Porsche and Peich families admitted to installing software to defeat emissions tests on its diesel engines. At the time of writing the issue had led to the resignation of the non-family chief executive although no suggestion has emerged that the controlling families knew anything about the issue.
[12] David Robertson *Brick by Brick* (Random House, 2013).
[13] The famous LEGO bricks were a later innovation.
[14] See *Family Business People Capital* (IFB Research Foundation Report with Cass Business School, 2013).
[15] *Coutts Family Business Survey 2005* provides an overview of the growing trend for family owned businesses to be led by women and the annual report of the Davies Commission published in March 2015 confirms that only five of the top FTSE 100 companies have female chief executives.

1.1.3 The family business and the UK economy

Overview

The contribution of family businesses to the UK economy is enormous. Key points emerging from a more recent study[16] commissioned by the Institute for Family Business (IFB) included that:

- there are approximately 4.6 million family businesses in the UK, comprising 87% of all private sector firms;
- UK family businesses provide an estimated 11.9 million jobs, 47% of total private sector employment and 36% of overall employment in the UK;
- family firms generated revenues of £1.3 trillion in 2014, or 35% of private sector turnover. On these revenues, family firms made a £346 billion value-added contribution to UK GDP, or nearly a quarter of the total;
- family businesses are estimated to have contributed £125billion in tax receipts to the UK Exchequer, or 19% of total government revenues in 2014.

Family owned businesses make an equally significant, if not greater contribution to the economies of most countries throughout the world. A European Commission report suggests that 70–80% of enterprises across Europe are family owned.[17] The Family Firm Institute place the figure at 65–80% worldwide.[18]

Family business sectors

Although family firms are to be found across all sectors of the economy an earlier IFB survey found that these were concentrated most strongly in particular sectors, the highest sector concentrations being in in agriculture and extraction (89%), hotels and restaurants (85%), and in wholesale and retail (77%).[19] Various explanations have been given for this. Some attribute this concentration to the culture and service ethos of family owned businesses. Our personal belief is that the core factor that businesses in these sectors have in common is that they are location or property based. Businesses based on a key property or real estate asset provide a stable foundation for a family firm to weather the storms it will inevitably face, at key stages of its evolution, in particular during phases of succession from one generation to the next. Whilst, for example a hotel business might suffer during a difficult or protracted succession the core business can continue. This is less likely be the case with, for example, an engineering or high tech company.

---

[16] *The State of the Nation: The UK Family Business Sector 2015–16* (IFB Research Foundation with Oxford Economics, 2016). The IFB reports work partly by analysing data from the Department of Business Innovation and Skills Small Business Survey. This now classified all owner managed small businesses as family businesses. Previously the survey allowed for self-classification. This has led to a degree of inconsistency between numbers in the later IFB surveys and earlier reports. The definitional issue is explored in more detail in 1.2.

[17] *Overview of Family Business Relevant Issues, Final Report* (2008).

[18] *Tharawat Magazine* July 2014 contains an article summarizing the concentration of economic contribution of the family firms worldwide and includes references to various source surveys.

[19] *The UK Family Business Sector: Working to grow the UK economy* (Institute for Family Business and Oxford Economics, November 2011).

Family business geography

Similarly large numbers of family firms can be found throughout the UK. Whilst the South East (499,000) and London (466,000) have the highest absolute number of family businesses, family business represent the largest proportion of overall firms in the East Midlands and Northern Ireland (78%), while the West Midlands has the lowest concentration (58%).[20]

Family business size

A common perception is that family businesses are small businesses. Certainly, according to the 2015–2016 IFB survey[21] the vast majority, over 3.6m concerns would be classed as micro businesses, employing fewer than 10 people. Walking down a typical UK high street one is likely to pass many such businesses, shops and pubs that may have been fixtures of their locality for decades or longer. What is claimed to be Britain's oldest family business, butchers RJ Balson & Sons of Bridport, Dorset has recently celebrated its 500th anniversary.[22] But any such walk will also include national and international household chain store still in family ownership. For example the Zara fashion stores with over 6,700 outlets world-wide employing in excess of 140,000 staff,[23] owned by the Spanish Ortega family,[24] Top Shop still owned by the Green family,[25] Clarks Shoes, or the Entertainer, all in the ownership of British families. By the time of this later 2015–2016 IFB survey, there were 735 larger family businesses, defined as those employing more than 250 people, across the UK, providing over 1 million jobs.

Age of family firms

The position on the age and survival of family firms as family owned entities in the UK is more complex. Notwithstanding examples of long standing family firms such as RJ Balson & Sons, such family firms are atypical, with comparatively few UK businesses staying in long term family ownership. There does seem to be a disparity between the UK and continental Europe, where older family firms are much more prevalent. According to research[26] 'in Continental Europe if the firm survives then it is expected to remain family controlled throughout time' whereas in the UK there is only a 75% probability of a business remaining in family ownership after 40 years. It is suggested that various features of the UK economy are the cause of this, including the centralised and unsupportive commercial banking system,[27] the highly developed mergers and acquisitions market and efficient stock markets in the UK. All of these mean that a successful family firm is comparatively more likely to be sold or floated in the UK than in, for example, Germany.

---

[20] *The UK Family Business Sector: Working to grow the UK economy* (Institute for Family Business and Oxford Economics, November 2011).
[21] *The UK Family Business Sector* (Institute for Family Business and Capital Economics, 2008).
[22] *The Telegraph*, 23 September 2015.
[23] *The Guardian*, 17 September 2015.
[24] Who also own a number of other High Street brands including Massimo Dutti and Pull and Bear.
[25] Although there are now gaps in most high streets and Sir Phillip Green has attracted significant adverse publicity and parliamentary censure following the sale of BHS and its subsequent collapse into administration under new ownership leaving a significant pension fund deficit.
[26] Franks, Mayer, Volpin and Wagner 'The Life Cycle of Family Ownership: International Evidence' *Review of Financial Studies* 25, 1675–1712, June 2012.
[27] See Colin Mayer *Firm Commitment – Why the corporation is failing us and how to restore trust in it* (Oxford University Press, 2013).

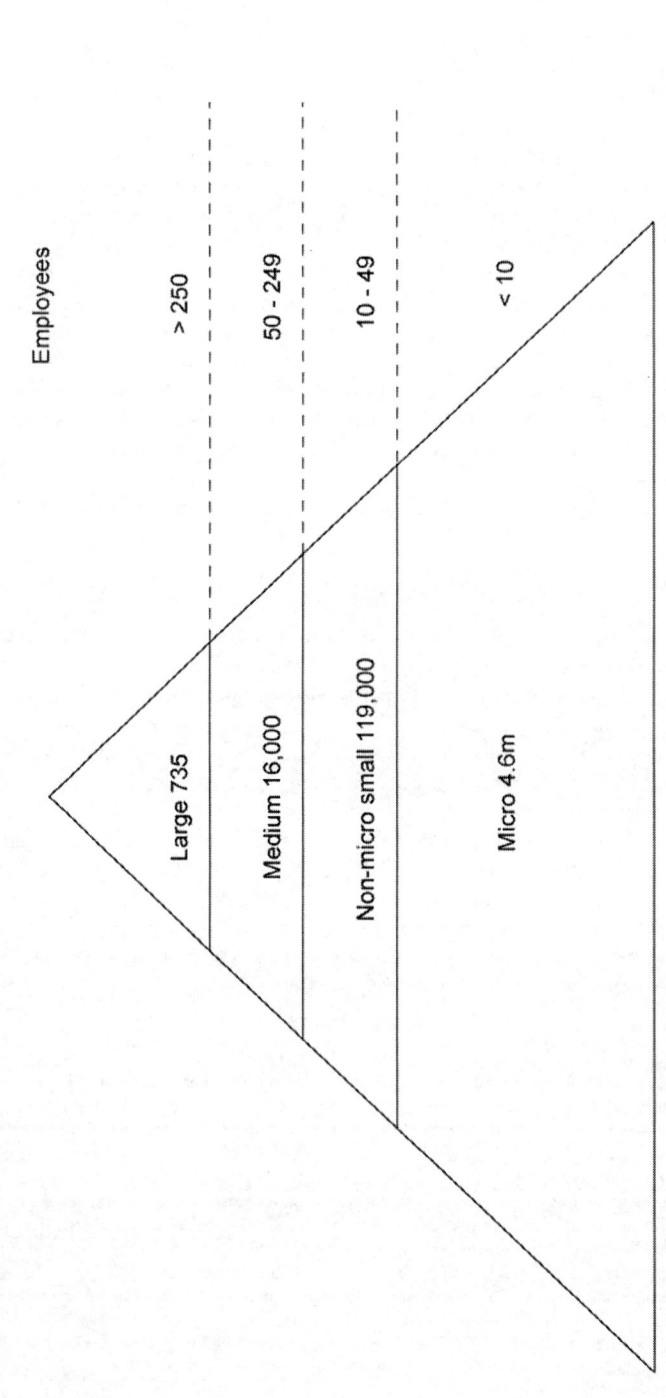

Figure 1.1: Number of family businesses by size of firm

Category	Count	Employees
Large	735	> 250
Medium	16,000	50 - 249
Non-micro small	119,000	10 - 49
Micro	4.6m	< 10

Source: The State of the Nation: The UK Family Business Sector 2015–16 (IFB Research Foundation with Oxford Economics)

Family business structures

The 2015–2016 IFB research also looked at the profile of family businesses by size and legal structure. It found that the vast majority of family firms (3.1m or 68% of the total) still traded as unincorporated sole traders. Almost invariably family businesses using this structure were concentrated in the micro sector, employing less than 10 employees.

A much smaller proportion, 7%, but nevertheless substantial in overall numbers, 336,000, traded as partnerships.[28] Companies were the second most prevalent form of family business structure, comprising 24% of the total and approximately 1.2 million businesses.

Parts of this book deal specifically with small early stage family firms. Chapter 13 looks at a particular issue thrown up by the use of partnerships as an ownership structure. But the vast majority of the book deals with issues relating to the family owned company. Nevertheless most of the points made in relation to smaller family companies apply irrespective of the legal format of the business.

1.1.4 Family business survival: the 30:13:3 'rule'

A frequently quoted statistic is that only 30% of family businesses survive through a second generation of family ownership, with 13% making it through the third generation and 3% beyond that. This statistic is often referred to as the '30:13:3 rule'.

This so-called rule is frequently used as evidence in support of an argument that the family business model is inherently weak. It has academic echoes of the well-known family business aphorism 'clogs to clogs in three generations'.[29] So it is worth exploring the background to the statistic and unpicking the argument in a little more detail.

This 'rule' has its origins in research carried out by John Ward in 1987 who looked at the generational profile of 200 manufacturing businesses in Illinois.[30] This is obviously a relatively small sample size and limited to one industrial sector in a single US state nearly 30 years ago. But that is not really the issue. Later academic researchers refer to John Ward's work as 'largely unchallenged' and also praise the thoroughness of his methodology.[31] Other, later, research seems to broadly replicate Ward's findings.[32]

The issue is not with the validity of the original research or its replicability. Partly the problem lies with how Ward's research has been interpreted. Frequently the 'rule' is misstated as only 30% of family businesses survive to their second generation rather than through that generation. Taking a generation as 25 years this makes an enormous difference to the perception of the fragility of the family business model suggested by the

---

[28] It is not immediately obvious from the research whether this included Limited Liability Partnerships or related purely to unincorporated partnerships. At the time the research was carried out LLPs were a relatively new form of business structure.
[29] Alternatively expressed as 'shirtsleeves to shirtsleeves in three generations' and various other permutations.
[30] Reported in detail in John L Ward *Keeping the family business healthy* (Jossey-Bass, 1987). Basically Professor Ward and his research team went back in history to identify a group of family firms in business in 1924 and traced what had happened to them by 1984 when the research was carried out.
[31] Zellweger Nason and Nordqvist 'From Longevity of Firms to Transgenerational Entrepreneurship of Families: Introducing Family Entrepreneurial Orientation' (2011) *Family Business Review*.
[32] For example the 2015 Credit Suisse survey referred to above 32% of the quoted family companies surveyed had survived into their third generation of family ownership.

alternative interpretation. In fact 73% of the businesses in Ward's sample survived longer than 35 years (although not necessarily in family ownership).[33]

Neither is the issue that the mortality rate of family firms is higher than non-family businesses. In fact the converse appears to be the case.[34]

1.1.5 Business families

Zellweger et al[35] argue that the key issue is that, by looking at longevity simply at the level of a single family business, we miss out on the wider range of entrepreneurial activity at a family level. In other words we need to concentrate our attention on business families and not individual family businesses. Their research suggested that a business family would, on average control 6.1 businesses over the course of family entrepreneurial involvement and that the business family would change their main industry 2.1 times during this period. Often the original family business provides family members with the capital to branch out into other businesses.

The Cadbury family are a case in point. Although clearly best known for their involvement in their chocolate company, the founding brothers, Richard and George Cadbury were the third generation of the wider family who had been involved in family businesses. The family started out with drapers businesses. John Cadbury, the father of Richard and George then set up a shop dealing in tea, coffee and cocoa next door to the drapers business and financed by a small sum of money from its profits. John then moved into rudimentary manufacture of cocoa before Richard and George joined him in that business. The rest is history.[36]

1.1.6 Family business success?

But perhaps the biggest issue to take with John Ward's approach in *Keeping the Family Business Healthy* is the standpoint that simply because a business passes out of family hands this should be seen as a failure. A business leaving the family control of its founding family will inevitably be a watershed moment. When judged against an ambition that 'this business shall last forever' which Ward suggests is 'every family business owner's dream' there will inevitably be some element of disappointment.

Returning to the Cadbury's story, which includes floatation on the London Stock Exchange, and a merger with Schweppes before the company was eventually taken over by Kraft in 2010. That takeover is frequently cited as a sad day for British industry let alone the Cadbury family. This may well be so. Yet this should not obscure the many thousands of jobs, the iconic brands and the contribution to the UK economy made over 150 years or so made by this world-class business whilst still in family hands.

---

[33] The Franks et al research referred to above seems to be consistent with this more optimistic interpretation of the prospects of survival of family firms in the UK suggesting that there is a 75% chance of survival after 40 years.

[34] The 2011 IFB research on the UK family business sector suggested that over a 3-year period family firms suffered a lower percentage of insolvencies than other businesses. This was irrespective of business size. Also fewer family firms dissolved for non-insolvency reason. The exceptions to this were for large family businesses (broadly those employing 250 or more people) where for 2008 and 2009 a slightly higher proportion of family firms dissolved for non-insolvency reasons.

[35] Zellweger Nason and Nordqvist 'From Longevity of Firms to Transgenerational Entrepreneurship of Families: Introducing Family Entrepreneurial Orientation' (2011) *Family Business Review*.

[36] As told in Deborah Cadbury *Chocolate Wars* (Harper Press, 2011).

Less high profile, but nevertheless, when judged against most criteria, success stories, will sit behind huge numbers of other family businesses which do not even make it into a second generation of family ownership, let alone last for all eternity. Most advisors will be able to identify family business clients who sold out for millions. Of John Ward's original cohort of 200 family businesses 20% still survived as independent companies 60 years later with 13% still owned by the original family whilst 5% had been sold to third parties and 2% had been publicly listed.

Of the 80% that no longer remained as independent businesses after 60 years the overwhelming majority, 67%, had lasted in business for over 35 years. This is quite a long time to be providing an income for the owning family, employment and paying taxes. It is hardly evidence of the fragility of the family of the family business model. Yet, often based on a misconception of the 30:13:3 rule, many commentators suggest that family businesses are inherently doomed.

1.2 FAMILY BUSINESS – A DEFINITION?

So far we have used the terms family business, family firm, family company and family owned business interchangeably and many times over, but without saying precisely what we mean by those terms. Most of us think that we know what a 'family business' is. The truth is that there is no universally accepted definition. A 2008 study commissioned report by the European Commission[37] identified more than 90 separate definitions in use. It is certainly not our intention to comment on all of these, much less to suggest a 91st. Various academics and commentators have come up with their own formulation. Different surveys use different definitions of family businesses, making it correspondingly harder to compare results and research. We will look at some of the main definitions in this section.

The world leading family business advisory network, the US based Family Firm Institute (FFI) tell us that a family business:[38]

> 'may consist of one or more activities, such as an operating business only; alternatively the enterprise might include real estate leased to the business. Another possible configuration is an operating business with a diversified wealth portfolio held for the benefit of the family, often referred to as a family office.'

This is not so much a definition but more of a recognition that a family business can take of various forms and therefore the complexity, bordering on the impossibility, of arriving at a single, succinct but comprehensive definition of family business.

One approach could be to break the expression family business down into its component parts.

The logical starting point would be first to look in detail at the definition of family. But this apparently simple concept is itself fraught with difficulty and so will be considered as a stand-alone topic in the next section of this chapter. For the time being it will be

---

[37] *Overview of Family Business Relevant Issues*, Final Report (2008).
[38] *Family Enterprises: Understanding Families in Business and Families in Wealth* (The Family Firm Institute Inc, Wiley Inc, 2014), glossary at p 147. This book devotes a whole chapter of 38 pages to the subject of 'Defining the Family Enterprise'.

sufficient to think of a family as the founder of the business, their spouse or partner together with the founder's direct descendants.

1.2.1 European Commission definition

The above study led to a final report by a group of family business experts drawn from across Europe, recommending a formulation which appears to be gaining traction[39] as a leading definition and is recommended for use by the European Commission. According to them:

> 'A firm, of any size, is a family business, if:
> (1) The majority of decision-making rights is in the possession of the natural person(s) who established the firm, or in the possession of the natural person(s) who has/have acquired the share capital of the firm, or in the possession of their spouses, parents, children or children's direct heirs.
> (2) The majority of decision-making rights are indirect or direct.
> (3) At least one representative of the family or kin is formally involved in the governance of the firm.
> (4) Listed companies meet the definition of family enterprise if the person who established or acquired the firm (share capital) or their families or descendants possess 25 per cent of the decision-making rights.'

We will adopt the EU Commission definition as our basic starting point. We will also explore some of the issues raised by the expert group definition, many of which have historically caused family business commentators to grapple with alternative formulations.

1.2.2 Large businesses

The expert group make it clear that their definition of a family business applies to 'a firm, of any size'. Larger companies such as Clarks potentially qualify. The descendants of the founder brothers, James and Cyrus Clark, still hold the vast majority of the shares in the company. Whilst no Clark family members currently hold senior executive positions there are family appointed non-executive directors and many more family members are involved in the family council and therefore 'in the governance of the firm'.

Similarly with News Corp. Although the business is listed on the New York Stock Exchange the Murdoch family, control in excess of 25% of the voting rights, largely through the separate class of shares held by them carrying weighted voting rights. Press speculation[40] has been rife for years as to which of Rupert Murdoch's children, James, Lachlan or Elisabeth will emerge as the heir to Rupert (who himself took over a much smaller Australian based newspaper business founded by his own father).

But there are many other businesses, which technically fall within the European Commission definition but simply do not feel like they are family owned. The Credit Suisse survey referred to above uses a similar definition of family business but with a 20% shareholding threshold for quoted companies to qualify. On that basis Google and Facebook are both treated as family businesses, presumably because of the retained

---

[39] The first trace we have of this definition comes from The Family Entrepreneurship Working Group set up by the Finnish Trade Ministry in 2004 but the definition was adopted in the *European Commission Final Report Of The Expert Group on Family Business Relevant Issues* in 2009.
[40] See, for example, 'Rupert Murdoch's eldest son emerges as most likely heir, *The Guardian*, 26 March 2014.

shareholdings and continued involvement of their founders. But neither Google nor Facebook[41] look and feel like they are family businesses. Why not?

1.2.3 Owner managed or a family business?

There will be many businesses where the EU Commission fits both the technical circumstances and the look and feel of the family business concerned, for example smaller family owned farming partnerships or family companies with two generations or siblings working side by side.

The basic structural difficulty with the European Commission definition is that, by simply looking for a majority of voting rights, all single-founder controlled owner-managed businesses will automatically be treated as family businesses. This fits with the intention of the expert group[42] who were keen to focus on simplicity and to arrive at a definition that was 'operational'.

Many such businesses will remain very much their founder's. They may never pass any part of the ownership to or employ any other family members. Can such businesses truly be said to be family businesses? Most commentators would say not. Something else is required. Exactly what the missing ingredient is has led to the other 89 definitions and consumed countless hours of debate in the family business world.

1.2.4 Wider ownership

It may help in getting closer to that a more precise definition if at least two family members participate as owners or if a large percentage of the business is held by the wider business owning family. But this is not decisive.

A business may clearly be seen as a family business under all other criteria even if it is owned exclusively by a founder or a single current generation family shareholder. For example a family farm where the senior generation retain ownership but the next generation also live and work full time on the farm.

But wider family ownership might not be decisive in capturing the essence of a family business. Handing on shares may be the start of an ownership succession process. Conversely it might simply be a tax planning exercise, with the intention of the founder, always being to sell 'his' business as and when they thought the time and price was right.

1.2.5 Multi-generational

Is it necessary for at least one intergenerational transfer or succession to have taken place before a business can truly be seen as a family business? Although some academics take this approach[43] this is very much the minority view.

---

[41] Indeed the founder of Facebook, Mark Zuckerberg, has recently announced an intention to put 99% of his Facebook shares into a charitable foundation. His, as yet, very young daughter will not therefore be inheriting the Facebook family firm.
[42] See p 10 of the report.
[43] Some commentators suggest that a family business cannot truly be defined as such unless it has undergone at

1.2.6 Succession intention

Is the missing ingredient therefore that the founder or current generation intend to pass the business on to the next generation?

Dr Peter Davis[44] suggests that this is so. He argues that some additional ingredient is required before an entrepreneur can be regarded as the founder of a family business:

> 'Founders are typically intuitive and emotional people. They obviously have the drive and ambition to build a great business, but they also have a feeling about the place, a love of what they have created that makes them want to perpetuate it through the generations.'

John Ward also sees an element of succession intention as crucial and defines a family business as:[45]

> '... one that will be passed on for the family's next generation to manage and control.'

Of course intending to pass the family firm to the next generation and actually doing so are two different things. This issue of uncertainty inherent in Ward's formulation can be sidestepped by introducing the qualification that a family business is one that the family **intend** will be passed onto the next generation. But even such a revised definition still disqualifies businesses, currently run by a wide coalition of family members, where there is either a positive intention for the business not to pass to the next generation or even an open mind as to whether or not that is a good idea.

1.2.7 Family involvement in management

So is the crucial question how many family members are involved in the business? The European Commission definition requires that 'at least one family member is involved in the formal governance structure of the business' so the test would be satisfied by the presence of a founder alone.

Again that definition could be modified for example by requiring the involvement of at least two family members. But there will be a number of businesses where the decision-making and management rests with a single-family member but where there is a clear intention to pass the business on to the next generation and to involve them in management when they are ready for this. Again many farming businesses will fall into this category, with the next generation already earmarked for their roles as successors before they have started school.

Conversely the mere presence of other family members in a notional governance capacity will do little to create or maintain a true family business. Chapter 8 (Directors' Duties) looks at the position of what we have termed 'family director' and highlights the perils of that position.

---

least one generational succession. See for example, CM Daily and SS Thompson 'Ownership structure, strategic posture, and firm growth: An empirical examination' *Family Business Review* (1994) Vol 3, 237–250.
[44] Peter Davis 'Three Types Of Founders – And Their Dark Sides' *Family Business Magazine* (1990).
[45] *Keeping the Family Business Healthy* at p 252.

Mere token family presence is therefore not enough to capture the essence of what it takes to be a family business. In their seminal article introducing the three-circle model Tagiuri and Davis define family businesses as organisations where:[46]

> 'two or more extended family members influence the direction of the business through the exercise of kinship ties, management roles or ownership rights.'

Active involvement and participation in day-to-day management by the wider family could therefore be part of the missing ingredient. But this is not really necessary.

1.2.8 Family owned and family managed business

A key distinction to make so far as family businesses are concerned is between, on the one hand, family managed businesses and, on the other, family owned businesses. In the former, family managed business, the business family will, in addition to owning all or most of the business, perform the vast majority of senior management roles. These tend to be early stage or smaller family businesses.

The term family owned business usually implies that, whilst the business family have made a commitment to retaining all, or the vast majority of ownership rights, many, and in some cases all, of the senior executive management positions, are occupied by non-family managers. Larger and later stage family business conforming to this description are more typically described as family owned.

The distinction between ownership and management is one of the key concepts in family business work. Achieving the right blend between family involvement, thereby leveraging the advantages of the family business model referred to above and non-family expertise, to help dispel or dilute the corresponding disadvantages, remains a central and perennial challenge for the business owning family. This key theme of professionalisation is explored in the following chapter and generally throughout the book.

Other academic commentators argue that it is necessary to take a more detailed look at a combination of family involvement in ownership (FIO) and family involvement in management (FIM) to obtain a rounded view of a family firm.[47] Their work suggests that there is an adverse correlation between the number of family members involved in management and family firm performance. We would argue that whilst this research may highlight a potential defect in the family business model, it should be seen as signposting potential traps to avoid, rather than exposing any fundamental flaw in that model. Any potential negative impact of over-reliance on family management can be overcome by an investment in non-family professional managers and governance.

Most of the elements of the definition of family business we have discussed so far have been quantitative. Some have been simple threshold tests such as those contained in the European Commission definition. Other quantitative measures like the FIM FOM analysis look at degrees of involvement.

---

[46] Renato Tagiuri and John Davies 'Bivalent Attributes of the Family Firm' *Family Business Review* (1996), Vol 9(2). This key article is discussed in more detail in chapters 2 (Themes) and 3 (Tools, Models and Theories).

[47] Salvatore Sciascia, Pietro Mazzola 'Family Involvement in Ownership and Management: Exploring Nonlinear Effects on Performance' *Family Business Review* (2008), Issue 4.

1.2.9 'Familiness'

Is there an additional intangible element which is also needed before a business can truly be classed as a family concern? For want of a better word, 'familiness'. This is hinted at by reference to active language such as 'influence' and 'exercise' in the Tagiuri and Davis definition. It is also implicit in concepts such as succession intention. If so the European Commission definition could be seen as an entry point or as a provisional qualification for treatment as a family business. Some further characteristics would then need to be present to confirm that family business status.

As these intangible factors are not absolutes but a collection of variables, the relative strength or absence of the various factors will determine how securely (or otherwise) any qualifying business can be seen to qualify as a family business. In some cases the absence of many of the factors comprising familiness may mean that, a founder managed enterprise will, on closer analysis, lose its provisional family business status.

Although they do not use the familiness expression this is essentially the argument employed by Astrachan *et al* in developing their F-PEC Scale of Family Influence.[48] Their approach is to look at the influence of the family in three areas, power experience and culture. The higher a business scores on their F-PEC scale the more that it can be seen as a family business. Looking at the elements of the scale in a little more detail.

- **Power.** Power is itself broken down into three separate elements assessing the involvement of the wider business owning family in ownership, management and governance.
- **Experience.** By which the authors mean how long has this family been in business together? The more generational transitions it has survived the higher its F-PEC factor.[49] For example many family farming businesses have been through a sufficient number of generational successions that they can be said to have developed a succession gene.
- **Culture.** To what extent do the family share a common view on the strategy and values of their family firm and above all a commitment to it remaining in family ownership?

The F-PEC scale attempts to quantify what might otherwise be seen as unquantifiable, intangible elements of family business life. But as the starting point of the model is a questionnaire based on the inevitably subjective views of family members, even a methodology as complex as the F-PEC scale might not deliver an absolutely robust analysis of the relative degree of familiness of any particular family business.

However the approach does move us way beyond the simple analysis of ownership thresholds and family governance participation into an examination of the contribution made by the wider business owning family to their family business. In this way it could be a useful tool to examine the relative strengths and weaknesses of the family as a business family. Does the family hope to remain in business together for the foreseeable future? If so an analysis based on the F-PEC approach may allow them to identify weaknesses and build on strengths and thereby to turn that dream into a reality.

---

[48] Joseph H Astrachan, Sabine B Klein and Kosmas X Smyrnios 'The F-PEC Scale of Family Influence: A Proposal for Solving the Family Business Definition Problem' *Family Business Review* (2002) Vol 15(1) at pp 45–58. The family business questionnaire used by the authors is included as an appendix to the article.
[49] Although this runs contrary to the 30:13:3 rule discussed above.

1.2.10 Self-definition

A number of studies allow participants to self-define whether or not they are family businesses.[50] This affects the robustness of survey results. A number of businesses that would otherwise qualify as family businesses might exclude themselves from the survey.

Peter Leach, a leading UK family business consultant, also introduces self-definition as a component of his own definition of family business, which he sees as one that:[51]

> 'is influenced by a family or by a family relationship and that perceives itself to be a family business.'

Recognition by a family that they are working together in a family business is clearly helpful. The family are more likely to appreciate both the benefits and challenges of this. But relying exclusively on self-definition may cause difficulties for family businesses and their advisors.

We have encountered many businesses that certainly qualify as family businesses under the criteria of the European Commission test but do not see themselves as such. Instead they see themselves as corporates who just happen to have some family shareholders. It might be that such businesses would score low on the F-PEC scale in terms of their family involvement. Nevertheless family dynamics will still apply. For example the next generation might have an expectation that they will be able to work in or even own what they see as 'the family business'. By failing to recognise the reality of their family business situation the family are at a greater risk of ignoring the inevitable tensions arising from family business dynamics.

The most graphic illustration we have encountered of this relates to the sale of a medium sized business some years ago. In addition to the first generation founder both his son and daughter worked in the business, occupying senior management positions. The founder's initial instructions were that the son and daughter were not to be told about the proposed until after completion. Those instructions were soon revised.

The maxim goes that one can never take the family out of the family business.

1.2.11 Is Dyson's a family business?

To conclude our discussion on the definition of a family business we will look at the Dyson appliance business founded by Sir James Dyson in 1978 and with a public image that is still very much synonymous with its founder. The company is described on the Dyson website[52] as a 'technology company with over 1,000 engineers worldwide'. The business is privately owned and whilst ultimate beneficial ownership of the shares is not readily apparent from public records it is understood that this sits with Sir James and his family.

---

[50] See, for example the Institute for Family Business/Capital Economics report on the UK Family Business Sector February 2008. As referred to above removing this option and following the EU definition seemed to add a significant number, approximately 1.5 million to the UK family business population overnight.
[51] Peter Leach *Family Businesses – The Essentials* (Profile Books, 2007).
[52] See www.dyson.co.uk (accessed 6 October 2015).

The company has a non-family CEO but, its public image is inextricably linked to Sir James, who features on advertising etc. In addition to Sir James, various members of the Dyson family occupy board positions within the overall company structure. Dyson therefore clearly falls within the European Commission definition of a family business.

But can Dyson truly be seen as a family business, rather than Sir James' business, or a technology company in which the wider family have an interest and occupy governance roles?

The argument for family business categorisation may have been strengthened by the acquisition by the parent Dyson business of Dyson Lighting, a business set up by James Dyson's son Jake supplying high end LED lamps which led at least one business commentator to conclude that this acquisition 'puts Jake in pole position to succeed his father'.[53]

Whilst it would seem that Dyson would clearly qualify as family business under the European Commission definition it remains to be seen quite where Dyson would be placed on the F-PEC scale.

1.3 A DEFINITION OF FAMILY?

1.3.1 EC expert group – the bloodline family

Returning now to the definition of what constitutes as 'family' as a key component of the definition of a family business. As stated above the EC expert group saw a family for this purpose as:

> 'the natural person(s) who established the firm, or ... the natural person(s) who has/have acquired the share capital of the firm, or ... their spouses, parents, children or children's direct heirs.'

This approach therefore concentrates on the 'bloodline' starting with the original founder.

This may be seen as the standard approach in family business thinking. The same or similar formulations are often used to decide who is, and who is not a family member, for example for the purpose of deciding to whom shares in a family company can be transferred by will or gift,[54] or who is entitled to attend family assemblies[55] convened as part of the governance processes of larger family businesses. This formulation does however raise a number of issues and questions.

1.3.2 CA, s 253 – the nuclear family

The Companies Act has its own definition of a family, which is essentially used to work out who should be seen as connected to a director for the purpose of various statutory company governance provisions. CA, s 253(2) defines a director's family as:

---

[53] *The Guardian*, 3 September 2015.
[54] Discussed in chapter 11.
[55] See chapter 18.

(a) the director's spouse or civil partner;
(b) any other person (whether of a different sex or the same sex) with whom the director lives as partner in an enduring family relationship;
(c) the director's children or step children;
(d) any children or step-children of a person within paragraph (b) above (and who are not children or step-children of the director) and have not attained the age of 18; and
(e) the director's parents.

Here it will be seen that the definition concentrates very much on the nuclear family unit, the family of choice rather than the family of origin. This is emphasised by the fact that CA, s 253 excludes wider family members from the definition of a director's family, even those living with the director.[56] Of course the purpose of CA, s 253 is to look at those family members most closely connected to a director, so as to be more likely to be influenced by them and therefore needing to be grouped with that director for governance purposes.

The contrast between these two definitions does bring out a number of key issues. Many of these will resurface at various stages of this book.

1.3.3 Divided loyalties

The first issue is the potential conflict that may be caused for a family business member in trying to find an appropriate balance between loyalty to their family of origin, represented by the family business and looking after the interests of their own immediate family of choice.

For example pushing for a pay-rise, a greater share of ownership or promotion to a key leadership role, may be challenging for any young business person. Doing so may also be necessary to achieve their immediate ambitions or needs, for example, to provide a house big enough for their own growing young family. But those difficult conversations become harder still if they involve competition for scarce resource with wider family members. Of course some family businesses might be sufficiently successful, so as to be able to provide more than adequately for the material needs of all those involved. But there will only be so much status, recognition and ownership to go round, irrespective of the size and prosperity of the family business concerned.

1.3.4 In-laws

It will be seen that spouses and other in-laws are excluded from the EC expert group definition of family. So if this definition were adopted for the purposes of determining to whom shares in a family business could be left by a will, in-laws would be excluded.

But in-laws will often play a significant role in the management of a family company. Should they be deprived of the right of direct ownership, in circumstances where a

---

[56] The director's grandparents, grandchildren, sisters, brothers, aunts, uncles, nephews or nieces are excluded from the CA, s 253 definition of family. Quite why these more remote family members actually living with a director are presumed to be immune from influence is not immediately obvious.

bloodline family member, who contributes nothing to the day-to-day success of the family enterprise is allowed to participate fully in ownership?[57]

Even if they are not working in, or participating as legal owners of a family business, spouses are capable of exerting considerable influence over their family business member co-spouse who does work or own shares in the family firm. This can be seen as the mirror image of the logic underpinning CA, s 253. Closely connected non-owners can clearly influence owners.

The extent to which in-laws are embraced within or rejected by family firms will vary from business to business. The key figure in the survival of Clarks shoes as an independent family business was an in-law to the Clark family, the late Roger Pedder.[58] He initially served as a non-executive director. He was a key figure in keeping Clark's in family ownership and also the prime architect of the company's family business governance system. Latterly he served as chairman of the company.

The ultimate recognition of in-laws is to be found in the Japanese practice of mukoyōshi, where, in the absence of a suitable blood-line successor, an in-law is formally adopted as the son of the business leader, assumes the family name and leadership of the family business. Many household name Japanese companies, including Toyota and Suzuki have used this practice to help preserve family ownership and leadership of their companies.[59]

Other family businesses, particularly in the West, have a less welcoming attitude to in-laws, sometimes expressly prohibiting the employment of in-laws in the family business. In some cases in-laws might be treated as 'part qualified' family business members. They could be allowed to work in the business, but not own shares in it, with ownership being reserved for bloodline family members. Alternatively in-laws may be allowed to hold shares but subject to divestment provisions, whereby any shares held have to be transferred to bloodline family members in the event of divorce. Sometimes the transfer will be on unfavourable terms but permitted transferees are likely to include the bloodline children of the in-law who is moving beyond the pale of the business owning family circle on divorce.

A key question to answer as part of family business governance is therefore the status and rights of in-laws. Often this will lead to in-laws having some form of partially recognised status within the governance process itself. For example being allowed to attend social functions organised in conjunction with family assemblies but being excluded from participating in the business part of the family assembly itself.[60]

Again there is no universally correct or accepted answer to this question. In many cases, the influence of in-laws will be hugely beneficial. They may have valuable skills and experience to contribute. Whilst being close enough to the core business family to appreciate relevant underlying issues and dynamics they might still be able to remain sufficiently detached and objective and to mediate between bloodline family members. As such they may be capable of forming part of the solution rather than adding to any difficulties that there may exist between the bloodline family members.

---

[57] This aspect of family business ownership philosophy is explored in detail in chapter 18 (The Family Business and Marriage).
[58] For an obituary see *The Times*, 7 October 2015.
[59] See David Landes *Dynasties: Fortune and Misfortune of the World's Great Family Businesses* (Penguin, 2006).
[60] Family assemblies are discussed in detail in chapter 17 (Governance).

On other occasions the influence of the in-laws may be seen as much more pernicious and even the source of branch factionalism that breaks out within the business family. The Harding family farming business case is discussed in length in Part E. Although it is impossible to apportion precise responsibility for the breakdown of family and business relationships between the three sisters involved, Elizabeth' husband emerges as a strong ally of his wife. The husband had control over the accounting function of the business and seemed to have been instrumental in entrenching the dispute between the sisters.

1.3.5 Second marriages and step-children

Further complications arise with second and subsequent marriages in relation to the children of those marriages. Whilst the EC expert group definition includes step-children within its definition of the family, many definitions actually used by business families themselves do not. This may result in children who have grown up together, some of whom were children of the 'full business family member' from a previous marriage being treated differently from children of the 'in-law' spouse.

1.3.6 Modern family units

It will have been noted that those responsible for the drafting of CA, s 253 have made attempts to recognise the reality of modern family life. In addition to civil partners any person 'with whom a director lives as partner in an enduring family relationship' will be treated as a member of the director's family. This expressly includes same sex relationships.

The expert group definition, on the other hand, concentrates on 'spouses', presumably envisaging some form of traditional religious or civil wedding ceremony. Whilst the expert group definition is not legally binding it does reflect the prevailing position in the articles of association or other formal governance documents of many family businesses, which of course are. More to the point issues such as whether unmarried or same sex partners should be treated as family members, at least to the same extent as married, opposite sex partners, have historically been capable of causing considerable friction or embarrassment in some business families.

1.4 FAMILY BUSINESS CHALLENGES

The difficulties surrounding the definition of a family business, or even in deciding who is and who is not a family member for the purposes of a family business, illustrate just how complex the family business world can be. Those complexities breed challenges. It is now time to turn briefly to some of the challenges facing family businesses.

Of course family businesses face much the same business pressures as their non-family counterparts operating in the same industry. It is widely accepted that a huge percentage of new start-ups will fail in the first few years of their existence.[61] In his Illinois study John Ward effectively screened his survey sample for survivability by excluding all businesses less than 5 years old. Many of these businesses will be concentrating too hard on survival to think overmuch about what comes next. They may well perish before the

---

[61] For example see 'Half of UK start-ups fail within five years' *The Telegraph*, 21 October 2014.

additional element that makes them true family businesses, such as intention to pass the business on to the next generation has fully crystallised.

There may be commercial reasons why the business does not pass to the next generation, such as:

- The business failing to adapt to changing market or economic conditions. This may partly be because the founder resists change, as they refuse to believe that what once worked for the business is no longer the best approach.
- Technological or other changes mean that the products or services which the family business provides have been superseded.
- Competitors catch up with the technological, or other leads, which the business had when it started.

It is probably not surprising that there are more family businesses in the agricultural and construction sectors where, although there have been major changes in the method of operation these are not radical as those in, for example the technology sector.

Some family businesses will adapt and change as a result of commercial factors. The business inherited by the second generation may be totally different from that set up by the founder. It may be in an entirely new sector.

This book does not and cannot look at business, management, financial or strategy issues in any detail. In any event these commercial challenges are faced by family and non-family businesses alike. What challenges are unique to family businesses or disproportionately affect family owned firms?

1.4.1 EC expert group

The EC expert group believed these fell into the following categories:

Environmental

By which they meant largely the tax and regulatory environment in which family firms operate in their own jurisdictions. Arguably the UK environment is relatively benign with relatively generous business property relief against inheritance tax available in most situations to facilitate the transfer of ownership to the next generation.[62]

It is however a long-standing grievance of larger family business that this relief is not available for quoted company shares thereby, it is argued, providing a huge disincentive for family owned companies to list their shares, in effect denying them access to capital markets and thus inhibiting growth.

Similarly the expert group point to the debt-averse nature of lower geared family companies and the comparatively generous tax treatment of interest on borrowed money arguing that most tax systems, including the UK effectively, penalise lower leveraged family businesses.

---

[62] See chapter 16.

A detailed analysis of these policy issues is beyond the scope of this book.[63]

1.4.2 Succession planning

Unsurprisingly succession planning was identified as a key challenge by the expert group. This included the need to plan transfer of ownership early and an acknowledgement of the complexity of the process, including as it does, the transfer of 'social and cultural capital'.[64]

As management and ownership succession planning are covered in detail in chapters 7 and 15 respectively we will say no more at this stage.

1.4.3 Governance

Similarly the expert group recognised the benefits to a business family from engaging in the governance process. But they identified the lack of awareness of the family business community of governance and its importance as a key challenge. The report highlighted the close, almost inextricable, link between succession planning and governance saying that the object of governance to 'minimise potential tensions' within the business owning family was particularly important as these 'risks heighten as intergenerational transfers take place'.[65]

Again, and as one of the predominant themes of this book is the importance of family business governance we will say nothing more at this stage.

1.4.4 Attracting and retaining a skilled workforce

Notwithstanding the observation made in **1.1.2** above and the survey results referred to there the expert group suggested that:[66]

> 'the negative image of the family business in the labour market is also considered to be one of the biggest challenges that family firms face.'

To an extent this image may have been earned by those family businesses which display a clear family first policy when hiring or promoting. It is not uncommon to find family members, in many cases, inexperienced, unqualified or otherwise unsuitable occupying all senior positions in a family business. A clear objective of family business governance is to control nepotism of this nature.

But not all family firms operate in this way. The expert group believed that for this, we would hope, majority of family companies, a key challenge was to communicate the positives of family business employment to the labour market and to persuade potential employees to join them.

---

[63] But within the remit of the Institute of Family Business which has a clear lobbying function including supporting the All-Party Parliamentary Group for Family Business with a remit to 'promote and facilitate communication and understanding between the UK family business sector and members of both Houses'.
[64] See p 15.
[65] At p 16.
[66] At p 15.

1.4.5 Training

The final challenge identified by the expert group was the lack of entrepreneurship training and education on family business specific issues available for business owning families.

1.4.6 Family members?

To a large extent the challenges identified by the expert group mirror those noted by many other advisors and commentators. But with one notable omission. It will have been noted that the expert group did not specifically highlight the personalities, behaviour and relationships of individual family members as a key challenge facing family businesses. This may seem to be a curious omission. A considerable part of this book is devoted to disputes between family members where personality clashes appear to be at the core.

Peter Leach identifies three categories of issues that cause difficulties to family businesses. First business issues. Secondly structural issues, 'where something is malfunctioning in the structure of how the family relates to the business which undermines family dynamics and decision making'. Thirdly personality 'such a person is impossible, unreasonable, illogical, irrational'. Leach argues that in the 'great majority of cases', although often presented as personality or business related, the real cause of family business difficulties will be structural.

This, argues Leach, provides the real opportunity for family businesses:[67]

> 'because structural issues are to a large extent predicable to family businesses, they have the opportunity, not enjoyed in other businesses, to effectively resolve these problems before they arise.'

Taking this approach a failed family business succession does not need to be reduced to the personalities of the family members concerned, the dominant entrepreneur founding father who won't let go of the business, or the weak and incompetent next generation family member who lacks the skills and drive to take the family business forward, or the interfering non-working sibling who is a disruptive influence. To be sure these are highly relevant issues. But, so the argument goes, they are also sufficiently common to be seen as predictable themes and structural issues of family business dynamics, rather than fatal character flaws of the family member concerned. By concentrating on the key challenges of education, governance and succession planning, as identified by the expert group, the hope would be that the effects of these structural issues could be identified and compensated for.

To paraphrase Fisher and Ury we need to be hard on the problem and soft on the person.[68]

---

[67] Peter Leach *Family Businesses – The Essentials* (Profile Books, 2007) at p 5.
[68] Roger Fisher, William Ury *Getting to Yes: Negotiating an agreement without giving in* (Penguin, 1981).

1.5 FIVE FAMILY BUSINESS STORIES

Many of the concepts and much of the terminology used in this book is fairly abstract. To place some of this in context we will look briefly at the stories of five family businesses, in a variety of industries and of different ages and sizes. One of these stories features a business that is an international household name. However four of the stories have been found from the pages of legal case reports and cannot therefore be presented as tales of outright, unqualified family business success. There is a strong argument that the difficulties that these businesses encountered could be seen as structural issues, a product of the family business environment, rather than the result of any basic personality defect of the family members concerned.

These case studies will be used to provide reference and anchor points throughout the book.

1.5.1 The early stage founder led family business: Park House Properties and the Carters

The case of *Re Park House Properties Ltd*[69] provides a familiar scenario. The case concerned a company set up to manage buildings (Park House) on an industrial estate leased in his own name by the father and business founder, Mr Carter. He comes across in the case report as a typical serial entrepreneur. We learn that he built up and sold one successful business and then became involved in 'a succession of companies, some of which were successful and others unsuccessful'. Mr Carter was a director of Park House Properties Ltd and held 45% of the shares personally.

The rest of Mr Carter's immediate family were also appointed directors and held shares in the company. Their roles varied.

Mrs Carter (who held 10 shares) played no part in the company whatsoever. Indeed, in cross examination Mr Carter frankly admitted that if his wife had raised any relevant detailed business issues over breakfast he would have 'choked on his cornflakes'.

Mr Carter's son, Ivan and his daughter Alexandra, did work in the business. Ivan was responsible for the maintenance work at Park House and Alexandra for marketing and finding occupiers. Although Mr Carter involved his children in meetings with the company's accountants, neither acted in any real managerial capacity. The judge in the case found that Mr Carter was 'effectively solely responsible for all management and financial decisions'.

It will be seen that Park House Properties clearly qualifies as a family business under the expert group definition above. It would also qualify as such under most of the other definitions considered above.[70]

The founder, Mr Harrison personally held only 45% of the shares in the company. In theory his voice was one of four on the board. Notwithstanding this the key question is

---

[69] The court case from which this case study is obtained was reported at [1998] BCC 847. The legal issues arising from the case are considered in chapter 8 (Directors' Duties).
[70] The exception being the requirement suggested by Daily and Thompson that at least one generational transfer should have taken place before an organisation assumes full family business status.

to what extent could Park House Properties truly be seen to be a family business with the rest of the family participating fully in it, rather than Mr Harrison's business in which he happened to have given shares and directorships to his immediate family? Put differently how far up the F-PEC scale would Park House Properties sit? In reality not very far.

1.5.2 First generation succession: the Davies family

The Davies family case concerns a farming family and their struggles with the first succession, in this case father to son. The family business was a small Welsh farm, less than a hundred acres which initially been rented by the parents, Tom and Ellen Davies, but after a lot of hard work and effort, had been bought by them outright.

Although all of their five children worked on the farm during their spare time when they were up growing, only their middle child, a son, James appears to have shown any real interest in farming. His brothers and sisters left the farm to pursue their own lives and careers but James gave up any thought of an alternative career.

When James was just about to leave school and considering his future he faced a choice between joining the police force and going to agricultural college and joining the family farm. James chose the latter and devoted his life to working on the family farm.

He was influenced in doing so by promises made to him by Tom that if he stayed to work on the farm the place would be his.[71]

In some ways matters went well in the Davies family business. There is no evidence of friction in the working relationship between James and Tom. The business was run as farming partnership (and kept separate from the underlying ownership of the land). James was admitted to the partnership and, in due course became sole proprietor, when his parents retired from active farming. They went to live in a bungalow that they had built on land forming part of the farm, leaving James and his young family in occupation of the main farmhouse.

The business prospered under James' stewardship and he was able to expand the farm and to make fairly substantial capital investments, for example, in a new milking parlour.

But in other ways the Davies family were far less successful.

Tom's relationship with James' long-term partner, Cindy was initially good. But this deteriorated over time with Tom recording in his diary 'that he felt that Cindy bossed his son and did not care for him or the farm'.[72] Relationships were sufficiently poor within the family that when James and Cindy eventually married they did so without inviting any guests.

Secondly the Davies family were spectacularly poor at talking to each other. The detail of their ineffective communication will be explained in the next chapter (Themes).

---

[71] See para 4 of the judgment in the case, reported as *Davies v Davies* [2015] EWHC 1384 (Ch). Although the rest of the family disputed James' version of events this was accepted by the court.
[72] At para 33 of the judgment.

As mentioned above Tom and Ellen had four other children apart from James. Notwithstanding the early promises made to James (which were repeated subsequently and also confirmed by Tom to his own friends and confidants) the position of their other children does not seem to have been far from the minds of the couple and, in particular of Ellen. Tom and Ellen appeared to have been greatly troubled by the great debate of fairness and equality discussed in a little more detail in the next chapter and generally throughout the book.

Add in the fact that none of the discussions concerning ownership of the family business were ever recorded in formal documents to the above issues of attitude to in-laws, communication and the pressure towards equal treatment, these combined to provide the ingredients for an inheritance dispute that eventually came before the High Court.

1.5.3 The second-generation sibling partnership: the Cadman Developments Ltd

In contrast to Park House Properties, Cadman Developments can be seen as a family business, whatever definition is used. The case also introduces two key family business themes. First, the personality of the founder and its impact on the survival prospects of a family business. Secondly ownership philosophy: should ownership of a family business be for the wider family or just those who work in the business?

Described in the law report as a 'sad breakdown in family relationships' Cadman Developments Ltd[73] concerned a second-generation property company, initially set up in 1961 by James Cadman as a vehicle for carrying on a building and property development business. James had three children Janis, Cedric and Rodney. At about the time the business was set up James and his wife Edith, moved from the West Midlands to Stamford in Lincolnshire, taking with them their two sons, who joined their father in the business. Until their deaths James and Edith acted as directors of the company alongside Cedric and Rodney.

Janis, who was married with children of her own by the time the rest of her family decamped to Lincolnshire, remained behind in the Midlands. It is clear that she remained emotionally close to her parents. Although she played no role in the family company her father James gifted her 200 shares, at the same time as making a similar gift to his sons, who did work in the business. A property was also bought through the company at Hagley in the West Midlands. In effect this was a holiday home so that James and Edith would have somewhere to stay close to their daughter (referred to as Mrs Fisher throughout the court judgement) when they returned 'home' to visit her and their grandchildren.

Under James' leadership Cadman Developments appears to have been a highly successful small family business. The judgment refers to a 'number of successful building and housing developments'. The company had also built up a small portfolio of investment properties, presumably by reinvesting profits from the main building business.

---

[73] Reported as *Girvan Janis Fisher v Cedric Cadman, Rodney Cadman, Cadman Developments Limited* [2005] EWHC 377 (Ch) and usually referred to as *Fisher v Cadman*. The legal points arising from the case are considered in Part F.

James comes across as a strong and domineering character, who 'maintained a firm grip on the company' and also on his sons. For example James insisted that his sons carry out repairs and undertake the day to day running of the property portfolio without payment. As a question of fact the trial judge found that the brothers:

> 'Cedric and Rodney Cadman had long had a sense that they had been treated harshly by their father, by not being paid remuneration for their day to day running of [Cadman Developments Ltd]. In my judgment, they felt inhibited about doing anything about that while their father and mother were alive, but once their mother died they decided that an opportune moment had come to rectify what they regarded as an injustice from the past.'

The Cadman family story is further complicated by the fact that in 1969 Cedric and Rodney set up their own building and property development company, Cadman Homes Limited (CHL). Although James Cadman was 'unhappy about this development' he made a small investment in CHL as did the in-laws of both Cedric and Rodney. The two brothers continued to work for both CHL and Cadman Developments Limited (CDL) and both companies entered into various transactions with each other over the years.

Notwithstanding this fairly complex business and ownership position, little or nothing was done by way of formal governance. The affairs of CDL 'were run with considerable informality while James Cadman was alive' which the trial judge found to be 'unsurprising, in view of its nature as a small family company'.

The concept of a sibling partnership; where, most typically the '... & Sons' in the second generation take over the running of a family business created by their father is widely used in family business circles and is also frequently referred to in this book. There appears to be no doubt that Cedric and Rodney were operating their own company, CHL, as a sibling partnership. Equally the sibling partnership label seems to apply to their own participation in CDL after James' death. The issue was the extent to which Janis was excluded from this partnership.

Janis gave evidence that it was intended that she should take an active part in the running of the company. The judge found that, although her participation was supported by their father, the brothers had opposed their sister's involvement so that:

> '... there was never any mutual understanding between Mrs Fisher and any other member of the family that she should be involved in the management of the company.'

James Cadman died in 1994 followed by Edith in 1997. James left half of his shares in CDL to Edith and the other half equally to his three children. Edith also left those shares equally to the three children. So, following Edith's death, CDL was owned in roughly equal shares by the three siblings. Janis also inherited a small interest (3.7%) in CHL, representing part of her father's initial investment in that company.

Following the death of their parents the state of uneasy equilibrium that had hitherto prevailed between the three siblings disintegrated and the trial judge noted 'episodes in the past between them that have generated a good deal of ill-feeling and upset'. By 2002 relationships had disintegrated to the point that proceedings had been issued and in 2005 three siblings, each in their sixties, faced each other in court. Why?

Clearly there was a legal reason. Janis had issued an unfair prejudice petition based on her brothers' attempt to exclude her from participation in CDL.

Were there behavioural or psychological factors creating or exacerbating the dispute? Possibly but we can only speculate about such matters as they will not emerge from a legal case report. Were there structural reasons, relating to family dynamics that made such a dispute predictable and therefore to an extent avoidable or containable? Almost certainly, and we will pause from time to time as we go through this book to point these out.

1.5.4 The later stage 'cousin consortium' family business: Saul D Harrison plc and the Harrison family

The next family business to introduce is Saul D Harrison plc. As one of the two leading cases on unfair prejudice and one directly concerning a family owned business it is of considerable significance and is discussed in detail in Part E.[74]

This family business was based in the East End of London, founded by Saul Harrison and historically had been engaged in making industrial cleaning cloths. By the time the case came to court the management of the company was in the hands of the third and fourth generations of the Harrison family. Although the company was (at least in a non-technical accounting sense) a medium sized business with turnover of £5m and approximately 100 employees and was registered as a public company, this was a historical anomaly relating to a previous investment. The High Court judge dealing with the case, Mr Justice Vinelott, described the business as 'a classic example of a private family company'.

By the time the matter came to court in the 1990's the business had already been through two generational transitions. Ownership and management roles were spread between the third and fourth generations of the Harrison family and between various family branches. We are now looking at a large business owning family, what is usually labelled a 'cousin consortium,' in family business circles. Saul D Harrison plc, had a complex ownership structure. Whilst by no means unique in later stage family companies, the structure in this case was more complex than most. In 1960 the share capital of the company had been re-organised to create three classes of shares, each with different rights relating to voting and entitlement to income and capital.

The Saul D Harrison business had struggled for some years, veering from modest profitability to minor losses, but with a significant loss of £336k being recorded in the year immediately before the matter reached the Court of Appeal. The root cause of this could well be attributed to second generation of management who appear to have been reluctant to let go of the reins and allowed the business to stagnate, keeping faith with out dated products and manufacturing processes.

As family businesses go down the generations, the family tree is likely to grow ever wider. Even based on modern demographics with everyone having, on average, just less than two children each it becomes virtually impossible for a family business to accommodate the 8 or so children who will comprise the third generation. Of course not all children in the third generation might want to join the family business as employees. But they may well retain an economic interest in or emotional attachment to that business.

---

[74] The case is reported at [1994] BCC 475.

Saul D Harrison & Sons plc, could be seen as a classic case of 'haves' and 'have-nots'. One of the third generation was a director. Two of the fourth generation were employed in the business and had just joined the board. The working family directors had reasonable salaries, pensions, private medical insurance and company cars. Their wives were employed on modest salaries and also had cars. The insiders also had access to information about the family business.

The wider family members, including the petitioner had no dividends, nor given the current performance of the business, had they any reasonable prospect of receiving dividends. Neither did they have a viable exit route or any means of unlocking the value, including valuable freehold property, tied up in the family company and forming part of the wider family wealth and inheritance.

A key fact in the case was that the company's factory premises were wanted for redevelopment as part of the Jubilee Line extension project. The board decided to take the relocation compensation (in excess of £2m) and reinvested this in new premises.

A petition for unfair prejudice was presented by Rosemary, one of the great-grand-daughters of the founder Saul Harrison. She held about 8.25% of the C shares, which carried no voting rights and only limited rights to receive dividends. Her argument was that the company was being run for the benefit of the 'haves', the working family members rather than in the best interests of the wider family. In particular she complained that the board or controlling shareholders had missed a golden opportunity to cash in, wind the business up and distribute capital to the family when the old premises were sold. Instead the board had chosen to put their own interests in receiving salary and other benefits of employment first. The petitioner argued that, in doing so, the board were acting in bad faith and in breach of their duties as directors.

In many ways it might be thought that the position of the non-working family members could indeed be seen to be unfair. That part of their inheritance represented by their interest in the company was effectively worthless.

But, as explained in detail in Part E the legal claim failed dismally, leaving the petitioner marooned in the family company and no doubt with an embittered set of relatives and a substantial legal bill to boot.

The legal aspects of the Saul D Harrison story are considered in more detail in Part E. But there are many aspects of the story that draw out wider family business themes. The most obvious of these is the difficult position of remote family shareholders, the have-nots or outsiders, together with the related need to introduce governance processes and ownership practices to recognise the position of family members in such a position. These issues are dealt with in more detail in chapter 17.

Other family business themes include the commitment of Saul D Harrison to its workforce and the community in which the business was based. A significant factor in favour of the majority family shareholders was the backing of the court for the director's decision to keep the business going partly for the benefit of the employees, including a number of employees with special educational needs.

But there does appear to be a happy ending of sorts to the Harrison family story. The business itself survived its trip to the Court of Appeal, continues under the leadership of

Stephen Harrison, profitable, still providing 35 jobs and, as proof positive of the suggestion that family owned businesses tend to have lower gearing, with almost £1m cash in its bank account and very little borrowings.[75]

1.5.5 The large family owned business: Clark's Shoes and the Clark family

A business that needs little introduction is Clark's Shoes, a fixture of most British high streets and an iconic British brand. Clarks is still largely family owned and now with a turnover of £1.49 billion and annual pre-tax profits in excess of £120 million.[76]

The business was started in 1825, by brothers Cyrus and James Clark in Street, Somerset. Notwithstanding the aphorism that family businesses go from clogs to clogs in three generations Clarks now have an eighth generation of family shareholders.

But, like Saul D Harrison, the path has not always been smooth for the C&J Clark family business. The most notable recent hurdle that the family have had to overcome, a dispute over whether to accept a take-over bid from Berisford, a US company, is dealt with as a detailed case study in chapter 17 (Governance). Other, less well-known difficulties encountered by the Clarks family business are discussed at various stages of this book.[77]

1.6 CONCLUSION

Having emphasised the importance of the family owned business, not only to the UK economy, but also worldwide we have attempted to grasp the essence of what it is that makes a business a family business. We have done so by looking at the definition of a family business, by attempting to identify the key advantages and challenges presented by the family business model and also by looking at the stories of a number of individual family businesses at various stages of evolution.

In the next chapter we drill down a little deeper into the nature of family business life and identify some key themes relating to family business dynamics.

---

[75] Statutory accounts to 31 March 2015.
[76] Statutory accounts for year ending 31 January 2015.
[77] The Clarks' story is told in Mark Palmer's book *Made to Last* (Profile Books, 2013).

CHAPTER 2

THEMES

2.1 INTRODUCTION

Every individual is unique. Every family is therefore comprised of unique individuals. Each business is different. So it must follow that no two family business situations can ever be identical. Nevertheless certain common themes emerge from looking at both family business literature and also the cases of individual business families that have found themselves before the British courts.

The two core and universally acknowledged issues facing family businesses are succession and governance. Succession related issues include the vulnerability of the family owned business during the process of intergenerational transfer. The closely related topic of governance emphasises the importance for a business owning family in investing time, effort and thought in family business governance, for the health of both their business and family relationships. Those twin key topics are both subjects of chapters in their own right. Succession and governance can also be seen as core threads running right through the middle of this book.

But underlying those two core issues there are another set of issues and themes frequently encountered in family business life. In this chapter we will introduce some of those sub themes.

We will look at:
- The role of the founder including letting go and the entrepreneurial mind-set.
- Ambivalence.
- Fairness and equality.
- Communication and taboos.
- Conflict.
- Fairness and equality.
- Insiders and outsiders.
- Father and son relationships.
- Father and daughter relationships.
- The psychological status of the family business.
- Sibling rivalry.
- Professionalisation.
- Myths.

- Scripts.

2.2 THE FOUNDER

The biggest paradox for many family businesses is that their greatest strength, their founder, the source of life, creation and inspiration for the family firm can also be their greatest enemy, presenting the main obstacle to the continuation of their own creation.

Entrepreneurs can be found at any stage of the life of a family business. But entrepreneurialism is more typically found in and associated with the founder of a family business. Indeed Dr Peter Davis suggests that 'all founders of family businesses are entrepreneurs'.[1]

2.2.1 The Ford story

Perhaps the most graphic illustration example of the above proposition is the early story the Ford motor company. That the company is still going strong is both because of and despite its founder, Henry Ford.

Much has been written about the drive, vision and zeal of Henry Ford, who is frequently credited with introducing the modern mass-produced motor-car. Less well known is how aspects of Henry's personality and, in particular his relationship with his son, Edsel, almost destroyed the business that Henry had created. Henry Ford had appointed his son Edsel as President of the, by then, already highly successful motor company and transferred about 40% of the shares in the company to Edsel when his son was still in his early forties. Although a very different character to his father, by all accounts, Edsel was an extremely capable individual. He attempted to introduce various innovations to the Ford products, marketing and labour relations and was generally admired for his ideas and management approach.

But Henry remained as Chairman of Ford. Through a mixture of voting control, force of personality, riding roughshod over management lines and organisational structures, Henry continued to dominate the business and still exercised all the real power. In particular Henry sought to dominate Edsel. All of Edsel's important ideas were overruled by Henry, who portrayed his son as weak and incompetent. Edsel persisted notwithstanding his father's opposition and:[2]

> 'drove himself to exhaustion and illness in the face of repeated contradictions and scoldings by an old man who ran the show from retirement.'

Tragically this all led to the premature death of Edsel. His widow had little doubt that much of the blame for her husband's death could be laid at Henry's door.

---

[1] Peter Davis 'Three Types Of Founders – And Their Dark Sides' (1990) *Family Business Magazine*.
[2] David Landes *Dynasties: Fortune and Misfortune in the World's Great Family Businesses* (Penguin, 2006) at p 139.

Against Henry's wishes the rest of the family used their voting control to appoint Edsel's second son Henry Ford II, Henry's grandson as vice president. By this time the Ford business was on its knees. On appointment Henry II visited the main Ford plant and:[3]

'was stunned to find the company was as decrepit and senile as the old man himself.'

The Ford Motor Company has obviously survived and thrived. Equally clearly the Ford story is extreme. However elements of that story (thankfully usually heavily diluted) are present in innumerable family businesses, which have reached the second generation and beyond. For example in *Fisher v Cadman*[4] we learn that James Cadman was a successful entrepreneur, responsible for building a successful construction company and accumulating, by most people's standards, a large portfolio of investment properties. We also get a picture of a tyrannical father, particularly in his dealings with his sons Cedric and Rodney, one who was quick to demand that they contribute to the family enterprise, but reluctant to acknowledge that contribution, in financial or other terms.

2.2.2 Letting go

Frequently difficulties within a family business are attributed to the reluctance on the part of the founder to let go of what they have created and to pass their business on to the next generation. In many ways this is understandable. The founder has never had to deal with succession planning before, and so they do not know how to deal with the process.

Some of the obstacles to the founder letting go that are more readily attributable to external factors rather than the personality of the entrepreneur founder. These could include that:

- the founder has not made provision so as to be financially independent from the business;
- a reluctance to chose a successor, because of fear of being seen to favour one child against another;
- there is no family member in the next generation genuinely ready or capable of leading the business.

But equally many examples of the founder hanging on to power and control can be properly seen as a factor of their mindset. The reluctance of the founder to let go could be for a variety of reasons:

- A misplaced belief that no-one else is capable of running the business – particularly the case with a dominant founder.
- Dealing with succession is an admission of their own mortality.
- The business is their 'baby', and they do not want to let go because of the sense of loss and purpose.
- The relationship between parent and offspring (and more often than not that of father and son) is so poor that the father does not want to pass over control.

---

[3] David Landes *Dynasties: Fortune and Misfortune in the World's Great Family Businesses* (Penguin, 2006) at p 139.
[4] The story of Cadman Developments Ltd as told in *Girvan Janis Fisher v Cedric Cadman, Rodney Cadman, Cadman Developments Limited* [2005] EWHC 377 (Ch) and usually referred to as *Fisher v Cadman*. More detail is provided in chapter 1 – as one of five core family business stories.

- As a result of previous friction, the potential next generation successor has left the business.

This failure on the part of the founding entrepreneur to let go is one of main reasons why family firms fall at the first hurdle, failing to make a successful transition from first to second generation. It is therefore worth looking at the entrepreneurial mindset in a little more detail.

2.2.3 Entrepreneurs and founders

So far we have used the terms 'entrepreneur' and 'founder' pretty much interchangeably. Dr Peter Davis disagrees and distinguishes between the two terms. He argues that whilst all those who start up a business are entrepreneurs they do not necessarily also become founders. Some additional ingredient is required before an entrepreneur becomes the founder of a family business:[5]

> 'Founders are typically intuitive and emotional people. They obviously have the drive and ambition to build a great business, but they also have a feeling about the place, a love of what they have created that makes them want to perpetuate it through the generations.'

But even after an entrepreneur has made the shift in their mental gearing so as to want to pass the business they have created onto to the next generation it still might not be a smooth ride. Henry Ford had clearly become a founder under, Dr Davis' categorisation, intending to pass the Ford business to Edsel. By the time he was 40 Edsel had 40% of the shares and the title of president. So what stopped Henry?

Dr Davis identifies three types of founders:

- **Proprietors**. For these individuals ownership, rather than mere control, is the most important. Their identity and that of the company are generally intertwined, and they don't have much trust in anybody else to make decisions. They will also dominate their children and other family members involved with the business.
  Both Henry Ford and James Cadman seem to be have been proprietors. This can lead to the children becoming dependent and submissive. Cedric and Rodney Cadman seem to fall into this category.
  Alternatively the offspring become rebellious. There may be a stage of fighting back against the founder, with deterioration in the relationship and an ultimate parting of the ways. In the case of Fords this came about as a result of Edsel's tragic death.
  Davis believes that which category the offspring fall into depends a lot on the character and personality of the founder's spouse. A meek and submissive spouse is likely to produce equally dependent and submissive children. The role of Edith Cadman is notably passive. On the other hand if the spouse regularly stands up to the founder it is more likely that children in the family business will do likewise. Henry Ford's wife Clara played a pivotal role in his removal from the Ford business, in favour of his grandson, Henry Ford II.
- **Conductors**. Conductors are also keen to remain firmly in control, but they are more open to allowing the development of good staff. They will delegate some responsibility and try to develop harmony in the business. As a result they like the idea of developing a family business and allowing their children to join them.

---

[5] Peter Davis 'Three Types Of Founders – And Their Dark Sides' (1990) *Family Business Magazine*.

Often conductors will encourage their children to take over different divisions or operations of the business. Whilst they are proud of the family and want to create a common purpose, conductors still want to remain firmly in control.

In the early stages, when the rest of the family are prepared to take direction from the conductor all can work well. But as the business matures and the conductor ages there might be a wrestling match between the children to claim the conductor's baton. Unwilling to choose between his children the conductor might prefer to sell the family business instead.

Tom Davies may well be seen as a conductor. He seemed to have little difficulty passing over the day-to-day management of the farm to James.

- **Technicians.** Technicians build businesses based on their own technical or creative skills. They can be obsessive, and are happiest when working on new designs or products. Generally they will try to avoid administration and management matters. They will only succeed by delegating these aspects, either to non-family managers or to family members. Technicians typically believe that they have special knowledge and they will be reluctant to pass this on to their children. Consequently the children tend to take alternative roles where they can create their own niche.

All types of founders have positive characteristics. These can be harnessed during the earlier part of their career in building a successful business. But Davis argues that each also has a 'dark side' which will emerge as the founder approaches retirement age.[6] The success of the transition to the next generation and the survival of the family business will depend on the ability of the founder to do so.

Logically it would appear that conductors have the greatest prospects of success. Proprietors and technicians are inherently more ego-centric. But Davis believes that, even in the case of a conductor founder, a successful transition is likely to be achieved at considerable cost, including the emotional cost to the conductor consequent upon making difficult choices. The choice might be between family members, or perhaps between family members and third party managers. Perhaps this will result in family members leaving the business. According to Davis the consultant is also likely to engage and incur the cost of paying for an army of consultants and advisors to help with the transition process.

2.2.4 The psychology of the entrepreneur

The drive and vision of the founding entrepreneur forms the foundation for the success of the family firm. Much has been written about entrepreneurship. De Vries and colleagues devote a whole chapter in *Family Business on the Couch* to the psychological profiles of entrepreneurs. Bivalence (considered as a separate theme later in this chapter) comes to the fore.

The good news is that adjectives typically attached to entrepreneurs include creative, imaginative, risk taking, energetic, 'contagious enthusiasm', 'achievement-orientated'. As de Vries sees it:[7]

---

[6] This theme of ambivalence is explored in detail in the next paragraph of this chapter.
[7] Op cit at p 112.

> 'By conveying a sense of conviction and purpose, they persuade others to follow them. Whatever it is – seductiveness, gamesmanship, theatre, or charisma – entrepreneurs know how to build an organisation and give it momentum.'

But, according to de Vries et al and the sources they cite, that entrepreneurial drive may well have been fuelled by difficulties in the entrepreneur's childhood (including death, poverty, illness and desertion). Therefore, whilst outwardly appearing to manifest extreme confidence, many entrepreneurs are in fact deeply troubled and much of their entrepreneurial behaviour can be seen as a product of low self-confidence and insecurity.

According to Levinson an entrepreneur:[8]

> 'characteristically has unresolved conflicts with his father ... He is therefore uncomfortable when being supervised and starts his own business both to outdo his father and to escape the authority and rivalry of more powerful figures.'

Detailed aspects of the 'inner theatre', of the entrepreneur which have the potential to derail the family business include:

- a need for personal control and with it a rejection and distrust of management structures and third parties, both within and outside the family business, capable of diluting the entrepreneur's control;
- distrust of the abilities and also motives of others, at times bordering on paranoia;
- excessive mood swings where the entrepreneur veers between exhilaration and despair at the state of their business. According to De Vries this can often be counter-cyclical or 'cyclothymic'. So paradoxically the entrepreneur, feeling unworthy of success and fearing that their luck is about to run out appears to be least happy when things are objectively going well but most enthused and driven when their backs are against the wall; and
- attention seeking behaviour.

De Vries identifies and labels a number of aspects of typical entrepreneurial behaviour which flow for this including:

- **Splitting** a defensive behaviour whereby the entrepreneur sees events and people in entirely black and white terms, either all good or all bad and, particularly so far as people are concerned, a tendency to swing from one extreme to another. So that, for example an employee or family member who has been quickly placed on a pedestal is just as quickly torn down.
- **Projection** or the tendency to blame others for our own failings or weaknesses. Rather than facing up to these, the blame is allowed to fall elsewhere, leading to insularity and political infighting.
- **Flight into action** or responding to stress and anxiety by taking impulsive and ill-thought action that allows the entrepreneur to maintain an illusion of control but which may ultimately prove to be destructive.

The challenge for any entrepreneur is to engage the positive aspects of their psychological tool kit, whilst managing these negative tendencies in a way that does least damage to their business. The additional challenge for the founding entrepreneur of a family firm is to do so in a way that causes least damage to the rest of their family.

---

[8] Levinson 'Conflicts that Plague Family Businesses' *Harvard Business Review* (March 1971).

2.2.5 The balanced entrepreneur

This theme is taken up by Lucia Ceja Barba.[9] Amongst other personality traits[10] she identified narcissism as a defining characteristic of many entrepreneurs. At an extreme or 'unbalanced' level narcissism will be manifested in arrogance, egocentricity and lack of empathy on the part of the entrepreneur. However in the less extreme form of the 'balanced narcissist' these less attractive traits will be subdued, leaving a confident ambitious and inspirational entrepreneur.

It is those balanced entrepreneurs who, coupled with the desire identified by Peter Davis to become founders, build the foundations of the many successful multi-generational family businesses in the UK today.

2.3 AMBIVALENCE[11]

It can be seen that Henry Ford had a deeply ambivalent attitude towards Edsel. At one level he clearly wanted Edsel to succeed and to take over from him as business leader and majority owner. But at another level Henry appeared resentful of Edsel's achievements as a manager and seemed to see his son as a rival and a threat.

Such ambivalence is a characteristic feature of family business life. Other similar words or concepts often employed with regard to the family business situation are, ambiguous, duality, paradoxical, dichotomous, opposed, contradictory, equivocal, mixed and tension.

Ambivalence can be found across the full spectrum of family business life and is certainly not confined to succession related tensions between fathers and sons. Another key example would be the relationship of siblings, especially brothers in a family business, who can by degrees be both the closest of collaborators or the most bitter of enemies.

What is seen as the main root cause of this ambivalence, that there are three separate systems operating in any family business (family, business – or management, and ownership), and the well-known three-circle model, which illustrates this phenomenon is explored in detail in the following chapter. But the basic features of ambivalence are examined in some detail in the seminal article first suggesting that model; *Bivalent Attributes of the Family Firm*[12] by Harvard academic Renato Tagiuri and John Davis.[13]

The primary argument of Tagiuri and Davis is that family firms possess 'several unique, inherent attributes' which are simultaneously a 'source of benefits and disadvantages' for the stakeholders of a family business.

---

[9] 'Balancing Personality Traits: Capitalizing on the strengths of our "true self"' *FFI Practitioner*, 23 April 2014.
[10] The article suggested that the other personality traits often found in entrepreneurs were that they were antisocial, histrionic, dependent, obsessive compulsive and schizoid. Again in unbalanced form these were unhelpful. It is argued that in balanced form these are potential sources of strength for both the entrepreneur and their business.
[11] Defined in the Concise Oxford English Dictionary as the 'coexistence in one person of the emotional attitudes of love and hate, or other opposite feelings towards the same object or situation'.
[12] *Family Business Review* (1996), Vol 9(2) at pp 199–208.
[13] Then of the Owner Managed Business Institute in California.

The trick (and it is indeed a difficult one to pull off) for those involved is therefore to reap the benefit of those advantages whilst recognising and seeking to minimise the effect of the corresponding disadvantages. Tagiuri and Davis warn that it will not be possible to fully eliminate the negative aspects believing that these, as well as the positive attributes, are an inevitable feature of family business life, which arise from the overlap of the various systems in play.

In detail Tagiuri and Davis identified the following as 'bivalent attributes':

- **Simultaneous roles.** This attribute is at the heart of systems thinking and the three-circle model. Key individuals in a family business will occupy multiple roles as a family member, owner and, often, as a director or manager. This can enhance co-operation, loyalty and trust. It can streamline decision-making and promote efficiency.
  But the fact that family members are also colleagues can be problematic. Tagiuri and Davis note that 'families traditionally seek internal unity and try to repress or deny rivalry' whereas businesses 'often strive for a healthy level of internal competition'. Difficult performance related issues might be ducked to avoid conflict. Either the business or family relations are likely to suffer in these circumstances.
  Also the existence of simultaneous roles creates the likelihood of role confusion and the potential to 'move in and out of roles'. The authors suggest that in a conflict situation a father/managing director is likely to revert to whichever role gives them the greatest power over their subordinate/son.
  Conflicts and disputes that do arise become harder to resolve because of the complexity created by these simultaneous roles.
- **Shared identity.** Over time a family business will develop its own culture and identity. The business owning family will become associated with this family firm identity, potentially gaining credibility and respect in their community.
  But the converse is true. Reputational damage caused by the poor conduct of either the business or by a family member can then leak across the divide between the two systems.
  Alternatively a 'gold-fish bowl' effect might be created whereby members of well-known business families feel themselves to be permanently 'on-duty' as guardians of the family business reputation.
- **Lifelong common history.** Family members will have grown up together. They will have an instinctive understanding of each other's strengths and weaknesses. This can promote superlative teamwork.
  However the potential for family members to outgrow an earlier adverse reputation is diminished, such and such 'has always been like that ever since he was a child', just as the potential to become trapped in behaviour patterns having their roots in family interactions grows.
- **Emotional involvement (and confusion).** Clearly family members involved in a family firm will have a much closer emotional involvement than colleagues who are not related.
  Again this can lead to increased loyalty, motivation and trust which can be a huge source of strength for the family firm. The converse can apply. Family relationships can be fractured to a much greater extent than would typically be found between colleagues, poisoning the working atmosphere and substantially detracting from the efficiency of the family firm, and in the worst cases jeopardising its survival.[14]

---

[14] See for example the Harding family farming case discussed in Part E.

The emotional landscape of a family firm can rarely be painted as black or white or static. It is likely to be much more nuanced and variable. At times relatives who basically get along well will find themselves filled with a violent hatred of one another. Whilst the trigger for this might arise in a business context, often the root of this strong emotion can be traced back to an earlier family cause. The source of that emotion might be sufficiently deeply buried as to be invisible to the family members concerned. Even if the issue is capable of being recognised and articulated the family culture might prevent the problem from being aired and discussed. Tagiuri and Davis believe that 'there are generally strict psychological prohibitions against open conflict among family members'.

The complexity of the emotional landscape of the family business and the resulting potential for damaging conflict is explored in much more detail later in this chapter.

- **Private language.** Family members who have grown up together may well have developed their own form of communication shorthand, both verbal and non-verbal. This family language can give the family business a significant advantage in terms of the depth, clarity and speed of communication.

  But a private family language can also be a barrier to entry, for example to non-family executives. The efficiency of a family firm can be jeopardised if subtle signals, embodied in the private language of the family members, are missed by the non-family manager concerned.

  Private language can also be a trigger for negative emotions and confusion discussed in the previous paragraph.

- **Mutual awareness and privacy.** Family members working together will have a very clear idea of each other's personal circumstances. This may be directly communicated between family members or it may be gathered from the unspoken private family language referred to above or gleaned indirectly via the family grapevine.

  This can be a source of strength, for example allowing the rest of the family to offer support and understanding to a family member with a sick child, over and above what could be expected in a non-family setting.

  But the ability of the family member to keep their private and work lives separate is correspondingly compromised.

  The issue of privacy can be compounded in settings where work and home are virtually inseparable, for example agricultural, hotel or leisure family businesses where the family members often 'live on top of each other'.

- **Meaning of the family company.** Finally Tagiuri and Davis note that the family firm itself can have a strong meaning for family members.[15] This can be both positive in terms of attachment and pride. Alternatively the relationship between the family members may be more complex and capable of giving rise to difficulties. The psychological status of the family firm is explored in more detail in **2.10** below.

2.4 COMMUNICATION AND TABOOS

The theme of communication, or more precisely ineffective communication, is hugely significant for business families. There is an understandable concern about offending fellow family members. But that concern can quickly lead to difficult subjects being avoided altogether.

---

[15] This seems to have been a factor for Janis Fisher in the Cadman family case.

US psychologist Steven Hendlin identified the 'inheritance taboo' as having a powerful grip on families generally and not just those in business together.[16]

Certainly the Davies family were affected by the inheritance taboo. Although Tom promised James that the family farm would pass to him if he worked on the farm this was not discussed with the remaining children. Indeed a suggestion emerges that Tom might not have discussed this promise even with his wife, Ellen.[17] Neither did James mention his expectations of inheritance to his brothers and sisters. Nor apparently did the siblings ask their parents who would be inheriting the farm, even at the time the parents moved out of the farmhouse, leaving James and his family in occupation.

The inheritance taboo appears to have over-ridden the inevitable curiosity of the Davies children, even when they were aware that their mother and father had made wills. Indeed in James' case it was some 12 years after his father's death before he learnt the contents of his father's will and that, after all the farm had not been left to him alone but to the wider family equally.[18] Shortly afterwards the family found themselves in court.

On the basis that governance involves 'the right people talking about the right things at the right time' it must follow that the failure by a family to talk at all or to the wrong people or at the wrong time is a failure of governance; alternatively a governance application point missed. The link between communication and governance is clear and strong. The Davies story can be seen as a catalogue of governance application points missed.[19]

Although powerful, the inheritance taboo is not the only taboo in family business circles. Other taboos include questioning the competence, performance or even remuneration of family managers[20] or, more challengingly, substance abuse or psychological difficulties of family members. Indeed it would be rare for a business owning family not to have at least 'one elephant in the room'.

Of course taboos are not the exclusive property of business families. The difficulty for family businesses arises when the effects of the taboo, having at its root a desire to avoid family conflict begin to be felt within the business system. According to Kets de Vries and colleagues taboos persist:[21]

> '... because they are such good social defence mechanisms (with their unspoken objective of keeping the family together), they are not easily challenged. In corporate culture, employees question the myths at their peril.'

---

[16] Steven J Hendlin *Overcoming the Inheritance Taboo: How to preserve relationships and transfer possessions* (Plume, 2004).
[17] The concern could well have been that Ellen would have objected to James taking the farm on the basis of Ellen's wish to treat all of the children equally. See para 8 of the judgment in the case, reported as *Davies v Davies* [2015] EWHC 1384 (Ch).
[18] It appears that James had (incorrectly) understood that he was already the legal owner of the farm, having bought his parents out of the farming partnership – which, in fact, did not own the land. Ellen, together with at least two brothers who were named as executors in the will choose to keep silent about its contents to preserve family harmony. In particular Ellen was concerned that the inevitable upset might mean that James and Cindy would prevent her seeing her grandchildren (see para 33 of the judgment).
[19] This argument is revisited and expanded in chapter 17 (Governance).
[20] For many years it seemed difficult for Pauline to question the remuneration of her brother in law Ian in the Irvine case (discussed in Part E).
[21] See Kets de Vries and Carlock with Florent-Treacy *Family Business on the Couch* (Wiley, 2007) at p 105.

In the following chapter, Tools, Models and Theories, we introduce some aspects of communication theory, in an attempt to help chart a path through the maze of missed communication.

Rather than being a social defence mechanism, in the long run, ineffective communication and family taboos run the risk of exposing the business owning family to more serious long-term conflict. It is to the theme of conflict in the family firm that we now turn.

2.5 CONFLICT

2.5.1 Conflict: in perspective

Conflict is an inevitable fact of family life. The late Harry Levinson was a Harvard psychology professor and one of the pioneers in bringing a behavioural dimension to the study of business organisations. Echoing Catullus[22] from two millennia previously he suggested that family members should accept that 'since there is love and hate in all relationships, theirs cannot, by definition be pure'.[23]

Family business commentators often quote Tolstoy's observation from *Anna Karenina* that whilst 'all happy families are alike; each unhappy family is unhappy in its own way'. Given the mind blowing complexity of potential combinations of systems, situations and personalities to be found in any family, let alone one in business together, this may well be the case. Nevertheless some themes and commonalities do emerge.

It is absolutely not our intention to attempt a detailed psychological analysis of family business dynamics or to suggest that lawyers, accountants or other professionals dealing with business families should attempt to identify or deal with such issues. Family therapy is a highly specialised and skilled process. Instead our aim is to illustrate that there are often powerful psychological forces at play within the family system. These can create a subtext beneath the presenting issue, be this about succession or employment policies. A practitioner must be aware that something else is being said even if he or she lacks the skills to decipher the hidden message precisely.

What unites happy families and what successful business families have in common is successful communication. That they are able to deal quickly and successfully with their inevitable differences, so that any ill feeling between family members can be swiftly dispelled and the normality of affection restored.

Notwithstanding the inevitability of conflict families can go to extra-ordinary lengths to deny its existence. Expressions of frustration and disappointment, much less anger towards family members become proscribed and family taboo subjects to preserve 'the myth of harmony'.[24]

In the case of the Davies by the time of James' marriage to Cindy, Tom so thoroughly disapproved of Cindy and relationships between the young couple and James' parents were so poor that neither he nor the rest of the family were invited to the wedding. At

---
[22] 'I hate and love. Why I do so, perhaps you ask. I know not, but I feel it, and I am in torment'.
[23] Levinson 'Conflicts that plague family businesses' *Harvard Business Review* (March 1971).
[24] Kets de Vries and Carlock with Florent-Treacy *Family Business on the Couch* (Wiley, 2007) at p 105.

around this time Tom caused a solicitor's letter to be sent to James unilaterally increasing the rent James paid to his parents for the farmland. Tom had not discussed the matter with James beforehand. Neither father nor son mentioned the letter to each other afterwards.[25]

In many ways a family businesses can be seen as breeding ground for conflict. As Nigel Nicholson observes:[26]

> 'In most families, the conflict dissipates as offspring enter adulthood. In family firms, it is kept alive by continual co-dependence around the shared investment of power and wealth that is locked into the firm.'

But Nicholson nevertheless puts forward an argument, based on evolutionary psychology that, as the family business is the closest economic unit to fit with the natural state of human organisation, 'family firms can claim an advantage in that many of their forms are more congruent with human design than are nonfamily firms'. In particular (and following a similar line of reasoning to Tagiuri and Davies in their discussion of the inherent ambivalence of the family business) that the trust and understanding stemming from family relationships creates a powerful potential for co-operation between family members, allowing family owned businesses to out-perform their non-family owned counterparts.

So whilst much of this book concentrates on conflict and disputes in family businesses, it is important to maintain a sense of perspective. There are very many families working happily in business together.

2.5.2 The presenting issue

What typically categorises disputes involving business families is that an issue, which initially seemed to be about business, has clearly become a deeply personal matter for the family members concerned. An experienced mediator and family business commentator, Ian Marsh, suggests that, 'it is never just about the money' and that 'all conflict has its irrational/emotional component'.[27]

That is not to say that all conflict in a family owned business is inherently bad. A level of constructive conflict, focused on achieving the best solution to any given business problem is both healthy and necessary for the long term good of the business and the family. Indeed one of the perceived difficulties facing family owned businesses is that their tendency to homogeneity and introspection creates an inherent conservatism, which will impede such constructive challenge.

It is therefore helpful to begin by looking at various categories of dispute.

---

[25] See para 35 of the judgment.
[26] 'Evolutionary Psychology and Family Business: A New Synthesis for Theory, Research and Practice' *Family Business Review* Vol XXI No 1, March 2008.
[27] *Business Families and Family Businesses* (STEP Handbook, Globe Business Publishing, 2009).

2.5.3 Categories of conflict

Analysing conflict and attempting to distinguish between helpful and destructive conflict Jehn and Mannix[28] identify three different types of conflict which we have applied to a family business context:

Task conflict

Task conflict is where the family members disagree about business decisions, what needs to be done, business decisions and strategy. As such task conflict is the most likely to be seen as constructive conflict.

Process conflict

Process conflict is about the decision making process, including who decides what tasks the family should undertake, the decision making process itself and who will be involved in any implementation. Here the potential for unhealthy conflict grows. If the decision making process is seen to be autocratic, obscure or based on favouritism the seeds for future family disputes may have been sown. Many succession and inheritance disputes fall into this category. In the Davies family case relationships between the five siblings were described as initially good. What categorises the case is a complete absence of anything that could be termed a succession process.

Conversely commentators have argued that a commitment to fair process can greatly reduce the potential for conflict in a family business.[29] In other words family members will accept unpopular decisions, provided that these can be shown to have been arrived at fairly and have been properly communicated. Procedural justice is paramount.

Relationship conflict

Relationship conflict in a family business is where the conflict has more to do with emotions and the dynamics between the family members concerned than the underlying business problem. The dispute may be fuelled by antipathy, jealousy, distrust and other negative emotions. Clearly disputes based on relationship conflict are hugely damaging and destructive, for the family business, the individuals most directly concerned and the wider family.

This may all sound very neat. But in practice there may be elements of more than one type of conflict and potentially all three in any dispute. Take, for example, a disagreement between a son (who is in favour) and a father (who is against) about whether their family business should expand into new markets.

The disagreement is perfectly capable of being wholly, or more realistically largely confined to being one of task conflict. This will be so if the dispute can be categorised by a robust but rational and civilised debate about the benefits and risks of the proposed

---

[28] K A Jehn and E A Mannix 'The dynamic nature of conflict: A longitudinal study of intragroup conflict and group performance' *Academy of Management Journal* (2001), 44(2), 238-251, reviewed in FFI Practitioner 25 January 2015 by Anthony Devine. The underlying study by Jehn and Mannix is based on a sample of MBA students carrying out work place assignments and is not specifically related to family owned businesses.

[29] Blondell, Carlock and Van der Heyden *Fair Process: Striving for Justice in Family Firms*, INSEAD R&D Working Paper 2001.45/ENT.

expansion. This may result in a decision to approve the expansion in principle but to postpone implementation until more favourable market conditions return. Both the relationship of father and son and the family business benefit from the positive process and sensible outcome. But that decision is perfectly capable of seeping over into process conflict. Perhaps the son's carefully thought out business proposal has been peremptorily rejected by the father, without any appearance of due consideration.

Most problematic of all is where the presenting business issue spills over into, or is a symptom of a deeper relationship conflict. The rejection (or postponement) may follow a similar pattern. Perhaps the father has relied on other siblings, perceived by the son to be more favoured, in arriving at his decision. It is then easy to see how existing feelings of frustration or resentment or sibling rivalry could be re-enforced.

Whilst an outcome might be accepted as primarily a rational outcome to a task conflict, this might be tinged with an element of process conflict and relationship conflict. Reflecting on the outcome in the above scenario the son might conclude that 'thinking about it I see that the old man was right but I wish he wouldn't just shoot from the hip like that, it makes it difficult for me to feel listened to'.

The difficulty for both families and their advisors is identifying whether the matter in question has crossed the line and whether the dispute is now less about task or process but now mainly about relationships. In some cases this will be obvious. In Part E, in the context of bad faith in the conduct of family business disputes, we discuss the case of *Burry & Knight Ltd*.[30] At face value Dr Knight's issue could be seen as task conflict, based on concerns about corporate governance and tax compliance in his family business. But the courts had little difficulty in concluding that, 'Dr Knight's real purpose was not that asserted in his request but that of conducting a vendetta against members of the two families' concerned.[31] In other words that relationship conflict had taken over as the driving force. Perhaps a relatively easy conclusion to draw given letters from Dr Knight including phrases such as:[32]

> 'I believe that there is a much bigger problem ... faced with the choice of supporting her dishonest brother or companies or her honest son she chose to lie to the Board thus betraying me as a director and as a mother.'

2.5.4 Conflict symptoms

In many, if not most family business cases, the presence or extent of process conflict and especially relationship conflict may not be immediately obvious to advisors, or even to the family members concerned. Here are some suggested indicators:

Proportionality

To what extent is the degree of conflict and the perception of its importance proportional to the issue at stake?

---

[30] *Burry & Knight and another v Knight* [2014] EWCA Civ 604.
[31] See para 53 of the judgment.
[32] See para 44 of the judgment.

Clearly Dr Knight's statement that he was dealing with 'matters of national importance' which he would seek to bring to the attention of the Charity Commission, the Lord Lieutenant of Hampshire and his MP along with 'other parties likely to be interested' betrayed a lack of proportion.

Tell-tale signs that matters have moved beyond task conflict into the area of relationship conflict include phrases such as 'this was the straw that broke the camel's back'.

Appropriate audience

Is the issue being aired before an appropriate audience? It is clearly part of human nature to let off steam and to talk to friends and spouses about difficulties at work. When this becomes ingrained and habitual, even if the subject matter is about business related task conflict, the sub-text will almost certainly be about relationship conflict.[33]

When a family business member discusses an issue with their accountant. Perhaps the father in the above example talking about the proposed expansion, to what extent are they seeking objective professional expertise on a business issue and to what extent are they seeking an ally or validation of their own supremacy as family business leader? Perhaps the acid test is whether the accountant still retains instructions having agreed with the son.

Some lawyers will have attained the coveted status of trusted advisor to the family business concerned. They may be approached for informal advice on an issue of task conflict. If that approach turns into formal instructions, for example from the son to assist in challenging his father's refusal to expand, then almost invariably the matter has moved into the realm of process and relationship conflict.

The courts have consistently said that they are not the appropriate forum to review business decisions.[34] By extension the legal process does not work to air what, on a proper analysis, are process and relationship related grievances.

The main issue before the courts in *Saul D Harrison & Sons plc*[35] was whether, in deciding to continue the family business and invest in new premises, rather than to shut up shop and distribute the proceeds of sale of the previous premises of the long-standing family business to the family shareholders, the directors had acted to the unfair prejudice of the wider family who were not then receiving any dividends or other return on their interest. That this was on the face of it an example of task conflict, relating to a business decision, does not obscure the reality. That the dispute proceeded as far as the Court of Appeal is a clear indication that the matter was fuelled by process and relationship conflict. In a well-functioning family system there must have been opportunities and mechanisms to prevent the escalation of the conflict if not its origination.

Terminology

The terminology and language used by the family members concerned might be a give-away. Listen carefully. Does the family member sound as though they are discussing

---

[33] Triangulation is discussed at 3.6.3.
[34] This reluctance is long standing. For example see *Carlen v Drury* (1812) 1 Ves & B154 at p 158. Also the more relevant and recent cases involving family business disputes discussed in Part E.
[35] [1994] BCC 475.

a pure business related task conflict or are there clear sounds emerging of feeling badly treated (process conflict) or resentment and hostility (relationship conflict).

Presenting issue

Almost inevitably, if lawyers are instructed to intervene, for whatever reason this will be driven by process or relationship conflict.

That is not to say that there will not be elements of each type of conflict present in any family business dispute. It will be impossible to say with precision how the mix is made up in any given family business conflict. But that does not mean that it is an idle academic exercise to attempt to do so. It is only by honestly and robustly exploring the underlying causes of a family business dispute and the motivations of the parties for pursuing that dispute that the true interests of the family members concerned can be identified and the possibility of a satisfactory resolution opened up.

By focusing on the task conflict, the symptom but not the cause, there is a danger of both exacerbating the problem and losing the opportunity to use more appropriate tools, to alleviate the underlying tension.

Commentators warn that:[36]

> 'Relatives rarely fight openly about what they are really fighting about. Fights or arguments usually go on at one content level and mean something else, especially in families with a long history of bickering. The conflict will continue to recycle if the underlying process issues are not identified, examined and resolved.'

In other words the sub-text cannot be ignored. If it is the opportunity to explore the causes, rather than the symptoms of the dispute, through family business consultancy (or facilitation) or mediation will be lost. We will return to this in Part F.

2.5.5 Conflict resolution strategies

So far we have talked a lot about conflict in family firms but have said little about strategies for dispute resolution. An American academic, Ritch Sorenson,[37] building on earlier research[38] which categorised dispute resolution styles or strategies, studied the approach of about 60 family businesses to assess the effectiveness of these strategies in terms of both family relationships and business performance.

The dispute management strategies identified were:

Competition

This is an outright fight between the family members concerned, categorised by a selfish focus on each individual's own aims and concerns. These disputes are most often

---

[36] Moore *The mediation process: Practical strategies for resolving conflict* (Jossey-Bass, 1986) discussed in *Family Enterprise – Understanding Families in Business and Families of Wealth* (The Family Firm Institute, Wiley 2014).
[37] Sorenson 'Conflict Management Strategies Used by Successful Family Businesses' *Family Business Review* (1999) No 4.
[38] Thomas and Kilmann *Thomas-Kilmann conflict MODE instrument* (Xicom, 1974).

resolved in favour of the majority owners. This approach is least productive in terms of both family harmony and, because of the ensuing damage to relationships, business performance. Unfortunately Sorenson believes this to be the prevailing style of dispute resolution in the family businesses he studied.

Accommodation

Basically this is the opposite approach to competition. Here the parties to the dispute pay high regard to the concerns of others and less to their own. As the conflict is recognised and articulated this strategy can be distinguished from avoidance. Accommodation should produce a good family outcome but may ultimately mean that the business suffers as 'hard', but, in business terms, necessary decisions are deliberately not taken in order to preserve family harmony.

Avoidance

Here the family members actively avoid conflict. This is the classic 'elephant in the room' situation. Because unresolved tension is allowed to build up it is likely to resurface somewhere. Perhaps family members will complain to spouses. Alternatively tension might build for years before resulting in an explosion of anger within the business family. Avoidance might damage the mental health of the family members involved.

Avoidance is associated with high sibling rivalry and low levels of trust. Accordingly it is likely to be damaging to both family and business relationships. This was borne out by Sorenson's findings. According to Sorenson, avoidance would seem to be the second most common conflict management strategy for business families.

Compromise

Compromise is where the family members both recognise a conflict and go some way to meeting the needs of the other family members concerned, thereby giving up some ground from their own ideal position. For example a son wants to take over the management of the family business at age 35 when his father is 60. The father wants to stay on until he is 70. A compromise based on the father leaving at the age of 65 is eventually agreed.

Sorenson refers to this as a 'fixed pie' strategy. Although less bruising than outright conflict and less damaging in the long term than avoidance, neither party will have got what they wanted and so some damage to family relationships (and perhaps the business) could be anticipated.

Collaboration

Here the family members are working positively and creatively to find a solution that meets the needs of all concerned. This is not about giving in, but rather an active attempt to achieve the proverbial 'win win solution'. As such it will require a high level of communication skills from the family members concerned, both in articulating their own concerns and in listening to and understanding those of other family members.

Returning to the management succession example, collaboration might involve the son expressing his need for immediate increased responsibility but understanding his father's desire to stay actively involved in the family business in the short to medium term. This might result in the son being appointed managing director immediately, with the father becoming chairman and retaining some clearly defined but reducing responsibilities until he reached 70.

Not surprisingly, whilst by no means a widespread conflict management strategy, Sorenson found collaboration to be the most effective method, both for building the business and for maintaining family relationships.

Sorenson recognises that many families will adopt different conflict management strategies at different times. It might be that a father and son will compete or compromise over some matters, perhaps decisions over business strategy or investment, but avoid altogether the big questions such as ownership or succession.

The message from Sorenson's research is nevertheless clear. Those families whose prevailing approach to conflict is collaboration are most likely to achieve both business success and positive family relationships.

2.6 FAIRNESS AND EQUALITY

Although they are closely related concepts, fairness and equality are different words. The avowed intent of most parents is to treat their children equally.

In the Cadman Developments case it is clear that the two brothers, Rodney and Cedric, did all the work in managing the property portfolio held by the family company. Their father also expected them to do so without pay. It is equally clear from the evidence in that case, in particular how Mr and Mrs Cadman senior structured both their wills and the lifetime disposition of shares that they believed that their daughter, Janis Fisher, had a right to share fully in the ownership of the family company.

This might, or might not, be unfair in a family business context. The answer depends partly and, perhaps largely, on the perspective of the family member concerned but partly on the ownership philosophy of the business family. Similarly in the Davies case the competing claims of James, who had worked all of his life on the family farm and their other four children seems to have been a source of trouble Tom and Ellen Davies for approaching 40 years.

There is no universally correct or widely acknowledged answer to the question of whether ownership of a family business is a factor of family membership or working in the family business.[39] What is clear however is that failure to address that question is capable of causing huge resentment, particularly between the next generation. In the case of both the Cadman and Davies families, that resentment surfaced in the High Court. A key plank in the family business governance boat is to shape and articulate the ownership philosophy of the business family concerned.

---

[39] The issue of fairness and equality is discussed in more detail in chapter 11 (Ownership Overview).

2.7 INSIDERS AND OUTSIDERS

Inequality in the family business world is not confined to ownership. It can also apply to employment opportunities.

A consistent theme is the different perspectives of family business 'insiders' and 'outsiders', broadly family members who have jobs in the family business and those who do not.[40] The outsiders may or may not be owners, but in the case of non-owning family members, irrespective of the three-circle model analysis,[41] may actually see themselves as being completely outside the family business system.

Sometimes we express this distinction as being between the 'haves' and the 'have-nots', because the difference goes beyond between simply having jobs in the family firm and extends to such matters as, access to information, status and fringe benefits, such as private use of family company assets.[42]

Accordingly immediate family members of controlling family insiders may be seen as quasi-insiders because their close connection to the insider gives them indirect access to some of these insider benefits. For example the children of the insider family business leader will inevitably know more about the family firm than their outsider cousins even though their parents may have equal shareholdings.

There will be an inevitable difference in perspective between insiders and outsiders. This can be illustrated by the three-circle model.

As John Tucker[43] puts it:

> 'The outsiders often regard the insiders as plunderers of their legacy. They might view their shares in the family business as poor investments because they lack liquidity, offer too little return, and are subject to too much control by insiders who divulge too little information and pay too little in dividends.
>
> Insiders, on the other hand might see outsiders as parasites, detached investors, uninterested in the growth of the business, too interested in distributions, too vocal with advice and criticism and too willing to inject family concerns into business decisions. These differences ... can breed resentment that can be destructive to the effectiveness of the ownership group as a whole or harmful to personal relationships in the family. Regardless of how well the family gets along now, old rivalries, new in-laws, or something completely unforeseen can trigger a conflict between parasites or plunderers.'

One of the primary functions of family business governance is to redress the insider/outsider imbalance before the tensions inevitably created degenerate into outright conflict.

A number of commentators therefore argue that only those members who work in the business should own shares and those family members that do not should be gifted or

---

[40] The expressions insider and outsider are widely used in family business circles and can be traced back to Aronoff and Ward in *Family Business Ownership: How to be an Effective Shareholder* (Family Enterprise Publishers, 2002).
[41] Explained in detail in chapter 3.
[42] For example use of a holiday home acquired using family company funds.
[43] John Tucker, *Living in the Family Business* (ICFIB, 2011).

bequeathed other assets. Other commentators distinguish between ownership and control and argue that whilst family members who do not work in the business may be owners. It is vital to keep the control of the business in the hands of those working in it. Others go further and suggest that the family business leader or leaders must have ownership control. This is explored in more detail in chapter 15 (Ownership Succession).

2.8 FATHER AND SON RELATIONSHIPS

Perhaps the most complicated continent in the family business world is the relationship between fathers and sons. Some undercurrent of tension or rivalry will be present in most father/son relationships. We have explored one factor contributing to this complexity, the entrepreneurial mind-set, in **2.2** above.

If that were not sufficient, one only needs to add a pinch of father son rivalry, to make the archetypal succession scenario a truly combustible mix. Levinson identifies the bivalency of the father's position who:[44]

> '... consciously wishes to pass his business on to his son and also wants him to attain his place in the sun, unconsciously the father feels that to yield the business would be to lose his masculinity.'

The issues arising from this complexity are many and varied and cannot be conveniently be captured in any one place. Instead this theme crops up regularly throughout this book.[45]

2.9 FATHER AND DAUGHTER RELATIONSHIPS

In contrast father and daughter relationships do not seem to produce the same volume of disputes. Nevertheless bitter father/daughter disputes do arise. For example, the lengthy litigation concerning Eirian Davies ('the Cowshed Cinderella') and her father discussed in detail in chapter 19 (Inheritance Disputes).

Partly the perception of relative harmony of father and daughter business relationships might be due to the relative infrequency of '... and Daughters' family businesses as compared with the typical '... and Sons' model. Although there are strong suggestions that this demographic is changing with gender forming an increasingly less common criteria for succession.[46]

Perhaps an equally or more likely explanation is the different dynamics at play in father and daughter relationships. Whilst many of the structural issues will be the same in father to daughter successions Dumas[47] suggests that these are less prone to conflict than father son transitions.

---

[44] Conflicts that Plague the Family Business, op cit.
[45] See for example chapter 7 (Management Succession) and Part E (Family Business Disputes).
[46] See Jimenez 'Research on Women in Family Firms: Current Status and Future Direction' *Family Business Review* (2009) at pp 53–64 for a summary of and further reference to this research. The author identified 48 academic articles, 3 doctoral theses and 23 books dealing with the subject.
[47] Dumas 'Understanding of father-daughter and father-son dyads in family-owned businesses' *Family Business Review* (1989) at pp 31–46.

Although historically fewer in number, later research[48] points to mother-daughter successions as also being fraught with tensions. The issue of gender and succession is considered in a little more detail in chapter 7 (Management Succession).

2.10 PSYCHOLOGICAL STATUS OF THE FAMILY BUSINESS

The family business itself is capable of being seen as part of the cast in the drama of a business family. Later in chapter 3 we talk about the possibility of the family business itself being used a scapegoat for all the ills of a business family.

The potential for emotional attachment to the family business is obvious. According to Levinson[49] 'an entrepreneur's business is simultaneously his "baby" and his "mistress"'. Although this may seem uncomfortably Freudian, this analysis has been picked up and developed by Tagiuri and Davis,[50] who suggest that, particularly in the case of a founder/ father, the family business 'often represents a wife, mistress or child'.

The argument goes that the next generation, in particular sons, involved in the family business may also develop a psychological relationship with the family firm seeing themselves as its 'guardian, sibling or suitor' potentially giving rise to confrontational dynamics and father-son succession battles, categorised by de Vries as an 'Oedipal struggle'[51] (presumably one in which the role of Queen Jocasta, Oedipus' mother is taken by the family firm).

Tagiuri and Davis believe that the potential for such damaging struggles and the psychological status of the family firm itself diminishes with succeeding generations of ownership.

They also argue that a family business is capable of being treated as a 'transitional object' by family members – in effect a teddy bear representing comfort and a safe haven from the harsh world outside: 'a place where one does not really have to grow up'. Certainly we have experience of a client who, when asked to consider their relationship with their own family business concluded that it was in fact their 'X-Box'.

Again there may be significant positive aspects arising from this analysis in terms of creativity, a sense of fun and belonging and an environment providing a sensible work life balance. These are capable of benefiting the business as much as the business family. The dangers to the business of over emphasising the aspect of the family business as a plaything will be obvious. The dangers to family members of what may be seen as an inappropriate relationship with the family business itself may be less obvious. Taking Levinson's dual analogy both mistresses and favoured younger children are capable of diverting attention from the rest of the 'real family' creating potential for envy and resentment and, so far as the younger generation are concerned, potentially sowing the seeds of further cycles of abandonment.

---

[48] Vera & Dean 'An examination of the challenges daughters face in family business successions' *Family Business Review* (2005) at pp 321–346.
[49] Levinson 'Conflicts that plague family businesses' *Harvard Business Review* (March 1971).
[50] 'Bivalent Attributes of the Family Firm' *Family Business Review* (1996), Vol 9(2) at p 206.
[51] *Family Business on the Couch* at p 143.

But there is hope for the business family, particularly one with a strong family system providing 'adequate security and abundant nurturance' in which case Tagiuri and Davis suggest that the family firm will not be perceived as a 'threatening rival or interloper'.

2.11 SIBLING RIVALRY

2.11.1 Overview

Sibling rivalry may be seen as one of the defining characteristics of family business life and can have a devastating effect on the business and its success. Whilst this might be so in many cases, it would be quite wrong to lose sight of the counterpart, the powerful and compelling business proposition that can be created by siblings, working in harmony and in partnership. Cyrus and James Clark are a clear and well-known example, as are Richard and George Cadbury.

What is the reason for this rivalry? Psychologists believe it comes from a deep desire for the love of the parents to the exclusion of siblings. So if a parent appears to show love to one child, the other child can consider the sibling is valued more highly, and they are worth less. The eldest can dominate by virtue of age, size and ability, and this can cause resentment with the younger siblings. Historically a boy might have been considered of more value in the business, solely through being a male. Although the youngest, they may use their preferred status to try and control older sisters. A middle child may feel a lack of love, especially if the older child is of the same gender, but the younger child is a different gender.

It is normal for a degree of rivalry to exist between siblings. As the children leave home and create their own roles in life, and families, then the effect of this rivalry will usually become dissipated. However if the siblings continue to be closely involved with each other through engagement in the family business, the rivalry can continue into adult life. So children will compete for, say, the father's blessing in relation to the business. This can allow the rivalry to have an adverse effect on decisions regarding the running of the business, and management decisions. This can lead to the business stagnating, particularly if, say, one sibling refuses to agree a particular course of action because of the deep-seated rivalry.

It is often the case that the sibling who becomes managing director tries to pressurise the parents into giving them a controlling shareholding in the company so that they can exercise control over their siblings. However if the parents want to be seen to be fair to all their children, they may decide to split ownership equally between all of their children. This then leaves the sibling rivalry locked into the company structure.

Sibling rivalry exists, and it is rare to totally avoid the problems that can arise. But family businesses do survive and deal with these tensions. Membership of a family business can be a driver to develop the skills to resolve the issues. Those families will tend to show the characteristics of a strong and coping family, and may go on to develop a long lasting business.

As the first stage in a family dealing with these issues, the family members have to understand the psychological basis for the rivalry, and how that is being manifested. This is no easy task. But armed with this understanding it should be possible to begin to reduce some of the emotional intensity, and then to analyse what is happening. This in turn should help in working out ways of dealing with the issues. Obviously this involves the siblings talking to each other openly about their feelings, and explaining why they react in certain ways. They may then be able to work out a code of behaviour that recognises they are stronger as a team, and develop procedures for resolving disputes. This may involve the use of independent board members, trusted advisors or family business consultants.

Practical steps to accommodate siblings and other family members in a family business is discussed as part of the management succession process in chapter 7.

2.11.2 Adidas, Puma and others

Family Wars contains a whole chapter on disputes between siblings in well-known family businesses. The examples include the Dassler family. There the family dispute led to the creation of the rival sports brands of ADIDAS owned by Adolf (Adi) Dassler and the breakaway PUMA brand set up by his brother Rudolph.

Family Wars also explains that, notwithstanding their recent advertising campaigns, harmony has not always reigned supreme between the Gallo brothers in their wine business. Similarly many of the most bitter feuds that have found their way into the English courts and are referred to in later chapters were between siblings. These include the Shah brothers, the Harding sisters and, (to add balance) the Brownlow brothers and sisters.[52]

2.11.3 Predictive factors

So are there any pointers or factors that might make disputes between siblings more likely?

Birth order

It is often suggested that there is a relationship between birth order and conflict in a family owned business. The argument goes that the 'natural order' is for the oldest child, or following the logic of primogeniture more strictly, the oldest son to take on the mantle as designated successor. According to Levinson:[53]

> '... the eldest child is earlier and longer in contact with the parents, and their control efforts fall more heavily on him. Consequently, older children tend to develop stronger consciences, drive themselves harder, expect more of themselves, and control themselves more rigidly than younger ones.'

Alternative explanations are that the eldest child is more likely to develop compliant and competitive behaviours as a way of competing for their parent's attention and approval on the arrival of their younger siblings. Those behaviours naturally translate into the skills required for business leadership. The younger siblings are, on the other hand, expected to be subservient and to play supportive roles.

---

[52] Discussed in detail in Part E.
[53] Levinson 'Conflicts that plague family businesses' *Harvard Business Review* (March 1971).

All may be well if the siblings are given and assume their 'natural' roles. The case report of the *Irvine*[54] family dispute is, from the perspective of a family dynamics analysis, both fascinating and frustrating. The case reports tell us that Malcolm Irvine joined his brother Ian's business, that he played a supporting role and that whilst the two brothers owned the company equally they had a private agreement to share profits in the ratio of four sevenths/three sevenths in Ian's favour. It is also clear that this arrangement worked well up until Malcolm's death. What the report does not tell us is the age of the two brothers. But we would be surprised if Ian was the younger.

But problems may arise if this 'natural' order is not followed. It might be clear that younger children are in fact the more talented and best suited to be business leaders. Whilst promoting them may logically represent the best business decision, it is likely to require exceptionally cohesive family dynamics and strong characters from relevant siblings for this not to cause significant difficulties from a family perspective. These difficulties can then of course start to infect the business.

Resentment of the older sibling may be fairly obvious and predictable. Less obvious might be that 'the younger brother is faced with feelings of guilt for having attacked the elder and usurped what so often is accepted as the senior brother's rightful role'.[55] Perhaps this will be manifested in the older brother being allowed to coast unchallenged in a senior role in the family business, albeit one that is subordinate to their younger sibling.

Even if the elder child is preferred problems may still arise. It is clearly difficult for young adults working in their family business to be on the receiving end of adult-child transactional communication.[56] It is doubly difficult when the 'adult' in the transactional analysis is an older brother rather than an actual parent. As Levinson explains it 'being already, therefore, a harsh judge of himself the, the eldest is likely to be an even harsher judge of his younger siblings'.

Younger siblings may of course fight back, resenting their place in the family and the business pecking order. Perhaps their doing so will create a healthy challenging atmosphere of competition, largely focused on task conflict,[57] so that both the family business and their relationship, forged in steel, emerges stronger. But the relationship between the siblings may be categorised by more damaging sibling rivalry, such as point scoring, empire building and back-biting. Each business problem will always be the fault of the other's department. Alternatively the younger sibling might accept and assume the role of permanent little brother, notwithstanding a wallet full of business cards suggesting a more responsible position.

Parents, seeking to minimise the potential for conflict between their children might attempt to divide the family business into separate divisional fiefdoms, giving each responsibility for their own empire. This might work on a day-to-day basis but if there is common family ownership the potential for unresolved sibling rivalry to resurface as disputes over business strategy or competition for investment or other resources is ever present. One of the case studies in *Family Wars*[58] is that of the Ambani family. There

---

[54] Discussed in detail in Part E.
[55] Levinson 'Conflicts that plague family businesses' *Harvard Business Review* (March 1971).
[56] The concept of transactional analysis is briefly introduced in chapter 3 (Tools, Models and Theories).
[57] The difference between surface level or task conflict and deeper relationship conflict is explained in 2.5.3.
[58] See *the Reliance Story – The Myth of Unity* at p 42.

dividing operational control of the Reliance business representing 3% of the total GDP of India, between two brothers, could not prevent a bitter and public struggle breaking out between them.

Age spacing

Possibly the effects of siblings rivalry might be diluted by long age gaps between the siblings directly involved in the business. It is less likely that younger siblings will push against the 'natural order' of the authority of the elder if there is an age gap of 10 years or so. The greater the age gap the more likely it is that elder siblings will have assumed 'quasi-parental' roles in the lives of younger family members, for example by baby-sitting etc.

Family size

It is also suggested that the effects of sibling rivalry may be diluted in larger families. The argument being that in larger families competition for resources, including the love and affection of parents, is the natural order of things. Accordingly family members realise from an early age that not everyone can have everything all the time and that all things are in finite supply, including leading positions in the family business. This may also lead to a dynamic where a degree of family meritocracy is also tolerated, so that the best family member for the job may be allowed to fill the role.

Gender

The theory also goes that conflict and sibling rivalry is less likely between sisters, or between brothers and sisters, than the classic situation of sibling rivalry between brothers. However cases such as *Harding* and *Fisher v Cadman* show that even if this is the case such conflicts nevertheless occur and with sufficient severity as to find their way to the courts.

Prodigals

In an ideal world a capable and talented family member whose experience and career aspirations fit with a return to the family firm could be an ideal recruit for a growing and increasingly successful family business. The recruitment of this family member strengthens the management team, is welcomed by both parents and siblings and provides the returnee with an additional level of engagement that they have not been able to find in a corporate environment. Examples of such fortuitous family recruitment clearly exist. Equally there are occasions when family considerations prevail, so that jobs are created without a corresponding business need. The problem, for all concerned is identifying the real reason for the return of the sibling. This often will not be acknowledged or fully articulated between the family members involved. There might be a number of competing explanations or stories.

The return of a sibling to the family business fold can cause huge resentment on the part of those siblings who have toiled patiently in the family field in the meantime. One or both parents will almost inevitably have championed the return of the prodigal. This can be for a variety or combination of reasons.

First, as part of the 'fairness and equality theme' the family business could be seen as common family property, the fruits of which are to be enjoyed by all and not just those who have historically worked in the business. Tensions arising from this will be exacerbated if the prodigal is simply given a share in the ownership of the family firm upon joining, when the stay-at-home siblings believed that their share was as a result of their long-term commitment to working in the business.

Secondly need. If, just like the biblical prodigal son, the family member has somehow failed in the outside world the parent might want to find a way to accommodate the prodigal in the family business simply to take care of them. For a whole host of reasons, including divorce, redundancy, illness, the family member concerned might need a job.

Thirdly the prodigal could be seen as the 'white knight', the outwardly successful and perhaps favourite child, who has done well in the wider world and who is encouraged to return to the family firm to fill perceived gaps in management or to compensate for weaknesses in the skill set of their siblings, if not to 'save the family firm'. It is not difficult to see why, in each of the above cases, the return of the prodigal can cause bitterness and resentment, when viewed from the perspective of those who have remained in the family business. To what extent should the years they have spent working loyally for the family firm be taken into account to provide some form of accrued ownership expectation, the equivalent of vested share-options in non-family businesses? How fair would it be if a family member walked into a senior position, perhaps one created especially for them and on a similarly high remuneration package to family members who have learnt the job the hard way, especially if the prodigal then failed to pull their weight?

Finally even if the family member entering the business is objectively more capable how hard will it be for the existing family employees to acknowledge this and how understandable is it that would jealousy and insecurity could arise?

Parental death

Even if they have nominally retired from the family business the founder or other senior generation former business leader may nevertheless cast a long and substantial 'generational shadow' over the business.[59] Often that influence can be helpful and benign, providing leadership, wise counsel and moderation. In other cases the 'family glue' will be provided by the non-working parent, typically the mother. Clearly one of the most significant events in the evolution of any family will be the death of a parent. This will be especially the case in a family owned business with the death of a parent playing a significant role in the business. The death of the most significant parent in terms of family business harmony may then cause cracks already present in the relationships between members of the next generation to develop into a full-blown split. The death therefore should be seen as the catalyst rather than the cause of the ensuing family dispute.

This loss of family glue appears to be a key factor in a considerable number of disputes. The death of the founder, Dhirubhai, in the Reliance story, is a clear example. But a similar pattern emerges from many, probably the majority of family business sibling

---

[59] The concept of generational shadow comes from Davis and Harveston 'In the Founder's Shadow: Conflict in the Family Firm' *Family Business Review* (1999) No 4 and is discussed in more detail in chapter 3 (Tools, Models and Theories).

disputes reported in the legal cases,[60] for example the death of the father in *Fisher v Cadman* and *Harding* or the mother in *Singh*.

Later stage family businesses

Notwithstanding the potentially combustible cocktail of ingredients in first and second-generation family businesses, typically categorised as founder led and sibling partnerships, research suggests that the incidence of conflict is 'significantly higher' in older family business in their third generation and beyond.[61] The research rules out 'generational shadow' as a contributory factor, analysing this as a markedly less significant factor in the cause of conflict on the transition between second and subsequent generation family business leaders to the next generation than on the first transition from founder to second generation.

So if the research is correct why is it the case that conflict is more likely to arise in later stage family owned businesses? The answer may be a combination of increased complexity and reduced cohesion in such businesses. As the size of the family grows accommodating every family member in the business becomes impossible. The potential grows for a schism between the 'haves' or insiders, those with jobs, management control and perhaps on the basis of branches or alliances, overall ownership control, and the 'have-nots' or outsiders. The parallel question of whether the rewards from the family business should follow the effort and participation in the business by the haves or should be seen as a matter of inheritance allowing the wider owning family, the 'have-nots', to participate, is brought into sharp focus.

Many of these factors might also be present in second-generation family businesses, particularly those where only some family members from that generation work in the business. But if the family business has reached the third generation of family ownership it is likely to have grown in value. The cousins will have grown up in separate households so family cohesion is likely to have diminished. The seeds for disputes about remuneration, levels of dividend, mismanagement and nepotism could well have already been sewn. A family script may have been handed down from previous generations centered on an inherited grievance, along the lines of 'that lot get everything, it's not fair and it's not what grandfather would have wanted'. Perhaps this will be combined with the death of a key figure in the senior generation, who had hitherto provided the family glue, or at least allowed the myth of family cohesion to be perpetuated. Their death allows those seeds to take root and develop into a full-blown conflict.

Of course neither the presence of these complications nor the absence of family cohesion guarantees that the family will fall into serious dispute. Sometimes the relative indifference of the have-nots will mean that matters only reach the stage of vague discontent. On other occasions early stage disputes will be prevented from escalating by some combination of buy-outs of the have-nots, pruning the ownership tree[62] to a manageable size and the introduction of family governance mechanisms.[63]

---

[60] Discussed in Part F.
[61] Davis and Harveston 'In the Founder's Shadow: Conflict in the Family Firm' *Family Business Review* (1999) No 4.
[62] See chapter 11.
[63] See chapter 17.

2.12 PROFESSIONALISATION

2.12.1 Overview

A further family business theme, and one of the greatest significance to long-term growth and survival, is that of professionalisation. This can be seen as the gradual evolution of the entrepreneurial start-up business, reliant on the drive and energy of the founder, backed up by the commitment of others family members into a family owned corporate entity, run according to accepted best business practice and usually with professional management, who are wholly or largely responsible for the day to day operations of the business.

One of the key functions of governance is helping business families make this long and difficult journey towards professionalisation. The topic of governance occupies a large part of this book.

Family firms are often seen as lifestyle businesses, not run on strict business principles with the aim of maximising profit and growth, but to provide the business owning family with an enjoyable and ideally financially secure life. There is nothing inherently wrong or morally repugnant in this. A good number of family firms are set up by 'refugees' from the corporate world with the express objective of working alongside loved ones to build a good business, but not at all costs. The sacrifices in terms of lower and slower business growth are anticipated and accepted by the business family. To the extent that growth is constrained this can be seen as part of the conscious governance processes of the family.

In other cases the failure of a family firm to grow or thrive can be attributed to the unconscious failure of the family to professionalise their business. This can be for a variety of reasons including the overbearing control and inability to delegate of the founding entrepreneur, nepotism in allowing unsuitable family members to occupy key roles, or the allied failure to introduce non-family managers and best practice business systems where necessary.

Of the five main family business case studies introduced in chapter 1, only Clarks shoes, can be clearly seen to have successfully completed the journey from family run start up to being a family owned corporate business.[64] Of the other businesses Mr Carter singularly failed in the task of introducing basic financial discipline, and, as a direct result the Park House Properties business was lost, with fairly dire consequences to the wider family. Cadman Developments survived into the next generation but the operation carried on by Rodney and Cedric could barely be labelled a business, much less a professional one. The brothers relied on passive property inflation in the value of the property portfolio they had inherited from their father rather than taking any active steps to improve the value of the portfolio. Although the court rejected the argument of their sister, Janis that this failure amounted to actionable mismanagement, could a more pro-active approach to management and professionalisation in particular and governance in general have prevented the dispute from arising in the first place?

---

[64] Although the Davies family farm continued into the next generation, and appears to be successful as a farming business. The problems there related to ownership.

A similar situation could be found in Saul D Harrison plc, at least at the time that case came to court.[65] By then the business had been in existence for over a century and was employing over a hundred people. But there were no non-family members on the board. The evidence was that the senior generation of the family leadership had stayed on well beyond normal retirement date and had failed to modernise the operations of the business so that the company 'under the control of the older generation had in short got stuck in a groove in a business declining profitability'.[66] In the circumstances no dividends could be paid to remote family members, which in turn led to proceedings being brought against the controlling shareholders. Those proceedings failed. But could they have been avoided in the first place by greater and continual attention being shown to business fundamentals, in short professionalisation?

2.12.2 Components of professionalisation

There is much more to professionalisation than simply engaging non-family managers and following perceived management best practice. A number of John Ward's '50 Lessons Learned from Long-Lasting Successful Families in Business'[67] can be seen to fall within the professionalisation bracket. These include:

For early stage – owner-managed family businesses

- **Irrevocable retirement** – having a fixed retirement for everyone, including the founder. As a factor of failing to let go it is not uncommon to find family business leaders well into their seventies and in some case beyond.
- **Voluntary accountability** – where business leaders submit themselves to accountability and scrutiny, for example by independent directors, notwithstanding that they in fact control their family company so that this investment in governance cannot be justified under traditional agency theory.[68]
- **Principle of merit** – so that rewards from the business are allocated on the basis of merit not nepotism. That is not to say that family members should be barred from holding senior management positions. In many cases family members, with a deep commitment to the family firm and an understanding of the business acquired over a lifetime might be best suited to assume those positions. But the question needs to be asked whether this is indeed the case. The requisite support and training needs to be provided to ensure that the family member concerned is properly equipped to discharge their responsibility.
- **Attract the most competent family members** – rather than provide jobs for all.
- **Many non-family executives** – in recognition that much of the management talent needed for the family firm to thrive is likely to be found outside the business owning family.

For second generation and later stage family businesses

- **Business bias** – on the basis that what is good for the business should ultimately prove good for the family.

---

[65] But the business has survived and is now managed by a mixture of family and non-family directors.
[66] At p 483 of the case report.
[67] John Ward *Perpetuating the Family Business* (Palgrave, 2004).
[68] In other words that mechanisms for the scrutiny and control of management are necessary to protect the interests of shareholders.

- **Selective family employment** – including developing specific policies on recruitment, promotion and remuneration of family members so that only the most talented family members become employees.

2.12.3 The family business: at the wrong end of the professionalisation spectrum?

In a more recent article other academics, Alex Stewart and Michael Hitt, suggested that professionalisation had a number of components and referred to the 'stereotypical dichotomies', unfavourably contrasting family owned businesses with their non-family counterparts. But Stewart and Hitt did not take their stereotypes from popular perception. Instead they referred to a body of other family business studies and literature, which they saw as supporting an unfavourable contrast between family and non-family owned business across various dimensions.

Stereotypical Dichotomies Regarding Non-family and Family Businesses[69]

Feature	Non-family business	Family business
Rewards	Achievement, merit based. Employees: Based on performance. Universal criteria	Ascription, nepotism based. Family members indulged. Specific criteria
Management	Delegation to professionals. Rational and analytic. Innovative. Formalised, command and control	Autocratic. Emotional, intuitive, rent seeking, stifling innovation. Organic, mutual accommodation.
Ownership	Diverse	Concentrated, family based
Governance	Ownership and control split. External influences on the board. Transparency and disclosure	Ownership and control united. Internal dominance of the board. Opaqueness and secrecy.
Networks	External ties based on business connections	Based on family and kinship networks
Leadership	Highly educated, high turnover	Entrenched, long term, trained on the job
Careers	Short term horizons	Long term horizons
Returns	Economically defined	Non-economic goals important

Of course many of us will be able to identify family businesses that do not conform to these regressive stereotypes. In chapter 1 we questioned whether Dysons should be classed as a family business. Irrespective of the answer to that question that business would inevitably exhibit more of the characteristics of a non-family business as listed above.

Is there any evidence to show whether highly professionalised family businesses are atypical or that family involvement in management is necessarily so detrimental? Certainly one study suggests that there is a 'negative quadratic relationship' between the

---

[69] Based on Table 1 in Alex Stewart and Michael A Hitt 'Why Can't a Family Business Be More Like a Nonfamily Business? Modes of Professionalization in Family Firms' *Family Business Review* (2011) Vol 25(1) at pp 58–86.

number of family members involved in the management and the performance of unquoted family firms, with businesses with the most family members involved in management assessing themselves as being the worst performing. In other words too many family cooks spoil the business broth.[70]

2.12.4 The case for professionalisation

Taking listed company status as a proxy for professionalisation most evidence suggests that listed family firms outperform the market.[71] On the other side of the coin the evidence from studies of the comparative performance of non-quoted family and other firms is much more equivocal, with perhaps the majority of studies suggesting that non-quoted family firms (particularly those no longer run by the founder) perform worse.

Looking at the core elements of professionalisation, basically introducing best business practices, procedures and systems into a family business and ensuring it is managed and led by the most competent and best trained people available (irrespective of whether they are members of the business owning family), the arguments for professionalisation seem obvious and inescapable. Conversely the various cases discussed in chapter 8, albeit viewed with the benefit of hindsight, illustrate just what can go wrong for a business family in the absence of professionalisation.

2.12.5 Barriers to professionalisation

So why do so many family firms fail to professionalise? Or to repeat the question posed by Stewart and Hitt 'Why can't a family business be more like a non-family business?'[72]

The authors offer various explanations, all of which can be traced back to the particular 'mental model' of the family business leader concerned, which, so Stewart and Hitt argue, give rise to a number of categories or 'modes of professionalisation' so far as family firms are concerned. They identify the following:

- **Minimally professional family firms.** The argument is that many family firms simply cannot professionalise. This can be as a result of 'cognitive, cultural, emotional or managerial barriers'. Some family business leaders simply fail to see that a more professional approach is needed or have an over inflated sense of their own management ability. Probably Mr Carter of Park House Properties fell into this category. Certainly this was so for Tom Patterson in the Listowel Trading case, discussed in chapter 8 (Directors' Duties).

    Other family business leaders have a touching but misplaced faith in their offspring, who they prefer over objectively better qualified external candidates for senior management positions. This will not necessarily, and perhaps rarely, be out of conscious nepotism, but more likely from a genuine belief that their children are indeed the best for the job concerned, perhaps notwithstanding an academic or employment record that might suggest otherwise.

---

[70] At least in Italy where the survey was carried out: Salvatore Sciascia and Pietro Mazzola 'Family Involvement in Ownership and Management: Exploring Nonlinear Effects on Performance' *Family Business Review* (2008) No 4 at pp 331–345.

[71] See for example Anderson and Reeb 2003 Founding family ownership and firm performance: Evidence from the S&P 500 *Journal of Finance*, 58 1301–1328.

[72] Alex Stewart and Michael A Hitt 'Why Can't a Family Business Be More Like a Nonfamily Business? Modes of Professionalization in Family Firms' *Family Business Review* (2011) Vol 25(1) at pp 58–86.

In some cases non-family managers will be recruited, but their appointment will quickly end in failure because of the inability of those concerned to appreciate the complexities of the family business situation and the incapacity of the non-family manager to 'navigate through idiosyncratic family culture'.

- **Wealth dispensing family firms.** Wealth dispensing family firms will have grown to a sufficient size as to be highly cash generative. But the family business leaders see their business as a cash cow and are motivated more by extracting as much as possible by way of salary and other benefits than improving and growing their business.

  Consequently non-executive directors, governance and all the other paraphernalia of professionalisation are dismissed as an unwelcome hindrance to this extraction process, as are family members with minority interests, particularly outsiders from other branches of the family.

  Disputes between the 'haves,' those in control of the family business and the 'have-nots', the more remote family members are 'notoriously common'.

  The essence of the claimant Rosemary's argument in Saul D Harrison was that the company was being run as a wealth dispensing family firm, and unfairly so. But neither the High Court nor the Court of Appeal agreed. Much clearer examples of wealth extraction can be found in such cases as *Irvine*[73] and *Samuel Weller and Sons*[74] discussed in more detail in Part E.

- **Entrepreneurially operated family firms.** Some businesses simply work better when operating on an entrepreneurial, flexible basis. This third group of family owned businesses will reject full blown professionalization, in the sense of business school, one size fits all 'generally accepted management principles, or GAMP' (which the authors do not seem to use as a wholly positive expression) on the basis that doing so will jeopardise the entrepreneurial character and with it the competitive advantage of the business concerned.

  The authors point to research which suggests that founder led businesses outperform successor led businesses.[75]

  In the best of these businesses the leaders will find a way to mix management disciplines with family drive and values 'to energise the medium sized family business'.[76]

  But in some cases the informality and failure to balance the, at times competing demands of family and business can mean that the business ultimately suffers.

- **Entrepreneurial family business groups.** These are groups of businesses owned or controlled by a large family or network of connected families. The idea is that such groups are common in jurisdictions with poor investor protection and weak commercial law systems. Families therefore band together to form networks to protect and promote their own commercial interests.

- **Pseudo professional public family firms.** Here the idea is that the controlling family use the façade of listed company status to expropriate an unfair share of the profits or assets of the business for their own benefit, to the detriment of external shareholders. Again the problem will be particularly acute in jurisdictions with poor shareholder protection.

  The problem need not be confined to listed companies. Larger family controlled unquoted companies, including unlisted PLC's may have a veneer of good governance but in fact be poor stewards of wider stakeholder interests. The

---

[73] [2006] EWHC 406 (Ch).
[74] [1990] Ch 682.
[75] R Fahlenbrach 'Founder CEO's, investment decisions and stock market performance' *Journal of Financial and Quantitative Analysis* (April 2009) Vol 44, Issue 2 at pp 439–466.
[76] Stewart and Hitt at p 71.

clearest example of this phenomenon is the Luqman Properties case discussed in chapter 8 where the company concerned was clearly used as a vehicle for a major fraud by the controlling members of the Luqman family.

- **Hybrid professional family firms.** This last category of family firms combine an element of family ownership with a recognisably professional approach. The residual family influence helps provide stability and reinforce core values. The presence of external shareholders, investors and management on the other hand should prevent expropriation by the controlling family and introduce best management practice.

Whilst warning that it is difficult to determine a 'golden mean of family influence' Stewart and Hitt tentatively postulate that firms with families holding about 15% of the equity may have achieved the best balance between family and external ownership, at least in terms of achieving optimal financial performance. As of 2012 the Sainsbury family owned just less than 15% of the eponymous supermarket chain.[77] But a 15% ownership (absent any weighted voting rights) will take the firm concerned below the 25% family ownership threshold necessary to qualify as a family business under the European Commission definition discussed in chapter 1.

Of course many families will simply be unwilling to relinquish any significant level of control to outside shareholders.

2.12.6 Stakeholder focused family firms

It might be possible to add a further sub-category of professionalisation to those listed by Stewart and Hitt, the 'stakeholder focused family firm'. These are family businesses that instinctively do the right thing by the various stakeholders or constituents of their business in addition to the owning family. These stakeholders would include the employees, customers and suppliers of the family business concerned. Often stakeholders would include also the local community in which the business is based and perhaps the local environment. Section 172 of the Companies Act 2006 set out a shopping list of stakeholders whose interests directors have a statutory duty to consider in promoting the success of the company.[78]

But the stakeholder focused family firm does not need to refer to any statute, written HR policy or Corporate Social Responsibility document to determine what course of action it should or should not take. Rather such family firms instinctively do the right thing as a product of their deeply ingrained culture. Here the family firm is acting as what Professor Colin Mayer terms a 'commitment device'.[79]

2.12.7 Professionalisation – conclusion

Just like entrepreneurially operated family firms, stakeholder focused family firms might be doing exactly the right thing for the success of the family business, the business owning family and their wider stakeholders. Problems arise when the business family believes this to be the case but the reality is that the family firm concerned is, on a proper analysis closer to a minimally professional family firm.

---

[77] Source: Franks, Mayer, Volpin and Wagner 'The Life Cycle of Family Ownership: International Evidence' *Review of Financial Studies* (June 2012) Vol 25, Issue 6, 1675–1712.
[78] Discussed in more detail in chapter 8 (Directors' Duties).
[79] Colin Mayer *Firm Commitment; why the corporation is failing us and how to restore faith in it* (Oxford University Press, 2013).

Probably the only way to differentiate is for the business family concerned to at least undertake make some sensible level of 'governance audit' to assess what level of professionalisation or governance process is appropriate for their own family firm or, on the other hand how much can safely and sensibly be disregarded on the basis that we genuinely 'do it differently and better round here'.

2.13 MYTHS

There is an element of mythology inherent in most organisations, where the image of aspects of the organisation concerned, or key figures in it differ from objective reality. This can be especially so in family firms.

Kets de Vries and colleagues[80] identify family myths, defined as 'beliefs and assumptions shared by members of the family to explain the way that things are done within the family', as a 'powerful navigating force'. Sometimes these family myths will be helpful in promoting cohesion within the family and presenting a common face to the outside world. But the greater the gap between myth and family reality, the greater the potential for conflict. This is particularly the case when the family members have bought into their own family mythology rather than having an objective view of that reality.

Kets de Vries and colleagues identify a number of common family business myths. Of most relevance to family business disputes is 'the Myth of Harmony'. Where despite evidence of conflict and tension, family members 'hang on to the fantasy of family togetherness'. Tagiuri and Davis talk about the 'generally strict psychological prohibitions against open conflict'.[81] Such denial or a cultural climate which prevents tensions and concerns being aired by family members may work in the short term, in the sense of preserving a façade of togetherness. But ultimately the absence of authentic communication will erode the foundations of family relations. So when conflict does come to the surface it becomes correspondingly harder to contain.

2.14 SCRIPTS

A closely related concept is that family members accept clearly defined roles within the drama of the family system and follow the script written for that role. As the pioneering British psychiatrist RD Laing put it in relation to our families:[82]

> 'We are acting parts in a play we have never read and never seen, whose plot we don't know, whose existence we can glimpse, but whose beginning and end are beyond our imagination and conception.'

Some of those roles and their associated scripts may seem like good roles to play. For example the heroic entrepreneur who regularly sacrifices time and family for the good of the business, or who steps in to rescue crises caused by others, including family employees, or the dutiful son who has given up his own independent career aspirations to take on the family business.

---

[80] *Family Business on the Couch*, op cit.
[81] 'Bivalent Attributes of the Family Firm' *Family Business Review* (1996), Vol 9(2) at p 204.
[82] RD Laing *The Politics of the Family* (Penguin, 1971).

Other scripts will be harder for the family member chosen for the particular role to accept, but nevertheless central to the overall family drama. These could include the 'problem child,' perceived as a failure at school, then taken into the family business because there was no other option available, where the family script prevents their contribution from being recognised.

The more closely the family members are expected to follow their scripts, without the potential to ad-lib on appropriate occasions or to rewrite the script in the light of changed circumstances, the greater the potential for family conflict.

The greater the gap between the assigned role for a family member and their true nature the greater the requirement for them to engage in what Oliver James[83] describes as 'emotional labour' to bridge that gap and with it the greater the potential for this to result in both intrapersonal and family conflict.

2.15 CONCLUSION

In the previous chapter we provided a basic overview of family businesses and their importance to the UK economy. This chapter, introduced some key themes that are prevalent in the day-to-day life of family businesses. The picture is undoubtedly one of considerable complexity. The next chapter, the final chapter in the introductory part of this book, introduces some theories, tools and models that can be used by families and their advisors in an attempt to make sense of this complexity and to help analyse and explain the situation of individual family businesses.

---

[83] Oliver James *Office Politics* (Vermilion, 2013).

CHAPTER 3

TOOLS, MODELS AND THEORIES

3.1 INTRODUCTION

The first two chapters provide an insight into the complexity of family businesses. This chapter is intended to introduce some key tools, models and theories to help understand and deal with that complexity. It was previously suggested that the circumstances of family businesses are infinitely varied. No two family businesses will be exactly the same. Therefore the models we describe will not capable of providing a precise and fully lifelike depiction of the reality of any particular family business. Instead the models can assist by providing an overview or perspective of that complex reality.

Similarly the theories we describe, both in this chapter and in various places throughout the rest of this book, are not put forward as universal truths, capable of explaining the circumstances of each and every family business. Rather they are offered as possible explanations, which may or not be seen as useful in looking at the situation of any given family firm and the associated business family.

Amongst other subjects we will look in detail at:

- **Genograms** and their use and application to provide an overview of a business family.
- **Systems theory** and its application to the family business, particularly through the three-circle model, referred to in the previous chapter.
- **Life cycle theory** and the stages of growth and evolution both of the family firm and the individual family members at the core of the family business.

3.2 GENOGRAMS

3.2.1 Know your client

The simplest form of a genogram is a family tree.

Preparing an organisational chart, showing the positions of the key members of the management team of a business is an entirely standard management practice. Notwithstanding the central importance of the business owning family to a family business, preparing a genogram to explain the relationships between family members is much less common.

Obviously, in almost every early stage family business the family members will possess a detailed understanding of the family and their relationships with each other. This will be second nature. But in the largest and most complex later stage family business, where a hundred or more family members can be involved, knowledge of third and fourth cousins can be sketchy at best. It is fairly common practice for the company secretariat of a family company of this type to maintain a detailed family tree, which sits alongside the more formal statutory registers of shareholders.

Similarly it may be second nature to most private client advisors to obtain detailed background information on their client's family, although this is perhaps more likely to be captured in note form rather than diagrammatically as a genogram.

For advisors engaged to deal with corporate or tax affairs wider details of the composition of the board and the ownership may well be relevant and form part of a thorough information gathering exercise. However, for many business advisors a detailed knowledge of the business owning family may at first sight appear irrelevant to the job at hand, particularly if that job is ostensibly business task related, such as choosing an new accounting system, taking on a new lease or appointing a distributor for a new product or venture.

One of the threads running through this book is that in a family business, family and business issues are irrevocable intertwined, giving rise to the maxim that 'you can't take the family out of a family business'. It can never do an advisor any harm to learn about that family.

Moving to the example of corporate instructions, for example tax planning, arrangements for transfers of shares or a new shareholders' agreement in connection with succession planning arrangements. All the advisor strictly needs to know to advise on the letter of their instructions may well be details of existing and proposed shareholdings, the board and possibly, for tax purposes the relationships between the shareholders. Again what a genogram might illustrate is the presence of other children not working in the family business, divorces and second younger families of the senior generation of the family business leader, or of one of the next generation potential successors. All of these factors would be included in a comprehensive genogram. Any of these factors might explain an apparent reluctance on the part of the senior generation to progress the succession plan or the transfer of shares. A feature of the family business bivalency referred to in the previous chapter is the distinction between the formulation of plans, often conceived in the business domain and the execution and implementation of those plans, frequently due to family related constraints. The management theorist Chris Argyris categorises this as the difference between 'espoused theory' and 'theory in use'.[1]

We are not suggesting that it would always be practicable for advisors involved in routine business transactions to obtain all information necessary to complete a full genogram or even to attempt to do so. But it may well be possible to begin the process or to obtain and capture information from elsewhere within the advisor's organisation.

The simplest justification for the use of genograms when dealing with all family business and all family business issues is as a tool to know your family the business client and

---

[1] Argyris and Schon *Theory in practice: Increasing professional effectiveness* (Jossey-Bass, 1974).

thereby to help identify and manage any disconnects that might be encountered between espoused theory and theory in action in the family business concerned.

3.2.2 Understand your client

A basic genogram or family tree is therefore a useful tool to understand and summarise the basic composition of the business owning family. The symbols most typically used are:

Figure 3.1: Genogram symbols

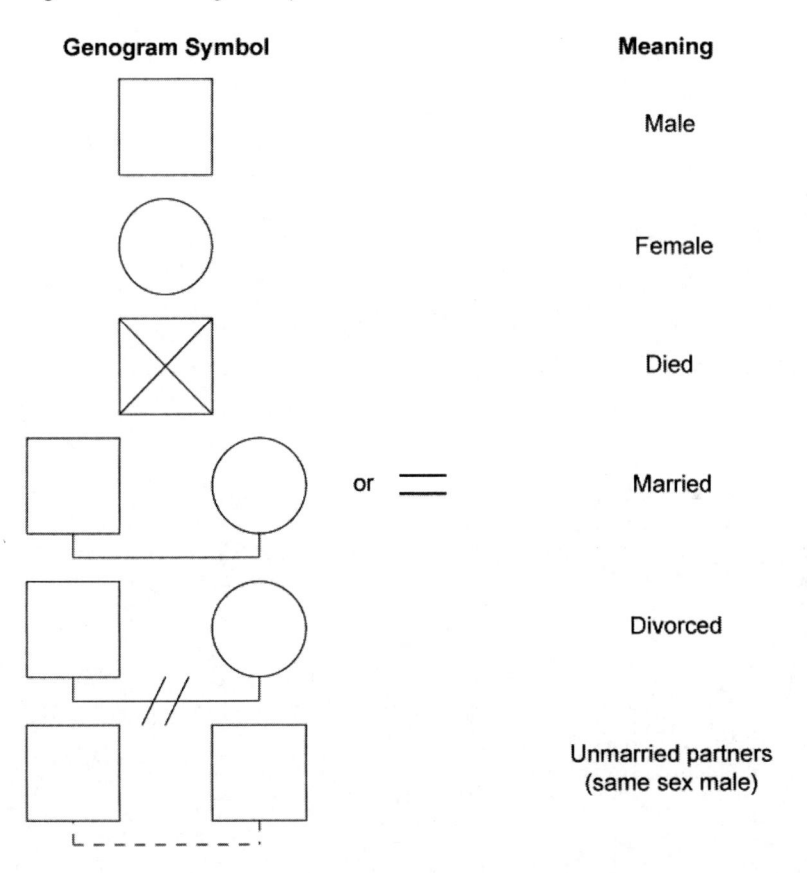

Genogram Symbol	Meaning
□	Male
○	Female
⊠	Died
□—○ or =	Married
□—○ (with //)	Divorced
□ □ (dashed line)	Unmarried partners (same sex male)

Returning to the case study of the Cadman family the basic picture would look like this.

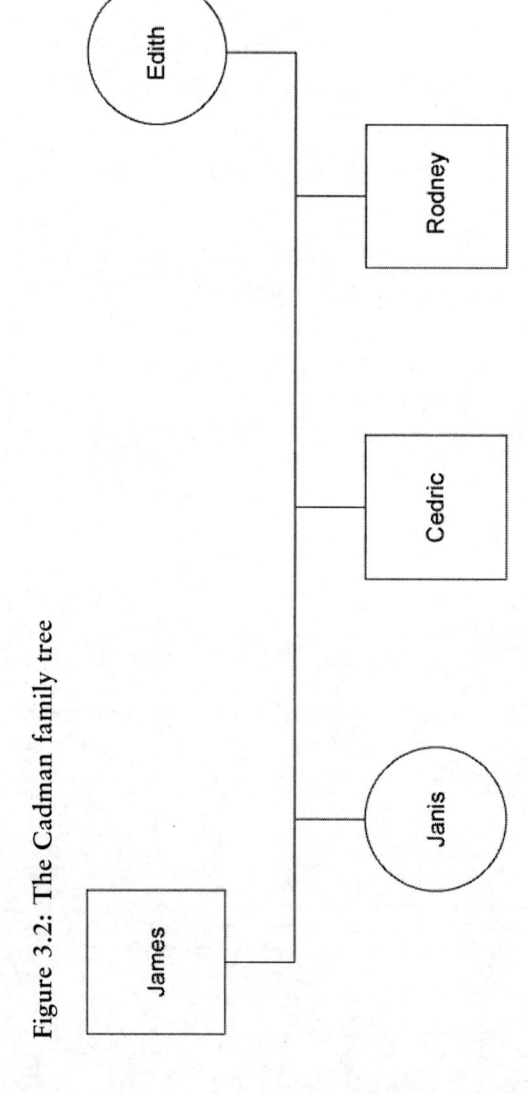

Figure 3.2: The Cadman family tree

In the case report we are not given any details about the respective ages of the family members other than the dates of death of the mother and father, James and Edith Cadman and that when the case came to court the warring siblings were all in their sixties. This might be helpful in understanding whether any of the factors traditionally associated with sibling rivalry and referred to in chapter 2 were present. So the genogram here contains a degree of guesswork (based on clues from the judgment) that Janis is the oldest followed by Cedric and Rodney. Similarly, whilst the case report refers to each of the siblings being married and having children of their own, no information at all is provided about the wider family.

In many ways the case report can be seen as an echo of a typical advisory file. But, as explained below, a full genogram could conceivably reveal information that would be useful in explaining and perhaps helping resolve a dispute such as that in Cadman Developments well before the matter reached the High Court.

The use of genograms in the context of family business advisory work stems from the family therapy profession. There the genogram is used to provide a full and detailed overview of the family history. The recommendation is that at least three generations should be explored to look for patterns of behaviour, recurring family themes etc.

A full genogram will also include representations of significant life events, such as death, divorce, starting the family business etc. By going back over time patterns might emerge. For example in a case involving a stalled or delayed succession a full genogram populated with all relevant information might show that in the two previous generational successions the senior generation waited until they were in their eighties before transferring ownership of the family firm to the next generation. The current incumbents might well feel that they have only just taken over the firm and not be at all ready to hand over the reins.

A genogram can also be used to capture information on the quality or otherwise of relationships between the family members. Full genograms can also be used to record additional biographical information and key events in family life, such as the dates of divorce or serious illness. In a family business context this can include information about the family business, a key piece of information being who actually works in the business.

Other information that may emerge from looking back over the generations of a business family are matters such as the use of key names or naming patterns, especially the use of names that are significant in the context of the family business. This can include middle names. For example there may be a pattern that the oldest son is named after the founder of the business? If so, does this indicate an expectation that the son would be expected, literally from birth, to take over leadership of the business? In effect does the genogram point to an assumption of primogeniture?

Some of the more important additional symbols traditionally used in a genogram to capture this information are as follows:

Family therapists use other more detailed genogram symbols to show other significant life events, such and family issues such as substance abuse, mental health issues, physical and sexual abuse, adoption and the birth of twins.[2] Obviously most of these issues will go well beyond the scope of instructions of most financial professionals.

---

[2] For more details of the use of genograms and relevant symbols see Jane Hilburt-Davis and W Gibb Dyer Jr

Figure 3.3: More complex genogram symbols

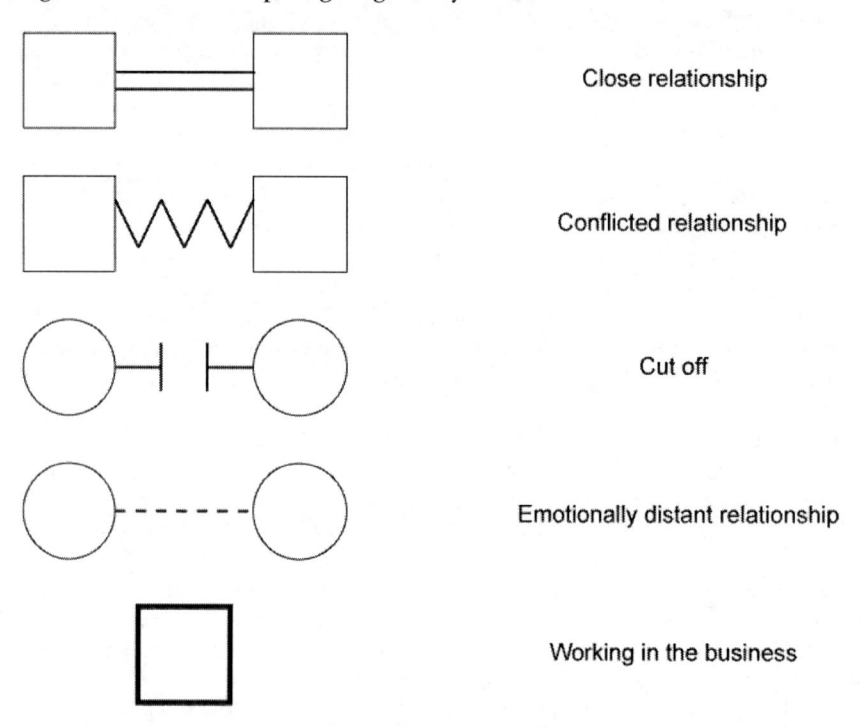

Close relationship

Conflicted relationship

Cut off

Emotionally distant relationship

Working in the business

So a more detailed genogram of the Cadman family would look like Figure 3.4 below.

It will be seen that the relevant symbol to reflect the clearly conflicted relationship between Janis and both of her brothers have been added, also that the close relationships between the two brothers Cedric and Rodney has now been recognised.

The case report also suggests that Janis had a close relationship with, at least, her father, which has also been reflected in the genogram and possibly her mother. Conversely the case report suggests that the brothers struggled with their authoritarian father, James, although not necessarily with their mother.

Consulting to Family Businesses (Jossey-Bass, 2003) at p 46 and Kets de Vries et al *Family Business on the Couch*, op cit at pp 166–172. The symbols shown above are an amalgamation of suggested symbols taking from those two sources together with one or two others in fairly common use.

Tools, Models and Theories 77

Figure 3.4: The Cadman relationship tree

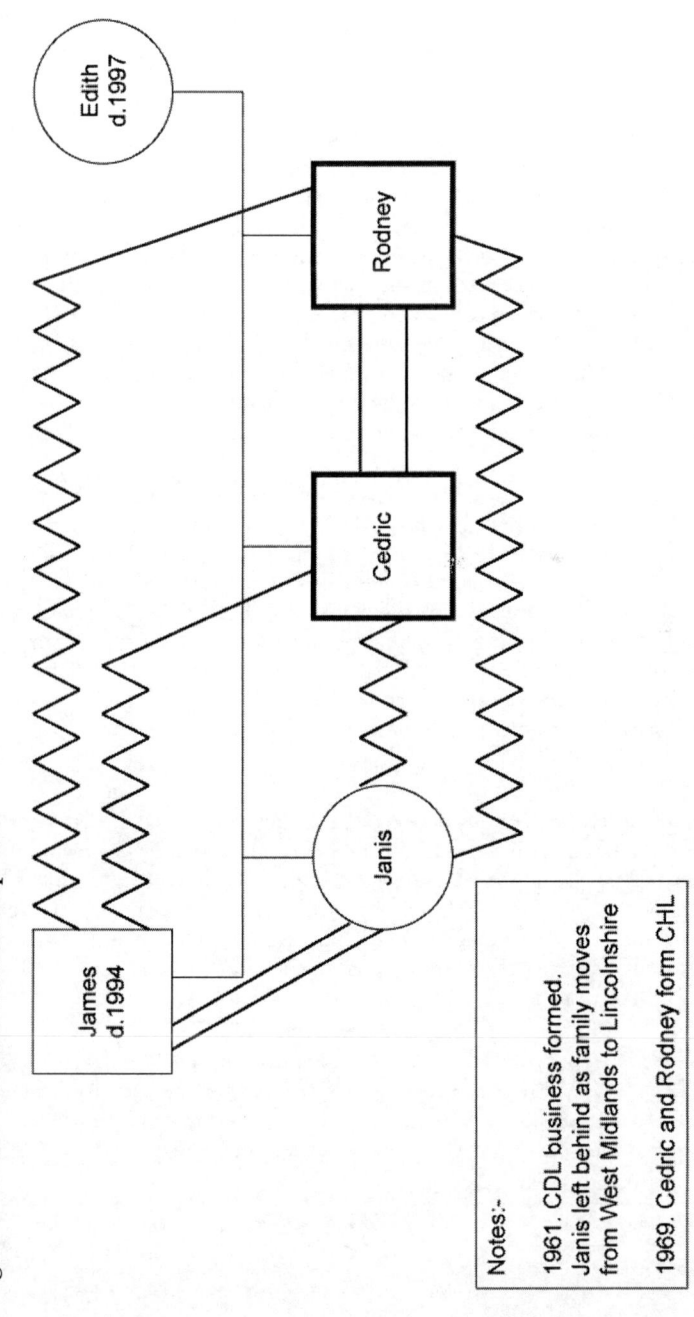

Notes:-

1961. CDL business formed.
Janis left behind as family moves
from West Midlands to Lincolnshire

1969. Cedric and Rodney form CHL

3.2.3 Helping your client

So where does all of this lead? Possibly focusing on the nature of the relationships between the father James Cadman, and each of his three children might help illustrate to the next generation, after his death that the root cause of their dispute lay not in whether or not the brothers were managing the business properly or were entitled to charge high management fees but a deep dissatisfaction at what they perceived to be favouritism shown by their father to Janis. Difficulties in their relationship with their overbearing father appear to have been a key factor in Rodney and Cedric deciding to set up Cadman Homes Limited (CHL), a separate building company controlled by them but with some element of family ownership.

In the early stages of the dispute between the siblings that realisation might have helped a negotiated settlement through mediation, conciliation or otherwise. What seems obvious is that, at the time the wills of James and Edith Cadman were giving instructions for their wills useful information could have been captured in a detailed genogram on the basis of a simple question from the advisor concerned such as 'and how do they all get along?'. Of course the question might not have been accurately and honestly answered by the senior generation concerned. If it had been this would have shown two brothers with a difficult relationship and considerable resentment towards their sister. The risks of leaving a family company comprising a substantial property portfolio and effectively controlled by the brothers in common ownership of all three siblings would have been more obvious, as would the solution of a partition of the portfolio.

In fact it appears from the case report that tensions between the siblings were evident to the advisors after James's death and whilst Edith was still alive. The family solicitors were instructed by Edith to write to all three children with a proposal that the shares in CDL were divided equally with Janis also being appointed a director. This was opposed by Cedric and Rodney.[3] Shortly afterwards a meeting took place involving all three siblings and the family solicitors at which a proposal from her brothers that Janis take a larger share of cash under her mother's will but give up both her existing shares in CDL and any expectation of receiving more under her mother's will. Janis rejected this proposal on the basis that she believed her father had wished her to hold onto the shares in CDL.[4]

So, at least at some level, the tensions between the siblings, in particular that Cedric and Rodney had absolutely no wish to be in business with their sister, was visible to both family members and advisors whilst Edith was still alive. Could the use of a genogram made any difference? It is no doubt fanciful to think that simply having the difficult family relationships illustrated in diagrammatic form would, on its own, have made any meaningful contribution to improving those relationships.

Used as a private tool by the family solicitor the vivid depiction of the family relationships might have provoked a more interventionist approach with the succession planning and Edith's will. However Kets de Vries argues that the primary benefit of a genogram is its use as a collaborative tool where advisors and family members work jointly to produce and interpret the genogram and thus provides:[5]

---

[3] See *Girvan Janis Fisher v Cedric Cadman, Rodney Cadman, Cadman Developments Limited* [2005] EWHC 377 (Ch) at para 26 of the judgment.
[4] See para 27 of the judgment.
[5] At p 278.

'a unique opportunity to discuss, interpret and hypothesise interpersonal relationships involving both living and dead family members.'

At first sight it might seem embarrassing to introduce the idea of a genogram at a meeting of a family such as the Cadmans. However once that has been overcome the genogram does have the advantage of seeming 'semi-scientific' and therefore to an extent, depersonalising the deeply personal issue of discussing the strengths and weaknesses of family relationships.

Ultimately the Cadman case was resolved only after a full High Court hearing. The court provide, in essence, provided for the solution initially suggested by Cedric and Rodney to their sister approximately 10 years earlier and before the family had expended a considerable amount on legal costs. This was that the brothers buy-out her interest in Cadman Developments Limited. To put it no higher introducing a genogram into the equation 10 years earlier could just possibly have facilitated a deeper and more realistic discussion between the siblings. On that basis what is there to lose for a family and their advisors from trying to introduce a genogram in a similar situation?

3.2.4 Genograms summary

A genogram can be used as a pictorial summary of all key information concerning a business family. Developed in collaboration with the family client genograms can be used not only to capture basic information but as a focus for detailed questions about the family. Especially in a smaller or earlier stage family business, the family members concerned will have a ready and instinctive understanding of family relationships, in the sense of who is who and how they get along. What is harder for family members is the ability to see long term patterns in relationships or to see these in systemic rather than personal terms.

Genograms can also reveal information going to the root of the instructions concerned and illustrate potential traps relating to family relationships so that possible solutions can be developed for the family business client. Whilst in the first instance it might be perceived as intrusive, if properly explained and implemented, a genogram can provide an essential tool to help a family client appreciate the realities of their family business situation.

3.3 SYSTEMS THEORY

3.3.1 Overview

In a nutshell, systems theory, as applied to family owned businesses, explains that there are a number of separate but inter-related systems in operation in any family business. These are the family, the business (or management) and the ownership systems. In an attempt to understand what is happening in a family business it is necessary to consider each of the systems separately and also the inter-relationship between the three systems.

Each of those systems will have their own characteristics and values including:
- **Business system.** An emphasis on 'hard values,' such as profit, rewards linked to performance and participation, competiveness, business strategy, management structures and processes and organisational structure.

- **Family system.** A corresponding emphasis on so-called 'soft values' such as stability, long-term ownership, inclusiveness, lifetime membership, equality, shared values, relationships and commitment to the wider community.
- **Ownership system.** Based on capital value, income, ultimate control and legal rights.

The overlaps between these systems can often be a source of strength for the family owned business. For example if a family prizes its long term ownership of the family business and their commitment to the local community, the family owners may be much more ready to endorse a long term investment strategy, rather than insist that the board focus on short term profitability and cost cutting to increase or maintain dividend income. It will be seen that many of these values are in conflict. The success of the family business and the happiness of the business family will depend on how well these inherent conflicts are managed and reconciled.

3.3.2 The three-circle model

The clearest illustration of family business systems theory can be found in the three-circle model developed by Harvard academics Renato Tagiuri and John Davis and referred to in their article, *Bivalent Attributes of the Family Firm*,[6] which has already been discussed in the previous chapter. Tagiuri and Davis provide little by way of introduction or explanation in their article, leaving it for others to interpret and comment on the model. That opportunity has not been lost. The three-circle model is probably the most discussed concept in the study of family business, and features in just about every book on the subject. According to Barbara Murray the 'three-circles model has been universally accepted as the guiding theoretical framework for conceptualising family business systems'.[7]

It is the most useful tool in the family business advisor's toolbox. Similar to genograms the three-circle model can be completed privately by the advisor to provide a quick overview of who sits where in the three systems of a family business. Also, as in the case of a genogram, the three-circle model is at its most powerful when used and developed collaboratively with a family business client. By working on their own three-circle model a business family can identify which positions family members and other key stakeholders, such as non-family management, occupy in the model, identify and debate any relevant questions and, in doing so begin to gain an insight into systems theory and the positions and perspectives of other family members involved. In an ideal world use of the three-circle model can help demonstrate that whatever problems the family firm is facing these are have their root in the structures and systems of the family business rather than the character and personality of the members of the business family. Using the three-circle model is a good place for any advisor or business family to start the transparent dialogue that needs to take place to address change and transition in a family owned business. Basically the model looks like this:

---

[6] *Family Business Review* (1996), Vol 9(2) at pp 199–208.
[7] From Denise E Fletcher (ed) *Emotional dynamics of family enterprises* in *Understanding the Small Family Business* (Routledge, 2002) at p 77.

Figure 3.5: Three-circle model of family business

1. Family owner and manager
2. Family shareholders, not employed in the business
3. Family employees
4. Non-family shareholders, employed in the business
5. External shareholders
6. Family members with no direct involvement in the business
7. Non-family employees

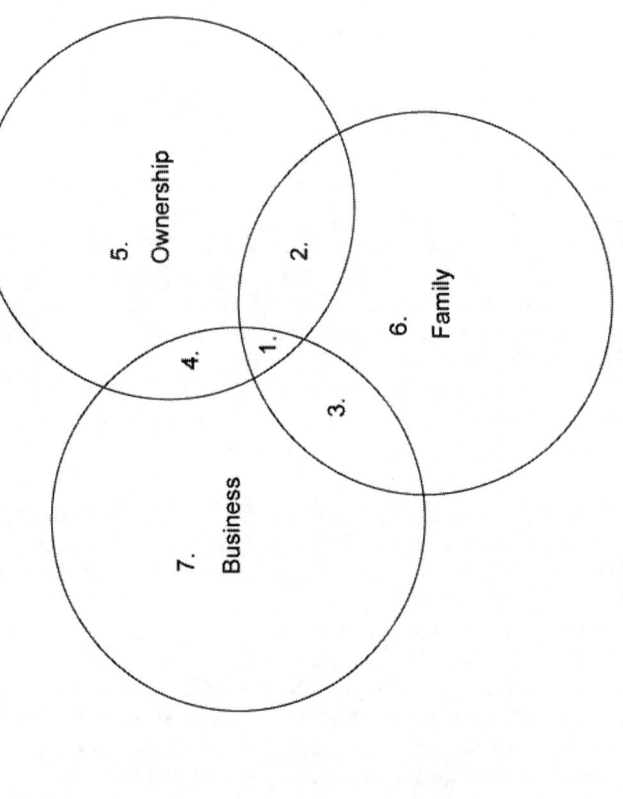

Note Tagiuri and Davis use the label Managers and Employees for the circle we have labelled 'Business'

Adapted from Tagiuri & Davis (1985)

Based on these three-circle systems we can see the family owned business represented by using three interlinked circles, one for the family, one representing the business[8] and one showing ownership. This illustration highlights the interdependence of the three overlapping. The interdependence of the three systems becomes more evident when the people within each system are identified. It quickly becomes clear that the roles of individuals within the three circles (systems) often overlap. For example, at the intersection of the three circles, Zone 1, in the diagram[9] are people who are at the same time members of the family, employees and shareholders. At the intersection of family and business circles, Zone 3, you find people who are family members and employees of the family company, but who do not own shares in the company. Continuing this approach the three-circle model contains seven different, but linked and overlapping zones into which each person linked to the family business, can be placed.

Each individual can occupy one, and only one place in the model. However there are certain matters of judgment as to what that place should be. For example should non-executive family directors (assuming that they do not also own shares) be shown in Zone 3, at the overlap between the family and business systems? Or, if the reality is that they have little real involvement in the management of the business is it more realistic to categorise their role as being a family member only (Zone 6)?[10] Similarly there might be family members who are, in theory employees of the family firm, but in reality hold pretty much pure sinecures, rarely being seen anywhere near the actual business. How should we categorise these? In the Davies case we are told that all five of the children worked on the farm during their school holidays and at weekends. Another brother Peter did occasional work when he was living at home but had a full time job elsewhere. Does temporary or casual work of this nature move family members from Zone 6 to the more involved position of family employees in Zone 3?

What about in-laws? In chapter 1 we raised the potentially ambiguous position of in-laws in the family business. On one hand they may have huge influence over family members, including major shareholders. On the other hand in-laws may be prohibited from owning shares in the family company or from participating fully in family assemblies or other parts of the family business governance mechanism. Should in-laws be recognised in the three-circle model or ignored?[11] Tagiuiri and Davis give no guidance in the parent article giving birth to the three-circle model. In fact the article introducing the model contains very little discussion about it. Practice will vary. But merely raising these questions illustrates the power of the three-circle model to spotlight the systemic strains, difficulties and potential conflicts facing individual family firms.

3.3.3 The three-circle model and the Cadman family

Applying the three-circle model to the Cadman family, after the deaths of James and Edith, the position would look like this.

---

[8] Tagiuri and Davies actually use the labels: (1) Family members, (2) Managers and employees and (3) Owners.
[9] Again Tagiuri and Davies use complex symbols rather than numbered or labelled zones to depict positions on the three-circle model.
[10] Neubauer and Lank use a more complex 'three-circle model with tie' depiction with the three circles being ownership, business and board, which are overlaid by a family tie. This creates 15 separate dimensions including a zone for 'family and board only'. See *The Family Business* (MacMillan, 1998) at p 15.
[11] Our preference is to include in laws in both the three-circle model and genograms.

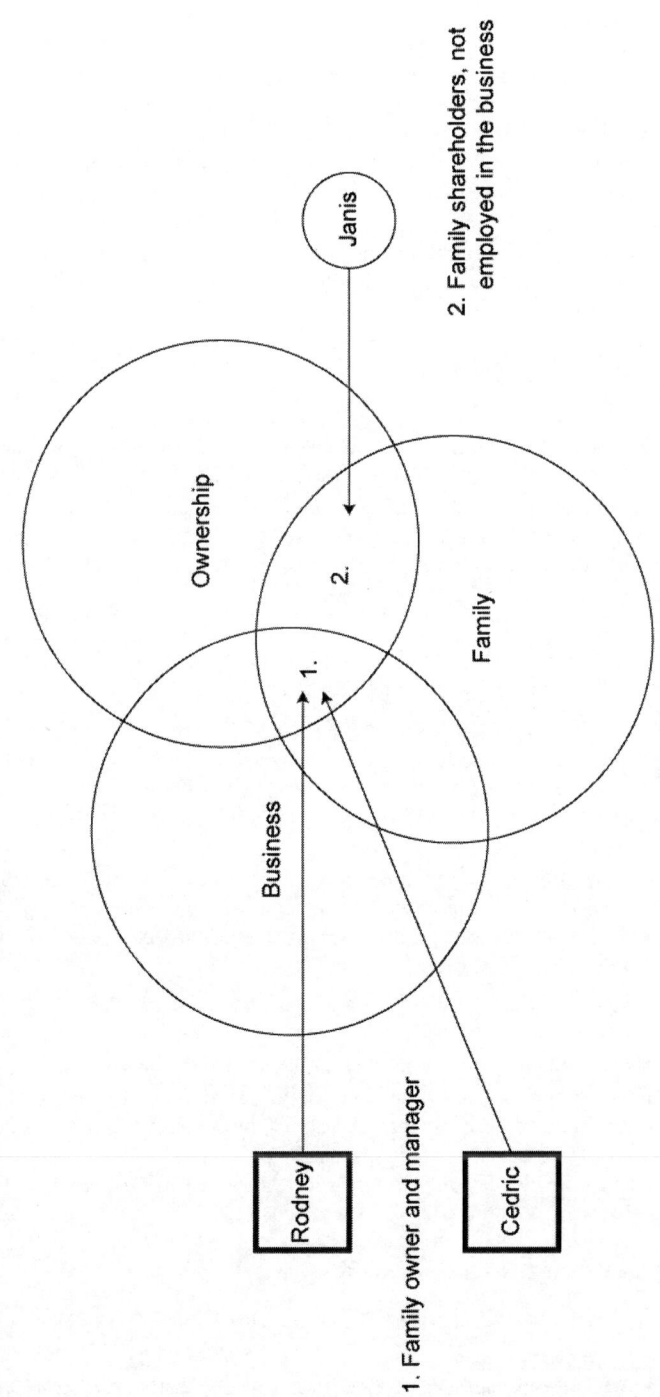

Figure 3.6: Three-circle model and the Cadman family

Placing each individual involved within the circles helps to better understand their behaviour, which is often linked to the advantages and disadvantages of their position.

It will be immediately be seen that, in the case of the Cadmans, whilst Cedric and Rodney occupy the central, Zone 1, positions of family owners also employed in the business, Janis is one stage further removed, as a family owner positioned in the overlap between the family and the business systems. Shown this way the potential for conflicts of interest between the siblings becomes obvious. Every pound taken out of Cadman Developments Limited by way of dividend must be split three ways. Each pound taken as salary, or extracted via payments to their own company, Cadman Homes Limited can be shared between the two brothers equally to the exclusion of Janis.

Factor into the equation the poor relationships between Janis and her brothers, add the resentment borne out of years of domination by their father and the dispute between the brothers and Janis hardly seems surprising.

3.3.4 Systems clash

The systems analysis would be that, in the case of the Cadmans family business, the business system was in conflict with the family and ownership systems. A similar analysis can be applied to the Saul D Harrison case and to that of the Davies family. Viewed this way family business disputes can be seen not so much tales of the personal avarice and obstinacy of individual family members but rather of individuals being caught in the clash of the family business systems.

The three-circle model is usually used to illustrate the potential systems clash inherent in the family business model. The analysis being that such clashes are most likely to occur in the areas of overlap between the three systems as shown on the model. For example between:

- **Business and family** – in relation to employment matters such as family recruitment, policies, nepotism, promotion and remuneration of family members, family-branch favouritism.
- **Ownership and family** – for example in relation to family business trusts or whether exit mechanisms should be introduced to help more remote family members who no longer want to be part of the family company to exit on reasonable terms.
- **Business and ownership** – over dividend and remuneration policies.

But systems analysis goes beyond merely predicting where disputes may arise in a family owned business. It is capable of illustrating one of the fundamental challenges of the family business model. This is the basic incompatibility between the nature, values and characteristics of two of the core systems concerned, the family and business systems. Leading family business academic and commentator Randel Carlock summarised the position thus:[12]

> 'families are about caring and businesses are about money.'

---

[12] Randel S Carlock *When Family Businesses are Best*, Insead Faculty and Research Working Paper 2010/42/EFE.

In many families decisions can be taken (or avoided) as a result of this systems clash that can damage the family business, or, at the very least substantially impede its progress. This need not be as a result of tensions or antagonisms amongst the business owning family. Quite the reverse. In the most loving and caring families decisions might be made within the business system that, on closer analysis, are driven wholly by concerns arising in the family system. The classic example would be creating a job in the family business for a family member who needs employment.

In more detail the values stemming from the family and business systems can be shown as follows:

Figure 3.7: The system 'clash' in the family business

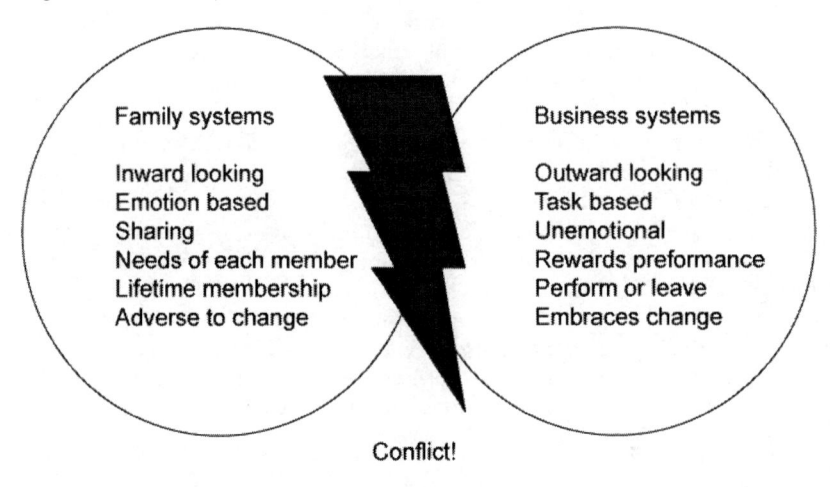

Family systems

Inward looking
Emotion based
Sharing
Needs of each member
Lifetime membership
Adverse to change

Business systems

Outward looking
Task based
Unemotional
Rewards preformance
Perform or leave
Embraces change

Conflict!

3.3.5 ... or systemic cohesion

Although usually presented as an inherent flaw in the family business model these differences between the family and the business systems are in fact also capable of providing a source of strength and cohesion for a family business. This is the 'bivalency' at the heart of the Tagiuiri and Davis article, *Bivalent Attributes of the Family Firm*.[13]

Let us return to the example of family employment. In an ideal family business world, rather than taking a family member on board as a passenger, the family business will be engaging a hugely committed employee, with an innate and deeply embedded loyalty to the family business and their fellow family members and with a deep understanding of the family business, its values and workings. Any shortfall in the skill-set and experience of the family member concerned can easily be addressed by training and will be more than offset by the additional qualities brought to the business by that family employee. There are many family business stories about family members who were prepared to take pay cuts, work voluntary overtime or even go without pay altogether for long periods to ensure survival of their family business during difficult times.

---

[13] *Family Business Review* (1996), Vol 9(2) at pp 199–208.

3.3.6 Systemic equilibrium

Keeping an appropriate balance between the values stemming from the family system and those from the business system is probably the hardest task for any family business. Too much attention to business values and the family system suffers. Logically the worse the family relationships the harder it will be for those concerned to focus on business issues. Alternatively an unduly inappropriate 'family first' approach may mean that whilst family relationships are placed at a premium and preserved in the first instance the business suffers. Key non-family employees may be lost to the curse of nepotism. The business might become generally uncompetitive. In extreme cases this can lead to financial pressure and even business failure, which will inevitably rebound on family relationships.[14] Some commentators distinguish between business owning families who take a business first approach and those who put family first. John Ward effectively comes down in favour of 'business bias' arguing that ultimately 'what is good for the business also serves the best interest of the family'.[15]

Others take a more nuanced and flexible approach arguing that at times and for certain decisions a more business focused approach will be needed, at other times the needs of the business family should be placed first.[16] The family business is a fragile eco-system and subtle balances are needed to keep it in equilibrium. What is needed is a constant and careful evaluation of the health of all three systems at play. The trick, for a family business is, according to Carlock is to be 'professionally emotional'.[17] By which he means finding a way to leverage the positive attributes arising from the family system in a way that does least damage to the business system. The means to achieve that balance is through the family business governance process, especially in Carlock's view by following the Parallel Planning Process, developed and advocated by him and John Ward which is described in detail in chapter 7 (Management Succession).

3.3.7 The three-circle model and the family business leader

The three-circle model provides an excellent way of illustrating interpersonal conflicts between individuals located in different systems comprised within the family business. As the greatest complexity and therefore the greatest potential for conflict is to be found where the circles representing the separate systems intersect the model also shows that those occupying 'Zone 1' are potentially the most conflicted. It is relatively easy to see, particularly in a more mature family business, potential conflicts of interest arising between family members occupying different positions within the three-circle model. For example, between family members employed in the business and those who are not, but would like to be. Or between family employees seeking to maximise their remuneration and family shareholders wanting to receive dividends.

What is less obvious simply from looking at the model, but is brought out in the text of Tagiuri and Davis' article itself is the potential for the inter-locking family business systems to create internal psychological conflict for individual family members. In earliest stage family businesses, the so called 'one circle family business' the entrepreneur founder will have various roles. They may be the sole or main employee, the majority

---

[14] For example the Listowel Trading restaurant case discussed in chapter 8 (Directors' Duties).
[15] John Ward *Perpetuating the Family Business* (Palgrave, 2004), Lesson 15 (Business Bias) at p 74
[16] See for example, Collins McCracken Murray and Stepek 'Strong governance: a result of evolutionary and revolutionary processes' *Journal of Family Business Management* (2014) Volume 4, No 2.
[17] Op cit at p 21.

owner and also a family member. The internal psychological conflict caused by these clashing roles form the basis of the 'bivalent attributes' of family owned businesses identified by Tagiuri and Davis. As they comment: 'Even in the best of cases we find the owner-manager-relative periodically suffering from the anxiety that results from what we call 'norm confusion'.[18]

What the model struggles to illustrate, although this comes through strongly in the Tagiuri and Davis article is that those subject to the greatest pressures of role conflict is not necessarily between individuals positioned in different parts of the system, inter-personal conflict. Rather the most difficult conflicts are likely to be for those with multiple roles and therefore facing pressures from different parts of the system. In other words, intra-personal conflict.

Role conflict is therefore most likely to be felt by family business leaders sitting in Zone 1 and, as such positioned in the vortex of the family business systems clash. Returning to the Cadman family and considering the position of the father, James Cadman, in relation to his daughter Janis. James and Edith caused the family company CDL to buy a residential property close to Janis in the Midlands. Clearly he and Edith wanted to have a base when visiting their daughter and grandchildren. That decision can therefore be seen to have been taken by James more in his role of father/ grandfather than as a shareholder or director. Equally we learn that James was keen for Janis to be an owner of CDL and to be more closely involved as a director of that business. There is no suggestion that Janis had any skills or experience to contribute to CDL. Again James would appear to have been motivated by a desire to see his daughter remain attached to the family, notwithstanding the move to Lincolnshire and using the family business as a mechanism to achieve this. Whilst there is no evidence that James was even aware of this duality, much less troubled by it, the consequences of this tension were felt elsewhere and later, in the systems clash between business, family and ownership manifested in the court case.

Tom Davies seemed to be affected by subtly different intra-personal conflicts. Whilst he seemed quite content to surrender his place in the business system to James his dual role as owner of the farmland and head of the Davies family caused him to vacillate between succession options of full family ownership and passing on the land to James. This ambiguity or intra-personal conflict will remain with the family business leader, albeit in an increasingly obvious way, as the family business matures. Even in larger and later stage family businesses one individual may simultaneously be managing director, majority owner and a senior family member. As such they may be called on to make employment decisions which call for choices between their own children or nieces and nephews or dividend policies that may compromise either their own family's lifestyle or that of their siblings' families.

3.3.8 The three-circle model and systems change

The family business and the separate systems comprised within it are not static. So the positions of individuals within the three-circle model will also change. Take, for example the position of a next generation family member. On joining the family firm at a relatively young age it is quite likely that they will not have any direct ownership of the family firm and that they will occupy a position within Zone 3 of the three-circle model;

---

[18] Op cit at p 202.

that of a family employee. As the model illustrates that position is complicated enough in its own right. All the tensions and issues associated with the employment of family members will need to be negotiated.

Assuming that the next generation family member stays with the business and progresses to a senior management position,[19] considerations of ownership are likely to arise. At what stage could the next generation reasonably expect to become owners of the family firm? Too early and the financial needs of the senior generation might not be properly catered for. If ownership transfer is delayed too much tensions and conflict might arise.[20] These issues relating to family business life cycles are considered in more detail in the remainder of this chapter but can be illustrated and explored, exposed even by the use of the three-circle model.

3.3.9 Homeostasis

Notwithstanding that change is inevitable in any organisation there will often be countervailing forces seeking to resist that change. An important theoretical concept relevant to in family systems theory is homeostasis. This is the ability of the family system to develop mechanisms to maintain a self-correcting and constant state.[21] Perversely, on occasions this will include mechanisms to keep a conflict alive, if relationships in the family have deteriorated to such an extent that the natural state of the family is one of strife and conflict. People do what comes naturally, even if this is to fight. The organisational and development thinker Peter Senge talks about positive and negative feedback loops or 'virtual and vicious cycles'.[22] The considerable challenge for a family business locked into a vicious cycle of conflict is how to break that cycle and escape the gravitational pull of their systemic homeostasis.

3.4 FAMILY BUSINESS LIFE-CYCLE THEORY

3.4.1 Overview

Notwithstanding the force of homeostasis all family business systems inevitably change with time. For those family businesses that survive through the generations the features and characteristics of the business will inevitably alter as the business matures through its various life stages.

As the business owning family and the family business develop the layout of that family's three-circle model will change. That change will itself be the composite of the changes

---

[19] Some commentators advocate a variant of the three-circle model by dividing the business or management and employee circle into two parts, management or directors and employees, thereby creating a four circle model. The four circle model is really only of relevance for larger family businesses and is not widely used or discussed. Various other variations on the three-circle model and alternative approaches and models that have been proposed by a number of academics are discussed by Torsten Pieper, Sabine Klein in 'The Bulleye: A Systems Approach to Modeling Family Firms' *Family Business Review* (2007) Vol 20(4). The authors also introduce their own 'Bulleye' model arguing that family business can only be understood as an 'open system' with a fluid interchange between the individual, the three circles or systems identified by Tagiuri and Davies and the environment (by which they mean a combination of the culture, economic and regulatory systems) in which the family business concerned operates.

[20] For example in the case of Eirian Davies, the cowshed Cindrella, discussed in detail in chapter 19 (Inheritance Disputes).

[21] See Kets de Vries and Carlock with Florent-Treacy *Family Business on the Couch* (Wiley, 2007).

[22] Senge *The Fifth Discipline – The Art & Practice of the Learning Organisation* (Random House, 2006).

that are taking place in the lives of individual family members. In the case of the founding entrepreneur as they move from founding energetic business visionary, through to respected business leader and then to senior statesman. In parallel their children are growing from infants, who only occupy the family circle in the model, to, in the case of children who join the business, junior subordinates, now with a foot in the business circle also. This creates a need for recognition in terms of status, role and remuneration. Meanwhile those children who do not join the family business will be building their own independent careers and lives but will remain in the family dimension of the model. Meanwhile in the family system the next generation will be moving away from their family of origin, forming life partnerships and starting their own families bringing a further set of complexity into the business family mix in the form of partner or spousal influence and loyalties and responsibilities to the new next generation of their own nuclear family.

An understanding of the relevant stages of this evolutionary process and the key features and challenges of each of these is therefore important for a business family and their advisors. Families who recognise this development process and adapt to it are more likely to achieve their aims and objectives, and to make the transition from one generation to the next. The challenge for the family business advisor is to help the business family navigate through this evolutionary process. The categorisations used most often are those suggested by John Ward[23] who sees the evolutionary process as follows:

- **Stage 1 – The owner-managed business.** This is the typical early stage founder led family business, highly reliant on the entrepreneurial zeal of the founder. Indeed in many cases these owner-managed businesses will have been established with no clear idea of family succession. It could be argued that it is only towards the later part of this stage that such businesses can truly be seen as family firms.[24] Others use the term 'controlling owner'[25] but essentially follow the same model. The key challenge at this stage of evolution is survival. Establishing the family firm, battling for customers for the goods or services it provides, financial management and obtaining funding, recruitment of good employees, both family and non-family. But in the later part of this stage, family and ownership issues will also be jostling for attention.

- **Stage 2 – The sibling partnership.** The first major stage in the evolution of a family business will be the first intergenerational succession event, the transfer of the business from first to second generation. In Ward's typical model the family firm will then be run jointly by the founder's children as a sibling partnership. The siblings will face a fresh series of challenges. Not only will they have to find a way of working together, they will also need to take the business onto the next stage without the involvement of the founder. Almost inevitably the business will have outgrown the founder's rough and ready, seat of the pants style of management and will need to introduce a more professional approach if it is to survive and thrive.

- **Stage 3 – The cousin collaboration.** After the second inter-generational succession the family firm will be owned by the grandchildren of the founder. Even if the business has grown to a considerable size it is most unlikely that the business could accommodate all concerned, always assuming that each of the cousins wanted to

---

[23] See John Ward *Perpetuating the Family Business* (Palgrave, 2004).
[24] See the discussion on the definition of a family business in chapter 1.
[25] See for example Gersick, Davis, Hampton & Lansberg *Generation to Generation: Life cycles of a family business* (Harvard Business School Press, 1997).

work in the family business and were qualified to do so. Although other terms are sometimes used for this stage[26] such as a 'cousin consortium', Ward prefers the term 'collaboration,' which, he argues emphasises the need for the cousins concerned to co-operate and work together if their family business is to thrive or even survive in this increasingly complex form. Instead to take the business forward it will almost certainly be necessary to supplement the family gene pool by recruiting more non-family managers, perhaps moving to the position where the majority of executive director posts are filled by non-family, always assuming that this professionalisation of the family firms did not take place during one of the earlier stages. The position of the more mature family business that has reached this stage is therefore one of growing complexity. The challenge for the third generation is two-fold. First how to manage this transition from a family run to a family owned family business. Secondly how to organise their cousin collaboration in a way that accommodates the various roles that the cousins will occupy, some as family employees, others as family shareholders and some perhaps simply as family members. Attention to formal family business governance becomes paramount.

The classic family business life cycle model therefore looks like Figure 3.8 below. Indeed in a later article[27] Ward looks at various permutations and complications that do not fit easily into the earlier and basic model. He suggests a number of 'best fit' compromises so that the model can remain useful. For example he recognised that smaller cousin collaborations (those with four or fewer cousins) will have many of the features of a sibling partnership and suggests that they should basically be treated as such, even though there will be key differences such as the fact that the cousins will have grown up in different households and will therefore have undergone different socialisation processes. Of course the position is more complicated in real life.[28] Some family businesses will be established as sibling partnerships. Clarks, for example, was initially set up by Cyrus Clark, who was soon joined by his brother James, to establish a sibling partnership. Cadburys was started by Richard and George Cadbury, although the business was closely related to other family concerns. Many businesses are started by just one individual, and initially there may or may not be other family members involved. In many cases other family members will not be brought in until a later date. In other cases the husband and wife may be involved from the beginning, or else it may be a parent and child who found the business.

In other cases the family business may pass to a single owner for a number of generations. The business family might only have one child, or only one child interested in taking the business over. The business family ownership philosophy might be based on single ownership, such as a form of primogeniture. Outsider branches may have been bought out, either following a dispute, or as part of a more strategic ownership pruning exercise. So either or both of the cousin collaboration or the sibling partnership stages might be delayed for several generations or missed altogether.

---

[26] See for example Gersick, Lansberg, Desjardins and Dunn 'Stages and Transitions: Managing Change in the Family Business' *Family Business Review* (1999) Vol 12(4) at pp 287–297.
[27] John Ward and Christina Dolan 'Defining and Describing Family Business Ownership Configurations' *Family Business Review* (1998) Vol 11(4) at pp 305–310.
[28] See Gersick's Three-Dimensional Development Model discussed at **17.7.1** which captures and depicts some of this complexity.

Tools, Models and Theories 91

Figure 3.8: Family business stages

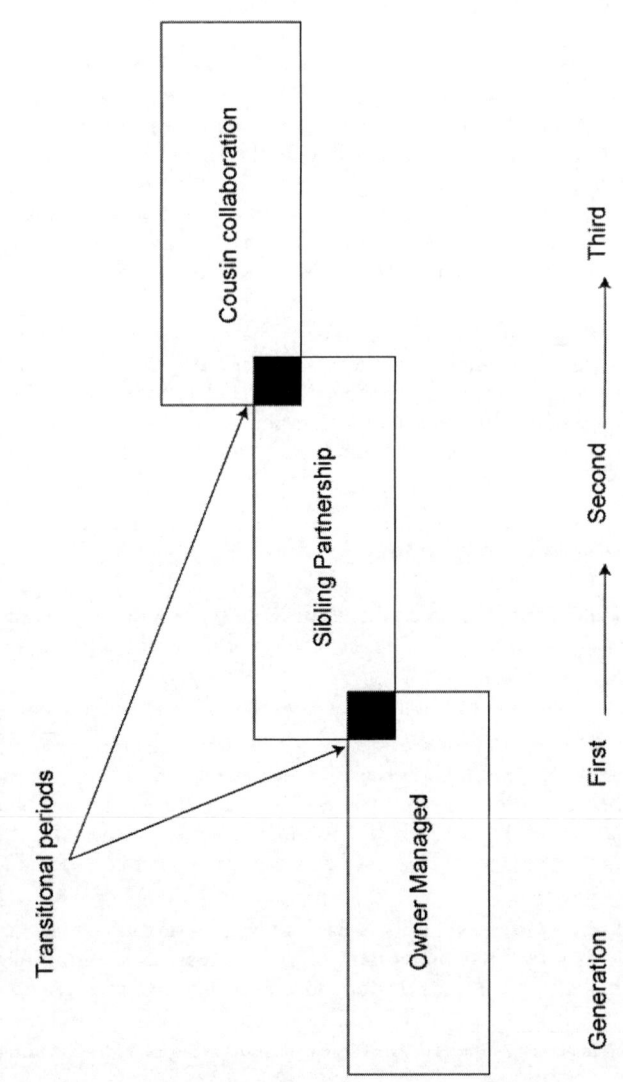

The life cycle model works more as a series of generalisations, with many variants, rather than an absolute single, one size fits all, description of family business organisation.

3.4.2 Transitional periods

A family business will be particularly vulnerable in the transition periods between generations. In the Cadman case, difficulties and tensions over ownership and the role of Janis in the family business which surfaced shortly after the death of the father James, remained unresolved at the time of the mother's death approximately 3 years later and developed into a full blown dispute between the siblings afterwards.

Transition periods are discussed in more detail in chapter 7 (Management Succession).

3.4.3 Parent-offspring or intergenerational partnerships

Others commentators introduce an intermediate stage between the owner managed family business and the sibling partnership. This is the parent-offspring or intergenerational partnership. The idea being that, as part of the transition between generations, the next generation will grow from being the employees or helpers of the senior generation into jointly leading and owning the business with them. This sophistication reflects the evolving nature of family business relationships. Analytically the intergenerational partnership can either be seen as part of an extended transition phase between the generations, or alternatively as a stage in its own right.

Perhaps the most obvious examples of intergenerational partnerships can be found in the agricultural sector, where it is common for the next generation to progress from farm employees, to entering into a formal partnership with their parents, where both generations work side by side, with the senior generation gradually stepping back from active work into the role of overseer, before leaving the farming partnership and eventual retirement.[29]

3.4.4 An alternative life cycle model

An alternative, but similar, approach to family business life cycles looks at the dominant characteristic of the business rather than the composition of the business owning family.

This approach sees the evolution of a family firm as taking place in phases, as follows:
- **The entrepreneurial stage.** This is a critical and necessary stage for every business. The new enterprise is energised and driven by the personal vision and goals of the entrepreneur. The development of the business is characterised by an opportunistic and intuitive trial and error pursuit of the founder's dream. The founder is at the centre of everything, works incredibly hard and expects others to do the same, and from this loyalty follows.
- **The managerial stage.** After the business has survived its start-up challenges, and shown that it can grow, the limitations of the entrepreneurial stage become evident. The founder's passion, hands-on, controlling, intuitive involvement in all

---

[29] The Davies family case and also that of the Ham family cases, discussed in chapter 13 (Family Partnerships) illustrate this.

aspects can become obstacles to growth. There may be a period of frustration, but the entrepreneur will, perhaps with reluctance, recruit outside expertise to help in the next stage of growth. One of the first outside appointments is likely to be a finance director to bring financial discipline and administrative structure to the business. Afterwards the founder appreciates the value of the change, but chafes at some of the constraints. The ability of the entrepreneur and the newly recruited non-family management team to work together and encourage each other is key to the continued success of the business.

- **The professional stage.** Not every family business gets beyond the managerial stage, either through choice or limited potential. But many family businesses have the potential for greater growth. Their owners may have a strong desire to exploit that potential to the full. However to achieve that success means the business has to take a more professional approach to its future. This involves strategic planning and goal setting. If the resulting goals are to be successfully implemented then sound and adequate internal structures and systems are required. Most importantly leadership and management must be based primarily on capability, character and commitment rather than family ties. The necessity of family members to conform to this professional culture can be a source of tension. The initiative for this process may come from the second generation.

The advantage of this developmental model is that it applies to the state of development of the underlying business rather than the progression of the business through various generations and changes of ownership succession. Accordingly a high growth early stage family business, such as Dysons, will reach the professional stage, during the lifetime of its founder.

This second model also deals in abstract concepts rather than absolutes. The transition from one stage of business to another will be an evolutionary process, rather than a clear and distinct set event. The path might not be smooth or linear. For example it might take several false starts and failed recruitments before non-family managers are successfully integrated to work alongside the entrepreneurial founder.

Many highly professional family businesses will somehow retain elements of entrepreneurial zeal.[30] Others family businesses have found a need to reintroduce this at a later stage of the life of the family business to ensure its very survival. After several years of professional management the LEGO family business was facing bankruptcy. Handing leadership to Jurgen Vig Knudstrorp, who introduced a programme of highly focused entrepreneurial 'disruptive innovation,' revolutionised the fortunes of the family firm and turned out to be a masterstroke by the family owner Kjeld Kirk Krtistiansen and turned LEGO into one of the biggest business success stories of recent times.[31]

An alternative view is that, rather than the entrepreneurial, managerial and professional phases being distinct stages of a family business evolution, elements of the first two, need to be continuously present in any successful family firm. Based on the observation that:

> 'only a minority of family businesses nurture growth ambitions and expand to become, first medium sized companies and then, possibly global corporations.'

---

[30] Indeed Gersick argues that a degree of re-invention is necessary otherwise a business simply stagnates and dies.
[31] For more on the LEGO story, see David Roberston *Brick by Brick* (Random House, 2013).

Bengt Johnnanisson[32] attempts to identify the ingredients that make growth and expansion possible. Rejecting the traditional view that growth calls for 'more professional management and less family involvement' he argues that the continued influence of the family system and continual entrepreneurship are necessary to rub up against 'mangerialism' and to create the 'friction energy' necessary to power growth.

3.5 INDIVIDUAL LIFE-CYCLE THEORY

3.5.1 Overview

Just as the family business involves a number of members of the business family, the overall family business life cycle is made up of the individual life cycles of the members of that family. Particular problems can arise when these individual and family business life-cycles are not in harmony. In practice, it will be comparatively rare that the timing is perfect for any business family. Figure 3.9 illustrates this.

Figure 3.9: Individual and family business life cycles

Father				
Age	35	45	55	65
Role	Founder	Leader	Overseer	Supporter

Current Generation — Next Generation — Transitional period

Next Generation				
Age	10	20	30	40
Role	None	Helper	Manager	Leader

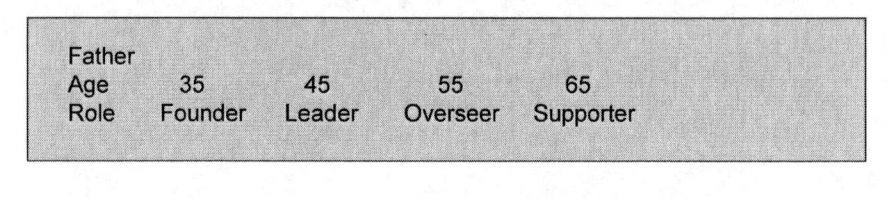

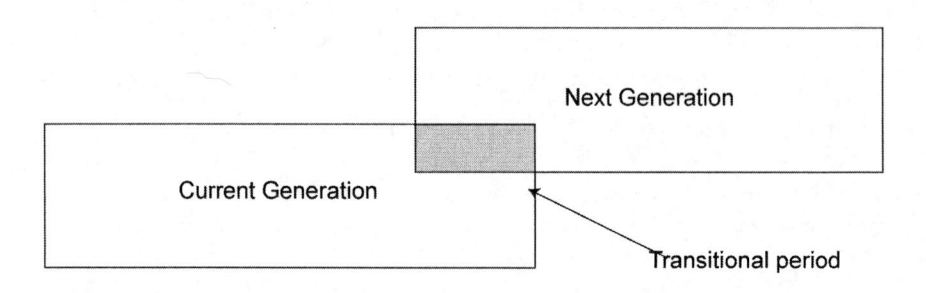

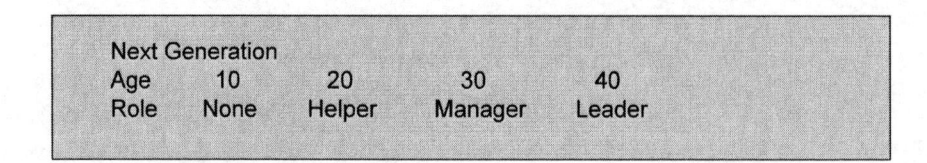

The model assumes that a family business was founded by a 35 year-old father, with a child then 10 years old and the father retires from a formal role in the business at the age of 65. Assuming that the child joins the business at some stage between their late teens

---

[32] Denise E Fletcher (ed) *Energising entrepreneurship* in *Understanding the Small Family Business* (Routledge, 2002) at p 46.

and mid-twenties and following a typical career progression the next generation would hope to be assuming managerial role in their thirties and leadership of the family business at around the age of 40.

A few years either-way and the life cycles of the business family and the family business are out of kilter. If the senior generation put off starting a family until their mid to late thirties, perhaps to concentrate on their business it will be seen that the next generation would be asked to assume leadership of the family firm at a very early age if the founder still wished to retire at a typical age. Conversely (and perhaps more typically) if the 25 year age gap remained what if the current generation business leader, in the absence of a compulsory retirement age in their family firm decided to remain in position for just an additional 10 years or more? This would take them to 70 or beyond. The next generation family member would be 45 or older before assuming overall leadership. Their career would be in danger of stagnation.[33]

3.5.2 The eight ages of man

In chapter 4 of *Family Business on the Couch* Kets de Vries and colleagues look at a number of models of human development, including the thinking of Freud, and consider their relevance to the context of the family owned business.

Of particular interest is their discussion of Erik Erikson's *Eight Ages of Man*.[34] The basic concept being that the successful psychological development of any individual depends on them satisfactorily navigating each particular stage of development, like a series of canal locks; the 'epigenetic principle'. Failure to pass through each stage will result in some form of arrested development. Most of the stages concern development from infancy to early adulthood. But two final stages have clear implications for those involved in family business. These are the adult stage, defined as from 20's through to 50's and late adulthood, from 60 onwards.

According to Erikson the primary life struggle in the adult stage is between, on the one hand, 'generativity', encompassing establishing a career and family, working out how to make the best use of one's life and how to contribute to the development of others and, on the other hand 'stagnation' by which Erikson means self-absorption. The final life stage, of late adulthood, from 60 onwards, is seen as a struggle between 'ego integrity.' In essence a struggle between on the one hand gracefully accepting senior statesmanship and, on the other hand, 'despair,' kicking back against the march of time and mortality, which is manifested in the senior generation refusing to let go of control of their family business.

It will be seen that in most family businesses, two generations will simultaneously be undertaking their life struggles. The bivalent potential of the family business structure once more comes to the fore. The senior generation family member, approaching the end of a satisfactory career may, gradually and gracefully step back, support and mentor the next generation and allow their careers and potential, and with it the family business, to develop. Equally there is the possibility that the senior generation, trapped in the lock of

---

[33] Sometimes referred to in family business circles as 'The Prince Charles Syndrome'.
[34] Erikson *Childhood and Society* (Norton, New York, 1950).

a classic mid-life crisis and perhaps psychologically pre-disposed to do so, might attempt to retain absolute control of the family enterprise and fail to give the next generation room to grow.[35]

3.5.3 Differentiation

So far we have tended to focus on the situation of the senior generation business leader. Young adulthood is also a key developmental stage for the next generation. Another life cycle theory model, developed by Carter and McGoldrick,[36] also discussed in the *Family Business on the Couch* emphasises the need for the next generation to establish their psychological and physical independence from their parents: or differentiation.

Usually this involves the young person leaving home and developing an independent life at university or through their careers. For those joining the family business, particularly straight from school this will not be the case. The potential arises for the psychological development of the next generation to be thwarted and for them to be trapped in a pre-adult developmental stage, in other words to be permanently infantilised by their very presence in the family business.

The theory is that this is much less likely to happen if earlier stages of the development of the next generation family member concerned have been satisfactorily navigated. In particular that the family member was able to develop a sufficiently robust sense of self in early childhood, or, in the jargon had become 'differentiated' from their parents.[37]

Paradoxically the more support received in early childhood the greater the confidence and sense of independence developed by the child. Conversely the less secure the child, perhaps because one or more of the parents is significantly distracted by the demands of an early stage family business, the less likely that proper differentiation will have been achieved. The more a poorly differentiated next generation family member is pitched back into an environment, which encourages infantilisation, without the mechanisms and boundaries to recognise naturally his or her adult status, the greater the potential for age and role confusion.

On the other hand, in addition to perpetuating a state of infanthood the family business environment is also capable robbing the next generation of their opportunity to grow up naturally. Often the imagery used in connection with the family business world involves children in adult roles, playing at business, or perhaps a photograph of a son literally stepping into his father's shoes or wearing his suit. Much has been written about the 'Sunday lunch time board meeting' or other ways in which the next generation are immersed in the family business from an early age. This may have many positive features, including fostering a sense of involvement and a deep and instinctive understanding of the operations and culture of the family business.

The phenomenon may continue after the next generation actually join the business. Often the next generation will be promoted to senior positions, including directorships, before their age and experience would have made this a realistic possibility in a

---

[35] The Ford story provides a classic example.
[36] Carter and McGoldrick *The Expanded Life Cycle; Individual, Family and Social Perspectives* (New York, 1999).
[37] From Winnicott 'Transitional Objects and Transitional *Phenomena*' *International Journal of Psychoanalysis* (1953) and Bowlby *Attachment and Loss* (Penguin, 1992).

non-family firm. Again there may be some positive aspects to this. However this 'family first' approach is capable of weakening the business in various respects.[38] It is also capable of damaging the development of the next generation by robbing them of the opportunity to develop their careers and independence under their own steam and at a natural pace.

Arguably the fact that university education, often away from home, is becoming the norm rather than the exception for next generation family members will assist in the differentiation process. One of the consistent messages from the family business world is the wisdom of the next generation obtaining outside experience in other businesses before returning to the family firm. Although this is often more on the development of the CV's of the next generation there must be some benefits in terms of cementing the differentiation process.

3.5.4 Black spots and purple patches

Tagiuri and Davis look more deeply into the concepts of individual life cycle theory and the consequences of this for the relationships between fathers and sons working together in family firms.[39]

Based on various sources about life cycle theory[40] they identify a number of periods where, for different reasons, the challenges thrown up by life can prove particularly challenging for many men. This has a knock-on effect for the quality of their interpersonal relationships including work relationships. These are typically:

- **From seventeen to twenty-two.** When young males are trying to complete the separation process from their parents and establish their own identity.
- **Thirty-four to forty.** The time when, typically, males are battling to achieve at work, build homes and families and achieve status in their communities.
- **Forty-one to fifty.** The classic period of mid-life crisis when males wonder whether the battle was worth it and start to contemplate their own mortality.
- **Sixty-one to seventy.** Erikson's age of *ego-integrity* as males get to grips with the fact that their economic role is almost at its end.

Notwithstanding that these periods do seem to take up the vast majority of the male working life Tagiuri and Davis do identify two periods of relative calm which can make the average male comparatively easy to live with and work alongside:

- **Twenty-three to thirty-three.** When the next generation is beginning to build a career and their relationships. Life seems exciting and full of possibilities.
- **Fifty-one to sixty.** When the senior generation begins to think seriously about their legacy in the working world, is willing to pass on their knowledge and experience and is best placed to act as a mentor to the next generation. The end is in sight but perhaps not frighteningly so.

---

[38] The legal pitfalls of acting as a 'family director' are discussed in chapter 8 (Directors' Duties).
[39] John A Davis and Renato Tagiuri 'The Influence of Life Stage on Father-Son Work Relationships in Family Companies' *Family Business Review* (1989) Vol 2(1).
[40] In addition to Erikson the authors refer especially to D J Levinson *The Seasons of a Man's Life* (New York, 1978); 'The Phases of Adult Life: A Study in Developmental Psychology' *American Journal of Psychology* (1972) 129(5) 521–531; and G E Valliant *Adaptation of Life* (Little Brown, Boston, 1977).

Taking the father and son working relationship as the most prevalent in the family business world, the authors theorise that whilst there will be many 'black spots' in that relationship when, due to their respective ages, both father and son are in potentially difficult phases in their life cycles, there will be some 'purple patches'[41] when each of them will be in a 'good place', resulting in periods of close and harmonious working relationships.

Plotting the age of the father on the horizontal axis of a graph and the age of the son on the vertical the cross correlations of their ages the result should show periods when the life stages are in opposition or alignment as in Figure 3.10 below.

It will be seen that there is a period where the relationships are shown as mixed, when the son is in his late teens to early twenties and the father is in his fifties. This can be explained by the fact that although a young man joining the family business straight from school or university is 'extending his father's control over his life at a time when, according to these life cycle theories, he can least tolerate it,' conversely a father in his fifties is most able to be supportive and to act as a mentor for his troubled son. But the mixed element of this relationship cross over provides further justification for the frequently made suggestion that the next generation should delay their entry into the family firm until they have gained sufficient experience in the wider world and that their 'identity formation' is complete.

The authors surveyed a large (200 plus) sample of father and son relationships in American family businesses by asking each to rate the quality of their relationships across four dimensions, ease of work interaction, enjoyment of their work relationship, accomplishment and learning and found their hypotheses to be broadly supported. On the assumption that this research holds good for father and son relationships generally it has significant implications for understanding and working on family business dynamics. The 'purple patches' provide windows of opportunity when the harmonious working relationships can be maximised, both for development of the family business, but also to lay down foundations for future succession plans and for working on governance structures designed to support both those plans and also to help the family firm weather the almost inevitable storms that will be encountered in the next relationship 'black spot'. Equally charting potential relationship 'black spots' could provide each generation not only with an understanding of their own position but also that of the other party and thereby foster greater understanding and tolerance. Each becomes better equipped to steer a careful and sympathetic course through potentially troubled waters.

Significantly the research confirms that otherwise 'fathers and sons both seem to attribute the downturn in the quality of the relationship to the other person'. The possibility of improved communication and understanding can be supplemented by family business training and succession planning to provide structural solutions to the relationship risk of the black spots. For example, there might be a need to provide the greatest independence and to minimise the potential for conflict during the period when a father might be in his sixties and the son in his late thirties or forties. Suggestions include providing the son with a clearly defined and separate area of responsibility within the business, or as the father approaches retirement age, him assuming the role of non-executive chairman with the son having day-to-day operational responsibility as managing director.

---

[41] These are our terms not the author's.

Tools, Models and Theories   99

Figure 3.10: Black spots and purple patches – intersection of individual life cycles

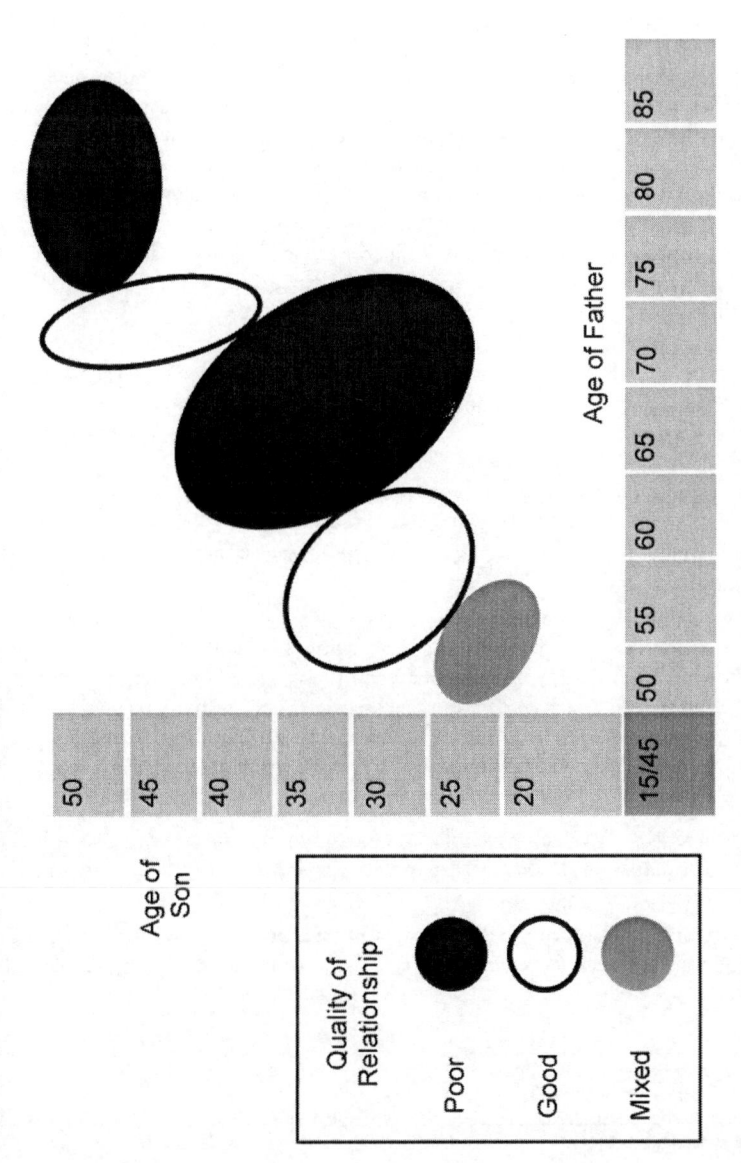

Source: adapted from Figure 9: The Influence of Life Stage on Father-Son Work Relationships in Family Companies (John A Davis and Renato Tagiuri)

3.5.5 Personality

Further layers of complexity are added to the psychological picture of the family firm when one begins to add in the separate personalities of the individuals involved. The jury seems to be out as to the extent to which personality traits are, on the one hand, genetically inherited or, on the other hand, determined by the environment, upbringing and life circumstances of the individual concerned. Nigel Nicholson and Grant Gordon take the view that 'more than 50 per cent of our character comes from our genes'.[42] Psychologist Oliver James on the other hand is firmly of the view that 'what makes us different from each other is that only very occasionally is it a case of 'entirely or largely genes'; mostly it is largely 'environment'.[43]

If James is correct then it might be thought (particularly by non-geneticists) that siblings who grew up together and work in the family business ought to have pretty much identikit personalities. In essence James' answer is that whilst siblings may have grown up in the same house, in the sense of a physical building, they will almost inevitably have grown up in different households. Their parents' circumstances may be radically different in terms of their, age, the state of their marriage, financial position and, not least in the context of our discussions, the demands and situation of the family business. These factors and especially issues such as gender and birth order (discussed below) will all mean that whilst most parents will claim that 'we treat our children the same' the reality will be that this is never the case. The difference in household environments will, in the view of James and others of his school of thought, have the potential to create radically different personalities.

Others[44] argue that personality is made up of two components. Temperament, which is largely genetic and unchangeable and character, which is based on experience and can, to an extent, be changed.

For our purposes we do not need to take sides in the nature versus nurture debate or even to consider this further. It is sufficient to note that, whichever school of thought is correct, or even if the answer is a bit of both, the possible personality mixes are pretty much infinite.

To make sense of this psychologists have attempted to isolate key personality traits, labelled the 'big five'. The idea being that each the traits can be seen as separate scales and each of us will fit somewhere along each scale. The 'big five personality traits' are:

- **Introversion/extroversion.** In addition to how 'outgoing' we appear to be this also includes factors such as whether we gain stimulation from social interaction or prefer solitary activities.
- **Agreeableness.** By which psychologists mean whether we are nurturing, inclined to want consensus and socially orientated as opposed to tough, judgmental and self-centred.
- **Conscientiousness.** How performance and task orientated we are rather than easy going and laid back for example in relation to deadlines, meeting times and to do lists.

---

[42] *Family Wars* at p 32.
[43] *They F*** You Up* at p 12.
[44] See Lucia Ceja Barba 'Balancing Personality Traits: Capitalizing on the strengths of our "true self"' *FFI Practitioner* (23 April 2014).

- **Openness.** In the sense of willingness to experiment and to accept new ideas, concepts and ways of working as opposed to preferring traditions, rigid structures and rules.
- **Emotional.** The extent to which we wear our heart on our sleeve and are seen to be anxious, pessimistic or prone to mood swings rather than stoical and solid.

Similar terms and concepts will be familiar to anyone with experience of the various psychometric testing and personality profiling frameworks such as Myers Briggs.

It will be seen that this level of complexity provides an incalculable number of permutations for the various personality profiles to either conflict with each other or co-exist in a state of harmony. But, notwithstanding the presence of potentially combustible material on many occasions family members manage to rub along together without uncontrollable sparks flying. In other circumstances seemingly harmonious families disintegrate into bitter conflict.

3.6 COMMUNICATION THEORY

Much of this book concerns, at root, breakdowns and failures in communication between family members. We repeatedly argue that the key success factor for family business governance systems is good communication. Indeed that must be seen as a common feature of happy families. The converse must also be true.

In this section we will briefly look at some key concepts in communication.

3.6.1 Transactional analysis

The basic idea of transactional analysis is that in any two-way communication each party can adopt one of three roles, parent, child or adult. Accordingly there are various possible permutations for any piece of communication, or transaction. There is a direct link between transactional analysis and the roles adopted by family business members.

A conversation between a parent asking a child or teenager to tidy their room is likely to be conducted on the basis of an adult (scolding, demanding or, especially in the case of younger children, helping) transacting with a child (guilty, helpless, submissive, defensive or defiant).

Equally one would expect a communication on a business issue between the same people, now as adult family members engaged in a family business to be conducted as an adult-to-adult transaction. Take an example of a discussion about following up sales leads. The expectation would be that the parent business leader would seek and evaluate information, which would be properly delivered by the son, with a balanced and professional discussion about any follow up action required.

Both of the above interactions would be seen as 'complementary' transactions, in other words appropriate to the situation and roles the family members now occupy. But when the transaction between the father and son is analysed the language, (including the use of words such as 'should', 'always', 'typical' 'never', 'not fair', or 'you are always on at me' possibly combined with corresponding body language) this may suggest that in fact the transaction seemed more typical of that between a parent and child (albeit one in a suit and driving a BMW). In which case the analysis would be that a 'crossed transaction' had occurred, one that is inappropriate for the relationship of a managing director and their sales director.

Perversely and most confusingly, the adult role is not always assumed by the eldest participant in a crossed transaction. Many advisors (and perhaps especially bank managers) can identify clients in senior leadership positions in their family business who, on closer analysis frequently transact from the position of child. For example by treating requests for timely delivery of financial information in a manner similar to a teenager being asked to tidy their room. Crossed transactions may occur in any interaction and are not confined to the family owned business. However the potential for family members to revert to inappropriate transactional positions, or 'ego-states', and with it the likelihood for the next generation to be infantilised, must be greater in a family owned business.

Davis and Tagiuri argue that the assumption of transactional roles by in family members is not fixed or static. Rather that:[45]

> 'Because of the overlap in the social system, relatives can retreat into whatever roles will give them the greatest power in conflict situations. An owner-father-president can retreat into his role as father, and treat his son-subordinate like a child, for example, to maintain his position or power'.

This can make family business disputes harder to understand and to resolve:[46]

> 'The movement in and out of roles can obscure the reasons underlying disagreements and prolong and inhibit the resolution of conflicts. Nonrelatives doing business together are less able to retreat into non-business roles and more likely to handle business decisions objectively.'

3.6.2 Double bind communication

The argument that a considerable part[47] of communication is non-verbal is well known. A double-bind communication occurs where the overt spoken message, what Paul Watzlawick[48] terms the 'content component' conflicts with the unspoken message conveyed by body language, reaction, context or otherwise: the 'relationship component'.

The example given in *Family Business on the Couch* is of a father who consistently berates his son for his poor performance as a sales director in following up sales leads. However the father clearly seems to take pleasure in stepping in, doing the job and saving the day. What does the son do? Try to improve his performance and thereby undermine his father's hidden message and his underlying need for relevance? Or not bother to improve, routinely collect dressings down but covertly feed his father's ego?

---

[45] Op cit at p 202.
[46] Op cit at p 202.
[47] Estimated at 89% see B Pease, A Pease *The Definitive Book of Body Language* (Bantam Books, New York, 2004).
[48] Watzlawick *How Real is Real? Confusion, Disinformation, Communication*, (Random House 1976), discussed in *Family Business on the Couch*.

3.6.3 Triangulation

Triangulation is the process whereby a third party is drawn into a conflicted relationship between two other people.

Put simply it is when someone who is struggling in their relationship with someone else starts 'talking about rather than talking to'. One party, often the one who perceives themselves as the weaker party in the primary relationship, seeks to build an alliance with a third person; alliance triangles. An example would include be a feuding sibling who seeks to air their grievances and enlist the support and sympathy of a parent in their struggles with their sibling. But triangulation can occur across the generations, perhaps a son seeking support from his mother against a domineering father, or, alternatively a parent with a poor relationship with their spouse seeking to enlist a child as their ally or confidant. Attempts may also be made to draw non-family employees or advisors into the triangulation process.

Of course some degree of triangulation is a normal part of human interaction. Everyone moans about somebody else sometime. Neither is the process confined to the family business. However given the closed and complex nature of family business systems the consequences of triangulation in this setting are potentially more acute.

3.6.4 Scapegoating

A more complex form of triangulation is where two parties with a conflicted relationship join together to blame a third party for the problems in the family business rather than acknowledge the difficulties in their own relationship; 'scapegoating triangles'. Perhaps a husband and wife who have grown apart find it easier to blame the ineptitude of their son as the cause of the husband needing to spend so much time in the family business rather than to acknowledge that is where the husband would prefer to spend his time.

Scapegoating can go wider and deeper than scapegoating triangles. It is a game that the whole family and indeed an entire family business can play. Often sub consciously parents can decide that one of their children is the 'problem child,' perhaps because of early academic struggles or due to a withdrawn or volatile temperament. Although the problem may be rooted in reality it is allowed to grow out of all proportion. The unfortunate recipient of this perception then becomes seen as the cause of all the ills of the family business. They were only given a job in the first place because they could not cut it in the 'outside world'. Just look at the difficulties they have caused in the business and the opportunities that have been lost. The parents will never be able to retire.

It has been suggested that in some circumstances the family business itself can be the scapegoat chosen by the business family. Perhaps this can be seen as the most benign form of the phenomenon.

At its most invidious this scapegoating becomes part of both the mythology of the business family and, most sadly, the personal script of the scapegoat themselves.

3.7 FAMILY FIRM TYPOLOGY

Another leading commentator, W Gibb Dyer Jr, offers an alternative model to categorise family firms which can be applied to differentiate family businesses in terms of their degree of professionalisation and also their commitment to family cohesion. He argues that these factors will in turn influence family business performance. This will necessarily vary from family to family. In some cases the defining characteristics of the family business concerned, for example nepotism, will create a tendency towards family harmony but tend to produce poor financial performance.

Dyer[49] divided family firms into four broad categories as follows:

- **The clan family firm.** These family businesses have the best of both worlds. The business is run on a successful and profitable basis. This is with the support of the wider business owning family, the clan, whose wider family goals are taken fully into account. As a result the clan family firm is able to leverage all the advantages of family ownership but without needing to over invest in governance systems to police the activities of the family managers. In economic jargon it also enjoys low agency costs.

- **The professional family firm.** Professional family firms are run on business first lines and performance is correspondingly good. But these firms lack the family cohesion of Clan Family Firms so need to incur high agency costs and invest heavily in governance to prevent the family insiders riding roughshod over the interests of more remote family members, whose interests they will not instinctively take into account. As a result they might be more bureaucratic and not as light on their feet as clan family firms.

- **The mom and pop family firm.** These firms, by contrast, operate on a family first basis. Whilst family cohesion might be high this is often at the expense of professionalism, for example over hiring polices, which will typically be operate on a jobs for all basis. So the business may suffer to the extent that the family effect can be categorised as a liability.
  Here Dyer's terminology can be a little confusing. He suggests that 'this type of family firm is likely to be represented by small 'mom and pop' enterprises such as family owned restaurants or family farms'. However we would suggest that in many cases considerably larger family businesses have strong mom and pop family firm or, perhaps more accurately family first characteristics. Whilst the larger family first firm might employ a number of managers, promotion to the top management team is skewed in favour of family members.

- **The self-interested family firm.** As the title suggests the self-interested family firm offers provides the worst of all combinations, at least for the more remote family have-nots or outsiders. The main motivation of the insiders will be to enrich themselves, or their immediate family. The interests of the have-nots or outsiders will fall by the wayside. These businesses will be most unlikely to have formal governance processes. The introduction of such processes will be opposed by the family insiders, who will see them as impediments to their wealth extraction.

Dyer depicts these categorisations thus:

---

[49] G W Dyer Jr 'Examining the "family effect" on firm performance' *Family Business Review* (2006) Vol 19(4) at pp 253–273.

Figure 3.11: Family firm typology

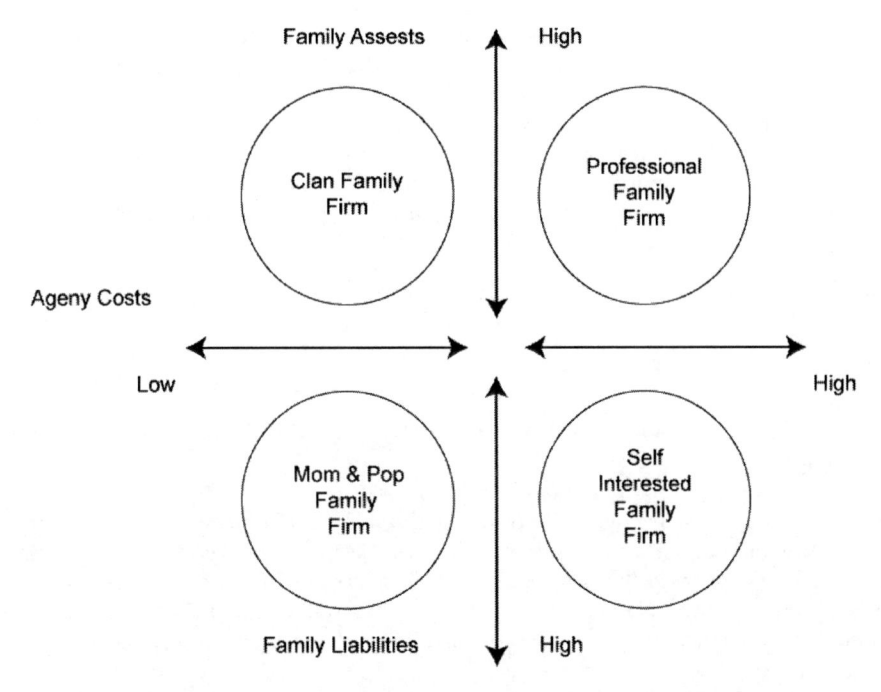

```
                    Family Assests    ▲ High
                                      │
              ┌─────────────┐         │         ┌─────────────┐
              │ Clan Family │         │         │ Professional│
              │    Firm     │         │         │   Family    │
              │             │         │         │    Firm     │
              └─────────────┘         │         └─────────────┘
  Ageny Costs                         ▼
              ◄─────────────────────► ◄─────────────────────►
        Low                           ▲                           High
              ┌─────────────┐         │         ┌─────────────┐
              │  Mom & Pop  │         │         │    Self     │
              │   Family    │         │         │ Interested  │
              │    Firm     │         │         │   Family    │
              └─────────────┘         │         │    Firm     │
                                      │         └─────────────┘
                    Family Liabilities ▼ High
```

Source: based on Figure 3: Examining the 'family effect' on firm performance (G W Dyer Jnr, 2006)

These typologies are not fixed absolutes and can vary over time. There will be borderline cases. Well run clan family firms might, on occasions prefer a marginally less qualified family member for a job over a non-family candidate. But if this occurs too often the family business concerned is in danger of drifting towards and, eventually even over, the demarcation into the mom and pop family firm. A family business may have become a mom and pop family firm or even a self-interested family firm. More optimistically there is the potential for such a firm to redeem itself by returning to either a more business focused or wider family focused way of operating. The introduction of formal family business governance systems may be a key factor to assist in this transformation.

3.8 SAUL D HARRISON – REVISITED

3.8.1 ... as a sibling partnership

The *Saul D Harrison* case can be used to illustrate many of the points discussed in this chapter.

The business was founded in 1891. For the first two generations it was a classic '... and Sons' family business with ownership of, what was then an unincorporated partnership, being passed down from the founder, Saul Harrison, to his four sons. We are not told whether any daughters were ignored in terms of business ownership, or whether Saul simply had no daughters.

Following incorporation of the business in 1947 one of the sons died, without leaving any children. He left his shares in the company equally to his surviving brothers. At this stage the evidence points to the business operating as a tight and functioning sibling partnership. In particular, as a result of the 1960 re-organisation, the three surviving brothers took the voting A Ordinary Shares. This left ultimate management control of the business firmly in their hands.

The case report does not contain much information of non-shareholding members of the wider Harrison family. Neither are we given some fairly important information about the ages or dates of birth or death of the first two generations of the *Saul D Harrison* business leaders, or the circumstances of the transfer to the next generation. A detailed life cycle analysis cannot therefore be undertaken. But on the basis that the business was almost 50 years old by the time that it was incorporated and two of the surviving brothers went on to serve a further 40 years, it does appear that the practice had been for the incumbent generation to remain in post to a fairly advanced age. On Eriskson's analysis questions might be asked about stagnation of the incumbent generation and the corresponding denial of generativity to the next generation.

An abbreviated genogram, based on the information in the case report of the early stage Saul D Harrison business would look like this:

Tools, Models and Theories 107

Figure 3.12: Saul D Harrison genogram as a sibling partnership

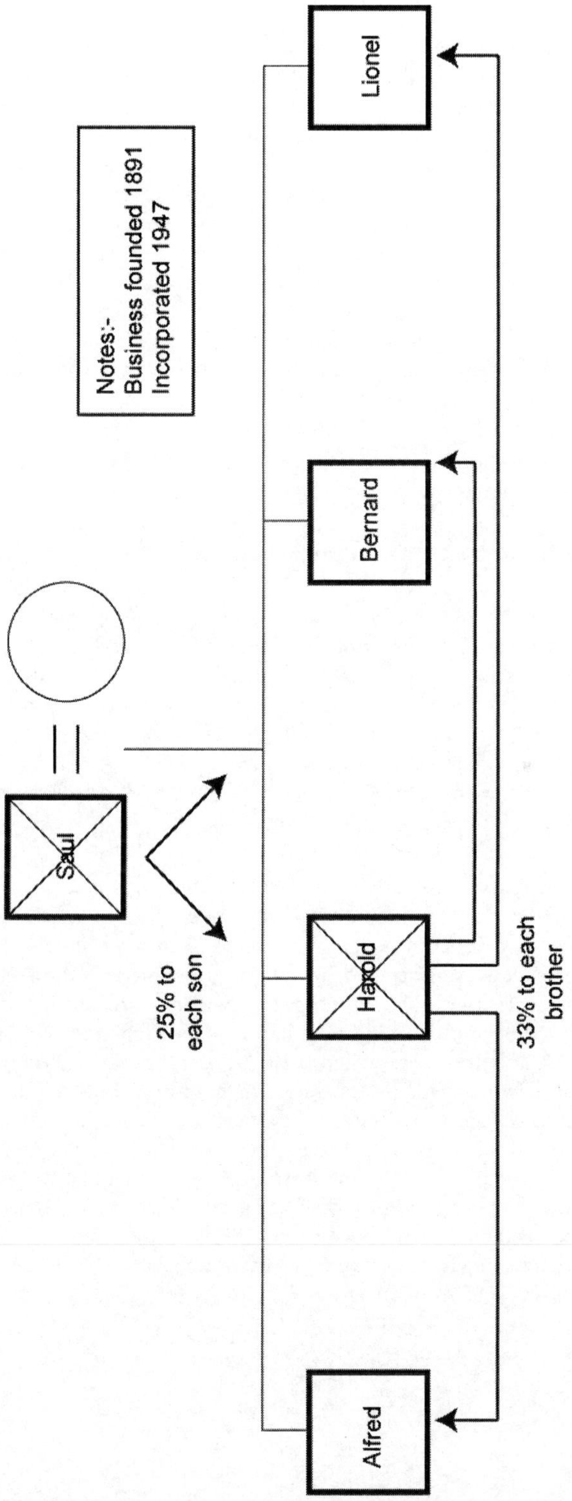

3.8.2 ... as a cousin consortium

But, following the 1960 re-organisation the position had become much more complex. Whereas an early stage owner-managed business or sibling partnership has psychological and relationship issues to contend with in addition to business challenges, the cousin collaboration has all this and more. By the time the *Saul D Harrison* case came to court the business had evolved into a full-blown cousin consortium. We struggle to use Ward's term cousin collaboration in the context of members of a family engaged in litigation. Leadership of the business had recently transitioned from the second to the third generation of the Harrison family, although this more or less coincided with the introduction also of members of the fourth generation into the management team. The transitional period appears to have caused difficulties with the senior generation appearing slow to make way for the next generation and their new business ideas, leading to a stagnation of the business. This may well have been the root cause of the dispute leading to the court case. Almost certainly it was a contributory factor.

As can be seen in Figure 3.13 the genogram of the Harrison family at this stage had now become considerably more complicated.

Some additional commentary might assist to explain the genogram.

Clearly the business and the family suffered considerable trauma in the mid 1980's with the deaths not only of two second generation brothers, Bernard and Lionel (the third surviving brother Alfred having died in 1977) but also the loss of Alfred's third generation son, Seymour in 1987. Leadership of the business was then split between the third and fourth generations with directorships being held by Lionel's son Alan, his own son Stephen, Seymour's son David and also Seymour's widow Marian. As explained above the A Shares in the company carried the voting rights and therefore control. We have used the genogram to plot the movement of these shares.

Marian's position is particularly intriguing. From the remainder of the genogram it will be seen that Saul D Harrison had remained a male dominated '... and Sons' family firm so far as management was concerned. Neither, until then had in-laws assumed prominent management roles. Marian had not been appointed a director of the company, and is no evidence that she played any day-to-day role in the company. However, Marian inherited Seymour's voting A Shares in the company. This contrasts with the deaths of other family members, when their A Shares were transferred to male bloodline family members working in the business, including on one occasion across branch lines and ignoring female blood-line family members. Thus when the second generation brother, Bernard died leaving a daughter but no son, his shares were transferred to his nephews, who were working in the business, Seymour and Alan who also inherited their own father's holdings of A Shares. Sisters were also similarly excluded. These included Seymour's sister, Bernice, whose daughter Rosemary eventually brought the court proceedings against her aunt, Marian and Alan. Alan's sister, Susan was equally absent from the A Share register.

Tools, Models and Theories 109

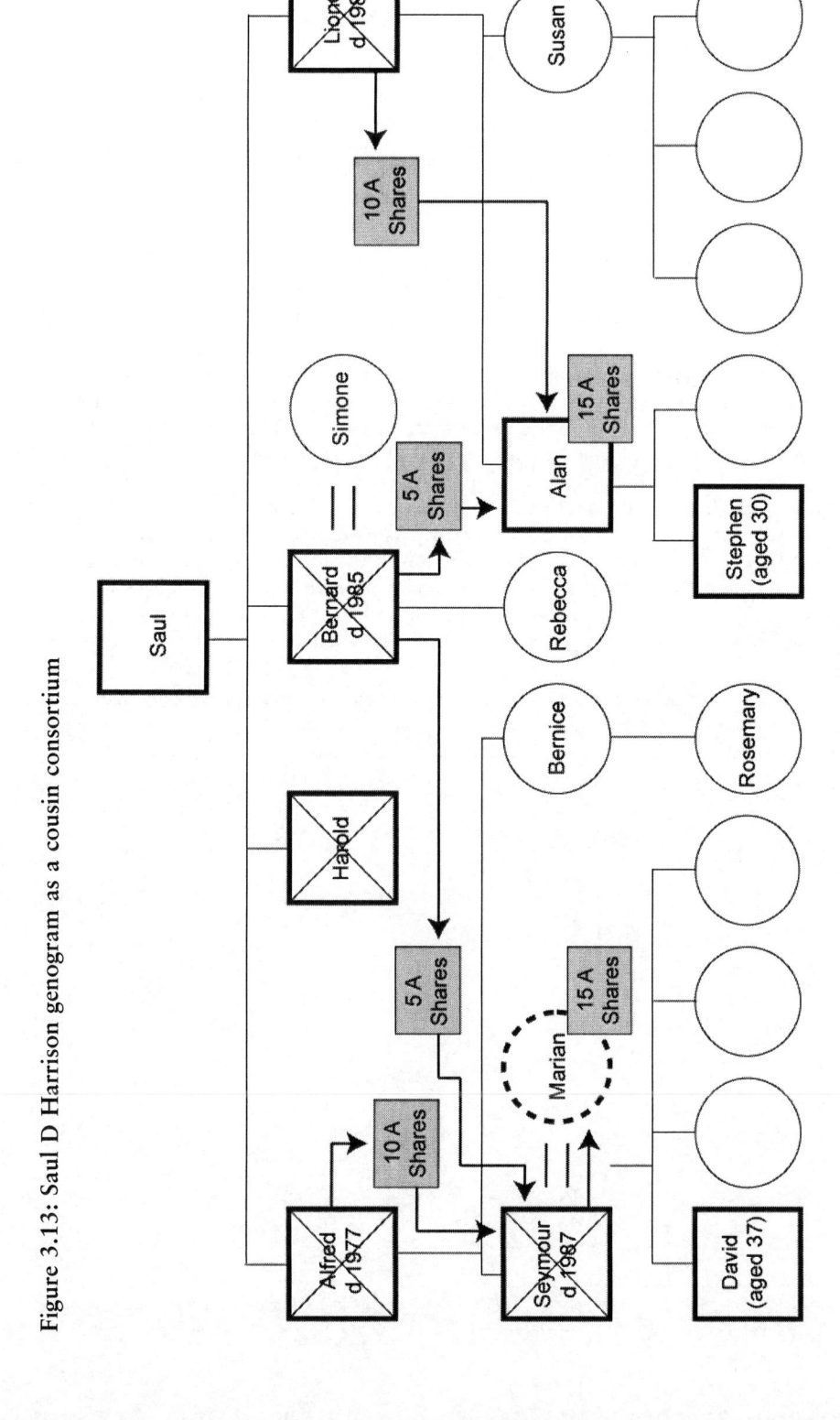

Figure 3.13: Saul D Harrison genogram as a cousin consortium

It will be seen that the practice of passing the controlling A Shares to male bloodline family management that had previously prevailed in the *Saul D Harrison* family business broke down after the death of Seymour and the transfer of his A shares to his widow Marian. Hence Marion's particular status in having some voting control over the family business is shown bold broken border around her name in the genogram.[50] This raises several questions for the family business practitioner that are not answered in the case report. Why was the previous practice abandoned? What role did Marian actually play in the business? How could the relationships between Marian and her sister-in-law Bernice, and that between Bernice and her brother Seymour be categorised? Did the family dispute have its roots in the treatment of Marian? To what extent was this a contributory factor?

As can be seen from a three-circle model (Figure 3.14 below) showing the *Saul D Harrison* family business at the time of the court case, the wider ownership position of the *Saul D Harrison* family company had also become quite complex by this stage.

In addition to the A Shares, there are the B and C Shares. The B Shares, carried preferential income rights. They were beneficially owned by members of the third generation, including in the case of Bernice, Saul's granddaughter and in the cases of Simone and, again Marian the non-bloodline widows of other grandchildren of the founder. A further complication is introduced by the fact that legal title to some of the B Shares are held by the professional executors of Lionel's will. The C Shares, with secondary income rights but preferential rights to capital on winding up are basically widely spread across the great grandchildren in the fourth generation, with no single individual holding a large share. The claimant Beatrice held only about 8% of the C Shares. The exception to this being that over 50% of the C Shares were held by the Royal Bank of Scotland as trustees under a trust for Saul's granddaughter Rebecca.

Viewed through a combination of the genogram and the three-circle model, the potential for conflicts of interest in the business become obvious. Those conflicts are not only between, those like Alan, David and Stephen, who occupy the central 'Zone 1' position of family owners and managers and more remote family shareholders, but also given the share structure of *Saul D Harrison*, between different generations and branches of the Harrison family and between family shareholders and professional trustee or fiduciary shareholders.

---

[50] Our own symbol for non-executive 'family' directors. This is not found in conventional explanations of genograms.

Tools, Models and Theories 111

Figure 3.14: Saul D Harrison – three-circle model circa 1994

[Three-circle Venn diagram with circles labeled Ownership (5.), Family (6.), and Business (7.), with overlapping regions numbered 1., 2., 3., and 4.]

1. *Family owner and manager*
Alan (A Shares)
David, Stephen (C Shares)
and Marian (A and B Shares)

2. *Family shareholders, not employed in the business*
Bernice, Simone (B Shares)
Rosemary (approximately 8%, David's three sisters, Stephen's sister and Susan's three children (C Shares)

5. *External shareholders*
Royal Bank of Scotland as trustees of a trust for Rebecca (over 50% of C Shares)
Lionel's executors (B Shares)

6. *Family members with no direct involvement in the business*
Rebecca

7. *Non-family employees*
Over 100, some presumably in management roles

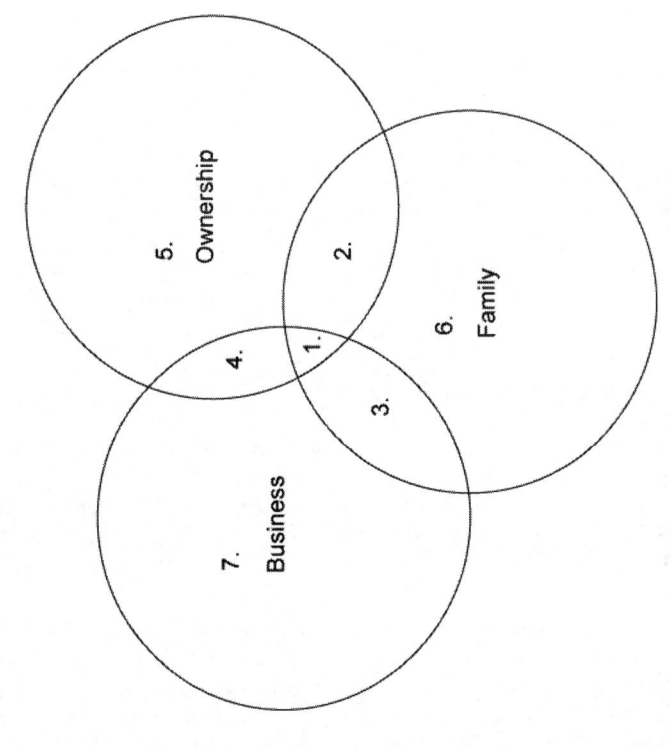

3.8.3 Family business typology

How should we analyse the *Saul D Harrison* business in terms of Dyer's family business typology?

Certainly by the time the matter came to court the Harrison family could not be seen as a wholly cohesive clan. Perhaps the claimant, Beatrice was an outlier, an outsider within an otherwise basically cohesive family? The courts rejected any suggestion that the A Shareholders and directors, the family insiders, had taken excessive remuneration from the business, thus logically removing it from classification as a self-interested family firm.

A possible analysis could be that, whilst initially operating a clan family firm, as a result of some combination of the senior generation remaining in post for too long and other failures to pay attention to the needs of the business, the business, although large, drifted into the quadrant of a mom and pop family firm. Whilst the corresponding lack of professionalism could be tolerated by the family in the short term, eventually the business pressure began to tell on family cohesion, at least so far as Rosemary was concerned.

3.9 CONCLUSION

The genogram and the three-circle model are key items in the tool-box of the family business advisor, as the application of these to the facts obtained from the *Saul D Harrison* case illustrate. By using these tools to supplement the more traditional forms of written notes used by most advisors a more detailed and accessible picture of the separate systems comprising a family business may emerge, prompting further questions and lines of exploration and enquiry that in turn are capable of providing both the advisor and the business family with a greater insight into relevant issues.

When combined with an understanding of key theoretical concepts, such as family business and life cycle theory, family business typology and an appreciation of some of the core family business themes discussed in the previous chapter these tools can help make sense of the complexity of a particular family business issue. Once analysed in this way it becomes correspondingly easier to see relevant issues as having a structural systemic root, arising from recognisable patterns and dynamics rather than fundamental flaws in the character and personality of the members of the business owning family themselves.

3.10 FURTHER READING FOR PART A

- J A Davis and R Tagiuri 'The Influence of Life Stage on Father-Son Work Relationships in Family Companies' (1989) *Family Business Review* Vol 2 No 1. We discuss this article in some detail in the chapter above. It is well worth reading in full.
- De Vries, Carlock and Florent-Treacy *Family Business on the Couch* (Wiley & Sons Ltd, 2007). A key work on family dynamics with comprehensive coverage of entrepreneurial psychology, sibling rivalry etc. Provides a detailed analysis of family business life cycle and systems theory from a psychological perspective. The book also contains explanations of genograms and the three-circle model.
- *European Commission Final Report of The Expert Group on Family Business Relevant Issues* (European Commission, 2009). A fairly short report explaining the significance of family businesses to the European economy and providing an overview of key family business issues and challenges.
- Gordon and Nicholson *Family Wars* (Kogan Page, 2008). A highly readable book with case studies of disputes in many well-known family businesses but also with a useful introductory section on family business dynamics.
- J Hilburt-Davis and W Gibb Dyer Jr *Consulting to Family Businesses* (Jossey-Bass, 2003). A detailed introduction to family business consulting. The book contains a good explanation of the use of genograms and their application to family business life cycles.
- O James *They F*** You Up – How to Survive Family Life* (Bloomsbury, 2002). A lay introduction to psychological development (but fully cross referenced to academic sources) written from a 'nurturist' perspective by a leading British psychologist and writer.
- P Leach *Family Businesses – The Essentials* (Profile Books Ltd, 2007). A general and accessible overview of family business issues written by one of the most senior and respected consultants operating in the family business field.
- I Macdonald, J Sutton *Business Families and Family Businesses* – The STEP Handbook for Advisers (Globe Law and Business, 2009). A handbook aimed at the professional advisor, again providing a detailed overview of key issues and concepts in family business practice with contributions from various practitioners, including a number of 'founding fathers'.
- R Tagiuri and J A Davis 'Bivalent Attributes of the Family Firm' (1996) *Family Business Review* Vol 9(2), pp 199-208. The original article introducing the three-circle Model but containing so much more about the essential ambiguity of family business life. Short and readable, well worth taking the time to read this seminal article in full.

PART B

BUSINESS MATTERS

CHAPTER 4

TAX BASICS AND THE FAMILY BUSINESS STRUCTURE

David Pierce

4.1 INTRODUCTION

Much of this book concerns family dynamics; the inter-relationship between the family, business and ownership systems comprised within the three-circle model, as introduced in chapter 3. But the family business model also has implications for the tax and financial arrangements between the business and the family, as business owners. The purpose of this chapter is to outline some of the basic issues concerned, particularly in relation to structure and internal operating arrangements of a family business. Chapter 16 looks at tax issues and transfers of ownership.

Of approximately 4.6m family businesses in the UK it is estimated that 68% were sole traders, 7% were partnerships and 24% operated as companies.[1] Although there are a number of different trading structures that can be used and which are briefly outlined in the next paragraph, this chapter will concentrate on limited companies and sole trader or partnership structures (including LLPs).

4.2 CHOICE OF FAMILY BUSINESS STRUCTURE

The decision on which is the most appropriate structure can depend on a number of factors, such as commercial reasons (wanting limited liability protection for the family against business claims), and tax treatment (discussed below). On occasions the structure adopted by some family businesses has less to do with detailed planning and more to do with historical accident.

Any family business has a number of different structures which can be used, being:

4.2.1 Sole trader

Under this structure the business owner is personally exposed to the liabilities of the business. As referred to above, this is the most common family business trading structure in the UK. Virtually all the businesses operating as sole traders employed less than 9 people. So that structure dominates the micro business sector, and as will be explained,

---

[1] *The State of the Nation: The UK Family Business Sector 2015–16* (IFB Research Foundation Report with Oxford Economics, 2016).

this is what one would expect from a tax perspective. Sole traders are less likely to be found in later stage family businesses as they do not provide easy vehicles for succession planning.

4.2.2 Partnership

Partnerships consist of two or more individuals. Here there is also the commercial exposure to the business debts. There are no formalities involved in setting up in partnership. The partnership relationship can arise automatically, by operation of law.[2] The question of whether or not a partnership exists, and if so, what are its terms can give rise to considerable uncertainty in the context of family business relationships.

4.2.3 Limited partnerships

Limited partnerships will, in most respects regarding taxation, operate in the same way as a partnership or LLP. So far as liabilities limited partnerships are a hybrid between the two. The liability of some partners is limited but under this structure there must be one or more general partners who have unlimited liability. The general partner can be a limited company. This provides the individuals with protection from the business debts, but they need to ensure it is the limited liability company which manages the partnership. Limited partnerships have much less relevance for family businesses now that LLP's have been introduced. Their use is now confined to historic family business structures and more esoteric family business tax planning arrangements.

4.2.4 Limited liability partnership (LLP)

LLP's also involve two or more individuals, whose personal assets are protected from the business creditors, unless they have guaranteed any of the debts. It is possible to have a limited liability company as a partner in an LLP.

4.2.5 Limited company

Limited companies are different from the other alternatives in a number of regards. First there is a separation between the owners of the business, the shareholders, and those who are responsible for management, the directors.[3] Secondly, the company is considered to be a separate entity for tax purposes, as it is taxed on the profits earned, and the directors and shareholders are taxed on what they receive from the company. Thirdly the shareholders' liability for the debts of the company is limited to the amount they subscribe for their shares, so provided the latter are fully paid up, there is no further liability. The directors are not liable for the debts of the company provided they have properly fulfilled their legal responsibilities in running the business. The exception to this position for both the shareholders, and directors, is if they have given any guarantees in respect of debts or commitments (eg leases on property or assets).

---

[2] Under the Partnership Act 1890, s 1, a partnership automatically arises when people 'carry on a business in common with a view to profit'. Some particular difficulties of family business partnership structures are discussed in chapter 13.

[3] Many of the difficulties encountered by family companies can be traced back to a failure on the part of the director insiders to make this distinction to the detriment of the outsider owners.

The separation of ownership from management in a company situation means that it tends to be the most common structure for family businesses looking to transition to the next generation.

When it comes to succession planning, generally a limited company structure is better because it allows the separation of ownership from management, and therefore gives greater flexibility for passing ownership control in different proportions, between members of the family, and also allowing for family members not involved in management to share in the success of the business.

An exception where limited companies are used less often in multi-generational family firms is with the agriculture sector, where often the business will operate as a sole trader or, more likely, a partnership, with possibly the land held outside the business structure.

4.3 OVERVIEW OF BASIC TAX ISSUES

4.3.1 Tax and choice of structure

At certain profit levels, generally lower profits, there is a lower tax cost for the owner/manager by operating as a sole trader or partnership, including an LLP. Generally, if it is decided to start the business as a sole trader or partnership, or an LLP, it is possible to transfer the business to a limited company with little or no tax cost using the reliefs contained in s 162 TCGA 1992 (gift of business assets); s 165 TCGA 1992 (transfer of a business to a limited company) and s 266 and s 267 CAA 2001 (transfer of plant and equipment at tax written down values between connected parties).[4]

However the reverse is not true. There are not the same reliefs for the disincorporation of a business, although for the period from 1 April 2013 to 31 March 2018 some disincorporation reliefs were introduced by the Finance Act 2013. If a limited company is used, it must generally be viewed as being the structure that will be retained for the remainder of the life of the business.

The tax treatment of the different types of structures can be divided into two groups.

- The tax treatment for the sole trader, or individual who is a partner in a partnership, limited partnership, or LLP is the same, in that he/she pays income tax and Class 2 and 4 national insurance on their share of the business profits. Class 2 national insurance will be abolished from April 2018.
- A company, however, will pay corporation tax on its profits, and the family members who are directors, employees or shareholders will pay tax on payments made to them, and benefits provided, by the company. For the employee/director there will be income tax to pay on these amounts, as well as employee's national insurance on, principally, salary payments. The company will also have to pay employer's national insurance on salary payments, and a large number of benefits provided to the individual, such as car benefits, private medical insurance, etc. The shareholders will generally receive payments from the company in the form of dividends. The individual has a dividend allowance of £5,000.
- Thereafter the tax rates work within bands as set out in the table below.

---

[4] This is explained in more detail in chapter 16 (Tax and Family Business Ownership).

Income tax rates

Income tax and national insurance rates for 2016–2017

	Taxable income	Income tax rate	Dividend rate
Starting savings rate/dividend rate	£0–£5,000	0%	0%
Basic rate	£5,000–£32,000	20%	7.5%
High rate	£32,001–£150,000	40%	32.5%
Additional rate	> £150,000	45%	38.1%

(* the starting rate only applies to savings income. If an individual's taxable non-savings income is above the starting rate limit the 10% rate will not apply.)

National insurance rates

Class 1 – employers and employees

Employers	on earnings in excess of £156 per week – 13.8%
Employees	on earnings between £156 and £827 per week – 12%
	on earnings in excess of £827 per week – 2%
Different rates apply for members of contracted out pension schemes, and for those who qualify for the married women and widows rate	
Class 2	Flat rate per week £2.80
Class 4	Self Employed
Lower limit	£8,060
Upper limit	£43,000
Rate on profits between limits	9%
Rate above upper limit	2%

Corporation tax rates – year ending 31 March 2017

The main rate is 20%. It has been announced that for the year ending 31 March 2018 the tax rate will reduce to 19% and to 17% from 1 April 2020.

4.3.2 Tax and cash flow

As part of their cash flow management, the family business member needs to be aware of the timing of their tax payments.

For the sole trader, or individual, who is a partner, the relevant dates are:
- Class 2 national insurance – generally paid monthly.
- Income tax and Class 4 national insurance – Two equal payments on account (which are generally based on the tax paid for the preceding tax year) are payable

on 31 January in the year of assessment, and 31 July after the year of assessment. Any further income tax or national insurance due is then paid on 31 January after the year of assessment.

A company generally has to pay its corporation tax, 9 months after the accounts date. There is an exception to this if the company in the preceding accounting period paid, and expects in the current accounting period to be making taxable profits at or above £1.5m.

4.3.3 The family company and tax deductions

Income tax and employee's national insurance is deductible by the company from any salary payments made to family members, and paid to HMRC, together with employer's national insurance, twenty two days after the end of the month when the salary was paid (or 19 days if paying by post). There are special rules for calculating the national insurance due by directors. Any under or over payments of income tax on salaries are dealt with under the tax return system.

If the shareholder has any further tax to pay on dividends, then this is due on the 31 January and 31 July payment dates.

4.3.4 Family businesses and close companies

The tax legislation introduces a concept known as 'close companies'. This is highly significant for family companies, as most will fall within the definition. In simple terms a close company is one under the control of five or fewer shareholders, or any number of shareholders who are also directors, ie controlled by director – shareholders.[5] For these purposes any shares held by an associate of a shareholder are attributed to that shareholder. An associate is defined as any business partner, or relative of the shareholder (such as parent, spouse, children both minors and adults, brothers and sisters).[6] Also shares held by trustees of a trust set up by the participator (or one of his/her relatives), or a trust in which the participator has an interest are treated as held by an associate.[7] Shares held by a nominee are also attributed to the shareholder.[8] This can be a complex area, and it is not intended that all the circumstances in which persons may be considered to be associates should be considered in this book.[9]

One or more people are considered to have control of a company if they have, or are entitled to have, more than 50% of the issued share capital, votes or company's assets on a winding up. So one needs to be careful with share options, or loans to the company. In the latter case the possible repayment of the loan is added to the shareholder rights to capital to determine what an individual could receive on a winding up.[10]

The legislation mainly refers to ownership when determining control, however, it also treats a person as having control if they exercise, are able to exercise, or entitled to

---

[5] CTA 2010, s 439.
[6] CTA 2010, ss 451, 448.
[7] CTA 2010, s 448.
[8] CTA 2010, s 451.
[9] Further reading on the definition of an associate can be found in the case of *R v CIR, ex p Newfields Developments Ltd* (2001) STC 901.
[10] CTA 2010, s 450.

acquire, direct or control the company's affairs. HMRC interpret this as management control as well as shareholding control. So the person who exercises control in the boardroom also needs to be considered.

In view of the definition of an associate it may be difficult for many family businesses to avoid being classified as a close company. The tax implications for them are:
- the close company loan rules apply (see below).
- if the company incurs any expense or provides any benefit to a non-working shareholder or associate, this will be treated as a distribution (ie effectively a dividend) and the recipient will be taxed on the amount;[11]
- if the company is a close investment holding company it will pay corporation tax on its profits at the full corporation tax rate and will not be able to use the small company rate;[12]
- if any shareholder makes a loan to the company out of borrowings, and the company is a close investment holding company, they will not be entitled to tax relief on the interest cost.[13] If the close company is a trading company then interest relief will be available.

4.3.5 Close company loan rules

One factor of family business informality is the frequency with which loans are made by the family company to directors and other participants. These are basically treated as dividends. A 32.5% tax charge arises on any loan or advance made to a shareholder of the company, if it is not repaid within 9 months of the end of the accounting period in which it is made.[14]

This tax will then be repaid in whole or part to the company 9 months after the end of the accounting period in which the loan is reduced. In addition the individual will have a benefit in kind charge unless interest is paid on the loan at a rate at least equivalent to the official rate of interest.

4.3.6 Family companies and corporation tax rates

Companies are, in simple terms, associated with each other if one controls the other, or both are under the control of the same person or persons.[15] In considering whether companies are under the control of the same persons HMRC will look to see what is the minimum group of persons who control a company. If that group is the same as the minimum group which controls another company, then those two companies are associated. For these purposes individuals are attributed the rights of their associates in the same way as when considering whether the company is a close company (see below).

There was an exception in that by Extra Statutory Concession HMRC did not attribute to an individual the rights of any relative except those of the spouse and any minor children, provided there was substantial commercial interdependence between the

---

[11] CTA 2010, ss 1064 and 1065.
[12] CTA 2010, s 18.
[13] ITA 2007, s 392.
[14] CTA 2010, s 455.
[15] CTA 2010, ss 25, 450 and 451.

companies.[16] This has now been put on a statutory basis.[17] However, it has also been extended so that now, provided there is commercial independence the rights of a spouse, relative, partner, settlement or company are not attributed to the individual.

Two points to note are that dormant companies (including those only receiving bank interest[18]) are not treated as being associated, but companies not resident in the UK are associated if they fall within the control definition.

The impact of this legislation for family companies can be as follows:

(1) If the family company sets up a subsidiary, then there are two associated companies. A new subsidiary could be set up to operate a new venture, or the trading activities of the existing business could be transferred, with the property interests left in a holding company to protect then from the risks of the commercial activities.. The number of associated companies no longer has any impact on the rate of tax paid but it can impact upon the timing of payments. The £1,500,000 limit for Q1Ps mentioned in 3.2 above is divided by the number of companies in the group eg for three associated companies it falls to £500,000. Therefore if consideration is being given to setting up a new subsidiary for commercial reasons, the potential impact on the timing of tax payments needs to be considered.

(2) A parent may, perhaps because of sibling rivalry, set two children up with their own companies. In these circumstances careful thought will need to be given to how the shares are held, as trading between the companies or support from one to the other, or any loans between the companies or from family members; may make them associated companies. One should also consider any relationships with any company controlled by the parents.

(3) Depending on expected profit levels and the overall tax payable, if another business is set up by a family member it may be more tax efficient to use a non-corporate entity, such as an LLP.

4.4 LIMITED COMPANY OR SOLE TRADER / PARTNERSHIP?

With the small profits tax rate of 20% and income tax being payable at 40% on taxable income of over £43,000 (being the basic rate tax band of £32,000 plus the personal allowance for £11,000) it might, on first reflection, seem that in the majority of cases the family business should operate through a limited company. However that is too simplistic an assessment because one also needs to consider the tax effect of the income which the family member takes from the business, and also the national insurance costs. Rewards can be taken from the company as either salary or dividends, but each has tax implications for the recipient. Also the way in which the rewards are taken affects the tax position of the company. Salaries and the national insurance cost reduce the company tax liabilities, but the company cannot claim a tax deduction for dividend payments. At lower profit levels (up to about £50,000 to £60,000 per individual) if the individuals needs all that income to live on, it is more tax efficient to operate as a sole trader or partnership. This is the probable reason why so many of the micro family businesses operate as sole traders. The overall tax cost tends to be about the same on profits above these lower levels if all profits are withdrawn from the company.

---

[16] Extra Statutory Concession C9.
[17] CTA 2010, s 27.
[18] *Jowell v O'Neill and Brennan Construction Limited* (1998) STC 482.

Other factors which can determine the most tax efficient structure to use are:

- Debt which needs to be repaid out of profits. In a corporate structure if say corporation tax is payable at 20%, there is 80% left to repay the capital element of the debt. However if income tax is payable at 40% on sole trader or partnership profits, only 60% is left. So where there is significant debt in the business a corporate structure can ease the cash flow.
- Shares can be held by a spouse or other family members, and so dividends can be paid to utilise the £5,000 tax free band which might otherwise not be used.

Ultimately, to determine the most tax efficient structure it is often the case of doing the calculations for the specific circumstances of the family, because it will depend on a number of factors.

When the business is initially set up, if there are likely to be losses in the first year, because it, say, seeks to establish itself and so there are a lot of initial costs, or capital allowances are claimed on plant and equipment needed for the business, a sole trader or partnership can a useful structure because of the ability to offset these tax losses in the first 4 years against income from other sources in the 3 prior years.[19] If after this initial period it then becomes more tax efficient to operate through a company the business can be transferred to a company, generally with no tax cost because of the tax reliefs available.[20]

Partnerships will operate and have the same tax issues as an LLP but will not provide the partners with limited liability protection.

4.5 FAMILY LLPS

4.5.1 Comparison of LLPs and companies

The family business has a choice of a number of legal different structures through which to carry on the family enterprise. The choice can depend on the nature of the activity, tradition, taxation or the aims of the family members involved in the business. However if the family want personal protection from the risks of the activity being carried on, then one is normally just considering two alternatives, either a limited liability partnership (LLP) or a limited company (company). Both are equally as effective in terms of limiting the liability of the family, but in either case third parties dealing with the enterprise may want personal guarantees, or the security of assets owned personally by family members. These are typically required by landlords, bankers and in some cases by financial institutions providing lease or hire purchase finance.

The way in which LLPs and companies are governed and managed are different and when it is a family business this difference can have an impact on the family's relationship to the business. In the case of an LLP the owners will be partners in the entity and will collectively manage it. A members' agreement will set out the decision making process, but if the family members are the only members and partners then it

---

[19] ITA 2007, s 72.
[20] See TCGA 1992, ss 162 and 165 and CAA 2001, ss 266 and 267.

tends to operate on a less formal basis. This can mean that unless there are clearly defined roles and responsibilities for each family member, there can be confusion and the potential for conflict.

In the company structure it is the directors who are responsible for the day-to-day management of the business. They are technically appointed by the shareholders to run the company for their benefit. The board of directors can include some, or none, who are also shareholders. That is not to say that smaller 'quasi partnership' family companies are not without difficulty so far as roles and responsibilities are concerned.

Perhaps the area where it is easiest to understand the distinction between LLPs and companies, and why one structure would be chosen over the other, is taxation. The members of the LLP are assessable to income tax on their share of the profits. For that reason one would expect them to be actively involved in the management of the business. In the case of a company:

- the directors are subject to income tax on the salaries and bonuses they take from the company;
- the company pays corporation tax on its profits after deducting the salaries paid to the directors; and
- the shareholders pay income tax on any dividends paid to them out of the post tax profits, but if no dividends are paid then the shareholders have no tax liability in respect of their interest in the company.

Therefore one would only expect to see an LLP being used in a family business context where those who are the members/owners are also actively involved in the management.

This means that an LLP structure is not conducive to succession planning where the retiring generation wants to split their business interests between all their children, where some will not be actively involved in the business. Also there are not the two aspects of management succession and ownership succession to consider. This can mean that in a LLP situation the older generation remains actively involved longer, because they need the ability to draw income from the business, and to achieve that they need to continue as a partner.

With a company it is possible to create a legacy, if that is the aim of the current generation, because of the separation of management and ownership. Shares can be passed down through succeeding generations, so that ownership remains within the family, and is always there to support the family. This can though create issues in terms of governance which do not exist for LLPs, because shares become spread amongst a wider group, particularly at the cousin consortium stage and beyond, who may, or may not, feel any connection with the business, and who may have divergent views on the family business.

There may be tax reasons why a business which initially started as an LLP converts into a company, being primarily to reduce the overall tax burden. The partners in the LLP will pay income tax at up to the highest rate on the LLP profits, but profits in a company may only be taxed at 20% (17% from April 2020).

It is relatively easy to convert from an LLP into a company with tax reliefs available to avoid tax arising solely because of the conversion. However there are no similar reliefs available to convert from a company to a LLP. So the conversion should be considered to be a non-reversible step.

A company structure also creates the opportunity to bring in non-family expertise at a senior level, either as executive or non-executive directors, without giving them a significant ownership share in the company. In addition, where perhaps there is not the ability in the family to take on the managing director role, or the family relationship with the business has become more of an investment one, a third party individual can be recruited to run the business.

4.5.3 Tax implications of changes in ownership of LLPs

Turning to the tax implications on the change in ownership of an interest in a partnership. Whether the partnership is carried on through an LLP, or a partnership, is irrelevant for these purposes.

When one member of the family retires from the partnership and is replaced by another family member there are income tax implications for both:

- **Retiring member.** In the tax year of retirement the individual will be assessable on their share of the partnership profits from the end of the period which was the basis of assessment in the preceding tax year, to the date of cessation. So if for example the normal accounting date of the business was 30 June and the individual retired on 30 September 2016, for the 2016–2017 tax year the assessable profits would be those from 1 July 2015 to 30 September 2016. If the individual has any 'overlap profits' (see below regarding the taxation of the joining member) then these are deducted from the assessable profits.

- **Joining member.** There are special rules which determine the amount of assessable profits in the first three tax years. In the first year the assessable profits are those from the date of joining the partnership to the following 5 April. In the second year, if there are accounts made up to a date in that year, which are for a 12 month period from when the person became a partner, then the share of the profits from those accounts are used, otherwise the profits for the first 12 months from the individual becoming a partner are used. In the third year the assessable profits are those shown by accounts for a 12 month period ending in that tax year. This method of calculating the assessable profits means that some profits are brought into tax twice. For example, if a partnership prepares accounts to 30 June and a family member becomes a partner on 1 July 2016, for the 2016–2017 tax year that person will be assessable on profits from 1 July 2016 to 5 April 2017. Then in 2017–2018 they will be assessable on profits for the year ended 30 June 2014, which will again include the period from 1 July 2016 to 5 April 2017. The profits which are taxed twice are known as 'overlap profits'. Relief is given for these overlap profits either, on a change in accounting date, or when the individual ceases to be a partner.

These rules can have a significant impact on the tax payments, and cash flow, for the retiring and new partner. In the case of the retiring partner they may be assessable on more than a year's profits in the tax year of retirement. Although this will be partly offset by the use of their overlap profit. In the case of the new partner, there will be a period of time from when they become a partner, until they have to pay tax on their profit share.

The calculation of assessable profits for incoming partners is easier, and the cash flow impact can more easily be predicted, if partnership changes happen on the first day of a new accounting period for the partnership.

The other main aspect of tax which needs to be considered on partnership changes is capital gains tax. When a partner retires they dispose of their interest in any capital assets owned by the partnership, typically any property and goodwill. Equally when a partner joins, or there is a change in profit sharing ratios, there is a disposal by some partners of their interest in these assets and an acquisition by others. Partnership changes do not fit easily into capital gains tax. For that reason HMRC have a Statement of Practice (D12 together with amendments as set out in Revenue and Customs Brief 03/08) which gives guidance in dealing with transactions between partners. D12 allows partners to reallocate their base costs of assets subject to capital gains tax, rather than treat it as a disposal, except where actual consideration is paid; or the assets are revalued in the partnership accounts; or one of the partners contributes an asset to the partnership. Also HMRC will accept that transactions between partners are not between connected persons provided they are part of bona fide commercial arrangements. However D12 may not apply where the parties are connected, other than being partners. So if they are members of the same family, it is likely they will be connected, and HMRC say in those circumstances the transaction will be considered to have to be at market value, which may mean any gain being calculated by reference to a different consideration figure than the amount paid. But the Statement of Practice goes on to say that if nothing would have been paid, or if any amount was paid it would have been the same, in the event the persons were not connected by reason of being members of the same family, then they will not seek to say the actual consideration should be replaced by the market value for capital gains tax purposes. This means that provided family members, coming into partnership or leaving, pay the same (or nothing if appropriate) as other partners who are not family members, when they are involved in partnership changes, then HMRC will accept those amounts for tax purposes. The difficulty comes with this when all the partners are family members because there is nothing to compare against to assess whether the amount is what would have happened if it was a third party. However if the transaction is considered to have taken place at less than market value then provided the asset concerned is a business asset, or an interest in a business asset, an election can be made under TCGA 1992, s 165 to avoid any tax liability arising on the retiring partner in respect of the difference between the market value and the consideration paid. Therefore by reason of one of the above provisions it is possible that there will not be any capital gains tax cost when family members join or leave partnerships, or profit sharing arrangements are changed.

If the LLP owns land or property a change in membership is likely to create an SDLT liability. However, certain reliefs may be available to reduce or extinguish any SDLT charge but those reliefs must be worked through. The relevant rules are complex and beyond the scope of this book.

4.6 TAX EFFICIENT EXTRACTION OF PROFITS FROM A COMPANY

Operational tax planning for family companies often involves a choice between taking income as an employee or as an owner. Analytically it can be seen as arbitrage between, on the one hand the business and on the other hand ownership or family systems of the three-circle model. Whilst this will often be accepted by HMRC as legitimate, the choices made for tax reasons can have repercussions elsewhere in the family business system. For example if family employees were remunerated by dividends and the employment relationship subsequently broke down this could cause complications in any employment or shareholder dispute. Often the trade-off for tax efficiency will be added complexity in the family and ownership systems.

Those family members who are both employees and shareholders will have two options to extract profits from the company, either by salary and benefits, or by dividends. One might think that as dividends do not carry a national insurance cost, they are a more tax efficient method of extraction. However as salaries and national insurance are tax deductible, the net tax cost of this method of extraction can in some cases be a cheaper route. Which is the most tax efficient method depends on the corporation rate paid by the company, and the tax rate payable by the employee. For example if the company only pays tax at the current small profits rate (20%) and the employee is a higher rate tax payer (40%) then paying rewards by dividends is more tax efficient.

If spouses have different income levels, for example, say the spouse who works full time in the business pays tax at the higher rate, but the other spouse has no income, then there will be tax savings by paying dividends to that spouse. This could be achieved in a number of ways, but there are tax pitfalls with some of the options. HMRC have taken some cases to the courts where they have considered share arrangements have been made to provide dividend income to the wife. They have attempted to use the settlement legislation[21] to challenge the arrangements.[22] The conclusion which can be drawn from these cases is that provided the shares held by the spouse have the normal features one expects to find with ordinary shares, such as voting rights and capital rights on a winding up, then any dividends paid will be treated as their income, and not allocated to the other spouse under the Settlements legislation. So one spouse can give shares to the other spouse, or the lower income spouse can subscribe for new shares, to enable dividends to be paid.

Under company law when a dividend is declared, the same rate is paid on all the shares in that class. When shares are held by spouses, or the family has decided to reward family employee shareholders by dividends, it is probably going to be the case that the plan would be for each shareholder to receive different dividend rates. This can be dealt with in two ways:
- **Dividend waivers.** So some shareholders would waive their right to particular dividends. The waiver has to be made before the right has accrued, and has to be by deed. To ensure the waiver is not treated as a transfer of value for Inheritance Tax purposes the waiver must be made within the 12 months before it becomes payable.[23] HMRC may challenge some dividend waivers under the settlements

---

[21] ITTOIA 2005, ss 620–628.
[22] *Young v Pearce* (1996) STC 743 and *Jones v Garnett* [2007] UKHL 35, [2007] 1 WLR 2030.
[23] IHTA 1984, s 15.

legislation.[24] However provided the dividend rate being paid on those shares where the waiver has not been made, is not such that if the same rate was paid on all the shares, there would not be adequate reserves, then it should be possible to resist any challenge. HMRC would certainly challenge a circumstance where a dividend could not be paid out of reserves unless the dividend waiver was made.

- **Alphabet shares.** This involves designating the shares held by, say, each shareholder as a separate class. For example the shares held by one spouse would be classified as 'Class A' and those held by the other spouse as 'Class B'. One dividend rate would then be paid on the Class A shares, and a different rate on the Class B shares. This would be a simpler solution to the use of dividend waivers. Alphabet shares are an area where HMRC are increasingly seeking to challenge arrangements made. Detailed advice should be sought.

Two other possible arrangements which could be considered in respect of spouses are:

- **Employing the spouse in the business** – the issue which needs to be considered in this scenario, is whether the salary which is being paid can be justified on commercial grounds for the work being performed. If the spouse is actually doing very little in the business then a significant salary would be difficult to justify. A higher salary would be possible if the spouse is a director of the company, because being a director involves taking on certain responsibilities. If the level of salary and benefits cannot be justified then HMRC may seek to disallow part of the cost on the grounds that it is not 'wholly and exclusively' for the purpose of the trade.
- **Holding shares jointly** – since introduction of independent taxation for married couples, unless an election is made for a different treatment, income arising on jointly owned assets is split equally between them, even if the capital ownership is not equal.[25] This arrangement is useful to avoid some of the issues regarding waivers and the settlement provisions.

Some other people, for example the parents, may want to pass income to their children, because they may have little income, and so could use their personal allowances and lower rate tax band to reduce the overall tax cost on the family. However a gift of shares by the parent to a child who is a minor on which a dividend is paid will be caught by the parental settlement provisions.[26] These provisions also apply to step children and adopted children. The effect of the provisions is that any tax benefit is nullified as the dividends are assessed on the parent who made the gift. Once the child is 18 the settlement provisions do not apply, and dividends paid will be treated as belonging to the child. So this can be useful in providing income to pay costs for, say, university education.

The settlement provisions in respect of minor children only relate to gifts of shares by parents. There is nothing to stop another family member making a gift of shares to the child. In those circumstances the dividends arising are treated as belonging to the minor child. That child cannot, as a minor, give valid receipt and so the dividend could be paid to the parent as bare trustee, and they then use it to pay expenses for the child, like school fees.

With any gift of shares it is important to also consider the capital gains tax and inheritance tax implications. These will be considered at a later stage.

---

[24] ITTOIA 2005, ss 620 and 648.
[25] ITA 2007, s 836.
[26] ITTOIA, s 629.

Alphabet shares are also a useful means of providing income to retired family members, and other family members, who the family has decided should be helped by the profits of the family business.

4.8 OVERVIEW OF BASIC ACCOUNTING AND FINANCIAL MANAGEMENT ISSUES

4.8.1 Accounting requirements

Normally on an annual basis the family business will need to prepare accounts. This can either be a legal requirement, or at least will be required to determine the tax liability for the period.

Companies and LLPs have to file accounts made up to an accounting reference date and file them at Companies House. This means that they are available for public inspection.

Sole traders and partnerships which are not LLPs do not need to file accounts, but they will be required for tax purposes, as well as good practice. If companies are concerned about their information being publically available it is possible, if they are a 'small company' to file abbreviated accounts. These accounts exclude a lot of the information which is found in full accounts, such as the profit and loss account. In order to qualify as a 'small company' it must meet at least two of the following criteria:

- annual turnover of £6.5m or less;
- the balance sheet total of assets (fixed and current) must be £3.26m or less;
- the average number of employees must not exceed 50.

If it exceeds the limits for one year it can continue to claim the exemption for that year, but cannot do so for the following year if it still exceeds the limits. An LLP can also file abbreviated accounts if it is within the limits for a small company.

There are also legal requirements regarding the information which should be disclosed, and the format of accounts for companies and LLPs. Accounting Standards also set out the policies which should be adopted in preparing the accounts for these two types of entities, and prescribe other disclosures which need to be made.

Companies and LLPs are also required to have their accounts audited by a registered auditor if for accounting periods ending on or after 1 January 2016 they meet at least two of the following:

- have a turnover of more than £10.2m; or
- have a balance sheet total of assets of more than £5.1m; or
- have an average member of employees of more than 50.

If it is a member of a group which exceeds the audit exemption limits then an audit will be required. An audit can also be required if members holding more than 10%, by value of the issued share capital or of a class of shares, request an audit.

Subsidiaries will also be exempt from audit for accounting periods ending on or after 1 October 2012 if the parent company guarantees all their liabilities.

4.8.2 Good financial management for family businesses

It is good practice for all family businesses to prepare management accounts on a monthly basis, as soon after the end of the month as possible. These will help management to monitor what is happening, financially, in the business and to take steps to make improvements or changes. This can be necessary if the business is growing faster than expected, or is not achieving the performance levels expected, or there is overspending in certain expense areas. The cash position can give a general indication of what is happening in the business, but it often lags behind the actual performance, if, for example, finance is effectively taken by delaying creditor payments. If the business is growing the need for additional working capital can be identified earlier if there is good financial information. It will be seen that many of the family business failures discussed in chapter 8 can be attributed to poor financial management in general and a lack of management accounting information in particular.

The management accounts should include a balance sheet for the business at the month end date, and an updated cash-flow forecast. The latter will show whether the business needs additional working capital compared with what was expected. This will enable early discussions with the bankers to the business, if necessary, or for other action to be taken.

As part of the management accounts reporting there should also be reports on the key performance indicators (KPIs) for the business. Which indicators are appropriate will depend on the business, but some typical ones would include:

- Gross profit in both monetary and percentage terms for each main product line; division; or contract.
- Wages cost as a percentage of turnover.
- Any significant cost area of the business.
- Debtor days – an increase in debtor days may indicate a need for more working capital.
- Stock turnover levels.
- Creditor days.
- Unused financial facilities, including headroom against agreed overdrafts.

The accounting system of the business should be capable of providing explanations at the detailed level, for any unexpected changes in the KPIs.

The business should also at the beginning of the financial year prepare budgets and cash-flow forecasts. These should reflect management's realistic view of what they expect to happen. Ideally some sensitivity analysis should be undertaken so that risks, as a result of under or over performance, can be identified.

The management accounts should include a comparison of actual results against the budget, and a variance analysis of any significant differences. If, during the course of the year, it becomes apparent that the actual performance is going to be significantly different from the original budget, then the budget should be revised.

4.8.3 Business plan – unifying business and family plans

As the family business develops and passes down through the generations it becomes more important that there is communication between the family, and the management of the business. This needs to be more formalised with each generation. In the early stages of the family business the owners and management will be the same, but as this situation changes so the family plans and the business plans need to remain unified. The family will have views on the long term goals for the business, for example how large they want the business to become; and whether they want it to remain a family business. They should also consider the values and mission which they want adopted by the business, and aspects such as:

- Whether the best interests of the family or the business are to be put first, or a combination of the two?
- Whether family members want to work in the business and what should be the criteria for entry?

These matters are explored in detail in chapter 18.

It is good business practice to prepare a business plan each year. The management team should be working to achieve the goals set out in the business plan which it will have prepared. If its business plan is not looking to achieve objectives which fit with the family plan then there is the potential for conflict. For example if the family decide they want the business to remain about the same size, because of their views on how the business should support the family, but the management's plan is to grow the business to say double its current size in the next 5 years, then the family could well be uncomfortable with the risks being taken on and the impact on their aim of the business supporting the family. So, the two plans need to be unified in achieving the agreed purposes.

The communication on the plans should be two way. So management needs to make the family aware of its business plan, just as the family needs to make management aware of its aims and objectives.

From the early stages of the family business development, to the later stages, when management becomes more professionalised, it is good practice to prepare a management plan which looks at a three to 5-year period. The plan will be more detailed for the first year and be more an outline for the subsequent years. Each year the plan should be updated and rolled forward a year. When putting the plan together consideration should be given to the following matters:

- The long term aims and goals of the business.
- An assessment and review of the marketplace in which the business operates. This will include an assessment of the major competitors.
- An identification of the unique selling points (USPs) of the business, and USPs which should be adopted.
- A realistic assessment of the strengths, weaknesses, opportunities and threats (SWOT analysis) of the business. This should lead to identification of areas which need to be addressed in an action plan.
- Profit and cash flow forecasts – these should as a minimum be in detail for the first 12 months even if they are only in more summarised form for subsequent years.

- Production and sales processes, and changes which need to be made. The financial implications of any changes need to be considered and included in the financial forecasts.
- Sources of any additional funding which might be required to achieve the plan.

4.8.4 Financial controls

When the business starts everything will be controlled by the owner/manager who will be involved in all significant decisions and all financial matters. For example they may well place all the orders, check the invoices from suppliers, and sign the cheques for payment. As the business grows they no longer have the time to perform all these functions, and other people have to be brought in. There is a danger that in a family business these new people soon become trusted and are viewed as 'part of the family', and so the financial controls which one would see in a larger public company are not introduced. As the business grows it should continually review the systems which operate, and as far as possible introduce processes which ensure a segregation of duties. This will create checks and balances on the financial management of the business. It should also help to prevent fraud, and reduce financial risk in the business. Also it can help avoid possible conflict between family members involved if for example, there are procedures which require certain financial decisions to need a family discussion and agreement, such as remuneration levels.

The business will need to develop controls over all its financial areas such as:

- Ordering systems – these will specify which personnel have authority to place orders, and to what financial limit.
- Approval of suppliers' invoices – this should involve checks to ensure the goods have been received, prices are correct, and the goods were properly ordered. The systems will also specify who has the authority and/or is required to approve certain invoices.
- Credit control – this will include checks on new customers; approval; setting credit limits for new customers; and checking that orders from existing customers and new customers do not exceed the limits originally set.
- Cheque signing – normally cheques above a certain limit should require two signatures, and the larger the payment the more senior should be the signatory. In this electronic age with more payments being made through computer systems the need for adequate controls over this area has become more important.
- Stock control – to ensure that there is a record of all stock received, and when it is sold, or used in the business, and what the stock holding levels are at any point.
- Wages – with controls to check the wage rates being paid, and the net amount being paid to employees.

This is not a comprehensive list, but it does demonstrate that as the family business grows the owner/manager cannot exercise the same control as when the business started. As the management of the business becomes more professional, one of the first outsiders to be recruited tends to be somebody with financial skills.

4.9 WEALTH PLANNING

4.9.1 Building wealth in the business and for the stakeholders

Successful family businesses have the potential to build wealth for all the stakeholders, with that wealth increasing as it passes to subsequent generations. The wealth can come from a variety of sources. The way the family deals with its wealth may depend on how the current wealth has been created. It can come from:

- Being internally generated by the success of the trading enterprise. In which case the wealth comes from the inherent value of the business, and over time from the accumulation of resources surplus to the trading activities. The latter may take time because the business will initially need to reinvest in the operational side to continue to grow the business.
- A sale of the original business by the company, so the proceeds of sale are still retained in the corporate entity, and the family have decided that the wealth created should continue to be retained in that structure for the benefit of the whole family.
- A windfall, such as a property being sold for development at a price which generates more funds than are needed for the ongoing trading business.

The family will want to protect the wealth created from claims by creditors and the commercial risks of the trading activities. Some of the commercial risks can be insured against but not the financial failure of the business. To grow the business, finance will be required and the family will have to accept that assets will need to be pledged as support for say bank overdrafts and loans. Also guarantees may need to be given, which will put assets, and perhaps assets in a company where it has invested its surplus wealth, at risk.

A couple of steps which the family can take to protect the accumulated wealth from the commercial risks of the trading activities are:

- To set up a group structure, which could be just a holding company and a subsidiary, or a holding company with several subsidiaries, and to carry on the trade through one subsidiary, with the 'surplus' assets which the family want to protect, being held by another subsidiary, or the holding company. If Inheritance tax is likely to be an issue in the near future then the implications of this restructuring on the potential liabilities will need to be considered.
- To demerge, using an Insolvency Act 1986 (IA), s 110 type reconstruction, the assets the family want to protect into a separate company which is independent of the trading company. Demergers are explained in more detail in chapter 11 (Ownership Overview).

If there is accumulated wealth within the business it may be the case that the family decides it wants to extract that value. This can be achieved in a number of ways:

- For those working in the business rewards can be taken as remuneration and benefits in kind. If they are also shareholders then wealth can be extracted as dividends. These will be subject to income tax.
- If they are shareholders then dividends can be paid. These will be taxed as income in the hands of the shareholder, and there may be higher rate and additional rate tax payable.

- Another option, to return value to shareholders is for the family company to buy back their shares. Pruning of the ownership tree is also discussed in chapter 11.

There will be key employees in the business, some of who may be family members. The loss through death or a serious illness of a key individual can have a dramatic effect on the business. In order to protect against this scenario, by providing funds to the company to help it financially through an interim phase until, say, a new person has been recruited and established in the business, consideration should be given to key man and/or critical illness cover. This will help to preserve the wealth created in the business.

Often, because of the financial need to reinvest back into the business, little thought is given to the need to provide an income on retirement, until the date draws near. At that stage the soon to be retired family managers may view the company as their pension pot. This can give rise to a number of issues for the family business:

- The older generation continues to be involved in the management because they are concerned to protect their income requirements. This creates frustration for the next generation.
- The older generation are unable to enjoy the life they feel they are entitled to from all the years they have devoted to the business, because of constrained financial resources within the company, or its need to reinvest in the business.
- The financial constraints on the business from providing the income the retired generation needs, means it cannot take some of the commercial risks it needs to in order to continue to be successful. The danger is that this can become a spiral to decline from which the business cannot escape.

All of the above can have an impact on the preservation, and generation of wealth through the family business.

The financial needs of the retired generation may be provided for, and protected, by separating the investment assets from the trading activities. However a more sensible approach is for the company to start making pension provision for those family members working in the business, as early as possible. This creates a pot for the future, protected from the risks of the company, and not dependent on the company, to provide income in retirement for both the working family member and their spouse, which can continue to provide income for the spouse after the death of the individual.

Pension planning is closely linked to succession planning. Too many family employees view the company as effectively their pension scheme, one which should provide for them once they have retired. This can cause difficulties as the next generation look to take the business forward, because of the financial commitment that entails, and the potential concern the retired generation in wanting to ensure the company will continue to fund their retirement. If there is a sizable pension fund at retirement, then these pressures can be reduced or hopefully removed. With the current limits on maximum annual allowable contributions it is even more important that pension funds for family members are started as soon as possible, to ensure they have adequate income in retirement which is not dependent on the company.

In the past it has been possible for the company to make large contributions to pension schemes and obtain a tax deduction. This meant that pension planning could be left to nearer retirement. However from 6 April 2014 it has only been possible for tax relief to be claimed on contributions of up to £40,000. If the £40,000 limit has not been utilised in any of the preceding three tax years then the unused amount can also be used. This means that if contributions have not been made in the previous 3 years a contribution of £160,000 could be made in one year. However where an individual earns over £150,000 the £40,000 annual allowance will be abated to as little as £10,000. In a family business one would normally expect the company to make the contribution to the pension scheme for the benefit of the individual. The alternative of paying a bonus to the individual to enable them to make the contribution will involve a national insurance cost. Also if the individual makes the contribution they need to have earned income of at least the amount of the pension contribution in the same tax year.

4.9.2 The family's purpose in wealth planning

Where the family business has built up wealth, then the family needs to decide how it will manage that wealth. The approach taken will depend on the nature of the wealth, whether it is mainly related to a trading business, or whether the historic trading business has gone, and now the wealth is related to a portfolio of investments. In either case, the family needs to decide on its relationship to the business; its vision as far as the wealth is concerned; whether as a family it wants to stay connected collectively, or whether there are members who do not want to stay connected, to the family wealth/business; and the purpose of the wealth which has been created. A family charter or constitution can be useful to set out the family's views. The approach to the creation of such a document has been considered elsewhere in this book. The principles covered there can be adapted to a situation where the wealth constitutes a portfolio of investments. Some of the specific questions which the family will need to address in the latter circumstances are:

- What are the family's capital and income needs?
- Does the family want capital growth or preservation of capital?
- What is the family's attitude to risk?
- Does the family have views on the type of assets which should be invested in?
- How do we prepare the next generation for the responsibilities of managing the wealth?
- What are the time frames for the family?
- What is the *mission* the family is trying to achieve? For example, wanting to safeguard the inheritance, and providing a solid financial base from which the current and future generations can develop successful lives?
- What is going to be the family's approach to *governance*? As the family grows in complexity it will need to establish decision making structures that ensure a fair process is seen to be taking place.

4.9.3 The family office

Often family wealth is managed in separate individual portfolios for each family member, although the family may well share the same IFA or other financial advisor.

Where the family wealth is a portfolio of investments, and it has been decided by the family that they want to collectively manage that wealth for the benefit of the family, then if the portfolio is large enough, there is merit in considering whether a family office may be appropriate. Historically the concept of a family office has come from the USA, where they have grown out of the need to look after family matters such as the administration and accounting for family assets, and the management of the family wealth. In the UK one has seen estate offices performing some of these functions, having developed from just looking after the management of the estate to dealing with, organising and administering a whole range of matters for family members.

In a fully developed family office there will be a team who will deal with administrative and accounting issues and others whose skills will be bought in, as and when required, such as lawyers, investment managers, accountants, tax advisors, and property experts. In some cases this can be formalised, but in others it may be that specific family members take on the function of managing particular aspects on a less formal basis. The formalised structure continues to predominate in the USA, but we are seeing an increasing number of family offices being established in the UK and Europe.

The major reason why we are seeing this growth, is that co-ordination of all the professional disciplines required to manage the family's financial affairs results in a more efficient and effective management of the family's wealth. In the past families have tended to rely on one financial institution, but the increased specialisation and fragmentation that has been seen in the financial services market, means there are opportunities for the family's management of its wealth to be improved if it moves away from that single provider.

Part of the family office function can also be to manage the business interests in which the family wealth is invested, and effectively provide a link, or barrier between the family and the business.

The family office becomes a way for the family to maintain control over the manner in which they preserve and grow their wealth, whilst also being a focal point of contact for the family and their advisors.

There are three main types of family offices:

- **The single family office (SFO)** – this is the traditional model looking after a single family. In some cases this can operate on a 'do it yourself' (DIY) basis where perhaps the family want to maintain control over the investment of the wealth, and the individual(s) may have had some investment experience. They may then call upon some outside expertise. In this scenario the role can be time consuming and challenging. This DIY approach to the SFO is probably unlikely to provide the family with administrative and accounting services. It may also become increasingly rare because of the complexity of today's financial markets, and the need to bring in outside consultants to advise in certain areas, such as asset allocation; manager selection; and risk management. The writer has seen instances where the family has set up its own unit trust to manage the investment portfolios of a range of family trusts, pension schemes for family members and personal portfolios. The management of that unit trust as regards investment decisions is by a couple of family members.
- **The multi-family office (MFO)** – as the name implies MFOs offer services to more than one family. This has the advantage of spreading costs, and risks, across a larger asset base. An example of an MFO is the Bessemer Trust based in New York which is owned and controlled by descendants of the founding family, and grew out of the family's SFO.

- **The multi-client family office (MCFO)** – this is where existing family office consultants take a small number of their existing clients, and create a vertical business model of deeper relationships, rather than a horizontal model with a large number of clients with smaller assets.

As the sector has matured we have seen large institutions such as JP Morgan, UBS and HSBC Bank competing in the family office market. This competition has led to some consolidation, resulting in larger MFOs such as Pictet in Europe. One of the largest UK MFOs is Fleming Family and Partners. Its origins are the investment business of Robert Fleming, and its family office client base includes the Fleming family.

As with any decision about management of the family's wealth, when deciding on a MFO the family should review the services being offered, and undertake a full due diligence of the MFO's attributes. A good MFO will have stable and committed ownership; compatible clients; the ability to pursue the best solutions for clients on an independent basis, and transparent fees. They should also have systems which ensure integrity, discretion and confidentiality.

4.10 LIQUIDATION AND THE FAMILY BUSINESS

4.10.1 Liquidation as the only exit

In chapter 1 we discuss the mortality rate of family businesses. Many will be sold, others will transition to the next generation. Some will end in business failure.

But sometimes solvent liquidation of the company may be the only exit for the business owner, because there is no family succession, and a buyer cannot be found. Part of the reason for this may be because technology, new services or products, or changes in society's tastes, mean the business is no longer viable. This can be quite a difficult decision to make, because of the emotional attachment to the business.

Normally the route is going to be by the appointment of a liquidator by the shareholders, if the company is solvent, and able to pay all the creditors. There had been previously been an informal process for winding up a company known as Extra Statutory Concession C16. This allowed a company to apply to HMRC for confirmation that they would treat the distribution of the assets to the shareholders as a capital distribution, rather than as income. Following this distribution, an application would be made to the Registrar of Companies to strike off the company. This saves the cost of a formal liquidation. However there are a couple of issues:

- It is possible for a creditor to make a claim against the company, after it has been struck off, and then to have the company reinstated, so that the claim can be pursued. Only a formal liquidation process will prevent a creditor making a claim once the company is no longer on the register.
- The distribution of the share capital as part of the dissolution process is an unauthorised return of capital. The company has the right to recover that money from the shareholders. Where the company is dissolved, rather than liquidated, this right passes to the Crown. The Treasury Solicitor had confirmed that it would not pursue these amounts where the amount of the share capital is less than £4,000. Then in November 2011, they stated that they wouldn't pursue any claims in respect of share capital.

4.10.2 Tax and solvent winding-up

In December 2011 it was announced that legislation would be introduced, which would mean distributions after 1 March 2012 would be covered by legislation, and the concession would be withdrawn. From 1 March 2012, only if the distribution does not exceed £25,000 will it be treated as capital.

Distributions made by a liquidator to individuals who are shareholders will be liable to capital gains tax, if the amounts received are greater than the base cost of the shares. The base cost will normally be either the price paid for the shares, or the value at the date they were received as a gift, unless any latent gain was held over on that event. The capital gain is assessable in the tax year in which the liquidator makes a distribution.

If at the time of the liquidation of the company, the shareholder would have qualified for entrepreneur's relief, they can still claim the relief in respect of distributions made within 3 years of the company ceasing to trade. There is no restriction in the relief because the company has ceased to trade.

For some shareholders it may be more beneficial for them to receive a distribution, which is taxed as income, rather than as a capital gain. In those cases it may be appropriate to change the rights on some shares so that they receive a special dividend, which extinguishes all their capital rights except the nominal value of the share. This special dividend is then paid prior to the liquidation.

4.10.3 Tax consequences of an insolvent liquidation

If the shareholder receives a distribution in the liquidation which is less than the amount they paid for the share, then they will have a capital loss for tax purposes. This loss can be set off against other capital gains in the same year. If there are no gains in the year then the loss is carried forward.

It may be the case that there is a capital gain in the year before the company goes into liquidation. In those circumstances it may be worthwhile considering whether a negligible value claim can be made under TCGA 1992, s 24(2) in the earlier year. Whether a claim can be made will depend on the circumstances, and financial position of the company.

If the person who incurs a loss on ordinary shares was the person who originally subscribed for them, then the loss may, instead of being set off against a capital gain, be relieved against income in the tax year of the loss, and/or the preceding year.[27] In order to be able to make this claim:

(1) The individual must have subscribed in money, or money's worth, for the shares, or they were transferred to them by their spouse who had similarly subscribed for the shares.
(2) They must be ordinary shares in a qualifying trading company, which for shares issued after 5 April 1998 is defined as:
    (a) a trading company on the date of disposal, or ceased to be a trading company within 3 years before that date, and had not since cessation been an

---

[27] ITA 2007, s 132.

investment company, or one which mainly traded as a dealer in land, commodities, futures, shares, securities or other financial instruments; and

(b) been a trading company for a continuous period of at least 6 years prior to disposal (or the cessation of trading), or been a trading company for a shorter period, and not previously been an investment company or traded as a dealer in land, commodities, futures, shares, securities or other financial instruments; and

(c) has carried on its business wholly or mainly in the UK throughout the period from incorporation, or the date of the issue of the shares if later, to the disposal date.

(3) The company must meet the qualifying conditions for Enterprise Investment Scheme purposes, as regards the trading activity it carried on, and gross assets test at the time of the issue of the shares. From 6 April 2012 gross assets must not exceed £15m before the share issue and £16m after the issue.

In an insolvent liquidation an individual may in addition to being a shareholder, also be a loan creditor. If that loan is not repaid in full, then a claim may be possible for a capital loss.[28] In order to qualify for relief:

- the loan must have been used by the company wholly for the purposes of the trade it carries on; and
- the company has to be resident in the UK; and
- the debt must not be a debt on security as defined in TCGA 1992, s 132.

A claim for this loss can be made at the time the company goes into liquidation, or when a distribution is received which is expected to be the final distribution, or at an earlier time which is specified in the claim. In the latter case the loan must have been irrecoverable at that time. But the claim cannot be made for a date which is more than 2 years before the beginning of the tax year in which the claim is made.

In addition to any loan, or instead of, a family member may have guaranteed a bank loan. If as a result of the insolvent liquidation the bank make a claim under that guarantee, and a payment is made, then a claim can be made for a capital loss.[29] The bank loan has to meet the same conditions as for the loan by the individual, except it can be a debt on security.

HMRC have confirmed that a capital loss can also be claimed if the guarantee was in respect of an overdraft, but not if it was in relation to a hire purchase agreement.

The guarantee payment has to be made in respect of a formal claim, and not a voluntary payment. Therefore it will be important that there is documentation to show a formal claim.

Whilst the ability to claim for a capital loss on the non-repayment of a loan, or in respect of a guarantee payment, the value of the loss will depend on whether there are any capital gains.

It might be thought that there is an opportunity to convert a capital loss into one which can be relieved against income, in circumstances where it is known that the company

---

[28] TCGA 1992, s 253(3).
[29] TCGA 1992, s 253(4).

may fold, by converting a loan into share capital. However HMRC will deny a loss claim on the new shares, because they will contend that it was unlikely the loan would be repaid and therefore full value has not been paid for the shares.

4.11 EMPLOYING FAMILY MEMBERS – TAX AND ALTERNATIVE METHODS OF REWARD

For the reasons explained in chapter 7, best practice suggests that a market rates should be used to determine the remuneration of family employees. This applies to basic salary bonus schemes and benefits including pension contributions.

If there is to be a bonus paid as part of the remuneration package then the same approach needs to be adopted. In other words the system needs to be clearly set out, be fair and seen to be fairly determined against objective measures.

Nevertheless it may be decided to pay discretionary bonuses to family employees on top of any performance related ones. If the employed family members are also the only shareholders then this will often not lead to conflict, provided all those involved agree on the allocation between them. In these circumstances the question which needs to be considered is which is the most tax efficient method of extraction, as a bonus or as a dividend? As discussed above this will depend on the corporation tax rate payable by the company, and the income tax rate for the individual. If the dividend route is the most tax efficient method of extraction then if the amounts which are to be paid to each shareholder are not in the same ratio as the shares are held, then it will be easier if the shares are designated as alphabet shares, 'A', 'B' and 'C' etc. to enable different dividend rates to be declared, rather than to have to prepare dividend waivers.

If one spouse works in the family business, and the other has no income, then a common question is whether part of the remuneration can be paid to the one with no income to reduce the overall tax burden on that family. Whilst this arrangement would reduce the overall tax burden, it is possible that HMRC may challenge the salary paid to the low income spouse, and not allow the company to claim a tax deduction for the cost on the grounds that it has not been paid 'wholly and exclusively' for the purposes of the business. A deduction would only be allowed if it can be argued that the salary paid is commensurate with the duties performed. If a person is a director of a company then that position carries with it certain responsibilities, even if it is not a full time role, and that can then justify a reasonable level of salary, and at a higher level than if the person is just treated as an employee. So if spouses are paid a salary and their duties are limited, it is worthwhile considering whether they should also become a director with all the obligations that this imposes.

It may be decided to include benefits as part of the reward package. The cost of providing these rewards should normally result in a tax deduction for the company, provided it can be argued the complete package is appropriate for the duties. The actual tax deduction will depend on the nature of the benefit. For example the payment of, say, health insurance will give a tax deduction the same as the cost, whereas the provision of a car for use by the family employee will give a deduction based on the capital allowances rules. The tax advantage to the family employee of a benefit being provided, if it is an expense they would otherwise have to pay out of taxed income, is that it reduces the after tax cost to them.

For most benefits in kind, where expenses are paid by the company but the employee receives a benefit, they are taxed on the employee at their highest income tax rate, and the company pays employer's national insurance on the cost. The company will claim a deduction for the cost of the benefit and the national insurance against its taxable profits. Examples of these types of benefits are health insurance; home telephone; the cost of work done on the employee's home.

There are special rules which apply to the provision of certain benefits in kind, typically where an asset is provided for the use of the employee, such as a car (which includes the company paying the insurance and maintenance costs); a van; accommodation; or other asset (eg motorcycle, yacht or aeroplane). Another area where special rules apply is where the company pays for private fuel. A brief outline of the taxable benefit position for the employee in these areas is set out below. This is not intended to be an exhaustive explanation of the tax treatment in these areas, but is only a brief overview.

4.11.1 Cars, fuel and vans

The car benefit is calculated by multiplying the list price (not necessarily the same as the price paid for the car) of the car by a percentage that is dependent on the level of approved CO_2 emissions of the car. If the CO_2 emissions are 110g/km or less the company can claim a 100% capital allowances deduction. With the low benefit in kind charge and the capital allowances claim cars which fall into this latter category can be a very tax efficient benefit.

In family businesses it is not uncommon for both spouses to be provided with a car. In these circumstances a strict interpretation of the main tax legislation might indicate that if both are employed, then both are assessable to a benefit on both cars. However, if the cars are provided as part of their employment packages then they are only assessed on the individual to whom the car is provided.

If fuel is provided for private mileage the taxable benefit depends on the type of car. If the amount of private mileage is small then it is worthwhile reimbursing the company for that element.

The taxable benefit for the provision of a van for private use is £3,000. This has made them an attractive benefit. But the question whether particular vehicles which one might treat in some respects as a van, should be classified as a car for benefit in kind purposes is a complex one.[30]

4.11.2 Accommodation

If the company provides accommodation for private use the taxable benefit in kind is based on the excess of the acquisition cost over £75,000, multiplied by the 'official rate' as announced by HMRC. If the company pays rent for the provision of the accommodation then the benefit is kind is the rental paid.

---

[30] See HMRC Manuals 36.

4.11.3 Other assets

Other assets provided by the company for use by an employee, such as a motorcycle, yacht or aeroplane will be subject to a benefit in charge of 20% of the value of the asset when it was first provided. In addition any expenses in respect of the asset paid by the company will also be taxable as a benefit in kind.

4.11.4 National insurance

In relation to all the above categories the company will have to pay employer's national insurance on the taxable value of the benefit in kind.

4.12 EMPLOYEE OWNERSHIP AND TAX

4.12.1 Tax benefits of share schemes

The use of share incentives has been a growing trend in the recruitment, retention and motivation of key employees over the last 20 years. Their relevance to family businesses is considered in chapter 6. This section looks in a little more detail at the tax issues involved.

Share schemes and equity incentives will, if properly structured, deliver value to senior employees in a tax efficient manner. This will generally arise from an ability to tax gains made by participants in the scheme under capital gains tax rules, rather than taxing those gains as earned income. Whilst this benefit is not always available, it is very often at the heart of designing an appropriate and attractive scheme. In addition, there are opportunities for family companies themselves to benefit from tax deductions related to the provision of share scheme benefits.

There are a broad range of plans and schemes available to provide equity incentives to employees and they can be separated into two broad groups. Approved schemes are those which are recognised in tax statute and capable of being approved by HMRC.

These will typically provide considerable tax advantages which are set out in statute. By their nature, approved schemes are governed by complex legislation and require careful drafting. Very often, prescribed requirements must be met before approval will be granted and this can result in a degree of inflexibility which may not make an approved scheme appropriate in all cases. Later in this section the key characteristics of the approved schemes most suitable for family companies are described.

Unapproved schemes are not subject to such requirements and as a consequence, considerably more flexible. In general, they do not attract the same tax reliefs as their approved alternative, but with careful structuring, can provide substantial benefit within a tax efficient environment.

4.12.2 Family member or family employee?

The primary tax issue is that, in general terms, an employee will be subject to income tax on the value of any benefit received from the issue of shares to them by reason of their employment, unless one of the exceptions mentioned below apply.[31] The starting point is that shares acquired from an employer or a connected person (including a controlling family member) are deemed to have been acquired by reason of employment.[32] But what about shares acquired by family members?

There is an exception where the shares have been acquired or the right arises in the normal course of domestic, family or personal relationships. At first sight this would appear to apply to family business succession planning. HMRC claim that they will:[33]

> 'take a common-sense view of this exception. It would clearly apply if a father, on reaching retirement, hands over all the shares in his family company to his son and daughter *simply because* they are his children, even if they are both also employees of the family company.'

However HMRC go on to warn that there are circumstances where the primary driver will be the employment rather than the family relationship. They also comment that this might be the case if family members, who are employees, are given shares, or the right to acquire shares at the same time as other employees. Therefore it is advisable to separate in time, opportunities given to family members, from those given to employees if it is hoped to claim the exclusion from the employment related share provisions.

One scenario not canvassed in the HMRC manual is where, in pursuance of a 'business first' ownership approach shares are given only to family members working in the family company to the exclusion of other siblings who do not do so. It might be difficult to argue that the gift is made '*simply because*' of family membership. Employment would be an additional qualification. Nevertheless it would still be the case that the primary determinant was family membership.

4.12.3 Basic tax rules and valuation

As discussed in chapters 12 (on sale) and 16 (for other purposes, including tax), the valuation of shares in a privately held company is a complex matter. Where an equity incentive is to be used in such a company then a method for determining value must be found not only for commercial reasons but also to establish the tax position of the employee and employer.

Unfortunately given the importance of the valuation of a share to the tax position of the employee HMRC will not provide an advance valuation and will only discuss one once a transaction has actually taken place. The only exception to this is where approved schemes are used as they will often provide for the agreement of a value with HMRC in advance of the grant of any award, thereby establishing the tax position and providing certainty for both the employer and participant.

If an employee or director of a company acquires shares they must do so at market value if they are to avoid suffering an income tax liability on any discount they have enjoyed. Furthermore in certain circumstances it is possible for such a liability to become subject to PAYE with the attendant cost for the employing company. In addition to the potential for income tax charges on acquisition the Employment Related Securities legislation will operate to tax the employee and employer unless appropriate care is taken at the outset.

---

[31] ITEPA 2003, ss 421B (1) and 471(1).
[32] ITEPA 2003, ss 421B(1) and 471(3).
[33] See HMRC Employment Related Securities Manual (ERSM) 20220 – emphasis added.

These rules are complex and cannot be covered in detail here but the advisor of any company providing shares to employees will need to be conversant with them if a successful incentive is to be created.

4.12.4 Direct acquisition

A company can look at some different alternatives where immediate share ownership is desired. If the value of the shares is substantial then funding of some kind may be required. The company may offer a loan to the employee to fund the acquisition or assist in securing funding from a third party. Often though this route is unattractive as employees may not wish, or be able to borrow substantial sums. Additionally where loans are made available on a beneficial basis by the employer benefit-in-kind charges can arise, although if the loan is to an employee who spends the greater part of their time in working for the company, or an associated company; or the loan is to acquire more than 5%; and the company is not an investment company, but is a close company, then no benefit in kind charge arises. Loans to employees who are directors to acquire shares will also give rise to a tax liability under s 455 CTA 2010, of the loan, which will be repaid when the loan, or part of it is repaid.

An alternative but more complex approach is to create a new employee share class with rights designed to reduce the value of the shares at the point of acquisition. This can be a very effective way to reduce the market value of a share and make it more affordable for an employee to purchase. The employment related securities regulations will seek to tax to income changes to shares that artificially pass value to an employee, but if the shares simply grow in value due to the success of the business then the gains made should be subject only to capital gains taxes.

4.12.5 Other considerations

Whatever the approach taken to letting employees acquire shares directly it should not be forgotten that care must be taken to ensure that the company's articles and shareholders' agreements are adapted to cope with the issues that come along with employee ownership such as employees' rights on leaving employment.

A key aspect of designing an effective incentive will be the method by which the employee's holding can realise their value. Obviously the timing of this will be important and should align with the achievement of the desired goal or objective. In practical terms however this can be particularly problematic in a family business where the ultimate sale of the company may not just be unlikely but anathema to its owners. In such circumstances the use of a purchase of own shares or employee benefit trust can be very effective in providing a means for the employee to turn their equity into cash.

There are also a number of reporting requirements that arise when an employee is granted the opportunity to acquire a share. In particular HMRC Form 42 must be completed by the employer for each tax year and submitted on-line to HMRC.

4.12.6 Options

Where it is not deemed appropriate to allow employees to acquire shares immediately but perhaps at some point in the future or on the achievement of a particular objective a share option is often used. Put simply an option is the right to an option and has the benefit of providing the certainty of a contract between the employee and employer that in the event that certain criteria are met the option may be exercised and shares acquired.

There are two kinds of approved share option plans that are most commonly used which are the enterprise management incentive or 'EMI' which is the most popular and the company share option plan or 'CSOP'. The phrase unapproved option or 'USOP' covers all options that do not fall within one of the approved schemes available and is widely used due to its flexibility.

4.12.7   Enterprise management incentive (EMI)

The EMI is a tax advantaged share approved option. They were introduced to help smaller, higher risk companies recruit and retain employees.

The tax advantages of using such a scheme are that:
- There is no income tax charge on the exercise of the option.
- Any gain made on the shares will be subject to capital gains tax. Shares acquired under an EMI scheme which meet the other qualifying conditions for entrepreneur's relief, will benefit from the 10% tax rate even if the individual holds less than 5% of the issued share capital and voting rights, which Is normally a requirement for entrepreneur's relief. Also the one year holding period for entrepreneur's relief starts from the date of the grant of the option in the case of qualifying EMI shares rather than from the date the option is exercised and the shares acquired. The other qualifying conditions for entrepreneur's relief, such as being an employee or officer of the company, also have to be met.

EMI options with a market value of up to £250,000 may be granted to each employee who meet certain criteria subject to a total share value of £4m.

To qualify for EMI an employee has to be employed by the company whose shares are the subject of the option, or by a subsidiary. They must spend at least 25 hours a week working for the company or the group or if they are part time they must spend at least 75 per cent of their working time working as an employee for the company or group.

EMI options can be issued to just one or a small group of key employees. Also, the targets to be achieved to enable the option to be exercised can be very flexible.

The company issuing the EMI must also meet specific requirements in order to be a qualifying company. It must an independent trading company meaning essentially that it must not be owned by another company and must not have a substantial investment activity. It must also have gross assets of no more than £30m at the time an EMI option is granted.

Amongst other requirements are that the company must have fewer than 250 employees, and carry on a qualifying trade. Certain trades, including many where family business are often found, are excluded.[34]

---

[34] These include dealing in land; property development; farming or market gardening; forestry activities or

In addition there must be a permanent establishment in the UK.

As with most approved share incentives the qualifying criteria can appear numerous and complex but despite this the EMI is a very popular and effective share option scheme. Whilst these criteria are prescriptive the scheme offers great flexibility in determining when and how an employee can exercise their option and acquire shares. More over a properly structured EMI scheme will provide the opportunity of realising a gain upon which only capital gains tax will apply.

4.12.8 Company share option plan (CSOP)

The company share option plan or 'CSOP' allows options to be granted to selected employees over shares with a maximum value per individual of £30,000 at the date of the grant. Importantly exercise is only allowed 3 or more years after the date of the grant but at that point will be free of income tax and national insurance contributions.

The CSOP is a more restrictive scheme than EMI but can be useful where for example the company is carrying on an excluded trade or is simply too large to meet the employee or gross assets tests.

As with EMI the company must neither be a listed company nor controlled by another company. The shares under option must meet certain conditions and most importantly in family companies they must not be subject to restrictions other than those attaching to all shares of the same class. This can be problematic if it is desired to create an 'employee' class of shares separate from the family ownership.

CSOP options must be granted with an exercise price which is equal to or exceeds the market value of a share at the grant date. Any growth in value is usually income tax free if the option is exercised more than three years after grant. When the shares are eventually sold the gain made by the employee will be subject to capital gains tax.

The option may specify performance criteria that must be met before exercise is allowed much in the same way as an EMI.

The CSOP is less flexible than EMI, requires advance HMRC approval and cannot deliver the same level of incentive, however it is useful in certain circumstances and can be utilised where EMI is not available.

4.12.9 Save as you earn share option plan (SAYE plan)

One of the conditions for a SAYE Plan is that all employees who have worked for the company for a qualifying period not exceeding 5 years, have to be eligible to join the scheme. In these circumstances it will have little application to family companies, and will not be covered in this book.

---

timber production; operating or managing hotels or comparable establishments; and operating or managing nursing homes or residential care homes. There are other categories of non-trading businesses, including banking.

4.12.10 Unapproved share options

If an option is not granted under one of the above approved share option schemes then it will be an unapproved option, and the favourable tax treatments will not be available. Any EMI, CSOP or SAYE options where there is a breach of the conditions for approval will also be treated as unapproved options.

For the purposes of this book the normal, and simple situation, of a share option being granted to an individual who then exercises that option at some time in the future will be considered.

The employment related securities tax provisions apply if the person who acquired the right or opportunity to acquire shares does so by virtue of their past, present or prospective employment. The family exception discussed above also applies.

If an employment related option is potentially within the charge to tax on exercise, no income tax liability arises on receipt of the option, but an income tax charge does arise on the exercise of the option. At the latter point the chargeable amount is the excess of the market value of the shares over the consideration given for the shares acquired. This is assessable in the year in which the option is exercised. The market value for this purpose is determined as for normal capital gains tax purposes, so discounts for minority shareholdings can be taken into account. This means that employees can potentially benefit from future growth in the value of the company if, for example, it were sold a number of years after the option is exercised, at which point the employee shareholder would take a proportionate share of the total company value. So whilst there may be an income tax charge on the exercise of unapproved share options, they can still be seen as an incentive. The issue though is often one of how the employee pays the option price, and the tax liability if the exercise price is less than market value. If the employee waits to exercise the option until immediately before a sale, then arguably the market value at that time is the amount which will be received on a sale, and not a discounted amount, and hence the whole of the growth is taxed as income.

The benefit to an employee, and hence the incentive is if the share sale is taxed as a capital gain rather than as income. The tax rate payable could be nil% (if the gain is less than the annual capital gains exemption); or 10% (if the qualifying conditions for entrepreneurs' relief are met, one of which is that the shareholding must be at least 5%); or 18% (if the taxable gain plus other income in the year is not greater than the basic rate band); or 20% in other cases. In any event these rates will be better than 40% or 45% income tax payable by most senior employees as higher rate tax payers. In calculating the taxable gain, for options exercised on or after 10 April 2003, the cost of acquisition is the price paid for the shares, any consideration given for the grant of the option, plus any amount charged to income tax on the exercise of the option. This means that the full market value of the shares at the time of the exercise of the option is a deduction for capital gains tax purposes.

The alternative to issuing a share option is to issue shares directly to an employee / director. However this means the employee has to pay at least nominal value for the shares. If nominal value is less than market value then if they are employment related shares, there will be an income tax charge in the same way as for share options. An alternative is for the individual to be gifted, or sold shares by another shareholder. These situations also give rise to employment related share issues, if the opportunity for the gift, or purchase, is by reason of employment. A gift gets around the issue of the employee having to pay for the shares, but there will again be an income tax charge on the value of the gift. If the shares are sold at under value there will also be an income tax charge.

In the case of a gift, or sale at under value, the vendor will also have to consider their own capital gains tax position, as they will be subject to capital gains tax based on the market value of the shares. This liability can be avoided if an election can be made under s 165 TCGA 1992 to holdover the gain (see chapter 16). However some points to be aware of are that the company must be a trading company; the gain held over is restricted if the company holds non business assets; and the gain crystallises if the done becomes non-resident or ordinarily resident in the UK within 6 years of the end of the year of assessment.

As with share options, the employment related share provisions for income tax purposes do not apply if the shares are acquired in the normal course of domestic, family or personal relationships.

In the HMRC Manuals they recognise that personal relationships can include friendships, and that it is not unknown for a proprietor to pass the ownership of a business to a long term employee with whom he has built up close personal ties.

If one wants to reduce the tax cost for the employee, and the amount they have to pay for the shares, it may be worthwhile considering issuing 'growth' or 'hurdle' shares. A 'growth' share could be one which currently only has nominal value, and has no interest for capital purposes in the current value of the company, but it is able to participate in the future growth. Therefore the issue of the share becomes an incentive to the key employee to assist in the growth of the company. A 'hurdle' share will again be typically issued for nominal value, and is used as an incentive, and a way of rewarding if the value of the company exceeds a specified figure within a period of time. For example the company might currently have a value of £1m, and 'hurdle' shares might give an individual a right to say 5% of the capital value in the event of a sale in excess of £10m within 10 years. Because of the current uncertainty in being able to achieve that target the share may well be worth no more than nominal value when it is issued. By creating a separate class of shares for the 'hurdle' or 'growth' shares, it may be possible to issue just one share, but with rights to a greater pro rata share of the assets, say 5%. But if one also wants the individual to benefit from entrepreneurs' relief, they will need to have at least 5% of the ordinary share capital, and at least 5% of the voting rights, then at least 5% by nominal amount may need to be issued.

Another common method of reducing the value of shares on issue has been for them to carry restrictions. The type of restrictions which might apply are:

- Provisions for the transfer, reversion or forfeiture of the shares if certain circumstances do, or do not arise, so that the holder ceases to be beneficially entitled to them and will not be entitled to at least their unfettered market value. Good and bad leaver provisions are the most obvious example.
- Restriction on the freedom of the holder to dispose of the shares, or retain the proceeds if they are sold.
- Provisions whereby the disposal or retention of the shares, or the exercise of a right conferred on the shares results in a disadvantage to the holder, or employee or a connected person.

There are exceptions and exclusions to the above list, but they will not be covered in this book.

The value of the shares could then be enhanced by removing the restriction at some future date. Any restriction will be deemed to have been removed when the shares are sold. To counter this potential income tax free benefit legislation was introduced which taxed the uplift in value on the removal or variation of restrictions, or the shares ceasing to be restricted shares, or the disposal of the shares for consideration by an associated person otherwise than to another associated person, at a time when they are still restricted. Arguably, normal commercial restrictions might catch some shares, and therefore result in gains being taxed as income rather than capital. To avoid this situation it is possible to make an election under s 431 ITEPA 2003. By making the election the provisions on restricted shares are disapplied, and as a result any restrictions attaching to the shares are ignored when calculating their value on acquisition. The election is effected by an agreement between the employer and employee, in a format approved by HMRC. The election has to be made no later than 14 days after the acquisition of the shares, but it does not have to be submitted to HMRC. It is generally thought to be good practice to make the election, as in most cases if there is no intention to fall within the restricted shares legislation, nothing is lost my electing to disapply the provisions.

4.12.11 Share incentive plans

A share incentive plan (SIP) is a company established plan approved by HMRC, which provides either 'free shares' (where shares are allocated to employees without payment); and/or 'partnership shares' (where deductions are made from salaries to buy shares. Where there are 'partnership shares' it is also possible to have 'matching shares' (where shares are allotted to employees for free in proportion to their 'partnership shares'.

An approved SIP has to provide that only a qualified employee is eligible to participate. In order to qualify the employee has to have been employed by the company, or group if it is a group scheme, for a minimum period which cannot be longer than 18 months. There is also a requirement that all employees who meet the eligibility tests may participate, and must be invited to do so. For this reason it is thought to be of only limited use in a family company scenario and will not be covered in any further detail.

4.12.12 Employee shareholder shares

The Finance Act 2013 issued a new form of share incentive scheme, which is being referred to as employee shareholder shares.

For an individual to qualify for shares under this approved scheme they must enter into an agreement with the company and sacrifice some of their employment rights including:
- unfair dismissal rights (apart from the automatically unfair reasons, where dismissal is based on discriminatory grounds and in relation to health and safety); and
- rights to statutory redundancy pay.

Under the agreement the company must allot or issue fully paid up shares worth at least £2,000 to the individual, who does not pay for these shares. This value applies at the first day of the share issue, so if for example the minimum amount was being issued, they cannot be issued on two separate days. In determining whether the shares are worth the minimum amount, the shares have to be valued taking into account any restrictions, whether or not an election has been made under s 431 ITEPA 2003. The valuation also has to be market value by reference to the meaning in ss 272 and 273 TCGA 1992, which will mean applying any discounts for the size of the shareholding. In the case of smaller family companies, after applying a discount to reflect the number of shares being issued, it may be difficult to obtain the right balance between the nominal amount willing to be offered and this minimum value requirement.

As far as the employee is concerned, there will be no liability to income tax and NIC (nor employer's NIC) on the first £2,000 of value received, but the excess will be subject to a liability. Value for this purpose is based on the unrestricted value if a s 431 ITEPA election has been made.

When the employee comes to realise the shares, there is no capital gains tax to pay on the gain provided the total value (market value ignoring any restrictions) of qualifying shares immediately after acquisition is not greater than £50,000. Also the individual, and persons connected with them, must not have a material interest in the company or its parent, at the time of issue of the shares and in the preceding 12 months. A material interest is defined as a holding of 25% or more of the voting rights.

It is generally thought that the scheme will have only a narrow market for family companies. The advantages for the employee are limited when compared with what they are being asked to give up. Where there may be more scope for use will be with those senior employees who may be are, or are becoming, minority shareholders and are not family members.

4.12.13 Corporation tax

The company itself is likely to qualify for a corporation tax deduction when the option is exercised by its employees. Tax relief is given as a deduction from company profits of an amount equivalent to the benefit received by the option holder. This deduction can, in some circumstances, be quite substantial and will enhance the value of the family company when it is sold to a third party.

CHAPTER 5

EMPLOYING FAMILY MEMBERS

5.1 OVERVIEW

This chapter deals with issues arising from employing family members. The following chapter looks at the position of non-family employees working in a family firm. Both categories of employee are covered by the same employment law and identical tax rules. Commentators are clear that best family practice is for family and non-family employees to be treated alike. Why therefore treat family and non-family employees as distinct categories?

The main reason is that the situations of the two groups are systemically and structurally different. As a matter of family business theory they occupy different zones within the three-circle model.[1] As a result, whilst all employees are, in theory, equal under the law, different employment issues may be more relevant to family employees. Notwithstanding the theory that non-family and family employees should be treated alike, these structural pressures mean that, this ideal will often be unattainable in real family business life. The following chapter looks at some of the implications of this, both for the non-family employee and also the family business itself.

There are clear and positive benefits of employing family members. The family business can recruit knowledgeable employees who have grown up with a deep understanding of it. They are likely to be highly motivated and committed to its long-term success. The family have an opportunity to spend time working together to build something for the benefit of the wider family. Individual family members can make a lasting personal contribution to that success that will provide more personal satisfaction and is more likely to provide a better work life balance than an equivalent corporate career.

But there are equally clear and powerful negative factors relating to the employment of family members. On the part of the family member joining the business there may be a sense of entitlement that they are assuming their birth right. Conversely joining, or remaining with the family business out of a sense of obligation can be highly corrosive to both the individual and to family relationships. For the senior generation leaders the challenge is to steer an appropriate middle course; to avoid both favouritism and victimisation of family members. The ideal being that their employment in terms of salary, promotion, expectations of performance and treatment generally are neither too generous, nor too unfavourable when compared with non-family employees.

---

[1] Explained in detail in chapter 3 (Tools, Models and Theories).

The remuneration enjoyed by family member employees is a perennial source of tension in family businesses, which are partly owned by outsider family members not working in the business.[2] Especially so when the family business is struggling and unable to pay dividends to the outsiders, as in the *Saul D Harrison* case.

For non-family employees there will be a concern that their working lives, careers and promotion prospects will not be blighted by lazy, incompetent or family members appointed or promoted beyond their capability: in short nepotism.

One of the greatest challenges of a family business governance system is to promote a culture where the benefits of employing family members triumph over the negative. If the family business fails in this task it stands little chance of attracting and retaining talented non-family employees. The growth of the family business will be constricted to the size and capabilities of those within the family gene pool.

This chapter looks at some of the issues of structural and family business dynamics relating to the employment of family members. It also emphasises the role of the governance system in regulating family employment issues. In many ways this is the most important consideration. Once family members are examining their detailed legal rights something has gone wrong with the dynamics of family relationships.

There are a number of other areas where the family employment relationship creates a particular risk of legal claims. There are two separate factors that make this so. The first is the tendency of family firms to informality, particularly where the employment of family members is concerned. Informality is particularly characteristic of smaller family businesses but is by no means confined to them. The second is the perennial issue of family dynamics and the danger of family issues crossing the boundary from the family system and being played out within the business system in the context of the employment relationship, with the attendant risk of tribunal and other legal claims.[3]

The chapter is divided into three broad, but overlapping and linked parts:
- A discussion on family employment in the context of family business systems and dynamics (5.2–5.6).
- A broad outline of employment legislation. This is not intended to detain anyone with a working knowledge of employment law. Instead the aim is to provide some background and context for those who are not familiar with this increasingly complex and procedural subject. The bulk of this outline is in 5.7–5.12 but some issues are dealt with in context.[4]
- A discussion on some specific applications of employment law and procedure to family business situations towards the end of the chapter.

This chapter is followed by a (much shorter) chapter dealing with employment issues relating to non-family employees, especially senior non-family managers in family businesses. Of course the broad outline of employment legislation is generally applicable to their situation.

---

[2] This issue is considered in detail in chapters 11 (Ownership Overview) and 21 (Unfair Prejudice).
[3] The *Papier* case provides a graphic example of this and is discussed in detail towards the end of the chapter.
[4] For example the discussion on age discrimination, succession and retirement ages at 5.6.

5.2 FAMILY EMPLOYMENT TERMS AND THE FAMILY BUSINESS SYSTEM

In many ways the employment relationships of family members could be seen to be the fulcrum on which the family business system rests.

Adapting the model for the clash of family business systems it will be seen that most of the features previously identified[5] can be traced back to employment issues. For example, the link between the lifetime membership of the business family and the potential for this to translate into a 'jobs for life' mentality so far as family employees are concerned. This sharply contrasts with the requirements of the business for a continuing and acceptable level of performance.

Figure 5.1: Employment and systemic balance in the family business

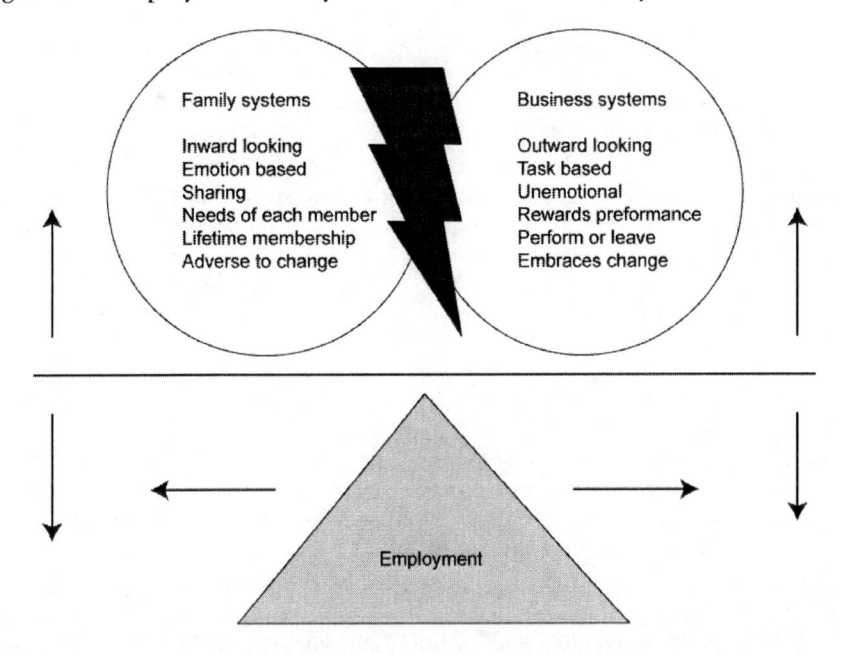

Family systems	Business systems
Inward looking	Outward looking
Emotion based	Task based
Sharing	Unemotional
Needs of each member	Rewards preformance
Lifetime membership	Perform or leave
Adverse to change	Embraces change

Employment

If the fulcrum of employment terms is moved too far in the direction of the family system the business system becomes weighed down by the operational inefficiencies created. Conversely if too much emphasis is placed on the needs of the business so that, for example family members are expected to work for below the market rates and to work long and unsociable hours as part of their family business bargain, family cohesion could well suffer.[6]

A similar case could be made for the importance of balance in employment terms so far as the relationship between business and ownership systems are concerned. If those terms are too favourable to the family employee, then resentment can build up within

---

[5] See Figure 3.7 and the discussion of family business systems theory in chapter 3.
[6] Consider the example of Eirian Davies and James Davies who both worked long hours for low pay on their respective family farms. These cases are discussed in detail in chapter 19 (Inheritance Disputes).

the ranks of the family outsiders.[7] But asking family members to invest too heavily in the business system, by working to unfavourable terms, inevitably puts strain on the ownership system, as was the case for James Davies.

In theory, achieving balance should be simple. Family business books are full of exhortations to treat family and non-family employees alike. It should be relatively easy to spot situations where family members are receiving preferential treatment. There are plenty of benchmarks and market comparators to aid this exercise. Certainly this book joins in advocating this best practice approach. But we are also realistic in accepting that this ideal may well be hard to achieve against the backdrop of family dynamics.

So the ideal situation is achieving parity of employment between family and non-family employees right across the employment spectrum, from recruitment, to remuneration, to promotion, to performance evaluation and to discipline.

The worst situation must be when the family business leadership is blind to or refuses to acknowledge any actual inequalities in practice. If the reality of a particular family business situation is that, with a nod to George Orwell, 'family animals are more equal than others', it might be preferable to acknowledge this, if not explicitly, at least tacitly.[8]

It might then be possible to take some form of corrective action, through governance procedures or by bolstering the position of non-family employees. If all else fails the family business leadership can at least consciously lower their expectations of business performance and accept this as a consequence of being a family first or lifestyle business so far as family employment is concerned.

5.3 FAMILY EMPLOYMENT

Whilst there are clear benefits of employing family members, there are corresponding drawbacks and challenges. The advice from commentators is clear. Family employees should be treated just the same as any non-family employee[9] and that non-family employees should be made are aware of this policy.

In practice this might be considerably easier said than done. Logically employment is, at root, a pure business relationship. This best practice advice assumes that family employment issues can be confined fairly and squarely within the business system. The reality will be that the other systems present in the family business, both family and ownership have the potential to intrude and to create complexity and tension. The success, or otherwise, of the family in recognising, containing and dealing with these forces can be the difference between harmonious employment relationships, both family and non-family, and with that, a thriving family business, or the opposite.

This tension has a number of symptoms. The most obvious is nepotism.[10] Here the influence of the family system on the employment relationship in the business system is obvious. Slightly less obvious, but usually fairly readily apparent when subjected to the

---

[7] See for example the case of *Samuel Weller* and the other excessive remuneration cases discussed in chapter 21.
[8] The issue of a family fast track is discussed in chapter 6.
[9] See for example John Ward *Perpetuating the Family Business; 50 Lessons Learned from Long-Standing Successful Families in Business* (Palgrave 2004) Lesson 4 (Principle of Merit).
[10] Explored in chapter 2 (Themes).

analysis of the three-circle model, is the capacity of employment issues to flow backwards and to permeate the barriers between the family and ownership systems and to pollute the purity of the arm's length employment principle.

Particularly in early stage and small family businesses the business and ownership systems become irretrievably linked when family members are underpaid and/or overworked. This level of commitment might simply be expected as a condition of family membership. Alternatively the commitment could be justified on the basis of eventual ownership expectation: 'one day all this will be yours'. The farming industry, further complicated in many cases by low profitability, is a classic example of this phenomenon, which is manifested in the stream of proprietary estoppel claims discussed in chapter 19. Less dramatically this can mean that this person feels undervalued and not appreciated.

Ultimately this can lead to a very able family member, who perhaps could have one day become the management successor, leaving the business. Arguably this is as damaging to the family business (although perhaps not family relationships) as a full-blown proprietary estoppel claim.

The growth in size and profitability of the family firm also carries with it the potential for the confusion between the family business systems through the medium of the employment relationship.

The most frequent area of tension is remuneration. This is discussed in detail in 5.5 below. However, the whole basis of family employment is a key topic for family business governance.

5.4 GOVERNANCE AND FAMILY EMPLOYMENT POLICIES

It is usual practice for the family charter to document the policy of the family in relation to employing family members.[11] Often this will be in response to the realisation that the family business cannot provide employment opportunities for every member of the next generation of an expanding family. Equally the family business may have reached a stage of sophistication such that its needs cannot be met by the skill set of the family members alone and the family believe that their commitment to full professionalisation needs to be reflected in the family charter.[12]

Ideally the approach taken to family employment in the governance system will help with achieving the crucial balance between allowing the values and vision of the business owning family to survive and thrive, leveraging the loyalty, knowledge and commitment of individual family members, whilst protecting the business from negative effects of over-reliance on family management.[13] Often the family charter will begin and end with

---

[11] See chapter 17 for a general discussion on family business governance, including family charters. Employment policies and family charters are considered in 17.5.
[12] See for example John Ward *Perpetuating the Family Business; 50 Lessons Learned from Long-Standing Successful Families in Business* (Palgrave 2004) Lesson 16 (Selective Family Employment), where Ward argues, that to make room for good non-family employees who are necessary to fuel the growth of the family firm, only the most talented and capable family members should be given jobs.
[13] See chapter 7 for a more detailed discussion on practical aspects of recruitment and promotion of family members.

general statements that family members have no automatic right to employment in the family business and that recruitment will be based on merit.

Sometimes the enthusiasm of the family to be seen to do the best thing by the business will cause the language of the charter to over-reach the true intentions of the family so far as employment of family members is concerned. Phrases may appear in the charter such as 'family members will be only considered for employment if they are the best qualified person for the position concerned'. At first sight this appears a laudable and sensible principle. However is it really the intention of the family to reject adequately qualified family members for all positions in favour of marginally better external candidates? To what lengths should the business go to seek out the best qualified person in terms of salary offered and the robustness of their recruitment process? Must all positions be open to competitive external recruitment?

Sometimes discussion on family employment policies will be conducted against the background of recent difficulties caused by family members being employed in positions for which they were unsuitable. A perception may have arisen that one branch of the family have been unfairly favoured so far as employment opportunities are concerned. These factors may lead to more restrictive employment policies being included in the family charter. The most extreme we have seen is a rule that there should be a complete moratorium on the employment of family members and that management should rest exclusively in the hands of professionals. This was in a multi generation family business that had been blighted by poor relationships between working family members for two generations.

Equally there may be hopes and aspirations amongst family members that their own children will have employment opportunities within the family business. The family might in practice wish to encourage this as part of a general 'family first' policy. In this case a family charter that raises the bar to family employment too high would not reflect the true intentions of the family. The charter would soon lose its effectiveness as a guiding document to steer recruitment policies. At worst the disconnection between the reality of the employment policies and the rhetoric of the charter could itself be a cause for friction and discontent.

In practice family employment policies are one of the most sensitive and difficult areas to cover in any family charter. Accordingly there are many examples of these issues receiving detailed and extensive consideration with a correspondingly detailed output.[14] Whilst family employment policies might be painful to negotiate this is preferable to glossing over this difficult subject with anodyne language that does not do justice to the real intentions of the business owning family and the underlying issues.

Many of the details of family employment policies are also relevant to management succession planning and are considered in chapter 7. However the overlap is, or should be, by no means complete. One of the key issues for any family business to deal with is promotion of family members, especially to positions of leadership. To what extent is it legitimate for family members to explicitly, or implicitly be fast tracked for promotion and for the managing director's office to be reserved for a family member. This issue is considered in chapter 6, from the perspective of other senior, non-family managers and in chapter 7 as part of the management succession process.

---

[14] Sometimes family employment policies are set out in a separate document, rather than the main family charter.

5.5 FAMILY REMUNERATION

5.5.1 Remuneration and the early stage family firm

Arrangements to determine the remuneration of family members are a crucial family business governance consideration.

Frequently advisors concentrate on how the remuneration package for a family member can be structured, and how to make it tax efficient.[15] But the first question is how the remuneration is to be determined?

In early stage, founder led family businesses everything is usually very informal. The owner often takes whatever salary they want or need for their lifestyle, subject to there being adequate profits to support that level of payment. If there are inadequate profits then the owner may well take less than the market rate for the role they are performing to help the business through a difficult or development stage. Alternatively, there may be large dividends/bonuses taken at the end of the year when the profits have been determined, with these being decided in the light of the future needs of the business.

The owner is likely to expect the rest of the family working in the business to be equally flexible. The application of the national minimum wage to family employment is considered below.

5.5.2 Informality, the later stage family enterprise and conflict

It is easy as the family business evolves from this early stage, into a fully-fledged family business, employing a number of family members, to continue this same informal and unstructured approach to remuneration and rewards. This can lead to tension between family members, the work force and key employees. The tension can take many forms.

- First, simple excessive remuneration being paid to the family insiders working in the family business. This can be the business leader, the next generation or other family members. On one analysis anything above market rate remuneration could be seen to be an ownership premium and therefore more properly distributed through dividends to the ownership group, including family outsiders.
- Salary paid to a spouse who makes little or no real contribution to the business. The spouse might previously have worked in the business but gradually withdrawn. The salary could be a pure (and questionable) tax-planning device.
- All family members being paid the same, regardless of what they contribute to the family business. This can occur because it is felt this will avoid the conflict of making a decision about what is an appropriate salary.
- More complex situations where the family business and its payroll is being used to consciously subsidise the family system.
  For example a son or daughter could be deliberately overpaid for the role they perform, because the parent 'wants to look after them' and to support their lifestyle, perhaps to allow for the private education of children/grandchildren.
  More extreme examples are often found of family members on the payroll of a family business, when the reality is that they do little, if any real work. Here remuneration is used to look after family members who are not actively involved

---
[15] Briefly discussed in chapter 4.

in the business. Perhaps this is because the controlling family member feels they should be looked after perhaps because the family member concerned is in need or has limited financial resources.

In complex situations remuneration can be used as a carrot, or stick, to obtain the desired action from a family member. For example that continuing pay from the family company is conditional on attending some form of rehabilitation for substance abuse, or less dramatically participation in family activities.

It might simply be that the family business leader believes that family fairness dictates that all family members should share equally in the success of the family business. We certainly know of examples where business leaders have arranged for their adult children who are not working in the family business to receive identical remuneration to those devoting their working life to the family firm.

Leaving aside the tax implications, such arrangements can affect the equilibrium of the family business system. The implications are many and varied but, depending on the precise circumstances these can include issues, such as:

- Resentment by outsiders. Excessive remuneration of insiders can be the source of significant family disputes and eventually finding their way to court.[16]
  A family member, who is a shareholder but not an employee, could feel that those family members employed are rewarded for more than they contribute to the business, because they do work in the business and this is at the expense of the dividend return. The non-employed shareholding family members may be unable to influence the dividend policy.[17]

- Resentment by family insiders. The capacity for resentment on the part of working insiders, who feel that they are working hard to subsidise the life style of other family members is obvious.

- Resentment amongst key employees. They see a person they suspect is overpaid, or who they believe does not make a full contribution to the business, or who has been over promoted simply because they are a family member. This can lead to the non-family executive feeling correspondingly under-valued and that they will not have the opportunities to progress, because key positions will be retained for the family. Ultimately competent employees (including in extreme circumstances good family performers) may choose to leave, so the family firm has to fall back on weaker family management.

- Relationships can also break down between the family business leadership and the non-working outsider, who has been treated as an employee. Ascertaining their true employment position and corresponding rights can be complicated and this complexity is in turn capable of adding to the family tensions and conflict.

- The informality might have been allowed to continue up until the death of the senior generation, giving rise to potential claims against not only the family company but also the estate of the business leader.[18]

---

[16] This was at the heart of the leading unfair prejudice case of *Saul D Harrison*. This and various examples of other excessive remuneration cases are discussed in chapter 21.
[17] The position of family outsiders in relation to dividend is considered in chapter 21 (Unfair Prejudice).
[18] Inheritance Act claims are discussed in chapter 19.

5.5.3 Systems, boundaries and governance

As suggested above, applying a three-circle model analysis, the position is clear. All of the above situations can be attributed to confusion between the business, family and ownership circles. The boundary between these has become blurred.

The remedy is equally clear. At least in theory. All of these problems can be avoided by restoring the boundary around the business system and by treating family employment issues, to the maximum extent possible, as purely business matters. This involves identifying any family or ownership influences on remuneration and other employment matters and disregarding these as extraneous considerations. There should be a separation between reward for employment and ownership. So non-working family members and lifestyle should be catered for through dividends not remuneration.[19]

5.5.4 Market rate remuneration

A family member needs to be paid a market rate for the role they perform within the business. This means assessing the role performed by the family employee, comparing the salary with the rates paid to other employees, and also with market rates. Considerations include the market in which the company operates, the size of the company, rates paid to people in similar positions, the level of responsibility and the contribution of the individual to the company's performance.

In addition to these quantitative criteria, qualitative aspects of the role may also be relevant such as leadership abilities, an understanding of the bigger picture as far as the business is concerned, the extent to which the relevant family member promotes the business in the local community and their relationship with key third parties who deal with the business.

It is common in well run businesses with a motivated workforce, to have a performance appraisal system.[20] Partly this is designed to assess the above factors.

5.5.5 Remuneration and governance

The degree of formality required in relation to remuneration will depend on various factors. These include the development stage of the family business. Later stage large cousin consortia, with a large number of family outsiders will need to invest in more formal procedures and policies, documented in family charters. If trust is low and family dynamic poor legally binding arrangements on pay restraint might be needed.[21]

There should be an open discussion and communication of the principles which are adopted in determining the remuneration levels amongst both the family and key employees. This will also make it clear to those family members thinking about joining the business, how their pay will be determined, and that they cannot expect any preference because they are part of the family.

---

[19] Dividend policies are explored in chapter 11 (Ownership Overview) and tax planning aspects of remuneration planning in chapter 4 (Tax Basics and the Family Business Structure).
[20] Discussed in chapter 7 as part of the management succession process.
[21] So for example insider pay rises might be pegged to inflation, or objective business performance targets, unless outsiders agree to higher amounts being paid.

Remuneration committees are an important feature of quoted company corporate governance. They can be useful in enhancing the level of objectivity in determining remuneration levels. Remuneration committees also have a role to play in larger family enterprises. Serving on this committee can be a useful part of the role of the non-executive director. Family directors will often also participate. Sometimes consultation with the family council is involved. The basic idea is to increase the objectivity the remuneration setting process and to reduce the potential for this to be unduly influenced by family dynamics. The committee should also, ideally, consider the salaries of at least all the key non-family employees. This will confirm to everyone that there is an objective approach being adopted.

In the interests of transparency the decision process should be communicated to the outsider family shareholders.

5.6 LETTING GO AND COMPULSORY RETIREMENT AGES

Many family business commentators[22] recommend a compulsory retirement age for all employees, and especially senior generation family business leaders. The reluctance of the senior generation to let go of control of the family business is a recurrent theme in this book.[23] A commitment by the senior generation to step aside at a set and pre-agreed time is therefore seen as a key component of any family constitution. Of course one of the key advantages of the family business format is flexibility. This could be compromised by set retirement dates. But the corresponding uncertainty is potentially more dangerous for the family business and for family relationships.

Would such a provision contravene age discrimination legislation, which, broadly put, frowns on compulsory retirement provisions? This is a risk, but there is case-law to the effect that such provisions might be justified if the retirement age is a proportionate means of achieving a legitimate business aim. In the case concerned factors identified were succession planning, promotion opportunities for younger members of the business, and maintaining a collegiate workplace by avoiding performance management of older workers. The relevant case[24] concerned retirement of senior partners in a law firm. Given the wealth of literature on the damage caused to family firms by the senior generation refusing to let go,[25] it is suggested that such arguments are more powerful in the context of a family business. This damage can be to the business, including failure to adapt and modernise,[26] and to the careers of both family and non-family employees. Ultimately this can lead to a loss of key management thus compounding the business risk.

Various factors may mean that in practice a compulsory retirement age may be binding in honour only so far as the senior generation are concerned. The retirement age might only be specified in a non-legally binding family charter. If the set retirement age has been translated into formal legally binding employment agreements the senior generation family member could well still hold a controlling interest in the family business, as it is less likely that ownership will have passed before management control.

---

[22] See, for example John Ward *Perpetuating the Family Business; 50 Lessons Learned from Long-Standing Successful Families in Business* (Palgrave 2004) Lesson 2 (Irrevocable Retirement).
[23] Explored in detail in chapter 2 (Themes).
[24] *Seldon v Clarkson Wright and Jakes* [2012] UKEAT 0434/13.
[25] A prime example being the Ford motor company.
[26] A factor in both Fords and in *Saul D Harrison*.

Even if other family members control the family company and were in a position to enforce the compulsory retirement provisions, it would need exceptional circumstances[27] to persuade them to do so against the wishes of the senior generation family members, possibly their parents who founded the business.

Nevertheless, set retirement ages, even if in practical terms these fall short of compulsory retirement provisions, remain valuable family business governance and succession planning tools. They provide clear evidence of the intentions of the family. They are a key part of management succession planning.[28]

5.7 EMPLOYMENT LAW AND EMPLOYMENT CLAIMS

On comparatively rare occasions employment issues relating to family employees spill over into legal confrontation. More by way of highlighting the potential risk areas, we will quickly summarise the main areas of potential employment claims.[29]

Whilst the family relationships are intact the possibility of employment claims will not present any real problem. But once those relationships fall apart it is by no means uncommon for claims to surface.

Given the complexity of family business life it is fairly common, once family relationships have deteriorated badly, for employment claims to arise. These will often exist alongside other, potentially more lucrative claims relating to ownership. Even though there have been recent changes to employment tribunal procedures, including the introduction of fees, employment claims can often be more straightforward and cheaper for a family employee to bring than ownership based claims. So employment claims can sometimes be used, typically by a next generation family employee, who finds themselves outside the family pale, to score an early win and to build a fighting fund, at the expense of the family business, to finance these more complex claims.

The next few paragraphs are devoted to providing a basic overview of the main areas of employment law and relevant claims, loosely discussed in the context of family business situations.

5.8 UNFAIR DISMISSAL

5.8.1 Overview

Protections against unfair dismissal have been around for approaching five decades and are now contained in the Employment Rights Act 1996 (ERA 1996). Only employees can claim unfair dismissal[30] and, save for some limited exceptions (referred to below), they must have 2 years continuous service in order to bring a claim.

---

[27] Such as in *Re Harmer* discussed in chapter 21.
[28] We return to the subject of compulsory retirement ages in chapter 7.
[29] For a more general guide to employment law see *Tolley's Employment Handbook* (30th edition, 2016).
[30] The implications of informal employment practices in relation to family members are considered below at 5.19.

If a qualifying employee is dismissed then an employer will be vulnerable to a claim for unfair dismissal unless:

- it can show a potentially fair reason for the dismissal;[31] and
- the employer acted reasonably in treating that reason as sufficient to justify dismissal.[32] Treating an employee fairly has been taken by the tribunal to mean that the dismissal was both procedurally and substantively fair.[33]

There are some instances where a dismissal will be automatically unfair with no need for a qualifying period. For example to dismiss an employee for refusing to work longer than the prescribed limits on working time set out in the Working Time Regulations (WTR 1998)[34] or to dismiss an employee for enforcing their right to the national minimum wage.

5.8.2 Dismissal and constructive dismissal

In order to bring a claim for unfair dismissal, an employee must have been dismissed. A dismissal will occur if the employer terminates the employment, either summarily or on notice, or the employer does not renew a fixed term contract on the expiry of that fixed term.

A dismissal will also occur if an employee resigns (with or without notice) and can establish that they were constructively dismissed. In order to show constructive dismissal an employee must establish that there was a fundamental (or 'repudiatory') breach of contract by the employer and that the employee resigned promptly because of that breach.

The rough and tumble of family dynamics leads to a tendency, on occasions, for family members to behave differently and worse towards one another, when compared with non-family employees. Arguably this makes family businesses vulnerable to constructive dismissal claims. At least in theory. Employees need to resign in response to the breach of contract and to do so without unreasonable delay. Quite often family members will simply put up with the situation (at least until some cataclysmic event occurs).

More obviously the relevant behaviour will consist of outbursts, shouting, swearing, abuse[35] and, on occasions, physical violence.[36] Less obvious is the situation where relations between family members are so poor and communication so stymied that the normal interaction necessary for a functioning employment relationship is absent. The 'last straw' doctrine is relevant to constructive dismissal cases. This is where an employee resigns in response to series of less serious breaches, which when taken cumulatively, amount to a fundamental breach.

In the *Bunning* case[37] Suzanne Bunning was employed as a welder in a third generation family agricultural machinery manufacturing business. When she discovered that she

---

[31] Section 98(1) and (2) of the ERA 1996.
[32] Section 98(4) of the ERA 1996.
[33] See 'Reasonableness of Dismissal' at 5.8.4 below.
[34] Working Time Regulations 1998, SI 1998/1833.
[35] As in the case of *Papier v (1) Formara Print Ltd (2) Phoenix Offset Ltd (3) Steven Ball* discussed in detail below.
[36] As in the Eirian Davies case discussed in chapter 19.
[37] *Suzanne Bunning v GT Bunning & Sons Ltd* [2005] EWCA Civ 983.

was pregnant she was convinced she needed to change to a less hazardous working environment. Initially she enlisted the support of her father, one of three sibling directors. Her father felt unable to make a decision in relation to his own daughter without the support of the other directors, so Suzanne spoke to her aunt the following day in the office. The aunt in turn involved a firm of health and safety consultants, who made a 'superficially and cursory' risk assessment. This resulted in a letter to Suzanne from her uncle in an 'inappropriately formal tone', telling her that 'there is no reason why you should not continue to do the type of welding work which you are already employed to do'.[38]

A stand off resulted. Suzanne did not turn up for work. About three weeks later the family directors had a change of heart and offered Suzanne a job in the factory stores, again following a cursory risk assessment. She accepted this changed role. Tragically Suzanne suffered a miscarriage, which she blamed on her treatment by the family. She wrote to the directors asking for a meeting and to be paid in full (strictly her entitlement was to statutory sick pay only) whilst she was off work following the miscarriage. When the family directors failed to respond in accordance within the tight deadlines Suzanne had set, she resigned claiming constructive dismissal.

The employment tribunal, Employment Appeal Tribunal and Court of Appeal all agreed that, in accepting the job in the stores, Suzanne had waived any initial breach by the family company and also that she had been premature in treating the failure to respond to her letter as a further breach. She had not been constructively dismissed.[39]

5.8.3 Reason for dismissal

There are five potentially fair reasons for dismissal. These are conduct, capability, redundancy, breach of statutory restriction and 'some other substantial reason'.[40]

The conduct reason will relate to any misconduct on the part of the employee, whether it be a single act of gross misconduct, such as an act of violence or a series of less serious offences, such as repeated poor attendance. The capability ground relates to the employee's qualifications or their ability to do the job. Redundancy situations will arise where the employee's dismissal is:[41]

> 'wholly or mainly attributable to ... the employer either ceasing or intending to cease to carry on the business for the purposes of which the employee was employed by it; ceasing or intending to cease to carry on that business in the place where the employee was so employed or having a reduced requirement for employees to carry out work of a particular kind or to carry out work of a particular kind at the place where the employee was employed to work.'

A breach of statutory restriction reason may justify a fair dismissal, if the continued employment of the individual would contravene any duty or restriction imposed by or under any enactment, for example if an employee lost their driving licence but needed to drive to do their job.

---

[38] See paras 6, 7 and 8 of the Court of Appeal judgment.
[39] She had nevertheless been treated unfavourably as a result of her pregnancy, which amounted to direct discrimination. See below.
[40] Section 98(1) and (2) of the ERA 1996.
[41] Section 139 of the ERA 1996.

There is no further statutory guidance on what is meant by the term 'some other substantial reason' (SOSR), but it is designed to catch potentially fair dismissals which do not fall within the definition of any of the other potentially fair reasons. To establish SOSR as a reason for dismissal it is only necessary to show that the reason could justify dismissal, not that it actually did.[42] Common examples of SOSR dismissals are business reorganisations or a failure by the employee to accept a change to their terms and conditions (following due consultation).

Until 6 April 2011 retirement was also a potentially fair reason but this ceased when the default retirement age was abolished.

5.8.4 Reasonableness of the dismissal

Once an employer has established a potentially fair reason for dismissing the employee[43] it is then for the tribunal to decide if the employer acted reasonably in dismissing the employee for that reason. The test for reasonableness is set out at s 98(4) of the ERA 1996:

> ... the determination of the question whether the dismissal is fair or unfair (having regard to the reason shown by the employer) -
>
> (a) depends on whether in the circumstances (including the size and administrative resources of the employer's undertaking) the employer acted reasonably or unreasonably in treating it as a sufficient reason for dismissing the employee, and
> (b) shall be determined in accordance with equity and the substantial merits of the case.

This test is an objective one. It is for the tribunal to decide whether the employer's decision to dismiss fell within the range of reasonable responses that a reasonable employer could adopt.[44] The important point to note is that the tribunal does not necessarily have to agree with the employer's decision to dismiss, only that the decision was within the range of reasonable responses open to that employer.

5.8.5 Fair dismissal procedure

In order to dismiss an employee fairly, an employer has to follow a fair procedure. What amounts to a fair procedure will vary depending upon the reason for the dismissal. When dismissing an employee on the grounds of conduct or performance, a fair procedure will include following the ACAS Code.[45]

The case of *Polkey v AE Dayton Services Ltd*[46] established the principle that when a dismissal is procedurally unfair, the tribunal can reduce the amount of compensation, to reflect the chance that there would have been a fair dismissal if a fair procedure had been followed. This reduction is known as a Polkey deduction. The deduction can be substantial, in some cases up to 100%.

---

[42] *Willow Oak Developments Ltd v Silverwood* [2006] IRLR 607.
[43] Under s 98(1) ERA 1996.
[44] *Iceland Frozen Foods Ltd v Jones* [1982] IRLR 439.
[45] ACAS *Code of Practice on Disciplinary and Grievance Procedures* (March 2015).
[46] [1987] IRLR 503 (HL).

Procedurally unfair dismissals potentially represent the biggest Achilles' heel for family owned businesses. The tendency of family firms, particularly early stage, entrepreneurial businesses, to shun procedures and bureaucracy is noted many times in this book. There are countless examples where family owned firms have fallen foul of procedural fairness so far as the dismissal of non-family employees is concerned. The tension between the formality required by the employment relationship and the informality of family business life is considered in detail below.

5.8.6 Remedies for unfair dismissal

If an employee is found to be unfairly dismissed then the tribunal may make any of the following awards:

- reinstatement;
- re-engagement;
- compensation.

Although the tribunal can order the employer to re-engage or reinstate the employee this remedy is only awarded in a small minority of cases. Most often the tribunal will award compensation.

The compensation consists of two awards: the basic award and the compensatory award. The basic award is calculated in a similar way to a statutory redundancy payment and is based on a formula that takes account of age, length of service and the amount of a week's pay (which is capped at a statutory maximum).[47]

The tribunal may then go on to award a compensatory award under s 118 of the ERA 1996. The objective of a compensatory award is 'to compensate, and compensate fully, but not to award a bonus'.[48] There is no prescribed formula for the compensatory award, but s 123 of the ERA 1996 provides that the award shall be:

> 'such amount as the Tribunal considers just and equitable in all the circumstances having regard to the loss sustained by the complainant in consequence of the dismissal insofar as that loss is attributable to action taken by the employer.'

This gives considerable scope to the tribunal when making a compensatory award but the sum awarded cannot be arbitrary.

There is a maximum that can be awarded for the basic award, which under the formula is 30 weeks' pay and the employee's weekly pay is subject to the statutory maximum referred to above. The compensatory award is also subject to a statutory cap.[49] This means total compensation for an unfair dismissal is usually capped. However, there are some unfair dismissal claims, such as a dismissal for whistleblowing or for raising health and safety concerns, for which compensation is uncapped.

In contrast there is usually no cap on awards for successful discrimination claims and an individual will be compensated both for financial loss (for example lost earnings) and

---

[47] £479 per week from 6 April 2016 to 5 April 2017: s 227 of the ERA 1996.
[48] *Norton Tool v Tewson* [1972] ICT 501.
[49] Since 29 July 2013 the maximum compensatory award is the lower of the statutory cap (£78,962 for the period 6 April 2015 to 5 April 2017) or 52 weeks' pay (which is actual gross weekly pay).

non-financial loss, notably injury to feelings. In determining how much to award an individual for their injured feelings a tribunal will have reference to specific guidelines, known as the Vento guidelines.[50]

5.9 THE LAW ON DISCRIMINATION

The law on discrimination was consolidated by the Equality Act 2010 (EA 2010), which sets out nine protected characteristics in relation to which discrimination and harassment are prohibited in varying degrees. The protected characteristics are age, disability, gender reassignment, marriage and civil partnership, pregnancy and maternity, race, religion or belief, sex and sexual orientation.[51]

The EA 2010 contains several types of discrimination and unlawful conduct that apply to most and sometimes all of the protected characteristics: direct discrimination, indirect discrimination, harassment, victimisation, and instructing, causing, inducing and aiding discrimination. There are also two additional types of discrimination that apply in the case of disability discrimination. These are discrimination arising from disability and failure to make reasonable adjustments.

5.9.1 Direct discrimination

Direct discrimination occurs where, **because of** a protected characteristic, A treats B less favourably than A treats or would treat others who do not share the protected characteristic.[52] The comparator to test how others are or would be treated can be a real or hypothetical person. Direct discrimination cannot be objectively justified except in the case of age. In such a case the burden of proof will be on the employer to prove that the discrimination was justified.

This can include less favourable treatment of a person because they are associated with a person who has a protected characteristic (except for marriage or civil partnership). For example, a claim of disability discrimination could be brought by a mother of a disabled child, because of less favourable treatment she has received as a result of being the mother of a disabled child.

Direct discrimination also includes less favourable treatment because A perceives B to have a protected characteristic (except for marriage or civil partnership) even if B does not actually have that characteristic. For example if an employee of Asian origin had been discriminated against by someone who wrongly believed that they were Muslim they would be entitled to bring a claim for religious discrimination on the basis of that conduct.

5.9.2 Indirect discrimination

Indirect discrimination occurs through acts or decisions which are not intended to treat any group less favourably, but have in practice the effect of disproportionately

---

[50] *Vento v Chief Constable of West Yorkshire Police (No 2)* [2003] IRLR 102.
[51] Section 4 of the EA 2010.
[52] Section 13(1) of the EA 2010.

disadvantaging a group which share a particular protected characteristic. If this act or decision cannot be objectively justified then it may constitute indirect discrimination. The test set out in the EA 2010 is:

- A (normally the employer) applies to B (normally the employee) a provision, criterion or practice (PCP);
- B has a protected characteristic;
- A also applies (or would apply) that PCP to persons who do not share B's protected characteristic;
- the PCP puts or would put persons with whom B shares the protected characteristic at a particular disadvantage compared to others;
- the PCP puts or would put B to that disadvantage;
- A cannot show the PCP to be a proportionate means of achieving a legitimate aim.

An example of possible indirect discrimination would be a requirement for all employees to work full time. Although this is not obviously discriminatory, this PCP could prove to be indirectly discriminatory on the grounds of sex as it may have a disparate impact on women, due to the fact that it is widely accepted that, on a statistical basis, women are more likely to have childcare commitments, which prevent them from working full time (although it is worth noting that changes in societal norms may make it increasingly difficult to prove a disparate impact in some industries and workplaces).

Indirect discrimination does not apply to the protected characteristics of pregnancy or maternity. Discrimination on these grounds will be covered by direct sex discrimination.

As in cases of direct age discrimination, the burden is on the employer to prove justification of the discrimination. In order to justify indirect discrimination it will be for the employer to show that the PCP was a proportionate means of achieving a legitimate aim. The term PCP has been construed widely and does not have to be a formal policy put in place by the employer.

5.9.3 Harassment

The EA 2010 sets out three types of harassment:[53]
(1) Unwanted behaviour relating to a relevant protected characteristic which has the purpose or effect of:
 (a) violating a person's dignity; or
 (b) creating for that person an intimidating, hostile, degrading, humiliating or offensive environment for that person.
(2) Unwanted conduct of a sexual nature which has the effect of creating for that person an intimidating, hostile, degrading, humiliating or offensive environment.
(3) Less favourable treatment because an employee submits to or rejects sexual harassment related to sex or gender reassignment.

Marriage and civil partnership, and pregnancy and maternity are not relevant protected characteristics for the purpose of harassment, however they may be protected by

---

[53] Section 26 of the EA 2010.

different types of discrimination legislation. The unwanted behaviour does not have to be specifically aimed at the person who finds that it violates their dignity and a one off incident may amount to harassment.

When considering whether behaviour amounts to harassment the tribunal will consider whether it was reasonable for the conduct complained of to have that effect. As with direct discrimination a person may be harassed on the grounds of being perceived to have a protected characteristic.

5.9.4 Victimisation

Victimisation occurs where an employee is subjected to a detriment as a result of having done (or the employer believing the employee has done) a 'protected act'. A protected act is:

(1) Bringing proceedings under the EA 2010.
(2) Giving evidence or information in connection with proceedings under the EA 2010, regardless of who brought those proceedings.
(3) Doing any other thing for the purposes of or in connection with the EA 2010.
(4) Alleging (whether expressly or otherwise) that the respondent or another person has contravened the EA 2010.

However, giving false evidence or information, or making a false allegation, will not be a protected act if done in bad faith.

5.9.5 Instructing, causing, inducing or knowingly helping unlawful acts

Under the EA 2010, A must not:
- Instruct B to do in relation to C anything that contravenes the EA 2010.
- Cause B to do in relation to C anything that contravenes the EA 2010.
- Induce B, directly or indirectly, to do in relation to C anything that contravenes the EA 2010.

For this to apply, the relationship between A and B must be one in which discrimination, harassment or victimisation is prohibited, such as an employment relationship or other relationships governed by the EA 2010. For example, a line manager giving an instruction to a more junior employee.

A must not knowingly help B to do anything that contravenes the EA 2010. For example, one employee providing information to another employee that allows that employee to discriminate.

5.9.6 Disability discrimination

As mentioned above, there are two types of discrimination claim that only apply to disability discrimination. Unlike other protected characteristics, in order to pursue a claim of disability discrimination, an individual needs to establish they have the protected characteristic, ie that they are disabled within the meaning of the EA 2010.

The test is that the person suffers from a physical or mental impairment that has a substantial and adverse impact on their ability to carry out normal day to day activities.

That impairment must have lasted, or be likely to last for a period of 12 months. There are some impairments, such as cancer, that will automatically qualify for protection. Conversely, there are other conditions, such as addiction to alcohol that are specifically excluded (although disabilities arising from excluded conditions may be covered).

It is for ultimately for the tribunal to decide whether an individual is disabled within the meaning of the EA 2010 but in arriving at their decision they will usually have reference to medical and witness evidence.

5.9.7 Discrimination arising from disability

Under s 15(1) of the EA 2010, 'discrimination arising from disability' occurs where both:
(1) A treats B unfavourably because of something arising in consequence of B's disability.
(2) A cannot show that the treatment is a proportionate means of achieving a legitimate aim.

For example, if an employee's visual impairment means that he cannot work as quickly as colleagues, and his employer dismisses him because of his low output, this dismissal will be discrimination arising from disability unless it is objectively justified.

5.9.8 Failure to make reasonable adjustments

The EA 2010 imposes a duty on employers to make reasonable adjustments to help disabled job applicants, employees and former employees in certain circumstances.

The duty can arise where a disabled person is placed at a substantial disadvantage by:
(1) An employer's provision, criterion or practice (PCP).
(2) A physical feature of the employer's premises.
(3) An employer's failure to provide an auxiliary aid.

However, an employer will not be obliged to make reasonable adjustments unless it knows or ought reasonably to know that the individual in question is disabled and likely to be placed at a substantial disadvantage because of their disability.

The EHRC Employment Statutory Code of Practice (the EHRC Code), which tribunals must take into account if it appears relevant, contains a non-exhaustive list of potential adjustments that employers might be required to make. Adjustments might include adjustments to premises, adjusting working hours or providing a specific piece of equipment.

It is for an employment tribunal to objectively determine whether a particular adjustment would have been reasonable to make in the circumstances. It will take into account matters such as whether the adjustment would have ameliorated the disabled person's disadvantage, the cost of the adjustment in the light of the employer's financial resources, and the disruption that the adjustment would have had on the employer's activities.

5.10 INFORMALITY AND FAMILY BUSINESS EMPLOYMENT PRACTICE

As a general proposition family firms are often much more informal in their approach to employment matters and to have less developed HR systems and procedures than their non-family counterparts.[54] Whilst this approach can sometimes extend right across the employment spectrum, covering family and non-family employees alike, observation from practice suggests that it is more likely that the engagement of family members will be undertaken much more casually.

The relationship between employer and employee is heavily regulated, not only through common law (ie the oral or written contract of employment between the parties and the law of tort) but also statute law, regulations and (at least for the time being) European Law as summarised above.

Ensuring compliance with all different sources of employment law can be a daunting task for any business, but can be more problematical for the family business, especially in relation to family employees. This can often be down to the difficulties the parties have in divorcing the emotional side of the relationship from the professional side. Typically the informality of the family relationship is allowed to carry through into the working relationship with both parties often choosing to 'turn a blind eye' to their respective legal obligations. When relations sour this frequently results in the employee seeking to formalise the relationship and enforcing their legal rights against their family employer.

Frequently family employees will not have been issued with or asked to sign employment documents, whether simple statements of the main terms of employment, issued under ERA 1996, s 1, or full blown executive service agreements, containing detailed provisions to protect the family business including post employment restrictions on competition, use of confidential information and ownership of intellectual property rights relating to their employment. This is often so, even for large and fairly sophisticated family businesses. The appropriate paperwork might be in place for non-family employees. But somehow the need for this has been overlooked so far as family members are concerned.

Some potential consequences of this informality are examined in the next few paragraphs.

5.11 FAMILY MEMBERS AND EMPLOYMENT STATUS

Sometimes the level of informality is such as to cast doubt on the employment status of the family member concerned.

---

[54] See W Gibb Dyer Jr 'Integrating Professional Management into a Family Owned Business' *Family Business Review* (1989) Vol 3 at pp 221–235.

Employment law recognises a number of different categories of worker. It is important to identify the correct category into which an individual fits, as this will affect the statutory and common law rights available to them. Unfortunately, determining the status of an individual is not necessarily an easy process. There is no clearly defined checklist which allows an employer to definitively determine an individual's status. Broadly speaking, individuals fall into one of three categories: employees, workers and self-employed, although other more specialised classifications do exist.

5.11.1 Employees

The broadest scope of legal protection is available to 'employees'. For example employees have the right not to be unfairly dismissed whereas workers and the self-employed do not. Under s 230 of the ERA 1996 an employee is defined as:

> 'an individual who has entered into or works under (or, where the employment has ceased, worked under) a contract of employment.'

The starting point, then, in identifying whether a family member is an employee is to look at the contract they work under. Importantly however, the courts will look at the substance of the relationship, rather than the labels that the parties have attached to it.

The legal test for identifying a contract of employment was originally set out in *Ready Mix Concrete (South East) Limited v the Minister of Pensions and National Insurance*.[55] The key elements are:

- personal service – generally speaking an employee cannot provide a substitute to do their work;
- mutuality of obligation – the employee must be required to carry out their work and the employer must be required to pay their salary;
- control – an employer is generally required to control the activities of the employee; and
- the other elements of the contract must be consistent with it being a contract of employment.

There is a large body of case-law dealing with these factors, and how they interact with each other in determining employment status. The courts and employment tribunals will look at each case on its own facts.

It will be seen that in family faux employment situations the reality of the position could be that one or more of these elements might be absent. There might be no real requirement or expectation that the family member concerned actually carries out any work. This might be so even if they have been issued with an employment contract containing, on the face of it, the usual provisions one would expect to find in an employment situation.

Hybrid situations could prove the most problematic to categorise, for example, where a family member is on the face of it employed and remunerated as a full time employee, but in reality performs only occasional duties. The classic hybrid situation is where salary is paid to a spouse, who makes little or no real contribution to the business. Issues

---

[55] [1968] 2 QB 497, [1968] 2 WLR 775, [1968] 1 All ER 433.

can arise if the marriage breaks down, including employment claims from the spouse. Whether or not the spouse should be regarded as having real income is obviously a factor on divorce. However it should ultimately be possible to look at the overall reality of the situation and assess the means of both parties accordingly.

Putting the tax issues to one side[56] the precise employment status of the family member concerned, for example an adult child who receives an allowance through the business, may well not be too much of an issue when family relationships are sound. The case is otherwise if a dispute erupts. The family member might rely on the income. They will struggle if the family tap is turned off and with no clear means of redress. Their position could have been much better if they had been in receipt of regular dividends as an owner.

From the perspective of the family business, what might at root be a family dispute may nevertheless give rise to employment rights such as unfair dismissal or the right to a redundancy payment. It may be difficult for the family firm to resist such claims, on the basis that the family member claimant is not really a proper employee, if the family business leadership has initiated this fiction in the first place.

To state the problem at its lowest the uncertainty and bitterness associated with such claims or potential claims must make the underlying family conflict harder to resolve.

5.11.2 Workers

If an individual does not satisfy the test for being an employee, he or she may still be a 'worker'. This might be particularly relevant in smaller and early stage family businesses where family members are engaged to work on a casual basis, for example, in the agriculture, retail, hotel and leisure industries.

Section 230 of the ERA 1996 defines a worker as:

> an individual who has entered into or works under (or, where the employment has ceased, worked under):
>
> (a) a contract of employment, or
> (b) any other contract, whether express or implied and (if it is express) whether oral or in writing, whereby the individual undertakes to do or perform personally any work or services for another party to the contract whose status is not by virtue of the contract that of a client or customer of any profession or business undertaking carried on by the individual ...

This definition was considered by the Employment Appeal Tribunal in *Byrne Brothers (Formwork) Ltd v Baird and others*.[57] The EAT noted that the definition of worker is intended to lower the 'pass mark' so that individuals who do not pass the test for employee will qualify as workers.

It is clear from part (a) of the definition that all employees will also be workers. Part (b) goes on to widen the group of individuals who will qualify as workers to include those who perform personally any work or services for others. The genuinely self-employed are excluded from the definition.

---

[56] In particular the difficulty of claiming a full deduction from corporation tax for an expense that has, in reality not been wholly and necessarily incurred by the family business.
[57] [2002] ICR 667, [2002] IRLR 96.

The key to being a part (b) worker is personal service. As a result, an unfettered right in the contract to send a substitute and for that right to be actually exercised may mean that an individual does not qualify as a worker.

For practical purposes, the main differences between workers and employees is that workers do not benefit from the right not to be unfairly dismissed or the right to receive a statutory redundancy payment. Workers do, however, accrue annual leave and benefit from the national minimum wage. Both workers and employees are protected under discrimination law.

5.11.3 Self employed

It is also important to consider the category of self-employed in light of the above tests. An individual may not have the same status for all purposes. For example an individual may be treated by HMRC as self-employed for tax purposes. However an employment tribunal may still decide that the individual is an employee or a worker when determining eligibility for protection under employment legislation. This is an important consideration for businesses who may have consultants working for them who claim to be self-employed for tax purposes.

5.12 CONTRACT OF EMPLOYMENT

On a mundane level family businesses often fall at the first hurdle by failing to issue a written contract of employment to the family employee at the start of their employment. This may be an oversight, or because of an inherent reluctance to formalise the employment relationship. This might not cause any real problems when relationships are good but the lack of clarity can be problematic if they break down.

It is important to set out clearly in writing the parties' respective entitlements, duties and responsibilities. Failure to do so at the outset can lead to later disagreement and confusion about the terms of the employment relationship. This in turn can lead to the employee raising a grievance or even bringing a tribunal claim. If the employee wins a claim for unfair dismissal the tribunal can order the employer to make an additional payment for the lack of a contract. A lack of clarity in the contract about pay structures such as bonus schemes, for example, could lead to an employee claiming unlawful deduction of wages and/or breach of contract. In an extreme case, where there is no contractual documentation in place recording the individual's duties, for example, a fundamental disagreement about this could lead to a claim for constructive dismissal.

5.12.1 Section 1 statements

It is not only best practice to issue a contract of employment at the start of the relationship there is also a legal requirement to do so. Under s 1 of the ERA 1996 employers must provide all employees whose employment is to continue for more than one month with a written statement of certain basic terms of their employment.[58] This is often known as a 'written statement' and takes the form of a basic contract of

---

[58] The written statement must contain the following:
   (a) the names of the employer and employee,
   (b) the date when the employment began, and
   (c) the date on which the employee's period of continuous employment began (taking into account any

employment or letter to the employee. The written statement must be issued to the employee no later than 2 months after their employment begins.

If an employer fails to provide a s 1 statement, provides an inaccurate or incomplete statement or does not provide an employee with a statement of changes under s 4 of the ERA 1996, an employee may make a complaint to an employment tribunal while the employment continues or, if it has terminated, within 3 months of the date of termination. The 3-month period can be extended if the tribunal is satisfied that it was not reasonably practicable for the employee to present the application within that period.

Where the employee has a successful substantive claim, in addition to a declaration of particulars of employment, they may also be eligible for compensation if the tribunal finds that at the time that the claim was brought, the employer was in breach of its duties under s 1 or s 4 of the ERA 1996. The additional compensation will, unless there are exceptional circumstances, be 2 or 4 weeks' pay, subject to the statutory cap on a week's pay.[59]

5.12.2 Detailed contracts of employment

The above is only a minimum requirement and would form the basis of a contract of employment for a junior employee. If employing a family member in a senior role a more detailed contract of employment would be strongly advisable, covering issues such as intellectual property, restrictive covenants, confidentiality obligations and garden leave. A disgruntled family employee can be a dangerous commercial competitor. Again the family business world has a number of high profile examples where, following a dispute, a family member has left to set up in direct competition to the original family business.[60]

---

employment with a previous employer which counts towards that period).
(d) the scale or rate of remuneration or the method of calculating remuneration,
(e) the intervals at which remuneration is paid (that is, weekly, monthly or other specified intervals),
(f) any terms and conditions relating to hours of work (including any terms and conditions relating to normal working hours),
(g) entitlement to holidays, including public holidays, and holiday pay (the particulars given being sufficient to enable the employee's entitlement, including any entitlement to accrued holiday pay on the termination of employment, to be precisely calculated),
(h) incapacity for work due to sickness or injury, including any provision for sick pay, and
(i) pensions and pension schemes,
(j) the length of notice which the employee is obliged to give and entitled to receive to terminate his contract of employment,
(k) the title of the job which the employee is employed to do or a brief description of the work for which he is employed,
(l) where the employment is not intended to be permanent, the period for which it is expected to continue or, if it is for a fixed term, the date when it is to end,
(m) either the place of work or, where the employee is required or permitted to work at various places, an indication of that and of the address of the employer,
(n) any collective agreements which directly affect the terms and conditions of the employment including, where the employer is not a party, the persons by whom they were made, and
(o) where the employee is required to work outside the United Kingdom for a period of more than one month – (i) the period for which he is to work outside the United Kingdom, (ii) the currency in which remuneration is to be paid while he is working outside the United Kingdom, (iii) any additional remuneration payable to him, and any benefits to be provided to or in respect of him, by reason of his being required to work outside the United Kingdom, and (iv) any terms and conditions relating to his return to the United Kingdom.

[59] Which is currently £479 from 6 April 2016 to 5 April 2017.
[60] One of the most high profile examples is the dispute in the Dassler family in Germany. Conflict between Adolf (Adi) Dassler and his brother Rudolph (Rudi) led to the separation of the initial family sports shoe

Of course fair competition cannot be prevented. Over restrictive provisions against competition will not be enforced by the courts, as a matter of public policy, as being restraints of trade. But proportionate and reasonable provisions, designed to protect the legitimate business interests of the original family business, will give the leaders of that business time to regroup and to consolidate customer and employee relationships that might otherwise be lost in the wake of the departure of a senior family member.

The related issue of who is entitled to use the family name in such circumstances is considered in chapter 9.

5.13 EMPLOYING YOUNG FAMILY MEMBERS

It is to be expected that in a family business, more so than in other businesses, that the children of the family will become involved in the business from an early age. Stories of the current business leader helping out in the family firm from a very young age are legion.[61]

The distinction between 'helping mom and dad' and employment of young children needs to be made, particularly in smaller family firms. Family businesses must be cautious as the employment of children is a highly regulated and complex area of law, which places restrictions on employers regarding children in the workplace. Although detailed discussion about the employment of children is outside of the scope of this book we note some points below which the family business should be aware of.

In general, children under 14 years old may not be employed. However, this rule can be relaxed by local authority bye-laws to allow 13-year-old children to be employed in certain capacities, such as delivering newspapers or stacking shelves. If the child can be employed then additional rules will apply to their employment, with those rules being more stringent if they are defined as a 'child' (broadly under school leaving age) as opposed to a 'young person' (under 18).

Children may only be employed to carry out certain types of 'light work', which is work that is unlikely to be harmful to the child's safety, health or development, to their school attendance or participation. There are no statutory restrictions on the rate of pay that can be offered to children, so the rates of pay for children do not have to meet the national minimum wage requirements. Additionally, children do not benefit from a statutory right to receive annual leave under the WTR 1998 but must be given a two week break from employment each year.

The hours that a child may work are more restricted than those of an adult, although these rules can be relaxed by local authorities. For example, a child cannot be employed to work before the end of the school day or for more than two hours in a day on which they have to go to school.

---

business into two separate and rival companies, Adidas and Puma. The story of this dispute is contained in Gordon and Nicholson *Family Wars* (Kogan Page, 2008).
[61] For example the story of Gotdfred Kirk Kristiansen, the son of the LEGO founder in chapter 1.

5.14 NATIONAL MINIMUM WAGE/NATIONAL LIVING WAGE

The national minimum wage (NMW) was introduced in 1999 through the National Minimum Wage Act 1998 (NMWA) and the detailed rules of the regime are contained in the National Minimum Wage Regulations 2015. This legislation applies not only to employees but also workers (see above). This created for the first time a minimum wage across the UK and depends on the age of the worker.[62] Any attempt by an employer to enter into an agreement with the individual that the NMW will not apply will be void. From April 2016 workers and employees aged 25 and over qualify for the National Living Wage of £7.20 per hour.

5.14.1 Family workers

The NMW does not need to be paid to workers who participate in the running of the family business, provided that they are family members and live in the family home. However, if the family employee resides outside the family home the NMW will apply.

It is not unusual for a family employee to be provided accommodation by the family business to reside in either free of charge or for a rent. If this is not the family home where other members of the family reside but a second home (for example investment property owned by the family business) then the family workers exemption (see above) is unlikely to apply. Issues of interpretation can arise in the setting of family farms, hotels and leisure businesses. For example is self-contained accommodation occupied by a next generation family member, on the same site as, but separate from the main hotel building where the rest of the family live, part of the family home?

5.14.2 Accommodation allowance

The provision of accommodation is the only non-cash benefit which can be used by the employer to offset its obligations in respect of NMW. This can be a fairly important exception in a family business context. Therefore, where the family business provides the family employee with accommodation it can count some of its value towards NMW. The family business cannot count more than the accommodation offset rate which is in force at any time.[63]

Where the employee pays rent to the family business (whether or not deducted directly from wages), any rent up to the value of the accommodation allowance can be disregarded for the purposes of the offset but any excess will be treated as a deduction so as to reduce the pay for NMW purposes.

---

[62] NMW rates from 1 October 2016:
25 and over: £7.20
21 to 24: £6.95
18 to 20: £5.55
Under 18: £4.00
Apprentice Rate: £3.40
The provisions relating to the NMW are contained in the NMWA and in the National Minimum Wage Regulations 1999 (the NMW Regulations).

[63] From 1 October 2016 the maximum amount which an employer can count towards NMW pay as accommodation offset is £6.00 per day or £42.00 per week.

5.14.3 On call

In order to ensure compliance with NMWA the employer needs to know which hours worked by the employee will trigger NMW. An area of contention has been the time which a worker spends 'on call' and whether this counts for the purposes of the NMW.

> *Example*
>
> Rosa's mother and father operate a farming business in Cornwall. Over the past 4 years the business has diversified. As well as being a fully functioning dairy farm, it now operates a restaurant, shop, cafe and children's soft play area. Rosa manages the café and restaurant between 9 am and 5pm and receives the NMW for these hours. She also lives on her own on site in a small cottage. Rosa is available on call out of office hours and through the night in case of burglaries, flooding of farm buildings etc. She also checks the herd at 10pm and 6 am every day. Should Rosa receive the NMW for any of these out of office hours?
>
> It will depend on whether Rosa is 'available for work' or actually working. In practice this can be a difficult distinction to draw. In this scenario, it is likely Rosa will only be entitled to the NMW for the hours she works between 9am and 5pm, for the period when she checks the herd at 6 am and 10 pm every day and for any periods during the night when she is awake dealing with any emergency issues. However, this can be a tricky area where it would be advisable to obtain specialist advice in any given circumstances.

There might also be implications under the Working Time Regulations if a worker is required to be 'on call' and this should also be considered.

5.14.4 Enforcement

Notwithstanding that the rules are widely known, family workers are frequently paid less than the NMW. Again smaller family businesses in the agriculture, leisure and retail sectors are the typical culprits. This might simply be accepted by the family member concerned. It could be a topic of significant contention. As NMW claims can be backdated 6 years, these can often leave the family firm facing a significant cash call. There are usually two schools of thought within the business family as to whether these claims represent an unmerited windfall for the family employee, or their long overdue and just deserts.

A family employee may appear quite willing to work on an informal basis for less than the minimum wage. However issues can arise if the parties fall out at a later date and the individual suddenly decides to enforce his entitlement to NMW. NMW claims can be brought either by the family employee. In this case the individual can bring either a claim for:

- Unlawful deductions from wages in the employment tribunal – this needs to be brought within 3 months of the date of the deduction (ie the failure to pay the NMW) or the last in a series of deductions. There used to be no limit on the length of arrears that can be claimed, provided it is all part of the same series of unlawful deductions. However, for claims issued after 1 July 2015, a 2-year limit will apply.[64]
- Breach of contract either in the employment tribunal or the county court. In the county court a claim can be brought up to 6 years after the breach. In both venues

---

[64] Section 23(4A) and (4B) of the ERA 1996.

arrears can be claimed going back up to 6 years prior to the claim. However employment tribunals can only hear a claim for breach of contract if the individual's employment has ended and the claim is brought within 3 months of termination.

A worker may also bring a claim to an employment tribunal for unfair dismissal or victimisation if the employer dismisses them or takes some other action against them for trying to ensure that they are paid the NMW, or simply because the worker is, or is going to become, eligible for the NMW. State officials can also enforce the employee's claims.

5.14.5 Pay records

The employer is legally obliged to keep certain records in relation to the hours worked by, and the payments made to, workers. It is a criminal office to fail to keep records, keep false records or produce false records. It is also a criminal offence to refuse or prevent an enforcement officer from seeing the necessary records. All of the offences are punishable on summary conviction by a fine not exceeding level 5 on the standard scale.

5.15 WORKING TIME REGULATIONS (WTR 1998)

Another area of vulnerability for family businesses can be compliance with the WTR 1998. The purpose of the WTR 1998 is to regulate hours of work. As with the NMW (above) the WTR 1998 apply to the wider category of workers as well as employees.

WTR 1998 impose a number of obligations on employers. The key obligation relating to the '48 hour week' is well known.[65] In more detail this is to take all reasonable steps in keeping with the need to protect workers' health and safety to ensure that each worker's average working time (including overtime) does not exceed 48 hours per week. This is over a reference period of 17 weeks which means that short busy periods such as Christmas can be accommodated. A reference period of 26 weeks applies to a number of sectors, including tourism and agriculture where there are recognised seasonal surges in activity. However the worker can choose to opt out of this maximum week, provided a valid opt out is signed by the employee. The worker can cancel the opt-out by giving at least seven days' notice unless the opt-out agreement provides for longer notice (which cannot exceed 3 months).

With family employees there can be a sense of everyone 'mucking in' and working whatever hours may be needed to ensure success of the family business. Insisting on taking formal breaks, all holiday entitlement and not working in excess of the 48 hour working week may all be frowned on in a family business context.

---

[65] Subsidiary obligations under the WTR 1998 include:
– to keep and maintain records showing whether the limits on average working time, night work and provision of health and safety assessments are being complied with in the case of each worker;
– to allow workers the following rest periods unless they are exempt, in which case compensatory rest will usually have to be given: 11 hours' uninterrupted rest per day; 24 hours' uninterrupted rest per week (or 48 hours uninterrupted rest per fortnight) and rest break of 20 minutes when working more than six hours per day;
– to allow workers 5.6 weeks' paid holiday a year (equivalent to 28 days (5.6 x 5 = 28) for a full-time worker).

There are a wide range of sanctions available against an employer under regs 28–32 of the WTR 1998, depending on the breach in question. These include compensation for workers in the Employment tribunal, as well as possible fines. Workers who are dismissed or suffer a detriment as a result of taking their entitlement to rest breaks may also complain to a tribunal.

5.16 DISCIPLINARY AND GRIEVANCE PROCEDURES

5.16.1 Overview

The theory that family and non-family members should be treated alike extends to disciplinary and grievance procedures.

A story frequently cited in family business circles, presumably apocryphal, is of a father and business leader with a wayward son, who was proving to be a most unsatisfactory employee in the family firm. When asked for guidance by the son's non-family line manager the father made it clear that his son should receive no special treatment. He did not and, as a result the son had lost his job by the end of the day. When he came home from work, the father, who had now taken off his hat as business leader and was ready to assume his family role as father said (or so the story goes) something to the effect of:

'I hear that you have had a hard day at work at son. What can I do to help?'

Practice might be very different.

At one end of the scale senior generation business leaders might see work based issues as an extension of family control and treat family members more as children than as business managers and accordingly be correspondingly less respectful and react more severely to any perceived failings. The next generation might simply put up with this. Their performance and health could be adversely affected, like Edsel Ford. They might walk away from the family business and pursue a career elsewhere, simply regarding their situation as untenable. If the departure is against the background of serious confrontation claims, including for constructive dismissal, might follow.

At the other end of the scale, family employees may be seen as above and beyond the usual performance and disciplinary process and effectively untouchable. This might be as between non-family members and more junior family members, who are seen to have the protection of family business leaders. It could be that family leaders in senior positions are reluctant to confront family members, perhaps siblings or cousins, in notionally subordinate roles, for fear of igniting family confrontation. If the issues are ignored for too long the family business might suffer, perhaps from the departure of senior non-family line managers, whose ability to manage family employees properly is undermined. What might happen is that, having ignored the problem for so long, a catalytic incident will occur. This might be relatively minor in its own right. But some combination of family dynamics and the tension relating to past conduct might create a complex and dangerous cocktail.

So what are the difficulties of applying the theory of disciplinary and grievance procedures to the reality of the family business situation? Successfully managing disciplinary and grievance issues is a challenge for any employer. For the family business however, there is a further layer of complexity due to the individual relationships and dynamics involved. It might be almost impossible to work out where business and employment issues end and family begin. Family members may genuinely want a conciliatory outcome in order to protect their personal relationships. However, even with the best of intentions, the family element can heighten emotions and make it difficult to find solutions where a working relationship has become troubled, or has broken down.

5.16.2 Fair procedures and communication

It is crucial to use appropriate and fair procedures to address disciplinary and grievance matters. Failing to do so will not only affect relations with the individual employee but also increase the risk of them bringing a tribunal claim against the family business. The cost and resources of defending a tribunal claim can be substantial. Where the employee is a member of the family, the repercussions for personal relationships and ramifications throughout the wider family and the family business can be significant.

5.16.3 Communication

By encouraging open communication amongst employees of all levels the family business is more likely to create an atmosphere whereby staff feel they can air and resolve issues without needing to resort to making a formal grievance. Likewise, where there is good communication within an organisation, performance and conduct issues are more likely to be satisfactorily resolved informally, without the need to instigate a formal procedure.

Naturally, one size cannot fit all in terms of effective communication styles, as much depends on the size and organisation of the family business. The family business should take time to consider how to keep communication channels as consistent as possible between family and non-family employees. Whilst family members might feel comfortable enough with the senior management to circumvent official communication channels when faced with an issue, careful thought should be given to ensure that non-family employees feel equally comfortable doing so. Whatever its size, the family business should consider how to keep lines of communication open between all staff. For example this may be through having weekly team meetings with all staff where any issues or concerns can be raised. Alternatively regular social get-togethers or team away days for both family and non-family members can engender team spirit and promote good communication in the workplace.

Where the family business employs both family and non-family members, thought should be given as to who is best placed to engage in different types of communication. Where the structure of the business allows, it may be more effective to ensure that a family member is able to speak openly with a more senior non-family employee. This will be the case particularly where a matter is sensitive for any reason, or where there is a traditional hierarchical family structure that translates to the family business.

5.16.4 ACAS Code

The existence of the ACAS Code[66] and its basic requirements are fairly well known.[67] The ACAS Code seeks to promote the fair and satisfactory handling of disciplinary and grievance matters. Although the code is not strictly legally binding this is a narrow point, as an employment tribunal will consider the degree to which the ACAS Code has been followed when deciding whether an employee has been unfairly dismissed for misconduct or poor performance.

Where the ACAS Code is not followed, employers risk being penalised by the tribunal. Incorrectly applying or disregarding the ACAS Code can result in compensation awards being increased by up to 25%. Equally, if an employee fails to adhere to the ACAS Code, for example, by jumping straight to a tribunal claim without exhausting internal avenues, they can see their compensation reduced by up to 25%.

5.16.5 Family charters and employment procedures

In addition to adhering to the ACAS Code, the family business must remember to also take into account its own grievance and disciplinary procedures to ensure that it is not in breach of these (particularly where these are contractual). In practice most internal procedures are modelled on the ACAS Code but are not usually contractual.

Whether any relevant employment related aspects of the family business governance system, such as family charters, would be taken into account by employment tribunals, does not appear to have been tested. For example it is conceivable that a family charter might require some form of consultation with the family council before a family member is dismissed from employment.[68] If the family business does not want to be bound to follow any relevant provisions of a family charter when it comes to dismissing an employee, it would be beneficial to state that such provisions are non-contractual. It might be thought entirely inappropriate in business terms for family members to be involved in management and employment issues. On the other hand the family dimension cannot be ignored. It might be almost impossible to differentiate between family and business issues as the source of any conflict. But wider family intervention, or involving family business consultants, could well assist in this process.

Broadly speaking the more formal the procedure, the more damaging this is likely to be for family relationships. As will be seen from the next sections it is almost surreal to attempt to reconcile most employer's disciplinary procedures with family reality. Once the formal process has started the family relationship has finished.

The alternative to informal resolution of conflict and tension in family employment relationships might be to for the courts or employment tribunals to undertake the difficult task of deciding where family relationships end and the more formal relationship of employer and employee prevails.

---

[66] ACAS *Code of Practice on Disciplinary and Grievance Procedures* (March 2015).
[67] The Code and relevant guidance can be accessed via the ACAS website http://www.acas.org.uk.
[68] Such a provision is probably not desirable as this could be a fetter on managerial discretion.

5.16.6 The law relating to disciplinary and grievance procedures

A family business needs to make itself familiar not only with the ACAS Code, but also with the law surrounding disciplinary and grievance matters.

Conduct is one of five potentially fair reasons for dismissal under s 98 of the ERA 1996 along with capability, redundancy, breach of statutory restriction and 'some other substantial reason'. A fair procedure must be combined with the imposition of a reasonable sanction in conduct cases. Where the reasonable sanction is dismissal, provided the family business has acted fairly and reasonably, it will be in a strong position to defend any subsequent tribunal claims.

5.16.7 Separation of powers

The Code recommends that, so far as possible, different managers should be appointed to deal with internal investigations, chairing disciplinary meetings and any appeals. This is subject to the employer's own internal procedures. This separation of decision-making processes is designed to ensure maximum fairness.

ACAS acknowledges in the introduction to the ACAS Code that:

> 'Employment tribunals will take the size and resources of an employer into account when deciding on relevant cases and it may sometimes not be practicable for all employers to take all steps set out in this Code.'

Full separation may be difficult to achieve, particularly in the small family business for purely practical reasons.

In a larger family enterprise, junior family employees may be reporting to non-family line managers.[69] Even if they are not it might be preferable for non-family executives to be asked to handle any disciplinary process to keep family and business issues as separate as possible.

Alternatively a family business may choose to appoint an external third party to carry out the investigation and/or sit on the disciplinary or grievance panel or chair the appeal stage of the process. This is a role offered by a number of independent HR providers.

There can be many benefits to using an external third party. Where the matter involves a family employee it can be seen by the employee, other non-family employees and also other family members as the most impartial way of handling a disciplinary or grievance procedure.

However careful consideration needs to be given by the family business before using an external resource in such a sensitive context. By doing so it is effectively choosing to be bound by the decision of a third party and the family business may not ultimately be happy with the decision which the third party reaches. Further it would be problematical for the family business to overturn the findings of a third party and choose to proceed with a disciplinary procedure despite the recommendation of the third party.

---

[69] This is recommended best practice anyway.

5.16.8 The right to be accompanied

Any worker (ie employee or worker) who is required or invited to attend a disciplinary or grievance meeting is entitled to be accompanied by a fellow worker of their choice or a trade union official even if the family employer does not recognise a trade union.

A worker is not entitled to be represented by a family member but sometimes employers will agree to this. Particular sensitivity will be required if the disciplinary procedure cuts across family branch lines where there has been a history of conflict. Allowing for example an outsider sibling into the meeting to support their child/ nephew/ employee subject to the procedure, might lead to an inappropriate row between the senior generation insider and outsider. Saying no might be added to the pile of family resentments.

5.16.9 Third party mediation

In some circumstances it may be appropriate to consider mediation as a means by which to resolve workplace disputes in the family business. The foreword to the ACAS Code advocates the use of mediation where possible.

Mediation is a form of alternative dispute resolution (ADR) and typically involves a third party (the mediator) to assist the parties to negotiate a settlement.[70] Mediation can be particularly beneficial for a family business where relationships are not just of work but also close family ties. Due to the emotions involved family business disputes can often be protracted and costly. Keeping disputes out of tribunal can help preserve both work and family relationships as well as keeping costs down.

Mediation can be helpful for family businesses of all sizes. For example where a small family business comprises solely of family members and a dispute arises mediation can be beneficial in preserving relationships. Mediation can be equally helpful for larger family businesses which comprise family and non-family members. Even if the family members most directly concerned might struggle to accept the outcome, the wider business owning family might be reassured by the involvement of an independent and objective third party. Relying on family members to deal with the dispute internally could exacerbate existing frictions and stoke the fires of family branch factionalism.

ACAS and a number of private companies offer workplace mediation services. The foreword does not comprise part of the ACAS Code itself and is therefore not compulsory.

However, the family business that takes all forms of guidance into account when seeking to resolve grievances is likely to be able to more effectively demonstrate to a tribunal that it has genuinely sought to resolve the issue.

5.17 CAPABILITY AND PERFORMANCE

One of the most difficult areas to deal with in any employment relationship are concerns about capability and performance. This is especially so in family businesses.

---

[70] The use of mediation in the context of wider family business disputes is discussed in chapter 25.

Commentators argue that family employees are often conditioned to work demonstrably harder and to outperform their non-family counterparts.[71] However this will not always be the case.[72] Underperforming family employees can pose particular problems. The family manager might not consider performance by other family employees to be a particular problem. There could be a natural reluctance to tackle the issue with close relations or there may be an insufficient distinction between work and family life.[73] The underperforming family member may also feel protected by virtue of their family status.

The effect on non-family members should also be considered. If an underperforming family employee is seen as 'getting away with it', this can have a significant impact on overall workplace morale. Careful and consistent management of performance is therefore central to the successful running of the family business.

5.17.1 The importance of handling capability issues fairly and effectively

Failing to tackle effectively underperformance at an early stage can also make it difficult for the family business to then raise it as an issue at a later stage. All of these issues are potentially compounded in the family business by close relationships, emotions and the increased risk of allegations of favouritism. It is therefore important to deal with under-performance promptly and in a fair and consistent manner with all employees, regardless of whether or not they are family or non-family members.

5.17.2 Managing performance before a problem arises

Prevention is always better than cure and the family business should ensure that every employee is clear about what is expected from them in their role. A well drafted job description and contract of employment will help an employee understand from the outset the standards which are required of them.

Probationary periods can also be a useful tool to allow an employer to assess an employee's suitability for the role, to appraise performance at an early stage and affirm the standard required. A probationary period will usually last three to 6 months and provide for each party to terminate employment on a shorter notice period. However many family businesses will feel uncomfortable subjecting family employees to a probationary period.

Regular appraisals are a useful tool to motivate good employees but also provide invaluable evidence of poor performance, which can be used later to support a fair dismissal (or indeed used as evidence to defend an unfair dismissal claim).

---

[71] See for example John Ward *Perpetuating the Family Business; 50 Lessons Learned from Long-Standing Successful Families in Business* (Palgrave, 2004) Lesson 4 (Principle of Merit).
[72] For example in the matrimonial case of *Cowan*, discussed in chapter 18 the brother of the business founder, was known by the non-family employees as 'The Golfing Director'.
[73] It is suggested that whereas parents and older siblings may be prepared to exercise parental or quasi-parental authority over younger family members, on the occasions where younger family members have been preferred to older for leadership positions, the younger family managers can, experience a form of guilt that the natural birth order has been subverted in their favour and therefore allow the older family members to have an easier ride.

5.17.3 The law relating to under-performance

As stated above, capability is one of five potentially fair reasons for dismissal under s 98 of the ERA 1996. ERA 1996, s 98(3) includes competence, health and qualifications within its definition of capability whilst s 98(2)(a) states that if the reason for the employee's dismissal 'relates to the capability or qualifications of the employee for performing work of the kind which he was employed by the employer to do' it will fall within this subsection.

Provided capability (or one of the other potentially fair reasons for dismissal) applies to the dismissal in question, it will depend on the reasonableness of the employer's decision in the particular circumstances and the fairness of the procedure followed whether the dismissal is adjudged to be fair.

The employer should establish whether the issue is capability or misconduct. The issue may be misconduct where the employee is well qualified and properly trained but is negligent or has willful failed to perform their duties.

Whether the family business' decision is reasonable in the circumstances requires the tribunal to consider whether the employer held a reasonable belief in the employee's incompetence when it took the decision to dismiss. This requires the family business to hold an honest belief based on reasonable grounds of incapability.

5.17.4 Addressing a capability issue informally

Often a quiet word is all it takes for an employer to address concerns about an employee's performance. This informal approach is advocated by ACAS in the foreword to the ACAS Code. However it is recognised that if this does not prove successful, formal steps will need to be taken.

Where a capability issue does arise it is important that an employer avoids being openly critical of the member of staff on in front of their colleagues.[74] There are a number of cases where employees have been severely reprimanded, humiliated, intimidated and degraded in front of other workers about their performance and this has been sufficient to breach the implied term of trust and confidence, leading to constructive unfair dismissal claims. This can be a particular problem for a family business where the boundary between family life and a formal work setting may become blurred, leading to inappropriate language and comments being made between family colleagues in front of other members of staff.

Professional and carefully chosen language should always be used even when addressing the family employee privately. Again this may prove difficult to family business employees who are used to using more informal language (including swearing) in the home environment.

---

[74] The process of triangulation, or involving third parties in family conflicts, is discussed in chapter 3 (Tools, Models and Theories).

5.17.5 Following a fair capability procedure

Where the capability issues cannot be resolved informally, a formal capability procedure should be followed. Compliance with the ACAS Code will be key. The core elements will be a thorough investigation, fair opportunities for the employee to improve (often supported by training and other measures) and, usually a minimum of two warnings. A fair procedure will therefore usually be a protracted process.

5.17.6 Ensuring a fair capability procedure for family members

There are no hard and fast rules about whether and if so how family members in the family business should be treated differently to ensure fairness. However a good rule of thumb is to treat family employees as far as possible in the same way as non-family employees, however artificial this may seem to the respective parties. The exception is likely to be where family members are line managers, or would otherwise be involved in the disciplinary process.[75]

In terms of underperformance this involves following a fair procedure discussed above. It is important to avoid allowing personal family issues to impact on the procedure. If the family business employs senior non-family members it can be a good idea to involve them in the capability procedure to help demonstrate objectivity and ensure fairness. Family dynamics will almost inevitably complicate an already sensitive situation.

5.17.7 Dismissing fairly for capability

Before moving to dismissal (if appropriate) a fair procedure must be followed. This will involve ensuring full compliance with the ACAS Code. Capability procedures tend to be very time consuming, as they involve allowing sufficient periods of time to the employee to improve their behaviour and also in terms of the management time needed to follow a fair procedure, agree and set targets with the employee and monitor improvement.

Once a fair procedure has been followed and the employee's performance has failed to improve it is a good idea to consider alternative employment or demotion before moving to dismiss.

If this is not realistic, or if alternative roles are not available, then the employer may dismiss the employee. Dismissals are rarely risk-free and capability dismissals are often the hardest to justify as reasonable. It is therefore vital that the employer feels confident that its decision to dismiss was reasonable in the circumstances, was based on the honest belief of incompetence and that a reasonable and fair procedure was followed before reaching the dismissal.

5.18 ILL HEALTH

One would expect a family business to provide the most supportive environment possible in the unfortunate event of the long term or serious illness of a family member. But ultimately such a situation might prove one of the hardest tests of finding the balance between the needs of the family and business systems.

---

[75] See the discussion above. However there appears to be no case authority for this proposition.

One of the hardest things for a family to deal with is the long-term sickness of one of its members. Where that family also has its family business to consider, the situation is made even more difficult as the family business seeks to do the right thing not only commercially but in order to protect the family member.

Dealing with long-term sickness can be difficult enough with a physiological illness, but when this involves a mental illness (such as stress or depression) especially when this can, at least in part attributed to the family member's job or to add even more complexity, the family background, the business can feel under even more pressure to look after the sick family employee. As with conduct and capability issues the tendency with family employees will often be to let matters go on longer. When action is eventually taken this can be rushed and not properly thought through. In cases such as this, in addition to the risk of a claim for unfair dismissal, the bigger risk to the business will be a claim of disability discrimination under the EA 2010 and/or a claim for personal injury. There is a high procedural burden on the employer in such cases. This includes obtaining medical reports, considering work place adjustments, including phased returns to work and alternative duties. If the employer concludes that dismissal might be an appropriate response the ACAS code needs to be carefully followed, taking into account the effect of the illness on the employee's ability to participate.

5.19 FAMILY DYNAMICS; BEHAVIOUR AND BOUNDARIES

One area of risk is the behaviour of family members towards one another in an employment setting. It is by no means uncommon for family members who are studiously polite, considerate and professional in their dealings with non-family employees, to behave entirely otherwise in their interactions with other family members. Highly offensive and inappropriate language may feature. Physical violence is not uncommon.[76] Such behaviour might be a continuation of family behaviour patterns. It will undoubtedly have links to long-standing family relationship issues. But it can have serious ramifications in the employment context. The boundaries between private family issues and family business employment need to be respected. Employment tribunals are likely to require family members to behave professionally towards one another in an employment setting.

5.19.1 Family disputes and employment tribunals

The case of *Papier v (1) Formara Print Ltd (2) Phoenix Offsset Ltd (3) Steven Ball*[77] clearly illustrates this point.

Steven Ball was the owner and founder of printing business. His wife, a senior civil servant, took a four-year posting in the USA. Steven asked his older sister, Linda Papier, to take over the leadership of the business so that he could join his wife in the States. Linda resigned from her position with a firm of legal recruitment consultants in order to do so. The business continued to prosper under Linda's leadership. Steven returned

---

[76] One of the more salacious details of the Eirian Davies case discussed in detail in chapter 19 was a physical fight involving the mother, who poured water over the daughter, the father and daughter who wrestled with each other, resulting in the daughter biting her father's leg.
[77] An unreported but reserved decision of the employment tribunal (Case No 3202018/2003).

home approximately once a year to meet with Linda and attend business meetings etc. Linda continued to work in the businesses alongside Steven when he returned to the UK permanently in August 2002.

So far Steven seems like a model modern man. According to Linda, of all her five brothers and sister, she was closest to Steven. It might therefore be surprising that brother and sister found themselves before an employment tribunal, which made findings of fact that:

- Steven said to Linda, in front of a senior business contact from a supplier another: 'Listen to me, you know nothing about business and how businessmen behave, we don't repeat things told in confidence, keep your mouth shut and don't tell anybody about what was said'.
- In another meeting with a client a year or so later Steven said 'don't listen to her John, she's just an old dog'.
- A month or so after that meeting, following an argument about a mislaid quotation, Steven summarily dismissed Linda saying 'you are the most obnoxious bitch I have ever worked with. Fuck off and get out of here!' He then went towards her with his fists clenched and his left arm raised and said: 'Get out of here you cunt, you're fired!'

So what went wrong? The employment tribunal believed that they had identified the problem, or at least an opportunity missed to take preventative measures. When Steven returned from the States he wanted:[78]

> '... to be fully hands on and to take control over matters he had previously left in Linda's hands. Unfortunately it seems that [Steven and Linda] never sat down to discuss what their respective roles in the business were to be in the future. Had they done so the tragic sequence of events that unfolded may never have got as bad as they did.'

In other words a governance application point was missed.

Steven's counsel[79] tried to find explanations a little deeper in family dynamics regarding the overall situation as 'an object lesson in the folly of mixing roles'. He pointed to the fact that Linda was 13 years older than Stephen and would inevitably have difficulty in accepting the authority of her much younger brother. He argued that she had difficulty in accepting their employer/employee relationship, which, counsel suggested, she treated as 'secondary to the brother/sister relationship'. Perhaps tellingly Steven's counsel found it significant that Linda referred to the firm as a 'family business' whereas Steven was, at all times the sole owner and seemed to resent his sister's presumption.

All this seems to ring true, or at least to have the potential to do so. No doubt this was Steven's perception. Linda might have seen matters otherwise, perhaps believing that Steven was insecure as to his status and too prone to see her as a domineering elder sister when she merely wanted to offer support.

The detailed job and role descriptions suggested by the tribunal would undoubtedly have helped. Whether they would have indeed been enough to prevent the family tragedy

---

[78] At para 15 of the decision.
[79] See para 30 of the decision.

unfolding is however a moot point. The decision, including the evidence of the other brother working in the business, Alan, points to continual and long running tension in the relationship between Steven and Linda.

But if not, Steven and Linda what other possibilities to deal with the conflict were open to the siblings?

Conflict is an inevitable part of family business life. The key issue is how the business family deal with this. They could have looked at a family business consultancy intervention[80] to help deal with the issues identified by Steven's counsel at an early stage. If difficulties still persisted there would have been an opportunity to agree to go their separate ways. Logically resulting in some form of departure package for Linda. Although we examine, and indeed advocate, the use of protected conversations and settlement agreements in the context of family employment disputes below, if both Linda and Steven had played their cards differently such formality might not even have been necessary in this case.

Instead the tribunal heard evidence[81] of the deep ambivalence of Steven towards his sister in the form of a message left on her answering machine, saying:

'I am phoning to apologise for my outburst on Thursday. It was unnecessary and a lot of things were said that shouldn't have been said. I still love you as a sister but unfortunately darling I cannot work with you.'

He then went on to tell Linda that he was sorting out a severance package for her before concluding with a warning that:

'... if you get in touch with any clients ... to say how badly you have been treated the offer will be withdrawn and you can take it to an Industrial Tribunal. I still love you and that's my final word.'

Linda did of course take the matter to a tribunal. What was the legal analysis against this factual background?

5.19.2 Discrimination

First the tribunal found that Steven had subjected his sister to unlawful direct sex discrimination by verbally abusing her and then dismissing her. Clearly Linda had been treated unfavourably. To make a finding of discrimination the tribunal needed to be satisfied that this was on the basis of her sex, rather than their family relationship. They needed to find a comparator. There was also a brother working in the business. But he had only recently joined and lacked Linda's seniority. The tribunal therefore constructed a hypothetical comparator, an imaginary brother of Steven:[82]

'who had been managing the business for him for as long as [Linda] had and of similar age to [her].'

---

[80] Family business consultancy is explained in more detail in chapter 25.
[81] See para 25 of the decision.
[82] At para 12 of the decision.

The transcript refers to the 'roles' of Steven and Linda before the tribunal, those of 'third respondent' and 'applicant' respectively. This further emphasises the chasm that had developed between their roles as brother and sister as a result of their relationship employer and employee.

The tribunal found that Linda had indeed been treated less favourably than this hypothetical male comparator would have been.

It did not help Steven that he denied making the comments and could accordingly give no explanation for the treatment of his sister. His own evidence also illustrated less favourable treatment. In the meeting with the (male) supplier he directed his words to Linda only; suggested it was inappropriate for her to be listening to the conversation even though she had been dealing directly with the supplier for 4 years; and suggested, without evidence, that she had a loose tongue. The treatment was to her detriment since Linda was humiliated. The tribunal found that, the use of the term 'old dog' about a woman was tantamount to calling them slovenly or unattractive and was satisfied that this was less favourable treatment on grounds of sex. Compensation for unlawful discrimination is not subject to the statutory limits that apply to unfair dismissal.

5.19.3 Unfair dismissal: are family relationships 'some other substantial reason'?

The tribunal also found that Linda was unfairly dismissed.

Steven contended that he had not dismissed his sister. His counsel argued that there was a precedent to allow an employer to recant words said in the heat of the moment and to retract words otherwise indicative of dismissal to try to repair the employment relationship. The tribunal dismissed this argument. The tribunal felt that when considering an employer's ability to recant, the implied duty not to act in a way that could destroy the relationship of mutual trust and confidence that exists between employer and employee needed to be borne in mind. In any event, on the facts of the case they simply did not accept that Steven wanted to repair the relationship. All the evidence pointed to dismissal.

Steven's counsel sought to argue that the issue between Steven and Linda was, at root, a personality clash, between brother and sister and accordingly that the dismissal should be seen as fair under the residual category of potentially fair reasons for dismissal, 'some other substantial reason' justifying dismissal. Employment tribunals do recognise that a breakdown in relationships may justify a fair dismissal on the grounds of some other substantial reason. But this cannot be used as a pretext to conceal the real reason for dismissal.

The tribunal could decide that a family business was not big enough for both siblings and therefore one of them had to go. Logically that would be Linda as the non-owner and less senior employee. Generally speaking, it will be quite difficult for an employer to successfully persuade a tribunal that dismissal on the grounds of 'some other substantial reason' is justified. Usually, an employer will need to have shown that they have done all in their reasonable power to fix the situation. On the facts of the case no such steps had been taken. There had been no attempt at job demarcation. There had been no disciplinary action. There had been no express recognition by Steven of the difficulties in his relationship with Linda, much less any attempt to resolve or mediate these.

Even if the employer falls the wrong side of the line of being able to justify a dismissal of an employee as being for 'some other substantial reason', the tribunal might nevertheless agree that the employee concerned has, by their approach and conduct in the employment relationship, contributed to their own downfall. In which case the compensation otherwise due to the employee can be reduced appropriately.[83] Here the tribunal found no fault on Linda's part. There was simply no evidence of reluctance on her part to bow to her brother's authority.

In terms of cases making their way to tribunals this is perhaps an extreme and unusual case with particularly humiliating and offensive language being used by a brother against his sister. Sadly, in terms of what goes on behind the closed doors of family businesses the case is by no means unique.

Perhaps Steven's behaviour can be understood. He grew up in the shadow of a much older sister, who perhaps exercised quasi-parental authority over him. Having built a successful business it must have been difficult if (at least in his perception) his big sister was not according him the respect he believed was his due as business leader. Perhaps, on the basis of the theory that the family business is capable of being a transitional object,[84] he could have felt that the big sister was trying to steal little brother's toy.

But to explain is not to accept.

In considering the reasonableness or otherwise of an employer in relation to a dismissal a tribunal is required to take into account the size and administrative resources of the employer concerned, not their emotional resources.

So Steven and Linda's case is a useful reminder that appropriate, professional language and conduct should always be deployed in the workplace regardless of whether the individuals are related or not.

5.20 PROTECTED AND WITHOUT PREJUDICE CONVERSATIONS AND SETTLEMENT AGREEMENTS

The steps and procedures that would be necessary to fairly dismiss a family employee for a performance or capability related reason can be seen to be incompatible with anything approaching normal family interaction.

This is particularly so with early stage family businesses, where any family employment issues are likely to arise between immediate family members and the business may lack the administrative resource to allow any resulting disciplinary or grievance procedures to be handled by non-family line management. But even in larger and later stage family companies there is still likely to be a significant personal element attached to any formal employment procedures. There is a danger that the wider business family will be drawn into the matter, with family members being forced to take sides, often along branch lines.

---

[83] Usually this is done on the basis of a rough and ready of assessment of proportionality. So that if an employee was seen as 50% to blame (but the employer had nevertheless acted unfairly, perhaps by dismissing before giving a final warning) the compensation would be halved.
[84] See chapter 3 for a discussion on the psychological status of the family business.

The wise business family (and their advisors) will therefore usually recognise that any difficulties that arise in family employment relationships can often be attributed to the complexity of that relationship, rather than any basic character flaw of the family members concerned. If so there are clear benefits from frank communication, resulting in an acknowledgement that the employment relationship has broken down and that a parting of the ways accompanied by a suitable severance package is in the best interests of both the employee concerned and the family business.

Even if employer or employee strongly believes that the other side is at fault, there is a clear risk of damage to family relationships in pursuing, or defending employment proceedings, rather than achieving a negotiated outcome. Any such discussions could be undertaken on without prejudice basis or as 'off the record' 'protected conversations' (also called pre-termination negotiations') and, assuming a suitable outcome, formally documented in legally a enforceable settlement agreement. With effect from 29 July 2013 new legislation was introduced aimed at enabling employers to have frank discussions with an employee with the aim of agreeing to terminate their employment on agreed terms.

Prior to July 2013 employers still did have conversations with employees with a view to bringing their employment to an end but, if subsequently challenged, had to rely on the 'without prejudice' principle to assert that it could not be referred to and was confidential. However in order to for an employer to have the protection of 'without prejudice' there must be a pre-existing dispute. This will not be the case in many employment situations. There was previously no similar protection for employers in situations where there was no existing dispute. Accordingly, broaching conversations with employees brought the risk that what was said was subsequently referred to in tribunal or court proceedings. This may mean that any subsequent process could be challenged as a sham and pre-determined, or an employee could use the conversation as a trigger to resign and claim constructive unfair dismissal. If previously the employer took the risk of broaching the subject of the employee's departure and an agreement was reached, employer and employee could then enter into a formal agreement, previously known as a compromise agreement (now, settlement agreement), to bring an end to the employment relationship.

We now have legislation which prevents 'pre-termination negotiations' from being referred to in evidence in any subsequent tribunal proceedings for ordinary unfair dismissals.

It is important to note that this does not replace the without prejudice principle which still applies in appropriate cases in conjunction with these new confidentiality rules.

Settlement agreements are legally binding contracts, which can be used to end the employment relationship on agreed terms, ie a negotiated exit. Under a settlement agreement an employee is required to waive their rights to make a claim to a court or tribunal in relation to the matters that are specifically covered in the settlement – for example, the right not to be unfairly dismissed. The employee generally waives their rights/complaints in exchange for a payment. The provision of a reference by the employer is frequently included in the terms of a settlement agreement and so it can provide the employee with more than a purely financial incentive. In order to be valid settlement agreements need to be in a prescribed form, which meet certain conditions.

There are many reasons why a family business might consider entering into a settlement agreement with an employee in order to bring about an end to an employment relationship. It can be used as an alternative to a formal procedure and as such, it can often be a commercial way of ending an employment relationship without following lengthy and stressful formal procedures. Settlement agreements will also include a term as to confidentiality and they can therefore be a useful mechanism for bringing an end to a relationship in a confidential manner – both in respect to other staff members and in appropriate cases the wider family or the general public. Settlement agreements can also offer a 'clean break' for both employers and employees.

Although settlements agreements can provide a means of avoiding the management time and cost of following formal procedures, there are still a few strict rules that must be complied with in order for a settlement agreement to be legally binding and it is recommended that specialist advice is sought to ensure compliance with these.

A pre-termination negotiation provides a useful method by which employers can raise with an employee that they should consider mutually agreeing to bring their employment to an end through a settlement agreement. They can be used in situations where the employee is already aware of existing issues with their employment (for example, where they have already been spoken to about their conduct or performance), or they can be used as the first step in broaching an issue.

It is important that in order to have the benefit of confidentiality the negotiations must be raised in an appropriate manner. There is an ACAS Code of Practice which must be complied with.[85] An employment tribunal will have regard to whether employers complied with this Code of Practice when determining whether the negotiations should be confidential. There is also a broader guidance note which is not legally binding but which a tribunal will have reference to.

The conversation loses its confidentiality protection if there is any 'improper behaviour' on the part of the employer. Improper behaviour is not defined but is likely to include bullying, harassment, intimidation, Physical assault or threat of this, victimisation, discrimination or undue pressure – insufficient time, advising that dismissal will be the alternative etc. It is therefore fundamental to the negotiations that the proposal is presented as an option and never as an ultimatum. There is no obligation on the employee to engage in the process or to accept the proposal – or any proposal – to end their employment. It should be made clear to the employee that the outcome of the discussions will have no bearing on any formal proceedings which follow. It is legitimate and usually appropriate to inform the employee that the employer will follow alternative formal procedures if this is the case in order that they might fully consider their options.

It will not be considered to be 'improper behaviour' to: factually state the consequences of not reaching agreement; state that the terms will not be available in future; not agree to pay legal fees to the advisor; not agree to provide a reference. It is essential to note that this 'confidentiality protection' does not apply to automatically unfair dismissals, discrimination claims, or other claims – such as wrongful dismissal claims. Accordingly, additional care must be taken in these cases and an awareness that the discussions may be referred to in subsequent proceedings. Depending on the circumstances, however, discussions may be protected (ie confidential) under the 'without prejudice' principle.

---

[85] ACAS *Code of Practice on Settlement Agreements* (July 2013).

5.21 ACAS AND EARLY CONCILIATION

Before an employee or worker can bring a claim to an employment tribunal they must register their claim with ACAS within 3 months of their dismissal or other event giving rise to their claim such as an act of discrimination or breach of contract. For one month ACAS will conciliate between the employee/worker and the employer to try to settle the claim. The practice of some employers is not to take part in conciliation but to wait to see if the employee/worker goes on to make a tribunal claim, because they will have to pay a tribunal fee. Statistics show that tribunal fees have discouraged many potential claimants. However as the services of ACAS are free and they act as go between it can be worth-while for the employer to take part in conciliation at least to find out more about the potential claim at an early stage. It is likely to be the last chance to preserve family relationships.

5.22 CONCLUSION

Employing family members is one of the key ingredients, if not the essence of, a family owned business.[86] The employment relationship also sits at the pinnacle of the systems clash between the business and family systems. The modern workplace is based on roles, systems and professionalism and is supported by employment legislation, which places great emphasis on following clear, careful and consistently applied procedures. This contrasts sharply with highly personal, emotionally charged and (often) largely or partially submerged issues of family dynamics.

The consequences of this systems clash can be very bloody indeed. So, although this chapter has been a long one, its concluding message is really very short and simple. This is that business owning families must do all in their power to avoid that clash. In the first instance, by investing in early stage and informal conflict management where family members are concerned and in the family employment specific aspects of family business governance generally.

Secondly, if conflict persists and cannot be resolved, to recognise this and move quickly to a resolution, usually involving the departure of a family member under agreed terms, based on protected conversations and settlement agreements. This could well involve the family business by-passing all or most of the procedural steps of approved disciplinary procedures.

That is absolutely not to say that HR and employment practices generally of the family business should not apply to family members. Ensuring, both compliance with best practice and consistency of treatment, of family and non-family employees is clearly good governance. It is likely to reduce the potential for clashes with family members and by helping to retain and motivate non-family employees, will be in the best interests of the family business. This is largely the theme of the next chapter.

---

[86] Even if later stage family owned businesses have few or even no family employees they will have passed through the stages of family employment at some stage of their evolution.

CHAPTER 6

NON-FAMILY EMPLOYEES

6.1 OVERVIEW

Although significant numbers of micro family businesses rely exclusively on family members to provide their labour force any family business with pretensions to growth will need to look beyond the family for employees. One of the main themes of this book has been the professionalisation of the family business, the introduction of management disciplines and processes that are necessary to sustain the growth of a family enterprise. That will almost certainly involve the recruitment of non-family managers. A key challenge for the family firm then becomes how to attract and retain key family managers, whilst also providing opportunities for the next generation of the business owning family to also build their own careers in the family business.

This chapter looks at some of the dynamics of non-family recruitment. It also provides a basic overview of management incentive schemes, including share options.

As shown in the previous chapter, there are, perhaps comparatively rare occasion when family businesses have to deal with employment claims from family members. Probably much more frequently family businesses find themselves before employment tribunals facing claims from non-family employees, although we are not aware of any research or statistics suggesting whether family firms are more likely to suffer this fate than other businesses. Modern employment legislation requires a highly procedural and, at times, formal approach. There is a possible connection between the informality with which a lot of family business affairs are conducted and the potential for such claims. This might be counter-balanced by the proposition that, notwithstanding a typical abhorrence of procedural matters, family businesses are seen to provide an inherently fairer working environment than their non-family counterparts.[1]

In any event, there are very few areas where the fact that the employment setting is a family business materially affects the legal situation of the non-family employee. The issue of nepotism and its relationship to unlawful discrimination is examined below. Although we go on to examine the legal consequences of nepotism, for most practical purposes there are really none. In most cases the consequences of family favouritism, if not addressed, will be felt in reduced non-family employee motivation, potentially resulting in key employees leaving in search of a more level playing field and ultimately in sub-optimal business performance by the family firm.

---

[1] See chapter 1 and *Family Business People Capital* (IFB Research Foundation Report with Cass Business School, 2013).

We have taken the view that general employment claims by non-family employees are the province of specialist employment works and not this book.[2] However, as employment settings, family firms differ from their non-family counterparts. This will inevitably affect the working life of the non-family employee. The bulk of this chapter examines some of the underlying dynamics.

It would be very easy to fall into the trap of portraying employment in a family business as a career graveyard, only accepted by untalented and terminally unambitious employees. Nothing could be further from the truth. There are a number of surveys and much literature pointing to family firms as providing a preferable employment environment for non-family employees.

So, on average, a non-family employee, should be happy with their family business lot. If so the majority of this chapter and this paragraph in particular can be seen to be directed at the atypical non-family employment situation.

6.2 INTRODUCING NON-FAMILY MANAGERS

6.2.1 Why introduce non-family managers

The family will not have all the skill sets to cope with the various roles required by the business as it grows, hence the need for non-family members in key positions. Initially, for most growing family businesses, these individuals will typically be managers but may subsequently become directors. Often the first senior non-family member recruited will be one with financial skills. This will be a key function in the business, because of the need to have reliable financial information and tight financial controls.

The recruitment of marketing specialists and HR professionals are also closely identified with the professionalisation of the family business. However, until later in the evolution of a family enterprise, these roles will often be filled by non-specialist family members.[3] Various cases featuring family business failures, discussed in this book can be seen as warnings of the dangers of relying on unqualified family members to fill gaps in the managerial skill set.[4]

Being a non-family member in a business closely managed by the family, may not be easy. Talented people may become frustrated by the lack of opportunities, the politics and emotional cross-currents and could eventually leave. But, those who can work in the environment can become an important member of the team, one who is respected by all the family, and, over time become trusted for their impartial advice, as well as being seen as (almost) one of the family.

Other, more complex reasons to hire non-family managers have been suggested by Dyer.[5] One is to change the 'norms and values of business operations', where the business owning family perceive the need to change, for example by introducing

---

[2] For example *Tolley's Employment Handbook* (LexisNexis, 2016, 30th edn).
[3] One or more of these roles will be often be assumed by a spouse. See chapter 18 for a more detailed discussion.
[4] These include *Park House Properties* and perhaps most graphically, *Listowel Trading*, both of which are discussed in chapter 8.
[5] W Gibb Dyer Jr 'Integrating Professional Management into a Family Owned Business' *Family Business Review* (1989) Vol 3 at pp 221–235.

organisational efficiencies to address falling sales or profits, but the paternalistic approach of the family prevents them from making these changes.

A further reason suggested is to prepare for leadership succession, where there are no immediately suitable family candidates.[6]

It will be seen that many of the difficulties in introducing non-family managers stem from a basic culture clash between the idiosyncrasies of the individual family business and the more generally accepted management practices of the wider corporate world. To overcome, or at least minimise the impact of this culture clash there are strong arguments for balancing the introduction of non-family managers with the training and development of existing managerial resource within the family business. Both family members and non-family employees could be considered.

6.2.2   Effectiveness: limiting factors

Some of the factors which may limit the effectiveness of non-family managers are:

- **Vision.** The family has not set out a clear vision and set of values or policies defining the family's relationship with the business.[7] By extension there is no family charter capturing these fundamentals to guide the non-family management team. This makes it difficult for the manager to properly understand the family context in which they are being asked to perform their function. It is possible for there to be a lot of family interference from those not involved in the business management, or by those involved, stepping outside what should be their role.
- **Ambiguity.** The non-family employee is not given a fair chance. Sometimes this is because the family are not all agreed on the appointment. This can either be on the question of why an outsider is needed in the first place, or on the level of seniority or identity of the eventual appointee.
  More subtly the senior generation business leader may demonstrate ambiguity towards the appointee (or often more accurately the appointment). The family business leader's head might acknowledge the need for the introduction of financial disciplines. But resentment may nevertheless be directed at the financial professional who tries to instil these.
- **Remuneration package.** Possibly the family business will identify a key individual whom they wish to recruit but cannot compete with remuneration levels paid by larger corporate non-family businesses. Some commentators advocate family businesses paying above market rates to attract talented non-family managers. This is discussed in more detail below.
- **Leadership succession and the family glass ceiling.** Enhanced remuneration packages are also sometimes justified to compensate for the possibility that the career progression of non-family managers could be limited by an implied, or, on rare occasions, express and articulated assumption that family candidates will be preferred for the most senior roles within the business.
- **Ownership.** Senior and talented non-family managers will often want to have the ability to acquire shares in the business they work for. This may be a difficult issue for a family, with a pure family ownership philosophy, which dictates that ownership should be reserved solely for family members. There are compromises solutions. Employee share ownership is considered in more detail below.

---

[6]   Considered as part of management succession in chapter 7.
[7]   See chapter 17 for a discussion on family charters and other family business governance issues.

- **Decision making.** Mangers may be reluctant to join if they feel that the family, or the family business leader, will always have the final say on significant decisions, without the chance for an open discussion.
- **Management style.** The attitude of the owner and their style of management can also be a critical factor. For example if they are autocratic, then this can inhibit the development of others. It may also lead to the lack of succession planning, which the manager sees as a risk to the business and to their own job.
- **Family dynamics.** A non-family manager can become the person that some family members turn to and dump their problems on, rather than having an open discussion with the person they are complaining about.[8] The non-family manager/director loses a lot of management time and get sucked into the family dynamics.
- **Family interference.** One of the growing pains of a family business, moving from being family run to family owned is the recurring tendency of family members, especially those in the senior generation to interfere in day-to-day business and management decisions. Sometimes these family members will still hold directorships of the family company. In theory the positions might be non-executive. These family members might still hold significant ownership stakes. It is accordingly very difficult for the non-family manager to stand up to such interference.

6.2.3 Family firm positives

However there are a lot of good reasons why a non-family member should join the right family business in a key role, including:

- The ability to work in a close team, with a lot of trust on all sides.
- The ability to see their decisions being implemented and change/improvements occurring because of those decisions.
- Escaping the bureaucracy and corporate hierarchy of a large multi-national organization.
- The large amount of job satisfaction that comes from, knowing that they are respected and trusted by the family. This can include fulfilling an important role at the time of management succession acting as a mentor to the next generation.[9]
- The opportunity for significant financial rewards because the family business is less bureaucratic than a larger organisation, and so on occasions could pay more or make discretionary payments to key non family members above market rates.

In many cases key managers/directors will join the family business after experience in a larger organisation, but then stay with the family business until their retirement.

6.3 NON-FAMILY MANAGERS AND PROFESSIONALISATION

As the business grows, and particularly as it reaches the third generation, it will have created its own identity, separate from the founder, although some of their

---

[8] This process, triangulation, in psychological terms, is discussed in chapter 3 (Tools, Models and Theories).
[9] See chapter 7.

characteristics and legacy may still be seen in how the business operates. There are likely to be more family members who will have a stake in the business. Also there are likely to be more non-family members in key roles.

The suggestion that family members should gain experience working in other organisations[10] ideally applies also to non-family managers. This will enable them to bring a more objective view to what they find in the family business, rather than accept practices that remain in place simply because 'that is the way we have always done things round here'. Also proven success elsewhere should translate into respect for from both the family and other key employees of the business.

However these arguments have marginally less force when applied to non-family managers than to family members. First the lack of respect issue is less likely to be a concern when decoupled from the suspicion of nepotism attached to family favourites. Secondly non-family employees are prone to share distrust of outsiders and their ideas and methods with the family.

There are many successful family businesses with a management team that includes both indentured non-family insiders, who are capable of interpreting the idiosyncrasies of the family firm and in effect acting as ambassadors of the family to the non-family outsider managers, who can in turn, introduce the insights and practices they have learnt in their travels to wider corporate lands to the family firm. It can initially be difficult for the non-family person joining a family business because of the long established culture, and the reluctance to change. This means that the right individual will need to be sensitive to these aspects and the family's attachment to the business. If the family has decided, and set down on paper, its values and vision in respect of the business then this can be useful in attracting the right executive, as they can see and understand from the outset the family's views, and that the family has recognised the need to define its role with the business.

The presentation of the appointment of the first non-family executive will need to be carefully handled, and in particular its presentation to the family. Both those already involved in the management, and those outside, especially if they are hoping to join the business, may have views on the possible appointment. Some family members may be disappointed and see the non-family appointment as thwarting their own ambitions. But there will be others who will see the move as a step towards professionalisation. So the possible appointment, and the business need, should be discussed with the interested parties and the wider family. It will be useful for both that discussion to define the role, the potential for career development, the goals that will be set and the appraisal process.

It is important for the individual being recruited that they can see there will be the opportunity for advancement which will be on a merit basis, and that the route to the top will not be blocked by the presence of family members. The extent to which this utopian position might be frustrated by the presence of a family glass ceiling is discussed below.

---

[10] See chapter 7.

6.4 THE FAMILY BUSINESS CULTURE CLASH

In his article *Integrating Professional Management into a Family Owned Business*, W Gibb Dyer Jr[11] looks at the difficulties of non-family professional management joining the idiosyncratic world of the family business. In essence Dyer identifies a fundamental culture clash, which has parallels with the clash between the family and business systems described in chapter 3.

The following table illustrates some of the differences between professional or managerial culture and family business characteristics, as perceived by Dyer and others[12] and how this translates into different approaches and mind-sets of family and non-family managers.

Professional Management	Family Business
External training and qualifications, generally applicable	Learning on the job
Management based training	Technical and highly specific training.
Status based on accomplishments	Status based on family membership
Membership of professional organisations	Family membership
Mobile and varied career	Family business for life
Professional detachment and objectivity	Driven by vision and sense of mission
Professional and balanced commitment	Unconditional and full commitment
Reliance on systems	Belief in flexibility
Embrace change	Committed to the status quo
Expect promotion on merit	Expect leadership as a birth right

Of course these are stereotypes. Increasingly many family businesses recognise the value of formal management training for family members.[13] Nevertheless some of the features listed above are observable realities, both from the perspective of professional non-family managers and from businesses families.

Commentators talk about potential clashes in style and personality between the entrepreneur founder and newly introduced non-family managers in early stage family

---

[11] *Family Business Review* (1989) Vol 3 at pp 221–235.
[12] Including Schein, Gersick and Sonnenfeld.
[13] Some families even include requirements that family member entrants should have an MBA or equivalent business qualification. One of the interesting issues is what effect the next MBA generation of family business leaders will have on the development of the in the family business world.

businesses. The tendency for entrepreneurs to put new managers on a pedestal and just as quickly tear them down has been noted in chapter 1. Many famous names[14] in the US car industry worked at Fords, before being driven out by clashes with Henry Ford. Partly this stems from the entrepreneur seeing talented non-family managers as rivals, otherwise called the 'tall poppy syndrome'. Partly this stems from a failure to appreciate that a family business moving into its managerial phase needs different talents to those required to get the business off the ground and embodied by the entrepreneur. This is coupled with a tendency on the part of the entrepreneur to see these differences as weaknesses.[15]

Much pain and suffering could be avoided if, in addition to examining their technical skills and experience, non-family managers could also be recruited on the basis of their ability to make the cultural leap into family business life. More precisely attention could be paid to ensuring that potential recruits appear to have the psychological maturity to accept the ambiguities of the family situation, and are prepared to embrace the positive aspects of this, whilst living with the negative.

This assessment could be reinforced by offering non-family management training in family business dynamics. In short the family business leadership could take step to ensure that the rest of the workforce and in particular senior management 'get the point' of a life in their family business. However, whilst some degree of reshaping of both the non-family manager and the family business might be possible (and indeed necessary), there are likely to be limitations to the extent that a square corporate manager peg can be refashioned to fit a round family business hole.

The potential culture clash between family business and corporate life goes deeper than the issues stemming from personality clashes between the entrepreneurial and managerial mind-sets. One of the distinctions made above is between the family system, which broadly seeks to maintain the status quo and the business practice of continual change and improvement. Again sensible balance needs to be achieved between preserving the culture and values of the family firm, which can represent a unique strategic strength and, on the other hand, the need to evolve and adapt. Dyer notes that 'some professional managers see their role in the family firm as one of killing sacred cows'.[16] A wholesale cull is likely to lead to clashes with the business owning family and possibly the early exit of the professional manager, whether by dismissal or their frustrated resignation. A more gradual process of change should lead to a more valuable herd.[17]

6.5 MOTIVATING NON-FAMILY MANAGERS

For the non-family executive to be effective then they need to be properly motivated. This will mean that there should be appraisal systems, objective setting, and career paths for the individual, equivalent to those in well-managed larger organisations.[18] Also financial rewards will be an important part of the motivational package.

---

[14] Of whom Horace Dodge remains the most best-known.
[15] Sonnenfeld provides an interesting example of this in an extended case study anonomised as Flowtrol Inc. See Sonnefeld *The Hero's Farewell: What Happens When CEO's Retire* (Oxford University Press, 1988), ch 10.
[16] Op cit at p 231.
[17] In a conversation with one former (and successful) non-family leader they used almost the same language as Dyer, but with they added that the family sacred cows should be 'shot one by one'.
[18] Commentators have identified a reluctance to embrace HR systems and practices as a typical family business weakness.

The professionalisation of the family business should therefore mean the non-family executive has:

- An employment contract with all the terms and conditions one would expect to see with a well-managed business. This should include provisions for the protection of the family firm, including restrictions on post employment competition and the use of confidential information and intellectual property.

- A financial reward package, based on fair market principles, including comparison with third parties and which is clear and transparent.[19] This can include both monetary rewards, and other benefits. It should also include the opportunities for performance related bonuses. The package should be seen as being objectively determined. Best practice dictates that family members in the business should also be assessed on the same basis and that this should be transparently so. If the family has clearly separated the financial rewards that derive from employment, and those which arise through ownership, then this will help in the development of reward systems that are motivational to the non-family workforce. This is also a key element of family business governance.

It might be that the family business leadership take a conscious decision to pay key non-family employees above the market rate in an attempt to recruit and retain them. This might be sensible in an environment where realistically their expectations to fill senior or top management positions may be limited by family incumbents. Arguably there is a lingering stigma attached to employment in the family business sector. Although this is may be entirely unfair, there could be an argument to compensate non-family managers for the possibility that their CV might be tainted by a spell in the family business world.

Using shares to compensate managers (family and non-family) is a tempting idea (and is discussed in some detail below). It is an obvious way to tie compensation to the long-term value of the business; an idea many family businesses find appealing because of their long-term orientation. Also, handing out shares can, at least superficially and in the short term, seem a cheap way to reward key people. It is also a device that is widely used in public companies.

However, unless the family business has liquidity (ie adequate cash resources to redeem shares) or is sold it is unlikely that managers will realise the rewards for their efforts. In addition 'when push comes to shove 'most family business usually want to restrict ownership to family members.

Incentive schemes are an alternative to share ownership for rewarding family and non-family managers for their efforts and performance and examples of such schemes include bonuses, profit share schemes, 'phantom' or 'shadow share schemes' and 'golden handcuffs' or deferred compensation, rewarding long term commitment to the family firm.

---

[19] Even if bonus schemes and allocations under share option schemes are discretionary this should be clearly stated.

6.6 EMPLOYEE OWNERSHIP

6.6.1 Overview

An important and potentially difficult issue is the question of share ownership. The debate about the admission of employees to the ownership register sits at the fulcrum of the balance between business, family and ownership systems. Again this may well be opened up as a result of work on a family charter.[20]

The executive may see an opportunity to acquire an equity stake as a key incentive, but the family may be reluctant to release shares. Some families will see share ownership, and the effective binding of the individual to the business as a positive, and encourage the family management to offer it as part of the package. Even if the family are not so welcoming of non-family members the board might be acutely concerned about the ability of the family company to recruit and retain talented senior employees in the absence of equity incentives.

6.6.2 Employee ownership and the early stage family firm

So far our discussion has focused almost exclusively on family ownership, on the assumption that an intention to create a family firm already exists. In many cases the position will be much more confused. In the early stages, key employees may well have been admitted to the ownership circle, alongside the founder and perhaps other family members. As discussed in chapter 1 it will often take some years before a fully-fledged and recognisable family business emerges.

6.6.3 Employees and ownership approach

The business owning family may have developed a family only ownership policy. This may be absolute. They may nevertheless regard a number of senior or long term employees as quasi-family members. Sometimes a separate class of shares is created for employees, in effect designed to provide them with temporary membership of the family firm, with full membership being reserved for family members.

As a first stage it is necessary to understand the family's views on share ownership for the executive and any objections, as well as the reason why ownership is important to the executive.[21] Often any conflicting views can be catered for. For example, if the family is concerned about the shareholding being spread across a wide base of family and non-family, with many former employees, or their families, owning shares, then the rights attaching to the executive's shares can include a condition that on their retirement, or departure, from the company they are required to sell the shares. This represents best practice in any event.

Sometimes the result of the ownership debate will be to allow full membership for a limited number of employee shareholders. However this would be comparatively rare, especially for a family committed to structured long-term family ownership. More often hybrid solutions emerge to recognise the status of employees. In practice the family

---

[20] See chapter 17.
[21] See chapter 11 (Ownership Overview).

charter is only likely to contain broad statements of principle of the family's attitude to employee share participation. The details will be contained in separate shareholder agreements, articles of association or option agreements.

6.6.4 (Not quite) one of the family

The next question is what happens if the employee leaves the company and thereby ceases to be one of the family? The family are unlikely to want too wide a share ownership base developing. So the family are less likely to want any shares issue to employees to then be passed on to members of that employee's family. They may also want to use the pruning tools discussed later to buy back existing employee shares.

Even if the family's ownership philosophy is not fully formed at the time it would be sensible to address this point at the time shares are issued or transferred to employees. Provisions should be included to:

- Restrict further share transfers by employee.
- Require the employee to sell their shares when they retire from or otherwise leave the family business.[22] The employee shares would then come back into the family fold.

If the relevant rights to acquire the departing employee's shares (usually structured as call options) are not exercised by the family business the former non-family executive (and possibly their family members) will remain as sleeping shareholders in the family firm. More than one family business has been severely caught out by a failure to include, or to police and enforce, these arrangements when a senior shareholding employee has left the family business. If the departure has been in acrimonious circumstances the employee may use the leverage provided by their holding to extract some form of revenge.[23]

Complications can arise even in circumstances when an employee has retired on good terms after long service. Particularly in larger multi-generational family-owned businesses the shareholder register often contains the original employee's own children and grandchildren who have no clear continuing connection with the company and whose presence can complicate the governance and cohesiveness of the shareholder group.

Whether to provide the outgoing executive with parallel rights, structured as put options, enabling them to realise the value of their holding is a different question and is discussed in the context of share options below.

---

[22] In rare circumstances the family might be prepared for an employee to retain shares after retirement, to provide an income via dividend streams or perhaps to allow the employee to retain their attachment to the family firm. It would nevertheless be important to include provisions obliging the employee's estate to sell the shares on death.
[23] And many family firms have lived to regret their presence, particularly if the family business is to be sold later (see chapter 12).

6.6.5 Employee ownership solutions

There is a large amount of flexibility in developing share schemes, and the rights that attach to shares. Often an arrangement can be created which meets both the needs of the family and the executive.

The range of employee ownership solutions include:
- **Full ownership.** Providing employees with full shareholding rights whilst employed. Best practice dictates that there should be compulsory buy-back arrangements, binding on (at least) the employees on leaving the employment of the family company.
  Any such offer should be accompanied by buy-back arrangements, allowing those shares to be reacquired by the family shareholders once the employee's temporary family status has been surrendered on leaving the family business.
- **Employee share class.** Issuing a separate class of non-voting shares to employees usually accompanied by similar buy-back provisions.
  Restrictions can be incorporated into the ownership rights attached to those shares. For example they may only have capital rights, and no voting rights.
- **Option schemes.** Setting up share options schemes. These will need to be carefully crafted to provide value and appropriate incentives for the employee concerned. Usually, in most non-family business situations, value is created for employees under share option schemes on sale or flotation. Those exit routes may well be blocked by the family's long-term family ownership philosophy. Alternative triggers will need to be created if the employee is to realise value, usually on leaving employment.
  Options can be priced at the market value at the time of grant so that employees benefit from the uplift in value created during their time with the company, thereby creating a strong incentive to help the business grow.
  Sophistications can also be added, such as performance criteria (either individual or collective) and good and bad leaver provisions, so that long term employees retiring or leaving because of ill health will benefit in full. However employees leaving after a shorter period of service or those bad leavers departing under a cloud will see their benefits scaled back or eliminated altogether.
- **Phantom option schemes.** It is possible to set up a shadow or phantom option scheme, if there is a greater reluctance for employees to participate in ownership, but still a desire to create incentives by linking financial rewards to long term company performance and growth in share value. The complications of full ownership, including the complexity of retrieving shares from departing employees are avoided. Under phantom share schemes the executive does not actually acquire shares. Instead, at some stage in the future, they receive a reward that is linked to the increase in the value of the business, or perhaps a part of the business over which they have control. A phantom share scheme is therefore a species of long-term bonus arrangement that mirrors actual share ownership. As no actual shares will be issued any resulting payments are treated in the same way as any other employment related bonus and will be taxed as income. The tax benefits of structuring employee share incentives under EMI option schemes will not available.

6.6.6 Employees and exit routes

If employee shares are to have real value as incentives key questions are who will buy those shares and how will the buy-back of shares of non-family executives, whether held directly or pursuant to rights under share option schemes be financed?

Potential buyers are:

- **The family company.** There are legal and tax implications and requirements of this alternative, which will be considered at a later stage when looking at pruning the share ownership tree.[24] However many of the technical company law restrictions on buy-backs discussed in chapter 11, do not apply to employee share schemes.
- **Family members.** The buyer could be an individual family member, or group of family members, or a family trust.
- **Other employees.** Shares can be sold directly between employees. The sale could be from a departing manager to their replacement. However it may be sensible for the incoming employee to serve some form of qualifying period, typically 3 years, in which both parties can assess whether they will fit into the family firm with all its cultural idiosyncrasies.
- **Employee share ownership trust.** The shares can be bought an employee share ownership trust (ESOT) set up by the company as discussed below.

Often the viability of the exit route will come down to hard economic realities including supply and demand and cash-flow. So considerations such as payment by instalments, discussed in the context of family exit provisions,[25] apply equally to shares and options held by non-family employees. This is with one key difference. This is that the less generous and more uncertain the exit route is for the executive, the lower is the incentive actually provided by share ownership in the family firm in the first place. Whilst the business owning family might agree that it is appropriate for family members to have a viable exit route from ownership, they might not feel that it is sensible for family members to have an incentive to use that route. However employees leaving a family firm after many years of loyal service would undoubtedly expect to be treated as good leavers with the benefit of a fair, viable and well thought out exit route for the sale of their shares.

6.6.7 Employee share ownership trusts

In simple terms this is a discretionary trust that is initially funded by a contribution from the company. The basic purpose of the ESOT is to buy shares from and sell shares to employees.

ESOTs can also acquire shares from other shareholders, including family members, who are in search of an exit route from their family company. The trusts could provide a marketplace for such share transactions. But the consequence will be a shift from family ownership to employee ownership of the business. As well as buying back shares from retiring employees, it can also 'warehouse' these to create a pool from which an employee, who has been granted an option to acquire shares, buys their shares.

---

[24] See chapter 11 for a discussion on pruning generally and chapter 16 for the related tax implications.
[25] See chapter 11.

ESOTs are usually part of sophisticated employee incentive and remuneration schemes, with carefully thought out eligibility criteria. The board control which employees benefit from the shares held under the trusts and put documents in place to make sure that the shares are reclaimed once employment has finished.

6.6.8 Employee ownership and tax

All share schemes have tax implications. Some share schemes are tax efficient and others, which are 'unapproved' have limited tax benefits. The tax implications of the various types of share schemes will be considered at a later stage.[26]

6.7 FAMILY EMPLOYEE AND SHARE OWNERSHIP

It will be readily appreciated that family employees occupy at least two, if not all three systems in the family business three-circle model. In addition to any shares they own as family members, there is an argument that family employees should be entitled to participate in any employee share scheme arrangements on identical terms to non-family employees. This would include divestment provisions on leaving the family company, including on retirement.[27]

Treating family employees in this way has a number of potential advantages. In governance terms it is helping to show a level playing field between family and non-family employees. In terms of ownership philosophy it provides a possible bridge between whole family and insider ownership approaches.[28] Finally, in terms of succession planning, it provides a potential pot of cash to senior generation family employees on their retirement.

6.8 NON-FAMILY MANAGERS AND GOVERNANCE

As part of the professionalisation of the business, if shares are issued then consideration should also be given to the preparation of a shareholders' agreement. This will give the family some protection and comfort in, say, a potential sales situation, with, say a 'drag along' clause.

The starting point for creating a governance structure is in agreeing on the family's views on the purpose of the business and the values that it should adopt. Best practice suggests that these should be captured in some form, most typically in a family charter.[29] The detailed governance structures can be formal or informal, depending on various factors, including the size and sophistication of the business, the size of the business family and the quality of the underlying family dynamics.

The governance system and in particular the values of the business owning family, as articulated in the family charter need to be clearly understood by the non-family executive. If the executive is to be effective and motivated then they need to understand,

---

[26] See chapter 16.
[27] Logically the divestment provisions would apply only to those shares held by virtue of employment rather than family status.
[28] See chapter 15.
[29] See chapter 17.

as thoroughly as possible, the family culture and environment in which they are expected to operate. If not, there is a danger that decisions they make will be overruled by the family. Best practice suggests that some form of 'family acclimatisation', including access to the family charter, should form part of the induction process for incoming executives.[30]

Within the business system good governance points to the need to move towards the more formal, and regular management systems, processes and meetings, which would operate in the professional manner one would expect to see for public and larger companies. Some movement in this direction is likely to be necessary, both for the successful integration of the non-family executive and to enable them to do the job for which they have been hired. The challenge for family enterprises is how to introduce these systems in a way that does not create undue tension with senior generation family members and, most importantly does not sacrifice the flexibility, creativity and responsiveness that may have been a core strength of the family firm to date.

The primary business governance forum will of course be the board of directors[31] but the general points about the need to develop systems and procedures hold good across the management spectrum. A key reason is to ensure, so far as possible, an even flow of information and opportunity between family and non-family employees.

6.9 DISCRIMINATION AND NEPOTISM

In the previous chapter we mentioned the nine protected characteristics recognised by the Equality Act for the purposes of the discrimination legislation. These are age, disability, gender reassignment, marriage and civil partnership, pregnancy and maternity, race, religion or belief, sex and sexual orientation.[32]

At first sight positive discrimination in favour of a family member, nepotism in plain language, does not appear to fall foul of any of these. It might be clearly shown that family members were treated more favourably in terms of hiring, promotion, higher pay and other employment terms. This may seem unfair. It conflicts with recommendations as to family business best practice. But in the absence of a protected characteristic, there is no obvious legal remedy for the disadvantaged non-family employee.

The same argument could even extend to dismissal. For example if there was a severe and unresolvable personality clash between a family and non-family employee, such that it was clear that one must leave. It could be argued that, all other things being equal, it would be within the range of reasonable responses for family management to favour the

---

[30] As explained in chapter 7, this is for both family and non-family executives. The reason for this is more obvious in the case of non-family entrants. However there are strong arguments for family members joining the business to receive an equivalent briefing as a foundation for a level playing field.
[31] Discussed in detail in chapter 17.
[32] Section 4 of the Equality Act.

family member and dismiss the other[33] relying on the SOSR (some other substantial reason) to do so.[34] Similar arguments could apply in the case of selection for redundancy.

But what of the situation where the other candidates for the job, the pay-rise or the promotion in question, or dismissal was of a different gender, from a different racial group or disabled? In this scenario, there is a risk that the unsuccessful individual could try to argue that the decision was discriminatory. Here the family could argue that the presence of a protected characteristic was purely incidental. The dominant reason for the choice was to prefer family members. In essence the family firm would be pleading nepotism as a defence. This might not seem to be an over-attractive argument. In certain situations identified below it would by no means be guaranteed to succeed before an employment tribunal.

6.9.1 Discrimination and recruitment

In a family businesses, where the workforce includes non-family employees, recruiting a family member directly into a position, without considering a wider pool of candidates can inevitably have a negative impact on staff morale. It may appear that the business places the needs of the family above that of the business. Being seen to go through a fair recruitment process, including advertising the position, can go some way to mitigating these negative perceptions. However in practical terms, if the family member is successful, even at the end of an entirely fair recruitment process, there may be some sense of inevitability about the business's recruitment choice. In practice it may always be difficult to wholly dispel negative perceptions of favouritism so far as the rest of the workforce is concerned.

In legal terms there is no requirement to advertise positions either internally or externally. In the majority of cases a family business will recruit a family member without advertising the position. However recruiting family members automatically, where there is a potentially wider pool of applicants from which the business can choose, can increase the risk of discrimination claims (see below). Also, in terms of best employment practice, it is generally considered that by advertising the position the pool of potential applicants is widened, thereby ensuring equality of opportunity.

The Equality Act 2010 Code of Practice (EHRC Code) specifies that before deciding only to advertise a vacancy internally, an employer should consider whether there is any good reason for not advertising externally as well. If the workforce is comprised of, for example, a particular sex or racial group then advertising internally will not help diversify the workforce. If there is internal advertising alone, this should be done openly so that everyone in the organisation is given the opportunity to apply.

---

[33] Although we have absolutely no authority for this proposition similar arguments have supported the retention of a senior employee and the dismissal of the more junior. Conceivably arguments such as the relative difficulty of family members finding alternative employment, damage to other family relationship within the business, could all be used as supporting arguments.

[34] Some other substantial reason dismissals are discussed and, explored in the context of the *Papier* case discussed in chapter 5.

Not advertising available posts at all or undertaking selective advertising to certain individuals may give rise to complaints of unlawful discrimination. The Equality and Human Rights Commission (EHRC) in its Guidance on the Equality Act gives the following example:

> 'A large employer recruits workers to driving jobs through word of mouth. This results in everyone who has a driving job being a member of the same few families or a friend of these families. All the family members and their friends are white, despite the workplace being in an area of high ethnic minority population. Unless the employer can objectively justify the way drivers are recruited, this is likely to be indirect discrimination because of race.'

However, in the day-to-day life of a family business it is questionable whether such claims are likely or would succeed. In early stage and small family businesses, perhaps where the existing workforce comprises only family members, the chances of a discrimination claim being brought as a result of a decision to recruit another family member is relatively remote. In practical terms it may be safe to assume that the wider world would be unaware and largely unconcerned about any such recruitment decision.

The issue was considered in the case of *Coker and Osamor v The Lord Chancellor and the Lord Chancellor's Department*,[35] in which the then Lord Chancellor's decision to appoint an individual who was known to him, rather than advertise the post, was held not to be discriminatory. Although strictly the case deals with positive discrimination in favour of friends and acquaintances, the same logic ought to apply to preferment of family members.[36] In *Coker* the Court of Appeal suggested that:[37]

> 'Making an appointment from within a circle of family, friends and personal acquaintances is seldom likely to constitute indirect discrimination.'

The Court of Appeal also questioned whether, in taking a decision to appoint (in that case a friend or acquaintance) an employer has, in the true sense, applied a 'requirement or condition' that a protected group will be disproportionately less likely to satisfy (as required by the ERA 1996. Instead the employer 'has simply offered someone known to him a job'.[38] When dealing with family leadership appointments there must be an argument as to whether a recruiting exercise, in the proper sense of the word is taking place at all.[39] However the Court of Appeal in *Coker* did not need to decide that point.

In addition a requirement that is potentially indirectly discriminatory, may nevertheless be found to be justifiable. Although this aspect was not explored in any detail by the Court of Appeal it could possibly be argued on behalf of family businesses that some of the positive features of family leadership, including continuity and commitment, could provide justification for the appointment of family candidates. However the Court of Appeal added the caveat that:[40]

---

[35] [2001] EWCA Civ 1756.
[36] There are various references made to recruitment of family members in the text of the judgment. The proceedings were funded by the Equal Opportunities Commission and the Commission for Racial Equality who made it clear that the object was to 'challenge the practice of closed, or internal recruitment' (at para 7 of the judgment) and that the outcome of the proceedings had potential impact not only for the 'practice of substantial undertakings' but also for 'every small business where staff are recruited from family friends or acquaintances that share a common racial grouping' (see para 8).
[37] At para 39 of the judgment.
[38] At para 23 of the judgment.
[39] See para 51 of the judgment.
[40] At para 53 of the judgment.

'It does not follow that this practice is unobjectionable. It will often be open to objection for a number of reasons.

It may not produce the best candidate for the post. It may be likely to result in the appointee being of a particular gender or racial group. It may infringe the principle of equal opportunities.'

6.9.2 Discrimination whilst in employment

Similar issues arise in relation to discrimination once the employment relationship has commenced, for example in relation to promotion, benefits and bonuses. Where non-family members are already employed and known to the family business, it is more likely that they will feel disgruntled if a family member is given preferential treatment, particularly in circumstances where the non-family member is, or believes themselves to be, an equal or better performer. In these circumstances, disgruntled family members may be more likely to try to rely on a discriminatory reason for their perceived unfair treatment.

Example

The position of line manager at Smiths Family Bakers becomes available. Tom Smith, the son of owners George and Mavis Smith, is given the position. Tom has only recently left school and apart from working during some holidays in the bakery has no other relevant experience. Jane Thompson has worked in the business for 5 years and is suitable for the role. When Jane hears that Tom has been given the role she brings a claim for direct and indirect sex discrimination.

In the above scenario Jane will allege that she has been treated less favourably than Tom on the grounds of her sex. Direct discrimination cannot be justified (with the exception of direct age discrimination). However Smiths would look to defend such a claim on the grounds that Tom was the most suitable person for the role based on his particular skills and attributes, although his relative inexperience would obviously be problematic in establishing a successful defence.

Jane could also try to allege indirect sex discrimination on the grounds that Smiths Bakers has applied a 'provision, criterion or practice' (PCP) that the successful candidate must be a male member of the Smiths family. However Smiths could look to defend such a claim on the grounds- that the PCP was not related to sex and could extend equally to a female member of the Smiths family. In other words the decisive criteria was family membership.

6.9.3 Discrimination and equal pay

As with its predecessor legislation, the Equality Act implements the fundamental principle that men and women should receive equal pay for equal work.[41] Equal pay is a complex area and a detailed explanation of the law surrounding equal pay is outside the scope of this book.

Equal pay claims can be brought by either gender. An individual employed under a contract personally to do work is legally entitled to enjoy contractual terms that are as

---

[41] Equal pay is a very complex area of law, the detail of which is beyond the scope of this book.

favourable as those of an opposite sex comparator in the 'same employment' if they are employed on equal work. Equal work is defined as 'like work' 'work rated as equivalent' or 'work of equal value'.

The law works by implying an 'equality clause' into every contract of employment. This operates to replace the less favourable terms, for example in a woman's contract, with the equivalent more favourable terms of a man's contract.

Material factor defence

It is a defence to an equal pay claim to demonstrate that the difference in pay is due to a material factor which is relevant and significant and which does not directly or indirectly discriminate against the female worker because of her sex. In the case of indirect sex discrimination the employer will need to be able to objectively justify the provision, criterion or practice which is ostensibly non-discriminatory but has a disproportionate adverse impact on women as being a 'proportionate means of achieving a legitimate aim'.

Remedies

An individual must bring a claim to tribunal within 6 months of the end of their employment or bring a breach of contract claim in the civil courts within 6 years. Where the individual is successful in their claim a tribunal can make a declaration of their rights under the equality clause, require payment of any arrears (in the case of pay) or damages (in the case of a non-pay contractual term) going back up to 6 years for breach of the sex equality clause.

Risk areas for the family business

A family business could, theoretically find itself inadvertently falling foul of equal pay legislation through practices which it considers entirely acceptable and lawful.

> *Example 1*
>
> A family care home business 'Primrose Place' is run by a group of four brothers. They decide to recruit June Day, a female non-family employee, into a senior management role in the business. June has 15 years' experience in the private care home sector and is hired to work alongside the four brothers carrying out a similar role to them in terms of developing the business, assisting in marketing and overall strategy of the business. The brothers choose to pay her significantly less salary than they are each paid (£30,000 compared to £50,000 they each receive). June discovers this discrepancy in pay, resigns and brings an equal pay claim.
>
> It will be necessary for June to use one of the brothers as a comparator in her claim. The Family Business will have a successful defence to the claim if it can demonstrate that June's work is not 'equal work' to the work which her chosen comparator carries out (ie 'like work' 'work rated as equivalent', or 'work of equal value'). Alternatively the business will need to prove that the variation in pay is due to a material factor which is not direct or indirect discrimination. The Business may try to plead market forces as a material factor, namely to pay her more would have involved paying significantly more than the local 'going rate'. Alternatively it may try and rely on the fact that in order to earn the higher salary one must be a family member of the business and that sex is an irrelevant consideration. For example the Business would pay a sister or female cousin the higher rate of pay but a male non-family member the same lower hourly rate paid to June.

Using family as a material factor defence to an equal pay claim is as yet untested. It remains to be seen whether this defence would be successful.

Example 2

> Take, for example, the 'Primrose Place' scenario above but instead of the brothers recruiting a female non-family employee they choose to recruit their sister into the business. However they pay their sister £20,000 less than the salaries they each receive. Assuming the sister could point to a successful comparator, we suggest that it may be more difficult to establish a material factor defence. In this scenario it would not be open to the business the 'family' defence mentioned above.
>
> The brothers could have structured their pay differently to reduce the risks of an equal pay claim in these cases. Assuming that the brothers are each shareholders in the business they could choose to pay themselves additional amounts by way of dividend payment.
>
> This might be more tax efficient anyway.[42] It also makes more sense in a three-circle model systems analysis. The additional remuneration would clearly be seen to flow to the brothers in their capacity as owners.

6.10 NON-FAMILY MANAGERS AND THE FAMILY BUSINESS GLASS CEILING

The advice of commentators is pretty much universal and unequivocal; that family members should only be recruited and promoted to positions they are qualified to fulfill, and that this advice applies especially to the role of business leader.[43]

Commentators also speak of the need to ensure that the family business can attract and retain a pool of talented non-family managers. They assume that this can be achieved by a mixture of restricting family employment to only the crème de la crème of the next generation,[44] and that the continuing growth of the family enterprise will provide sufficient opportunities for all.[45]

Nevertheless the same commentators also advocate a family firm setting up specific programmes for the development of family leadership.[46] Clearly these are based on the working assumption that family leadership is to be preferred. This positive discrimination in favour of family insiders can inevitably have repercussions so far as the recruitment, motivation and retention of senior non-family managers are concerned. In practice the realistic prospects of advancement for senior non-family managers are inhibited by the presence of a family glass ceiling. The question then becomes to what extent should the existence of this de-facto glass ceiling (together with associated elements of this, such as the family fast track) be explicitly acknowledged and even articulated to non-family employees?

---

[42] This is considered in more detail in chapter 4.
[43] See for example John Ward, Lessons 4 (Principle of Merit) and 5 (Attract the Most Competent Family Members) from John Ward *Perpetuating the Family Business: 50 Lessons Learned from Long-Lasting Successful Families in Business* (Palgrave, 2004). Neubauer and Lank suggest that the key criteria for family business leadership 'must be competence not blood'. See Neubauer and Lank *The Family Business: Its Governance for Sustainability* (Harvard Business School Press, 1997) at p 150.
[44] See Lesson 16 (Selective Family Employment), John Ward, op cit.
[45] See Neubauer and Lank *The Family Business: Its Governance for Sustainability* (Harvard Business School Press, 1997) at p 149.
[46] These are discussed in chapter 7.

Based on the authority of *Coker* the legal risks of discrimination claims would appear to be quite low. Arguably expressly acknowledging a family first policy provides an opportunity for the business owning family to consider the commercial wisdom, extent and limits of such a policy. Any implicit but inappropriate assumptions can then be refined. Attempting to justify a family first policy also provides an opportunity to cross-check the application of the policy against the residual legal risks referred to above.

Assuming that the family first policy has been tested and survived closer scrutiny by the family business governance processes there seems to be much to recommend making this clear to non-family employees. This is certainly so, when compared with the dangers of offering positive reassurances that the family firm represents a level playing field when the reality is that non-family members are playing permanently uphill. Non-family recruits will inevitably arrive with a degree of scepticism and concern about the existence of a family glass-ceiling in any event.

Arguably an express discussion about the implications of family ownership on career development will mean that those recruited are more likely to appreciate the positive aspects of this referred to above[47] and correspondingly more likely to last the family business course. As referred to above it might be that the family business leadership take a conscious decision to pay key family employees above the market rate in an attempt to attract and retain them. Share based incentives, as discussed above could also be considered.

6.11 CONCLUSION

The successful recruitment and retention of non-family employees, especially senior management, is likely to be one of the key factors for a family business to survive and thrive. As with many family business challenges difficult balances need to made. Recruits need to be sufficiently dynamic to help drive change and growth, yet flexible enough to appreciate and work within the unique culture of the family firm concerned.

But the most difficult balancing act concerns the tension between the needs of the business, those of senior non-family managers and the presence of the next generation of family managers. Taking the presence of family leadership as one of the main elements in most family businesses (although not necessarily a defining characteristic[48]) the central challenge becomes how to reconcile the health of the business, with the presence of family managers and the careers of non-family managers.

This issue is encountered at various stages, each of which present different challenges. When non-family managers first join to work alongside the founding entrepreneur, when the next generation family and non-family managers need to be integrated to produce a cohesive and effective management team and, most crucially, at the stage of leadership succession. This topic forms the subject matter of the next chapter.

---

[47] And in chapter 1.
[48] See the discussion on the definition of family businesses in chapter 1.

CHAPTER 7

MANAGEMENT SUCCESSION

7.1 INTRODUCTION

The defining characteristic of family business success is often seen to be how well succession is handled. Usually that is measured by the number of generations that a business stays in the hands of the business owning family. But that does not necessarily have to be the case. Whilst succession within the business owning family may be the preferred option there are other, equally valid alternatives, which are mentioned below,[1] the most significant of which is likely to be a sale.

There is a lot at stake. Obviously on a micro level the wealth, careers and happiness of the members of the business owning family are on the line.

The efficiency or otherwise of the succession process has significant macro-economic consequences for the UK as a whole. According to a report produced in 2010 by the Institute for Family Business in conjunction with Oxford Economics[2] there are approximately 3 million family businesses in the UK, generating revenues of £1.1 trillion. It is estimated that 172,000 of these will leave the control of a generation each year, through sale, passing on ownership to the next generation or simply closing the family business. A back of the envelope calculation suggests that this translates into revenues of about £63 billion that are exposed to the risks of the succession process each year.[3] In more human terms the same study suggested that family firms provided approximately 9.2 million jobs. Applying the same logic this means that about 530,000 people will be employed in family firms concluding a succession process. If that process has gone well those jobs should be secure. Employment might increase. If not the jobs are at risk.

Most family firm will have a working bias towards family leadership succession. But that is not the only option and will frequently not be the most appropriate.

The true measure of a successful transition for a business owning family is to choose the most appropriate alternative and to implement the transition in a way that provides the best outcome, or, more precisely, the best balance of outcomes for all stakeholders in the

---

[1] And discussed in detail in chapter 15.
[2] *The UK family Business Sector: Working to grow the UK Economy* (Institute for Family Business with Oxford Economics, November 2010).
[3] Any errors in the maths are ours but the argument and approach is borrowed from Martin Stepek, deployed when seeking to demonstrate the significance of succession to the Scottish economy and the corresponding need for academic institutions to include family business content as a core part of their business school curricula. See Martin Stepek 'No visible means of support' *Journal of Family Business Management* (2011), Vol 1, Issue 2 at pp 174–180.

three systems comprised within the family business. These are the business itself, including employees, customers and suppliers, secondly ownership (as evidenced by the wealth of the business owning family) and, last but by no means least, the happiness and harmony of the business owning family and its individual members. As one commentator put it the goal:[4]

> '... should not be to increase the number of family businesses that survive into the next generation, but to **narrow** the number to only those whose family businesses enhance their lives.'

This is no small task. The rest of this chapter will look at various aspects of the succession process. Because succession is such a pervasive theme running through the heart of family business life and, with it, this book as a whole, this chapter serves partly as a summary and a source of cross references.

Succession is multi-faceted. The two core elements nevertheless remain ownership and management succession. These are usually considered together. The two issues are, of course, very closely related. But the overlap is not fully complete. Without a desire to keep the business in family ownership, the question of family management succession becomes pretty much irrelevant. The converse is not necessarily true. It may be possible to retain family ownership of a business but under non-family management. That approach will take great courage and commitment on the part of the business owning family. So, although management succession will often be the first to occur, in many ways the more important and strategic question is whether the family want to retain ownership of their business into the next generation? This is explored in chapter 15. This chapter will concentrate on the first of those issues, management succession.

7.2 SUCCESSION DISSECTED

There is no single and widely accepted definition of succession in the context of family business. Whilst the Family Firm Institute (FFI) define 'succession planning',[5] they do not attempt a definition of succession itself. As suggested, above succession is often seen narrowly, as being confined to the transfer of ownership from one generation of the business owning family to the next.

Alternatively succession is seen in terms of the transfer of management responsibility from one generation to the next, the day on which the next generation family business leader moves into the big office of the managing director, previously occupied by their father.

The dictionary definition,[6] 'following in order', is much broader and more general and fits with the wider concept referred to above. Succession is also a much more complex process and involves not only the transfer of ownership and management but also the more subtle elements as shown below.

---

[4] K Kaye 'Happy Landings: The opportunity to fly again' *Family Business Review* (1998) Vol 11 at pp 275–280.
[5] As 'the process and content of preparing for a successful transition of leadership in a family enterprise, often from one generation to the next' see *Family Enterprise; Understanding Families in Business and Families of Wealth* (Wiley, 2013) at p 151.
[6] *Concise Oxford English Dictionary* (Oxford University Press).

Figure 7.1: Elements of succession

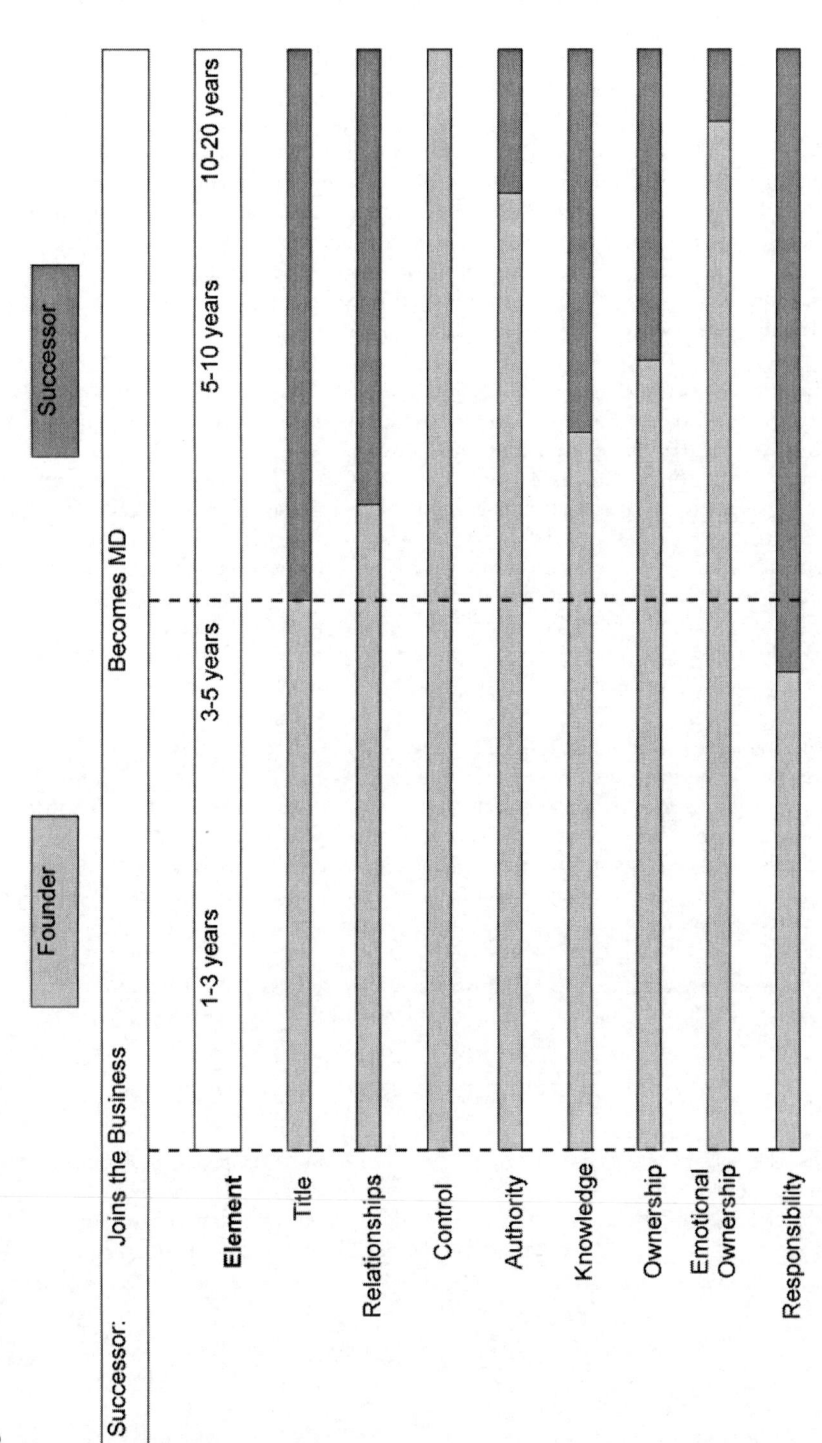

The purpose of Figure 7.1 is to illustrate some broad points about the succession process rather than to paint a precise picture. Just as there is no typical family business, so there is no typical succession process. The figure is meant to show the simplest succession scenario, that of a founder to a single child, following the traditional stereotype, most typically a son. It shows the son being appointed as managing director some years before ownership is transferred to him. This would be quite usual.

The illustration also suggests that notwithstanding the transfer of ownership, the father continues to exert influence and control over the family firm. This might be through strength of personality or the founder's position within the business owning family. The clearest example would be Henry Ford. Henry had passed over majority legal control of Fords to Edsel and to family trusts at a comparatively early stage, but continued to rule the roost well into his eighties. This distinction between legal and real outright control of a family business is referred to in chapter 11.

The model also suggests that, although the son had been appointed as managing director, the father still enjoyed greater technical and business knowledge until after that transfer, also that the key business relationships, with senior employees, suppliers and customers continued to reside with the father, well beyond the point of theoretical management hand over. Indeed there will often be a significant disconnection between theoretical titles and the real power and control in a family owned business. The senior generation former business leader may have resigned have as a director but nevertheless remain involved in key decisions. Alternatively the senior generation could in theory be acting as chairman, but still taking most of the day-to-day management decisions, so that the role of the next generation, although nominally that of managing director is correspondingly reduced so as to be almost indefinable.

We can argue about the detail. Indeed this will differ from succession to succession. We can certainly point to one example where a second generation son, revolutionised a family business to such dramatic effect that all of the elements, including knowledge and also the relationship with the main non-family manager, who had previously been the father's loyal lieutenant, could be seen to have transferred to the son at a very early stage. The exception was legal ownership, which, in that case was very closely connected to ultimate control.

What the diagram does clearly illustrate is that succession is a complex and involved process, which can take many years to fully evolve.

7.3 FAMILY BUSINESS LIFE STAGE AND SUCCESSION

We introduced the concept of the life stages of family businesses in chapter 3. This has implications for the succession process. As the business grows and matures through the typical stages of owner management, sibling partnership and cousin collaboration, a different approach to management and ownership will be required.

Figure 7.2: Stages in a successful multi-generational business

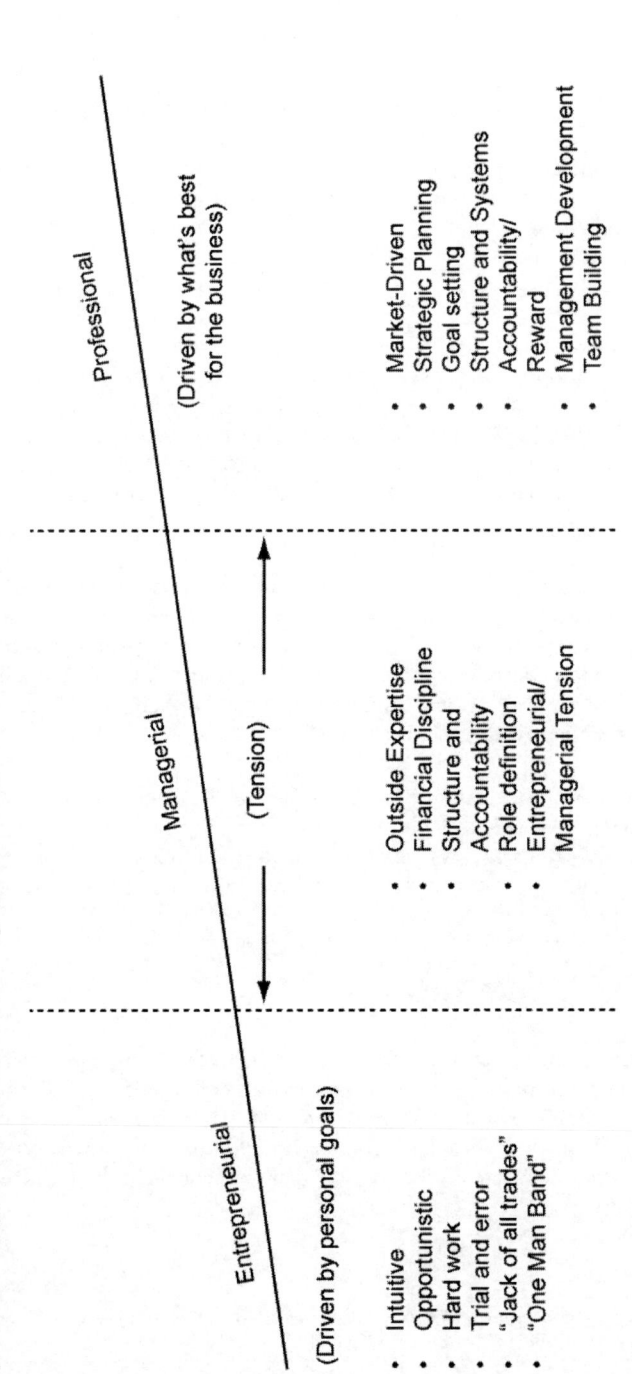

Entrepreneurial — Managerial — Professional

(Driven by personal goals) — (Tension) — (Driven by what's best for the business)

Entrepreneurial:
- Intuitive
- Opportunistic
- Hard work
- Trial and error
- "Jack of all trades"
- "One Man Band"

Managerial:
- Outside Expertise
- Financial Discipline
- Structure and Accountability
- Role definition
- Entrepreneurial/Managerial Tension

Professional:
- Market-Driven
- Strategic Planning
- Goal setting
- Structure and Systems
- Accountability/Reward
- Management Development
- Team Building

Source: Swartz, 2004

In the early days of the entrepreneurial start up, the founder is likely to hold all the shares, take all key decisions and to lead a small group of employees by sheer force of personality. Decisions will be made on the hoof and instinctively. Seat of the pants will prevail over systems. If the family business is to survive and thrive this management style can only be sustained for so long. The founder won't be able to do everything. Almost certainly there will be gaps in their skill set that need to be filled. The temptation might be to fill those gaps largely with next generation family resource. That might work to an extent. Other parts of the evolving management structure are likely to require suitably qualified and experienced non-family managers, for example financial expertise.

Almost inevitably this shifting of the tectonic plates within the family business system will create friction. The founder's ambivalence will come to the fore. Logically they may understand and even champion the need for change. Some deeper part of their being might miss the sense of excitement of earlier years, resent the constraints of the new systems and see the new management (both family and non-family) not as allies but as rivals.

Ivan Lansberg, in turn quoting Max Weber, suggests that the process of introducing management structures, but without losing the essential entrepreneurial characteristics that define the family firm, as 'the institutionalisation of charisma'.[7] This move to a managerial system might take place sooner or later, depending on the growth of the family business concerned, but it could well be occurring at a crucial time in the succession transition process.

In contrast to the revolutionary disruption likely to accompany the move from entrepreneurial to managerial stages, the progression of a family business into its professional stage is likely to be smoother and evolutionary. In many ways it is more of the same. More detailed structures and processes underpinned by strategic planning may have created a recognisably professional environment, one where handing managerial control to non-family management becomes a possibility.

At this stage of the evolution of the family business the core challenge might well move into the ownership system. How will the business owning family balance the interests of insiders and outsiders?[8] Governance systems will come to the fore.[9] If the business is to be managed by non-family directors how will the family ownership and influence be felt?

7.4 BARRIERS TO SUCCESSION

In chapter 2 we introduce, as part of the examination of the psychology of the entrepreneur, the distinction made by Peter Davis between entrepreneurs and founders; the idea that whilst all family businesses will have an entrepreneur at their root not all entrepreneurs are family business founders. There is an additional ingredient present in founders 'a love of what they have created that makes them want to perpetuate it through the generations'.

---

[7] Ivan Lansberg 'The Succession Conspiracy' *Family Business Review* Vol 1(2), 119–143, at p 119, referencing Weber *The Theory of Social Economic Organization* (Oxford University Press, 1946).
[8] See chapter 15.
[9] See chapter 17.

Often that realisation will grow over a period of time. The entrepreneur becomes a founder. It is comparatively rare that in establishing a business the entrepreneur sets out to create a family business dynasty. The business moves further towards the stricter definitions of a family business[10] once passing this onto the next generation becomes the preferred option. Yet the family business survival rates from generation to generation are low. Many founders fail in their mission to perpetuate their creation. Why is this? What are the barriers to a succession?

They are many and varied.

7.4.1 Managerial barriers

Sometimes the difficulties with the succession process relate to the management structure of the family business. For example:

- the dependence of the business on the owner manager;
- that there is no natural successor to the current generation;
- difficulties in selecting the next business leader.

7.4.2 Ownership issues

There might be unresolved questions relating to the ownership of the family business, which in turn lead to delays in the management succession process. These include questions over:

- who should own the business in the future?
- whether all children should own the business equally, whether or not they work in business?
- how to reconcile the interests of family members who work for the company, and those who pursue other interests, particularly if there are insufficient transferable assets held outside the business.

7.4.3 Financial barriers

The senior generation might simply not feel that they have the financial security to retire. This can be attributed to various factors:

- historic business performance;
- financial dependence of the senior generation on the business;
- failure to plan adequately for retirement, including re-investing surplus funds in the business or funding the lifestyle of the senior generation rather than their pensions.

7.4.4 Psychological barriers in the senior generation

Often the obstacles are much more difficult and personal and require the senior generation to address difficult issues and questions such as:

---

[10] See chapter 1.

- their own reluctance to let go and the underlying reasons for this including fear of what comes next in retirement;
- the entrepreneur's instinctive aversion to planning.

Most of these issues will be explored in more detail below.

7.5 SUCCESSION AND THE SENIOR GENERATION

7.5.1 Letting go

Difficulties with the succession process are often attributed to a failure or reluctance on the part of the senior generation family business leader to let go of managerial control. What Gersick et al[11] label the 'passing the baton' stage becomes impossible if the baton remains firmly in the grasp of the senior generation, who seem much more intent on running the next leg of the family business relay race themselves anyway.

Some of the barriers to succession referred to above (although clearly not all in every case) can be overcome through foresight and planning. The fact that they have developed or preserved a family firm to the stage that succession is under consideration can be taken as evidence for the proposition that family business owners are basically clever and successful people.

Advice that family business owners should invest time in succession planning at an early stage is so widely broadcast by advisors and the business media to be almost a cliché.

So why do so many business families fail to undertake adequate succession planning?

The answer is that succession planning is difficult. And the reason for that difficulty can often be traced to ambivalence.[12] Although all stakeholders in the family have a role to play in the succession planning process, the lead actor will almost inevitably be the founder or other senior generation business leader. As Lansberg puts it:[13]

> '... the fact remains that the founder has the power to make or break the dependency cycle, since he is largely, though not entirely, responsible for perpetuating it.'

The senior generation business leader might genuinely want to see both the next generation and the family business succeed in the future. On occasions they will, at least partly, welcome the idea of retirement. But they are caught by powerful countervailing currents. Those currents could be intra-personal. Chapter 2 talks in detail about the entrepreneurial mind set and also about the psychological status of the family firm as a surrogate child or mistress. Jeffrey Sonnenfeld[14] writes powerfully about the 'heroic mission' of business leaders to build a lasting business monument. All of these factors can contribute to reluctance on the part of the business leader to let go of control. This reluctance is likely to be more pronounced in the founder than in later generation family business leaders.

---

[11] Gersick, Davis, Hampton & Lansberg *Generation to Generation: Life cycles of a family business* (Harvard Business School Press, 1997).
[12] Explored in detail in chapter 2.
[13] *The Succession Conspiracy*, op cit.
[14] Sonnenfeld *The Hero's Farewell: What Happens When CEO's Retire* (Oxford University Press, 1988).

However some succession processes will proceed smoothly. Others will be horrendous, characterised by delay, disputes and tensions that damage both the business and relationship with the next generation. Sonnenfeld argues that the personality and departure style of the senior generation is the crucial determinant.[15] He categorises[16] and distinguishes between the departure styles of business leaders as follows:

- **Monarchs.** Here the leader will continue in office, clinging to their crown, until they are forced to give this up, whether by death, illness, a palace revolution led by other family members or perhaps the invasion by a neighbouring state in the form of an unwelcome takeover of a, by then, ailing family firm.
  Family business founders are particularly likely to fall into this category.
- **Generals.** Generals are equally reluctant to let go. However they take a more strategic approach. They are more likely to accept defeat by the forces of age, time and change and withdraw from office. However that surrender is more tactical than absolute. Generals will regroup their forces on the nearest high ground and look to retake command. Perhaps they will act as chairman of a family firm but constantly challenge the authority of the next generation, even secretly wishing for some state of emergency to be declared so that they can return to re-impose their authority.
- **Ambassadors.** Ambassadors on the other hand have a more statesmanlike and diplomatic approach to power. They accept that their tenure will not be forever. They see their primary role as serving their state (in our context the family enterprise) and aim to pass over office with relationships preserved and enhanced to the maximum extent possible. Ambassadors are prepared to make their accumulated contacts, knowledge and wisdom available to their state and to mentor their successors.
  Ambassadorial management successions are more likely to be found in later stage family enterprises.
- **Governors.** Governors accept that they have fixed terms in office, which will be vacated with the minimum of fuss when that term expires. The governor will move on to other things, with little or no continuing contact with the business.
  Non-family leaders are likely to fall into this category.

One of the most well-known and graphic illustrations of a monarch's departure is that of Henry Ford and the Ford Motor company. The story is told at 2.2.1. Sonnenfeld contrasts Henry's ousting with the carefully planned ambassadorial departure of Henry Ford II, aged 63, when Ford's first non-family leader assumed control.[17]

Monarchial or general like resistance to succession can take a range of forms. At its crudest, avoidance can take the form of outright resistance. The senior generation might simply refuse to discuss succession, becoming angry if the subject is raised. The efforts of the next generation could be frequently denigrated. Tensions and arguments could be frequent. This is more or less the story of Henry Ford and his son Edsel.

The response of the senior generation to these difficult succession questions could be avoidance. It is never quite the right time to get down to succession planning. More

---

[15] Sonnenfeld emphasises that departure styles might be different from leadership styles when in office. Again Henry Ford presents a prime example. Many commentators suggest that his considerable achievements from earlier in his career were undermined by the way he clung to power later in life.
[16] Sonnenfeld's study is based on a series of detailed interviews with approximately 100 business leaders, both family businesses and non-family, of various sizes, in the USA.
[17] Sonnenfeld, op cit at pp 252–259.

subtly, the succession process can be started and ostensibly pursued. But it can hit obstacles that stall or derail the process. There might be business issues that must be dealt with in priority. Complex tax problems could arise, for which equally complex solutions need to be found. There could be concerns over the financial security of the senior generation. Succession planning is to a large extent a process of identifying, confronting and overcoming these obstacles.

The concerns raised might be valid and reasonable. Or they could just appear to be so. In reality they might be bound up with other deeper psychological barriers to the succession process. The reasons given for not proceeding with the process are really excuses for not confronting these far more difficult obstacles. The senior generation, have both the primary responsibility to drive the succession process and the clear ability to stall or halt it.

7.5.2 The succession conspiracy

However Lansberg argues that it is often unfair to lay all the difficulties with a stalled succession process at the door of the senior generation business leader. The position is far more nuanced and complicated. All of the stakeholders in a family firm might join in an unspoken conspiracy against succession. As Lansberg puts it:[18]

> 'each of the constituencies that make up the family firm experiences poignantly ambivalent feelings about the inevitable succession transition.'

If there is indeed a wider conspiracy against succession, who are the co-conspirators?

The next generation

A lot of the writing about barriers to succession assumes that the progress of keen and ambitious next generation family members is blocked by the senior generation. This is not always the case. The next generation may have grown up in the shadow of a powerful entrepreneur. They might lack confidence. Although they could hold the nominal title of managing director, the notional next generation family business leader habitually defers to the 'old man' so far as anything approaching a major decision is concerned.

The clear view is that outside experience is highly desirable, if not absolutely necessary, for the success of the next generation as business leaders. One key reason is that, by proving themselves in the outsider world, the next generation gain significant confidence. Research carried out some years ago at Bournemouth University Business School by Gatrell & Kiely showed that 38% of identified successors had only worked in the family business.[19]

Lansberg sees the problem for the next generation as potentially having far deeper psychological roots, than a mere superficial lack of experience and confidence. He argues that:[20]

---

[18] *The Succession Conspiracy*, op cit.
[19] Since this research the proportion of young people gaining first degrees has increased so arguably next generation horizons will have broadened at least to some extent.
[20] *The Succession Conspiracy*, op cit.

'the younger generation sometimes avoids succession planning because it arouses strong fears of parental death, separation and abandonment'.

So, whilst the next generation may be keen for their own careers to develop, they too are afflicted by ambivalence at the loss of their parent. Alternatively they may simply think it rude to make too much of a fuss over their own advancement and to force their parent out of a business that they have founded.

Non-family managers

Few people really welcome and embrace change. Senior non-family managers may well have grown up alongside the senior generation business leader. They might have a strong personal relationship with them, which they will naturally be reluctant to relinquish. These non-family managers might therefore be ready and willing allies of the founder in any rear-guard actions he may be fighting against the march of time led by the next generation. The ultimate example of this is Henry Ford's henchman Harry Bennett.

The spouse

Commentators also suggest that, on occasions, the non-working spouse can provide a barrier to succession. They might be instinctively more cautious about financial security and correspondingly more reluctant to pass over capital and to forego income. They might relish the status that accompanies being the leader's wife. Whilst ostensibly welcoming the opportunity to spend more time together, the reality might be that, after years of leading quasi separate lives, the prospect of a spouse in the house is, frankly disturbing.

Taboos and the wider family

For many business owning families key succession questions on the minds of the next generation, such as 'when are you going to retire?', 'who is going to take over the management?', 'how are the shares to be left?', 'what about me?', are taboo subjects and never articulated. Sometimes this is because previous attempts to raise these questions have resulted in arguments. Often it stems from a sense of embarrassment of talking about money issues. In a recent informal survey of approximately 100 rural family business owners (who between them controlled many millions of assets) were asked about the their succession planning practices and in particular when they last met as a family to talk about succession planning. Almost as light relief we included an option for them to answer by saying that 'we are really not that sort of a family'. 30% of those surveyed confirmed that this option indeed best described their approach.[21]

According to Lansberg this is not a purely English phenomenon and is to be found in most Western cultures which:[22]

'have norms regulating family behaviour that discourages parents and offspring from openly discussing the future of the family beyond the lifetime of the parents. This is particularly true

---

[21] See also Steven J Hendlin *Overcoming the Inheritance Taboo: How to Preserve Relationships and Transfer Possessions* (Plume, 2004), discussed in chapter 15 in the context of ownership succession.
[22] *The Succession Conspiracy*, op cit.

of economic and financial matters, such as estate planning, an open discussion of which is typically viewed as a breach of etiquette or as denoting self-interest and a lack of mutual trust.'

More subtly members of the wider business owning family might exert pressure on the senior generation. Perhaps everything is pointing towards a transition of both management and ownership to family insiders. But the outsiders may expressly ask 'what about me.' By their demeanour, attitude or otherwise, the outsiders could convey the clear but implied message that 'it's not fair.' The end result could be that issues over ownership succession frustrate the transfer of management control.

7.5.3 Continuing role

A key element in any succession plan is to determine what, if any, role the senior generation business leader will play in the family enterprise going forward.

A governor might prefer complete separation, perhaps focusing their energies on voluntary work. However governors are less likely to be found amongst family business leaders. Pursuing Sonnefeld's classification the aim is likely to be to achieve an ambassadorial hand-over, with the senior generation being available to provide advice and support to the next generation. This can be on business issues, including strategy, helping consolidate relationships with and build the confidence of customers, suppliers and other key stakeholders such as banks in the next generation of leaders. Help might be needed in dealing with other family members, especially outsider owners. Possibly there might be discrete and separate projects that could be overseen by the former senior generation leader. Ideally these would be distinct from the rest of the day to day operations.

Clearly a smooth transition is much less likely with departing monarchs or generals. The greater the continuing role, the more the potential for interference arises. To an extent the adverse effects of this might be tempered by close attention to governance processes including establishing carefully delineated role and responsibilities.

7.5.4 Chairman

Probably the most common continuing role of former family business leaders is to become chairman, with the next generation taking over as managing director or chief executive. Such a move is frowned on in the quoted company context.[23] As the overwhelming majority of families owned businesses are unquoted they are not subject to even the 'comply or explain' principle and so do not have to justify the progression of business leader from chief executive to chairman, other than possibly to other family shareholders. The IOD Code for unlisted companies[24] is less prescriptive.

In practice there may well be many things to recommend this progression from managing director to chairman in any event.

---

[23] See the UK Corporate Governance Code Provision A.3.1, which recommends that a chairman should be independent on appointment (i e having no current or recent material connection with the company). If the board wishes to go against this recommendation they are supposed to consult with major shareholders and to explain their reasons.

[24] Discussed in chapter 17.

- The senior generation leader is likely to have built up a lifetime's experience of the business and the market sector in which it operates. They might be extremely well connected and well respected by customers, suppliers and bankers. They may hold other relationships that are crucial to the family business concerned.
- The senior generation leader still has a contribution to make. Crucially the leader remains keen to remain involved in the business. The remainder of the family are either equally keen or prepared for this to happen.
- There may be concerns as to the capability of the next generation to take over the business.
- Perhaps the family are sensitive to the needs of the senior leader to remain closely involved in the business that has formed a key part of their life.

There is a potential difficulty in the progression of senior generation business leader from managing director to chairman that can be more acute for family businesses than their non-family owned counterpart. There may be reluctance on the part of the senior leader to let go of the real control of the management of the business to the next generation or professional management team. For various reasons the family may be unable or unwilling to tackle the issue. Those reasons can include that the senior generation leader still controls the business through a large ownership stake, their sheer force of personality or, at a more personal level, a humane recognition that 'the business is his life' and that 'retirement will kill him'.

In the most extreme cases, the change or role from managing director to chairman is a purely nominal change of title, without any real corresponding change or role or behaviour. The next generation family member may have the title of managing director, together with the legal responsibilities and weight of expectations that this brings. However all real authority and decision-making power remains vested in the chairman. Employees and other key stakeholders still look to be chairman for their lead. In extreme cases decisions taken by the next generation managing director and their management team are reversed by or at the chairman's behest.

This puts the next generation leadership, together with the remainder of the executive management team in the family business concerned, in an almost impossible position and, in the most extreme cases, can seriously compromise the health and potentially the survival of the family business.

So, if the senior generation business leader is to remain in the family business in the role of chairman as part of succession planning, how does the family business make the most of the experience, guidance and support that their chairman can bring? How does the family business avoid the Henry Ford effect?

Using Sonnenfeld's classification, in reality it might nevertheless be difficult to distinguish between an ambassador, and a general, using the office of chairman to retain military rule over the family firm. However some practical and structural governance steps can be taken to help avoid this.

Possibilities include:
- Except in the largest and most complex family businesses making the chairman's role a non- executive position.

- Symbolic gestures of handover of the chains of office. For example the new next generation leader moving into the managing director's office, previously occupied by their father. A classic example in the farming sector is the senior generation leaving the main farmhouse for the occupation of the next generation successor and their family.[25]
- Having very clear and well documented 'demarcation agreements' making it clear what roles responsibilities and decisions fall within the executive bailiwick of the managing director and where the (non-executive) role of the chairman begins and ends. These can be documented in some combination of shareholders' agreement,[26] family charter, board terms of reference, job descriptions or director's letters of appointment. This may all seem like unnecessary bureaucracy and pointless paperwork. However the key point is to recognise that a key stage in the succession process has been reached and that a governance response is called for.
- The senior leader taking some form of extended holiday, sabbatical or a career break on their retirement, as managing director, before assuming the chairman role. This allows for the symbolic retirement the senior leader and for their contribution to be recognised.
  It also allows the new managing director some time and space to establish their own presence and regime. Crucially the business can demonstrate that it is not 'business as usual' in management and governance terms, with merely a change in title. The family business world abounds with stories where the senior generation business leader has retired one Friday only to return to the office the following Monday to 'finish a few things off'. Those few things then take the best part of several years to deal with, leaving the next generation business leadership, employees and other key stakeholders deeply confused as to the governance and control of the family business concerned and the realities of the succession process.
- The presence of a well-respected senior independent director[27] specifically mandated to referee the demarcation line between chairman and managing director and who will be prepared to flag the occasions on which the chairman has, usually inadvertently, and with the best of intentions, strayed offside.

7.5.5 Simultaneous transfer of ownership

The final and perhaps the most telling point so far as the letting go is concerned is the timing of the handing over ownership. Ideally this should be at the same time as the leadership transition occurs. Often the two are kept separate, with management control passing first.[28] Ownership confers ultimate control. Without a transfer of ownership a general has the power to return and overthrow the new regime. After ownership has been transferred the general is reduced to operating as a guerrilla leader, able to snipe from a distance, but unlikely to do real and lasting damage.

---

[25] Which happened in James Davies' case. The problems there, as discussed in chapter 19, related to ownership succession.
[26] See the discussion on restricted matters in chapter 11 (Ownership Overview).
[27] A concept borrowed from the listed company world and the UK Corporate Governance Code.
[28] This is especially so in the farming world as the various cases discussed in chapters 13 and 19 illustrate.

7.6 FAMILY MANAGEMENT SUCCESSION AND THE NEXT GENERATION

So far we have concentrated almost exclusively on the internal mind-set of the senior generation business leader (at times aided and abetted by the other participants in the succession conspiracy) as the primary obstacle to succession. But that is only half the story. The other ingredient for a smooth family management transition is a next generation, ready, willing and able to take up the baton and run with it.

There could also be many questions relating to the abilities of the next generation that create additional barriers to a smooth succession process. Sometimes the questions will be legitimate. They could be in addition to the internal psychological obstacles affecting the senior generation. On other occasions there will be little of real substance to those concerns. They are really smokescreens to obscure the internal concerns of the senior generation. The position is therefore complex.

7.6.1 The key question

Working on the basis that the preferred option of the senior generation will usually be to keep family business leadership in family hands, there is really only one main question to ask. In theory it is quite simple, and has a yes or no answer. This is 'are the next generation the best people to manage this business going forward?' In some cases we know of the answer has been unequivocally, yes, the next generation are indeed the best and that judgment has been proved right by the subsequent success of the family business under the leadership of the family members concerned. In other cases the answer has been, equally clearly, no. The supplementary question, assuming a wish for the business to remain in family ownership, then becomes 'how will we make non-family management work?'

But in a huge number of cases answering (or even asking) the question of the competence of the next generation, properly and fully can be spectacularly difficult. As a result the management succession process stalls or is never really properly started in the first place.

It is therefore worth examining some of the potential responses to the key question of competence. Each response corresponds to a widely acknowledged barrier to the succession process.

7.6.2 'What do you mean by best?'

This is a good question. Best does not necessarily mean the manager who has the best CV in terms of experience and qualifications. Other factors such as loyalty, understanding of the business and the business owning family and consistency with ownership plans are clearly relevant. In these areas next generation family insiders have a clear head start. These factors might tip the balance in favour of a marginally less qualified family insider candidate.

Best therefore means, best in all the circumstances. Certainly it means, at least, good enough. Gaps and weaknesses in knowledge and skills might, at least to an acceptable extent, be plugged by some combination of on-going training, mentoring, business coaching, support networks, by supportive family members and by investment in non-family management and non-executive directors. Almost inevitably this will be a long-term and continuing process. Identifying those gaps and a willingness on the part of the next generation family leader to accept long-term support will be crucial.

7.6.3 'Yes but I don't want to admit it'

The proposed next generation family leaders might be perfectly well qualified to take over, but the senior generation might be reluctant to acknowledge this. Partly this might be due to a reluctance to let go and to trust others, explored above. This is of particular relevance to founders.

It could also be due to a failure to recognise the changing nature of the business and the different managerial requirements as the family business goes through its own life cycles. Very different qualities will be required to manage a growing business in its second generation, from the entrepreneurial zeal of the early stage first generation business set up by the founder. The ability to recruit, motivate and retain a management team and to introduce systems and processes capable of supporting growth will be required. These may not be qualities that the founder respects or prizes. But these skills might clearly be present in one or more of the next generation family members.

This inability to respect differences might also lead to a stalled succession process. The senior generation could interpret the failure on the part of the next generation to be more like themselves as a sign of unfitness and therefore a justification for delaying management handover.

7.6.4 'Possibly, but not yet'

Sometimes the life cycles of the business owning family might be out of kilter. The senior generation might be well past their sell by date but the next generation, although showing promise, are simply too young or lacking in experience to take over. In which case a non-family leader could be appointed as a caretaker manager on an interim basis. In addition to preserving the business, a key role of the caretaker manager[29] will be to oversee the development of the prospective next generation family leaders. It obviously takes a special type of manager, or someone at a particular stage of their own career, who is prepared to devote, possibly several years, to the task of holding the fort for the next generation.

On other occasions the senior generation will feel that they have no choice other than to remain in position, effectively acting as a family bridge, until, usually in the judgment of the senior generation, the next generation are ready to take over. Particular projects might need to be completed. The business might be judged to be going through especially difficult times. All too often the reasons given are hollow. The reality is that the senior generation simply do not want to let go.

---

[29] Sometimes the caretaker manager is referred to as 'a bridge' as they help to cross the gap between the senior and next generations of family management.

7.6.5 'No but it's going to happen anyway'

In many cases there might be serious doubts about the ability of the next generation in general, or a particular candidate, to take over and lead the family firm.

The most extreme example of this are families committed to primogeniture, where, even if there is strong evidence to suggest that the eldest, or eldest male child, is not the most able business leader, they are nevertheless groomed for leadership and often given sole or majority ownership of the family firm.[30] In the research referred to above, Gatrell & Kiely found that whilst 56% of the family business owners they surveyed would like to pass their business on to the next generation and about half of these had identified a successor, less than 10% of those senior generation business leaders had confidence in that successor.

Was that lack of confidence justified? Often insufficient attention has been paid to the development of the next generation.

The family might nevertheless choose to install a family leader. This can be for various reasons, including family tradition, family expectations or a misguided perception of the abilities of the next generation. The family might want to retain ownership, but not be ready to put in place the complex governance and control systems necessary if they are to successfully cede control to outside management.

The right to appoint management is of course a fundamental right of ownership. But if the business owning family choose to make key management appointments based on family considerations, the potential for the business system to suffer is clear and obvious.

Positive discrimination in favour of family insiders can have repercussions in the business system so far as senior non-family managers are concerned. This issue is considered in chapter 6.

How much damage is done is down to a mixture of luck and circumstances. But there is considerable potential for the business owning family to help themselves and to rebalance the family business systems.

That process starts with a realistic assessment of the capabilities of the family business generally, but the next generation in particular. We will look at some assessment tools later in this chapter. On the basis that no individual and no organisation is perfect, this approach should logically be the same for all family firms undergoing management transition. Some firms might be reassured that they have many more strengths than they might instinctively perceive. Others might identify weaknesses and areas for development in family managers and management teams, that would otherwise have gone unrecognised. Any weaknesses and shortfalls can then be addressed by training, support and the recruitment of management, non-executive directors, consultants and others. Ideally the weaknesses will be all but eliminated and the optimum balance

---

[30] Of course the cultural context of the family business concerned could be highly relevant. These complex issues are beyond the scope of this book but have been explored by various academics and commentators including by Vipin Gupta and Nancy Levenburg 'A Thematic Analysis of Cultural Variations in Family Businesses: The CASE Project' *Family Business Review* (2010) 23(2) 155–169.

between the family and business systems restored. In any event the business family will have tried to make the best out of a less than perfect situation.

7.6.6 'But who do I choose?'

Businesses often pass out of family control, notwithstanding a strong desire to retain family ownership, simply because there is no next generation family member ready willing and able to take on the mantle of management and leadership. Those families may regard other business families, where there are a number of potential candidates for leadership, as unnaturally blessed. It might not feel this way for a senior generation leader having to choose which of their offspring should take on the leadership role for the next generation. In a later stage cousin consortium family business, the choice might be harder still, with the candidates, including, not only the leader's own children, but also nieces and nephews from other branches of the family.

The advice of the commentators is unequivocal. Only the most competent family members should be working in the family firm in the first place and the foremost of these paragons of virtue should be preferred for leadership roles.[31] This is undoubtedly much easier for us to write than for a family business leader to recognise and to put into action. It is not an easy task to tell an ambitious child that the managing director's office will in the future be occupied by their cousin and not by them, or in a family dominated by traditions or assumptions of primogeniture, that in fact the youngest daughter is the chosen candidate.

But the consequences of making the wrong call are potentially huge. If a single family leader is chosen in preference to an objectively more qualified non family candidate, the business will be the main system to suffer. It might be possible to rebalance the effects of this by support, including from the rest of the management team.

When the choice is between family members, the effects of a poor choice are likely to be felt in the family and ownership systems also.

The need for strong governance systems (for example the presence of non-family non-executive directors helping bring objectivity) to facilitate good and fair choices becomes paramount.

7.6.7 'How do I tell?'

Various commentators have noted the difference between perception and reality where the ability of the senior generation to judge the talents and potential of their offspring is concerned.

This perception bias can operate either in favour of, or against the abilities of the next generation. Both are problematic. So how does a naturally biased senior generation family business leader make a halfway objective judgment on a matter of such crucial

---

[31] See, for example John Ward's lessons that Stage 1 owner managed firms should 'attract the most competent family members'; John Ward *Perpetuating the Family Business: 50 Lessons Learned from Long-Lasting, Successful Families in Business* (Palgrave, 2004) Lesson 5 at p 52.

importance to their family firm? There is no sure fire or fail-safe answer. It will come down to a mixture of intuition, supported or not, by as much objective evidence as can sensibly be obtained.

Some possibilities are explored below.

7.6.8 'Why does a business have to have a single leader anyway; is there a case for co-leadership?'

Co-leadership, where rather than appoint a single designated business leader, the roles and responsibilities of leadership are shared between two or more joint managing directors is probably most likely to be found in a family business context. Co-leadership is explored in more detail below.

7.6.9 Insurmountable barriers to succession

Sometimes the answer to the questions raised above will point to a fairly obvious outcome. The questions raised might be incapable of a satisfactory answer, consistent with the family retaining ownership. The family business will often need to be sold. The difficulty might be for the business owning family to accept this, especially if the business has been in the family for generations, like a family farm.

Tragedy for a family in these circumstances can often arise when the family, notwithstanding the evidence to the contrary, choose to retain both family leadership and ownership. But perhaps the saddest situations are where the difficulties in addressing the undoubtedly difficult succession questions and to follow an appropriate process to formulate a succession plan, result in a failed succession in circumstances where a workable solution could have been found.

7.7 CO-LEADERSHIP

7.7.1 Overview

It is possible that the next generation family management might work as a naturally cohesive and collaborative team; as a genuine sibling partnership. One sibling (or cousin) might take the lead on some issues, another might come to the fore in other areas. For key decisions the next generation instinctively consult and usually arrive at consensual decisions.

In these circumstances why is it necessary to recognise one of the next generation as 'first among equals' by formally appointing them CEO or managing director? In reality it isn't. Co-leadership is a recognised management concept. It is probably the case that proportionately more family firms are co-led, for example, by joint managing directors than any other form of business organisation.

Unless the chosen route is to stay with, or return to the simplicity of the single owner manager,[32] both the sibling partnership and cousin collaboration models contemplate a

---

[32] As Gersick's model contemplates. See chapter 17 for a discussion of this.

high degree of co-operation, at least at ownership level, even if this falls short of full and outright co-leadership at management level.

Whilst co-leadership may seem initially attractive, it is in fact extremely difficult to work in practice. Roles need to be very clearly defined. One individual is likely to need to take the lead on business critical relationships, for example with bankers or with key customers and suppliers. Co-leadership places a hugely high premium on the cohesion of the family management team.

If the main reason for choosing a co-leadership structure is, in fact, the wish for the senior generation to avoid having to make a choice, or to be seen as preferring one family member over another, problems are likely to arise. This is especially so if the underlying dynamic between the next generation is one of overt or suppressed competition. Sometimes the senior generation attempt to deal with intra-generational rivalry by giving competing siblings or cousins their own discrete area of operations. In a larger family enterprise this can be a subsidiary or a business unit. Family business commentators recommend this, or at least establishing clearly defined roles, as best practice anyway. But sometimes even the largest family enterprise will not be big enough to contain fierce sibling rivalries.[33]

If the relationships between the next generation family members are truly cohesive, it would be hoped that these would continue, relatively undamaged, irrespective of the formal titles taken by the family management team. It might just be that the family firm makes slower but steadier and safer progress as a result of a more consensual decision making style of a co-leadership team than if a single designated leader had been chosen.

There is always the potential for a 'first among equals' to emerge as the natural leader, albeit with a highly consultative management style, from what remains as basically collaborative co-leadership group. Carlock and Ward nevertheless suggest it is sensible to revisit and if necessary revise and strengthen family codes of conduct relating to behaviour of family members towards each other and support of management processes and decision making as part of the transition to more complex forms of management and ownership.[34]

Co-leadership has no chance of working if it is a fudge or a fiction.

7.7.2 The chair as a co-leader

So far the discussion on co-leadership has assumed some form of 'job-share' of the managing director's desk, by two or more family members both working full time in the business. However, there are potentially two key roles in a family leadership structure, those of managing director and chairman. The most common model is for the chairman role to be filled by a senior generation figure. Often this is the outgoing family managing director, as a part-time non-executive role. On other occasions a senior non-family figure is chosen for their industry experience and to add balance to the family influence. In

---

[33] One of the most graphic examples is the story of the Reliance Group in India, where even a family business with turnover equivalent to 3% of the country's GDP could not contain the rival ambitions of two brothers. The story is told in *Family Wars* (Gordon and Nicholson *Family Wars* (Kogan Page, 2008) at pp 42–50).
[34] See p 115.

some, perhaps comparatively rare cases, the family are able to leverage wider family resource and recruit a younger chairman, to work in partnership with their sibling or cousin.

The business logic behind such arrangements is often that the full time family managing director, whilst being strong operationally, benefits from the support of the chairman in strategic areas. There is the added advantage that this arrangement can cement wider family involvement, particularly if chairman and managing director, come from different branches of the business owning family. Of course collaboration, rather than competition, is the key to making such arrangements work, especially where the role holders are of similar age. But, at its best a good managing director and chairman relationship can be seen as a species of co-leadership.

7.8 NON-FAMILY LEADERSHIP

7.8.1 Overview

There might be no appropriate family candidate to take on the mantle of leadership. In which case the alternatives for the business owning family boil down to sale, closure or retaining family ownership, but under non-family management.

This alternative will only be a viable option in a minority of cases. Usually these will be larger more established family enterprises, which are well down the road of establishing professional management and operating systems. In addition, to make non-family leadership work, a significant degree of sophistication and understanding will be needed on the part of the business owning family. Successful examples of family owned but non-family run businesses do clearly exist. Clarks' shoes provide a prominent example, with no Clark family members currently involved as executive directors.

Occasionally special and unforeseen circumstances will arise. For example we dealt with one family business which, following the death of the founder, was managed for many years by a trusted family friend on behalf of the widow and young children. The individual concerned acted as a caretaker leader for, in effect almost a generation, during which time the next generation, who were in their infancy at the time their father died, matured into adults, joined the family business and, eventually, assumed management positions.

But usually this structure of a split between non-family management and family ownership will be a difficult trick to pull off except in larger family firms, which are dedicated to remaining in family ownership. It might appear that separating the two systems of ownership and management returns a family firm to the clarity and simplicity of the classic Victorian company model, without the complications and complexities of overlapping family systems, as illustrated by the three-circle model. In practice successful models of split of family ownership and non-family management will usually have two features.

First, high agency costs. These will be both sticks, in the form of highly evolved governance and supervision structures[35] and carrots,[36] such as bonuses and share-option plans designed to align the interests of the family owners and the non-family management.

Secondly, an exceptionally high level of commitment will be required from the family to act as responsible and involved owners. They will need to police the governance systems. Even if they are not part of the day-to-day management team, the business owning family will need to maintain a very high presence. If not, they will, in effect, be absentee landlords of their own family business property. In chapter 12 (Selling the family business) we look at the concept of effective appropriation of the business by non-family management. This is the most extreme consequence of the absence of a proper presence by the business owning family.[37] The *Bartlett* family business trust case discussed in chapter 14, provides a prime example of the damage that can be inflicted by, even well-meaning management operating in an absentee landlord environment.

In the case of Clarks, their governance arrangements include two family members acting as non-executive directors, operating alongside a fully functioning family council.

7.8.2 Non-family outsiders or insiders

If non-family members are to be appointed to manage and lead a family business, where are the most suitable candidates to be found?

Peter Leach[38] counsels against the appointment of existing members of the management team, arguing that they are likely to be too set in their ways, resistant to change and in the shadow of the founding entrepreneur, who they have worked alongside for a number of years. He argues that more radical change might be required for the business, which can only be initiated by a complete outsider, who has not become institutionalised in the family firm concerned and can bring a fresh perspective.

This might be the case. But many non-family management CV's have been spoilt by unsuccessful attempts to change family businesses too quickly. Family firms are highly idiosyncratic and individual institutions. At least in the early stages of transition to non-family management, there are likely to be highly interested and committed family members in the background. This is much more likely to be so than in other corporate businesses. There could be family members who are resentful about being passed over for leadership. Change might well be needed but too radical a prescription of reform could well alienate large sections of the business owning family.

The change will also involve the family in making the transition from being a family managed business to being solely an owning family. This will involve a change in their

---

[35] See chapter 17.
[36] See chapter 6.
[37] A fairly graphic example of the absentee family landlord can be found in the trust case of *Bartlett v Barclays Bank Trust Company* [1980] 1 All ER 139 discussed in chapter 14 (Trusts).
[38] See *Family Business: The Essentials* at p 166.

relationship to the business, and how the family communicates with the business.[39] This can be an easier transition if the first managing director is a trusted non-family member.[40]

In practice an understanding of the business owning family, the culture of the family business and a tolerance of the ambiguities of the family business condition might be much more helpful than a track record of implementing best practice business change in record time. Neubauer and Lank tend to agree, suggesting that only approximately 30% of family businesses appoint new leaders from outside. They also suggest that those that are appointed from outside have only a 50% prospect of success.[41]

This level of understanding and sensitivity might well be found within the ranks of the existing family business management team. If not it will need to acquired exceptionally swiftly by the non-family outsider. As chief executive of LEGO, Jorgen Knudstorp is widely credited with turning round the company's fortunes. His background was in management consultancy, rather than as a company insider. However he grew up close to LEGO's headquarters in rural Denmark and is quoted as saying that:[42]

> 'I was keenly aware of LEGO's heritage, so the call [to work for the company] represented a kind of homecoming.'

Part of Knudstorp's turnaround strategy involved abandoning peripheral diversifications, such as theme parks and interactive games and returning to innovations based on LEGO's core legacy building brick products.

7.8.3 Non-family interim leaders

Non-family leadership might be used as a temporary solution. This could be as a 'bridge' between generations. Perhaps where the current managing director wants to retire (or due to a sudden death) and the next generation are not yet ready to take on the reins of full leadership. A non-family manager can then step into the role for a period of time as a bridge, until the successor is ready. During that period they can help to develop the successor and act as a mentor after the handover.

A manager assuming this role will almost certainly be a business insider. There may often be a degree of urgency about the appointment if the senior generation were forced to retire through ill-health or death.[43] There will need to be a strong degree of mutual trust between the manager and the business owning family. It is difficult to see that capable executives would be prepared to join a family business form outside on the basis of such a limited tenure.

---

[39] If the family do not want to make this transition and instead decide to sell, there may be an opportunity for the non-family person to lead a management buyout. They may well be viewed as a preferred bidder, because of their relationship to the family and the business. See chapter 12.
[40] Many of the points made below about training and development of family leaders apply equally to non-family managers.
[41] See p 158, although the claims are quite unspecific. For example it is unclear how success was measured.
[42] Quoted in Robertson *Brick by Brick* (Random House, 2013) at p 65.
[43] One of the tests of the preparedness.

7.9 FAMILY LEADERSHIP

The role of the family (as opposed to business leadership), often termed Chief Emotional Officer, is discussed in chapter 18. This is in the context that the role is often filled by the founder's spouse. John Ward suggests that an important part of the succession planning process is to identify 'a successor to mom'.[44] Writing later with Carlock, Ward suggests that the most likely candidates for this role in the next generation would be either a sibling or 'the oldest son or daughter not employed in the family business or another family member with special skills in human behaviour'.[45]

The role of Chief Emotional Officer will not be advertised, rarely formalised and often simply assumed. According to Carlock and Ward the job description is to:[46]

> '[work], usually quietly, at the critical tasks of family leadership. She interprets the behaviour of one family member to another, keeps communications open, makes sure that feelings are considered.'

The role is readily recognisable in family business practice. Sonnenfeld gives an example of the mother helping to smooth sibling tensions on the transition of Corning Glass, a large American company then with a turnover of $1.5bn, from the CEO (as in chief executive officer) to his younger brother.[47] In practice there is a close relationship between this role and the role of any chair of the family council.[48] It is another matter whether the succession process can recognise the importance of the role whilst, at the same time, jettisoning the gender stereotyping above.

7.10 THE SUCCESSION PROCESS

It is often said that 'succession is a process not an event'. It will be clear from the complexities and issues outlined above why this is so. The transition process is likely to last a number of years. According to some commentators up to 20 years. It might be unclear when the process starts. Perhaps this is when the senior generation first start seriously thinking about what will happen to the family business in the future. Neubauer and Lank argue that 'at the very latest' the process should be considered as starting the minute a new business leader is appointed, on the basis that the process will continue throughout their reign.[49] Certainly the thinking underpinning the transition process is likely to have started well before advisors are consulted about tax and other technical issues. Based on Figure 7.1 it might be equally unclear when the transition process has been fully completed, especially in the case of some of the more intangible elements identified in that model, such as emotional ownership and ultimate control over the family firm.

Commentators agree that family firms are at their most vulnerable during transition periods from one generation to the next. Taking Neubauer and Lank's argument that the process is almost continual, the greatest vulnerability would be closer to handover of

---

[44] See Lesson 26 (Perpetuating the Family Business).
[45] At p 99.
[46] Also at p 99.
[47] See *The Hero's Farewell* at p 248.
[48] See chapter 17.
[49] Neubauer and Lank *The Family Business: Its Governance for Sustainability* (Harvard Business School Press, 1997) at p 150.

management or ownership control, especially whilst key decisions, including as to the choice of business leader and the timing of handover of management control remain open.

It will be equally clear how close the links are between management succession and other key topics discussed in this book. Ownership succession, obviously.[50] Also family employment policies.[51] The overarching theme is family business governance.[52] Given the complexity of the subject it will be obvious that there is no, one size fits all family firms, template solution available to follow for the management succession process. This is even without bringing in the issue of ownership succession considered in chapter 15. What follows is therefore a series of comments and pointers on certain aspects of the process.

We have separated the process into three stages. This is obviously artificial as many of the stages are not distinct and will overlap. Indeed the first two stages will be applicable to the employment of family members generally, even if they do not progress to leadership of the family firm. However both of the earlier stages need to be completed before leadership becomes a possibility. So for that reason they have been included as part of the discussion of the management succession process.

7.11 THE MANAGEMENT SUCCESSION PROCESS: STAGE 1 – OPENING THE DOOR

7.11.1 The family socialisation process

Family business commentators are united in recommending that succession planning should begin early. This is often interpreted, especially by those in traditional advisory professions, in terms of a low number of single digit years. Enough time to plan and implement tax saving strategies, to recruit and hand over the business to a non-family manager, or to prepare it for sale.

But, if family management succession is to be an option, the behaviourists are really thinking in terms of decades. Their concern is the link between the early socialisation process of the next generation and the later willingness of the children concerned to consider a career in, or leadership of, the family business in the future. If the impression that a young child gains from their parents of the family business is largely negative, for example 'if it is the founder's style to bring home the frustrations and problems of the firm'[53] it should be no great surprise if, later in life, the family firm is not seen by them as a positive career choice. Equally Gersick et al argue that the physical absence or emotional distance of a parent pre-occupied with the family business can lead to feelings of resentment towards the business and exclusion on the part of the next generation.

---

[50] See chapter 15.
[51] See chapter 5.
[52] See chapter 17.
[53] Gersick et al, op cit at p 145.

But a positive impression of the family firm, particularly the 'pioneering or adventurous aspects of the founder role' whereby the children build an image of their parent as 'part cowboy, part pirate and part king or queen'[54] can lay the foundations for future family business leadership.

There is some suggestion that the process of socialisation and subtle pressure to join the family might be felt more by younger members of the next generation. Whereas the older children receive more general encouragement to choose their own way in the world, by the time the youngest need to make career choices, the senior generation are approaching retirement age. Both time and available candidates as management successors are reducing, so the youngest family members receive more encouragement (often unconscious on the part of the parents) to make a career in the family firm as the 'youngest in the family [...] seemed in some cases to represent the last chance for succession'.[55] In effect a form of semi-conscious or subconscious ulitmogeniture comes into play.

7.11.2 Family business work experience

By the time the next generation enter their teens the possibility of them joining the family firm becomes a more real and overt consideration. Either informal or structured work experience in the family business needs to be considered.

The next generation is often exposed to the family business at an early stage, as part of the extended family business socialisation process. The children can be found working in the business at evenings, weekends and in school holidays from early teens onwards. There are many stories about being around the business from a much younger age, playing in the corner of the office, or doing homework whilst parents worked late or children helping out with menial tasks in the business.

Some families actively encourage this and say so in their family charters. Occasionally there is a formal requirement for family members to have spent some time with the family business on work experience or as an intern before they will be considered for a full time position.

As with all family employment policies there is a difficult balance to be made. On the one hand providing the next generation with as much exposure to the family business, helps them make an informed choice as to whether or not a career in the family firm is for them. Legitimate choices can be enhanced. Costly mistakes can be avoided. On the other hand the boundary between providing experience of the family business and creating an expectation that the next generation will join is a fine one and dangerous in circumstances where family employment will benefit neither the family business nor the next generation family member.

---

[54] Gersick et al, op cit at p 146.
[55] See Dumas, Dupuis, Richer & St-Cyr 'Factors that Influence the Next Generation's Decision to Take Over the Family Farm' *Family Business Review* (1995) Vol 8(2) at p 110. This is a study relating to succession in Canadian farming, which found that management succession was skewed towards younger family members. Arguably the wider picture is that ultimogeniture is more likely where the family business is not an obviously attractive career proposition or earlier stage family business, where a family succession tradition will not have been established.

7.11.3 Family business training

Commentators recommend that this informal socialisation process is supported by more formal next generation training programmes, covering both specific aspects of the family's own business and more general family business and general business training topics.[56]

7.11.4 Genuine occupational choice

For the financial health of the family business and the mental health of the next generation it is crucial that any decision to join the family firm, much less to take over its leadership, is based on a genuine desire to do so, rather than a sense of obligation. There is a suggestion by Carlock and Ward, based on separate research that the majority of college students would prefer to work for a business owned by their family.[57] There are many examples where family members successfully work in the family enterprise in a variety of roles but are genuinely and perfectly content to leave the leadership and other top management roles to others whether family or non-family.

Gersick et al argue that, paradoxically a sense of obligation is more likely to arise in enmeshed families, those that are more tightly drawn, where family members are seen to be special than in more remote disengaged families.[58] The worst of all situations would be where the dynamics are such that refusal to join the family firm will amount to effective banishment from the business owning family.

Whilst the possibility of joining the family firm might be canvassed at a relatively early stage, it will almost never be appropriate to contemplate the putative family member recruit as a potential business leader until much later, when they have joined the business and established their leadership credentials. The same is likely to apply to promises of ownership based on an insider ownership approach.[59]

7.11.5 External work experience

The next generation gaining external experience of working outside the family business before joining is strongly recommended by most commentators.[60]

Should the governance system nevertheless be flexible enough for family members join straight from school or university? This might be the tradition of the family business concerned. But most commentators recommend that there should be a requirement for family members to have obtained 'real life' experience (in a related business or otherwise) before taking up a position in the family business. Somewhere between 2 and

---

[56] See Carlock and Ward at p 93. Family business training is discussed in more detail in chapter 17, as one of the main roles of the family council.
[57] At p 103 citing Covin 'How Young Graduates Rate the Family Business' *Family Business Review* (1994) Vol 5(4) at pp 42–43.
[58] See pp 163–164.
[59] Arguably the root of the family disputes in both James Davies' and the Ham cases (discussed in chapters 19 and 13 respectively) was the premature linkage by the senior generation concerned of the next generation working on the family farm and its ownership.
[60] See Neubauer and Lank at p 153. Some commentators suggest that a relevant business qualification, such as an MBA would be an adequate substitute for external work experience. Some of the largest family enterprises insist on both external work experience and a management qualification as minimum entry requirements for family members.

5 years is often stipulated. Other commentators concentrate on the quality, rather than the quantity of the outside experience, recommending criteria such as the next generation family member should have gained at least one or two promotions, worked for two or more bosses and have led a project in a non-family business setting, before they are ready to come into the family firm.[61]

There are advantages in the next generation being able to bring new ideas into the family firm, thus guarding against insularity. But the main benefit is to help the family member to complete their individuation. External success should help to confirm the credibility of the next generation, in the eyes of the senior generation, the wider business family and the non-family managers who they will be joining and who will inevitably regard the new family member with a degree of sceptiscim. Most importantly success in an external business environment will help the self-confidence the next generation family member concerned.

7.11.6 Role

Are family members only to be considered for employment if there is a genuine business need? This can either be as a replacement for an existing role or for a new role. This is the position adopted in most family charters. However the reality might well be that in practice roles will be created if family members need jobs. In practice this is a two way process involving continually appraising both family business needs and opportunities alongside the aspirations and circumstances of the next generation, especially their possible appetite for a career in the family business. Occasionally charters specify that family members will be given preference for entry level jobs (or even that these will be found for family members) but that promotion must be earned on merit.

7.11.7 Recruitment process

Are family members only to be appointed as a result of a fully competitive external recruitment process? Alternatively is it sufficient for family members to be able to prove that they meet the requirements of an objectively prepared job description for a genuinely needed role?

7.12 STAGE 2: FINDING THEIR FEET

7.12.1 Induction

Assuming that the family member is now through the door of the family business, the first stage will be their induction process. As the new family employee will have been immersed in the family firm from an early age, this could seem like overkill. However it is important that the new family recruit is, to the greatest extent practicable treated like other new employees. Also the socialisation process and attitudes of the family members will have been acquired in the setting of their family of origin. It is sensible for them to be re-educated about the family firm from the perspective of the business system.

---

[61] See Carlock and Ward at p 106.

7.12.2 Trial period

It is almost invariable practice to recruit non-family employees on the basis of a probationary period of between 3 and 6 months. In a minority of cases either the family business management or the non-family employee themselves will conclude that there is no real prospect of establishing a satisfactory working relationship and that the employment should not continue. That will be traumatic enough for both parties.

In a family owned business the arguments for a vigorous and genuinely searching trial period are far more compelling. The long-term damage to family relationships caused by unsatisfactory working relationships cannot be understated.

Even the most functional and balanced family relationships may not stand the test of working together. There are numerous examples of previously harmonious and balanced working relationships between parents and next generation or between two siblings being knocked out of kilter by the arrival in the family business of another sibling; the prodigal son syndrome. In joining the family business the next generation may well have given up careers elsewhere and relocated back home to join the family business. With the sense of responsibility this creates in the mind of the business leaders there is a strong temptation to live with an unsatisfactory situation, one which would not be tolerated in a non-family employment situation. We can think of few examples of family members successfully returning to non-family corporate careers after joining the family business. Further and serious damage to family relationships becomes almost inevitable.

A genuine trial period may therefore avoid the twin perils of the family business becoming both a career graveyard and a family battleground. We have heard of one 6th generation family business speak about their policy of both welcoming the next generation to try working in the family business but insisting that this is on the basis of an honest and searching appraisal of whether things are working out. If not the next generation member concerned can return to non-family employment with damage to long-term family relationships minimised. Expectations have been managed. It was never meant to have been forever. It will have been worth a try.

These trial periods can be aligned to times of genuine business need, for example a family member providing maternity leave cover or replacing a departing employee. The trial periods can also, at least to some extent, be structured around the career development of the next generation. One next generation family member in the business referred to above decided to combine wider career development with a trial period in the business by dividing his time between pursuing an MBA and working part time in the family business. Perhaps a trial period in the family business could be arranged at a time when the career elsewhere of the next generation family member has reached a natural crossroads. It should be relatively easy for a next generation family member, seeking to re-enter the 'mainstream' employment market to explain a sojourn of 12 months in the family business if this was to undertake a particular project. Longer periods in the family business, followed by a sudden departure could be harder to justify. We suspect that this is the case even where the length of stay with the family firm would be considered unremarkable for non-family members.

It will be seen that a trial period policy such as this relies on highly evolved communication between the business leadership and the potential family recruit.

7.12.3 Promotion

Most of the above issues apply to all family employees. They are nevertheless barriers that need to be successfully negotiated if family management succession is to occur. The topic of promotion of family employees is getting closer to the question of leadership succession.

Non-family employees will usually be recruited for a specific role. Others may join a business with a strong indication that, if all things go well, promotion will follow. There is nevertheless a clear understanding that criteria need to be met and promotion must to be earned. Does the family really believe that promotion in a family owned business will be strictly on competitive merit? Alternatively is the reality that the family are keen to retain and encourage family leadership where this is realistically possible? In which case how is the parallel business imperative of retaining and motivating good non-family management to be achieved?

Some family businesses have what amounts to a family fast track policy, whereby family members undergo dedicated training programmes and are exposed to high level management positions and projects, on the working assumption that they will one day take up senior positions in the top management team of their family business. The key point is that this remains an assumption, not a self-fulfilling prophecy, until the next generation family member concerned has proved their capability. One extremely difficult issue to confront is the extent to which the existence of the family fast track is made known to other non-family employees. This issue is explored in chapter 6.

7.12.4 Mentoring

Especially in businesses committed to family leadership there will often be special arrangements in place designed to mentor and develop the next generation of family members, who may possibly assume key leadership roles in due course. These arrangements can also operate to provide a safeguard as part of the overall governance arrangements. Younger family members[62] receive guidance not only about their business performance but also about their behaviour and attitude. Warnings can be provided about anything that may be seen as inappropriate by other employees.

One area of potential sensitivity is the next generation claiming family privileges; expecting different and favourable treatment simply because of their family status.[63] In practice most next generation employees will be acutely conscious of their family status and the perception of nepotism that this carries. They will feel the need to work harder and to demonstrate greater commitment and competence to dispel this. Yet, at the same time they will remain conscious of a distance between themselves and other similarly placed colleagues. Being related to the general they will never be quite one of the troops. A more subtle purpose of mentoring is to offer support and reassurance to the sometimes isolated and insecure next generation family member, rather than taking the presumptive upstart down a peg or two.

---

[62] The suggestion is that after a few years the next generation should be sufficiently established to have outgrown the need for formal mentoring. See Carlock and Ward in *Parallel Planning* at p 108.
[63] The founder's brother spending so little time at work that he became known as the 'golfing director' in the *Cowan* case discussed in chapter 18 is a good example.

Some larger family owned businesses have well-developed mentoring programmes. Often a respected senior non-family executive acts as mentor to the next generation family members. The best of these arrangements manage to achieve a balance whereby promotion and senior leadership roles for family members are, on the one hand, a genuine opportunity, available to be grasped but, on the other hand, not seen as a pre-ordained right.

7.12.5 Supervision

Sometimes policies are put in place to ensure that younger family members are not supervised directly by close relatives. Partly this is to preserve objectivity and business focus. It also helps to guard against the adverse effects of family dynamics, be they intergenerational, branch related or sibling rivalries. Clearly the larger the family business, the more practicable this is to achieve.

7.12.6 Relationship dynamics

Unsurprisingly it is argued that the quality of family relationships can positively or negatively affect the outcome of the management succession process. Lansberg and Astrachan identify family cohesion and the quality of relationships between the current and designated family business leaders as key factors.[64] Carlock and Ward inject a note of realism saying that:[65]

> 'it is unrealistic for the family to expect that siblings or cousins who have had a conflicted relationship will suddenly work together for the good of the family and business.'

In fact intra-generational conflicts could well increase after the succession process once the senior generation are no longer able to exert a moderating influence, either through their ownership or, after they have died, their presence. Cracks may appear in the family structure once the glue that holds it together is no longer there.

7.12.7 Gender and succession dynamics

Much has been written about the potential difficulties in father to son transitions arising from relationship dynamics, in particular the apparent need for the two generations to compete with each other for the prize of the family business. Although historically fewer in number, later research[66] points to mother-daughter successions as also being fraught with tensions. However there is some suggestion that 'cross gender' father to daughter or mother to son transitions tend to be comparatively smooth.[67]

---

[64] See Lansberg and Astrachan 'Influence of Family Relationships on Succession Planning and Training: The Importance of Mediating Factors' *Family Business Review* (1994) Vol 7(1), 39–59.
[65] Page 114. The case of *Cadman Developments*, discussed in detail in chapter 21, presents a prime example of this.
[66] Vera & Dean 'An examination of the challenges daughters face in family business successions' *Family Business Review* (2005) at pp 321–346.
[67] See Sonnenfeld at p 262.

7.13 STAGE 3: PASSING THE BATON

7.13.1 Life cycles and breathing space

Realistically the course of a family business succession process is unlikely to run smooth. In chapter 3 we talk about the complications caused by the juxtaposition of two individual developmental life cycles of the senior and next generation. These purple patches and black spots have particular relevance to the succession planning process.

Ideally progress can be made during the purple patches, when the typical life cycles of both generations are in a benign phase. If this is not possible an understanding of the underlying life cycle theory can mean that allowances can be made for any anticipated relationship difficulties in the life cycles of either generation that could affect the intergenerational dynamic. Allowances can also be made for the delays in the progress of the succession process. Life cycle theory is another reason to allow for plenty of time in the formal succession planning process.

7.13.2 Fixed retirement dates

Returning to the senior generation and the issue of letting go, the solution is logical, obvious and endorsed by leading commentators.[68] This is to have a fixed retirement date, applicable to all, including family members and especially the business leader.[69] This helps deal with the letting go issue in a relatively sensitive way. The retirement date is part of agreed family policy. This certainty will bring clear benefits to the business and the next generation, allowing both to move forward. In the absence of such a policy uncertainty will prevail. This uncertainty will permeate through the family firm, to employees and then outside to customers, suppliers and bankers. The business could be in danger of stagnation. Put at its starkest if a fixed retirement date is unworkable the succession planning process has failed. If planning was started early enough and has been followed through the desk of the senior generation should be clear by the time the designated retirement date has been reached. If there are things remaining that only the senior generation can handle or if they need to stay around 'just in case', this is really an indication that, at least they believe, their successor is not up to the job.

All of this might sound a bit brutal so far as the senior generation are concerned. Much of this chapter is about the next generation. To the extent that the senior generation has been mentioned it has largely been in negative terms, either as megalomaniacs clinging to power, or as terminally indecisive, unable to choose the best management succession option. Sonnenfeld's approach is much more sympathetic and understanding of the senior generation position. Lansberg also suggests that the starting point in any succession planning exercise must be the senior generation:[70]

> 'given the centrality and influence of the founder, his willingness is a necessary, though not a sufficient condition for effective succession planning to take place.'

The suggestion is that a mixture of support networks, including other senior generation family business members, counselling and consultancy, can all contribute to help the

---

[68] See, for example John Ward *Perpetuating the Family Business; 50 Lessons Learned from Long-Standing Successful Families in Business* (Palgrave 2004) Lesson 2 (Irrevocable Retirement).
[69] The implications of this in terms of age discrimination legislation are discussed in chapter 5.
[70] *The Succession Conspiracy*, op cit.

senior generation resolve their inevitable ambivalence towards the succession process, so that they become more committed to the change and transition. Glen Ayres argues that the basic starting point in the process needs to be an examination of the financial needs and security of the senior generation.[71] Good independent financial planning is therefore an important early step.[72]

7.13.3 Evaluation tools

One of the enemies of the succession process is subjectivity. This can cut both ways. For some senior generation leaders nothing the next generation do can ever be quite good enough. For others their anointed successor can do no wrong. Of course, in reality neither of these polar opposites will serve to plot the true position of the next generation on the map of leadership competence. Everyone will have strengths and weaknesses.

The aim is therefore to get as much objective evidence on the performance and capabilities of the next generation. This could come from informal observations and feedback from trusted senior management, non-executive directors or other family members. This might lack candour or specificity.

There are various evaluation tools available which aim to provide a more balanced and objective view of the successor's true capabilities.[73] Usually these are based on some form of 360 degree appraisal, whereby the next generation complete a form of self-evaluation which is then compared the evaluations of a number of others. These are likely to include the individuals mentioned above. If the process is being followed rigidly it is also likely to include, for example, direct reports of the next generation manager.

7.13.4 Next generation career development programmes

Commentators also suggest that successor evaluation processes and support from a non-family mentor should be supplemented by specific career development programmes for family managers. Some of the development could include more generic training, such as attendance at courses on family business dynamics,[74] or more general training on leadership responsibilities[75] or financial awareness. Highly specific issues might have been identified, such as a weak understanding of certain areas of the family business operation. If so, secondments, projects or training relevant to the area could be required.

The evaluation or mentoring process could have revealed behavioural issues, for example concerning the communication skills of the next generation or their ability to deal with conflict. Again specific counselling or coaching could be arranged.

Of course the family firm might be open to the criticism that similar efforts to the above are not being made for non-family managers in theoretically similar positions. In an ideal world family and non-family managers will have equal access to career

---

[71] See Glenn Ayres 'Rough Corporate Justice' *Family Business Review* (1998) Vol 11(2).
[72] See chapter 26 for a discussion on inter-disciplinary collaborative practice in the context of family business advisory work.
[73] See, for example the Successor's Assessment and Feedback Form including as part of Appendix D in Carlock and Ward *Strategic Planning for the Family Business: Parallel Planning to Unify the Family and Business* (Palgrave, 2001).
[74] The Institute for Family Business run training programmes aimed at the next generation family members.
[75] For example the programmes run by the IOD.

development opportunities. If this is not so and career development programmes are clearly part of a next generation family management fast track, at least the family firm will be taking steps to address weaknesses that would otherwise cause operational difficulties.

7.13.5 The ideal leader

Carlock and Ward identify seven core characteristics of the ideal management succession candidate,[76] the '7-Cs, namely conscience, competence, communication, credibility, coaching[77] and capability. Of these they see conscience as the central and most important characteristic.

7.13.6 Succession working groups

Most of the suggestions made in this paragraph are equally applicable to the development of the careers of all family members (and, by and large, non-family members) working in the business. Sooner or later, what was once a background possibility that the next generation would take over leadership crystalises into a firm plan to make this happen. In some circumstances, most obviously a family with a tradition of primogeniture this possibility quickly becomes the working presumption. There will be an optimal rate of progress towards the formal anointment of the management successor. This will differ slightly for each family business. But there are potential difficulties if the possibility becomes a firm plan too soon. Equally there are difficulties if finalising or implementing the management succession plan is put off for too long.

Neubauer and Lank's suggestion is to set up a succession working group. This should increase objectivity, reduce the reliance on senior generation intuition and also reduce the potential for inter-generational conflict.. The group would be comprised of non-family senior management, non-executive directors and possibly external advisors. The role of this group will vary. Often it will include work on developing the detailed aspects of a formal succession plan. Sometimes it will include providing advice and recommendations as to the suitability of next generation leadership candidates.

Family members will rarely be part of this group, although part of the remit could be to liaise with the family council. Alternatively the senior generation business leadership will undertake this task of family liaison. The whole point is to inject an element of business objectivity and to remove family bias and influence. On very rare occasions, usually if the family has been affected by branch factionalism in the past, the governance system might give this succession planning group the power to make a binding choice, or perhaps vest them with a power of veto over the next business leader.

7.13.7 Advisor support

Professional advisors are also often involved in the succession planning process. The support they are able to offer goes far beyond matters such as tax planning advice

---

[76] See pp 112–113.
[77] By which they mean the ability to coach and develop other people within the business.

offered by the typical content professional or expert advisor.[78] Process trained consultants, such as family business consultants, are skilled in providing support over the wider process, including helping business families whose succession process has stalled at one of the succession barriers identified above.[79]

7.13.8 Next generation competition

Further complexities abound when is more than one next generation family leadership candidate.

Carlock and Ward argue that a degree of healthy competitive tension is good for a family business.[80] Where there are a number of leadership succession candidates Neubauer and Lank also talk of family firms setting up a 'horse race' whereby, over several years in advance of the anticipated leadership succession date, the candidates are given projects or tasks, such as the leadership of a subsidiary or the introduction of a new product. The runners and riders in the family leadership stakes are then judged, as objectively as possible, in terms of their business performance on these tasks.

A formal process of this nature will be rare and in practice only available in the largest of family enterprises with multiple opportunities for the next generation to prove themselves. Instead, using the same analogy as Gersick, Neubauer and Lank suggest that a 'relay race' would be much more common, with the heir presumptive being positioned to receive the baton of leadership, but on the basis that they stand to be removed from the leadership race if they show signs that they will not be able to run their leg of the race.

The difficulty here is if the remaining candidates attempt to trip up the front-runner. The line between healthy competition between the next generation and destructive family conflict can be a fine one. The stakes are likely to be high. The family ownership philosophy might be skewed in favour of the business leader taking complete ownership or at least a much larger share. Even if ownership is to be evenly spread individual and branch pride is at stake. In these circumstances, avoiding choosing a single leader and opting for some form of co-leadership (as discussed above) has both temptations and potential pitfalls.

Ultimately Neubauer and Lank believe that choosing a business leader 'cannot be done with the help of formal analytical tools" and that the "choice has to be largely intuitive'.

The main trick is not to ignore what evidence is available or genuine intuition. If the senior generation choose to go ahead with a family appointment where they have serious and legitimate misgivings as to the capability of the next generation some level of problem must be anticipated.

---

[78] These terms and the respective approaches and roles of the content and process advisory professionals are explored and explained in chapter 25.
[79] As Gersick puts it 'the best advisors help manage the process, not just schedule the event'; – see *Generation to Generation* at p 271.
[80] At p 114.

7.13.9 Conclusion: fair process

Above all the succession planning process must be seen to have been a fair process by all concerned. Blondel *et al*[81] identify a number of component elements to this:

- **Communication.** This involves not only the senior generation making their views on management succession clear, but also providing the next generation with an opportunity to actively participate in the process.
- **Clarity.** Including setting out clear procedures for the selection of the next generation management leader and the criteria under which they will be chosen.
- **Consistency.** To the greatest extent possible treating family and non-family members alike and within the family eliminating subjective criteria such as birth order, gender and family branch from the leadership succession decision.
- **Changeability.** Being prepared to adapt and change the succession process from generation to generation to fit the changing needs of the business and the family.
- **Commitment to fairness.** The suggestion here is that it is necessary to have an over-riding sense of fairness and justice built into the succession process. This will often be rooted in the core family values, identified and captured through the governance process.[82] This over-riding commitment to fairness sits on top of and prevails over the procedural aspects of the succession process.

The argument is that, even though unpopular decisions could well need to be taken as part of the management succession process, these are much more likely to be accepted by all relevant stakeholders, including any 'losers' in the succession stakes, if the result has been arrived at as a result of a demonstrably fair process.[83]

7.14 FORMAL SUCCESSION PLANS

Failure to engage in succession planning on the part of the family business community is something of a cliché. There is also some evidence to suggest that it is a fact.[84] Conversely there is some evidence to suggest that the link between succession planning and family business performance forms a virtuous circle.[85]

The term succession planning is often used. It will be seen from the above that management succession is much more about an evolving and unfolding process from which a plan or, more precisely a series of plans, will emerge than the product of the typical business planning session.

---

[81] Blondel, Carlock and Van Der Heyden *Fair Process: Striving for Justice in Family Firms* (INSEAD Working Paper 2001/45/ENT, 2001).
[82] In family charters etc. See chapter 17.
[83] Glen Ayres takes a similar view. See 'Rough Corporate Justice' *Family Business Review* (1998) Vol 11(2).
[84] Carlock and Ward refer to research in the USA suggesting that almost two-thirds of CEO' approaching retirement age have no designated successor and slightly more than that do not have written strategic plans (see *Parallel Planning* at p 8, referring to a 1997 survey by Arthur Andersen & Mass Mutual). Similar results have been found in the UK, with a Barclays Banks survey in 2002 (*A Family Affair: Today's Family Business* finding that 61% of family business owners had no idea of their succession route, whilst only 16% had a designated successor.
[85] A survey of the UK dairy industry found that the farming businesses with an identified successor 'were considerably more likely to be looking to increase production' whereas those without a successor were more likely to be considering leaving the dairy industry. See Dairy Co Summary Report on *The Structure of the GB dairy farming industry – what drives change?* (The Andersons Centre and the University of Nottingham, January 2013).

Nevertheless the strong recommendation is that the output from the succession process is captured in writing. This is for reasons of clarity, certainty and precision. Having a formal succession plan is therefore accepted best practice. Or more precisely, a series of plans. The key argument of Carlock and Ward's *Parallel Planning* is that planning as the family and business systems are inter-related, intertwined, but nevertheless distinct, it is necessary to work simultaneously, but separately on succession as it relates to both the family business and the business family:[86]

> 'The Parallel Planning Process integrates and balances the family's and the business' interests. It promotes a continuous, interdependent dialogue between management and family ownership around the issues of family and business continuity.'

Writing elsewhere[87] Carlock argues that the process allows a business family to take a 'professionally emotional' approach to the key issue of succession.

Following the Carlock and Ward parallel planning approach gives rise to a requirement to work on two core plans:

- **Family enterprise continuity plan.** This is the outcome of the process whereby the family commit to keeping the business in family ownership.[88] It includes elements such as exploring the commitment of the family to the business, developing their ownership philosophy and an understanding of how they will work together as effective owners.[89]

  There will be a need for related plans, such as retirement plans and inheritance tax planning for the senior generation[90] (estate plans).

  Carlock and Ward also place some of the planning relating to the development of the next generation, for example career development plans within the umbrella of the family continuity plan.

- **Business strategy plan.** Here Carlock and Ward are really proposing using the transition period between the generations as an opportunity to have a long hard and high level strategic look at the family business. Various commentators make the point that, what has served the current generation well, might be out dated by the time the next generation are ready to take over, indeed that this might be a source of tension between the generations during the transition process.

  The assessment of the potential of the family business and the markets in which it operates will, in turn, affect the approach of the family to ownership.[91]

  The overall business strategy plan will need to be supplemented by a succession implementation plan, a detailed plan for the actual transfer of management control.

7.15 MANAGEMENT SUCCESSION: CONCLUSION

The importance of the succession process to the wealth and happiness of the business owning family cannot be underestimated. Neither can the level of complexity and challenge involved. Management succession can undoubtedly present a difficult

---

[86] At p 227.
[87] See Carlock *When Family Businesses are Best* (INSEAD R&D working paper 2010/42/EFE, 2010) at p 21.
[88] Assuming that to be the eventual outcome of the process.
[89] Various aspects of this are explored in chapters 11 (Ownership Approach), 15 (Ownership Succession) and 17 (Family Business Governance).
[90] Estate plans, in the US terminology used in much of the literature.
[91] This is explained and explored further in chapter 15.

challenge for many family businesses. The key options have been considered in this chapter. They are basically to pass leadership to a designated family member, to a non-family leader or to a group of co-leaders. Otherwise the family firm will need to be sold or closed.

Management succession will inevitably occur. Sometimes commentators list an additional succession option for the senior generation; to do nothing. They do not really mean that this is a viable option. Whilst succession might be postponed it will eventually be triggered even if this is by some catastrophic event, such as the death or the serious ill-health of the senior generation business leader, or possibly a cataclysmic dispute within the business owning family. In the meantime deterioration in the business will be almost inevitable. In *Parallel Planning* leading family business academics Ward and Carlock argue that the whole purpose of the succession planning process is for a business owning family to generate as many viable strategic options for succession as possible. To do so the family will need to make the best use reasonably possible of the available transition period from one succession to the next.

The most common reasons for delay and indecision on the part of the senior generation in relation to the succession process have been noted above. They are real and understandable reasons. There are difficult decisions to be taken. The senior generation have formidable personal barriers to overcome. Their approach and the decisions they take will affect the future of the business and the family for many years to come, if not for ever.

Succession is an awesome responsibility, which is borne chiefly by the senior generation. However, as Figure 7.3 shows, it is one of the great ironies of family business life that failure to make best use of the transition process and the longer key decisions are put off, the greater the likelihood that the strategic options for the business will in fact diminish. Whilst there might be dreams of family continuity, in terms of ownership, management or both, preconceptions can be dangerous. One of the key objects of the succession process is to explore viable alternatives before settling on the most appropriate. A successful process will require a huge amount of patience and compassion but also drive purpose and planning. Whilst the primary responsibility for driving this process rests with the senior generation, as the incumbent holders of power, status, control and ownership of the family firm. But everyone comprised within the family business system has a role to play, be they next generation, management insiders or outsiders, non-family management. Communication is key. Families that take the approach that 'we are not that sort of family' and avoid talking about succession issues are seriously limiting their prospects of achieving a successful outcome.

A successful transition, retaining both family management and ownership, could take many years to plan and implement properly, when the development needs of the next generation family management are taken into account alongside establishing any governance processes that will be required to balance the interests of family insiders and outsiders. Likewise, if the business is to be sold there will be an optimum time to do so, if the best price if to be achieved. This is most unlikely to be when the current generation of management have, like Henry Ford, 'past their sell by date'.

Pursuing the 'do nothing option' for too long may leave the senior generation no other option than to 'turn out the lights' and close the family firm.

Figure 7.3: Succession options and the transition period

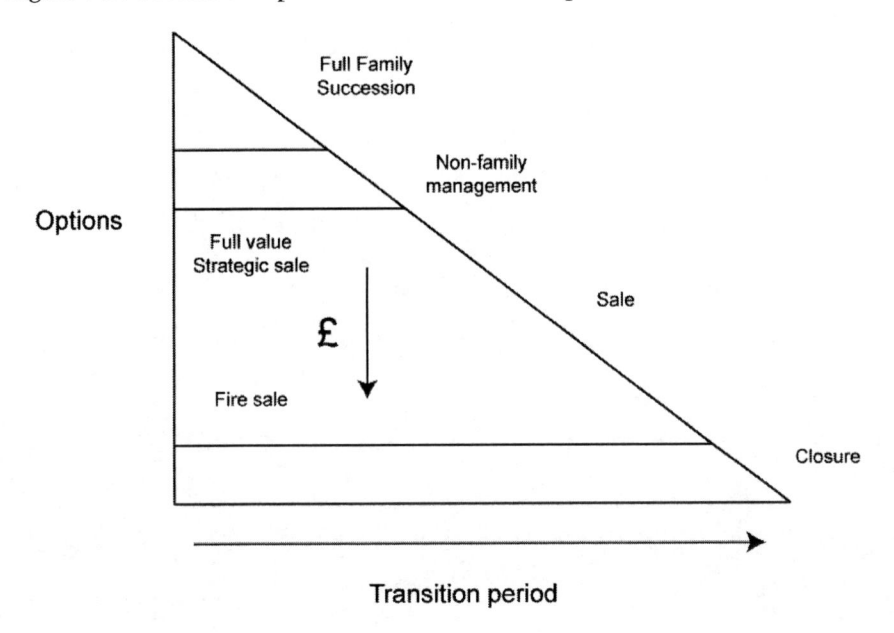

Options:
- Full Family Succession
- Non-family management
- Full value Strategic sale
- Sale
- Fire sale
- Closure

£ ↓

Transition period →

CHAPTER 8

DIRECTORS' DUTIES

8.1 INTRODUCTION

Much has already been written about directors' duties, particularly in the context of the codification of these duties in the Companies Act 2006.[1] We do not intend to duplicate that effort by attempting a comprehensive treatment of the subject in this chapter. Instead we will provide a basic overview of the topic, highlight a number of issues of key relevance to family owned businesses and signpost the reader to sources containing a more detailed coverage of this key issue.[2]

Our consideration of directors' duties will be limited to a narrow range of 'core duties' largely contained in Chapter 2 of the Companies Act 2006 (ss 170–179). Directors also have much wider obligations, for example to ensure that a whole host of filing and compliance requirements contained elsewhere in the Act are dealt with, tax compliance, health and safety and data protection, along with any specific regulations relating to the industry in which the business concerned operates. The detail of these wider duties are both encyclopedic and beyond the scope of this book. But as will be seen failure to comply with accounting requirements feature heavily in cases where directors have found themselves in wider difficulty.

8.1.1 The relevance of directors' duties

Why is the subject of directors' duties so important? It is probably fair to say that almost every company will at some stage in its corporate lifetime have been in breach of some requirement of the Companies Act, however minor. Indeed there has been judicial recognition of the fact that this is to be expected in the case of smaller owner managed businesses.[3] Many such breaches are criminal offences and, at least in theory, expose the directors to criminal sanctions.[4] But in practice sanctions for breaches of filing requirements as stand-alone offences are almost unheard of.[5] Whilst in no way diminishing the importance of statutory compliance we do not intend to deal with the detail of this in this chapter.

---

[1] That is summarising previous case-law and turning it into statutory form by an act of Parliament.
[2] See further reading recommendations for this part.
[3] For example in *Fisher v Cadman* [2005] EWHC 377 (Ch), an unfair prejudice case, discussed in detail in chapter 21, the judge acknowledged that 'the affairs of [the family company] were run with considerable informality while [the founder] was alive. This is unsurprising, in view of its nature as a small family company' (at para 20 of the judgment).
[4] For example failure to maintain an up to date register of directors as required by CA, s 162.
[5] They are nevertheless taken into account as relevant factors in, for example director's disqualification proceedings.

Other more substantial duties, which usually give rise to civil rather than criminal sanctions, for example, the duty of directors not to place themselves in positions where their personal interests conflict with those of the their family company (discussed in detail below), may, in some family businesses, be more honoured in the breach than the observance. Yet such breaches may go unchallenged, unremarked or even accepted on the basis that 'it is all in the family'. Maybe those concerned will be unaware that how they operate their family business is in breach of directors' duties, it is simply 'the way we do things round here.' Potentially this situation will prevail for year after year. If indeed no-one minds, why should the directors of what is a privately owned family business be over concerned about duties that might seem to sit more in the public arena? Michael Griffiths and Matthew Griffiths put the challenge more graphically: 'if, for whatever reason a duty cannot be enforced then it really is a semantic nonsense that it should be called a duty'.[6]

Whilst recognising that many, if not most cases breaches or directors' duties will not be enforced, they do identify circumstances where action may be taken against directors. Most relevant for our purposes are:

- **Insolvency.** It might be possible for a family to run their family business in their own way and to pay scant regard to the requirements of the Companies Act whilst the business is solvent. But any serious breaches will come under scrutiny following insolvency. As will be seen, many of the successful breach of duty cases against family business directors have been brought by insolvency practitioners. Other cases have been brought by the Disqualification Unit of the Insolvency Service, seeking disqualification orders against the directors concerned. It is of course one of our contentions that family owned businesses are, on the whole, more prudently run, and therefore less likely to encounter the insolvency regime than their non-family owned counterparts.

- **Insider claims.** By insider claims we mean claims against family directors made by other family members. On comparatively rare occasions an individual family director with few if any shares may do something sufficiently heinous to provoke the rest of the board, backed by the majority of the family shareholders, to take action against the wrong-doer. This would, under basic principles of company law, be taken in the name of the company.[7] A much more likely situation will be that, for whatever reason,[8] family cohesion has broken down and one or more family members find themselves on the outside the family tent. Breaches of duty that have previously been tolerated now become the cause of major discontent, leading to the issue of legal proceedings. This seems to explain the litigation in *Harrison Properties*[9] discussed below.

Occasionally, as in *Harrison Properties*, the relevant breach will be litigated as a stand-alone issue. But it is more likely that the breach of duty will form part of a claim for unfair prejudice under CA, s 994. As explained in chapter 21 serious beaches of duty by directors are a fairly fruitful source of successful claims when families fall out.

---

[6] Michael Griffiths and Matthew Griffiths *A Director's Guide to Duties* (Jordan Publishing, 2014) at p 110.
[7] The rule in *Foss v Harbottle* [1843] 2 Hare 461 – otherwise known as the 'proper plaintiff rule'. The basic idea is that as the wrong has been done to the company concerned so it is the company that should sue.
[8] Conflict in family owned businesses is explored in chapter 2, Themes and generally throughout the book.
[9] *JJ Harrison (Properties) Ltd v Harrison* [2001] EWCA Civ 1467.

Less likely, but still relevant, will be the possibility that the directors in breach face derivative claims instigated by the minority, but brought in the name of the company. The issues surrounding derivative claims are explored in more detail in chapter 24.

8.1.2 The link to governance

Nevertheless it must be the case that the occasions where family business directors face legal proceedings represent very much the tip of the iceberg of breaches of duty.

Compliance with directors' duties and the general corporate governance are inextricably linked so that often, such compliance is seen as a part of overall governance, alongside wider aspects of risk management, business planning and, particularly in the quoted company arena, compliance with the UK Corporate Governance Code. We would suggest that the most compelling reason to pay attention to directors' duties is that, along with other aspects of governance, it makes both business and family sense.

Take, for example, the case of a controlling shareholder wishing to use company funds to buy a holiday home. This is not an infrequent occurrence in the family business world.[10] Rather than assume that the rest of the family won't mind, or taking the view for whatever reason that such a purchase should go ahead anyway,[11] a much better result may be obtained by following the thought process and procedures that form part of the package of directors' duties.

To follow the example through, a full governance process might be seen to involve a series of steps and questions as follows:

- Why is it sensible to use company funds to buy a holiday home in the first place? Put in terms of directors' duties how would such a purchase be consistent with the general duty in CA, s 172 for directors to promote the success of their company, especially when considered in terms of the interests of the various stakeholder groups mentioned in that section? Rather is this not a classic example of a business owning family mixing business considerations with family wishes? Put into family business theory terms it is an example of a systems conflict.
- Assuming that the proposal to buy a holiday home survives proper scrutiny by the board (and it is difficult to see how this could be so; the usual reason that 'it will be good investment' is most unlikely to stand up to scrutiny), good governance would suggest that consultation with the wider family membership would be in order. If that consultation provides a positive result the directors have insulated themselves from internal attack.[12]

---

[10] And featured as an issue in the unfair prejudice case of *Sam Weller and Sons* [1989] 5 BCC 810 discussed in chapter 21.
[11] The purchase by the family company of a holiday home for use by the sons of the controlling shareholder was one of the factors in *Same Weller and Sons Ltd* [1990] Ch 682.
[12] Although not necessarily from external attack by insolvency practitioners and others in the case of business failure, particularly if this occurs in the short to medium term future. Of most concern may be that rather than creating a family asset for mutual enjoyment the business family have probably created a source of future tension and dispute over rights to use the property and responsibilities for its upkeep and maintenance and administration. A significant number of family business disputes have family holiday homes as a complicating factor if not a direct cause.

- An opportunity to rethink. If the business can afford it they might consider paying out dividends as an alternative way of privately funding the purchase by the controlling family with the minority family members taking their proportionate share.
- Even if the reaction of the wider family is negative those controlling the family business may nevertheless choose to go ahead anyway, even in the absence of a compensating dividend. At least the purchase will have been made with transparency and a degree of compliance with the more formal, if not the substantive, aspects of corporate governance. This might not prevent claims from the wider family membership. But at least these should not include accusations of secrecy and underhand behaviour.

A similar process can be applied to many other governance situations, particularly those involving conflicts of interest between the controlling family members and the wider family membership. The basic point being that by pausing to ask, and honestly answer, the question 'should we be doing this?' the controllers have an opportunity to test the wisdom and propriety of their proposed course of action before too much damage is done.

8.1.3 Key issues for family owned businesses

Clearly all of the duties discussed in this chapter, together with the whole raft of regulatory and compliance legislation referred to above, apply just as much to family owned businesses as to their non-family counterparts. However there a number of areas where the directors of family owned companies are particularly prone to get into difficulties. The following key issues are explored in more detail later in this chapter.

- **Family directors** (see 8.6). There is no legal recognition of the concept of the family director. Nevertheless family directors, by which we mean family members occupying (usually) non-executive positions because of their status as a family member, rather than because of their experience and contribution to the business, are a clearly observable phenomenon in many family companies. The problems this can cause for 'family directors' are explored below.[13]
- **Conflicts of interest** (see 8.7). All directors need to be wary of conflicts between their own personal interests and those of the company (usually seen through the eyes of other shareholders). Family owned business include the additional dimension of wider family interests. They often feature complex ownership structures. These complexities make conflicts of interest both more likely and particularly difficult to deal with.
- **Remuneration** (see 8.8). One of the most sensitive issues in any family owned business, if not the most sensitive issue, is the level of remuneration to be enjoyed by those in control of the family owned business. This paragraph looks at the extent to which the 'have-nots' are able to control the remuneration of the 'haves'.
- **Balancing stakeholder interests** (see 8.9). CA, s 172 contains a general duty for directors to promote the success of their company. The section also provides a shopping list of stakeholder groups whose interests the directors must 'have regard to' when discharging that duty. Especially in more mature, diversely held family owned businesses family members may have strong, but differing views about where the true interests of their family business lie. What happens if the view of the

---

[13] The position of family directors in the family business governance system is also discussed in chapter 17.

Directors' Duties

board is radically different to that of a proportion of the wider family membership, particularly in relation to one of the mandatory considerations listed in CA, s 172?

- **The sinking ship – insolvency claims** (see **8.10**). The interests of creditors will inevitably be damaged with every insolvent company failure. The insolvency regime contains a number of remedies a liquidator might be able to use against directors to help repair that damage.

Of course whether those remedies are available and used will depend on the precise circumstances of the case concerned. Two primary factors will include the funds available to the liquidator to pursue any action and the prospects of success, not only the legal strength of the claim but also whether the director concerned has any assets to satisfy any judgment. For this reason many breaches of duty, including provisions specifically relating to insolvency go unpunished.

This section takes a brief look at insolvency in the context of the family owned business and seeks to examine whether there are factors relevant to family businesses that make insolvent failure more likely.

The cases on this subject also illustrate that whilst third party creditors, may lose out on the failure of a family company, including HMRC in terms of unpaid Corporation Tax, VAT and National Insurance Contributions; so called 'Crown debt'), those most likely to suffer could well be the family members themselves.

8.2 OVERVIEW

8.2.1 Directors: a definition?

Before looking at the duties of directors in any detail it is sensible to pause and to examine exactly what a director is. The answer to this question is by no means obvious. The Companies Act is not much help, simply stating that the meaning of director:[14]

'... includes any person occupying the position of director, by whatever name called.'

In effect we will know a director when we see one. So it is necessary to look at various categories of person who might fit the description of a director.

8.2.2 *De Jure* directors

The first and most frequently encountered species of director is what is frequently called the *de jure* director.[15] This term applies to a director who has been validly appointed under the company's internal procedures and continues to hold office. Their appointment will have been properly recorded at Companies House. There will usually be little or no doubt about who are the *de-jure* directors of a company.

As will be seen *de jure* directors will still be seen to be 'occupying the position of director' and therefore subject to a full range of directors' duties even if their position is pretty much nominal and their contribution to the business limited to non-existent.

---

[14] CA, s 250.
[15] Latin: of right, by right, according to law.

8.2.3 *De facto* directors

A *de facto* director is someone who has not been validly appointed as a *de jure* director but in practice, can nevertheless be seen to be acting as a director.

There is no definition of *de facto* director in the Companies Acts, although the concept has been widely recognised by the courts for well over a century. All will turn on the particular facts of the case. Sometimes this will be because the company intended to make a formal or *de-jure* appointment but the appointment was procedurally flawed. Often such individuals will be held out as a director and can be clearly shown to have 'taken their seat around the board table'. They will usually struggle to hide behind the invalidity of their appointment to escape scrutiny for their conduct as a director.

The second and, especially for those concerned, more unfortunate category of *de facto* director is where an individual, who whilst never intended to be formally appointed as a director, nevertheless gives every appearance of being one. The courts will look at each case on its own facts.[16] No single fact will be decisive. But there will be some key indicators. Holding out someone as a director, in other words allowing them to assume the title of director internally or in business dealings with the outside world, will be a significant, but not a decisive indicator.

Conversely simply occupying a senior management role in the day-to-day operations of a business will not, in and of itself, be sufficient for someone to be seen as a *de facto* director. Something more will be required.

This will be participation in core 'director like' activities, for example a high level participation in key decisions and negotiations on strategy, sales and acquisitions of businesses or key assets, negotiations with funders or on 'business critical' contracts, or having a say in the appointment of other directors or senior employees. Basically activities of such importance that only a director could properly be undertaking them. It is not necessary for someone to be found to be a *de-facto* director that they participate in each and every director type decision. It may be sufficient that they can be shown to have participated in certain key decisions.

As discussed in the context of succession[17] there may be a significant disconnection between theoretical titles and the real power and control in a family owned business. So that a senior generation ex-director, who has in theory resigned as a *de jure* director may nevertheless remain involved in key decisions to such an extent as being treated as a *de facto* director. Similarly the more informal management structures and less bureaucratic procedures seen to be characteristic, particularly of smaller and medium sized family businesses, could open up questions whether certain individuals, possibly including highly influential senior employees, are *de facto* directors.

8.2.4 Shadow directors

A shadow director is defined by CA 2006, s 251(1) as 'person in accordance with whose directions or instructions the directors of the company are accustomed to act'.

---

[16] For a detailed discussion in relevant factors and references to both UK and Commonwealth cases see Andrew Keay *Directors' Duties* (Jordan Publishing, 2nd edn, 2014) at pp 13–21.
[17] See chapter 7.

The concepts of *de facto* directors and shadow directors overlap. So a notionally retired senior generation family member who in practice exercises a power of veto over key business decisions taken by the next generation *de jure* directors could also be seen to be a shadow director.[18]

Shadow directors, as the name implies, are however more typically to be found lurking behind the scenes of a smaller family business, leaving the operation to be fronted by a family stooge who has taken on the formal *de jure* directorship appointment. Often there are factors such as a director's disqualification order (or an undertaking given not to act as a director to avoid formal disqualification proceedings) or a disqualifying event like personal bankruptcy, that prevents the driving force behind the family business from stepping out of the shadows and being seen to be in control.[19]

Companies Act 2006, s 170((5) provides that the general directors' duties contained in Part 2 of the act apply to shadow directors.

8.2.5 Executive and non-executive directors

It is standard practice both in corporate governance and in wider business speak to distinguish between executive and non-executive directors. The Companies Act makes no such distinction. The directors' duties discussed in this chapter apply to all directors. This is irrespective of whether they work full time for the company concerned and earn a small fortune in the process or whether they occupy a board position out of a sense of family obligation and are not even reimbursed their expenses for doing so.

8.2.6 Family directors

Conversely the concept of family directors is rarely recognised. Family directors can be seen to fall into various broad categories.

- First directors who are executives, usually working full time, operating at a full director level but who 'just happen' to also be members of the business owning family.
- Secondly non-executive directors, who play a full role in the life of the board and satisfy most of the tests of a good non-executive director emerging from the corporate governance literature, but who again are also family members.
- Thirdly formally appointed *de jure* directors, who also work in the business but, notwithstanding their title as director, for a wide range of reasons, including age, ability or having been side lined as a result of family politics, actually cannot be said to take any real role in the actual direction of their family company.
- Finally family non-executive directors, who play no real role and make little practical contribution to the board. They occupy their positions for reasons of convenience or family tradition.

---

[18] It used to be important to plump for either *de facto* or shadow directorship when considering a claim against a non *de jure* director because the English courts initially said that there was no overlap between the two concepts. This has now been reversed by the Supreme Court in *Revenue and Customs Commissioners v Holland* [2010] UKSC 51 where it was accepted that the two concepts overlap.

[19] *Cohen v Selby* [2000] BCC 275 (and on appeal [2002] BCC 82 discussed in detail below), where a 17-year-old son took on the mantel of *de jure* directorship is a case in point.

The appointment of directors in the first two categories can be fully justified by reference to business criteria.

It is the last two categories we are primarily concerned with in looking at family directors at 8.6 below. The common factor between them is that, absent their formal appointment as *de jure* directors, their lack of true involvement in the direction of the company would not be seen as sufficient for them to be classified as *de facto* directors.

8.2.7 Courtesy director titles

Finally individuals holding courtesy titles as directors but who have neither been formally appointed to the board nor can be seen to be 'occupying the position of director' for the purposes of CA, s 250. These individuals may be held out, particularly externally, as directors and carrying business cards with, for example titles of 'Sales Director' or 'Regional Director'. They may have some explaining to do in the case of business failure as titles and holding out will be seen as a strong indication of *de-facto* directorship. But as this is not a decisive indicator.[20] If the individual concerned can show that they did not really operate at director level they will escape scrutiny as a director.

Having now explored who will be treated as a director and introduced some relevant terminology we now turn to look at the actual duties of directors.

8.3 DIRECTORS' DUTIES – AN OVERVIEW

8.3.1 Codification and the relevance of case-law

The Companies Act attempts to codify the core general duties of company directors. Those duties have been analysed and developed by the courts over at least two centuries and are contained in a considerable body of case-law. The relevance of this body of case-law is complicated.

CA, s 170(3) provides that the new codified duties 'have effect in place' of 'common law rules and equitable principles' as they apply in relation to the general duties of directors. However CA, s 170(4) says that the new codified rules are to be 'interpreted and applied in the same way' as these rules and principles and that 'regard shall be had' to this body of law in trying to work out the extent of directors' duties. Mason's view is that this approach the courts 'are required to regard ss 171–177 more as principles set out in a very authoritative judgment or textbook than as statutory rules'.[21]

Whatever the academic arguments, having their core general duties set out or summarised within the space of a few sections, easily accessible to anyone with an internet connection[22] must be of considerable help to those directors who are keen to understand the key principles under which they should operate their family business. It

---

[20] *Re Sykes (Butchers) Ltd* [1998] 1 BCLC 110
[21] *Mason French & Ryan on Company Law* (Oxford University Press, 33rd ed, 2014).
[22] At http://www.legislation.gov.uk.

is clear from the body of case-law that arguments based on ignorance of those duties cut little ice with the courts in the past and presumably will cut less still under the new codified regime.

Whilst there might be hundreds if not thousands of cases on directors' duties decided before codification there is, little case-law interpreting the new codified duties. Inevitably attempts to reduce this body of previous case-law to the nine sections contained in CA, Chapter 2 will throw up many questions for the courts in the future.

8.3.2 Duty to act within powers – CA, s 171

The first general duty listed in the Act is for directors to ensure that their company acts within its powers. In full the relevant section, CA, s 171, provides:

Duty to act within powers

(1) A director of a company must –

    (a)   act in accordance with the company's constitution, and
    (b)   only exercise powers for the purposes for which they are conferred.

This is self-explanatory and little more needs to be said. Except perhaps to note that family owned businesses often have undergone little or no change of control from the founding family nor taken any major venture capital or other external investment. Both these events are likely to cause a review and updating of the constitution. Older family businesses may therefore find that their constitution has not been updated since the formation of the company and will be operating under older versions of Table A from previous Companies Acts. These will include a number of anachronisms eliminated under subsequent versions of Table A or now the Model Articles.[23] They may not include various modern developments taken for granted in modern corporate practice, for example, the ability to hold remote telephone or electronic board meetings.

8.3.3 Duty to promote the success of the company – CA, s 172

The provision that has received the most attention is perhaps the new summary of the obligation for directors to promote the success of their company. CA, s 172(1) provides that:

(1) A director of a company must act in the way he considers, in good faith, would be most likely to promote the success of the company for the benefit of its members as a whole, and in doing so have regard (amongst other matters) to –

    (a)   the likely consequences of any decision in the long term,
    (b)   the interests of the company's employees,
    (c)   the need to foster the company's business relationships with suppliers, customers and others,
    (d)   the impact of the company's operations on the community and the environment,
    (e)   the desirability of the company maintaining a reputation for high standards of business conduct, and
    (f)   the need to act fairly as between members of the company.

Various aspects of this duty, as they relate to family companies, are considered below in **8.9** (Balancing stakeholder interests).

---

[23] Companies (Model Articles) Regulations 2008, SI 2008/3229.

8.3.4 Duty to exercise independent judgment – CA, s 173

CA, s 173(1) required a director to 'exercise independent judgment' in other words maintain their independence, to stand upright and be true to the company, rather than any third party or factional interest that might have been responsible for their appointment, for example a holding company or investment institution.

Recognising the potential conflicts of interest caused by such appointments CA, s 173(2) contains an 'institutional opt-out', whereby the strictness of this duty may be tempered by formal arrangements. The duty of independent judgment will not be infringed by a director acting either:[24]

(a) in accordance with an agreement duly entered into by the company that restricts the future exercise of discretion by its directors, or
(b) in a way authorised by the company's constitution.

In a family business context, by custom and practice, or by constitutional right, branches of a family are sometimes able to appoint family directors with an express or implied understanding that the appointee is to police the interests of the appointing branch. It would seem that if the terms and extent of such an understanding is carefully spelt out, in the articles of the family company concerned, or in a shareholders' agreement, the family director can suspend his independent judgment and use his position to promulgate the views of their particular branch of the family.

Whether having family branch appointees to the board in the first place is a different question (and answered in the negative in chapter 17 (Governance)). But if the opposite approach is followed, the family concerned may wish to go the whole hog and attempt to protect the position of the branch appointee, by fully documenting and thereby recongnising, the limits on their obligation to exercise independent judgment and excusing what might otherwise be construed as breaches of this obligation.[25]

8.3.5 Duty to exercise reasonable care, skill and diligence – CA, s 174

Directors owe a basic duty of care to their company. If they are negligent they risk being sued by the company. The more likely scenario is that proceedings will be brought by a liquidator, following the collapse of the family company. Directors also risk being disqualified from acting as a director in the future. The position is confirmed in CA, s 174 which provides that:

Duty to exercise reasonable care, skill and diligence

(1) A director of a company must exercise reasonable care, skill and diligence.

(2) This means the care, skill and diligence that would be exercised by a reasonably diligent person with –

(a) the general knowledge, skill and experience that may reasonably be expected of a person carrying out the functions carried out by the director in relation to the company, and

---

[24] CA, s 173(2)(a), (b).
[25] The general duties of directors overlap. Even a fully mandated family branch director might still have difficulty in justifying partisanship under CA, s 172 – the general duty to promote the success of the company.

(b) the general knowledge, skill and experience that the director has.

This duty, including the dual standard of competence contained in CA, s 174(2), is considered in detail below in **8.6** below (the family director).

8.3.6 Duty to avoid conflicts of interest – CA, s 175

The duty on directors to avoid conflict of interest is central to company law. The duty is simply but widely stated in CA, s 175(1) which reads:

> A director of a company must avoid a situation in which he has, or can have, a direct or indirect interest that conflicts, or possibly may conflict, with the interests of the company.

It will be seen that the provision covers potential as well as actual conflicts and indirect conflicts or interest in addition to direct conflicts. Much of the case-law is concerned with directors taking advantage of their position by engaging in improper property transactions, taking advantage of confidential information and diversion of business opportunities. CA, s 175(2) focuses on these evils (although not to the exclusion of all others) and emphasises that the duty to avoid conflicts of interest applies:

> ... in particular to the exploitation of any property, information or opportunity (and it is immaterial whether the company could take advantage of the property, information or opportunity).

There is effectively a defence of foreseeability so directors will not be in breach of duty if they are involved in a transaction or arrangement involving the company which 'cannot reasonably be regarded as likely to give rise to a conflict of interest'.[26]

Of course many dealings between a company and its directors will involve an inherent conflict of interest. For example the terms of that director's appointment, service agreement or remuneration, a lease by the company of premises belonging to a director or business dealings between the company and another company in which a director holds shares.

Recognising this commercial reality the Act provides approval mechanisms. If properly followed, these will authorise a transaction or arrangement, which would otherwise amount to a breach of the duty to avoid conflicts. CA, s 180 confirms that 'a transaction or arrangement is not liable to be set aside' on the basis of breach of either the duty to avoid conflicts of interest under CA, s 175 or the duty to declare interests under CA, s 177, provided that the approval procedures contained in those sections have been followed.

Briefly summarised a conflict situation may be authorised by the directors, provided that such authorisation does not conflict with the express provisions of the company's constitution.[27] Also the conflicted director cannot be counted in the quorum for the relevant director's meeting and (broadly) that their votes are disregarded.[28] There is nothing to prevent the director concerned attending at and speaking at the relevant board meeting.

---

[26] CA, s 175(4)(a).
[27] CA, s 175(5)(a) – for private companies. For public companies the opposite position applies, ie the constitution must expressly allow the approval by directors.
[28] CA, s 175(6).

A key point is that conflicts of interest involving transactions or arrangements directly involving the company are not covered by the duty in CA, s 175.[29] This issue is discussed in 8.7 below.

Some arrangements with directors are so inherently conflict ridden and or commercially significant that the authorisation of the rest of the board will not be sufficient. The approval of the members will always be required. These are:

- service agreements;
- severance payments;
- substantial property transactions;
- loans to directors.

8.3.7 Duty not to accept benefits from third parties – CA, s 176

CA, s 176 contains a stand-alone prohibition on directors accepting benefits from third parties. The section operates alongside the criminal law provisions of the Bribery Act 2010 but is a 'private' protection for the benefit of the company and gives rise to civil claims if breached. The provision is clearly intended to reinforce the general duty to avoid conflicts of interest contained in CA, s 175. Unlike the conflict of interest provisions there is no express procedure for directors to obtain approval of any third party benefits actually offered.

There is a defence 'that acceptance of the benefit cannot reasonably be regarded as likely to give rise to a conflict of interest'.[30] So, although there is no formal *de-minimis* exception, it would be surprising if accepting routine corporate hospitality from suppliers or customers would place a director in breach of this duty.

8.3.8 Duty to declare interest in proposed or existing transactions or arrangements – CA, s 177 and s 182

A fundamental requirement is that directors who are interested in a proposed transaction involving their company must formally declare that interest to their fellow board members in accordance with CA, s 177. There is a largely parallel procedure under CA, s 182 relating to declarations of interest in existing transactions or arrangements. The principal difference being that it is a criminal offence[31] not to disclose interests in existing arrangements. The requirement is to declare the 'nature and extent' of a director's interest. Therefore a full declaration needs to be made. This is explored below in the discussion of *Harrison Properties*.[32]

---

[29] CA, s 175(3).
[30] CA, s 176(4).
[31] CA, s 183. Failure to disclose an interest in a proposed transaction or arrangement has purely civil consequences. The transaction is unlikely to be enforceable against the company and the director may be liable for any losses suffered by the company or profits the director makes. Logically an undeclared proposed arrangement, once consummated becomes an existing arrangement covered by s 182.
[32] JJ Harrison (Properties) Ltd v Harrison [2001] EWCA Civ 1467.

8.4 RATIFICATION

8.4.1 Basic principle

In the real world directors will frequently be in breach of both the procedural and substantial aspects of corporate governance. Usually this failure will be innocent and inadvertent. Examples could include issuing shares without following the pre-emption procedure in the articles of association or a director buying or selling property to the company without obtaining the approval of the members under CA, s 190.

As directors owe their duties to the company[33] the theory goes that the company, acting through its members may also forgive[34] or ratify breaches of duties. But behind that simple proposition there sits a considerable complexity and a large body of case-law.[35]

8.4.2 Limitations and issues

That case-law makes it clear that there are limitations to what may be ratified. The problem, particularly for those advising minority shareholders, is determining from the case-law exactly where those boundaries lie. It is well beyond the scope of this book to attempt to map out those boundaries. Indeed academic commentators have suggested that the task is impossible.[36] Instead we will simply flag up the key issues and areas where ratification might not be possible.

- **Insolvency.** If a company is insolvent, its creditors rather than the shareholders have the real economic interest in its assets, including any possible claims against directors. Of course in a family or other owner managed company there will be a considerable overlap between the directors and shareholders. It would be entirely inappropriate if, at a time when the company was insolvent, the membership could forgive directors their breaches of duty to the detriment of creditors.[37] The same position probably applies at a time when a company is in financial difficulties or approaching insolvency.[38]

- **Fraud on the minority.** A key principle of company law is the internal management rule, the idea that if proper procedures are followed, including those relating to the ratification of a previous breach of procedure, then the courts should not intervene. A further key principle is that of majority rule; once the appropriate majority has been obtained, and usually for ratification of most breaches of duty this will be a simple majority, again the courts should not interfere.[39] But this potentially leaves minority shareholders in an invidious position. By definition the company will not have been managed in accordance with the rules of its own constitution or wider company law, or both. Those breaches may go well beyond the merely technical. Must the minority simply sit back and allow all breaches to be ratified if the majority want this to happen? The answer is no. Certain breaches will not be capable of ratification, as so to do so would be seen as a 'fraud on the minority'. However that concept is itself extremely difficult to define. Certainly it

---

[33] CA, s 170(1).
[34] See Harman LJ in *Bamford v Bamford* [1970] Ch 212.
[35] For a more detailed discussion see Andrew Keay *Directors' Duties* (Jordan Publishing, 2nd edn, 2014), chapter 16, Part III.
[36] Paul Davies *Gower and Davies' Principles of Company Law* (Sweet and Maxwell, 7th ed, 2003) at p 439.
[37] *Bowthorpe Ltd v Hills* [2002] EWHC 2331 (Ch).
[38] *Dilmun v Sutton* [2004] EWHC 52 (Ch).
[39] *Bamford v Bamford* [1970] 1 Ch 212.

is not meant in the criminal sense that only outright dishonesty will be constrained. The concept has its roots in the jurisdiction of equity, so fraud is to be interpreted in the equitable sense of unconscionable conduct. But case-law suggests that in some circumstances, conduct by the directors in bad faith and for an improper purpose not in the interests of the company may nevertheless be capable of ratification by the majority.[40] One of the key areas of difficulty for minority shareholders in family owned businesses is understanding where the boundaries lie between conduct supported by the majority which, in the absence of a viable exit route, they must simply put up with and, on the other hand, matters that go beyond the pale of majority rule giving rise to remedies actionable by a derivative claim, unfair prejudice proceedings or otherwise.

- **Misappropriation of company property.** Perhaps the clearest area where majority rule will not prevail and where a fraud on the minority will be easiest to establish is where the directors misappropriate company property (including corporate opportunities and information) in breach of duty.[41] Even if the majority are prepared to stand by and see this happen the minority should be well placed to challenge the loss to the company and with it the damage to the value of their own shareholding of the relevant asset.[42]

- **Dishonesty.** It is doubtful whether outright dishonesty, in the criminal sense, can ever be ratified, even by the unanimous agreement of all shareholders. There are clear public policy reasons against this. The company is a separate legal personality and will still have been wronged by the dishonest actions of the directors.

8.4.3 Who is bound by ratification?

Whilst a company is a separate legal personality it must nevertheless operate through the agency of its human members.[43] Is any purported ratification binding only on the members at the time or will it hold good for all time? Of most interest will new shareholders or any liquidator be bound by a purported ratification? Although there is some uncertainty and academic debate the better view appears to be that, subject to the limitations in terms of solvency, fraud on the minority and dishonesty have been identified above, the members at the time of ratification have the ability to bind their successors in title.[44]

8.4.4 Statutory procedure

At common law a valid ratification of a director's breach required a high degree of transparency and procedural compliance. Members must clearly understand that they

---

[40] In *Bamford v Bamford* the directors issued shares to a sympathetic third party as part of a strategy to defeat a take-over bid. Although, on the facts of the case, the court did accept that this had been done in what the directors believed to have been the best interests of the company, the Court of Appeal nevertheless suggested that, provided the action was supported by the majority of the shareholders it was still binding on the minority even if undertaken on the basis of an improper motive, for example to cement the position of the directors on the board.

[41] *Cook v Deeks* [1916] AC 554.

[42] *Aveling Barford Ltd v Perion Ltd* [1989] BCLC 626; *Re Halt Garage (1964) Ltd* [1982] 2 All ER 1016 (an insolvency case where the remuneration taken by the husband and wife in a small family company without proper authorisation was successfully challenged by the liquidator).

[43] Including the actual people sitting behind any corporate members.

[44] See the *obiter dicta* of Lord Russell in *Regal Hastings v Gulliver* [1967] 2 AC 134 at p 150.

are being asked to forgive a particular breach. CA, s 239 now contains a statutory procedure for ratification. This adds to earlier common law procedural requirements. The key features of the new procedure are:

- **Application** – CA, s 239(1). The new procedure applies to ratification of conduct by a director amounting to 'negligence, default, breach of duty or breach of trust' in relation to the company.
- **Resolution** – CA, s 239(2). A formal resolution will now always be required for ratification to be binding, although this can be a written resolution.[45]
- **Directors and connected persons.** Crucially the common law position has changed so that directors can no longer vote on any resolution to ratify their own breaches,[46] or be treated as an eligible member to approve any written resolution in this regard.[47]

  The ban on interested voting extends to persons connected with the director. Under CA, s 252 this will include close family members broadly those forming part of the director's household together with parents and adult children.[48] Directors of a family company will not therefore be able to rely on their own immediate family members to secure ratification.

  Crucially, in a family business context, the definition of connected persons will not extend to wider family members, including siblings, much less cousins. The potential for ratification to operate on the basis of wider family and branch allegiances therefore remains.
- **Participation** – CA, s 239(4). Whilst an interested director is not allowed to vote in favour of ratification of their own breaches, the Act nevertheless makes it clear that they are entitled to attend and participate at any meeting called to consider ratification. The potential for influence, undue or otherwise, of dominant family members therefore remains.
- **Unanimous consent** – CA, s 239(6)(a). It remains possible for ratification to take place by the unanimous consent of all members outside the requirements of CA, s 239. Therefore first generation family companies where all family members are both directors and shareholders can still secure ratification of previous breaches of duty.
- **Formal release** – CA, s 239(6)(b). The act also confirms that formal decisions by the board of a company 'not to sue, or to settle or release' any claim that the company has against board members are outside the scope of the ratification procedure. Quite how any decision not to pursue a fellow board member will square up against the basic duties owed by the rest of the board, especially the duty to promote the success of the company under CA, s 172, without creating a further breach on their part will remain a highly relevant question.
- **Common law rules and acts incapable of ratification** – CA, s 239(7). Significantly all of the previous common law rules limiting the extent of what will constitute a valid ratification are retained, with the attendant uncertainties.[49]

---

[45] CA, s 239(3).
[46] CA, s 293(4).
[47] CA, s 293(3).
[48] CA, s 253.
[49] See Keay, op cit at pp 506–524.

8.4.5 The *Duomatic* principle – informal unanimous consent

Company law compliance has a strong procedural element. This does not necessarily sit well with the informal way many family owned businesses operate. What is the position when it is clear that all relevant shareholders are perfectly happy with a decision taken by a family company but it is equally clear that few or any of the procedural requirements that should have been followed to put that decision into effect have been followed?

For example a decision for the company to acquire the freehold premises from which the family business operates from the founder. As explained in more detail below this should be approved by the members in accordance with CA, s 190 as a substantial property transaction.

The answer is that, notwithstanding that a formal members' resolution may not have been passed, the transaction might nevertheless be saved under what is known as the '*Duomatic* principle'.[50] Simply stated the principle is that the unanimous informal consent of all members entitled to attend and vote at a general meeting of a company to authorise a matter is as effective as a formal resolution would be.

The principle can therefore often provide a 'get out of jail card' for a family owned business which need to defends a particular transaction in the absence of formal approval to the matter concerned. This can often be at a time when ratification is no longer possible. For example because the family company has gone into liquidation or a dispute has arisen between family members so that the requisite majority to ratify the breach in question could no longer be obtained.

But the *Duomatic* principle is not a panacea for all procedural shortcomings. It has various limitations:

- **Evidential**. The first is that in the absence of any formal resolutions or minutes the family might have difficulty showing that all shareholders did in fact consent to a transaction that occurred many years ago.
  Perhaps in the example of the freehold transfer all relevant shareholders were involved in the conveyancing process and signed contracts or other transfer documents. On other occasions all shareholders might also be directors and have approved the transaction at a board meeting[51] or perhaps signed board minutes approving the transaction (but not the resolution also required).
  This difficulty will be heightened if family members are now in dispute.

- **Unanimous consent**. For an informal procedure the *Duomatic* principle is strictly applied. So it must be shown that all of the shareholders have agreed to the relevant matter, not simply a sufficient majority to pass the relevant resolution. This is so even if the majority hold the vast majority of the shares and the remaining shareholders have a token shareholding and would almost inevitably have provided actual approval if they had been asked.[52]
  Fully informed consent must be shown. The members must be seen to understand what they are approving. So simply asking a remote shareholder to sign a transfer of a freehold to the company, without a detailed explanation will not be enough.

---

[50] Taken from the leading modern case on the point – *Re Duomatic Ltd* [1969] 2 Ch 365.
[51] *Re Conegrade Ltd* [2002] EWHC 2411 (Ch).
[52] *Re D'Jan of London Ltd* [1993] 1 BCC 646.

However acquiescence, as opposed to objection, might be treated by the courts in the same way as express consent. There will be a need to show that the shareholder concerned was fully aware of the matter under discussion. But relying on acquiescence has its limitations.[53]

- **Third party rights.** Some procedural requirements can be seen as introduced only for the benefit of the members of the company. Taking an informal approach to these under the *Duomatic* principle can therefore be regarded as a purely internal matter. However other procedural requirements can benefit or protect non-member third parties. In these cases the *Duomatic* principle cannot apply to over-ride the protection offered to these third parties by the relevant procedural requirement.

  It can often be difficult to analyse the underlying purpose of any given procedural requirement. So some procedural failings may be excused under the *Duomatic* principle whilst others fail. Sometimes these can be in related subject areas.

  For example, a requirement to approve a long-term director's service contract under CA, s 319 has been seen to be for the benefit of the members only.[54] However the procedural requirements to remove that director, giving special notice, allowing opportunities to put their case in writing or speak at the meeting, must be for the benefit of the director personally, so any failure to follow the prescribed procedure for removal cannot be saved under the principle.[55]

- **Share buy-backs.** Share buy-backs[56] are frequently used to provide shareholders in a family company with an exit route, following retirement, disputes or otherwise. However the buyback procedure is highly technical. Mistakes are frequently encountered and which are often unearthed many years after the original buy-back, perhaps in connection with a sale or financing transaction. This creates doubts over the true ownership of shares.

  To what extent can the *Duomatic* principle be relied on to patch up these procedural irregularities?

  Instinct may suggest that given the highly prescriptive nature of the buy-back procedure and that, particularly where the buy-back is out of capital, the interests of creditors are involved, so *Duomatic* is unlikely to help. This is the basic approach taken by the courts.[57]

  But examined more closely some of the individual procedural requirements relating to buy-backs can be seen to operate only for the protection of members, rather than creditors or wider stakeholders. So a failure to display a buy-back agreement at the company's registered office[58] for 15 days before the resolution to approve the buyback, defects in the drafting of a resolution approving a buy-back,[59] and failure to formally approve a buy-back agreement in accordance with CA, s 694 before entering into it in circumstances where it was clear that the members did in fact all approve the buy-back,[60] have all been saved under the *Duomatic* principle.

---

[53] *Schofield v Schofield and others* [2011] EWCA Civ 154 – where a family member abstained from voting on a decision to remove them from the board at a meeting which had been convened without the proper period of notice the Court of Appeal thought that the silence of the director concerned was by no means conclusive as to their consent to their own removal.
[54] *Atlas Wright (Europe) Limited v Wright and another* [1999] EWCA Civ 669.
[55] *Bonham-Carter and another v Situ Ventures Ltd* [2012] EWHC 230 (Ch).
[56] Under CA, Part 18 – discussed in more detail in chapter 11.
[57] See *RW Peak (King's Lynn) Ltd* [1998] BCC 596.
[58] *BDG Roof Bond Ltd v Douglas* [2000] BCC 770.
[59] *Kinlan v Crimmin* [2006] EWHC 779 (Ch). But a resolution is still required.
[60] *Dashfield and another v Davidson and others* [2008] EWHC 486 (Ch).

Whilst no substitute for full procedural compliance the *Duomatic* principle is therefore capable, in many circumstances, of coming to the aid of a family company provided that the family can show that they were in harmony in relation to the matter concerned.

8.5 CLAIMS AND CONSEQUENCES

The final part of this overview deals very briefly with the consequences of breaches of directors' duties and the claims that can be made against the directors concerned.[61] These fall into three broad categories:

- Criminal consequences.
- Civil claims.
- Directors' disqualification.

8.5.1 Criminal

Failure to comply with most of the many filing and other procedural requirements of the Companies Act is a criminal offence. For example, and taken almost at random, the requirement under CA, s 707 to send a return to the Registrar of Companies following a buy-back or purchase by a company of its own shares. Whilst in no way counselling or condoning non-compliance it is fair to say that criminal proceedings based on single acts of non-compliance with filing requirements are almost unheard of. In practice failure to comply with filing requirements, particularly serial failures and those relating to filing of accounts are more likely to come home to roost following a business failure in connection with director's disqualification proceedings.

So far as the more substantial directors' duties are concerned, whilst the consequences of breach are usually civil, it must not be forgotten that a family company is a separate legal personality from the controlling family members. As such it is perfectly possible to steal from one's 'own company'.[62] However any detailed examination of the criminal law in relation to family owned businesses is well beyond the scope of this book.

8.5.2 Civil

Because the duties of directors have largely been developed through the system of equity, often based on trust principles, many of the associated remedies for breach are also equitable remedies. As such they are much more concerned with restitution and ensuring those in a fiduciary position are not seen to have benefited from their breach of duty, than a strict analysis of the damage actually suffered by the family company, as victim, associated with common law remedies, for example, following a breach of contract. CA, s 178 expressly preserves the application of these historic remedies to the breach of the newly codified directors' duties.

The position is extremely complicated and we will not attempt to go into any real detail here. Andrew Keay devotes a chapter of his book to the subject,[63] albeit against a similar

---

[61] See Keay, op cit, chapter 15 for a more detailed review.
[62] See, for example the *Luqman* [2009] EWCA Civ 117 case discussed below.
[63] See chapter 15 of *Directors' Duties*, op cit.

disclaimer. For a full examination of remedies following directors' breaches reference will need to be made to specialist legal works.[64]

Civil claims might be made by the family company, perhaps following a change in leadership[65] and, or, some form of family dispute, by a disgruntled remote family member through a derivative claim, or by an insolvency practitioner following the failure of the family business.

Briefly the main remedies for the family company, or looked at from the other angle, consequences to the director in default are as follows:

- **Damages or equitable compensation.** In cases of negligence (breaches of the duty in CA, s 174 to exercise reasonable skill and care) damages are likely to be the only remedy available to the family company.[66] These are likely to be assessed on common law principles so issues such as remoteness of loss or causation will arise.[67]
  Breaches of other duties give rise to the possibility of equitable compensation. Basically this is more flexible than common law damages. Rules on causation are not applied so strictly. The courts have more flexibility to provide appropriate compensation to without unjustly enriching the family company.
- **Account of profits.** An alternative remedy where directors have taken advantage of business opportunities or have exploited property belonging to the family company is to ask for an account of profits made by the director concerned.
- **Restoration.** On occasions the errant director might still be in possession of property acquired in breach of duty.[68] It might then be beneficial for the family company to ask for the relevant property to be transferred to or held in express trust for it.
  This remedy is closely linked to the concept of constructive trusteeship,[69] the idea that as a fiduciary a director holds any company property, including information and opportunities as a trustee for the company.
  From a practical perspective if the company can establish a proprietary interest in a particular asset this will provide a form of quasi –security allowing the family company to jump the queue of creditors if the errant director has subsequently become bankrupt.[70]
- **Rescission.** A family company may also wish to rescind a contract, for example to sell property to a director made without full disclosure of development potential.[71] The usual bars to rescission would need to be taken into account including delay or affirmation on the part of the family company and the intervention of innocent third party rights.
- **Injunctions.** Injunctions may also be considered in cases of threatened breaches of duty, particularly if subsequent financial remedies will not provide adequate relief for the family company.

---

[64] For example, *McGregor on Damages* (Sweet and Maxwell, 19th edn, 2015).
[65] As in *Harrison Properties* [2002] 1 BCLC 162 (CA) discussed in more detail below.
[66] CA, s 178(2) excepts breaches of CA, s 174 from the general principle that breaches of directors' duties should be seen as a breach of fiduciary duty and therefore leading to equitable remedies.
[67] See for example *Cohen v Selby* [2002] BCC 82 considered in more detail below.
[68] For example the commercial property acquired by the directors in *Re Bhullar Brothers Ltd* [2003] EWCA Civ 424.
[69] See Keay, op cit, chapter 16, Part III.
[70] See Keay, op cit, chapter 16, paras 15.53–15.54.
[71] As in *Harrison Properties* [2002] 1 BCLC 162 (CA) – discussed in more detail below.

8.5.3 Relief from civil liability – CA, s 1157

CA, s 1157 provides a mechanism whereby directors who have or might be found to have been in breach of duty to apply to court for relief.

There are three basic requirements:

- **Honesty.** First, the court must be satisfied that the director has acted honestly. The case-law on whether this is an objective, subjective or some form of hybrid test is a little confused. But the consensus appears to be that if the director has fallen short of the 'ordinary standards of reasonable and honest people' he will not be able to satisfy this test simply because the conduct fitted into his own moral scale.[72] However honesty will be presumed unless the contrary is shown.

- **Reasonableness.** Secondly the director must show that they have acted reasonably. It may seem paradoxical, that particularly in cases of negligence, a director may have fallen short of the standards of a reasonable director, so as to be in breach of CA, s 174, but at the same time have acted sufficiently reasonably to be relieved from liability under s 1157.
But this approach has been applied in a number of family business cases.[73]

- **Court discretion.** Once the first two conditions have been satisfied the court must consider whether 'in all the circumstances of the case ... [the director] ought fairly to be excused'.[74]

Relief can be full or partial. Each case will be judged on its own facts. But factors such as personal benefit by the director from the breach or the onset of insolvency, particularly if caused by the breach, will make relief less likely.[75]

8.5.4 Director's disqualification

The final topic to look at in this overview is disqualification of directors under the Company Directors Disqualification Act 1986 (CDDA 1986). The conduct of all directors of companies that enter into formal insolvency procedures[76] will be reviewed by insolvency practitioners as a matter of course and the Secretary of State acting through the Disqualification Unit of the Insolvency Service may decide to bring disqualification proceedings under the CDDA 1986 in appropriate circumstances.

There are various grounds for disqualification under the CDDA 1986 but all involve some breach of duty on the part of directors in its broadest sense, including breaches of filing requirements. The key question will be is the director concerned unfit to act as so that the public need some protection in the future? In practice financial mismanagement, trading whilst insolvent to the detriment of creditors, especially crown debt and serious failures to file accounts are likely to be the most fruitful sources of applications. But as will be seen below, simple inactivity on the part of family directors will also count.[77]

---

[72] *Royal Brunei Airlines Snd Bhd v Tan* [1995] 2 AC 378.
[73] Including *D'Jan of London Ltd* [1993] BCC 646 and *Cohen v Selby* [2002] BCC 82.
[74] CA, s 1157(1).
[75] *Re Marini Ltd* [2003] EWHC 334 (Ch).
[76] Other than solvent members' voluntary liquidation.
[77] See *Park Properties* discussed below.

Routine commercial misjudgement is unlikely to lead to disqualification, even if creditors lose out, although gross negligence might do so. Usually some lack of commercial probity is needed.[78] But this need not be dishonesty.[79]

We will not deal with the topic in any detail but key points in relation to directors' disqualification are:

- **Independent proceedings.** Disqualification proceedings can be taken entirely independently of any civil action.
- **Disqualification undertakings.** To avoid the costs to both sides of formal court proceedings, directors often agree to give formal undertakings[80] not to act as a director in similar terms to orders that would likely to have been made by a court.
- **Period of disqualification.** The leading case on directors' disqualification, *Re Sevenoaks Stationers (Retail) Ltd*[81] sets out a tariff or series of bands for disqualification, depending on the seriousness of the case. These are:
    - a top bracket of over 10 years for particularly serious cases. These will in practice involve fraud or other serious dishonesty or repeat offenders who have been disqualified previously;
    - a middle bracket of 6-10 years for serious cases that do not merit the top bracket;
    - a lower bracket of 2-5 years for less serious cases. The minimum period of disqualification is 2 years. In practice this seems to be given in cases of failure to act on the part of family directors, with a disqualification towards the upper end of this range applied to the driving force behind a culpably failing business.[82]
- **Leave to act.** It is possible for a director who has been or who faces directors' disqualification to apply for leave to act as a director during their period of disqualification. Leave will only be given after serious consideration by the court and then only on terms that closely police the director's activities so as to best protect the public including future creditors.
- **Concerned in the management.** It should be noted that disqualification goes beyond simply acting as a director and covers taking part in the management of a company. This itself has been widely interpreted. But the idea of disqualification is not to render the director concerned economically inactive. Disqualification will not itself prevent someone setting up business as a sole trader or in an unincorporated partnership. It would also seem that token family directors are more likely to be granted relief than the driving force behind family business directly responsible for the loss suffered by the family company.[83]

8.6 THE 'FAMILY DIRECTOR'

8.6.1 Introduction

The position of a family director is a precarious one.

---

[78] *Re Lo-Line Electric Motors Ltd* [1988] Ch 477.
[79] *Park House Properties* – discussed below.
[80] Under CDDA 1986, s 7(2A) or s 8(2A).
[81] [1991] Ch 164, per Dillon LJ at p 179.
[82] See *Park House Properties* also *Westmid Packaging Services Ltd* [1998] 2 All ER 124 – a non-family business quasi-partnership.
[83] See *Cohen v Selby* [2002] BCC 82.

Many, if not most, family members who are directors of their family companies play a full role in the strategic direction of the business concerned, whether as working executive directors or as non-executives. They are well equipped to discharge their directors' duties and to protect the interests of their family company, their fellow family members as shareholders and other stakeholders.

But there are many directors of family companies who whilst having all the responsibilities of directors lack the influence, skills, knowledge or ability to properly discharge those duties. It is this category of 'family director' with which this section is primarily concerned. In many cases the sins of their fathers clearly have been visited on their offspring.

The main area of exposure for such family directors is under CA, s 174, the duty to exercise reasonable care, skill and diligence, or the director's duty of care. Usually this exposure will arise because of the inability of the family director to act as an effective counterbalance to check the actions of the family member or members primarily responsible for driving the family business into difficulties.

Historically comparatively little was required from directors in terms of commitment and aptitude. The courts were content to regard non-executive directors as amateurs and part timers and to set the performance bar at a correspondingly low height. The courts, in various cases, excused various 'lords on the board' for their lack of attention following the failure of larger companies to which they were supposed to add credibility.[84] This position also historically offered a degree of protection to family directors.

However towards the end of the nineteenth century and by the early part of the twentieth there was a noticeable tightening of standards by the courts.[85] This has continued up to the present day, with the courts expecting an increasing level of attention and performance from all directors, including family directors. Certainly any view that a family director's lack of attention to the affairs of their family company will be excused by the courts on the basis that they have a token or nominal role and have left matters to the family members running the family business on a day-to-day basis is hideously out of date. All directors are expected to play an active role in the supervision and direction of their company. That does not mean that non-executive directors need to be involved in the day-to-day management. Rather that they have a key role in monitoring and supervising those that do. Participation is key. As will be seen from the cases referred to below where a family director is concerned fitness is very closely linked to exercise. Lack of participation on the part of family directors is likely to be found in two broad circumstances.

First the early stage, owner managed family business. These businesses tend to be dominated by founder entrepreneurs. Their personality and characteristics are discussed in chapter 2. Whilst other family members, typically spouses and children, may have been appointed as *de jure* directors, the controlling personality of the founder is such that the other family members will struggle to assert any real influence. It is these family directors that have most often found themselves before the courts answering allegations of breach of their directors' duties.

---

[84] See for example *Turquand v Marshall* [1869] 4 Ch App 376 or for an excoriating fictional account of this phenomenon Trollope's *The Way We Live Now*.
[85] *Re City Fire Insurance Co* [1925] Ch 407.

The second category of family director who are of concern are those who occupy board positions in larger and more established family businesses but, when viewed objectively whose contribution, in business terms, would not justify that appointment. Instead the appointment must be seen as wholly or largely attributable to their position as a family member. Often the family director will be acting as a non-executive director, perhaps because of a family tradition that there has always been a director from a particular branch of the family on the board. There will be occasions where the family director is, at least notionally, a full time executive. In theory, and by reference to other cases involving, typically non-executive directors in failed larger non-family companies,[86] family directors in this second category are also vulnerable if they are incapable of exercising proper supervision of those directors actually driving their family business or fail to do so. However it is fair to say that it is harder to find examples of reported cases where family directors in this second category have fallen foul of the courts.

8.6.2 *De facto* directors – *Re Gemma* and *Mumtaz Properties*

Before examining the family director's duty of care in more detail we will look at the contrasting cases of *Re Gemma Ltd*,[87] and *Re Mumtaz Properties Ltd*[88] which illustrate the importance of the distinction between *de jure* and *de facto* directorship.

Re Gemma concerns an early stage construction business, which failed and went into liquidation. The business had previously traded as a husband and wife partnership, which was incorporated to carry out a more ambitious project, a new build of a £1m+ house. The company collapsed as a result of judgments for defective work on this contract. Both husband and wife faced a number of claims from the liquidator of the company, including that company funds had been used to pay off the couple's mortgage and preferences[89] had been made in favour of key creditors of the company with whom the husband needed to trade for the purposes of a new business. The judge had little difficulty in upholding most (but not all) of the claims against Mr Davies who had been validly appointed as a *de-jure* director and was clearly the driving force behind the business.

Mrs Davies had not been validly appointed as a director. Was she a *de facto* director? There was some evidence that she had been held out as such. Her name appeared on the company notepaper, she counter-signed cheques as a director and she was named as a director in key legal documents. But her role in the company was minimal. She kept the company books, which the court saw as a 'purely clerical task involving no decision making at all'.[90] Approving a statement from an earlier case that 'what is important is not what he called himself but what he did'[91] the court accepted that Mrs Davies in fact did very little. Certainly it could not be shown that she undertook functions that could only properly be discharged by a director[92] or that she exercised any real influence in the

---

[86] For example *Equitable Life Assurance Society v Bowley* [2003] EWHC 2263.
[87] *Gemma Ltd v Davies* [2008] EWHC 546 (Ch), [2008] BCC 812.
[88] [2011] EWCA Civ 610.
[89] Contrary to s 239 of the Insolvency Act 1986. Preferences are considered in a little more detail in 8.10 below.
[90] [2008] BCC 812 at p 823.
[91] Lewison J from *Re Mea Copr Ltd* [2007] BCC 288 at para 82 – quoted in [2008] BCC 812 at p 822 of the *Gemma* judgment.
[92] *Re Hydrodan (Corby) Ltd* [1994] BCC 161.

corporate governance of Gemma Ltd.[93] The evidence was that Mr Davies took all the decisions and that Mrs Davies 'simply went along with what her husband wanted to do'.[94]

Accordingly no order was made against Mrs Davies, who, by the time the matter had come to court was divorced from her husband. All other things being equal some of the matrimonial assets may well have been preserved for her benefit, free from the claims of the liquidator of the family company. Her position may therefore be contrasted with that of the validly appointed *de-jure* family directors in the cases referred to in **8.6** below.

Her position may also be contrasted with that of a third generation family member, Zafar Ahmed, in the case of *Mumtaz Properties*. The business was a property management and letting company, one of a series of businesses run by the wider family 'with a high degree of informality'.[95] So although Zafar had not been formally appointed as a director of that company it was significant that he was recorded at Companies House as a director of 20 or so other companies in which the wider family were interested so that it was 'a matter of chance whether a person was formally given a title or not'.[96]

The main business activity of Zafar appeared to be negotiating with suppliers and local authorities. It was argued on his behalf that this was work that a senior manager could do rather than a director and that accordingly one of the key tests of directorship[97] had not been met. But the High Court and the Court of Appeal identified various other factors pointing towards directorship, including that Zafar had responsibility for the company's accounts and records (which went well beyond the pure book-keeping like that of Mrs Davies in *Re Gemma*), that he held a company credit card and had effectively invested in the company. Crucially he was shown as chairman of the meetings placing the company into liquidation.

Accordingly Lady Justice Arden in the Court of Appeal (upholding the decision of the High Court) concluded that Zafar was 'one of the nerve centres from which the activities of the company radiated'.[98] The outcome was that Zafar, along with his father and uncles, was found to be jointly and severally liable for the aggregate amount of all overdrawn directors' loan accounts, rather than solely for the amount of his own personal loan account. The directors, both *de jure* and *de facto* were collectively in breach of duty for allowing the situation of overdrawn accounts to develop.

8.6.3 The dual test – CA, s 174(2)

A key part of the tightening of standards so far as the duty of care owed by directors is concerned was the introduction in CA, s 174(2) of the so called 'dual test'.

The starting point under that test is that directors will need show that they have displayed, at least, a basic level of competence if they are to be seen to have discharged their duty of care, skill and diligence. That section defines the duty of care as:

---

[93] *Re Kaytech International plc* [1999] BCC 390.
[94] At p 824 of the *Gemma* judgment.
[95] At para 17 of the judgment.
[96] At para 45 of the judgment.
[97] *Re Hydrodan (Corby) Ltd* [1994] BCC 161.
[98] At para 47 of the judgment.

... the care, skill and diligence that would be exercised by a reasonably diligent person with –

(a) the general knowledge, skill and experience that may reasonably be expected of a person carrying out the functions carried out by the director in relation to the company, and

(b) the general knowledge, skill and experience that the director has.

The test therefore has both an objective and a subjective element.

The objective test, contained in CA, s 174(2)(a), imposes a level of care commensurate with that of 'a reasonably diligent person' fulfilling the role of director. Previously there was a strong suggestion in the cases that the courts would only look at the subjective abilities and experience of the director concerned.[99] This would have suited unworldly or uncommitted family directors well. Now it is quite clear that an objective minimum standard of performance will be required to satisfy the duty of care.

It is sometimes suggested that CA, s 174 now imposes an identical duty of care on all directors, whether executive or non-executives. This does not appear to be correct. Whilst all directors are subject to the same statutory duties the extent of those duties will still vary from case to case. The test in the section clearly refers to a 'person carrying out the functions carried out by the director' concerned. It would therefore be reasonable to expect a higher standard of attention to detail and day to day matters from an executive director, and in particular a managing director, than from a non-executive.

But this might operate against family directors. It is often the case that in smaller family companies family directors have fairly grand titles bestowed on them, which little reflect the actual role and experience of the family member concerned. It is by no means uncommon to find a wife who 'looks after the books'[100] rejoicing in the title of finance director, a son as sales director or a daughter as HR director. Those with financial titles may be particularly vulnerable. It would be rare for a company failure not to be accompanied by some form of failure of financial oversight. The duty of care required, even from an unqualified and inexperienced part time family director will be that of a 'reasonably diligent' finance director.

In fact the trend appears to be towards expecting all directors, not just those with specific financial responsibilities, to have some degree of financial competence and to pay attention to the financial position of the company.[101] Whilst the preparation of accounts and financial statements is delegable, understanding, interpreting, questioning or challenging (if necessary) and acting on this financial information, appears to be a non-delegable duty for all directors.[102] This part of the director's duty of care; to pay close attention to the financial position of the company will come to the fore when the company is in financial difficulties.

---

[99] Re City Fire Insurance Co [1925] Ch 407, per Romer J at p 429. Although academic opinion differs on the exact extent of this proposition. Keay, for example, suggests that in later cases such as Dorchester Finance Co Ltd v Stebbing [1989] BCLC 498 the courts had begun to look for certain minimum standards from all directors, including non-executives.

[100] Like Mrs. Davies in Re Gemma discussed below.

[101] Re Westmid Packing Services Ltd [1998] BCC 836.

[102] See the discussion in Keay at pp 223–233 and the various (largely Australian) authorities referred to there. Especially the leading Australian case of ASIC v Healey [2011] FCA 717 where Middleton J said that 'a director, whilst not an auditor, should still have an enquiring mind'.

That is not to say that the directors of a small family company need to exhibit the same level of competence expected of highly paid directors of major corporate entities such as banks or other financial institutions. The test does apply to the function of the director concerned 'in relation to the company'. It may well be that the suggestion made by Romer J in *Re City Fire Insurance Co*[103] that the standard of care will differ between a small business and a large corporate still holds good under the new statutory test. But the basic standard of care expected from directors even of small family companies nevertheless remains high, as will be demonstrated by the cases discussed below.

The second part of the dual test adds an additional subjective element. In addition to showing a duty of care that would be objectively expected of anyone occupying the role of the director concerned the duty is 'topped up' so that performance is also judged against 'the general knowledge, skill and experience' that the director concerned actually has. The more experienced and qualified the director the more that will be expected of them.

This subjective element potentially carries a sting in the tail for non-executive directors of family businesses with wider experience and qualifications. For example qualified accountants or lawyers or those with main board experience on major or quoted corporates. Such individuals may have agreed to join the board of their family business, as non-executives, to provide support to the family members having the day-to-day conduct of the business. They will no doubt be capable of fulfilling a full non-executive role. Certainly the second part of the dual test will expect this of them. However circumstances may conspire against delivery against this standard. Perhaps pressure of work from the non-executive's primary career might prevent them paying proper attention to the family business. Possibly family dynamics may render a proper contribution impractical. Circumstances may mean that otherwise experienced and talented family non-executives may be operating in the narrower and pejoratively limited sense of a family director as referred to above.

Nevertheless they will be judged against a full and increased standard of care that comes with their skills and experience under the second limb of the dual test.[104]

8.6.4 *Luqman* – directors' duties and family ties

In many ways *Lexi Holdings plc v Luqman*[105] is an extreme and surprising case. But it offers a clear illustration of just how far family directors will be required to put family loyalties to one side to fulfil their directors' duties.

Lexi Holdings plc was what a client once termed a 'private plc', in other words an unlisted public company with the 'plc' format being chosen to add credibility, in the case of Lexi, for what was essentially a vehicle for fraud. The business of the company consisted of taking loans from a syndicate of banks, led by Barclays, for the purpose of providing short-term property bridging loans. The syndicate lent a total of £120m. But

---

[103] [1925] Ch 407 at p 426.
[104] See for example *Re AG (Manchester) Ltd* [2008] EWHC 64 (Ch) where a finance director with 'big company' experience as a financial controller was disqualified for failure to implement appropriate financial control systems not necessarily expected to be found in a smaller company such as the one he was then working for.
[105] [2009] EWCA Civ 117.

the managing director, Shaid Luqman, fraudulently misappropriated approximately £60m of this. The thefts took place over a 5 year period and through about 100 separate transactions.

The beneficial owner of Lexi was Shaid's sister Zaurian who was also a director from when the company started trading in 2001 until it was placed into administration in 2006. Other directors subsequently joined the board. In addition to a second sister, Monuza, who was appointed in 2003, three non-family members were involved. These were two non-executives, a former corporate banker and an individual with considerable 'city' experience, as a director and chairman of a major international property company, appointed in 2003 and 2004 respectively. An experienced property professional was also appointed in an executive capacity also in 2004.

In addition to the misappropriations, Shaid also committed various other breaches of duty. These were the provision of unauthorised loans and property transfers and, most significantly, false accounting in that Shaid caused the company's accounts to show fictitious loans introduced by him and Zaurian fluctuating between £4m and £22m.

There was no suggestion, either in the High Court or the Court of Appeal judgments that either Zaurian or Monuza were personally involved or had any actual personal knowledge of Shaid's activities. However what they did know about was Shaid had previous convictions for offences of dishonestly, including one resulting in a two-year prison sentence.

The evidence was that neither Zaurian nor Monuza took any active role in Lexi. Theirs were breaches of omission rather than commission. Accordingly the High Court judge concluded that:[106]

> 'by reason of their total inactivity while directors [they] breached the fiduciary and common law duties of care which they owed to Lexi.'

In more detail Mr Justice Briggs thought that the sisters had, in particular failed to:
- Pay any attention to the accounts of the company. These would have revealed the fictitious loans credited to Shaid and Zaurian herself. Zaurian in particular, with knowledge of the family's and Shaid's financial circumstances, would then have realised that there was no way that Shaid had access to this level of funding and personal wealth.
- More contentiously tell their fellow non-family directors about Shaid's track record of dishonesty which the judge thought was 'special knowledge which, despite their family ties, their duty to Lexi required them to communicate with their colleagues on the board'.[107] A director's duty can therefore be seen to outweigh family loyalty, misplaced or otherwise.

There would be little doubt that neither Zaurian nor Monuza would have been able to successfully defend any director's disqualification proceedings brought against them. But they faced proceedings brought by Lexi, through its administrators, seeking to hold the sisters liable for their brother's misappropriation. It was therefore necessary to show that these breaches of duty caused the loss suffered by the company.

---
[106] Quoted at para 3 of the Court of Appeal judgment.
[107] Quoted at para 21 of the Court of Appeal judgment.

The company's case failed in the High Court on this basis. There were a number of factors that could be argued to have broken the chain of causation so that, the sisters' breaches of duty could not be said to have directly led to the company's loss. These included that the banks continued to lend notwithstanding being alerted to the resignation of the company's previous auditors over VAT irregularities which were drawn to the bank's attention on the direction of the court in connection with other proceedings, and reports from a 'big 4' accountant pointing to breaches of facility letters. This is to say nothing of the involvement of the replacement auditors and the experienced professionals on the board of Lexi.

Most significantly Briggs J drew attention to the character and dominance of Shaid finding him to be a 'persuasive, sophisticated, charming and highly intelligent liar' who had been able to 'talk his way out of tight corner' with Barclays previously so that pulling the wool over his sisters' eyes would 'have been for him a relatively easy task'.[108]

The Court of Appeal accepted that this was so. However rather than being an excuse they thought that this was in fact a further breach of duty on the part of the sisters. Basically directors have a duty not to be fooled or dominated by the driving force of their company. The Chancellor Sir Andrew Morrit quoted with approval Lord Woolf MR in *Westmids Packaging* when he said:[109]

> 'The appellants may have been dazzled, manipulated and deceived by [the driving force] Mr Griffiths, but they were in breach of their duty in allowing this to happen.'

The inactivity of the sisters meant that Shaid was never put to the test. Because his sisters knew of his track record of dishonesty they should have been hyper sceptical of any explanations he gave and then involved their fellow board members or the auditors in the process. As a result the rest of the board were thereby denied the opportunity to supervise Shaid more closely. In the view of the Court of Appeal the chain of causation was established and the Zaurian and Monuza were liable to compensate their family company for £41m and £37m respectively.

8.6.5 Park House Properties

Luqman is a case based on remarkable and unusual facts. In particular mind blowing dishonesty. It would be our contention that family owned businesses are fundamentally honest.

A much more familiar scenario came before the court in *Re Park House Properties Ltd*.[110] which reached a similar conclusion to the courts in *Luqman* so far as the inactivity of family directors is concerned. *Park House* was a director's disqualification case. Like *Luqman* it illustrates the dangers for 'family directors' accepting the responsibilities of directorship that they are, in reality not equipped to exercise.

The basic facts of *Park House* are set out in **1.5.1**. Basically, although the rest of Mr Carter's immediate family were also appointed directors of the company, the judge found that Mr Carter was 'effectively solely responsible for all management and

---
[108] See para 24 of the Court of Appeal judgment.
[109] Quoted at para 21 of the Court of Appeal judgment.
[110] [1998] BCC 847.

financial decisions'.[111] Crucially one of the decisions taken by Mr Carter was that the company should spend £173,000 on building an extension to Park House, notwithstanding that the company occupied the property under a bare licence[112] from him. We suggest in chapter 10 (Property) that complex and informal property arrangements are a common feature of family businesses. Often this will not cause any problem or, at worst, any issues that arise will be confined to the business owning family.

In *Park House* this expenditure took place in the context of the company being seriously undercapitalised, which seems to have led to VAT input tax being used to finance the extension. This was coupled with the company struggling to refinance its borrowings. As a result the company went into liquidation. Mr Carter was severely criticised for his decision to spend company money on the extension which the judge thought demonstrated:[113]

> 'a serious degree of neglect or incompetence in relation to the company's affairs, attributable to the fact that he has failed to distinguish between his own interests (as lessor) and those of the company.'

That alone justified a disqualification period of 4 years for Mr Carter. The primary purpose of this section is to consider the position of the family directors. The judge acknowledged that the rest of the family had not been paid any director's fees and significantly that:[114]

> '... any advice given to Mr Carter would have unlikely to have been acted on.'

Nevertheless the three other family members were also disqualified, albeit for the minimum period of 2 years on the basis that:[115]

> 'A person who knowingly is a director of a company and takes no part whatsoever in the management of the company no steps whatsoever to keep himself of herself informed of the affairs of the company and leaves everything to another director ... is ... unfit [to act as a director] in the absence of special circumstances.'

A similar approach was taken by the courts in the non-family business case of *Re Westmid Packing Services Ltd*[116] where two working directors who left all management and decision making to the driving force were disqualified for the minimum period and given leave to act as directors in a new company.

In contrast a disqualification case was also brought following a major business failure of a fully listed company, Polly Peck, against four directors (including the managing director and finance director). Curiously that case was described by the court as, 'at best speculative and very weak'.[117] This was on the basis that the court accepted that these directors were powerless to prevent the financial mismanagement of Asil Nadir.

---

[111] See p 854.
[112] And therefore had no formal property rights.
[113] See p 864.
[114] At p 868.
[115] At p 869.
[116] [1988] BCC 836.
[117] *Re Polly Peck International plc (No 2)* [1994] 1 BCLC 574, per Lindsay J at p 604.

8.6.6 Cohen v Selby

A third 'family director' case, *Cohen v Selby*[118] underlines the fundamental point, made in *Luqman* and *Park House*, that the total abdication by a director, however reliant they may be on the driving force behind the company, will be seen by the courts as a serious breach of duty. The case also provides a further perspective on the key issue of causation.

The family director concerned was the son of the driving force of the business and was only 17 years old when he was appointed as sole director of his father's gem dealing business, Simmon Box (Diamonds) Ltd. This appears to be because his father could no longer act as a director because of his personal insolvency. Two years later the father attempted to take approximately £400,000 of gemstones to mainland Europe for sale. The gemstones had been bought at auction on credit. Unfortunately the gems, which were in a holdall and uninsured, were lost or stolen on the cross channel ferry. The company was forced into liquidation.

The liquidator took proceedings[119] against both father (as a *de facto* director) and against his son as the only *de jure* director. The High Court had little difficulty in deciding that the father had been 'reckless to a high degree'[120] and found him fully liable for the value of the lost diamonds. The son had remained a full time student and, in practice, had nothing to do with the company. He acted merely as a nominee family director for his father. The High Court was also scathing in its criticism of the son saying:[121]

> 'he had not troubled to discharge any of his duties as a director. He simply left everything to his father ... He simply did what was asked.'

The High Court acknowledged that the son's position was hopeless, in that any attempts to influence his father were likely to be useless. However they found this to be more a source of additional criticism than an excuse saying:[122]

> 'If he had woken up to the problem it would probably have not made any difference, so abject was his willingness to defer to his father's wishes and his willingness to surrender control to a non-officer of the company.'

The son had also breached his duty of care.

Both father and son attempted to throw themselves on the mercy of the court and made applications under (what is now) CA, s 1157.[123] Again the High Court had no sympathy for the father's position but considerably more for that of the son as a teenage family director. The judge acknowledged that he could:[124]

---

[118] [2002] BCC 82.
[119] The proceedings were under s 212 of the Insolvency Act 1986, which provides that the liquidator of a company may apply to the court for compensation orders if a director has 'been guilty of any misfeasance or breach of any fiduciary or other duty in relation to the company'.
[120] See [2000] BCC 275 at pp 285B–285C in the High Court case report and p 85 of the Court of Appeal report.
[121] Quoted at p 85 of the Court of Appeal report.
[122] Quoted at p 85 of the Court of Appeal report
[123] See 8.5.3 above and for a detailed discussion of CA, s 1157 see Keay, op cit, chapter 17 (Judicial Excusing of Breaches).
[124] Quoted at p 86 of the Court of Appeal report.

'well understand why somebody, at the age of 17 when he was appointed as a director, would feel a close bond with his father, had seen outwardly his father's business apparently proceeding very satisfactorily that he would not question as vigorously as a more mature person who was more detached why he was suddenly becoming a director of the company. I can also well understand why, in his situation, he might feel reluctant to question his father's business where his father had many decades of experience with apparently no difficulties at all and where he had no experience.'

The son was accordingly granted partial relief for the consequences of his breach of duty but nevertheless ordered to pay £50,000 compensation to the company.

The son appealed to the Court of Appeal. He succeeded. But this was on a technicality,[125] not on the basis that the High Court was wrong to find him in breach of duty or not excusing him completely for that breach. The Court of Appeal also expressed concerns about the reasoning of the High Court on the issue of causation.[126] That concern being that whilst accepting the son had not acted as a proper non-executive director it might not have made much difference if he had been appropriately involved. Non-executives may delegate day-to-day business to senior management (the father). So provided that appropriate supervision was in place, the liquidators might therefore struggle to show a clear link between the son's breach of duty and the company's loss.[127]

8.6.7 Conclusion

What is the moral of these stories?

Early stage founding entrepreneurs may have a strong desire to involve the rest of the family in the business they have created whether as employees, shareholders or directors. A key characteristic of early stage family businesses is that they are driven by the enthusiasm, commitment and single mindedness and appetite for risk of the founding entrepreneur. Given, in particular the last two characteristics, before inviting family directors onto their board the founding entrepreneur, or their advisors, ought really to consider how much influence these family directors will, in all reality, be able to exert. In short will the founder listen to his family, or even be prepared to tell them what is going on in the family business?

The family director cases discussed above show that the driving force behind the family business will be held most to blame in the case of a business failure and will accordingly face the most severe consequences, whether in terms of length of disqualification as a director,[128] or in terms of being held fully liable for losses the company arising from their own breach of duty.[129] Whilst the risk may mainly reside with those family members steering the ship, the cases also show that the remaining family members cannot, as officers, assume that they are safe to sit back and simply act as passengers.

---

[125] That the case that his total failure to perform his duties had not been fully pleaded.
[126] In cases of negligence the claimant needs to show a causal connection between the negligence or breach of duty and the loss that was suffered.
[127] Perhaps supervision would mean showing that the company had generally appropriate insurance and security arrangements in place as part of the risk management role of the board. In practice the son could have struggled to show this anyway.
[128] As in *Park House Properties*.
[129] As in *Cohen v Selby* [2002] BCC 82.

The pliant and toothless family director will also face censure from the courts, albeit not necessarily to the same degree as the driving force. In the absence of a real ability to influence the affairs of their family business, the burdens of directorship for any family director could, given the wrong combination of circumstances, easily outweigh the benefits of carrying a director's business card.

8.7 CONFLICTS OF INTEREST

8.7.1 Introduction

Conflicts between a director's own interests and those of the company whose interests they are meant to serve are by no means confined to the family owned business arena. Many of the leading cases concern executive directors of non-family businesses who, having spotted a business opportunity in that capacity decide to form a second company to exploit that opportunity.[130] Such cases clearly establish that business opportunities are as much company assets as are its real estate. This is now confirmed in CA, s 175(2).

Perhaps what distinguishes these cases from those involving directors of family businesses is that, in the case of the latter, the directors concerned seemed not so much motivated by greed and opportunism, but rather blinded by an inability to distinguish between their own personal interests and those of their family company. Two factors of family business life make this understandable. First the complexity inherent in the overlapping systems of ownership, business and family as encapsulated in the three-circle model.[131] Secondly, partly as a consequence of this and partly as a factor of the innate entrepreneurialism of business families, larger and more established family owned businesses tend to have all their eggs in one family basket. The core family business may be surrounded by a portfolio of investment properties and non-core businesses, often with slightly different ownership mixes, forming a loose conglomerate but one still revolving around the core business family.

In these circumstances it is hardly surprising that conflicts of interest arise.

Whether those conflicts lead to trouble for, or within, the business owning family may, to a large extent, be a matter of chance. So far as conflicts within a business family are concerned, many of these may simply be accepted by the remainder of the business owning family as 'the way things are'. In the absence of family business failure, bringing into play duties to third party creditors and the scrutiny of outside agencies, the wider world is unlikely to become aware of any conflict of interest issues relating to the family business.

In this sense conflicts of interest could be seen as more of a theoretical than a real issue for the family owned business. But add a third factor, the tendency of family owned business towards informality and the potential for trouble arises. As will be seen 8.7 below the strictness of earlier rules against conflicts of interest have been modified in the interests of commercial pragmatism, so that, in most cases directors are allowed to proceed into conflict of interest territory provided that the relevant conflict has been properly disclosed to and authorised by either the board or the members in general

---

[130] For example *Cook v Deeks* [1916] 1 AC 554 and *Industrial Development Consultants v Cooley* [1972] 1 WLR 443.
[131] Explained in chapter 3.

meeting. Failure to follow those procedures properly may mean that if circumstances conspire against the director concerned and trouble does arise they will have lost the benefit of these approval procedures.

More significantly, for the interests of family harmony, failure to follow the approval procedures, may, in and of itself, be the cause of a family dispute. What might have been an awkward family conversation, but still one resulting in a valid authorisation of the relevant conflict, is avoided. Perhaps this is as a result of a failure to recognise the conflict issue by the director concerned. Perhaps they genuinely believe that the rest of the family won't mind. Perhaps there is a sense of embarrassment or entitlement. But given a change of family circumstances this failure to seek authorisation itself becomes a significant factor in a serious family business dispute.

These authorisation and approval procedures are a key component of corporate governance and found in a mixture of the Companies Acts and the constitution of almost any incorporated family business. The underlying requirement of communication as a key component is a central theme of this book.

We will now illustrate these points with reference to a selection of family business cases involving breaches by the directors concerned of their duties to avoid conflicts between their own interests and those of their family companies.

8.7.2 Authorisation

The starting point in looking at conflicts of interest is that directors have an absolute duty to avoid them. The old case-law and the text-books talk about the relevant rules, the no conflict rule, and the no profit rule and the strictness with which these rules are applied.[132] In real life, and perhaps particularly in family business life, where commercial property will often be held outside the trading company and commercial arrangements will exist between various businesses in which family members have cross interests, conflicts of interest abound.

The law has evolved to provide for a system allowing directors to proceed into a situation of potential conflict of interest, provided that the conflict has been fully disclosed and authorised by the board or, in some cases, the members. Whilst the origins of the no conflict rule cannot be forgotten, in many senses it has morphed from an absolute prohibition into a procedural requirement. For many years articles of association have almost invariably allowed directors, or in some cases the members, to authorise conflicts of interest.

In the cases discussed below the directors concerned got into trouble as a result of failure to follow the relevant procedures properly from a mixture of lack of awareness (*Park House*) failure to concentrate on the substance of the duty to disclose (*Harrison Properties*), or relying on incorrect advice (*Bhullar*).

---

[132] See Keay, op cit, chapter 9, paras 9.5–9.26.

8.7.3 CA, s 175(3) – transactions or arrangements with the company

The proposition that the no conflict rule has now been turned into a requirement to disclose is amply illustrated by the wording of CA, s 175(3) which provides that the core duty for director's to avoid conflicts of interest:

> 'does not apply to a conflict of interest arising in relation to a transaction or arrangement with the company.'

This may seem counter-intuitive. The transactions most likely to cause conflicts, in the normal sense of the word, between a director and a family company, are those areas where the director's personal interests most directly touch the affairs of the company, such as remuneration and property dealings. These are excluded from the ambit of the s 175 duty altogether.

The transactions discussed below in *Park House* and *Harrison Properties*, which involved direct land dealings with the family company, are therefore not strictly in breach of the primary duty to avoid conflicts of interest. Instead dealings between a company and its director are covered by separate general duties of disclosure, contained in CA, s 177, supplemented by specific provisions for the members to approve particularly sensitive transactions also, briefly discussed below.

8.7.4 CA, s 175(4)(b) – authorisation

It is a key theme of this chapter that the core duty of directors to avoid conflicts of interest does not operate as an absolute duty. Rather the duty requires directors to pause at the lights, think about their position and, if necessary, seek the consent of their fellow directors, or, on occasions the wider membership, before proceeding. If the relevant notification has been made or, where necessary consent obtained, the starting analysis is that the director can then proceed into what would otherwise be conflict-ridden territory.

For those cases where the source of conflict is external to the company CA, s 175(4)(b) provides that the duty to avoid conflicts is not infringed if the matter has been authorised by the directors. For private companies the board can authorise the relevant conflict of interest[133] unless the constitution of the company specifically prohibits this. So in a more widely held family business the non-director family members might wish to include a provision in their articles[134] that all or certain categories of conflicts, need to be brought back to the wider family for approval.

In an attempt to prevent a potentially conflicted director, or group of directors, from railroading their conflicts through the board CA, s 175(6) provides that the votes of 'the director in question and any other interested director' must be excluded. This is fine in theory but there are many scenarios where this could create difficulties in the context of the family owned company.

First there is no bar on the director concerned in attending and speaking at the meeting concerned. So a dominant individual, for example a majority shareholder founder, may

---

[133] CA, s 175(5)(a).
[134] Or include relevant provisions as reserved matters in a shareholders' agreement.

nevertheless secure a paper approval of an inappropriate conflict notwithstanding that they are on the minority of the board and the relevant minutes clearly record their abstention from voting. This issue can be seen as an example of a common theme, how to secure the true independence of thought and influence of the board as a whole.

Secondly and more subtly is the difficulty of determining who is and who is not to be treated as another 'interested director'. The term is not defined in the Companies Act. Is it wider or narrower than the concept of connected persons under CA, ss 252 and 253?[135] Take the example of a request to authorise a younger family director setting up a business where he would trade or even compete with the main family company. Even if their father or brothers on the board had no financial interest in the proposed new business, could they really be seen to be disinterested?

Thirdly what would the position be if a larger family business had several directors, all of who were interested in a conflict matter? An attempt to hold several meetings where the conflicted directors were authorised one by one would surely be rejected as a pure sham. Keay suggests that in such a case the directors could not rely on s 175(4)(b) and would need to seek approval from the members.[136] This must make sense.

8.7.5 CA, ss 177 and 182 – the duty to declare an interest

The strict no-conflict rule applicable to trusts and, by extension to directors, in the early stages of company law has now largely been displaced by a duty of transparency on the part of directors to make a full declaration of the nature and extent of their interest in any transactions or arrangements in which they are interested to their fellow directors. The detail of this duty is set out in two largely mirror image provisions. CA, s 177 deals with the authorisation of proposed transactions and CA, s 182 with those already in existence.

With the exception of four categories of sensitive transaction mentioned above there is no requirement for any transaction that has been disclosed to be approved by the board as such, much less the members, or even to be expressly notified to the members. So providing a valid notification has been given a director is free to proceed with the relevant transaction or arrangement notwithstanding their conflict of interest.

The theory is presumably that, once the declaration of interest has been made, the corporate governance mechanisms of the company will take over. With a properly balanced and independent board an arrangement that carries with it a significant potential for conflict of interest will be identified and, as a result of board scrutiny, either the transaction will be re-negotiated or the company will not proceed with it. Similarly, so the theory goes, for those transactions that need member approval, or which are otherwise of concern to the members of a widely held company, majority rule will prevail and inappropriate transactions involving directors will simply be voted down.

---

[135] Broadly close family members including spouses, non-married partners with whom a director lives in an 'enduring family relationship', parents and children, but not siblings, aunts, uncles, cousins, etc.
[136] Keay, op cit at p 282.

But what of the typical situation in the larger family company of the 'haves'[137] and 'have-nots'.[138] Even if the approval regime is properly followed there is little in the express provisions of the Act to prevent self-serving approvals for the benefit of the haves. Does the situation need to become sufficiently pronounced so as to enable the minority have-nots to invoke the protection of the unfair prejudice regime under CA, s 994?

8.7.6 CA, s 179 – overlapping duties

Perhaps the real or at least theoretical) answer lies in CA, s 179, which confirms that the general duties in CA, Chapter 2 overlap. The worse the conflict the harder it will be for directors to show that the relevant transaction or arrangement was consistent with their overall duty to promote the success of their company under CA, s 172. Conversely the more procedural and technical the nature of any failure to follow the declaration and authorisation process the less likely that the issue will result in practical difficulty and the more likely that the court will grant relief in any event under CA, s 1157 in appropriate cases.

8.7.7 Sole director companies

Many early stage 'one circle' family businesses will have only a single director and a sole owner, usually the founder. How does the disclosure regime work in such cases?

CA, s 186 still requires a sole director to make an appropriate written declaration of any conflicts of interest, which then forms a key part of the records of the company. This general duty of disclosure is supplemented by a requirement under CA, s 231 that any contractual arrangements between the company and the sole director are recorded in writing. In addition to the usual civil consequences surrounding the unenforceability of the relevant contract and the director's duty to account for personal profits made under it, failure to comply with the written record procedure will be a criminal offence.[139]

The new statutory regime may be more logical than that prevailing under the previous (1985) Companies Act, where case-law suggested that before entering into a contract in which they were interested, a sole director needed to hold a formal board meeting, to take time to evaluate the benefits of that contract and to minute that they had done so.[140] Whilst the provisions of the 2006 Companies Act may have removed the requirement for this fairy tale meeting, the question still remains, how often will those responsible for sole director companies or other early stage family businesses, both go through the thought processes necessary to identify and evaluate conflicts of interest and document that they have done so?

---

[137] Those in control of the family business and usually with jobs.
[138] The more remote family members, who typically do not work in the family business and are not directly represented on the board.
[139] CA, s 231(3).
[140] *Neptune Vehicle Washing Equipment) Ltd v Fitzgerald* [1995] 1 BCLC 352.

8.7.8 Conflicts and the early stage family business

Park House Properties[141] is discussed in detail in **8.6** above where we noted the criticism by the trial judge of Mr Carter's inability to distinguish between his own interests, as superior leaseholder of the Park House commercial property and those of the family company, as his sub-tenant or licensee. Similar factors seemed to be present in *Re Gemma*[142] where Mr Davies caused a substantial part of the first payment under the building contract to be applied in paying off the mortgage on his own property.

It is comparatively easy to understand the potential for those concerned in an early stage family business, and especially the driving force founder, to regard all assets and interests relating to the wider family business as being common to the family pot, irrespective of formal ownership structures.

It might be unrealistic to expect to eliminate such problems. But some mixture of awareness raising for early stage family business directors and challenge, especially from their professional advisors may help to reduce the instances of difficulty. It is not clear what steps, if any, the solicitor concerned in *Re Gemma*, took to question Mr Davies' instructions to apply company sale proceeds in this way. The case report does suggest that Mr Davies' accountant was instrumental in incorporating the business and regularly went to the couple's home to prepare accounts etc. What advice did he give about keeping family company and private family finances separate?

8.7.9 *Harrison Properties*[143] – disclosure of nature and extent of interest

The case of *Harrison Properties* concerns a company more towards the opposite end of the family business food chain than either *Park House* or *Re Gemma*, although also involved in property development. The company was established by a successful builder and property developer and then run by his son, Peter Harrison effectively as executive managing director. Three of Peter's sisters also sat on the board. They took part in board meetings and were consulted over key decisions. The sisters therefore appeared to be acting more as genuine non-executive directors than family directors (in the sense we have used that term in **8.6** above).

The company owned a considerable amount of agricultural and development land in the Yorkshire area. It was a subsidiary of a family holding company, the shares in which were held by various trusts for the benefit of the families of the founder's six children. These included two brothers who were not directly involved in the business.

The case revolved around the sale of a farm and land by the company to Peter Harrison for £8,400. Although supported by a professional valuation this did not take account of any development potential. In fact, by the time the sale went through planning applications had been submitted, at the company's expense, for a barn conversion and also to build a replica Elizabethan manor house on the land. Based on the advice of his (or more precisely the architect engaged by the company) Peter Harrison had every expectation that planning permission would be granted.

---

[141] [1998] BCC 847.
[142] *Gemma Ltd v Davies* [2008] EWHC 546 (Ch) – discussed in detail above.
[143] *JJ Harrison (Properties) Ltd v Harrison* [2001] EWCA Civ 1467.

Peter at least paid lip service to the authorisation procedure in the company's constitution. He arranged for a board meeting to be convened to authorise the sale of the land to himself. Only one his sisters (Theresa Harrison) had turned up to the meeting. The minutes of the meeting, which took place in 1986, record that:[144]

> '... Mr Harrison having an interest, did not vote and in order to obtain a quorum on this matter, [another sister], Mrs MC Farmer was contacted by telephone.'

Planning permission was duly obtained and Mr Harrison then proceeded to partially develop both sites before abandoning his plans and reselling the barn conversion for £110,300 and the manor house site for £112,500 in 1988 and 1992 respectively. The case came to court approximately 14 years later. By which time it was impossible to say with certainty exactly what each director was told or knew about the position at the time of the relevant board meting. There was some suggestion that Peter Harrison had deliberately tried to mislead his sisters, telling them that he wanted the land to plant trees, rather than to develop the land. The High Court judge did not accept this.

However the judge was not at all satisfied that Mr Harrison had told his sisters and co-directors about the development potential of the land, or about his plans to exploit this. But the judge did not think that this failure was due to bad faith on Mr Harrison's part. The judge believed that:[145]

> '... as often happens in these kinds of cases, Peter Harrison did not always distinguish sufficiently clearly between his own interests and the interests of the company.'

So far as the incompleteness of Mr Harrison's disclosure was concerned the judge found that:[146]

> 'Peter Harrison did not make a conscious decision to conceal his plans, or the developments in relation to planning ... from his fellow directors ... it did not occur to him that these were things which his fellow directors needed to be informed about.'

Nevertheless disclosure of the true extent of Mr Harrison's interest had not been made. Accordingly he was in breach of his duty to disclose his conflict of interest and the purported authorisation of that disclosure was invalid.

8.7.10 *Harrison Properties*: legal issues

Mr Harrison did not contest the trial judge's finding of inadequate disclosure. Instead a number of points were made on appeal and by cross appeal.

It is often said that the fiduciary position of directors is similar to that of trustees. First the Court of Appeal confirmed that, as a director, Mr Harrison must be regarded as a constructive trustee on behalf of the company as beneficiary, of the development opportunity, as a species of company property. Accordingly he was liable to account to the company for the full value of the proceeds he had received on the sale of the two

---

[144] See para 28 of the High Court judgment.
[145] At para 30 of the High Court judgment.
[146] At para 31 of the High Court judgment.

parcels of land (less allowances for the original cost price and any expenditure necessary to enhance or preserve the value of that land).[147]

There was an interval of approximately 12 years between Mr Harrison's breach of duty and proceedings being issued. The usual period of limitation is 6 years. However the Court of Appeal confirmed that because the company was in the position of a beneficiary and the action related to 'the proceeds of trust property ... previously received by a trustee and converted to his own use', no limitation period applied.[148]

The court also looked at a related point: the doctrine laches or and delay. It was argued on behalf of Mr Harrison that the company had access to the necessary facts about Mr Harrison's breach of duty at a much earlier stage and that it was most unreasonable that the company had taken so long to bring its action. Accordingly even if the company's claim was not statute barred under the Limitation Acts laches[149] should apply. Although this appears to have been a close call the High Court thought that a combination of the seriousness of Mr Harrison's breach and the fact that the company did not actually know about these (as opposed to having the ability to piece the picture together) until a year or so before issuing proceedings these factors should 'tip the balance' in favour of the company.[150]

Mr Harrison also pointed to references in a letter written by a solicitor to him on behalf of his sister, Theresa (Teri) Harrison (who had by then taken over as chair of the company) and suggested that the effect of this was the company had waived its rights in relation to any previous breach of duty. The passage he referred to said that he had:[151]

'... left the company in what might best be described as ignominious circumstances, Teri was most concerned that your reputation should not be tarnished and there should be no muck-raking about your stewardship of the company.'

The High Court also rejected this argument, as did the Court of Appeal.

8.7.11 *Harrison Properties* and governance opportunities

Of even more interest, from a family dynamics perspective, would be to understand what had changed in terms of the relationships between the family members between 1986 and when the letter before action was sent to Peter Harrison in 1997. As is often so the case report provides glimpses into the family issues but by no means a complete picture.

We learn that in 1992 the two brothers who were not on the board of Harrison Properties presented some sort of petition[152] alleging minority oppression in the holding

---

[147] See paras 25–30 of the Court of Appeal judgment and the cases reviewed there. The High Court judge had found that Mr Harrison was liable not as a constructive trustee but rather to make an account of profits or to pay equitable compensation. The distinctions between these remedies are beyond the scope of this book.
[148] Limitation Act 1980, s 21(1)(b). See paras 31–41 of the Court of Appeal judgment and the cases reviewed there.
[149] A defence in equity (and therefore at the discretion of the court) based on unreasonable delay by the claimant in asserting their rights.
[150] See paras 61–64 of the High Court judgment.
[151] See para 21 of the Court of Appeal judgment.
[152] See para 37 of the High Court judgment. Presumably the petition sought either relief from unfair prejudice or a just and equitable winding up, or both.

company. Later that year the family holding company was placed into voluntary (solvent liquidation) and, although the subsidiaries, including Harrison Properties continued to trade, Peter Harrison left the board. As can be seen from the above letter this was in less than auspicious circumstances.

There would therefore appear to have been an uprising of the 'have nots'; those without jobs in, or direct involvement in the management of the family business. It seems as though Mr Harrison's resignation was a condition of the family settling the wider litigation. Even so the court did not see the relationships between, in particular Peter Harrison and his sisters as being particularly strained, as late as 1997.

Mr Harrison believed the proceedings against him were motivated by his own opposition to the sale of other family land, which was near to his own home and needed as a motorway service site as part of the A1M motorway extension. The explanation preferred by the court was that proceedings followed soon after the new board became aware of the full factual background. No doubt there had also been a sea change in attitudes to corporate governance. By the time claims were made against Peter Harrison the family was controlled by liquidators, partners in a 'big four' firm of accountants. In the shadow of the family litigation, the new board of the company, with a non-family managing director and Teri Harrison as non-executive chairman, were presumably keen to do things by the book. Legal advice was sought into Peter Harrison's conduct and proceedings were issued.

Harrison Properties is a relatively rare case of someone in control of a family company being turned out by the rest of the family. Before moving on to the next case it might be interesting to pause and to speculate what might have happened if, back in 1986, Peter Harrison (or perhaps his advisors) had paid more heed to the spirit of his duty of disclosure as a director, rather than treating this as a minimal procedural formality.

The development land was in his home village. There was a clear element of risk and speculation about both projects, as born out by the need to sell-on both sites in a semi-developed state. Peter Harrison's relationships with his sisters, especially Teri, appeared strong at the time. There may have been every reason to suspect that a full disclosure of the development potential of the site would have resulted in an unimpeachable board approval. At worst for Mr Harrison a refusal, based on full communication, might have re-enforced the need for Mr Harrison to carefully distinguish between his own personal interests and those of the family company he was leading. Whether that lesson would have prevented the more global litigation and the wider enterprise being taken out of the hands of the family is impossible to say.

8.7.12 *Bhullar Brothers*[153] – whose opportunity is it anyway?

CA, s 175(2) makes it clear that a director will still be in breach of their duty to avoid conflicts of interest by exploiting an opportunity, even if the company was not able to take advantage of that opportunity. The section expressly provides that 'it is immaterial whether the company could take advantage of the property, information or opportunity'.

---

[153] *Re Bhullar Brothers Ltd* [2003] EWCA Civ 424.

Although only codified in the 2006 Act this concept has a long lineage and can be traced back to the eighteenth century where the then Lord Chancellor said that a trustee of a leasehold interest should have walked away from the opportunity to renew that lease, rather than taking it in his own name.[154]

That principle has been consistently upheld by the courts and was applied, almost three centuries later in *Bhullar Brothers*. There the impediment to exploiting a commercial opportunity was not a legal one as in *Keech v Sandford* (where the beneficiary was a minor who could not renew the lease in his own name) but the fact that relationships had broken down and split along branch lines in a second-generation family business. Based around grocery stores, the business had been trading for around 50 years and had obviously been successful as it also held a number of investment properties. These included a bowling alley, let to operators.

Relationships between the two family branches had broken down (although the case report does not say why) so that 'a state of considerable acrimony prevailed'.[155] The two families had been negotiating for 3 years to split the family business and its assets, but without achieving a resolution. In the meantime, at the request of the 'M' family (who were in a minority on the board) the 'S' family had agreed to a moratorium on the acquisition of new properties by the company.

A year or so after the moratorium was agreed one of the S family sons, Inderjit, who had taken time off from the business to entertain an uncle visiting from the USA, went bowling and noticed a 'sold' sign in the adjoining car park. Realising the value of the site to what we will term the 'wider family interest' Inderjit acted quickly. He persuaded the owner of the site, via their agents, to accept a higher offer from the S family pension scheme, pausing in the process to check with the company's solicitor whether this was in order in terms of conflict of interest. He was told that there was no issue.

The M family, who brought an unfair prejudice petition, disagreed with that advice, as did both the High Court and the Court of Appeal.

8.7.13 *Bhullar* - legal points – what is an interest?

Ultimately the courts confirmed the strictness and also the flexibility, in terms of lack of limits or rules as to the circumstances in which it will apply, of the fundamental underlying 'no conflict' and 'no profit' rules. Accordingly a director will be in breach of duty if the situation concerned presents 'a real sensible possibility of conflict'.[156]

It did not matter that the family company had no legal or beneficial interest in the opportunity to buy the site. That would be 'too formalistic and restrictive an approach ... flexibility of application is the essence of the rule'.[157] A reasonable man would clearly see the site as of potential interest to the family company. Neither did it matter that the M family had previously said they did not want the family company to buy any more

---

[154] *Keech v Sandford* (1776) Sel Cas t King 61.
[155] See para 10 of the judgment.
[156] Jonathan-Parker LJ at p 720 quoting and approving Lord Cranworth LC in *Aberdeen Railway Co v Blaikie Bros* (1854) 1 Macq 461. Companies Act 2006, s 175(4)(a) effectively provides for a defence in the mirror image of this test so that the duty to avoid conflicts will not be infringed 'if the situation cannot reasonably be regarded as likely to give rise to a conflict of interest'.
[157] Jonathan-Parker LJ at p 720.

property. By failing to seek their consent the S family had denied them, (to the prejudice of their interests in the company) the right to change their mind in the light of the new circumstances. The following points emerge from the decision in *Bhullar*:

- **A director is always on duty.** It certainly did not matter that Inderjit spotted the site on a day off. A director is always on duty so far as his director's duties were concerned. He could not argue that this was a private purchase. The S family 'had, at the material time, one capacity and one capacity only in which they were carrying on business, namely as directors of the company'.[158]

- **Legal advice.** Neither did it matter that Inderjit had sought and obtained positive legal advice that there were no conflict of interest issues. Although many of the cases talk about 'conscience' this is meant in a narrow legal (or more strictly equitable sense). Duties can be breached without any conscious sense of wrongdoing on the part of the director concerned. If the conscience of a reasonable man would have been troubled so should that of the director. Indeed the Court of Appeal saw the fact that Inderjit saw the need to ask for legal advice on the point as 'eloquent of the existence of a possible conflict of duty and interest'.[159]

8.7.14 *Bhullar* - investments and governance

Bhullar Brothers was, at least until the families fell out, an example of a fairly typical more mature family business phenomenon, the unstructured family conglomerate, where surplus funds and profits generated by the success of the core business, are reinvested in a diverse range of property and other business investments.

John Ward talks of the benefits of the benefits of shared investments including, trust building, demonstrating commitment and maintaining an equality of wealth between family members.[160] However he also talks about the benefits of the younger generation building 'by the time they reach young middle age ... their own substantial financial nest egg'.[161]

In his evidence in the High Court in *Bhullar Brothers*, Inderjit pointed to the fact that his cousin, a member of the M family 'had his houses', presumably as part of a personally owned private property portfolio. Inderjit implied that this justified his attempt to secure the benefit of the car park site on behalf of the S family.

Again we do not know what caused the family to fall out in the *Bhullar* case. At least one possible explanation could be a lack of coherence in the investment philosophy of the wider family.

8.7.15 Specific approvals

Given the complex arrangements often found between a family company, its directors and family members it is sensible to provide a brief overview of the categories of sensitive transactions involving directors that need the specific approval of shareholders

---

[158] At p 723. This does not mean that directors cannot have private interests or that they cannot be directors of other, even competing companies. However all relevant interests and appointments need to be fully disclosed and where relevant authorised.
[159] At p 723.
[160] See Ward *Perpetuating the Family Business* (Palgrave, 2004) Lesson 23 (Shared Investments) at p 91.
[161] See Ward, op cit, Lesson 22 (Financial Nest Eggs).

Directors' Duties 299

under CA, Chapter 4. The approval mechanism is simple in that, unless the company's constitution provides otherwise, only a simple majority is needed for approval to be given. There are no provisions preventing the directors concerned from exercising their own votes or for disregarding the votes of their immediate family members or other connected persons.

These categories of sensitive transaction are:

- **Long term service agreements – CA, ss 188-189.** As a starting point directors are in a position to determine their own employment terms. To prevent self-dealing long-term entrenchment company law has, for some while, restricted the length of service agreements that directors can agree to without resorting to the members. The maximum notice period or guaranteed fixed term is now 2 years.[162] Any longer period will be void.[163]
- **Payments for loss of office – CA, ss 215-222.** Related provisions require payments of compensation for a director's loss of office also to be approved by the members. These are broadly defined under CA, s 215 and require member's approval under CA, s 217. The key distinction is between payments for loss of office as director, which require approval, and a genuine payment for compensation for loss of employment under a properly approved employment contract. Employment compensation is exempted under CA, s 220(1)(c). 'Golden parachutes', payments of compensation for directors losing their positions on takeovers[164] also require members' approval. CA, s 222(1)(a) provides that unapproved payments will be held by the director concerned on trust for the company. Also any directors involved in authorising the unlawful payment will be jointly and severally liable to the company for the amount paid.[165]
- **Substantial property transactions – CA, ss 190-196.** Substantial asset dealings between a company and a director also require members' approval under CA, s 190. Although the title to that section refers to "property" its application is certainly not confined to real estate and applies to dealings, whether acquisitions or disposals, of any 'substantial non-cash asset'. Intellectual property, for example, would clearly be covered. Substantial effectively means[166] the lower of £100,000 and 10% of the company's net assets.[167] It is possible to obtain subsequent affirmation of a substantial property transaction by the members under CA, s 196 provided that this is sought within 'a reasonable period' of the transaction itself. Consequences of breach of the substantial property transaction provisions are that the relevant transaction is voidable.[168] Also any directors concerned, including family members and other connected persons who may have benefited from the property transfer and any fellow director who authorised the transaction without members' approval, are liable to account to the company for any gains made.
- **Loans to directors – CA, ss 197-214.** Prior to the Companies Act 2006 loans by a company to its directors were, subject to minor exceptions, illegal. However that law was more often honoured in the breach than the observance by very many

---

[162] CA, s 188(1). Previously the maximum period was 5 years. This was reduced to reflect both market trends and current corporate governance thinking.
[163] CA, s 189. That is unenforceable against the company.
[164] Whether by asset sale (CA, s 218) or share sale (CA, s 219).
[165] CA, s 222(1)(b) and s 222(1)(a).
[166] CA, s 191.
[167] As ascertained from the last statutory accounts, but subject to an effective *de-minimis* of £5,000.
[168] CA, s 195(2). That is the company can apply to have the transaction set aside unless restitution of the property cannot be made, third parties have become involved after the original transaction without actual knowledge of the breach or unless the company has received a proper indemnity.

owner managed businesses. Parliament pretty much accepted this reality, and changed the position from one of absolute prohibition to one where loans to directors require member's approval under CA, s 197. There are exceptions for small loans, of less than £10,000,[169] for company expenditure[170] and for directors facing proceedings.[171] The consequences of unlawful loans are similar to unauthorised substantial property transactions. They can be set aside as voidable at the instance of the company,[172] the director concerned and any family members who have benefitted, together with any other directors who have authorised the payment, have a liability to the company to repay the loan.[173] There is also a similar ability for otherwise unlawful loans to be ratified by the members within a 'reasonable period' under CA, s 214. The 2006 Companies Act also removed the criminal sanctions, previously applicable for unlawful loans to directors.

8.8 REMUNERATION

8.8.1 Overview

Perhaps the most frequent source of real conflict in more mature family businesses is the level of remuneration taken by the working directors, often accompanied by a history of paying low or no dividends. *Saul D Harrison* is a case in point.[174]

As a matter of legal theory directors, as office holders have no entitlement to be paid for acting.[175] The theoretical starting point is that directors as fiduciaries should not profit personally from their position (the 'no-profit rule'). Directors are required to exercise 'self denying loyalty'.[176] In practice this self-denial on the part of directors rarely needs to extend to their own remuneration. As a matter of course a company's articles almost invariably allow directors to take directors fees and to determine the level of these as a board.[177]

As explained above employment terms will not be subject to the duty in CA, s 175 for directors to avoid conflicts of interest. Instead the terms of a director's employment will be excluded from the ambit of that section by CA, s 175(3) as a 'transaction or arrangement' between the director concerned and their family company. Executive directors are usually also employees of their family company. Similarly the board can agree employment terms amongst themselves. This is subject only to disclosure of the proposed arrangements under CA, s 177, the obligation to keep details of director's service agreements and to make these available for inspection[178] and for long term arrangements, exceeding 2 years to be approved by members.[179]

---

[169] CA, s 207(1).
[170] CA, s 204.
[171] CA, s 206.
[172] CA, s 223(2).
[173] CA, s 223(3) and (4).
[174] See for example *Saul D Harrison and Sons* [1994] BCC 475 discussed in detail in chapters 20 and 21.
[175] *Guinness v Saunders* [1990] 2 AC 663.
[176] Andrew Stafford and Stuart Ritchie *Fiduciary Duties: Directors and Employees* (Jordan Publishing, 2nd edn, 2015) at p 16.
[177] See, for example Art 19(2)(a) of the Model Articles for Private Companies SI 2008/3229.
[178] CA, ss 227–230.
[179] CA, ss 188–189.

This general rule that the directors can pay themselves what they wish may be subject to challenge by the members, but realistically, as we will show this will be only in the more extreme cases. Far better for family companies to remove this potential source of actual conflict through a mixture of open communication on the expectations of both the directors and the wider family and to have the result fully documented in appropriate remuneration policies. This topic is discussed in more detail in chapter 5.

8.8.2 Procedural irregularity

The first potential area of challenge for the aggrieved minority is to examine whether the proper procedures under the company's constitution have been followed to approve the relevant remuneration. In practice this does not create a high hurdle for the directors to jump. Under Art 23 of the Model Articles[180] 'directors are entitled to such remuneration as the directors determine'. The board can simply determine their own remuneration.[181]

Even failure to comply with these simple 'self-approval' mechanisms will not necessarily be fatal to the majority. However they will be on the defensive. The court will then have jurisdiction to decide whether the amounts taken as salary are reasonable.[182]

Directors could be ordered to repay amounts taken in breach of procedural requirements as director's fees, as opposed to salary. As an office holder directors have no automatic right to be paid and accordingly are not entitled to be paid on a *quantum meruit* (reasonable sum) basis for work actually done as a director (rather than an as an employee).[183]

On occasions the constitution of the family company may stipulate that the remuneration of directors has to be approved by the members. In such cases the courts might be doubly reluctant to interfere. As a matter of company law theory not only would the court be reviewing a management decision, they would be interfering with majority rule. But in practice in most family companies the majority of the shares are likely to be held by the directors and their sympathisers, even if they are not treated as connected family members under CA, ss 252 and 253.

8.8.3 Collateral purpose

In rare cases it may be possible to show that the remuneration is based on irrelevant or aberrant considerations and therefore cannot possibly have been arrived at by a proper exercise of directors' powers.

For example in *Fisher v Cadman*[184] provisions for directors' remuneration had been included in the accounts of over £50,000. This was in a year when the Cadman brothers had done very little with the property portfolio, compared with remuneration of only £6,000 taken in a year when the brothers had been much more active in selling off a couple of properties. Whilst making a primary finding that Mrs Fisher had an

---

[180] SI 2008/3229.
[181] This is subject to duties to formally declare their interest in their own remuneration under CA, s 177, the need to obtain members approval of long-term service agreements under CA, s 188 and to payments of compensation for loss of office under CA, s 217.
[182] See *Irvine (No 1)* [2006] EWHC 406 (Ch) at paras 309–325.
[183] *Guinness plc v Saunders* [1990] AC 663.
[184] See 1.5.3 for the basic facts.

expectation that her brothers would look after the portfolio without any remuneration the trial judge found little difficulty making a secondary finding that the proposed payments were objectionable.[185]

Similarly in *Re Tobian Properties Ltd & Maidment v Attwood*[186] where the majority shareholder had fixed a level of remuneration to meet his personal needs, without reference to the interests of the company, the Court of Appeal had little difficulty in confirming that this was a breach of duty. The Court of Appeal took the same approach in *Lloyd v Casey*[187] where pension contributions were increased significantly to help fund the acquisition of the company's trading premises by the controlling shareholder's personal pension scheme.

8.8.4 Disguised returns on capital

In some instances it might be clear that, although labelled remuneration, payments received by a director or someone else connected with the majority, are in fact and on a proper analysis something else. This may be labelled as a gift, a disguised dividend payment or return of capital. In *Halt Garage Ltd*,[188] a claim brought by a liquidator against the husband and wife directors of small family business succeeded against the wife, who had become ill and was unable to work but for 4 years until the company was wound up had taken a reduced salary. As she had not worked she could not be entitled to remuneration so the payments to her were seen as improper. However payment of small salaries and benefits to the wives of the 'haves' did not appear to trouble either the High Court of the Court of Appeal in *Saul D Harrison*.

8.8.5 Remuneration and the duty to promote the success of the company?

In many cases it will not be possible to show that amounts paid as remuneration are invalid as, in essence, mislabelled breaches of the no-profit rule. But the minority may nevertheless remain concerned that the directors are simply paid too much. To position an overpayment of salary as a breach of duty the minority would need to show that the level of pay is so extreme that it in agreeing to it the directors have breached their fiduciary duties, especially their duty to promote the success of the company under CA, s 172. Although excessive remuneration has been considered in a number of unfair prejudice cases we are not aware of any authority to show that this argument has been successfully pursued as a stand-alone breach of duty.

8.8.6 Remuneration and derivative claims

If the directors can be shown to be in breach of the duties they owe the family company by awarding themselves excessive remuneration the question becomes how do the aggrieved minority do something about it?

In theory they could make a derivative claim. The procedure and the difficulties with this are explained in chapter 24.

---

[185] See para 47 of the judgment.
[186] [2013] BCC 98, CA.
[187] [2002] 1 BCLC 454
[188] [1982] 3 All ER 1016.

8.8.7 Remuneration and unfair prejudice

The more likely scenario, if the issue of excess remuneration is to be pursued at all is that this will be the subject of unfair prejudice proceedings.[189]

- **Market rate or what the company can afford?** The general approach of the courts in unfair prejudice excessive remuneration cases is examined in detail in chapter 21.

  Basically the courts seem to accept that, even in the context of insolvent companies and provided that the company concerned has not entered into wrongful trading territory,[190] then directors are entitled to be paid at market rates for their services. Cases such as *Irvine (No 2)* suggest there may be some considerable latitude to go beyond market rates for directors who have made an exceptional contribution to, or whose continued employment is vital to their family company.

  But there is some authority to suggest that what is appropriate remuneration must be judged in the context of the performance and ability to pay of the company concerned. Market rates will be a relevant but not a decisive factor. Criticising the director concerned for a number of matters, including taking excessive remuneration from a non-family futures trading business in a director's disqualification case the trial judge explained that 'A director must bear in mind what a company can afford as well as what is the going rate for the job performed by the director if he were an employee elsewhere'.[191]

- **A duty of restraint in family companies?** The decision in *Van Hengel* was in the context of insolvency, where it is often said that the primary duty of the directors switches from looking after the interests of the members of a company to safeguarding those of its creditors. Whether the concept of affordability of salaries is capable of extending to poorly performing but essentially solvent family company so as to prevent all available surplus funds being soaked up in paying market rate remuneration to the 'haves' in cases such as *Saul D Harrison* does not appear to have been explored in reported cases.

8.9 BALANCING INTERESTS – CA, S 172 AND THE DUTY TO PROMOTE THE SUCCESS OF THE COMPANY

8.9.1 Introduction

As explained above CA, s 172 contains a general duty for directors to 'promote the success of the company' but in doing so to 'have regard' to a number of factors and the interests of various stakeholders. These are set out fully in **8.3.3** above and can be summarised as follows:

- the long term consequences of the relevant decision;
- the interests of employees;
- relationships with suppliers, customers and others;
- impact of operations on the community and the environment;
- reputational impact; and
- acting fairly as between members.

---

[189] See chapter 21.
[190] See below.
[191] *Secretary of State for Trade and Industry v Van Hengel and Anor* [1995] BCC 173.

The factors listed in CA, s 172(1) are not exhaustive as the section makes it clear that those listed are 'amongst other factors' which directors should consider.

Turning now to consider the application of the general duty to promote the success of the company in the context of the family owned company.

8.9.2 Family branch factionalism

The primacy of members' interests is preserved by the introductory wording, which confirms that the reason the directors must promote the success of the company is 'for the benefit of the members as a whole'. This language, particularly when combined with the duty in CA, s 172(1)(f) to have regard to the duty 'to act fairly as between members of the company' ought to make it clear that directors in a family owned company should not act in a way that favours the interests of the members of one family branch over those of other branches.

More blatant cases of favouritism, for example, property dealings at an undervalue, may well give rise to an actionable breach, through a derivative claim[192] on the part of the disadvantaged minority. But one of the most common forms of branch favouritism in a family company will be in relation to employment opportunities. This may be much more difficult to directly redress as a breach of the general duty to promote the success of the company.

First it is unclear whether the duty to balance the interests of members relates only to their narrower interests as shareholders or whether wider interests including participation in employment opportunities should also be taken into account.

Secondly, and even if the courts adopt a wider construction of members' interests in the case of owner managed businesses, the section does not create an absolute duty to provide a fair balance between members' interests. It merely requires the directors to 'have regard to' this issue. It may often be the case that the directors could point to other factors, even factors that are a natural consequence of family business 'branch insidership' such as greater knowledge of the family company, as a business factor justifying the perpetuation of family branch employment inequality.

So it is likely to be only the most extreme or blatant cases of favouritism in terms of employment opportunities that could be pursued through the courts as a breach of the general duty to promote the success of the company. Even then it is less likely that this will be as a stand-alone breach of the duty itself. It is more likely that blatant branch favouritism in employment opportunities in a family business will be cited as a factor in unfair prejudice proceedings brought by the have-nots.[193]

---

[192] Explored in chapter 23.
[193] See chapter 21. However it is difficult to find an unfair prejudice case decided solely on the basis of branch factionalism so far as employment opportunities are concerned.

8.9.3 Stakeholder and long term interests

It is often suggested that family owned business are much better at taking a long-term view than their non-family counterparts.[194] Similarly it may be that family companies have a natural tendency to have regard to the interests of their various stakeholder groups, without the needing to be reminded to do so by the general duty to promote the success of their family business contained in CA, s 172. This may indeed frequently, or even usually, be the case. But it will not be invariably so. Where does CA, s 172 take us if there is a strong disagreement between the board and a significant proportion of the family membership in relation to factors covered by the list in that section?

For example a decision whether or not to close down the main manufacturing plant of the family company in the UK and to move production abroad. Whilst the decision might have a positive effect in reducing environmental emissions, it would almost certainly have a negative impact for the employees who would inevitably lose their jobs, for the wider community, particularly if, as is often the case, the family company is the main employer in the locality,[195] and for the locally based suppliers of the family company.

The board may have come to the conclusion, however reluctantly, that such a move would be in the best long-term interests of the business. Various family members who may live in the locality of the factory to be closed down, or otherwise be acutely aware of the legacy of the family business and its links to employees, suppliers and customers, may be vehemently opposed to such a material change.

The Act does not rank the factors that the board must consider in any particular order of importance. The board only has to 'have regard' to these in any event. There is a historic reluctance on the part of the courts to second-guess the business decisions of the board of directors and to interfere in the management of a company.

So, providing the board can demonstrate that they have been through the thought process of considering the impact of their decision to relocate abroad on employees, the community, suppliers etc., it is difficult to see how a court will find the board to be in breach of their duty under CA, s 172 in anything but the most extreme circumstances. In practice this will be where the board have reached a decision that no reasonable board could sensibly reach.

Or alternatively, to take an example of more venal family shareholders, the board may believe that, rather than relocating abroad, the best answer for the family company will be to substantially invest in improving the existing UK manufacturing base. This investment will inevitably soak up cash in the short to medium term that would otherwise be available to pay dividends to family members. As in *Re Samuel Weller and Sons Ltd*[196] family shareholders not on the board or connected to directors might object to this.

In this second example the board will be able to point to the express requirement of the Act for them to have regard to the best long-term interests of the company. There is

---
[194] For example John Ward talks about mature family owned businesses as having an 'infinite time horizon'. See *Perpetuating the Family Business* (Palgrave, 2004) at p 110 Lesson 31 (Shared Investments).
[195] Such as Clark's shoes in Street and surrounding towns in Somerset.
[196] [1990] Ch 682. The case is discussed in detail in chapter 21.

academic debate as to whether this allows the directors to now pretty much ignore short-term considerations such as maintaining dividend flows.[197] Even if these short-term considerations still need to be taken into account as factors 'amongst others' it becomes doubly difficult to see how a court will interfere and find a decision clearly based on a long-term assessment of the interests of a family company as being in breach of duty. In *Re Samuel Weller and Sons Ltd* the trial judge concluded that 'with some hesitation' he would allow an allegation of unfair prejudice based on significant capital expenditure to proceed to full trial because of the close link to a separate allegation of failure to pay dividends. It may well be that faced with similar facts today the requirement to consider the long term consequences of a decision contained in CA, s 172(1)(a) will mean that a court is more ready to strike out similar pleadings.

8.9.4 S 172 and company procedure

What do directors need to do to demonstrate that they have complied with the requirements of CA, s 172 and that, in particular, they have had regard to the list of statutory factors that should influence their decision-making?

Andrew Keay reviews the various schools of thought and guidance given both in Parliament, at the committee stage of the Companies Bill and by commentators and compliance bodies.[198] The consensus of opinion appears to be that the Act should not impose any additional burden of bureaucracy for the well-governed company.

Nevertheless there may be a distinction in the case of a number of family owned companies between those that are inherently well governed, in the sense that the family members in charge intuitively and instinctively give consideration and appropriate weight to the factors listed in CA, s 172, and those that are well administered, in the sense of being able to demonstrate, with reference to formal board minutes or other paper trails, that this was indeed the case. It would serve such companies well to pay attention to the more formal aspects of governance and, in particular to ensure that board deliberations for important and sensitive decisions which clearly involve these statutory factors are fully minuted.

8.9.5 S 172 – conclusion

There was concern that the introduction of the new general duty for directors to promote the success of their company under CA, s 172 would add considerably to the level of responsibility faced by company directors and, when combined with the new codified derivative claims under CA, s 260, lead to more claims for breach of duty being made against directors.

So far this does not appear to have been the case. This may be because major cases involving breaches of CA, s 172 have yet to find their way through the courts. Alternatively it might be that because of the structure of the provision, when combined with the reluctance of the courts to second guess business decisions of a board of directors, CA, s 172 has in practice added little to the burden of duties already faced by

---

[197] Mayson et al point to the fact that an earlier draft of the Companies Bill contained in the White Paper referred to the need for directors to consider both the short term and long term consequences of their decisions as support for the proposition that 'Parliament has clearly decided that it is the long term that is more important'.

[198] See *Directors' Duties*, op cit at pp 171–176.

directors. In a well-governed business the new section may even make it easier for directors to demonstrate that they have discharged their duty to the company and its various stakeholder interests. So rather than providing a sword with which disgruntled shareholders, including those in a family business, could attack the board, s 172 may have created a shield against such claims.

8.10 THE SINKING SHIP – INSOLVENCY AND THE FAMILY COMPANY

8.10.1 Overview

It has been noted that many of the claims against directors of family companies, either for breach of duty, or for disqualification, have been made in the context of insolvency. One of our primary contentions is that, when viewed in the round, family businesses are more conservatively managed than their non-family counterparts and therefore less likely to encounter insolvency. However given the sheer number of family businesses some failures are inevitable.

Any detailed consideration of insolvency law and procedure is well beyond the scope of this book. Instead we will dwell on one particular case. Partly because this neatly shows pretty much the full range of claims that can be made in the context of insolvency, but more because this case illustrates the catastrophic effect of the failure of a family business on the business family.

Before researching the topic we had expected to find family business insolvency cases falling into two broad categories. First cases relating to early stage family companies where a mixture of risk taking, lack of financial controls and disregard of directors' duties led the family into trouble generally giving rise to a multitude of claims. There are plenty of those. Some of which are considered in **8.6** above (the family director).

We also expected to find a number of cases featuring later stage family businesses, in particular concerning wrongful trading claims made under IA, s 214. Our hypothesis was that it would be particularly difficult for family management to accept that a multi-generation family company would sink on their watch so that the temptation to sail on into wrongful trading waters would prove irresistible. We are pleased to say that we have not been able to prove our hypothesis. Whether this is because fewer multi-generation family businesses fail, perhaps for the financial prudency reasons referred to above or whether we have simply failed to identify relevant cases we cannot say.

8.10.2 *Listowel Trading Ltd*[199] and the Patterson family – the facts

The *Listowel Trading* case does not contain any novel legal points. It is not reported in any major law reports. It does however show how much law can be thrown at directors who get things wrong. The case illustrates the application of many of the main insolvency remedies against directors. Above all it provides an object lesson on just how badly things can go wrong for a business family who do not comply with the basics of governance and financial housekeeping.

---

[199] *Hooper v Patterson* (unreported), judgment of 9 February 2008, High Court Case No 11688 of 2008.

The judge hearing the case[200] opens her judgment somewhat poetically, noting that 'The background of this application is one of broken dreams'.

The case concerns Raymond Patterson, an experienced and successful chef, who had worked for 12 years at the Garrick Club in London and whose dream was to open his own restaurant, working with his son Tom, who had just completed a hospitality management university degree. Tom and Raymond were the only directors but various members of the Patterson family also invested in and worked for the business.

The company traded for about 7 years. In terms of turnover it was successful, achieving sales in the region of £1.5m. In terms of financial management the business was a disaster. The first year of trading showed a loss. This would not be unusual for a new restaurant with fitting out costs etc. After that no accounts were ever filed for the next 4 years. VAT and PAYE returns and payments were spasmodic. No corporation tax filings were made. In many ways both Raymond and Tom Patterson could both be seen as family directors in the sense described in 8.6 above, that is lacking the skills training and experience to safely direct their family company.

Three sets of accountants were instructed by the family, although the court doubted that the Pattersons provided them with enough information to do their job. Indeed financial record keeping appeared to be seriously deficient. The last firm of accountants did manage to produce accounts showing that the business was making a net profit in the region of £250,000 on turnover approaching £1.5m.

But the business was clearly in cash flow difficulties. The recently prepared accounts showed current liabilities of nearly £500,000. There were other warning signs. For some time there had not been enough money to pay the Patterson family members who worked in the business. Those cash flow pressures eventually told. Following a pre-pack administration[201] of the restaurant business Listowel Trading Ltd went into creditors' voluntary liquidation. The deficit was eventually found to be in the region of £1.6m with huge amounts of unpaid tax.

Nevertheless the judge was quite convinced that Raymond (Mr Patterson senior) had 'by no means acted in a deliberate fashion to defraud creditors' and that he was 'a fundamentally honest individual'.[202] The problem was that Mr Patterson appeared to have been fundamentally incapable of taking the step from being a highly experienced chef to running a restaurant business. Likewise his son Tom's university degree in catering management did not appear to equip him to put the theory he had learned into practice.

Raymond Patterson faced a number of claims brought by the liquidator as a result of the collapse of the company. Many of these share common features with other early stage family business failures.

---

[200] Ms Deputy Registrar Jones.
[201] The procedure whereby an insolvent company enters into administration on the basis of a pre-arranged deal for the assets of insolvent the business to be sold by the administrator to a new company often (as in this case) one set up by the original owners or their family. In appropriate cases the purchase price paid can represent the best return for the creditors of the original company. However the pre-pack procedure has been much criticised and is now more tightly controlled.
[202] At para 17 of the judgment.

8.10.3 Wrongful trading – IA, s 214

In summary a director of a company that has gone into insolvent liquidation can be ordered to contribute to the shortfall if they allow the company to carry on trading and 'they knew or ought to have concluded that there was no reasonable prospect that the company would avoid' insolvency.[203]

As a general rule directors of an insolvent company are not personally liable to creditors. Wrongful trading is therefore an exception to that rule. Whilst there is no absolute prohibition against trading at a loss the logic of the wrongful trading provision is that limited liability privilege is being abused if creditors have suffered by directors carrying on regardless of the warning signs as to their company's doom.

The dual test[204] applies so that the test of whether a director ought to have realised that insolvency is inevitable is looked at both against the actual knowledge and experience of the director concerned but also the minimum standards that 'may reasonably be expected' from a hypothetical director in the same circumstances.

The usual order against directors will be for them to make a contribution based on the increase in creditors incurred between the period when the directors ought to have realised that their company was doomed and the time it actually went into liquidation.

There is a defence under IA, s 214(3) that the director took 'every step' to minimise loss to creditors after they realised that the company would fail. Because of the difficulty of showing that every step to minimise loss to creditors had been taken in practice most wrongful trading cases turn on identifying the point at which the director ought to have concluded that insolvency was inevitable. This will often require a degree of judicial discretion. In Mr Patterson's case the judge decided that this should be fixed at a date 3 months after the company's 2007 year-end. By this time a combination of statutory accounts that the judge thought should have been available by then and the day-to day affects of cash-flow difficulties ought to have 'fully alerted' Mr Patterson that his company was doomed.[205]

It could not help Mr Patterson that no accounts were in fact ever prepared for 2007.[206] That would be allowing Mr Patterson to plead one breach of duty to escape another. Neither would it help Mr Patterson that he had introduced more funding into the business during the period covered by those accounts. Whilst he might genuinely have believed that the company could be saved by his increased investment the judge thought that this belief 'was rather pie in the sky'.[207]

---

[203] Insolvency Act 1986, s 214(2)(b).
[204] See IA, s 214(4). The test is similar to that in the general duty for directors to exercise reasonable skill and care under CA, s 174. Indeed the test under CA, s 174 derives from the wrongful trading test so much of the case-law decided under IA, s 214 will also be relevant to matters under CA, s 174.
[205] See para 56 of the judgment.
[206] Although not expressly stated in the judgment the judge appears to be drawing a distinction between the time periods for filing accounts at Companies House (now 9 months but then 10 months in the case of a private company) and a reasonable period after the year end for directors to have prepared accounts for reasons of the internal financial management of their company. Good financial discipline suggests that reasonably reliable management accounts should be prepared monthly and certainly much more frequently than the statutory accounts. This point does not appear to have been taken against Mr. Patterson in the context of wrongful trading.
[207] See para 54 of the judgment.

So Mr Patterson was found to be personally liable for the increase in creditors over the period of 14 months between when he ought to have concluded that his dream had failed and eventually recognising this by ceasing to trade. These amounted to £463,046.28.

8.10.4 IA, s 212

Mr Patterson also faced a number of claims brought under IA, s 212 which, broadly, applies where directors have misapplied company funds or are guilty of a breach of fiduciary duty.[208]

The findings against Mr Patterson largely stemmed from his failure to keep proper accounting records and institute sensible financial systems and controls. The judge found that the accounting records 'such as they are, are clearly in chaos' that there appeared 'to have been no control over large amounts of cash', and that 'there was a remarkably casual attitude towards the financial affairs of the company' so that in summary:[209]

> 'Mr Patterson had no clue what was happening, what financial position the Company was in, where monies were or were not being applied or whether the Company was complying with its obligations to file returns [or] pay tax.'

This dereliction of duty was a breach of the fiduciary duties Mr Patterson owed to the company.

Mr Patterson had argued that he had relied on the company's accountants to deal with relevant matters. The judge was clear that this was no defence unless 'he had made enquiries and has satisfied himself that they were in fact doing what he had required them to do'.[210]

The court found that a number of defaults and circumstances on the part of Raymond Patterson fell under the general umbrella of IA, s 212. Many of these matters are commonly encountered in family owned businesses. They can be seen to stem from a basic failure to differentiate between the property of the family company and that of the family members. These matters included:

- **Mortgage payments.** Raymond had re-mortgaged his own house, mainly to inject funds into the company. However the new loan was also used to pay off Mr and Mrs Patterson's existing mortgage. Payments under the new mortgage were made from the company's bank account. Mr Patterson argued that this was part of a loan agreement between himself and the company.
  It may well have been possible to construct a proper loan arrangement. But in the absence of appropriate paperwork the court was not convinced and took the view that Mr Patterson regarded the arrangement as part of his (unauthorised) remuneration and that 'he was not entitled to treat a limited company as if it were

---

[208] IA, s 212 is, in essence, a procedural device, rather than imposing any separate duties on directors. The section provides a liquidator with the ability to bring breach of duty claims on behalf of company creditors. It is therefore similar to derivative claims considered in chapter 23, but is more flexible, wider and more general.
[209] At para 27 of the judgment.
[210] At para 25 of the judgment and citing *Re Barings plc (No 5)* [1999] 1 BCLC 433 (part of the fall-out from the Nick Leeson case) in support. The judge was also sceptical about whether the Pattersons had provided their accountants with the necessary financial information to prepare the accounts.

his alter-ego'.[211] Mr Patterson was ordered to repay the mortgage monies.[212] He and Mrs Patterson will also have remained liable to repay the new mortgage.

The *Litsowel Trading* case shares many features with the better-known early stage family business failure case of *Re DKG Contractors*.[213] These include a basic inability to distinguish between the assets and liabilities of the family company and those of the family members. Poor accounting and record keeping also feature. In *DKG Contractors* Mr Gibbons ran a groundwork contracting business. In practice the business was run as a single combined operation with common employees, plant and equipment. Mr Gibbons operated partly as a sole trader but also through a parallel limited company. Mrs Gibbons attempted to 'keep the books' for both entities.

Payments received from contracts entered into by the limited company were paid over to Mr Gibbons and used in his sole trader business. The sole trader business could well have supplied materials and labour to the limited company and *vice-versa*, but the records were sufficiently confused that no-one could really tell. The company faced cash-flow difficulties and key suppliers refused to advance further credit whereupon Mr Gibbons walked away from the company and left his wife to sort out the mess.

The court had little difficulty in finding that sums received on behalf of the company had been misapplied by both Mr and Mrs Gibbons as directors. An order was made under IA, s 212 that they should repay the full amount (which was approaching £420,000).[214]

- **Payments received.** Payments had been made from the company's bank account into the joint account of Mr and Mrs Patterson. These could not be fully explained. It was possible that Mr Patterson used some of the money for company purposes. The most likely explanation was that most of this was taken by Mr Patterson on an 'informal ad-hoc basis' in lieu of salary, the effective equivalent of drawings in an unincorporated partnership. Again the payments could easily have been regularised and taken as remuneration. Even though the judge accepted that Mr Patterson believed he was entitled to take these payments the lack of formality meant that he had: 'failed to exercise his responsibility as a fiduciary and [was] liable to repay the whole of the sum'.[215]

- **Unidentified cheque payments.** A number of cheques totalling £104,500 had been drawn against the company bank account but could not be explained. Although there was no suggestion that Mr Patterson had personally benefited from these payments there was equally no way he could prove that the money 'which appears to have been paid into the void' had been applied for proper company purposes. Mr Patterson's part in the collective failure of the directors to keep proper accounting records meant that he was ordered to repay the whole of this amount.[216]

- **Sums not paid into company accounts.** Similarly there was a shortfall of £18,427 of cash and cheques paid by customers that could not be shown to have been paid into the company bank account. Mr Patterson could offer no explanation for this. Notwithstanding that she accepted that Mr Patterson did not deal with 'cashing up and banking of the takings' the judge, thought that as a director he should 'at least

---

[211] See paras 32–34 of the judgment.
[212] It is unclear whether the order relates to the whole amount (probably the better reading) or just a proportion equivalent to the amount paid off the Patterson's previous mortgage.
[213] [1990] BCC 903.
[214] At p 408.
[215] At paras 36–37 of the judgment.
[216] At para 35 of the judgment.

- be aware of what was happening to these large sums of money'. Again Mr Patterson was ordered to pay this amount.[217]
- **Payments unaccounted for.** Conversely the company's records showed that almost £105,000 had been taken out of the company in cash either from the bank account or from unbanked cash takings which were unsupported by any evidence of expenditure. According to the judge 'it has simply it would seem disappeared into thin air'". Interestingly the judge accepted that Mr Patterson had received cash to buy food and noted that none of these payments what been recorded in the cash-book. Nevertheless, in the absence of proper records to show that this is how some or all of the cash was spent Mr Patterson was ordered to pay the whole of the unaccounted amount.[218]
- **Director's loan account.** A similar story applied to Mr Patterson's director's loan account, which was stated to have been overdrawn by about £66,000. Mr Patterson argued that the accountants had simply debited unexplained payments to his loan account and effectively treated this as a suspense account. The judge took the view that it was Mr Patterson's responsibility to ensure that the company's records were correct. He must live with what the records say and repay the amount stated.[219]
- **Filing penalties.** The company had incurred filing penalties of over £76,000 for failing to submit tax returns of pay tax on time. As Mr Patterson had a legal duty to ensure that the correct returns were made he was ordered to pay an amount equal to these penalties.[220]

8.10.5 Transactions at an undervalue – IA, s 238

Claims were also made against Mr Patterson under IA, s 238 on the basis that he had caused the company to enter into transactions at an undervalue. In essence, the remedy applies to reverse the effect of self-dealing between a company and directors,[221] typically where assets are transferred to directors at less than market value,[222] thus effectively taking value out of a company to the detriment of creditors. All transactions with 'connected parties' during the two-year period preceding formal insolvency are caught.[223] The court has discretion to make any order 'restoring the position to what it would have been if the company had not entered into that transaction'.[224]

In this case the claims related to the refinancing of the Patterson's house. Broadly the company seems to have been saddled with the full cost of servicing a loan used partly to repay Mr Patterson's previous mortgage. Because the judge had already found that in

---

[217] At paras 38–41 of the judgment.
[218] At paras 41–43 of the judgment.
[219] At paras 29–31 of the judgment.
[220] At paras 44 and 45 of the judgment.
[221] IA, s 238 is not limited to transactions between a company and its directors. Any transaction at an undervalue is covered. At least in theory. There is a defence in IA, s 238(5) that the company entered the relevant transaction in good faith provided that, at the time 'there were reasonable grounds for believing that the transaction would benefit the company'. So, for example a 'fire-sale' of stock in a retail business might be both at an undervalue and seen as reasonable attempt to save an ailing business.
[222] IA, s 238 is of broad application so could also cover services supplied at an undervalue, for example to a related company controlled by the directors concerned.
[223] IA, s 240(1)(a). The period is 6 months for non-connected party transactions.
[224] IA, s 238(3).

entering into this arrangement Mr Patterson was in breach of his duties and fully liable under IA, s 212 and to avoid double counting the court did not to explore this allegation further.

8.10.6 Preferences – IA, s 239

Preferences, where the directors apply scarce cash for the benefit of themselves or their associates, are a common feature of owner managed business insolvencies. Preferences can be seen to fall into three broad categories. Naked preferences where the directors simply cause their own debts to be paid first, for example loans that they, or close family members, have made to the business. Secondly, indirect preferences. For example, making strenuous efforts to repay an overdraft personally guaranteed by the director concerned. Thirdly, third party preference, where the directors give priority to certain trade creditors, perhaps key suppliers who they hope to use in a future business. Identical time periods apply to preferences as for transactions at an undervalue.[225]

It is perhaps a mark of Mr Patterson's fundamental honesty in his business dealings (some cynics might say naivety) that the claims against him did not include preferences. Mr Gibbons in *Re DKG Contractors* did face preference claims. The basic argument being that by ensuring that almost all of the money received by the company under its contracts was paid to him personally (whether for work or materials supplied, as a sub-contractor or otherwise) he was clearly preferring his own interests to those of other suppliers and creditors of the company.

The law relating to preferences can be difficult to interpret as the test is partly subjective. IA, s 239(5) provides that courts shall not make an order unless the company 'was influenced ... by a desire' to put a person into a better position in insolvency. If the person receiving the benefit of the preference is a connected to the company this is presumed.[226] So Mr Gibbons needed to convince the court that payments made to him by the company were in fact influenced by desires other than to place himself in a better position personally on liquidation. On the facts of the *DKG* case there was a point at which Mr Gibbons was attempting to complete ground-work sub-contracts. Payments made by the company to him in his sole trader, sub-contractor personal capacity that would allow employees and suppliers to be paid could be seen to have been influenced by a desire to complete those contracts for the benefit of the company. But payments made to Mr Patterson after the company had effectively ceased trading were clear preferences.[227]

8.10.7 Tom Patterson

The *Listowel Trading* case was brought against Mr Patterson senior only. He was stated to have:

> 'reigned supreme in the kitchen, managing the purchase of the food, the menus and the production of high value and quality dining.'

What then of his son, Tom, who 'appeared to be expected to deal with the takings, accounts etc'? Neglect of these areas was precisely what led to the failure of the family

---
[225] IA, s 240.
[226] IA, s 239(6).
[227] [1990] BCC 903 at p 910.

business. The answer appears to be that by the time the case came to court Tom was already bankrupt. Otherwise there would be little doubt that notwithstanding his lack of practical business experience he would have been criticised as severely, if not more than, his father.

Quite what Raymond thought of the wisdom of going into business with his son is not mentioned in the judgment other than the judge saying that she 'was impressed by the lack of self pity or of any attempt to lay the blame anywhere other than with himself'.[228]

8.10.8 Relief against liability and CA, s 1157

The power of the court to grant relief to directors in respect of the consequence of their breaches of duty has been mentioned above.

The total amount awarded against Mr Patterson for the claims under IA, s 212 was in the region of £500,000 to which must be added the £460,000 or so awarded under IA, s 214 and the liquidator's costs for bringing the court case. Many of the claims under s 212 were based on sins of omission rather than commission on the part of Mr Patterson, in particular his failure to ensure appropriate accounting systems were in place. This was an area for which Mr Patterson did not have direct responsibility.

Mr Patterson, who was not legally represented at the hearing, does not appear to have made any application for relief under CA, s 1157. Clearly any relief granted to Mr Patterson would have affected the recovery of the liquidator for the benefit of the creditors. But in various places in the judgment the judge expresses both sympathy for Mr Patterson's position and an acknowledgement that he was not directly responsible.

Might an application have succeeded, in particular concerning the use of the petty cash? Whilst Mr Patterson might have been in breach of his duty to ensure that proper accounting records were kept by the company, if there was a reasonable possibility that some or all of the missing cash was used by him to buy food for the restaurant, could he be seen to have acted reasonably in leaving the book-keeping to others so that he fairly ought to be excused?

8.10.9 Personal guarantees

The losses suffered by the Patterson family were not confined to the amounts awarded in favour of the liquidator. In addition to those claims Mr Patterson (along with Mrs Patterson) clearly faced claims from the mortgagee of their home. Perhaps Mr Patterson, along with Tom had given personal guarantees for other borrowing.

8.10.10 The family consequences

The consequences of any business failure can be devastating for the owner manager. In cases of family business failure the consequences can be felt throughout the wider family.

Mr and Mrs Patterson may well have lost their home as a result of the mortgage given to secure new investment into the failed business. Certainly the judgment transcript

---

[228] At para 59 of the judgment.

mentions that they were divorced by the time the case reached court. The transcript also refers to Raymond Patterson suffering heart problems. It also refers to investments made by the wider Patterson family in the business, the failure of which must inevitably strained wider family relationships.

Sadly the Patterson's case may not be seen as particularly unusual as owner managed business failure matters go. But a family business setting provides a context where the consequences of failure can ripple out to further damage wider family economic interests and relationships.

We do not know the precise reason for Tom's bankruptcy but the betting must be that this was directly related to joining his father in their family business. Governance wisdom has it that the next generation should gain some practical management experience elsewhere before joining their family business. Would things have been different if Tom had followed this advice?

The transcript suggests that Raymond Patterson refused to cast blame on others, at least in the public forum of the High Court. Was this true privately? It is difficult to think that the failure and the fall-out of their family business did not damage the relationship between father and son, but to what extent?

8.10.11 Advice and governance

So what, with the benefit of hindsight could the Patterson family have done differently?

Certainly the trial judge criticised Raymond for failing to take appropriate professional advice saying that it was 'very unfortunate that he did not obtain proper advice prior to the incorporation of the company'.[229] Clearly there were a number of failings in the Patterson case at a most basic governance level concerning financial records and accounting.

Obtaining comprehensive, accessible and cost effective professional advice on director's responsibilities is clearly a challenge for most small start-up family companies. Nevertheless there is a wealth of resource available from Companies House and other websites along with books and other publications or courses on directors' responsibilities provided by the Institute of Directors or otherwise.

But perhaps the most fundamental governance failing on the part of the Patterson family was not pausing to ask, why they should go into business together? Did they really believe that the family were capable of running a successful catering business in an industry where so many enterprises fail? Did Raymond and Tom really believe that, fresh from college, Tom had the capability to put in implement proper financial and management systems for the business?

A little more attention to these key business questions as opposed to not looking beyond the family dream of being in business together might have prevented both a business and a family failure.

---

[229] At para 59 of the judgment.

8.11 DIRECTORS' DUTIES – CONCLUSION

The subject of directors' duties might at first sight seem both a little dry and of limited application to the world inhabited by most family owned businesses. It is certainly true that many of the strictures of formal governance and compliance systems do not sit well alongside the more informal ways of operating of many family businesses. It is also the case that family members may be more inclined to accept informality and lapses than non-family shareholders.

So many duties for directors of family companies may arise and be breached without apparent consequence.

The problem for directors running family companies is that whilst directors' duties arise in real time they are enforced retrospectively. Usually this is when circumstances change. Sometimes this can be as a result of family disputes. More often enforcement follows upon the financial failure of the family company. When this happens, as the case studies considered in this chapter illustrate, the consequences for, not only the director primarily at fault, but also the wider business owning family can be extremely severe.

What the case studies also illustrate is a number of common themes running through many family company failures. With rare exceptions[230] outright dishonesty does not feature in these cases as opposed to simple ineptitude. Other common themes include failures of accounting systems,[231] failure to take or accept advice and the appointment of unsuitable 'family directors'.[232] But perhaps the single most common theme and therefore the greatest family owned business failing is the inability to distinguish between the corporate affairs of the family company and the underlying interests of the business owning family. This issue appears to affect the larger later stage family company[233] almost as much as it does the early stage founder led family business.[234]

Just as there appear to be common ills affecting family companies there also appear to be common cures. The judges in various cases bemoan the lack of awareness of their duties and responsibilities directors of the family companies including a lack of knowledge of the most basic elements of company law. Judges in other cases complain about the failure of directors to seek or take advice from appropriate professional advisors.

Clearly directors of family companies will be loath to forgo the benefits of flexibility and fun that the family business structure potentially provides and trade these in for bureaucracy and a corporate compliance environment. But some investment in the basics of governance, as covered in chapter 17, must provide directors of family companies with a good level of insurance against changes of circumstances such as family disputes and insolvency. Ideally that investment will contribute to both the financial health and the strength of family relationships in the business and thereby prevent such circumstances arising in the first place.

---

[230] Such as the Patterson family.
[231] The Pattersons and *DKG Contractors*.
[232] *Park House Properties, Cohen v Selby*, the Patterson case.
[233] Such as Harrison Properties.
[234] *In Re Gemma, Bhullar Brother, Park House Properties, DKG Contractors*, and the Pattersons.

Family dreams of working together in a successful business can often become a reality. Those dreams need not become a nightmare.

CHAPTER 9

THE FAMILY BUSINESS NAME

9.1 INTRODUCTION

In chapter 1 we suggest that the name of the business owning family, the name above the door, is a potential source of internal strength and cohesion for a family business. The family name will, of course, represent a considerable level of emotional attachment, loyalty and pride amongst the family members.

The family name can also have significant external value, as a brand and intellectual property asset. Again Clarks' shoes provide a good example. A family business will often trade under the family surname, as part of the formal company name (eg C & J Clark Limited) or as a trading name (eg Clarks). In both cases, a family business can build up a significant reputation and valuable goodwill in the family name.

The corollary is that this goodwill can be vulnerable, both to reputational damage caused by problems with the goods and services of the family company and to the activities of outsiders. Here we use the expression outsiders to include, not only unrelated third parties, but also outsiders in the sense used elsewhere in the book, members of the wider business owning family, not directly involved in day-to-day management.

In this chapter we look in more detail at the use of the family business identity as a brand. This includes the use of the family name as the business name. But it goes much further and includes how the connection between the business and the family is presented to the wider world. The main part of the chapter concentrates on some of the legal aspects of protecting the family business name, as intellectual property, both against third parties and where dissident factions of the business family break away from the original family firm and wish to use their family name in a competing enterprise.

9.2 THE FAMILY BUSINESS AS A BRAND

Much has been said in this book about family business values, including tradition, legacy, trust, continuity and commitment, whether to the quality of goods and services, employees, customers, suppliers or the wider community. Attempts are often made to capture these values and record them as part of family charters.[1]

---
[1] See chapter 17.

Theorists would see these internal values as part of the 'organisational identity' of the family business. This refers to the:[2]

> 'organisation members' collective understanding of the central, distinctive, and enduring character of the organisation.'

These values form a core part of the culture of a family firm and are instrumental for its internal cohesion. The same values also have significant potential appeal to third parties, in particular customers, but also suppliers and prospective employees. Many family enterprises, consciously choose to externalise their 'construct of identity'[3] by presenting some or all of these values as part of their 'corporate identity' to the outside world.[4]

One needs to look no further than Wharburtons bakers to illustrate this. Their logo reads 'Wharburtons – family bakers'. The tag line 'from our family to yours' appears not far below.[5] However the use of family based branding is much more likely to be adopted by small to medium sized family firms, since this provides a point of differentiation between them and larger competitors.[6]

Organisational theorists Micelotta and Raynard[7] identify various different ways that the family connection is used by family enterprises in practice. They argue that these differ from family business to family business depending on a number of characteristics including the nature and size of the family enterprise concerned. They identified[8] three distinct family brand strategies as follows:

- **Family preservation strategy.** By this the author's mean that the role of the business owning family in preserving the legacy of the founder is a central plank of the corporate identity and the marketing strategy of the family business. The family connection will appear prominently on its website and marketing materials. The family name and, often, that of the founder will be part of the business name.
  Businesses using this strategy see legacy, continuity and a connection with the past as a competitive advantage. The family will attempt to sell its history. This will often apply to luxury goods, hotel and leisure and food and drink businesses. Wharburtons again seem to be a good example of what the authors are describing.
- **Family enrichment strategy.** Here the family connection is important but less central to the corporate identity of the family business. The fact that the business is family owned is presented as relevant in order to establish longevity and experience in the relevant field. The family ownership history is the foundation of

---

[2] See Micelotta and Raynard 'Concealing or Revealing the Family? Corporate Brand Identity Strategies in Family Firms' *Family Business Review* (2011) 24(3) 197–216 at p 198 and the references to organisational theory cited there.
[3] Ibid at p 198.
[4] Micelotta and Raynard, op cit at p 198 suggest that there could be a difference between internal and external values and distinguish between 'corporate identity [which] reflects how identity is communicated and portrayed to outsiders, whereas organizational identity refers to how internal members conceive the identity of their organizations'. However much of the theory of brand strategy is aimed at achieving a congruence between internal and external values.
[5] See Wharburtons website – http://www.warburtons.co.uk, accessed 6 September 2016.
[6] J B Craig, C Dibrelland P S Davis 'Leveraging family-based brand identity to enhance firm competitiveness and performance in family businesses' *Journal of Small Business Management* (2008) 46, 351–371 and referenced in Micelotta and Raynard 'Concealing or Revealing the Family? Corporate Brand Identity Strategies in Family Firms' *Family Business Review* (2011) 24(3) 197–216.
[7] See Micelotta and Raynard 'Concealing or Revealing the Family? Corporate Brand Identity Strategies in Family Firms' *Family Business Review* (2011) 24(3) 197–216.
[8] The study was based on a review of the websites of approximately 100 of the world's oldest family businesses, from a list published by *Family Business* magazine.

the family business. However the key selling point is that the business has built on this foundation to develop products and services to modern 'best in breed' corporate standards.

Here the main focus is on the goods and services as now produced rather than the fact that the business is family owned or its legacy products. The family business is selling the present. Nevertheless the fact of family ownership conveys an important subsidiary message of trustworthiness and experience.

Clarks probably[9] fall into this classification. Although an early company logo and the phrase 'Shoemakers since 1825' appears on their website this is at the bottom of the home page, the remainder of which is much more focused on their latest products. Similarly an account of the history of the Clarks business is available from the website but the link is not prominently displayed.[10]

JCB are another example. The homepage of their website contains the following statement, alongside an old black and white photograph.

> 'Innovation is at the heart of everything we do. The story of JCB is one of innovation, ambition and sheer hard work. From small beginnings building agricultural tipping trailers in 1945, to the global force in manufacturing the company has become today.'

However this reference appears well down the homepage, which gives much more prominence to the machinery produced by the company today.[11] When the link is followed to the history of the company, although this mentions the family story, much more prominence is given to the 'innovation milestones' in the company's product history.

- **Family subordination strategy.** Here the focus is almost exclusively on the company and its products or services. The business is presented as a corporate entity. The fact that it is family owned is subordinated, in effect appearing as a footnote to the corporate story, if mentioned at all.

Family businesses in this category are much less likely to use the family name as a business name.

Dysons is a good example.[12] The front page of the website makes no mention of family ownership. Buried at the bottom of the front page is a link to a page describing the history of the company, which is simply described as a 'technology company with over 1,000 engineers worldwide'.[13]

9.3 PROTECTING THE FAMILY NAME

Many components of the overall family business corporate identity will attract separate individual intellectual property protection, for example copyright in websites or marketing and advertising materials. A discussion of these aspects is beyond the scope of this book. Instead we will concentrate on the family name itself. There are two main forms of legal intellectual property protection for the family name. These are:

- Trade mark registration.

---

[9] The authors of the study followed a particular methodology in arriving at their classification of family business corporate brand strategies in their study. This has only been partially applied for the purposes of the analysis here.
[10] See Clarks' main UK website http://www.clarks.co.uk, accessed 6 September 2016.
[11] See JCB main UK website http://www.jcb.co.uk, accessed 6 September 2016.
[12] With the obvious exception that founder's name has been retained. This of course pre-supposes that Dyson's can be seen as a family business. See the discussion on this point in chapter 1.
[13] See JCB main UK website http://www.dyson.co.uk, accessed 6 September 2016.

- Unregistered trade marks or passing off at common law.

There are likely to be occasions when the family business will need to enforce these rights against third parties, in order to avoid damage to the family business' reputation and goodwill. For example, a dissenting family member may set up a competing business, using his own identical family surname, or an unconnected individual with the same surname may set up a similar business under their own name.

But before taking any action the original family business must establish that they have protectable rights. Considering each of the above in turn.

9.3.1 Trade mark registration

The family business may acquire formal registered intellectual property rights by registering the family name as a trade mark.

Prior to 2005, it was not easy to register a common surname as a trade mark in the UK. Surnames were subject to special examination requirements under which common surnames were invariably found to lack distinctiveness under s 3(1)(b) of the Trade Marks Act 1994, and therefore failed to fulfil the essential function of a trade mark: to distinguish the goods and services of one undertaking from those of another.[14]

Following the ruling of the ECJ in *Nichols*[15] (concerning an application by the family business, Nichols plc, to register the surname 'Nichols' as a trade mark in the UK), surnames and other personal names are no longer subject to special examination requirements: they are examined in the same way as any other mark.

Before applying to register a surname as a trade mark, consideration should be given to any secondary meanings which could jeopardise the success of the application. For example, an application to register the surname 'Walker' in relation to goods such as walking sticks is likely to attract an objection as either lacking distinctiveness or being descriptive of the relevant goods under s 3(1)(b) and (c) of the Trade Marks Act 1994. Similarly, an application to register the surname 'Sparks' in relation to electrical services is likely to attract an objection under s 3(1)(c) and (d) (use consistent with established trade practice) of the Trade Marks Act 1994.

Personal names are still subject to special examination requirements in some other jurisdictions, and so specialist advice should be sought before seeking international trade mark protection for a surname.

9.3.2 Passing off

By using the family surname as the name of the family business, the business will accrue unregistered trade mark rights in the family surname.

In order to establish a cause of action under the tort of passing off, a claimant must prove the following three elements:[16]

---

[14] Trade Marks Act 1994, s 1(1).
[15] *Nicholls v Registrar of Trade Marks* [2005] RPC 12.
[16] *Reckitt & Colman Products Limited v Borden Inc* [1990] RPC 341, 406.

- **Goodwill** or reputation attached to the goods or services.[17] Goodwill has a geographic element. The goodwill or reputation must extend to the area where the competing goods or services are being sold. So Clarks would have little difficulty in preventing a rival shoe shop using the name throughout the UK.[18] Smaller and more locally based businesses would only be able to police the use of their family name in the area they operate;
- A **misrepresentation** by the defendant to the public (whether or not intentional) leading (or likely to lead) the public to believe that the goods or services offered by him are the goods or services of the claimant; and
- **Damage** to the claimant, by reason of the erroneous belief engendered by the defendant's misrepresentation that the source of the defendant's goods or services is the same as the source of those offered by the claimant. As quantifying damage might be difficult an injunction will often be the remedy sought.

9.4 WHOSE NAME IS IT ANYWAY?

The family business world has many examples of family schisms where, following a family dispute, one family member or branch have gone off to found a competing business.[19] To what extent can the family member concerned use the family name in the breakaway enterprise? This question needs to be answered in relation to both forms of business name protection.

9.4.1 Own names and passing off

First the situation where there are no registered trade marks, so the original family business will need to rely on passing off. This is more likely to be the situation where most smaller family businesses are concerned.

There is an 'own name' defence to passing off. This was established by a case in 1924 where Romer J explained that:[20]

> 'It is the law of this land that no man is entitled to carry on his business in such a way as to represent that it is the business of another, or is in any way connected with the business of another; that is the first proposition. The second proposition is, that no man is entitled so to describe or mark his goods as to represent that the goods are the goods of another. To the first proposition there is, I myself think, an exception: a man, in my opinion, is entitled to carry on his business in his own name so long as he does not do anything more than that to cause confusion with the business of another, and so long as he does it honestly.'

The two conditions described by Romer J mean that the defence can only apply in the narrowest of circumstances.

---

[17] The requirement to show goodwill does not apply in the case of breaches of a registered trade mark.
[18] In practice Clarks would not need to rely on common law passing off in any event. The company has a significant number of registered trade marks.
[19] One of the best known examples is that of Adolf (Adi) Dassler and his brother Rudolph (Rudi), where, following a split Rudi left to found Puma sports shoes, which has competed in the same town as the original family business Adidas since 1948. The story is told in Gordon and Nicholson *Family Wars* (Kogan Page, 2008).
[20] *Joseph Rodgers & Sons Limited v W N Rodgers & Co* (1924) 41 RPC 277, 291.

The first condition (that the defendant must do nothing to cause confusion beyond simply using his own name), is demonstrated in the analysis of the more recent case below.

Case analysis: Sir Robert McAlpine Limited v Alfred McAlpine plc[21]

The claimant and defendant are both well-known construction companies.

The McAlpine family construction business was set up in 1869 by Robert McAlpine (later Sir Robert McAlpine). The business grew and over time the running of the business was passed to the founder's three sons: Alfred, William and Malcolm. In 1935, the brothers agreed to split the business in two and agreed distinct trading territories in the UK for each business. The two businesses were sensitive to the need to distinguish each from the other, and agreed that the forenames 'Robert' and 'Alfred' should always be used in company and trading names in conjunction with the surname 'McAlpine'.

The two businesses coexisted relatively peacefully until 2003 when Alfred McAlpine plc dropped the name 'Alfred' and rebranded itself as 'McAlpine' – using a logo containing only the word 'McAlpine' on its letterhead, signs and vehicles, and changing its domain name from alfred-mcalpineplc.com to mcalpineplc.com. Sir Robert McAlpine Limited commenced passing off proceedings, seeking an injunction to prohibit Alfred McAlpine plc from using the name 'McAlpine' without any other distinguishing feature such as the name 'Alfred'.

The court held that Alfred McAlpine plc's activities amounted to passing off and granted the injunction. Although the two businesses jointly owned the goodwill in the name 'McAlpine', neither was entitled to monopolise it by adopting the jointly owned name as its principal identifier, thereby misrepresenting that it was in fact the sole owner of the goodwill in the McAlpine surname.

The court noted that although both businesses were successful and that each had a good reputation, circumstances could change and the lack of distinguishing marks between the businesses meant that any negative publicity for the rebranded Alfred McAlpine plc carried a real risk of damaging the goodwill of Sir Robert McAlpine Limited.

Although the 'own name' defence was not pleaded in the McAlpine case (as it revolved around the establishment of goodwill and whether Alfred McAlpine plc's actions amounted to a misrepresentation), it could not have provided a defence because Alfred McAlpine plc had done more than simply use its own name. Had Alfred McAlpine plc continued using 'Alfred' as a distinguisher, there would have been no passing off.

It is noteworthy that the businesses have now registered the names 'Alfred McAlpine' and 'Sir Robert McAlpine' as trade marks.

Romer J's second condition, honest use, is equally difficult to satisfy. Although the defence was established in 1924, Jacob LJ commented in 2004 that:[22]

> 'The Judge rightly observed that the passing off defence is narrow. Actually, no case comes to mind in which it has succeeded. Because the test is honesty, I do not see how any man who is in fact causing deception and knows that to be so can possibly have a defence to passing off.'

---

[21] *Sir Robert McAlpine Limited v Alfred McAlpine plc* [2004] EWHC 630 (Ch).
[22] *Reed Executive plc v Reed Business Information Limited* [2004] EWCA Civ 159.

In addition to the conditions set out by Romer J, subsequent judicial consideration has further eroded the scope of the own name defence in passing off. The defence does not apply to the use of a trader's own name on goods,[23] nor to the sale of goods under a trader's own name.[24] Equally, academics have argued that that the defence cannot apply to the supply of services under a trader's own name.[25] As such, it appears that the defence can only apply where a trader uses his own name as a company or trading name in such a manner that the name is not visible to the public. If this argument is correct the own name defence would appear to be all but extinct for all practical purposes.

The rationale for this judicial erosion of the already narrow-scoped defence was explained by Jacob LJ:[26]

> '... the "own-name" defence is indeed very limited. This makes sense – people are free to choose and use other names to trade under.'

It indeed makes sense, particularly when it is common for a business to trade under a name entirely distinct from that of its founder or proprietor.

9.4.2 Own names and trade mark infringement

A registered trade mark is infringed where it is used, without the proprietor's consent, in any of the four situations outlined in s 10 of the Trade Marks Act 1994:

> (1) A person infringes a registered trade mark if he uses in the course of trade a sign which is identical with the trade mark in relation to goods or services which are identical with those for which it is registered.
>
> (2) A person infringes a registered trade mark if he uses in the course of trade a sign where because –
>
> > (a) the sign is identical with the trade mark and is used in relation to goods or services similar to those for which the trade mark is registered, or
> > (b) the sign is similar to the trade mark and is used in relation to goods or services identical with or similar to those for which the trade mark is registered,
>
> there exists a likelihood of confusion on the part of the public, which includes the likelihood of association with the trade mark.
>
> (3) A person infringes a registered trade mark if he uses in the course of trade in relation to goods or services a sign which is identical with or similar to the trade mark, where the trade mark has a reputation in the United Kingdom and the use of the sign, being without due cause, takes unfair advantage of, or is detrimental to, the distinctive character or the repute of the trade mark.

The threats provisions set out in s 21 of the Trade Marks Act 1994 should be considered before any action is taken to enforce a registered trade mark.[27]

---

[23] *Wright, Layman & Umney v Wright* (1946) RPC 149.
[24] *Parker-Knoll Limited v Knoll International Limited* [1962] RPC 265.
[25] Mellor et al *Kerly's Law of Trade Marks and Trade Names* (Sweet & Maxwell, 15th edn, 2011) at p 683.
[26] *I N Newman Limited v Richard T Adlem* [2005] EWCA Civ 741, 274.
[27] Under that section a person making groundless threats of infringement proceedings could be liable to pay damages to the other party. For that reason, if the infringement claim is weak preliminary correspondence tends to be fairly guarded, often confined to 'drawing the attention' of the other party to relevant trade-marks and expressing concern over relevant aspects of the other third party's trading practices.

There is also an own name defence in relation to registered trade marks is set out in s 11(2) of the Trade Marks Act 1994:

> A registered trade mark is not infringed by –
>
> (a) the use by a person of his own name or address.
>
> ... provided the use is in accordance with honest practices in industrial or commercial matters.

The first condition has been interpreted widely, and the 'own name' of 'a person' has been held to include:

- the name on a natural person's birth certificate;
- the name by which a natural person is known;[28]
- the names of corporate entities;[29] and
- trading names.[30]

9.4.3 Honesty

However the second condition, honesty, narrows the scope of the defence.

The honest practices requirement is an objective test[31] and therefore the subjective honesty of the defendant in trade mark infringement proceedings is of no consequence. A competing family member will often feel entirely justified in re-using their 'own' name. They may believe that their business embodies the true faith of the family legacy. They could believe that those now using the family name, whether family members, or third party purchasers, have betrayed that legacy and that the family name is being tarnished by the activities of the original business. The point in demonstrated in the case analysis below.

> *Case analysis: Asprey & Garrard Limited v WRA (Guns) Limited and Asprey*[32]
>
> The Asprey family had traded in luxury goods (including jewellery and firearms) under the surname 'Asprey' for over two centuries. In 1995 the business was sold outside of the Asprey family, although members of the Asprey family remained employed in the business following the sale. They included William Asprey who managed the gun room. The claimant obtained a number of trade mark registrations including the name 'Asprey' for a range of goods including firearms in class 13 and jewellery in class 14.
>
> In 1999, William Asprey left the business and started his own retail business, selling luxury goods, including jewellery and firearms, under the name 'William R Asprey, Esq'. In a press release issued prior to the opening, the defendant made the following claims:
>
>> 'William R Asprey, Esq. was established in 1999 by William Asprey, 7th generation of the renowned Asprey family who established their first luxury business in 1781. Continuing his family tradition, William Asprey is now opening a new luxury goods store in Mayfair.'

---

[28] *Mercury Communications Limited v Mercury Interactive (UK) Limited* [1995] FSR 850 at p 861.
[29] *Anheuser-Busch Inc v Budejovicky Budvar Narodni Poidnik* (C-245-02) [2005] ETMR 27, 77–80.
[30] *Anheuser-Busch Inc. v Budejovicky Budvar Narodni Poidnik* (C-245-02) [2005] ETMR 27, 81; *Hotel Cipriani SRL v Cipriani (Grosvenor Street) Limited* [2010] EWCA Civ 110, [2010] RPC 16, 72.
[31] *Reed Executive plc v Reed Business Information Limited* [2004] EWCA Civ 159, 131–132.
[32] *Asprey & Garrard Limited v WRA (Guns) Limited and Asprey* [2002] ETMR 47.

Following pre-action correspondence in which the defendant refused to cease using the name 'Asprey', the claimant commenced proceedings for trade mark infringement and passing off. The Court of Appeal held that the defendant's use amounted to trade mark infringement and passing off, and granted an injunction restraining the defendant's use of the name 'Asprey'. In relation to the own name defence to trade mark infringement, Gibson LJ commented:

> 'However honest his subjective intentions may be, any use of his own name which amounts to passing off cannot be in accordance with honest practices in industrial or commercial matters.'[33]

The Court of Justice of the European Union has commented that the honest practices requirement embodies 'a duty to act fairly in relation to the legitimate interests of the trade mark proprietor'.[34]

9.4.4 Informality, complexity and honesty

It is difficult to see how the test of honesty could be satisfied where the use of the family name is by a breakaway faction of dissident family members. However two features of family business life, informality and complexity, are capable of giving rise to circumstances where the overall family brand is damaged by the honest use of the family name in similar or related, if not directly competitive businesses. The *Hotel Cipriani*[35] case provides a good example. There other members of the Cipriani family, having sold the famous and eponymous hotel in Italy, retained a food production business and restaurants operating under the family name in the USA and Europe. The family were prevented from using the Cipriani name to extend their restaurant operations to the UK.

In chapter 1 we talk about the concept of serial business families, the idea that family members engage in a number of separate ventures, rather than one single family business. Often these businesses will be in areas closely related to the original parent business. The underlying ownership of these satellite businesses may well differ. The use of the family name in these related businesses could have been tacitly permitted, or even encouraged by those in control of the main business.

All might be well for many years. However something could occur to disturb this equilibrium. The satellite business might start to trade more directly in competition with the original business. It could encounter product quality issues or financial difficulties, which cause reputational damage to the original business. There might be a wish to sell the main business and the presence of a related business, under different family ownership could prove to be a deterrent to a buyer.

In these circumstances use of the family name is likely to pass the test of honesty, that is 'use is in accordance with honest practices in industrial or commercial matters'.[36] Absent agreement between the two groups of family members concerned,[37] there would be little the owners of the original family business could do to prevent commercial or reputational damage caused by the satellite business.

---

[33] *Asprey & Garrard Limited v WRA (Guns) Limited and Asprey* [2002] ETMR 47, 49.
[34] *BMW v Deenik* [1999] ECR I-905, 61-62; *Gerolsteiner Brunnen v Putsch* C-100/02, [2004] RPC 39, 24; *Gillette v La-Laboratories* C-228/03 [2005] ETMR 67, 41.
[35] *Hotel Cipriani SRL v Cipriani (Grosvenor Street) Limited* [2010] EWCA Civ 110.
[36] Other defences or arguments could well be available to the satellite family business including consent, if the original business retrospectively sought to prevent the use of the name.
[37] Which of course remains a possibility whilst overall family relationships remain strong.

The answer to this difficulty? For those in control of the original business to pay as much attention to the use by the satellite of the family business branding[38] as if the same were being used by totally unconnected third parties. This could be achieved through a mixture of trade mark registrations and licencing agreements. This is essentially what happened on the original partition of the McAlpine business, as referred to above. It is also a matter of good governance.[39]

9.5 FAMILY NAME FOR SALE?

Upon the sale of a business, it is usual for the seller to give restrictive covenants preventing him from competing for a specified period.

It is also common for those covenants to also prevent the sellers re-using the business name in a competing business.[40] This is irrespective of whether or not the business sold uses the seller's family name. On occasions the covenant against re-use of the business name will be for the same duration as the main non-compete covenants. On other occasions (and we would suggest that this is the more usual practice) the re-use of name covenant will be absolute and indefinite.

It is also fairly common for some of the selling business family to become disillusioned with the sale.[41] On occasions they will to try to re-enter the market in competition with the original family business, often now in corporate hands. They may wish to leverage the strength and legacy of the family name to do so.

Generally, to be enforceable, restrictive covenants need to be justified as reasonable, in terms of policing a protectable interest, their scope and duration.[42] The courts have adopted an increasingly restrictive view of what will be enforceable.

How will the courts approach these situations where the family are re-using the family name? The short answer is with little sympathy for the competing family member. Rather than looking at the matter from the narrow perspective of the enforceability of restrictive covenants, the courts should be persuaded to apply the broader principles of passing off referred to above.

Even in the absence of a specific covenant against re-use of the family name as a business name by the sellers or after the term of any restrictive covenant has expired, the seller can be prevented from using his own name in competition. This is illustrated in the following case analysis.

---

[38]   Through the use and policing of trade mark registrations, trade mark licences and otherwise.
[39]   Similar considerations apply to informal family arrangements for the use of real estate property and are discussed in chapter 10.
[40]   Restrictions on the sale of a family business are discussed in more detail in chapter 12.
[41]   This appears to be what happened in the *Asprey* case.
[42]   This proposition dates back to the House of Lords decision in *Nordenfelt v Maxim Nordenfelt Guns and Ammunition Co Ltd* [1894] AC 635 and confirmed in more recent cases such as *RDF Media Group plc v Clements* [2007] EWHC 2892 (QB).

Case analysis: I.N. Newman Limited v Richard T Adlem[43]

In 1965, Mr Adlem began using the name 'Richard T Adlem' in connection with his business as a funeral director. In 1993, Mr Adlem sold the business and its goodwill and agreed to a restrictive covenant preventing him from competing with the business, within a ten mile radius, for a period of 5 years.

The purchaser continued the business under the name 'Richard T Adlem Funeral Directors'.

In 2000, the business (including its goodwill and the right to use the name 'Richard T Adlem') was sold to the claimant, I.N. Newman Limited. The claimant continued to use the name 'Richard T Adlem'.

In 2001, Mr Adlem recommenced trading as a funeral director under the name 'Richard T Adlem'. Mr Adlem advertised his business as 'the original Richard T Adlem', claiming that it had been established in 1965 and that the claimant had no right to use the name 'Richard T Adlem'.

The claimant commenced proceedings against Mr Adlem for passing off. The claimant sought an injunction to restrain Mr Adlem from trading as a funeral director under his own name. The Court of Appeal granted the injunction, finding that Mr Adlem's actions constituted passing off. In relation to the own name defence argued by Mr Adlem, the court held that Mr Adlem's advertising completely misrepresented the position so that 'There is no room for an own-name defence here'.[44]

It should be noted that even after the restrictive covenant had expired, Mr Adlem was not entitled to use his own name in competition with the business he had sold. Jacob L.J. commented that Mr Adlem '... had no more right to use his name for a competing business than if he had been a complete stranger with the same name starting for the first time'.[45]

When acting on the sale of a family business, the family should be given specific advice on this point. As suggested in chapter 12, it is not unusual for parts of the business owning family to be against a sale from the outset, or to become disenchanted with the way a corporate buyer has treated the legacy of the family business afterwards. The response can be to attempt to re-establish the 'real family business' and use the legacy of the family name to do so. This appears to have been a factor in both the Asprey and Adlem cases. A family business name can have real and significant value as intellectual property. Once sold, in broad terms, it is lost to the whole family forever.

9.6 CONCLUSION

A family business brand, can have significant, although intangible value.[46] The core, but not the sole, component of this is the name of the business owning family, when used as part of the overall brand.

---

[43] *I N Newman Limited v Richard T Adlem* [2005] EWCA Civ 741.
[44] *I N Newman Limited v Richard T Adlem* [2005] EWCA Civ 741 at para 47.
[45] *I N Newman Limited v Richard T Adlem* [2005] EWCA (Civ) 741 at para 31.
[46] The valuation and taxation of intellectual property and intangible assets are specialist subjects and beyond the scope of this book.

It therefore follows that protection of the family name should be seen as an important part of family business governance. This has both internal and external elements. Assuming that the external corporate identity of the family enterprise includes quality and customer service, the internal operations must be capable of delivering this brand congruence. On the basis that the business is potentially vulnerable to the activities of more remote outsider family members, all efforts must be made to keep the whole business owning family aligned and for any peripheral business activities undertaken by family members to be carefully controlled and monitored.

In broad terms, once the family name becomes associated with the family enterprise, the name is lost to individual family members (at least for use in competing or similar enterprises).[47] This provides further justification for maintaining family cohesion and for investing time and effort in the governance processes described in chapter 17 in order to do so.

---

[47] The most recent case to underline this point involved the fashion designer Karen Millen – see *Millen v Karen Millen Fashions Limited and Mosaic Fashions US Limited* [2016] EWHC 2104 (Ch).

CHAPTER 10

PROPERTY AND THE FAMILY FIRM

10.1 OVERVIEW

Property or real estate issues can sometimes be amongst the most complex for business owning families. Property is often a key asset of family businesses. Property ownership can be subject to a number of intertwining interests. Financially, family business property can be an important capital asset and can generate rental income for the business. Operationally, it can be used to accommodate the family business. The property can also be a home for some or all of the family members. Family members may have powerful emotional ties to land and property assets.

Inevitably tax issues associated with the ownership of major capital assets need to be taken into consideration. Property ownership can have substantial tax implications for the family business. It is important to ensure that the family members have obtained suitable tax advice and addressed these issues.[1]

But potentially the most difficult issues for a family business arise from the combination of complexity of property law and the informal treatment of property issues within the family business system. When all is well in the family, this complexity and the underlying technical issues remain buried within the overall system. But they are capable of surfacing with a vengeance when the family system comes under strain.

Sometimes this stems from the importance of property assets to the family business. Property can be the key asset of many businesses. In some cases, it is, in effect, the business. For example in the farming or hotel industries it is almost impossible to separate the family business from the underlying freehold assets.[2] A dispute about the business then becomes a dispute about land and *vice versa*.

Even where it is possible to separate land from the underlying family business, property issues are likely to be a significant factor in many family businesses. The inherent conservatism and financial prudence of family businesses noted above in chapter 1 means that family businesses are more likely to own their main operating premises and to have acquired surplus investment properties.[3]

---

[1] Which are mainly considered in chapter 16.
[2] See for example *Ham v Ham* (discussed in detail in chapter 13). But that is not to say that interests in the property cannot be split. This is discussed in detail below.
[3] For example although the original core family business in Cadman Developments was that of a building firm, the family company acquired a significant portfolio of investment properties and by the time the matter came to court this investment portfolio was the main business activity of the family company.

On other occasions problems stem from the complexities of property law, and the dynamic created, when different stakeholders within the family business system hold different interests in the same property asset. Property can simultaneously represent different things to different members of the business owning family. Property has surfaced at various stages in this book, and in different guises, often in the same family business case. For example in:

- *Saul D Harrison*[4] as the operating base of the family company, as a key business asset and as a significant part of the wider family wealth and inheritance.
- *Ham v Ham*[5] as the business itself, a home to the senior generation, the fruits of the career of the next generation insider, the primary asset of the wider family and a significant emotional symbol to all concerned.
- *Harrison Properties*[6] as an investment asset with development potential.

Property issues can therefore feature right across all three dimensions of the family business system, business, family and ownership.[7] Many difficulties stem from the tension between this complexity and the informality with which business owning families often approach property issues.

10.2 PROPERTY INSIDE OR OUTSIDE THE FAMILY BUSINESS

The key property related question for business owning families to consider is whether property assets should be owned by the main operating company, or by one, or a group of family members?[8] There are advantages and disadvantages to ownership by a family company and outside of the company.

As far as ownership inside a company is concerned the issues are:

- The property may be exposed to the financial failure of the trading business.
- Commercially it will create a stronger balance sheet for the company. From a lender's perspective both trading cash flows and other non-property assets are likely to be available to support borrowing, so company ownership is likely to be a lender's preferred solution.
- Any gain on the disposal of the property can be rolled over against the cost of replacement premises for CGT purposes.
- As the company tax rate is likely to be lower than the income tax rate for the individual, the cash flow from post tax income to repay the capital element of any borrowings will be greater and so the debt can be repaid quicker.
- Any gain on the property will effectively qualify for entrepreneur's relief, if the shares in the company are sold.
- The property will effectively qualify for 100% business property relief for Inheritance tax purposes, rather than perhaps only 50% if it was owned personally.

---

[4] See chapters 20 and 21.
[5] See chapter 13.
[6] Discussed in chapter 8.
[7] See also the discussion about the significance of the farmhouse in the James Davies case at 19.4.6.
[8] Hybrid solutions are available and are discussed below.

- There would be a double tax charge if the property were sold at a gain and it was decided to distribute the proceeds to shareholders, as the company would pay tax on the gain, and the individuals would pay tax on the amounts they receive.

If alternatively the property is owned personally the issues are:

- The property is protected from the financial failure of the trading business.
- Any gain on the disposal of the property can be rolled over, either under the reinvestment provisions where shares are subscribed for in a trading company, or in the acquisition of qualifying assets for use in the same company provided it is the individual's 'personal company' (one in which the individual has at least 5% of the voting rights).
- There will be less post tax income to repay the capital on any borrowings to acquire the property, compared with the company ownership position. Any shortfall on loan repayments as against rent received will need to be funded personally.
- Paying rent to the property owner will be a way of extracting income from the company without any national insurance cost. The rent can be used to repay any borrowings for the acquisition. Income tax will be payable on rent received but relevant expenses such as insurance, repairs and interest on loans can be offset.
- Paying rent on the property could also be a means of providing income to the retired generation or to other non-working family outsiders.
- If a commercial rent is paid for the use of the property entrepreneur's relief will not be available on the sale of the property. There will be some relief if the rent paid is lower than the commercial rate, and full relief could be due if no rent has ever been paid.
- When the property is sold, the proceeds go directly to the owner and there is no double tax charge.
- Business property relief of perhaps only 50% may be available for inheritance tax. This rate is only available if the owner has a controlling shareholding in the company that uses the property. In determining whether a controlling shareholding exists it is possible to take into account shares held by a spouse.
- Hybrid ownership solutions can be created if the property is held separately so there is greater flexibility for the business owning family.

There are some broadly neutral factors. For example interest on borrowings can be offset against either corporation tax or individual income tax, capital allowances and roll-over relief on sale can be claimed in either case. Whether it is appropriate to hold the property personally or through the company will depend on the family's personal circumstances, and views on the above issues.

Exactly how 'personal' ownership is structured is also another question. We have used the term to denote separate ownership outside the main trading company, but there are various alternatives to personal ownership by member of the business owning family. The chosen structure might be largely tax driven, although there are other factors to consider.

Commonly used property ownership structures include:

- **Holding companies.** Here the valuable property is held in a group holding company, which also owns all (or most) of the shares in the family operating company. This provides a degree of insulation against commercial risk and business failure.[9]
- **Associated companies and LLP's.** Here the property is also held in a corporate structure, but this time at arm's length from the operating business. The reason will often be to separate the trading and operating businesses from property ownership. In effect this creates a hybrid ownership structure.

Op-Co/Prop-Co structures are considered in the next paragraph. Tax is likely to loom large for any business owning family considering how to deal with acquiring or changing the ownership of property connected to a family business. Such property may well have a significant capital value so any tax triggered may be material. Secondly, and in the broadest terms, the UK tax regime is less helpful in its treatment of family property than it is over shares or trading assets used in connection with the family company.[10] But a business owning family needs to consider wider ownership issues alongside tax. Where the tax position is marginal these might tip the balance. Even if tax considerations point in one direction the business owning family need to 'price' these non-tax issues into their property ownership decisions.

10.3 PROPERTY AND HYBRID OWNERSHIP SOLUTIONS

In chapter 15 we highlight one of the key difficulties in succession planning, that of determining an ownership approach that reconciles the competing interests of the family insiders working in the business and the remaining family members, the outsiders who are not working in the business but whom the senior generation might want to share in the wealth represented by the family business.

Property based ownership structures are potentially capable of creating a bridge between the business first, insider fairness approach and the family equality argument.

If a family business owns its own freehold operating premises it might be possible to create an ownership structure whereby the operating business (Op-Co) is separated from the property, which then sits in a separate company (Prop-Co). The insiders would take ownership of all (or at least most of) Op-Co. Prop-Co would be in wider family ownership, possibly also including the insiders, possibly not.

The exact proportions of ownership of Prop-Co is likely to depend on two key factors. First the extent of purely personal assets outside the family business system, together with how these are allocated between insiders and outsiders. Secondly the ownership philosophy of the business owning family. If this philosophy is based on insider ownership and there are few free assets then the insiders are likely to receive not only ownership of Op-Co but also a large share of Prop-Co. Conversely the ownership philosophy may lean towards equal family ownership but there might be few free assets to achieve this. In which case the ownership of Prop-Co is likely to be skewed toward the outsiders.

---

[9] Although banks and perhaps key suppliers are likely to require property backed security as a condition of providing facilities, which will erode the level of protection.
[10] See chapter 16 for a general explanation of tax and family business ownership issues.

Key issues will be:
- Commercial terms.
- Family dynamics.
- Risk proofing.
- Emotional attachment.

The link between Op-Co and Prop-Co will be a commercial lease. Op-Co and the insiders will become the tenants of Prop-Co and the outsiders. There might be concern about future family dynamics between the insiders and the outsiders. If so the relatively static and simple landlord and tenant relationship might prove easier to regulate than that of co-owners of a fluid and evolving operating business.

Of course close attention will still need to be paid to the terms of the lease between Op-Co and Prop-Co. Rent will obviously be key. If the rent is too high this creates pressure on the insiders and the family firm. Conversely if the rent is too low, the potential for resentment by the outsiders becomes obvious. However, within broad parameters, market rents should be ascertainable. Certainly market rents should be less subject to debate than valuations of trading businesses, as data from recent transactions involving similar properties is usually readily available.

Possibly the business cannot easily afford to pay a market rent. In which case the business owning family need to address the question of why the business should continue? This might be for emotional reasons. Alternatively, as in *Saul D Harrison*, the family might be optimistic that the business can be turned round in the hands of the next generation. In which case perhaps some form of rent-free or reduced rent period would be appropriate, in terms of a family ownership solution, even if this could not be fully justified on the basis of the commercial rental market.

It might be appropriate to include other departures from 'institutional leases' typically entered into between landlord and tenant or additional arrangements between the wider family, as property owners. For example should the insiders have rights of first refusal if the outsiders wish to sell their interest in the freehold? Should either insiders or outsiders be able to force a sale of the property even if they own a minority of Prop-Co? Perhaps concessionary rents were agreed on the basis that Op-Co continued to provide significant employment in the area. If the family business relocated elsewhere should the concessionary rent be reviewed?

In summary Prop-Co will operate as a separate and parallel family business within the wider family business system. Identical governance questions, issues and solutions, including the use of shareholders' agreements and family councils considered in chapter 17 may apply to Prop-Co. The greater the involvement of insiders in Prop-Co and the further the arrangements between Op-Co and Prop-Co are from arm's length commercial property dealings the more that this will be the case.

10.4 PARALLEL INTERESTS

It can be seen from the above that property in a family business setting can be subject to a number of parallel intertwining interests between family members. So far we have assumed that the interplay between those interests has been carefully thought through and fully documented. In practice this is most unlikely to be the case.

The implications of these intertwining interests can include the following:

- One property can sometimes be used by more than one family business or occupied by more than one household. For example, a second-generation family business may operate from a property that separately houses the founders and their children, some of whom now own and manage the business. The farming and leisure industries provide many examples.
- The distinctions between personal and business use can be blurred. Meetings might be held around the kitchen table, or family members might use the business premises for personal purposes, including peripheral businesses.
- Occupational and ownership arrangements are often developed ad-hoc to suit the needs of the family, rather than being formally documented. Whilst this flexibility can be a strength, in that it encourages full exploitation of available property assets, it can also lead to uncertainties regarding rights of ownership and occupation.
- Contributions to improvements, capital works or to payments of capital or interest on borrowings by one family member, often in occupation of land, the legal title to which is held by the family company or in the names of other family members.
- Informal rights of way and other easements.
- The family business and individual family members can each be tenant or landlord or both. The property can be subject to business or residential tenancies which may be written or unwritten. Identifying the nature of any leases is essential to correctly advise on security of tenure, succession rights, rental obligations and responsibility for the condition of the property.

Farming and diversified rural business are particularly prone to most of the above issues but the issues are by no means confined to such businesses.

A first governance step, when dealing with family business property is therefore to identify all relevant interests in the property. This is essential if the land or business is being sold, or divided between family members. This process will assist the family business in dealing with it appropriately, in terms of maintaining the property, collecting any payments and obtaining possession when appropriate or necessary. The complexity of the interests is also a potential source of disputes between family members.

10.5 INFORMALITY AND FAMILY BUSINESS PROPERTY ISSUES

When advising family businesses, it is common to encounter land that has not been sold for many years, because it was inherited by the current owners. Difficulties can arise where family business property has been passed from generation to generation without having been sold. Again this is particularly common with farming businesses.

Family businesses are less likely to borrow than their non-family counterparts. As a result the regular review of title and other property matters that occurs as part and parcel of third party sales or borrowing is less likely to happen in family property situations. A property sale or secured borrowing brings scrutiny, and the absence of this can often mean that title defects and other issues go unnoticed. These issues can then cause problems when the property is sold or re-financed or if a dispute arises within the family business. Neglect of these issues could reduce the value of the property, and lead to further avoidable expense in the longer term.

A further consequence is that property in family businesses is more likely to be unregistered. Familiarity with dealing with unregistered property is key. Clients owning unregistered land should be encouraged to register it voluntarily, as this should reduce the risk of fraud and gives greater protection against adverse possession claims. It is also likely to simplify any future transactions involving the land.

Over time, the use of land changes. Planning permissions may be out of date. For example on a farm retail operations may have grown gradually from the sale of a few eggs many years ago to the position where the farm shop dominates the farming operation but the requisite change of use consents might not have been obtained.

Legal documents may no longer reflect the position on the ground, boundaries may have moved, footpaths may have been re-routed or land outside the title may be used for storage or parking. Rights of way might be informal and undocumented. If a property has not been sold for many years, issues like these are more likely to have gone unnoticed. For example, a business may have no formal right of access to its land, and individuals may need to cross another site to reach it. This may have been going on for years without any problem. However, if the issue is not identified before the sale process, the most likely solution would be an expensive insurance policy. If the issue had been identified earlier, it could well have been possible to gather information and implement a cheaper solution, such as the registration of the relevant right.

Issues such as these are not unique to family businesses. However, they are more likely to lurk unnoticed and unidentified where land has been in the same ownership for several generations and there has been no review of the legal title. Practitioners should therefore encourage family businesses to invest time in reviewing their title to their land. This allows problems to be identified whilst there is time to find solutions.

Ideally, such a review would include:

- Checking the extent of the property. The owners should check that the title boundaries reflect the position on the ground. Who looks after the boundary structures? Is any land occupied which is not within the legal title?
- Who is in occupation of the land? Are relevant rights of occupation suitably documented?
- Consideration of whether to make an application to the Land Registry for first registration of the title.
- An analysis of how the land is used? Are planning consents in place for the current use, and for the buildings on the land?
- Do any third parties use the land, for example for business or recreation? This can be particularly relevant to agricultural land.

If possible, the whole family should be engaged with this process. Very often the older generation of a family will have direct knowledge about the land that is very helpful and could be lost. This information should be gathered and recorded if at all possible. Many title problems will be easier to solve where detailed information can be provided about the background and history. However, this takes time to gather.

In practice few family businesses will be prepared to commit time and cost to what they might see as a bureaucratic and pointless exercise in relation to property that has been in the family for generations. The best realistic hope that such advice will be heeded might be if the family were contemplating a sale or fund-raising using the land as security. In which case they might be persuaded of the benefits of a property pre-sale due diligence exercise.[11]

This still leaves one very significant risk factor exposed. This is that an informal approach to property matters, in particular occupation rights, become the subject matter of a family dispute or that occupation rights become harder to resolve in the context of a wider family dispute. This is more the norm than the exception, so far as family business property arrangements are concerned.

Often one or two members of the family business will be permitted to occupy a space on an 'informal' basis. This often means that there is no paperwork and that over time the parties have agreed various points, but kept no record of what has been agreed. Furthermore, the recollections of the parties will often differ as to what has been agreed.

There is usually no incentive to formalise these arrangements whilst family relationships are working. However, it is much easier to put in place documentation at a stage when the parties are cooperating and points can be agreed. The position becomes much more difficult and will often result in the need for the intervention of the courts or a mediator to deal with the issues if there is a dispute. The advice must be that it is most sensible for both parties for the arrangement to be documented as soon as possible.

If there is a dispute, much of it will revolve around who said what and who promised what, when. This is best avoided. If a family business considering allowing its members into occupation of different spaces, it is most sensible for the arrangement to be fully documented. Ideally both parties should be separately represented in these circumstances. The question of conflicts of interest and separate representation is discussed in more detail in chapter 26.

The only sensible antidote is to treat family property as an integral part of the family business governance system and, in particular, to carefully consider and document the rights of occupation agreed for each family member. This in turn relies on the business owning family accepting the validity of the central message of this book: the wisdom of investing in comprehensive family business governance.

10.6 TYPES OF INTEREST

Before giving detailed property advice to a family business on any particular issue, it is helpful to form an overview of its land interests and superior or derivative interests.

The following example illustrates some of the issues that can arise in relation to family business owned property.

---

[11] Pre-sale vendor due diligence is discussed in more detail in chapter 12 (Selling the Family Business).

Property and the Family Firm 339

Figure 10.1: Complexity of family business property interests

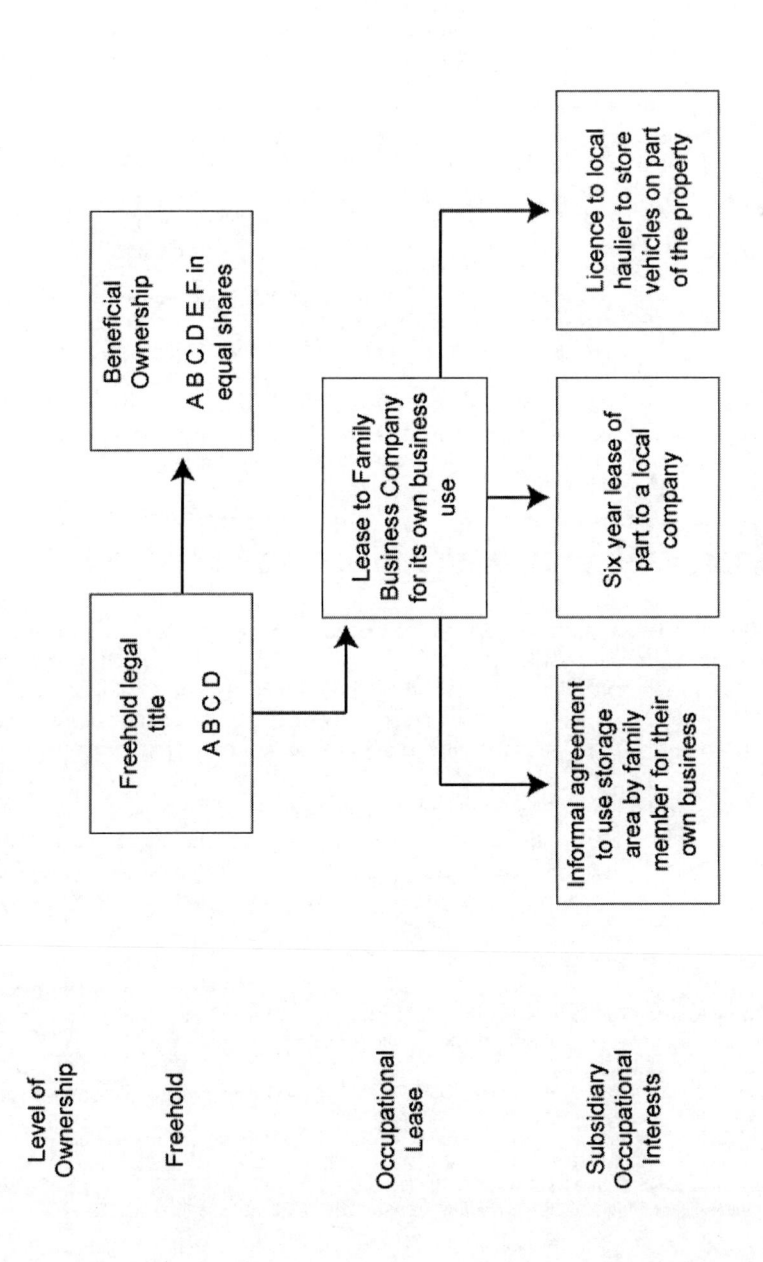

Level of Ownership	
Freehold	Freehold legal title **A B C D** → Beneficial Ownership **A B C D E F in equal shares**
Occupational Lease	Lease to Family Business Company for its own business use
Subsidiary Occupational Interests	Informal agreement to use storage area by family member for their own business • Six year lease of part to a local company • Licence to local haulier to store vehicles on part of the property

It will be noted that the diagram stops short of including rights of way or other easements in the already complex picture.

Example

In the example, a property is subject to the following interests:

- The legal title in the freehold is owned by four family members, who are owners and managers of the family business. There is a separate trust document which records that the beneficial interest in the property is in fact shared equally between six family members.[12]
- The business is an incorporated company and occupies most of the property for use in its operations. This is documented by a business lease, which expired some years previously. The company continues to pay a rent to the individual owners. In these circumstances, there is a danger that the lease would have been drafted solely to create the obligation to pay the rent (perhaps for tax reasons), without further consideration being given to its terms. If the terms of the lease are not appropriate to the wider circumstances of the family or the business, then this should be addressed, particularly if the ownership of the family business changes.
- The business lease is then subject to a series of subsidiary interests as follows:
  - A family member uses a building on the property as a workshop and for storage. There is no written agreement.
  - A six-year lease to a local company to use a lock-up workshop unit on the property for a small manufacturing business.
  - A licence for a local haulier to store vehicles and equipment on the property at weekends.

All of these arrangements exhibit a high degree of informality. Accordingly each is capable of giving rise to uncertainty and difficulty against the pressure of a family dispute or a sale or borrowing transaction.

10.7 LICENCES AND FAMILY BUSINESSES

True licences between parties at arms-length are relatively rare. Many purported licence arrangements in fact meet the criteria for a lease[13] and will be treated by a court as a lease. This can be particularly relevant in the context of the Landlord and Tenant Act 1954, where attempts to avoid giving security of tenure by granting a licence, rather than following the formal contracting-out procedure, are particularly risky[14].

However, in arrangements between family members, it is more likely that a genuine licence can be created. The court will often consider the arrangements in such circumstances to be licences because the arrangement was based on an act of generosity because of the family relationship. In an old case Denning LJ (as he then was) explained that:[15]

> 'in all the cases where an occupier has been held to be a licensee there has been something in the circumstances, such as family arrangement, an act of friendship or generosity, or such like, to negative any intention to create a tenancy.'

---

[12] Please see below for further commentary on the issues that can arise in relation to joint ownership.
[13] See for example *Street v Mountford* [1985] AC 809.
[14] See s 38A Landlord and Tenant Act 1954 and Sch 2 of the Regulatory Reform (Business Tenancies) (England and Wales) Order 2003, SI 2003/3096 and *Mann Aviation Group (Engineering) Ltd (In Administration) v Longmint Aviation Ltd*) [2011] EWHC 2238 (Ch).
[15] See obiter dictum of Denning LJ in *Facchini v Bryson* [1952] 1 TLR 1386 (CA) at 1389.

An act of generosity will counter the assumption that there was an intention to create a legally binding relationship (which is one of the essential ingredients of a lease). However, a family relationship will not always lead to the implication of there having been no intention to create a legally binding relationship. For example, in *Ward v Warnke*[16] a mother and father allowed their daughter and her husband to move into a cottage. The daughter's marriage failed and the daughter moved out, leaving her husband in occupation with one of the four children of their marriage. The daughter and her husband paid for the water, electricity and phone rates and a nominal rent. On the application of the mother for possession of the property, the court found that a tenancy had been created, despite the family relationship, as there was exclusive possession at a weekly rent and an intention to create a legally binding relationship.

It is always important to consider the situation as a whole, as a court will not assume that a family relationship has led to the creation of a licence. The other issues to bear in mind when deciding whether or not a licence or a tenancy has been created will include an analysis of whether:

- exclusive possession has been granted;[17]
- there was capacity to grant a tenancy, although a contractual relationship may still be formed if there is no capacity to grant a tenancy;[18]
- there was an intention to grant a legally binding relationship (eg is rent paid and payable).

The above issues can arise both in the context of commercial and residential premises.

10.8 COMMERCIAL LEASES AND PART II OF THE LANDLORD AND TENANT ACT 1954

10.8.1 Security of tenure

Part II of the Landlord and Tenant Act 1954 contains the main statutory provisions relating to security of tenure and the right to renew business tenancies. This act gives business tenants a statutory right to renew their tenancies, unless the landlord is able to show that certain grounds of possession apply. It is outside the scope of this book to discuss in detail the right to renew or the grounds of opposition.[19] However, the potential application of the Act should be considered whenever there are business occupants on family business property.

Again the point is of primary relevance in the context of family disputes.

10.8.2 Contracting out

The procedure for contracting-out of the security of tenure provisions of the 1954 Act[20] is somewhat bureaucratic. This formal procedure is at odds with the informal nature of

---

[16] [1990] 22 HLR 496.
[17] *Street v Mountford* [1985] AC 809.
[18] *Tower Hamlets London Borough Council v Sherwood* [2002] EWCA Civ 229.
[19] For further reference see Barnes et al *Hill & Redman's Law of Landlord and Tenant* (LexisNexis, 2015).
[20] Under Landlord and Tenant Act 1954, s 38A and Sch 2 of the Regulatory Reform (Business Tenancies) (England and Wales) Order 2003, SI 2003/3096.

many of the occupation arrangements and decision-making processes that can arise in relation to family owned property. This increases the likelihood that business occupants of family property will have security of tenure. The implications of this should be considered carefully.

10.9 AGRICULTURAL HOLDINGS

Similar considerations arise in relation to occupation of agricultural property.[21] Again a detailed consideration of agricultural holdings and security of tenure is beyond the scope of this book.[22]

10.10 RESIDENTIAL LEASES

It is not uncommon for individuals to live on the family business property. This is particularly likely to arise in agricultural businesses, in businesses with an agricultural heritage, such as food processing and in the leisure industries. It is also fairly common, once a family dispute has arisen, for this to extend to rights of occupation of residential property by a family member.[23]

It can be difficult to determine which statutory regime applies to a particular occupant and particular care is required when dealing with residential occupation. Furthermore, residential arrangements can be difficult to terminate. There are many potential pitfalls for lawyers used to dealing mainly with commercial property or with residential conveyancing.

The following is a list of the most common types of tenancy that arise in the family business scenario, given that the family business will be a private sector landlord/property owner. This is intended only as a brief guide to some of the potential issues of which practitioners should be aware. For an analysis of the nature of the rights that can arise, a specialist text should be consulted:

10.10.1 Rent Act tenancies

Until 15 January 1989, most residential tenancies were Rent Act tenancies and regulated by the Rent Act 1977. Rent Act tenancies are subject to rent controls and tenants have security of tenure. On the death of the tenant, the tenancy may be transferred by succession. There are two sets of succession rights. A landlord is only entitled to possession in very limited circumstances. Once a tenant is protected by the Rent Act, the rights will transfer to other properties that the tenant moves to, if the landlord and tenant remain the same.

---

[21] For example in James Davies' case (discussed in detail in chapter 19) an alternative argument, if his claim for proprietary estoppel failed was that he had obtained a protected agricultural holding.
[22] See *Scammell, Densham & Williams' Law of Agricultural Holdings* (LexisNexis, 10th edn, 2015).
[23] The proceedings in the Eirian Davies proprietary estoppel case discussed in detail in chapter 19 started life as a possession action, brought by her parents against Eirian in relation to the farmhouse she occupied.

10.10.2 Assured tenancies

Assured tenancies are regulated by the Housing Act 1988, which came into force on 15 January 1989. There is one set of succession rights. Although the rent can be increased by the landlord if he complies with a set procedure, there is a mechanism to refer the rent for independent assessment. Possession can be obtained if a landlord proves a relevant ground and in some cases, the court will have to exercise its discretion even if the ground can be proven.

10.10.3 Assured shorthold tenancies (ASTs)

ASTs are also governed by the Housing Act 1988 as amended by the Housing Act 1996. Before 28 February 1997, ASTs had to be for a term of not less than 6 months and a s 20 notice confirming that the tenancy was an AST had to be served before the tenancy was entered into. If the paperwork is in order, possession can be claimed, without having to prove a ground, once the term has expired. Since 28 February 1997 most residential tenancies in the private sector will be ASTs and there is no longer a requirement that the term be for at least 6 months and no s 20 notice now needs to be served. It will therefore be easier for the landlord to recover possession of the property.

10.10.4 Service occupancies

Service occupancies can arise frequently in family businesses and it is important to be fully aware of these arrangements. If an employee is in occupation of property belonging to his employer the employee may be a service occupier. This will be the case if either it is essential for the employee to live in the relevant property for him to be able to perform his duties as an employee, or if the contract of employment requires the employee to live in the relevant property and this arrangement enables the employee to better perform his duties as an employee. A service occupancy will end when the relevant employment ends.[24]

If a family member, employed in the family business, lives in a property owned by the business, the possibility of a service occupancy should be considered. For example is the occupier of the house an employee of the family company which is the owner of the freehold? Was the occupier asked to occupy the premises in order to perform his employment duties? Was that obligation set out in his or her contract?[25] If so there may be a service occupancy in place which will terminate with any employment.[26]

However, if the employment ends and the occupation continues, then it is only a matter of time before the court will assume that a new arrangement, possibly with protected rights of occupation, is in place.

10.10.5 Other residential protections

In residential situations, there are a number of statutory provisions that may apply to the arrangements, particularly if the occupant is paying a rent. These are separate from any arrangements that may have been agreed between family members. These may not be

---

[24] See *Ivory v Palmer* [1975] ICR 340.
[25] See *Langley v Appleby (Inspector of Taxes)* [1976] 3 All ER 391, 415.
[26] See *Norris v Checksfield* [1989] 1 WLR 1241.

considered in connection with family owned property, but could prove significant, particularly if there is a falling out between family members.

- **Repairs and services.** Landlords of residential premises can also be responsible under statute for the upkeep of the property and some services.[27] There are also regulations relating to health and safety eg servicing boilers etc. The sanctions for ignoring or simply being unaware of these obligations can be severe.
- **Protection from eviction.** Regardless of their status, residential occupiers benefit from greater protection from eviction than commercial occupiers. Particular care must be taken when considering how to terminate any residential occupancy. It is important to comply with the Protection from Eviction Act 1977 which requires in most circumstances at least four weeks' notice to be given to residential occupiers.[28] Furthermore, the notices must usually be served in a statutory form.

10.11 ESTATE MANAGEMENT (OR PROPERTY GOVERNANCE)

Generally, it may be tempting not to consider estate management in a family business situation. However, there are good reasons why this issue must be kept in mind. If family owned or occupied property is seen as part of the overall family business system, the logic for including property as part of comprehensive governance arrangements becomes inescapable. It will be seen that a considerable number of the family business disputes considered in Part E have property issues at their root.[29]

If the landlord of any property that is subject to a tenancy is a trustee, it will have obligations to the beneficiaries to ensure that it obtains an appropriate income.[30] It is also necessary to keep in mind estate management to ensure that the properties are maintained, repaired and the income is preserved.

Good estate management is also prudent, as a dispute will often involve suggestions that one family member has received more than their fair share of property related benefits, or a family member has been allowed into occupation without paying a full rent.

10.12 OCCUPATION BY AND SHARING WITH THIRD PARTIES

All family members should consider not only the current arrangements in place, but the situation should there be a need to terminate the arrangements. The legal and family position may be quite complicated if property is occupied just by a bloodline family member, but this could be even more so for property occupied by 'in-laws' and 'partners'.[31]

The parties must consider and agree what will happen if others begin to share the property with the family member. It is not at all unusual for family disputes to arise when a son or daughter begins a relationship with an individual who is not liked by the

---

[27] See for example s 11 of the Landlord and Tenant Act 1985.
[28] Section 5(1)(b) of the Protection from Eviction Act 1977.
[29] For example in *Saul D Harrison* (see chapter 21) a central issue in the dispute was whether the proceeds of sale of the original operating premises should be reinvested in new premises or returned to shareholders, *Harrison Properties* and *Bhullar Brothers* (both discussed in chapter 8) together with *Daniels v Daniels* (chapter 23) all concern disputes relating to the exploitation of family property opportunities.
[30] See chapter 14.
[31] See chapter 1 for a discussion on the different approaches to treating in-laws as family members.

parents. Consideration should be given when drafting any lease, residential tenancy or licence arrangement, whether the arrangement is to subsist if others move into the property and also if the family member leaves the premises, leaving behind children, step children partners etc.

Even if in-laws are accepted as family members and given rights of occupation of property during the currency of a relationship with a blood-line family member, it is much less likely that family property owners will be prepared for rights of occupation to continue once that relationship is over.[32] Complications can also arise following the death or illness of the family member concerned. For how long should their partner be allowed to remain in occupation?

If these issues are relevant care needs to be taken over the termination provisions in any lease or licence. Arrangements need to be regularly reviewed, especially if new individuals take up occupancy of the building. It will be necessary to make sure that those new individuals are aware of and agree to the basis upon which they take up occupation.

10.13   JOINT OWNERSHIP WITHIN THE FAMILY BUSINESS

10.13.1   Corporate ownership

It is common for property owned by family businesses to be owned by a family company.

At first sight this may seem to simplify matters for the property lawyer and for the family business. In fact it might complicate matters, as many of the same issues of principle which apply to shared ownership will also be relevant to property owned by a family company and will need to be addressed, either in a shareholders' agreement, joint ownership agreement relating just to property matters or some other governance document.[33] In practice family property issues will call on the interdisciplinary teamwork, as discussed in chapter 26, between corporate and property professionals (to say nothing of tax colleagues).

10.13.2   Individual ownership

However, whether for tax planning or historic reasons, land owned by family businesses will often be owned by a number of individuals. In later generations, the number of beneficial owners can increase, often to an unwieldy number. This can lead to complications.

10.13.3   Legal and beneficial ownership

The owners of the legal estate in property are the persons registered as the owners at the Land Registry (or in the relevant title document, if the property is unregistered). In the simplest situation, the legal owners will also own the whole of the beneficial interest in the property in equal shares.

---

[32] See for example *Ward v Warnke*, op cit.
[33] See chapter 17.

However, the legal and equitable interests can diverge. The maximum number of legal owners is four,[34] but there may be many more individuals with a share in the property, which means some will have only a beneficial interest. In these circumstances a trust of the equitable interest will arise and the beneficiaries have equitable rights in relation to the property. This can either be regulated by an express agreement between the parties or by the applicable law.

10.13.4 Joint tenants and tenants in common

The equitable interest may be that of joint tenants or tenants in common. This can be difficult to establish.[35] The distinction is of course relevant to succession. Where co-owners are joint tenants, if one dies their share will pass automatically to the other joint tenants.

10.13.5 Joint ownership agreements

It should be a priority to ensure that, so far as possible, the legal and beneficial interests in the land are identified and that the relations between the various owners are expressly agreed and documented. In all cases where property has more than one owner, the owners should be advised to consider entering into a joint ownership agreement to regulate the relationship between the co-owners.

Many of the same issues apply to such an agreement as to the negotiation of a shareholders' agreement.[36] When preparing a joint ownership agreement, consideration should be given to the following issues:

- **Legal ownership.** Who will be the legal owners? The maximum number of legal owners is four.[37] If there will be more than four beneficiaries, some thought should be given to the identity of the legal owners. It is often helpful for the legal owners to represent each branch of the family that has a beneficial interest in the property. Similarly if the main operating business has family insiders and outsiders there are strong arguments that, even if they are not directors of the main family company, outsiders should have a role as legal owners of property, essentially as guardians of the family silver.
  The position is not dissimilar to having family branch representatives on company boards or on family councils.
- **Decision making.** How will decisions relating to the land be made? The default position is that the legal owners can enter into any disposition of the land.[38] They are subject to the duties, to obtain the best price etc. as set out above. In practice this will mean that the legal owners will have substantial practical control. If the equitable owners are unhappy with the legal owners' decisions, their remedy will be limited to a potentially difficult and expensive damages claim for breach of trust.

---

[34] Section 34(2) LPA 1925 and s 34(3) Trustee Act 1925.
[35] See *Pettitt v Pettitt* [1970] AC 777.
[36] See chapter 17.
[37] LPA 1925, s 34.
[38] TLATA, s 6(1).

- **Restricted transactions.** On other occasions, where the group of beneficial owners is not too large and unwieldy, it might be appropriate to allow the legal owners to manage the property on a day-to-day basis but to ensure that the beneficial owners are involved in more major decisions.

    For example joint ownership agreements could restrict the ability of the legal owners to enter into transactions (or a particular class of transactions, for example freehold sales or leases of more than, say, 10 years) without the consent of the beneficial owners. This can be enforced by the registration of a restriction at the Land Registry (see below).

- **Sales of interests.** Will the owners be allowed to transfer their shares in the property to third parties? The default position is that shares in the equitable interest of land are assignable to third parties. Family members may be reluctant to allow this or may only be willing to permit transfers to other family members.

Will the owners be able to sell their shares? The provision of viable exit rights is recommended best family business practice. However there may not be a market for an individual's share in the land. The owners should at least consider granting mutual rights of pre-emption. There are various well-known methods for agreeing the value in these circumstances.

If the owners wish to ensure that they can withdraw from the arrangement altogether then they may need to include in the agreement a right to trigger a sale on the open market.[39]

10.13.6 The default position: TLATA, ss 14 and 15

In the absence of a joint ownership agreement, much of the applicable law is contained in the Trustees of Land and Appointment of Trustees Act 1996 (TLATA). Sections 14 and 15 are of particular importance.

Section 14 provides that anyone who has an interest subject to a trust of land may apply to court for an order relating to the exercise of the trustees' powers or relating to the nature etc of the beneficiaries' entitlement. Applications are often made to deal with premises where a co-ownership arrangement has broken down and perhaps one party wants to sell but the other does not. In making any order under ss 14 and 15 of TLATA requires the court to consider the following:

- the intentions of the person who created the trust;
- the purpose for which the property is held;
- the welfare of any minors;
- the interests of any secured creditors or other beneficiaries.

The court may also need to decide, as part of these proceedings, the percentage shares of the property to which the beneficiaries are entitled if that is not clear. This default position will often not be appropriate for the family business. Reliance on TLATA is uncertain and requires litigation. It is far preferable to minimise the uncertainty and potential for disputes by entering into a joint ownership agreement, which deals with as many of these issues as possible.

---

[39] Many of the considerations concerning ownership approach and transfers of shares in family companies are equally relevant to interests in family owned property. See chapters 15 and 11 respectively. A coherent governance system aims to deal comprehensively with both family business and family property issues.

10.13.7 The protection of beneficial interests at the Land Registry: notices and restrictions

Beneficial interests in land are largely left unprotected under the land registration regime, and are vulnerable to overreaching.[40] If the beneficial interest is overreached, the beneficial owner's interest transfers to the proceeds of sale. However, this is of little comfort to a co-owner who finds they have to proceed with expensive and stressful litigation to recover monies from the trustees. A beneficial co-owner may not even be aware that a sale has taken place.

Protecting beneficial interests at the Land Registry can be difficult. Interests under a trust for land cannot be protected by an agreed or unilateral notice.[41] Restrictions can be a useful tool. A beneficiary under a trust for land may apply for a Form A restriction if one has not already been entered in the register. This gives some limited protection by providing that any capital money must be paid to two trustees or a trust corporation.

More robust protection is possible. With the agreement of the legal owners, beneficiaries under a trust for land can be given a similar level of control to the legal owners by the registration of a restriction preventing the disposition of the land without the written consent of each beneficial owner. A restriction to ensure that the person named in the restriction receives notice of the disposition could be entered, giving the beneficiary the opportunity of pursuing the proceeds of sale.

Any restriction other than a Form A restriction will only be registered if the Land Registry, having considered the evidence and the nature of the restriction applied for, considers it appropriate. In practice it is difficult to persuade the Land Registry to enter other restrictions.[42] The Land Registry will be mindful of the intention of the relevant legislation[43] that overreaching should be permitted to take place. The entry of a restriction should therefore be provided for in any joint ownership agreement.

10.14 JOINT OWNERSHIP CASE STUDY

The following case studies[44] may assist in illustrating some of the pitfalls of neglecting the issues associated with joint ownership.

Case Study A

A family owned a substantial former industrial site on the edge of a large town. The land had formerly been used as part of the family manufacturing business but had been vacant for a number of years. The land was originally held in the joint names of the husband and wife who founded the business. For a number of years, a developer had expressed interest in entering into an option agreement to provide for the residential development of the site. The parents transferred the property into the joint names of themselves and their three children.

---

[40] Overreaching is where the interests of beneficial owners of land are transferred to the proceeds of sale on disposal. This means that a buyer does not have to concern themselves with the underlying beneficial ownership, only that certain conveyancing formalities have been complied with and accordingly facilitates the transfer of land.
[41] LRA 2002, s 33(a)(i).
[42] See Land Registry Practice Guide 19 *Notices, Restrictions and the Protection of Third Party Interests on the Register* (Appendix A, Beneficiaries under a trust of land).
[43] LRA 2002, ss 42(1)(b) and 44(1), and LPA 1925, ss 2 and 27.
[44] The case studies are loosely based on a real life scenario.

All five family members entered into a deed of trust to provide that the parents would jointly own 40% and each of the children would own a 20% share of the property. The Land Registry only registered the first four family members listed on the TR1 as owners, leaving one of the children unregistered. This went unnoticed for a number of years. Relations between the family members deteriorated during this time.

An agreement was reached with the developer and an option agreement was entered into. The third child, who was not registered as an owner, did not agree with the terms or timing of the agreement. However, as he was not a registered owner he had no control over this. His remedies were limited to a risky and potentially very costly claim for breach of trust.

In addition, he was concerned that he would not know when a sale pursuant to the option completed and so would not know if the proceeds of sale had been paid to his co-owners. He was concerned that he would not receive his share of any sale proceeds. He would in these circumstances be able to bring a claim for payment of any monies due but would still face the challenge of enforcing any judgment.

All of these issues should have been addressed at the time of the original transfer and an appropriate agreement entered into to protect his interest as a beneficial owner (for example by registering a suitably worded restriction on the title to the property).

Case Study B

In another example, two brothers owned a caravan park, which had been left to them by their father. There was no joint ownership agreement between the brothers.

The younger brother was not particularly involved in the running of the caravan park, leaving the elder to operate the business. The vehicle for the business was a limited company, owned and managed by the elder brother. As joint owners of the land, the brothers granted to the company a business tenancy. The rents were collected in a fairly haphazard fashion and substantial arrears accrued. The physical condition of the property deteriorated.

The younger brother wanted to deal with these issues and in particular, to recover the arrears of rent from his brother's company. However, he would need the elder brother, as his joint freehold owner, to join into any action against the company. Obviously, as owner and manager of the company, the elder brother was unlikely to agree to this. The older brother also wanted to mortgage the site in order to raise funds to develop his business. This was frustrated by the younger brother who would not agree to a charge.

In the absence of agreement, the only practical option for either brother was to consider an application to the court under s 14 of TLATA 1996. In practice, this would be likely to take the form of an application for an order for sale, as the existing position was untenable. In these circumstances, a court has a wide discretion and can make any order. It needs to bear in mind s 15 of TLATA.[45] The court may for example give the elder brother a period in which to raise funds to buy the younger brother's share or decide that the property be put into an auction where the other party may bid. In this case, the court could also order that account be taken of the income and decide whether any rental sums are due to the other party.

All of these remedies are likely to be costly for both of the owners. The original arrangements between them were inadequate and the majority of the issues could have been avoided had an appropriate join ownership agreement been entered into at the outset.

---

[45] See **10.13** above.

10.15 FAMILY BUSINESSES AND PROPERTY OWNERSHIP: CONCLUSION

Family businesses are more likely than their non-family owned counterparts to own their own land. They are also more likely to own interests in property not directly used for operational purposes, whether previous and now redundant operating sites, or investment property. This is a product of the innate conservatism of family firms.

Further factors of family business life are complexity, in particular the likelihood of a variety of differing interests between family members, especially in later stage family enterprises and also informality, which can often apply to property dealings between family members and the family firm.

These ingredients can often make for an uncertain and complicated legal position so far as family property arrangements are concerned. Whilst, with the key exception of tax, this is unlikely to cause significant difficulty, whilst family relationships are harmonious, particularly in the absence of third party sales or borrowing, considerable problems can arise if relationships deteriorate.

It therefore follows that the general message of this book, the need for family business owners to pay close attention to governance arrangements applies equally to family business property matters. The precise detail of those arrangements will be driven by a combination of the family ownership approach, commercial factors and last, but not least, tax considerations.

10.16 FURTHER READING FOR PART B

- M Barnes et al *Hill and Redman's Law of Landlord and Tenant* (LexisNexis, 2015). A comprehensive reference source on tenancy issues covering everything from general common law rules to business tenancies and from private and public sector housing to agricultural tenancies.
- Carlock and Ward *Strategic Planning for the Family Business* (Palgrave, 2001). Again although we explain some of the principles of parallel planning in this chapter the book is full of helpful insights and practical suggestions to implement succession and strategic planning for family owned businesses. Although much of the content might be aimed more directly at larger and later stage family enterprises, the basic principles can be adapted and applied to earlier stage and smaller firms.
- Michael Griffiths and Matthew Griffiths *A Director's Guide to Duties* (Jordan Publishing, 2015). Aimed at a non-legal audience, this book uses an extended case study of a fictional second generation family owned business to explore not only the narrower topic of directors' duties covered in this chapter but also wider aspects of company administration and legal compliance.
- D Impey and N Montague *Running a Limited Company* (Jordan Publishing, 8th edn, 2013). This general work on the legal issues relevant to owner managed businesses contains a short section on intellectual property rights more generally.
- A Keay *Directors' Duties* (Jordan Publishing, 2nd edn, 2014). A highly readable text-book, aimed at legal practitioners, which provides a comprehensive treatment of the topic of directors duties.
- I Lansberg 'The Succession Conspiracy' (1988) *Family Business Review* Vol 1 No 2, pp 119–143. A key article from one of the leading family business consultants, academics and commentators. Although we have made extensive references to this article in the main body of this chapter, the article as a whole is insightful and merits reading in full. The key point that emerges is that paradoxically the leading members of the business family are also the chief co-conspirators with the senior generation business leader in preventing the successful transition they all really wish to achieve.
- Mellor et al *Kerly's Law of Trade Marks and Trade Names* (Sweet & Maxwell, 15th edn, 2011). Widely acknowledged as the trade mark practitioners bible and frequently referred to in court.
- J Sonnefeld *The Hero's Farewell: What Happens When CEO's Retire* (Oxford University Press, 1988). A thoughtful study, from the perspective of the senior generation of the issues involved in relinquishing management control. The book is based on 100 in depth interviews with retiring chief executives in the USA, many of whom had previously led family enterprises. Although the business climate and (to a certain extent) the social context in which the book is written may be a little dated, the insights into the psychological issues involved certainly are not.
- Tallon and Howard *Tax Planning for Owner-managed Businesses 2015-16* (Tolley, 2016). A detailed guide to tax issues affecting owner-managed businesses generally.

PART C

OWNERSHIP

CHAPTER 11

OWNERSHIP OVERVIEW

11.1 THE IMPORTANCE OF OWNERSHIP

All three systems comprised within a family business,[1] family, business and ownership are crucial to its functioning and operation. But the ownership system can lay claim to being the central system around which the other two revolve. Ownership is at the root of most key family business issues.

Whilst succession has many elements that stem from the family and business systems the fundamental issues in this core topic relate to ownership. When will ownership be transferred, to whom and how? Similarly although the causes of family business disputes are many and varied, for example sibling rivalry, the resolution such disputes will ultimately usually boil down to a question of whether the ownership of a family business will change and, if so, how and on what terms?

Understanding the ownership position will therefore be a key starting point in looking at any family owned business. This will include not only the current ownership structure but also the plans, expectations and hopes of all relevant members of the business owning family for the future.

This deeper look at ownership as a key component of ownership succession planning and is contained in chapter 15. This chapter is concerned with the more basic mechanical elements of ownership. But, as this includes some aspects of implementing the family's ownership philosophy, or ownership approach, developed as part of that succession process, the two chapters are inter-dependent. In particular this chapter leans heavily on the two basic approaches to ownership developed in chapter 15. These are the whole family ownership approach, where all family members, both insiders working in the family business and outsiders who do not, are encouraged to become and remain owners and the opposite approach, insider ownership.

Ownership has a number of elements, which are explored below. Some are financial. However the most significant element of ownership, especially in a family owned company where there is no prospect of sale, is the ultimate ability to control the company through the exercise of voting rights attached to shares. Although, in theory operational decisions will be taken by the board of directors, operating in the business system of the three-circle model, in most family businesses there will usually be a

---

[1] See chapter 3 (Tools, Models and Theories) for an explanation of systems theory and its application to the family business together with the three-circle model.

considerable overlap with the ownership dimension. Even if this is not the case, the ultimate means of control, that of removing the directors, will remain with the owners.[2]

More often than not these rights are bundled together into a single class of ordinary shares. However, as has been seen in the case of *Saul D Harrison*, it is perfectly possible, by the use of different share classes to separate control and the rights to income and capital. Broadly speaking, the ownership structure of a family company can be tailored to fit the preferred ownership approach of the business owning family.

11.2 BASIC SHAREHOLDER RIGHTS

Before looking in detail at ownership in the context of the family business tailoring it is worth recapping on some basic principles on the rights attached to ordinary shares in limited companies.[3] As will be seen the actual legal rights of an individual minority shareholder are really very limited. For ownership to be meaningful such a shareholder would need to rely on other factors to gain any real degree of control or security.

In a UK limited company the basic rights attached to owning shares are as follows:

11.2.1 Dividends

Ordinary shares will usually carry the right to receive dividends. But this is only if the directors declare a dividend. There is therefore no *prima facie* right for shareholders to obtain any income.[4] Dividend policies are discussed in more detail in **11.7** below.

11.2.2 Capital

In theory ordinary shareholders are entitled to their pro-rata share of any surplus capital on the winding up of the company after debts have been paid. Obviously this capital will have disappeared in an insolvent winding up. Solvent winding up is rare.

11.2.3 Sale

Of much more practical significance is the right to receive a share of the proceeds of sale if the family firm is eventually sold. If the intention is to keep the business in family ownership this can be seen more as a theoretical than a real right.[5]

In theory, a shareholder can sell their own shares, independently from the sale of the family company. But, as discussed in detail below, provisions are often included in family business constitutions preventing or restricting the ability to sell, other than to family members. Even if transfer restrictions are not included, the market for unquoted shares in a small to medium sized family firm is likely to be very limited indeed. In practice this would usually be confined to family members anyway (or perhaps employees).

---

[2] Under CA, s 168. This is subject to any weighted voting rights designed to entrench the director's position.
[3] Subject to modification, where this is possible. There are some limited circumstances where it is not. These are discussed in chapter 20.
[4] The (limited) extent to which minority 'outsider' shareholders are protected by the unfair prejudice legislation is considered in chapters 20 and 21.
[5] Discussed in more detail in chapter 15 (Ownership Succession). The sale process itself is covered in chapter 12.

11.2.4 Voting

Shareholders have the right to receive notice of, attend and vote at general meetings of a company.[6] As the table below shows, the control that a minority lone voice shareholder can exert is really quite limited. The right to attend and vote applies to general meetings of shareholders only. There is no right for a shareholder to participate in board meetings, which is where the overwhelming majority of business and operational decisions are (or should be) taken.

11.2.5 Accounts

Shareholders are entitled to receive a copy of their company's statutory accounts.[7] They are not however entitled to receive any further management or financial information.

11.2.6 Notices

Similarly shareholders are entitled to receive formal notice of key matters relating to the regulation of their company in addition to notices of general meetings and proposed resolutions.[8]

11.2.7 Shareholder democracy

Shareholders with comparatively small shareholdings are entitled to exercise the shareholder democracy provisions of the Companies Acts, including requisitioning general meetings (see table below).

11.2.8 Legislative protection

A number of provisions of the Companies Act are designed to protect the rights of shareholders. The most important of which is protection from unfair prejudice under CA, s 994. These provisions are considered in detail in Part E.

11.3 LEGAL CONTROL

It is usually said the most important right attached to holding shares in a family business is control. In practice control for legal purposes is a graduated concept. Once the shares held by a shareholder and their voting allies[9] reach certain thresholds they gain different levels of legal control. Below that threshold the relevant control is absent.

In basic terms the position so far as private companies are concerned looks like this:

---

[6] In the first instance voting is on a show of hands but if a poll is demanded voting will be on the basis of percentage of shares held Companies Act 2006, Appendix 1 Model Articles, Art 42.
[7] CA, s 423.
[8] For example copies of any representations made by a director protesting against a resolution to remove them – CA, s 169(3).
[9] In a family company logically these are likely to be close family members and family members in the same branch. But family dynamics, including sibling rivalries can often upset this assumption.

Shareholding Threshold	Level of control	Statutory Provision
100%	Absolute control	
90%	'Statutory squeeze out' rights can be invoked allowing the majority to force the remaining shareholders to sell	CA, s 307
75%	Can pass a special or extra-ordinary resolution. These include:	CA, s 283
	• altering the Articles of Association	CA, s 21
	• winding-up the company	IA, s 84
	• changing the name of the company	CA, s 78
	• agreeing a buy-back of shares (other than one's own)	CA, s 694
	• waiving pre-emption rights (for existing shareholders to take their pro-rata allocation of new shares)	CA, s 569
50% +	A simple majority have ordinary control of a company. This has positive aspects. They can pass an ordinary resolution. For example to increase the share capital and allot new shares.	CA, s 282
	The same majority also have negative control. They can block ordinary resolutions proposed by other shareholders and therefore have both positive and 'negative control' over the company. For example an ordinary resolution to remove directors could be defeated	CA, s 168
25% +	Can block a special or extra-ordinary resolution. Therefore have limited negative control. In practice this provides a right of veto over most major corporate transactions, for example sale or major investments, which are likely to require a special resolution.	CA, s 283
10% +	Have the ability to resist statutory squeeze out provisions.	CA, s 979
	Some limited governance powers emerge, including the ability:	
	• to block consent to short notice of a general meeting	CA, s 307
	• to require an audit (if a company would otherwise be exempt)	CA, s 476
	• to demand a poll (if the articles otherwise restrict this)	CA, s 321
5% +	'Shareholder activist rights', for example the ability to:	
	• requisition extra-ordinary general meetings of shareholders	CA, s 303
	• require written resolutions to be circulated.	CA, s 292
	• require a company to circulate a statement in support of a resolution	CA, s 314
	• prevent the deemed re-appointment of auditors (in which case this would then simply be put to the members as an ordinary resolution)	CA, s 488
	Without more support these rights amount to little more than the ability to make a noise and possibly embarrass the board.	
>5%	Basic shareholder rights as set out in **11.2** above only	

11.4 OWNERSHIP AND CONTROL

Appropriate levels of ownership will usually carry with it the ultimate ability to control the destiny of the family firm. That is not to say that other factors will not be relevant to the question of control on many occasions.

We have briefly looked at the treatment of ownership and control for legal purposes in the paragraphs above. The definition of control under the Companies Acts is quite narrow, focusing on directors' ownership of equity share capital and their ability to exercise voting rights.[10] The interests of 'connected persons' are taken into account.[11] Although these include members of the director's family the definition of family for these purposes is not widely drawn.[12]

But the issue of control in the context of family firms has more subtle connotations, the implications of which go well beyond the legal and tax sphere.

What about family members without formal shareholdings but who nevertheless are able to exert considerable influence over their family firm, for example, by providing or guaranteeing loans, or allowing the family firm to use premises, or other key assets, owned by them outside the formal company structure?[13]

In many cases it will be the influence of the family system itself that acts as a balancing factor, providing a check or restraint, so that those in legal control of the family business do not exercise their ownership rights to the fullest extent. Instead the legal controllers of the family firm show restraint in matters such as personal remuneration for reasons rooted in family stewardship.

To what extent does habitually deferring to the senior generation as a result of their dominant personality, family tradition, or otherwise, mean that in reality the senior generation control the family firm even though, in terms of strict voting rights, they are in a minority? Returning to the example of Fords, it took many years (and the death of his son Edsel) before the rest of the family, including Henry's wife, Clara, were prepared to exert their legal control over the Ford business and challenge the authority of Henry.[14]

So, in many family business situations, there will be a disconnect between ownership, giving theoretical control over the family firm and the actual day-to-day exercise of authority. Both ownership and control need to be understood and analysed. However, just as in Fords, in various cases, pressures emanating from the family system will provide the catalyst for ownership rights, that have lain dormant, to be exercised. For example in one case of 'stuck succession' the senior generation business founder was reluctant to hand over full ownership to his son. The succession process was freed when it became clear that the wife of founder was ultimately prepared to vote alongside the

---

[10] CA, s 255.
[11] CA, s 252.
[12] CA, s 253 – which includes spouses, live in partners, children and parents but does not include siblings or more remote family members. The definition of control for tax purposes is wider – see chapter 4.
[13] Since April 2016 companies have been obliged to maintain a register of Persons with Significant Control. This goes beyond shareholding and directorships.
[14] See chapter 2 (Themes) for more on the Ford motors story.

rest of the family and against her husband. The alternative was for her son to leave the family business and the area in which it was based, thus resulting in loss of contact with her grandchildren.

Ultimately ownership will prevail.

11.5 OWNERSHIP STRUCTURES

A detailed discussion on the use of ownership structures to regulate the ownership interests of insiders and outsiders is contained in chapter 15 (Ownership Succession).

11.6 EMPLOYEES AND OWNERSHIP POLICY[15]

The question of employee ownership adds a further raft of complexity to ownership policy. In the early stage family firm employee ownership is likely to have developed on an ad-hoc basis. Refining this into a definable employee ownership policy and the important point of buying back employee shares are discussed in **6.6**. The pruning tools discussed later in this chapter are equally applicable to buy back existing employee shares.

11.7 DIVIDEND POLICIES

There are various reasons why a family business may want to pay dividends, particularly for those outsider shareholders who are not employed in the business including:

- supporting immediate family members who have little other income.
- a wider agreed purpose that the business is there to support the whole family, and the descendants of the original founder.
- corporate responsibility to the shareholders to provide a return on their capital.
- loyalty to any ex-employees shareholders or their dependents to support them in retirement.

Arriving at a suitable dividend policy is a difficult issue. As a matter of company law and good governance practice it is for the directors to recommend and for the members to approve dividends. Any fixed dividend policy can be seen to usurp the role of the board.

Profitability and the needs of the family enterprise for reinvestment clearly should be considered.

Dividend policy can often be a source of tension where significant numbers of the owning family are not employed in the business and where dividends are low. Most obviously this can be created by where the remuneration practices of those that have jobs in the family business are perceived to be unfair by the have-nots.[16] As far as the directors and other family employees are concerned, it is important to realise the difference between employment returns and investment returns. In other words, the salary and bonuses received in return for the services provided to the business should not

---

[15] Explored in detail in chapter 6.
[16] The clearest example is the *Irvine* case discussed in detail in Part E.

include an extra amount because they are also shareholders. If it does, and there is a wider shareholder group this can lead to conflict. It is vital that the return which family employees receive should be seen to be fair. This may mean some formal procedures to assess performance and rewards, perhaps involving external benchmarking. Dividend policies can therefore be seen as the other side of the coin from remuneration policies discussed in 5.5.

Difficulties can also arise where, even if remuneration of employed family members is modest, the board are adopting a policy of heavy reinvestment of profits in the business at the expense of dividend payments. Outsiders may still feel that they have the worst of all worlds. They have no salary, little say in the business and no real income from it. The outsiders' shares are illiquid but may also represent a large proportion of their theoretical net worth. To an extent, these concerns can be managed by other features of the governance programme. For example share redemption procedures[17] and the general communication process through the family assembly.[18]

Sometimes polices are introduced to pay a set minimum proportion of profits as dividends. Fixed dividend policies of this nature are often thought to be too constrictive. Certainly it would be inappropriate to allow the family or the family council to subvert the role of the board and to control dividend policy. However and as a minimum requirement consultation between the board and the family council over dividend policy will often be enshrined in the family charter.

Alternatives include providing a guide to directors, which falls short of a binding legal obligation. Also setting a basic and conservative level of regular dividend with the directors able to top this up if performance is good.

The dividend cover of quoted companies (ie the number of times that post tax profits cover the dividends paid) can provide some indication of a suitable policy for a comparable family firm. However quoted companies may be paying a high dividends for reasons of market pressure.

Shareholder needs and expectations cannot be ignored. If regular dividends have been paid this expectation can cause problems in years when difficult trading circumstances mean dividend levels cannot be sustained. Again family and business needs have to be balanced.

There is no simple answer to the question of what dividend policy should be adopted. Ultimately, the approach (if not the actual level of dividend) the board, the family and the shareholders need to collectively discuss and agree an approach. Consultation should reduce the potential for conflict.

Typically the agreed dividend policy would be included in a family charter, if one is prepared as part of the governance structure. Sometimes dividend policies are contained in a legally binding shareholders' agreement. On occasions this will be because of low levels of trust between insiders and outsiders, perhaps where the dividend policy is being introduced after a dispute. Alternatively the dividend policy might take a legally binding form simply because this is what lawyers have recommended.

---

[17] Considered below.
[18] Discussed in chapter 17.

11.8 OWNER CONTROLS

Company law theory is that the management control the day-to-day business of a company subject to the oversight of the board of directors. Owners have a very much background presence. In practice this theory is prone to become blurred in family companies. Owners and non-executive family directors often interfere in management decisions. On other occasions outsiders can feel powerless to influence the board.

Most shareholders' agreements (for both family and non-family businesses) contain a list of matters that cannot be implemented by the directors without the approval of shareholders. These are alternatively termed restricted matters, veto rights or negative pledges. This list of restricted matters will often cover most key business decisions including:

- Hiring firing and changing the employment terms of senior employees, including family employment matters.
- Entering into significant contracts.
- Major borrowing.
- Property transactions, including transactions involving family insiders.
- Mergers and acquisitions.
- Changes to company structure including issuing new shares, changing the constitution etc.

In theory, approval of many of these restricted matters could, usually be given by the board, without reference to shareholders. On the basis that the primary responsibility for making business decision rests with the board, the inclusion of restricted matters represents a fetter on the powers of the board by the shareholders and runs contrary to basic corporate governance principles.

Restricted matters provisions can therefore send a message that the board are not trusted to run the company. Equally they can hamper the decision making process and prevent a family owned business from being able to move quickly, thereby losing what is perceived to be one of the key advantages that family businesses hold over their non-family counterparts.

The justification for inclusion of restricted matters needs to be carefully considered. But that justification may well exist.

Reasons could include:

- Allowing the senior generation (or same generation outsiders) a greater degree of control and comfort, during the early stages of the next generation's insider management of the family business, to allow trust to be built. The same logic applies to a new non-family management team.
- Paradoxically lists of restricted matters could lead to less interference with day-to-day management decisions. If a list of matters that the senior generation believe that they need to have a say in emerges from dialogue between the generations, by definition, anything not on the list should be within the bailiwick of the next generation managers.

- Risk management, particularly if a large proportion of the wealth of the senior generation or other outsiders remains tied up in family business. Similar provisions are often found in banking and investment agreements.
- Encouraging communication between the board and the remaining family shareholders in particular around sensitive areas such as family employment.
- Responding to history and circumstances. Shareholders' agreements and restricted matters are sometimes introduced as part of a compromise where trust has broken down and disputes have arisen. This may be because the board have in the past taken decisions that have led to problems, or have been unpopular, with some or all of the remaining shareholders. The board may remain in place but subject to increased control and accountability so far as the remaining shareholders are concerned.

Once including negative pledges has been accepted in principle, the question becomes how long should the list of restricted matters be? Some shareholders' agreements contain long lists of 20 or more restrictions. Depending on the approach taken by the business owning family the list might cover:

- Only core decisions that go to the root of the family business identity such as a sale of the business (see below), dropping use of the family name or perhaps changing location from the birthplace of the business in which the family have a strong presence and identity.
- Shareholding and ownership issues, including changing share rights or issuing new shares (although in all probability these matters will be dealt with in detailed provisions relating to ownership, discussed below, which will form a key part of the agreement.
- The remuneration of the family board members or the employment of other family members.
- Other sensitive areas where the interests of insiders and outsiders are in potential conflict, such as dealing in property.
- Key strategic borrowing and investment matters, 'bet the ranch decisions' that could drastically affect the wealth of the wider family if they go wrong.
- More routine operational matters. However as discussed the more of these that are included the more the role of the board is being undermined.

The next question becomes, if negative pledges are to be included, what level of buy in from family members must the board secure before from family members before proceeding to implement a restricted matter?

It is fairly common practice (in drafting shareholders' agreements generally) to provide that unanimous consent of all shareholders needs to be obtained. In other words, full veto rights.[19] This might be appropriate in smaller family businesses, particularly if accompanied by workable exit provisions (see below). Whilst providing short-term protection and possibly a cooling-off period, unanimous consent provisions can be open to political abuse, remove the incentive to compromise and frustrate the development of the company.

---

[19] Clearly this is the polar opposite of the approach of allowing insiders full control over the family firm by devices such as voting and non-voting shares, as employed in *Saul D Harrison*.

Instead, particularly for larger family companies, some form of majority voting is likely to be more appropriate. This could be on a graduated basis, depending on the strategic significance or the sensitivity of the decision concerned.

At the lowest level there could be a requirement (or even a simple request or recommendation) that the board consult with the family shareholders or the family council on sensitive operational matters. In that way the constitutional role of the board is recognised and preserved but dialogue with the wider business owning family is encouraged.

For matters towards the more operational end of the scale, which have nevertheless been identified as shareholder reserved matters, a simple majority vote might be appropriate. In effect elevating what would otherwise have been a board decision into an ordinary resolution.

Decisions seen as more significant could be subject to a higher threshold. This could be so even if the decision could otherwise be taken by the board alone or passed by ordinary resolution. The next logical threshold supplied by company law would be the 75% required to pass a special resolution. However agreements can be structured around the circumstances of the individual family business concerned. For example, if the level of family executive remuneration was seen to be an issue, setting a threshold so that increases would need the approval of family members or family branches outside the insider executive branch.

For the most fundamental decisions, going to the root of the identity of the business owning family, such as the sale of the business, a higher super majority might be required to pass the necessary decisions.

Notwithstanding the common practice of including veto rights in shareholders' agreements[20] we cannot see any circumstances where requiring complete unanimity to pass shareholder resolutions will be sensible in a larger family business, even for the most significant decisions such as the sale of the company. At best such provisions create uncertainty and additional administration. On other occasions progress and the will of a large majority of family members may be frustrated a small minority. They might be acting from a deeply held and genuine belief that nothing should change. They could be motivated by a long held grievance. At worst the family is opening itself up to veto rights being used tactically to secure an inappropriate advantage.

11.9 WEIGHTED VOTING RIGHTS

Restricted matters limit the power of directors. Weighted voting rights increase them.

It is well-established law that there is nothing to prevent inclusion of weighted voting rights in the constitution. This can be of through weighted class voting rights allowing one class of shares extra votes either generally or on certain issues.[21] Although

---

[20] Often these are accompanied by 'Russian Roulette' provisions whereby if a deadlock develops and can't be resolved the company can be wound up.
[21] The most graphic example, albeit not under English law, is probably News Corp International which although fully listed on the New York stock exchange is structured so that the class of shares controlled by the Murdoch family although fewer in number carry substantially more voting rights than the other ordinary share class held by non-family members.

comparatively rare, we have seen a number of examples of articles that include weighted voting rights at board level, so that the votes of certain board members, typically a founding entrepreneur, or a powerful controlling family director will automatically outvote the remainder of the board.

The ultimate control of the members of a company is to remove the board. The most common use of weighted votes is to protect a director from removal from office; the so called *Bushell and Faith* clause named after a family business case.[22] In that case the articles of a family owned property company contained the following provision:

> 'In the event of a resolution being proposed at any general meeting of the company for the removal from office of any director, any shares held by that director shall on a poll in respect of such resolution carry the right to three votes per share ...'

Following the death of their mother, the 300 shares of the company were held equally by two sisters and their brother. They were all directors. For reasons that are not explained in the judgement the sisters became 'dissatisfied with the conduct of [their brother] as a director' and requisitioned a general meeting to pass a general resolution to secure his removal. Unsurprisingly the brother called for a poll[23] on the resolution.

The case needs to be set against the historical context, where directors for life were fairly common and developments in the UK corporate governance thinking[24] that this was not necessarily a good idea and that shareholders ought to have more control over boards of directors. These led to the introduction of s 184 of the Companies Act 1948 which provided that:[25]

> 'A company may by ordinary resolution at a meeting will remove a director before the expiration of his period of office, notwithstanding anything in its articles.'

The question before the courts was whether the article infringed the Companies Act and therefore the resolution for dismissal was carried by the 200 votes cast by the sisters to the 100 votes of their brother. Alternatively, if the article was valid did the triple voting potency attached to the brother's shares, trump his sisters by 300 votes to 200?

The issue came before the House of Lords via the High Court (where the sisters won) and the Court of Appeal (which found in favour of the brother). Despite a short but powerful dissenting judgement by Lord Morris (who dismissed the article because of its 'unconcealed effect is to make a director irremovable' which 'made a mockery of the law' the remaining law lords upheld the validity of the clause.

The majority judgements upholding the validity of the provision basically drew a distinction between, on one hand, parliament setting out a principle that directors can always be removed by passing an ordinary resolution and, on the other hand, leaving companies free to choose their mechanisms and procedures for voting on that ordinary

---

[22] *Bushell v Faith* [1970] AC 1099.
[23] A vote taken by reference to shares held rather than members present at the meeting.
[24] The Cohen Committee on Company Law Amendment (Cmd 6659/1945).
[25] The provision in the current legislation (CA, s 168 is slightly wider and provides that 'A company may by ordinary resolution at a meeting will remove a director before the expiration of his period of office, notwithstanding anything in any agreement between it and him' and therefore covers provisions in shareholders' agreements etc'.

resolution. In addition to the technical arguments around statutory construction the judgement of Lord Donovan contains a justification based on an understanding of family business dynamics:

> 'there are many small companies which are conducted in practice as though they were little more than partnerships, particularly family companies running a family business; and it is unfortunately sometimes necessary to provide some safeguard against family quarrels, having their repercussion in the boardroom.'

The decision in *Bushell v Faith* has been subject to a degree of debate and criticism in legal academic circles but remains generally accepted law. Does the practice of weighted voting rights represent good governance?

It is possible to understand the desire of a founding entrepreneur to retain control of the family business they have created and to secure their own position, perhaps at the time of starting, to give away shares to the next generation. Equally it is easy to sympathise with a founder who wished to protect each of their children from attack by their siblings and being forced out of the business after the founder has relinquished control.

However provisions of this nature are difficult to categorise as good governance. In practice they are much more likely to promote stalemate and entrenched attitudes. If the ultimate sanction of removal has been removed what incentive does a director protected by these provision have to co-operate and collaborate with the rest of the board or shareholders?

At most it is difficult to justify these provisions as anything other than providing a short term moratorium, perhaps whilst the next generation earn the respect and trust to be given full voting control, perhaps to create some form of deadlock, in effect a constitutional injunction, protecting the status quo, and preventing a director being forced out whilst a longer term solution is sorted out.

11.10 SALE OF THE FAMILY COMPANY

The most fundamental decision a business owning family is ever likely to take is whether or not to sell their family business.

As a matter of strict company law the assets of any business can be sold on the basis of a board decision without shareholder approval. It will be very rare that a buyer will be prepared to proceed in the face of family opposition. However most shareholders' agreement will seek to block this possibility, by including as a reserved matter the requirement for the board to secure the support of, at least, a majority of shareholders and, often a super majority, before the whole or a substantial part of the undertaking of a company is sold.

Many business-owning families will have given a commitment to remain together as a family business. Some families will be content to rely on a combination of fate, trust and an informal commitment, perhaps contained in a non-binding family charter to enforce this commitment. Certainly the vast majority of buyers of privately owned family businesses are reluctant to proceed with an acquisition that does not have the universal support of all shareholders.[26] This reluctance offers a degree of negative protection for the family ownership ethos. Some families choose to follow through their commitment to family ownership into formal legal documents. The practical mechanisms to implement the commitment and the extent to which it will be enforced (or not) will usually be found in their shareholders' agreement re-enforced by relevant provisions of the articles.

Some of those provisions are discussed in this chapter. For example pre-emption provisions requiring shares to be offered first to family members before outsiders. Perhaps share transfer restrictions preventing the registration of non-family shareholders. As articles including those provisions could ordinarily be changed by a special resolution, such restrictions might be contained in a separate shareholders' agreement, or otherwise given special protection, through weighted voting rights or otherwise.

Other families may not have the resource or the awareness or even see the need to follow this commitment through into legal documents.

11.11 SHARE TRANSFER PROVISIONS

Key provisions for inclusion in the constitution of any family company will be those relating to the transfer of ownership of shares. First the family need to determine their basic approach to ownership. This should be established as part of the succession planning process.[27] This then needs to be captured in suitable governance documents. The recommended starting point would be the family charter.[28] This will set out the broad principles that have been agreed. Given the central importance of ownership, the details should then be worked through and recorded in a legally binding documents, either articles of association or, more usually, private shareholders' agreements.

11.11.1 Discretion to refuse to register transfers

Provisions to prevent (or at least severely restrict the possibility) of shares being transferred to third party non-family shareholders are a must for a business committed to remaining in family ownership.

Even if it is thought unlikely in practice that third parties would seek admission to membership, including share transfer restrictions, does underline the commitment of the family to continuing family ownership.

There is long standing case-law to the effect that, in the absence of provision in the constitution allowing them to do so, the directors cannot refuse to register a transfer to a third party, even in a business which is clearly intended to operate as a family business.[29] The starting point or default position in the Model Articles (Art 26(5)) gives directors a general power to refuse to register a transfer. That power must be exercised

---

[26] This issue, and its solution, drag rights, are discussed in chapter 12.
[27] See chapter 15 (Ownership Succession).
[28] See chapter 17 (Governance).
[29] Re Bell Bros Ltd (1891) 65 LT 245.

properly in the interests of the company.[30] However where there is a clear intention to maintain exclusive family ownership it is likely to prove difficult to challenge a refusal to register a transfer to a third party.

It may be more likely that a share transfer proposed will be to a family member rather than a third party. Possibly the directors would have a genuine business reason for objecting to the transfer, for example a history of disputes with the transferee and a concern that they would be a disruptive presence on the shareholder register. The temptation is to put the share transfer which has been lodged to one side, until the wider issues can be resolved. But there is a trap. Discretions to refuse to register share transfers operate on 'use it or lose it basis'. If the directors do not positively refuse to register the transfer within any applicable time limits[31] the ability to refuse will be lost.[32]

In the earliest stage, of a first generation start up, a general power to refuse to register transfers may offer sufficient protection. However the family business will soon outgrow that provision and need to look at a bespoke solution, which reflects the ownership philosophy of the family.

11.11.2 Restrictions on share transfer

The safest route is nevertheless full clarity. The constitution of the family company should clearly spell out which transfers of shares are permitted, which are controlled[33] and to provide that any other transfers are prohibited. But any restrictions or prohibitions on share transfer need to be comprehensive and explicit, covering transfers of beneficial and other interests in shares, not just legal interests.[34]

11.11.3 Golden shares

The ultimate commitment to family ownership would be to include structures in the constitution to make the family business effectively unsalable to third parties. The method usually discussed would be some form of golden share (also known as trust shares or special shares) giving significant powers repel any third party attacks, even those made with significant insider family support. Those powers would include enhanced voting rights that would crush any resolution that would allow in outsiders eg to change the articles. It would usually be suggested that the golden share would be held subject to a single purpose trust, the trustees of which were obliged to keep the family ownership flame alive.

Whilst such structures may be discussed on occasions, they are, in practice, rarely implemented.[35] This is partly but not necessarily for reasons of complexity. More often it is because, however committed the current generation are to family ownership, they

---

[30] *Popely v Planarrive Ltd* [1997] 1 BCLC 8.
[31] These might be contained in bespoke articles. Article 26 of the Model Articles does not contain an express time limit but there are arguments that the discretion should be exercised within a reasonable period of time.
[32] *Re Swaledale Cleaners Ltd* [1968] 3 All ER 619.
[33] Through the existence of pre-emption provisions, discussed below as part pruning.
[34] In *Theakston v London Trust plc* [1984] BCLC 390 arrangements to transfer the beneficial interest, including control over voting rights to a third party where the transfer of a legal interest would be subject to pre-emption provisions were upheld.
[35] It is more usual to see a species of golden share introduced where, to prevent deadlock, for example in a sibling partnership, a small number of shares, in effect carrying a casting vote, are vested in a trusted and neutral shareholder, either a family member, an advisor or a trusted family friend. This structure was adopted

accept (in some cases after some time and debate) that there is a limit to how far they can completely control the future ownership and destiny of their family business. A combination of a business that has been made too difficult to sell and poor performance (whether caused by declining markets, poor management or otherwise) may mean that the wealth of the business owning family becomes imprisoned in the family business and ultimately declines. Realistically the option to sell must always be kept open.

Instead even the families most wedded to continuing family ownership will settle for a compromise of making their family business difficult to sell, but not impossible, if circumstances dictate. Indeed many families take the approach that, if they are to surrender family ownership of their business to a third party, the surrender should be honourable, clean and efficient, executed with dignity and on the best terms reasonably available. Once the point has been reached when family ownership should cease it will be damaging to the business, to the family's business, wealth and relationships for the sale to be frustrated by, typically, senior generation, family members who refuse to join in the sale for reasons more deeply entrenched in family sentiment than commercial reality.

The mechanism to achieve this will be drag and tag provisions and these are considered in more detail in chapter 12 (Selling the Family Business). The key issue for the family will be what percentage of the family can trigger drag rights, forcing the remaining family members into a sale?

11.11.4 Permitted transfers

If shares cannot be sold to non-family third parties (at least in the absence of an outright sale of the family company), then the only logical buyer or transferee would be a family member. This brings us back full circle to the definition of family member,[36] which is likely to feed through into a further definition of permitted transferees, to whom shares can be transferred as a matter of absolute right, free from pre-emption provisions.

It would be usual for family trusts (whose beneficiaries are confined to family members entitled to hold shares in their own right) to be included within the class of permitted transferees.

Often a family will choose to adopt a fairly narrow permitted transfer regime whereby shares may be transferred freely down to lineal descendants along the branch line of separate 'sub families'. Transfers across the branch lines to siblings, nephews and nieces will often be excluded from the classes of permitted transfers. Instead transfers across branch lines would be subject to pre-emption provisions (options or rights of first refusal to other shareholders).

To the extent that any thought has been applied to this approach the logic is usually to help prevent one of more branches of the family being able to build disproportionately high stakes in the family company, marginalising other branches. This is of particular concern if tensions and difficulties between one or more branches of the family are creeping into business and family dynamics. A dominant insider branch might be able to acquire shares held by disinterested or economically disadvantaged outsider branches.

---

in the old Scottish family business case of *Symington v Symington Quarries Ltd* [1905] 8 F 121 discussed in chapter 22. That the case ended up in court is evidence that this solution failed in that case.

[36] Introduced in chapter 1.

However close family permitted share transfer provisions might often be the result of simply slavishly cutting and pasting precedents rather than a carefully considered ownership approach.[37]

Other families take a more liberal view allowing free transfer of shares between family members across the wider family, bloodline or otherwise.[38] Often this is based on a whole 'family free float' ownership philosophy. This is that the priority is for shares to gravitate to those family members most committed to the family business. This approach is more likely to provide an exit route for less committed family members, thus preventing a build-up of frustration. In that way it is more likely that the wider family will retain long-term ownership of the business. Of course the relative wealth of various family members or branches will be a crucially relevant factor. In cases where that wealth has arisen largely as a result of the remuneration paid to working family members their ability to mop up surplus shares as a result, may further inflame an already tense situation.

Still others adopt a hybrid solution where gifts of shares (both lifetime and on death) can be made to wider family members, but sales fall into the net of the pre-emption provisions. The logic being that increased influence in the family company can be earned as a result of loyalty and affection between wider family members (recognising that close relationships are not necessarily confined to branch lines), but that such influence cannot be bought or sold (at least without the opportunity for the wider family to join in the process).

So far this discussion of permitted transfers has made no distinction between insiders and outsiders. Logically, if a business family adopts a narrow 'insider only' ownership approach, transfers would only be permitted between family members working in the business. However this approach is rarely taken.[39]

The permutations are many and varied and can take considerable time and effort for the business owning family to explore.

11.11.5 Pre-emption provisions

Pre-emption provisions, basically call options, giving other shareholders preferential rights to acquire any shares that are available for sale, are discussed in detail in **11.16** below.

---

[37] Typically permitted transfer provisions allow transfers to spouses, children and family trusts. The accidental inclusion of a spouse would be problematic in a family with a 'bloodline only' ownership philosophy.
[38] Again this sometimes happens accidentally. A typical provision allowing permitted transfers between existing shareholder might operate to allow cross branch transfers between existing family shareholders.
[39] At least deliberately. Insider only transfer provisions are discussed in more detail below.

11.12 THE OWNERSHIP TREE

11.12.1 Growth of the ownership tree

As shares are passed from one generation to another, and as the business develops, so the shareholding in a company can become more widely spread.[40] Family members will have less close connections, both to one another and to the family company.

This can create a number of issues, some of which can be alleviated if there is a governance structure in place, which maintains and encourages involvement of the shareholders, with the business and with each other, as a business owning family.

Some of the issues which can arise with a widely spread shareholding are:

- **Cohesion.** Understanding and interest in the business can weaken for minority shareholders, especially if none of their immediate family are actively involved. Outsiders might not respond to opportunities to connect with the company, even if efforts are made by the insiders. The outsiders become disenfranchised. This may in turn at some stage in the future lead to a galvanising of the minority shareholders into taking some form of disruptive action.[41]

- **Interference.** Conversely the outsiders might attempt to interfere in the management of the business. They might feel that, as a family member, they have a right to be heard, and to participate in management, to a much greater extent than the notwithstanding they have no formal role in the governance process.

- **Economic disenfranchisement.** Outsiders might see no economic value in their shareholding, and have little appreciation of the legacy associated with ownership of the family firm. Such shareholders may prefer to see value realised from the shares, but there is no market where they can be sold, and no third party would be interested in buying them. This can lead to constant pressure on the directors to pay dividends or find an exit route for them.
There could be shareholders whose ancestors had a connection with the company, but there is no longer any active family involvement. Their shareholding may represent a significant portion of the equity.

- **Investment fetters.** One part of the family could be actively involved insiders, but their cousins are only outsider shareholders. The insider side of the family want to take the business forward and invest heavily in the family enterprise. However they feel constrained there in doing so because of their responsibilities to the outsider shareholders to also provide dividends. This creates inertia in the development of the business.

If governance structures are present and working as they were intended, and consequently there is interaction and positive dialogue between the family shareholders and management, then a wide family shareholding can still be beneficial for the business.

---

[40] The position can be further complicated by the presence of employee shareholders. Their situation is discussed in chapter 6.
[41] *Bartlett v Barclays Bank Trust Company* [1990] 1 All ER 139 discussed in chapter 14, provides a prime example.

11.13 PRUNING THE OWNERSHIP TREE: THE CASE FOR PRUNING

The classic model of family business evolution embraces all members of the family, in some shape of form. By the time the business has reached the stage of a cousin collaboration, more often than not, the numbers of family members involved will have reached double figures. This is well illustrated in the *Saul D Harrison* business with 10 fourth generation cousins in the picture,[42] as well as various members of the third generation and a number of family trusts.

Whilst attempts may have been made to restrict the share ownership, it can still become widely spread. There may be many reasons why the ownership tree of a family company has become unmanageable and why there may be a need to reduce the number of shareholders. These include, in summary:

- Some family shareholders have different views on the values and purposes of the business, and this is causing conflict or a lack of focus.
- There is no longer any real connection between the family member and the business.
- Some shareholders, perhaps younger family members, would prefer to see value realised from the shares they have been gifted.
- A family shareholder is now retiring and wants to realise value for their retirement.

Lambrecht and Lievens,[43] question the basic model of family business life stages.[44] They argue that many family businesses consciously choose the simplicity of a limited ownership model, in preference to the complexity brought by wider family ownership. These families choose to prune back ownership rather than allowing the branches of the family business tree to grow in an unmanageable way.

The pruned back family business should have a number of advantages. There will be a much closer correlation between ownership and management. More resource should be available for re-investment, or, for that matter management remuneration, without the requirement to balance the needs and expectations of family outsiders to dividends. The need for governance systems will be reduced, so agency costs will be lower. The risk of damaging conflict should also be reduced.[45] Indeed the authors argue that restricting ownership is a key factor in family business longevity citing other commentators,[46] in support of their proposition that:[47]

> 'family businesses that are more than a century old owe their great age to pruning, among other things. They limit the number of family shareholders.'

---

[42] See Figure 3.13 in chapter 3.
[43] Johan Lambrecht, Jozef Lievens 'Pruning the Family Tree: An Unexplored Path to Family Business Continuity and Family Harmony' *Family Business Review* (2008), Vol 25(4) at pp 295–313.
[44] As outlined in chapter 3, these are owner managed, sibling partnership and cousin collaboration. As explored in chapter 15, Gersick also question the classic 'linear succession model' and identifies 9 different possible succession permutations.
[45] Or at least one species of conflict, that between family business insiders and outsiders as in the *Cadman* and *Saul D Harrison* cases. Plenty of scope remains for conflicts between sibling participators – see chapter 21 for examples.
[46] Gallo 'Why do 100 year-old family businesses get so old?' *Family Business Advisor* (2006), 15(7), 4.
[47] At p 299 of the Lambrecht and Lievens article.

The authors argue that pruning can create a family business owned by highly motivated and cohesive family members, with shared and identical interests, a clan family firm within Dyers classification.[48]

There are of course disadvantages to the simplified, restricted ownership model resulting from pruning the family business tree. One of these could be the loss of liquidity to the family business itself. Business cash used to buy back a relative's shares is inevitably lost for reinvestment or other business purposes. But the authors argue that the distraction of conflict, that could otherwise ensue, more than makes up for the lost liquidity.

Perhaps the greatest single disadvantage to pruning is the loss of the ideal. The founder's dream may have been for long-term participation of the whole family in the business. For that reason alone many business-owning families will attempt to follow a wider ownership model, at least in the first instance.

Ideally these issues will be explored a part of the ownership succession process. But frequently they surface after that process has been completed. The ownership succession could have been based on a wider family ownership approach. Despite initial optimism that this could be made to work, problems have subsequently arisen, so that some pruning of the ownership tree becomes necessary.

Although pruning to create restricted ownership is available to the business family as part of their succession planning exercise Lambrecht and Lieven's research suggested that:[49]

> 'the assumption of the simpler form generally does not occur during the generational transfer. The family tree is pruned only after several family members of the same generation have become owners and/or managers of the family business.'

In most of these cases it appears that something happened that persuaded the business owning family to abandon their previous wider ownership philosophy. Even the most traditional proponents of the inclusive model of family business evolution recognise that it is unrealistic for every family business member to share the founder's dream of full family participation for all eternity and that, accordingly pruning has its place. Lesson 32 from John Ward is that cousin collaborations should have a policy of 'Fair Facilitated Redemption Freedom',[50] so that an exit route is available for a family business member who wants to cash in their shares.

One of Ward's key points is that even after the individuals concerned have sold out, and are therefore no longer part of the ownership system, they still remain part of the family system and should be recognised and embraced as such. Accordingly exiting family members should remain on the invitation list for family assemblies and other forms of wider family communication.

So there appears to be a universal consensus that pruning has an important role to play in family business ownership and should therefore form a key component of any family business governance system.

---

[48] See chapter 3. Although it must be said that one of dictionary definitions of 'clan' is 'a family holding together' which does seem to imply the opposite of pruning.
[49] At p 304.
[50] John Ward *Perpetuating the Family Business* (Palgrave, 2004) Lesson 29 at p 111.

11.14 PRUNING AND TREE SURGERY

There is of course the opportunity for the current senior generation to adopt a restricted ownership model as part of their succession planning arrangements. This opens up the possibility of compensating the outsiders by letting them have a proportionally larger share of the non-business assets held by the senior generation.

Leaving this aside, and assuming that the inter-generational succession has taken place based on a wider inclusive ownership model, there are two levels of pruning. The approach taken depends on how deep seated the tensions and difficulties referred to above are.

11.14.1 Buy-outs of individual family members

The first approach is where one or more individual family members sell some or all of their shares. This can properly be categorised as pruning: routine maintenance of the family business ownership structure.

Pruning might be needed as a result of some level of tension or conflict. But this need not be the case. Family members, especially younger outsiders, might simply want to raise capital for their own private purposes, deposits on houses etc. The Ward approach works on the basis that if there is a fair way out of the family firm, the family member concerned will be more likely to take that route at an early stage, before tension has built up and conflict has occurred. They are therefore correspondingly more likely to remain as a participator in the family system. They could even re-enter the ownership system later on when they have accumulated more surplus capital.

The purchaser will usually be either other insider family members (or sometimes non-family shareholders including employees) or the family company itself. Some of the technical considerations for pursuing either approach are considered below. Some alternative buyers are considered below.

Buy-outs can be of individuals or larger groups of family members, often separate branches or groups of outsiders. Large-scale buy-outs can be seen more as fairly drastic tree surgery. Third party borrowing might be required and the family business ownership system will be radically changed afterwards, possibly returning to the simplified form of a sibling partnership or even an owner-managed enterprise.

Pruning can take place as an informal ad-hoc response to situations that have arisen within the family firm. Alternatively, in anticipation that pruning and exit routes are likely to be required at some point in the future exit and buy-out arrangements can be incorporated into family business governance documents, including articles of association, shareholders' agreements, or what the Americans call 'buy-sell agreements'.

The key message is that for a buy-out arrangement to work, in the sense of having the best hope of maintaining or restoring family relationships, the process must be seen by all parties to have been transparent and fair. This is especially the case in terms of arriving at a fair price.

Lambrecht and Lievens[51] explain that:

> 'The theory of procedural justice or a fair process derives from the research of Thibault and Walker (1975). They determined that people find the justice of a process just as important as the outcome itself. A fair process is based on the combination of three principles: involvement, explanation, and clear playing rules.'

Arguably these requirements are much more likely to be satisfied if the exit arrangements are contained in governance documents, discussed and agreed in advance of the exit event. Even if the selling family member did not participate personally in negotiations it is likely that one of their immediate family members did. Exit will have been discussed as an abstract concept by the family, rather than a response to a real issue. Any family member could be either a buyer or a seller. As a matter of negotiating theory the end result is more likely to be a balanced and fair agreement.

The most dangerous position would be if either party and, more often, but not always, the seller, believes that the remaining family members have somehow exploited their position. For example, the insiders have used the seller's need for ready cash and lack of access to funds to pursue a dispute, to acquire the seller's inheritance on the cheap.[52]

The mechanics of buy-backs, which are a widely used tool in regulating family business ownership are discussed below in **11.17**.

11.14.2 Re-organisations

In some cases buy-outs of individual family members will not be possible or practicable. In these cases some wider re-organisation of the family business will be required. This is definitely tree surgery. Although it is not practicable to look at re-organisations in any great detail, one or two of the more frequently used mechanisms are briefly examined at the end of this chapter.

We now turn to examine some common pruning tools.

11.15 COMPULSORY DIVESTMENT PROVISIONS

Compulsory transfer provisions can be seen as a type of pruning tool.

If entitlement to membership of a family company is based on a particular criterion, it is entirely logical that the right to membership should cease if that condition is no longer satisfied. There can be various qualifying conditions for holding shares in family companies. Sometimes these remain implicit. How far should a family go to make these conditions both explicit and legally enforceable?

Compulsory transfer provisions almost invariably operate as call options, allowing the remaining members to buy. Whether that option is exercised will depend on various factors that are discussed below in the context of pre-emption provisions.

---

[51] At p 309.
[52] There were suggestions of this in the Harding farming family dispute discussed in detail in chapter 22.

11.15.1 Non-family transferees

As discussed above it is extremely common for business families to restrict permitted transfer of ownership to bloodline family members. Occasionally transfers will be made in breach of these provisions, for example leaving shares directly to a spouse in a will. Once the principle of defining who is a family member has been established provisions requiring the company to refuse to register the transfer and requiring any interest in the spouse to be re-allocated to a permitted beneficiary, for example children, can be seen as simple drafting competence.

11.15.2 Family employment

Similarly provisions requiring non-family employee shareholders to sell, or at least offer to sell, their shares when leaving employment are entirely standard, highly recommended and largely unobjectionable.

On occasions these will appear to apply to family employees. Almost always this is an accident of drafting.[53] Compulsory divestment for departing family employees would be an absurdity in a family that encourages wide family share ownership.

But what about the opposite situation, where a family has established a strict insider ownership policy? If a family member leaves employment they will no longer satisfy this primary ownership condition. In which case why should departing family insiders not be subject to the same logic as that applied to non-family employees? At first sight this appears to be a fairly simple question to answer. Why not? In a sibling partnership the continuing partners would have the right to acquire the departing insider's shares. They would then join any other non-owning, non-employee siblings in the outsider encampment. This question does raise one of the fundamental issues of ownership approach: how conditional or absolute is a gift of ownership in a family business intended to be?[54]

The inclusion of insider compulsory transfer provisions can also expose the family business to the law of unintended consequences. Assuming the insider's interest to have reasonably significant value, the incentive for self-interest to override what is best for the family business takes over. The potential manifestations of this are many and varied. Nepotism could be encouraged. If the insiders want to keep value within their own branch, they are incentivised to turn their own offspring into insiders. The next generation concerned might be entirely unsuitable and have no real wish to join the family enterprise. They may have a miserable career as a result. Sibling rivalry and factionalism is difficult to avoid in a family business. The potential for problems must increase if driving out a family insider carries a financial benefit for the remaining insiders.

Finally and paradoxically such provisions could operate to prevent the sale of the family business. This point is explored further in chapter 15.

The question of whether compulsory transfer provisions should apply to family employees is perhaps rarely asked. If it is, for the reasons suggested above, our view is

---

[53] See chapter 26.
[54] See the discussion on Gifts with strings? in chapter 15 (Ownership Succession).

almost certainly not. Instead the business owning family needs to invest their effort in examining their approach to ownership as part of the governance and succession planning process. Fair and viable voluntary exit routes provide a much better alternative.

11.15.3 Divorce

The controversial question of whether compulsory share transfer provisions should apply to any non-bloodline spouses who might have acquired shares in a family company on divorce is considered in chapter 18.

11.16 PRE-EMPTION PROVISIONS

Most family business constitutions will include pre-emption provisions, giving options or rights of first refusal to other shareholders, if shares are being offered for transfer. These provisions need to dovetail with the permitted transfer provisions and operate alongside and sequentially immediately, after the permitted transfer provisions have been worked through.

The wider the permitted transfer regime (see **11.11.4**) the lesser the scope and relevance of pre-emption provisions.

Pre-emption provisions will also apply to re-allocate any shares that are subject to compulsory transfer provisions.

The first question to answer in structuring pre-emption provisions is who are shares to be offered to? The second question is in what order? Some families, in an attempt to move as far away from branch and other factionalism have no, or very narrow, permitted transfer provisions (perhaps allowing gifts to children only), so that all or most shares available for transfer are offered to the wider family. Yet again other families adopt hybrid pre-emption procedures so that shares are first offered to family branch members, before being made available to the wider family.

11.16.1 Key issues

Once the question of who should be offered shares has been addressed it is necessary to move onto the question of how the process should operate. Pre-emption procedures can be fairly complex and need to address these key issues:

Price

The starting point is usually that the price at which shares are to be offered can be agreed between the selling shareholder and the board. The default arrangement will usually be some form of third party valuation (see below). In the case of employee shareholders 'good and 'bad' leaver clauses are often included in share documentation, so that if they leave under a cloud, the price paid for the shares is reduced, but if they leave for good reasons, say through retirement then the employees receive full value for their shares.

It would be extremely unusual for good leaver and bad leaver provisions to apply to family employees.

In the case of some transactions, particularly for larger shareholdings, or where family dynamics are poor, it may be appropriate to include in the agreement some 'anti-embarrassment' provisions. So that, if there were a sale or flotation of the family company within a short period of time, that values the company at a significantly higher amount than the transaction which has taken place, then the former shareholder receives some proportion of that uplift in value.

Valuation principles

Because there is no ready market for the shares, it is in effect impossible to arrive at a precise valuation of an unquoted family company. Various methods of valuation can be adopted which can produce radically different results. Occasionally a formula for the valuation is set out in the agreement, based on historic profits, net assets or a combination of the two.

In larger companies family, with employee share option schemes, valuations, of some description, are likely to have been obtained for the purposes of those schemes. These could possibly be used for valuing family shares also. These last two approaches may be especially relevant in dealing with small parcels of shares, where the cost of a full valuation process can easily outweigh the value of those shares. More often than not a separate valuation will be needed.

Discounts

A key question is whether the shares being sold are to be valued as a proportion of the overall value of the family company, or at a discount, to reflect that a minority interest is being sold. The most common arrangement is however for shares to be valued on a full enterprise basis. Under usual valuation principles significant discounts would be applied for minority shareholdings[55] in (even large) unquoted companies. It will usually be expressly provided that these should be ignored for family exit valuations.

Valuation procedure

If a price cannot be agreed to avoid an impasse when it comes to the shares being sold, the articles, shareholders' agreement or buy and sell option agreements, should contain provisions for the valuation process. Options often seen are that:
- the value is determined by the company's auditors;
- the parties agree an independent third party to determine a value;
- the President of the Institute of Chartered Accountants is asked to appoint an independent expert to determine the value, usually if the parties cannot agree who should carry out the valuation.

Occasionally, and in an attempt to demonstrate to the departing family member that fairness can be seen to have been done multiple valuations may be obtained. The price chosen will be the average of these.

---

[55] These discounts on usual valuation principles can be as much as 90%.

Overall, families need to find a balance between, on one hand, the cost and complexity of operating their share transfer system and, on the other hand, the need, which we have previously identified, for all concerned to see that a fair process has been followed.

Costs of valuation

The costs of the valuation can be significant. There are various approaches as to how those costs should be borne:

- The crudest approach is to split them equally between the seller and the company.
- Often the family company will bear the costs of an auditor's valuation, on the basis that this is simply a cost of governance.
- The most sophisticated approach is to apportion costs based on outcome and conduct so that any third party valuer has some discretion to penalise any party that has caused unnecessary costs to be incurred, either by taking an unrealistic approach to value or behaving unreasonably in the way they have conducted the procedure.

Timescale

Timescales for the operation of pre-emption provisions in non-family owned private companies tend to be quite short with, perhaps 30 days, allowed for the remaining shareholders to decide whether or not to take up their allocation. We would usually recommend longer timescales for family owned business. If the object is to encourage family ownership, extra time might be needed to allow family members more time to raise funds etc., before committing to buy. This is especially important if sales to third parties are permitted (see below). Shorter timescales could disadvantage (or even eliminate) possible family purchasers. If ownership is confined to family members, longer timescales are to the benefit of both buyer and seller as it gives more time for the main (or perhaps only) voluntary realistic exit option to be explored.

Payment terms

Similar considerations apply to payment terms. The approach in non-family owned companies is often to provide for cash to be payable in full on completion. To encourage sales to family members payments by instalments over 2 to 5 years are often included.

Waivers and variations

Particular in the case of smaller business owning families, it is always open for the family to agree different timescales and variations to the pre-emption procedure. Indeed in the vast majority of cases share transfers take place on the basis of informal agreements and discussions between buyers and sellers. The board (or possibly the family council) often act as facilitators to help agree price, identify buyers and obtain confirmation that the non-buying family shareholders are content to stand back. This acceptance would then be confirmed in short documents formally waiving pre-emption rights. In this way the formal pre-emption procedure can be seen as a fall back or starting position. It is nevertheless vitally important.

11.16.2 Secondary pre-emption rounds

Is it sensible to encourage the take up of shares through further, secondary, pre-emption rounds? These give existing family members a second chance to acquire any shares that were not taken up in the first round of pre-emption. This adds to the complexity of the process.[56] But it might create a viable exit route.

11.16.3 A family trust

There may already be family business trusts in existence that would agree to take more shares. Some families set up and fund trusts specifically to acquire and effectively 'warehouse' unwanted shares until a buyer can be found.

11.16.4 Wider family offers

Although rare, mechanisms are sometimes included to allow family members, who are not currently shareholders, to be offered surplus shares in a second round of the pre-emption process. One family took this approach based on a clear philosophy that ownership should be encouraged amongst the widest group of bloodline family members possible.

If the primary purpose of pruning is to restrict and simplify the ownership tree, this approach could have the opposite effect. It could increase the number of shareholders. But the better analysis is that by offering shares to wider family non-members new shoots are being encouraged to grow on the family ownership tree.

Inevitably wider family pre-emption provisions pose drafting issues and problems of procedure and certainty. For example, just how far need the family company secretariat go to track down estranged family members to offer them surplus shares without invalidating the process?[57]

11.16.5 If not the family, who else?

Of course even after an exhaustive secondary pre-emption round, there might still be no buyer found. The final and perhaps the most significant question to address in drafting pre-emption provisions for family owned businesses is, who else, if anyone, can shares be transferred to if the current family members do not wish to buy?

For families with a pure family ownership philosophy the answer will be nobody. But the family ownership base may well provide few or no buyers leaving the seller with no

---

[56] Although not necessarily the length of the process. It is possible, in terms of drafting to ask for indications or commitments to take up surplus shares not taken up in the 'first round' of the pre-emption process at the outset.

[57] The case of *Tett v Phoenix Property and Investment Co Ltd* [1986] BCLC 149 (Court of Appeal), discussed by Andrew McGee *Shares and Share Capital under the Companies Act 2006* (Jordan Publishing, 2009) provides a good illustration of this. In that case the secondary pre-emption round required the ownership appetites of spouses, children an parents of members to be tested. The pre-emption process was messed up. The court indicated that notice to an actual member might be sufficient constructive notice to their wider immediate family, on the basis that members could be expected to pass on details of the pre-emption offer to their own relatives. It is suggested that this is not really a safe approach. Instead the obligations of the secretariat should be relegated to making 'reasonable endeavours' to involve wider family members.

real market for their shares. In which case both fairness and received wisdom dictate that serious consideration should be given to creating an 'off family market' exit route (as discussed below).

11.16.5 Employee offers

Some constitutions allow employees (or in some cases senior employees approved by the board) to step into the pre-emption procedure as default buyers if the family do not take up their full allocation. In effect these employees are seen as having the status of quasi-family members.[58] Including employees in the pre-emption process in this way is part of a planned process.

11.16.7 Third party transfers

The default provision in most non family business articles is to allow a shareholder to sell any shares not taken up by existing shareholders to a third party. This will be entirely inappropriate for any family with a pure family ownership philosophy. Often there will be no real likelihood of a third party being prepared to buy the shares on offer and to become an unwelcome, minority shareholder guest at the family shareholder table. There is no real possibility that family ownership will be diluted. The drafting issue is entirely theoretical.

Employees are one potential exception. Here the scenario is that a senior employee surfaces as an opportunistic buyer, rather than as part of a plan for the employees to provide a more general secondary market for family shares as part of the pre-emption process.

So what are the indicative factors that would create a climate for a sale to a third party? These would include larger, multi-generational family businesses, with a wide family shareholder base, particularly a business struggling with business performance and financial issues. The wider family might have little direct involvement in management of the business, which is led by increasingly influential non-family managers. A large proportion of the shareholder base might be disenfranchised or disengaged. In short the family grip is weak. These circumstances can allow the non-family management to obtain a strategic stake as the first stage of an expropriation sale.[59]

In a much smaller number of cases acquiring a minority stake may have strategic value to competitors or others seeking to acquire the business. A weak commitment to the family business, coupled with a lack of either dividends or an alternative exit route has been known to leave the back door of the family business open to unwelcome non-family shareholders.

---

[58] Employees share ownership is discussed in more detail in chapter 6.
[59] The concept is discussed and explained in chapter 12.

11.17 EXIT ARRANGEMENTS

11.17.1 The case for exit arrangements

Here we are using the term 'exit arrangements' in the sense of additional mechanisms and provisions that will kick in to help a family member exit the business, if the usual and voluntary pre-emption provisions have failed to find a family buyer.

There may be no natural or voluntary market for family business shares. Any possible buyers could be excluded because of share transfer restrictions. If so, to what extent should a market be created or stimulated to provide an effective exit route for a family member who, for whatever reason, no longer wants to remain as an owner?

Broadly put if the exit arrangements are non-existent or too restrictive unwilling family shareholders are help captive in the family business and tensions will inevitably build. Too liberal an exit policy and the stability of the business as a family owned operation is placed in jeopardy. The approach taken to this balance will differ from business family to business family.

This gives rise to a corresponding need for flexibility and creativity in drafting appropriate exit provisions to support the chosen approach in articles and shareholders' agreements. The next few paragraphs look briefly at some of the tools that can be used to create this internal market or exit route.

11.17.2 Dealing periods

Families with a larger shareholder base may wish to add provisions to create or stimulate an internal family market for the shares of those wishing to exit. These arrangements will often involve the board arranging a share valuation at a set time each year and then administering a system inviting interested shareholders to offer to either buy or sell shares from each other at that price. Clarks shoes employ such as system.

11.17.3 Put options

Ideally the voluntary exit process will match willing sellers with family buyers who are willing to pay a fair price to increase their own stake in the family firm. However a combination of low dividends[60] and little prospect of capital gain if the family are committed to long-term ownership will rarely make acquiring more shares an attractive investment proposition. If buyers are found they will often be motivated, to a significant extent, by non-economic considerations.

Shares can therefore remain unsold. Some families are fully committed to offering a viable exit route, so that ownership is gradually concentrated in family members genuinely interested in long term ownership, a fully committed family business clan in Dyer's terminology. These families may choose to underpin the voluntary transfers with provisions giving the seller the right to ask to be bought out. In effect creating an artificial market through compulsory purchase provisions through the use of put options.

---

[60] Which might relate more to re-investment and prudence than the financial weakness of the family firm.

This can be in situations where third party sales are expressly prohibited. Equally the introduction of put options might be based on a realisation that for many, if not most, family owned businesses it is extremely unlikely that a third party purchaser will be found (except possibly from amongst employees). Put options are fairly rare and would usually sit underneath more routine pre-emption provisions.

11.17.4 ... on other shareholders

If there are to be put options upon whom should the sellers' shares be put?

This is a difficult question to answer. The first and most logical candidates would appear to be the other family shareholders. But it is likely to be a step too far in the direction of creating an exit route to oblige the remaining shareholders to buy the leaver's shares. First they would need to find funds to fund the buy-out. Secondly a compulsory purchase would increase the risk profile and decrease the liquidity of those remaining in the family firm. It could also create instability in a struggling family firm, with a tactical advantage being afforded to the 'first rat' to leave the sinking family ship. A put option could also be used tactically against other shareholders if a dispute had arisen.

The put-option need not operate at full market value. To mitigate against these factors, creating an exit route through put options, could carry with it a discount to full pro-rata market value.[61] Even this might impose too much of a burden on the remaining shareholders. They would be still be obliged to find funds privately to buy shares in circumstances where, although committed to stay with the family company, they might have no wish to increase their stake and the wealth they have at risk in the business. Also unless the shares were in high demand amongst family members, there would be little incentive to bid for the departing shareholder's interest in a normal pre-emption round.

Price differentials could also be seen to be penalising a family member who simply want to leave the ownership circle, for entirely legitimate and understandable reasons.

11.17.5 Compulsory buy-back provisions

The other alternative would be the family company itself. If buyers were not found for the seller's full stake through the usual pre-emption process the company would be obliged to buy back the remainder. The mechanics of buy-backs are considered in a little more detail in **11.18** below. This may seem extremely complicated. Nevertheless some default position, whereby the company acts as a purchaser of last resort, may offer the only realistic guaranteed exit route for a minority family shareholder.

The presence of provisions such may offer a degree of defence or protection to the majority against unfair prejudice petitions brought under CA, s 994. Usually the remedy sought will be the compulsory acquisition of the shares held by the minority.[62]

---

[61] Or looked at otherwise, some or all of the discounts that would be attributable to sales of minority interests in unquoted shares in a family company on normal valuation principles could be recognised in the put option price.

[62] For a more detailed discussion on unfair prejudice see chapter 21.

Again there is an issue of balancing the interests of the family member wishing to exit and the collective interests of the remaining family members represented through the balance sheet of the family company. A compulsory buy-back will not require individual family members to contribute personal funds to buy-out the departing shareholder. The buy-back will nevertheless divert money otherwise available for distribution as dividends, or cash that could be reinvested in the growth of the company. To achieve an appropriate balance of interests the family might wish to explore amendments to dividend policies so that, for example, 50% of dividends (that would otherwise be paid under the usual dividend policy) could be paid out to the shareholders generally, but the remainder withheld and diverted to fund the buy-back.

Other variables that can be adjusted to achieve the desired balance include:

- Price and in particular whether activating the compulsory buy-back carries some form of discount.
- Timescale for the buyback.[63]
- Restrictions on the exercise of the buy-back, with reference to numbers of shares, shareholders or time periods (for example that the procedure can only be used to force the family company to buy back a maximum of 10% of the capital in any 5-year period).
  In practice drafting a workable buy-back option is complicated. The buy-back regime under the provisions of CA, ss 690–708 works on the basis of conditions that must be satisfied at the time the buy-back takes place. The most significant of these is that the company has sufficient distributable reserves to finance the buy-back. The company would also need to go through the buy-back procedure set out in the Companies Acts. However a workable mechanism, whereby all shareholders commit to put these precise statutory procedures into effect can be created.

In addition, if the seller activates the buy-back put option, they cannot be guaranteed favourable tax treatment.[64] Possibly the seller could seek the appropriate clearance from HMRC that capital treatment will apply before deciding whether to activate the put option buy-back procedure. Equally a recognition that HMRC clearance would be desirable could be built into the procedure.

As company buy-backs are also a primary tool used in 'voluntary' restructurings and pruning exercises we will now briefly look at some of the technical issues involved.

11.18 COMPANY BUY-BACKS

11.18.1 Overview

Buy-backs, or purchases of own shares, are probably the most widely used tool in exit planning by family owned companies.

Often no family member will want to step in and buy the shares of those who want to exit. In these circumstances another method of buying out these shares may need to be

---

[63] Although any installment arrangements will need to take into account the requirements in CA, s 691(2) that 'where a company purchases its own shares, the shares must be paid for on the purchase'.
[64] Explained in more detail in chapter 16.

found. In many cases the family may want to use cash reserves in the company, or its borrowing potential rather than their own personal resources. Fortunately in these circumstances, company law allows a private company to buy back its own shares.

Buy-backs also have a potential tax-trap. This is that the starting point under tax legislation is that the most of the proceeds of sale would normally be treated as a dividend and taxed as dividend income. This obviously can create a larger tax liability for the shareholder than if they had to pay capital gains tax. A clearance from HMRC allowing capital treatment may be available. This issue is considered in detail in chapter 16.

11.18.2 Basic legal requirements – CA, ss 690–708

There are certain basic legal conditions that need to be met to validly authorise a buy-back of shares. These are set out in CA, ss 690–708, the most important of which being:

- The shares must be fully paid.[65]
- The Articles must not restrict or prohibit the purchase of own shares.[66]
- Financing of the buy-back must be strictly in accordance with the provisions of CA, s 692. Usually this will mean having sufficient distributable reserves to cover the purchase price. This point is explored in more detail below.
- The full amount due, must be paid on completion and cannot be deferred.[67] This requirement is also discussed in more detail below.
- The purchase must be authorised by a special resolution of the members.[68]
- The purchase must be in accordance with a contract between the company and the seller the terms of which have also been approved by the members.[69]

There are strict procedures to be followed set out in the detail of the above sections. In chapter 12 (Selling the family business) we suggest that defects in buy-back procedures are one of the most common issues raised by buyer's lawyers as part of their due diligence, potentially de-railing the sale.

11.18.3 Financing the buy-back payment

A core principle of company law is the capital maintenance rule. Shortly and simply put this is that the capital of a company, represented by its cash and other assets should not be returned to shareholders, unless it is clear that the creditors of the company can be paid. So dividends can only be paid out of distributable reserves.

---

[65] CA, s 691(1).
[66] CA, s 690(1)(b). Previously the opposite applied. The articles of a company needed to expressly authorise a purchase of own shares. Most did, other than those of very old companies.
[67] CA, s 691(2).
[68] CA, s 693A.
[69] CA, s 694.

As a buy-back has the effect of returning capital to shareholders it will usually be necessary to check that the company has distributable reserves (in other words profits that could otherwise be used to pay dividends), at least equivalent to the amount of the payment being made for the shares.[70]

There are some other payment routes, but payments from distributable reserves are by far the most usual method of financing a buy-back. The other methods allowed are:

- **Small buy-backs.**[71] CA 2006 introduced a *de-minimis* exception to the capital maintenance rule which is potentially helpful in buying back small holdings. Payments can be made out of cash providing these do not exceed the lower of £15,000 or 5% of the company's capital in any one financial year. However the articles must include an express ability to make these payments.
- **Proceeds of a fresh issue of shares.**[72] Buy-backs can also be financed by the proceeds of a fresh share issue. This is logical. The capital being withdrawn on the buy-back is replaced by that injected into the company by the proceeds of the fresh issue.
- **Capital.** There is a complicated route to buy back shares out of capital contained in CA, Chapter 5, ss 709–723 is to be followed. However the procedure calls into question the basic solvency of the company. The directors' must prepare detailed statements of solvency, supported by reports from the auditors. The proposed payment out of capital must be publicised in a national newspaper. As their interests would potentially be affected by the payment, express notice must be sent to creditors.[73]
  Whilst buy-backs out of capital do occur with reasonable frequency they are nowhere near as common as buy-backs from distributable reserves.
- **Reduction of capital.** Under the Companies Act 2006 it is now easier to obtain a reduction of capital than under previous legislation so this route could be considered as an alternative to a buy-back out of capital.[74]

11.18.4 Timing of buy-back payment

CA, s 691(2) requires the purchase price for the shares bought back to be paid on completion of the buy-back. Instalments are not allowed.

Frequently buy-backs are as a result of some form of dispute of conflict involving the exiting family member. Often this is set against a backdrop of a poor or deteriorating financial position of the family business. Whilst the business may have the distributable reserves on its balance sheet, it is simply not in a position to finance the buy-out of the family member concerned and to find the cash available to do this in one lump sum. In theory the buy-back could also be financed by the proceeds of a fresh issue of shares. But the only realistic candidates as subscribers for such a fresh issue are likely to be other family members. Those family members may simply not have the cash to subscribe. Even if they do they might lack the appetite to tie up further private cash and increase their risk exposure to the family business. The only realistic option might therefore be a

---

[70] CA, s 692(2)(a)(i).
[71] CA, s 692(2)(1)(b).
[72] CA, s 692(2)(1)(a).
[73] CA, s 719(2)(b).
[74] For a more detailed explanation see Andrew McGee *Shares and Share Capital under the Companies Act 2006* (Jordan Publishing, 2009).

payment in instalments by the family company. However the provisions of CA, s 691(2) and its predecessors make it clear that the purchase price has to be paid 'on purchase' and therefore in a single lump sum.

A device often employed to reconcile this statutory requirement with the commercial reality of the family business, is for the price to be paid over to the exiting family member, but on the basis that a significant proportion of the sale proceeds are then loaned back to the company. Some commentators support the validity of these sale and loan back arrangements and take the view that a buy-back structured in this way complies with the strict requirements of the Act.[75] However there does not appear to be any decided authority on this important practical point.

11.18.5 Key procedural points

The buy-back procedure set out in CA, ss 690–708 must be followed precisely. This commentary is not intended to provide a line by line analysis of the requirements[76] but to highlight some of the main failures to follow the statutory approval procedures that arise in practice:

- **Selling member.** It is important that the family member whose shares are being bought back does not join in the voting and approval process. The natural inclination is to include all members in relevant resolutions. However CA, s 695 provides that a buy-back resolution is invalid if voted on by the exiting shareholder and the resolution 'would not have been passed if he had not done so'. The intent behind this provision is presumably a form of minority protection. In effect to prevent majority shareholders barging onto the life boats leaving the minority shareholders behind on the sinking family ship. However the practical effect is often to create a technical trap in structuring buy-backs (and a mathematical headache for lawyer reviewing their validity as part of due diligence exercises).

- **Display of the buy-back contract.** One of the more unusual features of the buy-back regime, is that the buy-back contract must be available for inspection at the registered office for 15 days before the meeting to approve that contract takes place.[77]
  This trap has much less practical significance since the written resolution regime has been available to approve buy-backs. This simply requires that a copy of the contract is attached to the written resolution approving the buy-back.[78]

- **Stamp duty.** A buy-back operates to cancel the relevant share rather than transfer them. Accordingly a stock transfer form is not needed in relation to the shares bought back (although some practitioners prefer to adopt a belt and braces approach and still produce a form). Stamp duty is nevertheless payable on the buy-back. This is collected by Companies House, at the time the return relating the buy-back (form SHO3) is filed. As with most filings, the failure to file the relevant return is criminal offence on the part of both the company and its officers.[79]

---

[75] See, for example Dougherty and Fairpro *Company Acquisition of Shares* (Jordan Publishing, 6th edn, 2013) at pp 57–58. The key point is that there must be an actual payment and loan back.
[76] For a more detailed analysis of buy-back provisions Dougherty and Fairpro *Company Acquisition of Shares* (Jordan Publishing, 6th edn, 2013).
[77] CA, s 696(2)(b)(i).
[78] CA, s 696(2)(a).
[79] CA, s 707(7).

11.18.6 Tax and buy-backs

This is considered along with other ownership tax issues in chapter 16.

11.19 RE-ORGANISATIONS

Re-organisations imply a more root and branch change to the structure of the family firm than buy-outs. Having said this the dividing line between a large-scale buy-out and a re-organisation is thin.

We will look briefly at two of the main forms of re-organisation used in practice.

11.19.1 Partition of the family firm

The partition of the family firm into separate businesses envisages root and branch surgery. Whereas buy-outs will leave the basic family business intact, albeit with a changed ownership, partitions split the business into two parts.

Partitions are often employed in circumstances of extreme tension, if not outright conflict, within the business owning family. The dream of family togetherness will have been shattered, large cracks will have appeared in that vision. Usually one branch of a business family will split off taking a part of the family business with them.

On occasions the partition can provide a relatively neat technical solution to difficult family circumstances. Perhaps siblings with a conflicted relationship have been given separate operating businesses or divisions to look after, in the hope that keeping them apart operationally will prevent outright warfare from breaking out. If this hope proves unfounded, then it could be a relatively simple matter for each to take the business they have been responsible for and run it as an independent concern.

Alternatively a later stage family business could have developed a large portfolio of investment assets. If tension has arisen between the outsiders and the insiders it might be possible to partition the overall business so that the outsiders take the investment properties and the insiders the operating business.

Often the main capital asset of the family firm will be the freehold properties used in the operating business. There might not be sufficient liquidity or third party borrowing available for an outright buy-out of the outsiders. The solution chosen may then be to partition the assets into a separate operating company or 'Op-Co', owned by the insiders and a property holding company or 'Prop-Co' owned by the outsiders. As the partition would involve substituting a fractious relationship of co-owners, for that of landlord and tenant, such an arrangement can often be a less than ideal solution. It may nevertheless be the best available.

On occasions 'Op-Co/Prop-Co' structures are undertaken as re-organisations rather than partitions and on the basis that all family members retain an interest, direct or indirect in both businesses. Often this can be in response to perceived risk, so that valuable property assets are kept apart from riskier trading operations. In this way tensions over the level of risk, which can often be a proxy for a lack of confidence by the outsiders in the ability of the insiders can be accommodated if, overall, the family want to remain in business together.

The method of partition most often used is the demerger.[80] Although there are a number of variations the most common format is for two new companies to be formed, one of which will ultimately be taken by each branch of the family. A liquidator is then appointed for the original family company. The family shareholders then agree with the liquidator to accept a transfer of the relevant assets each branch is to acquire under the partition or demerger to their respective new company in satisfaction for their claims to share in the surplus assets on winding up of the original family company.

This type of reconstruction can normally be achieved without any corporation tax or capital gains tax implications for the company or the shareholders. However there is likely to be a stamp duty cost.[81]

11.19.2 Share for share exchanges

An alternative route is to effectively abandon the old family company as an ownership vehicle and to carry out a reorganisation where a new company is formed to purchase the shares from those who wish to sell. This would involve the following steps:

A new company would be established ('Newco').

- Newco would acquire all the shares, of those shareholders who are going to continue to be involved in the target company in a share for share transaction.
- Newco would acquire the shares of the disposing shareholders for cash, which it would either borrow from a bank secured against the assets of the target company, or borrow from the target company.
- The target company can subsequently pay a dividend to Newco to eliminate the loan it has made to Newco, if that is the method chosen to fund the purchase.

This reorganisation should not create a capital gains tax liability for those shareholders exchanging their shares in Newco by virtue of the provisions of TCGA 1992, s 127. Share for share exchanges can often be used in circumstances where buy-backs are not available because of lack of distributable reserves. Borrowing can be introduced into Newco from banks or other sources, secured on the assets of the target company, which can be used to pay out the departing family members. If new shareholders are being introduced, for example employees to re-energise the business that borrowing will reduce the value of the shares being acquired and so reduce any employment related securities issues.

If it is likely that over a period of time, there will be a number of purchases of shares in the family company then the reorganisation route, described above, will create a significant amount of professional costs and disruption on a regular basis. Costs would also be incurred in connection with purchase of own shares arrangement, but as buybacks are more common and simpler, without the need for exchanges of shares or the creation of new corporate structures the costs of buybacks should be much lower.

---

[80] Under IA, s 110.
[81] These tax issues are briefly discussed in chapter 16.

11.20 OTHER METHODS OF ADJUSTING THE BALANCE OF OWNERSHIP

Before leaving this subject it is worth mentioning two further, but similar methods of addressing the issue of relative degrees of commitment amongst members of the business owning family. It would be difficult to categorise these methods as pruning, as both involve the issue of new shares. Nevertheless both methods can allow ownership of the family business to be focused on the most committed family members.

In both cases some incentive in terms of price, discount or other benefits could be considered for those family members who are prepared to increase their investment in the family company. But any incentives have to be carefully thought out and justifiable on commercial terms.[82]

11.20.1 Scrip or cash dividends

Scrip dividends are where shareholders are given a dividend in the form of additional or bonus shares rather than cash. The distributable reserves that that would otherwise be used to pay the dividend are in effect converted into share capital.

It is possible to give shareholders a choice between, taking a dividend in the usual cash form, or participating in the bonus offer. If they choose the latter cash is preserved and the balance sheet of the family company is strengthened.

The logic behind this approach is that commitment to the family firm may be relative rather than absolute. Some family members might want to remain as shareholders, for various reasons, including a wish to remain within the ownership circle. They might not feel it appropriate to actively sell shares in the family company. But neither may they want to increase the amount they have tied up in the family business. Other family members might be more whole-heartedly committed and prefer a marginally increased stake in the business to cash dividends. The axis of ownership shifts gradually to the more committed group.

The use of scrip dividends could therefore offer a mechanism to allow the gradual and subtle transfer of ownership and control to the latter, more fully committed group of family members, whilst still allowing the remaining family members to remain as owners. The family firm then has the potential to become increasingly like a family business clan (in Dyer's terminology).

11.20.2 Rights issues

Rights issues, where all existing shareholders are given the right to buy new shares. Logically only the most committed family members will invest further cash from their own resources to do so.

Both rights issues and scrip dividends are not without their difficulties. Those family members who do not participate may become more marginalised from the rest of the family. At some stage further pruning might be required. The directors will need to

---
[82] See chapter 21, and the discussion on 'wrongful rights issues'.

consider whether there is a true business need for the additional capital that will be provided for the company. They will also need to be sure that the subscription price and other terms of the rights issue can be fully justified commercially. If the real motive or effect is to dilute the influence of what they see as a troublesome group of family members, or to take commercial advantage of the outsiders, the share issues could be attacked by those family members.[83]

11.21 CONCLUSION

The ownership system is a key dimension in any family owned business. Because family members will often occupy different positions within the three-circle model their perspectives on ownership will often differ. The family business advisor has an important role to adopt and modify ownership rights and structures of family companies so that these are suitable for the circumstances of individual business families.

Exit provisions are a crucial element of ownership structures but these have to be tailored carefully, to achieve an appropriate balance between the needs of individual family members to obtain a fair and viable exit route and the requirements of the family company for stability.

---

[83] See, the discussion of 'wrongful rights issues in chapter 21 – for example *Sunrise Radio Limited; Geeta Kohli v Dr Avtar Lit, Ravinder Kumar Jain, Surinderpal Singh Lit, Sunrise Radio Limited* [2009] EWHC 2893 (Ch).

CHAPTER 12

SELLING THE FAMILY OWNED BUSINESS

12.1 INTRODUCTION

It is often assumed by the business owning family that their family businesses will remain in their family ownership forever. Yet every week many family businesses are sold to third parties. This chapter begins by looking at the reasons stemming from family dynamics underpinning this disconnect. It then goes on to provide a basic and general overview of a sale transaction.

Much of the sales process will be common to both family and non-family owned businesses and will not be discussed in any detail. However a number of issues and factors have particular relevance for family business situations and these are highlighted below.

12.2 FAMILY DYNAMICS AND SALE

As seen above, in fact only a minority of family businesses will stay in family ownership beyond the end of the second generation.[1] Of those that do not remain in family ownership a large number of family owned businesses are sold to non-family third party owners, including the management team. That sale may be influenced by a whole combination of factors and circumstances including some of the following:

- A premium offer received out of the blue, that the family believe they simply can't turn down. This could be from a competitor, perhaps based on a key strategic advantage of the business to the purchaser.
- Market conditions – perhaps making it difficult for, typically smaller, family owned businesses to compete effectively with larger publically quoted or multi-national businesses. Alternatively the family might perceive that the market has reached its peak.
- Exceptionally strong financial performance of the family business, creating a window of opportunity to sell when core maintainable earnings are high.
- Alternatively, deteriorating financial performance.
- A wish to diversify the investment and risks for the family away from a single family business.
- The family wish to pursue alternative opportunities to work together as a business owning family.
- Lack of liquidity or access to capital.

---

[1] See chapter 1 for a discussion on the mortality rates of family enterprises.

- Lack of family or other suitable management successors.
- The age of the business leader (where family succession is not an option).
- Alternative land use values of the operating premises of the family business, offering greater return than carrying on the business.
- Lack of pension of other financial resources away from the business to look after the senior generation in retirement.
- Insufficient non-business assets where the senior generation want insiders and outsiders to benefit equally.
- Differing levels of interest and commitment between family members to the business.
- Disputes or poor dynamics between family members.

There is often a further assumption, by the family and others, that a sale of a family business to a third party in some way represents a failure on the part of the business owning family. As suggested above, in practice there are a wide range of circumstances and factors leading to sale. Some of these are clearly positive, others much less so. At one end of the spectrum the sale might be the culmination of a carefully planned strategic process, fully supported by the business owning family, as a way of generating considerable personal wealth. At the other end of the scale the sale may indeed be forced upon the family as a result of failures in the business, management or family systems.

INSEAD based academics Klein and Blondel[2] looked at a number of family business sales in the UK and Germany and separated these into three categories:

- **Entrepreneurial.** In these sales, notwithstanding a degree of involvement on the part of the wider family in ownership or management, the leadership and decision making in relation to the family business, rested fairly and squarely with a single dominant family member. Just as these key individuals exhibited 'an autocratic pattern of decision making' in running the day-to-day operations of their business, they also dominated the decision making in relation to the sale. In these situations it will be the key entrepreneur who decides to initiate the sale, based on a mixture of personal, business and opportunistic reasons. Similarly it will be this key individual who controls the sale process including leading negotiations, agreeing price, appointing advisors etc. The remaining family members will play, at most, supporting, if not entirely passive roles in the process, notwithstanding that they hold management positions or, usually, minority stakes. What the business leader says goes. Klein and Blondel see strategic entrepreneurial sales as characteristic of relatively early stage (first to third generation) family businesses.
- **Strategic.** These sales often take place against a background of a more dispersed pattern of ownership, management and decision taking across the wider business owning family. Typically found in medium to older family businesses (third generation onwards) the family as a whole, employing their governance processes, fully involve working family managers, working and non-working owners in both the decision to sell and the sale process itself. Strategic sales are based on a carefully considered analysis that the sale is in the best overall interests of the business family. This is notwithstanding the long term emotional ties between the family and the business or that a number of family members are employed in the business. The decision to sell is often due to structural changes in the market that the family business operates in, lack of diversity, market concentration, etc.

---

[2] The Sale of the Family Business – Entrepreneurial Project, strategic Decision or Expropriation – INSEAD Working Paper Series 2004/25/IIFE.

- **Expropriation.** The most surprising and saddest category of sale identified by Klein and Blondel were what they termed 'expropriation cases'. They do not mean that the family business is taken from the family illegally. Rather that, due to a breakdown of family dynamics, the decision to sell the family business is in effect taken away from the business owning family and made by third parties. The study does not go into the specifics of exactly how this was achieved in any of the cases concerned. However the basic implication is that a combination of poor management, disputes and breakdowns of communication prevents the family from paying proper attention to their family business. The business either deteriorates or becomes over reliant on external third party management or shareholders. The family are no longer in a position to shape their own destiny and become vulnerable to outside market forces or over reliant on third party insiders, management or external investors. Ultimately the business itself or at least the decision to sell is removed from the hands of the family.
  Paradoxically, elaborate governance structures introduced to help control family disputes, such as pre-emption rights, can provide mechanisms making it easier for third parties to exploit differences between family members and to gain control of the family business.[3]

Equally there may be compelling reasons against sale. Sometimes these will be financially based. In other cases the reasons against sale may be more rooted in the emotional attachment of the family to the business. Reasons against sale include:

- The long-term total financial return for the family. This might be much greater than any realistic alternative investments could reasonably be expected to provide.[4]
- Loyalty to employees, the local community and other stakeholders.
- The extent to which family identity is bound up in family business ownership, with associated issues of legacy, tradition and stewardship.
- Employment opportunities for future generations.
- The potential for the business to provide a common sense of purpose and act as the glue to keep a family together.

Clearly few of the above factors are quantifiable and measurable in cold, analytical financial terms. Choosing to keep the business in family ownership may indeed result in the loss of other financial opportunities. What is clear is that a family that makes a decision to retain a business in family ownership based wholly or partly on non-financial factors, without addressing and finding adequate answers to compensate for the reasons pointing to sale; or, perhaps even more so, a family that puts its head in the sand and fails to address or even recognise these issues, will be heading for trouble. At best they might be postponing the inevitable day when the business needs to be sold, but then at a lower price. At worst they might be heading for gradually increasing discontent and disputes between family members, eventually leading to an expropriation sale.

In short a family that wishes their business to remain in family ownership long term has to create the conditions in which this can be happen. Asking and answering the question, 'do we want this business to remain family owned and, if so, how can we achieve this' is the key question for any family business governance process.[5]

---

[3] For example if the pre-emption procedure allows third parties or employee shareholders to buy unallocated shares.
[4] See for example the analysis in *A Look at the Numbers: Don't Sell* – FFI Practitioner November 1995.
[5] Discussed in detail in chapter 15 (Ownership Succession).

This issue is explored in detail by Carlock and Ward in *Strategic Planning for the Family Business*[6] where the authors advocate a 'parallel planning' process which looks simultaneously at business and family issues. The aim of the process is to arrive at the optimum overall strategy for the family business, which may include sale, by balancing:

- the commitment of the family to the business;
- against the internal capabilities of that business (including management and financial resources; and
- the external environment (market conditions and competition).

The decision may be to sell. If so it could prove crucial to the success of the transaction for any professional advising the family on the sale to develop not only an understanding of the main drivers for the sale but also any the reasons against, or objections to, the sale, together with the underlying family dynamics. Particularly if the transaction is taking place against a background of family discord or has elements of an expropriation sale extra steps and safeguards may need to be built into the sale, process.

12.3 SALE PROCESS – OVERVIEW

A detailed examination of the mergers and acquisitions or sales process goes beyond the scope of this book. However the process can be seen as having three distinct phases.

(1) Phase 1 – Pre-transaction which can last anything up to 3 years but rarely less than 6 months. This phase can include:

(a) *Strategic planning*. The process whereby the family arrive at the strategic decision to sell their business as referred to above.

(b) *Maximising the value on sale*. See **12.4** below.

(c) *Seller preparation*. See seller due diligence (**12.14** below).

(d) *Tax planning*. This is a huge topic in its own right and largely beyond the scope of this book. However an overview of the key topics can be found in chapter 16, including the hugely important issue of entrepreneur's relief against capital gains tax.

(e) *Selection of advisors*. There may be much to recommend using the existing advisors of the family business in terms of knowledge of the business, the family and also established teamwork with the family business leadership and also possibly between the advisors themselves. But family members leading a sale of their family business will be acutely aware that the transaction is likely to be the most significant event in the life of the family business. They will be equally aware of their responsibility to the wider family. It is fundamental to the success of the transaction that advisors have experience of sale transactions.

(f) *Marketing of the family business*. Frequently family businesses, are sold as a result of unsolicited approaches from trade competitors or suppliers. The obvious suspects may turn out to be the best buyer, offering the best price. Clearly this will not always be the case. The alternative approach is a full and professional marketing campaign for the business led by a corporate finance professional. This will involve detailed research into the market, often including potential international buyers, using proprietary databases. A 'teaser', containing basic

---

[6] Palgrave, 2001.

details of the family business or 'target', but without identifying the business concerned, is then sent to likely candidates to solicit interest.

(g) *Confidentiality agreement.* Also known as a non-disclosure agreement or NDA. Before disclosing detailed information about the target it is sensible to obtain a legally binding commitment from potential buyers not to use, or disclose further, any information provided to them by or on behalf of the seller. Ultimately this is only a piece of paper and the seller will be reluctant to face the costs, evidential burdens and risks of enforcing the agreement in the courts. Sellers should therefore be very wary of disclosing key, 'crown jewels', confidential information that could damage the family business if the transaction with the buyer does not proceed. This is of particular concern if potential purchasers include trade competitors.

(h) *Information memorandum or IM.* This is a detailed document, usually prepared by a corporate finance advisor sent to interested buyers who have signed a confidentiality agreement, to provide fairly detailed information about the family business including its financial position, market and opportunities and, usually on an anonymous basis, an overview of customers and employees. Effectively it is the equivalent of sales particulars for a property. Typically, IM's are between 10 and 25 pages long.

(i) *Negotiations.* Discussions with seriously interested buyers may stretch over many months. A corporate finance advisor will often take the lead in these negotiations. However key family members should expect to be fairly heavily involved and, on occasions, may take the lead in the process.

(j) *Selection of buyer.* The ideal position for the seller will be to keep as many potential buyers involved in the process and interested in the business for as long as reasonably and sensibly possible. One of the key roles for corporate finance advisors will be to stimulate competition between potential purchasers. Ultimately the family will need to choose the buyer who will take their business forward. This is discussed in more detail in **12.7** of this chapter below.

(k) *Price.* Of course the key term to be agreed in negotiations is price. Frequently buyers will attempt to proceed to advanced stages in negotiations without a firm commitment to price. This is dangerous for any seller. For a family business, for the reasons referred to above, the risks are arguably greater. Earn-outs, where part of the purchase price is payable after completion and dependent on the performance of the business, are an increasingly common feature of transactions. Again, the nature of family businesses raise particular concerns about the viability of earn outs, which are discussed in **12.6** below.

(2) Phase 2 – Transaction, typically 3–6 months and including:

(a) *Exclusivity or lock out.* Eventually a seller will need to commit to a single preferred buyer. That buyer will be committing significant internal resource and external costs incurred with advisors to the transaction. Almost invariably a buyer will want to agree a period of exclusivity, where the sellers agree to take the business off the market and do not to continue discussions with any other interested buyers. Exclusivity arrangements may be contained in legally binding provisions in the heads of terms (see below). Alternatively these might form a separate agreement signed at about the same time. This is a key stage for the selling family. Realistically their negotiating position is likely to decline from this point. The sellers will also be incurring costs. It will be difficult to retain interest from other buyers if the transaction does not proceed with the chosen buyer. Notwithstanding that there may be many legitimate reasons why the initial transaction did not proceed, the family business may be tainted by the initial failed transaction. The seller may have disclosed details of the proposed transaction to key employees, customers and suppliers. Despite the existence of non-disclosure agreements and attempts to keep the transaction under wraps transactions have an inconvenient habit of leaking. This can be damaging for any business. For a family business, especially one that has hitherto traded, expressly or impliedly on its tradition of family ownership as a core strength, the damage can be significantly greater.

(b) *Heads of terms or letter of intent.* It is fairly common practice to document the agreement between the buyer and the seller on the key terms of the transaction in this document. The heads serve a both as a reference point of key terms to remind the parties what has been agreed, and also as a briefing document, especially for lawyers, who are often instructed at this stage of the transaction. Usually heads of terms are not legally binding and represent an agreement in principle to proceed with the deal. Signing heads is nevertheless a key stage in the transaction. Even if the family business leader has not engaged specialist advisors before this stage, now would be a good time to do so. This will enable the family, before signing, to get an objective benchmark of the overall transaction against market practice. Even though they are not in most cases legally binding, it will be difficult for the family to renegotiate points contained in the heads at a later stage after signing. Apparently innocuous phrases can contain hidden meanings in the context of transactions. If these are accepted by the family at face value this can place them at a significant negotiating disadvantage during later stages of the transaction.

(c) *Tax and revenue clearances.* Frequently the structure of the transaction will mean that the parties are advised by their tax professionals to obtain pre-transaction tax clearances from HMRC.[7]

(d) *Due diligence.* Due diligence, often abbreviated to 'DD', is a detailed investigation by the buyer into the accounts, financial, tax, legal and trading position of the target family business. Under English law, the principle of *caveat emptor* (buyer beware) applies. Businesses do not come with any implied guarantees. Therefore, in most acquisitions, the prospective buyer will want to undertake detailed due diligence to obtain sufficient information about the target to enable the buyer (or other parties with an interest in the transaction, such as the funding bank) to decide whether the proposed acquisition represents a sound commercial investment. Effectively, due diligence is an audit of the target's business; commercial, legal, tax and financial. Due diligence is a key part of the acquisition process. It can also be a laborious and frustrating time. The transaction remains highly uncertain. There will sometimes be uncertainties over the buyer's funding whilst due diligence continues. The terms of the transaction documents will usually be under negotiation in parallel with due diligence, often with significant differences of opinion between the parties or their lawyers over the terms of these. The sellers will often be asked to provide a huge volume of information whilst at the same time seeking to maintain the confidentiality of the transaction and to keep the business running. Frequently the same or similar information will be demanded from different members of the buyer's due diligence team. Sometimes information will be requested in a format or in a level of detail that the systems of the family business cannot really provide. Often the need for the information requested will be questionable so far as the sellers are concerned.

(e) *Sale and purchase agreement (SPA).* Also called a share purchase agreement in a share acquisition or alternatively, in a business acquisition known as a business purchase agreement or (BPA) or an asset purchase agreement (APA). This is the

---

[7] Some common tax clearances are briefly mentioned in chapter 16.

main document that sets out the key terms of the transaction, including, details of the consideration and how it is to be paid, including earn out provisions (discussed at **12.6** below), post completion restrictions on sellers, and warranties and indemnities (also explained and discussed in detail at **12.15** below). The SPA is usually prepared by the buyer's lawyers.

(f) *Disclosure letter*. The disclosure letter is closely linked to the acquisition agreement. It is probably the second most important document in the transaction. It is normally prepared by the seller's solicitors on the basis of information provided by the sellers, and makes disclosures qualifying the warranties contained in the acquisition agreement. In general terms, to the extent that a matter has been disclosed in the Disclosure Letter (or the accompanying bundle of disclosure documents), the buyer will be prevented from bringing a warranty claim against the sellers.

(g) *Tax covenant*. A highly technical document, often forming a schedule to the SPA, under which the sellers agree to be responsible for any unforeseen tax (broadly tax liabilities not provided for in the accounts) in the target company that relate to the period before completion.

(h) *Ancillary documents*. In addition to the SPA and the disclosure letter, there are likely to be a number of other key legal agreements involving members of the family, for example employment or consultancy agreements for family members who will continue with the business, either on a long-term basis or for a short handover period. Conversely the buyer may see some family employees as surplus to their requirements. Those family members may nevertheless value their role in the family business. Delicate negotiations may be required before the family employees concerned are prepared to sign settlement agreements, agreeing to resign and to waive any rights that they may have to bring employment claims against the business or the buyer. Less controversially, it might be necessary to put in place new leases of premises occupied by the family business but owned by one or more family members to provide the buyer with security of tenure for the operation.

(i) *Completion* (increasingly called '**closing**' following US practice). This is the day on which the business will pass out of family ownership. The buyer will pay, typically, the bulk of the purchase price, although it is increasingly common for part of the consideration to be payable in instalments, sometimes subject to earn out arrangements. There will usually be a significant volume of documents to be signed in addition to the SPA and the disclosure letter. Frequently there are final points outstanding on the transaction documents which need to be finally resolved between the parties before they can proceed to the actual completion. Traditionally completions have been structured as formal meetings, usually at the offices of one of the lawyers with all, or most, parties present. Sometimes family members with minority interests will have provided powers of attorney allowing family business leaders or major shareholders to negotiate these final details on their behalf. Increasingly completions take place remotely, without a completion meeting and lawyers co-ordinating signatures by e-mail. This will deprive the transaction of an element of ceremony that is often helpful to mark the occasion for the family. If the business has been under family control this can be a hugely emotional milestone for the family. The advisors involved should not underestimate the significance of the event for the family members concerned. It is by no means unheard of for family members, particularly those not centrally involved in the negotiations to raise final objections to the sale or even have a last minute change of heart – see discussions below.

(3) **Phase 3 – post completion,** including:

(a) Handover periods where key family employees will be required to remain with the business, perhaps on a consultancy basis, for a period of time, typically 3 to 12 months, to ensure a smooth transition from family ownership to the buyer.

(b) Investment of sale proceeds. In many cases family members will receive their own share of the sale proceeds and invest these separately and privately. In the case of larger sales and where the family wish to re-invest collectively they may decide to set up a family office, either on a single family basis or to join an established multi-family office.[8]

(c) Earn outs where part of the purchase price will depend on the future performance of the business in the buyer's hands over a period, usually between 1 and 5 years. These will need to be monitored and, so far as possible, policed, on behalf of the selling family. The issues involved are discussed further below.

12.4 MAXIMISING THE VALUE ON SALE

An ideal business would have a unique product, or be a market leader in its sector, with growing turnover and profitability and also the scope for that growth to continue. Very few businesses can satisfy all these criteria, but by meeting some of them the potential seller will have increased the value of their own business.

The principal message when it comes to maximising value on the sale of a business is to plan ahead, and that generally means up to 3 years before the intended sale. During that period the owners / senior management should be addressing all the factors which will make the business more attractive to a buyer, and factors which would reduce its value. Some of these factors are:

- **Unique selling points.** What are the unique selling points (USPs) of the business? The business needs to be clear on the reasons why customers will use them rather than their competitors, and those need to be points which are difficult to replicate. Price can be matched by others willingly to undercut to achieve a sale. But selling points based need quality to be built up through consistency over time, and have more value.
  Does the business have unique products which give it an edge over its competitors? If it is one of the market leaders in the country in its sector, or for a particular product or service, then this will enhance the value of the business.

- **Management.** The quality and experience of management will be key consideration for the buyer. If all the management skills are with the family owners who are selling, then the business may have less value then one with a wide base of management ability and a good second tier management level. If relationships with customers, suppliers or the technical skills rest with management who will leave shortly after the business sale then this will reduce its value. This can often be the case if people are selling because they are reaching retirement age. Planning ahead and recognising this weakness, allows time to bring forward second tier management.

- **Margins.** A buyer will be more wary of a high turnover low gross margin business, because its profitability is so dependent on achieving those sales levels.

---

[8] Family offices are briefly discussed at 4.8.3.

- **Consistency.** A consistent set of results with improving profitability over the previous couple of years, is more attractive than a business with flat or falling profits.
- **Barriers to entry.** How easy is it for others to enter the marketplace? A distributor may only need to set up supply agreements with the same or similar suppliers compete so a buyer is not going to pay a high premium/goodwill for the business when they could easily set up their own business from scratch. But if a distributor deals in products with a good reputation in the market and has an exclusive supply agreement this will enhance the business value.

  Conversely sometimes even tired and underperforming family businesses will be of interest to a buyer, especially new market entrants from abroad, if the business has a skilled and experienced workforce and market presence. It could be almost impossible difficult for the buyer to replicate this quickly.
- **Accounting systems.** Buyers are reassured to find robust and accurate accounting systems. These should ensure that the financial information is timely and gives a correct representation of the business. The systems should also be capable of analysing how the parts of the business are operating, and the profitability of different products or product ranges. A potential buyer, before making a commitment, will want to thoroughly understand the weak and strong points of the business from a financial perspective. If a business does not know, for example the profitability of a product, or the true value of stock, then the buyer will be more cautious, and may seek to discount the price they are willing to pay because of that uncertainty.

  A buyer should always be expected to carry out a thorough review of the accounts. So any aggressive accounting policies which are used to enhance profits, for example low depreciation rates, will be factored back into a maintainable profits calculation to determine an appropriate price. Also if there are any "skeletons" on the balance sheet, then it is better to clear these up at the beginning of the planning for exit stage, rather than leave them for the buyer to find, as they may then use that factor to negotiate a reduction in the price.
- **Intellectual property.** What protection exists in respect of the intellectual property of the business? The more difficult it is for others to copy what the business produces, the more valuable it is. Also make sure the intellectual property is actually owned by the business. It is not uncommon for say patents to be in the name of the individual rather than the business.

These are only some of the factors which will affect the value. Experienced advisors will be able to work alongside the business owners over a period of time to help them to address these and other issues which will be relevant for that particular business. They will also help to identify who are likely to be appropriate potential buyers. These could be varied, and can range from trade buyers who are looking to expand their share of the market, to those who are looking for vertical integration in the market and are wanting to move into sectors which complement their existing business, to those looking to run their own business from a lifestyle perspective or want to grow a business with the aim of a gain at some stage, or to management who want to take over the operations.

It is important to recognise that not all businesses are saleable, and may only have one potential group of buyers, who are probably the management. Each group of buyers will have different criteria which are important to them. Hence by identifying the potential buyers during the planning stage, it is possible to address those issues, so that the best picture of the business can be presented.

12.5 VALUING THE FAMILY BUSINESS FOR SALE

This leads on to the question of the value of the family business for sale.[9] Because the valuation of a private business is often very subjective, an advisor will often give a range of values at the start of the sale process. It is important to have an idea of the potential sale price at the beginning, in order to assess any offers received. It is frequently said that the valuation of a business is an art and not a science. This is because the valuation process involves a number of subjective judgments. It is a truism that ultimately the value is what a willing buyer will pay to a willing seller. In the case of a sale, one is normally looking at valuing the whole business.

The normal starting point in the valuation is to calculate the future maintainable level of profits. That is what can one reasonably expect the level of profitability to be in the future? This involves analysing the past results, and adjusting them for any unusual income or costs. This could also include adjusting to market rates the amount of remuneration taken by the owners and family members or any other family specific factors. The potential buyer is paying out a capital sum and their return is going to be the profits which the business makes in the future. This is why an assessment of the likely future profit level is important.

Having determined the future profitability, there are a number of accepted approaches to valuing the business:

12.5.1 Net assets

This involves taking the current net asset value of the business as shown by the accounts with an adjustment to market value of any assets where that is appropriate, normally land and buildings. The balance sheet is then restated to include those market values. In some cases it may be appropriate to provide for the tax which would be payable if the assets were sold at those revised valuations.

If it is an investment company, or a loss making company, or one where maintainable earnings are uncertain, then no value would usually be included for goodwill. If the business is profitable a figure for goodwill could be added to the net assets figure. There are various views as to how goodwill should be valued for this purpose. A normal approach is to take the average of the last 3 years profits, adjusted for unusual items and multiplying by 1 or 2. Sometimes the average profits are calculated on a weighted basis.

12.5.2 Price/earnings (P/E)

This tends to be the most common method used, and involves applying a P/E to the post tax future maintainable profits figure to arrive at a business value.

The subjective element in this valuation approach, is in choosing an appropriate P/E ratio. There are P/E ratios for all quoted (including AIM listed) companies and for industry sectors. It can be argued that these give a market view of those sectors, and

---

[9] Valuations can also be required for other purposes, when only a portion of the shares are being valued, such as a shareholding held on death, shares being sold because one shareholder is exiting for whatever reason, an employee share scheme, or a gift of shares. Some comments on valuing the family business for other purposes, including for inheritance tax on death, are contained in chapter 16.

therefore bring an element of objectivity to the process. However the private company being valued will be different in terms of its size and operations to the quoted company; and its shares are not freely tradable; and will be different in many other regards. But the quoted company ratio does give an indication.

Another useful indicator is the BDO Private Company Price Index. This is an index produced every quarter which looks at private company sales and calculates the average P/E ratios for deals completed. This is often lower than the average P/E ratios for quoted companies, and can therefore be used to discount a quoted company P/E ratio to what may be appropriate for the private company being considered. The valuer then has to make a subjective judgement as to the appropriate ratio. This would take into account factors such as the position of the company or its product in the marketplace, profits growth, barriers to entry, strength of management team etc. After valuing the business using a P/E ratio it is then useful to compare that value with the asset value of the company. Any excess is effectively goodwill. If the value is less than the asset value then this means the business is not making what the market considers to be an appropriate return on the assets employed in the business.

12.5.3 EBITDA

An EBITDA based valuation takes the earnings before interest tax, depreciation and amortisation (EBITDA) and multiplies by a factor in a similar way to the P/E valuation. This method is effectively valuing the business on the basis of its cash flow generation.

12.5.4 Discounted cash flow (DCF)

Purists would say that this is correct way to value a business because the method involves discounting future profit levels back into today's value. Therefore it is expressing the present value of the future profit stream, which is precisely what is being bought. However the big problem is in forecasting the future profit streams. A business finds it difficult to forecast, with any degree of accuracy, profits for the coming 12 months. What chance is there of forecasting profits in say 10 years' time?

In addition to this element of subjectivity DCF valuations are relatively complex and accordingly difficult for non-specialists.

12.5.5 Industry standard approach

Some industries will have methods of valuation which are accepted as being the norm. These can often involve applying a multiplier to turnover or gross profit.

12.6 PRICE AND TRANSACTION STRUCTURE

Whatever method is used to calculate the 'headline price' how the payment is structured can make a significant difference to the transaction for the family business seller. We will look at three frequently encountered issues.

12.6.1 Cash and working capital adjustments

Family businesses often have significant cash reserves on their balance sheets. It would be a huge mistake not to take this into account in profits based price calculations. Against this purchasers will increasingly expect a basic level of working capital to be left in the business. Although there is often a degree of negotiation over the exact amount of genuinely surplus cash, this can usually be added to the purchase price.[10] Both the level and value of stock is a frequent issue in family business sales. Often a mixture of prudence, surplus cash and outdated buying practices mean that a family business will be carrying much more stock than industry norms. The buyer will be reluctant to pay for the surplus above what is really needed and can be used. Similar arguments for adjustments also apply to freehold property which is in the family company books at below market rates.

12.6.2 Earn-outs

The seller and buyer may have very different views on the value of a business. Earn outs can potentially bridge this gap. If the business performs well the seller will (or should) extract the maximum value. If the business performs less well the seller will have extracted a reasonable price on completion (or perhaps by way of agreed and ascertained deferred consideration) and the buyer will not have overpaid.

The seller will always prefer as much up-front cash as possible. The buyer will always face a risk that the business will not perform to expectations after completion. This may be for a variety of reasons, including uncertainty over whether forecasts of future (and increased) profit and turnover, or anticipated profit, based on the introduction of new products or contract wins can be met. There is also the difficulty of integrating the business into the buyer's operations.

Ideally the seller will be able to argue that their family business can demonstrate long term stability so most of the factors justifying an earn-out do not apply. But this may not be possible. There is the back drop of the general economic climate. Since 2008, the continuing reduction in bank funding available to buyers to fund cash transactions, to which must now be added the uncertainties of Brexit.

For these reasons transactions with an earn-out element have become increasingly the norm in recent years. Structuring part of the consideration as an earn-out can significantly de-risk the acquisition for the buyer. Conversely the seller is at greatest risk under earn out arrangements. Arguably this is even more so for the sellers of family businesses.

Partly the risks relate to the structure of earn outs, and who has the ability to affect the earn-out, positively or negatively. The buyer may want to make management charges to reflect costs incurred in providing support from group resources. The buyer may also want to invest in new employees, fixed assets, marketing activity, all of which can affect 'the bottom line' and, depending on how this is structured, the earn-out.

---

[10] HMRC may challenge the availability of entrepreneur's relief if they suspect that cash has been hoarded in expectation of a sale so as to avoid paying income tax on dividends.

However the greatest risks may be cultural. In particular, bridging the cultural divide between the corporate world of the buyer and the idiosyncratic, highly individualised cultures often found in family owned businesses. The buyer will be in control of the business after completion. Even if key family members remain working in the business during a hand over period. Things will inevitably change. The buyer will have their own views on how the business they have bought should be run. Despite what is often said in negotiations, changes might be necessary to bring the business in line with the buyer's corporate procedures. The sellers will often disagree and will hold equally strong views that the proposed course of action will damage the culture of the family business (and with it the previous levels of profitability and the earn-out).

Buyers will usually agree to accept restrictions on artificial manipulation of an earn-out. They will often agree not to take management charges or to add back obvious additional costs flowing from the acquisition. Buyers will almost never agree to ring fence the family business from change during the earn-out period.

Given that earn outs are increasingly a fact of transactional life we would suggest that an earn out is more likely to produce a satisfactory outcome (roughly defined as an amount that the seller is happy to receive and the buyer happy to pay) in circumstances where:

- the maximum amount of consideration has been paid in cash or certain fixed consideration so that the earn out can genuinely be seen as a bonus;
- the seller will retain a high degree of day-to-day control of the business throughout the earn out period;
- the target will remain a distinct stand-alone entity;
- the earn out is simple (ideally focused on turnover rather than profit); and
- the buyer is also a family owned business and therefore more likely to share common cultural similarities with the target.

12.6.3 Security

If any of the purchase price is to be deferred, whether as an earn-out, or staged payments of a set purchase price, the seller needs to consider the possibility of obtaining security from the buyer to protect their future entitlement.

Some form of assessment of the risk of the buyer defaulting needs to be undertaken. This can take the form of some, usually limited, 'reverse due diligence', by the seller's advisors on the buyer's financial position. Parent company guarantees will often be agreed if the actual legal buyer is a relatively poorly capitalised subsidiary. Third party bank guarantees are comparatively rare.

Security over the assets of the target family company may also be agreed but these are prone to structural and enforcement difficulties. Often the buyer's bankers will require first charges over any core assets, including properties. Secondly enforcing security might involve the sellers having to step back in to run a business, which would probably now be in a worse financial position than when they originally sold it.

12.7 CHOICE OF BUYER

The choice of buyer can be almost as important as headline price.

Many family business sellers do not necessarily choose to deal with the buyer making the most attractive financial offer. Often families choose to sell to the buyer who they perceive will be the best custodian of 'their' family business. The buyer most likely, for example, to keep the business in its current location for the long term, to look after employees (who may include continuing family members) and other stakeholders generally, or to maintain use of brands closely associated with the family. Indeed selecting a buyer, at least partly based on these considerations, may help to overcome some of the reasons against sale referred to above.

Often a buyer selected on this basis will be a larger, sometimes international, family business themselves, perceived by the sellers to have similar values, culture and long term time horizons. In other words perceived family business fit.[11] Of course a selling family needs to remain aware that talk is cheap, and that assurances made by a buyer during the 'courting phase' to secure the target family business may be difficult to secure legally and in practice are sometimes broken.

Nevertheless there are many successful examples of family business targets being nurtured under the stewardship of larger family owned buyers. The selling family might be able to investigate the track record of the buyer on other similar family business acquisitions. It may also be possible to build in structural incentives for the buyer to keep to their promises into the fabric of the transaction, for example long-term lease commitments by the buyer to premises retained by the family. On some occasions we have seen the concerns of the family dealt with much more overtly, for example by creating buy-back options exercisable if the buyer decided to relocate. However these are comparatively rare, and may significantly affect price if insisted upon. Ultimately the family will need to accept that the family business will no longer be theirs and that to a significant extent they will need to trust that their chosen buyer will be an appropriate custodian of that business. Custodianship nevertheless remains a legitimate agenda item for negotiations.

12.8 FBO'S AND MBO'S

A suitable buyer might be found much closer to home. The possibility of the next generation of the business owning family, usually insiders, buying out the senior generation through a family buy-out (or FBO) is considered as an ownership succession option in chapter 15.

Sales to the management team through a management buy-out or MBO are much more common than an FBO. In the absence of family management insiders, the business owning family may prefer to sell to non-family employees rather than to a third party buyer. Often the business family will agree to proceed with a management buy-out team even if theirs is not the best offer on the table. The family might believe that this will protect the position of the employees or the heritage and values of the family business.

Less constructively the family owners could be faced with little choice, other than to sell to the management team. The family might have become too remote from their own family business, playing little role in its governance. In effect the family become absentee landlords. The role of the management team is likely to have expanded to fill the

---

[11] The importance of cultural fit and post completion cultural integration is highlighted by Vanessa Williams in chapter 6 of *Due diligence: A Practical Guide* (Jordan Publishing, 2nd edn, 2013).

vacuum created. Relationships with key customers and suppliers (including banks) have become firmly embedded in the management team. The management team has begun to resent the 'rent' in the form of dividends paid to the family owners. Certainly the management will not support a sale to a third party that could undermine their own security, whilst enriching their family landlords. But at the same time the business is over-reliant on the non-family management and effectively unsalable to a third party, without their support. An MBO becomes the only sale option. But, in Blondel and Klein's terms, this should be categorised as an expropriation sale.

FBO/MBO hybrids also occur, with the next generation insider leading or supporting a management bid with significant involvement from the rest of the non-family management team.

12.9 MINORITY INTERESTS

The first factor from the sales process of particular relevance to family businesses is the position of minority shareholders.

A buyer will almost invariably want to purchase 100% of the share capital of a privately owned family business.

Non-family owned private businesses are much more likely to have a natural coherence in terms of their ownership perspective than their family owned counterparts. Private equity backed businesses will usually be working to a pre-agreed exit timetable. Quasi partnerships established by colleagues of similar age are likely to have similar views about the right time to exit, usually around their retirement ages. Exits from entrepreneurial businesses driven by a single founder, but with minority shareholders will be driven by the ambitions of that founder.

As identified by Klein and Blondel, entrepreneurial businesses of this nature overlap into the family owned business arena (with minority interests being held by family members rather than, typically non-family managers).

But there are many more complex situations in the family context. This is especially so in more mature family businesses, where majority ownership and family employment may have divided along branch lines. There might be pressure for a sale from the more distant branches, who see little of the benefits of retaining the family business and whose emotional ties to the business are correspondingly weakened. Conversely, free from the day-to-day realities of running the business and perhaps independently wealthy, typically older, minority family shareholders might have a strong emotional antipathy to the sale of a historic family business. Even in younger, second generation family enterprises, conflicts of interest may arise between the older generation looking to raise capital on exit and the next generation expecting either a long-term career in the business, or eventual ownership of that business, or indeed both.

Certainly almost no buyer will be prepared to buy a stake in a family business leaving a resident minority of passive shareholders, much less family members who are actively opposed to a sale.

Yet many older family businesses have failed to prune their ownership tree and, as a result, have a large and disparate share register. This is a hugely significant factor in approaching a family business sale for all parties concerned, but especially the sellers.

As Peter Leach puts it:[12]

> 'Many advisors have found themselves in the situation where the sale of the family business has been agreed ... the contract is about to be signed and the phone rings. It is uncle Mortimer, who owns a few shares inherited from his mother, saying, "I don't think the price is enough", effectively holding the process to ransom.'

This type of 'greenmail' is clearly particularly unsavoury in the context of a family business. Hopefully it is also a rare occurrence. The more common situation will be where family members are genuinely opposed to a sale, simply because they are reluctant to see the business pass out of family hands.

The reluctant minority shareholder could also be a former employee, perhaps a 'bad leaver' from the family business in circumstances, where either there were no compulsory sale provisions available to the company or, for whatever reason, these were not enforced or policed at the time they left employment.

In other cases shareholders may simply have languished on the register and they can either no longer be traced or have since died, leaving it unclear who now is entitled to be registered as shareholder in their place.

12.9.1 Drag rights

Drag rights might provide the family with a 'get out of jail' card. These are provisions, in either the articles or a shareholders' agreement, entitling a specified majority of shareholders to require the remaining shareholders to join in a sale approved by the majority. In effect the majority can disarm the last members of the family resistance to facilitate a dignified surrender of the family business into third party ownership.

Drag provisions are an extremely sensible component of the constitution of any family business, even where the family are heavily committed to family ownership. The best time to discuss and negotiate these provisions is likely to be as part of general governance discussions when the sale of the family business is an abstract future consideration, rather than at a time when a sale is a real possibility. Drag rights are considered as part of ownership governance at **17.21**.

There is a significant statistical possibility that the target family business for sale does not have drag rights included within its constitution. What then?

12.9.2 Statutory squeeze out – CA, ss 974–991

If the reluctant minority represent (broadly) less than 10% of the equity some help might be obtained under the statutory squeeze out provisions contained in CA, ss 974–991. Corresponding rights for minority shareholders to be bought out, in effect statutory tag rights are contained in CA, s 983. The provisions, in particular those relating to setting

---

[12] Peter Leach *Family Businesses – The Essentials* (Profile Books, 2007) at p 180.

up trust accounts contained in CA, s 982, can be used in cases where the share register of the family business has become so outdated that contact has been lost with shareholders.

Although these provisions are mainly discussed in the context of large quoted company takeovers, they do apply to private company sales.

The provisions can, at least in theory, be used to provide, in effect, statutory drag rights to squeeze out against reluctant sellers from a family owned business. Whilst the majority may occasionally threaten to use the statutory squeeze out procedure against a minority it is rarely employed in practice in a private company context. There are a number of reasons for this.

- The threat of becoming embroiled in this compulsory purchase procedure (or perhaps financial incentives negotiated in parallel) might persuade the minority to agree voluntarily to a sale. However, contrary to the usual rules, no costs may be awarded against a shareholder challenging a squeeze out notice in the courts unless that shareholder has behaved improperly, frivolously or vexatiously, has delayed unreasonably in bringing the application, or conducted the application unreasonably.[13] In effect the buyer must show that the application by the minority shareholder was an abuse of process.

- The right of the minority to challenge the squeeze out notice in the courts under CA, s 986. That section appears to give the courts wide discretion whether to uphold the squeeze out notice or not or to determine the terms of acquisition. However case-law shows that the onus is on the applicant to convince the court that it is proper to interfere in the squeeze out mechanism and that the burden of proof will be high. In effect not that the offer is questionably unfair but that it is 'obviously unfair'.[14] This is consistent with the objectives of the statutory squeeze out right, to inject an element of shareholder democracy into a company's constitution. After all 90% of the shareholders will have agreed to the sale. Examples of areas where the court might be persuaded to interfere would be conflicts of interest or rather a substantial identity of interest between the buyer and the majority shareholders,[15] or failure to provide adequate information to the minority to properly consider the squeeze out offer,[16] or that the information actually provided to the minority was misleading.[17] Nevertheless the right of the minority to appeal to the court must inject a degree of uncertainty into the process.

- The inherent complexity of the statutory squeeze out process. In essence an acquisition relying on the squeeze out process needs to be structured like a public company takeover, rather than a traditional owner managed business private sale. The entry point to the procedure is that the buyer has made a takeover offer within the meaning of CA, s 974. A key point is that in calculating the 90% threshold that the buyer must achieve to trigger the process, any shares already held by them, or which they have contracted to buy, including under conditional contracts are disregarded.[18] A buyer cannot therefore acquire 90% or more of the shares and then mop up the remainder under the procedure. The 'already held rule' does not however apply to '... shares that are the subject of a contract ... intended to secure that the holder of the shares will accept the offer when it is made' and entered into

---

[13] Companies Act 2006, s 986(5).
[14] Re Sussex Brick Co Ltd [1961] Ch 289.
[15] Fiske Nominees Ltd v Dwyka Diamond Ltd [2002] BCLC 123.
[16] Chez Nico Restaurants Ltd [1992] BCLC 192.
[17] Re Lifecare International plc [1990] BCLC 222.
[18] Companies Act 2006, s 975(2).

by deed, for token consideration or a promise on the part of the buyer to make the takeover offer. So the buyer can secure irrevocable undertakings on the part of 90% or more of the shareholders to accept a takeover on agreed terms and then initiate the squeeze out process. There are also strict time limits in which to invoke the process, 3 months from the date the takeover offer closes together with obligations to notify the company that squeeze out notices have been served and statutory declarations confirming their validity.[19]

Also within one month of reaching the 90% threshold, buyers must either issue a squeeze out notice or serve formal notice on the minority of their right to be bought out.[20] It is a criminal offence not to do so. Simply ignoring a 10% minority is therefore not an option for the buyer in any circumstances.

- Perhaps the main reason why the statutory squeeze out process is seldom used in a private family business context would be reluctance on the part of buyers, who have to make most of the running under the squeeze out procedure, to accept the risks and cost of becoming involved in a complex process. They would be doing so to sort out what is essentially the sellers' problem; a breakdown in family business governance resulting in a failure to keep family members aligned on the most fundamental question of ownership.

12.9.3 Pre-sale alignment

What can keen sellers do in the absence of drag and tag provisions in the constitution of the family business, or if the statutory squeeze out procedure is either not available (for example because more than 10% of the sellers are opposed to a sale), or unlikely to appeal to buyer?

Do the majority sellers simply proceed with the proposed transaction and hope for the best? In other words that the minority who are or may be opposed to a sale can ultimately be persuaded to join in. This may work in the case of an entrepreneurial sale. Any minority shareholders may well be swept along by the dominance of the controlling shareholder. Such sales tend to be characteristic of earlier stage businesses and those with fewer family shareholders, or where there is a lower level of emotional attachment to the family business.

In strategic sales the family will reach consensus based on family cohesion and fair process (although Blondel and Klein noted that family businesses falling into this category exhibited a high degree of adherence to best practice family business governance in any event).

Concerns are much more likely to arise with later stage family businesses with either a minority actively opposed to sale, or, who are so out of touch that their position is unclear to the majority. It may well be tempting to leave consideration of such shareholders to one side until the transaction is much more advanced. However the later in the transaction, the more likely it is that the transaction will be widely known amongst employees and other stakeholders, and therefore the greater the risk to the family business of the damage that could be caused by a transaction collapsing. Costs will also have been incurred.

---

[19] Companies Act 2006, s 980(2).
[20] Companies Act 2006, s 984.

Conversely by engaging with the minority at an early stage in the sales process the majority are best placed position to evaluate the position of the minority, to plan the overall sales process accordingly, and to build in appropriate measures to cater for the minority. Those measures may include:

- **Communication.** The logical and simple first stage would be for the majority to engage in a consultation exercise with the minority. Better late than never. Ideally this re-engagement will reveal a willingness to sell, in which case the majority are free to focus on the main aspects of the transaction. If not, negotiations with the minority can take place in parallel with the main transaction. This is likely to give a better result for the majority than if discussions are left until immediately pre completion. At worst it might become apparent that the minority are likely to present a major obstacle to sale. The sale might need to be abandoned, or postponed. But if that becomes clear at an early stage it might be possible to formulate alternative plans. Relations may be sufficiently strained between the various groups of family members so that discussions are best facilitated by a specialist family business consultant or other independent advisor.

- **Rectification of the register.** It might be that the exercise reveals a number of areas where the shareholder register needs to be brought up to date with amendments to shareholder details. This may simply be to update addresses of shareholders. In other cases the registered shareholders may have died, perhaps leaving no eligible family members who are entitled to be registered under the articles. Sometimes the provisions of wills conflict with the articles. This could bring pre-emption provisions into play. On other occasions shares remain registered in the names of executors under bare trusts for adult beneficiaries. In any case, tidying the shareholder register would be useful piece of pre-sale planning.

- **Powers of attorney.** Even if the majority believe that the minority will be perfectly happy to join in the proposed sale, it is well worth obtaining powers of attorney (sometimes called transaction powers) whereby minority holders appoint one or more of the major shareholders as their attorney for the purposes of signing any transaction documents. Usually this is done to make completion arrangements easier so that there is no need for all shareholders to personally sign documents or attend completion meetings, and so as to avoid delays caused by holiday absences etc. Willingness to provide powers of attorney is also a good early indicator of the level of support for the sale. It is worth noting that powers of attorney to cover the possibility of lack of capacity are covered by separate rules and that all powers of attorney cease on death.

- **Buy-backs.** Where cohesion and levels of trust are low it might be sensible for the majority to buy-out the minority in advance of any proposed sale. However the majority, particularly those holding directorships, will need to be exceptionally careful about exploiting any knowledge relating to a possible sale, especially any information relating to price or value to the detriment of the minority. The minority might prefer to wait and see how a sale unfolds before making any commitment. Anti-embarrassment provisions, entitling the minority to a share of any uplift on resale could be considered if a third party sale is more of a remote possibility.

- **Options.** The majority might not have sufficient cash to finance a buy-back. In which case, as an alternative to buy-backs, call options could be considered obliging the minority to sell if certain conditions, eg as to price, are met.

- **Deal structure.** It might be that opposition to a sale is sufficiently entrenched to make an agreed sale of shares unlikely, or so widespread as to prevent drag rights or squeeze out provisions from being implemented. The majority sellers could consider structuring the transaction as an asset sale, which, in theory, could be approved by the board of directors without resorting to the shareholders. However there are a number of obstacles and drawbacks to this. If the assets of the family business to be sold include its corporate name a special resolution to change the name will need to be passed by at least 75% of voting members. Secondly a potential double charge to capital gains tax arises.[21] Thirdly depending on the circumstances the minority may have a claim for unfair prejudice on the basis that their family business has been removed against their will.[22] At least, the buyer may have concerns that such claims might be made. It will therefore only be in extreme circumstances that asset sales are used to bypass minority opposition.

- **Constitutions.** There is always the possibility that discussions relating to a possible sale may be a catalyst to introduce wider governance processes and constitutions into a family owned business.
- **Unfair prejudice.** At least in theory, the majority are free to petition the court under CA, s 994 on the basis that, in opposing a sale the minority are unfairly prejudicing the rights of the majority. However we are not aware of any decided case in support of the point. Again in theory, an order forcing the minority to buy-out the majority or to sell to the majority or a third party buyer are within the discretion of the court. Given the availability of the separate statutory squeeze out remedy we suggest that orders based on unfair prejudice to the majority would only be available in the most extreme circumstances, where the minority can be shown to be using their refusal to sell vexatiously to disadvantage the majority rather than for any real commercial purpose.
- **Just and equitable winding up.** It has been established that an order for the just and equitable winding up of a family business under IA, s 122(1)(g) may be granted in circumstances where a family dispute has effectively made the business unmanageable.[23] Logically this could include the situation where the business is both unmanageable and unsalable. However we can trace no decided case on this point. It is also highly debatable whether the interest of a potential buyer could be retained for long enough for the remedy to be invoked and pursued through the courts. Double taxation issues would also need to be overcome.

12.10 FAMILY EMPLOYEES

Having considered the position of outsider family members as minority shareholders we now turn to the situation of insider family employees.

As discussed in chapter 5 a disconnect may be found between how family members are treated in relation to employment matters and normal market practice. This could be a sticking point for buyers. A change of ownership will also be a major event for all employees of a family business. The impact of that change is likely to be particularly significant for family employees.

---

[21] There would be a charge made for any gain made by the family company on the sale of the assets. There would then be further tax to pay when the capital is extracted and returned to shareholders on the winding up of the family company.

[22] There are cases where minority shareholders have successfully challenged the sale of assets agreed by the majority as a species of unfair prejudice (see for example *Re London School of Electronics Ltd* [1986] Ch 211). However in these cases the majority have retained some continuing interest in the assets which have been put beyond the reach of the minority. Arguably an asset sale, agreed by the board and entered into for genuine business reasons should be left intact under the internal management rule (whereby the courts should not interfere in the internal management of a company).

[23] See, for example the Harding family case discussed in chapter 22.

Frequently encountered issues include:

- **Employment documents.** There is often a lack of formal documentation for family employees. Non family employees may be subject to appropriate employment documents ranging from simple statements of terms of employment complying with the Employment Rights Act, through to formal service agreements for directors and senior employees, containing detailed protections in favour of the family business over intellectual property, confidential information and post-employment restrictions. Frequently there are no corresponding documents applicable to family employees.

- **Non-market remuneration.** Family members may be engaged on employment terms that do not reflect arms-length market terms. Family members may be over remunerated for the job they do. On some occasions, particularly in smaller businesses, younger family members remuneration will be below market rates on the basis that 'you are part of the family' or 'have enough for what you need' or, particularly dangerous in the circumstances of a sale 'one day all of this will be yours'. It is not unknown for family members to be paid less than the national minimum wage.

- **Potential redundancies.** Often buyers approach the acquisition of a family business with a degree of scepticism about the roles and value of family members engaged in the business.[24] On occasions that scepticism can be fuelled by the frequently unwitting and inadvertent approach and comments of the business leader. Concerns may include whether the family member concerned is overpaid, or, looked at another way, performing a role suitable for the job title they hold (over titled). In extreme cases there may be concerns over whether the family member has any real role in the business going forward. Sometimes those concerns will be legitimate and even readily shared and acknowledged by everyone, including the family member concerned. The classic example would be the spouse of the business leader who might have looked after the, human resources or financial affairs of the family business in its early stages and retained the title of HR or finance director after the business had matured sufficiently to engage non family professionals to undertake all or most of the day to day work within the role. The spouse may have no expectation, or indeed wish to continue in the family business after the sale or departure of the business leader. On many other occasions, the perception or presumption that the family member concerned is not undertaking a full role will be both entirely unfair and difficult to dislodge. The family employee may be performing well and keen to remain in the business after sale.

- **Expectations of family employees.** Family employees, particularly in the next generation may have been expecting to remain in the business long term, perhaps eventually to take over leadership. They may therefore not be fully committed, or even opposed to the sale, perhaps without having articulated that opposition to the business leader.

- **Work practices.** One of the potential advantages of working in a family owned business is the potential for greater flexibility, in particular over work life balance issues. If there is a basic trust that a family member will do what is necessary to 'get the job done', flexibility over working hours will often be the reward.
  It might be fairly easy for the next generation to negotiate flexible working arrangements with senior generation grandparents, on both a short term and long term basis, sometimes without this affecting remuneration, status or prospects.

---

[24] Other than perhaps the family business founder.

There may well be a greater willingness to allow next generation family employees to pursue other business ventures.

These arrangements might not sit well within the more rigid corporate culture of the buyer. The more embedded the arrangements the greater the concern about the impact of change of ownership, both for the buyer and the family members concerned.

12.10.1 Family business leaders after completion

Similar cultural considerations apply to the family business leader, after completion of the sale. Buyers may insist on the continuing involvement of the family business leader to achieve orderly handover and integration. Other family sellers may want the business leader to remain in place to help secure the best earn out achievable. The business leader may themselves be reluctant to let go of the day to day management of the family business.

Realistically the prospects of a family business leader remaining in post for an extended period after sale may not be great. Particularly for older leaders, and especially founding entrepreneurs, who have been used to running the family business their own way for many years, accepting the cultural, operational and reporting changes entailed in being part of the buyer's group may be too much. A more realistic option might be to accept that long-term involvement with the family business post completion is unlikely to work, even if this is at the cost of a reduction in overall purchase price by the removal of an earn out element and securing the maximum possible fixed cash payment.

12.10.2 Conflicts of interest

There are therefore potential conflicts of interest in relation to family employees on the sale of the family business. These are not only between buyer and seller, but also possibly amongst the business owning family themselves. The buyer will want to ensure that they will be inheriting a business with a stable, capable and committed workforce, especially so far as the senior management team are concerned, and without being burdened by excessive cost or working practices that are at odds with the buyer's own operations. The family on the other hand will be simultaneously interested in achieving the best price on exit, and also protecting the interests and lifestyle of family employees.

How can these potential conflicts be resolved? Ultimately the aim is to achieve fair treatment of family employees. That may be a continuing position in the business, objectively appropriate in terms of remuneration, position and performance. Alternatively, for those family employees who will not be remaining, fair and sensitive treatment as they exit at or after completion. Of course it is much easier to achieve fairness and objectivity when dealing with real estate issues than people. But the following pointers are relevant:

- **Governance and equal treatment.** The foundations for a successful transfer of family employees into non-family ownership are almost certainly laid in the long-term approach taken by the family business as part of its governance and family employment policies. The closer these are to arm's length market practice, with as little distinction made between family and non-family employees, the easier it will be to convince a buyer that it will be business as usual after completion of the sale. If family members are to remain with the business after completion buyers may well look for evidence of equal treatment of those family members when compared with their non-family counterparts. For example have they been subject to the same appraisal regime? Do family members have the same employment contracts? At its most basic, have family members been treated in compliance with legal requirements?

Equally the more family employees have been remunerated at demonstrably market rates, the less the scope for complaints on the part of the next generation that sacrifices made on the basis of expectations of eventual ownership by the family employees concerned have gone unrewarded.

- **Sale and the succession process.** A crucial question to be answered by the governance process is whether the business should remain in family ownership.[25]
If all family members, including any next generation employees, have been fully involved in arriving the decision to sell the transaction is likely to fall into Blondel and Klein's category of a strategic sale. The next generation will have been part of the process where the family have agreed to swap the benefits of continued ownership for cash.

  This level of involvement is less likely to be present in an entrepreneurial sale. It may be tempting for the business leader in such sales to want to explore the possibility of the transaction before involving the next generation. Certainly we have known instances of sellers, initially planning to tell their children working in the business about the sale, only immediately before completion. This may be driven by a mixture of concern to protect the children from uncertainty, the possibility that the deal might not happen anyway, embarrassment at the change of plan, or a conviction that whatever the entrepreneur eventually decides will be the correct option. It is difficult to envisage any circumstances where this level of secrecy is the best approach. Proposed sales have an inconvenient habit of leaking out. Whilst non-family employees may understand the business leader's approach in attempting to maintain secrecy, family employees almost certainly will not. Early communication and on-going consultation with family employees who will be affected by a potential sale is a must. The general rule we have advocated is to treat family employees no more favourably than non- family employees employed in similar positions. Early inclusion of family employees into the loop of confidence on a sale is an exception to that rule, and justifiable on the basis that the individuals concerned will be affected in their capacity as family members and possibly as owners, or potential owners, of the family business.

- **'Selling' family employees.** A more subtle factor is how family employees are presented and portrayed to the buyer, in particular, during informal conversations with the buyer?

  Are family employees involved in the process in a manner consistent with their job title? Alternatively is there a suggestion that they are being hidden from view? If there is a wish for family employees to remain with the business post completion it is important for the business leader not to inadvertently undermine their status, for example by employing 'parent talk' and referring to the sales director as 'my lad'. Equally there could be a strong desire on the part of the business leader to entrench and protect the position of family employees. Overstating their capabilities to the buyer is likely, at best, to provide short-term security.

  Buyers may be alive to the seller's concern and be quick to offer assurances that the jobs of family members will be secure in the long term. However this is most unlikely to be accompanied by (non-market) long-term service agreements or any other form of legal guarantee. Whilst we have known many examples of the careers of next generation family members surviving and indeed thriving in their

---

[25] Discussed in chapter 15 (Ownership Succession).

former family business, there are plenty of cases where things have not worked out. Often this is not really the fault of anyone concerned. But the change in culture from family ownership to corporate control cannot be underestimated.

- **Surplus next generation family employees.** The buyer might not want family employees to remain with the business. They could have their own management who they wish to introduce into the business. They might have serious concerns about the capability of family employees to discharge their duties inherent in their job title. Of course the family employees concerned have employment rights, just as non-family employees. The buyer might insist on the family employees concerned agreeing to waive those rights by signing legally binding settlement agreements.
- **Key next generation family employees.** Conversely the buyer may regard the continued involvement of key next generation employees as integral to the success of the business after completion, particularly if the business leader is to go into retirement. In which case the buyer may look for the relevant family member to commit to a long-term service agreement (although this is becoming less common). The family member concerned may be less keen to provide this commitment, particularly if their own ownership ambitions will be thwarted by the sale, or if they joined the family business to escape a more corporate culture. Their preference could well be to seek fresh challenges elsewhere.

12.10.3 Bridging the conflict gap

It will be seen that a sale will potentially create tensions and conflicts of interest not only between the next generation in their position as family employees and the potential buyer, but also with the senior generation in their position as exiting owners with a strong interest in the deal proceeding. The ideal is to avoid this conflict by communication and agreement between the generations to arrive at a strategic sale fully supported by all concerned. Support may also be strengthened or even obtained by the approach adopted by the family to the structure of the transaction and the division of the proceeds of sale. Possibilities include:

- **Ex gratia payments** or settlements to family members who are losing their jobs and being asked to sign compromise agreements. In most circumstances the first £30,000 of any settlement could be paid free of income tax as a non-taxable payment of compensation for loss of office.
- **Pre sale structuring** so that family members who will forgo potential future ownership in the family business are brought in to become actual owners in anticipation of the sale, ideally qualifying for entrepreneur's relief.[26]
- **Leveraging the structure of the sale.** For example, if the next generation are to remain with the business and the sale structure includes an earn-out element, arranging for those concerned to receive a large share of the earn out notwithstanding that they might have a small share of the equity.
- **Reallocation of sale proceeds.** The sale might have been driven to provide for the needs of the senior generation in retirement. Every penny of the proceeds might be needed for this purpose. If not there is nothing to prevent the senior generation diverting surplus proceeds of sale to the next generation at the time of the sale. This can either be by way of allocating the sale proceeds disproportionately to the next generation, or by making cash gifts out of the proceeds of sale.

---

[26] Which will require the next generation employees concerned to hold shares for 12 months prior to the sale. So early planning is crucial. Entrepreneurs' relief, IHT and BPR are all discussed in chapter 16.

There is no time like the present. In most cases the long-term intention will be to pass the proceeds onto the next generation by will on death. But the favourable IHT treatment of business assets (broadly exempt from IHT) disappears at the moment of sale, so that cash held in the estate at death becomes taxable at the full IHT rate. Passing over the surplus proceeds immediately after sale at least starts the 7-year clock of potentially exempt transfers ticking. As mentioned previously in the context of ownership approach, one of the key debates for any family business with a mixture of family members working in the business and those not is whether fairness dictates equal treatment between the members of those two groups. That debate has potential application to the division of the proceeds of sale on exit from the family business. Have those working in the business demonstrably made sacrifices of salary, or lifestyle or career for the good of the family business? Will the sale prevent legitimate ownership expectations from being met? Have the family employees made an exceptional contribution to the business and accordingly the sale price achieved that will not be reflected in their individual share of the equity? If any of these factors are present is it appropriate to deviate from the natural starting point of parents that fairness and equality are synonymous?

Alternatively have those working in the family business been fully rewarded (or over rewarded) for their efforts or input compared with siblings who have forged their own career path in the wider world? They are difficult questions but, if ignored, they are capable of creating resentment within the next generation of the family and of disturbing the hoped for peaceful retirement of the senior generation.

12.11 FAMILY OWNED PROPERTY

We suggest in chapter 10 that family owned businesses are more likely to hold real estate interests, than their non-family counterparts. We also suggest that those arrangements are more likely to be informal, ad-hoc, undocumented and not on arm's length terms. A review of those property arrangements as part of a seller due diligence exercise should reveal what issues need to be addressed, either as part the sellers pre-sale preparations, or in negotiations with the buyer.

Issues commonly encountered are:

- **Wider family ownership.** Properties, both core operating properties and land more peripheral to the operations (for example used for storage, car parking, access, or to provide staff accommodation) might be owned outside the business. Often ownership will be in the hands of family members closely involved with the business, or perhaps by a pension fund for the benefit of the family. Occasionally the relevant property rights will be held by more remote family members or, in a worse case by family members in dispute with the majority or opposed to a sale.
- **Investment properties.** Similarly family businesses may hold investment properties, or surplus property, no longer needed in the operation on their balance sheets. A buyer is unlikely to want to tie up capital in acquiring these. They will usually need to be removed to present the business for sale. The process, including tax planning, will need to be started well in advance of the eventual sale.
- **Arms-length terms.** Property arrangements in family businesses are often not on arm's length terms. A family business could occupy property owned by a key family members without payment or pay a rent at considerably below the market level. Less frequently a family business will pay over the market rate to the property owning family member.

- **Family use of business property.** This can include family members occupying residential properties owned by the family business. This is particularly so in agricultural, hotel and leisure businesses but is also found in other businesses where residential properties have been acquired as investments.

    On other occasions family members may use surplus business property for their own enterprises.

    In each case buyers will be concerned to establish that they will acquire unfettered use of business premises, free of these complications. The sellers might need to come to separate arrangements with the family occupiers so that this can happen.

- **Undocumented arrangements.** More often than not family business property arrangements will be undocumented, so that the precise nature of the respective interests of the family and the family business in the relevant property, is unclear. Leases and other documents will probably need to be put into place to regularise the position to the satisfaction of the buyer.

The range of potential issues relating to property that may be encountered in practice is very wide and potentially unlimited. So are the range of solutions. However there are two main considerations:

- **Value adjustments.** Any adjustments to transaction price or change to operating costs need to be identified and agreed at an early stage.

    Inevitably a buyer will be reluctant to pay over the odds to rent property owned and retained by the family. Equally the family will not want low rents contained in 'soft lease' arrangements to continue once the business has passed from family ownership. Any adjustments will affect the future profitability of the business.

    If these issues are not clear to a buyer at the time offers are made and price agreed at heads of terms stage, the selling family can find itself in a difficult position. A buyer may be quick to look for a reduction in purchase price or rent if they believe the business is paying below or above market rates respectively. However buyers are not likely to be so quick to agree to an increase in rent or purchase price, to reflect the true market circumstances if these only emerge as part of the due diligence process. They are likely to argue that these factors were within the knowledge or control of the seller at the time the heads of terms were concluded.

- **Formalising arrangements.** The buyer will likely insist on typical arm's length arrangements being negotiated and documented as part of the completion arrangements. Clearly the closer the relevant family members are to the sale the easier this will be to achieve. The sellers may wish to put relevant arrangements in place to tidy up the business pre-sale. If the arrangements are of continuing benefit to the family, the preference may be to leave things as they are until there is more certainty that the deal will proceed to completion. In any event an early recognition that there are property issues to be addressed should assist with a smoother transaction. If the family members concerned are more remote or, worse hostile to the sale process, similar considerations will arise as for minority shareholders and will need to be considered carefully before embarking on, or proceeding too deeply into, the sale process.

12.12 CAPACITY ISSUES

With the exception of bankruptcy, capacity of shareholders is rarely a concern in the sale of a non-family business. Two situations are sometimes encountered in the context of family business sales where capacity of the sellers to enter into the sale documents may need to be considered. These sit at opposite ends of the age range of family members.

- **Elderly shareholders.** It is more likely that a family owned business will have elderly family members on its shareholder register, than a non-family owner managed entity, where the participators are more likely to be looking for an exit on or before normal retirement age. The risk of a transaction being de-railed by a lack of mental capacity on the part of an elderly shareholder is therefore correspondingly greater.

  Again analysis and planning is key. Ideally governance processes would include encouraging elderly family members to provide lasting powers of attorney to other family members.

  If not early recognition of the incapacity and lack of a suitable power of attorney should allow appropriate applications to be made to the Court of Protection so that any lack of capacity does not derail or delay the eventual sale.

- **Minors.** It is fairly common for shares in family owned businesses to be held for the benefit of children of the business owning family under trust arrangements. On rare occasions shares will have been transferred directly into the name of minor children. This will cause significant difficulties on sale. The initial transfer will be prima-facie valid (assuming that pre-emption provisions and stamping requirements etc. have been complied with), as minors have capacity to hold shares. However as minors do not have full capacity to enter into contracts they will not be able to give full title to the shares they hold to the buyer on completion. The buyer will face a risk that the minor concerned may seek to set aside the sale transaction on achieving their majority on reaching the age of 18.

12.13 PROCEDURAL ISSUES

Many owner managed businesses pay scant attention to statutory corporate compliance. Family owned business are no exception. Family businesses may be particularly prone to difficulties due to factors such as longevity, complexity and frequency of ownership transfers, by sale, gift and on death and the absence of third party investment, when checks are likely to be made and any issues dealt with there and then. Any resulting irregularities are likely to trouble the buyer (or more precisely their lawyers). Some frequently encountered procedural issues are highlighted in this paragraph.

12.13.1 Buy-backs

It is fairly common in multi-generational families for a degree of pruning of the ownership tree to have taken place over the years, with shares held by more distant family members in remote branches of the family, having been bought back in by the controlling family.

The legal mechanism to do this will often be the purchase by the company of its own shares using the procedure contained in what is now Chapter 4 of CA (ss 690–700). Buyer's lawyers will be concerned to make sure that this highly technical statutory procedure has been followed precisely. If not the buy-back may well be invalid.[27] At its most extreme the family member everyone has long since treated as a former shareholder and part of the family history may still be technically a shareholder.

Frequently encountered difficulties include:

---

[27] See **8.4.5** for a discussion on the extent to which the *Re Duomatic* principle can provide a get out of jail card.

- Failure to check (or to be able to evidence) that at the time of buy-back there were sufficient distributable profits[28] to finance the buy-back. Payment from distributable reserves being the most typically used method of completing a buy-back.
- Prior to the Companies Act 2006 coming into force, and particularly for older family companies, where such provisions were less common, the buy-back not being authorised in the articles of association.[29]
- The purchase price paid for the shares bought back not being paid in full on completion.[30] It may be clear from the face of the buy-back document that the price has in fact been paid in instalments.[31]

  Sometimes the family company was party to loan-back arrangements and provided security in connection with buy-backs.

  Arrangements of this nature were particularly problematic before the abolition of the restrictions on financial assistance for private companies for the purchase of their own shares. This is because they needed to be authorised under the 'whitewash procedure', contained in earlier Companies Acts. A detailed consideration of that procedure is beyond the scope of this book, but the issues will remain relevant to the due diligence process for a number of family owned businesses for some years to come in relation to historic buy-backs.
- The family member whose shares are being bought back joins in the voting and approval process. The natural inclination is to include all members in relevant resolutions. However CA, s 695 provides that a buy-back resolution is invalid if voted on by the exiting shareholder and the resolution 'would not have been passed if he had not done so'. The intention behind this provision is to provide a form of minority protection, on top of the solvency protections for creditors inherent in the buy-back procedure. However the practical effect is often to create a technical trap in structuring buy-backs (and a mathematical headache for lawyer reviewing their validity as part of due diligence exercises).
- Failure to follow the statutory approval procedure as set out in the Act, including that the buy-back will be on the basis of a contract approved by the members as a special resolution. However one of the more unusual features of the buy-back regime, that the buy-back contract must be available for inspection at the registered office for 15 days before the meeting to approve that contract,[32] has much less practical significance since the written resolution regime has been available to approve buy-backs.[33]

  Failure to pay stamp duty on the buy-back. This is collected by Companies House, at the time the return relating the buy-back (form SHO3) is filed. As with most filings, the failure to file the relevant return is criminal offence on the part of both the company and its officers.[34] Under usual principles it also calls into question the validity of any alteration of the statutory books of the company to record the share buy-back.

---

[28] Companies Act 2006, s 692(2)(a)(i).
[29] Companies Act 2006, s 690(1) now contains a presumption that a company can buy back its own shares. But this authority might be removed or restricted by the company's articles. In practice it almost never is.
[30] Companies Act 2006, s 691(2).
[31] This requirement is discussed in more detail in chapter 11 (Ownership Overview).
[32] Companies Act 2006, s 696(2)(b).
[33] Companies Act 2006, s 696(2)(a) – under that section the proposed buy-back contract simply needs to be sent or provided to members along with the proposed written resolution to approve the buy-back.
[34] Companies Act 2006, s 707(7).

12.13.2 Pre-emption and transfer provisions

The older the family business, the greater the likelihood that a number of share transfers will have taken place over the years. A buyer will be concerned to check, so far as it is practicable to do so that these transfers have taken place in accordance with the constitution of the company. Family shareholders preparing their business for a third party sale will have similar concerns.

The articles may make this task easier. They might contain provisions allowing for free transfers, as of right between family members. Alternatively transfers might be permitted without any restriction, perhaps subject to the discretion of the board to refuse to register transfers. However it would be fairly common for the articles of association of a family owned business to contain pre-emption provisions requiring a prospective transferor of shares to offer these to the remaining shareholders before transferring their interest, in particular to a third party. If a transfer is made in breach of these pre-emption provisions the directors will be in breach of duty if they register the transfer. The transferee will not acquire legal title to the shares, merely an equitable right, which in turn will be subject to an overriding equitable interest for the remaining shareholders created by the articles to acquire the share transferred in breach of the pre-emption provisions. In effect the pre-emption provisions survive as a call option.[35]

This may not be a huge problem if the relevant transfer has been made comparatively recently and all the equitable option holders are joining in the sale. The remaining sellers can simply waive their equitable rights in relation to the share transferred in breach, either before or at completion. The analysis and solution may prove more complicated if only part of the shares are being acquired, or if third party rights have arisen on subsequent transfer or transmission of shares.

If a prohibited transfer is nevertheless registered, for example to a non-bloodline spouse any aggrieved party can apply to the court for rectification of the shareholder's register under CA, s 125.[36]

Perversely the family company could be in a better position if default has been made in applying pre-emption provisions applicable on the new issue of shares. In this case affected members must seek compensation form the directors within 2 years,[37] although the validity of the allotment itself does not seem to be affected.

12.13.3 Stamp duty

Fairly often stock transfer forms have not been stamped with the necessary stamp duty (roughly 0.5%). On other occasions stamp duty exemptions, for example on gifts will not have been validly claimed. Alternatively it might be clear that the relevant stamp duty formalities have been complied with. A share transfer should not be entered in the

---

[35] *Cottrell v King* [2004] 2 BCLC 413.
[36] That section also gives the court discretion to award damages to an aggrieved party, subject to a 10-year limitation rule in CA, s 128.
[37] The time period runs from when the return on allotment is delivered to the Registrar of Companies. The same regime applies under both the statutory regime CA, s 563, or pre-emption rights on new issues contained in the articles, CA, s 568. The position where pre-emption rights on new issues are contained in a shareholders' agreement is not immediately obvious from case-law. It is suggested that this is analogous with provisions contained in articles.

register of members unless the transfer has been properly stamped[38] However whilst the officers concerned may be liable to a penalty under the act an improperly stamped and registered transfer will nevertheless be valid to transfer title.[39]

12.13.4 Consequences of procedural defects

Obviously any family business seller will hope that all statutory and internal constitutional requirements will have been fully complied with, if not contemporaneously at least by the time of completion of the sale of the family business. The older the family business, the more share transfers and other internal dealings and transactions that have taken place, and the lower the resource that the family business has been able to devote to company secretarial compliance, the lower the likelihood that the sellers will be able to present a clean compliance sheet to a prospective purchaser.

How concerned should a buyer be about this? The nightmare scenario would be that, having parted with a significant purchase price someone with a better title emerges from the shadows and claim their rightful entitlement. We would suggest that in practice this should be seen more like a script from a soap opera and that selling family members should, in most circumstances, be able to convince a buyer that procedural irregularities should not be seen as deal breakers in practice.

This will of course depend on all the circumstances of the matter including:

- The proportion of shares affected.
- The overall purchase price.
- The existence of any disputes or disaffection between the family members concerned.
- Whether the issue is confined to selling shareholders or their predecessors in title or whether third party rights, particularly those under any form of disability are concerned.
- When the irregularity occurred and whether this has now been followed either by a long period of unbroken and unchallenged ownership or a number of further transfers.
- Finally, and potentially of most significance, the approach and attitude to risk of both the buyer and their lawyers.

Depending on the precise circumstances, a selling family would be reasonably hopeful that most buyers could be persuaded to proceed with the transaction based on one or more of the following approaches or arguments:

- Simply that, whilst procedural matters may not have been executed perfectly, the practical relevance and risks involved to the buyer in proceeding with the transaction are, in practice more theoretical than real. In other word that the buyer should 'take a view'.
- The principle in *Re Duomatic Ltd*.[40] This is that a decision, demonstrably approved by all of the shareholders of a company, will be treated by the courts a valid, notwithstanding procedural irregularities, including issues of statutory

---

[38] Stamp Act 1891, s 17.
[39] *Nisbet v Shepherd* [1994] BCLC 300.
[40] [1969] 2 Ch 365, [1969] 1 All ER 161.

compliance. The principle may be invoked, for example to affirm payments of salary (*Re Duomatic Ltd*), or dividend payments made in breach of formal approval provisions.

The application of the principle by the courts has in some situations been over-ruled by statute. For example CA, s 696(5) now expressly provides that a buy-back resolution 'is not validly passed' if the information requirements of that sections have not been complied with.[41] There are limits to the extent to which the principle in *Re Duomatic Ltd* can be relied on. The decision is of considerable importance in the context of family businesses and is considered in more detail in chapter 8 (Directors' Duties).

- The statutory presumption contained in CA, s 127 that the register of members is accurate and that anyone wishing to challenge the title of any registered shareholder would need to make an application to the court for rectification of the register under CA, s 125 within 10 years of the original entry complained of.[42]
- That the SPA will almost invariably contain title warranties, in effect assurances given by each shareholder that they have good title to the shares that they are selling. A buyer will often accept that these title warranties are given on a several basis (so that each shareholder guarantees the title to their own shares, but not that of other family members). However buyers will usually insist that title warranties are given on an absolute basis, rather than being limited to the extent of the seller's knowledge. Accordingly the risk of any unidentified procedural defects is likely to remain with the seller concerned.
- If specific issues have been identified but are seen as either unlikely to materialise or not to be significant in terms of cost, these can be covered by specific indemnities in favour of the buyer contained in the SPA. Indeed it may be difficult for the sellers to resist the inclusion of such indemnities.
- If relevant shareholders can be identified and are co-operative it may be possible to put in place paperwork including agreements, resolutions and waivers retrospectively correcting or ratifying actions or events. For example it might be possible to re-execute or rework the procedure in relation to a defective share buy-back where either the original procedure cannot be saved by the *Re Duomatic* principle or perhaps because the buyer's lawyer cannot be persuaded that this is the case.
- Specific retentions could be agreed, for a limited period of time, to give reassurance to the buyer that claims will not materialise, or, if they do that the buyer will not face enforcement difficulties.
- Applications could be made to the Court of Protection in the case of shareholders lacking capacity with either the transaction being made conditional on the outcome of that application, or a suitable retention being agreed.
- In other cases where serious doubts arise over capacity and title, for example, where shares are held by minors, other mechanisms could be used to obtain court approval. For example by using a scheme of arrangement under CA, s 899, providing for the cancellation, with the approval of the court (and therefore the protection of the buyer) of all of the existing shares in the family business and the issue of new shares to the buyer.
- The transaction could be restructured as an asset sale so that the buyer could take the business free from concerns about the underlying ownership of the family company. However, given the likelihood of a double tax charge arising and the

---

[41] Thus over-ruling the decision of the court in *BDG Roof-Bond Ltd v Douglas* [2000] BCLC 401.
[42] Companies Act 2006, s 128.

likely relative significance of title issues it is unlikely that the sellers would see this as an appropriate and proportional response.
- In theory any issues relating to procedural and title defects should be an insurable risk. However it is not common practice for title defect insurance to be underwritten (unlike property transactions).

Given that issues relating to procedural and title issues are really matters of risk rather than fundamental issues relating to the underlying operating business, it would be unfortunate if a buyer could not be persuaded to proceed based on some combination of the above suggestions. It is difficult to see situations where sellers should readily agree to price reductions as consequence of such matters. It would be doubly unfortunate to encounter situations where a buyer withdrew from a transaction based on such matters alone.

12.14 SELLER DUE DILIGENCE

12.14.1 Family business factors and transaction risk

Due diligence is usually seen as a buyer led exercise. Certainly the main due diligence exercise will be led by the buyer (perhaps encouraged by the buyer's funders). That does not mean that the seller need take an entirely passive and reactive role.

Family owned businesses have many strengths, typically including, high attention to quality and commitment to customers, suppliers and employees. These in turn lead to high levels of customer and employee satisfaction. But no business is perfect. There are a number of characteristics of many family businesses that unfortunately might lead a buyer to conclude that the particular family business they are considering buying is less perfect than most. These characteristics can include a tendency to insularity, with the result that some of the latest 'best practice' developments in the business world may pass the family business by or are dismissed as irrelevant to 'the way we do things round here', or as so much pointless bureaucracy.

Many family businesses have a low level of financial gearing, often using cash reserves on their balance sheet rather than relying on bank overdrafts. Such businesses are not beholden to banks or other financial stakeholders. This can often lead to a lack of attention to stock provisioning policies and other accounting issues. Other frequently encountered and less commercially significant examples include: a lack of, formally documented arrangements with customers, suppliers and employees: and having proper policies and procedures in place to demonstrate compliance with the more procedural aspects of health and safety and data protection regulation. Unfortunately if the buyer and its advisors are adopting a box ticking approach to due diligence, a lack of attention to these, arguably more peripheral, issues can obscure the fundamental soundness of the family business concerned. At worst these matters may persuade a risk averse buyer to withdraw from the transaction. They might also provide a less scrupulous buyer with leverage to renegotiate the purchase price. At the very least, black marks in the due diligence process will mean that the family business concerned is not presented in its best light. Often this is unnecessary and can be avoided.

12.14.2 Seller due diligence

The basic tool to do so is a process of seller due diligence. This involves the seller, working with their advisors, undertaking their own due diligence review in advance of the full transaction with the buyer. In effect to create a dummy run or dress rehearsal for the buyer's subsequent due diligence process. Any issues revealed can then be addressed privately by the family business. Each buyer and different advisors will place different weight on any given issue, so the process is not fool proof. Nevertheless, as most due diligence processes follow an industry standard approach, investing time and attention in a seller due diligence process should, at the least 'narrow the angle' and reduce the number and significance of issues arising from the full due diligence process undertaken by the buyer as part of the transaction. Information can be assembled gradually. The seller should be much better prepared for the full buyer due diligence process, which should proceed much more smoothly. The level of disruption to the business and the demands placed on the key family members are very significant and should not be underestimated. However a pre-sale due diligence process should lessen the overall burden and make the eventual transaction run more smoothly.

As a consequence of the factors referred to above, and also because on many occasions in smaller or mid-sized companies, the key family members might not have had any previous involvement in corporate transactions, family owned businesses may particularly benefit from a seller due diligence exercise.

Clearly each family owned business is different and each business will have its own strengths, weaknesses and idiosyncrasies. So it is impossible to generalise about what any particular seller due diligence exercise will reveal. However many of the common issues are referred to above.

12.15 WARRANTIES AND INDEMNITIES

12.15.1 Overview

Detailed warranties are usually contained in the SPA, often running to 50 pages or so. They are also extensively negotiated. The form of warranties is unlikely to differ over much in family business sales. However the effect of warranties could have different implications. This is due to the different categories and capacities of family business sellers, particularly in later stage family business sales.

Warranties are contractual statements made by the sellers about key aspects of the target family businesses. For instance, a sale agreement might include a warranty that there are no claims against by the business by present or former employees. A breach of such warranty would give risk to a claim for damages, but that would require the buyer to show a 'loss of bargain; that the business as a whole is worth less than it would have been if the warranty had been true. In practice, that might be hard to prove. Pursuing the example, let us assume that an undisclosed employment claim resulted in a liability for the business after completion of £25,000. However the profits of the business were more than anticipated, so that applying the price formula used in the transaction, would justify an additional payment of £50,000. In these circumstances it would be difficult for the buyer to argue that they have suffered any loss.

An indemnity, by contrast, is a promise made by the sellers to reimburse the buyer in respect of a particular type of liability, should it arise – there is no requirement to prove a loss of bargain.

Sellers will look to limit the scope of the warranties themselves, by deleting or qualifying the wording of various warranties. They will also provide a formal disclosure letter setting out any factual qualifications to the remaining warranties. Sellers will want to avoid providing indemnities to the greatest extent reasonably practicable. Usual UK practice is still that buyers will only be given indemnities for particular issues that have come to light during the due diligence process.[43]

Warranties and indemnities, together with the tax covenant (basically a complicated indemnity document whereby the sellers agree to pick up any unforeseen tax relating to the period before completion) are the main protections for the buyer. Accordingly they will usually be one of the most heavily negotiated parts of the SPA and indeed the overall transaction. Warranties and indemnities are a whole subject in their own right.[44] What follows is a brief overview highlighting a number of issues of particular relevance to family owned businesses.

12.15.2 Joint and several liability and three-circle model

In the vast majority of cases, buyers will require warranties and indemnities to be given on a 'joint and several' basis when there is more than one shareholder in the target. If the buyer claims under a warranty that is given jointly and severally, they have discretion to decide as to whom they claim against. This can be any one or more sellers. In practice the buyer would generally claim against all sellers, but may take enforcement action only against the sellers that they believe have the deepest pockets.

It is important to note that warranty claims can be made against all shareholders under the joint and several liability basis, whether or not the shareholder concerned was personally at fault, knew about, or even was in a position to find out about the relevant breach. So the starting point is that remote outsider family members, occupying Zone 2 of the three-circle model, will be equally liable with insider owners, in day to day control of the business in Zone 1.[45] On the other hand family insiders in Zone 3 who are not also shareholders might know the business (or even be responsible for the underlying business issue that caused the warranty claim) but, as non-owners, will not usually have any liability to the buyer under the warranties.

Whilst the buyer's usual approach will be to look for joint and several warranty and indemnity cover from all shareholders. However some limitations are customarily agreed, in particular that:
- **Overall aggregate limits.** The overall aggregate limit of liability should not exceed the purchase price (in some cases plus costs incurred by the buyer) – except where the breach is a result of fraud or wilful concealment.

---

[43] Although the position is gradually changing to move closer to the US approach where warranties are typically given on an indemnity basis.
[44] For a detailed treatment of the subject see Robert Thompson *Sinclair on Warranties and Indemnities in Share and Asset Sales* (Sweet and Maxwell, 9th edn, 2014).
[45] See Figure 3.5 in chapter 3.

- **De-minimis claims.** Minor warranty claims below an agreed de-minimis level will usually be disregarded. This is so that the parties do not spend time and cost arguing about insignificant claims.
- **Baskets.** Frequently the buyer will accept that no claims can be made until an agreed aggregate threshold (or 'basket') has been exceeded. The logic being that no business is perfect and that the buyer should be prepared to live with a certain level of problems that would otherwise be covered by warranties, before having recourse against the sellers.

It is rare for the latter two limitations to apply to indemnity claims.

12.15.3 Family risk profile

It will be seen that the risk remains for sellers that, on a joint and several basis, they will face claims substantially in excess of the proceeds of sale they have received personally. By the time claims are made they could well also have paid tax on the proceeds, so could (at least in theory) be out of pocket.

Under general equitable principles, selling shareholders will often have an implied right of contribution from the others. However the application of the equity of contribution doctrine is, at times, uncertain. It is still highly advisable for joint sellers to put in place a deed of contribution. This is a document that will provide for all joint and several claims to be shared in the manner set out in the deed. The liability is generally shared pro rata to the shares sold, but the sellers are free to agree, amongst themselves, the basis on which claims are shared. The deed of contribution will also usually deal with the procedural aspects of how claims are to be handled between the family shareholders with the buyer.

There are a number of family business situations where the principle of joint and several liability may be unacceptable to some family business sellers. How willing family members are to accept this risk will depend on a number of factors including:
- **Knowledge.** In the case of a family sibling partnership, with family members holding roughly equal numbers of shares, a high level of trust, and with all family members having a close involvement in the day-to-day affairs of the family business covered by the warranties this situation might be broadly acceptable. All sellers will sit in Zone 1 of the three-circle model.
  Conversely in more mature family businesses, with widely dispersed family shareholders, many of whom are remote, either geographically, or in terms of contact with the family management, it may be correspondingly harder for those shareholders to sign up to a set of warranties relating to a business they have long since lost touch with.
  Good communication with shareholders generally, both as part of routine governance, and also a part of the sale process, has a clear role to play in increasing the level of family shareholder knowledge and thereby reducing the level of discomfort surrounding the sale documents.
- **Trust.** To what extent do, in particular, the more remote family shareholders, trust the business leaders (and of course the chosen advisors) to have got the warranty and disclosure process right, so that the real level of risk in assuming joint and several liability under the SPA is, so far as possible, understood and seen to be acceptable? Good communication helps here also.

Conversely do the more visible family members, more likely to face claims from the buyer, whether as a result of closer involvement with the business, private wealth or otherwise, trust the remaining shareholders to honour implied or express obligations to contribute to claims made against them by the buyer?

In the case of an entrepreneurial sale, family members holding small amounts of shares might hope that either the entrepreneur will have negotiated a good deal, or that they will personally deal with any claims. Perhaps the minority shareholders have been given their shares and regard any share of the consideration as a windfall. The minority might simply be swept into the sale by the entrepreneur's strength of character without any real resistance, or thought to the implications of the documents that they are being asked to sign.

However trust will be lacking in an expropriation sale, where the sale of the family business is set against a background of mistrust ranging from a lack of confidence in the family management, to outright accusations of impropriety between family members or branches of the family.

- **Personal circumstances.** The personal and financial circumstances of the family shareholders may differ, so that on an objective assessment, some will feel they are taking radically different levels of risk by signing the same document. Certain family members may fear they will be first in the firing line when the buyer comes to enforce any claims under the joint and several liability principle. Examples include:
  - Independently wealthy minority family shareholders, who could in theory face large claims, considerably in excess of the proceeds of sale they received, leaving them to rely on collecting contributions from their more impecunious relatives.
  - If a family member could be facing a major personal financial crisis, such as a divorce, that will seriously erode their share of the sale proceeds. The remaining family shareholders become correspondingly more vulnerable.
  - Family members are likely to know and understand each other's personal characteristics, including financial prudence or otherwise. One family member may be known as a spendthrift or to have gambling or other addictions.
  - A family member, perhaps the founding entrepreneur, might have plans to relocate abroad after completion, making enforcement against them by the buyer difficult. The remaining family shareholders correspondingly more vulnerable to claims.
- **Trustees.** The issue of assuming risk under and SPA will be particularly problematic for trustees of family business trusts. The position of trustees in relation to family business sales is considered separately in **12.17** below.

12.15.4 Risk sharing

Negotiating the involvement of various categories of family shareholders in the sale and purchase agreement generally, and the warranties and indemnities in particular, is a potentially complex process. All too frequently the position of family minority shareholders is not considered until the eleventh hour, when a deal acceptable to the majority and the buyer has been hammered out. The potential for that deal to be derailed, or at least to be put in the balance whilst agreements with the minority are achieved is significant. Neither the majority sellers nor the family business need the resulting uncertainty and stress. The position of the minority needs to be catered for at the earliest possible stage of transaction planning. There are an almost infinite variety of arrangements that sellers can put in place to arrive at the position where all concerned are prepared to commit to the sale, albeit not necessarily on the same basis of collectively accepting joint and several liability under general principles. These include on or more of the following:

- **Deeds of contribution.** As explained above these will give family shareholders facing claims a right of counter indemnity or contribution from their fellow shareholders. Deeds of contribution will not remove any shareholder from the risk of enforcement action by a buyer. Therefore whilst being strongly recommended in any sale they may be seen as only a partial solution in some circumstances.
- **Negotiations with the buyer.** Even the first draft of the SPA produced by the buyer is likely to provide that the shareholders total liability for claims for breach of warranty and claims under the Indemnities or under the tax covenant will be limited to a specific amount, often the total amount of the purchase price. In some cases, it is possible to persuade the Buyer to accept further limitations. For example:
    - *Individual liability caps.* Under these each shareholder will have the benefit of a cap on their own liability – often equal to their percentage of the equity/purchase price. This money back guarantee will reduce the possibility 'wipe out claims' which could potentially erode private wealth. However, this only limits the seller's total liability for these claims. Any claim up to the individual cap could still be brought against one of the sellers, to the exclusion of the others. It would be most unusual for a buyer to agree to restrict themselves to pro-rata recovery against individual sellers in relation to claims. Sellers would need to rely on deeds of contribution (or other mechanisms discussed below) to ensure that claims were met by shareholders proportionately.
    - *Lower aggregate liability caps.* Whilst the usual starting point for a buyer is to insist on 100% cover for the purchase price (sometimes with costs on top) this is not necessarily the finishing point. Increasingly buyers are prepared to accept an aggregate liability cap less than this – often at around 50%. From the buyer's perspective the risk of a huge 'wipe out' claim that will exceed this reduced threshold, may be assessed as objectively small. Particularly in family owned businesses with freehold properties or other strong balance sheets, the buyer can be reasonably assured that they will still receive tangible value received from the deal. A reduced aggregate threshold leaves the sellers with some room for manoeuvre in their own negotiations as outlined below.
    - *Warrantor class.* Buyers may also be prepared to exclude, in particular trustees and minority shareholders, from giving warranties and indemnities under the SPA altogether, relying on the shareholders more closely concerned with the day to day running of the family business (together perhaps with their own immediate family) to shoulder responsibility as warrantors.
- **Risk premiums.** Whether the family business leaders will be prepared to shoulder responsibility and assume greater warranty risk is another matter to be resolved as part of negotiations between the sellers. The insiders might assess the risk of claims as low. They might be prepared to accept the risk as part of their wider family responsibilities.

Alternatively their view might be that, in addition to taking on the responsibilities of leadership and of building the value of the family business that is being unlocked by the sale, it is inappropriate to assume disproportionate risk under the SPA. Accordingly some form of risk premium, usually by way of an increased share of the sale proceeds could be demanded.

It might of course be the case that the majority shareholders or business leaders have a much greater interest in the deal proceeding to completion. The sale will be a major life-changing event. It might produce a much needed retirement fund. The sale might be necessary for health reasons. Conversely the stakes for the minority shareholders might be correspondingly lower. If relationships between the family shareholders are poor there might be an incentive for the minority to hold out for the best terms. So the major shareholder might ultimately also agree to take a disproportionate amount of risk, with great reluctance, simply to get the deal away.

- **Escrow accounts.** Many transactions feature escrow or retention accounts, where part of the purchase price, usually no more than 10%, is locked away in a deposit account for a period, typically between 6 months and 2 years. The escrow will provide the buyer with certainty that claims will be met. Sellers will usually resist escrow accounts if possible. This is on the basis that an available pot of money in escrow makes it more likely that a buyer will make claims. However escrows do have some collateral benefits for the sellers where there is a large and diverse group of shareholders, or where recovery under a deed of contribution would otherwise be uncertain.

  There is nothing to prevent the sellers from setting up their own escrow arrangements, irrespective of what has been agreed with the buyer. Basically under a sellers' escrow an agreed proportion of the sale proceeds would be held back to provide a kitty to meet warranty claims.

- **Warranty and indemnity insurance.** Insurance against warranty and indemnity claims has been available through specialist brokers for some years. There are two types of policy. Seller insurance, where the sellers insure themselves against claims brought against them by the buyer. Alternatively buyer insurance where, usually in return for a reduction in purchase price, the buyer insures itself against circumstances that would otherwise be covered by claims under the SPA and the sellers are excused from accepting risk under warranties and indemnities altogether. A buyer's policy might be the only practical solution available where a substantial proportion of the business is held by family trusts. Warranty and indemnity insurance is relatively expensive. Each transaction will need to be assessed separately. Insurers will insist on having, the costs of their own advisors paid in any event. Also as a third party needs to be brought into discussions, insurance arrangements need to be factored into the planning of the transaction at an early stage. For these reasons warranty and indemnity insurance tends to feature in only a minority of higher value and more complex transactions.

- **Risk management.** Perhaps partly because the process of due diligence and negotiating and disclosing against warranties is often both exhaustive and exhausting, the actual incidence of successful warranty claims is in practice comparatively rare. The business leaders and majority shareholders who are closest to both the family business and the sale process will be in the best position to assess the real level of risk involved. Factors that will give comfort that risk is low will include the extent to which warranties are focused on matters within the seller's knowledge (as opposed to operating to apportion risk) business history, robustness of governance procedures and risk management systems in the business itself.

- **Asset sale.** There is always the possibility of restructuring the transaction as an asset sale, so that the buyer takes the assets of the business, free from liabilities other than, in relation to employees, under TUPE and certain other clearly agreed and defined liabilities (eg to take on outstanding orders with suppliers or customers). This should reduce the need for or extent of warranties, which, absent personal guarantees by the family business shareholders, will be given by the company anyway. However proceeding by way of an assets transaction is likely to be a solution of last resort. First this is likely to expose the selling family to a double charge to capital gains tax (see above). Secondly if the sellers exhibit this degree of nervousness about providing warranties a buyer may well become concerned as to the level of risk inherent in the family business itself.

The above factors give rise to an almost infinite variety of arrangements that sellers can put in place to arrive at the position where all concerned are prepared to commit to the sale, albeit not necessarily on the same basis.

It will be appreciated from the above that negotiating the involvement of various categories of family shareholders in the sale and purchase agreement generally, and the warranties and indemnities in particular, is a potentially complex process. All too frequently the position of family minority shareholders is not considered until the eleventh hour, when a deal acceptable to the majority and the buyer has been hammered out. The potential for that deal to be derailed, or at least to be put in the balance whilst agreements with the minority are achieved is significant. Neither the majority sellers nor the family business need the resulting uncertainty and stress. The position of the minority needs to be catered for at the earliest possible stage of transaction planning.

12.16 POST SALE RESTRICTIONS AND THE FAMILY NAME

A related, but usually less contentious and complex issue, are post sale non-competition restrictions. The buyer will almost invariably expect the SPA to contain restrictions on competing with the business generally and against soliciting (and usually dealing with) customers, employees and suppliers of the family business. Those restrictions typically last for between 2 and 5 years, with 3 years becoming increasingly the norm.

Buyers will usually accept that only major shareholders closely involved with the day to day running of the family business will enter into these restrictive covenants as covenantors. Indeed the buyer might actually prefer this. The restrictions will be restraints of trade, and as a matter of common law a buyer will need to convince a court that the restrictions are reasonable in terms of protecting a legitimate interest, and also in terms of scope and duration.

Restrictions entered into by a seller are more likely to be enforceable than comparable restraints provided by an employee. It is well established law that a buyer, particularly one paying substantial sums, will have a protectable interest in the goodwill of that business.[46] However, even though they receive their proportionate share of sales proceeds, it is unlikely that family shareholders who are not engaged directly in the family business will be in a position to influence customers, employees or suppliers. Accordingly there is a greater the risk to the buyer that restrictions accepted by more remote shareholders, with little or no direct influence will be seen as unreasonably wide and potentially taint the restrictions entered into by the business leaders or perhaps other family employee sellers.[47] The position might be otherwise with outsider family members receiving substantial proportions of the consideration as there is a greater risk

---

[46] Dating back to the House of Lords decision in *Nordenfelt v Maxim Nordenfelt Guns and Ammunition Co Ltd* [1894] AC 635 and confirmed in more recent cases such as *RDF Media Group plc v Clements* [2007] EWHC 2892 (QB).

[47] Restrictions (albeit relatively short, of less than 2 years) have been enforced against employee sellers holding as little as 1.6% of the target company (*Systems Reliability Plc v Smith* [1990] IRLR 377).

that they might use part of the sale proceeds and also historic family connections with customer's suppliers and employees to compete against the former family firm.

So being bound by post sale restrictive covenants is likely to be one of the additional obligations that the family business leaders will need to be accept on a sale.

Two common restrictions usually sought by a buyer merit further consideration:

- **Family business name.** Buyers will usually look for a commitment on the part of the sellers not to re-use the business name or any similar or confusing name. For sellers of non-family business this is rarely contentious or problematic. However family members will often share their surname with the family business they are selling. The buyer might also have concerns that family members no longer active in the business but who previously played a key role might re-enter the market as competitors to the former family business. Accordingly the buyer might be more keen to secure the commitment of non-active and minority family shareholders in this particular covenant.

    The use of a family business name by family members in a competing business is discussed in more detail in chapter 9. Case-law suggests that the burden is on the competing family member to show that the use of the name is *bona-fide*. This is even absent express restrictive covenants by family members not to use their family name in a competing business. *A fortiori* it should be correspondingly easier to show use in breach of express restrictions, even those accepted by more remote family members, is not in good faith.

- **Family employees.** Again a common restriction is against sellers soliciting and, usually, also employing senior employees of the target business. In most business sales this is either non contentious or difficult to argue against. In the case of a family businesses sale the senior management remaining with the business will often include the next generation of family employees. They might be both key to the business. Because they are likely to feel the impact of the change in culture from family to corporate ownership, they might also be most vulnerable to become disenchanted with continuing employment under the new regime.

    The next generation might want to join the previous family business leader in new enterprises. These need not necessarily be in competition with the target. The safe drafting approach for buyers is to limit the application of restrictions to competing businesses. Does the buyer seek to extend the covenant to prevent relatives asking those next generation family members from joining them in any enterprise or capacity? Would a covenant, the effect of which would be to prevent father and children working together in a non-competing business be enforceable anyway? On the other hand the buyer has an interest in maintaining a stable workforce after the sale. Family insiders could be particularly vulnerable to approaches to join senior family members in alternative ventures. Case-law and commentary on these issues in specialist texts is thin on the ground.

12.17 FAMILY BUSINESS TRUSTS AND THE POSITION OF TRUSTEES

The use of trusts as ownership structures and the position of family business trustees is discussed in detail in chapter 14. Two particular issues arise in the context of the sale of the family business.

The first of those is whether the trustee should agree to the sale of the interest of the trust in the family business in the first place. That is considered in chapter 14. The second issue is, if the trustees agree that in principle the family business should be sold, the basis on which the trustees participate in the sale. That issue is discussed here.

Whilst the best position for family business trustees, at least from a commercial analysis, may well be the sale of the trust's interest in the family business, the trustees will need to exercise a degree of caution in relation to the basis on which they join in that sale.

There should be no question of the trustees being asked to join in restrictive covenants in their capacity as trustees).

However the position on warranties and indemnities, together with liabilities under the tax covenant may well prove more complicated. Whilst being attracted to the cash arising from the sale, trustees will be keen to avoid any associated risks arising under the sale documentation. The principal risk arises from the joint and several basis on which warranties are traditionally provided, as explained in **12.15** above.

Joining in an SPA prepared on the basis of personal, joint and several liability, is simply not an option for family business trustees. They cannot possibly risk even a remote possibility that claims that made against the trustees under the traditional full joint and several basis will exceed the proceeds of sale received by them, putting at risk any other assets within the trust, or even exposing the trustees to personal liability. This would be the effect of simply contracting 'as trustees'. Something more needs to done.

It would be difficult to conceive of circumstances where it was appropriate for the trustees to join in a sale relying solely on counter indemnities from fellow shareholders, even under an express deed of contribution. So what alternative options are open to trustees?

- **Exclusion from warranties.** The simplest solution is that trustees simply take the cash and do not accept any residual risk by joining in warranties etc. This is the approach often adopted in practice. Both buyer and the remaining shareholders, all with a vested interest in the deal going through should understand the trustee's position and find a solution to limit or share liability based on the other suggestions referred to in **12.15.4** above. But in some circumstances this might not work. The proportion of equity held by one or more trusts might be too large for the remaining shareholders to offer enough security for the buyer. The buyer may take an unusually hard line. The remaining shareholders may lack sufficient cohesion to formulate a reasonable alternative proposal acceptable to the buyer. Trustees will at least need to give warranties as to the title of the shares they hold.
- **Individual aggregate limits.** The position would be improved if the buyer agreed to limit (at least) the maximum exposure of the trust to its share of the sale proceeds. Whilst this would go someway to meeting the most fundamental concerns of trustees: that they would be accepting liability in excess of the amount received. Possibly the buyer would accept that the trustees liability should only be on a proportionate basis. Accepting a limitation equal to the gross proceeds of sale would still present trustees with considerable difficulties. These include:
  - *Lock up*. Whilst the claims period for commercial warranties is likely to be relatively short (between 18 months and 3 years), market practice is to allow the buyer 6 or 7 years to bring tax claims and up to 12 years (the usual limitation period for claims under a deed) to bring non tax indemnity claims.

During this period it would be unsafe for the trustees to distribute any of the capital realised by the sale to the beneficiaries of the trust, in case claims were made. Buyers will sometimes agree to limit the trustee's liability to the amount of proceeds held at the time of the claim. However the *quid-pro-quo* is likely to be an agreement to retain a large proportion of the proceeds.

– *Visibility*. Knowing that the trustees are holding funds the buyer may perceive the trustees as having, if not the deepest, at least the most accessible pockets, for the purposes of enforcing any claims. Unless the buyer had accepted proportionate liability the trustees would then need to fall back on counter indemnities. On this analysis the beneficiaries of the trust could be seen to enter the sale transaction in a weaker position than other shareholders.

– *Tax*. The trustees would need to account for any CGT due on the sale to HMRC within usual timeframes. Whilst any tax referable to a claim should ultimately be recoverable from HMRC there will inevitably be a cash flow exposure when the trustees are obliged to pay out to the buyer but have not recovered payment of the relevant tax.

– *Interest*. Similarly most SPA's give the right to the buyer to recover interest on claims, either from the date the claim is made, or, in some cases from completion. If all or most of the re-investment income has been distributed to beneficiaries the trustees could face a shortfall.

It might be that the trustees regard some of the above risks as more apparent than real. Their instinct may be that there is little risk of claims arising of sufficient magnitude to make these concerns a reality, particularly if the trustees make a prudent reserve. But we would suggest that those best placed to make that assessment will always be the business leaders. At the very least, trustees need to make a careful and considered analysis of the position before agreeing to proceed on this basis.

- **Buyer's escrow.** As referred to above it is fairly common for buyer's to ask for part of the sale proceeds, usually around 10% to be tied up in an escrow account to cover claims. It could be agreed with both and the buyer and the remaining sellers and that the trustee's liability could be limited to this amount. The remainder could be distributed. Trustees may conclude that agreeing to a higher escrow would be a reasonable if necessary to secure liquidity and to achieve certainty as to level of risk.

- **Sellers' escrow.** Participating in a sellers' escrow account would reduce the trustees' risk relating to recovery under counter indemnities from fellow shareholders. However unless the buyer has agreed to limit its claims against the trustees the primary risk, that under the joint and several principle the trustees' liability could exceed the proceeds of sale, will remain.

- **Insurance.** Again as suggested above, in certain circumstances, especially where a significant part of the equity of a family business is held by one or more trusts, obtaining warranty and indemnity insurance may be the only realistic way to provide the buyer with protection against the risks usually covered by warranties, indemnities and tax covenants. Ideally this will be the buyer's policy so that the sellers including the trustees, walk away from the business with the sale proceeds (albeit, in all likelihood, reduced by the premium and other costs associated with obtaining the policy). If a seller's policy is obtained this is likely to operate, analytically as a policy of re-insurance, with the sellers, including the trustees, in effect assuming primary liability as contracting party under the warranties etc.

Either way, insurance policies add an additional layer of cost and complexity, although they can provide trustees with some certainty as they contemplate the difficult prospect of personal liability.

CHAPTER 13

FAMILY BUSINESS PARTNERSHIPS

13.1 INTRODUCTION

So far our discussion on family business ownership has focused on corporate ownership structures. Many of the points made apply equally to other forms of family business structure, including family business partnerships, of which there were approaching 340,000, trading in the UK in 2014.[1]

At first sight family partnerships might seem much simpler to deal with than their corporate counterparts. They are the oldest form of family business ownership structure. Both the Cadburys and Clarks businesses started off as simple sibling partnerships, well before limited companies were commonly used as trading vehicles. Partnerships arise automatically by operation of law, without the need for any formality. However it precisely this informality that can lead to difficulties in family business partnerships.

Traditional unincorporated family business partnerships can create particularly difficult ownership, legal and governance issues. This is especially the case in businesses with significant property assets. Although the issues discussed in this section have potential relevance for other property rich family partnerships, for example nursing homes, hotels and retail businesses the issues are most acute and most frequently encountered in family farming partnerships. Indeed most family business practitioners we have spoken with have encountered at least one serious intergenerational family farming dispute at some stage in their careers.[2] This section will therefore concentrate on family farming partnerships.

A number of factors combine to create potentially complex and difficult situations:

- First, there will often be a disproportionate weighting towards land and perhaps other capital assets relative to the profitability of the family business. Return on capital employed may be low. Farming partnerships are typically said to be 'asset rich but cash poor'.

- Secondly, the same three systems, business, family and ownership identified in the three-circle model will be present in family partnerships as in any other family owned businesses. Whilst role confusion has been identified as a key feature for all family businesses,[3] we believe that it is especially difficult for those involved in family partnerships to distinguish between their various roles.

---

[1] See *The State of the Nation: the UK Family Business Sector 2015/16*: IFB Research Foundation with Oxford Economics, 2016). This survey is discussed in more detail in chapter 1.
[2] Often these take the form of proprietary estoppel and other inheritance disputes discussed in chapter 19.
[3] See the discussion on the three-circle model in chapter 3 (Tools, Models and Theories).

- This potential for role confusion places a high premium on family cohesion.
- Thirdly, if that family cohesion breaks down and disputes arise, various features of partnership law can make those disputes particularly difficult to resolve.

These propositions are vividly illustrated by the facts and outcome of the Court of Appeal case, *Ham v Ham*[4] discussed in detail below.

Although there are many other areas where family business partnerships have become embroiled in legal proceedings[5] this chapter will concentrate on issues surrounding the ownership of capital assets.

Also, as with any significant capital assets, tax issues need to be carefully thought through.[6]

13.2 THE HAM FAMILY

Briefly stated the story of the Ham family is that Ronald and Jean Ham farmed in partnership together and jointly owned a 440 acre West Country dairy farm. They had been farming for many years and the farm was worth considerably more than what they had paid for it.

They took their son John into partnership with them, making, him a joint one third partner when John was just 19 (at which time Ronald was 69). Unsurprisingly, given his age, John had no capital of his own to contribute. A formal partnership deed was put in place.[7] Everything went well for some years. Mr Ham began to do less around the farm. John's share of the profits was subsequently increased to 40%, presumably to compensate him for the extra work he was undertaking.

Unfortunately a dispute arose between John and his parents. 10 years or so after joining, John gave formal notice to terminate the partnership. This triggered an option contained, in the partnership agreement, for Mr and Mrs Ham to buy out John's share. They exercised that option. In the absence of agreement between the family members, the price was to be determined by the partnership's accountants, acting as experts.[8] A dispute arose between the parents and son over the basis on which this valuation was to be carried out, in particular over whether John's share was to be valued on the basis of the historic book value of the land or at current market value.

Before looking at the legal issues highlighted by this case, let us pause to apply some family business models to the situation of the Ham family.

---

[4] [2013] EWCA Civ 1301.
[5] For example the basis upon which the courts can dissolve partnerships based on the breakdown of family relationships. As discussed in details in chapter 20 the extension of the relevant concepts to 'quasi-partnerships' forms the foundation of many company law remedies.
[6] Some tax issues relevant to ownership are considered in chapter 16.
[7] See chapter 26 for further discussion of the efficacy of that agreement.
[8] In other words with a broad discretion to apply their own expertise on the basis set out in their instructions, usually contained in the relevant agreement to arrive at a final and binding decision. This is to be contrasted with arbitration where the arbitrator follows a much more judicial process, laid down under the Arbitration Acts.

13.3 THE HAM FAMILY AND FAMILY BUSINESS THEORY

As a matter of family business theory, an unincorporated partnership will, when compared with its corporate family business counterpart, typically have a greater degree of overlap and smaller separation between the family, business and ownership systems.

In larger family companies, such as in *Saul D Harrison*, the three-circle model can be used to highlight the different positions the various family members and other stakeholders occupy in the family business system. The three-circle model itself is harder to apply in the context of a partnership, when compared to a corporate counterpart, but the underlying thinking of Tagiuri and Davis about role confusion and the potential for conflict and tension between the various systems becomes more important and more instructive.

Figure 13.1: The Ham family – and three-circle model

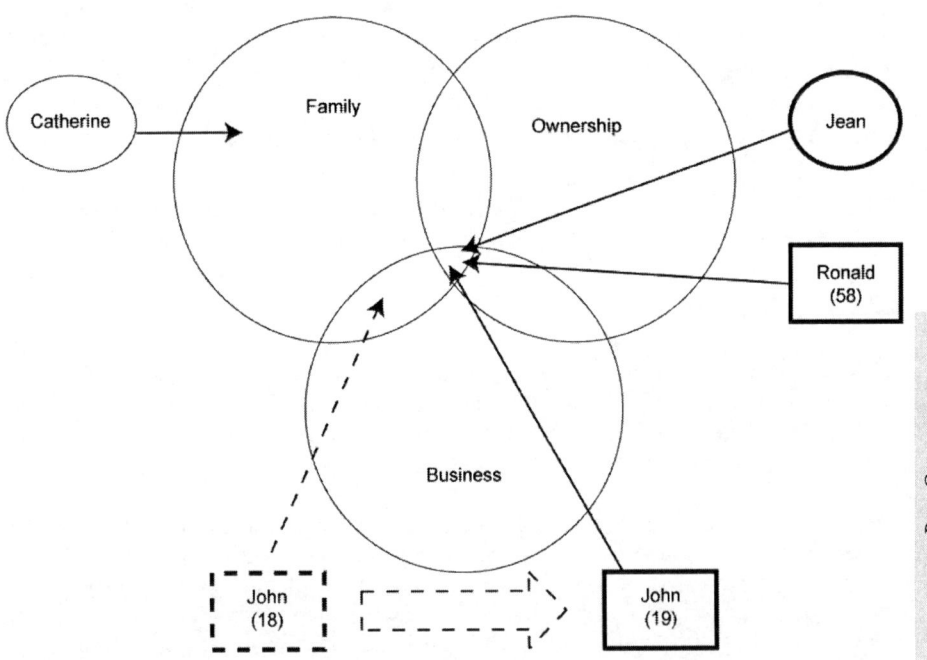

The Ham's also had a daughter, Catherine, but she played no role in the family farming partnership. Other than highlighting the position of Catherine as an 'outsider', the model simply confirms that, after John joined the partnership, and assuming that he had previously worked on the farm, all three partners occupied the central 'Zone 1' positions as family owners working in the business. But John will potentially be occupying that position with a very different perspective from his parents. So the influences of the business, ownership and family systems are capable of producing significant ambivalence. Further potential family dynamics emerge when life cycle theory is considered.[9]

---

[9] See chapter 3 for a discussion on family businesses and life cycle theory.

The age gap between John and his father is almost 40 years. Overlaying the Ham' circumstances on the model of a standard life cycle model, and assuming the generational gap to be 25 years, it can be seen that whereas, under the standard model at age 19, John's involvement (if any) could be expected to be that of a helper, in the Ham's case he was already an owner. Further points emerge if their respective ages are considered against Tagiuri and Davis' analysis of the different life stages of men.[10] It will be seen that both John and his father Ronald were of an ages where a potentially difficult patch in terms of personal development and conflict were concerned.

So family business theory might suggest that the Ham family could be facing troubled waters. But why should the fact that they were trading as a family partnership make those waters any more turbulent than if the same family had traded together through a family company? The family dynamics would surely have been the same. A dispute would be just as likely to have arisen. There would still be substantial property involved.

The answer is that, once family relationships have broken down, the complexities of partnership law can often make disputes harder to resolve than in equivalent circumstances where a family company is involved.

13.4 KEY LEGAL FEATURES OF PARTNERSHIPS

There are a number of features arising from the interplay of partnership law and the everyday business practice of family partnerships that can usefully be highlighted.

13.4.1 Informal creation

There is absolutely no formality needed to create a partnership. The relationship arises automatically by operation of law. The next generation family member will be deemed to have been taken into partnership with their parents once they can all be shown to have been '… carrying on business in common with a view of profit'.[11]

In a family company it will be entirely clear when the next generation family member has entered the ownership circle of the family business. They will be on the shareholder register. Conversely a younger family member working in a family company may remain within the intersection between the family and business circles in Zone 3 of the three-circle model for the time being, albeit that there may be an expectation that they will become an owner in the future and perhaps with increased status being marked by appointment to a position on the board of directors.

The complexities of partnership, often mean that the boundaries between being involved in the business essentially as a senior worker, entitled to a share of the profits and being a true business owner, occupying the crucial intersection between all three circles and entitled to ownership of the underlying assets are less clear cut.

Conversely in family partnerships there will often be no formal partnership agreement or other written evidence of a partnership. Disputes can arise as to whether or not a partnership relationship has arisen, in particular involving members of the next

---

[10] Also in chapter 3.
[11] Partnership Act 1890, s 1.

generation. Family partnerships often take an equally informal approach to employment matters. There is a relatively benign treatment of partners for PAYE and NI purposes. The term 'partner' and related partnership terminology may be used and inconsistently applied.

Often these disputes will turn on flimsy and sometimes conflicting evidence. Sometimes whilst the next generation had an expectation that they would become partners (and that expectation may be long overdue and unmet) the better view will often be that they are not actually partners in the partnership. In these circumstances the next generation family member concerned may need to rely on proprietary estoppel or, perhaps, and more rarely, claims under the Inheritance (Provision for Family and Dependents) Act 1975.[12]

13.4.2 Evidence of terms

Even if such family members can be shown to be partners, there may well be uncertainty surrounding the actual terms of the partnership. In the absence of evidence to the contrary, the Partnership Act 1890 will imply various terms. The partners, or their advisors, may well be scrambling round to find evidence of such a contrary intention.

In contrast every family company will have a basic constitution contained in its articles of association.

13.4.3 Stability and exit

It is often easier to exit a partnership than a corporate counterpart. As explained above, in the absence of special exit arrangements (or court remedies), a minority shareholder will be locked into a family owned company. There is an inbuilt bias towards stability of ownership. Conversely, in the absence of any express or implied agreement to the contrary, a partnership at will can be determined by notice from any partner at any time.[13]

Again whilst there is a presumption that a company will continue in existence until it is wound up, the default position on the exit of a partner is that, under the Partnership Act 1890, the partnership will be wound up and the underlying assets sold.

Farming partnerships therefore have an inbuilt structural bias towards instability. Of course it is possible to provide, as many farming partnership agreements do, for periods of notice and for the remaining partners to buy out the partner leaving. But given the capital structure of a family farming business those arrangements need to be very carefully thought out. Often this is not the case.

---

[12] Both of these areas of potential claims are discussed in chapter 19 (Inheritance Disputes).
[13] Partnership Act 1890, s 26(1) and 32(c). Although a highly experienced partnership practitioner suggested that this inherent legal instability can, in practice, often have the effect of bringing the parties to the negotiating table at an early stage of family conflict. The psychological forces are probably similar to the logic deployed in 'Russian Roulette' dissolution provisions used in shareholders' agreements, whereby parties in dispute can ask for the company to be wound up if they are unable to resolve their dispute. These provisions are rarely invoked but their presence persuades the parties to seek a negotiated alternative.

13.4.4 Partnership property

In contrast to corporate entities (including limited liability partnerships), partnerships are unincorporated and therefore do not have a separate legal personality.[14] Accordingly it becomes harder to determine issues of whether key assets, especially property, are held on trust for the partnership, typically by the senior generation, or in their private capacity. As it is more likely that part of the relevant property will also be the home of the senior generation in farming and similar family businesses and less likely that any formal rent will have been paid, these issues become harder to determine.[15]

13.4.5 Capital profits

Even if it is clear that the relevant property in the case of the Hams, the farmland and farmhouse, were intended to be treated as partnership property, the precise basis on which the property is held by the partnership and the underlying interests of the partners may well be unclear.

There is a key distinction to be made between income and capital profits. Income profits refer to profits arising from day to day operational trading. Capital profits are surpluses on the sale of fixed assets, especially freehold land. The entitlement to, capital profits, those surpluses on a sale or winding up is of crucial importance. The default rule is contained in s 24 of the Partnership Act 1890. The key provisions of that section provide that:

> The interests of partners in the partnership property and their rights and duties in relation to the partnership shall be determined, subject to any agreement express or implied between the partners, by the following rules:
>
> (1) All the partners are entitled to share equally in the capital and profits of the business, and must contribute equally towards the losses whether of capital or otherwise sustained by the firm.
>
> ...
>
> (4) A partner is not entitled, before the ascertainment of profits, to interest on the capital subscribed by him.

So the basic position is that, subject to contrary intention, the admission of a partner will give them an equal share of all capital profits. This is slightly different from saying that all partners have an equal share in the partnership. The capital initially introduced by the senior generation will still belong to them. So if the partnership is wound up and there is little difference between the capital and the value of the assets, the senior generation would still receive the greater share of the proceeds. But if there is a significant difference, as was the case with the Hams, between the initial cost, or book value, of the farmland and its current value, that difference will belong equally to all partners, both senior and next generation.

The question that arose in *Ham v Ham* was whether it really was the intention of Ronald and Jean Ham when they brought their son, John, into their partnership, aged 19, for him to have any interest in these asset surpluses or capital profits relating to the farm land? This would mean that if John decided to leave the partnership, even after a relatively short time, he would be entitled to receive one third of the difference between

---

[14] Although partnerships established in Scotland do have a separate legal personality.
[15] The complexity caused by informal property arrangements in family firms is discussed in chapter 10.

the book value and the market value of the property. The farm might need to be sold. Mr and Mrs Ham could then have to move out of the farmhouse that had been their home for over 50 years.

Alternatively was the intention simply that John would share in the income profits?

The treatment of capital profits can therefore make the difference between a family partnership continuing after the exit of a partner and the assets being sold and the business discontinued to fund their exit.

In the Ham's case there was an express partnership agreement. The terms of this could have rebutted the basic assumption under the Partnership Act 1890 that all partners would share equally in both income and capital profits. Before returning to the Ham's case we will look at one or two earlier cases where similar questions have come before the courts.

13.4.6   Re White[16]

The third generation of the business owning family in *Re White* family also found themselves before the Court of Appeal. In *Re White* is not a farming case but like *Ham* it also involves a dispute between a business owning family. The question was whether, following the death of one partner, his estate was entitled to a share of the key freehold property asset, an electrical engineering factory in Tottenham, based on the 1949 book value of £8,000 or the market value at date of the partner's death in 1993. There the key question before the Court was whether a requirement to produce accounts following the death, including the property at a 'just valuation', meant that the property had to be revalued?

The business of BE White was initially established as a sole proprietor electrical engineering business in or about the early 1900's by Bernard White who took his two sons, Dennis and Lawrence, into partnership in 1940, followed by his daughter, Jessie, in 1949. At this time a partnership agreement was signed. Bernard died in 1950 and Jessie left the partnership in 1961, leaving the two brothers to continue the business as a sibling partnership for another 30 years before they died in quick succession. Lawrence's son (also called Bernard White) had worked in the business for a number of years and it was:[17]

> 'not in dispute that both Mr Dennis White and Mr Lawrence White had for a long time envisaged that he would carry on the family business into the next generation.'

Shortly after Dennis's death, Lawrence brought Bernard into the partnership. The dispute was therefore between the two branches of the third generation, the outsiders, Dennis's family with no involvement in the business, and Lawrence's family through his son Bernard, as insiders, representing family business continuity.

Family business continuity won the day.

---

[16] *Re White (Dennis), Decd White v Minnis and Another* [2000] 3 WLR 885, CA.
[17] Chadwick LJ at para 15.

The provisions of the partnership agreement were in favour of the continuing partners in that the clause dealing with death or dissolution provided that:

> 'on death or dissolution for the purpose of ascertaining any partner's interest in the freehold property and land ... the figure appearing in the partnership accounts shall be deemed to be the value of a whole.'

The partnership agreement therefore expressly ruled out any revaluation on exit. The question before the Court was accordingly what figure should be included in the accounts.

The Court of Appeal were undoubtedly assisted by the factual matrix of the case including that:

- In two previous partnership changes, the succession from Bernard senior and on Jessie's exit, the parties concerned had valued the property at its book value.
- The property had been included at book value in every set of accounts from its acquisition until the last accounts prepared shortly before Dennis's death.
- Perhaps compellingly the Court heard evidence from the former book keeper who confirmed that the two brothers (who shared an office) had told her that keeping the property in the accounts at book value:[18]

> 'suited them both ... as it would enable the surviving partner to carry on the business if one of them should die and that their father had done the same thing before them ... the purpose of the partnership agreement was to ensure that the business kept going for future generations.'

The Court nevertheless had an interpretational hurdle to jump. What did the requirement to include the property at a 'just valuation' mean? On the facts of *White*, the Court thought that this meant something other than market value. It in fact meant fair value which in turn translated to book value because it was clear to the Court 'both from the terms of the partnership deed and the subsequent conduct of the partners' that that the brothers had seen book value as fair and just.

In doing so the Court noted that:[19]

> 'it was not unusual in a family partnership to find provisions designed to ensure that the business passed from one generation to another at a value that excluded goodwill.'

13.4.7 No presumption of continuity

However the Court did not go as far as saying that there should be a positive presumption that the deceased or departing partner should receive only book value for their share and accordingly the interpretation that is most likely to facilitate the continuation of the family business should prevail. Instead the Court of Appeal stated the opposite, saying that there was:[20]

---

[18] Peter Gibson LJ at para 76.
[19] Chadwick LJ at para 67 (albeit that the suggestion was that this practice was avoided the value of the estate being inflated for estate duty purposes rather than to benefit those continuing the business).
[20] Chadwick LJ at para 67.

'no room for a presumption (at least in the context of a family partnership) that the partners do or do not intend that a retiring or deceased partner should receive full value for his share.'

13.4.8 Scottish partnership cases

The Court in *White* considered a string of Scottish authorities (referred to in the judgment) which looked at similar issues of construction on whether exiting partners should do so on the basis of the book or market value of freehold assets. Typically they decided on the latter.

The Court of Appeal in *White* distinguished one of these cases, *Cruikshank v Sutherland*, on its facts.[21] As a House of Lords authority this would otherwise have been binding on the Court of Appeal. Other Scottish cases suggested that, in the absence of a provision to the contrary in the partnership agreement, there should be a presumption that open market revaluations should apply.[22]

13.4.9 A presumption of market value? The High Court in *White*

These cases were considered and applied by Park J in the High Court in *White* who came out strongly in favour of a proposition that the market value presumption that could only be displaced by clear provisions to the contrary in the partnership agreement:[23]

> 'the court leans to the conclusion that the agreement requires the amount payable to be ascertained by reference to the true current values of the assets, not by reference to their historic costs. That conclusion can be displaced by contrary provisions in the partnership agreement, but the provisions need to be clear. If the wording is broadly neutral as between taking current values or historic cost, it is very likely that the court will take current values.'

The Court of Appeal in *White* disagreed, saying that it was not appropriate that 'the Court leans one way or another'. Rather the court should take a neutral stance to construction and simply 'seek to ascertain what the parties intended by the words which they actually used having proper regard to the circumstances in which they made their agreements'.

13.5 THE HAMS IN COURT

13.5.1 The facts of *Ham v Ham*[24] have been outlined above

The point in dispute between the parents and son was over the basis on which the farmland should be valued, in particular over whether John's share was to be valued on the basis of the historic book value of the land or at current market value. This dispute turned on the interpretation of the termination provisions of the partnership deed. The key clauses provided that:

---

[21] [1922] 92 LJ CH 136 (HL).
[22] *Shaw v Shaw* SLT (Notes 94).
[23] Quoted by Chadwick LJ at para 66 of the Court of Appeal judgment.
[24] [2013] EWCA Civ 1301.

'4.1 The partnership may be terminated by any of the Partners giving to the others not less than three months' notice in writing at any time.

4.2 If the partnership is terminated in any way then the partners to whom notice is given ... may ... give notice to the other Partner or Partners ... electing either to have the partnership wound up under the Partnership Act 1890 or to purchase the share of the other Partner or Partners [at] the net value of such share.

4.3 The net value for the purpose of clause 4.2 shall be agreed between the Partners or their respective successors (as the case may be) or in default of such agreement shall be determined by the partnership accountants. In so determining the accountants shall act as experts and not as arbitrators and their professional charges shall be borne by the Partners in equal shares.'

Crucially the partnership deed did not give any guidance as to how the net value was to be calculated and that omission brought the family before the Court of Appeal where:

- Counsel for the parents argued that the correct approach to be followed and the clear intention of the parties in asking the partnership accountants to prepare the valuation was that this should be on the same basis as the annual accounts, without a revaluation of the land. As accountants are not land valuers, how could they be expected to prepare accounts on any other basis? This argument had been accepted in the High Court.

- John's counsel argued that, on the contrary, as clause 4.2 gave Mr and Mrs Ham senior, as the partners receiving notice of termination, the choice, either to have the partnership wound up or to buy John's share, then the parties must have intended the basis of valuation to provide a roughly equivalent outcome so that a valuation following exercise of the sale and purchase option should produce "a fair approximation" to a valuation based on the winding up route. As winding up would require the land being sold on the open market, then open market or fair land values needed to be included in the valuation.

The accountants could always turn to specialist surveyors to provide input on land values. As a buy-out without land revaluation would almost inevitably provide a lower valuation, Mr and Mrs Ham would never elect for winding up (even if they intended to sell up and close the farm down after John left). The parties must have intended clause 4.2 to provide a proper and viable alternative exit route. The interpretation favoured by the High Court meant that no real option existed. Accordingly that interpretation must be wrong.

The Court of Appeal agreed with John's counsel. In doing so the Court also looked in detail at the accounting practices and capital structure of the Ham family farming partnership and at the meaning of 'net share' and 'share' as a matter of partnership law.

13.5.2 Partnership accounting

The judgment explains that the last set of accounts prepared before John joined the partnership showed fixed assets consisting of freehold property, plant and machinery, motor vehicles, agricultural buildings and milk quota. After deducting liabilities, the net assets came to just over £1m financed by Mr and Mrs Ham's capital accounts. These showed the same balance of £1m standing to their credit. The land was recorded in the accounts at book value.

The judgment also explains the accounting treatment after John joined the partnership:[25]

> '... follow much the same format as the previous year's accounts. In other words having struck the balance between assets and liabilities, the net balance is shown. But this time, instead of simply being ascribed to Mr and Ham, part of the capital was ascribed to John. By reference to the notes to the accounts we can see that John's capital contribution was his share of profits after allowing for modest drawings. The bulk of the profits went towards increasing Mr and Mrs Ham's capital account. The land was, again, shown at book value. The same value was again carried forward from the previous two years' accounts. Clearly it had not been revalued.'

The argument of John's counsel turned heavily on the distinction in partnership law, between on the one hand a partner's capital account and, on the other hand, that partner's share in the assets of the partnership. He relied on the following passage from *Lindley and Banks*:[26]

> 'there is a fundamental distinction between a firm's capital on the one hand and its assets (sometimes confusingly called its capital assets) on the other ... the partner's capital will be unaffected by fluctuations in the value of the asset, which will represent capital profits or losses potentially divisible between the partners in their capital profit/loss sharing ratios.'

In other words whilst John's actual capital contribution (consisting only of several years undrawn profits) may have been fairly modest his share of the partnership (including his share of any capital profits on asset revaluation) will be much greater.

13.5.3 Current and capital accounts

It will be seen that like many family farming partnerships, the Ham partnership accounts did not have separate current and capital accounts for partners. Rather than using a separate current account to provide a reconciliation of (income) profits and drawings this adjustment is allowed to wash through into an annual adjustment appearing in the capital accounts of the family members.

In many partnerships (particularly professional partnerships without significant capital assets the distinction between current and capital accounts, whilst often made, is not overly significant in practice. The opposite applies in family farming partnerships. If the Ham family (or, more realistically, their advisors) had made a distinction between, on the one hand, income profits and the related current account and, on the other hand, capital accounts and ownership of the underlying assets including land and any capital profits arising on sale, this might have triggered a whole series of questions directly relevant to the governance and succession of the Ham family farming business.

The judgment explores these issues at length. It is not the object of this book to examine the decision in detail from the perspective of a partnership law practitioner (the sources quoted in the judgment do this). Instead we are interested in looking at the approach taken in the matter from a family business perspective.

---

[25] Lewison LJ at paras 10–14.
[26] *Lindley and Banks on Partnership* (19th edn) paras 17-01 and 17-02.

13.5.4 Ownership questions for family partnerships

Those ownership questions include, from the perspective of the senior generation:
- 'what do we really mean when we say that we want to take our 19-year-old son into partnership?'
- 'are we intending to give him a share of the land at this stage?'[27]
- 'would you expect us to sell off a large part of the farm to buy you out if you decided to leave the family business?'[28]

And from the perspective of the next generation:
- I will be working on long hours on the farm for low pay. Do I really want to do that? Why?
- what guarantee do I have that the farm will be mine?
- 'if I am not getting part of the land immediately then when will I?
- 'what happens if I want to leave?'
- 'what happens when you retire?'[29]

13.5.5 Governance investment

As with any family business governance exercise, answering these questions would have involved an investment of time, thought and cost on the part of the Ham family. It would have perhaps involved confronting difficult, contentious and uncomfortable issues.

Even without the benefit of hindsight this investment would appear to be justified on any conventional risk management approach. That is for any given risk, in the Ham's case, a damaging family business dispute, looking at the product of the consequences of that risk, in terms of damage to family relationships, costs and impact on the family business and its assets, multiplied by the likelihood of that risk materialising, which for reasons of family dynamics and practical experience, we would say were high.

13.5.6 Drafting issues

This clearly was the view of the Court of Appeal. Commenting on the lack of clarity over the valuation provisions, Briggs LJ said that:

> 'it is unfortunate that a matter of such importance should have to turn on an anxious and difficult consideration of factors pointing in different directions, in a context where it has throughout been common ground between counsel that the answer is by no means clear, and where reasonable minds have reached different conclusions. It is unhappily common for this type of issue not to be clearly dealt with in partnership agreements. It is an obvious problem

---

[27] It appears that Mr and Mrs Ham senior would say not. The judgment refers to a decision taken 2 or 3 years previously to remove the land from the partnership accounts with a corresponding reduction in the capital accounts of Mr. and Mrs. Ham. Whether this was done with or without John's approval was the subject of a separate dispute.
[28] Referred to as the 'Doomsday scenario' by counsel for Mr and Mrs Ham.
[29] The reciprocity factor ie appears to have weighed heavily with the Court of Appeal ie that if an exiting partner was not entitled to a share of any revaluation surplus Mr and Mrs Ham could be forced to retire at an artificially low valuation insufficient for them to fund their own retirement (see Lewison LJ at para 36 and Briggs LJ at para 44).

in relation to farming partnerships, where the land forms an asset of the firm. It is to be hoped that, in future, those preparing such agreements will take note of the anxiety, expense and delay which such unnecessary uncertainty can cause.'

It therefore fell to the High Court followed by the Court of Appeal to ascertain the intentions of the Ham family and the interpretation of the clause 4.2 of the partnership deed. We return briefly to the issue of drafting family partnership agreements in chapter 26.

13.5.7 The courts and family business context

Albeit to varying degrees, the members of the Court of Appeal expressly recognised that they were dealing with a family farming partnership.

At para 5 of the judgment Rimer LJ explained that:

> 'As in the case of any other contract the interpreter must take into account any relevant and admissible background which would help an informed reader in understanding what the contract means. One of the important background facts is that this was a family partnership. Another is that it was a dairy farming partnership and that, in the nature of things, a farming partnership is likely to be asset rich but cash poor.'

Notwithstanding this recognition of family business context, some initial leanings towards favouring the view of the High Court[30] and a clear sympathy for Mr and Mrs Ham's situation, Lord Justice Rimer found it necessary to join with the other members of the Court of Appeal in a unanimous judgment in John's favour confessing that he did so:

> '... with some reluctance because on the particular facts it may well be thought that John will receive a substantial windfall (subject to the outcome of the dispute about whether the land initially brought into the partnership remains a partnership asset). But that cannot alter the correct interpretation of the partnership deed.'

Briggs LJ on the other hand whilst expressing 'real sympathy for Mr and Mrs Ham' believed that the answer to the case was to be found 'entirely to be found in the true interpretation of the partnership deed ... read in the context of the partnership deed as a whole and with due regard being paid to admissible background fact' but without making any express mention of family business context.

Lord Justice Rimer, was openly hostile to the suggestion that the fact that the Ham case involved a family owned business should in any way affect the interpretation of the partnership deed. What is more he was convinced that 'the reasonable man'[31] would agree with him. He explained at para 67 of the judgment that:

> 'One should not leave a question of interpretation without first consulting the reasonable man for his view, for nowadays judges are in the fortunate position of being able ultimately to pass the buck to him. I consider that he would be surprised at the notion that, concealed in clause 4, was a provision to the effect that a potentially valuable element of the outgoing partner's interest in the assets of the partnership was to accrue to the other partners ... He

---

[30] See para 4 of the judgment.
[31] Apparently a classically educated passenger on the Clapham omnibus.

might also point out that equality is equity, that jus accrescendi inter mercatores locum non habet[32] and that it would be odd if there are any special, and different, rules for family farming partnerships.

The reasonable man would, as usual, be right.'

The approach taken, in particular by Lord Justice Rimer runs contrary to one of the key underlying themes of this book, that in a family farming partnership, family and business issues are inseparable, that you can 'never take the family out of the family business'. In other words that the case was really concerned with Ham family issues, rather than a dispute between John Ronald and Lorna Ham as business people.

Could the Court of Appeal have come to a different conclusion? For at least two of the Lords Justice of Appeal the case seems to have been a tight call. Although the Court expressly acknowledged that 'one of the important background facts is that this was a family partnership' (Rimer LJ) it is difficult to find much analysis in the judgment of the implications of this.

One of the key technical legal issues in the case is the distinction between the capital and assets of a partnership in the context of determining a share or 'net share' of a partner. The Court notes that:[33]

'by reference to the notes to the accounts we can see that John's capital contribution was his share of profits after allowing for modest drawings. The bulk of the profits went towards increasing Mr and Mrs Ham's capital account.'

13.5.8 Reciprocity and succession planning

Lord Justice Lewison acknowledges that, on the interpretation chosen by the Court of Appeal, it would have been possible for:

'John, had he wished to do so, to dissolve the partnership soon after his introduction, and after the introduction of the farmland by his very generous parents at a historic book value.'

However he was unable to 'derive any assistance' from this on the reciprocity point referred to above that:

'Mr. and Mrs. Ham are, of course, much older than John and might themselves have wished to retire from active farming, and to realise their share of the partnership property for the purpose of providing for their retirement and old age, or for the large resources necessary to deal with unexpected ill health.'

If the asset revaluation surplus would remain with the continuing partners:

'... John would upon receipt of a notice of dissolution from his parents have been able to buy out their shares in the partnership for a fraction of their real value. Furthermore, he would have been under no obligation to continue the farming business, and could thereafter have realised the full value of the former partnership's property for his own use and enjoyment.'

---

[32] (Roughly) the right of survivorship does not apply amongst business people.
[33] Lewison LJ at para 13.

That is precisely what happens in many family business situations. After a period of working in the business together, ownership is eventually transferred to the next generation. Ownership might be transferred on death, when, consistent with the decision of the court and the previous practice of the family in *White*, the estate and the rest of the family do not receive full (if any) value for the underlying assets of the family partnership.

The transfer of value might happen during the lifetime of the senior generation, on their retirement. This will not usually be on the basis of a significant capital payment by the next generation. In many farming family cases the transfer will be based on the contribution made by the next generation to the family business, usually made over many years. Often the transfer will be underpinned by an understanding (often informal and undocumented) that the senior generation would, in some way be 'looked after' by the next generation. Perhaps they would expect to occupy property on the farm. Possibly they would have some expectation to continuing income.[34]

What is less likely is that the senior generation would expect the farm to be sold, to fund their retirement, over the head of the next generation.

13.5.9 A family ownership explanation?

Is there an alternative explanation?

Simply that at the time they brought John into their partnership, aged 19, looking at the overall circumstances (rather than a narrow interpretation of the partnership agreement), Mr and Mrs Ham had absolutely no intention whatsoever that John should have any real interest in the farm land. That is an interest in any real common sense usage of the word, as understood by the hypothetical reasonable man as opposed to the partnership lawyer.

It appears that (at least Mr and Mrs Ham) subsequently decided to remove the land from the partnership accounts.[35] If Mr and Mrs Ham had intended to be 'very generous parents' so far as John was concerned why not make an outright gift of some of their capital which would include a relevant proportion represented by the present book value of the land? Did they really intend to retain their share of the present book value but to give away the revaluation surplus bearing in mind that surplus could only be realised by John, or the Hams themselves leaving the partnership?

13.5.10 Partnership Act, s 26 and contrary family intention

Section 26 of the Partnership Act requires express or at least some implied expression of contrary intention for capital profits are to be treated separately from income profits.

Perhaps it is almost inevitable that express contrary intention is least likely to be found in family farming partnership cases. A formal partnership agreement might not exist. In

---

[34] This was basically the outcome of James Davies' case, discussed in chapter 19. There was no partnership agreement and the court had to discern the intentions and agreement of the Davies family for the purposes of a proprietary estoppel claim.
[35] Whether this was with John's knowledge and agreement or whether the question of land ownership came into retrospective focus (perhaps because a deteriorating relationship between the family) was the subject of ongoing litigation at the time of the judgment.

fact the Hams did have a written agreement. But it will often be the case that costs constraints militate against a proper and full drafting exercise.[36]

Mr and Mrs Ham simply not having thought through (or having been advised) of the implications of failing to distinguish between capital and income profits would not amount to necessary implied contrary intention.

Would a full family business analysis point to reasonably compelling arguments that the intention of the parties all along was that John should be admitted to share in the income of the partnership (as a hard working 19 year old) but that the vast majority of the capital was to be retained by his parents at least for the time being?

An analysis of the judgment in the *Ham* case from the perspective of family business advisors does provoke a number of questions, comments and observations:[37]

- **Express discussions as to ownership approach.** Were there any actual discussions about exit arrangements, or what the Ham family believed were the reason and purpose for going into business together at the time of John's admission to the partnership?
  The judgment does not reveal anything. Perhaps any evidence was inadmissible.
  It might be that the discussions did not go beyond an agreement that John would be brought into partnership with little or no focus on the details. Equally it might be the case that there was a clearly stated or understood position that the farm was intended to stay intact and in the family for the foreseeable future.
  The farming industry has a long and rich tradition of family succession. Farms which have been in the ownership of the same family for a century or more are by no means uncommon. However, as has been noted in what was then the House of Lords in *Thorner v Major*,[38] the farming industry does not necessarily have a good tradition of clear communication when it comes to succession matters.
  Presumably any clear discussions would have been cited in evidence. Were there any background issues arising from family business dynamics that could have been relevant?
- **Custom and practice.** An outright gift of capital would be a fairly typical thing to happen as part of family business succession arrangements. In any event the senior generation would be reducing their assets through potentially exempt transfers for inheritance tax purposes.
- **Family business life cycle theory.** John was only 19 when he was admitted to the partnership. Family business life cycle theory would suggest that this is incredibly young for him to be entering the ownership circle (in the sense of an entitlement to underlying capital rather than income as a reward for work in the family farming business).
  Against this is the age of Mr and Mrs Ham when John joined the partnership. Mr Ham was 69. It could be argued that they were therefore of an age when it would be expected that they would be giving up a share in the underlying capital assets of the partnership.
- **Three-circle model analysis.** An intention for John to enter the business rather than the ownership circle seems to be supported by the fact that whilst receiving a full

---

[36] This point is explored further in chapter 26 (Advising the Family Business Client).
[37] However these arguments do not necessarily amount to admissible evidence to contradict the express terms of the partnership agreement.
[38] See Lord Walker at para 29 of the judgment.

share or more of the income profits of the partnership the accounting treatment was such that he was only gradually building a capital account through undrawn profits.

Also that John's share in at least the income profits of the partnership increased to 40% after 8 years of so in the partnership at the time he was in the mid 20's. The reasons are not explained in the judgment. Was this because he was undertaking increased responsibilities in the day to day business, and at the same time his parents were withdrawing from a hands on role? Did he now have a family of his own to support?

- **Fairness and equality**. Mr and Mrs Ham also had a daughter Catherine. So this would arguably make it less likely that there was an intention for John to take a full and outright share in the capital, particularly if he did not stay in the family partnership.

- **The farmhouse**. There is a key area of overlap between the family and ownership circles in nearly all family farming businesses. This is the farmhouse.

  It is to be assumed that there was a main farmhouse included in the land and that Mr and Mrs Ham lived there. If so had there been any discussions about their long-term occupation? Again these factors would make it less likely that the true intention of the family was to enter into partnership arrangements whereby it was likely that this would need to be sold if a partner left.

- **Retirement arrangements**. Had there been any discussions about Mr and Mrs Ham's retirement? The judgment makes much of the reciprocity argument. That is, that if John's entitlement on exit was to be calculated on the basis of the book value of the land, then the same would apply to Mr and Mrs Ham on retirement, forcing them to leave a large part of their wealth behind in the partnership for John's benefit.

  If Mr and Mrs Ham had other capital, pensions or assets outside the partnership this would be much less of an issue and accordingly a correspondingly much less reliable indicator of intentions.

  Equally was there an understanding and expectation (entirely common in the farming community) that Mr and Mrs Ham would gradually do less day-to-day work on the farm (whilst continuing to draw an income), John would do increasingly more on the basis that 'one day all of this will be yours'?

13.6 CONCLUSION

Inevitably with only the judgment to work from and without detailed knowledge of how the case was conducted we can raise, but not answer, these questions. We cannot know whether the questions posed above are simply irrelevant, have not previously been considered or have been considered but cannot be pursued because of issues of evidential admissibility or for other reasons.

Possibly these issues have been raised but dealt with as matters of fact in the High Court so do not form part of the case before the Court of Appeal. Equally it may be that our views on the relevance of family business dynamics in cases such as *Ham v Ham* may not be shared by the hypothetical reasonable man, who would agree that when John was taken into partnership he became less of a son and more a business person.

What cases such as *Ham v Ham* must clearly be seen to demonstrate is the complexity of ownership issues in family business partnerships and the potential, particularly in partnerships with substantial property assets for this complexity to lead to serious disputes. The position is further complicated if the next generation have been asked to make sacrifices in terms of earnings and lifestyle, in return for the express or tacit promise of eventual ownership.

Our concluding point is that robust governance needs a fully co-ordinated approach between the farming family, looking at both their family and business issues assisted by their advisors who are able to both understand and help the family articulate that approach and also crucially able to help the family document the resulting solution in a way that makes legal and accounting sense.

Certainly at least one commentator has speculated that:[39]

> '... if a succession plan had been implemented with the help of a family business advisor, the farm may have been saved for generations to come.'

---

[39] Debbie King TEP writing in the *STEP Journal* April 2014 at p 59.

CHAPTER 14

FAMILY BUSINESS TRUSTS

14.1 OVERVIEW

14.1.1 The relevance of family business trusts

Historically it would be relatively rare to find a large, later stage family owned business without some proportion of the shares being held under a family business trust.[1] That remains the case today.

However changes to the inheritance tax regime back in 2006 changed the status of family business trusts from being the ownership vehicle of choice for widely held family firms to being a more marginal consideration so far as the creation of new family business trusts are concerned. Nevertheless trusts still potentially have a role to play in particular to protect the family business and its members from claims relating to divorce, insolvency, business inexperience or challenges relating to diluted ownership.

It is a common misconception that trusts are only for the wealthy. Trusts, frequently including discretionary trust can always be considered for use in relatively small family businesses.[2] A trust can be set up by deed during the lifetime of the family business owner to take effect immediately, or by will to take effect on death. Certainly some degree of cost, complexity and tax leakage, may be anticipated, but this might be seen as a price worth paying for the advantages conferred by the trust structure from the perspective of the overall ownership objectives of the business family.

Trusts allow the transfer of assets out of an estate with the benefit of potentially retaining some control over them. Depending on the client's circumstances and objectives there are a variety of trusts to choose from. However, in order for it to be effective for IHT purposes, as with any gift, the settlor cannot retain a benefit in the property given away, and therefore should not be a beneficiary of the trust they create.

A particular attraction of trusts is that, by separating legal ownership of an asset, from its economic benefit, they can be as flexible or restrictive as the settlor wishes. For instance, the client may wish to create a fixed interest trust, so that the beneficiaries are prohibited from accessing the capital before a certain age by giving them contingent

---

[1] For example in *Saul D Harrison* the majority of C Ordinary Shares, those carrying capital value, were held under family business trusts.
[2] Other, less common types of trust, can also be useful in the context of a small family business, for example, a fixed interest trust (leaving a 50% beneficial interest to each of two children) could be a sensible way for a parent owner to pass an interest without risking disputes as to direction of the business (by leaving a trustee as 100% shareholder).

interests. The settlor can also determine the extent to which each beneficiary receives capital and income from the trust. This is particularly helpful in a family business when the beneficiaries are of different ages and therefore have various needs at various times.

14.1.2 Basic concepts and terminology

Turning now to some basic concepts and terminology.

A share in a company is essentially a package of rights, the most important of which are rights of control, to income, to capital and to receive information.[3]

At its simplest a trust is a legal arrangement artificially splitting these rights so that **legal ownership** of certain assets (**trust property**), carrying with it rights of control and to information, are transferred by the original owner or **settlor** to others, the **trustees**,[4] to be held by them on the basis that the economic benefit or **beneficial ownership** will be enjoyed by others, **the beneficiaries**. Similarly the beneficiaries are assumed to be members of the business owning family, although on occasions employees of the family firm can be swept up in trust arrangements.

Some trusts also have **protectors** in place. Protectors are not trustees but can be conferred with powers allowing them to exercise some supervision and control over the trustees (or, often, over who is appointed).

The terms of the trust will be documented in a **trust deed**. Often the trust deed will operate alongside a **letter of wishes**, a document where the settlor sets out his wishes about how the trust will operate. Although the letter of wishes does not replace or have the same binding effect as the trust deed, a trustee should give appropriate weight to the settlor's wishes as recorded in any letter of wishes.

Depending on the precise terms of the trust deed, trustees often pay the income earned on trust property, here dividends on shares in the family company, to the beneficiaries or otherwise apply those dividends for their benefit. The trust document is likely also to allow distributions of capital to the beneficiaries, either immediately or in the future, in certain circumstances or when the trustee considers it appropriate to do so. This could take the form of outright transfers of shares in the family company, of accumulated income, or, following the sale of the company the resulting capital proceeds.

The concepts of trusts and **settlement** are similar. However, private client practitioners tend to use the term settlement to refer to trusts created by wills, and trusts where lifetime trusts are concerned.

14.2 FAMILY BUSINESS TRUSTS AND TAX

Tax considerations (and, in particular, concerning inheritance tax) are often drivers behind the settlement of family business trusts. The approach we have taken is to separate the issue of trusts as an ownership vehicle from the underlying tax position.

---

[3] See chapter 11 for a more detailed explanation.
[4] Who will sometimes include the settlor. There are requirements for at least two trustees or a corporate trustee in relation to trusts of land (principally in relation to the need to give good receipts), but shares can be held by an individual trustee (although there may be good governance reasons for having more than one trustee).

This chapter therefore examines the place of trusts in the ownership philosophy of the business family, together with related structural and operational issues.

The tax treatment of trusts is considered separately, and briefly, in chapter 16 (Tax and Family Business Ownership).

Although the tax and non-tax issues are so often linked, neither should be allowed to dominate and each is important. A business owning family may choose to accept a modest degree of tax inefficiency which flows from the 2006 tax regime changes in return for a family business trust structure which meets their wider ownership objectives. In other cases business families and their advisors will need to consider alternative ownership structures, even though family business trusts may appear, at first glance, to meet their ownership requirements because the same tax bill might not be palatable to the family concerned. Each case will need to be carefully considered on its merits.

14.2.1 The inherent jurisdiction of the courts

A key historic role of the Chancery Court is the court's inherent jurisdiction to supervise trusts. There is always the possibility for trustees or beneficiaries to bring matters before the court to ask for directions and guidance. Indeed trustees will often be advised to take this course of action in circumstances where difficult technical legal issues, conflicts or potential conflicts between the trustees and beneficiaries or between beneficiaries are involved. This is particularly so if the sums at stake are high, either in absolute terms or relative to the value of the trust. Clearly there will be a cost involved in going to court for such guidance. However this can be considerably less than if the issue were to lead to full blown trust litigation.

14.3 DISCRETIONARY TRUSTS

14.3.1 Overview

We now turn to the types of trusts and their suitability for family businesses. The settlor might not always be able, or wish, to determine in advance the precise extent that he wants his beneficiaries to benefit under the trust. In such a case, a discretionary trust may be the most suitable trust vehicle. With a discretionary trust the settlor can nominate a category of beneficiaries or specific people. The settlor can also give their trustees the power to determine how much, if anything, each of the beneficiaries receive at any given time.

This flexibility is an important reason why discretionary trusts are usually the most popular structure for family businesses and succession planning. The following provides an outline of key matters to be considered in relation to when setting up discretionary trusts.

Other, less common types of family business trust are briefly considered in **14.22** below.

14.3.2 Income and capital

A settlor can combine the discretion to distribute income with a restriction over the distribution of capital to certain beneficiaries. Alternatively the discretion over income can be extended to capital. Clearly trustees need to be chosen carefully, as they can have extensive powers and ultimately influence over the beneficiaries' lives.

14.3.3 Trust assets

There is no restriction on the type of assets that can be put into a discretionary trust. The working assumption for this chapter is that the trust assets will consist wholly or mainly of shares in a family company. But family business trusts might also have as trust assets, property owned by the settlor and used by the family company, intellectual property rights, other investment assets or indeed other residual assets of the settlor.

14.3.4 Expectations not rights

Under a discretionary trust a beneficiary cannot claim any of the trust property as of right. Beneficiaries have only a right that the trustees will give appropriate consideration to exercising their powers of distribution in a beneficiary's favour.

Trustees have to exercise their powers in the interests of the trust or settlement as a whole (and have appropriate regard to the interests of all of those with an interest or potential interest in it). It therefore follows that the choice of trustees is crucial, in order to have the confidence of all of the beneficiaries and to be seen to hold the ring evenly between all of the family.[5]

14.3.5 Trustees' meetings

For this reason trustees' meetings should be held at appropriate intervals (including to consider any requests made by beneficiaries). Decisions regarding distributions should be fully minuted to record the proper exercise of their discretion. Annual accounts and tax returns also have to be prepared.

14.3.6 Primary beneficiaries

The assets can be held by the trustees for the benefit of a class of beneficiaries such as children, grandchildren, future grandchildren and anyone else the settlor wishes to include.

14.3.7 Default beneficiaries

The trust draftsperson might need to consider default beneficiaries, in other words a secondary class who would become beneficiaries if all the members of the class of primary beneficiaries died before all the capital and income has been distributed. This would mean that the trust would otherwise fail. If a default beneficiary is included then

---

[5] Choice of trustees is explored in detail in **14.10** below.

the trust assets would pass to that beneficiary, otherwise they will revert to the settlor on a resulting trust or the settlor's estate if they have died in the meantime. This should be avoided at all costs for tax reasons.

Logically, the narrower the class of primary beneficiaries, for example the next generation and descendants of a small branch of the business family, the greater the need for default beneficiaries to be considered, for example, the next generation and descendants of other branches of the family.

Trust deeds often include a power to allow trustees to add additional beneficiaries, either as a general discretion, or in particular circumstances, such as the absence of primary beneficiaries.

14.3.8 Distribution or accumulation

Usually the trustees will have an absolute discretion, either to accumulate income, which will usually be in the form of dividends received from the family company, or to pay it out to any one or more of a class of beneficiaries for a period of time which can extend for up to 125 years.

14.3.9 Discretionary payments of capital

During the period of the trusts the trustees will usually also have discretion to make payments of capital to the beneficiaries. At the end of the trust period the funds are distributed, either in fixed shares or again, at the trustees' discretion.

14.3.10 Termination of the trust

It might be that a family business trust outlives its purpose. In more extreme circumstance the beneficiaries might collectively want outright ownership, notwithstanding the wishes of the settlor and the views of the trustees. In principle all the potential beneficiaries could end the trust by joint agreement by directing the trustees to distribute all of the trust's assets, thereby bringing it to an end. However if there is a large class of beneficiaries this is not likely to be possible.

Also if the trust is a discretionary trust then it cannot be brought to an end in this way. It may be possible, however, to bring it effectively to an end by an application to the court for an order approving the distribution of all of the assets and, in effect, the winding-up of the trust, with minor, unborn or as yet unascertained beneficiaries represented by independent counsel appointed to act in their interests.

14.4 FAMILY BUSINESS TRUSTS AND THE THREE-CIRCLE MODEL

The legal analysis of trusts is that they split legal and beneficial ownership. From an economic perspective a trust separates out economic benefit from the control of a family business. Factored into the three-circle model,[6] a family business trust can introduce further complexities, but with added legal bite.

The key family business question of who should be included within the definition of a family members translates, in the case of family business trusts, to 'who should be the beneficiaries of the trust?' This is a matter of ownership philosophy. It also brings into stark focus issues such as whether non-bloodline spouses and partners should be treated as family members. This is explored in detail in chapter 11.

Analytically a family business trust divides the ownership circle into two parts with those family members who are beneficiaries under the trust falling into one part and the trustees as legal owners into another. The trustees can be non-family members, including institutional trust corporations such as the bank in *Saul D Harrison*,[7] trusted advisors or family friends therefore occupying only the ownership zone in the three-circle model.

On other occasions family members themselves will be trustees and will therefore sit in the overlap between the ownership and family systems. The settlor themselves can act in life time trusts, but sometimes other senior family figures will be appointed. In the case of will trusts it is fairly common for spouses and next generation family members to be appointed to joint roles of executor and trustee.

Here the three-circle model analysis is particularly useful. Family trustees may already be occupying the most conflicted and pressurised position in 'Zone 1' as family members, business leaders and though direct holdings of shares, as owners in their own right. By taking on the additional role of trustee family members in this position are adding to the pressure and potential for conflict and are assuming additional and potentially complex legal obligations in doing so. Often the trustee's immediate family members will be amongst the beneficiaries under the trust.

Returning to *Saul D Harrison* it may be recalled that a proportion of the B Ordinary Shares were held by the executors of one of the second-generation brothers, Lionel. The case report does not say who the executors were. But it would not be unusual if Lionel's son Alan were one of the executors. If so Alan would need to add the responsibilities arising from his role as trustee to those he already held as a director, employee, and shareholder of A ordinary shares, as well as his family roles of father, son, cousin etc.

But family business trusts do have potential to create a compensating simplicity so far as operational ownership is concerned. The directors in *Saul D Harrison* had something like 15 shareholders on their register, holding different classes of shares and occupying different positions within the three-circle model.[8] The share register would potentially grow in step with the growth of the generations. From an operational perspective life might have been considerably easier for the directors if ownership had been concentrated in a single family trust so the directors were only directly answerable to the trustees of that trust. The directors would have been free to manage the business. The responsibility for managing the family would then in effect have been 'sub-contracted' to the trustees, or, if one was in place, the family council.

---

[6] Explained in detail in chapter 3.
[7] See Figure 3.14 in chapter 3.
[8] See Figures 3.13 and 3.14 in chapter 3.

Although this might have been no easy task, if the trustees were supported by fully fledged family governance processes, including family charters, family councils and family assemblies there is the potential for a more coherent family solution to emerge from the use of family trusts as well. Possibly discontent from the family outsiders could have been avoided. Certainly direct legal action would have been much harder to sustain. We will explore this potential as this chapter progresses.

14.5 USES OF FAMILY BUSINESS TRUSTS

14.5.1 The traditional view

Trusts have traditionally been used in family businesses for some combination of the following reasons:

Stewardship

Where the settlor, or the business owning family generally, takes a long-term view on family ownership, adopting the philosophy that the family business belongs to the family as a whole. The responsibility of the senior generation is to preserve and enhance the capital of the family firm for the benefit of the next generation. In the meantime the current generation might be allowed to live, modestly, off the income generated by the family firm. Complete ownership of the family business by trusts can therefore be seen as the most extreme expression of a whole family ownership philosophy. Landed estates provide the clearest manifestation of this approach.

Asset protection

The settlor may have a more fluid approach to the next generation receiving the benefit of the capital of the family firm, in addition to income. The settlor might still have concerns that letting the next generation, or certain members of that generation, hold capital directly may place this at risk from claims from third party creditors on individual bankruptcy or from spouses following a divorce.

Multiple potential beneficiaries

A situation might arise, particularly in a later stage family business, where a shareholder in a family company has no children of their own but many nieces, nephews and more remote relations or, perhaps more frequently, multiple children between whom the settlor does not wish to discriminate in relation to passing on an ownership interest in the company. Their shareholding might not be large enough to divide into viable separate parcels. The concern might be that ownership would become too fragmented and unwieldy if their shares were divided up and allocated to the next generation. There could be other objections to outright ownership, such as concerns over the commitment and involvement of some members of the next generation. In such circumstances it is fairly usual for the parcel of shares to be left in trust for either selected members of the next generation or for the wider business owning family.

Lack of business acumen

On occasions one or more members of the next generation might be seen to be sufficiently lacking in worldly wisdom or business experience so as to make it unwise for them to hold shares directly and to be able to exercise voting control. There is a clear link to concerns about personal financial management and trusts being used for asset protection purposes against the consequences of insolvency or divorce.

Forced heirship

In theory placing family business assets into a lifetime trust will remove these from the settlor's estate[9] thus providing a measure of protection against claims by children and other dependents under the Inheritance (Provision for Family and Dependents) Act 1975.[10]

Incapacity

Some or all of those that the settlor wishes to benefit from the family business may simply be too young to exercise rights of ownership on their own behalf, for example infant grandchildren of the settlor. In which case a series of trusts, probably with the parents of each branch of the family as trustees, or, in some circumstances a single trust for the next generation may provide a vehicle to bridge the gap in ownership.[11]

In other cases a member of the next generation might be suffering from mental or other incapacity so their interest might need to be held under trust arrangements.

So family business trusts can be seen as driven from twin paternalistic motivations, the desire to look after dependents and the wish to offer them maximum protection.

14.5.2 Trusts and the ownership tree

In chapter 11 we talk about the importance of pruning the ownership tree. Partly this is to prevent the shareholder register becoming too unwieldy and populated by remote family members with small shareholdings and little or no interest in the family company as the family multiplies and ownership passes down the generations. With shares held in a family business trust there is an inbuilt restriction to the legal ownership tree. Only the trustees will be registered shareholders and able to exercise voting rights.

We also talk about the need to provide exit routes for family members who wish to extract their wealth and take this elsewhere. Otherwise there is a danger that remote family members will feel trapped in the family company. Beneficiaries might not be content with receiving occasional distributions of income, particularly if they perceive these do not reflect the value of the shares held by the trust.

---

[9] This must be a sufficient time before the settlor's death to avoid suggestions of depreciatory transactions in relation to inheritance and insolvency claims. Also the 7-year period for potentially exempt transfers for inheritance tax purposes could also be relevant.
[10] The implications of this act in the context of family owned businesses is considered in chapter 19.
[11] The consequences of omitting this bridge and passing shares directly to infants are discussed in chapter 12 (Selling the Family Business).

If that logic is sound, work may need to be done by the trustees to provide an equivalent exit route for beneficiaries. Possibly the trustees will be able to sell parcels of shares to other family members who are more committed to the family business and thereby raise capital to advance to those beneficiaries who prefer to exit.

Alternatively it might be possible for the trustees to mimic the operation of exit strategies discussed in chapter 11 by making larger immediate distributions to an 'exiting' beneficiary than those then made to continuing beneficiaries. The enhanced distributions could be of income, or income which has been accumulated as capital to those beneficiaries. The clear expectation would be that the 'exiting beneficiary' would be most unlikely to receive further benefit under the trust. In some ways this would be simpler than direct exit routes. There would be no need to alter share registers or to go through the formalities or pre-emption procedures or share buy-backs.

This strategy would probably have to be combined with an express power to exclude those beneficiaries from the exercise of future discretions that would have to feature in the trust deed and, ideally, a letter of wishes setting out the settlor's intention as to when the power would be exercised and/or the possible use of an exit strategy.[12]

In other ways using trusts as a proxy for exit routes creates more thought for the trustees. If the trust is wholly discretionary, it also creates challenges in terms of 'holding the ring' and acting equally as between different family members. A family shareholder with full capacity accepts an exit package their involvement in the ownership system ends there and with it the ownership expectations of their children.

The trustees always have the fall back of relying on the discretionary supervision of the courts, and the fact that. If the proposed exit concerned a major beneficiary and/or the distribution of a major part of the trust fund, a trustee may be advised to go to court to seek it's blessing to such a significant decision.[13]

Arguably, at least one main reason for needing an 'exit strategy' should not be present in a trust structure as with a disparate shareholding arrangement, since the scope for a family member to interfere in the business or otherwise be disruptive is much more limited. Nevertheless this approach could be very useful in the situation where a family member wants to extract capital for other reasons.

14.6 FAMILY BUSINESS TRUSTS AND BIVALENCY

Seen from other perspectives the motivations behind the use of family business trusts can sometimes be seen to be rooted in the darker side of family business dynamics and to embody some of the inherent issues of bivalency of family firms.[14] In some ways the term 'trust' is an odd one to use in the context of family business trusts. It can be argued that in many ways their use is driven by the exact opposite on the part of the settlor.

---

[12] It may also be worth the settlor considering the possibility of giving trustees a more general power to exclude beneficiaries. This could be something which a letter of wishes may often concern itself with (for example if any of my children becomes an alcoholic, or divorce they are to be excluded as a beneficiary).
[13] See, for example *Cotton and another v Brudenell-Bruce and others* [2014] EWCA Civ 1312.
[14] See chapter 2 (Themes).

For example asset protection trusts are based on a profound distrust of the ability of the next generation to manage their own personal finances or to form stable matrimonial relationships. The settlor may feel that this is justified in individual circumstances. The wider business family might conclude that general trust protections are justified on wider risk management grounds, particularly in the case of matrimonial breakdown.

But putting artificial barriers around the usual benefits of ownership might well create knock-on consequences elsewhere within the family system. For example tensions in matrimonial relationships. If non-bloodline spouses are expressly excluded from benefit under family business trusts how can they be convinced that they are truly embraced as a member of the business family for other purposes? Equally, to what extent will a family member, perhaps well into their twenties, thirties or even beyond, remain permanently infantilised, if a large part of their income and capital, is under the control of a third party trustee?

These issues go largely to economic rights otherwise attached to outright ownership. But they also relate to the potentially more complex issue of control and letting go. For example an entrepreneurial founder may have relinquished their formal board positions and business roles, so that, at least in theory the next generation are in management control. But if the founder has placed ownership in a family business trust, particularly one where they (or, perhaps, their close associates or confidantes) remain as a trustee or protector the trust may operate as a device for the founder to remain in control of 'their' business, notwithstanding the theoretical transition to the next generation.

Family business trusts can also be used to exert control or influence in the family system. Is the trust being used as a device to exert potentially inappropriate control in the family system, for example over choice of partners,[15] or less dramatically, to influence attendance at family events?

Family business trusts, can therefore have a dark side too.

14.7 FAMILY BUSINESS TRUSTS AND HYBRID OWNERSHIP APPROACHES

An alternative use of family business trusts can be to create a hybrid ownership approach.

Take an example where there are four children in the next generation, only one of whom is an insider working in the family business. The senior generation might lean towards an insider ownership approach but might nevertheless wish the outsiders to have some residual interest and involvement in the family business. This could be because there are insufficient assets held outside the family firm to provide a meaningful inheritance to the next generation outsiders. Alternatively the senior generation might simply want the outsiders to have some residual interest in the family business.

This could be for emotional reasons, perhaps because the settlor hopes that a shared interest in the family business will bind the next and future generations together. The

---

[15] *Davies v Davies* [2014] EWCA Civ 568 provides a clear example of the senior generation making crude but express links between family business ownership by the next generation and their choice of matrimonial partner, albeit outside of a family business trust position. The case is discussed in detail in chapter 19.

settlor might also want to hedge their management bets, believing that the next generation of family business leadership could just as well emerge from the grandchildren in the outsider family branches as from the insider's children.

In this example providing direct ownership interests in the family company could create structural difficulties. If each of the next generation had two children there would probably be six or so family members in the grandchildren's generation with outsider status. A large shareholder register could soon make the family firm unwieldy to operate. Even if some of the next generation became committed family business owners it might be too much to expect all of them to be so. Possibly other ownership approaches, such as pruning the uncommitted family members out of the ownership tree could provide a partial solution. But that removes the relevant outsider and their descendants from ownership and involvement in the family firm.

Creating family business trusts over minority interests can provide a solution to these issues. Ownership responsibilities would be exercised by the trustees but the remainder of the family could play an appropriate and flexible role in the family firm depending on their circumstances. Using family business trusts in conjunction with other governance processes, such as family assemblies etc, creates the potential for the remaining family members to retain both a sense of ownership in the family business and a more committed and active presence than would typically be the case for beneficiaries of a trust. At the same time the management of the family firm is simplified because the directors only need to deal with a small group of trustees rather than a fragmented group of minority family shareholders.

14.8 CHOICE OF BENEFICIARIES

14.8.1 Starting point: the whole business family

Obviously a key issue in setting up a family business trust will be to decide on the potential beneficiaries. Subject to one or two special situations this will largely be driven by the ownership philosophy of the business owning family, discussed in detail in chapter 15. One of the key questions will therefore be who should be regarded as family members for the purpose of ownership, in this case beneficial ownership under the family business trust.

As explained in **14.3**, whilst there are various types of family business trust, the most common is a simple discretionary trust. So often the starting point will be that all family members are potential discretionary beneficiaries. Sometimes this will include all family members during the period of the trust, potentially up to 125 years. It then becomes the task of the trustees, guided by any letter of wishes,[16] to decide how particular family members should receive direct benefit from the income and capital of the trust. The discussion in the remaining parts of this paragraph can therefore be seen to be about special situations and finessing the list of beneficiaries.

Turning now to look at a number the situation of a number of categories of potential beneficiaries.

---

[16] See **14.15** below.

14.8.2 Key exception: the settlor

Having the settlor as a possible beneficiary under the trust they established would be fairly disastrous in tax terms. Basically the trust would be treated as a gift with reservation of benefit and would be regarded by HMRC as remaining in the settlor's estate and therefore potentially subject to inheritance tax. On occasions the current business owning generation, perhaps a sibling partnership ownership group each with a number of children, might take the view that ownership is best regulated through trusts.

At the same time the current generation, whilst basically wishing to push on with succession and governance planning might also have concerns that they might fall on hard times and need some support from the family firm. In such circumstances it might be possible to establish a series of similar trusts, whereby each settlor was a potential discretionary beneficiary under their siblings' trusts, but not under their own. There would remain a risk that HMRC would seek to argue that the trusts, although theoretically separate, were in fact part of a single linked transaction and that each settlor had reserved a benefit (via their sibling's trust) in the entire scheme.

14.8.3 Grandchildren only

From a tax perspective, it might be tempting to by-pass the immediate next generation and to concentrate wealth, in particular capital, in the generation afterwards, the grand-children. Assuming that inheritance tax has been mitigated for the current generation, whether by life-time gifts, the availability of business property relief, or otherwise, this might postpone the next serious exposure[17] to inheritance tax for many decades.

The danger becomes that the next generation becomes a 'lost generation' so far as the family firm is concerned. Involvement of the next generation might be vital for the success of the family firm. This could be involvement of the next generation as working managers. In which case an appropriately rewarding (but not excessive) remuneration package might be sufficient.

The commitment of the next generation might also be needed to make sure that the family business governance systems function correctly, for example as family council members. Ideally the requisite commitment would be forthcoming through a mixture of natural dedication to the family company and concern to protect their own children's inheritance, as part of the grandchildren group. But the additional factor of the potential for personal economic benefit, which could be a clear motivational factor to secure that involvement, would be lost in these circumstances.

The question for any settlor considering by-passing the next generation through the use of generation skipping family business trusts is how much could the business be damaged if the next generation do not have a full economic interest in the family firm?

---

[17] The inheritance tax position of the trust is considered in chapter 16.

14.8.4 Whole family or branches?

If a family business trust is introduced at an early stage in the evolution of a family business, for example by a first generation founder it would be usual for a whole family approach to be taken with all of the family as potential beneficiaries.

If trusts are introduced later in the evolution of the family firm it would be more likely that beneficiaries will be confined to the family branch of the settlor concerned. This can create the potential for issues caused by disengaged owners (if the trustees concerned do not act as committed owners) and conflict of ownership philosophy. But these issues might be no worse and even less pronounced than if fragmented outright ownership had occurred. The effect of those issues can be diminished if any trust arrangements are part of an integrated family business governance system.

14.8.5 Spouses

The position of spouses in relation to family business trusts can be especially problematic. This is considered as a separate topic in **14.9** below.

14.8.6 Disabled beneficiaries

Sometimes a family business trust will be established solely to hold the shares of a family member subject to some form of mental or physical disability that prevents them from exercising direct ownership rights. In such cases the key issues affecting family business trusts, conflicts of interest and diversification, discussed below come into stark focus. The needs of the incapacitated family members might be very different from insider family members working in the family business.

14.9 TRUSTS AND MATRIMONIAL CLAIMS

14.9.1 Overview

We referred above to a wish to protect the family business from claims by bloodline spouses as a significant motivation for many settlors in setting up family business trusts. But do they achieve this? The short answer is not necessarily. Trust mechanisms might make interests in family companies harder to get at in the event of matrimonial breakdown. Nevertheless the UK courts will retain some degree of residual discretion to make orders benefitting the non-bloodline spouse and will be exercise that discretion in appropriate circumstances.

In practice, now that the UK courts are increasingly prepared to recognise pre-nuptial agreements,[18] these, rather than family business trusts, are likely to be a more reliable primary tool than when it comes to preserving the benefit of the family firm for the bloodline family. Even if asset protection on matrimonial breakdown may be less of a

---

[18] The position on pre-nuptial agreements is discussed in detail in chapter 18. However pre-nuptial agreements do require potentially delicate discussions with and the agreement of the new spouse. One of the beauties of trusts is that they do not require the new spouse's consent.

primary driver for establishing a family business trust, the implications of divorce are still highly relevant so far as existing trusts are concerned, particularly where no pre-nuptial agreements are in place.

14.9.2 In-laws and ownership philosophy

Pausing here to note that the discussion in this chapter presupposes that non-bloodline spouses will automatically be regarded as being beyond the family business ownership pale. Whilst this might often be the case it is not universally so. It all comes down to the approach taken by individual business families. The issue is explored in detail in chapter 11.

14.9.3 The international element

A huge part of trust work has an international element. Often this is tax driven. But the location of the family business trusts might also have implications for asset protection purposes on matrimonial breakdown, insolvency or otherwise. A detailed consideration of the international dimension of the trusts world and issues of conflicts of laws is well beyond the scope of this book.[19] As a rule of thumb the more benign the tax treatment of the relevant jurisdiction the more sympathetic and protective its legal system is likely to be of the interests of the trustees and beneficiaries as against third parties, including spouses.

Simply locating a trust in a sympathetic jurisdiction may add to costs and complications but also ultimately may not provide an impermeable barrier to intervention by the UK courts with jurisdiction to deal with a divorce, particularly where the trust assets consist of property in the UK, such as shares in a family company.[20]

14.9.4 The English courts and the Matrimonial Causes Act

As a logical starting point if a family member does not hold any personal shareholding in the family firm and is merely a discretionary beneficiary under a family business trust it would seem to follow that the value of the family company should be disregarded in assessing the extent of their assets available for redistribution on divorce. The English courts have long since moved past this point. They have used two approaches to do so, one technical and one broad brush:

Matrimonial Causes Act 1973, s 24(1)(c)

The technical approach is to use s 24(1)(c) of the Matrimonial Causes Act. This provision gives a court the right to vary 'any ante-nuptial or post nuptial settlement ... made on the parties to the marriage'. As explained in chapter 18, the term has been widely construed by the courts. So the question becomes in what circumstances could a family business trust fall into that category?

---

[19] See *International Trust Laws* (Jordan Publishing, loose-leaf) which has a chapter on each major trust jurisdiction around the world.
[20] See *C v C* [2003] 2 FLR 493. Another prime exposition of the power to vary trusts in foreign jurisdictions is *Charman v Charman* [2007] EWCA Civ 503.

There will basically need to be a connection between the marriage and the settlement so that the settlement is for the benefit of one or both spouses and relates to their matrimonial position. In other words it must be a nuptial settlement.

So if the settlement was made by a first generation family business founder with his spouse and children as discretionary beneficiaries it will be relatively easy for the courts to regard this as a nuptial settlement and then to order its variation to provide the wife with some absolute capital entitlement. Conversely if the family business trust relates to an older family company and the divorcing spouse is simply one of a number of discretionary beneficiaries along with a whole company of cousins, there is much less scope to regard the trust as a nuptial settlement.

This takes us back to whether or not spouses are regarded as members of the family. It might have been the case that when a trust was first set up only blood-line family members were included as beneficiaries. The trustees might have a discretion to add further categories of beneficiaries. This discretion could have been exercised to admit spouses as a class of discretionary beneficiary. Perhaps the initial approach of excluding spouses from full family membership was regarded as out of date by the business owning family. Maybe spouses were making a big contribution to the business (whether directly through involvement in its management or operations or indirectly through other valuable support) and it was thought that this should be reflected by confirming their eligibility to benefit under the family business. Under such circumstances the family business trust could be seen to be 'nuptialised' so that marriage became a central feature and therefore brought within the scope of MCA, s 24(1)(c).

In practice the threshold of establishing a nuptial settlement is quite low. In *P v P*[21] the High Court rejected the argument that the nuptial element was confined to rights to occupy a farmhouse provided to the husband and decided that the entire capital value was part of the nuptial settlement. This was notwithstanding the interests of the parties' children and more remote members of the husband's family as residuary discretionary beneficiaries. However the judge also recognised the need to give 'heavy respect' to the settlor's intentions to keep the property in the bloodline family. Accordingly the wife received a life interest in approximately half of the value of the property.[22] The Court of Appeal upheld the decision.

It would make no difference if the discretionary entitlement of the spouses were confined to life interests or even expressly terminable on divorce. Once within the scope of the nuptial settlement the power of the courts to order variation to confer greater and absolute rights where the courts think this appropriate will have arisen.

So paradoxically the more that a family business trust is set up to primarily to provide asset protection on divorce the less likely it is to achieve its aim. Conversely the fact that a bloodline spouse is one of many discretionary beneficiaries under a family trust established for a variety of reasons the less power the court have to intervene under MCA, s 24(1)(c).

---

[21] [2015] EWCA Civ 447.
[22] The position was complicated by the fact that the wife and husband had invested some of their own money in the property.

The big picture view

In many cases the view that in-laws should not be seen as full members of the business owning family will hold good. If the settlement cannot be regarded as nuptial does this mean that the trust will work to protect the assets of the family trust from claims by in-laws?

The answer is yes and no. Although the courts will not have power to make orders against the trustees or in relation to the trust property in a non-nuptial settlement the approach they take is to have regard to the overall circumstances of the divorcing parties.

If one party, although in theory, having few assets in their own name, is clearly enjoying a lavish lifestyle funded by a family business trust, the courts will not ignore this. They are perfectly free to look at the wider picture and make orders against the trust beneficiary spouse based on their apparent access to income and assets. It then becomes a matter for that spouse how to satisfy that order. Of course the expectation of all concerned, including the courts, would be that the spouse approaches the trustees and asks nicely for help.

The wider circumstances would include the apparent assets of the trusts, the historic pattern of payments and the number of other discretionary beneficiaries. The beneficiary spouse might, in defence, be able to provide evidence to suggest that the entitlement would not continue after divorce. Perhaps they could point to a strong disapproval of the settlor of divorce, maybe even evidenced in a letter of wishes or a pattern of cutting off divorced family members from benefit under the trust.

In *Browne v Browne*[23] the wife was a beneficiary under two offshore trusts. Significantly she appeared to be solely entitled. The High Court ordered her to make a substantial lump sum payment to the husband. It was clear that this could only be satisfied with the help of the trustees and that in effect the court order was designed to put pressure on the trustees to do so. The Court of Appeal approved this approach.

On other occasions the extent of the likely benefit under a family business trust may be significantly over-estimated by both the non-family spouse and the courts. In such circumstances the trustees may wish to provide more detailed information about the trust and the prospects of the beneficiary to dispel this even in circumstances when they could not be ordered to do so. The key question is whether co-operation and disclosure is in the interests of all of the beneficiaries of the trust? Demonstrating the relatively small interest of the divorcing family member or the competing claims on the trust funds of other family members at an early stage could well be in the overall interest.

14.9.5 Conclusion

Family business trusts remain of potential benefit to protect the value of the family business following divorce, particularly when used in conjunction with pre-nuptial agreements. But they are by no means fool proof. Whilst trusts might put the family silver onto a higher shelf it will not necessarily be beyond the reach of the courts.

---

[23] [1989] 1 FLR 291, CA.

It is almost inevitable that the presence of family business trusts will add to the costs and complexity of divorce and therefore the emotional trauma involved. The ownership philosophy underpinning the use of asset protection trusts and pre-nuptial agreements is, in essence, that non-bloodline spouses are not real members of the business family. Quite whether this damages family dynamics so as to make divorce more likely in the first place is another question.

14.10 CHOICE OF TRUSTEES

14.10.1 Overview

A key factor in determining the success or otherwise of a family business trust will be the choice of trustees. The most common categories of trustees are discussed below. Of course the key determinant will be the strengths, weaknesses and characteristics of the trustees actually chosen. But it will be seen that each type of trustee may have inherent advantages and disadvantages.

Overall the challenge for the settlor is to find trustees that will be sufficiently engaged – and suitably proficient and/or experienced – to act as committed and responsible owners and stewards of the family business. From a practical perspective, the trustees will need to find a balance between supporting the management team and avoiding the trap of interfering unduly in day-to-day management. If the trustees are too remote and disengaged the management team, be they family insiders or third party managers, will inevitably expand to fill the vacuum thereby created.[24] Too heavy an involvement by the trustees and the family business risks stagnation and becoming trapped in the values and approach of the settlor's generation, rather than progressing and adapting to the challenges of the environment that the family business is now operating in.

14.10.2 Trust companies

Many family business trusts have professional trust corporations appointed as the sole trustee. In the case of offshore trusts this might be necessary for structural reasons. In theory a professional trust company will bring complete independence and objectivity to the trust. Inevitably they will also bring a degree of expense. The challenge will often be remoteness. Can a large corporate organisation, albeit acting through individual trust managers, bring sufficient focus and understanding to their role to fully and properly understand the dynamics of both the business and the business owning family?

14.10.3 The settlor

The settlor, by contrast, will bring huge passion and commitment to their role if they are appointed as a trustee or protector of a family business trust established during their lifetime. But, as suggested above, they will also bring their prejudices and preconceptions, whether about individual family members or what the settlor perceives as the correct way to do business.

---

[24] This danger is vividly illustrated in the *Bartlett* case discussed in detail in **14.11** below.

14.10.4 Trusted advisors

It is fairly common for the trustees to include the senior generation's trusted advisors, for example, their accountants or lawyers. The challenge for the trusted advisors concerned, who might have spent many decades providing advice directly to the settlor, with the rest of the family more in the background, is to adjust their focus to take a wider perspective. Basically the goal will be to have regard to the family business system as a whole. At the very least the trustees will have a legal duty to consider the interests of all potential beneficiaries. The key issue of identifying the client in family business work is considered in detail in Part E.

14.10.5 Confidants

Alternatively trustees may be appointed from the ranks of the friends and confidants of the settlor, often individuals also with a family business background.

Being one step removed from the settlor, but also likely to possess a good working knowledge of both the family business and the business family, trustees drawn from this group seem to provide a good balance between additional objectivity and insight. The challenge may well be true independence and objectivity. Psychologists refer to socio-emotional selectivity theory:[25] the tendency, as individuals age, to select advisors and confidants from a narrower pool of friends and relations with whom one has close emotional connections and, with that a common world view. So senior generation settlors are less likely to choose as trustees, advisors or individuals who will challenge the status quo and champion new ideas and approaches.[26]

14.10.6 Family members

Family members are also often appointed as trustees of family business trusts. These can include surviving spouses, slightly younger members of the senior generation, or next generation appointees. Obviously family appointees have the advantage of detailed knowledge of the rest of the family and close identification with the settlor and the family business.

Lack of business experience may or may not be a problem, as might resistance to change. But the biggest challenge for family trustees is likely to be how to manage the additional role of trustee in addition to whatever roles the individuals concerned might already occupy within the family business system.

Often insiders are chosen as trustees, on the basis that they will possess the greatest understanding of the family firm. The settlor might also be reluctant to have family outsiders involved in business decisions, perhaps stemming from a fear that this could create conflict in the next generation or disruption to the on-going business. Analytically

---

[25] Socio-emotional selectivity theory or SEST and its application to family owned businesses is explained in more detail in Perry, Ring and Broberg 'Which Type of Advisors Do Family Businesses Trust Most? An Exploratory Application of Socioemotional Selectivity Theory' *Family Business Review* (2014), 1–16.
[26] For example Henry Ford's right hand man Harry Bennett was appointed by Henry as a trustee of one of the family business trusts in Ford Motors. Basically this was a voting trust whereby Bennett was given voting rights over Henry's shares during his lifetime and for 10 years after his death. Although Harry eventually voted with the remainder of the family in favour of change and against Henry this was not until much damage had been done both to the Ford family and the business by Henry's refusal to let go of control.

vesting significant ownership control in insiders upsets the balance between the business and ownership systems of a family business.

The potential for conflict of interest between the various roles held by the insiders is considerable. At first sight asking a family insider to act as trustee of a family business trust with outsider beneficiaries does seem akin to suggesting a fox should act as steward of a henhouse. It follows that the success or failure of family trustees will depend on the extent to which they are able to deal with this conflict of interest and properly discharge their duties as trustees. There are, no doubt, many examples where insider trustees have managed to reconcile this conflict of interest and to deal with the complexities of the additional role of trustee. But logic would question the wisdom of tempting fate in this regard.

Even at the most positive, by appointing family insiders as trustees the overall family business system loses the checks and balances to management that can be provided by committed owners. The concern could be that the management might be frustrated by the influence of outsider ownership, either directly or indirectly by family members acting as trustees of family business trusts. But relegating the influence of the outsiders to beneficial owners on the periphery of the ownership system will not remove this tension from the family business system. It will simply relocate it.

14.11 THE *BARTLETT* CASE AND OWNERSHIP VACUUM

One of the leading cases on the duty of care owed by trustees is *Bartlett v Barclays Bank Trust Company*.[27] The case concerned a family property investment company, established in 1920 as a vehicle for holding a considerable amount of commercial and prime London residential property. All of the shares were placed into trust with the trust company of a major bank being appointed as sole trustee.

Initially the board consisted of a mixture of property professionals, accountants, lawyers and family members with business experience. But in the 1960's the two family members on the board at that time were forced to resign because of ill health and were not replaced by other family members. The family then had no role in the business system and only a background presence as beneficiaries in the bifurcated ownership system created by the trust structure.

A functioning trust requires committed and engaged trustees, a factor markedly absent in the *Bartlett* case. An ownership vacuum therefore occurred. The role of the board expanded to fill this vacuum. Led by the managing director, a partner in a leading firm of surveyors and estate agents, the company changed the focus of its business from passive property investment to speculative property development with the attendant risks attached.

The board gambled heavily on a development at the Old Bailey in London, engaging in a joint venture, which took speculative positions on a complex project involving 20 separate sites and no planning permission for the development. The board caused the family company to borrow heavily, they flirted with floatation and no doubt incurred considerable fees in the process. Planning permission was not forthcoming and, as a result, the family company had to be sold to repay borrowings. The sale realised £4.49m

---

[27] [1980] 1 All ER 139.

(approximately £25m at 2016 values) so the family had hardly gone from 'clogs to clogs' in the three generations since the trust was established. Nevertheless this was 'less than they would have been brought if such a large sum had not been lost on the investment'.[28]

Give or take the managing director taking a lease of prime residential property in Chelsea owned by the company on favourable terms without the knowledge or approval of the bank as trustee shareholder, there is no suggestion that the board acted improperly much less dishonestly. As a general proposition the courts are reluctant to interfere with business decisions of directors.[29] The case was not concerned with the mismanagement of the board, but rather the lack of supervision and active exercise of ownership control by the trustee bank company.

In practice the trustee company appeared to be almost entirely absent from duty so that their manager 'placed complete confidence in the board and assumed they knew what they were doing'.[30] In detail the Court identified a cumulative and unfolding failures of supervision including failures to:

- seek additional information beyond statutory accounts;
- monitor investments and risk, even where there was evidence the board had strayed beyond recommendations laid down by the bank;
- respond to warning signs such as the need for additional borrowing;
- consider the suitability and experience of the board to undertake speculative property development as opposed to property investment.

As a result the bank was found to be in breach of its duty of care to the beneficiaries and was liable for obviously substantial damages.

The judges in the Court in the *Bartlett* case put forward a number of propositions so far as the duty of care of trustees is concerned.[31] These were:

- The starting point is that a trustee has a 'a duty to conduct the business of the trust with the same skill and care as an ordinary prudent man of business would extend towards his own affairs'.[32]
- This level of duty will apply to family trustees even if their trusteeship is 'unpaid and sometimes [accepted] reluctantly from a sense of family duty'.
- The duty will be enhanced in the case of professional trustees such as trust corporations which 'holds itself out in its advertising literature as being above ordinary mortals.'[33]
- More will be expected from trustees with a greater controlling interest and truly able to influence the board.[34]

---

[28] At p 438.
[29] This is discussed in chapter 20.
[30] At p 439
[31] The duty of care of trustees now stems partly from case-law and partly from statute (Trustee Act 2000, s 1). A detailed analysis of the differences between the common law and statutory duty of care and related topics such as exclusion and limitation of the duties is beyond the scope of this book.
[32] Brightman J at p 440, approving and applying earlier authorities noted in the judgment.
[33] Brightman J at p 443.
[34] At p 443.

- Although trustees with a controlling interest can consider requiring board representation this is not necessarily required if the trustees find other means to obtain information and to supervise the board.[35]
- Distinctions need to be drawn between a prudent business decision, that simply turns out badly and a reckless gamble. Trustees should not be totally risk averse.
- The greater the proportion of trust assets tied up in a single investment, such as a family company, the more the above factors come into play.[36]

In some ways the minimum standard of care expected from trustees can be seen to be higher than that required of directors. Certainly fully engaged and active ownership will be required.

Presumably alerted by the poor sale price achieved on the sale of the family company, some of the third generation, grandchildren of the settlor re-entered and challenged how well their interests had been served by their trust corporation trustees. The result was heavily contested litigation, culminating in a 40 day trial, with attendant risks and costs.

Obviously the primary problem was disengaged trustees who, rather than think too carefully about the trust assets, left it to other men in suits to do so. But the question remains, to what extent might all this have been avoided if the trust and wider family business governance arrangements had included mechanisms of some description to encourage the continuing involvement and interest of the family in the affairs of the trust?

14.12 PROTECTORS

14.12.1 Overview

So there might be occasions where the watchdogs need to be watched, for the trustees to be supervised, in a more delicate and simpler way than a (no doubt costly and time-consuming) application to court. This is where the concept of the protector can come into play. Sometimes called 'guardians', 'supervisors,' 'custodians', or 'appointed persons' protectors, typically have particular powers of supervision of trusts. Protectors are more common in offshore trusts and comparatively rare in UK trusts. They nevertheless have a role to play in fully formed family business trusts.

A protector is an individual, appointed under the terms of the trust deed, with particular powers (which may be fiduciary or non-fiduciary depending on the precise powers concerned). The protector is separate from the trustees. The concept of a protector is a creature of the draftsman's pen rather than statute or pre-existing case-law, so their precise powers and role can vary from trust to trust.

Protector powers are often found in lifetime settlements with the settlor acting as protector. But there is no reason why such arrangements cannot continue after the settlor's death, with the role of protector being filled by someone trusted by the settlor and seen by them to be like-minded so far as the strategy and approach to the family business is concerned.

---

[35] At p 443.
[36] At p 445.

The powers of a protector can be both positive and negative. Positive powers would include such matters as the over-riding ability to appoint or remove trustees, or even to amend the trust document itself. Negative powers are essentially powers of veto, reserved to the protector, over the decisions of the trustees. The most significant potential power of veto in family business trust is likely to be over the sale of the trust's interest in the family business itself and this is considered separately below.

As part of the machinery of trusts, protectors are subject to the inherent supervisory jurisdiction of the courts. Although they are not trustees, similar issues arise such as whether the protector should be entitled to indemnities from trust assets for expenses incurred, for pursuing litigation relating to their powers, or for the negligent misuse of those powers.

14.12.2 Extensive protector powers

Protector powers could extend well beyond the issues of whether or not the business is to be sold. In theory these could mirror the lists of restricted matters or 'negative pledges' commonly found in shareholder agreements.[37] They could cover any key ownership decisions relating to the interest of the trust in the family company, for example whether to support a major fund-raising or to confirm the appointment or support the removal of a director.

Potentially damaging in terms of family dynamics is the possibility of protector powers to be used as an instrument by the settlor to retain control of the family firm and to stifle its natural development. Is establishing a trust with extensive reserved protector powers a manifestation of reluctance to let go of the family business on the part of the settlor?

The issues of sham trusts and the place of trusts generally in the family business governance system are explored later in this chapter.

14.12.3 Protector powers and the family system

In the above paragraph we talk about the potential to use protector powers to control or at least veto business decisions. The settlor might want control over other key decisions relating to the internal operation of the trust so far as they relate to the family system.

It is possible to give the protector a positive power to add or remove beneficiaries, for example individual spouses, as discretionary beneficiaries or to veto the distribution of funds within the trust. A potentially interesting use of reserved powers could be to regulate the operation of family branch issues. For example the final apportionment of income between the discretionary beneficiaries of one branch of the family could be reserved to representatives of that branch.[38]

More controversially and straying into the danger zone of the overlap between the family and business systems powers to use the votes of the trust to appoint or remove a director from one family branch might be reserved to the 'other branches' of the family. At first sight this might seem to encourage the branches to co-operate. In practice it is

---

[37] See chapter 11.
[38] See *Vestey's Case* [1979] WLR 915.

capable of stirring up family branch warfare. It is far better for the trustees to act as committed and responsible owners so far as such issues are concerned.

14.12.4 Identity of the protector

The protector could be the settlor themselves,[39] a third party appointed by the settlor or the holder of some office or position from within the family business system. It is also possible, and indeed in some cases necessary for protectors to be able to appoint their own successor as protector. Certainly in cases where the protector has significant veto rights over the decisions of the trustees, for example over decisions to sell their shares in a family company, the administration of the trusts can become impeded if the position of protector remains empty.[40]

The personal characteristics of the proposed protector will be key but the structure and dynamics of the family business system may make some considerations relevant on more or less every occasion.

With the settlor their commitment to and deep understanding of the family business can be taken as a given. As mentioned above the concern would be whether the settlor could be sufficiently detached and avoid using their protector powers to exert undue influence over the trustees and, thereby, indirectly the board and the family company. Would the influence of the settlor cause imbalances in the family system?

Protectors appointed by the settlor have the advantage of being one stage removed and therefore more objective. But the risk might arise that the protector might feel obliged to exercise their powers on the basis of their understanding of what the settlor would have wanted. This might not be the same thing as the family business needs in the light of changed circumstances.

There is the possibility of tying protectorship, not to an individual but to an office. For example the chair of the family council. This would need considerable thought and great care would be needed to work out the extent of the protector powers and how they would be exercised in these circumstances. Giving the family council formal rights relating to ownership cuts across the basic premise that the family council is to act in an informal advisory role only. Any new officeholder would also need to agree to assume the role of protector.

In an ideal world it should not be necessary to introduce a third layer of protection of the family's interests. The board and the trustees should be enough. Nevertheless it is at least arguable that the situation in *Bartlett* could have been improved by the presence of a family council with both positive protector powers to appoint or remove the trustees concerned and negative or veto powers to prevent some of the more risky investment decisions.

Complex questions of law can arise where protectors have been appointed including deciding whether the powers bestowed on a protector are purely personal, so that the protector can decide issues how they choose without regard to the wider interests of the trust, or alternatively whether the protector has been appointed in a fiduciary capacity,

---

[39] This possibility and the associated risks, are discussed in the following paragraph.
[40] Although the court, under its inherent jurisdiction, would have the ability to appoint a replacement.

so must take the interests of all the beneficiaries into account (and of course disregard any personal interest they have in the matter) when exercising their powers. Where the issue becomes relevant each case will need to be considered in its own circumstances and in the light of the provisions of the trust deed. However, whatever the analysis of the nature of their powers a protector cannot go too far wrong by assuming that they are acting in a fiduciary capacity.

14.13 SETTLOR'S AND RESERVED POWERS

An alternative approach to using a protector is for the settlor, of a lifetime trust, to reserve the power to take certain key decisions for themselves. For this reason trusts where protector like powers have been reserved to the settlor are called 'reserved powers trusts'.

Reserved powers can either be full, for example where the settlor reserves the power to remove or add additional beneficiaries, or negative where the settlor retains power to direct that the trustees may only exercise certain powers with the settlors consent (ie a power of veto). However the more extensive the protector powers the greater the risk that the trust could face attack as a sham trust, on the basis that in reality the settlor, through their reserved powers, has retained almost full control of the shares in the trust.

Bestowing powers on a third party protector (rather than the settlor) may be an effective 'middle ground' between the settlor surrendering complete control (to, say, a trust corporation), and worrying about the consequences of that, and, on the other hand the settlor wanting to reserve powers himself or herself (with the risks referred to above).

14.14 REMOVAL OF TRUSTEES

Given the central importance of trustees to the successful operation of the trust and with that the protection of the economic interests of the beneficiaries what can be done if the trustees do not live up to expectations? Ideally there will be express and detailed provisions in the trust deed itself dealing with the appointment and removal of trustees.

There might be a protector involved with a positive power over appointment and removal. If there is no power or, if those holding the power are not prepared to exercise it, in theory, beneficiaries can always make an application to the court for the removal and replacement of trustees.[41]

As the protection of the beneficiaries and the trust assets are the primary considerations of the court[42] it might be presumed that in most cases where the trustees have fallen short their removal ought to be a relative formality. But each case will be turn on its own facts. Unrepentant trustees guilty of grave breaches of trust are likely to be removed. But just because a trustee is guilty of some breach of trust, including self-dealing, it does not always follow that the trustee will be removed if the court is satisfied that a repetition is unlikely.

---

[41] This can be under s 41 of the Trustee Act 1925 or under the inherent jurisdiction of the court. Almost identical considerations apply to the removal of executors or personal representatives during the winding up of an estate where removal is in accordance with s 50 of the Administration of Justice Act 1985 – see *Kershaw v Mickelthwaite and others* [2010] EWHC 506 (Ch).

[42] *Letterstedt v Broers* [1884] 9 App Cas 371.

In general terms that the touchstone for the court will always be what is in the best interests of the future administration of the trust?

There are two broad scenarios where this may be contemplated.

14.14.1 Disengaged trustees

First disengaged trustees.

As in the *Bartlett* case the trustees might not be exercising any real supervision or active management of their interest in the family company. In these circumstances it might be possible for the beneficiaries to performance manage the trustees and thereby secure a better level of engagement. The trustees might be persuaded to step aside so as to allow replacement trustees, in all probability chosen by the beneficiaries, to take over. This approach flies in the face of traditional trust theory. In effect it is suggesting that the beneficiaries acts as supervisors of the trustees. Clearly this will need an engaged and capable group of beneficiaries. But such a group are capable of emerging from a wider family business governance framework.

In these circumstances it might be comparatively easy to secure change. Few trustees, particularly trust corporations, would want to invest too much resource in retaining their trusteeship against the wishes of a committed and coherent cohort of beneficiaries. Even fewer would want to see the efficacy of their management and trusteeship debated in court.

Ultimately the beneficiaries might need seek replacement of existing trustees by way of application to court with new trustees who will act appropriately.

14.14.2 Removal of family trustees

If the main problem with non-family trustees can be said to be the risk of disengagement the core concern with family trustees could well be conflicts of interest. In the first situation family dynamics will be more or less absent. In the second case family dynamics are likely to be to the fore. By definition the family will be in the middle of a deep and serious conflict if one part of the family has gone before the court seeking removal of other family members as trustees. In practice it might prove difficult for the court to work out where family conflict ends and legitimate criticism of family members as trustees begins.

Mere hostility between beneficiaries and trustees may well not be enough to secure the removal of trustees, particularly where that hostility does not relate to the affairs of the trust.[43] In the High Court case of *Kershaw v Mickelthwaite and others*[44] Newey J noted that the fact that the case was the fifth piece of litigation between a brother and his sister over a portfolio of investment properties and property investment companies built up by their deceased father and now forming part of their mother's estate 'testifies to the

---

[43] It is arguable that hostility that derives from the administration of the trust and that is likely to impede future administration (such as where, for example, a beneficiary whose relationship with a trustee has broken down completely and the beneficiary is also an indispensable director of the underlying company) could be a reason why it would be in the best interests of the trust as a whole for the trustee to be replaced.

[44] [2010] EWHC 506 (Ch).

hostility which exists at least [between them]'.[45] Nevertheless, in the absence of any real evidence that the estate was not being administered properly – or that the present executors continuing would be likely to be against the interests of the trust in future – the Court refused the application of the brother to have his sister and the remaining executors removed.

The courts will be influenced by the fact that, in the case of the initial trustees, these have been chosen by the settlor. In *Kershaw v Mickelthwaite* the court heard evidence that the mother had taken what was clearly a difficult and deliberate decision not to appoint her son as an executor because of what she saw as his overbearing personality and a concern (subsequently borne out) that administration of the estate would be hampered by quarrels between the siblings. Additional costs incurred in replacing executors or trustees will also be a factor to be considered.[46]

But in other circumstances, such as where the relationship between family members has broken down to such an extent as to be entirely dysfunctional, so that the trust itself has no real possibility of operating properly, the court may order the removal of trustees. This is especially so where the management of the trust can be criticised even if this falls short of a breach of duty on the part of the trustees.[47] The touchstone is what is in the best interests of the trust?

Removal will be almost a formality if it can be shown that the interests of the beneficiaries have been put in danger by breaches of fiduciary duty or serious mismanagement on the part of the trustees. In *Thomas and Agnes Carvel Foundation v Carvel*[48] the High Court had little difficulty in ordering the removal of an executor who had ignored a probate of an earlier will in favour of a charitable foundation granted in the New York courts, obtained probate of a later rival will in England in favour of a second charitable foundation run by her mother who had in turn had consented to her daughter being re-imbursed some £8m in expenses from the estate and without notifying the first charitable foundation of the rival proceedings. Although Lewison J was unwilling to make findings of dishonesty against the executor during summary proceedings he was able to order her removal on the basis of an inference that she:[49]

> '... does not understand her responsibilities [as an executor] and is not willing to learn them.'

14.14.3 Case study

In theory the courts will be supportive of an application to remove a conflicted trustee who is clearly allowing their trust to suffer. Often real life will not be so straightforward. Few cases will be as clear-cut or have as much at stake for a single beneficiary as in *Carvel*. Even if the beneficiaries believe that they have a good legal case in practice securing removal might not be so simple. Consider this case study.

---

[45] At para 27.
[46] See *Kershaw v Mickelthwaite and others* [2010] EWHC 506 (Ch) at paras 33 and 34.
[47] *Kershaw v Mickelthwaite and others* [2010] EWHC 506 (Ch) at paras 7–9 discussing the earlier House of Lords authority of *Letterstedt v Broers* [1884] 9 App Cas 371.
[48] *Thomas and Agnes Carvel Foundation v Carvel* [2008] Ch 395 (a case concerning removal of a personal representative at odds with the charitable foundation who were principal beneficiaries under a will).
[49] At para 51.

Case Study

At first sight the structure of the family business concerned seems incredibly simple. After the death of the first generation founder the shares of the family company were placed into trust. All family members had a discretionary entitlement to income and the capital was held by the trust on behalf of the grandchildren. The widow Joan and the son Martin, who were the directors of the family company, were appointed trustees jointly with a former bank manager who was a long-standing friend of the founder.

A three-circle model for the family business immediately after the death of the founder is accordingly uncomplicated. Certainly this is so when compared with the three-circle model for the *Saul D Harrison* business (Figure 3.14). Similarly as a first generation family business the family tree is considerably less involved than in the *Saul D Harrison* case (see Figure 14.1).

Figure 14.1: Trusts and the three-circle model

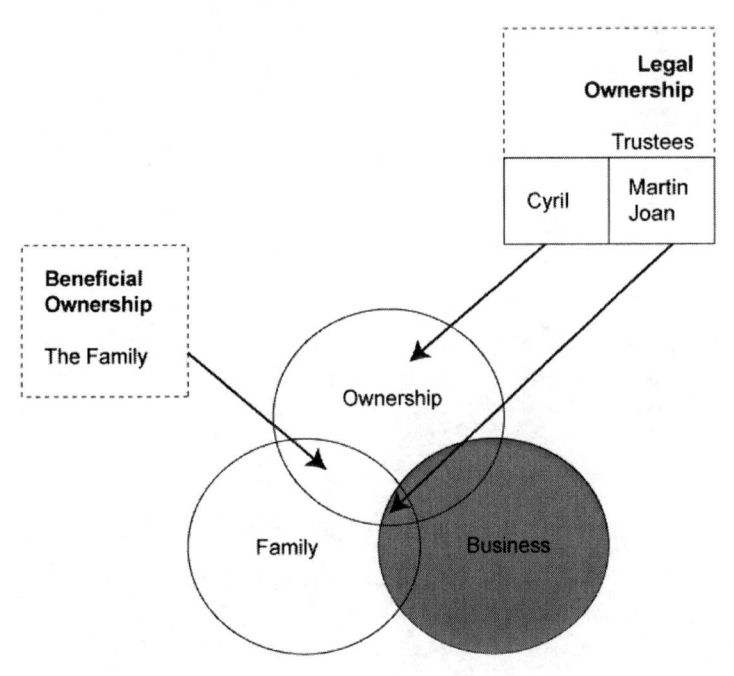

But factor in the family dynamics in the case concerned into a genogram a different picture emerges.[50]

---

[50] For an explanation of the uses of the genogram and the symbols used see chapter 3.

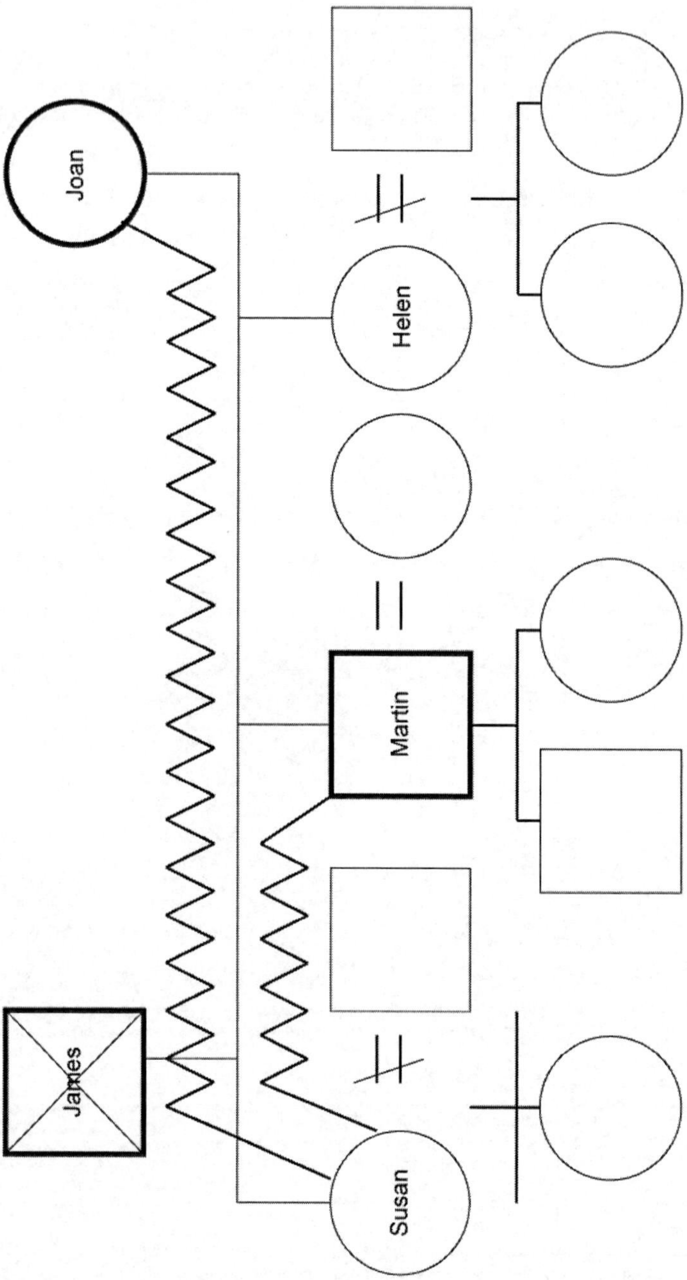

Figure 14.2: Family genogram

It will be seen from the broken lines that relationships between the eldest daughter Susan and her brother, Martin were conflicted and those between Susan and her mother much worse.

During his lifetime the founder, James, who had a strong relationship with Susan, doubled up his role as business leader with that of Chief Emotional Officer for the family, helping to mediate these tensions. James also ensured that his daughters, both of whom had been through divorces, were looked after financially. Displaying typical family business informality he did so by paying them an allowance directly out of the business, although neither daughter was actively engaged in the business.

With James' death the glue that held the fragile family relationships together disappeared. Things fell apart. In the business system Martin and Joan substantially increased their salaries, at a time when business performance markedly deteriorated. There were various examples of director's self-dealing over property matters. The trust received no income. In the family system Susan's allowance was stopped (whilst her sister, who adopted a much more conciliatory approach, continued to benefit).

Overall it looked as though an inheritance based on family business worth some millions in land values alone was in jeopardy, both generally and in particular so far as Susan's branch of the family was concerned.

This was certainly the view of the family friend and independent trustee. However in the face of opposition from Joan and Martin and with no access to funds he was advised to resign his trusteeship rather than to take or support any action for the removal of the other trustees.

Could Susan proceed on her own? Legally, yes. Although there were factors against her,[51] she appeared to have a good case for the removal of her mother and brother as trustees. Practically, no. Following her divorce and starved of benefit from the family firm she was in no position to finance even limited proceedings of this nature. Even if Susan had been able to secure the removal of her mother and brother as trustees and their replacement Susan would still have needed to persuade the new trustees to take proceedings against her family for example for breach of director's duty or for unfair prejudice. Assuming that any such proceedings could be financed and were successful Susan would still have no absolute guarantee of income from the discretionary trust.

So what appeared to several serious wrongs proved in practice to be irremediable.

14.14.4 The position of beneficiaries and shareholders compared

The above case study has many similarities to the unfair prejudice case of *Cadman Developments*.[52] If anything the position of Susan in our case study appears much stronger on the wider merits than that of Janis in *Cadman*. The crucial difference legally was that as an outright owner Janis was able to sue in her own right. Susan, on the other hand, as a beneficiary under a trust only had the right to ask the courts to use their

---

[51] Including that, as in *Kershaw*, her father had been passed her over as a trustee and it was difficult to separate pre-existing tension from conflict arising from the execution of the trust.
[52] *Girvan Janis Fisher v Cedric Cadman, Rodney Cadman, Cadman Developments Limited* [2005] EWHC 377 (Ch). The facts of that case are explained in detail in chapter 21.

residuary discretion to replace the trustees. It would then have been necessary to persuade the trustees to use trust funds to pursue proceedings against her brother and mother to restore depleted trust assets.

14.14.5 Trustees and family dynamics

It will also be seen that healthy family working relationships are key to the successful operation of a family business trust. A trust where the dynamics between trustees and beneficiaries is poor at the outset will be likely to fail.

14.15 LETTER OF WISHES

14.15.1 The basic position

It is common and recommended practice for the settlor to produce a letter of wishes at the time the trust is set up in which the settlor sets out his wishes about how the powers bestowed on the trustees of the family business trust should be exercised. Although the letter of wishes is not legally binding on the trustees it would be unusual for them not to pay close attention to its terms. One school of thought calls for the letter of wishes to be as detailed as possible.

14.15.2 Limitations

This might be relatively uncontroversial so far as the exercise of discretion by the trustees over the income and capital of the family business trust is concerned. For example the letter of wishes might confirm a preference on the part of the settlor for funds in a discretionary trust to be used to help family members in need, or to fund education, perhaps biased towards education which would be relevant to the family business, rather than for a general distribution of available cash to all family members.

There is the potential for the settlor to use the letter of wishes in an attempt to influence life-style decisions taken by future generations, which could be seen as having an inappropriate effect on the family business system. For example the letter of wishes might express a preference to benefit family members in conventional married relationships, potentially at the expense of unmarried couples, same sex partnerships or divorcees. However this level of detailed control over the family dimension would be fairly unusual.

What would be much more common, and indeed encouraged by some commentators, would be for the letter of wishes to deal in detail with business issues such as, business strategy including circumstances in which the family company could be sold, employment policies for family members and policies on dividends and re-investment.

At first sight this might appear uncontroversial. The settlor might be the founder of the family firm. They might have very strong views on the future of their creation. In family firms, and not just older businesses,[53] it is quite common for a belief as to what the

---

[53] For example in *Cadman Developments,* a second generation family business, both parties referred to the wishes of the founder, James. In the case of the claimant Janis, this was that her father wished her to participate in the family business. Her brothers on the other hand tried to dissuade Janis from pursuing her

founder would have wanted to be cited in support of a particular course of action favoured by one group of family business stakeholders. Often there is little evidence of what the founder would actually have wanted. Would it not be much more convenient if this was actually spelt out in a detailed letter of wishes?

To a point, perhaps. But there are potentially significant difficulties with adhering too closely to a detailed letter of wishes, even though trustees will need to think carefully before departing from these.

14.16 SHAM TRUSTS, LETTING GO AND BIVALENCY

With some lifetime settlements it might appear to the outside world that the family business remains under the control of the settlor even though the shareholder register would suggest that ownership and control lies in the hands of a trust.

The settlor's influence can take various forms. The trustees might act more like nominees and habitually defer to the settlor in all key decisions even though they have no formal role in the settlement.[54] The settlor could have reserved extensive protector powers for themselves. They might have given very detailed specific and wide ranging instructions to their trustees through a letter of wishes. The settlor might be seen to attempt to influence control the family firm from beyond the grave by the contents of their letter of wishes, their choice of trustees or replacement protectors.

In extreme cases there is a risk that the trust will be regarded as a sham, on the basis that, in reality, notwithstanding an elaborate trust structure and the presence of apparently independent trustees, the trust property is still under the *de-facto* control of the settlor. Life, or death, could then get very messy indeed. The logic would be that the settlor still owned the trust property. It would fall into the inheritance tax net. It would devolve under their last will, perhaps with a later wife as residuary beneficiary, drafted under the assumption that the interests of children from an earlier marriage are catered for under the trust.

The danger of attack will be correspondingly greater where the settlor is alive and where he is a trustee and in effect acting as the trust equivalent of a shadow director.

Attacks on sham trusts have traditionally been made by HMRC, usually on the basis that the arrangements are a fraud on the revenue, but challenge could come from any aggrieved party adversely affected by the alleged sham trust arrangements such as third party creditors or family members. The key element of a sham trust is pretence, an arrangement:[55]

> 'which in legal reality is one thing but is dressed up to pretend to be something else.'

Most of the authorities where trusts have been held up as shams by the court concern blatant attempts by the settlor to retain personal benefit for themselves whilst using the

---

unfair prejudice claim on the basis that this could lead to the break-up of the family business which they were convinced would have been a severe disappointment to James.

[54] This may be particularly the case if the trustee is a trust corporation and views the settlor who introduced them to the role of trustee as 'the client'.

[55] *Ramsay v Inland Revenue Commissioners* [1982] AC 300 at p 323.

sham trust to avoid tax or as a barrier against claims.[56] Some degree of conscious and deliberate pretence has been evident. In practice it is hard to allege successfully that a trust is a sham.

We would suggest that in most family business situations any pretence is much more likely to be sub-conscious and hidden even from the settlor themselves. Part of the time the intention will be to genuinely part with ownership as part of an overall succession plan but there are other forces at play. In essence these relate to the dark side of family trusts. To what extent is the family business trust generally, protector powers and the letter of wishes, in particular, being used by the settlor in a continuing battle to avoid letting go of the family firm? To what extent should the fact that family business trusts seem to be controlled by the settlor be seen more as evidence of the bivalency inherent in family business life, rather than of some carefully constructed sham?

14.17 TRUSTS AND GOVERNANCE

The settlor might be seen to be exerting an inappropriate level of control over the family firm, whether through their choice of trustees, the terms of a letter or wishes or a combination of these factors. The consequences are potentially severe.

Conflicts might arise between the trustees of the family trust and the managers of the family business. Harder to quantify is the potential for the family business to fail to adapt to changing market conditions because of constraints arising from within the trust system. Of course a letter of wishes will not be strictly legally binding. For example if the directors of the family company believe, that the employment or dividend policies suggested by the settlor is inappropriate they are not legally obliged to follow these. Such matters reside within their discretion as directors.

Similarly ownership discretion and the exercise of voting rights attached to shares in the family company resides with the trustees. Possibly the directors will be able to convince the trustees to exercise any relevant rights, for example to support an outside investment, even if this conflicts with the terms of the letter of wishes, if it is properly viewed as in the interests of the beneficiaries to do so. Outright conflict might be avoided. Nevertheless the settlor might still be seen to have exerted an inappropriate degree of control over the family company and probably based on outdated paradigms so far as the family system and business environment are concerned.

Is there any way to avoid this? Essentially family business trusts are ownership vehicles. Although they affect the family and business systems they operate principally in the ownership domain. The alternative approach is to see a family business trust as a component in an integrated family business governance system, rather than a stand-alone entity.

---

[56] For example *Midland Bank v Wyatt* [1995] 1 FLR 696 where the settlor executed a deed of trust in favour of his wife and children and locked this away in his safe whilst continuing to act as is he owned the trust property outright the court inferred that his intention was to create a flood defence against claims by his creditors if this were ever needed.

Case study

In chapter 11 (Ownership Overview) we talked about a family company that wrestled with their ownership philosophy before eventually deciding on a whole family ownership approach, using family business trusts as their basic ownership vehicle. Those trusts were only part of the overall governance system of the family concerned (see Figure 14.3).

As can be seen from the diagram, highly evolved communication channels were key to the success of the model. Family members enjoyed joint capacities as beneficiaries under whole family trusts and also as family members. They were entitled, once they reached the age of 18, to attend family assemblies where they could interact with members of the family council.

Family council members could engage with the trustees of the various family business trusts, who were in turn primarily responsible for maintaining a constructive dialogue with the board of the family company. The governance system was underpinned by a set of documents including, in the family domain, a family charter, in the ownership system articles and trust deed. The key document in the context of this discussion was the family charter.[57] Analytically this took the place of the letter of wishes, covering, as it did issues such as the long-term ownership of the family company, employment policies in relation to family members and their expectations as beneficiaries under the trust. However there is a key difference between a letter of wishes and a family charter. A letter of wishes is a one-off expression of the settlor's views on the future of the family business and liable to become out of date and, in the worst case downright dangerous. A family charter, on the other hand, is a living, breathing document capable of amendment to reflect changes in the view of the business owning family and the circumstances of the family company.

Via a letter of wishes the settlor is attempting to lay down a blueprint that will last for the duration of the family business. The role of the settlor is therefore much different so far as a family charter is concerned. There the settlor's role is to encourage the creation of flexible governance mechanisms that will stand the wider family in good stead for years to come and to encourage the wider business family to participate in those mechanisms. Inevitably, as a senior family member, the settlors' views will be reflected in the values embodied in the charter. But having played their role in establishing the governance system and possibly, in the early years participating in that system in some capacity or other, for example as chairman of the board, the settlor ultimately steps aside and allows the system they have helped to create to take over governance of the family company.

In short the settlor trusts the next generation (together with the trustees and any holders of any protector powers) to look after the family business.

---

[57] Family charters are explained in detail in chapter 17 (Governance).

Figure 14.3: The integrated family business governance model

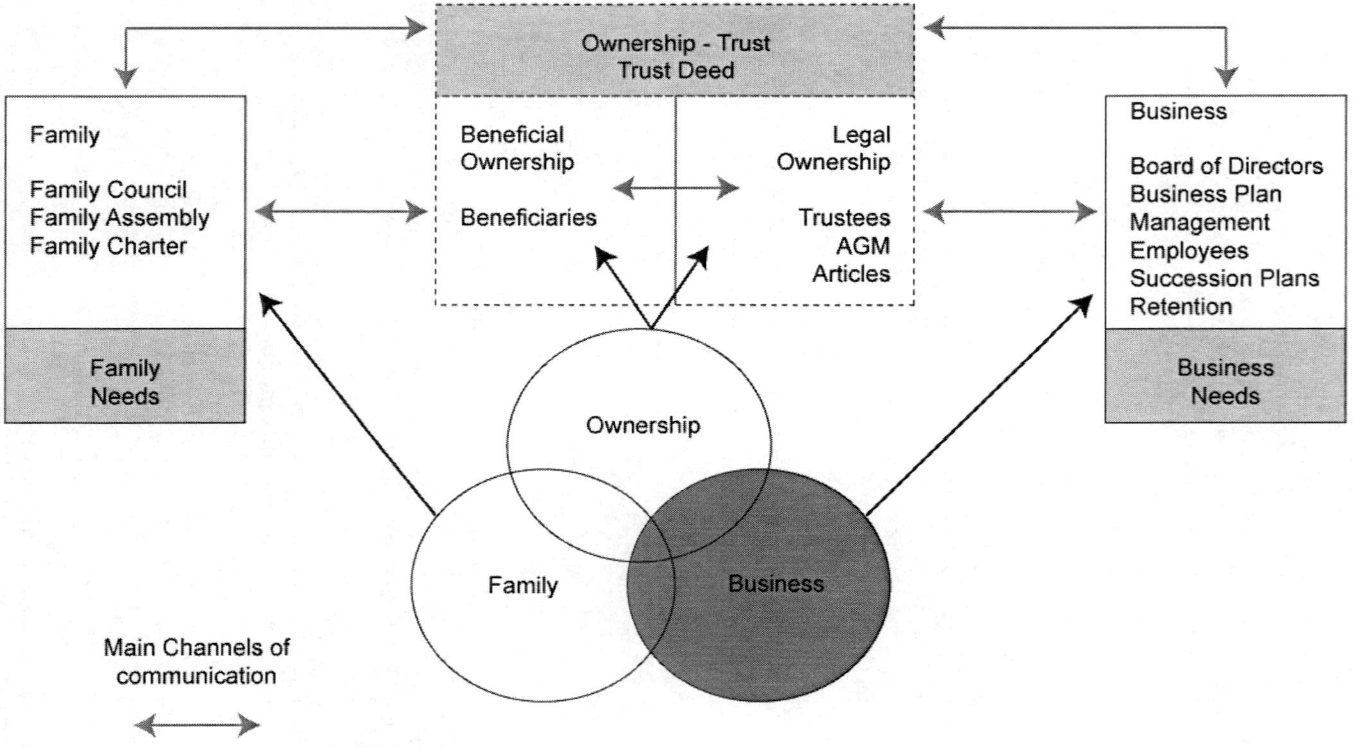

Source: adapted from ICFIB presentation

14.18 EMPLOYMENT POLICIES AND REMUNERATION

A key governance consideration is how to set and monitor employment and remuneration policies for working family insiders. The general considerations are discussed in chapter 5. Where family trusts are involved thought needs to be given to the mechanics of how these will operate.

If family insiders are also trustees will they be prevented from voting on this issue?[58] Alternatively will insider employment issues be subject to reserved powers to be exercised by a protector? If there are no insider trustees how will the remaining trustees be tied into shareholders' agreements or other relevant governance mechanisms dealing with remuneration issues?

14.19 INFORMATION

One fairly important issue is the question of the provision of information about the financial and business situation of the family firm first to the trustees and secondly to the beneficiaries.[59]

The mere fact the trustees are shareholders should not mean that the directors treat them any differently from any other shareholder (including in terms of information), absent express agreement to the contrary.

Rights to information can be broken down into three component parts.

14.19.1 The trustees and the family company

The first question concerns the trustees as legal owners. If it is anticipated that the trustees will have any greater right to information than the case under general company law, this should be catered for in some form of agreement between the family company and the trustees, particularly if the trustees are largely family outsiders or third parties. One of the main criticisms by the court of the trustees in *Bartlett* was their failure to use their controlling interest in the family company to require the supply of 'an adequate flow of information' to enable the trustees to protect the interests of the beneficiaries.[60]

14.19.2 The beneficiaries and the family company

The second question, the right of beneficiaries to information, is particularly pertinent where the trustees are dominated by family insiders as the information asymmetry has the potential to add more to any insider/outsider imbalance. In the absence of specific formal rights the beneficiaries, being one stage removed from legal ownership have no more automatic right to information from their family company than members of the public.

---

[58] For example in the case of estates the STEP standard provisions, para 9(2)(c) contain a mechanism for disclosure and approval by an independent trustee.
[59] Information as a component of family business governance is discussed in detail in chapter 17.
[60] At p 443.

14.19.3 The beneficiaries and the trustees

The starting point is that the beneficiaries of a family business trust have limited automatic rights to receive information about the trust from the trustees.[61] Ideally there will be a regular flow of information provided to the beneficiaries as a matter of good governance. This should be catered for in letters of wishes and family charters.

There is of course nothing to prevent a beneficiary asking the trustees for information. Indeed they should be encouraged to do so to play their part in keeping communication channels with trustees open. If the trustees refuse to provide information then the court might be prepared to compel disclosure under its inherent jurisdiction to supervise the administration of trusts. Being able to point to a good reason why the information is needed will be helpful. Each case will be looked at on its own merits[62] so there will always be some element of uncertainty for beneficiaries about how hard to push a request for information. Trustees also need to think carefully about refusing to provide information in their possession to beneficiaries. Whereas trustees can usually recover any litigation costs relating to the administration of the trust from trust funds the court will order trustees to pay costs personally where the trustees have unreasonably refused to provide information to beneficiaries. So costs risk should provide an incentive for collaboration.

There are also a number of general guidelines emerging from *Schmidt* and other cases of what the court is likely to consider is a reasonable request for information.

Information held by the trustees about the family company

As a general principle there will be a presumption that if trustees hold information relating to the family company in their capacity as legal owners this should be made available to beneficiaries who have a valid reason for wanting to see them.[63] It might be appropriate to ask the beneficiaries concerned to enter into confidentiality agreements as a condition of providing them with the information concerned.

On occasions commercial confidentiality might be an over-riding consideration and the courts will take the views of the directors into account. This is only likely to be a significant issue if there is some element of competition or some other commercial sensitivity as regards the beneficiary.

It will be seen that, in the case of family insider directors who are also trustees it may be almost impossible to determine whether the individuals concerned hold information in their capacity as directors[64] or trustees. This adds further uncertainty to the position. It is also another feature of the information asymmetry between insiders and outsiders which can be a significant cause of tension and disquiet in family businesses.

---

[61] At least under the law in England and Wales. The position is otherwise in some offshore trust jurisdictions.
[62] *Schmidt v Rosewood Trust Ltd* [2003] UKPC 26. The case was decided under the law of the Isle of Man but is basically considered to be the leading authority under English law.
[63] *Butt v Kelson* [1952] Ch 197, CA.
[64] See chapter 21 for a discussion on the (mixed) attitude of the courts to the provision or withholding of information as a species of unfair prejudice.

Information about trustees' decisions

Here the position is correspondingly pretty clear. The courts will almost never compel trustees to explain their reasons for exercising their discretionary powers, so a disappointed beneficiary under a discretionary family business trust is most unlikely to be told why another family member received benefit under the trust when they did not.

The inner workings of the trust is essentially a private matter so far as the beneficiaries are concerned.[65] The logic is that knowing the truth about why one family member has been preferred over another could 'embitter family feelings and the relationship between the trustees and members of the family'.[66] This approach is clearly contrary to the message of transparency and procedural justice preached by family business commentators, such as Carlock.[67]

Letters of wishes

Some settlors frame their letters of wishes as private documents to guide their trustees and include express requests that the content should be kept confidential so far as the beneficiaries are concerned. We believe that this is contrary to good governance principles.

The settlor's intentions will be a relevant but not the decisive factor. The courts may override this on appropriate occasions. The overall test is whether disclosure is in the best interests of the beneficiaries as a whole. On occasions the court might agree and compel disclosure, on other occasions not.[68] The distinction might be between situations where the letter of wishes can be seen as relevant to trustees' private decisions and situations where the letter can be seen more as a trust document and disclosure is required by the beneficiary to check that the trust is being properly administered.

Trust documents

Although beneficiaries have no automatic entitlement to see basic trust documents, including the trust deed itself, trust documents, including trust accounts should usually be provided to beneficiaries.

14.20 SELLING THE FAMILY SILVER

An almost inevitable component in a letter of wishes will be a statement from the settlor that their intention in setting up the trust is that the family business should remain in the ownership of trustees for the benefit of the family for generations to come. That might well be strongly phrased making it clear that the intention of the settlor is to found a dynasty.

---

[65] *Re Londonderry's Settlement* [1964] 3 All ER 855.
[66] At p 862.
[67] See, for example, Blondel Carlock and Van der Heydent *Fair Process: Striving for Justice in Family Firms* (INSEAD R&D Working Papers 2001/45/ENT).
[68] *Breakspear and others v Ackland and others* [2008] EWHC 220 (Ch). The case contains detailed guidance on the issue of disclosure of letters of wishes.

Whether that is wise is another question. An expression of hope is one thing. A clear direction to trustees via a letter of wishes is quite another. Even if the letter of wishes does not legally bind the trustees it will almost certainly be heavily persuasive.

How persuasive should the settlor's injunction against sale, expressed in a letter of wishes actually be? Particularly after the death of the settlor, when times and the business environment has moved on, the commercial context in which a previously successful business operated has fundamentally changed, or if the directors of the company have transformed the nature of the family business. It could be in the interests of the beneficiaries (albeit contrary to the letter of wishes) to sell off the business while it still has value.

The alternative approach, as advocated by Carlock and Ward in *Parallel Planning*[69] is to use the opportunity of generational transition to examine the commitment of the family to the business and the potential of the business in current market conditions. Would it not make more sense for a settlor to express a hope that the business stayed in the family for generations to come but give successive generations of the family both permission to make up their own minds and the governance framework for them to remain engaged and to take considered decisions over the future of the family firm?

In other words the trustees would take guidance on the key question of retaining or selling the family business not from a letter of wishes prepared by a long dead settlor but from the business owning family acting through its family council and other governance mechanisms.

14.20.1 The settlor's vision and trustees duties

In family business trusts, there could well be a tension between the duties of the trustees and the express or implied intention of the settlor in establishing the trust in the first place. This conflict manifests itself in the decision that the trustees need to make whether to sell (or even agitate for the sale) of the family business or to support the status quo of family ownership.

Trusts have traditionally been used as asset protection vehicles by settlors. Intentions vary, but often a primary motivation is to prevent beneficiaries from selling the assets that the settlor would rather remain in family ownership. However trust law operates on the basis of asset agnosticism, at least so far as general trusts are concerned. In other words, trustees should have little emotional attachment to the identity of the assets they hold, providing these generate the best return for the beneficiaries commensurate with an appropriate level of risk. Accordingly, trustees are under general duties to review the assets they hold and, depending on the terms of the trust and, taking into account the wishes of the beneficiaries as a whole, to diversify their investment risk.

As suggested, the express or implied intention of the settlor of a family business trust may well have been entirely inconsistent with this. The primary motivation of the settlor may be to protect the sole or primary trust asset itself, the family business, as a distinct and separate entity, in accordance with his wish that the business should continue in its present form after he has gone. By his choice of trustees, and often the express terms of

---

[69] Carlock and Ward *Strategic planning for the family business: Parallel planning to unify the family and the business* (Palgrave, 2001). The approach is discussed in detail in chapter 15.

the trust deed and accompanying letter of wishes, the settlor seeks to control the family business and its ownership from beyond the grave. In these circumstances, the nature of the family business trust that the settlor wishes to establish has more in common with a special purpose trust, which are unusual, (for example, to own and maintain an educational institution or historic building) rather than a commercial.

Careful attention therefore needs to be given to the structural basis on which the family business trust operates including:

- The terms of any letters of wishes prepared at the time the trust is established or any other relevant documents that evidence the settlor's intention, for example, family charters. These are not legally binding on the trustees and will not negate or serve as a substitute for the obligations of trustees to exercise independent discretion over how to manage the trust assets, including whether or not to sell their interest in the family business. The trustees should support a sale if this is manifestly the right thing for the beneficiaries. However, in more marginal cases following the letter of wishes may provide the trustees with a measure of protection legally and from criticism by beneficiaries keen for the trust to cash in its interest in the family business.
- The express provisions of the trust. The trust deed might well contain express provisions negating the general duties of the trustees and allowing (or obliging) them to retain the shares in the family business in circumstances where otherwise they would be obliged to sell or consider a sale. The trustees can take some comfort from case-law, in particular which suggests that trustees have a lower duty to consider sale and diversification of investments in relation to the original settled property of the trust than subsequently acquired routine investment assets

There will be some family businesses where the dividends received by the family business trust far outstrip any return on investment that could be achieved by any alternative investment of the capital that would be received on a sale of the family business. At the same time the underlying capital can remain safe and secure. Accordingly in this situation, trustees will generally be able to justify a *bona-fide* commercial decision that diversification, by selling the family business and reinvesting the proceeds is not in the best interests of the beneficiaries of the trust.

However we suggest that such occasions will be few and far between (and will require routine, regular reassessment by the trustees). In particular because the second assumption, that the underlying capital of the family business trust is safe, may well prove to be unfounded in the long term. Whilst the income stream received by the trust will be clear to the trustees the factors that may undermine the stability of the family business and with it the capital value of the trust are many, varied and may not be immediately obvious. These of course include external market factors that affect all similar businesses, but they also include the internal factors peculiar to family businesses with which this book is concerned: difficulties arising from the succession process: governance failures and; family disputes.

Commercial logic is therefore likely to suggest that the trustees of a family business trust should be agitating for a sale of the underlying family business. Even though the trustee's instinct may be against sale, this may be the only realistic option before business deterioration makes it too late. At the very least they should be keeping the overall position carefully and continuously under review, for example by active participation in the governance process. Yet frequently trustees take the opposite approach. Often it is the family business trustees who are most opposed to a sale. Sometimes this is from a concern that a sale would be against the wishes of the settlor or beneficiaries keen for family ownership to be preserved. On occasions the trustees will be family members or business colleagues, close to the settlor, and keen follow his wishes. Sometimes the settlor may still be alive and also a trustee.

The position of professional trustees may also be problematic. Original appointments may have been made on the basis of relationships between the settlor and individual trusted advisors. Those individuals may also have moved on. For various reasons, including budgetary constraints or the lack of formal governance channels through which non-family trustees can engage with the family business, trusteeship may have evolved into a passive administrative role, rather than active management of the interest held in the family business. Given the difficulties in contracting out of the basic duties of trustees, if professional trustees need to consider very carefully whether they are capable of exercising their duties properly. It might be possible, for example, for legal professionals to take advice from corporate finance or investment professionals to aid their decision-making. But if due to financial constraints, lack of expertise or relevant authorisations etc professional trustees cannot discharge their duties properly, serious thought needs to be given to resigning as trustees. At the very least professional trustees need to pay careful attention to the terms of their engagement, making it clear, if this is the case, that their role allows them to seek appropriate advice and devote sufficient time to the trust to properly exercise their duties as trustees.

What strategies can trustees adopt to manage this conflict and to reconcile the right result for the beneficiaries, their own duties and liabilities and the wishes of the settlor? We suggest the following:

- **Governance.** First trustees should participate actively and appropriately in the governance of the family business itself. As explained above this does not mean taking a role in the management of the family business. Rather the suggestion is that trustees should look to be active and engaged stakeholders. If the family business has highly evolved structures, such as family councils and family assemblies it will be correspondingly easier for trustees to leverage these mechanisms. In other cases it may be necessary for trustees to actively initiate and drive relevant governance processes, for example by suggesting and even organising meetings with managing directors, chairmen or other key shareholders of the family business.

- **Asset management.** Secondly by the trustees taking an active role in the governance of the family business, trustees are able to actively manage the family business trust. In particular, they should then be able to take active strategic decisions on whether to use their influence for the sale of the family business, or alternatively, its retention in family hands. Indeed it is suggested that constructive and active involvement, rather than passive uninvolved retention of shares by the family business trust, is capable of catalysing and supporting the sort of incremental improvements to the operation of the family business that make long term family ownership (rather than a medium term appropriation sale) a reality in accordance with the settlor's wishes.

- **Strategic options.** Just as one of the objects of family business governance generally is the 'generation of strategic options'[70] for the family as a whole, one of the objectives for the trustees in participating in that process should be seen as the generation of strategic objectives for the family business trust itself. These may

---

[70] Ward *Strategic Planning for the Family Business* (Palgrave, 2001).

well go far wider than supporting or rejecting an outright sale. It does not have to be all or nothing. Alternative options could include:
- the independent sale of all of the shares held by the trust, for example to non-family management, to establish an employee share scheme, to committed family members or to the company as part of a buy-back to prune the ownership tree and rationalise ownership. Clearly the trustees need to take great care over appropriate valuations in the absence of a third party, open market offer.
- partial sale of some of the shares held by the trust thereby providing for partial diversification, freeing up liquidity within the trust etc.
- conversely, and perhaps counter intuitively the trustees might feel it appropriate to increase the trust's holding in the family business, perhaps by buying in at relatively low values small parcels of shares on death or departure from employment of other shareholders
- actively supporting (but not participating) in proposals to buy out minority shareholders, perhaps to increase stability within the ownership group.

Clearly in the last two scenarios the trustees will need to be convinced that either increasing their stake or ignoring an exit opportunity is in the best long term interests of the trust.

14.20.2 Protections against sale

The arguments set out above might fall on deaf ears and the settlor might be determined to use the family business trust as a vehicle for their dynastic ambitions. Is it possible to include mechanisms to make it difficult to sell the family firm? In effect to structure family business trusts as a sort of National Trust, for the preservation of ancient family businesses? At first sight the answer would appear to be no, on basic principles of the law and practice of trusts. First as a general principle trustees have a duty to consider diversification of the trust assets. Trusts are primarily investment vehicles for the financial well-being of the beneficiaries. Having all their eggs in one family business basket is unlikely to be the best way for the trustees to ensure this. Secondly trustees have a basic duty to actively manage their investments. Simply assuming that the family business will remain unsold is inconsistent with this.[71] So something more needs to be done to the structure of the trust.

14.20.3 Golden shares

The most extreme solution would be to include provisions in the trust deed specifically preventing the sale of trust shares to non-family third parties. This can either be an outright ban or one that prevents a controlling interest from being transferred.

More sophisticated versions could involve a 'golden share' being created and held in a special purpose voting trust. Transfers of controlling interests could only be permitted with the agreement of the trustees holding the golden share. The terms of the trust would place heavy restrictions on the basis on which consent would be forthcoming. As the golden share would have little intrinsic economic value the investment duties of the trustees would be comparatively light.

---

[71] *Bartlett v Barclays Bank Trust Company* [1980] 1 All ER 139.

Whilst golden share arrangements are sometimes considered by clients, in practice, it is comparatively rare for these to be actually put in place.

On the other hand prohibitions or restrictions on the transfer of shares in family companies to third parties are comparatively common in articles of association. The key distinction with golden share trusts is that it is will usually be open for the family to change the articles by a 75% majority. Amending or dismantling the trust might be much more complicated.[72]

14.20.4 Protectors and veto

A less extreme and more frequently used device is to build protector powers to veto sales into the trust arrangements. The usual arrangement would be to include a provision in the trust deed to say that the consent of the protector needs to be obtained before shares in the family company are sold. The protection can apply to all shares, a specified threshold, say 10% of the trust's holding or to a key strategic stake, for example a sale that will mean that a non-family third party obtains a controlling interest.

The working assumption may well be that the protector will use their powers to veto any sale. However it would be unwise for the trustees to assume that this will inevitably be the case. The trustees' basic duty to consider diversification of investments will remain. So the trustees should undertake periodic reviews of the wisdom, or otherwise, of continued retention of the family business in the trust and be prepared to make recommendations for sale where appropriate.[73]

14.20.5 Self-dealing

Trustees owe strict fiduciary duties to their family business trust. These include restrictions against self-dealing, including personally entering into transactions relating to trust property and obligations to avoid conflicts of interest. The strict rule against self-dealing is often modified in the trust deed. The most obvious example is the inclusion of a charging provision, allowing professional trustees to charge for their services.

Some thought needs to be given to the position of family trustees. A blanket authorisation of self-dealing would be inappropriate as it would put the beneficiaries almost entirely at the mercy of trustees. However some degree of conflict of interest for a family trustee is almost inevitable. Some self-dealing might in fact be in the best interests of the beneficiaries. For example, it might be helpful if a trustee, or a close family member of a trustee, could buy shares in a family company from the trust in order to provide capital to release to beneficiaries, or to allow the trust to diversify. Also the precise scope of the rule against self-dealing is not beyond debate.[74]

---

[72] Both golden shares and transfer restrictions are discussed in more detail in chapter 11 (Ownership Overview).
[73] An interesting technical question Is whether any power to veto a sale would be construed as a fiduciary power as a matter of trust law, which would carry with it a higher duty of financial responsibility and must be exercised in the best interests of the beneficiaries as a whole, than if the power were to be seen as a purely personal one, in which case the power can be exercised as the protector wishes.
[74] See for example *Holder v Holder* [1968] Ch 353 where, in the special circumstances of that case, the Court of Appeal allowed a son who was a tenant of farm property under a lease from his father and who had also been appointed as an executor of the father's will to acquire the freehold from his father's estate.

For these reasons it might be better to anticipate and regulate potential self-dealing by trustees, by allowing this subject to safeguards. For example by insisting that transactions involving trustees or close family members have to be at properly evidenced market value and supported by the remaining, more disinterested and independent trustees. Again the practical implications of each individual case need to be carefully considered.

14.21 THE TRUST DEED AND MODIFICATION OF TRUSTEES' DUTIES

A mixture of statute and case-law provides a basic starting point so far as the duties of trustees is concerned. Suitable provisions can be included in the trust deed to modify this position to deal with various situations relevant to family business trusts, including the following.

14.21.1 Trustee voting

The basic position under the Trustee Act is that trustees need to act unanimously in the exercise of their powers. The group of trustees could have been chosen to represent various interest groups within the family business system. Appointing trustees from different branches of the family (and/or conferring on that branch the power to appoint or replace such a trustee) is the most obvious example. Other permutations could include trustees from different generations or insiders and outsiders. However there is always the possible tension between the need for legal duty for trustees to act in the interests of all of the beneficiaries, and the family business reality that certain trustees may be seen as, in effect, nominees of certain tribes within the family.

Whilst managing the trust by consensus is highly desirable, insisting on this is potentially dangerous. In the most obvious example the power of veto by a branch trustee could be used as a weapon in family branch warfare. More subtly conservatism by representatives of the senior generation could delay or prevent development crucial for the business itself, for example major refinancing. The ability for trustees to act by majority, or even a super-majority might therefore be important to counter these risks.

14.21.2 Investment and diversification

As a starting point the trust deed needs to contain a broad and general provision allowing the trustees to hold shares in companies, including private companies and to carry on business. Buying shares in a family company might be a very difficult to justify in bald investment terms. For this reason it is much more preferable for the shares to be placed in the settlement by the settlor at the outset, rather than the settlor providing the trustees with cash which is then used to buy shares in the family company. Under the former approach the trustees are simply given what they are given. In the latter situation they have a lump of cash and would need to consider how best to invest it. That might well not be in the family company concerned.

We have referred to the issues of diversification and spreading of risk above. It might also be the case that, whilst of potentially significant capital value, the dividend yield is at best uncertain and at worst pitiful. There might be various reasons for this. Some reasons might be seen as creditable, such as a policy of financial prudence and reinvestment by the board.[75] In other cases the reasons for poor dividends might be harder to justify on moral grounds. For example if a large share of potentially distributable profit is soaked up in paying excessive remuneration to the insiders, leaving little if anything for the outsiders, including the trust, to be paid out as dividends.

But from an investment perspective it makes little difference why an asset is not producing an appropriate return. If it is not the trustees should consider a sale.

Express provisions absolving the trustees from the need to consider diversification and to invest in income-producing assets would offer some measure of protection to the trustees from disgruntled beneficiaries, particularly family outsiders. Quite whether such provisions would provide full protection for trustees in all circumstances is a moot point. If trustees with a controlling interest in a family company ignore clear signs that the business might face future difficulties ignore the possibility of sale and allow the business to fall off a cliff the courts might still hold the trustees responsible for missing that opportunity.[76]

14.21.3 Duty of supervision

Without more, beneficiaries and courts would expect the trustees to exercise a reasonable degree of supervision.[77] Exactly what this would involve would vary from case to case. But it is clear that the greater the control conferred by the shareholding, the greater degree of supervision that would be required.[78] Similarly the courts would expect more from professional trustees than family members or other lay trustees.[79]

Consideration might be given to reducing the extent of the trustees' duty of supervision or limiting their liability for negligent failure to supervise the board. This approach might be justified where the expectations of all concerned are that the trustees will be acting purely as nominee owners for the beneficiaries, with all real day to day control of the family firm in the hands of the board.

14.21.4 Exoneration clauses

It is fairly standard drafting practice to include exoneration clauses in trust deeds, relieving trustees from personal liability for most breaches of trust. Most professional

---

[75] Lack of return on investment can be seen as essentially the problem in *Saul D Harrison* where the courts did not agree that the insiders had taken inappropriately high remuneration. There is no suggestion that the unfair prejudice position brought by Rosemary, one of the outsiders, had any support from the trustees of the various trusts concerned. It is unclear whether this was as a result of active support by the various trustees involved of the management position that the business would turn a corner, and that re-investment in new premises was justified, a reticence on their part to accept the risks of litigation or simply disengagement on the part of the trustees concerned.
[76] One of the criticisms of the trustees in *Bartlett* was their failure to cut their losses on a development project. Rather than accept an offer to buy out the interest of the family company at next to no loss, the trustees allowed the directors to invest further capital, which was ultimately lost on the failure of the project.
[77] *Bartlett v Barclays Bank Trust Company* [1980] 1 All ER 139.
[78] See chapter 11 for a basic summary of the degrees of positive and negative control relating to various shareholding thresholds.
[79] *Bartlett v Barclays Bank Trust Company* [1980] 1 All ER 139. So provisions diluting the duty of trustees to supervise the board are known as 'anti-Bartlett clauses'.

trustees will require a wide-ranging exoneration clause before agreeing to act. The courts have been generous to trustees in upholding exoneration clauses.[80]

A balance needs to be struck between the exoneration and involvement of trustees. The letter of wishes can assist by providing guidance on how involved and active the settlor would expect the trustees to be.

The basic approach we are advocating is for active trusteeship, so that the trustees use the votes and influence conferred by their shareholding to provide appropriate checks and balances to the board which, in all likelihood, will be dominated by family insiders. If this approach is accepted it would be entirely inappropriate to dilute the trustee's duties of supervision. Indeed it might be more apt if the duty of the trustees to be active shareholders was at least confirmed and restated in the trust deed, if not increased.

Quite whether, trustees, fully advised of their potential liabilities and common practice, would be prepared to accept appointments under the approach advocated above, is another question. In practice the compromise might be some form of exoneration clause, but accompanied by positive and detailed statements of the duties of trustees, provisions, all set within the context of active family and beneficiary supervision. This would be in the context of appropriate mechanisms providing for the removal of trustees. So, whilst underperforming trustees could not be easily sued, they could be efficiently replaced.

14.21.5 Trustee insurance

It would be sensible to include provisions allowing the trustees to take out indemnity insurance against their own negligence and for the premiums to be treated as an expense of the trust. This is especially so if trustees are to be subject to unrestricted or even enhanced duties of supervision.

14.21.6 Shareholder agreements

Much of chapter 17 preaches the virtues of comprehensive governance systems for family owned businesses, including the use of legally binding shareholders' agreements. Such agreements will almost inevitably contain restrictions on the freedom that would otherwise, at least in theory, attach to ownership interests held by the trustees such as restrictions on share transfer or sale to third parties and probably drag and provisions obliging the trustees to sell their shares if a certain threshold of shareholders wish to do so.

The conventional argument is that trustees should be wary of agreeing to such arrangements as they would be accepting fetters on their discretion.

But if the basic logic that comprehensive governance systems are good for the family business why should this not apply to interests held in trust? If the trust holds a controlling or significant interest in a family company and the trustees are in favour or are even encouraging a sale of that interest to enable them to diversify and spread risk, then drag provisions, in particular, might be a valuable tool for trustees to achieve this

---

[80] See *Armitage v Nurse* [1998] Ch 241 which makes it clear that whilst liability for fraud (on the part of trustees) cannot be excluded, liability for negligence, even gross negligence can be.

objective.[81] Absent a sale of the entire company the trustees could well have no real ability to sell their holding in the family firm even if they believed diversification was necessary.

The relevant provisions might already be in existence and contained in the articles or in an existing shareholders' agreement to which the trustees must adhere as a condition of registration of the transfer of the settlor's shares to them. In which case the provisions can be seen as part of the package of trust assets. The choice of the trustees then becomes simply whether or not to accept appointment.

New agreements or changes to existing arrangements might be proposed after the trust is established. Should the trustees, as a matter of policy, refuse to become party to these? We would argue not. Some provisions could be seen to fetter the discretion of the trustees, for example block voting agreements, or provisions entrenching the position of directors. Other provisions, such as minimum dividend policies, or provisions securing information rights could be very much in the interests of the beneficiaries. Each case (and indeed each provision) should be judged on its overall merits and with the interests of the beneficiaries in mind.

So an express power allowing the trustees to enter into whatever agreements or arrangements for the management of the shares or other trust property would appear to be sensible.

14.21.7 Power to enter into compromises and arrangements

Despite the most careful trusteeship and comprehensive governance systems serious and irreconcilable differences might arise within the trust between groups of beneficiaries, for example between those from insider or outsider branches of the family or between generations, where the older generation might be strongly in favour of the trustees retaining the family business and the younger in favour of sale. Alternatively disputes could arise between the trustees and other owners or with the board.

In all of these situations the trustees will need express and general powers to enter into compromises or arrangements concerning trust assets. Those powers could then be exercised, for example, to divide the trust into two funds so that a proportion of the shares in the family company could be sold and converted into a cash fund for those beneficiaries wishing to sell with the remaining fund retaining its investment in the family company.

The courts' have an inherent power, and also statutory powers,[82] to vary trusts on an appropriate application.

---

[81] Otherwise the trustees would need to rely on the 'statutory drag' provisions contained in CA, Chapter 3, whereby the holders of 90% of the shares can compel the minority to sell. These provisions are discussed in more detail in chapter 12.

[82] Depending on the nature of the trust statutory authority this could be under the Variation of Trusts Act 1958, the Trustee Act 1925, s 57 or the Settled Land Act 1925, s 64.

14.21.8 Sale agreements

Much of the discussion above has been about the need for trustees to remain alive to the possibility of selling the family firm. Of course that might not be so easy to achieve in practice, particularly if the business is seen to be heavily dependent on a retired or deceased settlor.

The position of trustees on the sale of a family business is discussed in chapter 12. Various aspects of the sale, in particular providing entering the warranties and indemnities could expose the trust assets to considerable liabilities there needs to be a specific power for the trustees to enter into a sale agreement and related documents.[83]

Ultimately the ability for the trustees to join in the sale and to give warranties and indemnities, particularly if the holding of the trust is large, might be the difference between being able to sell the family business for a half way acceptable price and all of the trust's assets being lost on the eventual insolvency of the family company. The difficulty of how the trustees protect their own position when they are not holding any trust assets still remains. The overall question for the trustees to satisfy themselves about, before using those powers, is whether this sale on these terms is in the best interests of the beneficiaries?

14.22 OTHER TYPES OF TRUST AND SIMILAR ARRANGEMENTS FOUND IN FAMILY BUSINESSES

Discretionary trusts are the main type of trust used in the family business context. It is worth briefly noting other forms of trust and uses of trust structures that might be encountered.

14.22.1 Direct bequests in wills

It is fairly common for shares in a family company or other family business property to be left to executors in trust for specified family members in proportions defined in the settlor's will. This is intended to be only a temporary holding arrangement until the estate can be fully administered. It is not a trust as such (as opposed to an on-going settlement established by a will).

Delays and complications can occur in the administration of the estate. Sometimes the position is complicated by the fact that some or all of the intended beneficiaries are minors,[84] so unless some other arrangements can be put in place, such as separate trusts with parents as trustees, the ultimate distribution might be delayed. However the issue might simply be delay in the administration of the estate. It is not uncommon to find executors still on the share register of a family company many years after the settlor's death.

---

[83] Most trust deeds will contain a power of sale.
[84] See chapter 12 for a discussion on the complications caused by minors holding shares directly.

The treatment of any dividends paid out and the exercise of voting rights in the meantime raise interesting questions, which are almost insoluble in retrospect. However such issues only usually surface against the background of a wider family dispute or a sale.

14.22.2 Bare trusts

Rather than executors continuing to hold shares for infant beneficiaries these might be given to, for example their parents, subject to bare trusts to hold these for the benefit of the children concerned until they reach 18, or some later date specified in the relevant will.

14.21.3 Constructive trusts

The complexity of family business dealings can give rise to various situations where implied trusts are created. These include constructive trusts and resulting trusts. Constructive trusts arise by operation of law in varied circumstances where a beneficial interest is deemed to have been passed to someone other than the legal owner of the property.

Constructive and resulting trusts can collectively be described as 'implied trusts'. A detailed examination of these implied trusts is beyond the scope of this book.[85]

On other occasions it might be harder to distinguish between a gift, a loan and circumstances giving rise to a constructive trust.

14.22.4 Resulting trusts

Resulting trusts, in a nutshell, also arise by operation of law, where money or property are provided by one person to another, other than by way of gift or investment.[86]

The classic example of a resulting trust is where one unmarried partner has contributed to the acquisition of a property owned by the other, through the payment of mortgage or financing improvements etc. A resulting trust will arise whereby the property owner holds a proportionate part of the property or its proceeds of sale on behalf of the non-owning partner. A similar situation will arise where a family member has made an investment in the family business. For example in one case a daughter sold her house, the proceeds of which were used to build a new property for her to live in on the family farm, which was legally owned by her parents. But, with typical family business

---

[85] See *Underhill & Hayton Law of Trusts and Trustees* – 2016 (LexisNexis, 2016) for a more detailed explanation.
[86] Lord Browne-Wilkinson in *Westdeutsche Landesbank v Islington* [1996] AC 669 suggested that:
'Under existing law a resulting trust arises in two sets of circumstances: (A) where A makes a voluntary payment to B or pays (wholly or in part) for the purchase of property which is vested either in B alone or in the joint names of A and B, there is a presumption that A did not intend to make a gift to B: the money or property is held on trust for A (if he is the sole provider of the money) or in the case of a joint purchase by A and B in shares proportionate to their contributions ... (B) Where A transfers property to B on express trusts, but the trusts declared do not exhaust the whole beneficial interest" (in the latter case, perhaps because it is implied that the money will be returned if, for example, an eventuality does or does not occur). A resulting trust arises from the presumption as to the parties' intentions'.

informality, nothing was documented. It was nevertheless comparatively easy to show that a resulting trust had arisen for the daughter based on her initial investment.

14.22.5   Interest in possession trusts (life interest trusts)

Under life interest trusts the beneficiaries have a right to income as it arises or the right to immediate occupation of any property. The right to capital is deferred either to a later age or perhaps bypasses the immediate next generation of children in favour of grandchildren in the generation after that. An example would be where property is put into trust for children for life with the capital passing to grandchildren.

These trusts are not as flexible as a discretionary trust due to the obligation to pay income to the beneficiaries as it arises. There is no option, for example, to accumulate income. Trustees can be given the right to advance capital to the beneficiaries at the trustees' discretion. The IHT treatment of interest in possession trusts is now the same as for a discretionary trust and the capital gains of the trust are taxed at the trust rate. Therefore, these types of trusts are becoming less common.

14.22.6   Trusts for persons with disabilities

There are special favourable tax rules that apply to trusts set up for the benefit of family members with a disability that qualifies them as a vulnerable beneficiary. Ideally, for investment reasons, any such trust would not hold shares in a family company.

14.22.7   Voting trusts

Shareholders might enter into arrangements to vote their shares in a particular way. Sometimes voting rights are transferred to others subject to specific trust arrangements as to how the shares will be voted, for example in accordance with the recommendations of the family council. These voting trusts can really be seen as a species of shareholders' agreement, rather than a full trust over the entirety of an ownership interest.

14.22.8   Insurance proceed trusts

It is fairly common, particularly in early stage businesses, for the business leaders to take out life insurance policies on each other's lives and to write the benefit of those policies in trust for each other. The policy proceeds will then be paid to the estate of the deceased once the supporting cross put and call options over the deceased's shareholding have been exercised.[87]

Although such arrangements might be more typically found in non-family quasi partnerships they are equally applicable to family business sibling partnerships. A considerable amount of grief, let alone three trips to the High Court could have been saved in the *Irvine* matter[88] if such policies had been in place.

---

[87]   A binding contract for sale will disqualify the estate from the benefit of business property relief.
[88]   The case is discussed in detail in chapter 21.

14.22.9 Employee share trusts and employee benefit trusts

Employee share trusts are considered separately in chapter 6. Of course there can be a crossover with the family system as family insiders might also qualify for benefit, or at least consideration under these trusts.

14.23 ALTERNATIVES TO FAMILY BUSINESS TRUSTS

Even without considering tax issues in any detail it will be seen that there are a number of potential drawbacks with the use of family business trusts. Are there any other arrangements that create similar benefits without the corresponding drawbacks?

14.23.1 Separate share classes

Separate share classes are often advocated as an alternative, whereby the family insiders working in the business take voting shares and the wider family including the outsiders receive the economic benefit. This is the structure adopted in *Saul D Harrison*. The logic is that this structure gives the family director insiders freedom to run the family business on a day to day basis, to the best advantage of everyone concerned free from interfering outsiders who know nothing about the business and are dividend grabbing vultures in any event.

There is a problem with such structures. It might be argued that such structures ought to create additional quasi-trustee obligations on the directors to look after the holders of other share classes, who, like beneficiaries under a trust have no direct voting rights. It is very difficult to define exactly what any enhanced duty should be and the courts have not accepted the argument that directors should be under any enhanced duty in such circumstances.

But at least outsider shareholders can get inside the doors of a court. In a trust structure with insider trustees they would have no direct right of action.[89]

14.23.2 Governance arrangements

We have talked at length about the need for family business trusts to be seen as only a component in wider family business governance arrangements. Can the trust be left out of the equation altogether? Of course, yes. Many family businesses operate perfectly well without the complications of trusts particularly in their early stages.

One of the advantages of trusts is that they concentrate formal ownership rights and especially voting control in the hands of trustees. If the trustees are carefully chosen they have the ability to work as active shareholders and to constructively work with the family board but also to exercise supervision and to hold the board to account. Without trustees the inbuilt restriction of the legal ownership tree, which comes as a natural part of the trusts package, would of course be lost.

---

[89] Although there are circumstances in which beneficiaries can be permitted, in effect, to pursue derivative claims against third parties on behalf of the trust where it would be inappropriate (perhaps because of a conflict of interest) for a trustee to pursue the claim (or where the trustees are reluctant do so).

There is no reason why a family council could not exercise a similar function. If, as in Clarks' shoes this supplemented by an optional voting trust, whereby shareholders agreed for the family council to act as their proxies, this informal supervisory function would be given additional legal bite.[90]

14.24 FAMILY BUSINESS TRUSTS: CONCLUSION

There are countless examples of family businesses that have successfully embraced family business trusts as part of their ownership structure.

Analytically a family business trust is a legal arrangement to look after an interest, shares, in an organisational fiction, a family company. Against the backdrop of real family dynamics such as greed, apathy, disenfranchisement the trust structure, is capable of producing highly undesirable results. Just like another artificial creature, Frankenstein's monster.

It is fairly common, particularly amongst older family businesses to find business leaders and other family members with a deep and pathological distrust of trusts. Often this is because the family still bear the scars of past failures and encounters with that monster.

To harvest the corresponding potential for good three key factors must be present. First carefully selected trustees chosen on the basis of both personal characteristics and their structural position within the family business system. Secondly the family business trust must operate as only one single component in a comprehensive family business governance system. Finally and most importantly a successful trust can only really operate well against the background of strong family dynamics. The other two factors will offer some protection if things go wrong and tensions and conflicts that are an inevitable part of family business life escalate. Individual trustees and governance systems can, by themselves, do little to repair seriously damaged family dynamics.

So the key to successful family business trusts is the quality and commitment of the trustees and the overall coherence of the family business governance system.

---

[90] These arrangements are described in more detail in chapter 17.

CHAPTER 15

OWNERSHIP SUCCESSION

15.1 INTRODUCTION

Chapter 7 is concerned with management succession, the transfer of day-to-day responsibility for the operation of the family enterprise. This chapter looks at the other side of the succession coin. Here the key question is 'who should own the shares in the family business in the next generation'?

The two issues of management and ownership succession are, of course, very closely related. But the overlap is not fully complete. Without a desire to keep the business in family ownership, the question of family management succession becomes pretty much irrelevant. The converse is not necessarily true. It may be possible to retain family ownership of a business but under non-family management. That approach will take great courage and commitment on the part of the business owning family.

So, although management succession will usually be the first to occur ownership succession planning deals with the more strategic questions of whether the family want to retain ownership of their business into the next generation and, if so, how that family ownership should be organised and structured.

The transfer of ownership of the family business to the next generation requires careful thought and detailed planning. Some commentators hold the view that ownership succession is more important than leadership succession.[1] Because of the control it provides ownership marks the ultimate seat of power. In the final analysis the continuity of the family business is in the owner's hands.

As will be seen the ownership succession process raises issues of significant complexity in terms of family dynamics. It is also emotionally sensitive one and has the potential to create significant conflict between parents and children, and between siblings themselves.

Much of ownership succession planning theory can seem abstract and, at least at first sight, mainly applicable to larger, later stage family concerns. To add focus, the chapter draws heavily on the story of the Davies family, first introduced in chapter 1. In that case there was only one possible candidate for management succession, James. The issues raised in the case therefore related only to ownership succession.

---

[1] See, for example, Kelin E Gersick *Generation to Generation: Life cycles of a family business* (Harvard Business School Press, 1997) at p 195.

15.2 FAIRNESS AND EQUALITY REVISITED

In some cultures, and times tradition dictated that wealth should be passed down to the oldest male. In the UK, the social norm is that, in the absence of powerful reasons to the contrary, wealth should be passed on to the next generation under arrangements that can broadly be described as 'fair'. But fairness lies in the eyes of the beholder and its application to passing down the family business is likely to be the source of an almost infinite variety of interpretations.

Leading family business advisor Glen Ayres believes that the 'honest advisor' would tell their family business clients that: 'absolute economic equality among your children is virtually impossible to achieve'.[2] Instead Ayres suggests that the senior generation should aim for: 'rough family justice: defined as equity, not equality, among members of the family system in a context designed to serve the best interests of the family business'.

Most other family business commentators also appear to agree, that equal is not always fair. In fact some would argue that equal is rarely fair in a family business context. Inheriting an equal share is not a right as such. Any inheritance is a gift. For the senior generation of many business-owning families, the goal of an ownership succession plan is not to pass on wealth *per-se*. It is about passing on the family business to those who value it and in a way that will safeguard its long-term survival. In other words custodianship.

15.3 OWNERSHIP SUCCESSION

At root there are really only four possible things that can happen to the ownership of a family firm, although there are a number of hybrids and variants. Three of these alternatives need only be mentioned briefly in this chapter. The options are:

- **A third party sale.** This is discussed in detail in chapter 12.
- **Floatation.** A floatation, the listing of the shares of a family business on a recognised investment exchange, such as the London Stock Exchange or on AIM[3] is clearly a positive outcome. Provided the business owning family retain 25% of the voting rights and some involvement in governance their business will remain within the European Commission definition of a family business.[4] Even though the family, through their voting block of shares, continuing family presence on the board or otherwise, may remain a hugely significant influence in the business, they will be submitting to third party control, through independent directors, the UK Corporate Governance Code, investor pressure and market forces. Many family firms, for example Morrisons supermarkets, Thorntons chocolates and Monsoon found these constraints uncomfortable at first, so much so that in the case of Monsoon the business quickly went back from public to private ownership in the hands of the Simon family.
  A floatation results in the forfeiture of favourable tax treatment in the form of business property relief. Shares in most trading family businesses can be passed

---

[2] Glenn Ayres '"Rough Family Justice": Equity in Family Business Succession Planning' *Family Business Review* (1990) Vol 3(1) at p 3.
[3] Strictly AIM is not a Regulated Market but instead falls within the classification of a Multilateral Trading Facility (MTF) as defined under the Markets in Financial Instruments Directive 2004 (MiFID).
[4] See chapter 1.

from generation to generation free from the burden of inheritance tax using BPR. This is not available for shares that can be traded on a public exchange.[5]

For these reasons, and also because of the relative rarity of floatation as an exit route, for any business we will not look at this succession option in any more detail.

- **Closure.** Many family businesses simply turn out the lights, either from the lack of a viable alternative succession option, or because of business failure (and often the two are connected). This will rarely be a preferred option. A lack of succession planning can contribute to closure being the only choice. Redundancy and other closure costs could well be incurred. The value of assets on a break-up basis on closure will inevitably be lower than on the sale of a business as a going concern. No goodwill premium will be obtained. Above all the dream of family business continuity will have died. We therefore do not propose to spend any more time examining the closure option.
- **Transferring ownership to the family.** For a significant number of business owning families transferring ownership to the next generation will be their preferred route. This will be the main focus of this chapter.

15.4 OWNERSHIP SUCCESSION TYPOLOGIES

In chapter 3 (Tools, Models and Theories) we introduce the concept of the life cycle of the family business, progressing from an owner managed start-up, through a sibling partnership, into a cousin collaboration.

Gersick[6] points out that in real life ownership successions are neither so linear, nor so simple or so prescribed. Business families can choose to adopt the same business model for the next generation that has applied and worked for the current generation ('recycles'). Alternatively, if tensions have arisen in the current generation, which can be traced back to the complexities of multiple-ownership, the family can choose a 'recursive' succession model, where ownership is simplified and reverts back one or two stages.[7] Alternatively the current generation can adopt the classic 'progressive' succession model, whereby ownership devolves to an ever increasing group of siblings, then cousins.

As a matter of mathematical logic, with three broad categories of ownership mode Gersick argues that there are therefore nine possible types of succession.

---

[5] One of the long term campaign issues for the IFB has been to extend BPR relief to family owned quoted shares, previously held by family members in family owned businesses. The evidence that quoted family owned companies appear to out-perform the market suggests that there would be a wider economic benefit to this concession.

[6] See chapter 7 – The Diversity of Successions, Kelin E Gersick *Generation to Generation: Life cycles of a family business* (Harvard Business School Press, 1997).

[7] This appears to have happened in the Saul D Harrison family business, where only one family member, Stephen Harrison, now appears to be active in the firm. Recursive successions will clearly need close collaboration or compromise, at least in ownership terms. Ownership will have become more widely spread between siblings and cousins, as the case may be. Shares will have been given away and will need to be 'retrieved' from outsider branches of the family. In a minority of cases an aunt, for example might gift shares to a nephew insider, even in preference to her own children. But such cases must be rare. We would therefore argue that recursive ownership transfers can therefore be seen more as pruning or re-organisation exercises of the sort discussed in chapter 11, than pure ownership succession planning, where future ownership remains fully in the gift of the current generation.

Figure 15.1: Nine types of succession

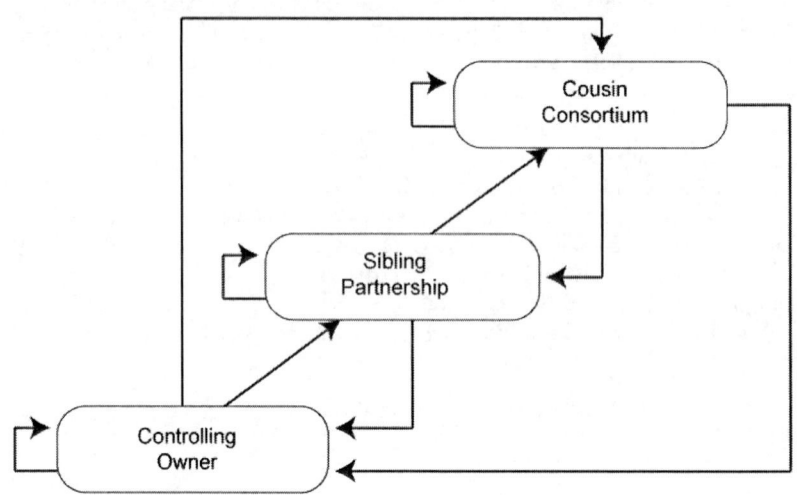

Source: based on Figure 7-1 from Generation to Generation: Life cycles of a family business (Kelin E Gersick, Harvard Business School Press, 1997)

Of course the current generation owners can only adopt one single ownership succession mode in any single case. The core problem in the Davies case was that, whilst Tom and Ellen Davies actually chose (in Gersick's typology) a progressive ownership succession model[8] transferring ownership to all five branches of the next generation, they let James believe that he would inherit outright under a controlling owner to controlling owner, recycle succession model.

Ownership successions from owner managed to sibling partnership businesses clearly involve increasing complexity. If only one of the siblings works in the business and the rest are outsider owners the potential for sibling rivalry might be diminished. But it will not be eliminated and has the potential to surface in a myriad of insider and outsider ownership issues.

However there are positive factors relating to stage one to stage two successions. There are fewer family members involved. They are likely to be closer in age and, ideally emotionally. They will have grown up in the same house and will have been subject to a similar socialisation process in relation to the family business.[9] It becomes correspondingly easier to develop a shared vision of the future of the family firm and the respective roles of the next generation in this.

Sibling partnership to cousin collaboration ownership transitions are, almost certainly, more complex and difficult. The sheer numbers likely to be involved mean that insider and outsider distinctions are both necessary and inevitable. Even if all of the cousins wanted to work in the family enterprise and were qualified to do so it probably could

---

[8] In fact the will gave outright shares to the four other children and 'generation skipped' James leaving his children, Tom and Ellen's grandchildren, to share the remaining fifth, subject in each case to allowing James to remain in occupation until he was 60. See para 3 of the judgment *Davies v Davies* [2015] EWHC 1384 (Ch).

[9] Complications inevitably arise in the case of second marriages with a new set of younger children.

not accommodate them all. The cousins will have grown up in different households, with parents who have varying relationships with the family firm. Different perspectives will abound, making it correspondingly harder to arrive at a shared vision for the future that is relevant across the cousin consortium. The sheer weight of numbers mean that informal communication between owners will not be sufficient and that some formal governance procedures will be desirable. The potential for sibling rivalry remains within individual branches. It is also possible that unresolved issues between sibling parents may affect relationships between corresponding offspring cousins. A strong shared belief in the family firm, underpinned by a commitment to governance is therefore needed for a cousin collaboration transition to succeed. Many do.

15.5 SUCCESSION DECISIONS NOW AND FOR FUTURE GENERATIONS

Transitions from sibling partnerships to cousin consortiums (typically second to third generation transitions) typically first to third generation transitions) can be more complex than transitions from an owner-controller to sibling partnership (typically first to second generation transitions), particularly where the branches have unequal numbers of offspring.

A difficult question in designing an ownership structure for the cousin consortium is whether to pass shares down by branch also referred to as distribution *per stirpes*, or to reallocate shares so that, *per capita*, each of the cousins controls an equal amount of shares, maintaining an equality of individual ownership. It will be appreciated that if the number of cousins differs in each branch of the third generation the cousins could have radically different levels of voting power. A *per capita* arrangement could well be very difficult to put in place the future.[10]

15.6 FAMILY OWNERSHIP SUCCESSION AND PLANNING

The classic family business ownership cliché is of the business owning family sitting in their lawyer's office, following the death of the senior generation business leader and waiting with bated breath to discover who, amongst the next generation, will inherit the family firm.

This might happen occasionally.[11] But it will almost inevitably be a disaster for both the family and the business. In the absence of some form of communication process during the lifetime of the senior generation, disappointment for, either the insiders, the outsiders, or both can be pretty much guaranteed. The uncertainty over the future ownership of the family business will almost certainly have had a detrimental effect on its trade. Insiders and key employees may become demotivated, even to the extent of

---

[10] As this would involve members of the branch with fewer cousins (therefore holding a higher number of shares) transferring some of these to the more densely populated branches on some basis. In practice this would have to be by agreement. Compulsion would be almost impossible. But what price should be paid? Issues concerning family branches and branch dominance are discussed in more detail in chapter 17 (Governance).

[11] One of the most extreme examples can be found in the Davies case where James, as the son working on the family farm, was not actually told the contents of his father's will (which left the farm equally to the wider family) until some years after his father's death.

leaving the business to further their careers elsewhere. Major customers and suppliers could have scaled back their dealings with the family business because of concerns over continuity.

15.7 A SHARED DREAM?

Much of family business literature talks about dreams, missions and visions.[12] The first question to ask in ownership succession planning is an abstract one. Does the family have a shared dream for the future of the business?

This will often not be an easy question for many business-owning families to answer immediately, with conviction and with unanimity.[13] Indeed, for many families, including the Davies family, even raising the question might seem too difficult. Talk of dreams, vision and mission could well seem too airy fairy and business school for many down to earth business owning families. If so, alternative and more appropriate language needs to be found.

Alternative questions could be 'do we want to continue in owning this business, as a family? If so why?' These questions needs to be borne in mind when looking at the myriad of subsidiary questions posed in this chapter. The absence of a compelling answer to these big picture questions opens up the wider issue of whether the business should remain in family ownership, in the first place, rather than pursuing the other main succession option, the sale of the family firm.

A key component of the ownership succession process is to make sure that the expectations of all family members in the next future generations are fully articulated and reconciled to form part of a fully shared dream (captured as part of the governance process). What absolutely cannot be allowed to happen[14] is for the ownership transition to take place on the basis of an unarticulated and unexplored assumption that the business owning family all want the same thing for the future.

The most obvious champion of continued family ownership is likely to be the next generation business leadership elect. Gersick talks about the heroic next generation business leader with a vision to drive the family firm forward. That leader will often expect a controlling ownership stake as a reward for doing so. However other family members might be equally keen for the business to remain in the ownership of a wider family group. These could be family employees working in the family enterprise but not part of the senior management team. Family members not employed in the business might also be keen to become involved as supportive and committed owners.

The business leadership designate might, or might not, welcome the opportunity of involvement in the family enterprise and of working together with siblings and cousins to ensure both its success and family continuity.

What could emerge is that, to the extent there is a commitment to continuing family ownership, this is shared only by the senior generation and by next generation insiders.

---

[12] For example Gersick talks about the process of negotiating the shared dream; Kelin E Gersick *Generation to Generation: Life cycles of a family business* (Harvard Business School Press, 1997) at p 200.
[13] Commentators suggest that several meetings over an extended period of time, running to many months, if not years is likely to be necessary before the shared dream emerges.
[14] And the Davies case illustrates why not.

It was clear that, in the Davies case, James was the only one of the five siblings who displayed any real interest in the family farm and its continuation.

15.8 OWNERSHIP PHILOSOPHY

Against this background and given the central importance of ownership one of the key questions for any business family is to determine is its ownership philosophy. Who should be entitled to own shares in the family firm and why?

There are an almost infinite number of permutations available and a corresponding variety of ownership structures to accommodate those permutations. But these ultimately boil down to two key predominant approaches:

- **Insiders first.** One view is that ownership is the control and reward system for those working in the business; to family business 'insiders' in preference to 'outsiders,' the remaining family members, who have no day-to-day involvement with the family business. This approach could also be termed 'business first'. The argument being that clean, decisive decision making that is possible in owner managed businesses, without the complexity of wider family ownership, must be good for the business. A number of commentators therefore argue that only those members who work in the business should own shares and that other those family members should receive other assets. Further complications can arise if there is more than one family insider working in the business.
- **Whole family.** The opposite view is that the family business is a vehicle for supporting the economic needs and social well-being of the whole family, as well as offering possible employment opportunities for future generations. This second view, suggests distribution to all heirs.

These two approaches encapsulate the key family business theme of fairness and equality. Equal treatment would dictate splitting ownership of the family business between all siblings. But is that necessarily fair to those who have spent their working lives building up that business?

Other commentators distinguish between ownership and control and argue that whilst family members who do not work in the business may be owners, it is vital to keep the control of the business in the hands of those working in it.

It is rarely possible to satisfy everyone but establishing an ownership philosophy is a central part of both the family business governance and succession process. Even if consensus cannot be reached, at least discussing the issues with family members can reduce the risk of conflict.[15] The next generation will have a much better understanding of the dilemmas faced by their seniors in an attempt to be fair. They might form the view and that any economic 'inequality' has much more to do with the nature and amount of assets available for distribution, rather than any lack of or imbalance in love or affection.

In more detail the range of common ownership approaches can be shown as follows:

---

[15] Explored in more detail as part of the discussion of fair process below.

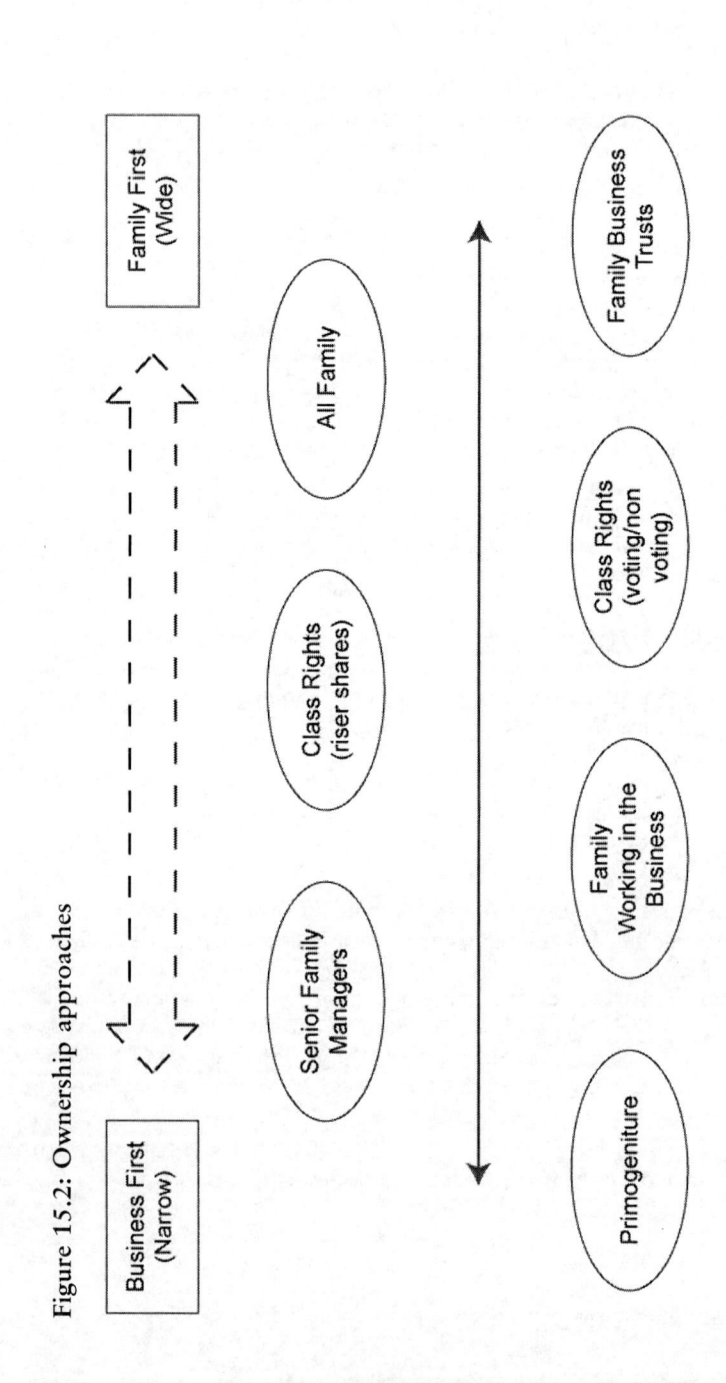

Figure 15.2: Ownership approaches

Business First (Narrow) ←—————————————————→ Family First (Wide)

- Senior Family Managers
- Class Rights (riser shares)
- All Family

- Primogeniture
- Family Working in the Business
- Class Rights (voting/non voting)
- Family Business Trusts

The structures associated with most of the approaches shown will need little explanation. The relevant shareholders will inherit simple ordinary shares. The control of the family company and the distribution of the wealth it creates will be a factor of the relative number of shares held.

There are a number of hybrid or compromise solutions. One of these is to introduce ownership structures where insiders and outsiders are treated differently. Another is a family buy-out or FBO. Both are discussed in this chapter below.

Family business trusts are dealt with separately in chapter 14. These can also be used as vehicles for primogeniture arrangements. Under some trust arrangements, whilst control of the family assets comprised within such a trust may vest in the first born male heir, ultimate beneficial ownership of the underlying capital assets will sit at the opposite end of the scale, as a widely owned family asset.

15.9 FACTORS INFLUENCING OWNERSHIP APPROACH

In theory once a business owning family have worked out their shared dream, they can define their ownership philosophy.

In fact ownership philosophy might be too grand a term to apply to the approach a business owning family takes to ownership decisions. The term philosophy suggests that this will be underpinned by some universal and permanent truth. In practice the approach of the business family to ownership decisions may be heavily influenced by pragmatic considerations. Some ownership configurations will not be viable until a family business has reached a certain size and sophistication. The approach to ownership may change from generation to generation. Indeed commentators[16] suggest that a key part of the transitional phase between generations is for a business owning family to examine whether the approach taken to ownership during the current generation remains valid for the next.

Ownership approach might be a better term. In deciding which ownership approach and which ownership structure is most appropriate for the family business, a number of factors need to be considered. These include:

15.9.1 The financial resources of the family firm

It might seem pointless adopting a family first approach if the business is simply incapable of supporting anyone other than those who work in it. Many farming businesses fall into this category.

The fairness and equality theme emerges with a vengeance here. Whilst equal treatment would dictate that all of the next generation share ownership, this might be simply unfair to the insiders, who have dedicated their working lives to the family farm (perhaps for little economic reward). But what about the underlying capital value.[17] Conversely if the business is able to adequately reward family members working in the

---

[16] See for example Carlock and Ward *Strategic Planning for the Family Business* (Palgrave, 2001).
[17] The compromise which seems to have been arrived at, at least in the heads of Tom and Ellen Davies, was to allow James to continue to farm and take the profits until he was aged 60.

business, produce surplus distributable profits, even after sensible levels of reinvestment, a business first approach may seem unfair to the remaining family members.

15.9.2 Insider employment packages

Many employees, including senior managers, go through their entire careers without ever having an ownership stake in the organisations that they work for. Why should family insiders be treated any differently, simply because they are family members working in a business owned by their parents or in wider family ownership? If family members have been remunerated at, or above market rates,[18] in their capacity as employees what is the basis of any additional expectation as to ownership? Especially if other senior non-family managers are excluded from the ownership circle it could be argued that such any such expectations of family insiders are incompatible with the business system.[19]

15.9.3 The extent of family assets outside the family business

The presence of significant family assets held by the senior generation outside the family business, might allow the outsiders to take a larger share of these and the insiders to assume ownership of the family firm. It is then correspondingly easier to take an insider first ownership approach with the family business and for this to be seen as fair to both insiders and outsiders. There are, however a number of complicating factors to be taken into account.

From the perspective of the insiders there is the degree of risk associated with having their wealth tied irrevocably to the fortunes of the family firm, particularly in a volatile trading business as opposed to an asset based business. There is also the issue of liquidity. How easy would it be to sell the family business, or alternatively raise cash if one or more of the insiders subsequently wanted to exit and to realise their share of the business? With this come associated questions of life choice. By taking their share of the family wealth in the form of ownership of the family business, the insiders might be committing themselves to a lifetime of service to it, whereas the outsiders are receiving more readily realisable assets to fund an independent lifestyle.[20]

The outsiders, on the other hand, might be concerned that the insiders would be taking not only the current value of the family firm but also its potential for growth. This is a complicated issue in itself. To what extent will that growth be created only by the continuing efforts of the insiders? Alternatively have the current generation, perhaps by decades of investment in the family firm already built that growth potential so that it will be a relatively simple matter for the insiders to unlock this in the future?

15.9.4 Need and the financial position of the outsiders

An associated factor is the current financial position of the next generation outsiders. Logically this has relevance. Bringing this factor into the reckoning is however fraught

---

[18] Of course the opposite is the case in many smaller family businesses, especially in the farming industry. This was a clear factor in James Davies' case. See para 47 of the judgment.
[19] See chapter 5 (Employing Family Members) for an analysis of family employment in the context of the three-circle model.
[20] These issues also surface on divorce and are considered in chapter 18.

with emotional danger. The next generation outsider might have been successful in their independent careers and have no financial need to inherit a share in the family firm. But is that a sufficient reason to be disinherited? Similarly, should the ownership expectations of the insiders be thwarted simply because a spendthrift outsider can't hold down a job?

15.9.5 The financial security of the existing generation

The existing generation may have a strong desire to pass on the family business to the next generation. But this might be an unrealisable dream. Some combination of lack of independent assets, poor pension provision or the low profitability of the family firm (so that the income generated could not support both the next generation and the senior generation in their retirement), could defeat the dream.

15.9.6 Familiness and emotional ownership

The question of approach to ownership of a family business goes well beyond purely economic considerations.

The family business might well have been the focal point of the business owning family, both insiders and outsiders, for many decades. It may have been the main topic of conversation at family gatherings. The outsiders could closely identify themselves with the family firm and have a strong emotional attachment to it. The business might be the outsiders' main link with the rest of the family and to their memories of their parents and grandparents. There will often be a significant emotional attachment to ownership.

The outsiders might have hopes of playing a role in the family firm in the future, possibly in some form of non-executive or governance role, or perhaps becoming an insider themselves as a 'prodigal' returning to the business after a career elsewhere. They might entertain similar hopes for their own children.

Ownership may carry external benefits, such as status in the community or the industry in which the family business operates, even for outsiders. The older and more established the family enterprise, the more that this is likely to be a factor.

Certainly the familiness factor featured in the decision of James Cadman to include his daughter Janis in the ownership of the Cadman Developments Limited and that of his wife to continue that approach. It also appeared to influence Janis, who rejected a proposal from her brothers that she should take a correspondingly larger share of the family's private assets, in return for allowing them, the insiders, to take ownership of the family company.[21]

Can the family find a way to foster emotional ownership of the family business but divorce this from legal ownership?

---

[21] See chapter 21 for a more detailed explanation of this case.

15.9.7 Tradition

In many older family businesses some form of ownership practice or tradition may have been established. The classic example would be pure primogeniture, whereby the eldest male offspring inherits ownership.[22] Many family farming businesses will also have a tradition of passing ownership to those working on the farm. Again James Davies is the obvious example. Historically this would typically be sons (although not necessarily the eldest) but daughter owners are increasingly becoming a part of the farming landscape.

Conversely many cultures have strong family first approaches, so that whilst leadership and legal ownership of a family business might traditionally be the preserve of male relatives, the benefits of the business are seen as a collective family asset.

15.9.8 Family definition

If a wider, family first, ownership approach is to be adopted this brings into play the question of who should fall within the definition of family member? This is considered in chapter 1.

Frequently encountered issues include the status of in-laws. Should ownership be restricted to the family bloodline? Alternatively should in-laws be entitled to own shares outright, including potentially, the ability to transfer these to children and future spouses outside the original founder's bloodline? Should distinctions be made between in-laws working in the family firm as 'quasi-insiders' and those not? Should any rights of ownership be restricted and conditional, so that the relevant ownership rights cease once the 'family condition,' be that working in the family business or being married to a bloodline family member, is no longer satisfied?[23]

Other, and it is to be hoped, increasingly less relevant and contentious, questions of family definition include the status of unmarried partners, same sex couples, step-children and adopted children.

15.9.9 Future proofing and flexibility

Business families will want to pay heed to the implications of the ownership approach that they adopt for the current generation will have for future generations.

A business first approach whereby ownership is confined to insiders working in the family business may alienate the outsider branches of the family. This could weaken wider family cohesion and potentially deprive the business of the wider and deeper talent pool of future generations of management and leadership in that wider family. Conversely a family first approach, with ownership spread across the wider family, including business outsiders might spread ownership too thinly and leave the business open to conflicts between the haves and the have-nots as in *Saul D Harrison*.

---

[22] According to one comparatively recent survey primogeniture was still seen as a the preferred ownership approach by the majority of landed estate owners, although the approach appeared to be diminishing (see *The Succession Project*, Saffrey Champness, 2004). But this is a more complicated question than it might first seem. Trust arrangements and wider stewardship approaches might place the first born male heir more in the position of a custodian of the estate concerned rather than an absolute owner.

[23] Discussed further in chapter 18.

But it is impractical to have more than half an eye to the long-term future. Changes in circumstances cannot be foreseen and must be accommodated. The ownership structure of the *Saul D Harrison* business might have made perfect sense at the time of the 1960 re-organisation when the business was prosperous. It made less sense, especially for C Shareholders, who were last in the queue for income, when the business was struggling financially. Flexibility and the need to respond and adapt to changing and evolving circumstances must form a key part of the succession planning process.

The temptation is for each generation of family business owners to lay down a blue print for the ownership approach intended to apply for all eternity. However commentators[24] argue that the transition period between generations offers the business family the opportunity to re-evaluate and, if necessary refresh or change that ownership approach. By sticking to rigidly to the past, the family squanders that opportunity and is often forced to re-evaluate in the face of conflicts arising after the transition has taken place.

15.9.10 Family dynamics

But perhaps the single most important determinant of ownership approach for a business owning family should be based on a cold, hard and realistic assessment of the quality of their family dynamics.[25]

Again the situation of the Cadman family offers a clear illustration. Notwithstanding the family first approach of James Cadman and his clear wish to see his daughter included within the fold of the family firm, it seems equally clear that, in the face of opposition from the insiders Rodney and Cedric, this was doomed to failure.

We discussed the four typologies of family firms described by Dyer[26] in chapter 3 (Tools, Models and Theories). It is helpful to return to that classification when considering family dynamics in the context of approach to ownership. Businesses that can be described as *Clan Family Firms*, clearly have the greatest prospect of successfully pursuing a wider family first ownership approach. The family management insiders instinctively recognise a responsibility to look after the interests of the wider clan members. In turn, the wider clan will be there to offer their support (through dividend sacrifices or more practical support) when the insiders or the family firm needs it. They will understand when family comprises need to be made for the long-term health of the family business.

Equally clearly businesses lacking in family cohesion, especially those with a history of conflict or strained relationships between the next generation family members, such as the Cadmans, seem much more likely to fall into the category of *Self-Interested Family Firms* and accordingly doomed to failure or conflict if a wider ownership approach is pursued.

---

[24] See for example Carlock and Ward *Strategic Planning for the Family Business* (Palgrave, 2001).
[25] An approach to assessing the quality of family dynamics and cohesion is contained in De Vries, Carlock and Florent-Treacy *Family Business on the Couch* (Wiley, 2007).
[26] G W Dyer Jr 'Examining the "family effect" on firm performance' *Family Business Review* (2006) Vol 19(4), 253–273.

15.9.11 Governance and ownership approach

What of Dyer's final classification, the *Professional Family Firm*, so far as ownership and family dynamics are concerned? The commitment to governance processes, including dividend, remuneration and employment policies, characteristic of such firms can play a role in re-enforcing family cohesion. Dispute resolution mechanisms, can provide a safety net to minimise the effect of conflict on both the family and the business if cohesion breaks down.[27]

Exit mechanisms are also likely to be of primary importance and are particularly applicable in the case of one or two disgruntled family shareholders. In more extreme cases, where discontent is more widely spread, a more radical pruning of the family ownership tree may be required. Both exits and pruning are as a separate topics in chapter 11.

Ultimately if family dynamics are poor at the outset it is most unlikely that any amount of investment in governance will ultimately operate as a sufficient safeguard against serious conflict, so as to make a wider ownership approach viable in the long term.

15.9.12 Tax

One ownership approach might result in a more favourable tax treatment, or at least open up some tax planning opportunities, for the business owning family. A basic overview of tax treatment in the context of ownership succession is provided in chapter 16. However we suggest that ultimately tax considerations should not be seen, as decisive in determining ownership approach.

15.9.13 The purpose of ownership

Finally and significantly, what do the family really see as the purpose or point of ownership? Is it the possibility of selling and sharing in the proceeds of sale of a valuable capital asset, even if that sale might not take place for many years? Alternatively is ownership more closely akin to custodianship? These key issues are explored in the following paragraphs.

15.10 GIFTS ... WITH STRINGS ATTACHED?

Assuming that ownership of the family business is to be gifted to the next generation an interesting hypothetical question is, what would be the reaction of the senior generation if the business is sold shortly after it was handed over?

Of course the reason for the sale would be important. It could be that poor family dynamics made a widely owned family business unmanageable. In which case the senior generation might regret not choosing a single insider successor. Or perhaps, notwithstanding doubts about their capability, a single insider successor was in fact chosen. The senior generation might then regret not selling, so that the whole family, including outsiders, could benefit from the proceeds of sale.

---

[27] Dispute resolution mechanisms are considered in chapter 26 (Advising the Family Business Client).

What about the situation where the family business was gifted to next generation insider owners, who simply decide to sell up and pocket the proceeds? Rationally the senior generation should receive the news with equanimity. After all one of the components of ownership of a capital asset is the right to sell it and to retain the proceeds of sale.

Let us suppose that Tom and Ellen Davies had followed through their promise (and presumably initial intention) and actually left the farm to James outright and also that, shortly after Tom's death, had James sold the farm. Just possibly the senior generation (in this case the surviving parent Ellen) might take the view that the insiders have already worked hard enough. Their early and wealthy retirement was well deserved. This is perhaps an unlikely reaction. More likely the senior generation will feel let down and that the next generation have betrayed a trust. This is an express or implied understanding that the family business will be kept in family ownership for as long as possible. In other words that the gift of the family firm came with some form of strings of custodianship attached to it.

15.11 STRINGS AND RED TAPE

The question then becomes do the senior generation attempt to reinforce their vision of family continuity in some form of legal structure? Alternatively, is the level of trust between generations sufficient to give the senior generation confidence that this vision is truly part of a dream shared with the next generation?

The senior generation, Ellen in our case, might be hurt and disappointed if James had sold the family business. She might also have been embarrassed to explain the situation to her other four children, the outsiders who will have lost out completely. Could some form of anti-embarrassment provisions, whereby the outsiders received a share of any subsequent proceeds of sale could be considered? Does even suggesting such arrangements betray a lack of trust in the insider's intention or ability to keep the business in family ownership? Anti-embarrassment provisions would also be a nightmare to structure.[28]

Some form of discretionary trust arrangement could be a possibility. With a letter of wishes[29] expressing a hope that the insiders (including those in succeeding generations) will receive preferential treatment, both in terms of income and capital, if a sale eventually takes place, provided that the insiders have demonstrably tried to turn the shared dream into a reality. This might sound fine on paper. But all sorts of practical questions arise.[30]

---

[28] As the descending spiral of questions and issue raised in this footnote illustrates. The starting point would be probably be some form of trust arrangements over the proceeds of sale. Other alternatives would be to provide the outsiders with rights of pre-emption, in effect options to acquire the family business in preference to outsiders. The expectation would be that the options would be waived in favour of the third party buyer in return for an appropriate share of the proceeds of sale. How long should these arrangements last? Too soon and they are easily avoided. Too long and they become absurd. Generations of outsiders would need to be identified and, in effect, credited with retrospective whole family ownership rights. Should the rights of the outsiders diminish over time? Would sales forced by market circumstances be treated differently from sales motivated by cash or caused by neglect of the business? How would the needs of the insider and their immediate family be catered for? Who could answer these questions? Most pertinently would the buyer be prepared to wait whilst these matters were dealt with? The danger is that a buyer is likely to walk away in frustration. The family business would become unsalable anyway.

[29] Letters of wishes and the strengths and weaknesses of family business trusts generally are discussed in chapter 14.

[30] Including who would be appointed as trustees. The insiders would be effectively reporting to the trustees as

The point is made elsewhere[31] that, notwithstanding the dream that a family enterprise will stay in family ownership forever, many family businesses reach their sell by-date. If the consequence of acknowledging this might be sharing wealth with the outsiders the temptation for the remaining insiders is to hang on to a perishing family firm.

But, if insider ownership is to be followed, most families will take the informal approach. After all the senior generation have known the next generation for all their lives. It might be thought simply inconceivable that the next generation would contemplate sale unless circumstances compelled this.

Problems, both family and operational can inevitable occur of the dead hand of the senior generation attempts to bind the hands of the next too tightly. The position in the Davies family, as in many other business families, could well have been that the possibility of James readily agreeing to a sale, much less initiating the sale process, would be almost inconceivable. The dream of continued family ownership is shared equally between the senior generation and the next generation insiders.

But to what extent is that dream truly shared by the outsiders?

15.12 VALUE AND OWNERSHIP

A refrain often heard from outsider owners in family firms goes something like 'my family own X% of this company, but little good it does us'.

It is certainly trues that, absent viable exit routes, or the realistic prospect of the family enterprise being sold and a reliable dividend stream in the meantime, the financial advantages of ownership to outsiders are minimal.

Glenn Ayres puts it graphically:[32]

> 'giving a child who is not also an employee a minority interest in a business may be analogous to giving her the urn containing grandfather's ashes. There is little she can do with it, it produces no income, and she cannot even get rid of it.'

A distinction therefore needs to be drawn between economic and emotional ownership when trying to answer the insiders first, or whole family, ownership question. Ideally the outsiders would receive some economic benefit from ownership in the form of dividends. But it is likely that this will need to be underpinned by strong emotional ownership of the family firm to make a whole family ownership approach worthwhile so far as the outsiders are concerned.

---

legal owners. Would this be too restrictive? Choosing family outsiders would seem to be a recipe for conflict. Appointing family trustees would have costs attached. Would trust arrangements provide sufficient incentive to the insiders to develop the business anyway?

[31] See chapter 12 (Selling the Family Business).
[32] *Rough Family Justice* op cit at p 7.

15.13 OWNERSHIP STRUCTURES

15.13.1 Overview

The task of the family business advisor involved in ownership questions is two-fold. First to fully and properly understand the actual approach of the business family to ownership, helping them to articulate this if necessary. Secondly (and this is the relatively easy bit) selecting or creating a structure to fit that approach. Broadly speaking a technical ownership structure can be devised that can accommodate almost any ownership approach or philosophy developed by a business owning family.

The legal structure of most family companies is unremarkable, with the majority consisting of simple ordinary shares. What is fascinating in practice is the interplay between the three systems in the business. To what extent does the family system counterbalance or conflict with the logic of ownership? What family or business conditions need to exist before ownership rights will be fully exerted? A minority of business families attempt to tailor their ownership and legal structure to fit their ownership approach or philosophy. Often these can be seen as hybrids or compromises between the two basic forms of insider or wider family ownership. We will now look at some possible examples.

15.13.2 Op-co / prop-co structures[33]

In family enterprises with significant property assets it might be possible to separate out ownership of the real estate, by the wider family, from that of the operating business, which can pass to the insiders. If the properties are surplus investment properties the division can be complete. But owners of property interests could also receive less favourable tax treatment when compared with owners of shares in family operating companies.[34] If the property concerned is a core-operating asset of the family enterprise, some form of tenancy arrangement will be necessary.[35] Many of the factors referred to in 15.7 above will remain relevant. These include the quality of next generation family dynamics. One question could be whether anyone, particularly the insiders would have sufficient incentive to develop and invest in the family enterprise to enable the family dreams as to its potential to be fulfilled? Alternatively with only a limited ownership interest, would the insiders act more like grudging caretakers for the outsiders, rather than custodians, carrying out the minimum of necessary maintenance.[36]

15.13.3 Voting and non-voting shares

Other solutions are achieved by creating separate classes of shares in limited companies. The senior generation might be powerfully drawn to equal treatment of their children,

---

[33] These are discussed in more detail in chapter 11, in the context of restructuring the family business by demerger, to resolve tensions outside the succession process. They can also be employed as a succession planning tool.
[34] See the overview in chapter 16.
[35] In essence the Davies family came close to adopting this solution. There had always been a distinction in the structure of the business between the operating farm, at one time run as cross generational partnership between James and his parents and latterly by James alone and the underlying farm and land, which had remained in the ownership of the senior generation. Rent was paid by James.
[36] Again a factor in James Davies' case was the extent to which he invested his own money in capital improvements to the farm, in the expectation that he would own this outright one day.

both insiders working in the business, and outsiders who are not. They could also be convinced that the insider business leadership needs a free hand to run the business, free from interference by the outsiders in management matters. A potential solution to this dilemma is to create separate classes of voting and non-voting shares. The insiders are given the voting shares and thereby control the operations. They are able to steer the direction of the family company. The outsiders take the non-voting shares, so are able to share equally in the economic benefits of the family business. Dual or multiple share classes with different voting rights are fully permissible in the UK but only for private companies.[37] Again it is possible to fashion this split in any number of ways. Rather than removing voting rights from the outsiders altogether, the insiders might be given weighted voting rights. In this way the outsiders are given a voice in general meetings. However the outsiders will have no real power or control under this structure.[38] The maths will usually work so that the outsiders can always be outvoted by the insiders, including on resolutions to remove the directors.

In terms of a family business systems analysis this has the effect of creating a separation between the management and ownership systems. The family-owner-management zone, Zone 1, at the centre of the three-circle model, is re-enforced.[39] If one of the objectives of family business governance systems is indeed to create 'boundaries not barriers' between the three systems in play, voting and non-voting share structures achieve the opposite. The insider management holding the voting shares can shelter behind the barrier created by the share structure, immune from any real hard legal influence, much less any form of control by the remainder of the family.

Voting and non-voting were introduced into the *Saul D Harrison* family business as part of the 1960 re-organisation. In more detail, the share capital of the company had been altered to create three classes of shares, as follows:

- 30 A Ordinary shares. These carried all the voting rights but no rights relating to income or to capital on winding up. These were originally allocated to the three second-generation brothers who were leading the business at that time. The intention appears to have been to allow them to retain management control. When the matter came to court the A Shares were held, in equal shares, by Alan, the third generation managing director and Marian, the widow of his elder brother.

- B Ordinary shares. These carried superior rights to income and priority but limited rights as to capital (ie a right to be paid any arrears of cumulative dividend and par value only). These shares were held largely by members of the third generation, the grandchildren of the founder.

- C Ordinary shares, with secondary rights as to income but entitlement to the remainder of any capital surplus. These shares were held mainly by the great-grandchildren of the founder, including the petitioner, along with a number of family business trusts.

---

[37] The position is different in other jurisdictions, including the USA, where even companies listed on the New York Stock Exchange are allowed to maintain dual share structures. The most notable example being News Corp where the voting rights attached to the class of shares held by the Murdoch family allows them to retain effective control of this major business, even though they do not hold a numerical majority of the equity of the company.

[38] Arguably this is consistent with John Ward's maxim that outsiders should have 'their noses in but fingers out' of a family business; John Ward *Perpetuating the Family Business* (Palgrave, 2004) Lesson 37.

[39] See chapter 3 for a full explanation of the three-circle model.

Figure 15.3: The effect of voting and non-voting share structures

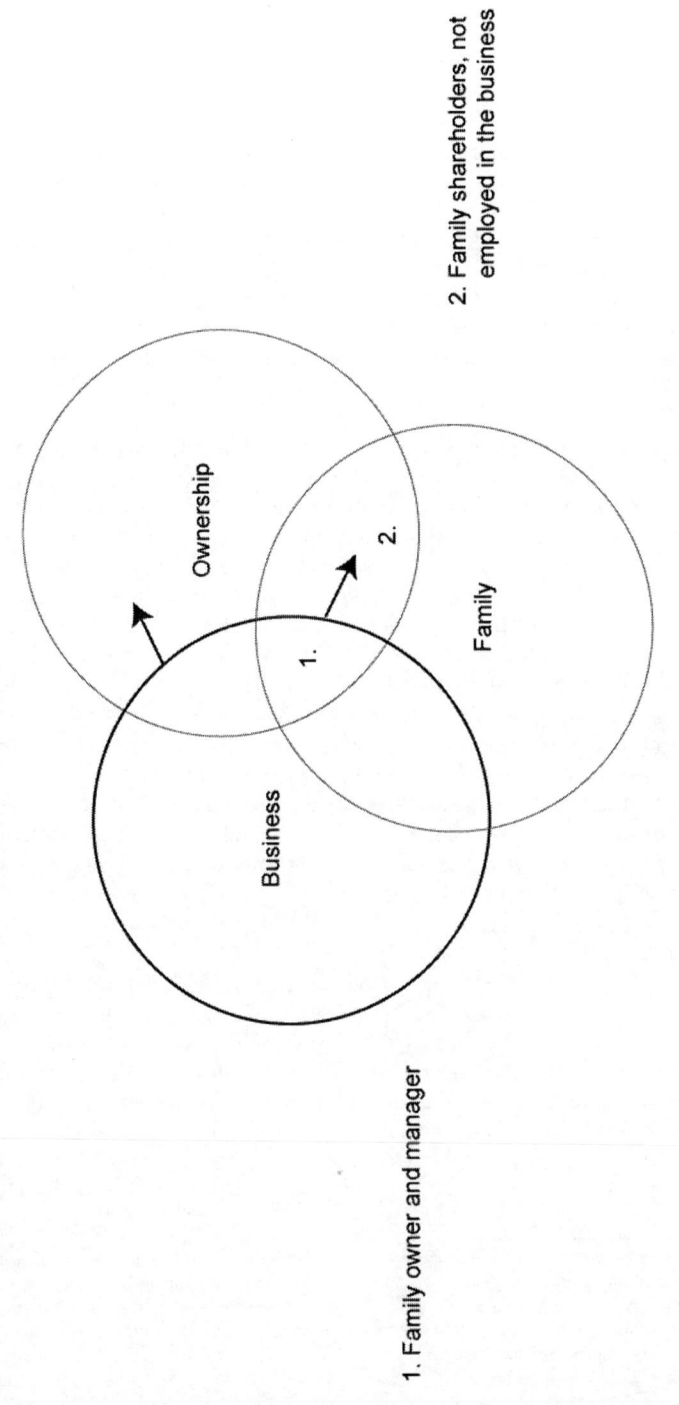

1. Family owner and manager
2. Family shareholders, not employed in the business

The idea behind the re-organisation appeared to be to concentrate voting control in the hands of Saul Harrison's three surviving sons, who at the time were all full time working directors but with value passing into the hands of the wider family. The next generation would receive the bulk of the income under the B Shares and the generation below would hold the capital value represented by the C Shares. It is unclear the extent to which this structure was introduced into the *Saul D Harrison* business as a result of the family business logic referred to above, for death duty (inheritance tax) planning reasons, or for some combination of the two.

The facts of the *Saul D Harrison* case vividly illustrate the potential shortcomings of a voting and non-voting share split. By removing voting rights from the outsiders the structure emasculates a central feature of ownership, the ability to control the board.[40] By removing the possibility of wider shareholder control, voting and non-voting share structures place a correspondingly high premium on the management abilities and stewardship credentials of the insider family management team. The system relies on those holding voting shares to, in effect, act as trustees of the family firm. However they do so without the raft of legal obligations associated with formal trusteeship to underpin this.[41]

Combining voting and non-voting structures with a comprehensive family business governance system, especially viable exit rights might help to create some form of counterbalance or safety net. But this will do well to fill the hole created by the removal of voting rights as a central plank of ownership. Restricted matters could also be introduced.[42] So, whilst the insider management could take decisions on most management matters, the outsiders would be able to vote on any major strategic decisions potentially affecting the financial stability of the family business, and on insider remuneration, or other matters where the interests of the insiders and those of the family business were in obvious conflict.

As this voting and non-voting share structure was introduced into the *Saul D Harrison* business by the three second generation brothers in their own lifetime it might be seen as an endorsement by themselves of their of their own management abilities. Alternatively it might be seen as evidence of their insecurity. If voting and non-voting share structures are introduced as part of ownership transition to the next generation this might be because the senior generation have concerns about the management abilities of the insiders.

Alternatively the senior generation might be worried about the current or future dynamics between insiders and outsiders. By effectively removing the outsiders from the general meeting of the family company, this cannot be used as a forum to play destructive family games. The next generation can then be allowed to get on and manage the family business without criticism and undue interference by the outsiders. This might work in the short term. But debate is being stifled and is likely to resurface at some stage.

---

[40] Given the extremely limited degree of control afforded to minority interests this should be seen very much as a residual ability in any event. On the facts of Saul D Harrison the claimant would have had very little personal influence with a shareholding of less than 10%, even if those shares had carried voting rights. She would have needed to convince many more family members and crucially the professional trustees, to join her crusade for the liquidation of the family firm.
[41] See chapter 14.
[42] See chapter 11.

The ultimate form of protection for the insiders would be to introduce weighted voting rights so that a family director under threat could always trump any cards played by the rest of the family seeking his removal.[43]

It is possible to take the opposite approach, that of curtailing the control of insiders and the board of directors by limiting the powers that would otherwise be available to them, by introducing restrictions (sometimes called 'negative pledges') in the articles or, more usually a shareholders' agreement. This approach is considered in more detail in chapter 11 (Ownership Overview).

15.13.4   Voting trusts and nominees

Voting trusts, whereby shareholders relinquish their voting powers to an appointed trustee or trustees but continue to receive a share of dividends, are an alternative mechanism to voting and non-voting shares.

Other larger families use proxy structures, whereby someone is appointed to represent the outsider shareholders and to vote their shares at general meetings etc. In the Clarks shoes structure family members can appoint the family council to do this.

These arrangements can either be compulsory or voluntary, revocable, or permanent.

15.13.5   'Freezer' and 'growth' shares

The basic concept of freezer growth shares

One argument for the distribution of ownership to the next generation equally is that the underlying wealth has been generated by the current (or past) generations and should be regarded as a family asset. All family members, both insiders and outsiders might have had to make sacrifices to the business as they were growing up. These could be lost holidays or a lack of attention from their parents, because family resources, both time and cash were concentrated on the family business.

The counter argument from the next generation insiders runs along the lines of 'that is all very well but from now on all further value will be created by our efforts. It is unfair that you, the outsiders, get a free ride off our backs'.

A combination of 'freezer' and 'growth or 'riser' shares attempt to reconcile these two positions. The basic approach is to draw a line over the current value of the family firm. Below that line the value is deemed to have been created by the current or past generations and can be seen as a family asset. So far as the wider family are concerned their expectation to share in the value of the family firm is frozen or crystallised at that level. All family members, logically including the insiders in their capacity as family members, receive their equal share of this value. Any further growth above that line belongs to the insider family management team as a reward for future effort.

---

[43]   A so-called *Bushell v Faith* clause after the case of the same name – see **11.9**.

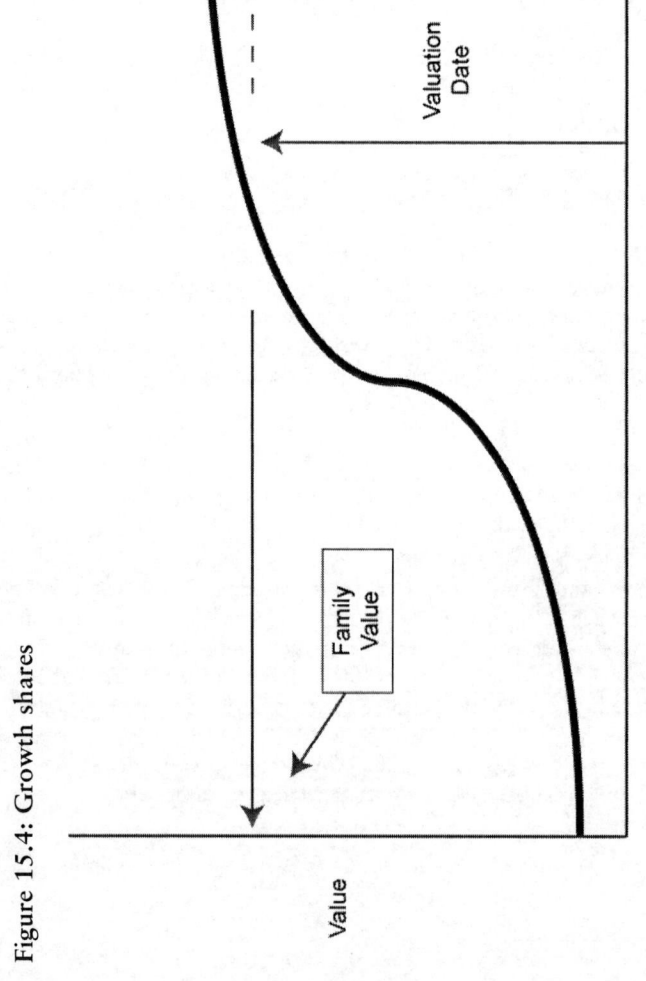

Figure 15.4: Growth shares

The same logic can be used for family buy-outs. For example where the senior generation want to receive market value for their shares, perhaps because their pensions are insufficient to fund retirement, or they wish to forestall future arguments from outsiders that the insiders have been given the family business.

An alternative application or refinement of the logic behind the growth share model can be obtained by creating a separate class of employee shares or share options. In this way insiders can hold two classes of shares. The main ordinary shares in their capacity as family members. Secondly shares or share options, attributable to their role in the business system, which can be awarded and justified where they can participate on equal terms with non-family management. These can include terms dealing with the return of those 'employees shares' if the insider leaves the employment of the family firm.[44]

Some issues to be addressed

The logic of growth shares may at first sight appear compelling, disposing as it does of both the fairness and free-rider issues. But there are a number of questions and issues to be addressed in its implementation:

- **Valuation.** It is often said that valuation is an art not a science. Goodwill and the future prospects of the family firm might prove especially difficult to value. We have not shown the value of the family business increasing in a straight line, or as a 'hockey stick' suggesting the probability of explosive growth under the leadership of the next generation. Instead we have suggested some tapering off of growth. This might be due the impact and loss of goodwill that will follow the departure of a charismatic entrepreneur founder. It could reflect that the family firm has, or the markets it operates in, have reached a certain level of maturity.

  Undervaluing the current value of goodwill undermines equal treatment, overvaluing it reinforces the fairness/ free-rider concern of the insiders.

- **Timing.** There is also the related but potentially much more difficult question of timing. Figure 15.4 shows a period of significant growth in the years just before the valuation date. Overlay the diagram of individual and family business life cycles in Figure 3.9 (chapter 3) and some interesting questions emerge.

  How does this period of growth correspond with the individual life cycles of the generations?

  The growth might have taken place relatively early in the career of the next generation insider. If so the growth can be fairly attributed largely to the efforts of the senior generation and the model is sound.

  But if the growth occurred during a period when the next generation were playing an increasingly prominent role in the business, a much more complex question of apportionment of contribution arises, if the free-riding concerns are to be dismissed.

  Often ownership succession planning or its implementation is delayed until after the senior generation have ceased to play any major day-to-day role in the business. If so the model becomes seriously flawed. Certainly we know of one case where, although the model was deployed to find a solution to a family conflict, the timing issue and its impact on valuation, meant that the next generation insiders retained a lingering resentment that they had paid the outsiders for the insiders own efforts.

---

[44] See chapter 6.

Again the risks associated with this timing issue can be ameliorated (if not eliminated) by some combination of early planning, attention to appropriate employment packages[45] and wider family business governance.

- **Economic benefit.** The disadvantages of the mechanics of riser shares are not experienced exclusively by the family management insiders. Whilst freezer shares allow the rest of the family to retain a carried interest in the family firm, more will need to be done for these to have any real economic value.

  Without more there will be no guarantee of a dividend. Certainly there will be no obvious exit route to enable real capital value to be unlocked. In each case the outsiders would otherwise remain at the mercy of the insiders.

  Again some combination of family cohesion, governance systems with exit routes and dividend policies are needed to provide a comprehensive answer.

- **Multiple insiders.** If there is more than one family insider working in the business the complications referred to in **15.8** also apply to the allocation of riser shares.

Mechanics

The alternative approach would be to build an answer to the economic uncertainties into the freezer / riser share mechanism. This can be done by structuring the freezer shares as preference shares and allocating these to the wider family. The insiders would take ordinary shares.[46]

Although widely used in corporate practice preference shares are not formally recognised under the Companies Acts. Their terms must be spelt out on a case-by-case basis. So, as with any preference share structure, one devised to implement riser shares will need to address a number of sub-questions:

- **Voting rights.** It would be unusual for preference shares to carry full voting rights. By removing voting rights altogether a riser share mechanism also creates a dual share voting and non-voting structure.

  If this is felt to be undesirable, there is no reason, in legal principle why preference shares cannot carry full voting rights.

  Alternatively the business family can leverage the logic of lenders and proceed on the assumption that whilst there is a high level of basic trust in the ability of the family management, there are certain 'bet the ranch decisions' when the wider family need to have some form of influence. A series of controls, similar to the negative pledges contained in shareholders' agreements[47] whereby the preference shareholders have veto rights, voting rights, or rights of consultation can then be attached to the preference shares.[48]

---

[45] The difficulties in the case referred to were exacerbated (if not caused) by the fact that the outsiders received significant remuneration from the family firm even though their day-to-day contribution was minimal.

[46] Whether this is achieved by converting into or exchanging the ordinary shares held by the current generation into preference shares, issuing new preference shares or new ordinary shares will be a matter of detailed planning in individual circumstances.

[47] See chapter 11 (Ownership Overview).

[48] A complicated sub-question is how should class voting rights operate? The working assumption is that the insiders will also hold a large proportion of the preference shares. A decision on whether or not allow postponement or waiver of preference dividend provides a good example. Should the votes of insiders be disregarded completely? Alternatively should they be taken fully taken into account, even if this overrules outsiders' votes? Should insider votes only count in some circumstances, for example where paying the preference dividend would damage the solvency of the family business? What about the effect on investment plans?

- **Income.** As the name implies, preference shares typically have first call on the income arising from the profits of a company. This is as of right, rather than at the discretion of the board.

  But how should the preference share rate be determined?

  Too high a rate and the family business is potentially denuded of income for working and investment capital purposes. Going back to Figure 15.4, if the preference share rate had been set on the assumption that the previous rate of growth would continue this would have proved to be over-optimistic. At extremes the outsiders would be able to exert lender-like influence and control over the family firm.

  Too low a rate and the economic benefit of the previous generation's contribution effectively transfers to the insiders.

- **Capital.** Preference shares also usually carry the right to preferential repayment of capital. In the absence of a sale or winding-up this is an empty right. So, should these be structured as redeemable preference shares, with provisions for automatic redemption? In this way the outsiders have more certainty that they will have a viable exit option.

  Redemption is usually structured as both an obligation of the company and a right belonging to it. If so the riser share restructuring will then also take on more of the characteristics of a vendor financed sale of the family business to the insiders and less of a continued carried interest for the outsiders in a widely held family firm. Is this what is intended? Alternatively should redemption only be at the option of the outsiders?

Tax treatment

Each of the hybrid ownership approaches discussed above will have potentially complex tax issues, relating to income tax on employee owned shares, inheritance and capital gains tax. Whilst it will rarely be the case that these are insurmountable it is beyond the scope of this book to examine these issues in detail. Specialist advice will be needed on a case-by-case basis.

15.13.6 Conclusion

Hybrid ownership approaches are complex and raise many questions. But, to finish this section on a note of optimism, they are by no means impossible to implement.

We can point to a number of business owning families where, as a product of good communication, structures were devised whereby the insiders took over not only responsibility for the direction of the family business, but also for the gradual and eventual payment to the outsiders of their share of the family inheritance. In most cases this might have taken some considerable amount of time to achieve. During the interim period when the hybrid arrangements were in place the insiders acted as responsible stewards, conscious of the interests of the outsiders. Equally the remaining outsider family members were content to leave the management of the family business to the insiders. They were the living embodiment of patient capital, remaining interested in and supportive of family management.

The key to success lies in a combination of advanced planning, effective communication and strong family dynamics.

15.14 CARRIED OUTSIDER INTERESTS

A simpler, but cruder, way of creating a hybrid ownership solution is for the outsiders to retain a residual or carried interest in the family enterprise. Usually this would be in the form of straightforward ordinary shares. Rather than a strictly equal division between all heirs, the insiders are given proportionately more, possibly enough to give them a controlling ownership position.[49] The larger the carried interest the less the departure from equality. Sometimes the remaining family members will want to remain as minority shareholders in the family firm. Often this will be for emotional reasons rather than a pure investment decision.[50] There is nevertheless still some residual price to be paid in terms of retained complexity of the ownership structure[51] and the corresponding need for governance[52] or agency costs.

15.15 SALE TO FAMILY MEMBERS OR FAMILY BUY-OUT (FBO)

15.15.1 Introduction

Family business buy-outs or FBO's are a sub species of management buy-out. It is just that the management are family insiders. The FBO term is not widely used but is nevertheless descriptive. There is nothing to say that, if the family business is to pass to the next generation of the family, this must be by way of gift. The next generation often buy the family business from their parents. There are many reasons why it might be appropriate for the including:

- **Pensions.** There might be insufficient pensions or other investment assets for the senior generation. This could be the result of re-investing surplus funds in the family business. It might have been due to unexpected events, such as divorce. The business might simply not have been profitable enough to provide for separate pensions. The lifestyle of the senior generation might have absorbed all of the surplus cash. In any event, whilst there is a will to pass the family business onto the next generation, the senior generation simply will not have enough to live on if they give the business away.

- **Fairness.** The family may wish to adopt a business first approach whereby ownership of the family business passes to insiders working in the business. The senior generation might also wish to achieve a measure of fairness so that the outsiders, not working in the business receive a larger share of assets held outside the family business. Even if the senior generation are adequately provided for in their own lifetime, they might not be confident that there will be sufficient surplus assets on their death to achieve this. The outsiders would in any event have to wait for their inheritance.

- **Self-worth.** On other occasions it might be thought helpful or even necessary for the pride and self-worth of the next generation for them to pay something for their

---

[49] At least a simple majority. See chapter 11 and the discussion of ownership thresholds.
[50] In pure investment terms, particularly if the senior generation are seeking to achieve a rough measure of economic equality the question arises whether notional discounts should be attached to the value of minority outsider carried interests in accordance with normal valuation principles. On the other hand should any credit be given to the insiders who may be assuming more risk in the family enterprise and with lower liquidity when compared with non-business assets allocated to the outsiders?
[51] See chapter 11 and the discussion on restricted matters.
[52] See chapter 17.

interest in the family business rather than having this 'handed to them on a plate'. This view could be shared (or sometimes suggested) by the next generation.

But this needs to be discussed and agreed. It might be disastrous for all concerned if the senior generation wait too long to find out if the next generation are prepared to pay for the family business. Again examples have been encountered in practice where next generation insiders, expecting to inherit the family firm, discover that, instead the senior generation expect to be bought at full market value.

Sometimes the issue of pride and self-worth sits with the senior generation. As a particularly complex example of conflicting aims, the founder might want simultaneously for their business to continue in family ownership, for the outsiders to receive their share of the family silver, to be fully provided in retirement and also for the value of what they have created to be formally recognised, by the purchase price paid for the family business. It might not be possible to accommodate all of these goals.

For these reasons an inter-generational sale, or family buy-out (**FBO**) will be preferable to an outright gift.

Turning now to the terms of the FBO. Usually the terms of an FBO will be somewhere in the middle of a scale between a fully negotiated arm's length agreement and a gift. Accordingly an FBO can be seen as one of those hybrid solutions referred to above.

15.15.2 FBO and price

Starting with price. This can be pitched anywhere on the scale from the full arm's length consideration, that would be paid by a third party purchaser, to a relatively nominal amount, if the senior generation wish to make the point to the next that it is inappropriate to get 'owt for nowt'.

Affordability needs to be considered, as does the primary purpose of employing an FBO rather than making an outright gift to the next generation. It may simply be beyond the means of the next generation to afford or finance an FBO at full market value. This might not actually be necessary. For example, if the primary purpose of the FBO is to finance the retirement of the next generation. Good and careful independent financial advice might show that this could be accomplished by a purchase price much lower than market value.[53] It could be much harder, if not impossible to structure an FBO if the primary reason for this is to achieve fairness, in the sense of absolute equality, between insiders and outsiders, or to pay market value to the founder. It might also be next to impossible, to arrive at a price that is fair to the insiders in the next generation if their pre-succession contribution is to be taken into account.[54] A combination of planning, communication and compromise will be necessary to navigate a path through this maze of considerations. It can be done. In one case involving all of these elements this was achieved by:

---

[53] In 'Rough Corporate Justice' (*Family Business Review* (1998) Vol 11(2)) Glen Ayres argues that the price paid to the senior generation in what we have termed an FBO transaction has to balance needs and the ability to pay. However he takes a 'business first' approach. Ayres argues that the starting point should be a high level examination of the needs of the family business, if it is to fulfill its strategic potential. Only then can the financial needs of the senior generation be taken into account.

[54] This point is considered in more detail in the context of 'freezer shares' in **15.13.5** below.

- A careful analysis of the financial needs of the senior generation in retirement. A good independent financial advisor, was engaged to help them understand what capital sum was needed to provide for these.
- A valuation of the family business. This was considerably higher than the capital sum needed to meet the financial needs as identified.
- A process involving family business consultants. This identified that the primary purpose of the FBO was the need to provide for the retirement of the founder and his spouse. Once these were satisfied, the clear secondary goal was to transfer ownership of the business to the insider son. Significantly a further goal was also identified as a result of the consultancy process. This was to formally recognise the economic value of the family firm and the corresponding lifetime achievement of the founder in creating that value.[55] By identifying and separating these primary and subsidiary goals a realisation emerged that the founder's contribution could be recognised by the wider family otherwise than by the payment of hard cash. In other words the purchase price could be lower than market value.
- Equally crucially the solution was underpinned by good and constructive communication between members of the next generation, both insiders and outsiders, supported by family business consultants. This led to a solution, driven by the next generation to the fairness and equality conundrum. The next generation acknowledged that it was virtually impossible to arrive at a mathematically precise answer to this issue. In practice they were happy to take the view that a rough and fair approximation of equality (with the outsiders receiving a larger share of the non-business assets) would suffice. The next generation were clear that family cohesion was a more important goal than fine-tuning the balance.

15.15.3 Payment structure

Once the price has been set for the FBO the next issue becomes payment structure. The main options are:

- **Commercial borrowing.** The FBO could be financed by third party commercial borrowing taken out by the family company. All the usual lending considerations will apply.

    There might be a reluctance to go down this route. Introducing heavy gearing might be against the conservative instincts of the business family. The business might not be able to obtain mainstream commercial bank lending. Even if this were available, introducing private equity or venture capital borrowing, might not fit with the ownership philosophy of the business family.

- **Next generation borrowing.** Borrowing could be taken out by the next generation purchasers, perhaps supported by a re-mortgage of their home. This could be to support company borrowing or instead of it. This might be necessary to make the finances work.

    It might be thought necessary for the next generation to have some degree of additional personal risk to demonstrate their commitment to the family business. But the next generation might argue that they have already made sacrifices in their careers by joining the family business and point to this as adequate evidence of their commitment.

---

[55] In his article the 'Ten Most Prevalent Obstacles in Family- Business Succession Planning' *Family Business Review* (June 1999) Vol 12(2) at p 117, Thomas Hubler listed 'lack of appreciation, recognition and love' as the most significant obstacle to a successful transition process.

- **Deferred payments.** It is fairly common for all or part of the purchase price payable under an FBO to be deferred and financed from the cash flow of the company.
  These could take various forms, such as payments under a loan-back arrangement to support a buy-back of own shares, instalments of consideration under a re-organisation whereby a Newco buys the assets of the original family company or redemption payments for freezer shares issued in the form of redeemable preference shares.[56]
  Exactly how much of the FBO consideration is deferred depends on various factors, both business and personal, including the risk appetite of both generations. One wise and experienced family business consultant, Steve Swartz (a past president of FFI) argues that asking the founder generation to accept deferred consideration is effectively asking them to risk their wealth and capital twice, first, in setting up and growing the business and then a second time, whilst the business is in the hands of the next generation and the senior generation are waiting for payment that might be needed by them in retirement.
- **Restructuring.** On other occasions it might be necessary, to look at more radical restructuring of the family business to free up funds. For example a non-core business, or surplus investment land could be sold.
  This could be to provide substantial capital for the senior generation on exit. Alternatively capital might need to be channelled in the direction of the outsiders, to satisfy a philosophy of fairness means equality.
  In one farming business the farm was left to the son working on the farm. This was on the basis that he eventually found some way to compensate his siblings. To do so the son needed to assume two roles, that of a farmer and also as a businessman. He built diversified businesses alongside the original farm. He became a part time property developer, sorting out planning permissions, developing and selling buildings on the estate (barn conversions etc). The son regarded his roles as farmer and wealth creator as equally important. It took many years to raise enough funds to pay out equal shares of capital to the non-farming siblings. But he did and the farm, family relationships and the equality principle were all preserved.
- **Carried interest.** See 15.14 above. The larger the carried interest the less that the insiders need to raise by way of FBO consideration.

In the example referred to in the previous paragraph most of the above payment structures were used:

- The next generation family insider re-mortgaged his own home. Although the sums raised were substantial in terms of his personal wealth, this provided a relatively small part of the overall purchase price. This was nevertheless seen as highly symbolic of his commitment to the family business and his ownership.
- Deferred consideration through a loan back of a large part of the buy-back proceeds.[57]
- A term loan from the family business bankers.
- A commitment to investigate the sale of the company's operating premises, to relocate the business and then to use the surplus sale proceeds to effect further buy-backs.

---

[56] These are all explained in a little more detail in the section on Pruning the ownership tree in chapter 11 (Ownership Overview).
[57] See chapter 11 (Ownership Overview) for a discussion of the technical issues involved.

Yes, the arrangements were complex, but they did achieve a bridge between the conflicting aims of allowing the insiders to own the family firm whilst simultaneously providing financial security for the senior generation and a share of the family wealth for the outsiders. The key point however is that this bridge was built on twin pillars. First good relationships between family members and secondly clear and cohesive communication, facilitated by skilled family business consultants. The technical legal tax and financial issues were, in comparison, routine.

15.16 FBO/MBO HYBRIDS

The possibility of sale to non-family management in an MBO transaction is discussed in chapter 12. FBO/MBO hybrids also occur, with the next generation insider leading or supporting a management bid with significant involvement from the rest of the non-family management team.

As a further variant management and other key employees might be given an incentive to remain with the family business, still in family control, as an extra element of planning and risk management to help the business negotiate the inevitable difficulties of the transition period. This will be especially relevant if a non-family leader is chosen as a result of the management succession process. Employee share plans are considered in a little more detail in chapter 6.

15.17 THIRD PARTY SALES

The sale of the family business is considered in detail in chapter 12. That chapter assumes an outright sale to a third party. As seen above, there are many variants and hybrids of sales, some involving family members, others not. The key point to emphasise here is that, ideally a third party sale should be seen as a legitimate succession option, one that can be considered as part of a succession plan, albeit an option that the business owning family might actively chose not to pursue. Sale does not necessarily mean defeat.

The most important word to highlight in the paragraph above is the word 'plan'. Sales of family owned businesses can also be placed on a continuum, ranging from well managed and planned strategic transactions, which extract the best overall terms for the business owning family, to reactive 'fire-sales,' where the family are forced to accept the best, or, in some cases, only offer on the table. Often the only other alternative will be liquidation and closure. The difference between the two ends of the scale can often be the presence or absence of proper and robust succession planning.

15.18 BARRIERS TO OWNERSHIP SUCCESSION

In chapter 7 (Management Succession) we referred to the barriers confronting a senior generation business leader who is facing a management succession process. Although some of the barriers are focused on other stakeholders in the family business system, for example the choice of the next business leader and their capability, many of the obstacles to the management succession process are inwardly focused on the founder themselves.

In the ownership succession dimension many of the barriers are external in the sense that they relate to the discomfort for the senior generation in dealing with the extremely difficult questions raised in this chapter and their impact on the next generation. Those questions include:

- who should own the business in the future?
- whether all children own the business equally, whether or not they work in business?
- how to reconcile the interests of family members who work for the company, and those who pursue other interests, particularly if there are insufficient transferable assets.

Core questions relating to future ownership, can therefore go unresolved or not even articulated for many years. The next generation may not do much to help matters. They might feel that they are not in a position to even raise the question of the future ownership of the family firm. Hendlin speaks of the 'inheritance taboo'.[58] Even asking about the future ownership could be seen as greed on the part of the outsiders or self-serving by the insiders.

That is not to say the members of the next generation might not exert subtle pressure on the senior generation. The insiders might talk about their plans for the future of the business. Or perhaps everything is pointing towards a transition of both management and ownership to family insiders. The outsiders might not expressly ask 'what about us?' But, by their demeanour, attitude or otherwise the outsiders could convey the implied but clear message that 'it's not fair'. The end result could be to stop the senior generation from following through on the original transition plan for insider ownership. This could well have been a factor in the James Davies case.

The primary obstacle to ownership succession can therefore be seen to be communication barriers. The Davies case of course offers a vivid illustration of this.

15.19 FAIR PROCESS

Whilst the primary responsibility for starting the ownership succession process rests with the senior generation, as incumbent owners and with current control of the family enterprise, the business owning family as a whole need to be involved.

The issues raised in this chapter are complex and difficult. Too often the senior generation shoulder the burden of finding the answers alone. This is unfair. After all the next generation will receive the benefit of ownership. It is also likely to be counter-productive. The allocation of assets is much more likely to be perceived as unfair by the next generation if they were not consulted as part of the decision making process and have no understanding of the reasoning behind their parent's allocation of assets.

The object of wider family consultation is first to explore the extent to which a shared vision for the future of the family enterprise can be identified. Secondly, to the extent that different views on ownership emerge within the next generation there is an

---

[58] Steven J Hendlin *Overcoming the Inheritance Taboo: How to Preserve Relationships and Transfer Possessions* (Plume, 2004).

opportunity to explore those differences, and considering the factors and approaches referred to earlier in this chapter, some possible solutions.

Commentators strongly argue that a fair process, where the next generation are fully involved in understanding the issues surrounding allocation of assets, can be vital to the next generation accepting the outcome of that process. As Ayres explains:[59]

> 'Even if there are not enough assets to go around "equally" the next generation will have a much better understanding of the fact that you did your best to be fair and that any economic "inequality" has to do with the nature and amount of the assets available for distribution, not any lack of love or affection.'

One of the key features of the matter referred to in **15.15** above was that the next generation siblings involved readily understood the impossibility of reaching an absolute economic equality in allocating family business and non-business assets. Not only that, they were able to agree a solution that they thought fair themselves and which their parents were happy to accept. This might seem idealistic. However Ayres believes that:

> '… many senior-generation owners will be pleasantly surprised at how their children react to such a discussion. Many children understand far quicker than their parents that absolute equality is simply not possible.'

Of course, despite the views expressed here, there is no guarantee that engaging in a fair ownership succession process will produce a result accepted by all and that family harmony will prevail. There remains the risk that conflict will break out within the next generation. Indeed this might be anticipated in the short term and can be seen as an integral part of the succession process. But Ayres argues that the whole family fair process approach remains valid notwithstanding the risk of more serious conflict. He reasons:

> 'So many clients say, "I could never have such a discussion with my family; it would be World War III." That in fact may be true, but if you fail to have the discussion while you are here to mediate—with love and your special insight and experience—the chances of it becoming World War III when you are gone go up dramatically.'

All this is not to say that the senior generation have nothing to lose. In the short term they risk upsetting family equilibrium. But the long-term damage of ignoring ownership succession questions, or of not involving the next generation in formulating the answers, potentially risks much more serious long term conflict.

Would a fair process ownership succession have prevented family conflict in the Davies family? We can never know. They simply failed to communicate. What we do know is that relationships between all five siblings were good until James discovered the contents of his father's will.[60] We also know that a short while afterwards the family were in court.

---

[59] Glenn Ayres 'Rough Family Justice: Equity in Family Business Succession Planning' *Family Business Review* (1990) Vol 3(1) at p 12. See **7.13.9** for comments on fair process in the context of ownership succession.
[60] See para 38 of the judgment.

15.20 PARALLEL PLANNING

So far in this chapter we have mentioned succession planning on numerous occasions. We have talked about the elements of succession planning. We have also discussed the potential consequences of delaying the process for too long. What we have not done is talk in any detail about succession planning tools and techniques. We will conclude the chapter by looking at one main approach, that of parallel planning, as advocated by Carlock and Ward in their book *Strategic Planning for the Family Business*.[61] The logic underpinning their approach is that, because the business and family systems are irretrievably intertwined, any succession planning process needs to operate simultaneously in both dimensions. It would be as pointless developing a business plan if the family had little real support for the business as it would be producing a plan for long-term family ownership of an enterprise doomed to failure in a struggling industry. Accordingly the 'goal of the Parallel Planning Process is to identify family and business plans that are mutually supportive of the other's needs and goals'.[62] The process involves checking the alignment of the business owning family and the management team in four key areas as shown below:

Figure 15.5: The parallel planning process

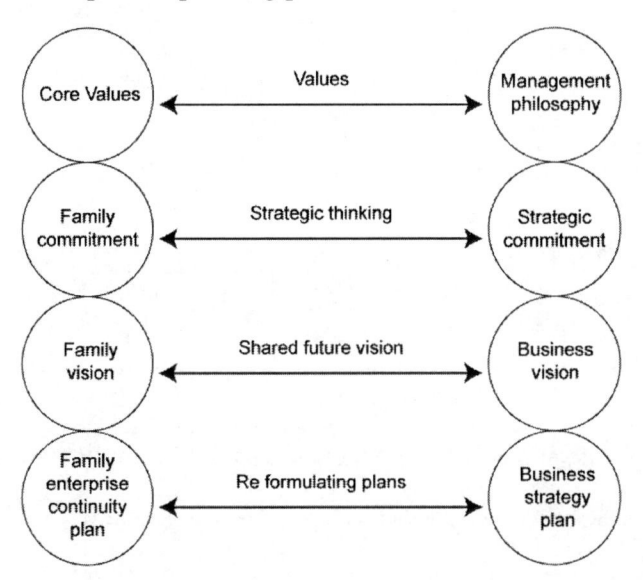

```
Core Values  ←― Values ―→  Management philosophy

Family commitment  ←― Strategic thinking ―→  Strategic commitment

Family vision  ←― Shared future vision ―→  Business vision

Family enterprise continuity plan  ←― Re formulating plans ―→  Business strategy plan
```

Source: Figure 1.7 Strategic Planning for the Family Business (Carlock and Ward, 2001 Palgrave, 2001)

The parallel planning process should provide a detailed examination of three dimensions:
- the internal capabilities of the family business, including the strengths of the family management team, and the available financial resources;
- the external environment in which the family firm is operating, in particular market conditions; and

---

[61] Palgrave, 2001.
[62] At p 13.

- potential family commitment to the business and its long term ownership.[63]

Shown diagrammatically the overlap between these dimensions represents the range of realistic strategic options available for the business owning family, balancing business realism and family ambition. The greater the degree of overlap, the more options that are available for the family business.

Figure 15.6: Strategic options

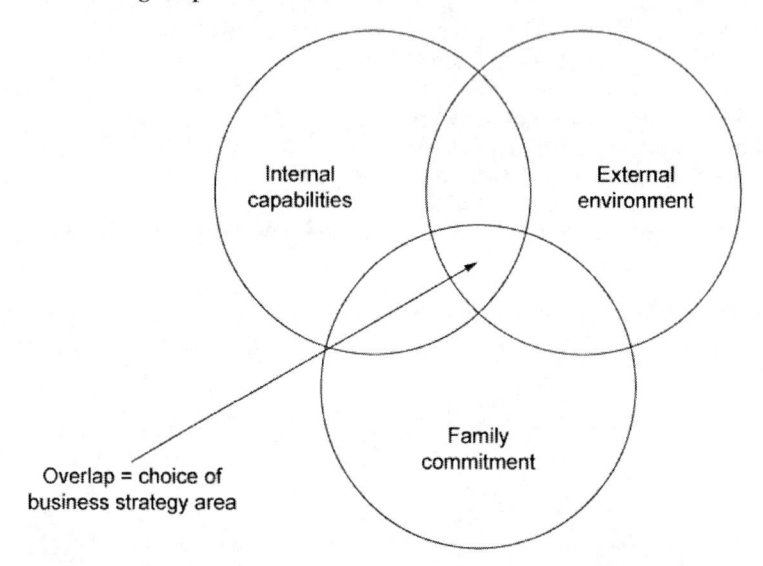

Source: Figure 9.1 Strategic Planning for the Family Business (Carlock and Ward, Palgrave, 2001)

The final part of the process is for the business owning family to decide what they are actually going to do, the 'reinvestment decision'. Ward and Carlock take the view that this should logically be the product of the strategic potential for the business (itself a combination of internal capabilities and markets) and family commitment.

Again, shown diagrammatically the options are as follows:

---

[63] The authors include tools, in the form of questionnaires to help a business owning family examine a number of ownership succession questions, including the overall situation of the family business, ownership philosophy and communication style.

Figure 15.7: The family business reinvestment matrix

management assessment of future prospects = internal capabilities + market conditions		Family Commitment	
		High	Low
Strategic Potential	High	Renew ++	Harvest **
	Medium	Reformulate +	Hold *
	Low	Regenerate +++	Sell ***

Investment needed		Capital released	
High	+++	High	***
Medium	++	Medium	**
Low	+	Low	*

Source: based on Figure 9.2 Strategic Planning for the Family Business (Carlock and Ward, Palgrave, 2001)

This is probably the most complicated diagram used yet, so some explanation of the less obvious terminology used by Carlock and Ward is in order:

- **Renewal** envisages a reasonably significant level of investment and is appropriate for a business owning family wishing to maintain their market position in an industry with good strategic potential.
- **Harvesting** is the approach to be taken by a less committed family with the same business. They will maximise the income they take from the business and minimise investment. They will treat the family business as a cash cow.
- **Reformulating** is where a committed business family re-invest a lower amount in a business whose best days might be behind it.
- **Holding** is where a less committed family continue to live off this business whilst they can.
- **Regeneration** involves a highly committed business family deciding to make a major re-investment, notwithstanding that the family business might be tired and the market in which it operates, highly challenging. It therefore represents the most brave and committed approach.[64]

---

[64] The UK dairy industry provides some good examples. Many dairy farmers are giving up business as a result

- **Selling** speaks for itself and is the logical solution for a family who have lost their commitment to family ownership, perhaps because of the difficulties faced by the business.

Applying this approach to the circumstances of the Saul D Harrison business it would appear that at the time the dispute arose the strategic potential of the business was, at best, medium, and probably best categorised as low. On the facts of the case it is possible to make the assumption that the claimant, Rosemary, was a lone voice of discontent and that the rest of the Harrison family were highly committed to the business. As explained previously the directors decided to re-invest the proceeds of sale of the original factory site in new premises. This would be seen as regeneration in Carlock and Ward's terminology, a major act of faith in and commitment to a struggling business.

Of course the parallel planning process was developed some years after the Harrison family faced their difficulties. There is no evidence that the Harrison family undertook anything approaching a comparable process. Was this an opportunity missed? With the benefit of both hindsight and more recent family business thinking, almost certainly, yes. Whilst there is evidence that the new board in *Saul D Harrison* had begun to formulate a new business plan to regenerate the family firm there is nothing to suggest that the wider family were involved in this process. Producing a parallel family enterprise continuity plan (to use the Carlock and Ward terminology) would have given an opportunity to explore the commitment of the Harrison family as a whole to that plan and the family business generally. If Rosemary was truly an outlier it might have been possible to include an element of partial pruning of the family tree in her case.

If Rosemary's concerns were more widely shared in the family, so as to place the overall family commitment into the low category, then both the parallel planning process and cold hard logic suggests that a more radical solution would have desirable. This could have involved the sale of the business as a whole, but not necessarily so. It might have been possible to arrive at some solution whereby the bulk of the proceeds from the freehold sale were returned to the discontents and a smaller, slimmer business, operating from rented premises and owned by a smaller committed family business cousin clan. Alternatively some form of partition could have been explored with the insiders owning the operating business and the outsiders, including Rosemary, owning the premises and renting these to the trading company.[65]

It will also be recalled that the dispute in *Saul D Harrison* came to a head in the aftermath of management transitions. These involved the introduction of the fourth generation of family management following deaths in the second and third generations which occurring at more or less the same time. This illustrates both the need to commence succession planning at an early stage and also the connection between governance and succession planning. It can be seen that whilst this in depth parallel planning approach has a particular benefit during a transition phase the approach has a much broader application and can properly be seen as part of the overall governance process of the family firm.

---

of the current market conditions. But a minority of farmers are choosing to invest heavily in machinery and in buying the herds of those farmers who are selling out.
[65] Demergers are considered in chapter 11.

15.21 CONCLUSION

The importance of the succession process to the wealth and happiness of the business owning family cannot be underestimated. Neither can the level of complexity and challenge involved.

Whilst there might be dreams of continuity of family ownership, preconceptions can be dangerous. One of the key objects of the ownership succession process is to explore both the commitment of the wider business family and viable alternatives, before settling on the most appropriate solution and structure for the next generation.

A successful process will require a huge amount of patience and compassion but also drive purpose and planning. The primary responsibility for driving this process rests with the senior generation, as the incumbent holders of power, status, control and ownership of the family firm. But the whole business family has a role to play, be they next generation, management insiders or outsiders.

Communication is key. Families that take the approach that 'we are not that sort of family' and avoid talking about succession issues are seriously limiting their prospects of achieving a successful outcome.

CHAPTER 16

TAX AND FAMILY BUSINESS OWNERSHIP

David Pierce

16.1 OVERVIEW

The tax aspects of succession planning for family owned businesses is a huge subject in its own right, or, viewed alternatively, a series of separate subjects covering all the main taxes. In this chapter we seek simply to provide a brief and basic overview of the issues.

Whilst all taxes need to be considered as part of succession planning, the two principal areas of concern will be inheritance tax and capital gains tax. This is regardless of whether one is dealing with sales by the senior generation, gifts to the next generation during the lifetime of the donor, or on death. Our starting point will be the reliefs that will be most relevant to any tax planning.

16.2 INHERITANCE TAX – BUSINESS PROPERTY RELIEF

Without business property relief (BPR) a gift of an interest in a family company would, unless some other relief, such as agricultural property relief applies, fall into the general inheritance tax net. So, unless the value of the interest gifted, when aggregated with other gifts made in the immediately preceding seven year period prior to the gift of shares, is less than the nil rate band[1] if the donor dies within seven years the chargeable element of the gift is added to the estate in determining the IHT liability. If there were no other gifts in the seven year period prior to the gift of shares, then this gift takes the first part of, or all, the nil rate band if an element of the gift is not eligible for BPR. Any tax payable on the balance is abated if the death was more than three years after the gift.[2] If the donor survives for 7 years the potentially exempt transfer becomes fully exempt and falls out of the inheritance tax net.

BPR is therefore likely to be the most relevant and useful relief so far as family business succession planning is concerned. This reduces the value of a transfer of value by a relevant percentage, either 100% or 50%, provided certain conditions are met. The relief is available on lifetime gifts, transfers on death and in relation to the provisions applying to trusts, the 'ten year charge'.

---

[1] £325,000 for tax year 2016–2017.
[2] The abatement is 20% of the tax if death was between 3 and 4 years after the gift, and then by a further 20% for each subsequent year which has elapsed. If there is a possible exposure to a tax liability if death occurs within 7 years, then consideration should be given to taking out life assurance to cover this potential liability.

In relation to companies, it should be noted that a company and all its subsidiaries are members of a group, and that 'holding' company and 'subsidiary' company have the same meanings as in the Companies Act.[3]

Therefore shares in holding companies which own shares in trading subsidiaries can qualify for the relief, although one needs to be aware that certain assets owned may be 'excepted' assets and so the amount of the relief could be restricted.

16.2.1 Types of business property and BPR rates

The types of business property which qualify for BPR, and the rates of relief are as follows:

- Unincorporated businesses – 100% relief.
- Unquoted securities which either by themselves or with other such securities or unquoted shares gave the transferor control – 100% relief.
- A holding of any size of unquoted shares in a company not listed on a recognised stock exchange (the AIM and OFEX markets are not recognised markets for this purpose) – 100% relief.
- Shares or securities giving control of a quoted company – 50% relief.
- Land, buildings, plant or machinery in a partnership, or in a controlled company, or in a settlement in which the transferor has a life interest – 50% relief.

16.2.2 BPR – qualifying conditions

In order to qualify for BPR:
- the business has to be a qualifying business; and
- the asset must be relevant business property (see above); and
- the asset must have been owned for a minimum period.

16.2.3 BPR and investment businesses

A business for the above purposes includes a business carried on in exercise of a profession or vocation, but does not include a business carried on otherwise than with a view to profit. But a business, or interest in a business (which will include an interest as a partner), or shares or securities in a company, do not qualify if the business (or the business of the company) 'consists wholly or mainly' of dealing in securities, stocks or shares, land or buildings or making or holding investments. There are exceptions to the latter category, which includes being a holding company of one or more companies whose business does qualify. A land holding, or dealing, business can qualify if its activities include building construction, or land development. The housing stock of a building business can qualify if it is regarded as trading stock.

In order to meet the definition of 'consists wholly or mainly' the business has to satisfy a quantitative test of 50% or more of its activities qualifying not excluded. A number of tax cases that have looked at this definition.[4] The conclusion that can be drawn from the cases is that one needs to consider all relevant factors, such as, the net profit generated

---

[3] Companies Act 2006, s 1159, Sch 6; IHTA 1984, s 103(1), (2), s 104.
[4] See *Farmer (Executors of Farmer Deceased) v IRC* (1999) STC 321; *Stedman's Executors v IRC* (2002) STI

from the various activities, turnover, asset values, net capital employed, management time involved in the activities, as well as considering the entire enterprise in the round.

In family businesses surplus funds are often built up, and invested in assets unconnected with the main trading activity, such as investment properties. These can become of significant value, and this can affect the ability to claim BPR. If the wholly or mainly qualifying business activity condition is not met, then no BPR can be claimed. A partial claim is not possible. If the non-business activities are significant then it may be necessary to consider restructuring he family company, for example, by transferring the assets to a new independent company, so that at least BPR can be claimed on the qualifying business element.

There is a provision in the legislation which says that an investment subsidiary does qualify for BPR[5] if the activity of the subsidiary is wholly or mainly the holding of land for use by other group trading companies. On a strict reading of the legislation this provision appears to only relate to subsidiary companies and not to holding companies. Therefore if the holding company owns property used by the trading subsidiaries that property could be considered to be an investment for the BPR test. The counter argument is that it would be wrong to consider the property as an investment, because it is held to facilitate the trading activities in the group. It is to be hoped that HMRC would not seek to use this anomaly in the legislation in a bona fide trading group situation.

Many family company groups have a holding company which owns both shares in the trading subsidiaries, and the property from which the trading subsidiaries operate. In a strict sense the holding company is an investment company as its only activities are holding the subsidiaries shares, and property which it lets to other companies. However there are special rules for holding companies,[6] which provide that:

> 'the investment condition does not apply to "shares in ... a company if the business of that company consists wholly or mainly in being a holding company of one or more companies whose business is not excluded by IHTA 1984, s 105(3)".'

Therefore provided all the subsidiaries are wholly or mainly trading, then the holding company will qualify for BPR.

16.2.4 Unquoted shares

Since a change in the legislation effective from 6 April 1996, any unquoted shares in a qualifying company, are eligible for BPR. This was an extremely valuable change as far as family businesses are concerned, as it enables any share owning family member to transfer their shares to the next generation, or other family member, without any Inheritance tax liability. There is no requirement regarding percentage shareholding to be held, or the need to be a director, or employee of the company. So even a 1% shareholding can qualify for BPR.

---

issue 33; *Phillips and Others (Phillips' Executors) v HMRC* (2006) STC SCD 639. See Toby Harris *Agricultural and Business Property Relief* (5th edn, Bloomsbury Professional) for a helpful discussion of these and other cases.
[5] See IHTA 1984, s 111(b).
[6] Inheritance Tax Act 1984, s 105(4).

16.2.5 BPR and preference shares

The legislation refers to unquoted shares, and does not specify that the shares have to be ordinary shares. Preference shares and redeemable shares are not specifically excluded from BPR. This may give some tax planning opportunities, and could be useful where the retired generation want some certainty regarding dividend returns and are issued with preference shares, leaving the next generation with the risk (and reward) associated with the ordinary shares.

16.2.6 Unquoted securities

BPR can also be claimed on unquoted securities, such as loan stock, in addition to shares, but they must on their own, or with other securities or unquoted shares give the transferor control of the company.

16.2.7 BPR, control and property

Whilst the 'control' definition has become of less relevance now that any unquoted shares qualify for BPR, it is still of importance when property used in the company's business is owned by shareholders personally. In these circumstances BPR at 50% can be available if the owner controls the company. In determining whether control does exist the individual can take into account shares held by their spouse, or civil partner, and a trust in which they have a life interest.

16.2.8 Binding contracts for sale

If shares, or an interest in a qualifying business, are to qualify for BPR there must be no binding contract for sale in place at the time of the transfer. A binding contract for sale is considered to exist if, for example, there is a binding obligation on other shareholders, or partners, to acquire the shares, or an interest in the business, on death. Therefore care needs to be taken when drafting shareholders' and partnership agreements. The simple solution to this potential problem is to use cross options. A call option then gives the ongoing shareholders / partners an option to be able to acquire the deceased's interest. The executors can also have a put option to sell their shares / business interests to the partners or remaining shareholders.

Although there is a clear expectation by all concerned that the options will be exercised, it is not certain that this will happen. In the circumstances HMRC will be prepared to accept that no binding obligation to buy and sell the relevant property has been created.

Cross options are the main device used in shareholder protection key man life cover arrangements.

16.2.9 Qualifying period

The final qualifying condition for BPR is that the relevant property must have been held for a minimum period of two years. If the current property has been held for less than two years, and it is replaced with other property that qualified immediately before its replacement, then the two periods of ownership can be aggregated to determine whether the two year ownership period condition has been met. This can be useful where there has, for example, been a restructuring of the company (to which the provisions of TCGA 1992, ss 126–136 apply) before any gift of shares, as part as the overall family succession plan.

16.2.10 BPR, family business partnerships and business property

A question for partnerships is whether the property should be held by the partnership or outside the partnership? If it is not part of the partnership assets, then only 50% BPR will be available. There is no requirement for the individual to 'control' the partnership as there is in relation to property owned by a family member and used by a family company. However if the property is on the balance sheet of the partnership as an asset then, provided the other conditions are met, 100% BPR is available. If the partners do not own the property in the same proportions as trading profits are shared, then there needs to be an agreement as to how the profits from any property disposal are to be shared. The simple inclusion of the property into the partnership can substantially increase the BPR available.

The tax treatment of family owned property is considered in detail at **16.10** below.

16.3 INHERITANCE TAX – EXCEPTED ASSETS

Even if the other qualifying conditions for BPR are met, there may still be a restriction in the amount of BPR that can be claimed because some of the assets are considered under IHTA 1984, s 112 to be 'excepted assets'. An asset will fall into this category if:

- it has not been wholly or mainly used for the purpose of the business during the previous 2 years, or its entire period of ownership if this is less than 2 years; or
- it is not required at the time of the transfer for the future use of the business.

Over the years family companies can acquire a number of assets that may be unconnected with the trading activity and are more in the nature of investments. These may be classified as excepted assets, and therefore create issues for inheritance tax purposes when it comes to passing on the share ownership of family companies.

The investment part of a mainly trading company is not automatically an excepted asset. For it to be an excepted asset it must not be part of the business. It is recognized that a company can have a hybrid activity which consists of trading and managing investments. However simply because a trading company owns investment properties does not mean they will necessarily qualify for BPR. It needs to be established that they constitute part of the business of the company. 'Business' for this purpose being the normal definition of what constitutes a business. Passive holding of land or property in anticipation of a rental income of some sort is invariably considered to be an investment activity[7]. So, for example, if properties are let on twenty-five year leases with five year reviews and all the company has to do is collect the rent and arrange the reviews, then this probably does not constitute a business. However if more active management of the property concerned is required, such as regular reviews of the properties, handling changes in tenants, and management of the properties, then this is more active then it

---

[7] See the Northern Ireland Court of Appeal case of *McCall and Keenan (as personal representatives of McClean Dec'd) v HMRC* (2009) STC 990.

could be classified as a business and BPR would be available. In the latter circumstances it would be advisable to minute the meetings, where decisions in connection with the active management are made.

So whilst a company may pass the wholly or mainly test for BPR, if there is investment property owned, then careful consideration should be given as to whether it is an excepted asset. If necessary a more active approach to the management of the property should be taken.

16.3.1 Surplus cash

HMRC will commonly look at the level of surplus cash within a business as being a potential excepted asset. This can be an issue for family companies that build up cash reserves before any reinvestment back into the business has been made. HMRC will want to know whether there are any plans to use for the excess cash in the future. This stance is supported by case-law.[8] In the particular case the executors were unable to argue that, because the cash may be needed, should an opportunity arise to use the cash in the future, it was required for the future use of the business. It is therefore important that family businesses keep evidence, perhaps by board minutes, or business plans, as to why it is holding surplus cash not required for day-to-day business purposes.

16.3.2 Investment activity

The investment part of a mainly trading company is not necessarily an excepted asset. HMRC do recognise that there can be hybrid companies with businesses comprised of partly trading, and partly investment activities. In such cases the investments are part of the business and so are not excepted assets. However it has to be established that the investment assets are part of the business. This can be difficult, and there is much debate on how that can be established. As with property, if there is active management of the investment, rather than a passive management, then there is a stronger case that it is part of the business. For example the investment of surplus cash may not take much time, if it is left on short-term deposit. Alternatively, if there is more active management of the cash by considering different rates available and regular transfers of cash deposits between accounts, then it may be possible to resist an 'excepted asset' claim by HMRC.

16.4 AGRICULTURAL PROPERTY RELIEF

Provided the qualifying conditions are met, agricultural property relief (APR) can be claimed at generally 100% of the agricultural value. In some circumstances the rate of relief is only 50%. The relief is also available in respect of shares or securities in a company, if part of the value is attributable to the agricultural value of agricultural property.

It is important to note that the relief only applies to the agricultural value, so any alternative use value, or 'hope value' in the land will not qualify for APR. There may be a potential claim for BPR on the excess value but this will depend on the circumstances.

---

[8] *Barclays Bank Trust Co Ltd v IRC* (1998) STC (SCD) 125.

An initial question to consider is the definition of agricultural property. This is land or pasture, and any building used in connection with the intensive rearing of livestock or fish (if the building is occupied with agricultural land, and the use of the building is ancillary to that of the land). It also includes cottages, farm buildings and farmhouses, which together with the land occupied with them, are of a character appropriate to the property. There have been a number of cases regarding farmhouses, and these should be reviewed if there is a doubt as to whether the farmhouse is appropriate in character to the agricultural activities.[9]

APR cannot be claimed unless:

- the property was occupied by the transferor for the purposes of agriculture for the 2 years before the transfer; or
- the property was owned by the transferor for the whole of 7 years before the transfer, and throughout that period was occupied by the transferor or someone else for the purposes of agriculture.

The relief is 100% if:

- the transferor had right to vacant possession, or the right to obtain it within the next 12 months; or
- the pre 1981 full time working farmer provisions apply;[10]
- the property was let for periods exceeding 12 months on or after 1 September 1995 under the Agricultural Tenancies Act 1995; or
- the property has been dedicated to wildlife habitats on or after 26 November 1996.

If the agricultural property qualifies under the other conditions but does not qualify for 100% relief, normally tenancies granted before 1 September 1995, then 50% relief should be available.[11]

As far as shares in family farming companies are concerned, where the value is partly attributable to the agricultural value of property, then APR will be available on that proportionate value if:

- the shares held gave the transferor control of the company immediately before the transfer (for the definition of control see above comments in **16.2.7** above); and
- either the property was occupied by the company for at least 2 years prior to the transfer, and the shares were held by the transferor throughout that period; or the property was owned by the company throughout a 7-year period before the

---

[9] See *Lloyds TSB as personal representatives of R Antrobus Deceased v CIR* (2002) STC (SCD) 468; *Arnander (Executors of McKenna Deceased) v HMRC* (2006) STC (SCD) 800 and other cases. Particular issues arise with small holdings and 'hobby farms' with a few acres surrounding large farmhouses.

[10] These provisions are complicated but (broadly) apply if the transferor has been beneficially entitled to their interest since before 10 March 1981; and if he had disposed of it by transfer of value immediately before that date, he would have been entitled to claim 50% relief between 6 April 1976 and 10 March 1981; and that relief would not have been restricted by reference to the limits of £250,000 or 1,000 acres; and the interest from 10 March 1981 to the date of transfer did not give him vacant possession rights, and did not fail to give those rights because of any act or deliberate omission by the transferor.

[11] In family farming businesses it is not unusual for the farming business to be passed on to the next generation but the land retained by the senior generation. This happened, for example in James Davies' case. As the arrangements are often informal there can sometimes be doubt as to the legal status of the property arrangements, for example whether an Agricultural Holdings Act tenancy has been created, which in turn cast doubt over the IHR and APR position.

transfer and throughout that period was occupied by the company or another for the purposes of agriculture, and the transferor owned the shares throughout that 7-year period.

There must not be a binding contract for sale of the property at the time of the transfer, otherwise APR will not be given. The comments in **16.2.9** above regarding options will also apply in this regard.

16.5 INHERITANCE TAX AND FAMILY BUSINESS TRUSTS

16.5.1 Overview: 2006, revolution or business as usual?

With effect from 21 March 2006 there was a major change in the tax treatment of trusts.

Initially it was thought that these changes would herald the end of the use of trusts. However they can still be of use in a family business, particularly in succession situations. Because of the various types of trusts and circumstances that can be encountered, it is inappropriate to undertake a full review of the tax treatment of all the types of trusts in this book.[12] However it is useful to consider some general principles, the basic types of trusts relevant to shares in family companies, the position for trusts set up after 21 March 2006 and how held by these types of trusts are affected by the 2006 changes.

16.5.2 Main types of trust

The principal types of UK based trusts relevant to family companies are as follows:[13]

Trusts set up pre 21 March 2006
- **Interest in possession** where one individual, or group of individuals, are entitled to the income arising from the trust asset, for example, dividends on shares held in a family company.
- **Discretionary trusts** where income is allocated between a group of beneficiaries at the discretion of the trustees.
- **Accumulation and maintenance Trusts** where income is applied at the discretion of the trustees to initially minor children, often grandchildren of the settlor, but they have to acquire an interest in possession in the underlying capital assets of the trust before they are 25. After 21 March 2006 many of these trusts reduced the age at which the children acquired an interest in possession, and also acquired their share of the capital, to the age of 18.
- If this change was not made then either the trust fell within the 18-25 trust regime, or became one of the new 'related property' trusts which started from 21 March 2006. It is thought unlikely there are many of these types of trusts which own shares in family companies, so their tax treatment will not be considered in more detail.

---

[12] For a more detailed review see Rayney *Tax Planning for Family and Owner-Managed Companies 2015/16* (Bloomsbury, 2016).
[13] See also chapter 14.

Trusts set up after 21 March 2006:

- **Relevant property trusts** – these may be Interest in Possession trusts or Discretionary trusts, but for Inheritance tax purposes they are treated in the same way.
- **Bereaved minors trusts** – these may attract similar reliefs to those previously enjoyed by Accumulation and Maintenance trusts. As it is considered that they will have little application in a family business situation, and it is likely that the flexibility of Relevant Property trusts will be more appropriate in most circumstances, they will not be considered in any further detail.

16.5.3 Pre-2006 trusts and inheritance tax: general principles

The general principles of the Inheritance tax treatment of trusts, as far as any shares in a family company which are held by the trust are as follows:

IHT on setting up

When a pre-21 March 2006 discretionary trust was set up there was potentially an Inheritance tax charge. This would have been calculated by taking the value of the assets settled on the trust, deducting any reliefs, such as BPR, and then the unused portion of the nil rate band of the settlor. The balance would have then been charged to Inheritance tax at the lifetime rate, of 20%. The unused portion of the nil rate band of the settlor is calculated by taking the nil rate band at the time of the settlement and then deducting the value of any chargeable lifetime transfers in the previous seven years. If the assets settled on the discretionary trust were shares in the family company and they qualified for 100% BPR on the full value of the shares then there would have been no Inheritance tax paid on the setting up of the trust.

No change in beneficiary

Provided there is no change in the beneficiary entitled to the life interest in a pre-21 March 2006 life interest trust then inheritance tax only needs to be considered on the death of the beneficiary, or on the termination of their life interest during their lifetime. On the death of the life tenant the value of the assets in the trust forms part of their estate, and the trust will have a potential inheritance tax liability. However whether any liability arises will depend on the extent to which BPR or APR can be claimed in respect of the shares. If 100% BPR is available on the full value of the shares then no Inheritance tax will arise on that proportion of the trust assets.

Gifts of life interests

If a life tenant of a pre-21 March 2006 life interest trust gives away their interest, or it is removed by the trustees, and the assets remain in the trust, this will bring these assets into the relevant property trust provision. There may be a charge to inheritance tax if BPR or APR is not available, or the value of the chargeable assets is greater than the nil rate band.

Death of life tenant

Also, if the former life tenant dies within seven years of the gift of their life interest, then the value of the life interest falls into the estate. If the value of the life interest is represented by shares in a family company, then whether there is any Inheritance tax payable will depend on whether the shares qualify for BPR. As in the situation on death, if 100% BPR is available on the whole of the share value there will be no tax payable in respect of the termination of the life interest so far as the value is represented by the family company shares. If the life tenant dies within the seven year period, the trust must still hold the shares and they must still qualify for BPR at the date of death.

Tax on appointment of assets

If assets are appointed out to a life tenant, or another beneficiary, from a pre-21 March 2006 life interest trust, and provided there has been no change in the trust which brings it within the relevant property trust regime from 21 March 2006, then there is no Inheritance tax charge on the appointment out of the trust of family company shares held by the trust. However there could be capital gains tax issues to consider and this will be considered at **16.6**.

10 year charge

A pre 21 March 2006 discretionary trust is subject to a 'ten year charge' for Inheritance tax purposes. This ten year charge is calculated by taking the value of the assets at the anniversary date, deducting any reliefs due, such as BPR, and then deducting the nil rate band at the time, or a proportion of that band. The excess is then charged to inheritance tax at 30% of the 'effective rate', normally the lifetime rate of currently 20%. This gives a tax charge of 6%. If the trust was set up after 26 March 1974 then one also has to take into account any cumulative transfers by the settlor in the seven years before the trust was set up. If there have been assets added to the trust in the previous ten year period then there are calculations to apportion the charge on those assets, based on how long they have been held in the trust. The nil rate band which the trust can claim for the ten year anniversary depends on whether there are any related settlements. Related settlements are settlements established on the same day by the same settlor. If there are none, which good planning should ensure is the case, then the trust will be entitled to a full nil rate band. Any undistributed and accumulated income is not treated as an asset of the trust for the purposes of the ten year charge. If the only asset of the trust is shares in the family company, which qualify for 100% BPR on their full value, then there will be no tax payable on the ten year anniversary.

Appointment out of capital

If capital is appointed out of pre-21 March 2006 discretionary settlements, then there may be a 'proportionate charge' on the value of the assets appointed out. There is no charge if the appointment of capital is within 3 months of the setting up of the trust or a ten-year anniversary. As with the ten year anniversary, if the trust was set up after 27 March 1974, in addition to the cumulative transfers of the trust, one also has to take into account the cumulative transfers of the settlor in the seven years before the setting up of the trust in determining the proportionate charge. If the trust was set up before 27 March 1974 then the settlor's cumulative transfers can be ignored. If it is before the first ten-year anniversary, then the proportionate charge, for a post 27 March 1974, trust is calculated on the basis of a complex set of provisions (a detailed description of which are beyond the scope of this book) taking into account the value of property in the trust, the settlor's cumulative transfers and the time that has elapsed since the trust was set up.

The important point to note in relation to shares held in family companies is that for the purposes of calculating the proportionate charge before the first ten-year anniversary, BPR is not deducted from the share value in determining the tax charge. So whilst there may have been no Inheritance tax to pay on setting up the trust there may be a liability on any transfer of capital out of the trust within the first 10 years.

16.5.4 Inheritance tax and post 2006 trusts

10 year charge

On the tenth anniversary of the commencement of a discretionary trust set up after 21 March 2006 and every relevant property trust (generally all other trusts set up after that date), there is also a ten year charge to inheritance tax. This is calculated in the same way as described above for pre 21 March 2006 discretionary trusts.

Appointment out of capital

If there is an appointment of capital out of a discretionary or relevant property trust after the first, or subsequent, ten-year anniversary, then there is a proportionate charge. This is calculated by using the rate of tax paid on the previous ten-year anniversary and then adjusting it to reflect the number of quarters that have elapsed since the ten-year anniversary. The rate of tax is adjusted if there have been any additions to the trust since the last ten year anniversary. The comments made above also apply to these trusts for any transfers of capital before the first ten-year anniversary.

16.6 CAPITAL GAINS TAX

If the shares of the current generation in the family business are transferred on death then, as far as the done is concerned, they will take over those shares at the value at that time, and there is no capital gains tax payable by the estate. Therefore there is an effective tax-free uplift of the share values.

If instead the shares are given away whilst the donor is still alive then this is treated as a disposal for capital gains tax purposes. The starting point is that the shares are deemed to have been transferred at their market value. This is not good news for the donor as they are faced with a tax charge without having received any consideration. Fortunately it is possible to holdover the capital gain in certain circumstances. There are two holdover reliefs available.

- gifts of business assets – under TCGA 1992, s 165; or
- gifts on which inheritance tax is chargeable – under TCGA 1992, s 260.

16.6.1 CGTA, s 165

The relief can be claimed under s 165 if the gifted asset is either:

- An asset, or an interest in an asset used for the purpose of a trade carried on by the donor, or his personal company (a company in which at least 5% of the voting rights are held), or a member of a trading group the holding company of which is his personal company; or
- Shares or securities of a trading company, or the holding company of a trading group, where the shares are not listed on a recognised stock exchange, or the company is the donor's personal company.

For the above purposes a trading company, or trading group is one carrying on trading activities that do not to a substantial extent include non-trading activities. HMRC have indicated that the non-trading activities must not represent more than 20%. They will look at turnover, profit, assets and management time in assessing whether the non-qualifying element exceeds 20% of these aspects. However HMRC do not indicate whether the business has to fail on all four accounts, or only two or three, or even one.

The test for holdover relief is therefore more restrictive than the 'wholly or mainly' for business purposes test applied for BPR.

16.6.2 Holdover relief and non-business assets

If the company holds non-business assets then there is a restriction on the holdover relief if the donor has held at least 25% of the voting rights in the previous 12 months, or within the same period it has been his personal company, ie he was able to exercise at least 5% of the votes. Voting rights do not for these purposes include the rights of associates or connected persons. Non-business assets are assets which on a disposal could give rise to a capital gain, which are not used for the purpose of the company's trade.

If there are non-business assets then the amount of the gain which can be held over is reduced by the following fraction:

Market value of chargeable non business assets / market value of chargeable assets

Chargeable assets are those where a gain accruing on a disposal would be a chargeable gain and includes plant and machinery. The goodwill of the business is also included even if it is not recognised in the accounts.

The restriction, if there are non-business assets, may mean that for some family businesses an election under s 165 will not relieve the whole of the potential capital gains tax problem. Also it cannot be used for investment companies.

16.6.3 CGTA 1992, s 260

In these situations s 260 may help. Relief can be claimed under this section if the gift is a chargeable transfer for inheritance tax. This does not include gifts which are potentially exempt transfers (PETs), and therefore does not include outright gifts to another individual.

It also, before 21 March 2006, did not include gifts to interest in possession trusts, however as since that date such trusts are now relevant property trusts, gifts to them can now be eligible for a claim. It is not necessary that Inheritance tax is paid on the gift, but only that it might be payable except for reliefs, or the value of the gift is covered by the nil rate band. Relief is generally claimed under s 260 on gifts into trust. There is no restriction on the type of asset being settled, hence its usefulness if under s 165 there would be a restriction, or it is shares in a non-trading company.

A claim under s 260 cannot be made if the trust is settlor-interested. Also a claim is not possible under s 165 if the gift is to a settlor-interested trust. This would be the case if the spouse, civil partner, or minor child is a beneficiary of the trust. In the case of a family businesses it is likely the intended beneficiaries will be the children. If they are minors at the time of the gift into the trust, then they need to be excluded from benefitting until they are at least 18 years old. The spouse can also be a beneficiary, but only when the settlor has died and they are then a widow or widower.

If a trust is not settlor-interested when a claim under s 165 or s 260 is made, but within 6 years of the end of the year of assessment when the gift was made, it does become settlor interested, then there is a claw back of the relief and tax becomes payable. A claim under s 260 can also be made when assets are transferred out of a trust, if that would give rise to a chargeable event for Inheritance tax.

16.6.4 Residence

If a claim has been made under either s 165 or s 260 and the donee ceases to be resident or ordinarily resident in the UK within 6 years of the end of the year of assessment when the gift was made, then the held over gain becomes assessable. HMRC initially look to the donee to pay the tax, but if they don't pay then they have recourse to the donor.[14] In these circumstances it is advisable for the donor, or trustees, to seek an indemnity. A claim cannot be made under either section if the donee is not resident or ordinarily resident in the UK.

16.7 ENTREPRENEUR'S RELIEF

16.7.1 The importance of entrepreneur's relief

Over the years we have seen various capital gains tax reliefs to benefit entrepreneurs when they either retire from the business or sell it.[15]

---

[14] Taxation of Chargeable Gains Act 1992, s 168.
[15] For many years we had retirement relief, this was then replaced by business asset taper Relief, which did not depend on the age of the vendor, and now we have entrepreneur's relief. Initially this relief meant that an individual had a lifetime allowance of up to £1m of gains which could be taxed at 10%. The relief now applies to up to £10m of lifetime gains.

There are various reasons why the retiring generation might want or need to sell some or all of their shares in the family company. They might need to realise some capital value from their shareholding. This could be because they have not made adequate pension provision, or they want the comfort of capital in their own names rather than be reliant on the continued success of the family business to provide income. The younger generation might want the freedom of not having the older generation continuing to have an involvement through their shareholding.

Ownership can be transferred in a number of ways, considered earlier in this part of the book, but it is useful to consider how any capital received will be taxed. If it is a capital receipt derived from a shareholding, then it will be subject to capital gains tax. Ideally the individual will want to claim entrepreneur's relief (ER) so that the first £10m of any gain (provided ER has not been claimed on any earlier disposal) is taxed at 10%. ER is also available on gifts.

If ER cannot be claimed, then the proportion of the gain which when added to other income in the tax year exceeds the basic rate band will be taxed at 20%. The proportion of the gain which effectively uses the balance of the basic rate income tax band is taxed at 10%. It is likely that in most family business cases, with relatively high earners, the difference, if ER can be claimed, will be between 20% and 10% on the first £10m of the gain, a potential tax saving of up to £1.0m.

16.7.2 Qualifying conditions

In order to qualify for ER the individual has to meet a number of conditions in relation to shares in a company, being:

- the individual must have held at least 5% of the ordinary issued share capital and voting rights for at least the 12 months before the sale; and
- the individual must throughout that 12-month period have been an officer or employee of the company, or a company which is a member of the group; and
- the company must be a trading company and not have non-trading activities which are substantial.

In calculating whether an individual holds at least 5% one does not take into account shares held by associates of the individual, such as their minor children, spouse or civil partner.

If the disposal of the business is not of shares, then to qualify for ER there must also be a material disposal of an interest in the business where the assets were used. The relief is not simply due on the disposal of business assets, in the case of a partnership or sole trader business. For example if a husband and wife carry on a business in partnership, and sell the premises from which the business operates, but continue the business as before in the same profit sharing ratios from leased premises, then ER cannot be claimed on the gain on the sale of the property. However if instead, in this example, the husband retired from the business at the time of the sale and their son became a partner, with the wife taking a substantially lower share of the profits as well, then ER could be claimed by both spouses if the property had been a partnership asset. A claim would also have been possible under the associated disposal rules by the husband if he owned the property personally, subject to any restriction on the relief if rent was charged to the partnership.

16.7.3 Entrepreneur's relief and spouses

These conditions raise a number of planning issues:
- If shares are held jointly by a husband and wife then they are each considered to hold one half of the shares. So for example if a couple hold 8% of the shares, then this is considered to be 4% each. If one of them works in the company and the other doesn't then neither of them will qualify for ER. However by the non-working spouse giving their shares to the other person at least 12 months before the sale, then the whole shareholding can qualify for ER, provided the other conditions are met.
- If a husband and wife each own shares, but only one works in the business, the shares held by the non-working spouse do not qualify for ER. In these circumstances either the non-working spouse can be appointed a director, or company secretary, or become an employee, at least 12 months before the sale, or the non-working spouse should consider giving their shares to the other spouse. Provided the working spouse already has a shareholding of at least 5%, this gift does not need to be more than 12 months before the sale.
- If the gain going to be made by one spouse is less than £10m, and the other spouse also has shares but does not qualify for entrepreneur's relief, then a gift of shares to the qualifying spouse can increase the relief claimed. This transfer does not need to be made more than 12 months before the sale if the qualifying spouse already meets the conditions as to having at least 5%, and being an officer or employee.
- If the total taxable gain on shares held by one spouse is likely to be more than £10m, and there are no shares held by the other spouse (who does not work in the company). In these circumstances they should consider gifting some shares to the non-working spouse and making them a director or employee of the company. Both these events must happen more than 12 months before the sale.

16.7.4 Tax planning and the wider family

Tax planning opportunities may also exist so far as the wider family are concerned.

A parent could gift some shares to a child, so that they had a shareholding of more than 5%. A claim under TCGA 1992, s 165 would have to be made in respect of the gift to holdover the capital gain, and it would be necessary for there to be no non trading assets, owned by the company. As with the gift to the spouse, this would need to happen more than 12 months before the sale, and the son or daughter would need to be an officer or employee of the company during that period. Depending on the age of the son or daughter it may be difficult to justify a position as a director. If they are made an employee then they must actually work in the business, and not just be paid a wage.

16.7.5 Trading company requirement

As far as the company is concerned it must be a 'trading company'. The definition of trading company is different than for business property relief, and is the same as for holdover relief under TCGA 1992, s 165, as described above, namely a 20% test.[16]

---

[16] Taxation of Chargeable Gains Act 1992, s 165A.

In the case of a group, which is the holding company and all its 51% subsidiaries, one or more of the members must carry on a trading activity, and when taking the activities of all the members together, they must not include substantial non trading activities. If a company has a shareholding in another company of 50% or less, then that will be treated as a non-trading activity unless it qualifies as a joint venture.

The holding will be classified as a joint venture if:
- it is a shareholding of more than 10%; and
- it is in a company which is a trading company, or the holding company of a trading group; and
  - 75% or more of the ordinary shares in the company are held by no more than five persons.
  - if the company meets the trading condition, but there are non-trading assets, there is no restriction on the amount of the gain that qualifies for ER.

Where the company has ceased to trade within three years immediately preceding the disposal, ER is still available if the 5% ownership, director or employee, and trading tests were met in the 12 months before the trading ceased.

16.7.6 Surplus cash

It is not uncommon for family businesses to build up large cash balances. This may be because there are large cash balances that as part of the ownership succession plan, it is decided to pass some of that cash to the retiring generation. However those large cash balances can mean that the company does not meet the trading test for ER purposes, if the excess cash is considered to be substantial. It is not the total cash figure that needs to be considered, but the amount of cash which is not required for trading purposes. Cash may be retained for working capital, genuine prudence or future trading plans. All of these are valid trading reasons. But whatever are the reasons for holding the cash then it is important that these are documented by way of board minute as a minimum. This evidence can be extremely helpful in refuting any claims by HMRC that there is excess cash in an attempt to deny an ER claim.

16.7.7 Entrepreneur's relief, sole traders and partnerships

If the business is carried on as a sole proprietor or in partnership, ER is also available in respect of any capital gain, provided it is a material disposal of business assets. So a buyout of a partner's share of the goodwill or interest in the business premises as part of their retirement from the business, will be a material disposal of business assets.

16.7.8 Independently owned assets

If assets are owned outside of the company, or partnership, and used in the business carried on by the entity, then ER may be available on the disposal of that asset. This would be the case if it qualifies as an 'associated disposal'. If the asset is used for the purpose of the company's business then the company has to be the individual's personal company (ie the individual holds at least 5% of the share capital and voting rights). There are a number of conditions which need to be met:
- the individual must dispose of all or part of his interest in the partnership or of shares in the company;

- the disposal must be part of a withdrawal process from the business;
- the assets must have been used for the purpose of the partnership or company business throughout the one-year period ending with the disposal.

There will be an adjustment to the amount of the gain which qualifies for ER if:
- the asset was only used for the business for part of the time it was owned; or
- only part of the asset was used for the business; or
- the individual was only involved in carrying on the business for part of the time that they owned the asset; or
- rent was paid for the use of the asset post 5 April 2008.

16.8 VALUING A BUSINESS FOR TAX AND OTHER NON-SALE REASONS

In non-sale circumstances, when a valuation of shares is required, this often involves only a proportion of the shares. The first question should be whether the shares are to be valued on a stand-alone basis, or as a proportion of the total company value.

If it is the former, then the value has to reflect the size of the shareholding and the influence and control it provides. A higher price per share would usually be paid for a shareholding of more than 50%, rather than if the shareholding is less than 10%. Even a 90% shareholding would not be valued at 90% of the whole company value, because the person does not have absolute control, there is still the 10% nuisance value of the other shares.[17]

In order to arrive at a share value when only a proportionate shareholding is being considered, the normal approach is to use one of the methods described in chapter 12, in the context of selling the whole business on the open market, to arrive at a whole company value, apportion that on a pro rata basis, and then to discount the value. The discount will primarily depend on the size of the shareholding. But it can also be influenced by other factors such as the size of the other shareholdings; the nature of the business ie an investment business would generally attract a lower discount for the same size shareholding, as there will be less risk because of the assets supporting the valuation; and dividend potential. The larger the shareholding being valued, the lower will be the discount.

Circumstances where a method of discounting the full company value for the size of shareholding would be appropriate are:
- on death for probate purposes;
- on a gift, perhaps to determine holdover relief, or any capital gains tax payable, or to determine if there is any Inheritance tax payable on a gift into trust;
- on a 10-year anniversary of a trust, or an appointment of capital by a trust;
- for the purposes of employee share options and share schemes;
- under shareholder agreements on the retirement, or exit of a shareholder;

---

[17] See chapter 11 for an analysis of levels of ownership and control.

- for the purpose of resolving disputes between family members. The approach of the courts to valuation and minority discounts, in particular in relation to unfair prejudice claims, is covered in detail in Part E.

Often the articles of association, or a shareholders' agreement, may state that the shares of a family company should be valued without any discount. Usually this will be to encourage wider ownership by family outsiders and employees.[18]

For smaller shareholdings it may sometimes be appropriate to use a dividend yield basis of valuation. This involves looking at the dividend history of the company, determining what level of dividends a shareholder might expect, then applying the yield rate someone would want.

16.9 TAX AND BUY-BACKS

16.9.1 The basic position – income treatment

The importance of share buy-backs as a family business planning tool, to be used as part of succession planning, dispute resolution and general governance is discussed in chapter 11. This section looks at the tax implications of share buy-backs.

Tax legislation normally means that any distribution in respect of shares is treated as a dividend and taxed as income. Any repayment of capital, unless on a winding up, in excess of the amount subscribed for the shares is treated as a distribution. This can often create a larger tax liability for the shareholder than if they had to pay capital gains tax, particularly if entrepreneur's relief is available.

However this may not always be the case if the amount payable to buy back the shares is not taxable at the additional income tax rate for dividends of (38.1%), and the shareholder would have to pay capital gains tax at (20%).

16.9.2 Capital treatment – the basic conditions

In many cases though, a capital gains tax treatment is going to be more tax efficient. Fortunately, there is an exception to the normal income tax treatment when a private company buys back its shares, if the transaction falls within the 'Purchase of own shares' provisions.[19] In order to fall within this legislation either Condition A or B has to be met:

Condition A requires that:
(1) The purchase must be wholly or mainly to benefit the trade of the company or one of its 75% subsidiaries.
(2) It is not part of a scheme or arrangement to avoid tax, or enable the shareholder to participate in the company profits without receiving a dividend.
(3) Certain other conditions are met, where applicable.

---

[18] However a provision requiring full pro-rata valuations contained in a shareholders' agreements etc could cause problems if the family want to argue that a discounted valuation should apply for other tax purposes.
[19] Corporation Tax Act 2010, ss 1033–1048.

(4) The shareholder, whose shares are being purchased must be resident and ordinarily resident in the UK in the tax year of the purchase.
(5) The shares must have been owned for the previous five years.
(6) If the shares were inherited, the period they were held by the deceased can be aggregated, and the ownership period is reduced to three years.
(7) If the shares were gifted to the shareholder by their spouse or civil partner who was then living with them, provided they are still their spouse or civil partner and living with them, then the period of ownership by the transferor can be aggregated.
(8) The shareholding of the vendor in the company and any relevant group must be substantially reduced. The interest after the purchase cannot be more than 75% of the previous interest in the shares, or the entitlement to distributable profits. The test extends to the seller's associates; broadly spouses, children under 18 and connected companies).
(9) The company purchasing the shares must be an unquoted trading company or the unquoted holding company of a trading group.
(10) After the share purchase the vendor must not be connected with the company. This is a 30% test and one has to include the interests of associates.

Condition B is that the shares are purchased from personal representatives, who must use the amount paid to settle an inheritance tax liability, and show that the liability could not have been settled without the sale of the shares or causing undue hardship.

Benefit to the trade

Under Condition A there is a requirement that the purchase of shares must benefit the trade. HMRC have set out in their Statement of Practice 2/82 their views on what that means. Some examples they give are:

- There is a disagreement between the shareholders over the management of the company, and that is likely to have a detrimental effect on the trade.
- An unwilling shareholder wishes to end their association with the company, and they do not want those shares sold to someone who may not be acceptable to the other shareholders.
- A controlling shareholder is retiring, and wants to make way for new management.
- The personal representatives of a deceased shareholder want to realise the value of shares held by the estate.
- A legatee of a deceased shareholder, does not want to hold shares in the company.

Any of these circumstances can arise in the case of a family company. A circumstance which is not covered in the above list, but which in the writer's experience has been accepted by HMRC is where a shareholder, who is not a controlling shareholder is retiring from management.

16.9.3 Retained shareholding

It may be the case that the company is not buying all the shares owned by the vendor. HMRC say that in those circumstances they believe it is unlikely the purchase will benefit the company's trade. However they do accept that there may be exceptions to this view, for example where the company doesn't have adequate resources to buy all the shares. In those circumstances, HMRC will accept the transaction provided there is the intention within a reasonable period of time, normally 5 years, for the remaining shares to be purchased.

The Statement of Practice[20] uses the word 'intention' but in some cases it has been seen that HMRC would like to see some form of agreement regarding the purchase of the remaining shares.

Does this mean that all the shares of the disposing shareholder have to be purchased at some stage? HMRC have said that they will accept that a retiring director can retain up to a 5% shareholding for sentimental reasons. But other than this small holding, all the other shares have to be bought despite the legislation only requiring the holding after the sale to be no more than 75% of the percentage holding beforehand.

16.9.4 Continuing directorship etc

The Statement of Practice also says that HMRC will not accept that the purchase is for the benefit of the trade if the vendor retains some connection with the company, such as being a director or consultant. So if a family member wants to realise capital value from their shares for their retirement, they cannot continue to be a director or draw an income from the company.

To the best of the writer's knowledge the position has not been tested, where a retiring senior generation family member retains a role but in the informal family business governance system, for example as a member of the family council.

It may be the case that the retiring family member does not want the full capital value of their complete shareholding, but the shares which represent the excess value may be more than 5%. In those circumstances HMRC have been known to accept that these other shares can be gifted to other family members, who will be part of the on-going management.

The requirement that there is a substantial reduction in the shareholding does not mean that the vendor has to dispose of 25% of their current shareholding. The legislation says that the shareholding afterwards must not be more than 75% of the amount of the previous shareholding. Mathematically the two can be different.

16.9.5 Continuing connection

After the transaction the vendor must not be connected with the company. This is defined[21] as the person being entitled to more than 30% of:
- the issued, ordinary share capital;
- the loan capital and the issued share capital; or
- the voting power.

---

[20] Statement of Practices 2/82.
[21] Corporation Tax Act 2010, s 1042.

For these purposes the rights and interests of associates have to be included. Associates are defined as a spouse or civil partner, children under 18, and any trust set up by the individual, or their spouse or civil partner. For this requirement it is necessary to consider any preference shares, and any loans immediately after the share purchase. So if part of the purchase price is loaned back to the company immediately afterwards to help the company's cash flow, this may breach this 'not connected' requirement.

16.9.6 Advanced clearance

The legislation[22] does allow an application to be made in advance to HMRC that the provisions for a Purchase of Own Shares will apply, so that there is a capital gains tax treatment, to a particular transaction.

16.10 PROPERTY AND TAX

16.10.1 Owning the property personally or in the company?

When property is bought for use in the trade carried on by a company, it can either be bought by the company, or by one or more of the family members (or possibly by a pension scheme). A general outline of the main commercial and governance issues relevant to this choice were considered in chapter 10. This section looks at the main tax issues relevant to property ownership in and the tax implications of the choice of ownership structure in more detail. As will be seen there are advantages and disadvantages with both scenarios. Each case needs to be considered in the light of the individual circumstances.

16.10.2 Inheritance tax

Individual

As far as inheritance tax is concerned, if the property is owned by the individual then the maximum business property relief (BPR) which can be claimed is 50%. The relief is available provided:

- the property is used wholly or mainly for the purposes of the company's trade;
- the individual must have 'control' of the company. 'Control' for this purpose carries its normal meaning, but one can also include votes exercisable by the trustees of a trust in which the individual has an interest in possession, and those held by a spouse or civil partner.[23]
- the company must qualify as one eligible for BPR (see above).

Company ownership

Provided the property is being used solely for the purposes of the business of the company at the time that an inheritance tax charge might arise, its value will form part

---

[22] Corporation Tax Act 2010, s 1044.
[23] See IHTA 1984, ss 269 and 161.

of the value of the shares, and in the case of most family businesses will effectively qualify for 100% BPR. This will obviously be better than the 50% relief if the property were owned by the individual.

16.10.3 Capital gains

Individuals

When the property is ultimately sold capital gains tax will be payable on any increase in value, after deducting costs of purchase and sale and any improvement expenditure.

In most circumstances (with higher or additional rate income tax payers) the taxable gain will be charged to tax at 20%. If the annual capital gains tax exemption has not been used against other gains in the same year then it can be used against the property gain.

Family company

If the property is sold, the company will have to pay corporation tax on the capital gain. The gain is calculated in a similar way as for an individual, namely sale proceeds less the original purchase price (assuming it was acquired after April 1982) any costs of purchase and sale and any improvements, but in addition the company can claim 'indexation relief' on costs, calculated from the date the cost was incurred. The resultant gain is then added to the other profits of the company in the accounting period, and taxed at the appropriate corporation tax rate. So the gain could, for example, be taxed at 10% or 20%, which if ER is not available to the individual may with the indexation relief, give a lower overall tax charge.

16.10.4 Double-tax charge

If the proceeds from the sale of the property are not required in whole or part by the company, then there will be a double tax charge if the surplus is distributed to the shareholders, as they will probably have to pay income tax, or less likely capital gains tax, on the amount received. This will be in addition to the corporation tax paid by the company. This would give a greater total tax charge on the amount ultimately received by the shareholders compared with the property being owned by individuals.

16.10.5 Entrepreneur's relief

It is possible that if a claim for entrepreneur's relief (**ER**) can be made then the gain may only be taxed at 10%. With lifetime qualifying gains of up to £10m now eligible for this relief it is extremely important to consider the possibilities of a claim if the alternative is a tax rate of 20%. However there are some conditions that need to be meet to qualify for a claim if the property is sold by the individual. Such a sale would be treated as an 'associated disposal' for the purposes of the legislation, and to qualify:

- the individual must also dispose of all or part of his shareholding in the family company, using the property; and
- the disposal must be made as part of a withdrawal from the business; and

- the building must have been used for the purposes of the company business throughout the period of one year prior to the disposal.

Even if the disposal qualifies on the above basis, a bigger problem is likely to be that if the company has paid rent for the use of the building, then the relief is restricted. If the rent was a market rate from 5 April 2008 then no ER will be due. If rent has been used as a method of extracting income from the company and/or to fund the loan repayments then ER will not be available. If less then a market rent ER will be available only on a proportionate basis using the following calculation:

(Market value rent – rent paid)/market value rent

However the gain only qualifies if the other conditions are also met. If they are met, the gain will still only qualify if the premises are not sold before the material disposal of shares.[24]

There are also adjustments to the qualifying gain for ER if only part of the building was used in the company's trade; or the individual was only an officer or employee of the company for part of the period prior to the disposal of the shares; or the building was only used for the company's trade for part of the period prior to the disposal of the shares.

Family company

If the shares in a family company are sold, whilst it owns the property, then provided all the conditions for entrepreneur's relief are met (see above), then up to £10m of the gain will be taxable at 10%. There will be no need to consider the market value rental levels that apply in the individual ownership situation.

16.10.6 Rollover relief and new premises

Individual

A building might be sold because the company needs larger premises. In these circumstances the individual could claim rollover relief by using the sale proceeds to acquire a replacement building.[25] To rollover the whole of the gain an amount equivalent to the whole of the proceeds must be spent on the new premises within one year before the disposal or three years after. It is not necessary that for the actual proceeds to be used.

For example, the old building may be sold for £1m and the new building costs £1.5m which is funded by a loan of £900,000 and cash of £600,000, so the individual keeps £400,000 to perhaps clear a personal mortgage or for some other purpose. If the cost of the new building is less than the sale proceeds of the old one, then a proportion of the gain may be rolled over. However the cost of the replacement building must be at least equivalent to the tax cost of the old building for any rollover relief to be claimed. If the old building has only partly been used for the purposes of the trade of the company, or

---

[24] See *Purves (Inspector of Taxes) v Harrison* (2001) STC 267.
[25] See TCGA 1992, Pt V, Ch 1.

for only part of the period of ownership, then the gain that can be rolled over is restricted. Other qualifying conditions which will need to be met include:

- the replacement building's first use after its acquisition must be for use in the company's trade;
- the company must be his 'personal company', which is defined as one in which he has least 5% of the voting rights;
- if the new premises are leasehold and the unexpired lease has less than sixty years to run then the gain is only rolled over for ten years, at which time it becomes taxable unless another qualifying investment has been made.

Company

A company can also rollover the capital gain by using the proceeds to acquire a replacement building. The rules work in the same way as for an individual. Special rules apply if the interest in the building is leasehold and the lease has less than 60 years to run and the amount of the gain which can be rolled over will be reduced if the property has not been used wholly for the purposes of the trade or throughout the entire period of ownership. There are other specified classes of assets against which the gain on the property can be rolled over.[26] An individual can also rollover their gain on the sale of the building against these other types of assets provided they are used in his 'personal company'.

16.10.7 Enterprise investment scheme deferral relief

An alternative to claiming rollover relief in respect of a gain on the sale of the property would be to claim enterprise investment scheme deferral relief[27] by investing in qualifying shares in a company. It is beyond the scope of this book to cover all the qualifying conditions, but some of the general principles are that:

- The company must be carrying on a qualifying trade. Most trading activities are eligible, but some involving property or those requiring a large property investment are excluded.
- The investment must be in ordinary shares.
- The investment must be made one year before the property disposal or within three years after.
- The net assets of the company before the subscription must not be more than £15m or more than £16m afterwards.

For the deferral relief there is no requirement that there must not have been a 'connection' with the company prior to the investment, as there is if enterprise investment scheme relief is being claimed for income tax purposes. So even if the individual owned 100% of the shares, if all the other conditions were met, deferral relief could be claimed.

A difference to rollover relief is that it is only necessary to invest the amount of the gain into shares and not the whole of the sale proceeds. This means that the individual can keep the remainder of the sale proceeds, and defer the tax liability until the shares are sold. When the shares are sold the deferred gain is crystallized.

---

[26] Taxation of Chargeable Gains Act 1992, s 155.
[27] See TCGA 1992, Sch 5B.

16.10.8 Tax relief

The company will be entitled to tax relief on the interest paid on any loans to buy the property.

The individual will be able to offset any interest on a loan to acquire the property against any rent received.

16.10.9 Capital allowances

In addition to expenses incurred in relation to the property, both individuals and family companies will also be able to claim capital allowances on any plant and equipment in the building, including integral features and fixtures, to offset against the rental income for tax purposes. If the expenditure qualifies as plant and equipment then the allowance is 18% from 6 April 2012 on the cost in the first period the building is acquired (assuming the individual does not have a capital allowances pool in respect of other let property).

In the subsequent tax year a further 18% can be claimed on the written down value brought forward from the previous year, and so on for each subsequent tax year until the whole of the cost has been claimed.

Any further expenditure in subsequent periods is added to the pool brought forward, before calculating the allowances claim. If however the item is classified as an integral feature[28] then the capital allowances rate from 6 April 2012 is 8%. Integral features include electrical systems such as lighting systems, cold water system and space or water heating systems.

If a used building is bought by or for use by the company, then part of the purchase price can be allocated to the integral features elements to enable the capital allowances claim to be made. From 6 April 2012 the amount on which a claim is made needs to be agreed within two years between the vendor and purchaser.

If a new building is constructed then it will save costs at a later date if at an early stage the costs are allocated, to identify the amount relating to those items which will qualify for a capital allowances claim. Costs which may qualify for a claim can often be 20% -25% of the total building cost, so they should not be ignored.

16.10.10 Removing property from the family company

There are various reasons why one or more family members of might want to acquire the property from the company. This could be because it is no longer needed in the trade, to raise funds for trading and investment activities, to help insulate the property from trading risk or to separate investment and trading assets as part of succession planning or governance.

Two possible ways in which the individual could acquire the property are:

---

[28] Capital Allowances Act 2001, s 33A.

Buying the property from the company

A transaction between the company and the individual shareholder will be one between connected parties, and hence HMRC will review the price payable to ensure it is market value. If too low a price is payable then it will either be treated as a distribution by the company,[29] or a benefit in kind.[30] In either instance there will be an income tax charge on the individual.

If such a transaction is contemplated then a professional valuation of the property should be obtained. Consideration should also be given to the inclusion of an 'adjuster clause' in the documentation, so that if the actual value of the property ultimately agreed with HMRC is different, the consideration can be adjusted and either the purchaser is repaid part of the price, or has a further amount to pay to avoid the income tax charge.

The purchaser may need to raise a loan to buy the property. If part of the price is left outstanding on loan account with the company then the company then the close company loan rules summarised in chapter 4 will apply and the company will have a liability to account to HMRC for 32.5% tax on the amount of the loan.[31]

There will be a stamp duty land tax charge on the purchase price of the property.

Distribution in specie

A distribution in specie will avoid the individual having to raise funds to buy the property, and there will only be a nominal stamp duty land tax charge of £5. The individual will be treated as receiving a dividend on which they will have an additional or higher rate income tax charge.

In either of the above instances the company will be making a disposal of the property and hence there may be a capital gain on which corporation tax will need to be paid.

In a family company situation any arrangements of this nature will need to be discussed and agreed with other family members who have an interest in the company, if conflict is to be avoided. It is unlikely the distribution in specie will be an acceptable route unless all the shareholders are involved in that distribution, or are compensated by an equivalent dividend. If the purchase route is used, then the other family members involved will want to ensure a market price is paid, and that if part of the price is left on loan account, that a commercial rate of interest is paid.

16.10.11 Transfer of property to the family company

The individual selling the premises used by the company to the company may be a tax efficient way of extracting funds from the company, because at worse they will pay 20% tax on the gain, whereas if the consideration was paid as a bonus or dividend then there could be 45% or effectively 38.1% income tax payable, respectively. The company will need to pay stamp duty land tax on the purchase.

---

[29] Corporation Tax Act 2010, ss 1000 and 1064.
[30] Income Tax (Earnings and Pensions) Act 2003, s 206.
[31] Corporation Tax Act 2010, s 455.

As in the case of the individual buying the property from the company, HMRC will be concerned to ensure the transaction takes place at market value. If too high a price is paid then the excess would be considered to be a distribution for income tax purposes. If too low a price is paid, the individual will be assessed for capital gains tax purposes on the market value and not the price paid.

16.10.12 Ownership of property inside or outside a family partnership

Inheritance tax and BPR

If the property is owned inside a family partnership then 100% BPR will be available for inheritance tax purposes, provided the partnership is wholly or mainly carrying on a business, and the property is used for the purpose of the business. Whereas if the property is owned by a partner in the partnership, and used wholly or mainly in the partnership business then the relief is only 50%.

Therefore there is considerable benefit in the business premises being a partnership asset. However the property purchase might be funded by only some of the partners, typically the senior generation. The next generation might be introduced into the partnership as 'junior' business trading partners but without any immediate intention of giving them a share in partnership property assets. In these circumstances the property should be recorded as a partnership asset, but it is agreed that capital profits in relation to the property are split in a different ratio to the trading profits.[32]

As there is this Inheritance tax advantage from treating the business premises as a partnership asset, then it is important that it can be treated as such. The rules concerning whether land is a partnership asset are complicated, but it is sufficient to say for the current purposes that if it is the intention of the parties who own the land, that it should be a partnership asset, then that should suffice. It is important that this intention is documented. Also the property should be shown in the accounts of the partnership. As regards any different profit sharing arrangements in relation to the property, then again these should be documented in the partnership agreement.

Agricultural property relief or APR will also be relevant to farming partnerships. A brief summary of the rules is set out above.

Rollover and capital gains

If the property used by the partnership for the purposes of its trade is sold, then it is possible to rollover any gain against the cost of acquiring replacement premises for use in the trade. The same rules apply as in relation to a company looking to rollover a gain. The gain can be rolled over regardless of whether the property is a partnership asset or owned personally by one of the partners, and used by the partnership.

---

[32] The root cause of the dispute in *Ham v Ham* and the similar cases discussed in chapter 13 is that no distinction was made between income and capital profits.

Entrepreneur's relief

If the vendors do not replace the business premises, then there will be a taxable capital gain. In order to qualify for ER on the disposal of the property, there must also be a 'material disposal of business assets'. To claim ER it is also important to ensure that the property is not sold before the disposal of the business interest.[33] There is no relief available if, for example, just the premises are sold, but the partnership continues just as before, but from new rented premises with profits being shared in the same ratios as before the sale. A 'material disposal of business assets' requires, in relation to a family partnership, for there also to be a disposal of the whole or part of a business and for that to be 'material'.

In relation to a partnership this means that either at the time of the asset disposal an individual who was carrying on a business takes on a partner or a partner disposes of all or part of his interest in the partnership.

Entrepreneur's relief and 'associated disposals'

If the property is instead of being a partnership asset, is owned by an individual and used for the purpose of the partnership's business, then to qualify for ER on its disposal it must qualify as an 'associated disposal'. The conditions to be met are:

- the individual must dispose of all or part of his interest in the assets of the partnership, and this is a material disposal;
- the disposal must be made as part of a withdrawal process from the business;
- the assets must have been used for the purpose of the partnership business throughout the period of one year ending with the disposal of the business.

Even if the disposal meets the above conditions then ER is restricted if the individual has charged a rent to the partnership for the use of the asset. The rules in this regard are the same as described above in relation to an individual owning a property used in a company.

16.10.13 Potential inheritance tax problems with investment properties in family companies

The value of business property relief (BPR) against inheritance tax is explained above as is the major requirement, that the company is 'wholly or mainly' carrying on a business. As also noted many family companies have substantial investment port folios.[34] As also explained above the concern is that if the investment property portfolio represents more than 50% of the activities then no BPR is available even on the trading part of the company's activities.

It is not uncommon in family businesses for investment property to be held in the holding company, to, say, protect it from claims or commercial risks in respect of the trading activities carried on in a subsidiary. If the value of the investment portfolio is greater than the value of the subsidiary (although asset values are not the only criteria,

---

[33] See *Purves (Inspector of Taxes) v Harrison* (2001) STC 267.
[34] For example the Cadman family, widely discussed throughout the book started off life as a building company but ended up as a property investment business.

but could in these circumstances be very influential) then BPR would be lost in respect of shares in the holding company. However in this situation there may be a simple solution to at least claim an element, or possibly 100% BPR on the holding company shares. Consider the following scenario:

Example

A family holding company owns £1.5m of investment property all let to third parties and has a shareholding in a trading subsidiary which is worth £1m. So the total value of the holding company is £2.5m.

In the above circumstances no BPR could be claimed in respect of the holding company shares as the investment property portfolio represents more than 50% of the company value and the wholly or mainly test is failed.

However if say £500k worth of investment property is transferred to the subsidiary, for say £1 it becomes worth £1.5m. The subsidiary is treated as a trading company because the investment property it owns is less than 50% of the value. As far as the holding company is concerned it now has £1m of investment assets and an investment in a trading company of £1.5m. It now meets the wholly or mainly trading test and so qualifies for BPR purposes. There may be a restriction on the amount of BPR which can be claimed because of the excepted asset legislation explained above. However, some BPR is better than none.

The investment property might all be owned in a subsidiary company. If that is the only activity of that company then the value of the subsidiary company shareholding will not qualify for BPR.[35] In these circumstances it will be worthwhile considering transferring the investment properties around the group to companies which with their trading activities, and the investment properties, will still qualify as wholly or mainly trading companies for BPR.

16.10.14 Some possible inheritance tax planning ideas for investment property companies

If the company is an investment property company, and therefore BPR will not be available the strategies available to reduce inheritance tax are reduced. This is partly because the normal strategy of giving away assets, and then surviving seven years is not possible without, in most cases, crystallising a capital gains tax liability if there has been a growth in the value of the shares. If the shares are in a trading company then except in a few cases, any capital gain can be held over on the gift under CGTA 1992, s 165.

A possible alternative approach to holdover a capital gain which might otherwise arise, is making an election is under TCGA 1992, s 260, where the gift is one on which inheritance tax is chargeable. In this case the held over gain is not capable of restriction, as under s 165. A gift into a trust is chargeable to inheritance tax, however if the value of the gift is less than the nil rate band then no liability arises on the settlement. Therefore provided the settlor does not have an interest in the settlement, and it is UK resident, a holdover election can be made for capital gains tax purposes. A trust is settlor interested if the spouse or minor children of the donor are beneficiaries. However if the children do not obtain any benefit until they are over 18, and the spouse does not obtain any benefit until the settlor has died, then it is not settlor interested.

---

[35] See IHTA 1984, s 111.

This gives an opportunity to pass some of the shares in a property investment company to the next generation, because it is possible to settle shares with a value up to the nil rate band on a trust for the benefit of say the children once they are at least 18, and to holdover the capital gain. As explained above the trust will be subject to the ten-year charge (currently 6% on the excess over the nil rate band at the time), and there will be an inheritance tax charge on the transfer of assets out of the trust.

This idea assumes that the settlor has not made any other chargeable transfers for inheritance tax purposes in the previous seven years, otherwise the value of the gift into the trust cannot be greater than the unused portion of the nil rate band, if there is to be no inheritance tax payable on the establishment of the trust.

If the spouse also has shares in the property company then they can also use this strategy. So at the current nil rate band levels, £650,000 of assets can pass to the next generation without any Inheritance tax or capital gains tax. The donors need to live for seven years after the gift for there to be no effect on their estates for Inheritance tax purposes.

One issue which the donors may have with the above strategy is that they are giving away shares and therefore dividend entitlements, which may be important to them as part of the income they require in retirement. An alternative approach which maintains the right to dividends, and is appropriate for family property investment companies is that of value freezing using freezer shares. The usual mechanics of this are explained in chapter 11. These new shares would carry the right to participate in a winding up, but only insofar as the net asset value then exceeds the value at the date of the issue of the shares. Therefore the new shares take all the future growth in the value of the company, and the existing shares take all the value up to the point of the issue of the bonus shares. The new shares can rank *pari passu* with the existing shares as far as dividends and votes are concerned. The new shares should be capable of blocking any resolution to wind up the company or alter the rights attaching to the shares, or to create any new share capital. This is necessary to counter any argument that the failure of the existing holders of the existing shares to cancel the rights of the bonus shares or to liquidate the company, is a transfer of value under IHTA 1984, s 3(3). The existing shares can be retained, but whilst the bonus shares have little value they are given away to the children. Depending on the value of the bonus shares at the time of the gift there may be a capital gains tax charge, but a gift into trust with a holdover election under TCGA 1992, s 260 could be an appropriate strategy.

This approach is possible in the case of a property investment company, because there is reasonable certainty on the value of the shares. The value will be related to the value of the property portfolio, with fairly standard accepted discount rates depending on the size of the shareholding. In a trading company situation the market value is more difficult to determine because it will depend on a variety of factors which will be more judgmental.

The value freezing approach is a long-term strategy, and its aim is to ensure the future growth of the property company does not continue to accrue to the existing shareholders. It has the benefit of the current shareholders retaining a right to capital, dividends and management influence. In a family business context this may be important to the older generation.

It is considered that the approach does not contravene the gifts with reservation provisions because the donor does not benefit from the property which is the subject of the gift. Any benefits which are continued to be received come from the original shareholding, which were already owned.

16.11 SOME TAX PLANNING IDEAS FOR OWNERSHIP SUCCESSION

Each family and family business is different, and so there is no single solution which will apply in all cases when it comes to ownership succession. Some of the following ideas which use the above outline of the relevant sections of the capital gains tax and Inheritance tax legislation may be appropriate, or a combination of them.

16.11.1 IDEA 1 – If the shares in the company qualify in full for business property relief, then hold on to them until death, and give them away under the will

This may be a reasonable answer from a tax viewpoint because there is no Inheritance tax on death because of BPR, and the donee takes over the shares for capital gains tax purposes at the value at the date of death. So in effect there is a tax free uplift in the 'cost' of the shares for capital gains tax purposes.

However from the family relationship viewpoint this may create problems. The next generation working in the business may want some certainty that they will be getting shares, and perhaps a controlling interest, in the business they are working hard to run. Whilst there may be the promise that *'all this will come to you one day'*, and the will may say that, there is still the chance, because the will can be changed, that it may not happen. Alternatively the child may not know what they are going to receive in terms of the business. Or they may see a sibling who has not joined the family business accumulating wealth from the career they have chosen, and without any immediate ownership passing to them, they may feel they are making sacrifices for the family business which are not being recognised.[36]

16.11.2 IDEA 2 – Give away some, or all, the shares now

If it is an outright gift and the donor doesn't reserve any right over the asset, provided the donor does not die within seven years then the gift is not subject to Inheritance tax. If the donor dies within seven years and the interest in the business qualified for BPR in full (ie there were no excepted assets) then there will still be no Inheritance tax to pay on death.

In making the gift, consideration should also be given to whether the gift is free of Inheritance tax, in which case if a liability on death arises, it comes out of the remainder of the estate, and the gift is grossed up to determine the value of the gift. If the gift is made on the basis the donee is responsible for any tax which may arise, they need to be aware of this risk.

---

[36] Possible remedies of proprietary estoppel are considered in chapter 19.

It will also be necessary to consider the capital gains tax position in respect of the gift. If a holdover election can be made under TCGA 1992, s 165 to cover the whole of the gain then a liability can be avoided. If there is a potential liability because there are non-business assets which would give rise to a capital gain in the company, or it is not a trading company then a gift to a trust as considered in Idea 3 may be necessary.

A lifetime gift will mean that the uplift of CGT base cost on death is lost, as the transfer under TCGA 1992, s 165 will be deemed to be at the acquisition cost of the senior generation, so any embedded latent capital gain will also be transferred. But the business family might think that this was a price well worth paying, to avoid the family tensions potentially created by Idea 1. This is particularly so if there is no realistic prospect of the family business being sold.

Giving away an interest in the business now may deal with some of the family problems which can occur with Idea 1. But the older generation may be reluctant to consider it because it may mean they are also giving up income which they need for their retirement, or the reluctance is because they still want to retain an element of control, which their shareholding gives them.

16.11.3 IDEA 3 – Give shares in the company to a trust

The possible benefits of family business trusts as a vehicle for wider family ownership are considered in chapter 14.

Any new trusts set up after 21 March 2006 which will be considered in a family business context, will be within the new legislation affecting trusts, and there will be a potential liability to Inheritance tax on set up. But this will not be so if the shares qualify in full for BPR or there is headroom within the donor's nil rate band. Trusts could be considered if a holdover election cannot be made for capital gains purposes under TCGA 1992, s 165. It would be possible to transfer shares in an investment company, with a value up to the amount of any unused nil rate band, to a trust for the benefit of the next generation. A holdover election could be made under TCGA 1992, s 260 to avoid the capital gains tax charge, and there would be no Inheritance tax charge because the value is covered by the nil rate band. The other spouse could do the same. This would mean that after 7 years £650,000 (using the 2016–2017 nil rate band limits) could be passed to the next generation with no Inheritance tax payable. If the shares were then appointed out of the trust before the first ten-year anniversary there would be no tax on that transfer, and another holdover election can be made for capital gains tax purposes.

If the older generation still have a reasonable life expectancy the basis of valuation can also be useful in planning. This is because if they survive the seven years, and the gift has taken them below the 50% shareholding level there are significantly higher discounts which then apply which mean the value of the shares they retain, on a pro rata basis to their previous shareholding, is significantly lower.

This idea might also be useful where the shares in the company qualify in full for BPR, but there are some investment assets with gains which will not qualify for holdover relief under TCGA 1992, s 165 if the shares were given directly to the next generation. In these circumstances a gift could be made to a trust and an election made under TCGA

1992, s 260 to avoid crystallising a capital gains tax charge. It will not matter what is the value of the gift in this instance because BPR is due on the full value provided the investment assets are not 'excepted assets'.

There is an income tax point to be aware of if gifting shares to trusts and dividends are going to be paid. This is that in the case of a discretionary trust, the dividend will be taxed on the trust as if it were an additional rate tax payer in the trust.

16.11.4 IDEA 4 – Buy out the older generation's shareholding to leave the younger generation with control of the company.

Buying out an older generation's interest in the family company may solve a number of issues:

- giving the older generation financial security, so that they are not reliant on the company profitability for their future lifestyle; or
- giving the next generation control of the company to make the changes which they feel are necessary without interference from the older generation; or
- giving the older generation capital to pass on to children not involved in the business, so that those who are involved have complete control; or
- extracting the value created, so that the older generation are rewarded for their efforts and possible sacrifices.

The two principal issues which arise are how to structure the buyout, and secondly the tax implications. As far as the first of these is concerned there are two options:

- a 'purchase of own shares' where the company uses its own financial resources, either accumulated cash or the ability to borrow secured against assets, to buy back in the shares. The qualifying conditions which will need to be meet to ensure a capital gains tax treatment will be considered in paragraph 16.9 above; or
- a new company is set up which acquires the retiring generation's shares in exchange for a cash payment; a partial cash and asset transfer 'payment'; or a partial cash payment now with the balance left on loan account. This may require an element of financial assistance from the 'target' company, if say cash is subsequently passed to the new holding company as a loan or dividend, or its assets are used as security for borrowings by the new company. Since the changes in company law introduced by Companies Act 2006 effective from 1 October 2008, this is a much easier process than it used to be. If the younger generation already have shares in the 'target' company then they will exchange those shares for shares in the new holding company.

In relation to the second option, if the younger generation are exchanging shares for shares in the new company this should not give rise to any capital gains tax charge by virtue of the provisions of TCGA 1992, s 127. It is always advisable to seek clearance from HMRC before the transaction for this share for share exchange under TCGA 1992, s 138, and under CTA 2010, s 748.

If the disposal of shares by the older generation qualifies for entrepreneur's relief then the first £10m of the gain will be subject to capital gains tax at 10% with the remainder of the gain taxable at probably 20%. This therefore gives a very tax efficient method of extracting value from the company.

The major tax impact of this idea, is that if the shares previously qualified in full for business property relief, and therefore effectively had no value for inheritance tax purposes, selling them immediately removes the relief as the individual now has cash rather than shares, and the full value is taxable as part of the estate. If part of the reason for the sale of shares is to allow some wealth to be passed to children not involved in the business, this should be done as soon as possible in order to give as much chance as possible to survive the seven years, after which point the gift can be ignored if death then occurs.

If the company does not qualify for BPR then there is no worsening of the inheritance tax position by the sale of the shares, but there would be no entrepreneur's relief on the share sale for capital gains tax purposes.

16.11.5 IDEA 5 – Reorganising the company and then splitting it into two separate companies one owned by the older generation and the other by the younger generation.

If the existing company has investment assets, or owns the business premises these could be transferred to a new company in which the older generation are the only or main shareholders and the existing company could effectively be passed into the control of the younger generation. This type of reconstruction could be useful if the older generation want some protection in terms of income in their retirement or the family want to protect the wealth created from the risks of the trading activities. Alternatively the Op-Co Prop-Co structures can be created to spread risk, for example between insiders and outsiders.

The family ownership logic and mechanics of these partitions or demergers are explained in chapter 11. Broadly they involved shareholders exchanging for their shares in the existing family company for shares in one of the new vehicles created for the purposes of the re-organisation.

Usually the exchanges of shares involved should not give rise to any capital gains tax charge by virtue of TCGA 1992, s 127.

If the question as to whether there has been any value shifting is to be avoided it must be ensured that the value which the A and B shareholders finish with, is the same as the value of the shares they started with. This may mean that some shareholders have to retain shares in the other company, or else there may need to be an inter-company loan account created which is subsequently cleared by a cash transfer.

Whilst the above idea may satisfy some of the family concerns, it does create an inheritance tax issue. Prior to the reconstruction it might be that the whole of the value of the family company qualified for BPR, with any investment assets being of a value not to affect such a claim, and/or they are not classified as excepted assets. However after the reconstruction whilst the shares in the operating company will still qualify for BPR, those in the property owning company will not qualify. If those shares are predominately held by the older generation then their inheritance tax exposure has been substantially increased. At that stage one then has to consider other strategies to reduce that potential costs by ideas such as transferring a portion of the shares to nil rate band discretionary trusts as explained above.

The trade-off for taking less risky assets is therefore the loss of tax reliefs tied to trading assets.

16.12 CONCLUSION

The object of this chapter has not been to attempt a comprehensive coverage of the tax issues relevant to family owned firms. Rather it is to highlight and introduce some key issues relevant to ownership and transfers of interest in those firms.

In chapter 1 we suggested that founding entrepreneurs in particular and business families in general will often hold diverse and multiple business interests, in addition to their main family trading business.

In chapter 10 we also suggest that business families are also likely to build a wide property portfolio, some of which may be occupied by family trading concerns, others held for investment purposes.

Often the overall family portfolio will have been assembled in an ad-hoc and piece meal fashion, with little or no regard having been paid to optimum tax structures.

As can be seen from above the combination of this diversity and complexity of interests, together with innate prudency of family business owners, could well present problems and tax planning challenges in qualifying for the various reliefs against IHT and CGT discussed in this chapter.

One of the key messages contained in this book is that succession planning should be driven by the wider ownership philosophy of the business owning family, rather than tax considerations. It nevertheless follows that, once the question of the primary ownership approach has been addressed, a key subsidiary question becomes how to establish the best tax structure to implement that approach.

16.13 FURTHER READING FOR PART C

- Glenn Ayres 'Rough Family Justice: Equity in Family Business Succession Planning' (1990) *Family Business Review* Vol 3 No 1. A wise and readable article which is now seen as a classic piece of family business thinking.
- R Banks *Lindley & Banks on Partnership* (Sweet and Maxwell, 19th edn, 2013). The leading work on partnership law, heavily relied on by partnership practitioners and frequently referred to in courts.
- P Beckett et al *Tolley's Property Taxation 2016-17–2016* (LexisNexis, 2016)
- Carlock and Ward *Strategic Planning for the Family Business* (Palgrave, 2001). Again although we explain some of the principles of parallel planning in this chapter the book is full of helpful insights and practical suggestions to implement succession and strategic planning for family owned businesses. Although much of the content might be aimed more directly at larger and later stage family firms, the basic principles can be adapted and applied to earlier stage and smaller organisations.
- N Dougherty and A Fairpro *Company Acquisition of Shares* (Jordan Publishing, 6th edn, 2013). A comprehensive explanation of the law and practice of share buy-backs.
- K E Gersick et al *Generation to Generation: Life cycles of a family business* (Harvard Business School Press, 1997). A classic work (if not the classic work) on succession issues in family owned businesses written by one of the leaders in the field.
- M Harper et al *International Trust and Divorce Litigation* (Jordan Publishing, 2nd edn, 2013). Covering the international trusts dimension for offshore lawyers, trust companies, private bankers and matrimonial lawyers who represent high net worth clients.
- T Harris *Agricultural and Business Property Relief* (Bloomsbury Professional, 5th edn).
- P Howard and P Tallon *Tolley's Tax Planning for Owner-Managed Businesses 2016-2017* (LexisNexis, 2016).
- Klein and Blondel 'The Sale of the Family Business – Entrepreneurial Project, Strategic Decision or Expropriation' *Insead Working Paper Series* 2004/25/IIFE. An interesting article dividing the family business sales into broad categories and exploring the positive and negative reasons for business owning families to sell.
- J Lambrecht, J Lievens 'Pruning the Family Tree: An Unexplored Path to Family Business Continuity and Family Harmony' (2008) *Family Business Review*, Vol 25, No 4, December 2008, pp 295-313. An article exploring the theoretical family business background to pruning and exit provisions.
- I Maston *Tolley's UK Taxation of Trusts 2016–17* (LexisNexis, 2016).
- A McGee *Shares and Share Capital under the Companies Act 2006* (Jordan Publishing, 2009). A detailed treatment of the technical legal issues relating to share capital.
- Charles Mitchell, David J Hayton, Paul Matthews *Underhill and Hayton Law of Trusts and Trustees* (LexisNexis, 19th edn 2016). Leading and authoritative text on the subject.
- S Singleton *Beswick and Wine Buying and Selling Private Companies and Businesses* (Bloomsbury, 9th edn, 2014). A leading practitioner text on private business sales.

- Tallon and Howard *Tax Planning for Owner-managed Businesses 2015-16* (Tolley, 2016). A detailed guide to tax issues affecting owner-managed businesses generally.
- R Thompson (ed) *Sinclair on Warranties and Indemnities in Share and Asset Sales* (Sweet and Maxwell, 9th edn, 2014).
- V Williams *Due diligence: A Practical Guide* (Jordan Publishing, 2nd edn, 2013). A detailed explanation of the due diligence process containing a significant number of practical tools and precedents (available on a separate CD Rom).

PART D

FAMILY MATTERS

CHAPTER 17

GOVERNANCE AND THE FAMILY OWNED BUSINESS

17.1 GOVERNANCE OVERVIEW

This chapter is concerned with the voluntary adoption of governance systems by family businesses. Traditionally corporate governance is thought of as a business matter. In a family enterprise governance issues are relevant to all three subsystems.[1] This chapter will look at the approaches and considerations applicable to each of these.

So far as the business system is concerned we concentrate on the evolution and operation of boards in a family business. In this chapter the emphasis is on the board as a collective. Chapter 8 (Directors' Duties) deals with particular issues faced by individual family business directors arising from general statutory and common law duties. We also look at family specific governance apparatus, including family councils, family assemblies and family charters. Our treatment of governance in the ownership domain is more concerned with an examination of the use of legal documents, such as shareholders' agreements in the context of a family company. The more strategic aspects of ownership governance are dealt with in chapters 11 (Ownership Overview) and 15 (Ownership Succession). Schematically the position looks something like the illustration below (Figure 17.1).

In practice a family business governance system cannot be confined to neat boxes and fixed boundaries. For example shareholders' agreements, although primarily a document between business owners, inevitably reach into the business and family sub-systems. Whilst some of the governance tasks are concerned with the internal regulation of the separate sub-systems, much of the underlying purpose is to encourage communication and interaction between the family members occupying separate positions within the overall family business system.

Equally a lot of family business governance theory is concerned with establishing structures and procedures. Ultimately the success or otherwise of these governance systems is likely to be a factor of the quality of the interpersonal relationships between individual family members; in short, family dynamics.

Much of the chapter will be refer to the increasing complexity of family businesses as they evolve through the family business life cycle and the corresponding need to introduce governance systems to provide structural underpinning to support family cohesion.

---

[1] See chapter 3 (Tools, Models and Theories), for an explanation of the three-circle model.

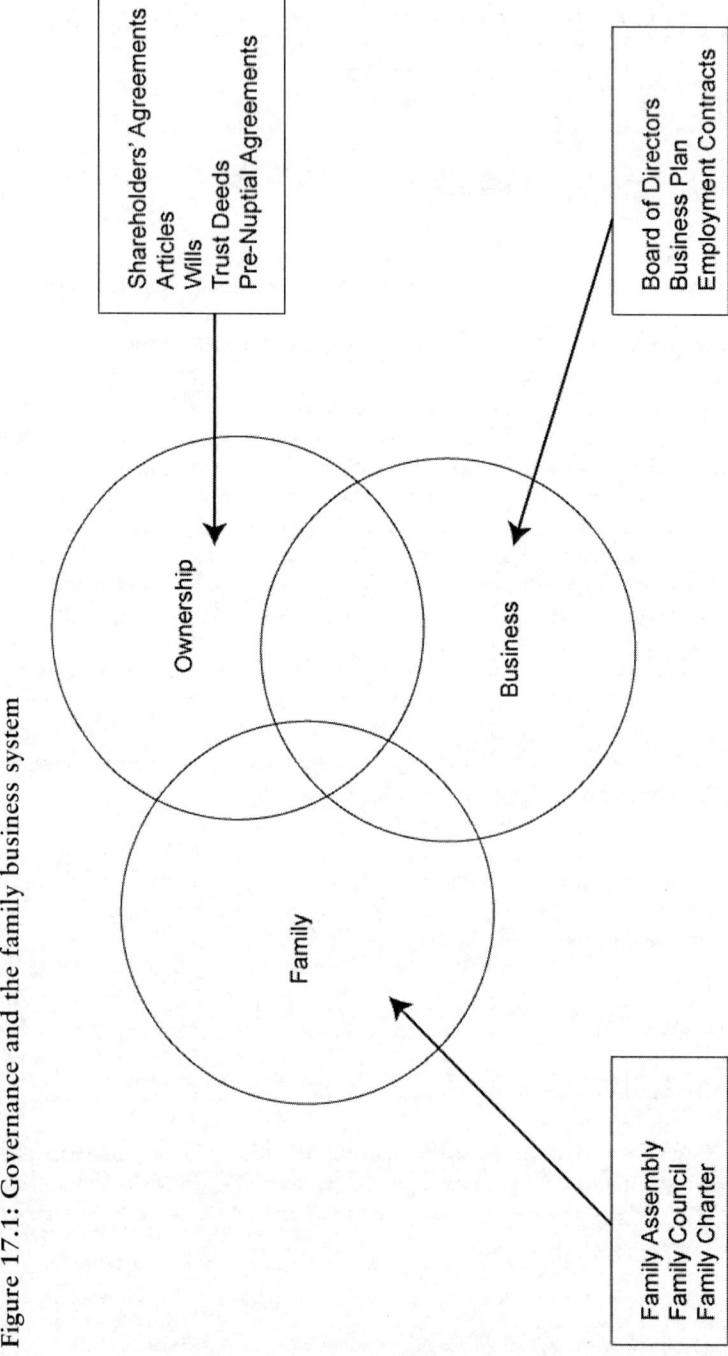

Figure 17.1: Governance and the family business system

- Shareholders' Agreements
- Articles
- Wills
- Trust Deeds
- Pre-Nuptial Agreements

→ Ownership

- Board of Directors
- Business Plan
- Employment Contracts

→ Business

- Family Assembly
- Family Council
- Family Charter

→ Family

Much of the logic for introducing family business governance systems is therefore to reinforce the positive elements of existing family cohesion. However as there is a natural reluctance on the part of families to invest in the considerable time effort (and cost) of establishing such systems when things are going well, the reality is that families often turn to governance as a response to family conflict. Whilst governance systems can support cohesion, they can rarely create it. The message must therefore be that early attention to the issues raised in this chapter is necessary, before conflict has the chance to grow into a full blown dispute.

Over the last 30 years or so a classic model of family business governance has evolved, involving the use of family charters, family councils and family assemblies. Whilst these are explained in some detail, they should not be seen as 'one size fits all' template solutions.[2]

Leading family business governance experts Neubauer and Lank[3] suggest that, as a matter of theory, any overall governance or control system can have a number of inter-related sub-systems that operate in different ways. They categorise these as follows:

- **Diagnostic and analytical control systems.** These include such traditional management tools as management accounting, reviewing performance against targets and key performance indicators. These tend to assess performance retrospectively and are quantative and business focused.
- **Boundary systems.** Boundary systems are particularly relevant to family owned businesses. They attempt to demarcate respective roles and responsibilities. Boundary systems can operate within the business sub-system, for example to establish demarcation between current and next generation executives, as part of a succession planning exercise, or between siblings to create a viable and functioning sibling partnership. Boundary systems also operate across the wider family business system, for example through family charters or shareholders' agreements marking out the limits of authority of the board, the family and the owner group.
- **Interactive control systems.** Interactive control systems operate at a higher level. They are more flexible and rely more on dialogue and communication between the stakeholders in a family firm than rigid rules and procedures, for example the interaction between the board and the family council.
- **Belief systems.** Belief systems can be seen as the highest level of control systems. Here governance is based on shared values and a common understanding of what good governance requires. Often language such as stewardship or custodianship is deployed. This common understanding can be developed or re-enforced by the investment of the business owning family in some of the governance apparatus discussed later in this chapter, especially family charters.

---

[2] See the discussion in Collins, McCracken, Murray and Stepek 'Strong Governance: a result of evolutionary and revolutionary processes' *Journal of Family Business Management* (2014) Vol 4, Issue No 2.
[3] Neubauer and Lank *The Family Business: Its Governance for Sustainability* (Harvard Business School Press, 1997) at pp 217–224.

17.2 THE CASE FOR GOVERNANCE IN THE FAMILY OWNED BUSINESS

The immediate reaction of many people may well be that formal governance systems have little or no place in family owned businesses. Certainly, available research does suggest reluctance amongst the family business community to adapt formal governance systems and procedures.[4]

So far as larger family owned corporates are concerned, one of the key advantages of remaining in private ownership, rather than listing on a public market, is to retain organisational flexibility and the freedom to operate without having to accept the strictures of the UK Corporate Governance Code.[5] Indeed (alongside the difficulties of running a business to the short term performance timescales of the capital markets) corporate governance compliance appears to have been a factor in the decision of high profile family businesses to de-list and return to private ownership.[6] In other cases, grappling with the requirements of corporate governance codes appeared challenging to larger family businesses, at least in the early stages following their listing.[7]

For smaller family businesses, the value of formal governance systems may seem even more escapable. Some may regard it as an irrelevance, bordering on impertinence, to suggest that close family members, who are working together, should have any need to formally document the fundamentals of their business relationship. Surely this is underpinned by the understanding borne out of a lifetime's shared experience, common interests, jointly held values and, above all, trust?

With a business based around close family working relationships it may well be the case that levels of trust will be high and that the possibility of disputes based on breaches of duty or dishonest practices will be correspondingly reduced. However it does not follow that the need for formal governance arrangements such as family charters or shareholders' agreements is eliminated. Indeed we would argue strongly that there is an increased need for such arrangements in a family owned business than for a non-family owned counterpart.

We would strongly argue that the adoption of governance systems represents a wise investment for the benefit of both the business itself and the business owning family. This is for a number of reasons:

- **Business performance.** First, for the better performance of the family business itself. A traditional perception and criticism of many family businesses is their insularity and resistance to change. The introduction of, for example, non-family

---

[4] In a survey carried out in 2008, only 12% of family owned business respondents confirmed that they had fully documented governance procedures and agreements in place to support their family business (*Praxity Family Business Survey 2008/2009* carried out by the International Centre for Families in Business). In a later survey and in response to a similar question, 63% of the respondents confirmed that they either had no governance structures or only informal arrangements in place so far as their family business was concerned (*2011 National Family Business Report*, University of West of England on behalf of Veale Wasbrough Vizards).

[5] Although this is not without irony, given that one of the key figures in the UK corporate governance landscape is the late Adrian Cadbury, architect of the Cadbury Report (which laid the foundations for the current code) and former chairman of the Cadbury Schweppes business which still fell within the definition of a quoted family business under his stewardship.

[6] Virgin Group and Monsoon Holdings, for example.

[7] For example, Morrison's Supermarkets and, to the extent that it should be seen as a family business, Sports Direct.

independent non-executive directors (see below) and non- family managers can help address this. At least to an extent the case for those family businesses with ambitions for growth and longevity adopting governance processes appears to be borne out by available research.[8]

- **Communication.** Secondly open communication is facilitated by governance processes. We believe that most disputes and failures of succession in family businesses can be traced back to a breakdown of communication. Time spent by a business owning family in devising and operating a governance structure should exponentially increase both the quantity and quality of communication between them.

  It is far more likely that the participators in a non-family business will have clearly agreed objectives for being in business together, for example building the business for a sale within a reasonably defined timeframe. The reasons for a family being in business together are often far less clear.

  Is it simply that there is a job to be done which might as well be carried out by a family member as a third party? If so does this mean that the business remains that of the founder to sell, retain or pass on, as they choose? Alternatively has a talented next generation member given up a promising career in the outside world to join and support the family business (often on a reduced wage) in the expectation that they would be given the business on retirement of the proprietor? The lack of clarity and transparent communication, with a resulting mismatch of expectations, represents a fertile ground for tension and disputes to arise. Ideally these fundamental questions will be debated and addressed as part of a wider governance process, including, in particular, through a family charter.

- **Family dynamics and complexity.** Thirdly, as explained in Part A, the dynamics of a family owned business, with more stakeholders and more roles to be considered, is almost inevitably more complex than its non-family counterpart. Out of that complexity flows the potential for conflict. The classic theoretical model of the family owned business is one of growing complexity, as the business passes down through the generations, from the first generation owner managed entrepreneurial start-up phase, through to the second generation sibling partnership, before moving on to the third stage cousin consortium, where the members of the third or later generations have significantly varied roles in the ownership and management of a (by now) large and complex enterprise.

- **Dispute resolution and prevention.** Finally (and ideally the least relevant reason) is that, in particular the more formal and legally binding outputs from governance processes, such as shareholders' agreements (see below), should assist considerably in resolving disputes that nevertheless arise between family members, notwithstanding the improved communication between the family flowing from their governance system.

  No governance arrangements can be omniscient and capable of providing a universal panacea for all ills that may befall a business owning family. Tensions and disputes can always arise. Indeed some level of conflict must be anticipated.

---

[8] There seems to be a correlation (if not in strict academic terms a causal connection) between the adoption of formal governance processes and the age and size of a family business. Surveys have noted that all large and 55% of medium sized family owned companies in the survey sample had adopted formal governance procedures. Equally, the adoption of formal governance process was seen to grow from 36% in the case of first generation family businesses to 57% in cases where the business was in its third generation or more of family ownership (*University of the West of England National Family Business Report 2011*). However in practice the research into the link between governance and performance in family owned businesses is fairly scarce. But what there is does suggest that there is a positive correlation. This is reviewed in T Pieper *Corporate Governance in Family firms: a Literature Overview* (INSEAD Working Paper Series, 2003) especially at p 16.

However we believe that, in almost every case, appropriate governance arrangements will help to lessen the impact of that conflict.[9]

The available research on family business mortality also suggests that relatively few family owned businesses make the journey through successive generations.[10] Our belief is that one of the key determining factors on whether any particular family business will survive that voyage and thrive in continued family ownership, is the extent to which the business successfully adopts governance systems and principles.

For those who are not yet convinced of the benefits of governance systems for family owned businesses and before leaving this introductory section on the case for governance systems in family owned businesses, we would offer two basic propositions:

- It is difficult to think of a single example where either a business or a family have suffered as a result of paying too much attention to governance issues.
- It is much better for a business owning family to adapt a system that is at least slightly over developed for the current needs of, in particular the family, so that both the business and the family can grow into that system, than for the family governance system to be put in place after the clear need for this has been demonstrated by unfolding events. In other words family governance is a species of insurance policy forming part of the overall risk management systems of the family business.

17.3 A DEFINITION OF GOVERNANCE?

So far, we have spoken about governance systems and procedures only in an abstract sense. What exactly do we mean by governance?

The short answer is that there is no universally accepted definition of governance, particularly in the context of family owned businesses.[11] Traditional approaches have concentrated on the relationship between the directors or managers of a company as agents of its shareholders or owners. These have focused on the rules and regulations that have been put in place to control this relationship together with related incentives (agency theory). Although codes of practice potentially have a contribution, the concept for all businesses, whether family owned or not, is now usually seen in the wider context so that:[12]

> 'more enlightened thinking in recent times has taken governance to include strategy (corporate and financial) as well as risk management. This broader meaning better reflects its importance to a company's prosperity.'

This is echoed by the OECD (Organisation for Economic Co-operation and Development) who believe that:[13]

---

[9] Attempts have been made throughout this book to identify various governance application points in many of the cases discussed. Chapter 2 discusses conflict theory in relation to family firms.
[10] See chapter 1 for a discussion on family business mortality statistics.
[11] T Pieper *Corporate Governance in Family firms: a Literature Overview* (INSEAD Working Paper Series, 2003).
[12] Mellor *Practical Corporate Governance for Smaller Companies and Private Companies* (Jordan Publishing, 2008), Introduction, p XX.
[13] OECD *Principles of Corporate Governance* (OECD, 2nd edn, 2004) at p 11.

'Corporate governance involves a set of relationships between a company's management, its board, its shareholders and other stakeholders. Corporate governance also provides the structure through which the objectives of the company are set, and the means of attaining those objectives and monitoring performance are determined. Good corporate governance should provide proper incentives for the board and management to pursue objectives that are in the interests of the company and its shareholders and should facilitate effective monitoring.'

Leading family business governance writers Neubauer and Lank, identify three core strands in their definition of corporate governance as:[14]

'A system of processes and structures to direct, control and account for the business at the highest level.'

In the context of the family owned business, the concept of governance needs to be wider still and cover not only the business operations and the relationship between management and owners, but also the wider relationship between the business owning family and their family business:[15]

'A family's governance structure is the family's rules and systems under which the family's business and wealth are held and preserved and under which a family and all of its members, fiduciaries and advisors can work together to give the family its own articulated decree and vision. Guidelines will be established for all family members to follow. A good governance structure would look to achieve organised accountability and a clear balance of power among the various interests and bodies that comprise a family and its business. This will include family members, shareholders and directors of the company ...'

More recently the language employed by family members, particularly in later stage, dynastic family firms, has seemed to distance family business governance from more mainstream or controls based forms of corporate governance and has talked about the business insiders or, at times, the current generation as custodians or stewards of the family business, on behalf of generations to come. One of the simplest and most accessible definitions and our favourite has been attributed to a leading family business academic, John Davis 'bringing the right people together at the right time to discuss the right things'. It therefore clear that current thinking about corporate governance goes well beyond a narrow set of rules. Governance is central to the strategy, success operation, continuity and well-being of a family owned business.

17.4 SOURCES OF GOVERNANCE

Based on a wide definition the sources of governance for a family owned business are many and varied. Later in this chapter we will examine the following.

Business governance
- IOD Guidance and Principles
- Family business boards

---

[14] Neubauer and Lank *The Family Business: Its Governance for Sustainability* (Harvard Business School Press, 1997).
[15] *Business Families and Family Business* (STEP Handbook, Globe Business Publishing Limited, 2009).

Family governance

Bespoke family business governance systems including:
- Family assemblies
- Family councils
- Family charters

Ownership governance

Constitutional documents including:
- Articles of Association
- Shareholders' agreements

However these formal governance structures serve to underpin and supplement the core sources of family business governance. These are both intangible and fundamental. They include shared values, a sense of legacy, family cohesion and stewardship. In other words Neubauer and Lank's belief systems.

Before turning to look in detail at these sources of governance, we will take a look at how one of the best known family businesses in the UK has approached the subject of family business governance.

17.5 CASE STUDY – C & J CLARK

17.5.1 Introduction

One of the best-known sayings from the family business world is 'clogs to clogs in three generations'. By 7 May 1993 C & J Clark Ltd, the well-known shoe business started by brothers Cyrus and James Clark in Street, Somerset was already into its sixth generation of family ownership. On that day a shareholder meeting took place at the Royal Bath and West Showground, at nearby Shepton Mallet, which would potentially change that forever. The meeting was to decide whether to accept a take-over bid from Berisford, a US company. The shareholders, over 80% of which were held by family members or family trusts, were deeply divided on the issue with substantial camps of family members for and against the sale. As one national newspaper[16] reported at the time:

> 'One of the few things that unites the two sides is an abhorrence of publicity. This intensely private Quaker Company is trying to keep the lid on a bruising row, but this may soon change. One director told the Independent on Sunday: "To say that we are unhappy is an understatement. People are beginning to express themselves freely. It cannot be nice when you have brothers ... taking opposing sides. They are both very charming and feel hurt at what has happened".'

So what lay behind this division? Arguably the root cause could be traced back to absences of or failures in the governance process of that leading family business. That is not in any way to remotely suggest any lack of propriety by any of the family members or directors concerned. Far from it. The picture that emerges from accounts of the

---

[16] *Independent on Sunday*, 28 March 1993.

company in general and the take-over battle in particular, is one of family shareholders and directors deeply committed to the business and anxious to do the right thing. Not only for their own personal financial interests but also for the employees and wider stakeholders of the business.[17] Rather it appears as though Clarks were suffering from the complexities inherent in the multi- generational ownership of a huge family business. Those complexities sewed the seed corn of a discontent, which had ripened and grown in the years leading up to the Berisford meeting.

17.5.2 Issues

Issues faced by the business included:

- A very large and diverse shareholder register with approximately 70% of the shares being held directly by more than 1,000 individual family shareholders, with the balance more or less evenly divided between trusts connected to the Clark family, employees and institutional shareholders.

- A lack of liquidity in the shares of the company. Attempts had been made to create an internal market for shares through bi-annual trading periods. Although these had been effective under good trading conditions, at times when the business was not performing well, the supply of shares for sale exceeded demand from buyers. At such times family members effectively had their wealth locked into the company.

- An absence of formal communication channels between this diverse group of family shareholders and the board.

- The company struggling to make the transition from being a family run, to a family owned business. Up to a few years before the takeover bid, the chairman, managing director, a significant number of board members and senior executives, all came from within the Clark family. Those struggles included the effective removal from the main board of three family directors in 1986. Later that year the former chairman, Daniel Clark made his frustration with the tension between the board and the family quite clear. In a letter written to a cousin in New Zealand, he said:[18]

    > 'there was a basic ownership instability in the business arising from the now wide dispersal of family shareholding and the fact that although most family shareholders' wealth is in the business very little of it is involved in a direct management or Board way. A couple of mediocre years allowed this instability to ferment.'

- The company faced difficult trading circumstances including high inflation, poor economic conditions, together with market pressures in the shoe industry. In particular cheaper imported shoes accounting for two thirds of the UK market at a time, when the company mainly manufactured its own shoes in the high cost environment of the UK.

- These economic pressures in turn lead to falling profits (in the year ending 31 January 1993 pre-tax profits had fallen by approximately one third to £19.7m from £28.8m in the previous year) and, with the fall in profits, cuts in dividends.

- The above factors caused further deterioration in the relationships between the board, which was split over the takeover, with a narrow majority in favour of sale.

---

[17] See in particular Mark Palmer *Made to Last* (Profile Books, 2013).
[18] Quoted in *Made to Last* at pp 287–288.

- Tensions between the shareholders and the board. This led to the formation of various shareholder activist and pressure groups, seeking to influence company policy and secure their own nominees to board positions.

Of most relevance to the Berisford take-over, was a group of family shareholders, drawn from various branches of the family (including board members) and operating under the acronym SHOES (Share Holders Opposed to Enforced Sale). SHOES issued a circular to shareholders dated 7 April 1993 making their case for the preservation of Clarks as an independent family owned business, arguing that:[19]

> 'it is important that our company is not sold at a low price which reflects the problems in the past rather than the future potential ... we believe that Clarks has a good future. Family ownership has proved responsible in the past and has considered the long-term view. The sale at this time and in this manner would seem to be short sighted and destructive.'

17.5.3 The vote

Ultimately the SHOES contingent found the support of sufficient shareholders to kick the takeover bid into touch. But it was no walk over. In fact the result was nail bitingly close, with the board majority recommendation narrowly failing to achieve the simple majority of shareholder votes it needed for the sale to proceed. On the day 47.5% of votes were cast in favour of a resolution facilitating the sale to Berisford and 52.5% of votes were against the sale.

17.5.4 The Clarks' family business governance system

A key element in the proposal of the SHOES group for the company retaining its independence was a commitment to adopt, within one year of the meeting, a governance system including the creation of a shareholder council.[20] The company then set about creating that governance system. The process was led by the late Roger Pedder, who took over as chairman of the company, following the Berisford meeting.

More than 20 years later that system remains in place and forms a key part of the governance arrangements of a major UK business, still largely family owned and now with a turnover of almost £1.5 billion and pre-tax profits of £35m in what was described as a challenging year.[21] Key features of this governance system include:

- **Shareholder council.** The creation of a shareholder council, intended to act as a bridge between the board of directors and the wider family owners. Representatives of the council are appointed for terms of 4 years and are drawn from all major branches of the Clark family. There is now a member of the seventh generation of the family with a seat on the council. The constitution requires council members to have the backing of shareholders representing at least 4.5% of the share capital of the company. Regular meetings to facilitate communication between the board and the council. There are four meetings a year between the council, and the chairman, CEO and finance director of the company to hear about company performance. These are supplemented by chair-to-chair meetings between, the chairman of the company and the chair of the council.

---

[19] Quoted in *Made to Last* at p 316.
[20] *Made to Last* at p 317.
[21] Source – based on statutory accounts for year ending 31 January 2016.

The council are then in turn responsible for communication with the wider family, including feeding back the views of the family to the board. This two way communication process provides a better level of information flow to shareholders and also a greater degree of accountability on the part of the board than would typically be the case in a widely held company, with many shareholders. Particularly so for shareholders with smaller individual holdings. In the words of Harriet Hall the first chairman of the shareholder council:[22]

> 'I saw my job as keeping the shareholders united and off the management's back, but at the same time the shareholder council was and is a way of holding the management to account.'

The council operates from within the structure of a company limited by guarantee Street Trustee Family Company (STFC). It has a professional secretariat paid for by the company. Family members wishing to participate in the formal governance structure must become a member of STFC. This is a fairly unusual feature. The majority of family councils operate more informally and automatically extend membership to eligible family members.

- **Family directors.** The council are able to nominate two family non-executive directors to sit on the main board.
- **Shareholder voting.** The provisions concerning voting are unusual. As a condition of joining STFC, family shareholders must provide the shareholder council with a power of attorney over their shares in the company. The council is obliged to give advanced notice to shareholders of how they intend to exercise the voting rights conferred by the power of attorney. If they wish to do so, individual family shareholders can withdraw their power of attorney from the council and vote their shares as they wish. Presumably this voting system is to encourage consensus, communication and planning and to prevent the possibility of a repeat of the drama of the Berisford meeting. The checks and balances included mean that the voting arrangements fall short of full abdication of voting rights by the shareholders, in favour of the council. Nevertheless the voting provisions can be seen to represent a highly engineered example of 'nudge architecture'.[23]
- **Education.** In addition to its more formal role the Clarks' shareholder council has a significant role in encouraging wider family engagement and education in particular to help younger generations of the family to learn about their family business.

The Clarks' family governance system has received widespread plaudits from family business commentators.[24] But the acid test of any system of governance must to be the degree to which it engages its constituents. It would appear that engagement in the Clarks' case is widespread. Those factions in the family previously in favour of the third party sale to Berisford joined STFC from the outset. There is also continued interest from younger family members in the 'next' seventh generation, family members in participating on the council and engaging in training activities. Harriet Hall explains that it was:[25]

---

[22] Quoted in *Made to Last* at p 330.
[23] As explained in *the Nudge* (Richard H Thaler and Cass R Sunstein, 2008).
[24] Including recognition as a Family Business Exemplar in the JP Morgan Private Bank Family Business Honours (2003).
[25] Quoted in *Made to Last* at pp 330–331.

'immediately encouraging that all those who wanted to sell the company opted to join the council rather than staying outside and sniping. Some people thought that once things had settled down councillors would stop attending, but this has never been the case. In fact, numbers have increased through allowing younger family members to attend so they can gain experience of looking at the company's performance.'

17.5.5 Clarks: conclusion

The best way to conclude this case study is probably to contrast the instability and uncertainty of May 1993, when something like a 2.5% margin of shareholder votes represented the difference between Clarks remaining in family ownership and sale to a US owned conglomerate, with the more recent attitudes of the shareholders:[26]

> 'in a 2012 survey of family shareholders, one question asked was, "How long do you intend to be a shareholder of Clarks for?" The response of 89 per cent of those polled was, "My lifetime".'

There appears to be little doubt that the family business governance system, pioneered by Roger Pedder in the wake of the Berisford crisis, has been a key factor in promoting this stability throughout a 20-year period which has seen the business expand its turnover, profits and international operations, whilst, at the same time, transforming its operations from a UK based manufacturer to an international retailer.

Given the historical background to Clarks, together with the size and complexity of the business and the number of family shareholders involved, it is easy to see the benefits of and needs for the governance system described above. How relevant are governance systems and procedures for smaller, more typical family owned businesses? Our view, clearly shared by the Institute of Directors (IOD), is that the underlying principles most definitely are relevant. The challenge is to tailor the structure to fit the size and circumstances of the family business concerned.

17.6 THE IOD CODE

17.6.1 Overview of the Code

The IOD (Institute of Directors) Corporate Governance Guidance and Principles for Unlisted Companies in the UK[27] (IOD Principles) sets out detailed guidance on appropriate corporate governance procedures that are applicable to all unquoted companies, including family businesses. The key point made by the IOD is that the level of process adopted by any business should be proportional to the needs, circumstances and ambitions of that business.

The IOD Principles, first published in 2010, are intended to set out guidance on best practice for governance of unlisted companies.[28] The IOD Principles are not intended to apply solely to family owned businesses, but rather to the full spectrum of unlisted

---

[26] *Made to Last* at p 331.
[27] 2010 Institute of Directors. The IOD Code can be downloaded from the IOD website: www.iod.com.
[28] The IOD Principles themselves have been developed from a wider European project and guidance, developed by the European Confederation of Directors Association (EcoDa), which have been translated into a UK context by the IOD.

companies. The IOD document nevertheless makes frequent reference to the family business situation and Principle 9 (discussed in detail below) is aimed specifically at family owned businesses.

Particularly for those not familiar with corporate governance concepts, or who wish to benchmark their own or their client's family business against best practice, the IOD Code is well worth reading in full. Nevertheless the level of the awareness of the IOD Principles, even amongst the professional community appears to be unfortunately low.

Even the full UK Corporate Governance Code applicable to listed companies in the UK does not have statutory effect. Rather, it relies on the 'comply or explain' principle whereby listed companies have to justify departures from the UK corporate governance code to the investor community. The logic being that an aversion to doing so will encourage a high level of compliance in practice.

The IOD refer to the concern of the OECD that applying 'an excessively formal approach in the case of unlisted companies would have adverse implications of costs and flexibility'.[29] Whilst having strong echoes of the UK Corporate Governance Code, the IOD are at pains to point out that:[30]

> 'the principles should not be viewed as a corporate governance code, but rather as a set of proposals aimed at increasing the professionalism and effectiveness of unlisted companies.'

The IOD Principles are entirely voluntary, without the underlying impetus of market pressure to encourage compliance. Neither have we seen any particular evidence of other stakeholders, for example bankers, encouraging adoption of the IOD Principles as a condition of lending.

17.6.2 Proportionality and the 'stepwise approach'

The IOD Principles recognise that the approach to governance taken by a business forms part of the overall picture of the transition, from an entrepreneurial owner managed start up business, into a fully governed corporate enterprise. Also that governance is not an end in itself but a key component in the success and survival of an enterprise. Accordingly the IOD code acknowledges that the approach to the adoption of governance systems needs to be gradual and realistic. The recommendation is to adopt a 'stepwise approach'. That is, a level of adoption that is proportionate to both the size and current circumstances of a company, but also its growth plans. This clearly sits well alongside the theory of evolution of family businesses from their owner managed phase, through into the second generation of sibling partnerships, into the more complex multi generation cousin consortium businesses in their third generation and beyond.[31]

Significantly the IOD code recognises the link between adopting formal governance process, as part of the professionalisation of owner managed businesses and their growth and survival. With this there is an inherent link between the governance and the succession process and in particular the need for the business founder to 'let go' of absolute control of the family business and move towards a more consensual model of

---

[29] Op cit at p 2.
[30] Op cit at p 2.
[31] See the discussion on basic family business evolution and life cycle theory models in chapter 3 and also the more complex model discussed below.

decision making.[32] Whilst the IOD code acknowledges the contribution of founding entrepreneurs it warns that building a business around a single individual '… is not a sustainable model for the longer term'.

Nevertheless the IOD code recognises that there is a danger of stifling entrepreneurial zeal and becoming unduly bureaucratic, so 'building the right checks and balances is therefore a delicate exercise …'.

The approach recommended by the IOD is for:
- Formal delegation of authority

    'The owner and/or the board should develop a systematic approach towards the delegation of authority and formalise this in writing. A schedule of matters reserved for the board and for executive management should be established, which sets out the parameters of the delegated authority (with attention for any financial thresholds regarding decision-making powers).'[33]

- Development of teamwork

    'A basic principle of good governance is that no one individual should have unfettered power over decision-making. There should exist 'checks and balances' that subject the actions of individuals to scrutiny, while the most important decisions should be taken on a collective basis.'[34]

- Chairman's leading role

    'The chairman has a particular responsibility in welding a group of capable individuals into *an effective board team*.'[35]

17.6.2 The fourteen principles

The IOD guidance operates through a set of 14 separate principles divided into:
- Nine 'phase 1' principles seen by the IOD as of general applicability to all unlisted businesses.
- A further five 'phase 2' principles applicable only to 'large and /or more complex unlisted companies'. The IOD do not attempt a definition of what they mean by a large or more complex company other, than to say that the phase 2 principles should apply to unlisted companies with significant external financing and all those aspiring to a public listing.[36]

Within each principle there is both an explanation of the key points underlying that principle and a discussion on the practical considerations and limitations relevant to a 'step wise' implementation.

In detail the 14 principles are:

---

[32] See chapter 7.
[33] IOD Code, Part 1 para 4(i).
[34] IOD Code, Part 1 para 4(ii).
[35] IOD Code, Part 1 para 3(iii).
[36] Op cit at p 36.

Phase 1 Principles – Applicable to all unlisted companies

- **Principle 1:** Shareholders should establish an appropriate constitutional and governance framework for the company.
- **Principle 2:** Every company should strive to establish an effective board, which is collectively responsible for the long-term success of the company, including the definition of the corporate strategy. However, an interim step on the road to an effective (and independent) board may be the creation of an advisory board.
- **Principle 3:** The size and composition of the board should reflect the scale and complexity of the company's activities.
- **Principle 4:** The board should meet sufficiently regularly to discharge its duties, and be supplied in a timely manner with appropriate information.
- **Principle 5:** Levels of remuneration should be sufficient to attract, retain and motivate executives and non-executives of the quality required to run the company successfully.
- **Principle 6:** The board is responsible for risk oversight and should maintain a sound system of internal control to safeguard shareholders' investment and the company's assets.
- **Principle 7:** There should be a dialogue between the board and the shareholders based on a mutual understanding of objectives. The board as a whole has responsibility for ensuring that a satisfactory dialogue with shareholders takes place. The board should not forget that all shareholders have to be treated equally.
- **Principle 8:** All directors should receive induction on joining the board and should regularly update and refresh their skills and knowledge.
- **Principle 9:** Family-controlled companies should establish family governance mechanisms that promote coordination and mutual understanding amongst family members, as well as organise the relationship between family governance and corporate governance.

Phase 2 Principles – applicable to larger unlisted companies

- **Principle 10:** There should be a clear division of responsibilities at the head of the company between the running of the board and the running of the company's business. No one individual should have unfettered powers of decision.
- **Principle 11:** All boards should contain directors with a sufficient mix of competencies and experiences. No single person (or small group of individuals) should dominate the board's decision-making.
- **Principle 12:** The board should establish appropriate board committees in order to allow a more effective discharge of its duties.
- **Principle 13:** The board should undertake a periodic appraisal of its own performance and that of each individual director.
- **Principle 14:** The board should present a balanced and understandable assessment of the company's position and prospects for external stakeholders, and establish a suitable programme of stakeholder engagement.

It will be seen that Principle 9 deals specifically with the need for family owned businesses to establish governance mechanisms to co-ordinate family and business governance. There is a growing body of practice around family councils and family charters aimed at providing these mechanisms. Clearly the Clarks Shareholder Council described in the case study above represents a highly evolved example of these mechanisms. Family councils and family charters are discussed in much more detail in 17.13 of this chapter below.

The IOD Principles place great importance on the board of directors as being the primary engine of governance of a company. This view is consistent with the views of academic family business commentators[37] and the principles of UK company law.[38] Later sections of this chapter therefore examine the composition and operation of boards in the family business context in detail.

17.7 STAGES IN FAMILY BUSINESS GOVERNANCE

17.7.1 Evolution and complexity

The Clarks case study, along with much of the literature on family business governance,[39] deals with a large and highly sophisticated family enterprise. Full governance systems will not be appropriate for smaller family firms. However something will be required.

The IOD Code recognises that the need for a family owned business to adopt increasingly complex systems of governance will evolve as a family owned business passes down through the generations from the first generation owner managed entrepreneurial start-up phase and beyond. The Code refers to 'step wise' growth.

What could those steps be in the context of the board of a family business? The short answer is that it is impossible to be prescriptive and to arrive at a one size fits all model for every family enterprise. Even if one works from the 'classic model' of family business evolution discussed in chapter 3, from an owner managed start-up, through a sibling partnership to a cousin collaboration, it will be seen that the situations of a family business and hence its governance requirements are different at each stage.

However one of the central points made by Gersick *et al* is that, family businesses grow and evolve in different ways, against the basic three dimensions of the family system.[40] They nevertheless argue that there are certain identifiable stages in each of the dimensions.

---

[37] John Ward *Creating Effective Boards for Private Enterprises* (Jossey-Bass, 1991).
[38] See chapter 8.
[39] In particular leading works such as Neubauer and Lank *The Family Business: Its Governance for Sustainability* (Harvard Business School Press, 1997).
[40] See Figure 17.2 which is based on figure 1.3 from Gersick, Davis, Hampton & Lansberg *Generation to Generation: Life cycles of a family business* (Harvard Business School Press, 1997).

Governance and the Family Owned Business 601

Figure 17.2: The three-dimensional developmental model

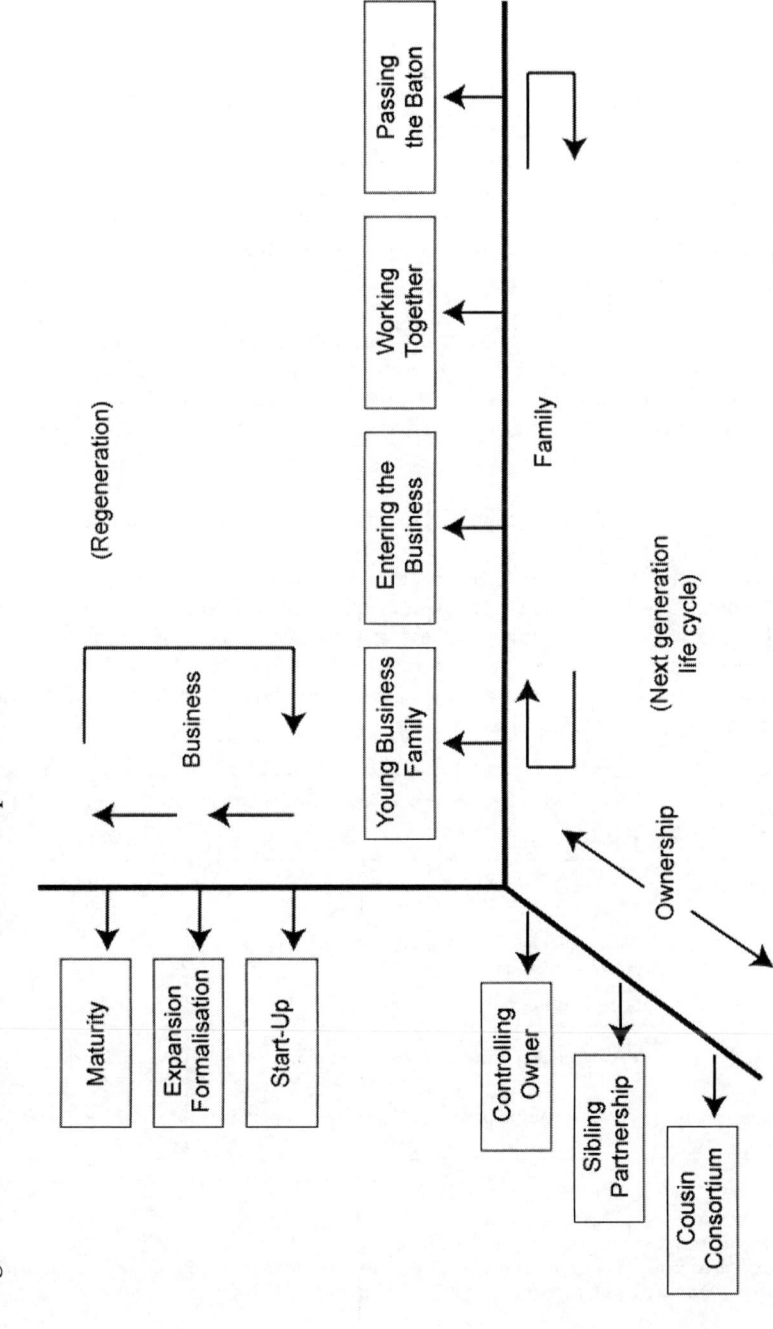

Taking the ownership dimension, some businesses[41] will continually recycle the controlling owner mode. This might be based on a concern that relationships between offspring are not robust enough to support a sibling partnership. There could be a wish to avoid the complexities of the cousin collaboration. Alternatively there could be a belief that a single strong ownership voice is best for the growth of the business.[42] Whatever the motivation, the ownership system will be simple, with a correspondingly reduced need for governance. However the business might grow rapidly and thereby create a requirement for more sophisticated management processes and systems.

Different combinations of circumstances can apply. For example a small family farm, which is run by a single sibling, but with the business or the underlying land in joint sibling ownership is likely to throw up few business governance issues, but will almost inevitably lead to a degree of complexity in the family and ownership dimensions. Neither is any movement that takes place along the dimensions necessarily linear. As discussed in chapter 11, more drastic pruning of the ownership tree can return a sibling partnership or even a cousin consortium, to the stage of an owner-managed business, with a corresponding simplification of governance requirements in the ownership system.

Less obvious is the potential for the business itself to move back through the life cycles. However Gersick *et al* argue that mature businesses need to find ways to regenerate their business offering, by entering new markets or producing new products and services. If not, they suggest that the stages beyond maturity are stagnation and death for the business.

It therefore follows that the appropriate governance system for any given family business will be dictated by the particular blend of evolutionary stages that business occupies along each of the three core dimensions. At least in part. There are also the issues of family dynamics and individual personalities to be taken into consideration. However, one of the functions of family business governance systems is to ameliorate and compensate, so far as possible, for the negative effects of these. Looking at the evolution in a single generation the business family, the key governance challenges, at the various stages of maturity can be summarised as follows:

Stage of family development	Three Circle Model System and Governance Challenges		
	Family	Business	Ownership
Young business family	Work life balance	Survival	Joint or sole ownership (ch 18)
	Sharing family responsibility (ch 18)	Risk management (ch 8)	
	Socialisation (ch 5)	Isolation	
Entering the business	Family expectations	Family employment policies (ch 7)	Managing ownership expectations (ch 19)
	Career opportunities (ch 5)	Recruiting non-family employees (ch 6)	

---

[41] This appears to have been the case within the Krtistiansen family as owners of Lego.
[42] There is some research to support idea that single ownership models prove most successful in terms of family business performance and longevity.

Stage of family development	Three Circle Model System and Governance Challenges		
	Family	Business	Ownership
Working together	Role confusion (ch 3) Insiders and outsiders (Part E)	Establishing roles and responsibilities (ch 7) Professionalisation Retaining non family managers (ch 6)	Examining ownership approach (ch 15)
Passing the baton	Letting go (ch 7) The 'succession conspiracy' (ch 7) Sibling rivalry (ch 3)	Management succession (ch 7)	Finalising ownership approach (ch 15)

Note the references are to chapters where particular issues are discussed in more detail.

At root the answer to most of these challenges is communication.

17.7.2 The early stage business – governance challenges

Looking at the stages in the classic model of evolution for the family business in more detail, starting with the early stage or start up business, the first step will be to establish an appropriate level of communication between the life partners concerned with the business (who may or may not also be business partners) appropriate to the level of involvement of the partners concerned and the impact of the success or failure of the business on the wider family, it's wealth and assets. Some suggestions are contained in the following chapter, which deals with the family business and marriage.

Gersick argues that a single controlling owner is entitled to exercise the sole 'voice of ownership ... a vocal solo. There is no ambiguity about the controlling owner's right to represent the ownership point of view'.[43]

However there is a strong argument that the financial security of the rest of the family could be damaged by any imprudence on the part of the controlling owner, so the spouse and older children have a strong interest in the implementation of a basic level of governance for risk management purposes.[44]

Most of the issues referred to in the table above are either fairly self-explanatory, or dealt with in more detail in the chapters referred to. However it might be helpful to elaborate on one or two matters at this stage.

- **Isolation.** Especially in family businesses led by a single founding entrepreneur, isolation and losing touch with wider business and market issues can be a risk. The demands of customers and limited resource, both financial and time can make such matters as trade shows, business networking and continuing business education

---
[43] At p 225.
[44] This theme is explored in more detail in chapter 17.

seem like a luxury. They are not. For an early stage family firm building a support network can be seen as both a necessity and the precursor to a more formal board structure as the business matures.[45]

Options for a support network include:
- Using some combination of accountants, lawyers, bankers, consultants and other advisors to provide periodic and objective advice on the wider position of the business and relevant issues it faces.
- Establishing an informal support network through relevant trade and general business organisations, networking, friends and contacts.
- Participation in formal business support programmes such as executive clubs and action learning programmes.
- Awareness raising and business skills training through workshops, training programmes, briefings and seminars such as those run by the IOD or local Learning Enterprise Partnerships.

- **Risk management.** As a related point, one of the core functions of governance is risk management. This is at odds with various entrepreneurial stereotypes. First, the entrepreneur as a risk taker. Secondly the entrepreneur a hero, one aspect of which is to stoically and silently shoulder the burden of financial and other business worries, shielding the rest of the family in the process. Thirdly the entrepreneur as a 'man of action', rather than reflection. As Gersick puts it: 'The founder is pre-occupied with implementing his or her vision, not reflecting on it'.[46] As the risk of family business failure will be equally felt by the whole family, good governance demands that discussion on the level of risk and its management are appropriately shared with life partners in young business families,[47] and with the wider family once the entering the business stage has been reached.[48]

17.7.3 Governance and the next generation transition

By the time that the next generation are contemplating entering the family business informal communication needs to be re-enforced by semi-structured family meetings of some description. Certainly these need to be in place by the time the oldest offspring are in their mid to late teens.

As Gersick puts it by this time 'the voice of ownership becomes a choir'.[49]

A few years later, when the working together and passing the baton stages have been reached, more attention will need to be given to formal and structured discussions about matters such as the roles of family insiders and ownership approach. These are discussed in detail in the chapters referred to above.

It is important that clear and consistent messages about the strengths and weaknesses of family business life and the attitude of the senior generation to careers in and ownership of the family firm are put on the table. Such formal family meetings are the precursor to

---

[45] Although the founder of Park House Properties, Mr Carter had his son and daughter working with him in the business, neither were old nor experienced enough to provide him with any meaningful governance support. The case is discussed in detail in chapter 8.
[46] Gersick et al, op cit at p 229.
[47] This issue is discussed in more detail in chapter 18. Risk discussion was singularly absent in the case of *Re Gemma* discussed in chapter 8.
[48] Again no real attempt to analyse risk and discuss relevant issues with the next generation was evident in *Park House Properties*.
[49] At p 226.

the family assemblies or family council meetings of the larger business owning family discussed below. They are intended to supplement, but not replace, the day-to-day communication about family business issues which lead to the high level of understanding of the next generation, which is a core strength of most family businesses.

It is equally important that this is done in an appropriate, clear and consistent way, so that ideally all offspring receive the same message at the same time. The exact opposite happened in James Davies' case,[50] especially in the case of ownership governance. As an inducement to join the family farming business, James was offered ownership by his father, at the inappropriately early age of 16. However that offer was not discussed with James' four siblings, or perhaps even his mother, Ellen. Equally when the father changed his mind and decided to leave the farm to the wider family, James was not told about this fundamental change of intention.

17.8 GOVERNANCE AND THE LATER STAGE FAMILY BUSINESS: BRIDGING THE DIVIDE

The terms insider and outsider have been widely used in this book to distinguish between owners who work in the business and owners or wider family members who do not. Once the family business reaches the stage where there two identifiable camps exist, complexity is a given. The need more structured governance becomes inescapable. Insiders and outsiders will typically have different perspectives on share ownership.

Ownership perspectives[51]	
Insiders	Outsiders
Have more access to knowledge and information	Less access to knowledge and information
Are so steeped in the business that they do not recognise that outsiders have less knowledge and understanding	Want to feel more connected to the business
Have power and status and can make important decisions	May be struggle with the boundaries and responsibilities of ownership
Work hard and carry a heavy burden	Often feel disrespected by the owner managers
May view owners outside the business as parasites	May suspect that owner/managers receive inflated salaries and perks

The table above might be seen as exaggerating the differences between insiders and outsiders. Nevertheless these factors emerge in many of the cases considered in this book. Governance in later stage family businesses is primarily focused on attempting to bridge the gap between insiders and outsiders. There are three key areas:

- Family employment policies.
- Dividend policies.
- Communication and information.

---

[50] Introduced in chapter 1 and explained in detail in chapter 19.
[51] Source: based on Aronoff & Ward *Family Business Ownership: How to be an Effective Shareholder* (Family Enterprise Publishers, 2002).

Ideally a fully functioning governance process will lead to deeper dialogue on more strategic issues, including the future development of the family company, so that the business moves forward in a direction that is understood, supported and informed by the views of the wider business family.

John Ward warns of the limitations to this ideal position and talks about the tension between those not working in the family business and those who are. He sees the two camps as caught between a rock and a hard place. If the outsiders do not take an interest in the business the insiders not only have to work out what they think is right for the business, but also whether their decisions will be approved by their wider family. On the other hand if the outsiders want to be too heavily involved and to be recognised as able to contribute equally in taking key decisions this can be seen as interference. The insiders could regard equal decision taking as devaluing the skills, knowledge and insight they have gained as a result of their full time commitment to the business. In Ward's words the full time family executives:[52]

> '… wish that their siblings understood more so that they could 'approve' [their] decisions they really don't relish any interference with their autonomy. In fact they would prefer passive, informed appreciation.'

Ward's solution? To rely on an outside (non-family) board of directors to provide checks and balances to the family insiders and with that reassurance to the wider family that the insiders are held accountable by the wider board.

17.9 THE FAMILY BUSINESS BOARD

17.9.1 Boards and the early stage family business

A similar evolutionary process can be identified in the primary organ of business governance in the family company: its board of directors.

As explained in chapter 18, at the start up or young business family stage the business could be directed, in the sense of full business leadership by a copreneurial couple or by a single business leader (even if the spouse is nominally also a director[53]). Once the entering the business stage has been reached, the founder may be keen to appoint next-generation family members to directorships and other positions of responsibility, often at a comparatively young age. The key questions become how deep and real is this change (and how appropriate is the appointment.[54]

Here there is a clear link between family business governance and succession planning.[55] A key question in any succession planning exercise is whether the next generation are ready to assume a high level or full management responsibility? The reverse side of this question is whether, in reality, the current generation are ready to let go of any real responsibility for the direction and control over the family business? Failure to address these issues will often mean that real decision-making resides firmly in the hands of the

---
[52] John Ward *Family Business Advisor* (July 1994).
[53] The risks of this are explored in chapter 8.
[54] Explored in chapter 5.
[55] See chapter 7. The UK Corporate Governance Code sees this as one of the primary responsibilities of the board.

first generation founder entrepreneur, with the remaining family members holding nominal positions and playing supporting roles.

17.9.2 Rubber stamp boards

In the absence of formal governance processes, debate and constructive challenge at board level may well be minimal. Indeed formal board meetings may not be held at all. It may be rare, if not unheard of, for the founder to be overruled by the remaining board members or for any decision to be taken without the express approval of the founder. Although a board of directors exists, at least on paper, it operates on the basis of what Peter Leach has referred to as a 'rubber stamp board'.[56]

The rubber stamp board phenomenon is not exclusively confined to the first stage, owner managed family business. Dominant controlling characters can often be found at the centre of second stage siblings partnerships or under third stage cousin consortiums where the brothers, sisters and cousins concerned, particularly those remote from day-to-day involvement in the family business, occupy board positions, but in reality do not assume any real responsibility for the discharge of director's functions.

The most striking example of a rubber stamp board we have encountered was in a fifth generation family owned business, with a significant turnover running to hundreds of millions of pounds. The company had a large board of directors. Changes to the board were frequent, particularly amongst the executive directors, but on average the company usually had 10 or so directors, made up of a fairly even mix of non-family executive and non-executive directors, together with family directors. The dominant character was a family executive chairman who presided over the board of the company with authoritarianism bordering on dictatorship. This chairman no doubt gained added confidence from a formal constitutional provision, contained in the articles of association of the company to the effect that:

> 'in the event that the Board does not vote unanimously on any particular matter those directors voting with the Chairman shall be deemed to outnumber by one of those directors of voting against the Chairman.'

That business is no longer in family ownership.

17.9.3 Advisory boards

The IOD Code canvasses the possibility of a family business creating an advisory board. Usually an advisory board would be an interim solution, between a fully family run board and a board with one or more formally appointed non-executive directors. Although there may be some cost advantages, this suggestion may well be driven primarily by a recognition that a founder often needs to be led gently along a path that leads to an increase, both in the formality of the way that their family business operates, but also crucially, the degree of accountability and challenge that the founder faces personally.

---

[56] Leach, op cit, p 109.

As that the name suggests the function of an advisory board is not to act on a statutory basis, but to provide a sounding board for the founder's ideas and concerns over the direction of the business. Almost literally a sounding board.

The concept of an advisory board is not recognised under English law. Great care will need to be exercised to ensure that the advisory board members are not classed as either shadow directors or de-facto directors, thus assuming all of the responsibilities of formally appointed board members but with none of the powers.[57]

Paradoxically, the more effective and influential the advisory board is in shaping and influencing the founder and the direction of the family business, the greater this risk will be. Conversely the more resistant to change and influence the founder is, the harder it will be to demonstrate that the advisory board members have exerted any real directorial influence. These issues will always remain one of degree and interpretation. However that interpretation would be assisted by relevant documentation, including clear terms of reference for the advisory board, minutes of meetings and most importantly board minutes demonstrating the independence and separate review by the actual directors of key issues that had been considered by the advisory board.

17.9.4 Functioning boards

The rubber stamp board is the polar opposite of the support offered by the model board of larger family owned businesses envisaged by commentators.[58]

What are the indicators of a functioning board of directors in later stage first generation or more mature family owned business? We would suggest the following:

- **Regular board meetings.** Regular board meetings, scheduled in advance and supported by board packs distributed sufficiently before the meeting to allow board members to arrive properly briefed and prepared to participate and challenge the executive directors. The board packs would include copies of all key financial information, briefing notes and other important documents relevant to the meeting. The frequency of board meetings will vary from business to business and depend on its size and complexity. Monthly meetings may be necessary for some businesses. Other factors will influence how frequently board meetings need to be held, such as the extent to which the executive family directors are supported by a good family or non-family full time management team. If so, the formal board can take more of a strategic and less of an operational role. In such businesses quarterly, biannual or, in rare and exceptional cases even annual meetings, may be sufficient. The less frequent the pattern of regular board meetings, the more it will be necessary to supplement these with emergency or ad hoc meetings to deal with key issues and decisions that simply can't wait until the next scheduled board meeting.

- **Strategic debate.** The key point is that whenever board meetings take place, a sensible, structured debate will ensue. Key indicators would be the full participation of all directors, both speaking and listening and crucially an absence of factionalism. Ideally the board should be able to point to at least some occasions where dominant family founders or business leaders change their position as a

---

[57] De facto and shadow directors are dealt with in chapter 8 (Directors' Duties).
[58] See for example Ward *Creating Effective Boards for Private Enterprises – Meeting the Challenges of Continuity and Competition* (Family Enterprise Publishers, 2001) and Carlock & Ward, op cit at pp 227–232.

result of debate at the meeting. Perhaps the acid test of a fully functioning board would be the ability to point to an instance when the dominant family member was outvoted.

- **Directors and family directors.** A board chosen on the basis of the skill set and experience of the directors concerned, rather than for family reasons, such as the need for each branch of the family to be represented on the board. Broad family representation on the board may be a necessary or even a desirable consequence of wider family ownership, to ensure that the voice of the owning family is heard. However for a board to be most effective, family appointed directors need to be able to bring independent value and richness to the family business board, rather than simply acting as spokespersons for a particular branch of the family. There are other ways for the voice of the family to be heard (in particular through family councils as discussed below) rather than use family directors as messengers for their appointing branch.[59]

- **Induction.** A formal induction programme for directors joining the board of a family owned business might seem to be an irrelevant concept borrowed from the world of the quoted company.[60] If family members are being appointed they are likely to have grown up with an awareness of the family businesses and be steeped in its complexities from a very early age. However that awareness may well have been instilled, at least in part by parents and other relatives, who no longer have an active role in the family business. The inherited dinner table knowledge may have passed its sell by date and have little relevance to the market conditions and challenges presently facing the family business. Worse still, the impressions that family members bring to the boardroom table may be coloured by a toxic combination of historical baggage and family myths. A structured induction programme, comprising briefings on key strategic issues, market conditions and business plans, combined with the opportunity for new directors to spend time with key managers and to observe the operations of the business at first hand, can be invaluable in creating a cohesive board. The alternative could be a factional board with, in particular new directors appointed at the behest of family branches, seen as outsiders sent to check up on the rest of the board and to pursue the agenda of their appointing branch.

- **Board training and education.** In many successful and growing family businesses family members and senior employees appointed to the board from within the ranks of the family business may well have grown their own capabilities roles and performance in parallel with the success of the business. They may have little outside experience and formal training. Making a commitment to formal director's training, in particular on financial, management and governance issues, may help those directors to carry on swimming with the tide of the continued growth of the business, rather than sink under the increased complexity that this creates.[61]

- **Evaluation.** A central plank of modern corporate governance theory is board performance evaluation. This applies to both the functioning of the board as a whole and the individual performance of the board members. This is one of the chairman's responsibilities. The former can often be dealt with as part of regular board 'away days' referred to below. Clearly this can be a sensitive subject, especially in a family company with a history of tension or which is beset by branch factionalism. Neubauer and Lank suggest a form of 360 degree appraisal,

---

[59] Some of the perils of acting as a family director are explored in chapter 8 (Directors' Duties).
[60] See main principle B.4 of the UK Corporate Governance Code.
[61] The IOD run various director's training programmes. For further details go to https://www.iod.com/training.

confined to fellow board members, to provide a measure of objectivity.[62] They also suggest that, if used sensitively, the process can promote the gradual strengthening of the board. Ideally the process will lead to better team and individual contributions. If not, they suggest that the process could help to, 'family directors', to realise that the time when they were most useful to the family firm has now passed and encourage them to step down in favour of more suitable candidates.[63] Nevertheless, the potential for such evaluation to expose weaknesses in family cohesion and conflict must nevertheless be present in many cases.

17.9.5 Two-tier boards

A number of European jurisdictions organise their corporate governance on the basis of a two-tier board system, with a management board having responsibility for the day to day operations and management of the company and a supervisory board assuming responsibility for the overall strategic direction, oversight and risk management of the company. Usually the supervisory board will have a majority of non-executive directors (and, in some jurisdictions, for companies over a certain size, compulsory employee representation). Many jurisdictions prohibit membership of both boards.

Some commentators[64] advocate the use of two-tier boards for UK and other common law jurisdiction family run businesses. Often the stability and historic success of the German mid-sized business sector, the Mittlestand, which is predominantly comprised of family owned businesses is cited as evidence in support of the benefits of the two-tier board system.

The use of a two-tier board system in family enterprises is based on two different justifications.

- **Policing.** First pragmatism and realism. This recognises the possible reluctance of the owning family to surrender full control of a business, to a management team, especially a non-family team. The business may have been in the family for generations and which may also represent a considerable part of the combined wealth of that family. In more mature family businesses ownership may be widely spread across the family. At the same time day-to-day management of the business is concentrated either in a narrower group of family members, or non-family executives, who perhaps do not command the full confidence of the wider family. In these cases the supervisory board would be dominated by family members. Its role would be very much to police the operating board and to make sure that they do not bet the family ranch. Nevertheless this arrangement does provide some potential to demarcate management and ownership decisions[65] and thereby give the management some room for manoeuvre, free from wider family involvement in day-to-day operational matters. A supervisory board of this nature would be most often found in and suitable for a mid-sized family business, often one at a relatively early stage of their journey from being family managed to family owned.
- **Strategic oversight.** The second school of thought is based more on a view of how the ideal board should operate. This is as a high level body, responsible for strategy and oversight, with a view on the big picture for the family business. The board

---

[62] See pp 118–121.
[63] Neubauer and Lank *The Family Business: Its Governance for Sustainability* (Harvard Business School Press, 1997) at pp 118–123.
[64] See Neubauer and Lank at p 98.
[65] For example through the use of carefully thought out and agreed lists of restricted matters (see **11.8**).

should be distinct from the management of the company and should not interfere in day-to-day operational matters. Instead the board should set overall policies, goals and objectives for the management team and monitor their performance and delivery against these. Equally the strategic board should maintain distance from the business owning family. It is not there to act on behalf of the family or represent the family viewpoint. That is the role of the family council (see below). Instead the board has a more neutral and objective brief, to exercise its judgment and skill in what it believes to be in the best long term interests of business and of the family as shareholders.

17.9.6 Holding companies and committees

As is the case with most common law jurisdictions, company law in the UK does not formally recognise the civil law two-tier board structure. However an equivalent structure can be created in practice by some combination of:

- **Holding companies.** A corporate group structure, with a holding company board can exercise many of the functions of a supervisory board. The day-to-day operations of the business would be carried on in one or more operating subsidiaries, with only the most senior management from these companies (who will often be senior family managers anyway) taking a seat from around the holding company board table.
- **Committees.** Alternatively board committees can be used within a single company structure. Here the board delegate operational matters to one or more committees, often termed operating boards or executive boards. The executive directors including, at least the managing director and finance director, would be joined by operating function heads. Often these would have courtesy titles, such as sales director, operations director etc, but would not be formally appointed *de-jure* directors.[66]

There would be minimal overlap with the full board, with perhaps just the most senior family executives and possibly the finance director sitting on both.

17.9.7 Board roles

Boards of family companies come in all shapes and sizes and make a range of contributions. Neubauer and Lank identify a range of influence from where the board run the company, through where the board have a detached and strategic role, to where the board provides a limited forum for the voice of outsider family shareholders to be heard. At the lowest end of this scale the board have no real influence.[67] Having looked at board structures we now turn to look at various categories of director and the qualities needed by them.

17.10 BOARD COMPOSITION

17.10.1 Overview

Under the model which regards the board as providing strategic overview, there is likely to be a majority of independent directors. That is neither executive directors nor family

---

[66] See chapter 8.
[67] Op cit at pp 101–104.

members. John Ward suggests that there should be at least three non-executive directors on a family business board, basically to encourage constructive challenge and dynamism within the board.[68] It has been suggested that the ideal size for a medium-sized family business would be no more than seven directors.[69] The recommendation goes on to suggest that there should ideally be an odd number of directors to prevent deadlock and stalemate on the board. It may well be that provisions found in the articles of many UK family businesses which provide a casting vote for the chairman,[70] are not likely to find favour with these commentators.

It will be seen that family owned business boards, structured and operating on the basis referred to in the previous paragraph, will be very much in the minority and, in practice, usually found only in larger family businesses which are further down the pathway of professionalisation and the journey from being family managed to family owned. For example, Clarks shoes as referred to in the case study above.[71]

The vast majority of family companies will have a board drawn largely from the ranks of the management team, both family and non-family, supplemented by a mixture of family and non-executive directors. The challenge then becomes to differentiate between operational and strategic matters and to ensure that both are adequately covered within the overall group. One possibility is to ensure that board have regular (at least annual) board 'away days' to focus on key performance and strategic issues for the company as a whole.

17.10.2 Non-family executive directors

A key stage in the evolution of most successful family owned businesses is the recognition that the gene pool of even the most gifted families is unlikely to provide a complete answer to all business challenges facing a growing and increasingly complex business. Acting on that recognition, the founder will seek to strengthen the operational capability of their early stage family owned business by recruiting, rewarding, motivating, developing and above all retaining non family managers, who can fill the gaps in the family skill set and equip the business to progress. The role of the non-family manager is considered in more detail in chapter 6.

Some of these key non family managers may go on to become valued executive directors, with positions on the family business board. They may be close confidants and contemporaries of the founder. Alternatively non-family directors may have grown up with the family business and have been promoted from the ranks. In either case, the possibility of non-family 'insiders' providing serious challenge to the founder and his world-view is not likely to be a strong. Alternatively, particularly in the largest family businesses, outsiders may have been recruited directly into executive director positions. Conflicts between the founder and especially senior executive directors brought from outside the family business are correspondingly more common. The successful family

---

[68] John Ward *Creating Effective Boards for Private Enterprises* (Jossey-Bass, 1991) at p 111.
[69] Neubauer and Lank at pp 109–113.
[70] Model Articles, Art 13(1).
[71] A number of commentators argue that this changes the system analysis of the larger family business, for example by introducing a fourth circle, the board or director system into the three-circle model – see for example *New Corporate Governance* (Hilb Springer 2005), Figure 1-14 at p 34. Other variations are to start with a general corporate governance model of three systems, ownership, management and business to which Neubauer and Lank, introduce the family dimension as a 'tie' between the systems – see p 15 of *The Family Business: Its Governance for Sustainability* (Harvard Business School Press, 1997).

businesses will be those with founders who have both the confidence and self-awareness to balance, on the one hand an adherence to their initial business vision and drive that has taken the business to a stage where it can afford to hire senior and highly competent non family executive directors with, on the other hand, a realisation that those directors have value to add. Part of that value is to provide constructive challenge to and, if necessary help in reshaping that vision.

17.10.3 Non-executive directors

Similar factors apply to the successful recruitment and integration of external non-executive directors. With one key difference. With the possible exception of finance directors, who may sometimes be appointed at the behest of the company's bankers, the founder will have identified a clear and obvious need to appoint an external executive director. The appointment will be primarily operationally driven. Any strategic value added by a good executive director will be an added bonus.

The reverse is true with the appointment of a non-executive director. Their appointment will be primarily strategically driven. This in turn requires the founder to acknowledge that their vision is not all seeing and all powerful and that this can be tested, refined and developed under the guidance of good non executive directors. A number of commentators have elaborated on the benefits good non-executive directors can bring to a family business, including the following:

- industry knowledge;
- contacts both in the relevant industry and the wider business world;
- adding prestige to the board;
- general business experience in some cases at a high level in major corporates. In others the experience might be as an entrepreneur and business leader in other successful owner managed businesses;
- knowledge of and experience in dealing with family business issues;
- mentoring of executives both family and non-family;
- appraising and supporting the founder;
- helping to deal with sensitive business issues with a family content in an objective and non-partisan way, eg recruitment of family members, remuneration and dividend policies.

However the benefit that is most often cited is the degree of objectivity and challenge that good non-executive directors can bring to the founder and the family business members. Their wider world-view can provide an invaluable antidote to the insularity of the family business environment.

The recruitment of independent external non-executive directors (as opposed to family members without day-to-day involvement in business) represents a key milestone in the evolution and professionalisation of a family owned business. Ideally the leadership of the family business will have both developed a vision and ambition for the future of the business and also come to the conclusion that neither the management team nor the support available from within the wider business owning family will be sufficient to achieve that ambition. As a result outside help is needed.

But where should that come from? Neubauer and Lank[72] have a list of those who are unlikely to prove effective non-executive directors for a family business. That list includes:

- The accountant, lawyer or other usual professional advisors of the family business. The logic being that their advice would be readily available under normal engagement terms. Also that their appointment may well give rise to conflicts of interest.
- Suppliers, customers and others with whom the family business regularly deals. These are also ruled out on the basis of conflict-of-interest.
- Retired employees, out of a concern that they are more likely to be focused on the past and not forward looking.
- Friends of the business leader. Here the argument is that they are likely to identify too closely with their friend to be sufficiently challenging and objective. In the worst case, friends of the business leader could be seen as too partisan by disaffected family factions.
- Those who need the money. The concern here is that appointees who are relying on their non-executive director fees to supplement their pension may not be sufficiently challenging to the leadership, either to foster the best climate of constructive debate, or at worst, to be truly independent.
- The time poor, including serial non-executive directors with a portfolio of appointments.

Instead it is suggested that non-executive directors are recruited from the ranks of retired or senior figures with experience in:

- The industry or sector in which the family business operates.
- Major corporate businesses who are therefore able to add credibility and insight and experience gained in these organisations.
- Finance or banking, particularly if the family business is contemplating expansion, acquisitions, a flotation or other major structural change.
- Perhaps most usefully, those with experience of running larger but still family owned businesses.

A number of organisations have lists of individuals interested in taking up non-executive appointments and there are a number of recruitment consultants and other organisations that specialise in the recruitment and placement of non-executive directors in various types of business. A key factor in the success of any appointment will be the extent to which the director 'gets the point' of the family business concerned and appreciates that the family influence will add a level of complexity (and ideally richness and quality) not found in similar non family businesses. The director may arrive with that appreciation deeply ingrained as a result of experience of working with other family businesses (perhaps their own). That appreciation may be supplemented by formal training and a willingness to understand more about family business dynamics, both of the business concerned and from a wider theoretical perspective. Above all success will be dictated by the personality, patience and innate empathy of the appointee.

After recruitment, performance and evaluation, a further question becomes how long should directors remain on the board? Assuming that both family and non-family executives will retain board positions for the duration of their employment (which will

---

[72] Op cit at pp 114–115.

typically be for longer than in a non-family business) this question is primarily relevant to non-executive directors and, to a certain extent family directors.

Corporate governance theory holds that one of the core components of non-executive directorship is independence and that this independence is compromised the longer the director is on the board. The director is more likely to adopt the mind-set of the executives, rather than constructively challenging this. Nuebauer and Lank therefore suggest that board tenure, for non-executives should be limited to 6 years.[73]

17.10.4 Chairman

The role of the chairman is vital in any company. This is distinct from that of the managing director. Often the difference is summed up as the chairman runs the board and the managing director runs the company. Aspects of the chairman's role will include some or all of the following:

- Chairing meetings of the board and of the shareholders.
- Responsibility for recruitment to the board.
- Performance evaluation of the board.
- Supporting challenging mentoring and holding the managing director to account.
- Acting as a figurehead or representative of the company.
- Acting as the principal point of contact and liaison between the board and the shareholders.
- Most importantly, in larger family owned businesses, working with the chair of the family council to form effective links and proper working relationships between the board and the family council (see below).

Corporate governance theory is keen to emphasise the separateness and independence of the chairman from the operation and management of the business. For example the UK Corporate Governance Code recommends that the role of the managing director or chief executive and chairman should not be combined and assumed by a single individual.[74] Most significantly, the Code frowns on the practice of the managing director 'moving upstairs' on relinquishing leadership of the management team, to take over the role of chairman.[75] The Code goes on to recommend an effective cooling off period of 5 years[76] during which a former executive director, including of course a managing director, should not return to occupy a non-executive role on their former board. The reason is that it is crucial to good governance that the chairman can be seen as independent of management.

There are plenty of exceptions to be found to this corporate governance principle in the quoted company sphere.[77] There the companies concerned are obliged to justify their departure from the recommendations of the Code under the 'comply or explain principle'.

---

[73] See p 118. This echoes the approach of the UKCGC, which suggests that after 9 years non-executive directors should no longer be regarded as independent.
[74] See UKCGC, provision A.3.1.
[75] See UKCGC, provision A.3.1 when read with provision B.1.1
[76] See UKCGC, provision A.3.1
[77] For example Stuart Rose at Marks and Spencer initially held the combined role of Chief Executive and Chairman before moving on to hold the Chairman role on the appointment of a new Chief Executive.

However for most family businesses, progression of the business leader from managing director to chairman is pretty much the rule rather than the exception. As the overwhelming majority of families owned businesses are unquoted they are not subject to even the 'comply or explain' principle and so do not have to justify the progression of business leader from that Chief Executive to Chairman, other than possibly to other family shareholders. In practice there may well be many things to recommend this progression in any event. This issue is explored in more detail in chapter 7. Non-family, non-executive, fully independent chairmen have worked well in many family enterprises.

Other possibilities are for a sibling or cousins to be appointed as chairman from the ranks of the family outsiders. This has particular merit if the business leader is not a family member. However it can be a considerable benefit if co-leadership at a strategic level can be established between a family insider, as business leader and an outsider family chairman. Again the key to making this relationship a success will depend on the skills and personal attributes of the chairman and the quality of the working relationship between the same generation family members concerned.

17.10.5 'Family directors'[78]

Of course many family businesses of any age or size will have non-executive directors, who are also members of the business owning family. The presence of such family directors can be an enormous advantage to the family business. At best appropriately skilled and experienced family members may provide many of the benefits of the non-family non-executive director. They should also be able to bring a lifetime's knowledge about the family business and wisdom in the workings of the owning family, all of which, when combined with huge loyalty and commitment to the family cause, can provide powerful support for the management. The target for the family business must be to recruit directors whose appointment to the board can be justified on merit, independent of family connection.

The contrasting position is where board appointments are made wholly or mainly on the basis of family membership. Rather than add value to the board, the director concerned acts as an unfortunate combination of messenger, shop steward, policeman and spy on behalf of the owning family or, worse still, branches or factions of that family. The more that the family member in question uses his position in one of these ways, the greater the risk of a dysfunctional board.

Appointments made on the basis of family criteria will mean, at the very least, that family directors occupy purely token positions on the board, add little value to the business, but do little harm either. This is particularly so if the influence of the family directors is out-weighed by a good management team, supported by effective independent directors. But too many family directors operating on the basis of family connection, rather than adding business value, will result in either a rubber stamp board or conflicted board. Of course, for the family members concerned, what they may regard, as a relatively token appointment, carries the full legal responsibilities associated with directorship.[79]

In its more serious form, the influence of family directors (even well-meaning individuals genuinely attempting to safeguard the interests of the family), can lead to the stagnation

---

[78] See also the detailed discussion on family directors in chapter 8.
[79] See chapter 8.

of the business, disputes, litigation and business failure. Symptoms that the presence of family directors are having a serious toxic effect would include, factional or tactical voting, the lack of proper discussion at board meetings, disrupted information flows so that the 'family director' is excluded from key briefings. Board meetings are pre-planned or rehearsed and the real discussion takes place between the actual business leadership outside of the boardroom. Often those pre-meetings include lengthy discussions on tactics for dealing with the family directors. In short the ideal position is to have family members who are directors in the full and proper sense of the term, not family directors.

However family business boundary theory suggests that there might be limitations on the role of family appointed directors. Mainstream modern corporate governance theory emphasises the need for non-executive directors to familiarise themselves with the company's operation, including site visits etc. Indeed Neubauer and Lank suggest that this 'management by walking about' could be a positive legal obligation under German law.[80] The question becomes how realistic is it for, in particular, family appointed directors to do this, before they are seen to have crossed the boundary into the business system and are seen to be interfering in operational matters?

All of this is of course not to say that the voice of the owning family should not be heard in the family owned business. Quite the contrary. We believe that many problems are caused in later stage family businesses because that voice is not heard, or at least is not heard sufficiently clearly and appropriately. The point is that communication between the family and the board is so fundamental to the health of the family business that it should not rest on the shoulders of 'family directors' (however broad and strong those shoulders may be). Instead business-owning families with any ambition for growth and longevity need to invest in family governance system to complement the business governance system centered on the board.

17.11 FAMILY GOVERNANCE SYSTEMS

17.11.1 Overview

So far discussion has concentrated largely on the management and leadership aspects of governance. In other words the business bit of family business governance. This next section will turn to the governance of the family. Most of the discussion will concern formal family governance systems. It will be immediately obvious why such systems are necessary in the largest family owned businesses, such as Clarks Shoes (discussed above), now with over 1,000 family shareholders on its register.

The applicability of such systems to early stage family businesses or businesses with a much smaller number of family members involved is much less obvious. The full range of bespoke family governance systems including family assemblies, family councils, family charters and the like may be seen as, at best, irrelevant over engineering for the vast majority of family businesses.

There is certainly something in that view. However the key point is that, analytically even the smallest family business has a family system and is subject to powerful family influences. Developing an awareness of these dynamics and finding some mechanisms to

---

[80] Neubauer and Lank *The Family Business: Its Governance for Sustainability* (Harvard Business School Press, 1997) at p 221.

recognise and deal with the resulting family issues is both more challenging and, if the business concerned is to beat the family business mortality statistics,[81] is arguably more vital in these smaller and early stage family businesses. In practice we believe that this can be achieved by family owned businesses:

- Of whatever size and shape developing an awareness of the issues, challenges and solutions that crop up in family businesses generally – by becoming family business aware. To an extent this has been helped by the growing coverage of family businesses in the mainstream media.[82]
- Joining the 'family business movement'.[83] In addition to a number of organisations dedicated to the support of family owned businesses there are general business and trade organisations that (as a result of the number of family owned businesses in their membership) take an interest in family business issues.
- Seeking out the support of appropriate advisors who can demonstrate a genuine commitment to supporting family businesses, combined with an understanding of key family business issues.
- Most importantly, as a result of the above, choosing the appropriate mechanisms and approaches from large family business best practice and applying these to the situation of each individual family business: in other words the IOD stepwise approach.
- Choosing a governance system fit for the medium term future of the family business concerned. Families should consider adopting a governance system, which may be slightly over elaborate for their current needs and circumstance, but is one for the family businesses 'to grow into'.

What therefore are the key elements of bespoke family business governance systems that business-owning families may wish to consider adopting?

17.11.2 Key elements and terminology

The evolution of most of the fully developed family business governance systems can be traced back to work done in the USA, in the last couple of decades of the twentieth century, by a leading group of academics and consultants. Their work was with mainly with large and complex American family owned businesses.

The key elements of those family business governance systems are as follows:

- **Family assemblies.** Also called family meetings, family forums, family briefings, family gatherings, family retreats or family conventions. Basically a family assembly will be a meeting of the wider business family. Attendance is usually open to all adult family members, irrespective of whether they work in or hold shares in the business.
- **Family council.** A family council is a representative body of the business owning family. The key role of the family council is to facilitate communication between the family and the board. The family council is one of the key building blocks for the governance of family businesses. The family council is an advisory and consultative body. The family council is not there to make business decisions. The family council will also usually organise family assemblies.

---

[81] With around two thirds of family businesses failing to make it through the second generation of family ownership. See chapter 1 for a discussion on the research about family business mortality statistics.
[82] Including the Fixer and more recently Britain's Oldest Family Businesses (BBC 4, 2014).
[83] A brief overview of the main family business organisations in the UK is contained in Appendix 2.

- **Family charter.** Also called a family constitution, family creed, family protocol or family agreement.[84] The family charter is the main document where the family set out their values, vision and commitment in relation to their family business. It is also use to record the agreement the family have reached on key issues such as who can own shares in or work for the family business. Family charters are rarely binding legal documents. Instead they record agreements in principle and the aspirations of the business owning family.

We will now turn to look at each of these three building blocks in bespoke family business governance systems. Before doing so it is sensible to sound a note of caution. This is that, whilst the above are the components of the classic family business governance model they are offered as possible suggestions rather than prescriptive requirements. John Timpson, for example, whilst endorsing at least some of family business governance theory, is no fan of family councils, seeing them as:[85]

> 'a democratic way of satisfying far-flung family that runs the danger of upsetting both business and family in one move.'

Other family business commentators suggest that 'there are no perfect formulas and template solutions' but nevertheless stress the need for business families to assess their governance needs on the basis of a 'more fluid, instinctive, intuitive, reflective type of change'.[86]

The governance needs of family businesses will depend on various factors. Some quantative, such as family size, business complexity and the balance between insiders and outsiders. Other factors will be qualitative, including the degree of cohesion and quality of communication between family members. It therefore follows that in smaller, more cohesive business families, an evolutionary approach may be adopted to governance, for example introducing more frequent family meetings as the family enters its first succession transition period. Other families of the same size and stage of growth that have experienced significant tensions and conflict might need a more revolutionary approach, including the negotiation of family charters and shareholders' agreements.

17.12 FAMILY ASSEMBLIES

17.12.1 Overview

Attendance at family assemblies is usually open to all adult family members, irrespective of whether they work in or hold shares in the business. One of the key purposes of the family assembly is to foster a sense of belonging and of emotional ownership amongst the wider family, many of whom are not involved in management and not (at least yet) shareholders. The family assembly would therefore include family members who are indirectly interested in shares through family trusts. Conversely, trustees would not usually attend family assemblies, purely in their capacity as trustees.[87] This is

---

[84] In fact Neubauer and Lank identify 15 labels that have been used to describe what we have termed family charters. See p 89.
[85] John Timpson *Ask John* (Icon Books, 2014).
[86] Martin Stepek in the discussion on *Strong Governance: a result of evolutionary and revolutionary processes* Collins. McCracken, Murray and Stepek – *Journal of Family Business Management* (2014) Vol 4, Issue No 2 at p 104.
[87] Trustees might also be family members and attend the family assembly in that capacity.

notwithstanding that the trustees might be the legal owners of shares controlling a large percentage of the voting rights of the company.

Often the threshold of adulthood is set quite low, perhaps at 16, so that the next generation of family owners or potential managers, at an early age, receive a semi-structured grounding in the issues and challenges facing the family business and some exposure to the dynamics of family business life.

Meetings are usually held on an annual or bi-annual basis. They are rarely held more frequently. The main purpose of the assembly is to promote family cohesion and inclusion and to bridge the gap between insiders and outsiders. A key component will be to facilitate communication between those in the business and the wider family. So briefings on the state of the business and key business issues from some combination of family and non-family executives and key advisors will often be a core component.

Family assemblies provide a process whereby the 'mood music' of the wider family can be captured and fed back to the board, usually via the family council. This is one aspect of a two-way communication channel. The wider family have a mechanism to provide feedback to the board and to raise questions and concerns. For example, the family might be unhappy with the level of dividends they are receiving. Or they might believe that some of the investment plans or business strategies the board are proposing are too risky. The wider family could be concerned that certain new products or perhaps the approach of the business to advertising and marketing, is at odds with the ethos and values of the wider family.

Family assemblies are informal, in the sense that no decisions or resolutions are tabled that will bind the company. For convenience family assemblies will often be held around the same time, often on the same day and in the same location as formal shareholder meetings. However the two meetings are clear and distinct gatherings, with the latter being restricted to duly registered shareholders (and their proxies), held to transact formal business and to pass binding resolutions.

Assemblies will often have a strong element of training and education, with activities aimed, in particular, at the next generation. There are a vast range of topics that can covered. Training could be used to raise the general business awareness of the next generation on matters such as accounting, financial and marketing issues. Training may include highly specific briefings on their own family business, including the part that the younger family members potentially have to play as next generation managers, owners or perhaps simply non-managing, non-owning supporters of the family business ethos and tradition.

Family assemblies also tend to have a strong social element, often including dinners, lunches, sporting and other activities. Although primarily intended to provide fun for the family, these also help the family develop teamwork, create bonds, cohesion and understanding between the family members. In larger family businesses, particularly where family members are widely scattered, the family assembly might mushroom into a full-blown family retreat, where the family take over a hotel or other venue for a full weekend. There are many different approaches that can be taken.[88] But the central purpose of the family assembly is inclusion.

---

[88] For example the Shepherds (Portakabin) family business in York deploy a range of tools and techniques to encourage the active participation of the fifth generation in their family business including issuing 'Family

17.12.2 Family assemblies and in-laws

A potentially thorny issue is whether partners should be invited to participate in the family assembly, or whether this is confined to direct descendants of the original founding family? Share ownership may be confined to blood relatives but the family assembly could possibly be opened out to include in-laws.

The family may take the view that the family assembly should be for family business, with attendance similarly restricted, to foster a sense of togetherness between the core bloodline family members.

The alternative, and perhaps preferable approach is to acknowledge the inevitable influence of partners on their family member life partners. This approach can also be based on an acknowledgement of the contribution that spouses and partners can make to the wider family business debate. With this comes the corresponding need for partners to understand as closely as possible the philosophy and the drivers behind the family business and to actively participate in the governance process that may well have a significant influence on their lives. These factors point to a more inclusive attendance.[89]

Sometimes families opt for a hybrid solution with the more formal, business focused parts of the family assembly being confined to blood relatives, but with spouses and partners participating in the social side of the event.

17.12.3 Family assembly, family council or both?

In smaller families there may be no family council in place. An annual family meeting, (supplemented by ad-hoc communication when the need arises), run on a fairly informal basis, may be all that is needed to ensure adequate communication and information flows between family members not involved in the business on a day to day basis and the family board members.

Alternatively, in sibling partnerships or smaller cousin consortia, there could be an organ termed the family council, but which operates informally, flexibly and inclusively, like a mini-family assembly.

In mid-sized businesses, with a family council there may be easy and clear access for family members to the family council. In these cases the more formal and business related aspects of governance can be left largely to the family council. The family assembly can then consist of a semi-formal briefing and question and answer sessions, to fill in any gaps of knowledge and understanding, but fulfilling a largely social function.

In the largest businesses with many family members involved, the family assembly will need to operate much more formally, with its own written constitution. There might be a need for procedures to mirror those of the company general meeting, including the ability to appoint and remove members the family council.

Member' business cards to all family assembly members, a family website and newsletter, producing a family values statement, an academically accredited and modular training programme and issuing formal questionnaires to the next generation to assess their level of commitment to and involvement in their family business.

[89] Neubauer and Lank are firmly in favour of in-law participation at family assemblies. See p 83.

17.13 FAMILY COUNCIL

17.13.1 Overview

The family council is one of the key building blocks for the governance of family businesses. Our view is that family council is little short of a necessity in family businesses with more than ten family members involved.[90] Experience suggests that a family council can also fulfil a valuable role in smaller families, including second generation sibling partnerships. Some families are natural communicators. Their family dynamics families allow for good, natural, free-flowing and constructive communication. They manage to deal with difficult and sensitive issues in a timely and appropriate way. This is not the case in all business owning families. Introducing a family council (however termed), with formal structures and rules of communication, is likely to provide a useful framework at an early stage of the evolution of the family business. This is particularly the case if some or all of these factors are present:

- communication between family members would otherwise be poor;
- the family has a history of disputes;
- ownership is widely spread between family members;
- a number of family members are remote from the day to day operations of the business, either geographically or because they do not have a full time executive role.

17.13.2 Role of the family council

So what is a family council? Broadly it is the primary vehicle through which the business owning family regulate family affairs relating to the family business. It is the main avenue of communication between the family and the board. Whereas the board manage the family's business, the family council manages the business owning family. The family council is an advisory and consultative body and not a decision making one. It is helpful to look at the question in the negative. A family council:

- is not part of the formal legal constitution of the family business. Indeed although a family council will often be constituted by the family charter, that document will itself usually be expressed not to have any binding legal status.
- has no voting powers either in relation to board matters or at general meetings (at least typically).[91] As the family council does not operate as a supervisory board, it does not therefore have a mandate to tell the board of the company what to do.
- has no role in setting the strategic policy for the company. This remains the responsibility of the board. However the strategic family policy must be aligned with the overall strategic ownership view of the business owning family.[92]
- should not interfere in operational matters.
- does not have the power to appoint or remove the board. Frequently mechanisms are in place, operating either through informal representations or in shareholders' agreements (or occasionally the legally binding parts of the family charter), for the

---

[90] Neubauer and Lank set the bar higher and suggest that 30 family members represents the appropriate cut off point. In practice the distinction between a family assembly and a family council in small to medium sized business families is a fine one. Sibling partnerships are unlikely to need both. More cohesive families with good communication may be able to rely on the less formal structure of the family assembly.
[91] The voting trust created by the constitution of the Clarks family council is an unusual exception.
[92] Discussed in detail in chapter 15 (Ownership Succession).

family council to nominate appointees to serve as family directors on the formal board of directors.[93] However such appointments apply only to the family representation element on the board rather than to the appointment and removal of the board as a whole, which remains the prerogative of the shareholders.

Instead the role of the family council is much more subtle and nuanced. It can be seen as the family's ambassador to the board. It is to act as the primary interface between the board and the business owning family. That communication channel operates in various directions:

- Sideways by allowing the policies, strategies, decisions and reasoning of the board to be explained and discussed with the family council. Possibly, as a result of consultation with the family council, policies and decisions will be revised or modified by the board. But the family council is not in a position to overrule the board.
- Sideways by the family council acting as the recipient of reasonably detailed financial and operational information which it would be impracticable for the board to disseminate to a larger group of family shareholders. Some of this might be commercially sensitive or confidential.
- Upwards by the family council taking steps, at family assemblies or otherwise, to pass on key elements of information about the direction and position of the company to the wider family group, usually both shareholder and non-shareholders.
- Downwards by the family council members receiving feedback and comments from their constituent family members about matters of concern including dividend policy, liquidity of shareholdings, appetite for risk, business practices and ethics, community social responsibility (CSR) or philanthropy issues and the level of family involvement including the quantity and quality of information provided by the board directly or indirectly via the family council, education, internship and employment opportunities in the family business.
- Sideways by the family council assimilating, editing and conveying this feedback to the board.

The interrelationship between the various family business governance bodies and the communication flows between them can be seen as follows:

---

[93] As in Clarks shoes.

Figure 17.3: Family business governance bodies and communication flows

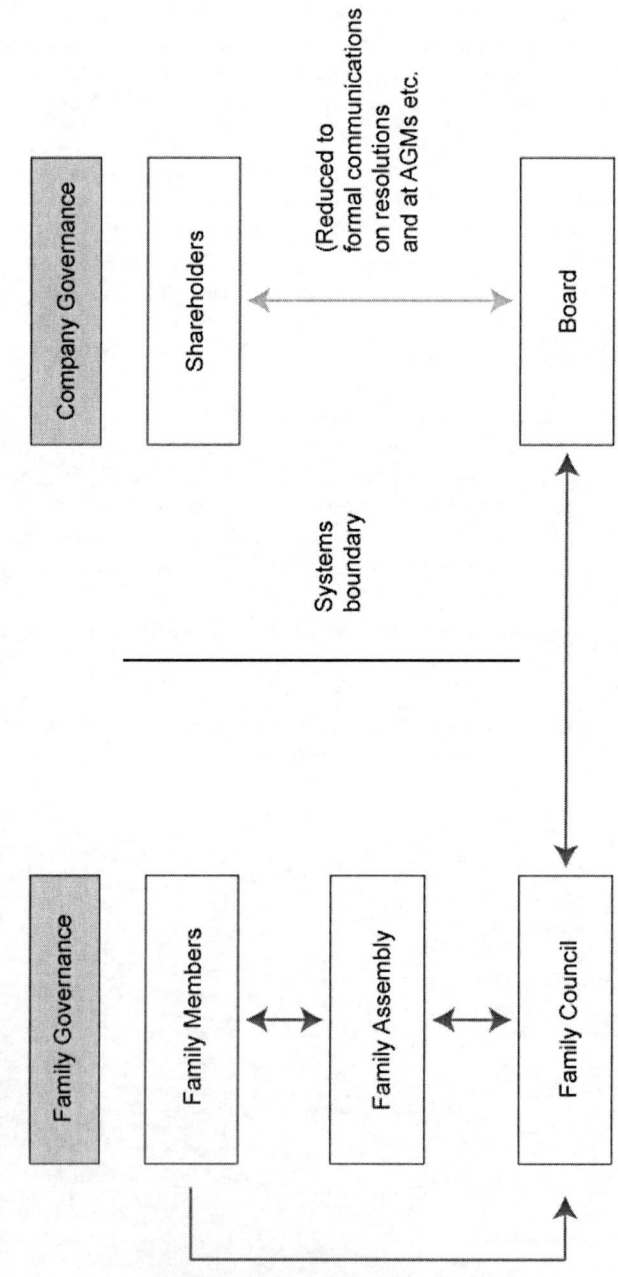

17.13.3 Membership of the family council

The charter will usually include procedures for choosing members of the family council. Overall the objective is to achieve a representative cross section, drawn from different generations, backgrounds and experience. Clearly, the larger the business owning family, the easier it will be to achieve this. To be effective the family council needs to be confined to a workable size. Neubauer and Lank recommend between five and eight members.[94]

In a smaller business owning family, members may simultaneously hold roles in a number of different governance bodies (for example as a major individual shareholder, a company board member and as a trustee of a family trust). This is not ideal. Particular problems may arise if executive directors and, especially the business leader are also members of the family council. The family council and the board perform separate functions. There are potential conflicts of interest inherent in membership of both.

However a shortage of personnel is not of itself a reason to dispense with the council altogether. Some duplication of roles might be necessary. Wearing separate hats, although superficially artificial, can, in and of itself, help otherwise conflicted individuals to recognise the different roles they have to play in the various family business sub-systems and to discharge those roles with more focus and precision.

A particularly important issue is whether family council representation should be based on the individual branches of the business owning family. Historical practice has been to do so. Probably this is based on the logic that as families progress down generations jobs and/ or shareholdings are likely to gravitate towards particular branches of the family and that branch representation helps ensure that the voice of outsiders or 'minor branches' of the family are heard.

More recently some families have moved to a single-family worldview, with branch mentality being seen as outdated and counter-productive. Here the approach is that the whole family pool needs to be explored to find the most committed and able representatives to look after the wider family's interests. Often this view is underpinned by a concern that past (and often still present) tensions and difficulties of the family business can be traced to family branch factionalism and that to avoid a curse on all of their houses a more unified approach is needed in the future.

In the largest families the work of the family council is sometimes delegated to various committees, with full family council members being supplemented by co-opted sub-committee drawn from the wider business family. Sub-committees include those concentrating on family employment, education, social and philanthropy matters.

Just as in the case of the board of directors, selection of the chair of the family council is of particular importance.

17.13.4 Chair of the family council

Often the bulk of this communication will fall to the chair of the family council. This role is therefore a pivotal position in the governance system of the family owned

---

[94] See p 83.

business. The candidate to fill the position will need a wide range of skills. These include sufficient business acumen to understand, assess and if necessary constructively challenge, the information provided by the board. The chair of the family council needs to be a skilled diplomat, with the communication skills to represent the board view to the family via the family council and vice versa. The chair of the family council needs therefore to be chosen with great care.

It also follows that developing a good working relationship between the chairman of the board and the chair of the family council will be crucial. The effectiveness of the family council will often depend on effective and constructive dialogue between the two chairs.

17.13.5 Changes to the family council

Changes to the family council and automatic rotation of family council members raise further issues. If council members remain in place too long, other family members are denied the opportunity to participate in the governance process. There is a risk that their relationship with the board develops into a set pattern, whether too confrontational or not sufficiently challenging. For this reason, some charters provide for the automatic rotation of the chair and at least part of the council, on an annual basis.

However some degree of continuity is also valuable, especially in the case of a good family council chair. The pool of suitable and committed family members might not be that large. Something mirroring current corporate governance practice, of set terms of 2 to 5 years, with the possibility of re-election to serve further terms, may be most appropriate.

The charter will usually spell out the process for electing new council members. This may be by nomination of the family assembly as a whole or the appropriate constituency (if positions are reserved for members of particular generations or family branches etc.). Alternatively membership could be by recommendation from the remaining council members, subject to ratification by the family assembly.

In the case where the family directors are appointed to the company board by the family council, the charter will usually contain the procedure for this.

17.13.6 Family council; additional roles

Particularly in larger businesses, the family council may also assume responsibility for aspects of the administration of the family side of the family business, including:
- Organising the family assembly both in terms of content and administrative arrangements.
- Taking responsibility for the education programme for the next generation of family members. In larger businesses this may be delegated to a separate committee of the family council.
- Leadership of the philanthropic activities of the family. Again often undertaken through a committee of the family council or, in the case of more established philanthropic activities, through the trustees of separately legally constituted foundations or trusts.

- Providing a family office function for the collective investments (and occasionally individual investment portfolios) of family members. Sometimes there will be a number of family trusts involved, with family council members also serving as trustees of those trusts. Detailed execution of the investments of larger investment portfolios, will usually be carried out by professional family offices.[95]

The family council will often rely on the administrative resource of the family company to help the council function. In the largest cases the family council may have its own separate and independent secretariat.

17.14 FAMILY CHARTERS

17.14.1 Overview

The family charter is the core document in the governance system of the family owned business. It is the foundation on which the governance system is built. Family charters are as varied in their structure and content as they are rare in practice.

Although the existence of family charters is slowly gaining recognition in the wider business community, these key documents were, until the last few years, almost unheard of outside the close confines of the specialist family business advisory community and their clients. Actual adoption and implementation of family charters remains low.

In essence a family charter is the document that records the relationship of the business owning family to their family business and the relationship of family members with each other, so far as the business is concerned.

It is rare for a family charter to be legally binding. The document is therefore much more concerned with values and principles than formal rules. Charters may therefore be distinguished from legally binding shareholder agreements. However in comprehensive governance systems the basic principles contained in family charters will be supplemented by detailed rules and mechanics, contained in legally enforceable documents, including shareholder agreements, option agreements and the articles of association. These documents will translate the principles of the charter, on key elements, such as ownership and transferability of shares, pre-emption provisions, voting agreements and dispute resolution procedures, into a legally binding form.

Occasionally family charters will contain a mixture of provisions that are not intended to be legally binding and those that are enforceable, for example provisions relating to the transfer of shares or perhaps dispute resolution procedures. These hybrid documents, perhaps better termed family agreements, are comparatively rare for various reasons including:

- **Authorship**. The preparation of family charters are very often facilitated by specialist family business consultants or on some occasions, by the family themselves. Legally enforceable provisions, for example detailed pre-emption provisions dealing with procedures for first refusal on a proposed transfer of shares, will almost inevitably be drafted by lawyers.

---

[95] Either multi-family offices, with one set of investment professionals working for a number of business families or, in the case of the largest portfolios single family offices with the family retaining its own dedicated portfolio management team.

- **Chronology.** In developing bespoke family business governance systems the almost invariable approach will be to use the family charter as a foundation. The principles and values set out in the charter are then, where appropriate, carried through into detailed drafting.
- **Convenience.** The family charter is intended to be a living document, the terms of which are easily accessible to and understood by the business owning family as a whole. The supporting legal documents could well be voluminous and relatively complicated. Our experience is that business owning family members will typically take a much more active interest in the drafting and negotiation of, for example shareholders' agreements, than their non-family business counterparts. To do so family members will often return to the principles in the family charter as a first reference point for governance issues.[96]

The difference between a family charter and other key family business governance documents can be summarised as follows:

Governance documents compared

Articles	Shareholders' agreement	Family charter
Legally binding	Legally binding	Not legally binding
Public document	Private document	Private document
Technical	Technical	Values based
Largely standard form	Bespoke	Bespoke
	Advisor driven	Family driven

17.14.2 What is the point of family charters if they are not legally binding?

The key point is that the process of putting together the family charter provides the business owning family with a structured mechanism to debate the main pressure points and touchstones that are likely to cause difficulty and conflict in the life of the family business. Family charters are therefore a catalyst to communication and, more significantly, pre-emptive and proactive communication.

Family charters also serve a subsidiary function as a document of record for the family of the output of that communication; a record of what has been agreed.

Whilst not legally enforceable as such, we would suggest that the contents of a family charter would nevertheless have strongly persuasive evidential value before a court in relation to a matter covered by it.[97]

It will be seen that all too often the courts are left to grapple with shreds of circumstantial evidence to divine the intentions of the parties to a family business

---

[96] Family charters can therefore be used in a similar way to heads of terms in corporate transactions.
[97] However we cannot trace any evidence of decided cases under English law to support this proposition. This might be because family charters are sufficiently rare that no litigation involving family charters has yet come before a court. It might also be that the presence of a family charter prevents serious disputes and litigation arising in the first place.

dispute, for example when considering, for example, unfair prejudice petitions relating to the link between share ownership and management participation.[98] Family charters will often contain clear statements that family members will be treated like other employees in all respects, and that they have no right to be employed or to participate in management. Cases are often brought by a family shareholder, who is no longer employed in the family business. That family member asks the court to order the compulsory purchase of their shares, based on an alleged right to participate in management. Although not strictly binding on the court, a charter expressly stating that there is no right to participate, must be of strongly persuasive value in convincing a court that the claim of the outgoing family employee should fail.

17.14.3 Format

There is absolutely no prescribed format for a family charter. The key point is that a family charter is very much the creation of the individual business owning family concerned. In practice family charters differ significantly in format and content. At one end of the scale some families operate on the basis of a limited set of unwritten but clearly understood family values. At the other end of the scale the family charter is contained within fully bound and illustrated books running to over 50 pages. In practice a typical family charter would, on average, be five to ten pages in length.

Legal publishers and know how content providers have recently introduced family charters as precedent documents.[99] However we use the term 'precedent' with significant caution. It will be appreciated from what has been said above that a family charter is not and cannot be a standard, one size fits all precedent document. Neubauer and Lank put the point forcefully and argue that:[100]

> 'A governance system deserving the name cannot be bought ready made in the market place.'

Although they have a role to play, the process of preparing a family charter cannot be driven by external advisors. Equally, for it to be fit for purpose, the document cannot be imposed by the business leader, even if having a family charter can be seen as best practice and for the clear benefit of the family.

The key point is that the end result should be very much a whole family charter. That is to say that the buy in of the whole business owning family has been secured in a manner that each relevant family member will feel that they have been involved in the process putting the charter together. This goes wider and deeper than simply being consulted about the contents. As a result, the whole family will consider themselves morally bound by the terms of the charter, notwithstanding its lack of legal effect.

17.14.4 Process

A family charter will usually be a comparatively short document, certainly when compared with most legal agreements. At first sight family charters do not appear to present any difficult drafting issues or to raise matters of technical legal or tax complexity. The issues covered are largely fairly obvious. The parties concerned will

---

[98] See chapter 20.
[99] For example see the short form and long form family charters produced by PLC.
[100] Op cit at p 236.

have long-standing relationships and in many cases will often be in day-to-day contact. In most cases they will have known each other since childhood. Many of the participants are likely to have grown up as part of the same household.

These factors would suggest that completing a family charter ought to be a fairly straightforward, speedy and painless process.

However, it is comparatively rare for family charters to be completed in less than 12 months. Occasions where the process has taken 5 years or longer are not uncommon. How can this be the case? The main reasons are:

- **Sensitivity.** When examined in more detail, it will be seen that each issue covered by the family charter raises difficult and potentially sensitive, if not highly divisive matters. Almost all of these matters are capable of leading to extensive debate. It would be dangerous to gloss over these issues. That is not to say that the process of debating the family charter creates problems as such. Rather the process highlights issues and latent tensions that could potentially surface in the family business at any time. To mix metaphors, rather than opening a can of worms, the process of preparing a family charter spotlights the elephant in the room.
- **Family history.** As a related point, comparatively few business families embark on the process of adopting a family charter as part of their strategic family business planning. The charter is not being discussed in an atmosphere of a calm, considered abstract debate. More often than not, work on a family charter is a reaction to a dispute having already arisen or, at least, awareness amongst family members that there are mounting tensions, capable of giving rise to a dispute. The family charter is therefore often being negotiated against the background of real life raw emotions or, in some cases, barely healed wounds.
- **Commitment.** The typical business family will have a significant financial and emotional commitment to their family business. They will care deeply about the contents of their family charter and will often be keen to discuss the document line by line and word for word.
- **Logistics.** There may be logistical issues of distance (particularly in the case of larger, more widely dispersed international business families). The work on the family charter will have to compete for attention with the day-to-day demands from the operation of the business. Family members who do not work in the business will have their own business, professional and personal commitments. However, and quite remarkably, once the family commitment to the charter process has been secured, these practical issues rarely impede progress.

The key point is however that, for the process to work and for the family charter to be an effective working document, it is necessary to secure the involvement and support of the wider business family.

17.14.5 Family champion

Behind every successful family charter lies a family champion. In the Clarks case that individual was clearly Roger Pedder.

It would be extremely unlikely that the entire business owning family arrive at a collective and simultaneous recognition that a charter is needed. So leadership is required from an identifiable process champion. This is likely to be an individual (or occasionally a small number of family members) who have developed an awareness of family business governance issues and recognise the value that a governance system, including a family charter can bring to the family business. The champion (or champions), through a process of leadership, diplomacy and persistence, secure the commitment of the remaining family members to prepare and adopt the charter. That is not to say that the family champion is the author of the family charter. The document needs to be a collaborative work of the entire business owning family.

On occasions a family champion will also be the business leader. However, this presents difficulties in and of itself. The family charter is the key document in regulating the family system in a family owned business. The business leader's primary responsibility is for the business system. One of the functions of the charter is to lay down boundaries between the business and family systems. The business leader has a conflict of interest as to where and how those boundaries should be drawn. Whilst the family charter must evolve in collaboration with the board, it needs to be driven by the family and not the board. Therefore, even if the initial impetus to adopt the family charter comes from the business leader, the sooner the baton of family champion can be passed to a family member not directly involved in the senior management of the business, the better.

Particularly in larger families, commitment to the family charter is often secured via the family council. More precisely the requirement for and the contents of a family charter will often be discussed with a broadly representative and generally respected group of family members. These form some sort of family council designate or family working party.[101]

17.14.6 Advisor facilitation

The process of formulating and adopting a family charter is often facilitated by a family business consultant or other advisor, specialising in family business work.[102]

Although relatively few in number, such advisors will have experience in dealing with sensitive and emotionally challenging issues in a sympathetic and supportive manner. They will not be unduly phased by any conflicts and tensions which arise between family members during the process. They will be trained and experienced in processes to maintain objectivity and neutrality, so that all family members are given a voice in the creation of the charter and that its contents are not unduly influenced by dominant characters, whether the family champion, the business leader or otherwise. Crucially, specialist advisors will be able to create a safe space where sensitive issues can be explored, including those raised by members not directly involved in management or with large shareholdings.

The process will differ from family to family, but an advisor facilitated process, will usually involve some combination of:

- **Education.** Initial awareness raising, where the purpose of the family charter is explained, sometimes alongside some form of education process led by the facilitator on family business issues, family business dynamics and management

---

[101] At this stage there will often be a family constitutional chicken and egg situation, whereby the initial task of the working group or family council or designate will be to agree a draft family charter, for adoption at a full family assembly. This will in turn give constitutional validity to the family charter that constitutes the family council.
[102] The role of a family business consultant is explained in more detail in chapter 25.

thinking, often illustrated by relevant case studies etc. There are a number of reasons for this. First to ensure, so far as possible, a level playing field in terms of knowledge and awareness of relevant issues. Secondly to illustrate that the issues facing the family are not unique but rather a predictable product of family business dynamics and structure.

- **One to one meetings**. A series of individual private and confidential meetings, so that each relevant family member has an opportunity to air their concerns and to contribute their views.
- **Family meetings**. Some form of feedback process, either through formal written reports or family meetings, identifying areas where the family are in agreement and those where they differ. Available options to resolve these differences will be explored and a process outlined to move forward to reach agreement.
- **Feedback loops**. Feedback loops at which outstanding issues and corresponding solutions are explored in an appropriate combination of private discussions and full family meetings.
- **Ceremony**. Some form of closing or adoption ceremony, often coupled with a meeting of the family council and a family assembly, when the family charter will be signed and adopted by the business owning family. The family can then celebrate this milestone in the evolution of their family business.

Each family business is unique and therefore must craft its own governance solution, including the form of its family charter. However it is likely that many of the issues and themes that surface during discussions will have been encountered by other business owning families. An ability to recognise these parallels and suggest range of solutions can help a business owning family regain its bearings and choose an appropriate direction. Equally the skilled and experienced family business advisor will be wary of imposing their own views and recommendations on the family.

The family charter must be a family driven, but can be an advisor guided, document.

17.15 CONTENTS OF FAMILY CHARTERS

Turning now to a discussion on the key contents and main issues relating these often encountered in working on a family charter.

17.15.1 Family values

Family charters will often begin with a statement of the core values and ethics of the business owning family. Words such as trust, respect, loyalty and commitment are likely to feature. The values statement may cover such matters as commitment to quality, customers, suppliers, employees, the environment and the local communities in which the business operates. The charter may also go on to document the commitment of the family to supporting charities and other philanthropic activity.

These statements may also cover the balance between short-term financial performance and sustainability, often with the family stating their commitment to taking the long-term view.

Values statements often cover the way that family members will deal with each other, confirming a commitment to treat each other with respect, fairness and integrity and to respect differences.

Clearly many of these matters are more statements of principle and intent. They would be incapable of enforcement, even if the charter is intended to be legally binding.[103] Equally clearly difficulties of interpretation can arise. One family member's robust expression of difference can easily be interpreted as a failure to observe the family's values of respect by the recipient. Nevertheless values statements of this nature will often have a strong moral effect and can be seen to have led to demonstrable changes of behaviour in many actual cases.

Often values statements will form part of the preamble or introductory provisions of more detailed family charters. In other cases, perhaps more strictly defined as family creeds, the family charter will consist only of a values statement.

17.15.2 Behaviour and conduct

Charters frequently reinforce the standards and behaviours expected of family members, such as treating each other with respect and act in good faith towards one another.

17.15.3 Long term family ownership intention

The default assumption will often be that the business will remain in family ownership for eternity. Very often family charters will contain a statement that 'the family wish the business to remain in family ownership for the foreseeable future' or words to that effect. Producing the family charter gives an opportunity to challenge this assumption. Indeed it is sensible to do so. A number of subsidiary questions can be asked, such as:

- **Motivation.** What are the individual and collective reasons for the family in making this declaration of dynastic intent? There may be a whole host of cogent and compelling reasons for the business to remain in family hands. These could include a strongly developed sense of legacy and desire to give the next and future generations of the family an opportunity to participate in the business. Perhaps the family believe that their family business has a long-term wealth generating capacity that can be harvested by successive generations. The family may recognise the relative sense of autonomy and purpose that a career in the family business can provide (when compared with a more traditional corporate counterpart). The family may see the business as a focal point that binds them together or want to acknowledge the genuine sense of enjoyment fun and friendship that family members gain from working together. The point is that if these reasons are explored and articulated, the process of producing the family charter in and of itself contributes to the cohesiveness of the family unit.
- **Other strategic options.** Continuation in family ownership is only one of a number of options open to the family. Why are other alternatives being discarded, particularly at the time of succession.[104] For example floatation, in the case of larger family owned business or, for most viable businesses, a third party trade

---

[103] Just possibly such statements could be capable of creating contractual duties of good faith between shareholders in circumstances where these would not usually be implied. See chapter 20.

[104] See chapter 15 (Ownership Succession), for a discussion on alternative options as part of the succession planning process.

sale? Is that refusal absolute, near absolute (so for example a super majority of family shareholders would be required to approve a third party sale) or conditional? In which case what are the circumstances where the family would consider selling out eg a compelling financial offer or perhaps the absence of suitably and qualified next generation family members, prepared to assume the leadership of the business? Are opinions divided? Perhaps the majority of family members are strongly in favour of retaining family ownership, but a minority have concerns about their own wealth being tied up in the family business for the foreseeable future. Work on the family charter can expose this tension and create an opportunity to address this by introducing the possibility of minority shareholder redemption programmes.[105]

17.15.4 Family share ownership

The family charter will also usually deal with the policy of who can own shares in the family business.[106] Should ownership be:

- Confined to blood-line family relations of the original founder?
- Alternatively and in the increasingly complex family situations caused by divorce and remarriage, should half children, step children and adopted children or children forming part of more informal family units be treated as family members eligible for share ownership alongside the blood line family members they may share a house with or have grown up alongside?
- Open to spouses? If so what happens in the event of divorce? Should the family have a policy of encouraging, or even insisting on pre-nuptial or post-nuptial agreements as a condition of ownership?[107]
- Available to unmarried partners? In which case, what degree of permanence is required in a relationship before the rest of the family will accept the partner as a full family member eligible to hold shares in their family business? Should this simply be down to the decision and discretion of the family member wishing to pass shares to their partner? Alternatively should each case need to be examined on its merits by the family council?

17.15.5 External shareholders

Work on a family charter creates an opportunity for the family to review their attitudes to third party external ownership. For example what is the attitude of the family to private equity and other investors? External investment may be highly desirable in helping the business achieve its short to medium term growth plans. The discipline and accountability that comes with external investment may have collateral business governance benefits. However external investment may change the dynamics of the family business forever. Private equity investors will be looking to drive the business toward a medium term exit to realise their investment, possibly pushing the business on the route towards eventual sale.

Recognition of the conflict between the short term time lines of private equity investment and the 'infinite time horizons'[108] of the committed dynastic family business,

---

[105] Pruning the ownership tree is explored in chapter 11 (Ownership Overview).
[106] Discussed in detail in chapter 11 (Ownership Overview).
[107] See chapter 18.
[108] Ward *Perpetuating the Family Business*, op cit at p 110.

may mean that the family are forced to accept that there limits to the growth potential or, at least the rate of growth, of the business.

17.15.6 Family employment policies

There are clear positive benefits of family employment. There are also corresponding dangers. In particular creating divisions between haves and have-nots. This is a core theme of this book.[109] Family employment policies will therefore be a key component of a family charter. They are also likely to be heavily discussed. Sometimes employment policies are sufficiently detailed that they are placed in separate employment policy documents. Detailed aspects of family employment policies are discussed elsewhere, especially in chapter 7.

It is likely to be highly inappropriate to document the employment policies as matters as formal contractual rights. This could cause employment difficulties both, between the family business and the family member concerned (perhaps arguing that they have a contractual or legal expectation to promotion) or between the family business and non-family employees arguing that they have been discriminated against.[110]

Many of the more detailed and family specific employment policies are likely to operate at the level of statements of principle contained in family charters or related documents dealing with family employment. Indeed they should do so. They could have potential evidential value, even if not strictly legally binding.

But, at best carefully thought out and worded policies on family promotion could help reassure non family employees that a level playing field exists between them and family employees. Clearly documented policies could at least help show that any discrimination is based on family membership, rather than an actionable form of discrimination. Equally clearly documented policies are likely to be helpful in resisting arguments from disgruntled family employees that failures to promote or increase remuneration etc. are in some way in breach of implied or express verbal agreements.

17.15.7 Dividend policies

The approach to dividends, as a key component of ownership is discussed in chapter 11. There is an inherent tension as soon as the outsider/insider dynamic arises. This is between the ability of the family company to distribute a sensible level of profits to family members, as a return on their investment or inheritance and, on the other hand the claims of the insiders to be adequately remunerated and also of the family business itself, to secure a sensible level of reinvestment.

17.15.8 Rights to information

As the family business grows, there is an inevitable information asymmetry between the insiders and the outsiders. In some situations information will be used as a form of family currency and will be deliberately hoarded by those in the know. Worse still

---

[109] This topic is explored in various chapters, including 2 (Themes), 5 (Family Employees), 7 (Management Succession), 8 (Directors' Duties) and 21 (Unfair Prejudice).
[110] See the discussion in chapter 6.

information will be shared only with chosen outsiders, perhaps from the same family branch, to the exclusion of the remaining outsiders.

In other, more cohesive or enmeshed families' information will flow naturally and spontaneously between family members. To the extent that those information flows are not perfect any omissions will be seen as accidental, inevitable and easily corrected. The larger the business owning family the harder it will be to rely on informal information flows.

Knowing what is going on in a family business is clearly a core component of inclusion. Statutory rights to information are extremely limited.[111] Family assemblies have a key role to play as forums for the provision of information. Family charters will therefore often specify a minimum level of information that will be provided to all members or, in some cases all family members entitled to attend the family assembly. Sometimes this will involve outsiders receiving copies of management accounts or briefings provided to employees. In larger families information will be shared through separate family newsletters or dedicated family member websites.

17.15.9 Owner responsibilities

Under UK company law shareholders have rights. It is difficult to identify any express responsibilities.[112] Sometimes shareholders in family owned businesses can undermine the success of the family business by interfering in the management process. Often the shareholders are acting with the best intentions and based on genuinely held beliefs that something is wrong and needs their intervention.

Family charters often reinforce value statements, by including express provisions to encourage family members to behave as responsible shareholders. Often these provisions are intended to reinforce the demarcation lines between family matters and the responsibilities of the board and management. These may include express responsibilities for family members:

- to observe both the letter and the spirit of the family charter;
- to respect and to work within the process embodied in the overall family business governance system, for example by raising concerns through the family council and not directly with board members or employees;
- to participate in the family democracy process, by attendance at family assemblies, company general meetings etc;
- not to air criticisms of the board, the company or employees in public. Or sometimes positive obligations to promote the reputation of the company.

17.15.10 Constitution of the family council

The formal constitution for the family council and rules for its operation and that of the family assembly will usually be set out in the family charter. The objectives role and

---

[111] Confined to receiving copies of the annual accounts in accordance with CA, s 423, together with notices of meetings resolutions and certain other circulars. Often even these basic information requirements are ignored in smaller family companies – see, for example the *Cadman* case considered in detail in chapter 21.
[112] Arguably there is are some implied duties, such as, not to unfairly prejudice the interests of other shareholders and, in some limited circumstances, to behave with good faith towards some other shareholders.

powers of the family council will usually be set out. Often these will be contrasted with the objectives, role and powers of the family assembly and the board.

17.15.11 Membership of the family council

The charter will usually include procedures for choosing members of the family council and any relevant changes.

17.15.12 Family assemblies

The charter will also deal with the procedure for dealing with family assemblies including:
- when where and how these are to be convened;
- in the largest of families policies and procedures for:
  - conducting business at family assemblies;
  - raising issues with the family council. However the governance and communication process has probably broken down if individual family members do not believe that they have a sensible level of access to the family council.

17.15.13 Dispute resolution

Some level of conflict and tension is an almost inevitable part of family business life. A good family charter will contain mechanisms to encourage the resolution of these issues before they become full-blown disputes. The emphasis will usually be on informal procedures, often involving the chair of the family council or other respected senior figure. Sometimes there will be an ability to seek the support of external facilitators, family business consultants or mediators if those informal procedures have failed. The charter will usually emphasise that involving formal legal process is to be heavily discouraged.

The legal mechanics of dispute resolution provisions are considered in detail at **17.22** below. Various forms of intervention and alternative dispute resolution are also reviewed in chapter 25.

17.15.14 Review

Last, but not least, the family charter, along with the overall governance mechanism will need regular and periodic review. Some aspects of the governance system may simply not have worked as anticipated. Other aspects will need to evolve as the family business moves through its natural life cycles. Concepts dismissed as irrelevant and overkill at the time the constitution was originally formulated, may have become highly desirable with the passage of time.

Reviews are recommended every 3 to 5 years. Indeed some families are converts to the idea that, to achieve maximum value from the family charter, as an organic living document and a key part of the family business communication system, the charter should be seen as part of the every day working life of the family business and as such should be under constant review.

One family business leader says that his copy of the family charter is in the top draw of his desk and is proud that to say that, after 15 years or so, this is now something like version 7.

Although the process of preparing the original family charter may have been protracted and at times painful, it should be easier next time around.

17.16 PHILANTHROPY

More detailed family business governance systems, particularly in larger multi-generational family businesses often cover wider issues beyond the operation and ownership of the family business and deal with the wider relationship between the business, the owning family and what they perceive to be their respective obligations to wider society.[113] Sometimes this will consist of little more than a statement that charitable giving is simply a matter of individual choice. This could be accompanied by a statement encouraging active philanthropy by individuals.

For other families' philanthropic activity is seen as a collective responsibility, either to be encouraged through the CSR and charitable activities of the family business itself or through the collective efforts of the business owning family. Family business related philanthropic activity is often seen to have the collateral benefit of engaging outsiders and providing them with a role in the overall enterprise. Treatment in the family charter may range from short statements of principle, through to highly detailed stand-alone policy statements, with philanthropic activity being administered by a separate committee. In its most highly evolved form, philanthropic activity will have been delegated to stand alone trusts or charitable foundations, administered by independent trustees albeit with a heavy family influence.

17.17 FAMILY VENTURING

Some commentators draw a distinction between family businesses (based on the original business set up by the family founder) and business families (where the founders family have remained in business together, but have now diversified into a wider range of businesses, often bearing no relation to the original business that may well have long since been sold).[114] Gersick et al argue that it is necessary for mature family businesses to continually 'reinvent' themselves, by engaging in new and diversified activities, with the result that some part of the business should be involved in entrepreneurial or start-up activity. In their view the alternative for a mature family business, is stagnation, then death.

Other business owning families, whilst still concentrated around the core original family business, recognise the limitations of that business in providing opportunities for the next generation and place value on encouraging entrepreneurship within that generation.

---

[113] One study carried out by the Institute for Family Business and the Community Foundation Network in 2009 came to the conclusion that family businesses were 'Natural Philanthropists' (which was adopted as the title of their report).

[114] A classic example can be found in the Shepherds family business. Originally a large local construction company, based in York, a family member was supported in developing a business to supply temporary buildings. This became the world famous Portakabin business and the original core construction business was sold by the family to Wates, another family business, in 2015.

These families may choose to recycle wealth generated from their existing businesses, by investing in new business opportunities created by the next generation, by acting as a family equity house or by creating family joint ventures.

Again treatment in the family charter may vary from a very general statement that such ventures may be encouraged and supported by the family, through to detailed policy statements with set investment guidelines and administered by separate investment committees.

17.18 LEGAL DOCUMENTS

17.18.1 Overview

Family charters, family assemblies and family councils remain little understood and even less used. On the other hand the purpose and concepts behind most of the legal documents relevant to family business governance will be readily familiar to all company lawyers and to a lesser (but still considerable) extent to other lawyers, accountants, other professionals and to directors of family businesses. There are many detailed analyses of the general legal issues surrounding these documents, especially shareholders' agreements in other works.[115]

The purpose of this section therefore is not, beyond the briefest of introductions, to discuss the general aspects of these documents. Instead it is offer some comments on particular issues arising in family business practice.

The key message is that, irrespective of the nature of the document in question, this needs to be fit for the form and needs of family business concerned. Some examples of, fairly common situations where perfectly standard legal documents have failed to meet this basic test are considered in chapter 26.

17.18.2 Articles of Association

The base constitutional document for any company is its articles.[116] The articles are therefore the starting point in looking at the legal constitution of a family owned company.

Key points include that the articles:
- are legally enforceable and take effect as a contract between the company and its members[117] and between the members themselves;[118] they are, in effect, the rule-book of a company.[119]

---

[115] See, for example, Reece Thomas & Ryan *The Law and Practice of Shareholders' Agreements* (LexisNexis, 4th edn, 2014).
[116] Companies Act 2006, s 17 provides that references to the constitution of a company include the articles of a company and any resolutions or agreements amending the articles.
[117] Companies Act 2006, s 33(1)
[118] *Ely v Positive Government Security Life Assurance Co Ltd* (1876) 2 Ex D 88 (HL).
[119] The significance of the sister document, the Memorandum of Association, has been all but eliminated by changes in the Companies Act 2006.

- are available to the general public. This is because both the original articles and any amendments to them[120] must be filed at Companies House.
- can be amended by a special resolution of 75% or more of the shareholders.[121]
- often operate by a mixture of express provisions and by incorporating a set of general rules or default provisions now contained in a set of Model Articles.[122]
- subject to relatively few exceptions can be freely amended to form bespoke constitutions.

17.18.3 Shareholders' agreements

In contrast shareholders' agreements:
- are legally enforceable, but as a matter of private contract; they have no statutory effect;
- as a private documents do not need to be filed at Companies House;
- sit alongside and will usually supplement the articles.

In practice shareholders' agreements do not appear to be in widespread use in family owned businesses.[123] With a business based around close family working relationships it could be assumed that levels of trust will be high and that the possibility of disputes will be correspondingly reduced. This may often be the case. However it does not follow that the need for shareholders' agreements is correspondingly reduced. We have argued above that, in fact there is an increased need for shareholders' agreements in a family owned business, compared with a non-family owned counterpart.

17.18.4 Inter-relationship between articles and shareholders' agreement

The inter-relationship between the articles and a shareholders' agreement is complicated. Usually the intention will be for the provisions of the shareholders' agreement to override the articles. However the Companies Act requires any agreement actually amending the articles to be filed at Companies House.[124]

---

[120] Companies Act 2006, s 26.
[121] Companies Act 206, s 21. This is subject to any weighted voting rights. The CA 2006 envisaged the possibility for articles to contain provisions for entrenchment preventing the alteration of one or more articles, for example restriction on the admission of non-family shareholders. The implementation of those provisions was delayed. It is still possible to alter these articles with the unanimous agreement of the members at the time, or with a court order. Entrenchment provisions are incredibly rare and are covered in CA, ss 22–24.
[122] The Model Articles are contained in the Companies (Model Articles) Regulations 2008, SI 2008/3229. Companies Act 2006, s 20 provides that the Model Articles will apply unless they are excluded or modified by the specific articles of a company. They replace Table A from the Companies (Tables A-F) Regulations, which are still often relevant to companies formed before 1 October 2009. Indeed it is by no means unusual to find family companies still governed by previous versions of Table A contained in the 1948 Companies Act or even the 1927 version.
[123] Although no doubt more common than family charters given the fairly recent introduction into the UK of these documents.
[124] Companies Act 2006, ss 29 and 30. Exactly when shareholders' agreements amend the articles and need to be registered and how to avoid this is a complicated area of law. For a detailed discussion of this issue see Reece Thomas & Ryan *The Law and Practice of Shareholders' Agreements* (LexisNexis, 4th edn, 2014) at pp 59–64. This work also contains detailed discussions of other key technical issues, including the extent to which a company and its directors can validly join in shareholders' agreements without fettering their discretion and compromising their statutory duties.

To avoid falling foul of this provision, or filing the shareholders' agreement or, as a matter of pragmatism, spending too much time analysing the precise interplay between the two documents the usual practice is for shareholders' agreements to operate as voting agreements. Provisions are included in the shareholders' agreement to:

- Confirm that the intention is for the shareholders' agreement to prevail over the documents.
- Explain that, if the two documents are in conflict, the intention is not to amend the articles as such. Rather it is for the parties to the shareholders' agreement to use their voting power and other influence in the company to give effect to the shareholders' agreement.[125]

There is frequently debate amongst company law draftsmen as to whether detailed and key bespoke provisions should be contained in the articles of association of a company, a shareholders' agreement, or both.

Factors to influence this choice include:

- **Privacy.** Articles need to be filed at Companies House and therefore are easily available public documents. Business owning families may regard some provisions (such as who are to be treated as family members to qualify for ownership) as deeply personal family matters, which should not to be readily available to third parties. The same would apply to commercially sensitive provisions, such as dividend policies.
- **Family charter.** A business owning family could have invested time and effort in a fairly comprehensive family charter. This might take the form of a family agreement with at least parts of the document having legally binding effect. Alternatively the charter may give very clear guidance as to how discretions are to be exercised. In these (comparatively rare) cases it may be possible to miss out the shareholders' agreement and to rely on a combination of articles and charter alone.
- **Number of shareholders.** Once the shareholder register reaches a certain size, perhaps 25 or more members, but almost certainly if membership reaches 100, it becomes impracticable to administer a shareholders' agreement, for example, issuing and administering the execution and return of Deeds of Adherence.[126]
- **Amendments.** Amending the terms of governance documents is partly a factor of logistics and partly a desire to balance flexibility and privacy. Almost all shareholders' agreements require unanimous agreement to amendments. It would be rare for agreements to contain formal amendment procedures. We have worked with families who have been keen to maintain both privacy and flexibility and have therefore included bespoke amendment provisions into their shareholders' agreements, whereby the remaining family members would be bound by amendments to a shareholders' agreement endorsed by a super-majority of family members. However such situations are comparatively rare.

    Some families take a pragmatic view that, if the governance system as a whole is working, there should be no difficulty in securing appropriate amendments to a shareholders' agreement.

    Others take the view that, with a built in procedure both to amend the articles (via a special resolution of 75% of the shareholders) and to convene an extraordinary general meeting for the purposes of doing so, the articles are inherently easier to

---

[125] And to amend the articles, if necessary.
[126] Documents binding transferees of shares held by an original signatory of the shareholders' agreement to the terms of that document.

amend and should contain any key provisions that may potentially need to be changed, such as share transfer provisions.

There is no hard and fast rule. Our preference would in most circumstances be to keep the articles relatively brief, with the detail being contained in the shareholders' agreement. It therefore follows that most of the detailed provisions discussed in the next section could be included in either the articles or the shareholders' agreement.

17.19 CONTENTS OF LEGAL GOVERNANCE DOCUMENTS

17.19.1 Starting point

The whole premise on which this book is based is that family owned businesses have unique characteristics, not found in their non-family owned counterparts. But there is clearly a huge amount of shared structural DNA. As suggested above, business-owning families will vary significantly in their approach to key family business questions. Often their debate over issues they see as central to their unique situation will require bespoke solutions to be engineered. This presents corresponding drafting challenges. For these reasons it is not really practicable to arrive at universal family business precedent documents, suitable for use in every family business situation. Instead the starting point could well be generally available precedent documents,[127] but with key modifications and additions, to reflect the particular circumstances of the family.

The key themes and issues that generate those drafting issues are discussed elsewhere in this book. The rest of this section largely acts as a reminder that these issues create the need for corresponding provisions in legal governance documents.

17.19.2 Family member definition

The central issue of who is to be regarded as a family member (in particular in relation to the right to hold shares) is discussed in detail in chapter 11 (Ownership Overview). The result of that debate will need to find its way into the constitution of the family company to clarify whether, for example, non-bloodline in laws may hold shares. The drafting may also need to accommodate other aspects of the family's ownership debate. This may also have extended to whether un-married partners and step-children etc, fall within their own definition of family members entitled to hold shares.

17.19.3 Share transfer provisions

Once the definition of family members has been established this will lead on to related provisions about the transfer of ownership of shares in the family business. For a business committed to remaining in family ownership provisions preventing (or at least severely restricting the possibility) of shares being transferred to third party non-family shareholders are a must.

If shares cannot be transferred to non-family third parties on what basis will transfers between family members take place? Without a sensible balance between the need of the

---

[127] See, for example, the precedents supplied in Reece Thomas & Ryan *The Law and Practice of Shareholders' Agreements* (LexisNexis, 4th edn, 2014).

wider family for stability and the ability of individual family members to realise their investment, a key element of ownership, capital value, becomes pretty much illusory.

These central questions and relevant approaches are also examined in detail in chapter 11.

17.19.4 Exit arrangements

One of the key considerations in any family business governance system will be the introduction of appropriate exit arrangements. These are discussed in detail in chapter 11 (Ownership Overview). Broadly put if the exit arrangements are either absent or too restrictive, unwilling family shareholders are help captive in the family business. Tensions will inevitably build. Too liberal an exit policy and the stability of the business as a family owned operation is placed in jeopardy. The approach taken to this balance will differ from business family to business family.[128]

17.19.5 Appointment and removal of directors

The first directors of a company will be nominated at the time the company is formed, usually by incorporation agents. Subsequent directors will usually be appointed by the existing board.[129] There is a parallel inherent right for the members to also appoint directors by ordinary resolution. This right is also repeated in the same article. However, provided the wording used is clear, the right for the members to appoint directors can be excluded.[130] How appropriate would such an exclusion be for a family owned business?

Good governance would suggest that for a properly functioning and cohesive board, the directors need to be able to work together. This is less likely to be the case if a director has been foisted on the board by disgruntled family members.

Against this, large parts of the family may both have a long-term commitment to the family business and also feel disenfranchised and unrepresented on the board. Resentment might grow as the board recruit either insiders, from a particular branch of the business owning family, non-family employees or non-executive directors, with whom the wider family have no connection. It might be that the disgruntled group are in a minority in any event and unable to command the simple majority of votes necessary to pass an ordinary resolution to secure their preferred appointee.

Ideally the answer will be found elsewhere in a more highly evolved governance process with a mixture of the family assembly, the family council and the family charter (which might perhaps enshrine the principle that two or more directors can be nominated by the family council but must be approved by the board).

Hybrid solutions are often found, which recognise the need for board cohesion and to reconcile this with the need to recognise the interests of the wider business owning

---

[128] The Law Commission report on Shareholder Remedies (Law Com No 246, cm 3769) recommends model articles should include default exit rights so that a minority could ask to be bought out on the basis of a set valuation formula in certain circumstances, including on being removed as a director. The opportunity to include this provision was not taken when the current model articles (SI 2008/3229) were introduced as part of the commencement of the Companies Act 2006.
[129] Model Articles, Art 17(1).
[130] *Blair Open Hearth Furnace Co Ltd v Reigart* (1913) 108 LT 665.

family. These solutions might include a removal of the right of the members to appoint directors, but some form of consultation rights or even a power of veto over the appointment of directors nominated by the board.

Section 168 of the Companies Act gives the shareholders the right to dismiss one or more of the board by ordinary resolution. This is the ultimate right of the shareholders. This right cannot be removed by agreement between the company and the director concerned.[131] The shareholders can however agree between themselves to modify how and when they will exercise this right. For example by agreeing, in their shareholders' agreement not to vote for the removal of directors unless certain conditions have been satisfied.

17.19.6 Retirement by rotation

These are provisions, usually found in the articles, requiring directors, to offer their resignation to the members at the company's annual general meeting, usually every 3 years. The members can then choose to re-appoint the directors concerned (or not). Similar provisions require that new directors appointed by the board are presented to the members for validation at the annual general meeting immediately after their appointment.

Retirement by rotation provisions are standard for public companies.[132] The provisions are seen as an important part of shareholder democracy and are encouraged by the UK Corporate Governance Code.[133] For private companies, including of course the vast majority of family owned businesses, the practice is the exact opposite. Although predecessors of the current model articles did contain retirement by rotation provisions, these were routinely excluded in practice. The current version of the model articles does not contain retirement provisions.

For the early stage, first and second generation, family business this makes perfect sense. There would be absolutely no point in companies owned by a handful of family members in submitting to this regime. In the vast majority of cases re-appointment would be a pure formality and unnecessary bureaucracy. There might be a few cases where a director would not command enough support for re-appointment. However it is difficult to conceive of circumstances where the best way for the remaining family members to register their discontent would be to wait until an annual general meeting[134] and then, assuming the discontented family members command sufficient votes, block the re-appointment of the director concerned.

The logic for inclusion of retirement by rotation provisions in multi-generational family businesses with larger shareholder bases is worth further consideration. The issue is often raised in practice, particularly by outsider family members. It will be rare for other private trading companies to have as many shareholders on their registers as larger family businesses. In this sense the largest family owned businesses can be seen as quasi-public companies. The rationale for retirement by rotation provisions is

---

[131] Companies Act 2006, s 168(1). Although enhanced voting rights through a *Bushell v Faith* clause can entrench the director's position: see **11.9**.
[132] Article 21 of the Model Articles for Public Limited Companies (SI 2008/3229).
[133] The UK Corporate Governance Code requires all directors of FTSE 350 companies to submit themselves for re-election on an annual basis and for other premium listed companies to resign every 3 years and then annually once they have served 9 years.
[134] It might be necessary to reinstate the convening of AGMs in any event.

shareholder democracy and accountability. It will be comparatively rare, even with growing shareholder engagement, for directors not to be re-elected. Nevertheless avoiding the possibility that re-election could be anything other than a formality must be a driving factor in encouraging boards to engage fully and actively with their shareholders.

Shareholders in quoted companies have the fall back option and the readily available exit route of selling their holding on a public market. Members in a larger unquoted family business have a much less liquid asset.

These twins themes of accountability and illiquidity do mean that, in our view, family businesses with a larger shareholder base should give serious consideration to introducing retirement by rotation provisions into their constitution. This will introduce an element of risk that the board will be disrupted if one or more directors fail to secure the necessary majority to pass an ordinary resolution for their re-election. More realistically the board may face a high degree of embarrassment if a significant minority stage a protest vote against re-election.

Against this:

- The possibility of votes against re-election should encourage the board to take every reasonable step to secure and maintain family approval.
- Retirement by rotation provisions are only part of an overall governance mechanism, part of the checks and balances, including regular contact between the board and the family council.
- Ideally the operation of the retirement by rotation provisions will provide a positive endorsement of the work of the board. This is to be contrasted with an unquestioning or even grudging acceptance (falling short of positive discontent at a level that would cause resolutions for removal to be put) that the board should remain in place.
- If discontent is to surface it is probably better if this does so in the relatively planned environment of an annual general meeting rather than in an extra-ordinary general meeting convened to consider resolutions proposed by shareholders for the removal of directors. Better still the chairman has the opportunity to take soundings from the family council or key shareholder and to deal with any discontent in advance of the meeting.

17.20 SALE OF THE COMPANY

The most fundamental decision a business owning family is ever likely to take is whether or not to sell their family business.

Many business-owning families will have given a commitment to remain together as a family business. Some families will be content to rely on a combination of fate, trust and an informal commitment, perhaps contained in a non-binding family charter to enforce this commitment. Certainly the vast majority of buyers of privately owned family businesses would be reluctant to proceed with an acquisition that does not have the universal support of all shareholders. This reluctance offers a degree of negative protection for the family ownership ethos. Other families may not have the resource or the awareness to follow this commitment through into legal documents.

Less often families choose to follow through their commitment to family ownership into formal legal documents. The practical mechanisms to implement the commitment and the extent to which it will be enforced (or not) will usually be found in the shareholders' agreement re-enforced by relevant provisions of the articles.

These provisions are discussed in chapter 11.

17.21 DRAG AND TAG

A purchaser will usually look to purchase 100% of the share capital of a privately owned family business. Certainly almost no buyer will be prepared to buy a stake in a family business with a resident minority of shareholders who are opposed to a sale.

Once a decision to sell has been made, the actual sale process needs to be executed cleanly and efficiently. Drag rights, provisions entitling a specified majority of shareholders to require the remaining shareholders to join in a sale approved by the majority, provide an important safety net.

If the overwhelming majority of the business owning family are committed to a third party sale, but that sale is frustrated by a minority, the business, the wealth of the family and family relationships will almost inevitably suffer. The minority against sale may possibly be running the business on a day basis, perhaps protected by enhanced voting rights, and with a strong vested interest to maintain the status quo (including salaries). Alternatively (and perhaps more typically) the minority against sale may be senior generation members, who have little to do with the day-to-day operation of the family business. Their reluctance to sell may be based much more on sentiment, a view that the business should remain in the family as a matter of principle, rather than economic logic. Drag and tag provisions are a sensible component of the constitution of any family business, even where the family are heavily committed to family ownership.

The key question in structuring drag provisions is how high to set the bar?

Should a simple majority of family members be able to force a third party sale? This is justifiable in terms of family democracy. More subtly, those family members committed to family ownership will need to work that much harder on the day to day aspects of family business governance, if such a slender majority can require the business to be sold outside the family.

Many business-owning families will nevertheless decide that some form of super majority will be required for such a key decision. Perhaps this will be extremely high, for example 90%, mirroring the compulsory purchase provisions in the Companies Acts.[135] Ultimately this is one of key questions for the business owning family to debate. They need to balance all the relevant factors, in particular the family values emerging from the family charter and the practicalities of the composition of the business owning family, especially branch ownership and insider/outsider tensions.

Whilst drag options are legally enforceable obligations[136] in practice it will be very rare for proceedings to be issued. Drag provisions should be seen much more as part of an

---
[135] Contained in CA, Chapter 3, ss 974–991.
[136] Through applications to the court for specific performance, declarations and damages.

insurance policy. The real purpose of these provisions is to encourage dialogue between the majority shareholders, who will often be close to the management and the board, with the more remote family shareholders. Equally the board and the buyer will be conscious of the need to take their negotiations relatively cautiously and to make the overall sale proposition sufficiently attractive to the family as a whole. Whilst the threat of compulsion, under the drag provisions remains in the background, the real objective is to secure willing participation of all shareholders in the sale, albeit that this participation may be tinged with a degree of regret and reluctance on the part of some family members.

The best way to provide for long-term family retention is almost certainly to be for the business owning family to adopt and, most crucially, implement and maintain the wider governance processes referred to earlier. Even then the ambition of long-term family ownership needs to be tempered against the realities of family business mortality statistics[137] and the reasons conspiring against long-term family ownership.[138]

As the name suggests, most drag provisions are structured so as to allow the requisite majority to unceremoniously drag the reluctant minority into a sale. Time periods to comply with drag notices will typically be short, the rights of the minority to object or resist will be almost non-existent. The logic behind this approach is that once a deal has been struck between the majority and the buyer this needs to be executed with the minimum of delay. There would be a concern that the buyer might withdraw from the transaction if completion was unduly delayed. More particularly a takeover is a time of great uncertainty for a business. In practice it is extremely difficult to maintain full confidentiality, especially if drag provisions are being exercised. The longer the delay between a deal being reached and completion the greater the uncertainty for key stakeholders in the business including management, employees, customers and suppliers and therefore the greater the risk of damage to the business.

However there is nothing to prevent a business owning family from structuring drag provisions in a way that allows the family a final opportunity to keep the business in family ownership, encourages dialogue but ultimately facilitates a third party sale.

Some constitutions contain an absolute prohibition on third party transfers. More typically such transfers are allowed after a relatively short period of time has been allowed for shareholders to exercise pre-emption provisions. An alternative structure would be to combine a basic principle that shares are to be transferred only within the family, with a structure whereby the wishes of an agreed majority of the family shareholders to sell out to a third party would trigger a final option for the reluctant sellers to buy out the majority and retain family ownership. These enhanced pre-emption rights would contain a relatively generous timescale for the minority to exercise their option, as it would be necessary to raise funds, prepare business plans and to generally assess the viability of a reverse takeover by minority family shareholders.

Whether such provisions would be workable in practice would depend on the patience of the buyer. Would they be prepared to leave an offer on the table for perhaps 6 months whilst a minority of family shareholders opposed to sale tried to raise funds? There is a risk that heavily modified drag provisions of this nature may effectively negate the over-riding purpose of drag provisions and create a de-factor ability for a minority to

---

[137] See chapter 1.
[138] See chapter 3.

veto a sale. However discussions between buyer and sellers or private companies will usually take months and on some occasions, years to conclude, from first approach to completion. Arguably the knowledge that any offer will need to be acceptable to the wider family (who for example might be concerned about family legacy issues such as maintaining employment, retaining operations in particular locations or the preservation of the family name) may help to secure a transaction that is in the best interests of all the stakeholders of the family business.

All is not necessarily lost even in the extreme situation where a company does not have any express drag and tag provisions and a small minority of family members cannot be persuaded to join in a sale. Alternatively, in multi-generational family businesses with a large shareholder register situations have arisen where some family shareholders simply cannot be traced, to ask if they are prepared to join in a sale or not. If a significant majority of family members (in excess of 90% want to sell) and other family shareholders either refuse to do so, or in some cases cannot be traced. The statutory squeeze out provisions contained in CA, Chapter 3,[139] although mainly seen in the public company arena are, at least as a matter of law and theory, available in private family business situations. However, due to the complexity of the statutory squeeze out provisions, express bespoke drag and tag provisions remain by far the most preferable option.

Tag rights are provisions giving a corresponding right for the minority shareholders to join in a sale by the majority so that the minority are not left behind with an unsalable interest in what used to be their family business but is now under third party control. The introduction of tag rights will rarely be controversial. As discussed most buyers will want to obtain a 100% stake in any event. It is difficult to conceive of situations where the majority of a family could justify arranging their own exit on terms that other family members did not have the opportunity to sell at the same time.

Again the Companies Acts contain a statutory tag right or right of sell out.[140] Under CA, s 983 this is exercisable by minority shareholders only once the buyer has secured 90% acceptances to their proposed takeover offer.

There is absolutely nothing to prevent (and much to recommend) family owned companies including tag rights with a much lower exercise threshold in their articles or shareholders' agreement. Often the same threshold will be set for the exercise of tag rights as for drag provisions. This need not be the case. Indeed there are arguments for tag rights to apply as soon as a majority of family shareholders want to sell. The passage from family to non-family control will be a watershed moment. It will change the complexion of the business. The exit door should be open to all.

17.22 DISPUTE RESOLUTION

As has been explained elsewhere the reality for most business families is that conflicts and disputes will arise from time to time.[141] The issue is not therefore whether disputes will arise, but how these will be dealt with. In particular can the dispute be resolved in such a way as to preserve, rather than to destroy, family relationships?

---

[139] Companies Act 2006, ss 974–992.
[140] Companies Act 2006, ss 983–985.
[141] Conflict in family firms is explored in chapter 2. Chapter 25 talks about interventions and alternative dispute resolution.

For those business families with more detailed family charters, these will usually contain strong and fairly detailed exhortations for the family to do their utmost to resolve disputes informally. Most business families will not have family charters. Charters are in any event not usually legally binding. There is therefore a case for detailed dispute resolution procedures to be built into, in particular, shareholders' agreements.

The majority of shareholders' agreements pay comparatively little attention to dispute resolution procedures, often containing little beyond boilerplate provisions, confirming the jurisdiction of the relevant local law courts to hear disputes.

It is difficult, if not impossible, to think of an argument why shareholders' agreements for family owned businesses should not contain obligations on the family members concerned to do their utmost resolve disputes informally.[142] A hierarchy of gradually more formal procedures could be included. Parties could be required to attempt to resolve matters between themselves, then involve appropriate insiders such as the chairs of the family council or the board.

In some cases there will be an identifiable issue in dispute. Often that issue will be best seen as a presenting symptom of poor and deteriorating relationships between family members. Dealing with the dispute, as such, would therefore be dealing with the symptom not the cause of the underlying problem. Possibly an option could be included for the relevant chair to require the parties to participate in measures designed to deal with the cause itself. Relevant training could be useful, for example to explain the different roles of the family and the board. Possibly the chair could be empowered to bring in specialist outsiders, such as family business consultants, to work with the parties to restore working relationships.

If this does not work it may then be necessary to resort to formal third party mediation or possibly arbitration. Binding expert determination of valuation issues is routinely provided for. This could be extended to other financial matters.[143]

Whereas many dispute resolution procedures provide for strict timetables and a streamlined procedure, there is an argument that almost the opposite should apply in a family business dispute, with compulsory cooling off periods, before the parties escalate their dispute to the next step.

There may still come a point when, notwithstanding exhaustive attempts to resolve matters informally, it becomes clear that the family members concerned cannot realistically remain in business together. There are strong arguments for including family business divorce provisions in formal legal documents. This is particularly the case in earlier stage family businesses.

Occasionally shareholders' agreements contain provisions for the winding up of the company in the case of unresolved deadlock. Nuclear options of this nature are impossible to reconcile with a desire for continuity. It is easy to envisage circumstances where such provisions, essentially intended to 'bring the parties to their senses' can have

---

[142] It may still be wise to include provisions allowing emergency applications to the courts for injunctive relief etc in extreme circumstances.
[143] The role of mediators, arbitrators and experts in family business disputes are explored further in chapter 26.

unforeseen and unintended consequences for the stakeholders of a family firm, particularly if a severely disgruntled and malicious outsiders have the potential to press the red button.

There are a number of examples of deadlock resolution provisions to be found, particularly in joint venture agreements and sometimes in general shareholders' agreements intended for use in small company 'quasi partnerships', which are potentially capable of application in family businesses. These include the so-called 'Russian Roulette' and 'Mexican Shootout' provisions.

Under a Russian Roulette clause the party triggering the deadlock resolution procedure names a price at which they will, at the option of the other party to the dispute, either sell their own shares or alternatively buy those held by the other party receiving the notice. The incentive is therefore to specify a demonstrably fair price in the notice triggering the clause. More subtly as the party serving the notice has no real control of whether they will be staying in the business or being bought out there is a strong incentive to put the formal procedure to one side and renew efforts to find a mutually acceptable and ideally the best solution to the problem.

Under a Mexican (also called Texan) shootout one party serves a notice indicating the price at which they will be prepared to buy the other's shares. The recipient then has the choice of accepting that offer or alternatively buying out the other party at a higher price.

There always remains a danger that any provisions of this nature can be used tactically or improperly or that unforeseen results can apply. In some cases shareholders' agreements provide that the heavy procedures can only be used on the basis of, for example the certification of a third party such as the chair of the board or of the family council, that the relevant dispute seems otherwise incapable of resolution.

These provisions can only really be considered where family members have similar shareholdings (or at least similar borrowing power) and are equally engaged in the day-to-day management of the business. Where the family business has evolved much beyond the quasi partnership, with widely differing shareholdings or roles, provisions of this nature may well be of limited practical assistance and could potentially cause more problems than they would ever be likely to solve. Consider for example an outsider minority shareholder with no day-to-day management role at odds with the managing director with a significant shareholding. In practice there is only one realistic buyer, the insider managing director.

Alternatively consider a second-generation managing director son, with a smaller shareholding and little by way of other wealth, in dispute with his father, the senior generation founder. Absent a bank or private equity backed management buy-out (which might be the best solution) there is only one realistic seller, the son. But this will result in the father resuming control and will subvert the natural succession process.

Of course there are innumerable variations to the factual matrix of the examples given above relating to capability, financial and business performance, personal wealth and not least the psychology of those in dispute. This further illustrates the difficulty of drafting deadlock resolution mechanisms that are sufficiently flexible and far-sighted to accommodate these circumstances and to produce results that are likely to be fair and will not damage the later stage family business.

Perhaps the final permutation to consider is fault, on the part of one or more shareholders, or at least alleged fault. It is not uncommon for shareholders' agreements used in non-family business contexts to provide that a shareholder in breach, particularly serious repeated or un-remedied breach of the provisions of a shareholders' agreement are liable to have their shares compulsorily purchased under call options, sometimes on unfavourable terms.[144] Do such provisions have any place in a family owned company? Ideally exit provisions will be already be included for the benefit of minority outsiders in any event. Possibly these could be strengthened in the event of clear and serious breaches by insiders. For example relevant insiders could be made subject to personal put options. The provisions discussed in chapter 11 providing for generous payment terms could be accelerated.[145] But what of minority outsiders? Just possibly the family might consider adding call-options so that clearly dissident and disruptive minorities can be removed: in effect to as a 'bad family member'. This would be a drastic step and would almost certainly mark the end of the wider family cohesion. On a systems analysis the issue will often to seen as structural rather than fault based or personality driven. On a practical level it would often be extremely difficult to show that outsiders were in breach of the relatively general obligations they have assumed under shareholders' agreements.

The more complex and evolved later stage business are likely to be better served by a combination of:

- no fault exit provisions[146] allowing for the no fault, no reason required exit of minorities on fair terms;
- governance procedures allowing the board and the management room to manage;
- communication systems which allow for feedback and dialogue between the board and, in particular non-working family shareholders;
- sophisticated drag provisions under which a suitably large majority can procure that the family business is sold to a third party as the ultimate incentive for the board to make the governance system work.

Although the potential for dispute around substantive issues may be reduced by complex and comprehensive governance documents it becomes more likely that genuine disputes surrounding interpretation and implementation will arise. Although analytically any court application to resolve such issues could be seen as more of an administrative matter, it will in practice be extremely difficult for the family members involved to retain that degree of detachment. Almost inevitably taking or even threatening or canvassing court proceedings to resolve a dispute on interpretation when the parties have taken entrenched positions will be seen as one family member taking another to court, with equally inevitable long term damage to relationships between, not only the original parties, but in all probability branches of the family well into the future.

---

[144] There is also the related question of the bankruptcy of a family member. The usual treatment is to provide for the compulsory purchase of their shares. Complex questions of valuation arise. Would provisions requiring valuation to take into account minority discounts be acceptable as reflecting economic reality? Alternatively if transfers under other circumstances would be at full pro-rata value would a discounted valuation be unenforceable as a matter of public policy?

[145] Arguably these concessions might need to be made to frame a reasonable buy-out offer as a defence to an unfair prejudice petition. See chapter 24.

[146] Discussed in chapter 11.

This scenario emphasises the need for every effort to be put into early stage alternative dispute resolution.

17.23 OTHER FAMILY BUSINESS GOVERNANCE DOCUMENTS

In addition to the main governance documents discussed above, individual family businesses may employ a number of other documents that collectively ought to be seen as part of their overall family business governance structure. The type and contents of these documents are potentially as varied as family businesses themselves. However we will briefly list the main categories of supplemental documents.

17.23.1 Trust deeds

Any business owning family with formal trusts as part of their ownership arrangements will have formal trust deeds as part of their governance structure. Indeed for the vast majority of more traditional and long standing family businesses trust deeds are more likely to be in place than documents of more recent origin, such as family charters. In some cases trust deeds will be supplemented by letters of wishes, prepared by the settlor when setting up the trust setting out their views on such key issues as the sale of the shares held by trustees in the family business, and how income received from the underlying business as dividends is to be distributed and applied amongst the discretionary beneficiaries. The underlying trust issues are discussed in more detail in chapter 14. However the key issues relating to trusts from a family business governance perspective are:

- The use of trusts will add another layer of complexity to family business governance. This is particularly so if professionals or non-family trustees are involved as legal owners of shares in the family business. Where present, the primary role of the family council is to act as a channel of communication between the board and the wider business owning family. In highly evolved family business governance systems, with both trusts and family councils present, the family council will often have an additional function, to represent the views of some or all of the wider family as beneficiaries under relevant trusts, to the trustees concerned.
- As with most provisions in family charters, letters of wishes are not likely to be legally binding on trustees.
- Letters of wishes convey the views of one individual, the settlor (typically the entrepreneur or founder of the business) on how the family businesses should be governed. That view will be fixed in time at the date the letter of wishes was prepared. This can be contrasted with family charters which, at least in theory, should represent the views of the wider business owning family and, through a process of regular updating, reflect a more up to date perspective. Often conflicts can arise for the trustees, wishing to steer a path between remaining true to the original settlor's intentions, as expressed in the letter of wishes, the aspirations of the wider family as beneficiaries and their general duties as trustees.

17.23.2 Pre-nuptial agreements

As discussed in chapter 18 pre-nuptial agreements (and post-nuptial agreements) are increasingly likely to be recognised as legally enforceable by the English courts.

These agreements appear to be of significant interest to family business owners. Many family businesses will have a bloodline family only ownership policy. Family business owners, particularly those in the senior generation, will often have concerns that hard won family wealth can be lost to the family as a result of divorce. This concern is often given as at least one reason not to pursue succession plans and transfer shares to the next generation.

Analytically pre and post-nuptial agreements can be seen as a species of asset protection arrangement, similar to trusts. Clearly the introduction of pre-nuptial agreements (much less post nuptial agreements) will be an extremely sensitive issue, even as a discussion point. Equally clearly it will be for each business owning family to decide where they sit on the scale between, on the one hand a completely *laisser-faire* approach of embracing partners as fully fledged participants in the family business and letting the future take care of itself and, at the opposite extreme putting in place rigid rules about such agreements.

To put the point no higher, whether or not to encourage pre-nuptial (or post-nuptial) agreements should logically form part of the governance considerations of most business owning families.

17.23.3 Employment contracts

Although family employment policies should almost certainly remain in the family charter, as non-legally enforceable statements of principle, once family members actually join the family business it is important that they are subject to best practice employment procedures generally. This will include service agreements on identical term to non-family employees.[147]

The issue of equal treatment of family employees cuts both ways. Family employees are less likely to be subject to employment documents that would be routinely issued to their non-family counterparts. If the employment relationship breaks down, the family company will not have the protection of confidentiality provisions and restrictive covenants found in full service agreements. Disputes may arise at a more mundane level on exactly what terms the family member concerned was employed under.

17.23.4 Option agreements

Agreements in principle may have been reached between the senior generation and the next generation to transfer ownership at some point in the future. Perhaps that agreement will be conditional on some external event such as the performance of the business or the sale of surplus freehold properties, which will in turn generate funds to be released to the senior generation who need no longer depend on the business as their sole source of income.

Some families may be content to leave these matters as statements of intention. As recollections are apt to fade or differ, it may well be advisable for some form of note or minute to be produced to record exactly what has been agreed. Whilst a record of this

---

[147] This issue is discussed in more detail in chapter 5 and 7.

nature may well be of some assistance in avoiding disputes, arrangements recorded in an informal way are unlikely to be enforceable. At the very least doubts will clearly arise over whether this is the case.

Families will rarely choose to go further and to put in place detailed option arrangements, similar to those that would apply at the stage non family managers, assumed the status 'as owners or part owners designate' of the business concerned.

17.23.5 Partnership agreements

This chapter has dealt exclusively with the documenting the governance arrangements of family companies. Most of the underlying principles will apply equally to the situation of family partnerships. These, and especially the complexities of documenting ownership arrangements, are considered separately in chapter 13.

17.23.6 Connected party agreements

In various chapters we refer to the difficulties created by the twin factors of informality and complexity so far as dealings between family members are concerned.[148] The basic governance proposition is that such arrangements should be entered into on such terms and documented with the same degree of formality that would be appropriate to arm's length third party transactions.

17.24 GOVERNANCE CONCLUSION

Governance in the context of a family owned business is an all-embracing subject. It goes far beyond the traditional realm of corporate governance, which is firmly rooted in the business domain and extends into the family and ownership sub-systems.

The last 30 years or so has seen the development of family business governance systems and what can be described as the classic family business governance model. That is not to say that this model represents a blue print to be adopted by all family businesses as a panacea for all family business ills. Far from it. Just as all family businesses are, at least, subtly different so will be their governance requirements.

The key point for the business owning family is to establish a level of communication that can identify their own particular governance requirements and what systems and processes are necessary to serve these. The classic family business governance model can then be crafted and adapted as necessary. Governance case studies and advisors can also facilitate the process but ultimately the family must champion their own process.

---

[148] For example loan arrangements or property dealings considered in chapter 10 or in relation to the use of the family business brand dealt with in chapter 9.

CHAPTER 18

THE FAMILY BUSINESS AND MARRIAGE

18.1 INTRODUCTION

For some couples their pipe dream is the opportunity to work side by side in their own family business.[1] Extrapolating figures from research in the USA would suggest that for well over a million couples in the UK this dream has come true.[2] Most dreams fade. Some turn into nightmares.

Much of this book concerns the tensions and pressures associated with family business life. It is unclear whether these translate into a higher incidence of divorce and relationship breakdown for couples involved in family businesses. For various reasons, it would not be a great surprise if this was the case.

This chapter considers aspects of family business dynamics of particular relevance for couples working together as well as the legal issues relating the impact of divorce and marriage break-up on family businesses generally. The chapter is divided into two broad parts.

First we look briefly at the situation of so-called 'copreneurs', couples who are both domestic and business partners. Copreneurs are particularly found in smaller scale early stage family firms. There are inevitable complexities for couples working together. We point to factors and governance strategies that might help turn the dream those couples have of working together into a practical reality. We also consider the impact of divorce on such early stages copreneurial family businesses.

Small husband and wife family businesses have been around since time immemorial. The proverbial 'mom and pop store' and the pub landlord and landlady are prime examples. But there are suggestions that the copreneurship phenomenon is on the rise. Apparently the fastest rising categories of new business start-ups, at least in the USA, are those set up by couples and women.[3]

---

[1] Freud argued that the key to a happy life was 'lieben und arbieten' or love and work. If so, a couple working together in their family business should have the perfect package.
[2] Various surveys from the USA suggest that life partner firms represent about one third of all family businesses there (for example according to various surveys (FFI.org; National Federation of Independent Business). The IFB study referred to in chapter 1 (*The State of the Nation: The UK Family Business Sector 2015/16* (IFB Research Foundation with Oxford Economics)) suggested that there about 4.6m family businesses in the UK.
[3] See Jane Hilburt-Davis and W Gibb Dyer Jr *Consulting to Family Businesses* (Jossey-Bass, 2003) at p 184 and the sources cited there.

This is a due to a mixture of economics and demographics. The rise of information technology and the growth of entrepreneurialism have made it both easier and more on trend to set up a new family business. This development can be attributed to a combination of choice, in terms of positive work life balance, and necessity, in that, at more or less the same time, employees have increasingly rejected the corporate world and, equally, the corporate world has rejected swathes of employees through its vicious and continuous downsizing. This earlier part of the chapter is largely relevant to smaller, early stage family businesses.

We then move on to consider the position of spouses, not directly involved working in the family business. This will largely be with reference to larger and later stage family businesses. This will form the bulk of the chapter and will look at aspects of family dynamics and governance, including the position of in-laws. We also look at wider family business governance systems and, in particular, the evolving law and practice of attempting to control the impact of marital breakdown on family businesses by the use of nuptial agreements.

The courts in England and Wales have looked at the situation of business owning families on the breakdown of marriage on countless occasions. A significant part of this chapter is devoted to summarising the key points arising from those cases and explaining the evolving approach of the courts.

In the parts of the chapter dealing with family business dynamics we use the terminology of marriage quite loosely, to include not only legally married couples and those in a formal civil partnership but also any couple living together. That degree of imprecision does not work for those parts of the chapter, dealing with legal issues. The provisions of the key statute, the Matrimonial Causes Act 1973, relating to the redistribution of assets following the breakdown of a domestic relationship, only apply to couples in a formal legal relationship of marriage. In cases of civil partnership, the Civil Partnership Act 2004 applies, which broadly applies the same rules to civil partners or civil partnerships.[4] The position of cohabiting couples involved in a family business is both quite different and beyond the scope of this book.[5]

As the chapter concentrates on the effect of relationship breakdown on the family business, the legal content almost exclusively relates to the impact of divorce on the ownership of the family business. Accordingly huge swathes of basic matrimonial law and practice are not covered, including arrangements for the care and maintenance of children, the basic grounds for divorce, together with the important issue of the treatment of pensions on divorce. Obviously these matters are also of considerable

---

[4] The Civil Partnership Act 2004 is the key statue for civil partnerships. Same sex marriage is also a legal relationship but the statute determining how assets are distributed on divorce of same sex couples is awaited at the time of writing.

[5] But, put broadly, the matrimonial courts have no jurisdiction to interfere with the redistribution of property as between cohabiting couples. The position is quite different if this is necessary for the needs of children of the relationship. The courts may also be involved on the death of one of the partners (through the Inheritance (Provision for Family and Dependents) Act 1975 – discussed in the following chapter 19 (Inheritance Disputes)) or through equitable property or trust based claims, such as the doctrine of resulting trusts briefly explained in chapter 14. Claims for the benefit of children of cohabiting couples are brought under Sch 1 of the Children Act 1989 and are limited to lump sums, housing provision and maintenance top-ups during the child's minority.

importance to those involved in family businesses, but it is difficult to say that this is to any greater extent than for couples with no family business connection.[6]

18.2 COPRENEURS AND THE EARLY STAGE FAMILY BUSINESS

Just like the definition of family business there are various permutations or definitions of copreneur. Two academics, Barnett & Barnett,[7] are given credit for first coining the expression in 1988 as applicable to couples who demonstrate joint ownership, commitment, and responsibility to a family business.

Other more extensive and complicated formulations define copreneurs as:[8]

> 'married couples, or couples in a marriage-like relationship, who jointly own and operate a business or otherwise share ownership, responsibility, risk, and management of a business.'

Spread across the million or so family firms in the UK falling within these all-encompassing formulations there will be a huge range or degree of copreneurialism. Gersick et al[9] use the terms the 'marriage enterprise' as an umbrella term for the range of potential permutations in terms of role allocation and contribution to the twin domains of family and business comprised within the family business marriage partnership.

At one end of the scale there are out and out couple partnerships: family businesses founded jointly by life partners as genuine business partnerships, driven by a shared business dream and a wish to share both the benefits of the enterprise and the adventure of growing a business. These businesses are perhaps typified by couples who appear on Dragon's Den seeking funding for their business proposition or those who decide to give up their careers and homes in London to set up a rural food business.[10] Some of these husband and wife partnership teams go on to develop household name businesses. Anita and Gordon Roddick with Body Shop spring to mind.[11]

In these businesses the emphasis is on the word 'jointly' appearing in the above formulations, with each of the couple concerned acknowledged as making an equal (but different) contribution to the overall success of the family enterprise. Copreneurial businesses towards this end of the scale would appear to be in the ascendancy.

At the opposite end of the scale are businesses where one spouse, historically the husband (although history can point to a number of significant dynastic family businesses which have been founded by women) has pretty much exclusive conduct of the day to day business and assumes sole responsibility for all decision making. The Park House Properties and Gemma family businesses cases are prime examples.[12] Both

---

[6] For a more general and comprehensive treatment of many of these issues see Bird & King *Financial Remedies Handbook* (Jordan Publishing, 2015).
[7] F Barnett and S Barnett *Working together: Entrepreneurial couples* (Ten Speed Press, 1988).
[8] B S Hollander and N S Elman *Family-owned businesses: An emerging field of inquiry Family Business Review* (1988) Vol 1(2), 145–164.
[9] Gersick, Davis, Hampton & Lansberg *Generation to Generation: Life cycles of a family business* (Harvard Business School Press, 1997).
[10] Montezuma's Chocolate are a prime example. Set up and managed by a husband and wife team, who were previously City lawyers.
[11] Other, older examples include late Laura Ashley and her husband Bernard in relation to the eponymous UK clothing and furnishing chain and Estee and Joseph Lauder with their perfume and cosmetics business.
[12] Considered in detail in chapter 8 (Directors' Duties).

Mrs Carter and Mrs Davies were appointed as directors of the family companies concerned and (particularly in the case of Mrs Davies) they did some work in the business. However neither could be seen to have been jointly managing the family business with their husbands. Yet the coprenuer label is increasingly applied to all businesses where couples are involved, to some degree as an owner, employee or director of a family firm, irrespective of the relative or joint contributions of the partners.

In the middle of the copreneurship scale sit businesses with a whole range of circumstances where, depending on family and child care commitments, career and professional responsibilities, the complexity of the business and relevant skills and experience, a spouse works full time, but clearly in a supporting role. Alternatively, they might help out on a part time, temporary[13] or intermittent basis or act as a sounding board to guide the full time spouse on strategic issues.

All copreneurial businesses fall somewhere along this scale. Most of the available research suggests that the typical business would still be positioned closer towards the traditional business and gender role model.

Research suggests that historically copreneurial businesses will typically have been set up and be led by men, with women playing supporting roles, often unpaid or underpaid, juggling their support with other employment and taking primary responsibility for homecare.[14] Tellingly, it is suggested that the spouse, typically the wife, joining the business-founder does not make any material difference to the profitability of their family business.[15]

Similarly the research suggests that the typical couple-led business seems to conform more to the 'mom and pop store' stereotype than that of the thrusting innovative start-up. Typically couple led businesses are less profitable and more likely to be home based and located in rural areas than other businesses not run by couples.[16]

Of course many businesses are set up, owned and run exclusively by a single spouse. Whilst these businesses fall outside the copreneurship definition they come within the wide definition of a family business discussed in chapter 1. In any event the value of those businesses will be equally relevant on divorce.

But there are hopes and suggestions (although as yet little evidence) that the world is changing and moving towards a more balanced and equal model of joint copreneurship.[17]

---

[13] For example in *Cowan* (discussed in more detail below) Mrs Cowan ran the family business on a day to day basis until it was sufficiently established for Mr Cowan to give up his full time job. She worked for 10 years or so and then left to concentrate on the home, including supervising work on renovating the country mansion that the couple could, by then, afford.
[14] See for example Margaret A Fitzgerald, Glenn Muske 'Copreneurs: An Exploration and Comparison to Other Family Businesses' *Family Business Review* (2002), Vol 15(1), and also W Gibb Dyer, W Justin Dyer, and Richard G Gardner 'Should My Spouse Be My Partner? Preliminary Evidence From the Panel Study of Income Dynamics' *Family Business Review* (2012) Vol 26(1) 68–80.
[15] Dyer et al.
[16] Fitzgerald and Musk.
[17] Such as Montezuma's Chocolate.

18.3 MARTIN AND PAMELA WHITE

The couple concerned in the leading case on divorce and the family business,[18] Martin and Pamela White, fitted the joint copreneurship model. Before their marriage each had farmed separately, '... farming was in their blood. They both came from farming families'.[19] After they were married they bought Blagroves Farm and farmed this together in partnership. Pamela 'primarily brought up the children, and she also worked hard in all sorts of ways on the farm'.[20]

The Whites were successful farmers, acquiring land to more than double the size of their original farm to 337 acres. This land was owned by them jointly through their farming partnership.

The partnership also farmed a nearby farm, but there the underlying land was owned by Martin White personally. This land had previously been part of his late father's estate. Mr White senior had also helped the young couple with a loan to help acquire Blagroves farm at the start of their marriage.

18.4 MAKING IT WORK: GOVERNANCE AND COPRENEURSHIP

Peter Leach sounds a strong note of caution that if couples plan to work together they are entering a 'potentially disastrous emotional minefield'.[21]

If a couple has decided to take the plunge and work together in a family business, what are the tips and suggestions to help them reap the benefits and maximise the positive factors of this relationship, for the good of both business and family? Conversely what should be avoided if the business and the family relationships are to survive intact? The key factor will be the skill and determination with which the couple concerned approach their relationship. It is inevitable that being in business together adds considerable layers of complexity to a couple's relationship. Pointers include:

18.4.1 Boundaries

Much has already been said about the implications of the three-circle model[22] and the difficulties of recognising and respecting boundaries between the business and family systems. The danger of cross pollution between the two systems is particularly acute for coprenuers. Business issues can easily intrude into the home, almost to the extinction of a balanced domestic life. The needs of children can be eclipsed by those of the family business. Commentators talk about the need for couples to erect boundary markers between the two aspects of their lives. Sometimes these will be by explicit agreement, for example not to 'talk shop' at family mealtimes or on holiday. Other couples will put down non-verbal markers. An example cited is of a husband simply picking up the newspaper to signal to his wife that business talk is at an end for the day.

---

[18] *White v White* [2001] 1 AC 596.
[19] The quotation is from the speech of Lord Nicholls in the House of Lords judgment following the eventual breakdown of the White's marriage – *White v White* [2001] 1 AC 596.
[20] At p 602.
[21] Peter Leach *Family Businesses – The Essentials* (Profile Books, 2007) at p 25.
[22] See, in particular the explanation of the three-circle model in chapter 3 (Tools, Models and Theories).

The reverse situation, where unresolved domestic conflict is allowed to intrude into the workplace, is more obviously dangerous to the business, but may require a high degree of self-awareness on the part of the couple concerned, to identify when this occurring.

An interesting idea is that of 'boundary zones', a sort of no-mans land between business and family systems when work is being discussed at home or when domestic concerns are dominating the workplace and where:[23]

> 'incongruity between the physical and psychological transition states exists. In other words, an individual is in the boundary zone, or in between domains, when the subjective experience is that the psychological transition is still in process, while the physical shift is complete.'

Of course along with most professionals, family business couples will inevitably spend some time in this boundary zone. The trick is not to live there.

18.4.2 Conflict management

In chapter 2 we suggest that conflict is an inevitable part of family business life and that a key factor in the success of any family business will be how well conflict is managed. This is especially so for coprenuerial couples. One commentator[24] suggests that 69% of all marital conflict is never fully resolved.

So the success of any marriage and, by extension any family business run by a copreneurial couple, will be largely down to conflict management and how well they can accommodate each other and find workable compromises. This is also explored in chapter 2. The same commentator suggests that positive indicators and relevant skills include:[25]

- A ratio of 5:1 in terms of positive: negative interactions.
- Humour.
- Effective, quick repair after conflict.
- Expression of affection.
- Non-defensive listening.
- Recognition and censorship of 'hot thoughts'.
- Practice in 'better talk'.

18.4.3 Roles and responsibilities

Establishing clear roles and responsibilities for each of the copreneurs in the workplace (combined with flexibility in the home) can be an important plank in conflict prevention. Each of the couple understands what is, and what is not, his or her job. Duplication and interference is minimised. Employees know to whom they should turn on any given issue. Efficiency is maximised.

---

[23] From Kathy J. Marshack 'Coentrepreneurial Couples: A Literature Review on Boundaries and Transitions Among Copreneurs' *Family Business Review* (1993) 355–369 referring to the work of J Richter 'The Daily Transitions Between Professional and Private Life', unpublished doctoral dissertation, Boston University, 1984.

[24] J Gottman *Why marriages succeed or fail* (Simon & Schuster) cited in Jane Hilburt-Davis and W Gibb Dyer Jr *Consulting to Family Businesses* (Jossey-Bass, 2003) at p 188.

[25] More detailed lists are to be found in Jane Hilburt-Davis and W Gibb Dyer Jr *Consulting to Family Businesses* (Jossey-Bass, 2003) at p 190.

Logically establishing appropriate roles should include a proper assessment of whether the spouse is the best person for a particular role in the first place. Some combination of convenience, recruitment difficulties, or perhaps financial pressure prevents the hiring of a more suitable third party. The spouse becomes a default option for a role that they are not really suited to perform.[26] Whilst there is an inevitable element of needs must, too much reliance on spousal support (just as in employing any other family member) can delay the professionalisation and growth of a family firm.

18.4.4 Emotional leadership

Sometimes the role taken by one spouse is not directly business focused, but is nevertheless vital for the success of a family firm.

Family business writers often talk about emotional leadership in a family business. By this they mean someone who acts as a bridge between the family and the business and who takes responsibility 'to care for peace and harmony in the family and the firm'.[27] Often the role is to act as mediator between family members or to reduce friction between the family and business systems.

Sometimes the role is described as CEO or Chief Emotional Leader,[28] which underlines the importance of the role in a family firm and, perhaps, its ubiquity.

Although we can point to examples of the business leader fulfilling this role, more often than not, it will be the supporting spouse who acts as CEO, a role which Jimenez argues is 'much more difficult to replace than that of the [Chief Executive Officer]'.[29]

18.4.5 Positive gender issues

This is a more tricky subject. The sub-heading is borrowed from an academic article, discussed below, about how divorced coprenuers manage to continue to work together after divorce.[30] The issue is the interplay between traditional gender stereotypes, office politics, power and control in coprenuerial relationships.

There appears to be some evidence that female coprenuers may be more content to sit back and allow their husbands to assume the title of managing director and the trappings of being in charge, without the need for their own status to be recognised in badges of office. Often the husband had founded the business concerned in the research. But husbands were also held out as the nominal business leader where most factors pointed to a more equal partnership and even in cases where the family firm was initially founded by the wife, so that:[31]

---

[26] Typical roles assumed by the supporting spouse include looking after the accounts (variously described as 'doing the books' like Mrs Davies in *Re Gemma* to grander titles like 'Finance Director') or taking responsibility for HR matters.

[27] From Rocio Martinez Jimenez 'Research on Women in Family Firms: Current Status and Future Directions' *Family Business Review* (2009) Vol 22(1), 53–64.

[28] See, John Ward *Keeping the Family Business Healthy: How to plan for continuing growth, profitability and family leadership* (Jossey-Bass, 1987).

[29] Op cit at p 56. The role of the Chief Emotional Officer is discussed as part of management succession at 7.9.

[30] Patricia M Cole, Kit Johnson 'An Exploration of Successful Coprenuerial Relationships Postdivorce' *Family Business Review* (2007), Vol 20(3).

[31] Patricia M Cole, Kit Johnson 'An Exploration of Successful Coprenuerial Relationships Postdivorce' *Family Business Review* (2007), Vol 20(3).

'If wives held subordinate positions to their husbands, it was their choice rather than the result of a power struggle between the sexes.'

Quite whether this assumption of traditional gender roles extends to real power, control and decision making is a moot point. Dyer points to other research[32] on copreneurial decision making. This noted that 76% of husbands surveyed (who were generally the founder) reported that they 'often make important decisions concerning the business without consulting my spouse'. On the other hand 65% of wives were less willing to make important business decisions without consulting their husbands.

The alternative view is that real power and control will often be much more evenly distributed with wives being more comfortable and secure with their own roles, contributions and level of control, including the ability to subtly influence key decisions by using 'techniques or strategies such as patience, choosing battles, and timing to keep the waters smooth',[33] without the need to engage in constant power struggles with their husbands.

There are, of course, examples of positive gender roles being deployed by male copreneurs. In most of the well-known businesses noted above, including the Body Shop and Laura Ashley the public face of the business was very much associated with the female half of the respective partnerships.

So there does seem to be an argument that the working relationship of copreneurs is more collaborative and less conflict ridden than that of other family business dyads, such as father and son relationships, or that between siblings, especially brothers. Possibly this is as a result of a willingness to stick to old-fashioned gender stereotypes. Hopefully this is as a result of more subtle and positive influences, so that increasingly coprenreurs are able to avoid the need to compete in a head on battle of the sexes and manage to find a way to work together that enhances rather than compromises the emotional integrity of either partner.

18.5 EARLY WARNING SIGNS

If conflict is inevitable in any marriage and in any family business how do couples work out the difference between, on the one hand, routine disagreements or constructive conflicts and, on the other hand, deeper and destructive conflict pointing towards the need for some more radical intervention or the likelihood of divorce? In *Consulting to Family Businesses* Hilburt-Davis and Dyer refer to the 'four horsemen of the apocalypse' namely criticism, contempt, defensiveness and withdrawal as 'predictive over time of separation and divorce'.[34]

Conflict and its management is dealt with in chapter 2 (Themes). Hilburt-Davis and Dyer also suggest[35] a number of pointers of particular relevance to couples in business together. These include:

---

[32] L Ponthieu and H Caudill 'Who's the boss? Responsibility and decision making in copreneurial ventures' *Family Business Review* (1993) Vol 6, 3–17.
[33] Patricia M Cole, Kit Johnson 'An Exploration of Successful Copreneurial Relationships Postdivorce' *Family Business Review* (2007), Vol 20(3).
[34] At p 189. See also the sources and references quoted there. The analysis takes no account of more explosive events outside the family business system, such as the infidelity of either spouse.
[35] At pp 184–193.

- **Unresolved conflicts** – which can be about either home or work issues. The defining characteristic being that, if mentioned, the relevant issue sets off a 'land-mine'. These may escalate and be linked to other land mine issues.
- **Blame** – where each party blames the other for problems and accepts little or no personal responsibility.
- **Triangulation**[36] – whereby employees, advisors and possibly other family members are drawn into arguments between the couple or are used by one party as an audience for complaints about the other.
- **Distancing** – where the couple are remote and mutually cut off. Perhaps this will be characterised by poor communication, or by one or both parties keeping secrets from each other.
- **Pursuers and avoiders** – where one party reaches towards the other at an emotional level and the other withdraws or responds from a rational or intellectual distance.
- **Over-functioners and under-functioners** – where one party fails to pull their weight in an almost child-like way (either in the business or in the home) and the other is forced to compensate as a quasi-parent.[37]
- **Strategic disagreement** – between the couple on the vision and future of their family business. They no longer have a shared dream.

To what extent can governance help prevent the arrival of the four horsemen of apocalypse?

18.6 GOVERNANCE

Governance might seem to be too grandiose a word to apply to suggestions of how a couple could communicate with each other about the key issues relevant to their family business. Certainly we are not advocating that smaller and early stage businesses introduce, wholesale, the detailed mechanisms of the classic family business governance model such as family councils and family charters discussed in chapter 17. What we are suggesting is that some of the core principles from later stage family business governance can be distilled and applied to early stage family businesses.

The first step will be to establish a level of communication between the life partners concerned with the business (who may or may not also be business partners) which is appropriate to the level of involvement of the partner concerned and the impact of the success or failure of the business on the wider family, its wealth and assets.

As suggested above, copreneurship and the involvement of spouses and partners in first generation family businesses fall within a range. Different governance considerations apply at different ends of this scale.

At one end of the scale, the full joint corpreneurship, such as Montezuma's Chocolate, the business partners will be in constant communication about the details of their business. Their challenge may well be the typical one of finding time away from the all-encompassing burden of the day to day detail of an early stage family business (whilst at the same time juggling home and childcare responsibilities) to look at its strategic

---

[36] Explained in chapter 3 (Tools, Models and Theories).
[37] There is a clear link to transactional analysis – also discussed in chapter 3.

direction – to work on the business not *in* the business. On a three-circle model analysis both partners will be firmly entrenched in Zone 1, at the centre of the model as simultaneously family members, owners and business leaders.

At the other end of the scale the spouse might have a very much less involved role, for a whole host of reasons, including the demands of their own primary career, expertise or domestic responsibilities. There the arguments for classifying the business concerned as copreneurial or even as a family business are much more marginal. We have previously used the example of the Davies family *in Re Gemma*. The couple will occupy different places within the model, with more obvious potential for them to see life, as it applies to their family business, differently.

Nevertheless the assets of the Davies family were firmly on the line when the family business failed. In addition to the loss of family income, personal guarantees to banks, backed by security over the family home, are an unavoidable reality for many early stage family businesses. In such cases there is a powerful argument that a basic level of communication about business risks represents a minimum standard of acceptable family governance.

In these early stage family businesses appropriate governance could be some combination of building a wider support network, perhaps based on the suggestions in **17.7.2** supplemented by family centered governance mechanisms such as:

- Informal but nevertheless semi structured and briefings and discussions between partners on the trading, financial position, opportunities, challenges and threats facing the family business. These need to be on a regular basis. We would suggest at least twice a year.
- The family paying particular attention to both the initial decision to provide – and also the continuation and extension of – guarantees and security over property provided to banks and other financial institutions.
- Undertaking a periodic (and at least annual) review of the wider strategic options for the business, including whether to grow the family enterprise (if so how), or to sell, consolidate or even close the business. What will be the impact of each of those options on the wider life of the family?
- A careful analysis of the benefits and disadvantages of the supporting spouse working in the business and their roles and duties.
- Involvement of marriage guidance counsellors, family business consultants or other relevant professionals in early stage interventions once difficulties and warning signs are experienced.
- Most controversially pre-nuptial or post nuptial agreements spelling out what the partners have agreed will happen to the business and its assets if their personal relationship breaks down.[38]

Ultimately the aim is to establish an appropriately detailed and functioning system of communication which recognises that, even if life partners are not involved in an early stage family business as full business partners, they nevertheless have a deep interest in the success or failure of that business.

---

[38] Nuptial agreements are considered in detail in **18.18** below.

First generation family businesses also demonstrate a similar range of ownership philosophies. At one end of the spectrum fully copreneurial couples will share equally both day-to-day management responsibilities and also the rewards of ownership. At the other end of the spectrum ownership will remain firmly in the hands of the founding entrepreneur.[39]

In the middle of the range, day-to-day management may vest wholly or mainly in a single spouse, but ownership will be split. Often this will be driven by tax planning considerations including the possibility of paying dividends to spouses, or paying spouses salaries to make use of nil or lower rate income tax bands.[40] Perhaps less often, joint ownership will be driven by a carefully thought out and articulated ownership philosophy that, just as core non business assets such as houses and investments should be jointly owned so should the family's key income and capital producing asset, the family owned business.

Fully thought out shareholder agreements between business couples are even less common, sufficiently so as to be somewhere between a rarity and a theoretical consideration in most cases. But the received wisdom from the USA, where such agreements are much more commonplace, is that they are a sensible precaution for any couple with a family business. According to Hilburt-Davis and Dyer 'the longer divorce negotiations go on, the more acrimonious they become'. Anything that can be done to provide a starting point or to short-circuit those negotiations must logically be welcomed.

The approach of the UK courts to nuptial agreements and shareholder and partnership agreements (as nuptial settlements) is considered in more detail below.

18.7 DIVORCE: THE END OF THE ROAD?

So far this chapter has focused on how copreneurial couples can make both a family business and a marriage work. It has nevertheless been written with the spectre of divorce in the background. But many advisors will be able to point to examples where clients who, although no longer married, still work successfully in business together.[41] So the family business is not necessarily lost when a marriage fails.[42]

Based on in depth interviews with a number of couples who remained in business together post-divorce (in some cases for many years) Cole and Johnson[43] identified six factors that made this possible:

---

[39] But will nevertheless be regarded as a family business under the wide definition suggested in chapter 1 and, more pertinently perhaps as matrimonial property by the courts. This is discussed in detail below.

[40] See chapter 4. Perhaps more optimistically, the split could be based on the possibility of a sale of the family enterprise and a wish to maximise the lifetime allowance of £10m of each spouse for the purposes of entrepreneur's relief (see chapter 16).

[41] For examples see 'Why these divorced couples still do business together in the workplace' *The Telegraph*, 1 February 2016. Quite how large a proportion of divorcing family business couples these represent is another matter.

[42] Although, arguably the status as a family business might have been lost, if reliance is placed on definitions requiring a single family to be in control. This is on the basis that the former husband and wife are now two separate family units.

[43] Patricia M Cole, Kit Johnson 'An Exploration of Successful Copreneurial Relationships Postdivorce' *Family Business Review* (2007), Vol 20(3).

- **Trust** – by which they meant trust in the business integrity, financial probity and commitment to the business of the other partner. This was seen as absolutely key. Intriguingly all of the couples involved had been through bitter and difficult divorces, over half of which involved infidelity.
- **Compartmentalisation** – the ability to keep business and personal issues separate.
- **Emotional connection** – that somehow a friendship or respect survived the breakdown of marriage.
- **Synergy** – or complimentary skills and teamwork, 'the yin and the yang of their business relationship'.
- **Commitment to the business** – which was viewed 'in an almost parental way'.
- **Positive gender issues** – which we have discussed above in the general context of what makes for a successful working relationship between couples.

The key to the cases considered in this study was that all of the parties concerned wanted to continue in business together.[44]

Although there are cases where the courts in England and Wales have made orders binding the parties together in business,[45] this is fairly unusual. All of the difficulties for outsider shareholders in controlling the insiders, discussed in Part E, will be present, and with the vengeance of divorce in the background. Shareholders' agreements and the back-up of legal remedies such as unfair prejudice claims can only do so much to police the situation.

In the absence of a clear wish to continue in business together it will be much more common for one party to be ordered to buy the other out.[46] Forcing the parties to share an interest in a common asset will be confined to cases where lack of liquidity or high business risk make it unfair to do otherwise.[47]

18.8 DIVORCE: THE LEGAL STARTING POINT MCA 1973, S 25

If divorce occurs how will the English courts approach the matter when one or both of the parties have an interest in a family business and a court is tasked with making appropriate orders for financial provision? Relevant orders include periodical payments (maintenance), lump sum orders, in each case in favour or either a child or a party to the marriage[48] or property adjustment orders.[49]

The key provision is s 25 of the Matrimonial Causes Act 1973. In detail MCA, s 25(2) provides that:

---

[44] Interestingly enough the couples concerned achieved their continuing working equilibrium with minimal use of legal documents (even in the case of a business with a turnover in excess of $100m) and with minimal recourse to lawyers, family business consultants or other advisors.
[45] See *C v C* [2003] 2 FLR 493 and *G v G* [2002] EWHC 1339 (Fam) where the wife retained a beneficial interest in the family business but on the basis that voting rights were vested in the husband who ran the business on a day to day basis.
[46] *F v F* [2012] EWHC 438 (Fam) where a buy-out was ordered of the wife's shares. The husband who had set up the family business was 81. The marriage had collapsed into acrimony. The relationship between husband and wife, who was a board director, was in danger of damaging a successful family business founded by the husband well before he met his (third) wife.
[47] See *P v P* [2004] EWHC 2277 (Fam). Risk and liquidity are discussed in more detail at **18.10** below.
[48] MCA, s 23.
[49] MCA, s 24.

The Court shall in particular have regard to the following matters -

(a) The income, earning capacity, property and other financial resources which each of the parties to the marriage has or is likely to have in the foreseeable future, including in the case of earning capacity any increase in that capacity which it would be in the opinion of the Court reasonable to expect the parties to the marriage to take steps to acquire;

(b) The financial needs, obligations and responsibilities which each of the parties to the marriage has or is likely to have in the foreseeable future;

(c) The standard of living enjoyed by the family before the breakdown of the marriage;

(d) The age of each party to the marriage and the duration of the marriage;

(e) Any physical or mental disability of either of the parties to the marriage;

(f) The contributions which each of the parties has made or is likely in the foreseeable future to make to the welfare of the family, including any contribution by looking after the home or caring for the family;

(g) The conduct of each of the parties, if that conduct is such that in the opinion of the Court it would be inequitable to disregard it;

(h) In the case of proceedings for divorce or nullity of marriage, the value to each of the parties to the marriage of any benefit which, by reason of a dissolution or annulment of the marriage, that party will lose the chance of acquiring.

The first consideration for the court is the welfare of any relevant children.[50]

Once the needs of children have been catered for the courts can turn to the position of the divorcing couple and, with that, what will happen to any business interests within the family.

There are hundreds of cases, where the English courts have attempted to interpret and give guidance on the provisions of MCA, s 25. These can be seen to have veered between two broad positions. First that it is important for clarity and consistency for the higher courts to give clear guidance for lower courts, the parties and their advisors in order to make settlement more likely and litigation less so. Secondly, that any attempt to provide specific and binding guidance places a judicial gloss on the wording of the statute and thereby fetters the discretion of individual judges in a way that parliament had not intended. The position of a family business can accordingly be seen as strapped to the moving target of matrimonial law.

The overriding objective for the courts will be to divide the property of a divorcing couple in a fair way.[51] But, as Lord Nicholls observed, in giving the leading judgment in *White v White* 'fairness like beauty lies in the eye of the beholder'.[52] Nevertheless three key components of fairness have emerged from the House of Lords in the decision in *White* and in two subsequent leading cases.[53] These are:

- The **needs** of both parties.[54]

---

[50] MCA, s 25(1) – this will include any step-children.
[51] *White v White* [2001] 1 AC 596 Lord Nicholls at p 599.
[52] At p 599.
[53] *Miller v Miller* and *McFarlane v McFarlane* – reported together as [2006] UKHL 24. These were not family business cases but concerned two high earning individuals, in the case of Mr Miller with an interest in a non-family investment fund and Mr McFarlane a professional partnership.
[54] See practice guidance note released by the Family Justice Council entitled 'Guidance on Financial Needs on Divorce' June 2016. This is available on the FJC website and it is the result of the Law Commission consultation on needs and agreements in family law. It is a lengthy but helpful document that is intended to help the courts and parties when assessing what 'needs' actually mean.

- **Compensation for relationship-generated economic disadvantage,** in the sense that one party, usually the wife, might have given up their own potentially lucrative career to look after house, home and the children in it.[55]
- **Sharing** based on the principle that marriage is an equal partnership in which both partners can be assumed to have played a full, if often different, role and should accordingly be entitled to share in the resulting fruits.

Where family businesses are concerned it is often necessary to consider a further sub-component, the extent to which fairness dictates inherited family business should be excluded from the matrimonial pot so as not to be divided between the spouses but retained by and the inheriting blood-line family member concerned.[56]

18.9 THE FAMILY BUSINESS, NEEDS AND THE GOLDEN GOOSE

If divorce occurs during the early stages of a family business the financial needs of the parties might consume all available resources. The presence of children can steer the allocation of assets towards the parent who has care of the children, for example where the parent with care needs a larger home because of the responsibilities for the children, if there are insufficient assets to house both parties to a similar extent.

What is abundantly clear is that a family business will not be seen as in any way sacrosanct if its sale or break up is necessary to satisfy the needs of either party.[57] In *N v N*,[58] using a somewhat extended metaphor Coleridge J[59] explained that:

> 'those old taboos against selling the goose that lays the golden eggs have largely been laid to rest ... Nowadays the goose may well have to go to market for sale.'

Earlier distinctions between family assets, basically shared between husband and wife, and business assets, usually allocated to the spouse chiefly involved in its management, were put to rest by *White*.[60]

In *White* the High Court thought it 'unwise and unjustifiable to break-up the existing, established farming business' to provide Pamela White with enough money to buy her own farm. Instead the first instance judge gave Martin White the much larger share even of jointly owned partnership assets. This approach was overturned on appeal.

---

[55] See McFarlane – where, after the birth of their second child the couple agreed that the wife would give up her career at a city 'magic circle' law firm to enable the husband to concentrate on his at a 'big-four' accountancy practice.
[56] There is also the consideration in business cases of (a) how the court treats a business brought in to the marriage by one party and (b) how the court treats growth of a business after separation (and there may be a long gap between separation and the case coming to court). These issues are dealt with below.
[57] See *P v P (Inherited Property)* [2004] EWHC 1364 (Fam).
[58] [2001] 2 FLR 69.
[59] See *N v N (Financial Provision: Sale of a Company)* [2001] 2 FLR 69.
[60] But a different distinction, that between matrimonial property and non-matrimonial property retains its relevance in the case of family businesses. See below.

In cases of wealth, the needs of the other spouse will be generously interpreted.[61] An extreme example of a needs based award can be found in *NA v MA*[62] where the couple had previously enjoyed a lifestyle of 'unbridled extravagance' and the wife was awarded over £9m out of a fortune of about £40m, notwithstanding that this was entirely based on inherited wealth.[63]

It therefore follows that, whilst many business owning families will be comparatively well off, when judged against most standards, their situation will often be treated as a 'needs case' on divorce.[64] A 'needs case' may be one in which the assets run to many millions because need is judges according to the standard of living, financial resources and the length of the marriage. Inevitably this will mean that difficult balancing acts need to be undertaken. These will be complicated by the presence of other family members involved in later stage family businesses.

18.10 CLEAN BREAK LIQUIDITY, RISK AND REWARD

Of course many smaller and early stage family businesses may be effectively unsalable. There might be no goodwill to speak of, or any saleable goodwill might be irretrievably linked to the continuing presence of the main working spouse. In these cases, notwithstanding the clear preference for a clean break on divorce,[65] the courts will need to think about maintenance (periodical payments) or orders for lump sums to be paid in instalments.[66] If it is inappropriate or impossible to ascribe a capital value to a business shareholding and it the main source of income for the family, it may instead be proper to make a time-unlimited maintenance order in favour of the non-shareholding spouse. In that way, the non-shareholder can continue to benefit from the business in the future.[67]

These in turn raise difficult issues such as the vagaries of business valuation.[68] Traditionally, minority interests in companies are heavily discounted.[69] One of the main arguments for this is that, if sold separately, such interests will never achieve their pro-rata share of the full value of an enterprise. The courts will look behind this theory into the realities of a family business situation. In the Scottish case of *Hodge*[70] it was decided that a discount could not be justified on this basis. The husband was one of four family shareholders in a family farming company, run as a quasi-partnership, which in practice made key decisions jointly. It was unrealistic to assume that he would ever actually sell his shares separately.

---

[61] So called *Duxbury* calculations, of a capitalised lump sum to provide a given level of income will be regarded as 'a tool and not a rule' in appropriate cases.
[62] [2006] EWHC 2900 (Fam).
[63] The treatment of inherited wealth is considered in detail as part of the discussion of non-matrimonial in 18.13 below.
[64] For example in *P v P* [2004] EWHC 2277 (Fam) the parties' combined capital amounted to approximately £2.5m. This was thought to barely cover the needs of husband and wife.
[65] MCA, s 25A.
[66] *R v R* [2005] 2 FLR 365.
[67] See, for example, *V v V (Financial Relief)* [2005] 2 FLR 697.
[68] On various occasions the courts have recognised how difficult it is to put a precise valuation on an interest in an unquoted family company. See for example *Fields v Fields* [2015] EWHC 1670 (Fam). The difficulties in valuation can also extend to smaller quoted companies. In *Wells v Wells*, where the husband was the founder of a business listed on (what is now) AIM but with a minimal free-float and a highly volatile share performance, six alternative ways to value the husband's shareholding were put forward and all rejected by the court which came to the conclusion that the valuing the holding was 'impossible with any reasonable precision' (at para 70).
[69] On some arguments by as much as 90%.
[70] [2008] Fam LR 51.

But *Hodge* points to a parallel problem, the inherent illiquidity of interests in family firms. This can apply to later stage businesses, where the spouse might hold only a minority interest and the wider business owning family are committed to keeping the business in family ownership.[71] It is also relevant to early stage businesses, where the enterprise has not really reached a point where it could be sold for any real capital sum.

There is also the issue of business risk; how fair is it for one party to retain the greater share of the 'hard assets' especially the matrimonial home, if the other party is left with the risk of having their share of the matrimonial pot tied up in a family business? The courts have found different answers to this question.

On occasions courts will be prepared to either discount business valuations, to reflect their illiquidity or the reality that one party is bearing the greatest share of risk. Alternatively the party bearing the greater share of risk might be awarded a greater share, either of the risk bearing or the overall assets.[72] There is also authority to the effect that risk in relation to the valuation of an asset should, in general, be reflected in the valuation of the asset rather than by giving an increased share of the assets to the party retaining that asset.[73]

On other occasions, particularly where a business is performing poorly, and may have negligible value, the courts might be prepared to look for a more equal division of risk bearing and hard assets, even though this might have the effect of tying the parties together in business. In *Wells* the court thought that 'the separation of the family does not terminate the sharing of results' and that both sharing and a clean break could be achieved by a fair division of both the copper bottomed assets and the illiquid and risk laden assets'.[74]

A similar approach was taken in *P v P*,[75] where largely because of the lack of liquidity in the family business and the comparatively modest 'copper bottomed' capital represented by the matrimonial home, an order was made for the husband to transfer some of his shareholding in the family company to the wife. This allowed the husband to keep his pension and any liquid funds that could be extracted from the family company. If the resources of the couple are insufficient to allow a clean break, care needs to be taken to avoid double counting; where one spouse receives not only income arising from the profits of a family business but also a share in the underlying business itself.

Forcing a divorced couple to share ownership of a family business after their divorce cannot be a recipe for a trouble free business relationship. In *P v P* Baron J thought that the position of the wife could be adequately protected by a shareholders' agreement.[76] In *Wells* it seems that the court thought it sufficient that the wife would be entitled to receive routine shareholder information.[77]

---

[71] See the discussion on ownership philosophy in chapter 15 (Ownership Succession). One collateral benefit of documenting ownership philosophy in family charters and the like could be that this will support an argument of illiquidity in the unfortunate event that a family member is involved in a divorce.
[72] *G v G* [2002] EWHC 1339 (Fam).
[73] *SK v TK* [2013] EWHC 834 (Fam).
[74] At para 24.
[75] [2004] EWHC 2277(Fam).
[76] Which was left for the parties to sort out between themselves as part of the eventual court order.
[77] An additional measure of protection would have been provided to the wife by the need for the company to comply with the corporate governance requirements of (what is now) the AIM rules.

But what of the situation where one spouse wants to continue the family business relationship and the other does not? The court will consider the practicalities. In *AE v BE*[78] a substantial group of property investment companies had been built up, by the efforts of the husband. It was possible to partition the business and transfer one company that held a portfolio of residential property to the wife as a separate business. This was ordered by the court, notwithstanding that the wife was elderly and had no business experience and the husband preferred to keep the business[79] and raise finance to buy the wife out.[80]

On the other hand in *WF v HF*[81] where there was only one single business concerned and where the wife was at odds with, not only the husband, but also both the professional management and the children from the husband's first marriage, who worked in the family business, it was thought entirely impractical for the wife to remain connected to the family business as she wanted. An order was made, in effect ripping up a shareholders' agreement (which provided for the wife's participation in the company), transferring her existing shareholding to the husband, and removing her as a director.

The converse of risk is reward. In *FZ v SZ*[82] the husband was simply allowed to retain the benefit of offshore bonds, which were impossible to value, on the basis that the remaining matrimonial property was divided evenly.

In a minority of cases an early stage family business might have significant growth potential. But it would be comparatively rare for this to be seen as a matrimonial asset and for hope value to be taken into account.[83]

On occasions valuations used and accepted by the courts on divorce will prove to be highly optimistic, when the family business subsequently crashes and burns, or, alternatively pessimistic, if the business goes on to succeed well above expectations. It will be rare for the courts to agree to revisit a lump sum order.[84]

18.11 EQUAL CONTRIBUTIONS AND SPECIAL CONTRIBUTIONS

As will often still be the case with coprenruerial couples, Pamela White was seen to make both a full contribution to the farming partnership and to bear the brunt of looking after the home and children. So much so that in the Court of Appeal Butler-Sloss LJ thought that Mrs White should receive an enhanced share of the

---

[78] [2014] EWHC 4868 (Fam).
[79] The court thought the wife could either engage managing agents or ask the children, both of whom were engaged in the business and were on good terms with the wife to help.
[80] See also *C v C* [2003] EWHC 1222 (Fam) where the wife had some prior involvement in the running of the company concerned and where the company was now being run by non-family management.
[81] [2012] EWHC 438 (Fam).
[82] [2010] EWHC 1630 (Fam).
[83] *FZ v SZ* [2010] EWHC 1630 (Fam). The case also shows that contingent liabilities, in that case bank guarantees given to support failed property developments in Cyprus will need to be taken into account. However tax, including CGT on sale of assets retained as part of the court order will not, if payment of the tax is only a theoretical consideration, either because the relevant family business asset is unlikely to be sold or because realistic tax planning opportunities are available.
[84] *Cornick v Cornick* [1994] 2 FLR 530.

partnership assets to recognise that contribution.[85] This line of thought was not pursued either by the rest of Court of Appeal, or by the House of Lords.

In other cases the contributions of the couple concerned will be much more along traditional and stereotypical lines with one party, typically the husband, playing by far the major role in the family business and the wife playing little active part or a clearly subordinate role. In family businesses it would be entirely inappropriate to ignore the role of Chief Emotional Officer, referred to briefly above, which commentators suggest will usually be performed by the wife, irrespective of her degree of her day to day involvement in the business.

In chapter 2 we categorise entrepreneurs as being highly driven, often narcissistic, with a 'hero complex'.

It is necessary to dispel an illusion; that the courts are likely to consider the efforts of the spouse actually working in the family business as sufficiently special so as to justify, in and of itself, a greater share of the matrimonial pie.[86] In *White* it was stated to be a principle of universal application 'that there is no place for discrimination between husband and wife and their respective roles'.[87]

Nevertheless there are some cases where the courts have accepted that the contribution made by one party to the matrimonial assets is so great that it should quite properly be recognised. But these are rare indeed. The expressions 'special contribution', 'stellar contribution', and 'genius' have been used. There is at least one family business example that can found in the case of *Cowan* in which the husband is credited with introducing disposable bin bags into the UK before selling his family business for several million of pounds.[88] But this case was decided before the concept of special contribution was further constrained in later cases.[89] The case-law on special contributions has been summarised in the recent case of *G v W*.[90] Now it would appear that the contribution would have to be very special indeed: and will be founded on some 'exceptional and individual quality which deserves special treatment'.[91] The courts talk of in terms of a creative genius. Perhaps of the successful family business leaders discussed in this book only Sir James Dyson would come close to the requirements of a special contribution.

---

[85] See p 602 of the House of Lords judgment. But this could be seen as hang-over from the time that, almost invariably, the wife needed to show that they had made a significant contribution to the family business to rise above the 'glass ceiling' of an award to meet their reasonable requirements. The divorce of Terrence and Shirley Conran (founders of the now defunct Habitat business) provide a historic example. The logic now appears to be that as now special financial contributions are rarely recognised the courts should be equally slow to accept that a domestic contribution was truly so exceptional as to justify an increased share.

[86] In *Robertson v Robertson* [2016] EWHC 613 (Fam) the husband was the leading force behind an on-line fashion retailer and was instrumental in generating a family fortune in the region of £220m but this was not seen by the Court of Appeal as an exceptional contribution sufficient to make it fair to discriminate against the wife's contribution as a homemaker. The courts did however take into account the fact that, although the company had grown substantially during the marriage, it had been started by the husband beforehand so could, to an extent be seen as non-matrimonial property: (see **18.13.3** below).

[87] Lord Nicholls at p 605.

[88] *Cowan v Cowan* [2001] EWCA Civ 679.

[89] *Miller* and *Charman v Charman (No 4)* [2007] EWCA Civ 503.

[90] [2015] EWHC 834 (Fam) – a non-family business case where the husband generated a fortune of £144m from bonuses and commissions from trading in distressed Japanese debt. It appears that this case is subject to appeal due to be heard in December 2016.

[91] *Charman* at para 80 – quoted with approval in *G v W*. One rare and more recent example of a successful claim for special contribution was *Sorrell v Sorrell* [2005] EWHC 1717 (Fam) concerning the high profile divorce of Sir Martin Sorrell the founder of WPP (or more precisely the advertising agency that was reversed into the WPP shell).

Even if a stellar contribution is actually recognised, the Court of Appeal have indicated that it would be most unlikely for that special contribution to justify the division of matrimonial property (that would otherwise be divided 50:50) on anything more than a 66:33 basis.[92]

Now the working assumption of the courts is that any financial contribution to the family created by the hard work and dedication of one party to the family business will be matched by an equal and opposite contribution of the other party to the family.[93]

18.12 THE YARDSTICK OF EQUALITY: *WHITE V WHITE*

There is a further, and perhaps now more common illusion that needs to be dispelled. This is that the courts will invariably order an equal division of property between husband and wife. Although all three courts considering the White's case stressed the need to recognise the equal contributions of spouses as partners in a modern marriage they stopped well short of suggesting that equality of contribution should equate to equality of distribution, or even that there should be an assumption that this should be the case.[94]

Instead the courts need to apply all of the factors in MCA, s 25. Occasionally these will point to an equal division, in other cases not. The 'yardstick of equality of division' can then be used to sanity check the application of the statutory factors.[95]

Cases where the needs of children or one of the spouses will point to an unequal division in favour of the non-working spouse in an early stage or low value family business have already been discussed in **18.9** above.

In *White*, a case where the children were grown-up and the net assets of £4.6m were clearly more than sufficient to meet the needs of both parties Pamela was eventually awarded 40% of the overall assets.

The approach to equal division and the yardstick of equality was developed further by the House of Lords in *Charman* which suggests that the yardstick developed more into a principle: that the court should approach a case by defining matrimonial and non-matrimonial property with as much specificity as the case may allow and then to 'share' matrimonial property (broadly equally) unless there is a reason to depart from an equal sharing and only to share non-matrimonial property to the extent that needs require that.

Perhaps confusingly, the sharing 'principle' applies to both matrimonial and non-matrimonial assets, just that there is often much better reason not to share non-matrimonial property if the sharing of matrimonial property is sufficient to meet the parties' respective financial needs.

---

[92] See *Charman* at para 90.
[93] See Holman J in *G v W* at para 152.
[94] The position is different in Scotland where the Family Law (Scotland) Act 1985, s 10 provides that the net value of the parties' matrimonial property will be shared equally unless special circumstances dictate otherwise.
[95] See Lord Nicholls at p 605.

In *Charman* Potter P[96] said:

> 'To what property does the sharing principle apply? The answer might well have been that it applies only to matrimonial property, namely the property of the parties generated during the marriage otherwise than by external donation; and the consequence would have been that non-matrimonial property would have fallen for redistribution by reference only to one of the two other principles of need and compensation ... Such an answer might better have reflected the origins of the principle in the parties' contributions to the welfare of the family; and it would have been more consonant with the references of Baroness Hale in *Miller* ... to "sharing ... the fruits of the matrimonial partnership" and to "the approach of roughly equal sharing of partnership assets". We consider, however, the answer to be that, subject to the exceptions identified in *Miller* ... the principle applies to all the parties' property but, to the extent that their property is non-matrimonial, there is likely to be better reason for departure from equality. It is clear that both in White and in *Miller* ... Lord Nicholls approached the matter in that way; and there was no express suggestion in *Miller*, even on the part of Baroness Hale, that in *White* the House had set too widely the general application of what was then a yardstick.'

We now turn to the crucial distinction between matrimonial and no-matrimonial property.

18.13 THE FAMILY BUSINESS: MATRIMONIAL OR NON-MATRIMONIAL PROPERTY?

The main reason why the yardstick of equality provided only an approximate guide in *White* was the complication caused by the assets inherited by Martin White from his father. There is a considerable body of case-law which seeks to distinguish between, on the one hand, matrimonial property[97] and, on the other hand non-matrimonial property, including, potentially, inherited interests in family businesses. The degree of precision that should be achieved in distinguishing between matrimonial and non-matrimonial property will vary from case to case and, invariably, it does not require absolute precision.[98]

Put at its broadest, whilst matrimonial property will now, almost invariably, be divided equally, non-matrimonial property might escape the mixer and be retained wholly or to a greater degree by the contributing spouse. The distinction is therefore an important one. Several caveats and points need to be made.

18.13.1 Needs first

The needs of first any relevant children and secondly the other spouse must be fully and properly taken care of before any consideration will be given to allowing a spouse to retain an interest in a family business or other inherited or non-matrimonial property.[99]

---

[96] At para 66.
[97] The matrimonial home will almost always be treated as matrimonial property, even if provided from resources inherited by one spouse only.
[98] Lord Nicholls in *Miller* at para 26.
[99] *J v J (Financial Orders: Wife's long tem needs)* [2011] EWHC 1010 (Fam) where the bulk of the family wealth, of over £8.5m had been acquired from a family business set up by the husband's grandfather but the needs of the wife were assessed by the High Court at almost half this sum.

The concept of needs may be generously interpreted by the courts. For example in *AR v AR*[100] the needs of the wife were seen to include a house in a rural location (rather than living on an estate), a swimming pool and a gardener. The standard of living enjoyed by the parties before their marriage broke down is, of course, one of the factors that the courts must consider.[101] Nevertheless in *AR v AR* the husband was allowed to retain the bulk of the family fortune,[102] which had been derived from his father's manufacturing business but reinvested in land farmed by the husband.

18.13.2 The family business and the marital acquest

A family business started during a marriage will invariably be seen as part of the matrimonial property. The value of the business will fall into the joint matrimonial pot[103] and be subject to the sharing principle, particularly if the value of the business and other matrimonial assets are sufficient to achieve a clean break (with no on-going maintenance claims).

On the other hand a business started by a spouse before marriage may well be seen as non-matrimonial property.

But the distinction is by no means this clear-cut. At the time of the marriage the business might have been in its infancy but it may have grown in size and value by the time of the divorce: this growth may have been the result of the spouse working hard in the business combined with the freedom to do so created by the non-working spouse shouldering the bulk of domestic responsibilities. In such a case that the business growth will be seen as part of what is often termed the 'marital acquest'.

Alternatively one spouse might already own shares in a larger or later stage family business at the start of the marriage but play no active part in the management of that business.

All sorts of variations and complications will arise in practice. For example in *White*, Martin inherited the land at Rexton Farm from his father but this was farmed as part of the partnership with Pamela.

18.13.3 Previously owned businesses

A business might have been started by one spouse before the parties were married: in such a case, the court may permit experts to value the business both at the time of the divorce and at the date of the parties' marriage.

The courts (and any expert valuers concerned) will have the benefit of hindsight when it comes to placing a value on a business at the start of a marriage. So if a business has done well during the period of the marriage it might be possible for the business owning

---

[100] [2011] EWHC 2717 (Fam).
[101] MCA, s 25(2)(c).
[102] The wife retained or received £4.3m of total assets between £21–24m after a 25-year relationship which produced one child. The husband had three other children from his first marriage.
[103] See *Cowan v Cowan* [2001] EWCA Civ 679 where the couple were married for 35 years and set up a highly successful business. Although she worked in the business for the first 10 years or so after it was founded, Mrs Cowan then withdrew from active participation to look after their home and children. The yardstick of equality was applied and found to produce a fair result for Mrs Cowan.

spouse to argue that even at the start of the marriage there was inherent or latent potential in the business (effectively a hidden species of goodwill which would not be recognised under conventional valuation methodology,[104] but which nevertheless provided the 'springboard' for further growth.[105]

In early stage businesses much of the potential for future growth might, on closer analysis, be bound up with the knowledge, skills and experience of the entrepreneur, perhaps developed over the course of their business career to date, rather than the inherent attributes and assets of the new business they have created. In *Jones* the Court of Appeal overruled earlier decisions[106] that permitted the court to effectively capitalise the 'established earning capacity' of a spouse at the start of the marriage and treat this as non-matrimonial property. This capitalisation approach was both costly and artificial. Instead, in *Jones*, the Court of Appeal grappled with how to divide the valuation of a business that had both been started by the husband before the marriage and had increased in value after separation. The Court of Appeal attributed a value to the 'springboard' at the date of the marriage that doubled the expert's valuation of the business at that time from £2m to £4m. The value of the 'springboard' will normally be reflected in a professional valuation calculated by reference to future maintainable earnings[107] but, rarely, this might not be so. In those rare cases, the additional springboard value may also represent non-matrimonial property.

Certainly the reverse situation is easier to spot and deal with. This is where the owner of a business argues that much of its value is tied up with their personal goodwill and should accordingly be discounted to reflect the fact that they might leave. If there is no real possibility that this will happen no discount will be allowed.[108]

18.13.4 Post separation growth

The relevant date for the valuation of assets in a financial remedy case is always the date of the trial. It might be apparent, however, that by the time a matter comes to court, that a business has grown in value after the separation. Logically that growth should also be excluded from the marital acquest. However the courts are also prepared to apply the springboard principle at the end of the marriage and to attribute a proportion of any increase in value to the inherent potential built during the later years of marriage.[109]

In *Jones* the agreed valuation of the family business[110] at the date of separation was £12m but it was sold 15 months later for £32m, leaving net proceeds for the sole owner husband of £25m. In the circumstances both the High Court and the Court of Appeal were prepared to attribute the entire difference to inherent potential so that this fell within the marital acquest.[111]

---

[104] Such as valuations based on net assets or multiples of historic earnings.
[105] See *Jones v Jones* [2011] EWCA Civ 41 where the Court of Appeal were prepared to double the expert's valuation of £2m to £4m to take account of this factor. But they were assisted by the fact that an offer of £5m was received a year after the parties were married. Also, and rarely, the first instance judge found both experts' valuation of the business at the start of the marriage was wrong in principle and substituted his own assessment of a higher value. In *Jones* the business concerned was very much that of the husband. He had established this well before the marriage and remained sole owner, with the wife playing no active role.
[106] *GW v RW (Financial Provision: Departure from Equality)* [2003] EWHC 611.
[107] *Jones*, para 39.
[108] See *Sorrell v Sorrell* [2005] EWHC 1717 (Fam).
[109] See para 40 of the Court of Appeal judgment.
[110] But see the discussion on the definition of family business in chapter 1.
[111] It might be that the husband did himself no favours by dishonestly failing to mention negotiations were afoot

18.13.5 Active and passive growth

Having established an opening and closing valuation (as mentioned above) it is then necessary to apportion that growth between active and passive growth.

A distinction may be drawn between active and passive growth in family business interests. Passive growth of a non-matrimonial asset may be treated as non-matrimonial property, whereas increase in value attributable to the efforts of an actively working spouse during the marriage will likely fall into the matrimonial pot. At first this may seem counter-intuitive, with the hard working businessman who takes over the family firm from their parents being treated less favourably than the idle rich, who simply sit back and live on the dividends paid out by a later stage family company. But the key point is that the active growth of a family business during a marriage will be seen as the fruit of the marital tree.

In *Jones* Mrs Jones' counsel suggested that it would be sufficient to increase the valuation of the business at the start of the marriage by movements in RPI. This was rejected by Wilson LJ in the Court of Appeal, in favour of linking the initial valuation to increases in a basket of quoted shares.[112] Applied over the course of the Jones' 10-year marriage this had the fairly dramatic effect of more than doubling the initial pre-marriage valuation (itself already doubled for the spring board effect). The deduction from the marital acquest (which was then shared equally) was therefore substantial.

A similar example can be found in *Lilleyman*[113] where the evidence suggested that the family business had increased in value by about £550,000 during the period of the marriage. Although it was argued that this was largely down to passive growth attributable to increases in the market price of steel. Briggs J was nevertheless prepared to attribute £250,000 of this increase to the husband's activities and skill as a steel trader, giving a credit to the wife of 50% of this or £125,000.

It will be seen that the logical end-point of the attempt to distinguish between growth due to the activity of the family business owner and passive growth stemming from the market that the business operates in would be that the value of an underperforming business brought into a marriage by one of the partners would belong entirely to them. In *Jones*, Arden LJ accepted Lord Walker's approach, but appeared to do so with some reluctance. She struggled with the principle of passive growth in the first place noting that:[114]

> 'if only passive growth is taken into account the law rewards the spouse who buries her non-matrimonial assets in the ground rather than the spouse who actively manages them.'

In her view the correct approach was that at the end of a marriage a spouse with a non-matrimonial interest in a family business was entitled to:[115]

---

to sell the company for at least £2.5m at the time he completed his statement of assets (Form E) in which he valued the company at £3m (see para 9 of the transcript).

[112] The FTSE All Share Oil and Gas Producers Index.
[113] *Lilleyman v Lilleyman* [2012] EWHC 821 (Ch) an inheritance dispute case, discussed in detail in the following chapter 19, where the courts were applying the principles of a notional divorce to a claim by a widow for an interest in her late husband's family business.
[114] At para 60.
[115] At para 60.

'that element of the company at the end of the day which can fairly be taken to represent the fruits of the non-matrimonial assets that accrue during the marriage, even if the fruits are the product of activity by him or on his behalf.'

Less fundamentally Arden LJ struggled to accept Wilson LJ's choice of suggested index and thought that:[116]

'An allowance for growth in the manner proposed by Wilson LJ ... simply cannot be used unless the company's growth has far outstripped the index sought to be used.'

18.13.6 Length of marriage

One of the factors that the court is obliged to look at in every case is the length of the marriage.[117] In so called 'short marriage, big money' cases, this may well point to an interest in a family business being more or less entirely ring-fenced and treated as non-matrimonial property. This probably sits well with much of family business ownership philosophy. Ownership will be safeguarded for bloodline family members and protected from claims of in-laws. In the case of second marriages, the interests of next generation children of a first marriage will be preserved.

The longer the marriage the less likely it is that the ring fence will hold. In *White*, Martin's father made the young couple a loan of £14,000 in the early stages of their 30 year marriage. This was used to help them buy Blagroves Farm and for working capital purposes. Eventually the loan was written off by Martin's father. As Lord Cooke saw it:[118]

'the significance of this diminished because over a long marriage the parties jointly made the most of that help.'

In effect the loan could be seen to have been amortised over the length of the White's marriage.

In *White* Lord Cooke also thought that the loan 'was apparently intended at least partly for the benefit' of both Martin and Pamela jointly. He was not making a loan to his son for his own personal business. Similarly in *Rossi v Rossi*[119] it was said that the longer the marriage the more likely it was that 'non-matrimonial property will become merged or entangled with matrimonial property' whereas in a short marriage it is much more likely that non-matrimonial property will remain ring-fenced.

A number of cases such as *JL v SL*[120] have also looked at the 'intermingling' of assets. In that case Mostyn J referred to the treatment of pre-marital or other non-matrimonial property which has become 'part of the economic life of [the] marriage ... utilised, converted, sustained and enjoyed during the contribution period'. In *N v F*[121] the same judge suggested how pre-marital property and intermingling should be approached:

'It seems to me that the process should be as follows:

---

[116] See *Jones* at para 63.
[117] MCA, s 25(2)(d).
[118] At p 615.
[119] [2006] EWHC 1482 (Fam).
[120] *JL v SL (No 2) (Financial Remedies: Rehearing: Non-Matrimonial Property)* [2015] EWHC 360 (Fam).
[121] *N v F (Financial Orders: Pre-acquired Wealth)* [2011] EWHC 586 (Fam) at para 14.

i) Whether the existence of pre-marital property should be reflected at all. This depends on questions of duration and mingling.
ii) If it does decide that reflection is fair and just, the court should then decide how much of the pre-marital property should be excluded. Should it be the actual historic sum? Or less, if there has been much mingling? Or more, to reflect a springboard and passive growth, as happened in Jones?
iii) The remaining matrimonial property should then normally be divided equally ...'

18.13.7 Non-matrimonial assets and ownership philosophy

A related issue, particularly in the case of later stage family businesses and inherited family business wealth, is the extent to which the ownership philosophy of the wider family can influence the matrimonial/non-matrimonial property debate.

In chapter 1, in looking at the complexities involved in defining a family business, we suggest that one of the components might be succession intention, a wish to keep the family business intact, for future generations. There is some, perhaps scant evidence, that the courts will make an allowance for this in way they distinguish between matrimonial and non-matrimonial property.

In *Robertson* the fact that the husband had sold part of his holding in the publicly quoted company he had founded before the marriage and made the proceeds available as part of the family economy made it easier for the courts to find it fair to award the wife 25% of the remainder.[122]

On the other hand in *AR* the proceeds of sale from the sale of the husband's interest in the family company were re-invested in land and other investments, held by him in his own name alongside inherited land, so that the court thought that 'nothing has happened to the bulk of the wealth which has changed it into matrimonial property'.[123]

Similarly in *K v L*[124] the fact that the wife had kept shares, worth £57m and derived from the sale of her grand-father's company, ring-fenced, in her own name, helped persuade the court that a needs based award of £5m for the husband was appropriate and that the sharing principle should not apply. This was so, even though the wife had used the dividends and occasional sales of small parcels of these shares to fund the 'extraordinarily modest lifestyle' of the family, when neither husband nor wife had worked over the course of a marriage of 20 years or so.

Stewardship: the idea that family business assets are not really owned by the current generation, but are merely held by them on trust for the generations to come, is often a key component of family business ownership philosophy. But this will not necessarily be the over-riding consideration for the courts. For example in *P v P (Inherited Property)*[125] a farm, had been in the husband's family for four generations was jointly farmed by husband and wife for approaching 20 years. The wife's needs prevailed, so that she received 25% of the overall assets even though the free capital was much less and most

---
[122] The basis of the 25% award is explained below.
[123] [2011] EWHC 2717 (Fam) at para 81.
[124] [2011] EWCA Civ 550.
[125] [2004] EWHC 1364 (Fam). But landed estates, including stately homes and family heirlooms might be treated more sympathetically – see *Robson v Robson* [2010] EWCA Civ 1171. It is a moot point whether the effect of the various cases is that there is an inbuilt bias against 'new money', so that orders will be more readily made compelling the sharing of manufacturing businesses and non-landed estate agricultural businesses which would not be made where an 'old money' landed estate is concerned.

of the assets were non-matrimonial property consisting of the inherited land. This meant that the husband would have to sell some of the inherited land to satisfy the order.

18.13.8 A simpler approach?

Valuing any unquoted business is a hugely imprecise exercise; more art than science.[126] This might be thought especially the case when attempting to place a retrospective valuation on a business. The approach outlined above, of seeking to distinguish between active and passive growth, heaps complexity and imprecision on the uncertainties inherent in the opening and closing valuations. This is readily recognised by the courts.[127] So is there a simpler way to deal with the apportionment of value of a family business? By negotiation, of course, yes.

The yardstick of equality from *White* will always need to be applied. In *Jones* the Court of Appeal suggest that in cases where non-matrimonial property is involved it is sensible for the courts to put a further notch on the yardstick, in effect to indicate the judges gut-feel of where the relevant adjustment should be placed.[128] But in that case the suggestion was that this should by way of an additional cross-check to see whether the formulaic approach outlined above has produced an arbitrary result.[129]

Nevertheless, other cases suggest that a more broad-brush approach could and, indeed should be applied. These cases advocate a return to the language of MCA, s 25 and a more general discretion of the court to distinguish between matrimonial and non-matrimonial property.

This was advocated by the High Court and not only for lower value cases, where the dictates of proportionality required a less formulaic approach than that developed in *Jones*,[130] but also in a number of high worth cases. In *Robertson*[131] Holman J, having praised the thoroughness of a forensic accountant's expert report, chose to completely ignore its findings, on the basis that the calculation of the non-matrimonial element of the value of the business at the start of the marriage, as increased by the expert's calculation of passive growth, simply did not do justice to the husband. The judge treated half of the value of the husband's shares as non-matrimonial property and half as matrimonial property to be shared jointly. The net result was that the husband received about two thirds of the substantial overall joint wealth.[132]

---

[126] See comments in chapters 12 and 16
[127] For example see the remarks of Wilson LJ at paras 33 and 35 of *Jones*. For a more detailed discussion on the approach of the matrimonial courts to family business valuations see Bird & King *Financial Remedies Handbook* (Jordan Publishing, 2015) at pp 96–99.
[128] See Wilson LJ at para 52, Arden LJ at para 64 and Wall P at para 67.
[129] See *N v F (Financial Orders; Pre-Acquired Wealth)* [2011] EWHC 586 (Fam).
[130] *S v S* [2014] EWHC 4732 (Fam).
[131] *Robertson v Robertson* [2016] EWHC 613 (Fam) – which is not strictly a family business case and concerns the fortune of one of the co-founders of the ASOS on-line shopping site. As mentioned above, the husband was found not to have made a 'stellar contribution'.
[132] As mentioned above, the husband was found not to have made a 'stellar contribution'. If the adjustment from the 'yardstick of equality is effectively capped at a 66% share for such contributions, it would seem as similar result can be obtained by the application of judicial discretion to the question of fairness.

This more broad-brush approach has been applied in other cases.[133] A flexible approach is also consistent with the comments of Lord Nicholls in *Miller* where he said that:[134]

> 'where it becomes necessary to distinguish matrimonial property from non-matrimonial property the court may do so with the degree of particularity or generality appropriate to the case.'

18.14 THE FAMILY BUSINESS AND THE CORPORATE VEIL

Much of this book has been taken up with talking about the overlaps and boundaries between the business, family and ownership systems present in any family business. Particularly in a small or early stage family firm those boundaries might be very unclear. When will the courts recognise any boundaries that there might be? To what extent will the matrimonial courts ignore the boundaries and treat all assets within a global family business system as available for redistribution on the breakdown of marriage?

In most situations legal and beneficial ownership of interests in family businesses will coincide. But the question has particular relevance where this is not so.[135] Over the years the courts[136] had developed an approach, to the effect that, when a company was controlled by one person, whether or not they held shares, then the property of that company should be available for division in divorce. Family law had evolved fairly comfortably using that rough and ready approach.

But clearly property owned by a company is not the private property of the individual behind the company. So this approach attracted criticism in recent years until finally it fell to be dealt with by the Supreme Court, in the much discussed case of *Prest*.[137] As Lord Sumption noted:

> '... for some years it has been the practice of the Family Division to treat the assets of companies substantially owned by one party to the marriage as available for distribution under Section 24 of the Matrimonial Causes Act, provided that the remaining assets of the company are sufficient to satisfy its creditors.'

On the face of it Mr Prest seemed a prime candidate for an approach cutting through the niceties of company law. He was a hugely successful oil trader and appeared to be immensely wealthy. He appeared to control various high value assets including a number of UK properties. The courts wanted these to be transferred to Mrs Prest as part of a property adjustment order in her favour. The properties were, in fact, legally owned by a web of offshore companies, the precise structure, control and beneficial ownership of which was almost impossible to unravel, without the assistance of Mr Prest.[138] This left his former wife and her advisors floundering and unable to enforce a substantial property adjustment order against him.

It is clear in the first instance that Moylan J thought that he had the power to make orders against one of these companies ordering it to transfer some of these properties to

---

[133] Such as *AR v AR* [2011] EWHC 2717 (Fam) – combined wealth approximately £24m and *C v C* [2007] EWHC 2033 (Fam) – approx £22m.
[134] [2006] UKHL 24 at para 27.
[135] The position of family business trusts and divorce is considered in detail in chapter 15.
[136] Or more precisely the Family Division of the High Court in England and Wales.
[137] *Petrodell Resources Ltd v Prest* [2013] UKSC 34.
[138] Which he declined to give notwithstanding pressure from the court.

Mrs Prest, regardless of ownership, on the basis that there was some residual power in s 24 of the Matrimonial Causes Act 1973 which conferred on the Court a power to disregard the corporate veil in matrimonial cases. The various companies appealed on the basis that this was inconsistent with legal principle. The Court of Appeal and then the Supreme Court agreed and made it clear that:[139]

> 'Subject to very limited exceptions, most of which are statutory, the company is a legal entity distinct from its shareholders. It has rights and liabilities of its own which are distinct from those of its shareholders. Its property is its own, and not that of its shareholders.'

So in almost all cases a family company will be treated as a separate entity from its family shareholders. But there are exceptions where either:

- the corporate personality of the company is being abused for a purpose which is in some relevant respect improper; or
- on the particular facts of the case it could be shown that an asset legally owned by the company was held on trust for someone else.

The outcome in *Prest* was that, on the facts of the case, Petrodell did in fact hold the various properties on resulting trust for Mr Prest and, therefore, the properties were available for redistribution within the matrimonial regime.

Conversely it therefore follows that in other cases, for example where, a party holds no direct interest in a later stage more widely held family company, even if the entity as a whole appears to have significant value, it will be much harder for courts to disregard the boundaries between family, business and ownership.

18.15 IN-LAWS AND THE LATER STAGE FAMILY BUSINESS

It is most unlikely that senior generation family business owners would want to see family business assets being treated as matrimonial property so that former next generation in-laws benefit from these following a divorce from the bloodline spouse. As discussed in detail in chapter 14 the opposite philosophy of ownership sits behind the formation of many family business trusts as asset protection and ownership vehicles designed to protect family business interests against claims by in-laws.[140]

Often, in laws will be excluded from direct ownership of a family business. Sometimes in-laws have a conditional ownership status: in effect 'you can be treated as a member of the family business and also own part of it, provided that you remain married to X'.

This proviso will rarely be formally documented, remaining in the realms of implicit and unexpressed family understanding. If the relevant marriage falls apart ownership will remain with the in-law concerned[141] after divorce. But this might not be a huge disadvantage if the bloodline family member receives a correspondingly greater share of the non-business assets, or if the realities of remaining a minority owner in a family business controlled by hostile in-laws erode the theoretical value of that interest.

---

[139] Lord Sumption at citing with approval the leading and historic company case of *Soloman v A Soloman & Co* [1897] AC 22, and remarking that there 'the House of Lords held that these principles applied as much to a company that was wholly under control by one man as to any other company'.

[140] Whether or not such trusts work for this purpose is discussed in chapter 14.

[141] Subject to any property adjustment order that the Court might make under MCA, s 24 or, more likely the negotiations between the parties.

Rarely will the proviso of continued marriage be formally documented and translated into divestment provisions in articles of association or buy-sell provisions in shareholder or partnership agreements. The case for doing so is considered in **18.18** below.

18.16 BLOOD AND WATER: THE COMPETING CLAIMS OF FAMILY MEMBERS

A common feature of family business life is unfinished or delayed succession. Often this can be attributed to the reluctance of the senior generation, especially entrepreneurial founders, to 'let go.' Particular problems will arise if a divorce is interposed between unfinished succession business.

The courts will recognise the wish for a family business owner to provide an inheritance for their children.[142] In *F v F* the court recognised a 'moral or paternal obligation to provide for the children of his first marriage' on the part of the business founder as well as the younger children from his third marriage.[143]

But this will be seen very much as a subsidiary consideration, when compared with the claims of a spouse. In *White* Lord Nicholls refused to categorise Pamela White's wish to personally leave something substantial for the children as a need within MCA, s 25(1)(b). Instead he categorised this merely as a 'natural parental wish [and not] wholly irrelevant'.[144]

Certainly the genuine financial needs of one spouse will trump the desire of the other to use the resources of the family firm to look after other family members if this is framed as a need. But what if the expectations of those family members are such as to amount to an obligation or responsibility of the business owner?[145]

This was considered by the Court of Appeal in *Cowan* and thought to be a possibility. There, like many family companies, even large ones, the governance was in a mess. Mr Cowan had involved his two brothers, Graham and Jeffrey in the business as it grew, but neither had been entered on the shareholder register. On the somewhat complicated factual background everyone accepted that Graham (who performed a clear role) had a beneficial interest in one of the companies. The courts spent much time considering the position of Jeffrey, whose role was less clear[146] and whose claim to a beneficial interest (as advanced by Mr Cowan) was much more tenuous and rejected by the courts.

The Court of Appeal attached 'very little weight to Jeffrey's moral claim'[147] who the courts thought had been already been treated very well by Mr Cowan. So whilst the value of the matrimonial property was reduced to take account of Graham's interest, Mr Cowan was left to satisfy any residual moral claim that he believed that Jeffrey might have out of his own share of the matrimonial pot after division.

---

[142] See Lord Nichols and the discussion of the position of the next generation at pp 609–610 of *White*.
[143] *F v F* [2012] EWHC 438 (Fam) at para 48.
[144] See p 609.
[145] Also within MCA, s 25(1)(b).
[146] In evidence Jeffrey was described as 'the golfing director'.
[147] Lord Walker at para 104.

Cowan was a case of plenty. The scepticism of the courts towards ownership claims advanced on behalf of bloodline family members may be even more pronounced in cases of need. Certainly we can point to examples of share transfers, based on succession plans conceived and documented in draft form some years previously, but only implemented post-divorce, being set aside as depreciatory transactions.

In cases where the resources of the family firm are not sufficient to meet the needs of the other spouse, any family members concerned[148] will have an uphill struggle to persuade the courts, in a matrimonial case, to take notice of their interests.[149]

So the possibility of an interceding divorce further strengthens the arguments for senior generation business owners to progress succession or other ownership plans if they are not to forfeit the goodwill of their blood-line relations along with their marriage.

18.17 INTERVENERS

What if Jeffrey Cowan believed that he had a genuine claim to a beneficial interest in shares in the Cowan' family company? Could his claim be heard, or would this be drowned out by the noise of the matrimonial proceedings? There are provisions in the Family Procedure Rules (FPR)[150] allowing interested third parties or 'interveners' to join in the matrimonial proceedings.

These rules on joinder also apply in the opposite situation, where a party to the matrimonial proceedings believes that their former spouse has a beneficial interest in assets, but the legal interest is being held in the name of a nominee. The alleged nominee can be joined into the matrimonial proceedings so that the nature of the ownership can be examined and tested.

The matrimonial courts will deal with the position and claims of the third party who has intervened or has been joined in as a preliminary issue in the main matrimonial proceedings. This is entirely logical. The matrimonial pot cannot be divided until the court is clear whether this is to be reduced by legitimate claims from other family members, or augmented by assets really belonging to the other spouse but being sheltered from claims by their wider family.

The division of the matrimonial pot can be seen to be comparatively rough and ready, given the width of the court's discretion under MCA, s 25. However the approach to the determination of any right of other family members will be much more precise and forensic to be assessed: 'on exactly the same legal basis as if it were being determined in the Chancery Division'.[151]

The moral for all concerned is to act quickly, to identify any relevant wider family member or other third party who might have relevant claims or third party interests. Any issues arising and relevant parties must then be brought into the matrimonial

---

[148] For example, children from an earlier marriage.
[149] Unless there has been a preliminary hearing in which the claim of the non-spouse to a share of an asset has been determined by the court. In that case, the matrimonial court has no jurisdiction to make any award that is based on that third party's determined interest in an asset.
[150] FPR 2010, r 9.26B(1).
[151] *TL v ML (Ancillary Relief: Claim against Assets of Extended Family)* [2005] EWHC 2860 (Fam) per Mostyn J at para 34.

proceedings at the earliest possible opportunity.[152] It is possible the party may not have to formally intervene in the matrimonial proceedings. His or her evidence may be provided as witness to one of the parties. But the situation needs to be assessed at an early stage and the appropriate way of dealing with the third party claim ascertained. Costs penalties can be imposed if the parties do not do so.[153]

The actual strength of third party family member claims will be wide and varied in practice. Taking the case of next generation succession expectations, in the absence of an enforceable agreement to compel the transfer of the relevant interest, the next generation will probably need to intervene with something akin to a compelling case for proprietary estoppel.[154] Mere expectations or moral obligations will be unlikely, without more, to clear the hurdle of Chancery Court clarity.

Shield v Shield[155] provides a graphic example. The parties divorced after a 43 year marriage. In dispute was the beneficial ownership of the husband's shares in a family business. The husband claimed that the shares were held on trust for the son, who had returned home to run the family business after it got into financial difficulties. The son intervened in the matrimonial proceedings to assert his claim to ownership. Eventually the court concluded that, although the son had an expectation to inherit the family business on the death of his parents there was no trust or other binding legal arrangement. So the value of the husband's holding fell into the matrimonial pot.

Although the son's claim was heard as a preliminary issue the parties incurred costs in the region of £1m dealing with this. The judge suggested that these could have been reduced considerably by a different procedural approach. But the case raised a much more fundamental family business question. Could those costs have been eliminated (and the resulting damage to family relationships considerably reduced) if, at the time the son returned to the family firm, his expectations had been discussed and documented. This was a clear governance application point missed.

At the other end of the scale the rights asserted by wider family members might appear to be shams. There could be a strong suspicion that the bloodline family members have closed ranks in what is little short of a conspiracy to keep in-laws in penury and to shield the divorcing spouse from claims.

The difficulty for interveners is that what would in another context appear to be a legitimate expectation of inheritance might be treated with a high degree of suspicion in the context of a bitterly contested divorce. Particularly difficult issues can arise where cultural practices of wider family ownership might be inconsistent with the more structured approach to defining legal and beneficial ownership under western culture and business systems.[156]

---

[152] *TL v ML (Ancillary Relief: Claim against Assets of Extended Family)* [2005] EWHC 2860.
[153] *Fisher Meredith LLP v JH & PH* [2002] EWHC 408 (Fam).
[154] The difficulty of bringing these cases is explained in chapter 19 (Inheritance Disputes). However, in matrimonial cases the arguments based on the available evidence are likely to be reversed. The divorcing parent spouse who might otherwise be resisting the claims of their offspring could well be encouraging these. Although they might face a degree of scepticism. The next generation divorcing spouse will be correspondingly less keen to assert claims to ownership, at least for the time being. Their former spouse will have a very uphill struggle to establish a firm ownership entitlement.
[155] [2014] EWHC 23 (Fam).
[156] See *Gourisaria v Gourisaria* [2010] EWCA Civ 1019 where the courts were considering the implications of the concept of the Hindu Undivided Family but also wrestling with cross jurisdictional and other difficult issues.

18.18 ANTE AND POST NUPTIAL AGREEMENTS

Concerns about the consequences for a family business of marriage failure are increasingly captured in the use of nuptial agreements. Those concerns will often come from the wider family. Peter Leach refers to a family company, Rington Holdings, with a policy of requiring all family members to enter into pre-nuptial agreements on marriage.[157] Perhaps less often the impetus for nuptial agreements will come from the couple concerned, especially in the case of second or subsequent marriages. Nuptial agreements can either be made before marriage, the widely known 'pre-nup' or during the marriage itself, the less familiar post-nuptial agreement.

Over recent years the advice on the wisdom of pre-nuptial agreements has progressed from saying that they are not worth the paper they are written on (and it might annoy the judge),[158] to it cannot do any harm and might have persuasive value, through to the current situation where it might be thought silly for spouses with family business interests, whether inherited or self-made, not to have one.

18.18.1 The legal status of nuptial agreements

The advice will not go so far as to say that pre-nuptial agreements will automatically be enforced by the English courts.[159] The case of family business heiress Katrin Radmacher was widely covered in the press. The Supreme Court in that case[160] did not say that pre-nuptial agreements were binding in England and Wales, but rather that the courts would enforce such agreements if it was fair to do so.[161]

> 'The court should give effect to a nuptial agreement that is freely entered into by each party with a full appreciation of its implications unless in the circumstances prevailing it would not be fair to hold the parties to their agreement.'

It therefore follows that all of the component factors of fairness referred to above, including needs, sharing and the status of non-matrimonial property, will remain relevant. But one potentially crucial factor has been introduced into the equation. By signing the pre-nuptial agreement the parties to the marriage might be seen to be confirming their own assessment of what they thought to be fair at that time.

Since *Radmacher* the Law Commission has published a report recommending that what they have termed qualifying nuptial agreements should be enforceable, provided that certain conditions are met.[162] The Commission also put forward a draft Nuptial Agreements Bill but this has yet to secure its place in the Parliamentary timetable.

It is therefore helpful to look at the factors that will go towards enforceability of nuptial agreements, as identified by the Supreme Court in *Radmacher*, alongside the recommendations of the Law Commission for qualifying nuptial agreements. It will then

---

[157] See Peter Leach *Family Businesses – The Essentials* (Profile Books, 2007) at pp 130–131.
[158] As an attempt to exclude the jurisdiction of the English courts.
[159] This is the position at the date this chapter was edited in 2016. The enforceability of nuptial agreements varies from jurisdiction to jurisdiction with some recognising the legal status of these agreements, for example this is widespread in the USA and also in Germany.
[160] *Radmacher v Granatino* [2010] UKSC 42.
[161] At para 75.
[162] *Law Commission: Matrimonial Property, Needs and Agreements* (Law Com No 343, February 2014).

be open to the parties to either prepare nuptial agreements on the basis of the law as it stands or to attempt to 'future proof' these by anticipating and including the requirements of the proposed new regime.

18.18.2 Needs prevail

Both the current law, as interpreted by the Supreme Court in *Radmacher* and the regime proposed by the Law Commission, recognise that the financial needs of the parties and their children prevail over the terms of any nuptial agreement.[163] So there will be some protection against changes in circumstances creating real need, for example the loss of income from a previously well paid job, or even the collapse of a family business, which had not been foreseen at the time the agreement was entered into.[164]

18.18.3 Formalities

The proposed qualifying nuptial agreements regime introduces highly prescriptive formal requirements for nuptial agreements to be enforceable.[165] These include that the agreement takes the form of a deed, is otherwise contractually valid and contains a prescribed statement.

The current law after *Radmacher* does not lay down any such formalities but Radmacher does make it clear that fraud, duress or misrepresentation at the time the agreement is signed will vitiate its terms.

18.18.4 Cooling off period

A pre-nuptial agreement made within 28 days before the date of the wedding will be unenforceable as a qualifying nuptial agreement. Proximity to the wedding is but one of a number of factors that might point to the fairness, or otherwise of enforcing a nuptial agreement under the law as it now stands, following the decision of the Supreme Court in *Radmacher*.

---

[163] Although the issue of needs is approached differently. The approach in *Radmacher* is that the question of needs is one of a wide range of factors to be considered in deciding whether it is fair to enforce the agreement. Under the proposed qualifying nuptial agreements regime these must be enforced by the Courts unless the need of the parties or the interests of a child of the family dictate otherwise.
[164] See *Luckwell v Limata* [2014] EWHC 502 (Fam). Although Holman J said the submission that he profoundly disagreed with a submission that 'needs trump [nuptial] agreements' (see para 138) the agreement in that case was nevertheless not enforced against a husband in real need. Also in *WW v HW* [2015] EWHC 1844 (Fam) the court declined to enforce a pre-nuptial agreement, made after independent legal advice, providing for a clean break without any claims, against the husband whose business had failed and who had mismanaged his tax affairs, leaving him with no assets. However the court interpreted his needs narrowly and made an award that would mean some stepping down in standard of accommodation and lifestyle (readily rejecting the husband's claim that he should be provided with a country home, in addition to a central London property, in the process). There were children involved in this case, whose needs (including reasonable accommodation when they stayed with their father) also had to be taken into account as the primary consideration.
[165] Similar to the approach taken for enforceable settlement agreements in employment law.

18.18.5 Independent advice

Similarly whilst this is highly desirable to point to fairness under the law as it now stands,[166] to help show that the parties understand the implications of the agreement, independent advice is only a factor that goes to fairness. But it will be a strict requirement for a qualifying nuptial agreement.

18.18.6 Duress and undue influence

The formal requirements of the new regime are presumably intended to cater for undue influence and pressure on the parties to enter into unfavourable nuptial agreements. Under the law as it stands the age, maturity and economic position of the parties and any alleged or actual pressure to enter into the agreement[167] are all factors that the courts may look at retrospectively in deciding whether it is fair to enforce the agreement.

It is a moot point what the courts would make of any pre-nuptial agreements relating to a family business such as Ringtons, where bloodline family members who do not sign pre-nuptial agreements (or more pertinently persuade their betrothed to do so) are not allowed to hold shares directly.[168]

What about an ultimatum along the lines of 'sign this or the wedding's off'? In one case[169] where the husband had in essence said that he would end the marriage if the wife did not sign a post-nuptial agreement, this was not enforced against her. But there is a qualitative difference between threatening a divorce and introducing conditions to a proposal of marriage. Much will depend on the circumstances. The closer to the wedding, logically the more likely duress and undue influence might be found.

18.18.7 Disclosure

The same position applies to disclosure by the party seeking to enforce the nuptial agreement of their assets to the other party. Whilst a desirable factor to show fairness at the moment this will be a strict requirement for a qualifying nuptial agreement. After *Radmacher* the key point is that each party has received sufficient information about the other party's assets.

The Supreme Court's view on disclosure was as follows:[170]

> '... we consider that the Court of Appeal was correct in principle to ask whether there was any material lack of disclosure, information or advice. Sound legal advice is obviously desirable, for this will ensure that a party understands the implications of the agreement, and full disclosure of any assets owned by the other party may be necessary to ensure this. But if

---

[166] See *Kremen v Agrest* [2012] EWHC 45 (Fam) where a nuptial agreement was enforced against a husband who had not taken legal advice but was seen as financially sophisticated and also *WW v HW* [2015] EWHC 1844 (Fam) and *Y v Y* [2014] EWHC 1844 (Fam) and *SA v PA* [2014] EWHC 392 (Fam) where both husband and wife were international lawyers but the pre-nuptial agreement had been drawn up by a notary attached to a firm connected to the husband's father. There the wife was seen to have had 'the impartial but not strictly independent advice of the notary' (at para 57).
[167] Although pressure amounting to economic duress will prevent an agreement having contractual validity as a qualifying nuptial agreement.
[168] Although refuseniks might still benefit under family business trusts.
[169] *NA v MA* [2006] EWHC 2900 (Fam).
[170] At para 69.

it is clear that a party is fully aware of the implications of an ante-nuptial agreement and indifferent to detailed particulars of the other party's assets, there is no need to accord the agreement reduced weight because he or she is unaware of those particulars. What is important is that each party should have all the information that is material to his or her decision, and that each party should intend that the agreement should govern the financial consequences of the marriage coming to an end.'

In theory the disclosure required is not necessarily confined to financial matters.[171]

18.18.8 Review

The proposed qualifying nuptial agreements regime does not place any time limit on the validity of nuptial agreements. Neither did the Supreme Court in *Radmacher*. Nevertheless some practitioners suggest that nuptial agreements are periodically reviewed. The main concern would be that the agreement no longer meets the needs of the parties thereby failing the fairness test under *Radmacher* or justifying the courts refusing to uphold a qualifying nuptial agreement under the proposed new regime. The agreement can then be revised to cater for the changed circumstances of the parties and thereby increases the chances of the revised agreement being enforced.

The problem is what happens if there is a review but the parties cannot agree new terms? The original agreement could be drafted so as to continue in force until varied. But the fact that the parties cannot agree revised terms could possibly be seen by the courts as relevant to the question of fairness and enforceability on any subsequent marriage breakdown. Also the process of reviewing and revising a nuptial agreement is likely to be at least as emotionally challenging for the parties concerned as preparing the original agreement, if not more so. After all the parties will have been married for some years and would no doubt have expected greater trust to have been built between them.

18.18.9 Residual fairness

The key difference between the current law post *Radmacher* and the proposed new regime is that, at the moment courts have the residual ability to ask the question 'is it fair in all the circumstances of this case to enforce this agreement?'. Subject to the issues of need and the interests of the children, that question cannot be asked for a qualifying nuptial agreement if the procedural boxes have been ticked at the time of its formation.

18.18.10 Nuptial agreements and family dynamics

At the risk of leaving one of the main, if not the most significant considerations to last, how can nuptial agreements be reconciled with family dynamics? From a cold hard, business and ownership perspective the benefits and logic of deploying these agreements are pretty much inescapable. A (relative) degree of clarity and certainty can be obtained over what will happen on divorce. Family business assets can be protected. The consequence of matrimonial disputes minimised. From a systems perspective all nuptial agreements are trying to achieve is to establish appropriate boundaries between the family, business and ownership systems of a family business.[172]

---

[171] In *Hewett v First National Group plc* [2010] EWCA Civ 312 a husband decided not to tell his wife that he was engaged in an extra marital affair at the time he asked her to sign a post nuptial agreement – which was not enforced against her.

[172] For a fuller explanation and discussion of the three-circle model see chapter 3 (Tools, Models and Theories).

But this rhetoric may seem cold and unpersuasive when applied to the reality of family relationships and emotions. Even raising the question of a pre-nuptial agreement with a prospective in law highlights their outsider status so far as the family business and the business owning family are concerned.[173] Neither is asking someone to sign a pre-nuptial agreement a ringing vote of confidence in the prospects of a marriage succeeding.

The loudest objection might not however come from the prospective in law but from the bloodline family member who wants to marry them. By definition the remainder of the family by raising the question of nuptial agreements the rest of the business owning family are questioning their choice of partner and their ability to sustain a relationship.

Deeper issues might be triggered. Gersick[174] gives an example of a business owning family, who, having been involved in a lengthy legal battle to recover shares given to the husband of an older daughter following their divorce, attempted to close that particular stable door by proposing that the younger daughter's fiancé signed a prenuptial agreement. The sisters had a history of sibling rivalry, with the younger daughter being cast in the role of the underachieving and helpless baby of the family. Her opportunity to prove that she could 'beat' her sister by establishing a secure long-term marriage was undermined by the suggestion that she and the family needed the safety net of a pre-nuptial agreement. The family wedding was cancelled.

Of course this does not undermine the logic of pre-nuptial agreements. It merely highlights the huge sensitivity surrounding the subject and the need for careful, considered and timely introduction of the subject.

Possibly advisors could offer themselves up as suitable messengers to be shot.

If those involved in family businesses need further incentive to look at nuptial agreements they need look no further than the legal bills in many of the cases referred to in this chapter. For example the conduct of *White*, was described in the House of Lords as a 'very bad advertisement for the legal system'[175] these were 'estimated at the appalling sum of £530,000',[176] over 10% of the Whites aggregate net assets.

18.19 GOVERNANCE DOCUMENTS

The subject of nuptial agreements leads on to a consideration of the use of wider governance documents with relevant provisions covering marriage breakdown. Do such agreements have a role to play and to what extent will they be recognised by a court dealing with the breakdown of a marriage?

---

[173] Discussed in more detail in chapter 2 (Themes).
[174] Kelin E Gersick, John A Davis Marion McCollom Hampton and Ivan Lansberg *Generation to Generation: Life Cycles of the Family Business* (Harvard Business School Press, 1997) at p 69.
[175] Lord Cooke at p 615. Since *White* efforts have been made to improve the efficiency and reduce the costs of matrimonial disputes. These include the Pre-Action Protocol and Family Proceedings Rules 2010, Practice Direction 25A together with more general initiatives such as requiring parties to instruct single joint experts on valuation issues to avoid the significant costs incurred in instructing separate experts in many of the earlier cases. Also matrimonial lawyers were either pioneers or early adopters of many of the alternative dispute resolution approaches discussed in chapter 25 (The Family Business Advisor), including mediation and collaborative law. A detailed treatment of costs in family cases can be found in Wilkinson and Hunton *Costs in Family Proceedings* (Jordan Publishing, 2015).
[176] Lord Nicholls at p 612.

18.19.1 Early stage husband and wife partnerships

If the general proposition that governance documents are rare in family businesses generally,[177] then fully documented shareholder and partnership agreements, as between early stage family businesses, involving only husband and wife must be very rare indeed.

The Whites – governance application points?

There is no suggestion in the report of the case that Martin and Pamela White ever entered into a formal partnership agreement. Would it have benefited them to do so? Almost certainly, yes.

Notwithstanding that the couple had farmed in partnership together for almost 30 years with Pamela credited with having played an active role in that partnership, the outcome of the High Court hearing was that Pamela was awarded less than half the value of the partnership assets, leaving aside the value of the land Martin had inherited from his family.

How conceivable would it have been that the couple, whilst still on good terms and excited about being in business together, would have entered into a partnership agreement providing for an equivalent result if, unfortunately their marriage failed? It is not more likely that the couple would have suggested arrangements to partition their land, allowing both partners to carry on farming separately. Even if they agreed that Martins should buy out Pamela, would this have been at market value, perhaps payable in instalments? If this speculation is inaccurate and in fact the couple would have agreed that Martin would take over the business at least this would have been evidenced in the partnership agreement.

Even if they had not entered into a partnership agreement at the start of their business life together, other opportunities would have presented themselves. For example we learn that when Mr White's father wrote off his original loan this was originally credited to Martin's capital account, but that after a further 10 years the capital accounts of Martin and Pamela were merged into one. Did this have any significance to the couple in terms of confirming their copreneurial nature of their relationship? Of course the answer might be much more prosaic.[178]

The basic point being that most partnership discussions are likely to have led to something close to the middle ground which was eventually chosen by the House of Lords after much bitterness, many years of litigation and legal costs in excess of £500,000.

In chapter 2 (Themes) we suggest that a family business often assumes the status of a surrogate child.[179] If so, does it not make sense for a couple in business together to agree arrangements for the custody of that child in advance? The aim might not necessarily be to secure an absolutely legally binding agreement, which is guaranteed to be enforceable in the event of marriage breakdown. Rather it is to establish a starting point and a

---

[177] See chapter 17 (Governance).
[178] For example the White's accountant might simply have suggested the change and this could have been accepted without further thought.
[179] See Chapter 2 (Themes) at **2.10** (the psychological status of the family business).

reminder for the couple concerned of what they once thought reasonable. This might be seen as morally binding and may minimise the likelihood of serious dispute.

In any event business agreements made between husband and wife are always likely to remain subject to scrutiny by the courts if their marriage breaks down. Irrespective of how family business interests are allocated and dealt with by the parties during marriage the courts will always be able to vary ownership arrangements in any shareholder or similar agreement by using its powers to make property adjustment orders under MCA, s 24 and using its powers to vary settlements pursuant to s 24(1)(c) MCA 1973. This was the case in *F v F*[180] where the court[181] ordered a variation of a shareholders' agreement, in effect to transfer custody of the family company to the husband as being the only practical remedy in the circumstances of extreme acrimony then prevailing where husband and wife could no longer work together.[182]

F v F is interesting in that the case provides a picture of a couple whose marriage was clearly, in difficulties, attempting to use the shareholders' agreement to contain and regulate pressures within the overall family business system. The agreement provides for a clear role for the wife as a director. It also constrains the ability of the husband to extract cash for his own benefit or, tellingly, for the benefit of the children from his first marriage, some of whom worked in the family business. The agreement, combined with some family business trusts, effectively elevated the status of the children from this, the husband's third marriage, to that of preferential beneficiaries. Because of the value of the overall assets there was more than enough cash to look after the infant children from the third marriage. In these circumstances the court thought that it was 'entirely reasonable' that the husband should want to treat all of his children equally and to make further provision for the elder children, free from the constraints in the shareholders' agreement.

Neither, realistically, do nuptial agreements or governance documents, provide any absolute guarantee that fights will not break out between spouses over their terms and enforceability in the emotional turmoil of marriage breakdown.[183]

18.19.2 Later stage family businesses and divestment provisions

For larger and later stage family businesses relevant issues might be covered by any general governance documents, including employment policies in relation to in-laws.[184] Similarly family charters, shareholders' agreements or articles might contain provisions confirming whether or not in-laws are eligible to join the family ownership circle, participate in family councils and family assemblies etc.[185]

---

[180] *F v F* [2012] EWHC 438 (Fam).
[181] Using its powers to vary settlements pursuant to s 24(1)(c) MCA 1973.
[182] The case also debated whether provisions in the relevant shareholders' agreement dealing with salary and dividends were 'maintenance agreements' within MCA, s 34. As the agreement referred to the payment of salary and dividends into the parties joint bank account, the court thought that this implied that the agreement was not intended to apply when the parties were 'living separately' as s 34 requires (para 24) and therefore that as a shareholders' agreement between husband and wife it was 'poorly drafted' for failing to take into account the possibility of the parties separating (para 26).
[183] In *F v F* the parties had incurred costs of £2.4m between them, notwithstanding the presence of an agreement prepared against the background of and to help shore up their deteriorating marriage.
[184] In Ringtons Holdings in-laws were required to serve a 'probationary period' of 5 years after their marriage to a bloodline family member before becoming eligible for employment in the family firm.
[185] Discussed in detail in chapter 17 (Governance).

On the occasions that in-laws have been admitted to ownership this is most often in an unstructured way, usually based on their contribution as employees of the family firm and with little thought as to what would happen to those shares in the event of the breakdown of their marriage to their bloodline family spouse.

So formal divestment provisions, obliging an owning in-law to sell their shares, are a comparative rarity.[186] These could be contained in articles of association, or in separate buy-sell agreements or they could form part of more general shareholder or partnership agreements. Possibly departing and divorcing spouses might be accidentally caught by compulsory transfer provisions, generally applicable to all departing employees.

Divestment provisions bring into play all the issues relating to exit provisions discussed in chapter 11 (Ownership overview), including valuation and payment terms. And with a vengeance. Sometimes family business clients, particularly those in the senior generation, will be keen to make sure that the divorcing in-law does not leave clutching too many pieces of the family business silver and seek to ensure that any divestment provisions operate at a discount from market value.

As discussed in chapter 11, there is often a balancing act between providing a viable exit route for a family member and ensuring that this does not damage the family business on the other hand. Often this dilemma is resolved in favour of the family business and the wish to ensure its continuity. How do courts distinguish between a legitimate and enforceable commercial bargain and situation where they are able to intervene?

Penal divestment provisions might in any event be self-defeating as any reduction in the in-laws resources will be taken into account as part of the balancing act required under MCA, s 25. However such provisions might operate to transfer value from the departing in law to the wider business owning family.[187]

What about the position in later stage family businesses where children, cousins or wider family members have been brought into the ownership system and the divestment provisions concerned apply to all? Could divestment provisions in the relevant shareholders' agreements, potentially applicable to many marriages fall within the provisions of MCA, s 24? To be treated as a 'nuptial settlement' for the purposes of that section the settlement need only be one that makes some form of continuing provision for both or either of the parties to a marriage with or without provision for their children.[188] This is a very wide definition. Whilst arrangements relating to an early stage family business involving only the husband and wife could be seen to be linked to their particular marriage, it might be thought to be straining the language of that section to regard elements the constitution of a later stage, more widely held family firm, which apply to a number of nuclear family units as a nuptial settlement.

However this would not necessarily be so. The terms settlement has been very widely interpreted as any:[189]

---

[186] But a feature of the Ringtons governance system, with in-laws being obliged to surrender their shares to the bloodline family members on divorce.
[187] For example if pre-emption provisions allow all remaining family shareholders to buy their proportionate share of the former in-law's holding on favourable terms.
[188] DR and GR and Others [2013] 2 FLR 1534.
[189] Per Lord Nicholls in Brooks v Brooks [1996] 1 AC 375.

'arrangement which makes some form of continuing provision for both or either of the parties to [the marriage].'

If a settlement is made during the marriage with benefit to either party, it may well be nuptial in nature and, therefore, open to the absolute power of the court to vary it. This can include, for example, breaking the whole settlement and carving out assets for either party to meet their respective needs. In one case the court re-opened a discretionary trust of a farmhouse matrimonial home, set up for the benefit of the husband and children to effectively award the wife half of the value of that property.[190]

The court would then need to balance needs against the source of the assets within the settlement, which may bring into play inheritance and non-matrimonial property arguments again. If the arrangements subject to the settlement also relate to wider family members they would have the right to intervene, as explained above.

18.20 CONCLUSION

A huge number of couples create very successful life partnerships around family business interests. These may range from full-blown copreneurial partnerships, where both spouses are engaged in the business and domestically, to situations where one spouse contributes fully to family life but plays no active role in the family business. No discrimination will be made between the roles of the partners if they later divorce.

Against this broad proposition there are huge uncertainties, particularly surrounding the legal treatment of family businesses started before marriage and inherited family business interests.

This uncertainty carries with it the danger that the parties incur considerable costs in resolving this uncertainty. Inevitably this potential is compounded by the bitterness and high emotions surrounding many divorces. Ideally alternative dispute resolution procedures such as mediation or collaborative law approaches can help.

But preventing uncertainty is better than the cure of using the legal system to resolve it. Introducing the subject of nuptial agreements, or catering for divorce in more general family business governance documents such as family charters or partnership and shareholders' agreements are inevitably sensitive issues. Nevertheless this could prove a sound investment for the business families concerned.

---

[190] *AB v CB (Financial Remedy; Variation of Trust)w* [2014] EWHC 2998 (Fam).

CHAPTER 19

INHERITANCE DISPUTES

19.1 OVERVIEW: 'ONE DAY ALL THIS WILL BE YOURS'

Of all the clichés associated with the family business world the phrase 'one day all of this will be yours' is probably the best known. It is also capable of being the most invidious and dangerous sentence a senior generation family member can utter. Something to that effect was said to James Davies. Similar assurances were made to his namesake, Eirian Davies whose case[1] will be considered in much more detail below. As with many family business proprietary estoppel cases, and most of the cases referred to in this chapter both of the Davies cases concerned farming families.[2]

The problem is that whilst the senior generation may genuinely mean what they say at the time and a measure of reassurance might be given to the next generation recipient, such phrases are fundamentally vague, imprecise, subject to change and incapable of legal enforcement, at least under anything resembling usual contractual principles.[3]

Whatever reassurance was provided to the next generation family member at the time the promise is made will evaporate over time if the specifics of the promised succession do not materialise. Almost certainly their confidence will be severely shaken if serious conflicts begin to emerge between the generations in the interval between the promise of and actual ownership transfer. Really this chapter is about the consequences of unduly delaying and implementing succession plans.

So what does the next generation 'promisee' do in such circumstances? Do they hope that everything will turn out alright in the end? Do they press the next generation for more certainty? One of the phrases used in Eirian Davies' case was that she, as the next generation daughter who expected to inherit the family farm, should not 'kill the goose that lays the golden egg'.[4] There will be a huge concern for the next generation that pressing for more certainty as to their succession expectations will, if not kill the goose, at least severely annoy it. And senior generation family members, just like geese, have a reputation for being irascible creatures.

---

[1] *Evan John Tegwyn Davies & Mary Eileen Davies v Elizabeth Eirian Davies* [2014] EWCA Civ 568.
[2] In theory there is absolutely no reason why the main remedy discussed in this chapter, proprietary estoppel, should not apply to promises made in relation to ownership of non-farming family businesses. In practice it is difficult to find reported cases outside the agricultural industry.
[3] Especially the principle that the terms of a contract have to be sufficiently certain to be enforced by a court. It is also doubtful whether a senior generation family member would have any intention to enter into anything approaching a legal commitment when making 'promises' of this nature.
[4] At para 5 of the judgment.

The next generation therefore face a difficult choice between living with uncertainty over their position or initiating a difficult conversation with their parents. Of course it is to be hoped that the senior generation, remove the burden of this choice by leading the ownership succession discussion and ensuring that the process continues on track. Indeed, we would argue that it is their primary responsibility to do so. But, if not, does the next generation family member have any other choice available to them?

In the absence of a formal oral or written contract or agreement governing succession of a family business, any succession claims are, by necessity, brought by claimants based upon the principles of fairness. Claims are typically brought under the doctrines of proprietary estoppel, constructive or resulting trust, unjust enrichment or *quantum meruit*. It is beyond the scope of this work to consider each of these types of claim in detail and any other equitable principles potentially arising. Instead, as the most frequently occurring type of equitable claim brought in the family business context is proprietary estoppel, we have therefore focused our discussion on this remedy.

At the risk of giving the conclusion to this chapter in its introduction, if ownership expectations are, for whatever reason, not met, in the absence of formal contractual rights the position of the next generation is precarious indeed. The only hope might be to fall back on the discretionary remedies of the court mentioned above, in particular, proprietary estoppel, which, as this chapter shows, are highly uncertain. So much so that pursuing a claim must be seen as act of desperation on the part of the next generation family member, rather than anything that could legitimately be labelled a choice.

All of this, and much more, can be vividly illustrated by the cases of the Davies families.

We also consider the possibility of statutory claims under the Inheritance (Provision for Family and Dependents) Act 1975 (I(PFD)A 1975).[5] As such claims are relatively constricted in scope and also based on the courts assessment of the claimant's reasonable financial needs, I(PFD)A 1975 claims may provide an even less satisfactory remedy for a disappointed next generation family member.

Many disputes only come to fruition after the owner-manager's death, at the time the will is read. But succession disputes can also arise during the lifetime of the senior generation. The common factor is that if disputes are not resolved swiftly, they threaten both the function of the family dynamics and also the business performance.

Survey evidence consistently suggests that formal succession planning is the exception rather than the rule amongst many business families.[6] Yet, the senior generation will often have clear expectations as to who will inherit the family business. Usually, because of the informal family context, these expectations are not fully discussed with the next generation, much less recorded in a written contract or agreement with the would-be successors or other family members.

Typically, years pass before the matter is brought to a head; generally triggered by an event, such as the next generation's marriage to an individual who does not meet with family approval or struggles over the impending retirement of the senior generation,

---

[5] The chapter does not deal with the host of contentious probate disputes, which can affect business owning and other families to a similar extent. These include disputes relating to lack of capacity, lack of knowledge and approval and undue influence, together with disputes about the interpretation of wills.
[6] See for example *The UK Family Business Sector* (IFB and Capital Economics, 2008) at p 5.

typically based on a reluctance to let go and continuing interference in day to day operations.[7] But expectations of inheriting the business will have been raised with the next generation, which in the worst of cases, and as a result of this lack of formal planning, are never met. The scene is then set for a succession dispute.

19.2 CASE STUDY: AN EMERGING DISPUTE

Consider the following case study by way of illustration, which may serve to provide a glimpse behind the early stage scenes of some of the reported legal cases discussed later in this chapter.

The case concerned the failed succession of a second generation farming business from father and mother to their daughter. The farm was legally a partnership between the father and mother and its business originally comprised poultry, dairy, cattle and crops. In later years it had also diversified to include a coffee shop and over time also included a butcher's shop and farm shop selling groceries. The farm's property included farmland, a cottage, and a new farmhouse built by the daughter so that she could live near the business, and a bungalow, which was home to the parents. Other key family members were the daughter's former husband, with whom she had two children, her new partner and her sister, who was the only member of the immediate family who did not work in the business.

After many years of working well together, a hostile dispute arose when the father and mother changed their wills. The new wills effectively wrote both the daughter and her sister out of any entitlement to the farm to set up generation skipping trusts in favour of the grandchildren. The daughter had expected, after working on the farm for many years for very little pay, that she would inherit the business from her parents. As is almost inevitably the case, there were two sides to the story, which are set out below.

19.2.1 The daughter's story

The daughter's case was that she had worked hard on the farm since she was a child. She had always been close to her parents and enjoyed the work. When she left school and was considering her future career, she chose to remain on the farm and help her family make the business a success. Her mother welcomed this decision and her father made no objection to it, which was, in her experience, his usual way of indicating his approval.

She went on to work long hours on the farm; 6 days a week for very little pay. When she felt tired, she was told that she was working for the good of the family. On many occasions she put the business first before her own needs and when she went on to have her own family, she was often forced to prioritise the needs of the family business over those of her own children and husband. She did this because she believed that the family business should always come first. She did not object to the hard work and sacrifice because she believed that the business would be left to her when her parents retired and that, on their death, she would inherit most of the farm and all of the business from them.

She expected that the bungalow, where her parents lived, would be inherited by her sister, who had no direct involvement in the business. This seemed appropriate given

---

[7] Although this did not appear to be a factor in James Davies' case, nor a material issue in Eirian's.

that the bungalow played no part in the farming business and its value was roughly half that of her parents' combined estate. Her expectations were reasonable in her view because they were based upon the comments and promises her parents had made to her over the course of many years that, on their retirement she would take over the business. As a result of such expectation, the daughter made no separate provision for her financial future and sought no other employment.

As time went on, she took on more-and-more responsibility for the business, as her parents stepped back. Under her management, the business prospered, particularly in the diversified retail outlets overseen by the daughter. When her own children were born, she found the daily commute from her home to be too long as she spent many hours working on the farm. As a result, she and her husband sold their own home and with the encouragement of her parents, they built a new house on the farm site.

Her parents held legal title to the farm, including the new house, but the daughter did not worry about this because she expected that she would inherit the business and part of the farm. As relations had always been good between them, the daughter had no reason not to trust that her parents would not do what she believed they had promised. Relations between the daughter and her parents were good until the daughter came to divorce her husband. This was the first in a series of trigger events, which led to a full succession dispute.

19.2.2 Triggers for a succession dispute

As a result of her divorce, the daughter became aware of the lack of assets which she legally held in her own name. Her divorce lawyer advised her, as part of the financial order proceedings, that she had next-to-no assets of her own and she should consider her future financial security. This led her to want to formalise her legal succession to the family business.

Her parents commented at the time of the divorce that they were pleased they had not yet made their daughter's husband a partner of the business as, if they had, the divorce would have cost them a partial loss of the business to an outsider of the family. However, the daughter interpreted their comments differently. She considered them to be a form of assurance confirming that her parents' intended for her ultimately to become a partner in the business partnership.

The second trigger came when a family meeting was held to discuss formal succession plans. The meeting was attended by the parents' accountants and tax advisors as well as the family. At the meeting, the daughter asked for her role as an employee to be upgraded to her becoming a partner alongside her parents. She also requested that a share of the business assets be distributed to her. However, her parents did not agree to this. Instead, her salary was simply increased from a very low rate to a more reasonable one.

The third trigger came about 2 years later when the daughter's new partner, who was also working in the family business, had an argument with the father over a farming issue. This argument appeared to be the final catalyst for a full-blown succession dispute as following this, the parents made new wills stating that the daughter was not to receive any share of the business. Instead, their entire estates were to pass to their grandchildren, by-passing both of their daughters.

The parents also officially terminated the daughter's employment in the business, which led to her bringing a claim for unfair dismissal. She was forced to leave her home on the farm as the breakdown in their personal relationships made it impossible to stay any longer.

In the absence of any legal entitlement to the business and also to her home, which had been built on the farm site, the daughter had to consider her options.

19.2.3 Early attempts to resolve the dispute

Chapter 25 discusses various approaches to resolving conflict once this has arisen in a family business. The emphasis is on informal and alternative forms of dispute resolution. This is especially recommended in the case of inheritance disputes, given the huge level of uncertainty and the evidential difficulties surrounding such claims. That is to say nothing of the huge emotional strain and the damage to family relationships caused by a protracted succession dispute. These themes will be ever present throughout this chapter.

The daughter fervently wished to avoid litigation with her parents. This was despite the fact that the dispute had escalated to the point where the parties were not speaking and the father, in particular, was behaving very bizarrely. So early attempts were made to try and resolve matters within the family circle. A close family friend was called upon by the daughter to act as an informal arbitrator at a family meeting held to try and agree a way forward. Unfortunately, the parties were too entrenched to begin negotiations on this basis and the efforts of the well-meaning friend quickly failed.

The daughter recognised then that expert help would probably be needed to reach a resolution and she contacted a family business consultant for their help. Interviews with the individual family members were conducted by the consultant to draw out their individual perspectives and objectives. However, the elderly parents were reluctant to fully engage in the process and consequently, the consultant was not given the opportunity to help the family find a way forward.

It then became apparent to the daughter that she would require legal advice as the only means of helping her resolve this dispute. She was advised that one option was to wait until her parents' wills came into effect, after which she could contest their provision under the I(PFD)A 1975. As the adult child of her parents, she fell within the class of eligible claimants entitled to seek reasonable financial provision out of her parents' estates, subject to it being found that insufficient provision had been made for her in their wills.

A key advantage of waiting to bring an I(PFD)A 1975 claim would be that she was automatically eligible, as the adult child of her parents, to bring a claim. She would just have to demonstrate that the wills had made insufficient provision for her.[8] However, the disadvantage of waiting until this point was that she was deprived in the meantime, of her livelihood and also of her home. For this reason, she did not feel that she could wait until that point for a resolution.

---

[8] Further limitations of next generation claims in terms of levels of awards are discussed below.

The second option she discussed with her advisors was to bring a claim in equity during her parents' lifetimes. Given that the daughter's whole life was based around the family business and her role in it, she decided that she had little alternative but to pursue this claim during her parents' lifetime.[9]

19.2.4 The family dynamics

The case illustrates a number of factors common to many such family disputes. It is typical for parents to always want the final say over ownership, notwithstanding that their children may be undertaking more work and responsibility in the family business than they are by that time and notwithstanding previous assurances and expectations.

Inheritance is seen as a gift and not a right and this mind-set can prove too entrenched to be reversible in many cases.

Therefore, it was not uncommon in such claims, for parents to simply block out any efforts their children might make to negotiate with them. In this case, this was partly due to the fact that the parents were simply not susceptible to the same immediate losses as the daughter was; because their immediate livelihood and homes had not been endangered so far by this dispute, as hers had. Practically speaking, there was simply less urgency on the parents' part to resolve matters.

Finally, the parents had, over the course of the years, changed their minds about succession of the family business.[10] However, they appeared to consider that they were at liberty to change the plan as they saw fit. They did not perhaps appreciate that an obligation in equity could develop over the course of time to leave the farm to their daughter, which would potentially prevent them from reneging on their past promises to her.

19.2.5 Daughter's proprietary estoppel claim for the farm

The legal principles of establishing a proprietary estoppel claim are discussed in detail below. But the daughter's basic position was that it would therefore be unconscionable to allow the parents to rely on their strict legal rights of ownership and not to recognise that the daughter had obtained a beneficial entitlement to the farming business, the house she had built and most of the farm.

19.2.6 The parents' story

As is often the case, the parents' version of events was quite different.

Their story was that since leaving school, their daughter had simply been given a job in the family business. She had been allowed to pick and choose her hours and had been given many privileges over the years. These included the free use of farmland on which to keep her horses, help with loans to build a house on the farm and help for her and her husband to start new pig, poultry and horse-riding businesses on the farm.

---

[9] Proprietary estoppel claims can also be brought after a will has been proven but they are versatile in that they are also available as an equitable solution to disputes arising during the lifetime.

[10] Also factors in the case of both James and Eirian Davies.

In their view, their daughter's contribution to the family business was valuable but was limited to that of an employee who had worked as part of a team to make the business a success. Over the years, her contribution had started with her helping out in the farm shop after school. She had progressed on to helping out more, particularly in the retail side of the business. However, her parents had been the ones who were effectively managing the business throughout and they were still the active owner-managers of the business.

The parents considered that their daughter chose to work in the family business because it was easy and undemanding work and suited her own responsibilities as a parent. They did not accept that her efforts towards its success entitled her to become a partner or to ultimately inherit the business from them. They also denied that they had made the representations asserted by the daughter.

Their view was that they had not retired at all from the business, despite being quite elderly and had no wish to do so. Their attitude was that 'farmers don't retire' and that their work and life were inextricably linked. They said that it was never their intention to retire and therefore they would never have told their daughter that she would take over the running of the business at any point whilst they were still alive.

They had changed their wills due to the events which had taken place since the daughter's divorce and her subsequent relationship with her new partner, whom they disliked intensely. This animosity towards the daughter's new partner had culminated in the argument between him and her father, after which relations appeared to have been irrevocably damaged.

19.2.7 Issuing the daughter's claim

As we have already seen, the daughter had exhausted all informal means of resolving the dispute with her parents and was forced to take formal action. She was advised that her own claim in proprietary estoppel was strong and likely to succeed in part or whole, if she pursued it all the way to trial. Whilst a trial would be undesirable for all parties involved, and a potentially costly solution, she was advised that issuing proceedings formally against her parents would be strategically expedient to exert sufficient pressure on her parents to bring them to the negotiating table. In this particular case, the daughter decided that she had little choice but to issue proceedings.[11]

She was also advised to protect the property included within her claim, pending its resolution, by entering a restriction on the title at the Land Registry with reference to her proposed beneficial entitlement to the property.

Her solicitors advised her that, in these types of claim, the burden of proof is on the claimant to show that the necessary elements of assurance, detriment and consequential reasonable reliance can be found. Typically, assurances are made orally or by way of conduct. Inevitably, the parties will have different recollections of conversations held, often many years previously. Detailed witness statements were therefore taken from the daughter and from any other parties who could corroborate her version of events. In this case, many supporting statements were taken on behalf of the daughter.

---

[11] Under Part 7 of the Civil Procedure Rules (CPR) Details of the procedural aspects of issuing a proprietary estoppel claim are briefly described further below.

Equally, the parents both produced their own statements in defence of the claim and were also required to corroborate their version of events with a number of supporting statements. Whilst both parties no doubt hoped that a trial would be avoided, the preparation on each side had to be sufficient to stand up at trial, as there was no guarantee that the parties would agree to a compromise, particularly where both positions were so entrenched. The level of each party's costs inevitably rose with the number of statements which needed to be produced.

The exchange of witness statements was not the only significant cost to each side. The duty of disclosure of all relevant documents and amount of *inter-partes* correspondence between solicitors was also a significant consideration. The parties in this case were unable to agree directions ahead of the case management conference and it was therefore necessary to hold a case management conference 7 months after the daughter had issued her claim. This is not unusual in these types of dispute where, on both sides, emotions tend to run high and much is at stake in respect of the outcome, not only for the business, but also for the family.

19.2.8 Compromise by mediation

Finally, 17 months after the claim was issued, a mediation date was agreed for the parties to try and reach a compromise of the claim. Both parties were under an obligation to consider a form of alternative dispute resolution in accordance with the overriding objective of the CPR.[12] Indeed there are many factors that make cases such as these especially suitable for mediation. These include the costs, evidential difficulties and uncertainties of taking the matter to court.

The daughter was advised that a formal mediation, at which a trained mediator could facilitate a compromise, was the best opportunity to settle the case prior to a full and final hearing. The importance of engaging an experienced and able mediator was key to its potential success. Both parties instructed senior counsel to represent them on the day of the mediation. Position statements for each side were prepared by counsel outlining the cases of each side but also most importantly, these included detailed settlement proposals as to how the parties might reach an agreement as the focus was heavily on the compromise of the claim, rather than rehearsing the areas in dispute once more.

At the mediation, consideration was given to the way in which a settlement might work in practice. For example, the parties discussed possibilities, such as a transfer of land instead of monetary compensation being paid out to the daughter. Consideration was also given to the timing of any payments to be made between the parties and whether staged payments could be made or whether a clean break lump sum settlement would be more appropriate to both sides.

The importance of applying the terms of settlement to suit the particular circumstances were particularly relevant in this case where the parents were still alive. The parents for example were not necessarily in a position to surrender their own home, or a key asset of the business, which might deprive them of an essential part of their on-going livelihood. Equally, the daughter required the assurance of a future home and either a capitalised lump sum payment or on-going income from the business. It was therefore vital for the practitioners advising the parties to take a pragmatic approach and

---

[12] And in accordance with the case of *Halsey v Milton Keynes General NHS Trust* [2004] 1 WLR 3002.

remember the framework in which the family business might still operate after any compromise had been brokered, whilst still meeting the needs of the parties.

In summary, this particular dispute had a resolution in that ultimately, a practical, if not a happy ending, was achieved at the mediation for both the daughter and her parents. This solution, which took account of the factors described above in the best way achievable for both parties. The daughter received a substantial lump sum payment in effective recognition of her beneficial entitlement to the business.

However, the sad outcome for this particular dispute was that an irrevocable rift had developed between the daughter and her parents as a result. The impact this will have on future generations is still unknown. It is rare in such cases for the senior generation to maintain any sort of real relationship with their grandchildren let alone their child and former adversary.

19.2.9 The resolution of succession disputes where no formal agreement exists

The case study illustrates some typical features of early stage succession disputes where no formal agreement exists between the parties regarding succession planning. The matter was resolved by mediation but at considerable cost to the family both in financial and relationship terms. The impact of matters that proceed all the way to trial, or further, on appeal are therefore correspondingly more catastrophic to all parties, almost irrespective of the outcome.

19.3 *DAVIES V DAVIES*:[13] THE CASE OF THE COWSHED CINDERELLA

As with the above case study and many family business proprietary estoppel cases, Eirian Davies' case concerned a farming family. It is also, in many ways, typical of many such cases.

The case centres on the entitlement of the daughter, Eirian, to an interest in the family farm. However proceedings were in fact in initiated by her parents, Tegwyn and Mary, who sought to evict Eirian and her own family from the farmhouse where she and her family lived. After leaving agricultural college at 17, Eirian worked 'long hours on most days' on the farm. In return she received board, lodging and pocket money for clothes and entertainment. It appears that on occasions she asked to be paid a proper wage[14] but was told by her mother 'who held the family purse strings'[15] that she 'should not kill the goose that lays the golden egg'. The goose was in fact a quite substantial dairy farm, comprising what was originally three separate farms, Henllan, Caeremlyn and Glascoed, 200 acres in total, estimated by some sources to be worth £7m at the time of the trial.[16]

Eirian also had two sisters, Enfys and Eleri but it appears that they had little interest in farming. Press reports refer to Eirian missing out 'on going to Young Farmers' Club dances with her two sisters, as a teenager because she had to stay at home to deal with

---

[13] *Evan John Tegwyn Davies & Mary Eileen Davies v Elizabeth Eirian Davies* [2014] EWCA Civ 568.
[14] See chapter 5 for an explanation of the how the minimum wages legislation relates to family employees.
[15] From para 5 of the Court of Appeal judgment.
[16] See *Daily Telegraph* 10 March 2014.

her chores' and claims that 'her sisters once paraded through the poultry shed in their ball gowns while she prepared turkeys for Christmas'.[17]

The Court accepted Eirian's evidence that her father told her, on a number of occasions that 'the farm and the business would be hers one day'.[18] The press reported claims from her that she received promises of inheritance in lieu of birthday presents:[19]

> 'Even on my birthday, when the other girls were having things, they would say: "You will have the damn lot one day, it will all be yours".'

By the time Eirian was 21 her other two sisters had left home. It was in any event 'by this stage clear that she was the only possible candidate to take over the farm'.[20]

Prince Charming arrived at this time, in the shape of Eirian's fiancé, Paul. But here the story of the Davies family departs from the fairy tale. Tegwyn and Mary thoroughly disapproved of Paul leading to 'the first of many fallings out with her parents over what they regarded as her unsuitable choice of partners'[21] with the result that Eirian left the farm and stopped working there.

A while later[22] Eirian and her parents were reconciled, and Eirian returned to work on the farm.

Matters were further complicated by the fact that around this time, in 1990, Tegwyn and Mary bought an adjoining farm, Glascoed and sold part of the land to Eirian and Paul. Eirian was paid £15 a day to milk the Henllan herd but was not paid for her other work on the farm, which was substantial. On the other hand her father, Tegwyn, helped out, to a modest extent, on the smallholding Eirian and Paul had established on their part of the Glascoed land.

Ownership arrangements appeared to be progressing. In 1997 a draft agreement was prepared to bring Eirian into the farming partnership.[23] Although Eirian thought for some years her parents had signed the agreement, they had not in fact done so. The reason offered was uncertainty surrounding potential claims relating to a milk supply agreement.

Eirian and Paul sold their Galscoed property, moved into the Henllan farmhouse and carried out some improvements there. Family harmony was not to last long. In 2001 Eirian again fell out with her parents, moved out of the farmhouse, into rental property elsewhere. The parents let out the Henllan farmhouse but gave Eirian some of the rent they received.

---

[17] *Mail Online* 7 May 2014.
[18] From para 5 of the Court of Appeal judgment.
[19] From *Daily Telegraph* 10 March 2014.
[20] From para 5 of the Court of Appeal judgment.
[21] From para 7 of the Court of Appeal judgment.
[22] The High Court judge found this to be 2 years although the period was disputed by the parties.
[23] This appears to have been in respect of the farming business rather than conferring any ownership rights in relation to the farmland itself. Contrast the position with the Ham family discussed in chapter 13.

Tegwyn and Mary spoke to a solicitor about their wills at this time. They confirmed that although it was their overall intention to leave the farm to Eirian outright they were not prepared to do so whilst she remained married to Paul. In 2002 they signed wills leaving the farm to all three sisters equally.

Relationships between Eirian and her parents improved somewhat, so that in late 2005 or early 2006, she returned to work part time on the family farm. Unfortunately her relationship with Paul must have been deteriorating at the time. The couple separated in late 2006 and divorced the following year.

In 2007 a further family row occurred over a new relationship Eirian resulting in her again stopping work on the farm. Apparently Mary 'referred to a string of men, to whom she referred as "wretches", with kids behind them'.[24] But Eirian's absence was short lived. Tegwyn, repeatedly asked her to return to live and work on the farm and on Boxing Day of that year she moved back to live at Henlann, receiving promises from Tegwyn that this could be her home rent free for life.

During 2007, Eirian, who had often taken on other work to support her family, began working for a major agricultural company, Genus, on a freelance basis. She was significantly better paid for this than for her work on the family farm. The work-life balance was also much better allowing Eirian free time to take her two daughters to the beach when she would otherwise be milking on the family farm. Nevertheless, after she moved back to live at Henllan, Eirian began to do less work for Genus and more on the family farm.

Ownership discussions were resurrected. In 2008 a meeting took place between Tegwyn. Mary, Eirian and the family accountants and solicitors to discuss draft documents which providing Eirian with 49% of the shares in the, by then, incorporated farming company and appointing her a director. An increase in her pay was later agreed to provide Eirian with a salary of £18,000 per annum. The High Court judge accepted that in the following year, 2009, Eirian received promises on two separate occasions that the entire farm would be left to her and that she was shown a draft will to this effect.

But none of these documents were signed. One of reasons appears to be that Paul was pursuing matrimonial claims against Eirian. Tegwyn and Mary may also have had concerns about leaving nothing of substance to their other daughters because they continued to make changes to their wills culminating in a final proposal to place the farm in trust for all three sisters.

A further catastrophic row occurred in 2012 (it is unclear what this was about) during the course of which Mary poured milk over Eirian, who in turn ended up in a fight with her father, when (at least according to the press reports) she bit his leg. The eviction proceedings started shortly afterwards.

19.4 FAMILY BUSINESS THEMES

In many ways the facts of the *Davies* case might seem extreme. But it is by no means unique or freakish. Family tensions can often lead to violence. The case study in **19.2** above was, remarkably similar to *Davies* and involved allegations that the father had

---

[24] Floyd LJ but quoted in the *Western Mail*, 25 February 2015.

deposited a trailer load of manure on his daughter's doorstep. The reason is probably that farming inheritance disputes of this nature contain an unusually potent mix of the typical ingredients for family conflict.

The potential for family business systems confusion, uncertainty, delay, and poor communication present in many family business situations can be particularly acute in family farming cases, which are usually compounded by the parties living in close physical proximity.

19.4.1 Fairness and equality

In most family farming businesses the vast majority of the wealth of the family is tied up in the capital value of the farm. Often the farm will not be large enough to support two or more next generation family members, even if there was sufficient interest in farming amongst the next generation.

Historically the issue of who to leave the farm would be likely to have been solved by primogeniture, the oldest son was both expected to take over the family farm and had an expectation, generally shared by the rest of the family that they would do so. With primogeniture on the wane[25] the fairness and equality dilemma discussed in detail in chapter 15 can surface with a vengeance. Whilst there is no direct evidence to suggest that the position of their other daughters, Enfys and Eleri, was a major factor in the decision of Tegwyn and Mary to leave their farm to all three daughters it would be surprising if that was not at least a background concern.

The fairness and equality dilemma also featured strongly in James Davies' case.[26] There the father, Tom, was found to have promised the farm outright to his middle son, James, who had worked on the farm since leaving school. In fact Tom made a will creating a trust whereby James could occupy the farm up until he reached a retirement age of 60 and then leaving the farm in five equal shares. Four parts went to James' other brothers and sisters. The will 'generation skipped' James, leaving the remaining fifth share to his children, Tom's grandchildren. In the High Court HH Jarman acknowledged the parent's dilemma saying that:[27]

> 'I doubt very much whether Tom Davies regarded those provisions as unconscionable and he was always in the difficult position of balancing his strong desire to keep the farm in the family with a desire to be fair to all of his children.'

19.4.2 Ambiguity

The fairness and equality debate is closely related to the theme of ambiguity and ambivalence. Frequently it appears that the senior generation, either simultaneously or consecutively, want the insiders to inherit and for also for the whole family to share. Similar ambivalence can apply to management succession issues, and letting go. The

---

[25] One study of Canadian farming succession practice found that successors were increasingly women and the youngest or younger next generation family members, a form of ultimo geniture. See Dumas, Dupuis, Richer and St Cyr 'Factors that Influence the Next Generation's Decision to Take Over the Family Farm' *Family Business Review* (1995) at p 99.
[26] *Davies v Davies* [2015] EWHC 1384 (Ch). The case is introduced in chapter 1 and referred to throughout the book.
[27] At para 48 of the judgment.

resulting role confusions and tension between the senior generation and the next generation insiders, further undermine a plan to leave the business to the insiders.

19.4.3 Communication

Another family business theme, which features strongly in family farming proprietary estoppel cases, is communication difficulties. The classic example of this can be found in the leading case of *Thorner v Major*[28] discussed in more detail below, where the House of Lords accepted that in dealings between the two 'taciturn and undemonstrative men'[29] featuring in the case, communication would always be limited.

Although relationships between the family members in James' case appeared to be generally good during the lifetime of the father Tom, communication was clearly constrained. Crucially Tom had not told James about the contents of his will, which was based on a whole family ownership equality approach, so James still believed that he would inherit the family farm up until his father's death. Indeed, for some while after Tom's death, the mother and the two eldest sons, who were executors under the will, decided to hang onto the semblance of family harmony for as long as possible, essentially by supressing the contents of their father's will so far as James was concerned. Jarman J explained that:[30]

> 'By the time his father died, all of his children still got on with one another. No one mentioned the will. David and Peter accept that at their mother's request they did not proceed then to obtain probate and that accordingly they let "sleeping dogs lie." They understood that their mother was concerned that if probate were progressed there may be a family row and that she was particularly worried about not seeing James' children.'

Similarly in the other *Davies* (cowshed Cinderella) case, Eirian was in ignorance about the contents of her parent's wills and that they had not signed the agreement admitting her to the farming partnership.

Whilst communication difficulties feature in many family business situations they seem to be particularly acute in family farming cases. This might be due to the relative complexity and seeming intractability of the ownership and succession issues, in particular the fairness and equality debate. Considerable capital assets are likely to be involved, often against a background of few alternative assets and relatively low income. Communication difficulties might also be explained by the fact that the main protagonists, the senior generation owners, and the next generation heir apparent, will usually live and work in very close proximity. Even if the thought process of the senior generation is settled and clear the temptation to put off difficult and disruptive conversations must be considerable. A farm offers no escape for the protagonists if conflicts arise.

---

[28] [2009] UKHL 18.
[29] Lord Walker at para 59.
[30] At para 38 of the judgment.

19.4.4 Conflict

The more communication is supressed, the greater the risk that the underlying issues will surface in the shape of outright conflict. The *Davies* (cowshed Cinderella) case and the matter of the manure,[31] both provide fairly spectacular evidence of this.

In the much less conflicted Davies family in James' case, there is a reference to the father Tom causing a solicitors letter to be sent to James proposing demanding an increase in rent (James was by then farming the land for his own account) and threatening to charge for water supplied to the farm. Tellingly both father and son then ignored the letter and did not even acknowledge to each other that it had been sent, much less discuss the underlying reasons for Tom sending the letter.

19.4.5 Letting go

The core theme of the difficulty for the senior generation in letting go has been extensively discussed elsewhere. Those difficulties must be highlighted when farming is seen as a way of life. James attributed the solicitors' letter sent on his father's behalf as partly intended to show 'who was boss'.[32]

19.4.6 Systemic complexity and confusion

Most family farming businesses appear deceptively simple on a three-circle model analysis. The reality is often very different. There is considerable potential for confusion between the three systems comprised within the model.

For example one only needs to consider the position of the farmhouse. This will simultaneously be both the principal operating base of the farming business and the home of the farming family. The change of principal occupiers from the senior generation to the next generation will often be highly symbolic in terms of management succession, as in James Davies' case. The farmhouse may also be a significant part of the value of the family farm. Transfer of occupation may well not be divorced from transfer of ownership. Finally, as the farmhouse may well have been the family home where all siblings grew up it is likely to have huge emotional significance for the whole family.

An almost universal feature of the proprietary estoppel cases in particular and most farming life in general, is that the next generation work long hours for very low pay, even when compared with typical agricultural wages paid to non-family employees. Analytically the business system is being supported by sacrifices made in the family domain. Whilst disproportionally low pay might feature in other non-farming family businesses it is much more pronounced in the agricultural sector.

The compensating trade off, which of course lays the foundation for proprietary estoppel claims is that the ownership aspirations of the next generation are encouraged at a stage that would seem artificially early even in the context of the general family business population. Ownership noises were made to Eirian Davies whilst she was still a teenager.

---

[31] From the case study in para 2.
[32] However letting go of the day-to-day operation does not feature as a major issue in Tom's case.

Jarman J found that James Davies was also told he would inherit the farm shortly after leaving agricultural college. The judge offered this explanation, commenting also on the communication shortfall within that Davies family:[33]

> 'It is clear that his father was keen to keep the farm in the family and that James was the most likely candidate to promote this aim. Although he was very young when the promise was first made, it was at the time when young people have to make a choice about their future. Although he was very keen on farming, it is understandable why his father wished to maximise the chance of James coming to work on the farm, and continuing to do so, and should want to make his aim in this regard clear to him. It is also understandable that he should find it more difficult to discuss this with his other children who had chosen or were likely to choose other paths in life.'

But perhaps the single most significant clash within the family business system is between the family and ownership systems and, in particular, the place of in-laws within that system.

19.4.7 Family systems conflicts

A common feature in both of the *Davies* cases and also in the case study was friction between the generations relating to the next generation's choice of life partners. In James' case Jarman J explained that:[34]

> 'It is common ground that for the first few years after Cindy moved into the farmhouse, her relationship with her future in-laws was good. After the birth of their first son in 1993 the relationship became cold and by the time that she and James got married in 1997 had deteriorated to such an extent that his father was unhappy about the marriage so the couple decided to get married without guests. It is clear from diaries kept by Tom Davies that he felt that Cindy bossed his son and did not care for him or the farm. It is not necessary for me to decide who if anyone was to blame for this deterioration, but it is significant in my judgment that for whatever reason this view of Cindy had been formed by him.
>
> It was in this context that the first wills [leaving the farm to all five branches of the family] were drawn up in 1996, and in my judgment it is likely that his decision as to the provisions of it was informed at least to some extent by his worsening relationship with his future daughter in law.'

There often appears to be a close link between the perception by the senior generation that the chosen partner is not fit for family purpose and the close emotional attachment of the senior generation to the farm and land, which might have been in the family for generations. Honouring their promise to the next generation that the farm would be theirs involves, not only betraying the ownership claims of the rest of the family, but also opens up the risk that the spouse will get their unworthy hands on the family farm following their inevitable divorce from the next generation family member.

Recognising this dynamic the partner in the case study in **19.2** offered to enter into a pre-nuptial agreement expressly relinquishing any claim he might have on the family farm to ease transition to his partner, the next generation daughter.[35] That offer was insufficient to unlock the ownership impasse that had arisen between the daughter and her parents.

---

[33] At para 44 of the judgment.
[34] At paras 33 and 34 of the judgment.
[35] Nuptial agreements are discussed in chapter 18.

19.5 LEGAL COMPLEXITY

The principal legal claim we are concerned with in this chapter is proprietary estoppel but it can be seen that the complexity within the family business system of a farming family ownership dispute can give rise to a correspondingly complex collection of potential ancillary legal claims.

The *Davies* (cowshed Cinderella) case started life as a residential property eviction matter. There were allegations of assault against the parents. Employment issues such as minimum wage claims, unfair or constructive dismissal or sex discrimination could equally well have featured, as they did in the case study.[36] Sometimes, as in the case study, successful employment claims will provide funds, either to sustain the next generation family member whilst the main proprietary estoppel action is fought or to provide a fighting fund for legal costs to bring that action in the first place.

In James' case, an alternative claim for an agricultural tenancy was waiting in the wings, if his ownership claim fell through.[37] There, his older brother, David prepared the accounts of the family farming business. It would not have been difficult to envisage disputes arising between the siblings in relation to these.

Complex though these issues might be, they are relative sideshows when compared with the main act of proprietary estoppel, where the whole capital value of the family farm will usually be in dispute.

19.6 PROPRIETARY ESTOPPEL: THE KEY ELEMENTS

The principles of establishing a proprietary estoppel claim were set out in the leading case of *Thorner v Major*[38] where it was confirmed that three key elements must be present for a claimant to bring their claim. There must be:
- representations or assurances made to the claimant by the promisor; and
- reliance on such representations or assurances by the claimant; and
- detriment caused to the claimant as a result of his or her reasonable reliance upon such representations or assurances.

If the court then finds, as a result of the claimant proving the above, that it would be unconscionable for the promisor to rely on his or her strict legal rights, then the promisor will be estopped from denying his or her representations or assurances and equity will grant the appropriate relief.

Although we will now look at each of these elements separately the courts have emphasised that cases of proprietary estoppel will be looked at in the round without artificial emphasis being given to any individual element. A proprietary estoppel claim cannot be divided into watertight compartments.[39]

---

[36] For family employment issues more generally see chapter 5.
[37] For a general discussion on property issues in family businesses see chapter 10. However a detailed discussion on agricultural tenancies is beyond the scope of this book.
[38] See Lord Walker at para 29 of the judgment.
[39] *Henry v Henry* [2010] UKPC 3.

19.7 ASSURANCE

19.7.1 Nature of assurance

It will depend on the facts of the matter concerned as to what will amount to an actionable assurance. The reported cases show a wide range of express or implied assurances.

At the top of the scale,[40] so far as clarity of representations are concerned, are matters such as the two Davies cases. In Eirian's (cowshed Cinderella) case she was repeatedly told by her father that the farm and the business would be hers one day.[41] In James' case his father handed him the keys to the farmhouse and told James that 'its all yours now' at the time the father withdrew from active farming, went into semi-retirement and moved to live in a bungalow on the farm.[42]

The assurances relied on in *Thorner v Major* were much more oblique. Although Peter Thorner had made a will naming David as his residuary beneficiary this had been destroyed by Peter.[43] No replacement will had been put in place. Instead the courts relied on much more circumstantial evidence of Peter's assurance that David should inherit the farm. Much was made of Peter showing David a life insurance policy, which Peter explained was intended to cover the inheritance tax liability on the estate.[44] Also that Peter had showed David a particular cattle trough that never froze in winter,[45] which, the Court reasoned, encouraged David to think that he would have a continuing place on the farm after Peter had died and was no longer in a position to pass on such advice on farm management.

Perhaps more pertinently, although the point is not greatly emphasised in the judgment, Peter, in David's presence had made it clear to his solicitor that David would inherit the farm and that 'we wanted the deeds in one place as it "would be better" for David'.[46]

19.7.2 Subjective test

A representation does not need to be crystal clear. In *Thorner v Major* the House of Lords advanced the formulation that the representation merely needs to be 'clear enough'.[47] The test is subjective, in the sense that whilst a third party bystander, not used to the way the family members communicate between themselves, might not have realised a promise was being made, if the recipient reasonably believed that they had received an assurance as to future ownership that would be sufficient. Similarly it does not matter if the person making the assurance did not really intend the recipient to rely on it if they did and it was reasonable for them to have done so.

---

[40] There are still likely to be clear evidential difficulties, particularly where recollections differ and evidence is disputed.
[41] See for example paras 5 and 19 of the judgment.
[42] See paragraphs 4 of the judgment in James' case.
[43] Apparently because Peter had fallen out with one of the pecuniary beneficiaries named in the will.
[44] See para 42 of the judgment.
[45] See para 43 of the judgment.
[46] See para 87 of the judgment.
[47] Lord Walker at para 56, endorsed by Lord Rodger at para 26.

19.7.3 Subject of assurance

The courts will also take a reasonably flexible view about the precise extent of the subject matter of the promise. In *Thorner v Major* the more immediate family members who stood to inherit on Peter's intestacy, made much of the fact that since the initial assurances had been made to David, parts of the original farm had been sold off for development and new land had been acquired. The courts were clear that the promise made by Peter could be interpreted as that David would inherit whatever was comprised within the farm at the date of Peter's death. A similar approach was taken in James' case, where the fact that Mr Davies senior had sold off parcels of land for development purposes and kept the proceeds of sale without objection by James, was not seen as affecting James' claim to the remainder of the farm.[48]

However there can be a crucial distinction between the physical extent of property and the nature of the legal interest in it. In *Shirt v Shirt*[49] the court drew a distinction between a promise relating to the farming business and entitlement to the capital value of the underlying land.

19.7.4 Standing-by

In rare cases the senior generation, rather than making active promises of ownership to the next generation, will allow or encourage them to spend money or invest in the family business, conscious that the next generation are doing so in the expectation that they will inherit in due course. This was a feature in the case study in **19.2** above where, following her divorce and the sale of the matrimonial home, the daughter was encouraged to invest her share of the proceeds of sale by building a new home on the family farm. Acquiescence or 'standing-by', where the claimant has invested their cash in the asset in dispute, may be seen by the courts as equivalent to an active assurance of ownership in appropriate cases.[50]

19.8 RELIANCE

The recipient must be able to show that they have relied on the assurance that they have received and that it was reasonable of them to have done so. If that test is satisfied it does not matter whether or not the owner intended them to rely on the assurance.[51]

Thorner v Major was characterised by a long and unbroken pattern of David working for Peter without pay and without any reported conflict or tension between the two men. Other cases, such as Eirian's (and to a certain extent James') follow a more fragmented path, where an initial assurance will be followed by a family dispute and, often, withdrawal of the next generation from the family farm, in turn followed by family rapprochement and a return to work.

---

[48] See para 19 of the judgment.
[49] [2010] EWHC 3820 (Ch). The case is considered in more detail below.
[50] *Dann v Spurrier* [1802] 7 Ves 231. Although such cases could equally well be argued on the basis of a resulting trust.
[51] See Lord Walker at para 78 of the judgment in *Thorner v Major* overturning the Court of Appeal on this point.

In these cases it will be necessary to link a claim for proprietary estoppel to an assurance given (or confirmed) at the point of return to establish the necessary element of reliance. In Eirian's case the High Court found promises were made to her on Boxing Day 2007 that she would be able to live rent free in the farmhouse for life and that on two separate occasions in 2009 her expectations as to wider inheritance of the farm were confirmed.

19.9 DETRIMENT

The final element that must be established by anyone claiming proprietary estoppel is detriment. As the majority of cases concern family members working for little or, in some cases,[52] no pay, it might be presumed that this would be something of a formality, even in an industry where low pay might be the norm.

Whilst it is fair to say that it is difficult to identify cases which have failed as a result of the inability of the claimant to show detriment, this must nevertheless be proved to the satisfaction of the court. The claimant will need to show that they had alternatives, which in reliance of the assurance that had been made to them, they chose not to pursue. Eirian had previously tuned down a farm manager's job on another farm. In James Davies' case it was a possible career in the police force. In *Thorner v Major* the High Court was satisfied that David had one or more unspecified 'other opportunities which were then available to him, and which he had been mulling over'[53] at the time he decided to devote even more of his time to unpaid work on his cousin's farm.

Compensating benefits in kind such as free accommodation and food are part and parcel of life on a family farm. It is clear that these must be taken into account when assessing overall detriment.

There is a suggestion, emerging in particular from the Court of Appeal judgment in Eirian Davies' case that non-financial factors could also be taken into account and that 'estimation of the detriment suffered by Eirian was not an exercise in forensic accounting'.[54] Overall work/life balance might also need to be considered. Here the arguments could cut both ways. It is often said that farming is a way of life rather than simply a job. The vocational elements of farming have been emphasised in academic studies.[55] Vocational dedication could be cited in defence of a proprietary estoppel claim. If the next generation family member concerned is truly dedicated to the farming way of life where is the detriment to them in being allowed to pursue this?

A more attractive alternative may need to be shown by the claimant so that the assurance as to future ownership tips the balance and persuades them to choose a less favourable (in terms of both remuneration and lifestyle) life on the farm. In Eirian's case this was the alternative career of working for the major agricultural company Genus, which allowed her to earn more money and also to spend more time with her children on the beach rather than commit to the 'long hours she worked on the farm in a difficult working relationship'.[56]

---

[52] For example *Thorner v Major*.
[53] Quoted at para 16 of the House of Lords judgment.
[54] At para 51 of the judgment.
[55] See Dumas, Dupuis, Richer and St Cyr 'Factors that Influence the Next Generation's Decision to Take Over the Family Farm' *Family Business Review* (1995) at p 99.
[56] See para 52 of the judgment.

So it appears that having to put up with negative family dynamics might also be a factor to be considered in the overall detriment equation.

19.10 EQUITY AND CONSCIENCE

Establishing the three core elements of assurance, reliance and detriment, opens the door to the proprietary estoppel remedy. But the basis of the remedy is that it is unconscionable for the senior generation family member to deny ownership to the next generation: in legal terms that the conscience of equity has been invoked.

It is therefore possible that circumstances could have arisen where it would still be unfair to grant a remedy, for example to a claimant who had behaved extremely badly. For example if the claimant had clearly provoked their own exclusion. However it is difficult to find cases where proprietary estoppel had been denied on the grounds of the applicant's conduct alone. Clearly whatever blame could have been attributed to Eirian for a dispute which involved her biting her father's leg was not sufficient to do so.

The conduct of the applicant could, in theory, also be relevant to the extent of the remedy granted to them. However in Eirian's case the Court took a fairly pragmatic overview of the realities of the long running conflict within the Davies family and effectively refused to get drawn into apportioning blame between the family members. In the High Court remedies hearing Jarman J explained that:[57]

> 'Further allegations of conduct were raised on each side on the issue of relief. In my judgment taken at their highest these do not amount to the sort of misconduct which should impact upon the issue of relief, given the long history of the parties' dealing with one another. The conduct alleged arises in the context of a difficult and now a very bitter relationship between the sides, and in my judgment it is not necessary to make findings on these issues.'

But, in the comparatively rare circumstances where fault can be clearly attributed to one party, in particular the claimant, the principle of 'he who comes to equity must come with clean hands' could conceivably be invoked so as to adversely affect their remedy.

19.11 REMEDY: ALL THIS?

19.11.1 Overview: fairness

The logic is that, once the elements of proprietary estoppel have been established and the court is satisfied that the conscience of equity has been troubled, then, the appropriate remedy will be the minimum that which is sufficient to satisfy that conscience.

Following their outing to the Court of Appeal and notwithstanding the hopes expressed by Floyd LJ, that they 'might now be able to resolve such remaining differences as they may have in relation to Eirian's entitlement without recourse to further costly and divisive litigation'[58] the Davies family needed to return to the High Court for a further hearing to determine that entitlement. Matters did not rest even there. The Davies family needed a second visit to the Court of Appeal to deal with an appeal by Eirian's parents

---

[57] [2015] EWHC 015 (Ch), Jarman J at para 50 of the judgment.
[58] In the concluding para 59 of his judgment.

against the £1.3m awarded to Eirian in the High Court remedies hearing. The issue of remedies in proprietary estoppel is explored in the report of this second hearing.[59]

On occasions the conscience of equity might need the court to recognise and enforce the original promise or assurance. In some cases, such as those of *Thorner v Major* or James Davies, where 'the claimant will have performed his part of the quasi-contract' the 'assurances and reliance had consensual character not far short of a contract'.[60] Often in these cases the claimant will have based their whole life and working career on the promise of inheritance. On other occasions the conscience of equity, although clearly not the claimant, will be satisfied by much less.

The principles on which a court will assess remedies for the successful claimant were set out clearly by the Court of Appeal in Eirian's case. These broadly state that the court will look at the extent of the equity which has been established and then do the minimum necessary to satisfy that equity. The court will seek to achieve a proportionate result based upon the claimant's expectation and the actual detriment suffered. That is easier said than done, of course, as it may not always be particularly clear, from the evidence available, what those expectations and intentions were.

Simply put the court will do what it thinks is fair.

The core promise, consistently made to Eirian, was that the whole of the farm would be hers one day. At the remedies hearing in the High Court she was awarded, £1.3m, approximately a third of the net value of the farm. However this amount was reduced to £500,000 by the Court of Appeal, only a small fraction of what Eirian might at one time have expected. Why is the difference between the promise and the remedy so huge?

The key point is that although based on an assurance, an award in proprietary estoppel is based on very different principles to those that apply in determining damages for breach of a contractual promise. In the latter situation the promise is everything. In proprietary estoppel the assurance is but one factor which courts will need to consider in assessing overall fairness. That assessment:[61]

> 'is a retrospective exercise looking backwards from the moment when the promise falls due to be performed and asking whether, in the circumstances which have actually happened, it would be unconscionable for the promise not be kept.'

In *Jennings v Rice*,[62] which concerned a gardener's claim to his wealthy and elderly employer's house and estate, it was not entirely clear what was intended by the elderly employer when she told the gardener that 'this will all be yours one day' or words to that effect. The gardener claimed that she had intended him to have all her estate, which comprised her house worth £435,000 and further assets of around £865,000. In the alternative, the gardener's case was that, he was at least entitled to the equivalent value of the house as he had been living there for some time before his employer's death. The defence argued that the claimant's request may be the maximum award that could be made but that equity only permitted a proportionate award in view of the expectation and the detriment suffered. The court found, that the claimant could not reasonably have expected to receive the entire estate since the elderly employer had meant the house

---
[59] [2016] EWCA Civ 463.
[60] Lewison LJ at para 40.
[61] At para 38 of the Court of Appeal judgment.
[62] [2003] 1 P&CR 8.

when she said 'this will all be yours one day'. Whilst ample detriment could be found in this case, the award could not exceed the level of reasonable expectation.

It is apparent that the court has wide discretion in respect of orders for relief and its aim is to satisfy the minimum equity arising by examining the individual circumstances of each case.[63] A combination of all these factors gives the potential for much diversity in outcome, which should be borne in mind by practitioners, when advising their clients.

19.11.2 Factors

Other factors emerging from the remedies hearing in Eirian's case included:

- **Change in circumstances.** The relationship between Eirian and her parents was something of a roller-coaster ride. As a result Eirian's circumstances were constantly changing. There were times when she was away from the farm, working and living independently. At the times when she had withdrawn from the farm it must have been clear that Eirian's expectations were at best uncertain if they have not completely evaporated. So, as Jarman J observed:[64]

    'it cannot be said here ... that Eirian positioned her whole life on the basis of her parents' assurances.'

    Eirian's case can be contrasted with that of David Thorner, who worked on Peter's farm without interruption and for a number of years, after his own father had given up farming, exclusively. James Davies also worked without interruption on the family farm. The claimant in both cases received a much larger award than Eirian, These were based on a full share of the farm.

    A similar position applied in the Court of Appeal case of *Suggitt v Suggitt*.[65] In that case a father had assured his youngest child and only son that he would inherit farmland worth about £2.5 million as well as somewhere to live. The son relied on this assurance to carry out works of restoration, fencing and maintenance. He expanded the business and developed livery and poultry activities. The High Court judge held that the son had 'positioned his whole life on the basis of the assurances ...'. The son was accordingly awarded the farmland and a house.

- **Changes in expectations.** Just as, over time, there were fluctuations as to whether Eirian could expect to inherit anything at all, the precise extent of what she could expect to inherit also changed. Her eventual return to the farm was based on an express assurance of a home for life rather than an interest in the farm or the business.

    After her return, at various times she was offered, a one third share in the farming partnership, at others 49% of the shares in the farming company that took over the assets of the partnership. Exactly what was proposed over the farmland itself was unclear. So for a long period of time after Eirian's return to the farm:[66]

    'the position with regard to expectation was changing and somewhat uncertain.'

---

[63] *Plimmer v Wellington Corporation* (1883–84) LR 9 App Cas 699 at 714.
[64] At para 44 of the judgment.
[65] [2012] EWCA Civ 1140.
[66] [2015] EWHC 015 (Ch) at para 46 of the judgment.

Again the position in Eirian's case can be contrasted with that of David Thorner, James Davies and in *Suggitt v Suggitt*, which were characterised by consistent assurances of outright ownership.

- **Consequential benefits.** Consequential benefits, particularly in farming cases, board and lodging will be taken into account in establishing whether the claimant has suffered detriment in the first place. They will also be a factor in deciding how much to award in the final analysis.

- **Non-financial loss.** Non-financial elements can be taken into account in assessing detriment. This can lead to some complexity. In Eirian's case her passion for working with the Caeremlyn herd, rather than any other herd, or put broadly the way of life factor, was a countervailing consideration diminishing, or potentially extinguishing, detriment. But once 'net detriment' (together with the remaining elements of proprietary estoppel) had been established, the fact that Eirian would no longer be working with the 'her own' herd was a factor to be recognised in assessing the compensation due to her:[67]

    > 'That passion is also relevant to detriment, because the work which I have found Eirian carried out on the farm was work which she loved doing.'

    Although the Court of Appeal accepted that non-financial detriment needed to be taken into account one of the main reasons for reducing the overall award to Eirian was that this had been over stated by the High Court.

- **Capital contributions.** On some, perhaps relatively rare occasions, the next generation may have made relatively significant capital contributions to the family business. This was a factor in James Davies' case. It could be argued that these contributions would give rise to a resulting trust whereby the contributor was entitled to a pro-rata share in the relevant asset. However the better argument for the next generation family member might be that, in making these contributions, they had acted to their detriment.

- **Relative contributions.** The relative contributions, of the generations, both in terms of capital contributions and time spent working in the business will be also be relevant, particularly in cases where the senior generation are still alive.
    There might be occasions where the next generation have significantly added to the capital value by their efforts in developing a business legally owned by their parents.
    Certainly this factor proved to be a valuable negotiating lever in the case study in **19.2** where, despite her parents' arguments to the contrary, it was reasonably clear that the next generation daughter was primarily responsible for transforming what was in essence a farming small-holding into a thriving farm shop and rural business.
    Although we can trace no legal authority for this proposition, the claim of the next generation might also be enhanced in circumstances where the senior generation were themselves gifted the family business. Logically it becomes correspondingly harder for the senior generation who were gifted their inheritance, as opposed to investing their own capital in the family business, to deny the next generation their own inheritance (always assuming that the three key elements of proprietary estoppel have been established).

- **Other income and assets.** It would not matter one iota to the award of damages in a pure contract case if this left the defendants penniless. Conversely the courts will

---

[67] At para 40 of the judgment.

consider the effect of any award in a proprietary estoppel case on the remaining family members, even if to do so will have the effect of watering down the initial assurance made to the claimant.

Thus in Eirian's case the High Court looked at the alternative sources of income of her mother and father, apart from farming income[68] and the fact that they had a large farmhouse to live in, separate from the farm.

Similarly in James Davies' case there was a bungalow which could easily be separated from the operating farm, to eventually give his other brother and sisters some 'compsensatory' interest in the family wealth and to provide his mother with somewhere to live in the meantime.

- **Other family members.** The position of the remaining family members, not working in the family business, may also be relevant. On the basis of family equality, they might also have some background expectations as to inheritance. The Court of Appeal noted that:[69]

  > 'Eirian had two other sisters, for whom her parents might have wanted to make some provision.'

  However in James' case, whilst the High Court expressed some sympathy for Tom in his predicament over the fairness and equality debate, it was still thought appropriate for James to be awarded the greater share of the farm.

- **Life interests and tenancies.** A successful claimant would usually expect an outright capital award. Nevertheless, on occasions, it might be more appropriate, to achieve fairness, to make life time awards, such as life interests in properties or the payment of annuities.

  In Eirian's case the Court of Appeal thought that it 'would not have been least unconscionable' for her parents to have retained the freehold of the farm and to have granted her a tenancy to provide them with an income in retirement and (presumably) a continuing interest for her sister afterwards.[70]

- **Clean break.** Although annual payments were considered by the High Court in Eirian's case these were dismissed as impractical because the relationships between her and her parents were so strained. A clean break, through the award of a substantial lump sum was the only practical award, even though this would mean that the farm, or a substantial part of it would need to be sold so that Eirian could be paid out.[71]

- **Effect of an award being made against the family business.** The case of *Gillett v Holt*[72] is a good example of how an award in equity to a successful claimant can have a significant effect on the on-going performance of the business concerned.

  The case concerned a claimant who spent his working life as a farm manager for a friend, who was the first defendant in the case and the owner of a farming business. The court heard how the owner had made repeated and specific verbal assurances to the claimant over the course of many years, and on several occasions in public at family gatherings, that the claimant would succeed him in the farming business. The claimant had lived for some 25 years in the farmhouse with the permission of the owner.

  Relations deteriorated between the two and the claimant was dismissed from the business.

---

[68] In practice about £40,000 per annum from solar panels on the farm.
[69] At para 60 of the Court of Appeal judgment.
[70] Also at para 60 of the Court of Appeal judgment.
[71] See para 56 of the High Court judgment.
[72] [2001] Ch 21.

Finding for the claimant, on the basis that an estoppel was established, the court considered what was the minimum necessary to do justice and to provide relief for the equity which had arisen. There, the court ruled that the appropriate award was for the owner-manager to convey to the claimant the freehold of the farmhouse with some of its surrounding land plus a further £100,000 to compensate the manager for his exclusion from the rest of the farming business.

In making this order, the court took account of the appropriateness of achieving a 'clean break' solution for both parties, given the acrimony that existed between them. The court also made suggestions as to how the company assets could be reorganised in order to avoid, if possible, an outright sale or liquidation in order to pay out the claimant from his existing minority shareholding. In so doing, the court stated that it did not intend the equity awarded to the claimant to have penal consequences on the owner-manager defendant and his company. However, a significant payment was required to satisfy the equity owing to the claimant.

Gillett v Holt illustrates the threat which claims can have to the continuity of the family business, where equity gives rise to remedy or relief requiring the sale or transfer of company assets to claimants who may be inside or outside the immediate family circle.

19.11.3 Remedy: conclusion

It will be seen from the above that, even if the claimant can establish that the key elements of proprietary estoppel have been established, there will be great uncertainty about the precise extent of the remedy that they could expect to obtain. Courts have a difficult exercise in balancing all relevant factors, including those referred to above to achieve fairness between the parties. The High Court judge in Eirian's case concluded by accepting that:[73]

> 'it is clear that weighing all the above circumstances involves more than just arithmetical calculation, and justice is likely to lie somewhere between the polarised positions which the parties now adopt. It is not an easy exercise to determine the precise point where it does lie.'

It therefore follows that to combat this uncertainty and the attendant emotional and costs risk, any party to a potential proprietary estoppel action needs to consider their approach, including use of mediation and alternative dispute resolution very carefully indeed. Above all, on the premise that, as the above quote suggests, there are no real winners in proprietary estoppel and similar actions. Taking legal costs into account, both Eirian and her parents could well have been in a better financial position if the entitlement of the next generation had been clearly agreed and documented. Almost certainly family relationships would have been less damaged. Once again we return to the key theme of the importance of governance in family owned businesses.

19.12 VOLATILITY AND GOVERNANCE

Eirian's case and, to an extent that of James Davies, illustrate the volatility of family relationships, especially where family members are living in close proximity, as is usually the case in farming. As suggested above, other family business themes also come to the fore, such as the reluctance of the senior generation to let go, fairness and equality as

---

[73] See para 56 of the judgment.

regards other next generation family members and ambiguity, resulting in the blurring of family boundaries between the family, business and ownership systems.

This ambiguity begets a paradox. When things are going well and relationships are harmonious assurances of future ownership will be made in good faith by the senior generation and accepted at face value by the next. Neither generation will see the need to formalise matters. But barriers to communication will grow as relationships deteriorate. Rather than confirm the next generation family member working in the business as their successor, the senior generation are more likely to see them as undeserving, to seek emotional refuge in their relationships with their other children.

In Eirian's case, by the time the matter came to court, one of her sisters and her family were living with the parents in the family home. Another sister and her husband had taken over the turkey business forming part of the farming business but this had been discontinued and sold.

The senior generation may also start to have doubts about whether it is in fact fair to leave the family farm to the working insider after all. As a result they might shift their ownership approach back to one of family equality, or even exclusion of the ungrateful insider. Both Davies cases featured unsettled ownership patterns and new wills based on treating all children more or less equally. The next generation insiders will pick up on this change in the succession mood music and will inevitably become increasingly concerned about their own position. By this time they may well have invested many years in the family business, they might be approaching middle age, with increasing responsibilities to their own immediate family and decreasing opportunities away from the family business. The High Court judge in Eirian's case believed that the resulting frustration was a key reason for the eventual catastrophic breakdown in relationships within the Davies family saying that:[74]

> 'probably the major factor in the frustrations referred to above was that Eirian who was by then in her mid forties still had nothing in writing to confirm her position, apart from her father's will which he could change, as he had done previously.'

When trust between the generations is at its lowest ebb and tensions highest, the formal arrangements over ownership and wider governance arrangements are most at a premium. But these are precisely the circumstances when the senior generation are least likely to agree to put such arrangements in place. Instead tensions are more likely to boil over into outright conflict. In Eirian's case the outcome was a physical confrontation between Eirian and her parents where the judge found:[75]

> 'her father assaulted her and she assaulted him, and that this is likely to have been the culmination of frustration on the part of Eirian arising from the failure of her parents to formalise her role in the business despite indications that this would be done, frustration on the part of her parents that her relationship with men who had children and how that may impact upon their desire to keep the business in the family, and frustration on both sides arising from the difficult relationship over the years.'

So do families in general and next generation farming family members in particular simply trust to chance that their succession will work out alright in the end? Is there a realistic alternative?

---

[74] At para 42 of the judgment from the remedies hearing.
[75] At para 41 of the judgment from the remedies hearing.

Ideally ownership and succession arrangements will be agreed and implemented within a reasonable period after the next generation join the business. Care must obviously be taken about the detail of those arrangements to make sure that these are robust and fit for family purpose. The case of *Ham* family discussed in detail in chapter 13 shows the risks of conferring an outright ownership interest too early in the career of the next generation.

Realistically many business families will proceed on the basis of some combination of hope, expectation and assurances and will avoid, or not see the need for, formalising succession or wider governance arrangements. Some families will have simply never considered the possibility of 'writing anything down'.

On the basis that, as illustrated by both of the *Davies* cases, the path to succession seldom runs smoothly, there may well be a similar pattern of falling out and making up in many business families. A possibility could be that, forewarned by an initial falling out and when tensions are ebbing, the business family capitalise on these factors to make hay whilst the succession sun shines. Timing is everything.

Again advisors, trusted friends, the wider family and, especially in the farming industry, the wider agricultural community all have a role to play in encouraging this process. All of this is of course much easier to say, than to achieve in practice.

19.13 UNCERTAINTY AND THE LEGAL POSITION

Changes in circumstances present something of a challenge in terms of legal analysis.

As has been shown, the expectations of the next generation might ebb and flow with the tide of family relationships. In Eirian's case the High Court judge noted that 'in 2001 when Eirian left the farm after a row she had to an extent as she readily accepted in cross examination "given up" on [the farm]'.[76]

There is also likely to be a degree of express or implied conditionality so far as the representations or assurances are concerned. The most important of these is almost certainly to be an expectation that the next generation will continue to work in the family business. Again in Eirian's case: 'she also readily accepted, her expectation of the farm and the business was dependent upon her continuing to work in the business'.[77]

But for how long must the next generation work and on what basis before the assurances that have been made to them crystalise into an actionable right? What other factors can interfere with that expectation? In *Thorner v Major* the House of Lords speculated that Peter Thorner's personal situation might be one such factor, with Lord Walker questioning whether David would have any right to object to the sale of the farm, if this was necessary, for example, to fund Peter's nursing home fees.[78]

What if the next generation continued to work on the farm but also worked elsewhere? What if other members of the next generation suffered an adverse change in financial

---
[76] At para 33 of the judgment.
[77] Also at para 33.
[78] See para 20 of the House of Lords judgment.

circumstances, or became prodigals, and wished to return to the family business? The list of relevant factors is potentially endless.

The approach taken by the courts to the question of whether the remedy of proprietary estoppel will be available and, if so, the extent of that remedy can only be judged retrospectively. In what is thought to be a reference to Hegelian[79] philosophy Lord Hoffmann in *Thorner v Major* explained that:[80]

> 'Past events provide context and background for the interpretation of subsequent events and subsequent events throw retrospective light upon the meaning of past events. The owl of Minerva spreads its wings only with the falling of dusk.'

Again the huge uncertainty surrounding the proprietary estoppel remedy comes to the fore.

19.14 CONSTRUCTIVE TRUST

Although arriving at the same conclusion as his colleagues in the House of Lords in *Thorner v Major* that David should inherit the farm, Lord Scott was troubled by the application of the proprietary estoppel doctrine to the changing circumstance of family business inheritance cases, remarking that: '… it is an odd sort of estoppel that is produced by representations that are, in a sense, conditional'.[81]

Lord Scott suggested that proprietary estoppel should be confined to cases where the next generation have received an assurance of 'an immediate or more or less immediate interest in the property in question'.[82]

He suggested an alternative approach for inheritance cases where the relevant assurances are conditional and expected to operate some time in the future. This was to analyse these as constructive trust matters, so that in appropriate cases, such as *Thorner v Major* the courts would imply a 'remedial constructive trust' so that, based on the common intentions and understanding of the parties, and the detriment of the beneficiary, the senior generation are regarded as holding the relevant property on trust for the next generation.[83]

On the basis that the remainder of the House of Lords were content to apply proprietary estoppel to the facts of *Thorner v Major* and given the degree of overlap between the two remedies, the practical solution will usually be to argue for constructive trust as an alternative remedy.

19.15 FAILED CASES

It should be clear from the above that it would be a mistake to think that equitable claims for the ownership of the family business are easy to bring. Aside from the

---

[79] The concept that history can only really be understood at the time the world ends.
[80] See para 8 of the House of Lords judgment.
[81] See para 20 of the House of Lords judgment.
[82] See para 20 of the House of Lords judgment.
[83] For a more detailed explanation of the doctrine of constructive trusts see Dawn Goodman, Paul Hewitt, Henrietta Mason *Probate Disputes and Remedies* (Jordan Publishing, 3rd edn, 2014).

inherent risks of bringing any litigation, the outcome of proprietary estoppel claims are notoriously unpredictable, at best, as they will turn on the individual facts in each case, the credibility of the witnesses and the assessment of what the individual judge hearing the matter thinks is fair and how complex legal issues should be applied and interpreted.

There have been several cases since *Thorner v Major* which demonstrate this. These have produced quite different outcomes for claimants compared with that for David Thorner.[84] The most relevant of these to family business claims is *Shirt v Shirt*.[85]

19.15.1 *Shirt v Shirt*; the facts

Just how uncertain and therefore unreliable a remedy proprietary estoppel can be is well illustrated by *Shirt v Shirt*. The case confirms that the court will assess each claim on its individual facts and evidence. It featured a failed attempt in equity to establish entitlement to outright a beneficial ownership of a farming partnership by the claimant, Alan Shirt, who was the son of defendant, Stanley and his deceased wife Marie.

Stanley and Marie Shirt had formed a farming partnership with Alan in the 1970's. There were three other children. Geoffrey, who was briefly a partner too, but his involvement did not last for long, and Lynda and Jonathan, neither of whom worked on the farm. The partnership was technically dissolved on Marie's death some 30 years later in 2004. However, Stanley and Alan continued to work together on the farm in what then became a partnership at will.

In 1986 the business underwent severe financial difficulties and some of its assets were sold, including some of the land. Around the same time, Alan was forced to leave his existing home adjacent to the farm and, as he was homeless, Alan moved with his wife into a caravan on the farmland. The partnership then went into receivership but the business regrouped and a further farming partnership continued after this.

In 2010, following a dispute between Alan and Stanley over Alan living on the farmland, Alan claimed, in proprietary estoppel and in the alternative, under a constructive trust; that he had in fact, been promised the whole farm by Stanley and Marie over the course of many years and was therefore beneficially entitled to live there and to inherit all of the farm on Stanley's death. Alan gave evidence that, on a number of occasions over the years, such statements were made to him by both his parents, commencing in the 1970s and continuing on through the period of financial crisis in 1986 to the date of the claim in 2010. Alan also claimed that such statements had been made to third parties, by Stanley, such as the partnership's bank.

Alan claimed that, since he had worked hard for some 40 years on the farm from the 1970s through to 2010 when the case was heard, and in particular, because he had brought the farm through its financial crisis in 1986, receiving little pay for his efforts, he was entitled to rely on the assurances and representations given to him by his parents.

---

[84] For example, *Cook v Thomas* [2010] EWCA Civ 227 which featured a couple claiming that they had the right to remain in a property. The claim failed on the judge's finding of the facts against them, and the credibility of the witnesses did not help to support the claimant's case. Also see *Macdonald v Frost* [2009] EWHC 2276 (Ch), in which the court found against the claimant daughters of the deceased, who failed to argue successfully that payments made by them to the deceased relating to a property transaction proved to be grounds for a proprietary estoppel claim to the entire estate.

[85] [2010] EWHC 3820 (Ch).

In turn he was beneficially entitled to the whole farm as it was unconscionable to deny that, having had the benefit of Alan's continued labour for 40 years, that upon Stanley's death, the farm in its entirety should not go to Alan.

19.15.2 *Shirt v Shirt*: analysis

However, the court found against Alan, ruling that no proprietary estoppel or constructive trust claim was made out. The reasons given by Judge Perle QC are useful in analysing the way in which the court will approach the evidence given by parties. They can be summarised as follows:

The timing of the assurances given

The majority of Alan's evidence of assurances and representations given by Stanley and Marie related to the years before and up to 1986; the year of financial crisis in the business. The court found that there was very little evidence of assurances provided after this time. The court commented on the passage of time which had elapsed since these statements were allegedly made by Marie and Stanley and found that Alan's recollection of them was therefore more likely to be 'impressionistic … and not necessarily accurate'.

Sufficiently clear assurances: hopes and expectations distinguished

Judge Perle QC stated that he had no doubt that Alan harboured the very real hope that he would inherit the farm. However, he qualified this by saying that what he had to consider was whether there was a sufficiently clear promise or commitment on Stanley and Marie's part to give rise to an enforceable obligation by way of proprietary estoppel or constructive trust. Put another way, whether the hope became a firm expectation which Alan acted upon because of anything they said or did? The judge ruled that there had not been sufficiently clear assurances provided to Alan by Marie or Stanley as, 'whenever discussions took place about what might happen to the partnership after the death or retirement of Stanley and Marie; what the parties were talking about were the partnership assets other than [the] farm itself'.[86]

In other words, the court found there to be confusion between the parties as to what the assurances or representations related to. The partnership assets could therefore be distinguished from the farm, which included a farmhouse, in which Stanley had always lived (with Marie whilst she was alive). This confusion was apparent from discrepancies in the written and oral evidence presented by the parties.

Discrepancies in the written and oral evidence

Whilst the court found Alan to be a 'calm and measured witness' it was not persuaded to find in his favour. This was because Alan gave conflicting accounts in his oral and written evidence as to the meaning of 'the whole farm'. For example, in his written evidence, Alan's claim was for the 'whole farm' which included Stanley's house. However, in his oral evidence, Alan's claim appeared to be limited to 'some of the farm' (ie excluding his parents' house). Such discrepancies in his evidence proved fatal to Alan's claim.

---

[86] *Shirt v Shirt* [2010] EWHC 3820 (Ch) at para 18.

The credibility of the parties and witnesses

Equally, the court examined the credibility of the witness evidence heard on behalf of Stanley and Marie (albeit Marie was no longer alive and third party evidence was required on this point). On hearing this evidence, the court concluded that it was unlikely that, both Marie (who was described favourably in terms of her character in the evidence heard) and Stanley would be capable of reneging on clear promises, had they indeed been made, to leave the entire farm to Alan. The court also considered it unlikely that Marie and Stanley intended to effectively disinherit their other three children, by gifting the entire farm to Alan.

Detriment

Finally, the court considered that, Alan already possessed one-third ownership of the partnership, which was not in dispute, and further that he had received good remuneration for his work over the last 40 years, with the exception of the period of financial crisis in 1986. The court found that all partners of a business would expect to receive less remuneration during a financial crisis and that this was not persuasive evidence as to detriment. As a result, the court considered that this case was distinguishable from one where an adult child may have worked for no reward for many years in the hope of ultimately inheriting something or anything.[87]

Conclusion: no proprietary estoppel

Therefore the court ruled that, on the balance of probabilities, no such promises for the whole of the farm were made by Stanley or Marie to Alan, or, if they were, they were not made in sufficiently clear terms to form the necessary representations or assurances that would encourage detrimental reliance by Alan. Further, given that Alan had earned a reasonable income for his efforts over the years on the farm, it was not unconscionable to deny him the entire farm. The farm and all the freehold land belonged to the 1974 partnership and still did. Alan therefore had a one-third interest in the farm, subject to due dissolution of the 1974 partnership. The other two-third shares belonged to Stanley and to Marie's estate.

Constructive trust claim

Alan's claim in constructive trust also failed. The court did not spend much time elaborating on its reasoning for this. In summary, Alan's case for beneficial entitlement to the whole farm by way of constructive trust appeared to be that he had saved the farm from financial ruin in 1986 by arranging a business loan to pay off the partnership's debts as a result of the receivership. The loan had been secured against a life policy held in Alan's name. Alan's case for a constructive trust claim did not appear to be fully made out. The court, in any event, was swift to dismiss this, stating that, the savings which had been made to the business as a result of the loan being obtained by the partners were, in any event, distributed via the partnership capital accounts, which reflected a proper award to the partners. In conclusion, the court ruled that Alan's interest in the partnership was limited to one-third and dismissed Alan's claim to any further entitlement.

---

[87] Compare these facts with the case argued by the claimant in the daughter's case study cited at the start of the chapter.

19.16 EQUITABLE CLAIMS: PRACTICALITIES

It is clear from the above that cases, which appear on their facts quite similar, can produce quite different results. The House of Lords' decision in *Thorner v Major* widened the scope for a claimant to prove the first requirement of assurance or representation by a promisor, from just words to include conduct as well. Thus, the symbolic handing to David Thorner of the life policy, when viewed together with extrinsic evidence of intent, was sufficient for him to establish the necessary first part of the doctrine of proprietary estoppel.

However, subsequent cases show that such claims are prone to many pitfalls. It is necessary to critically appraise the quality of the evidence that can be produced from witness statements, oral evidence and third parties to support or deny the recollections a claimant may have of a representation or assurance. *Shirt v Shirt* is a good example of how a court may interpret recollections which are inconsistently presented at court through oral and written evidence and which may date back over the course of many years.

19.16.1 The importance of evidence

Proprietary estoppel and other equitable claims are highly fact specific. In non-contractual cases, which are the staple of family business arrangements, it appears that a claim or defence to a claim may be won or lost based on the impressions given by the parties in their evidence, and that the credibility of witnesses will also be key to the outcome of such claims. David Thorner presented as a credible and consistent witness, which no doubt contributed to his success as a claimant.

It should also be borne in mind that claims brought in the lifetime of an owner-manager will differ from those brought after the owner-manger's demise, given that a living witness should be able to give evidence to support or defend a claim in lifetime disputes. Accordingly the claimant's evidence is likely to be treated with more scepticism and caution.

Practitioners should advise their clients of the likelihood of needing to provide much extrinsic evidence and where available, third party statements to support or defend a claim in equity which will inevitably increase the costs to the client, but appear to be a necessary pre-requisite to a successful case. Whilst the process of disclosure between the parties may reveal some documents or information which significantly impact upon the case, it is more typical for the success of such claims to rest upon the strength of the evidence given, by way of witness statement and, if the case proceeds to trial, by way of oral testimony.

It is therefore particularly important to be aware that equitable claims in proprietary estoppel and/or constructive trust can prove evidentially difficult to bring, as they require the parties to cast back their minds to events and/or exchanges of conversation, which happened in the past. Sometimes, these will have taken place many years, maybe even decades beforehand, as was the case with the daughter and her parents in the case study from **19.2**.[88]

---

[88] For helpful guidance on how the court will treat evidence originating from a few decades prior to the claim being heard at court, see *Shirt v Shirt* [2010] EWHC 3820 (Ch) which is discussed above.

It is therefore important to consider what corroborating evidence is available from third parties, who can provide independent witness statements to support the client's case. Take care to check with a client whether any statements have been made or conduct observed in public, either at family gatherings or elsewhere, which will significantly strengthen or weaken their case and, if statements can be taken from one or more third parties, do so.

19.16.2 Procedure – starting the claim

Both equitable claims in proprietary estoppel and/or constructive trust are issued under Part 7 of the Civil Procedure Rules (CPR) and are subject to the pre-action protocols. CPR 7.2 and 16.2 specify what must be included in the claim form. Amongst other details, the claim form must contain a concise statement of the nature of the claim and specify the remedy that the claimant seeks. Particulars of claim are either contained in the claim form or more usually, served alongside it and must be served on the defendant within 14 days of service of the claim form if they are separate documents.

Once the claim form and particulars have been served on the defendants, they will serve and file their defence (if any) and set out any counterclaim within the defence. The claimant will then serve and file a reply to defence and counterclaim, if applicable. A party may not file or serve any statement of case after the reply without the permission of the court.

19.16.3 Case management

Following this initial exchange and both parties filing allocation questionnaires, the court will assign the case to a track and list a case management hearing, at which the court will set the timetable and make directions for the exchange of evidence, disclosure and any other matters, prior to trial.[89] As referred to above attempts to engage in mediation and other forms of alternative dispute resolution will be encouraged from the outset by the court[90] and will often be the forum in which the dispute is ultimately resolved.

19.17 INHERITANCE AND I(PFD)A 1975 CLAIMS

In addition to claims based in equity there is some possibility that disappointed next generation family members can make a claim under the Inheritance (Provision for Family and Dependents) Act 1975 (I(PFD)A 1975).

Claims made under the I(PFD)A 1975 can either be based on a will that fails to make adequate provision for the dependent concerned or where, the senior generation family member has died intestate, that the rules on intestacy have the same effect.

The I(PFD)A 1975 contains a two-stage test. First it asks whether the will of the deceased (or the rules on intestacy, as the case may be) make reasonable financial

---

[89] For a detailed description of the Part 7 procedure see Andrew Francis and Hedley Marten *Contentious Probate Claims* (Sweet & Maxwell, 2003) at ch 12.
[90] For general guidance on the obligation to give genuine consideration to the possibility of mediation see *Halsey v Milton Keynes General NHS Trust* [2004] 1 WLR 3002.

provision for the applicant?[91] If the court is satisfied that this is not the case it moves on to the second stage of the test, to ask what reasonable financial provision should be?

The statutory framework is sufficiently restricted so that claims by disappointed or disinherited children in relation to a family business are, in practice, a rarity. The I(PFD)A 1975 might however be of more relevance in providing a remedy to a spouse in the almost opposite situation, where the next generation have inherited the family business leaving the needs of the spouse inadequately provided for. The respective situations of offspring and spouses will be considered in turn.

19.18 THE I(PFD)A 1975 AND THE NEXT GENERATION; THE MAINTENANCE STANDARD

Section 1 of the I(PFD)A 1975 confers the right on, among others, a child of the deceased to apply for an order under s 2 of the I(PFD)A 1975 if the will of the deceased or the intestacy rules do not make reasonable financial provision for them. At first sight the I(PFD)A 1975 would appear to open the doors of the court for disappointed next generation family business members who, like James Davies were told that they would inherit the family business, but eventually, received nothing, or perhaps an equal share with their non-working outsider siblings. However this thought is quickly dispelled by s 1(2) of the I(PFD)A 1975 which provides that, in the case of a child, reasonable financial provision means:

> 'such financial provision as it would be reasonable in all the circumstances of the case for the applicant to receive for his maintenance.'

The remedy is, therefore, limited to awards which will meet the claimant's individual maintenance requirements. By contrast awards under the I(PFD)A 1975 for spouses or civil partners are not so limited. There the broader and more general test applies of what it is reasonable for the spouse to receive in all the circumstances of the case.

Returning to the test which applies for next generation claimants, what exactly is meant by maintenance? Earlier attempts by the courts to give a broad interpretation to the phrase as being equivalent to providing for the well-being or benefit of the applicant[92] were disapproved of in a later decision of the Court of Appeal[93] but it nevertheless appears that some regard may be had to the lifestyle of the applicant. According to Browne-Wilkinson J in *Re Dennis deceased:*[94]

> 'The court has, up until now, declined to define the exact meaning of the word "maintenance" and I am certainly not going to depart from that approach. But in my judgment the word "maintenance" connotes only payments which, directly or indirectly, enable the applicant in the future to discharge the cost of his daily living at whatever standard of living is appropriate to him.'

So an outright award of the family business to satisfy the hopes or even the expectations of the next generation as to inheritance is unlikely to be made. If the next generation is

---

[91] Note the different standard of maintenance for spouses explained below.
[92] *Re Christie (deceased)* [1979] 1 All ER 546, [1979] Ch 168.
[93] *Re Coventry (deceased)* [1979] 3 All ER 815, [1980] Ch 461. See also *Bahouse v Negus* [2008] WTLR 97 (CA) a cohabitee's claim.
[94] [1981] 2 All ER 140 at 145–146.

continuing to work in the family business and to draw a reasonable income from it, their maintenance needs would already appear to have been met. But the case of a next generation family member is not necessarily hopeless, where they can demonstrate a financial need that can be met by the estate's assets (typically that their outgoings exceed income).

Even though the relevant provisions of the Act are focused on maintenance the powers of the court are not necessarily limited to awards of income. Awards of capital sums have been made. Transfers of assets have also been ordered in cases where it was necessary for the courts to do so to ensure the maintenance of the claimant. In other cases awards have been made to enable the claimant to pay off debts so that their own independent income was then available to service their maintenance needs. Typically the parties to an I(PFD)A 1975 dispute will prefer a clean break, so commonly capital sum solutions will be explored by the courts, where practicable.

19.18.1 The statutory factors: s 3 of I(PFD)A 1975

Section 3 of the I(PFD)A 1975 contains the basic framework for assessing reasonable financial provision. It sets out the factors that must be considered in the particular circumstances of the case concerned.

The courts have emphasised that all relevant s 3 factors must be taken into account and that no particular weight should be given to any single factor.[95] Instead each factor 'may be of infinitely variable weight, on the particular facts of any given case'.[96] All the obvious factors are covered such as the size of the estate, the financial resources and needs of the claimant and of the other beneficiaries under the will or intestacy and also the conduct of the applicant.

The wishes of the deceased (including those expressed in the will itself) are not in and of themselves a s 3 factor. These might be taken into account by the court but will be a relatively low background factor compared with the needs of the claimant.[97]

19.18.2 The I(PFD)A 1975 and adult children: *Ilott v Mitson*

It is difficult to find I(PFD)A 1975 cases directly on point so far as claims by adult children involving family businesses are concerned. But the leading case involving an adult child, *Ilott v Mitson* might be helpful by analogy. In that case the mother left her estate of £486,000 to charity, making no provision for her adult daughter, from whom she had been estranged for over 26 years. The daughter lived in fairly straightened circumstances and had 5 children of her own, but by the time the matter came to court,[98] all but one of these were over the age of 18. The original court awarded the daughter £50,000. This was increased by the Court of Appeal to £143,000, which was enough for her to buy the house she was living in, together with a further capital sum of £20,000 for emergencies.

---

[95] *Ilott v Mitson* [2015] EWCA Civ 797.
[96] Briggs J in *Lilleyman v Lilleyman* [2012] EWHC 821 (Ch) at para 38.
[97] The conduct of the claimant could make the wishes of the deceased indirectly relevant as a s 3 factor. It would be more reasonable for the deceased to actively seek to exclude a patently badly behaved next generation family member from a will.
[98] Under the I(PFD)A 1975 the court must consider the s 3 factors at the date of the hearing.

In this case there were no other close family members whose needs were to be considered. Other key factors considered and ultimately rejected by the court were that the daughter had no expectation as to entitlement having been estranged from her mother for some years. The mother's wish was clearly that charities (with whom she had no real involvement during her lifetime) should inherit rather than her daughter.[99]

Perhaps of most relevance by analogy to family business situations the Court considered the relative responsibilities of mother and daughter for the estrangement as part of their assessment of the conduct of the applicant. The rift between the mother and daughter was caused by the elopement of the latter aged 17. Whilst not making any absolute findings as to ultimate and absolute blame the court did seem to think that this lay more on the side of the mother, Mrs Jackson. Arden LJ noted various attempts by the daughter to heal the rift, speculated that the mother was a difficult character and noted that the daughter, Mrs Ilott 'was deprived of any expectation primarily because Mrs Jackson had acted in an unreasonable, capricious and harsh way towards her only child'.[100]

Do cases such as *Ilott v Mitson* have any relevance to family business inheritance cases?

19.18.3   The I(PFD)A 1975 and family business claimants

The first point to make is that, whilst some of the key cases decided under the I(PFD)A 1975 establish legal principles, each claim will be considered on its own facts.

The Act would have been of no help to David Thorner. Claims under the I(PFD)A 1975 are not limited to close family members. Successful claimants have included cohabitees of more than 2 years and if the dependent is financially dependent on the deceased non-family companions and employees. But the key qualification for a non-family member or cohabitee is that, the applicant 'immediately before the death of the deceased was being maintained, either wholly or partly, by the deceased'.[101] David Thorner received no benefit for his 30 years of work on the farm of his first cousin, once removed.

But it is perhaps not fanciful to think of circumstances where the I(PFD)A 1975 could come to the aid of disappointed next generation insiders in circumstances where they both pass the eligibility test and secondly show financial need. For example in David Thorner's case if he received payment from Peter Thorner which, although short of a proper wages, represented his sole source of income.[102]

Consider, for example a late falling out just between the senior generation and the next generation family member who expected to inherit a family farm. Or even, as in James Davies' case, the situation where the next generation had hoped to inherit a farm outright but when the father's will came to be read, it left the farm equally to all brothers and sisters. It might be that in such circumstances there was no sufficiently clear

---

[99] However at the time of editing it is understood that the matter is subject to an appeal to the Supreme Court.
[100] Arden LJ at p 15.
[101] I(PFD)A, s 1(1)(e).
[102] It is nevertheless hard to trace decided I(PFD)A 1975 cases in favour of disappointed next generation family business claimants, whether children or more remote family members.

assurance that the next generation would inherit outright, so as to turn a hope of inheritance into an expectation.[103] A claim under the I(PFD)A 1975 could conceivably assist.

Relevant factors could include:
- The financial resources and financial needs of other beneficiaries.[104] Surviving spouses might be seen to have a greater claim than an excluded family business insider. Independently wealthy siblings less so.
- The size and nature of the estate[105] could be crucial. An award in the case of a capricious exclusion from a large estate could be relatively easy to contemplate. Whether and how to intervene where a small family farm is concerned may be much more problematic.
- The respective fault and conduct of the parties concerned that led to the breakdown of relationships.[106]
- The next generation insiders might have a significant role in caring for the senior generation, particularly in farming situations, where the generations will often live in very close proximity. In *Re Callaghan*[107] a stepchild had been very close to her stepfather and cared for him towards the end of his life to the detriment of her own circumstances. In that case the court awarded the stepchild the house in which the deceased had lived. But in that case the house had originally been left to him by the stepchild's own mother.

19.18.4 Limitations to the potential award

There are a number of limitations to I(PFD)A 1975 claims:
- A key distinction between a proprietary estoppel claim and a claim under the I(PFD)A 1975 is that where claims are made under the latter, other than by spouses, the powers of the court are limited to awards of reasonable financial provision for the maintenance of the applicant. Although the court has power to order lump sum payments and /or the transfer of assets to meet such needs, it would be unusual to see many circumstances where it was necessary to allocate anything approaching the whole value of a family business to a disappointed next generation applicant to secure their maintenance. Such cases might be confined only to the smallest of family businesses, having little or no capital value above the ability to provide a modest income for the next generation working in the business. Furthermore, a claimant who cannot demonstrate that they cannot meet their own needs will struggle to meet the second test of showing that the deceased failed to make reasonable financial provision for them.
- Unlike a proprietary estoppel claim, which can be brought in the lifetime of the senior generation, a I(PFD)A 1975 claim can only be made after their death.
- Finally there is a strict limitation period of 6 months from the date of the grant of representation in which to issue proceedings in relation to a I(PFD)A 1975 claim.

So a claim under the I(PFD)A 1975 might provide some measure of relief for a member of the next generation, arbitrarily excluded from inheritance from their parents. But that

---
[103] *Thorner v Major*.
[104] I(PFD)A, s 3(1)(c).
[105] I(PFD)A, s 3(1)(e).
[106] I(PFD)A, s 3(1)(g).
[107] [1985] Fam 1.

relief is likely to be basic rather than fully compensatory in nature. In essence the I(PFD)A 1975 might provide a lifeline. It is almost impossible to contemplate circumstances that it such a claim would be capable of giving effect to the great family business promise that 'one day all of this will be yours'. However I(PFD)A 1975 claims are simpler (and therefore usually cheaper), than proprietary estoppel claims, in that many of the evidential difficulties of the latter are avoided in I(PFD)A 1975 claims. So it may well be sensible to consider the possibility of a I(PFD)A 1975 claim, in addition to, or instead of a proprietary estoppel action.

19.18.5 The I(PFD)A 1975 and family outsiders

So far in this chapter we have been concentrating on the position of family business insiders, next generation family members who have devoted a large part of their working life to the family business and whose hopes of inheriting this have not been met. There is a converse situation to consider; that of the family business outsider,[108] who has been excluded from inheritance due to some combination of estrangement, an ownership philosophy, that insiders should inherit the family business and the fact that all or most of the family wealth is tied up in the family firm.

In *Gold v Curtis*[109] a son who was estranged from his deceased mother until shortly before her death, made a claim on the ground that he needed extra resources because he had mental health issues and had a daughter who also had mental health issues. The claim was opposed by his wealthy sister. The court made an order granting him a measure of financial provision despite the estrangement, but his share of the estate remained less than that of his sister.

There might be countervailing circumstances including the wishes of the senior generation and perhaps the conduct of the outsiders.[110] Family insiders will therefore need to consider very carefully the merits of any claim brought by outsiders, particularly those in reduced financial circumstances, and be prepared to compromise these in appropriate circumstances.

19.18.6 A brief note on procedure for I(PFD)A 1975 claims[111]

I(PFD)A 1975 claims are issued under Part 8 of the CPR and all evidence must be filed with the issue of the claim form. This is a requirement of CPR Part 8. See also Practice Direction 8 for further guidance.

Evidence is typically submitted by way of the claimant's witness statement, although third party supporting statements may be filed in addition if appropriate. Once served, the defendant will have 21 days in which to file and serve his acknowledgement of service and any written evidence in response. See CPR Part 57 and its associated Practice

---

[108] By which we mean family members, including children and other close family members, who do not work in the family business.
[109] [2005] WTLR 637.
[110] Other cases decided under the I(PFD)A 1975 involving adult children include see *Re Hancock (dec'd)* [1993] 1 FCR 500; *Re Goodchild* [1996] IWLR 694; *Re Pearce* [1998] 2 FLR 705; *Espinosa v Burke* [1999] 3 FCR 76 and *Myers v Myers* [2004] EWHC 1944 (Fam).
[111] For more detail on the relevant procedure and practice see Andrew Francis *Inheritance Act Claims: Law Practice and Procedure* (Jordan Publishing, looseleaf).

Direction for further detail in this respect. The claimant is then entitled to file and serve any evidence in response to that of the defendant.

I(PFD)A 1975 claims must be issued within a strict limitation period of 6 months from the date of the grant of representation. Any claimant wishing to issue a claim after this date will require the permission of the court to do so and will generally be required to show good reason for their application to be permitted once it is out-of-time.

After all the parties have filed and served their evidence, the court will typically list a case management cnference to set the timetable and make directions regarding any other matters raised by the parties in advance of a trial listing. Parties will be encouraged at all times to settle the claim through ADR and in practice, this is the most commonly used forum for the resolution of I(PFD)A 1975 claims.

19.19 SPOUSES AND THE I(PFD)A 1975

The position of spouses and civil partners under the I(PFD)A 1975 is different from that of all other eligible claimants, including the children of the deceased, in one crucial respect. The courts have to look at whether 'reasonable financial provision' has been made for the spouse and, if not, what this should be, as a general and wider question without the limitation, applicable in next generation cases, that this should be restricted to the maintenance[112] of the applicant. The idea is that the surviving spouse is elevated above all other claimants and is entitled to receive such financial provision as is reasonable in all the circumstances of the case.

As one would expect the court are obliged to take into account the age of the spouse, the length of the relationship,[113] and the contribution of the surviving spouse to looking after the home and family.[114]

One of the factors that the courts are obliged to look at is the so called 'divorce cross-check'.[115] This is to consider, as an additional indicative (but not necessarily decisive[116]) factor:[117]

> 'the provision that the applicant might reasonably have expected to receive if on the day which the deceased died the marriage, instead of being terminated by death, had been terminated by a dissolution order.'

These spouse specific elements will be taken into account in addition to the general factors set out in s 3(1) of the I(PFD)A 1975, including the needs of the claimant and the size of the estate.

So it would be fairly easy to foresee a successful claim in circumstances where a family business has been left to the next generation and there are few non-business assets for

---

[112] Maintenance in the context of divorce proceedings tends to refer to periodical payments of income. In the context of the I(PFD)A 1975 the term refers to the reasonable financial needs of the claimant. These can be satisfied by periodical payments, lump sums or the transfer of assets from the estate.
[113] Including any period of cohabitation before marriage.
[114] I(PFD)A, s 3(2A).
[115] Applying the test in *Lilleyman v Lilleyman* [2012] EWHC 821 (Ch).
[116] *Lilleyman v Lilleyman* [2012] EWHC 821 (Ch).
[117] I(PFD)A, s 3(2).

the surviving spouse, particularly after a long marriage. Where the family business is of modest value this might have the effect of disinheriting the next generation in favour of redistribution to the spouse, pretty much irrespective of the succession plans and wishes of the deceased senior generation family business owner.

It will no doubt be fairly unusual if the will of the deceased does not take adequate care of a long-standing spouse. Even if it does not, if the children inheriting the family business are those of the surviving spouse, or have been brought up by them, then the next generation may well choose to look after their mother (assuming that it is she who survives) irrespective of the terms of their father's will.

But family dynamics can be particularly complex where the children working in, and inheriting the family business are from a first marriage and the surviving spouse is party to a second or subsequent marriage. The family business might have provided a vehicle for the deceased to maintain a relationship with their children from the first marriage. The deceased might have had lingering guilt over the breakdown of the first relationship. The next generation children might harbour ill feelings or resentment towards the new spouse. So it becomes more likely that a second spouse will be excluded from benefit and less likely that the next generation will be accommodating towards their position.

As discussed if the second relationship is long-standing it may be relatively easy for the spouse to secure assistance under the I(PFD)A 1975, especially if the estate is comparatively small. But claims might be comparatively more difficult in so called 'big money short marriage cases'. The *Lilleyman* case had both these elements.

19.19.1 Lilleyman v Lilleyman

Roy Lilleyman was a successful businessman who had built a group of steel stockholding businesses. By the time of his death aged 63, following a long period of ill-health, the companies, although still owned outright by Roy, had been run as family businesses managed on a day-to-day basis largely by his sons.[118]

Roy's first marriage ended with the death of his mother. He had been married to his second wife Barbara Lilleyman, a divorcee of similar age, for just over 2 years, the couple having lived together for a short period beforehand. Under his will Roy gave various pecuniary legacies and gifts of specific items to his wider family including grandchildren. Barbara was given limited rights of occupation to the couple's main residence and a holiday home together with a relatively small annuity. Other than Roy's Dinky toy collection, worth about £17,000, she received nothing outright. Roy's shares in the family companies, valued at just over £5m, together with the balance of his residual estate (including the reversionary interest on the domestic properties) went to his two sons. Barbara claimed under the I(PFD)A 1975.

How did the court assess the various statutory factors in dealing with her claim?

---

[118] The father and sons jointly owned a third company.

19.19.2 The notional divorce or divorce cross check test[119]

Briggs J used the 'epoch making decision of the House of Lords' in *White v White*[120] as his starting point for what he termed the 'divorce cross check' and referred to the basic concept of the modern marriage as a partnership between equals. But the judge noted that: 'equality of treatment does not necessarily lead to equality of outcome'.[121]

He then referred to the subsequent House of Lords decision in *Miller v Miller*[122] and, in particular the judgment of Baroness Hale, as support for the proposition that 'the shortness of the marriage might justify a departure from the yardstick of equality of division'. The key distinction was between non-matrimonial property, usually brought by one party into the marriage, which might be retained by the original owner and matrimonial property, which would usually be subject to the principle of equal division.[123]

The judge offered the following as principles emerging from the matrimonial cases when looking at non-matrimonial property, particularly in short marriage-big money cases.[124] These were as follows.

- **Burden of proof.** This rests with the party seeking to argue that the relevant asset should be excluded as non-matrimonial property. By analogy, Roy Lilleyman's sons, as defendants to Barbara's I(PFD)A 1975 claim, bore this burden under the notional divorce test.

- **Matrimonial home.** The matrimonial home will usually be regarded as matrimonial property, even if this has been contributed only from the resources of one spouse. In the *Lilleyman's* case this would clearly point to Barbara getting the matrimonial home outright (to which she had contributed the proceeds of sale of her own house and as a result already owned part of the equity anyway).

- **Property acquired during the marriage.** Again the working assumption is that this will be regarded as matrimonial property. Exceptions may apply if the property was inherited or given to one spouse or where it was acquired other than for family use. On this basis Barbara would also get a holiday home the couple had bought.[125]

- **Previously owned property.** Property previously owned by one of the spouses will not usually be considered as matrimonial property unless it is 'then committed to family use'. Presumably a holiday home previously owned by one of the parties before the marriage and then used by the couple would usually fall into this category.[126] Equally, previously owned investment properties would be excluded. This was not a significant factor in the *Lilleyman* case.

- **Business assets.** Here a distinction is drawn between the value of a business at the time of the marriage, which is presumed to be non-matrimonial property and any increase in value during the marriage. In the latter case there may be an

---

[119] The position of spouses in relation to family businesses on an actual divorce (rather than the hypothetical situation envisaged by the I(PFD)A 1975) is considered in detail in chapter 18.
[120] [2001] 1 AC 596.
[121] See para 46 of the judgment in *Lilleyman v Lilleyman* [2012] EWHC 821 (Ch).
[122] [2006] 2 AC 618.
[123] See para 46 of the judgment in *Lilleyman*.
[124] See para 52 of the judgment in *Lilleyman*.
[125] There was a dispute as to whether this was acquired by Roy as a holiday home for the wider family or by Roy and Barbara as their own holiday home on the basis that the rest of the family could stay there on occasions.
[126] The Lilleyman's moved into a new home together.

assumption that the increase in value is attributable to the joint efforts of the parties to the marriage and therefore to be shared equally.[127] So the starting point would be that the value of the family businesses at the time of their marriage, which had been in Roy Lilleyman's ownership for 20 years or so before he met Barbara would be excluded. But any increase in value would fall into the matrimonial pot. Passive growth may however be excluded from equal sharing as matrimonial property.[128] The evidence suggested that the family business had increased in value by about £550,000 during the period of the marriage. It was argued on behalf of the sons that this was largely down to passive growth attributable to increases in the market price of steel. Briggs J was nevertheless prepared to attribute £250,000 of this increase to Roy Lilleyman's activities and skill as a steel trader, giving a credit to Barbara on the notional divorce of half the balance, or £125,000.[129]

- **Family businesses.** Interestingly Briggs J singles out the position of family business assets for special mention. He says that:

> '… where one spouse brings a pre-existing family business to the marriage, it may be positively unfair to have recourse to it for the purposes of equal sharing, in particular if to do so might cripple the business or deprive it of much of its value.'

The approach of the judge to detail of the family business issues in *Lilleyman* is considered below.

The limitations of the notional divorce test are explored in the leading big-money short-marriage case brought under the I(PFD)A 1975 of *Cunliffe v Fielden*,[130] where the Court of Appeal identified contradictory limitations to the quasi-divorce test.

On the one hand the I(PFD)A 1975 can be seen to modify the basic freedom of testamentary disposition so that:[131]

> 'a deceased spouse who leaves a widow is entitled to bequeath his estate to whomsoever he pleases: his only statutory obligation is to make reasonable financial provision for his widow.'

But this freedom must be counterbalanced by a caution in applying short marriage divorce case thinking to marriages cut short by death. As Wall LJ observed 'there is self-evidently a profound difference' between a marriage ending in divorce, where at least one party has decided to call time on the relationship and one ending on death, where the surviving spouse might have been prepared to continue to play their part in the partnership for many more years to come.[132]

So the 'blameless widow of a wealthy man is entitled to look forward to financial security throughout her remaining lifetime'.[133] In *Cunliffe v Fielden* this translated to a

---

[127] The counter-argument of 'exceptional contribution' argument and cases are discussed in detail in chapter 18.
[128] *Jones v Jones* [2012] Fam 1.
[129] See paras 77 and 78 of *Lilleyman*.
[130] [2006] Ch 361.
[131] Wall LJ at para 21 of *Cunliffe v Fielden*.
[132] At para 31 of *Cunliffe v Fielden*.
[133] At para 77 of *Cunliffe v Fielden*.

standard of living falling somewhere between the exceptional comfort enjoyed by the widow during the short marriage and her much more modest lifestyle before the marriage.

19.19.3 Other factors

The divorce cross check is only one of the factors that the court needs to consider under I(FPD)A, s 3. As such Briggs J, in *Lilleyman*, thought that a court considering an application under the Act did not need to apply a 'meticulous quasi divorce' analysis to the position. Rather they needed to consider the position in the round with the other factors in the section.

In *Lilleyman* these included:

- **The applicant's financial resources and needs.** Barbara Lilleyman had given up her part time jobs at Roy's request to look after him and their home. She had also sold her previous house. She clearly needed a roof over her head and a source of income.
- **The applicant's age and the duration of the marriage.** Although the marriage was short, about 4 years taking into account their previous cohabitation, this was longer than the year or so in *Cunliffe v Fielden*. Also, aged 66 at the date of the hearing, Barbara was considerably older than the widow in *Cunliffe v Fielden* and had no real earning capacity.
- **Financial resources and needs of the beneficiaries.** Roy Lilleyman's sons declined to provide evidence of their own needs and resources. Accordingly the court did not take these into account as a factor to reduce any award to Barbara. However the court did note that the family businesses had been sufficiently successful so as to have been able to fund pension contributions for the sons benefit in the region of £1m since Roy's death.[134]
- **Size and nature of the net estate.** This was in the region of £6m which indicated that there were potentially ample resources in the estate to make reasonable financial provision for Barbara without interfering with Roy's plans for the ownership of the family business in the next generation.

19.19.4 The family business factor

In practice, Briggs J positioned this under I(FPD)A, s 3(1)(d):

> 'obligations and responsibilities which the deceased had ... towards any beneficiary of the estate of the deceased.'

It is clear that for the purposes of the I(PFD)A 1975, obligations extend beyond pure financial obligations and include moral obligations and family responsibilities. So far as the next generation in the family business were concerned Briggs J thought that the founder, Roy Lilleyman:[135]

> 'had a degree of moral obligation not unnecessarily to undermine his son's future careers in the family business, to which he had encouraged them to devote their working lives.'

---

[134] At para 66 of *Lilleyman*.
[135] At para 67 of *Lilleyman*.

Notwithstanding that the sons, as defendants to Barbara's application had not introduced any evidence of their means, Briggs J was prepared to assume that their financial well being depended on the continued existence of the family business in their ownership (rather than after sale) observing that:[136]

> 'it is evident that the future careers and financial security of the defendants and the financial security of their families may well be dependent, to an extent which the court cannot precisely measure, upon preserving the three companies, whose shares constitute the most valuable assets in the estate from undue attrition by the consequences of any award made in Mrs Lilleyman's favour.'

So preserving the family business, irrespective of how it was analysed under the I(FPD)A, s 3 factors was a significant factor for the court in *Lilleyman*.

19.19.5 *Lilleyman*: conclusion

Briggs J made it clear that the over-riding factor would nevertheless be the obligation of the deceased, Roy 'to make reasonable financial provision for Mrs Lilleyman'. Although the court concluded that the will did not so, in that case there were ample non-business assets that could be transferred outright to Barbara, so as to leave the family business intact and in the hands of the next generation.

In other cases it might not be so easy to look after the needs of second spouses, without resorting to the value of the family business. This might necessitate its sale and with it the defeat of both the ownership expectations of the next generation and the wishes of the founder. Avoiding this risk and the resulting uncertainty for the next generation is a further factor pointing towards early succession planning. Such cases also point to the importance of financial planning. In particular the need to secure an adequate balance between business and personal assets so that neither the deceased, the surviving family members nor, as a final resort the courts are faced with the Hobson's choice of disappointing the succession expectations of the next generation or leaving the surviving spouse inadequately provided for.

19.20 PRACTICAL CONSIDERATIONS AND CHECKLIST FOR INHERITANCE CLAIMS

The reality of many succession disputes, irrespective of whether they are brought in equity or under the I(PFD)A 1975 often prove to be damaging for both the business and the family. Awareness of this likely aftermath at the outset should re-enforce the benefits of early resolution. We have included below a checklist of questions, which are not intended to be exhaustive, but can serve as a starting point for interviews with clients:

(1) What attempts have been made to facilitate an early resolution informally or formally before the parties' positions become irrevocably entrenched?

(2) What are the ultimate goals of both parties? (Here the need is to look beyond individual disagreements and differences of opinion over past events and to concentrate on the future.)

---

[136] At para 66.

(3) What room is there for compromise, if any, on those goals? All alternatives to costly and risky litigation and long-term damage to the family and business must be considered.
(4) If litigation seems inevitable – how will an owner-manager try to meet a claimant's settlement or award?
(5) Will payment of any awards ordered or agreed between the parties involve a sale of assets or security to be taken on business assets and/or property?
(6) How will the business be run without the role of the other party being involved anymore?
(7) Who will take the place of any exiting parties in the business? Will this involve bringing in an outsider or encouraging another family member into the business for the first time?
(8) What effect will the dispute have on the family dynamics?
(9) Will grandchildren and other family members be isolated or effected as a result?
(10) Is the dispute likely to cause an irrevocable rift in family relations?
(11) Is the dispute worth the results compared with the long-term effect on the family and the business?
(12) What written agreement(s), if any have been reached, and in what terms?
(13) Has the owner-manager prepared a will or previous wills which are now to be altered and if so, what advice have they received, if any, on the potential for future disputes arising out of this?

It will be seen that these questions are not confined to inheritance claims and have application to family business disputes generally.

19.21 INHERITANCE DISPUTES: CONCLUSION

It will have been seen that the informal and complex ownership and working patterns characteristic of many family businesses can give rise to equally complex legal positions.

Sometimes a mixture of inheritance traditions, for example in the farming industry generally or in individual farming families underpinned by strong and cohesive family relationships will mean that inheritance problems do not surface or are relatively easily resolved.

However the case studies and cases in this chapter speak eloquently of the dangers of leaving matters to chance. Any attempts family business owners, especially the senior generation, can make at succession planning during their lifetime, will stand the remainder of the family and the business in good stead. If succession is left until the point is forced by the death of the owner-manager, such unresolved issues will have an immediacy which can throw a family business into disarray if no particular plans have been set down. As a result, all owner-managers should ideally have a succession plan in place. Part of this should include a professionally drafted will.

The case study and cases discussed in this chapter show us how a dispute may finally be resolved legally within a family business context. However, it is also necessary to consider the effect that such a dispute can have on the family dynamics and on the functioning of the business. It is not an exaggeration to say that, in many cases, irreparable damage will be caused to one, if not both.

Disputes like the ones examined in this chapter, which become so entrenched, are likely to have the exact opposite effect of what a business family is usually seeking to achieve. That is, to ensure stability for future generations through their participation in an enduring family enterprise.

19.22 FURTHER READING FOR PART D

- R Bird and A King *Financial Remedies Handbook* (Jordan Publishing, 10th edn, 2015). A comprehensive coverage of financial remedies on divorce. The book includes detailed coverage of periodical payments, housing needs and the treatment of pensions, all important issues that can be relevant to the divorce of a family business couple, which are not covered here. The book also contains a number of useful appendices, including a full copy of the Matrimonial Causes Act.
- A Francis (ed) *Inheritance Act Claims Law, Practice and Procedure* (Jordan Publishing Looseleaf/Online). A comprehensive and regularly updated service for those dealing with 1975 claims in particular.
- Goodman, Hewitt and Mason *Probate Disputes and Remedies* (Jordan Publishing, 3rd edn, 2014).
- Neubauer and Lank *The Family Business: Its Governance for Sustainability* (Harvard Business School Press, 1997). A core text on family business governance, which concentrates on the larger, mature family enterprise.
- C Ryan and K Reece Thomas *The Law and Practice of Shareholders' Agreements* (LexisNexis, 4th edn, 2014). A detailed and comprehensive overview of the legal and practical issues surrounding shareholders' agreements, including a number of precedent documents, with related articles. Chapter 10 includes a discussion on the use of shareholders' agreements in family and other quasi partnership companies.

PART E

FAMILY BUSINESS DISPUTES

CHAPTER 20

FAMILY BUSINESS SHAREHOLDER DISPUTES – OVERVIEW AND KEY ISSUES

20.1 INTRODUCTION

Perhaps the most powerful and enduring warning about going to court can be found in the pages of *Bleak House* where Dickens warns that potential litigants in the Chancery Court should 'suffer any wrong that can be done to you, rather than come here'. Nevertheless, each year, a considerable number of families become embroiled in disputes where lawyers are instructed to advise and intervene on behalf of aggrieved minority owners in family companies. It is tempting to say that the law takes over when the family fails. But that is not strictly true.

One of the key themes and messages in this book is the importance, for the long-term health and prosperity of the family business of trust, underpinned by good communication. In chapter 17 (and indeed throughout the book) we advocate the desirability of business owning families investing in robust and appropriate governance systems, to improve communication between family members. Indeed (albeit with the benefit of hindsight and with only second hand knowledge of the individuals involved we would suggest that in almost all of the reported cases discussed in this section, governance interventions described in chapter 17 were capable of preventing those disputes arising in the first place.

Nevertheless it is clear that a considerable number of business owning families, are affected by disputes and difficulties. Chapter 2 examines the underlying family dynamics in relation to disputes. In particular it repeats the suggestion that disputes are 'never (just) about the money'.[1] There will always be an underlying emotional issue. That chapter also acknowledges that some level of dispute and disagreement, at least on occasions, is an almost inevitable fact of family business life. How families deal with those disagreements determines the success of their family business and the happiness of the business owning family.

Family business disputes cover a wide spectrum. They encompass, at one end of the scale, temporary disagreements, which are soon resolved. Sometimes issues are more long-standing but cause only relatively mild discontent and irritation. Often disputes cause serious difficulties for the family and the business, but nevertheless remain unchallenged unresolved and, on occasions, unacknowledged.[2]

---

[1] Made by Ian Marsh *Business Families and Family Businesses* (STEP Handbook, Globe Business Publishing, 2009).
[2] What de Vries and colleagues label as the 'Myth of Harmony'. See Kets de Vries and Carlock with Florent-Treacy *Family Business on the Couch* (Wiley, 2007) at p 104.

This part of the book therefore concerns a much smaller subset of family business disputes. Where members of a business owning family feel sufficiently aggrieved about a particular situation that they choose to issue proceedings to police their rights (and also have the finances to do so). Lawyers increasingly use the term dispute resolution, rather than litigation. But the use of the term in a family business context is usually euphemistic. Whilst some matters may be resolved by litigation (and still more by the threat of it), in the sense that a judgment is obtained or a settlement reached, it is almost inevitable that a business owning family who become involved in a court case will bear the scars and repercussions, not only for the current generation directly involved in the litigation but potentially for generations to come. Again in Dickens' analysis of *Jarndyce v Jarndyce*, 'whole families have inherited legendary hatreds with the suit'. It is for those families that the law truly takes over.

Even if this section does not persuade business families of the merits of investing in preventative governance measures it is to be hoped that the discussion of the family business cases contained in it and the prevailing message of uncertainty as to outcome will be sufficient to illustrate the wisdom of early stage intervention and the alternative approaches to dispute resolution advocated in chapter 25.

Fog is the prevailing metaphor used by Dickens in the first chapter of *Bleak House* when describing the workings of the Chancery Court. Although modern courts will try hard to actively manage cases before them, the complexity, lack of clarity and uncertainty relating to shareholders' remedies still makes it difficult for family business litigants and their advisors to see their way clearly through the various stages of most family business disputes.

It may well be that significant sums are involved in family business disputes making it difficult for the family members concerned to fully heed Dickens advice. But it must be the case that if they choose to embark on litigation, family business members must do so strategically and commercially and in the sure and certain knowledge that by doing so they will be irretrievably damaging relationships with their family adversaries. In other words to the greatest extent possible any litigation must be about the money but with full appreciation of the likely personal and family consequences and the time, stress and cost that litigation will entail.

There are perhaps thousands of reported cases concerning shareholder remedies. To the greatest extent we have been able to do so we have concentrated on cases directly concerning family owned businesses rather than their non-family counterparts. Broadly these family business cases fall into two categories. First, pure intra family cases, where the dispute is between members of the business owning family. Secondly cases where the family have closed ranks against third party shareholders.

20.2 OVERVIEW

The main remedies available to shareholders (all of which are discussed in detail in the chapters that follow) are:

20.2.1 Unfair prejudice – CA, s 994[3]

The principal and most used remedy is a petition brought by one or more family shareholders under s 994 of the Companies Act 2006, on the basis that those others have conducted the affairs of the company in a manner that is unfairly prejudicial to the interests of the minority.

The most usual remedy, following a successful unfair prejudice petition would be an order by the court under CA, s 996 requiring the majority to buy the shareholding of the minority at a fair valuation. This may be entirely appropriate if the minority are concerned that their wealth is trapped within the family owned company and that they are receiving little or no benefit from ownership. However in some cases an unfair prejudice petition will produce the remedy the minority family members least want. Their removal from the family owned business rather than a more active participation in the affairs of that business.

Think, for example, of a family business controlled by parents but with a son or daughter holding both a minority interest and an expectation, until relationships broke down, that they would assume outright control. Although orders for the purchase of majority holdings are within the scope of CA, s 996, they are rare.[4]

As will be seen, even if unfair prejudice is the main remedy for aggrieved family minority shareholders, it is by no means automatically, or even widely available. The remedy is closely policed by the courts. That a minority family shareholder feels aggrieved will not be sufficient. There is no concept of a no fault family business divorce.[5] Although the act uses general terminology of 'unfairness' this has been interpreted somewhat narrowly and in accordance with case-law precedent and pre-existing legal concepts.[6]

This is explained and explored in detail both in 20.3 below and in chapter 21.

20.2.2 Just and equitable winding up[7]

An alternative, and more drastic remedy, the nuclear option, would be a petition under s 122(1)(g) of the Insolvency Act 1986 for an order that the family company should be wound up on the basis that it is 'just and equitable' for this to happen. The family business will be sold or wound up, the family will take their respective share of the assets after liabilities have been settled and will each go their separate ways. This is very much a remedy of the last resort. However in a minority of cases the effects of the family dispute may be so severe as to prevent the effective operation and functioning of the family business. In which case winding up may be the only practical remedy.

---

[3] See chapter 21.
[4] This issue is explored in more detail in chapter 24.
[5] Lord Hoffmann in the House of Lords in *O'Neill v Phillips* [1999] 1WLR 1092 at p 1104.
[6] Hoffmann LJ in the Court of Appeal in *Re Saul D Harrison & Sons plc* [1994] BCC 475 at p 488.
[7] See chapter 22.

20.2.3 Derivative claims[8]

Both unfair prejudice and just and equitable winding up are proceedings initiated, usually, by minority shareholders, in their own name to claim personal remedies. Derivative claims under CA, s 260 are conceptually different. Here one or more minority family shareholders make an application to the court asking for permission to pursue a separate action on behalf of and in the name of a family company. Nowadays this will be against one or more of the directors whom the minority believe are in breach of their duty to, or have otherwise wronged the family company. The directors will be relying on some combination of their own control, the active support, or at least the apathy of other shareholders, as a shield to prevent a claim against them. The minority are saying, in effect 'this is wrong, and what's more I am going to do something about it'.

Both unfair prejudice and just and equitable winding up are proceedings likely to produce permanent solutions, either the cessation of a family business relationship or the end of the family business itself. Although claims may be based on a single act or omission (or more usually a series of acts or omissions) the primary objective in taking proceedings is not to correct the position as such. Derivative claims on the other hand are targeted at providing a remedy for particular breaches whilst (at least in theory) leaving the family company and the basic relationship between the family shareholders in place.

Derivative claims are extremely rare in practice.

20.2.4 Key concepts

The bulk of this chapter looks at a number of key concepts that are relevant generally to the conduct of shareholder disputes in family businesses and in particular to unfair prejudice petitions, just and equitable winding up and derivative claims. These concepts are explored throughout this chapter. They are:

'Quasi-partnerships' and the fairness approach[9]

First we look at the concept of the quasi-partnership in relation to the family owned business. In broad terms the worse the behaviour of the majority shareholders the more likely it is that the shareholder remedies, especially unfair prejudice will be available to the aggrieved minority. But in many family disputes whilst it is clear that there has been a serious breakdown of relationships between the family members concerned and whilst there can be seen to be a degree of fault on one or both sides, it is harder to establish that any breach of duty has occurred.

As explained in 20.2.1 above the mere breakdown of relationships will not be enough to qualify for a remedy. As also explained the concept of unfairness has been somewhat narrowly judicially interpreted. So behaviour or conduct that may, in a broad sense, appear unfair may not be sufficient for the purposes of invoking the legal remedy. Something more will be needed in such situations. Often this is summarised as a

---

[8] See chapter 23.
[9] See further 20.4–20.6.

requirement to show that the minority have been excluded from a quasi-partnership.[10] But, as will be seen, the position is considerably more complicated than this.

Failure to secure treatment of a family business as a quasi-partnership will also potentially mean that a successful petitioner in an unfair prejudice action will receive a lower exit price for their shares in the family company. This is because in most cases non-quasi partnership shares will be valued on the basis of a discount for the fact that those shares represent a minority holding.[11]

So establishing that a family business should be treated as a quasi-partnership can often be the key to unlocking unfair prejudice and just and equitable remedies. However a core theme of this chapter is that, by concentrating almost exclusively on the concept of quasi-partnerships, the courts can fail to achieve wider justice in a number of family business situations.

Remedies and the family business constitution[12]

This related introductory topic looks at the relationship between, on the one hand, the formal and informal governance mechanisms of the family business including its articles of association and other constitutional documents and, on the other hand the availability of supplemental shareholder remedies.

Bad faith[13]

Bad faith, or its opposite good faith is relevant in a number of ways.

It will often be the case that the conduct of both of the parties to a dispute can be subject to criticism. Arguably this is more likely to be so in family business disputes. First the conduct or bad faith of the respondent may be the primary cause of complaint. Secondly the conduct of the claimant themselves may be relevant to the availability or extent of relief available from the courts. These aspects of good faith are explored in the detailed chapters that follow.

As suggested above family business disputes will usually be driven by twin motives. Whilst there will usually be a financial or commercial element in any family dispute there will also almost inevitably be an underlying emotional driver, a desire to be proved right or to 'show the other side'. In some cases the latter element will appear to pre-dominate, almost to the exclusion of the financial driver. If so will a court refuse to allow itself to be used as an arena for a family fight? This second aspect of bad faith is considered separately in **20.5** below.

---

[10] See for example *Irvine v Irvine* [2006] EWHC 406 (Ch) at para 257 of the judgment.
[11] See *Irvine No 2* [2006] EWHC 583 (Ch). But see also the case of *Sunrise Radio (Sunrise Radio Limited; Geeta Kohli v Dr Avtar Lit, Ravinder Kumar Jain, Surinderpal Singh Lit, Sunrise Radio Limited* [2009] EWHC 2893 (Ch) where a much broader approach was taken to make an award of fair value, largely ignoring arguments about discounts. Indeed fairness could even involve the 'innocent party' receiving a premium on pro-rate value so that the guilty party cannot benefit from obtaining the shares of their shares 'by force'. This issue is discussed in detail in chapter 24.
[12] See **20.7**.
[13] See **20.8**.

Mismanagement[14]

Family owned businesses are in an unusual position in management terms. Most other owner-managed businesses will have a more or less complete symmetry between ownership and management. For businesses with outside investment this is likely to be on the basis of detailed investment agreements providing the ability for the investor to closely supervise the management team.

On the other hand, in the family business, management may be concentrated in the hands of a few individuals, often from a single branch of the family but with ownership spread across the wider family. Mismanagement is a frequent cause of concern, particularly for remote family shareholders in more mature later stage family businesses.

The court will not interfere with genuine commercial decisions, even if the court, or others, believed that better decisions could have been made.

20.3 REASONABLE OFFERS AND COSTS[15]

In practical terms the effect of launching the initial stages of litigation or threatening to do so is to provoke an offer by the majority to buy out the disgruntled minority family shareholders. This may well be the only practical and sensible solution available to the family. Indeed the courts will actively encourage the family members concerned to make and to accept reasonable offers. If a reasonable offer is made and refused this will usually take otherwise available remedies off the table. The logic being that it is a waste of the court's time to award what was on offer anyway.

At the very least a party who has either failed to make or to accept a reasonable offer will be in severe danger of suffering cost penalties. As the costs of shareholder litigation, particularly if the case proceeds to trial, are potentially huge deciding what constitutes a reasonable offer is therefore a key consideration for family members and their advisors involved in a dispute.

As this subject only makes sense in the context of what would be available if a matter proceeded to court this discussion appears after consideration of the substantive remedies in chapter 24, which also looks at particular costs issues relevant to the conduct of shareholder disputes.

20.4 'QUASI-PARTNERSHIPS'

Many family businesses will be treated as quasi-partnerships for legal purposes. For example the classic '... and Son Limited' company. Or, to use family systems terminology, the sibling partnership, with two brothers working together in a business. In each case, although the business trades as a company it has the look and feel of a partnership. As will be explained, the legal concept of the quasi partnership is broader and capable of applying to many situations beyond a working family partnership.

---

[14] See 20.9.
[15] See chapter 24.

In blatant cases of breach of duty remedies will be readily available irrespective of the background and circumstances of a company. Quite simply those controlling the company concerned have not played by the rules. For example in *Re London School of Electronics Ltd*,[16] a case where the family closed ranks against a non-family shareholder, a father and son held between them 75% of the shares in a training company. The remaining 25% was held by a non-family shareholder. When the father and son set up a second company and diverted the business of the first company to it, leaving the co-owner with a worthless interest, this was seen to be a clear case of unfair prejudice.

In other cases where bad behaviour amounting to a breach of duty is more marginal or absent, then it may be necessary for aggrieved minorities to show that special circumstances justifying court intervention exist. In practice this will usually depend on establishing that the family business should be treated as a quasi-partnership. This is in order to gain access to shareholder remedies, in particular unfair prejudice and just and equitable winding up in the absence of breaches of duty, or to make the most of an unfair prejudice remedy in terms of securing an exit without a share valuation discounted for minority holding.[17]

In the leading case on unfair prejudice, *O'Neill and another v Phillips and Others*[18] the House of Lords looked at certain underlying principles of company law and identified two key features:

- First the 'rules based' approach, derived from a combination of the constitution of the company, in particular its articles of association and any shareholders' agreement, as supplemented by relevant legislation including the Companies Acts and fiduciary duties imposed on directors. As Lord Hoffmann[19] explains:

    'a company is an association of persons for an economic purpose, usually entered into with legal advice and some degree of formality. The terms of the association are contained in the articles of association and sometimes in collateral agreements between the shareholders. Thus the manner in which the affairs of the company may be conducted is closely regulated by rules to which the shareholders have agreed.'

    This approach has been justified on the basis of the need to achieve commercial certainty and clarity in business dealings. Also, the courts have shown a reluctance to interfere in contracts. As such it closely echoes the values to be found in the business system of the three-circle model as explained in chapter 3 (Tools, Models and Theories).

- Secondly the influence of partnership law, based more closely on concepts of good faith and fairness:

    '... company law has developed seamlessly from the law of partnership, which was treated by equity, like the Roman societas, as a contract of good faith. One of the traditional roles of equity, as a separate jurisdiction, was to restrain the exercise of

---

[16] [1986] Ch 211.
[17] The logic appears to be that in actual partnerships if dissolution would be ordered based on equivalent conduct the assets of the partnership would be sold and each partner would receive their fully pro-rata share. Accordingly the courts are generally reluctant to order a winding up of a quasi-partnership company if the less drastic remedy of a buy-out would be available. But it would be unfair for a departing shareholder to receive a discounted valuation for their shares in such circumstances. An explanation of this is provided by Nourse J in *Re Bird Precision Bellows* [1984] Ch 419 at 430 (d)–(f).
[18] [1999] 1WLR 1092. A non-family business case.
[19] At p 1098.

strict legal rights in certain relationships in which it considered that this would be contrary to good faith. These principles have, with appropriate modification, been carried over into company law.'

These concepts much more closely relate to the characteristics of the family system, including fairness, equal treatment, need and inclusiveness.

In this chapter we use terminology such as 'fairness approach' in contrast to expressions like the 'rules based approach'. Of course it may be argued that cases decided under what we have termed the rules based approach have been decided perfectly fairly, on the basis that, in the circumstances of that particular case, it would have been unfair for the courts to look beyond the rules referred to above. We nevertheless will retain the fairness approach terminology. Mostly because this is a convenient shorthand way to differentiate between the two approaches.

Just as the three-circle model illustrates that there is an inherent tension between family and business systems in the day-to-day operation of a family owned business, there is a conflict between the rules based approach and the fairness approach in dealing with family business disputes. In some circumstances the first, rules based approach will apply to the exclusion of all other considerations. We need look no further than the constitution of the company to determine the rights and obligations the participators owe to each other. In other companies the rules based approach will be supplemented by considerations of over-riding fairness, arising from wider mutual understandings, good faith or mutual confidence. Here shareholders may be prevented from relying on or enforcing their strict legal powers and entitlements if it would be unfair to do so. This second category, where the fairness approach applies, are often said to be quasi-partnerships. What then is a quasi-partnership?

In practice the expression quasi-partnership is piece of legal shorthand rather than a clearly defined term. Earlier cases used the perhaps more helpful label of 'domestic companies' or 'family companies' when referring to family owned businesses generally.[20] Giving the leading judgment in the key House of Lords decision in *re Ebrahimi v Westbourne Galleries Limited*[21] Lord Hoffmann warned (at p 379) that:

'To refer, as so many of the cases do, to "quasi-partnerships" or "in substance partnerships" may be convenient but may also be confusing.'

This is especially the case when considering the position of family owned businesses. Here, arguably, the case for bringing equitable considerations into play may not really be based on partnership principles or business systems. Instead it could be seen that different considerations of fairness apply arising from family relationships. The basis of any such family based fairness considerations and the extent to which they will apply are difficult questions to answer.

Whilst recognising that equitable considerations apply to many family owned business situations (and in the process often applying the quasi partnership label to them) the

---

[20] For example *Loch v John Blackwood Ltd* [1924] AC 783, PC.
[21] [1973] AC 360.

courts have not explored these issues in any detail. Indeed in a leading case discussed in detail below, the court roundly rejected arguments that there should be a wider judicial recognition of family systems.[22]

We nevertheless offer some thoughts, suggestions and arguments for a wider recognition of a 'family business fairness approach' in 20.6 below. But first we will consider the *Ebrahimi* decision in more detail to see how the principles emerging from that case have been applied in subsequent decisions.

20.4.1   Ebrahimi v Westbourne Galleries Limited

Ebrahimi was a closing ranks case. The aggrieved minority shareholder was a non-family member and former director Mr Ebrahimi. The business was established in 1945 by Mr Ebrahimi and Nazar Achoury. Initially it was set up as an unincorporated trading partnership, in which they were both equal partners. It dealt in rare Persian carpets. The business was then incorporated in 1957 with both partners becoming directors and each holding 500 shares. Shortly after incorporation Nazar's son George joined and was made a director. At this time each of Mr Ebrahimi and Nazar transferred 100 of their shares to George so that the shareholdings were, Mr Ebrahimi 400 shares, Nazar 400 shares and George 200 shares. The business was successful. The policy had always been to extract the resulting profits by way of director's fees rather than dividends or salary.

In 1969 Nazar and George decided to remove Mr Ebrahimi as a director, using their combined 60% majority shareholding and following the procedure in what is now CA, s 168 and the company's articles. Mr Ebrahimi was accordingly deprived of any benefit from his interest in the company. It was clear that George and Nazar had followed the correct legal procedure to remove Mr Ebrahimi. There was no suggestion of any wrongdoing on the part of Mr Ebrahimi. The main justification given by the Achourys for removing Mr Ebrahimi was that he was 'perpetually complaining'. Initial allegations on the part of Mr Ebrahimi of oppressive conduct on the part of the Achourys made under s 210 of the Companies Act 1948[23] were dismissed by the High Court at first instance but the alternative remedy of just and equitable winding up was granted.

The House of Lords decided that Westbourne Galleries was a company where the second concept mentioned above, the fairness approach, should apply to supplement the strict rules in the company's constitution and confirmed that the winding up order should stand thus allowing Mr Ebrahimi to unlock his investment.

20.4.2   The *Ebrahimi* test

In doing so, the House examined, in detail, the concept of a quasi-partnership. Giving the leading judgment Lord Wilberforce acknowledged that many companies, even small trading concerns, will be covered exclusively by the rules based approach to the exclusion of wider just and equitable considerations:[24]

---

[22]   Patricia Mary Irvine, Michael Cleobury Thatcher, Patricia Mary Irvine as Trustees of the Accumulation and Maintenance Settlement Dated 6 August 1993 v Ian Charles Irvine, Campbell Irvine (Holdings) Limited (No 2) [2006] EWHC 583 (Ch).
[23]   The predecessor of the unfair prejudice remedy, which required the petitioner to satisfy a stricter test of oppression rather than unfairness.
[24]   At p 379.

'Certainly the fact that a company is a small one, or a private company, is not enough. There are very many of these where the association is a purely commercial one, of which it can safely be said that the basis of association is adequately and exhaustively laid down in the articles.'

But there will be other companies where Lord Wilberforce thought that a wider view needed to be taken based on:[25]

'... a recognition of the fact that a limited company is more than a mere legal entity, with a personality in law of its own: that there is room in company law for recognition of the fact that behind it, or amongst it, there are individuals, with rights, expectations and obligations inter se which are not necessarily submerged in the company structure.'

Westbourne Galleries Ltd was clearly a quasi-partnership. But Lord Wilberforce made it clear that it was not possible to arrive at a definitive formulation as to when the fairness approach would apply. He said that:[26]

'It would be impossible, and wholly undesirable, to define the circumstances in which these considerations may arise.'

Instead Lord Wilberforce identified various characteristics that would typically move a company from classification as a 'purely commercial one', governed exhaustively and exclusively, by the provisions of its articles of association and other relevant documents to one where additional requirements for the shareholders to act fairly and in good faith towards one another will be implied. In these latter set of fairness cases the court will:[27]

'... subject the exercise of legal rights to equitable considerations; considerations that is, of a personal character arising between one individual and another, which may make it unjust, or inequitable to insist on legal rights, or to exercise them in a particular way.'

Although not laying down a test Lord Wilberforce identified that the second concept, the requirement for overriding wider fairness and equity was likely to require 'one, or probably more' of the following:[28]

'(i) an association formed or continued on the basis of a personal relationship, involving mutual confidence – this element will often be found where a pre-existing partnership has been converted into a limited company; (ii) an agreement, or understanding, that all, or some (for there may be 'sleeping' members'), of the shareholders shall participate in the conduct of the business; (iii) restriction upon the transfer of the members' interest in the company – so that if confidence is lost, or one member is removed from management, he cannot take out his stake and go elsewhere ...'

According to Lord Wilberforce it is the above or 'analogous, factors' that bring considerations of fairness or equity into play. Not simply the existence or absence of quasi partnership characteristics.

It is therefore clear that, according to Lord Wilberforce, it is the wider background circumstances of a particular business that may (or may not) bring considerations of fairness and equity into play, not the structure of that business.

---

[25] At p 379.
[26] At p 379.
[27] At p 379.
[28] At p 379.

Forensic accountant Roger Issacs[29] has suggested that the following factors will point to the existence or otherwise of a quasi-partnership:

- The absence (or presence) of non-shareholder directors.
- Close working relationship between directors.
- Absence of formal shareholders' agreements (indicative of reliance on trust).
- Funding by directors.
- Funding of directors (such as the use of director's loan accounts to fund personal expenditure).
- Size (with smaller companies being much more likely to fall into the quasi partnership category).

20.4.3 *Ebrahami* and the family owned business

At first sight it would appear that most family owned businesses would satisfy Lord Wilberforce's test. At least nowadays, comparatively few family businesses may have been formed as partnerships and subsequently incorporated, as in Westbourne Galleries. But family businesses will almost invariably have been 'formed or continued on the basis of a personal relationship, involving mutual confidence'. Some level of wider family participation is likely to have been contemplated in most family businesses. An individual family member's shares will often be subject to formal written restrictions on transfer. Even if not, they will almost invariably be subject to de facto restrictions arising from the inherent unmarketability of a minority holding in a family owned private company.

Does this mean that the courts will automatically treat family owned businesses as falling within the second category of companies, that is, those where the formal constitution will invariably be seen as subject to over-riding considerations of fairness? In practice this is far from the case. The decisions are mixed. Whilst a number of cases can be seen to be 'family systems friendly,' adopting the fairness approach, the courts in other cases, including one of the leading unfair prejudice cases, the Court of Appeal decision in *Saul D Harrison*[30] (discussed in detail below), have not seen family factors as justifying a departure from a business systems rules based approach. Accordingly family members and their advisors will not be able to say with any real certainty what principles the courts will apply to their particular circumstances.

The next chapter, chapter 21, provides a more detailed analysis of the family business cases and the unfair prejudice remedy. The following sub-paragraphs look at a selection of cases on the application of the *Ebrahimi* principle to family business circumstances.

20.4.4 *Clemens v Clemens*

Early decisions followed the approach of Lord Wilberforce and refused to categorise or limit the circumstances where equitable considerations of fairness would arise. For example in *Clemens v Clemens Bros Ltd*[31] (considered in more detail in chapter 21 below). There, the claimant had inherited 45% of the shares in a family business and

---

[29] Writing in the Newsletter of the Network of Independent Forensic Accountants – *NIFA News* 30.
[30] The case is introduced in chapter 1 and referred to throughout the book, including in detail in the rest of this chapter.
[31] [1976] 2 All ER 268.

took no part in the day to day management of that business. Setting aside resolutions that would have diluted the niece's holding, the judge referred to *Ebrahimi* and said that the equitable principles in that case should apply. However he carefully avoided stating any rule or principle why this should be the case explaining that:[32]

> 'I think that one thing which emerges from the cases ... is that in such a case as the present, Miss Clemens is not entitled to exercise her majority vote in whatever way she pleases. The difficulty is in finding a principle, and obviously expressions such as 'bona fide for the benefit of the company as a whole', 'fraud on a minority' and 'oppressive' do not assist in formulating a principle.
>
> I have come to the conclusion that it would be unwise to try to produce a principle, since the circumstances of each case are infinitely varied. It would not, I think, assist to say more than that in my judgment Miss Clemens is not entitled as of right to exercise her votes as an ordinary shareholder in any way she pleases.'

So relief was granted on the basis of *Ebrahami* principles but without the need to categorise the business as a quasi-partnership. Certainly the principles in *Ebrahimi* have been applied in a number of subsequent family business cases. Some of these cases are classic sibling quasi partnerships, for example, *Brownlow v Marshall*[33] and *Shah v Shah*,[34] both of which are discussed in more detail in chapter 21 below.

20.4.5 *Harding*

Relief has also been granted in cases where the circumstances of the business concerned extend well beyond the situation of a typical trading partnership. In particular where the partners (or shareholders) are not all engaged working full time in the relevant partnership business.

For example, in the *Harding*[35] case, discussed in more detail in chapter 22, a low level of active participation and involvement in the actual conduct of the business was seen to be sufficient to bring the fairness approach into play. The case concerned an application for just and equitable winding up and was based on a complete breakdown of working relationships between three sisters in a family farming business. Although all three sisters were directors in the company none of them were involved in the day-to-day farming activity (which was undertaken by a non-family manager). They took very little part in the administration of the business. The evidence was that the role of the most active of the sisters, Mrs Edwards, (as a book keeper/administrator) occupied only about 3 or 4 hours a week which she fitted in around her full time job as a radiographer.[36] Another sister, Sally Harding had carried out book-keeping work in the business previously and her father had expressed a wish in his will that this should continue, but her practical involvement had ceased 10 years or so before the matter came to court. The third sister, Mrs Walton, lived in London but returned to the farm for occasional meetings allowing the judge to conclude that both she and Mrs Harding had 'involvement in the kinds of decisions that are normally taken by the directors and shareholders of a company'[37] and accordingly, along with Mrs Edwards were involved in a quasi-partnership.

---

[32] Also at p 282.
[33] [2001] BCC 152.
[34] [2010] EWHC 313 (Ch).
[35] Sally Harding, Rosemary Walton v Elizabeth Edwards, Janet Harding, the Executors of BM Harding (deceased), Brandon Harding Limited [2014] EWHC 247 (Ch).
[36] Paragraph 14 of the judgment.
[37] At para 14 of the judgment.

The judge in *Harding* quoted extensively from the judgment in *Ebrahimi*, including Lord Wilberforce's suggestion that the quasi partnership label 'may be confusing'.[38] The judge suggested[39] that to satisfy the test in *Ebrahimi*, it was necessary to establish that the business was intended to be and actually run as a quasi-partnership. The court found this test to have been satisfied by the fact that 'no third party outside the family has been involved in managing the Company and the sisters have all considered it their entitlement as well as their responsibility to be involved in the Company's affairs'.

20.4.6 The Gate of India[40]

The *Gate of India* concerns a restaurant on Tyneside of that name. This was one of a series of businesses run through a succession of unincorporated and limited quasi partnerships. The principals were two brothers, but other members of the wider family also worked in the business.

From time to time, each of the brothers returned to Bangladesh, but this did not effect their entitlement. Whether at home or abroad each brother was entitled to take the same money out of the business, each had an equal voice and, irrespective of who was actually looking after the day-to-day operations at any given time, each expected the other to consult them about and keep them informed and involved in any important decisions.

One of the brothers, Mr Rahman, retired from the business and returned permanently to Bangladesh. He passed his shares to his son, who was also appointed a director. The claimant's case was that at this time an agreement was reached with the other brother, Mr Malik for Mr Rahman junior to step completely into his father's shoes so that an expectation of participation in management had been passed from one generation to the next, along with the shareholding.

The judge followed the leading case on unfair prejudice, *O'Neill v Phillips*,[41] itself following *Ebrahami*, said[42] that:

> 'Lord Hoffmann emphasised (at p. 1098F–G) that context and background were very important. What was fair between competing businessmen might not be regarded as fair between members of a family. Fairness in the context of s 459 is not dependent upon the individual judge's notion of fairness but, as Lord Hoffmann further emphasised, rooted in principles established over centuries particularly by courts of equity which were prepared to step in to prevent a person relying on or exercising strict legal rights or acting or proposing to act in a manner where it would be contrary to good faith or against conscience to do so.'

The judge went on to make a finding of fact[43] that there was:

> '... an agreement or understanding between Mr Rahman Senior and Mr Malik to the effect that the former's share in the business in the fullest sense, that is as partner with a right and expectation of participation in the running of the business (whichever company vehicle owned and operated it), and of being consulted about all major decisions, was to pass to the

---

[38] See paras 7–9 of the judgment.
[39] At para 9 of the judgment.
[40] *Re Gate of India (Tynemouth) Ltd*, also known as: *Rahman v Malik* [2008] EWHC 959 (Ch), [2008] 2 BCLC 403.
[41] [1999] 1 WLR 1092. The case is introduced in chapter 1 and discussed in various places in the book.
[42] At para 56 of *The Gate of India* judgment.
[43] At para 78 of the judgment.

petitioner. It was further expressly or implicitly agreed between them that the petitioner would be appointed to the board of directors and that he was not to be a mere nominee for his father.'

Accordingly the *Gate of India* fell into the fairness category and the exclusion of Mr Rahman junior amounted to unfair prejudice.

The judge also emphasised that the family concerned were part of the Bangladeshi community, with a cultural tradition of family business succession explaining that:[44]

> 'it is also important to note, that the context was one of a Bangladeshi family tied by blood, religion, culture and tradition.'

Like many family business cases, the petitioner in *The Gate of India*, sought to preserve a right of active participation in family owned business, albeit an inherited right of participation or an expectation of succession. *The Gate of India* can therefore be seen as having been decided on the basis of an extended concept of quasi-partnership.[45]

20.4.7 Fisher v Cadman

Fisher v Cadman[46] concerned a second generation property company where a sister, Mrs Fisher was both geographically and operationally remote from her two brothers who ran the business following the death of their parents. Mrs Fisher argued that it was intended that she should take an active part in the running of the company. The judge[47] found that, although her participation was supported by their father, the brothers had opposed their sister's involvement so that:

> '... there was never any mutual understanding between Mrs Fisher and any other member of the family that she should be involved in the management of the company.'

In a judgment, invoking the core underlying spirit of *Ebrahimi*, the judge[48] explained that:

> 'It is clear that Lord Wilberforce was not intending to set out an exhaustive list of factors by reference to which one might conclude that the members in a company had become subject to equitable considerations between themselves in the exercise of their rights as members.'

And that:

> 'It is also clear that the term, "quasi-partnership", is only intended as a useful shorthand label, which should not in itself govern the answer to be given to the underlying question, whether the circumstances surrounding the conduct of the affairs of a particular company are such as to give rise to equitable constraints upon the behaviour of other members going beyond the strict rights and obligations set out in the Companies Act and the articles of association.'

---

[44] At para 11 of the judgment.
[45] There were also breaches of duty involved in the *Gate of India* case. The case is discussed in more detail in chapter 21.
[46] *Girvan Janis Fisher v Cedric Cadman, Rodney Cadman, Cadman Developments Limited* [2005] EWHC 377 (Ch). The background facts are set out in 1.5.3.
[47] Mr Philip Sales sitting as a Deputy Judge of the High Court – at para 20 of the judgment.
[48] At para 84 of the judgment.

Although the judge suggested that the quasi-partnership label could be applied to the family company in question he impliedly acknowledged that this would be straining that concept because:[49]

> '... it did not share all the features typical of a true partnership-type relationship as identified in Westbourne Galleries and In re Bird Precision Bellows Ltd. There was no agreement that Mrs Fisher should have a role in the management of the company. She did not herself provide capital for the company, but was given or inherited her shareholding in it from her parents.'[50]

Instead the core reason emerging from the judgment for applying equitable principles and adopting the fairness approach was that the business was a:[51]

> '... small family company in which the family relationship would be important alongside the relationship defined in the Articles of Association.'

However in other cases on similar facts with remote family shareholders the courts have declined to follow the fairness approach and found that *Ebrahimi* principles did not apply.

20.4.8 *Irvine v Irvine* – the widow's mite

In *Irvine v Irvine*[52] it was accepted that, on the facts of their case no quasi-partnership existed. Based on a reading of *Ebrahimi* that the existence or otherwise of a quasi-partnership is the main determinant to applying a fairness approach the judge, whilst granting unfair prejudice relief, based on a breach of duty, ordered the petitioner's shares to be valued on a discounted basis.

The case concerned a successful insurance broking business, run for over 20 years as a sibling quasi partnership and equally owned between two brothers, Ian and Malcolm. One brother, Ian, was very much the senior partner. He founded the business and was responsible for the key client relationships. Malcolm nevertheless played a valuable supporting role, looking after the finances and administration and clearly contributed to the success of the business over the long period that the brothers were in business together. Ian's contribution was recognised by Malcolm so although the shareholding was owned 50:50 there was a private agreement between the two brothers that the net profit would be shared in the ratio of four sevenths to Ian and three sevenths to Malcolm.

Malcolm died suddenly and left the bulk of his shares to his widow, Pauline. He had previously set up a trust for the benefit of their children. Although Malcolm had transferred half his holding to the trust (it would appear as a CGT planning device) the trust was otherwise dormant.

Crucially the will also provided for the transfer of a single share to the surviving brother, giving that brother a fractional overall majority.

---

[49] At para 89 of the judgment.
[50] At para 89 of the judgment.
[51] At para 89 of the judgment.
[52] [2006] EWHC 406 (Ch).

In the early years following Malcolm's death Ian appears to have been supportive to his sister-in-law and three nephews, ensuring that substantial payments, more or less in line with the previous profit sharing agreement, continued. After a couple of years this support declined and Ian used a combination of his de facto day-to-day control of the company and his voting control to determine his own, extremely significant remuneration. In later years Ian was shown to be taking approximately 95% of available profits. Nothing was left to pay dividends. Pauline received only a modest salary. By this time Ian appeared to treat the business as his own by survivorship. Ian was less than transparent in his dealings with Pauline, failing to explain the overall profitability of the business or the level of his own remuneration.

The widow, Pauline (along with Ian's wife) had been a director of the holding company for some time. After Malcolm's death she was appointed as a director of the operating company. Although it had initially been intended that Pauline would take some operational role in the business this never transpired. She was encouraged not to attend director's meetings. Her role as director continued to be purely nominal.

Nevertheless it was accepted by both parties that Malcolm's death had brought the quasi partnership arrangements between the brothers to an end. Instead counsel for the widow and trustees approached the case as a matter of family fairness. She:[53]

> '... laid stress on the fact that CIHL was a family company and submitted that what might be fair as between businessmen might not always be fair as between members of a family and that Ian should therefore have tempered the exercise by him of his powers and responsibilities as a director and shareholder of CIHL with this fact in mind.'

The High Court rejected this family fairness argument stating that, in the absence of any argument that the business was a quasi partnership, neither the widow nor the trustees had any expectations arising from participation in the family business nor:[54]

> '... any other legitimate expectation such as to subject the conduct by Ian of CIHL's affairs to any particular equitable consideration.'

In considering the relevance of the transfer of the single share the trial judge found that this was not intended to set up any form of family business trust imposing fiduciary obligations, as Pauline contended. Neither was it a signal for Ian to do entirely as he pleased with the company, as Ian argued. Instead it was simply designed to prevent deadlock so as to allow Ian to operate the company on a day-to-day basis.

Nevertheless unfair prejudice was established based on Ian's breach of duty in helping himself to what was seen to be excessive remuneration. Ian was ordered to buy the shares held by the widow and trust.[55]

The family also went back to court over a dispute as to whether the minority interest should be valued on a full pro-rata or, alternatively, a discounted basis. In that hearing (*Irvine No 2*)[56] the petitioners submitted that a pro rata basis of valuation should apply

---

[53] At para 257 of the judgment in *Irvine (No 1)*.
[54] Also at para 257 of the judgment in *Irvine (No 1)*.
[55] Explained in more detail below in chapter 21.
[56] *Patricia Mary Irvine, Michael Cleobury Thatcher, Patricia Mary Irvine as Trustees of the Accumulation and Maintenance Settlement Dated 6 August 1993 v Ian Charles Irvine, Campbell Irvine (Holdings) Limited (No 2)* [2006] EWHC 583 (Ch).

as, although since the death of Malcolm the company had not been run as quasi partnership in the strict sense, the company nevertheless remained a family company, the articles contained restrictions on transfer and there was no open market for their disposal. They further argued that it was only because of Ian Irvine's behaviour over several years that the family had been driven to seek an exit from the company through the unfair proceedings.

Counsel for the widow and trust again put the argument for family fairness and argued strenuously that:[57]

> 'If this was not a case where a pro-rata basis of valuation should apply, it would be difficult to think that any such case would ever arise, and there would be a risk therefore that the court's discretion in fixing the basis of valuation for a minority holding in a company which was not a quasi-partnership would be atrophied.'

The court rejected this argument explaining that:

> 'Short of a quasi-partnership or some other exceptional circumstance, there is no reason to accord to it a quality which it lacks. CIHL is not a quasi-partnership. There are no exceptional circumstances.'

There were no circumstances that would justify the winding up of the company on a just and equitable basis. As a consequence of the rejection of the fairness approach a discounted valuation was ordered. The absence of a finding of quasi partnership was therefore seen to be crucial.

20.4.9 Saul D Harrison & Sons plc

The most significant obstacle to establishing an argument that all family owned businesses are subject to overriding equitable considerations inherent in the fairness approach is the Court of Appeal decision in *Saul D Harrison & Sons plc*.[58] As one of two leading cases on unfair prejudice (the other being the House of Lords' decision in *O'Neill v Phillips*) and directly concerning a family owned business it is of considerable significance to us.

The facts of the case are set out in **1.5.4**.

The petition of the fourth generation claimant Rosemary (who held about 8.25% of the C shares) received very short shrift indeed both in the High Court, where the petition was struck out as an abuse of process and in the Court of Appeal where that decision was emphatically upheld, leaving the petitioner to pick up a no doubt substantial costs bill, including an order that the costs of the hearing be paid on an indemnity basis.

Why were the courts so dismissive of the claim? To a large extent this appears to be on the basis of the facts of the case, discussed in more detail in chapter 21 below. But most importantly the courts saw nothing in the circumstances of the Saul D Harrison & Sons

---

[57] At para 9 of the judgment.
[58] [1994] BCC 475.

family business to bring it within the second category of companies where equitable considerations apply. Indeed, as the High Court judge in the matter, Vinelott J, remarked:[59]

> '... the significant feature of this petition is that it is nowhere alleged that there is anything in the history of the company or the relationship between the shareholders which could be relied on as superimposing an equitable fetter.'

Counsel for the petitioner argued that the appropriate test of unfairness was whether 'a reasonable bystander would think that the conduct in question was unfair'. This argument was not accepted by the Court of Appeal. Hoffmann LJ (who also went on to give the leading judgment in the House of Lords in *O'Neill v Phillips*) gave the leading judgment. Whilst agreeing that the test of unfairness was indeed an objective one, Lord Hoffmann did:[60]

> 'not think that it helps a great deal to add the reasonable company watcher to the already substantial cast of imaginary characters which the law uses to personify its standards of justice in different situations. An appeal to the views of an imaginary third party makes the concept seem more vague than it really is.'

Instead, a more precise and legalistic approach was required. The starting point was the articles of association. The next question was whether the directors were in breach of their duty to the shareholders. After that comes the question of whether any equitable considerations arise which would justify a fairness approach. Explaining the basis for the application of these considerations Hoffmann LJ said:[61]

> 'Thus the personal relationship between a shareholder and those who control the company may entitle him to say that it would in certain circumstances be unfair for them to exercise a power conferred by the articles upon the board or the company in general meeting. I have in the past ventured to borrow from public law the term "legitimate expectation" to describe the correlative "right" in the shareholder to which such a relationship may give rise. It often arises out of a fundamental understanding between the shareholders which formed the basis of their association but was not put into contractual form ...'

The petitioner in *Saul D Harrison* had indeed argued that she had various 'legitimate expectations' in relation to the company.

Despite the judgment making frequent references to the family business context Hoffmann LJ was content to label this a 'commercial relationship'. He quoted the following passage from Lord Wilberforce's judgment in *Ebrahimi*:[62]

> 'It would be impossible, and wholly undesirable to define the circumstances in which these considerations may arise. Certainly the fact that the company is a small one, or a private company is not enough. There are very many of these where the association is a purely commercial one, of which it can safely be said that the basis of association is adequately and exhaustively laid down in the articles. The superimposition of equitable considerations requires something more.'

---

[59] Vinelott J in the High Court. See p 478 of the case report.
[60] At p 488.
[61] At p 490.
[62] Quoted at p 490 of the *Saul D Harrison* report.

Applying this analysis to the facts and arguments presented in *Saul D Harrison & Sons* Hoffmann LJ concluded that: 'In this case ... there is nothing more'.[63]

The governance scheme established in 1960 was seen as an exhaustive statement of the rights of the shareholders:[64]

> 'The petitioner was given her shares in 1960 pursuant to a reorganisation of the share capital which vested the entire control of the company in the A shareholders and the board whom they appointed. This scheme is binding upon her and there are no special circumstances to modify its effects.'

Accordingly the rules based approach applied. Any legitimate expectations of the shareholders of Saul D Harrison must be found in the articles of association, as supplemented by the Companies Acts and the general fiduciary obligations relating to the general conduct of the directors of a company.

Of course the courts must deal with the facts and evidence of the case before them as presented by the parties through their advisors. But might there be circumstances present in many, if not most, family owned businesses to enable arguments to be made that there is in fact 'something more' and therefore that the fairness approach should apply?

20.5 FAMILY OWNED BUSINESSES – 'SOMETHING MORE'?

It will be clear from the above that family ownership, in and of itself, will not be sufficient to found the requisite degree of trust and confidence necessary to bring equitable principles and the fairness approach into play. In shorthand not all family owned businesses will be treated by the courts as quasi-partnerships. Certainly nearly all family businesses will exhibit many of the features identified by Lord Wilberforce's in *Ebrahimi* (referred to in 20.3.3 above, in particular that they should be seen as 'an association formed and continued on the basis of a personal relationship involving a mutual confidence'. However, as has been shown, it would be going way too far to suggest that minority shareholders in family owned businesses will invariably qualify for equitable treatment:

(1) First Lord Wilberforce himself, in *Ebrahimi*, warns about creating: 'categories or headings under which cases must be brought ... This is wrong. Illustrations may be used, but general words should remain general and not be reduced to the sum of particular instances'.[65] Each case will therefore need to be argued and considered on its merits.

(2) Secondly, there are many larger family owned businesses where the shareholders will include employee shareholders, investors and other third parties, including publicly quoted companies with substantial family shareholdings. There the interests of third parties and certainty will require that a rules based approach should prevail.[66] Presumably there would be nothing to prevent equitable considerations being introduced into disputes between the family shareholders, provided these did not affect the position of third party non-family shareholders.

---

[63] At p 490.
[64] At p 490.
[65] At p 374.
[66] Following the logic in *Astec (BSR) plc* [1988] 2 BCLC 556.

(3) Thirdly, in family businesses with more sophisticated governance systems it may well be inferred that those systems were intended to be comprehensive and exhaustive. Accordingly the role of the courts to supplement express agreements between family members (whether or not legally binding) should be correspondingly limited. Indeed the governance structure set up in the 1960's formed a key part of the reasoning of the Court of Appeal in *Saul D Harrison* in applying a rules based approach.

(4) Fourthly, and related to the above, the circumstances of family businesses will change and evolve over time. There might well be factors present in an earlier stage family firm that would justify a fairness approach, which diminish over time, in the same business, as it gradually loses the characteristics of a quasi-partnership.

(5) Last, but by no means least, the decided cases, include cases such as *Saul D Harrison* and *Irvine* where on the facts, the courts have decided that the family business concerned the rules based approach should apply.

Aggrieved family members and their advisors will therefore need to point to something more than the fact that their case concerns a family owned business in order to secure a remedy based on the fairness approach.

That additional factor must be based on recognised equitable principles. It will not be enough to make an argument based on abstract concepts of fairness. For example what a reasonable bystander would regard as fair.[67] In *O'Neill v Phillips* Lord Hoffman[68] explained that, whilst the fairness approach (as we term it) can:

> 'free the court from technical considerations of legal right and to confer a wide power to do what appeared just and equitable. But this does not mean that the court can do whatever the individual judge happens to think fair. The concept of fairness must be applied judicially and the content which it is given by the courts must be based upon rational principles.'[69]

Lord Hoffmann went on to quote with approval the maxim of Warner J in *In Re JE Cade & Son Ltd*[70] that: 'The court ... has a very wide discretion, but it does not sit under a palm tree'.

Instead it will be necessary to demonstrate that the family member concerned has a legitimate interest arising from the context of their particular family business. Context is king.

> 'Although fairness is a notion which can be applied to all kinds of activities its content will depend upon the context in which it is being used. Conduct which is perfectly fair between competing businessmen may not be fair between members of a family. In some sports it may require, at best, observance of the rules, in others ("it's not cricket") it may be unfair in some circumstances to take advantage of them. All is said to be fair in love and war. So the context and background are very important.'

It will therefore be necessary to examine the background to the family business in some detail to determine the expectations of family members. Some expectations may have been created by the founder. Other expectations may be founded on express or implied

---

[67] *Saul D Harrison plc* at p 488.
[68] At p 1098.
[69] *O'Neill v Phillips* at p 1098
[70] [1992] BCLC 213 at p 227. See chapter 21 for a more detailed discussion of *JE Case & Son Ltd*.

agreements or understandings by other family members. They may arise from the way the business has been conducted and the language used by the family members themselves.

But we should use the term 'legitimate expectations' with a degree of a caution. Although the term was employed by Lord Hoffmann in the Court of Appeal in *Saul D Harrison*, by the time he considered *O'Neill v Phillips* in the House of Lords, he seemed to be regretting the potential use of that term, as potentially justifying a more liberal application of the fairness approach and with that the availability of the unfair prejudice remedy. He said in *O'Neill* that:[71]

> 'it was probably a mistake to use this term ... The concept of a legitimate expectation should not be allowed to lead a life of its own, capable of giving rise to equitable restraints in circumstances to which traditional equitable principles have no application.'

In particular Lord Hoffmann seemed troubled by the fact that although Mr O'Neill hoped to receive further shares in the company in question and this hope had been encouraged by Mr Phillips, such encouragement had fallen short of an unequivocal agreement to actually pass over control of the company.

Although there is no requirement for any promises or agreement to be strictly legally enforceable as a contract Lord Hoffmann suggested that:[72]

> 'A useful cross-check in a case like this is to ask whether exercise of the power in question would be contrary to what the parties by words or conduct actually agreed. Would it conflict with the promises that they appear to have exchanged?'

This approach may work in some family business contexts. Take the example of employment expectations. In some cases, such as in *The Gate of India* there might be a clear understanding between the senior generation that their children can join the family business as both owners and employees.[73] But in many cases, in particular in later stage family businesses, such as in *Saul D Harrison*, any agreements or understandings may be historic and incapable of being satisfactorily evidenced by the time a dispute arises. Even if the future generation family member can credibly point to tangible evidence of what their forbears agreed or intended, to what extent can this historic intention bind future generations?

In other businesses family members may have developed personal expectations, for example of employment, or participation in management or even ownership succession. Such expectations might be legitimate, in the sense of not being an unreasonable hope. However these expectations might not have been communicated or discussed with other relevant family members. So no argument can be made that the family have agreed the matter in question, even at the level of a non-legally binding common understanding.

---

[71] At p 1102 of the *O'Neill* judgment.
[72] At p 1101 of the judgment.
[73] This might be enforceable as between the sibling partners in the senior generation. However, on the basis of *O'Neill*, and in the absence of either unequivocal promises on the part of the senior generation to pass on ownership or, alternatively a recognition by the courts of wider family business factors, such an expectation likely to be un-enforceable via CA, s 994 so far as the next generation are concerned. The possibility of a proprietary estoppel claim is explored in more detail in chapter 19 (Inheritance Disputes).

The House of Lords in *O'Neill* were dealing with a dispute between two non-family members who had agreed to go into business together. They did not need to consider the complexities of family relationships or historical context. Lord Hoffmann quoted a formulation used in an earlier case where the judge said:[74]

> 'in order to give rise to an equitable restraints based on 'legitimate expectations' what is required is **a personal relationship** or personal dealings of some kind between the party seeking to exercise the legal right and the party seeking to restrain the exercise, such as will affect the conscience of the former.'

Lord Hoffmann approved this formulation, apparently on the basis that he thought the reference to 'conscience' was itself a reference to the jurisdiction of the 'long departed Court of Chancery.'

We therefore suggest that rather than concentrating on the structural form of a family business (and asking whether or not it is a quasi-partnership) or stopping at an examination of evidence of what the parties to the dispute have actually agreed, a better question might be 'are there any factors in this particular family business which point to the application of the fairness approach?'

Those factors might be any combination of agreements or understandings, historic or contemporary, communicated or implicit in the circumstances of that family business concerned. In various circumstances these factors would be re-enforced by support from principles derived from branches of equity other than partnership law. This approach, we would suggest would be consistent with the true spirit of *Ebrahimi* and in particular Lord Wilberforce's observation (referred to above) that:[75]

> 'It would be impossible, and wholly undesirable, to define the circumstances in which these considerations may arise.'

But Hollington provides a warning, elevated to the status of a principle that:[76]

> 'There is a deep rooted judicial caution in allowing fiduciary principles to intrude upon commercial transactions and relations.'

This discussion has echoes of the analysis of the differences between family and business systems contained in chapter 1,[77] with features of the rules based approach roughly corresponding to the business system and those referable to the fairness approach falling within the family system.

As has been seen the core legal remedies go some way towards the features of the family system. Informal agreements and understandings between family members may be respected and enforced if it can be shown that the formal documents governing their family business relationships do not fully capture their express understanding. So, to an extent company law can be seen to have relaxed the boundaries between the family business and ownership systems.

---

[74] Jonathan Parker J in *Astec (BSR) plc* [1998] 2 BCLC 556 at p 588 (emphasis added) – quoted in *O'Neill* at p 1101 of the judgment.
[75] At p 379.
[76] Hollington, op cit, Principle 16(2) at p 18.
[77] In particular see Figure 3.7. (The system clash in the family business.)

Figure 20.1: The rules and fairness approaches in the family and business systems

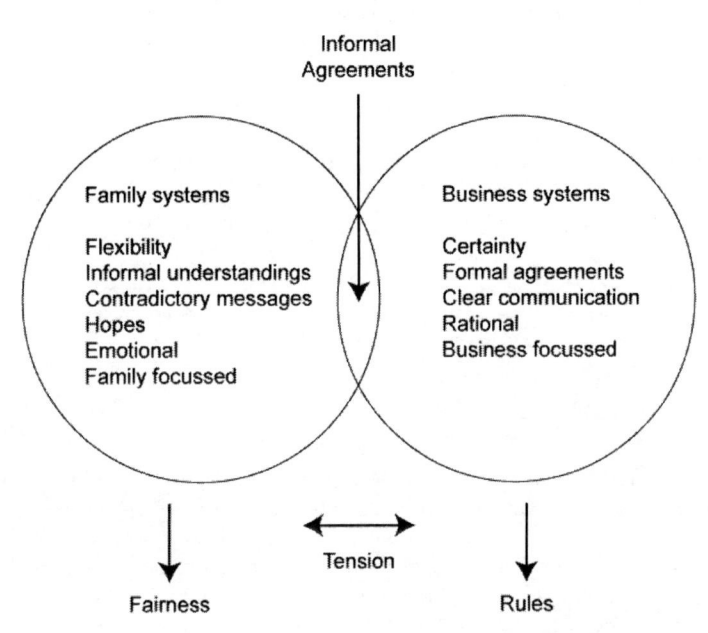

```
                        Informal
                       Agreements
                            |
        Family systems      |      Business systems
                            v
        Flexibility               Certainty
        Informal understandings   Formal agreements
        Contradictory messages    Clear communication
        Hopes                     Rational
        Emotional                 Business focussed
        Family focussed

              |            <--->            |
              v           Tension           v
           Fairness                       Rules
```

But much of family business life is founded on ambiguity, imperfect communication or unexpressed hopes and expectations. As explained above mere expectations, falling short of informal agreements or mutual understandings are unlikely to be protected. On this basis the law, as emerging from current cases, might be seen to have erected a barrier between those family expectations to protect the certainties of the business system.

But are there factors within the circumstances of certain family companies, which point to a further relaxation of the boundary between family and business systems and the wider application of the fairness approach?

20.6 FAMILY BUSINESS FACTORS

We are certainly not suggesting that the mere fact that a court is concerned with a family owned business, is a sufficient factor, in and of itself, to justify the application of the fairness approach. Circumstances such as the presence of non-family interests or comprehensive governance arrangements might make this entirely inappropriate. The argument is that, on closer examination of the family concerned, factors might emerge justifying a more liberal application of the fairness approach.

The approach of the courts to date has been to concentrate on the nature of express agreements, expectations and understandings between family members, rather than intervene simply because a family relationship exists. But our argument is that the existence of family relationships are likely to mean that other expectations and agreements are more likely to be present: albeit often stemming from the family system, rather than being driven by business considerations.

Often these arguments boil down to saying that the structure and context of the family business concerned may create an implied agreement between the family members, which is equally appropriate for recognition and protection under the fairness approach as an express understanding would be.

Some of these arguments have limited support from authorities. But it is accepted that many may only sit comfortably in the shade of Warner J's palm tree and could shrivel when exposed to the sunlight of judicial scrutiny. Nevertheless the concern persists that in concentrating on the business aspects of situations that have come before the courts to date, the wider context of the business family situation has not always received full recognition.[78]

Relevant family business factors and possible legal arguments could include the matters outlined in this paragraph. The arguments and factors overlap.

20.6.1 Proprietary estoppel[79]

Proprietary estoppel becomes relevant if someone has given a clear indication that they intend to follow a particular course of action and another person has relied on those indications to their detriment. Even if those indications fall short of a legally enforceable agreement the person giving the indications might be prevented from going back on their promises under the equitable principles of estoppel.

20.6.2 Participation

As has been shown above the courts will recognise an expectation of participation in a family business context. This may go beyond participation by working in or taking an active management role in a traditional sibling quasi partnership as in *Shah v Shah* or *Brownlow* and extend to wider participation in more general and remote management as family directors as in *Harding*. The *Gate of India* case suggests that expectations of participation by the next generation may be recognised by the court.

However, there are a number of circumstances where participation expectations have not yet been examined by the courts. These include matters such as the representation of family branch members as directors.

20.6.3 Senior generation's wishes

Where the senior generation gift shares to all of their children, rather than looking at alternative dispositions between private and business assets, are the senior generation expressly or by implication expressing a wish that the family as a whole should have a right to participate in the family company?

In the *Harding* and *Fisher v Cadman* cases reviewed above it is clear that neither Elizabeth Harding nor the Cadman brothers welcomed the participation of their siblings. In both cases they were nevertheless held to be subject to equitable constraints.

---

[78] Some modest comfort might be obtained from the suggestion attributed to Harman LJ that 'equity was not presumed to be of an age past childbearing' by Lord Evershed in *Simpsons Motor Sales London Ltd v Hendon Corporation* [1964] AC 1088 as quoted in *Hollington* at p 212.

[79] See chapter 19.

The rationale of the courts in these cases was that they were dealing with an extended form of quasi partnership. But in no sense can there be said to have been any agreement or mutual understanding by the family as a whole to create such a partnership.

Is there an alternative argument or explanation? This is that the children managing the family business could not accept the shares that they were given whilst denying their siblings their right to enjoy meaningful participation in the family business. Did the shares that the respondents were given therefore also come with equitable strings attached?

20.6.4 Succession

Again the *Gate of India* case suggests that wider agreements relating to succession may be recognised and enforced by the courts. Recognition of the wider ethnic and cultural context of the business concerned clearly was a factor for the courts in arriving at their decision.

But why shouldn't similar agreements and expectations arising as much from the internal values and culture of the family business be equally capable of enforcement? Certainly in *Ebrahami* Lord Wilberforce[80] criticised an earlier first instance decision[81] where the High Court refused to intervene in a case where two older brothers used a provision in the articles to refuse to register the transfer of shares left to their two younger brothers in their father's will, dismissing the younger brothers from employment into the bargain.

Employment

Again the *Gate of India* case suggests that active participation and an expectation of hands on employment in the family business may be protected under the fairness approach. In that case the courts found that there was a clear agreement between the two founder brothers that Mr Rahman junior would step fully into his father's shoes and would play an active role.

The courts have not specifically addressed the issue of employment expectations, in the context of branches of a later stage family business. The actual employment practices may favour a particular insider branch. Arguably, in the most extreme cases, this could amount to a breach of duty on the part of the 'haves'.[82] But could branch favouritism also be a ground for intervention on the fairness principle if a more general expectation of wider family employment could be demonstrated by the outsiders? Put more simply 'if my children are denied jobs in the family business offered to your children, then I should be entitled to ask you to buy my shares'.

---

[80] At pp 376–377.
[81] *Re Cuthbert Cooper and Sons Ltd* [1937] Ch 392.
[82] For example the duty against conflicts of interest discussed in chapter 8.

20.6.5 Expectations of information[83]

A frequent complaint from more remote family business members is that 'we don't know what is going on'. Often communication including the provision of information is one of the first things to suffer when family tensions rise. In *Irvine* the judge criticised Ian's failure to provide accounts and information about remuneration and takeover offers.

The gold standard would be that non-management outsider family members are, so far as practicable, kept fully informed about the family business. A possible yardstick could be that the more remote family shareholders in other branches of the family have access to the same level of information as the family members who do not work in the company but are seen as close to the family business management. Put differently information asymmetry should be kept to a minimum.

Perhaps the failure to provide a reasonable level of information could be seen as a species of exclusion. In other words withholding of information is a factor in exclusion from proper participation in the family owned business.

20.6.6 Provision of support

It would be highly unusual for non-family business shareholders or their dependents to have an expectation of financial support in retirement or in the event of death or ill health. In *Irvine* Ian seemed to regard any payments actually made for the benefit of his deceased brother's family as entirely discretionary, an 'act of emotion'[84] rather than being based on any legally enforceable legitimate expectation.

No evidence was put forward in *Irvine* that the brothers had expressly agreed to support each other's families if catastrophe struck. However in some family businesses, perhaps particularly those in the farming community (and also in some cultures) a more general expectation is created that family members will be 'looked after' in retirement or otherwise. Whilst this might not create a legally enforceable right to a set amount by way of, for example, annuity or fixed dividend, are such expectations capable of tempering the ability of those in control of a family business to increase their own salaries at the expense of paying dividends even where such increase in salary might not otherwise amount to a breach of duty?

20.6.7 Active dividend policies

The inter-relationship between failure to pay dividends and unfair prejudice claims is considered in more detail in chapter 21. *Re McCarthy Surfacing Ltd*[85] suggests that an absolute refusal on the part of the board to consider paying dividends may amount to a breach of duty. Often it will not be easy to show failure to pay dividends amounts to a breach of duty. Some family businesses will have clearly articulated dividend policies as part of their governance structure.

---

[83] Access to information as a key component of governance is discussed in chapter 17 and the relationship between information and unfair prejudice is explored at **21.6.11**.
[84] See para 176 of the judgment in *Irvine (No 1)*.
[85] [2008] EWHC 2279 (Ch). The case is discussed in detail in chapter 2.

In other later stage family businesses dividends will have been paid regularly. An expectation that the wider family are to benefit from the business through the payment of dividends will have been created. Simply stopping dividends for no good commercial reason may well amount to a breach of duty.

But financial circumstances may change so that maintaining the dividend stream becomes harder. If the board prioritise maintaining their own salaries, or less contentiously re-investment in the family business it will be correspondingly harder to show a breach of duty. However the non-working family members then will be receiving no income and will have no reasonable prospect of an exit route. Is there an argument that the fairness approach requires the board of such businesses to actively develop or explore policies or strategies to restore reasonable dividends, or perhaps provide an exit route? Accordingly failure to give active consideration to this should allow the intervention of fairness approach based remedies.

20.6.8 Family business sub-stratum

As explained in chapter 22 below, one basis for a just and equitable winding up order is that the basic substratum of a company, its underlying foundations, have been destroyed.

In *Symington v Symington Quarries Ltd*[86] one of the bases for granting a winding up order was that the foundation of the company had been destroyed. This had occurred because one of the brothers concerned effectively staged a 'coup d'état' to exclude his brother.

Commentators suggest that this ground is rarely relied on in UK (as opposed to commonwealth) jurisdictions nowadays.[87] Those cases, and the historic English cases, typically concern companies set up as 'single purpose vehicles', for example to exploit intellectual property or to manage funds where the initial purpose has disappeared but leaving the vehicle intact. What follows in this section is therefore highly speculative.

In *Saul D Harrison*[88] the petitioner, as an alternative to an unfair prejudice order, also asked for winding up order of the family business. However no basis for the intervention of equity was pleaded in the petition. It would be extremely interesting to understand what the key family members including the founder Saul Harrison and his three surviving sons would have said, if asked to explain t the foundations of their family business, particularly at the time of the 1960 re-organisation. It might be that the intention was always that the working directors as A shareholders would have full discretion to manage the business as they saw fit (subject only to over-riding fiduciary duties) free from the interference of non-working family members and that this power passed with the A shares. The B & C shareholders should have no right to interfere or question management and they were to regard any dividends and other benefits they received as pure bounty.

But it is perfectly possible that the three brothers talked about a common intention for the family business to provide collectively for the wider family as a whole. If so and if the financial position of the company had changed (or the family had grown so large) so

---

[86] [1905] 8 F 121: The Lord President and Lord Adam both at p 129.
[87] See *Hollington on Shareholders' Remedies* (7th edn) at paras 10.39–10.46.
[88] *Saul D Harrison & Sons plc* [1994] BCC 475 at p 476.

that it was no longer possible for the business to support everyone, can the family sub-stratum be seen to have been damaged thus bringing fairness considerations into play?

There is some limited support for this proposition to be found in the Commonwealth fund management cases referred to in *Hollington*. In particular the Cayman Islands cases referred to, suggesting that once the reasonable expectations of participating investors can no longer be met the corporate structures of investment funds should be wound up.

Although *Hollington* refers to funds cases from other jurisdictions taking a more restricted view of lost sub-stratum based winding up, these seem to envisage that investors will have an alternative exit route.[89] Applying this line of thinking to the context of a later stage family business in circumstances such as that in *Saul D Harrison* the argument would essentially be that 'when the founder left the business to the whole family the expectation was clearly that we would all benefit. Now that this fundamental foundation of the family business has been removed the fairness approach dictates that something must be done'.

Against this argument:

- It is clear from *Saul D Harrison* and *O'Neill v Phillips* that mere inference and speculation will not suffice. Some clear evidence of intention will be required for the courts to take a fairness approach.
- In the earlier English substratum cases the courts were wary about being asked to provide opinions 'as to the probable success or non-success of a company as a commercial speculation'.[90] In *Saul D Harrison* there were grounds for optimism that the fortunes of the family business might be restored and with it the potential for participation in profits by the minority may be resumed. In such cases the argument that the foundation of the family business has been lost cannot be made out. Conversely, by the time it becomes clear that the financial foundation has indeed been eroded it might be too late for the minority to salvage anything from the wreckage.
- Circumstances and, with that expectations might change. For example if significant external shareholders have been introduced to a family company, or one branch invests heavily in the business to see it through lean times, when other branches do not. The need for flexibility and departure from family expectations might be dictated by the business circumstances of the family company concerned.
- More fundamentally what is there to distinguish the lot of a shareholder in a poorly performing family business and their non-family business counterpart? Surely the risk of no return comes with the territory of owning shares in an unquoted company? The main counterarguments are that in a non-family private business the shareholders are both more likely to be either working members or to have taken a positive decision to invest in the business. Family members will not have had this choice. They will usually have inherited their interest.
- Most significantly the evidence that may emerge is that the founder or previous generations intended the business to remain in the family for the foreseeable future, if not for all eternity. The winding up of the family business to release capital and share out the family silver will be the last thing that the founder intended.

---

[89] See the discussion on British Virgin Islands case at para 10-46 in *Hollington*.
[90] *Suburban Hotel Company* quoted in *Hollington* at para 10-46.

However the point of the argument is not that the loss of family foundation should justify the drastic step of winding up the family business with all that entails. Rather that reference to the line of loss of substratum cases could be 'something more' to open the door for equitable intervention. In particular less drastic remedies under unfair prejudice may become available such as a purchase of own shares by the company under CA 2006, s 996(2)(e).

The basic argument is that just as the exclusion from participation in a quasi-partnership in the absence of an offer to buy the excluded quasi partner's shares will justify intervention so ought the removal of any family business foundation stone, without reasonable steps being taken to facilitate an exit.

20.6.9 Exit rights and routes

In *Ebrahimi* Lord Wilberforce identified that lack of exit rights was one of the characteristics of businesses where equitable intervention was likely to be justified. However in *O'Neill v Phillips* Lord Hoffmann made it clear that what is now CA 2006, s 994 was not intended to introduce an automatic exit right in the form of a 'no-fault corporate divorce'.[91]

Much of the rationale in relying on the rules based approach rests on a theory of voluntary association; that shareholders have agreed to join a company on the basis of its constitution. They have taken an informed and adult decision to invest in the company concerned. However in later stage family businesses family members will usually have had no choice in the matter, they will simply have inherited their shares and will have no choice but to inherit the governance position along with those shares. Equally those shares might constitute a large proportion of that family member's theoretical wealth. But, in the absence of a workable exit mechanism that wealth might be pretty much illusory.

In *Harries*[92] failure on the part of a one-time quasi partner to take an exit route available to them was held to amount to an election on their part to remain in the company concerned on the alternative basis as an investor, therefore not qualifying for the fairness approach and a non-discounted valuation of their shares when later unfair prejudice occurred.

Could the converse be true? Family businesses evolve through their life cycles and lose the look and feel of quasi partnerships, with greater divisions between insiders and outsiders. Is there an argument that the quasi partnership status of the outsiders could be preserved unless and until the outsiders are presented with a viable exit route? This could be a one-of exercise in 'pruning the ownership tree',[93] exit rights contained in formal governance documents, or, as was the case in *Harries* failure to act on earlier unfair prejudice, which would have created a clear exit right. This reasoning was employed in *Sunrise Radio*[94] where the fact that the petitioner had no real opportunity to exit on an undiscounted basis after ceasing to be an employed quasi partner was one of the factors which persuaded the court to apply a fairness approach.

---

[91] See p 1104.
[92] *Re A Company (No 005134 of 1986) ex parte Harries* [1989] BCLC 383.
[93] See chapter 11 (Ownership Overview) and the discussion on share buy-backs contained there.
[94] *Sunrise Radio Limited; Geeta Kohli v Dr Avtar Lit, Ravinder Kumar Jain, Surinderpal Singh Lit, Sunrise Radio Limited* [2009] EWHC 2893 (Ch).

In the above cases the presence (*Harries*) or absence (*Sunrise Radio*) of an exit route meant that the fairness approach was lost or preserved, respectively, for the original quasi partners. Our argument for preserved quasi partnership status requires taking this analysis one stage further. In a family business context that status, or more precisely the application of the fairness approach, would need to transfer with the quasi partners shares, in effect to be treated as a special right attached to family business shares. Looking at the main cases we have looked at in the chapter this would be for the benefit of the widow and children in *Irvine*. In *Saul D Harrison* the argument for inherited fairness treatment would have to be preserved for two generations[95] or, on the facts of the case approaching 20 years. But that does seem to be a more arguable analysis of the realities of family business life than the suggestion that the outcome 1960 re-organisation drew a line under Rosemary's wider equitable rights and expectations.

Even if this argument that rights stemming from a quasi-partnership can be preserved and inherited to justify a continuing fairness approach this only takes the outsider family member so far. The point made in *O'Neil* that no-fault corporate divorce is not recognised in English law will still hold good. On the facts of *Saul D Harrison* there were no grounds for divorce even though freehold premises had been sold any no attempt had been made to offer the outsiders an exit. Many of the other arguments raised in this paragraph can be seen as suggestions for additional grounds of divorce applicable to the suggested fairness rights inherited by family business outsiders.

As referred to above, some family owned businesses have created exit routes for family members who no longer want their inheritance to be tied up in the family business. Can the exit route argument be taken one stage further? Could a failure to provide such an exit route (or to actively seek to do so) be a relevant factor to justify a fairness approach? It could be argued that this would simply be taking the rationale in *McCarthy Brothers* (ie that the board of a company have an active duty to consider whether to pay dividends) one stage further. After all the question of whether or not to return capital by share buy-backs is ever present in the quoted company arena. There an aggrieved shareholder has the ability to sell their shares on the market.

20.6.10 A family business quasi-trust

Alternatively is there an argument that in some circumstances the non-management shareholders have in fairness and equity a legitimate expectation that their interests will be taken into account and properly and fully considered by the family members with management and shareholding control of their family business? Expressions such as 'stewardship', custodianship or being 'entrusted' to run the family business are fairly common in the context of family businesses. Is there an argument that, in appropriate circumstances, this should, receive some form of legal recognition?

In other words that the family business is subject to some form of 'quasi trust', under which the controlling shareholders have a fiduciary duty which goes above and beyond the duties that would otherwise be owed by directors of a pure commercial concern to their minority shareholders?

---

[95] The petitioner, Rosemary, was the grand-daughter of Saul's son Alfred, one of four sibling (quasi) partners. See genogram of the Harrison family at Figure 3.13 in chapter 3.

But this suggestion would cut across a basic principle of company law; that the directors owe their duties to the company itself, and do not hold the assets of the company as trustees on behalf of individual shareholders.[96]

20.6.11 Family business good faith

The concept of a family business quasi-trust is very similar to the concept of implied duties of good faith. Clearly family members who are also directors will owe fiduciary duties to all shareholders, whether family or not and irrespective of branch loyalties.

However, as a general proposition, shareholders do not have a duty of good faith towards each other and may exercise their votes as they please. The basic idea is that shares are property and the voting rights attached to them are therefore property rights. In many family business situations the exercise of those rights will be an inherent consequence of the decision of the senior generation as to whom their shares will be gifted, by will or otherwise.

The principal exception to this proposition are where that exercise would amount to a 'fraud on the minority. This discussed in detail in chapter 23 below (Derivative Claims). A further exception is where there is an express obligation of good faith, for example in a shareholders' agreement.

It may also be possible to argue that if family charters, creeds or other similar documents contain references to acting 'fairly' or in 'good faith' or some similar expression or if such language forms part of the underlying family culture, then the same position should apply. In which case the majority shareholders would be obliged, in exercising their voting rights on any relevant matter (for example a share buy-back proposed by the board to create an exit route) to undertake some form of balancing act between their own interests and those of the minority family member.[97]

Is there an argument that in some circumstances family members can stand in a fiduciary relationship to each other? What is the position in the absence of any express written or verbal understanding? In *Clemens v Clemens Brothers Ltd* (see 20.4.4) the judge relied on *Ebrahimi* principles to arrive at the conclusion that the aunt, Miss Clemens senior, was 'not entitled to exercise her majority vote in whatever way she pleases'.[98] However he declined to say exactly why this was the case. Could one explanation be that as majority shareholder in a small family company the aunt had an implied duty to act in good faith towards her niece, the granddaughter of one of the founders?

20.6.12 Change of equitable circumstances

One of the most difficult issues for family businesses is where circumstances change so that the business moves from classification as a straightforward and traditional quasi partnership into something else. Again *Irvine* provides a stark example of this. There was no doubt that during his lifetime a quasi-partnership existed between Malcolm and Ian. But in the absence of being able to show that some alternative equitable

---

[96] The rule in *Foss v Harbottle*.
[97] See *F&C Alternative Investments Holdings Ltd v Barthelemy* [2012] Ch 613.
[98] [1976] 2 All ER 268. This the following quote all at p 282.

circumstances had arisen on or after Malcolm's sudden death, justifying the application of the fairness approach, his widow Patricia was condemned to a discounted valuation.

Of course membership of a family owned business changes in much less tragic circumstances than in *Irvine* as a result of the natural evolution and succession process. The traditional family business model is for the children of the former 'sibling quasi partners' to evolve into a cousin collaboration.[99] But that model implicitly assumes a cohesive family with each party playing their agreed role under a coherent governance structure. It does not cater for the potential tensions that can arise, between the 'haves', those cousins with jobs and in day-to-day control of the family enterprise and the 'have-nots', those cousins more remote from either the business, the haves, or both.

The potential for such tensions will increase if there is a governance vacuum created by the absence of a recognisable governance system. The seeds for future tension may also be sown by a lack of interest and support for the family business on the part of the 'have-nots'. *Saul D Harrison* presents a prime example. At one stage that business was a clear sibling quasi-partnership between the four sons of the founder Saul Harrison. When the matter came to court the shares were widely spread between the family, including family trusts and the fourth generation. There is no way that the business could have been categorised as a quasi-partnership under any traditional interpretation of that term. Does this mean that, so far as the initial 'have-nots' were concerned the quasi-partnership rights of their fathers evaporated into the ether on their death-bed, simply as a result of the accidence of employment and control?

Alternatively were the rights of the fathers as quasi partners replaced by something else giving rise to an alternative basis for equitable treatment under *Ebrahimi* principles? For example could it have been argued that one of the key points of the 1960 re-organisation was for each of the family branches to have been represented on the board. When that was no longer the case did the remaining directors and 'A 'shareholders have some sort of additional duty towards the unrepresented branches, in particular to offer an exit route?

20.6.13 Equity and passivity

One possibility is that the 'have-nots' in *Saul D Harrison* remained a silent and passive minority until something stirred them into activity. This might have been the realisation that substantial capital sums had become available following the sale of the premises. As a general rule equitable remedies become harder to enforce the longer the interval between the wrong and the petitioner seeking remedy. The maxim is 'delay defeats equity'. However (as explained in chapter 21), even considerable delay will not necessarily defeat the availability of the main remedy of unfair prejudice.

Passivity on the part of more remote family members can arise for a number of reasons. Sheer lack of time or interest in the family business. Perhaps there will be a wish not to be seen to be rocking the family boat, at least whilst surviving members of the senior generation are still alive. Perhaps a sense of guilt because those in control are making career and financial sacrifices to keep the family business going (perhaps particularly relevant in the agricultural arena) whilst the 'have-nots' are not burdened by this responsibility. What is clear is that such passivity is most unlikely to benefit the minority family shareholder if a dispute does arise in the future.

---

[99] Family business life cycles are discussed in chapter 3 (Tools, Models and Theories).

This can be simply illustrated by the non-family business case of *DR Chemicals Ltd*[100] where it was held that a previous quasi partnership came to an end when the business moved from the premises of one of the shareholders. That shareholder then found out that his previous 'partner' had procured an allotment of shares to himself diluting the property owner from 40% to 4% of the equity. This was found to be unfair prejudice. Nevertheless the order was for the petitioner's shares to be bought back on a discounted basis, thereby providing the majority shareholder with some benefit from his own wrongdoing. The logic applied was that by remaining as a member once the quasi partnership had ended the petitioner had elected to remain as an investor.

20.6.14 The fairness approach – conclusion

It will be appreciated that the arguments for application of the fairness approach set out in this section become increasingly speculative and un-supported by authority as the list develops. Equally the above arguments, absent clear evidence that the family had actively enshrined the underlying principles may be seen simply as statements that 'family businesses are special'. As a stand-alone argument this proposition has received, at best, a mixed reaction in the courts.

It will also be clear that, whilst many of those involved in family businesses, in particular in traditional trading sibling quasi-partnerships may be well placed to obtain shareholder remedies based on the fairness approach, in many family business circumstances this is unlikely to be the case. Those involved in later stage cousin consortium family businesses seem particularly vulnerable.

Many if not all of the issues raised in shareholder remedies cases can be both foreseen and catered for in express family business governance structures. Family shareholders in such businesses would be well advised to push for the introduction of express governance structures before discontent and damaging disputes arise. It would be unwise to rely on the family management, whose position is already well protected by the law, as it currently stands, to provide adequate or assured protection.

20.7 REMEDIES AND GOVERNANCE STRUCTURE

A related topic to consider is the inter-relationship between the power of the courts to intervene to grant the various shareholder remedies discussed in detail in the chapters that follow and the formal and informal parts of the governance structure of the family company.

20.7.1 Remedies and the articles

Every family company will have articles of association. The key provisions on a breakdown of relationships will usually be the share transfer provisions. Does a member have a right of exit? Must he sell his shares if asked to do so when no longer employed or ceasing to be a director? If so, on what terms? The articles are the obvious starting point in considering shareholder rights and available remedies. Often the articles will be end point as well.

---

[100] [1989] 5 BCC 39.

In *Re A Company (No 004377 of 1986)*[101] Mr Justice Hoffmann (as he then was) took a restrictive approach and refused an unfair prejudice order sought by a former director in a non-family business quasi-partnership, holding him bound by the compulsory transfer provisions in the articles including those relating to the auditors valuation. Hoffmann J was concerned that the alternative of a court valuation would 'take longer and be far more expensive'. Accordingly:[102]

> '... in the normal case of a breakdown of a corporate quasi-partnership there should [not] ordinarily be any legitimate expectation that a member wishing to have his shares purchased should be entitled to have them valued by the court rather than the auditors pursuant to the articles.'

However the articles are by no means necessarily the end point. Often shareholder remedies are based on the principle that, as a matter of equity, it will be inappropriate for one shareholder to enforce their strict rights under the articles. In the above case Lord Hoffmann left the door open for claims which involved 'bad faith or plain impropriety in the conduct of the respondents', or cases where the articles 'provide for some arbitrary or artificial method of valuation'.[103]

The courts in other later cases have declined to follow the valuation mechanism in articles where there were legitimate grounds for questioning the independence an impartiality of the valuer appointed under the valuation mechanism contained in the articles, usually the auditor who was perceived as being too close to the majority shareholders.[104]

The background circumstances of the company may have changed so that the minority could fairly say that the provisions of the articles will not fairly operate in the new circumstances. In *Virdi v Abbey Leisure Ltd*,[105] a non-family business quasi partnership joint venture was formed to set up a nightclub. Mr Virdi, one of the shareholders had fallen out with the other two. They offered to buy out Mr Virdi in accordance with the articles. These contained an exit mechanism providing for the valuation of an outgoing shareholder's shares by the company's auditors but no stipulation that this should be on a full pro-rata basis. The High Court judge thought that Mr Virdi should be bound by the articles. The Court of Appeal disagreed. The night club had ceased to trade and the assets of the company consisted just of cash. In the circumstances of the case it was unreasonable to expect Mr Virdi to accept the risk of a discount when a just and equitable winding up, although more expensive, would ensure that he received a full pro-rata share.

The key question is whether these later cases, such as *Virdi* should be seen as having been decided on their own particular facts or whether, as *Hollington*[106] suggests should be seen as evidence of a more interventionist approach by the courts so that that the formal provisions of the articles are less likely to be seen as definitive.

The answer to that question will be of considerable concern to both majority shareholders wishing to frame a reasonable offer in relation to an unfair prejudice

---

[101] [1987] WLR 102.
[102] At p 110.
[103] At p 110.
[104] See *Re Boswell (Steels) Ltd* [1988] 5 BCC 145 and *Issacs v Belfield Furnishings* [2006] 2 BCLC 705.
[105] [1990] BCC 60.
[106] At p 304.

petition and to minority shareholders deciding whether or not they should accept an offer that has been tabled. We will return to this issue in chapter 24 (Shareholder Disputes).

20.7.2 Family charters

In *O'Neill v Phillips* Lord Hoffmann referred to the legitimate expectations of the parties and suggested that:[107]

> 'One useful cross check ... is to ask whether the exercise of the power in question would be contrary to what the parties, by word or conduct have actually agreed.'

Clear evidence of what a family have agreed, will therefore be highly relevant. That agreement could be evidenced by a family charter. Even though charters will usually be expressed to be not legally binding it will often seem appropriate that the court should give effect to the provisions of a charter. However no relevant case appears to have come before the courts. It is unclear whether this is because family charters are still sufficiently rare as not to have been litigated or whether (as we would hope) the existence of charters has removed, or considerably reduced, the need for litigation.

Certainly a number of cases have involved the courts attempting to retrospectively divine the intentions of a family based on, in both senses of the word, partial evidence. For example *Brownlow v Marshall*[108] turned on the significance of an entire agreement clause[109] in Mrs Brownlow's service agreement. Did this mean that once removed from employment she had no further expectations to participate in the family business? Rejecting that contention the judge came to the conclusion that:[110]

> '... it seems to me to have been a family expectation, growing over the years, that each of the children of Mr and Mrs Marshall Snr would, so far as possible and so far as personal circumstances allowed, be brought into the management of the affairs of the company. Once such status had been achieved (recognised by appointment as directors) it was expected that the relevant person would continue to be involved in the management. Throughout the various dissensions that I have recounted, it was recognised that if a family shareholder was to be dislodged from management, something would have to be done to realise the value of his or her shares.'

It must therefore follow that, to put it no higher, at least significant weight will be attached to family charters and similar documents to the extent that these supplement and do not directly contradict the provisions of formal binding governance documents such as articles or legally binding shareholder agreements.

There is however a paradox. The more detailed the governance structure of a family company the less scope for a court to intervene and rewrite or supplement those provisions.[111] This might be the case even though, absent the governance structure, some form of remedy might have been available.

---

[107] At p 1101.
[108] [2001] BCC 152.
[109] A common provision contained in the legal 'boilerplate' provisions at the end of an agreement to the effect that the agreement is a self-sufficient statement of the parties' agreement in relation to the subject matter concerned and stating that any previous or parallel agreements and understandings are to have no effect.
[110] At p 164.
[111] This was a compelling factor in *Saul D Harrison* where Hoffmann LJ was clear that the 1960 scheme of reorganisation was binding on the claimant (see p 390).

Often the articles will be supplemented by shareholders' agreements. As bespoke documents, which have usually or, at least, often been expressly negotiated between the family members in dispute, logically these will be even harder to displace than the articles. For example in *JE Cade and Sons Ltd*[112] the articles of a family farming company were supplemented by a separate agreement containing a call option allowing the majority shareholder to purchase the shares of the minority family member. However there was no corresponding put option for the minority shareholder to require that their shares were bought, or any other mechanism to compel the exercise of that option. The court refused to imply such an obligation in effect leaving the interest of the minority locked up in the family business.

It is therefore incumbent on family members and their advisors to ensure that any family business governance structure is both as comprehensive and also as balanced as sensibly possible.

20.7.3 Exclusion of jurisdiction of the courts

All three major remedies[113] are statutory rights. As such it might be thought that the right to go to court to pursue those remedies could not be excluded or contracted out of by family members.[114]

In *Fulham Football Club (1987) Ltd v Richards*[115] the Court of Appeal came to the opposite conclusion, at least so far as the enforceability of an arbitration clause in a shareholders' agreement was concerned. The court decided that there were no legal or public policy reasons that prevented enforcement of the agreement to arbitrate.[116] Although not necessary to decide the case Patten LJ also took the view that an agreement not to present a winding up petition based on just and equitable grounds should also, in principle, be enforceable.[117]

Part of the reasoning of the court was that, if the arbitrator, having heard the dispute, came to the conclusion that an award or remedy was justified, but that this lay outside the remedies that the arbitrator could make, then the arbitrator could, as part of his award, allow appropriate court or other proceedings to be issued. These could include leave to present a winding up petition, bringing into play the winding up regime of the Insolvency Act, or, on the basis of allowing an unfair prejudice petition, orders for the court to regulate the conduct of a company's affairs in accordance with CA, s 996(2)(a).

One of the key pieces of reasoning in the *Fulham Football Club* case was that, in most cases, arbitration was capable of providing an effective remedy for minority shareholders. Arbitration is of course highly regulated and the arbitrator has wide powers under the Arbitration Acts. What is unclear, following the case, is whether agreements to pursue other forms of alternative dispute resolution, to the exclusion of statutory remedies such as unfair prejudice, will also be upheld by the courts. Procedures

---

[112] [1992] BCLC 213. Discussed in detail in chapter 21.
[113] That is, unfair prejudice, just and equitable winding up and derivative claims.
[114] Re *Peverill Gold Mines Ltd* [1989] 1 Ch 122; Re *American Pioneer Leather Company Co* [1918] 1 Ch 556.
[115] [2011] EWCA Civ 855.
[116] But the High Court reached the opposite conclusion on the facts of *J&W Sanderson Ltd v Fenox Ltd* [2014] EWHC 4322 (Ch) – a case involving a joint venture company where a stay of unfair prejudice proceedings to allow arbitration to take place was refused.
[117] See para 83 of the judgment. Agreements to prevent winding up proceedings in the case of insolvent companies will be void as a matter of public policy.

could include mediation or determination by third parties, such as a family council. In these situations the third party charged with resolving the dispute will not have the wide statutory powers vested in the arbitrator. Nor will they be constrained by the rules applicable to arbitration. Minority shareholders could well be denied an effective remedy.

It might be that in these situations the courts will be ready to grant stays of court proceedings to allow these alternative dispute procedures to be followed but will ultimately assume jurisdiction if those procedures fail.

Interestingly enough there is an express statutory provision allowing members of an LLP to 'contract out' of the unfair prejudice regime.[118]

20.8 BAD FAITH

In this context we are not talking about bad faith on the part of the majority family shareholders towards the minority. That will be covered in the following chapters, in the discussion of substantive remedies. Rather we mean bad faith in the sense of the minority using the judicial process as a means of furthering what is at root a family dispute.

'Bad faith' is itself a difficult concept to define in terms of the underlying motivation to bring and continue family business disputes. It will be extremely rare to come across claimants who are motivated by a Machiavellian desire to cause damage to fellow family shareholders. Bad faith will not necessarily require conscious vindictiveness. On some occasions a strong desire for revenge will be present, for example as in *Barrett v Duckett*[119] discussed in 20.8.2 below. On other occasions family members will be driven by a genuinely held, but ultimately objectively unjustified, sense of the rightfulness of their cause. What we are concerned with here is bad faith in the sense that, viewed objectively, prosecuting a claim is motivated more by a sense of family grievance than the possibility of obtaining appropriate financial redress or other appropriate legal remedy. In other words proceedings are not being prosecuted for a 'proper purpose'.

We suggest in chapter 2 (Themes) that there will almost invariably be an element of family hostility, in any family business dispute. This may be inter personal, inter branch or otherwise. Indeed it can often be almost impossible to tell where the commercial element of any given dispute ends and where the family element begins. Judges have consistently stated the general principle that the courts should not be used as a forum to air family grievances. Some commercial substance needs to be present for a matter to get through the doors of, or more realistically remain in court.

Those controlling the family business may be absolutely convinced that the claims made by the minority are baseless and motivated by family issues rather than genuine commercial grievances. Nevertheless the dispute has the potential to prove costly, highly disruptive and destabilising for the business as well as emotionally draining for those most closely involved.

---

[118] The Limited Liability Partnerships (Application of Companies Act 2006) Regulations (SI 2009/1804), reg 48.
[119] [1995] BCC 362.

However the difficulty is that, given the inextricable link present between family and business systems, it may prove almost impossible for a court, in a family business dispute, to isolate commercial rights from private grievances. Accordingly cases with a relatively small amount of commercial content but with the appearance of a large degree of family antagonism may be allowed to proceed. The dispute will then not only consume cash and time that is wholly disproportionate to the commercial issues at stake, but also, in doing so exponentially increase that antagonism.

What follows below is an examination of a number of cases where the courts have expressly explored the motivation of minority family members bringing claims and the approach taken by the courts to dealing (or not) with those claims as a result.

20.8.1 Proper purpose – the statutory test

In *Burry & Knight Ltd*[120] the Court of Appeal was asked to look at the test of 'proper purpose' under CA, s 117(3) in connection with a request made by a minority family shareholder, Dr Knight, to inspect the register of members of his fourth generation family leisure parks business.

That section forms part of CA, Chapter 2 and is part of shareholder democracy, allowing shareholders, who might not otherwise know each other's details, to contact each other to discuss issues of mutual concern relating to the company, free from the interference by the board. To prevent abuse of this right by shareholder activists (for example in animal rights cases) CA, s 117 allows a company faced with a request under CA, s 116 to apply to court for appropriate orders on the basis that the request has not been made for a proper purpose.

The procedure is therefore only likely to be relevant to larger widely held family-owned businesses. Similar principles will apply to other provisions entrenching shareholder democracy. For example the right under CA, s 314 for members to require the company to circulate a written statement on matters relevant to a general meeting. This right is subject to a similar safeguard allowing applications to the court to be made under CA, s 317 on the basis that the right is being 'abused'.

The underlying issue in *Burry & Knight* related to historic allegations (by then over 10 years old) that family members had benefited from work done at their homes by a handyman on the company payroll, together with wider allegations of tax abuse. There is little doubt that Dr Knight took those issues most seriously, saying in a letter to the company's auditors that they were 'matters of national importance' which he would seek to bring to the attention of the Charity Commission, the Lord Lieutenant of Hampshire and his MP along with 'other parties likely to be interested'.

Dr Knight had made various attempts to pursue these issues over the years, including by reporting the company to HMRC. The allegations primarily related to his uncle but the dispute resulted in Dr Knight also falling out with his own mother. As part of an approach described by the Registrar of the Companies Court as 'increasingly intemperate and obsessive' Dr Knight wrote a letter to the auditors of the company concluding that:[121]

---

[120] *Burry & Knight and another v Knight* [2014] EWCA Civ 604.
[121] At para 41 of the judgment.

'my view is that this is not just a family company rotten at the core but a family whose morals are rotten at the core.'

When requesting access to the share register Dr Knight explained that his purpose in doing so was to study the current shareholders, to write to them 'detailing my written concerns about past conduct of directors' but also to raise concerns about share valuation methods under the articles.

The Registrar of the Companies Court refused leave to inspect the register of shareholders on the basis that, on the analysis of the Court of Appeal, 'Dr Knight's real purpose was not that asserted in his request but that of conducting a vendetta against members of the two families' concerned.[122] This was not a proper purpose.

Dr Knight's third reason, of communicating with fellow shareholders on share valuation issues was found to be a proper purpose but one capable of being dealt with by undertakings on the part of the company to circulate a letter to Dr Knight in appropriate terms and confined to this issue.[123] This would be sufficient to recognise Dr Knight rights.

However the registrar was concerned to make it clear that he did not believe that Dr Knight was acting in conscious bad faith but rather from an attitude he categorised as borderline 'solipsistic' which arose 'from the defendant's no doubt sincerely held conviction that he alone is in the right, that he alone occupies the moral high ground'.

Dr Knight appealed to the Court of Appeal. There appeared to be plenty of evidence from Dr Knight's own correspondence to support the registrar's conclusion. For example in a letter to his uncle, making one of many complaints about his mother, Dr Knight said that:[124]

'I believe that there is a much bigger problem ... faced with the choice of supporting her dishonest brother or companies or her honest son she chose to lie to the Board thus betraying me as a director and as a mother.'

Giving the leading judgment in the Court of Appeal, which unanimously upheld the decision of the registrar, and concluding that he was entitled to draw the inference that Dr Knight was acting to pursue a family vendetta rather than for a proper purpose in policing his rights as a shareholder, Arden LJ relied more on objective criteria. These included the lack of evidence of damage to the companies from the issues Dr Knight complained of, the lack of evidence in support of his claim and the fact that HMRC had done nothing to pursue the matter following Dr Knight's complaint to them. There was little or no benefit to Dr Knight in his capacity as a shareholder in obtaining access to the shareholder register.[125]

The registrar had also ordered Dr Knight to pay the company' costs on an indemnity basis. The Court of Appeal allowed Dr Knight's appeal on this point. They concluded that, in the circumstances, Dr Knight's conduct of the matter was not 'so unreasonable or out of the norm' as to oblige him to pay costs on an indemnity basis.[126]

---

[122] See para 53 of the judgment.
[123] A Pelling Order after *Pelling v Families Need Fathers Ltd* [2001] EWCA Civ 1280.
[124] See para 44 of the judgment.
[125] See paras 73–77 of the judgment.
[126] See para's 94–108 of the judgment.

Giving one of the supporting judgments in the Court of Appeal Briggs LJ confirmed that 'the Court will not lightly make serious findings of bad faith or dishonesty against a party who denies them and who has not been cross examined'.[127] Equally cases policing rights under the Companies Acts should be dealt with speedily and by avoiding a full trial if at all possible.

However this was a rare case where there was sufficient documentary and other evidence to support a view that Dr Knight rather than acting out of 'dishonesty or bad faith' Dr Knight 'had become sadly obsessed with what at heart was a family dispute' and that seeking access to the shareholder register to pursue this was not a proper purpose.[128]

20.8.2 Bad faith and CA, s 260 (derivative claims)

As will be seen in chapter 23, anyone seeking to continue a derivative claim must ask the court for to permission to do so.[129] One aspect that the court must consider under CA, s 263(3)(a) is whether the claimant is acting in good faith. If they are not then this gives the court discretion to refuse permission to continue.

The Court of Appeal decision in *Singh v Singh*[130] contains an interesting discussion on the difficult subject of bad faith in family business disputes in the context of derivative claims. There the claimant admitted that dispute over the will was the genesis of a derivative claim alleging breach of duty by his co-director brother. The judge in the High Court appeared quite satisfied that this amounted to bad faith saying that:[131]

> 'I am entirely satisfied on the evidence that the real motivation acting upon the claimant in seeking to continue this derivative claim is the feeling of animosity that he entertains towards his brother as a result of the change in the gift of the late mother's house ... he is seeking to strike at his brother rather than genuinely seeking to promote the best interests of the company. I would therefore refuse permission to continue the claim by reference to the discretionary ground in subsection 263(3)(a).'

This approach is consistent with earlier cases on derivative actions decided before the introduction of the statutory derivative claim remedy. As explained below, the Court of Appeal in the *Singh* case were however less convinced about the relevance of bad faith.

A reasonably clear example of bad faith can be found in the decision in *Nurcombe v Nurcombe*.[132] The case concerned a divorcing husband and wife where the wife was a minority shareholder in a company in which her husband had the majority interest. During the course of the matrimonial proceedings it was discovered that the husband had breached his fiduciary duty as a director of the company by wrongfully diverting a lucrative business transaction to another company in which he had a controlling interest. The wife continued with the ancillary relief proceedings after this disclosure and was awarded a lump sum, which took this improper profit into account.

---

[127] At para 112 of the judgment.
[128] See para 113 of the judgment.
[129] CA, s 261.
[130] Court of Appeal: *Sukhpaul Singh v Satpaul Singh, Singh Bros Contractors (Northwest) Limited* [2014] EWCA Civ 103. The *Singh* case is discussed in detail at 23.5.
[131] *Singh Brothers Contractors (North West) Ltd* [2014] 1 BCLC 649.
[132] [1985] 1 WLR 370.

Not content with this and after receiving two instalments of the lump sum, the wife started a derivative action claiming that the husband should pay to the company the improper profit he had made from the breach of fiduciary duty. Mr Nurcombe was therefore exposed to an element of double jeopardy. In essence he was being asked to pay twice for one breach of duty. Morally Mrs Nurcombe's claim may seem highly dubious. Having taken her share of the 'proceeds of crime' through the matrimonial proceedings she was now seeking further restitution, which would increase the value of her shares in the company. From a strict legal analysis the claim against the company seems at least arguable. A derivative claim is made on behalf of the company. The matrimonial claim was made in her personal capacity.

The High Court dismissed Mrs Nurcombe's derivative action on the grounds that by continuing the matrimonial proceedings after she had discovered the wrongdoing she had elected to treat the profit as belonging to the husband. She could not thereafter allege that it belonged to the company. The wife's appeal was dismissed by the Court of Appeal who were content to see through the derivative action as a mere procedural device. Mrs Nurcombe had previously chosen to pursue a remedy through the matrimonial courts. It was an act of bad faith to attempt a second claim through the cloak of the company.

Most family business claims, including derivative claims will, on paper at least, have the appearance of a financial dispute. Mrs Nurcombe would benefit financially through the increase in value of her minority shareholding. But almost inevitably a family business dispute will contain an element of personal animosity between the family members concerned. Family business disputes are 'never (just) about the money'.[133]

The courts may conclude that a derivative claim is being pursued primarily as a personal vendetta, rather than to protect commercial interests. If so, to what extent will the courts see this as bad faith and refuse leave to continue with a derivative claim under CA, s 263(3)(a)?

The case of *Barrett v Duckett*[134] concerned a second-generation bus and coach company, jointly owned by Mrs Barrett and her former son in law, Mr Duckett, but originally established by Mrs Barrett's husband. Mrs Barrett had been a director of the business but had resigned some years previously. She received no financial benefit from the business, perhaps creating a strong inference that this particular case had very little to do with the money.

Mr Duckett left his wife, Janet, Mrs Barrett's daughter, for a new partner, leading to acrimonious divorce proceedings. Mr Duckett had by then, remarried and had started a new company. It was alleged that he had diverted both money and business opportunities belonging to the original business into it. However what was clear was that whilst still married, Mr Duckett and Janet, who was at the time also a director, had improperly withdrawn considerable sums from the original company for their joint personal benefit in buying a second home.

There was therefore an arguable and disputed claim against Mr Duckett (and his new wife) and a clear claim against Mr Duckett and Janet. Whilst proceeding enthusiastically

---

[133] Ian Marsh – see chapter 2 (Themes).
[134] [1995] BCC 362.

against Mr Duckett and his new wife (to the extent of exhausting her own life savings) Mrs Barrett basically chose to ignore the claim against her daughter.

There was a history of obstructive conduct by both Mrs Barrett and her daughter in connection with the company's affairs, which had become inextricably linked to unresolved ancillary relief claims in the divorce proceedings. Mr Duckett applied to strike out the action, partly on the basis that as Mrs Barrett was motivated by a desire to punish him rather than protect the company she was not a fit and proper person to be representing the interests of the company in a derivative claim. The High Court disagreed.

But, in allowing the appeal the Court of Appeal agreed that Mrs Barrett's conduct had shown that the derivative action would not be pursued by her in the best interests of the company but rather would be pursued in order to further the disputes between her daughter and Mr Duckworth. In the view of Peter-Gibson LJ, giving the leading judgment, this ulterior motive, made her an inappropriate person to bring an action on the company's behalf. He was clear that 'personal rather than financial considerations would appear to be impelling her to pursue a course of action'.[135]

An alternative reason to strike out Mrs Barrett's derivative claim was the possibility of an alternative remedy, winding up the original company. In giving, what on the issue of bad faith, must be seen as a majority judgment,[136] Bedlam LJ relied on the alternative remedy argument. He was entirely dismissive of the bad faith arguments saying that:[137]

> 'it does not lie well in the mouth of those who have effectively ousted Mrs Barrett's family from sharing in the profits of the company to be critical of her, or to question her motives.'

Mrs Barrett's husband originally established the family business concerned. She was likely to have had an emotional attachment to the family business in its own right. Her actions might have also been motivated by her desire to protect the legacy of the business. This possibility and, if so, whether this would have been sufficient to dispel the allegations of bad faith does not seem to have been considered by the courts. Mrs Barrett had not personally taken money out the company for some years. Even so restitution would have potentially made capital available to be applied for her daughter's benefit. Even though they may not be just about the money most family business disputes will have a financial element. How are the courts to deal with this potential duality of motives for bringing a derivative claim?

This question appeared to trouble the Court of Appeal in *Singh*. Although the court upheld other grounds for refusal of leave to continue the derivative claim, Vos LJ was not at all convinced that the High Court were correct to refuse leave to continue on the grounds of bad faith saying that:[138]

> 'I do not think that a rejection of the application could properly be founded on a lack of the claimant's good faith. As I have indicated that is most problematic in an application of this kind. The conducting of a mini trial even where the legislation demands something that looks rather like a mini trial is not desirable even if required.'

---

[135] At p 372.
[136] The third Lord Justice of Appeal Russell LJ simply delivered a two line judgment concurring with 'all the reasons appearing in the judgment of Peter-Gibson LJ. See p 375.
[137] At p 373.
[138] Voss LJ at para 29 of the Court of Appeal judgment.

An application for leave to continue is, at least in theory, an interlocutory application. Questions of motive will be extremely difficult to establish on the basis of affidavit evidence usually relied on in such applications. It would therefore appear that the bad faith discretionary ground is likely to only be relevant in the clearest of cases of bad faith (such as *Nurcombe*) or as an additional discretionary ground to support refusal of leave where other discretionary grounds are present.

20.8.3 Bad faith and unfair prejudice

Certainly there was a strong suggestion in *Re a Company No 00836 of 1995*[139] which we will call the *Gippeswyck Case*, after the name of the family company concerned. The case was introduced in the judgment as 'the latest instalment in a long running feud between father and son ... conducted through the medium of the Companies Court'.[140]

The overall dispute had already cost the parties somewhere between £1-2m and had been running for approximately 15 years. The petition was struck out by the court, on the basis that a reasonable offer to buy out the petitioner's shares had been already made.[141] However the judge commented (strictly by way of *obiter dicta*) that:[142]

> '... behind the commercial aspects of this litigation there may well be personal reasons for continuing it. If that is so, that is not a proper matter for the Companies Court to entertain, and if such existed that might be an additional reason for striking out the petition.'

It will rarely be the case that a dispute finds its way to court, purely fuelled by a family feud. But it would appear that if the court conclude that the feud, rather than the underlying commercial considerations are, to any significant extent, driving the litigation this can be an additional ground for an unfair prejudice petition to fail. However whether continuance of a family feud could constitute a sole ground for striking out an action is unclear.

20.8.4 Bad faith – conclusion

It is almost inevitable that commercial rights and family grievances will co-exist and will be virtually impossible to separate. There are corresponding evidential and procedural difficulties in attempting to dos so. It will therefore be very difficult to persuade a court to dismiss a family business claim purely on the basis of suspicions as to the claimant's motive in bringing a case. This will be so notwithstanding a strong inference, in the case concerned, that the primary motivation for the claims may indeed be a sense of family grievance.

So what should the majority do when faced with potential claims from a vexatious family member? It must follow that the best advice for the majority family members wishing to avoid becoming embroiled in such disputes is that, rather than trying to win the dispute outright, it would be best to try to rise above them.

This can be achieved by approaching disputes tactically and strategically and (to the greatest extent realistically possible) with empathy for the claimant's position. Above all,

---

[139] [1996] BCC 432.
[140] Judge Weeks QC at p 432.
[141] See chapter 24 for a discussion on reasonable offers.
[142] At p 443.

by settling disputes on half way sensible, or at least only moderately disadvantageous terms, the majority might be taking a step or two backwards from their best (or apparent) legal position. However they might gain considerably in terms of conserving their own time and costs, avoiding the huge distraction of family business litigation and ultimately creating a climate where family harmony could conceivably one day be restored.

20.9 MISMANAGEMENT

Mismanagement is a frequent cause of concern, particularly for remote family shareholders in more mature later stage family businesses. There the ownership may be widely spread between family members but the control of the business is concentrated in a smaller number of family members or a particular branch. There may be strong views that the perceived mismanagement is damaging not only the economic interests of the 'have-nots' by eroding long-term shareholder value, even to the point of eliminating this by insolvency and, in the short term by making payment of dividends a non-starter. *Saul D Harrison* is a case in point. The outsiders may be convinced that it is unfair that their investment in the family business is in jeopardy and also that the incompetence of the insiders is such that it is unfair that they retain their jobs and directorships.

The outsiders may be able to catalogue a huge number of instances of alleged mismanagement by the insiders. Many of those allegations may have some substance.

As a general rule courts are extremely reluctant to get involved in the internal management of any business and to second-guess the board of directors at the behest of minority shareholders.

20.9.1 Mismanagement and unfair prejudice

Therefore the court will intervene and grant unfair prejudice remedies only in the most serious and obvious cases of mismanagement, in effect amounting to a clear and obvious breach by the controlling directors of their duties to exercise reasonable skill and care.

The difficulty for the outsiders and their advisors is that allegations of mismanagement will almost invariably be heavily contested leading to significant costs in obtaining and analysing evidence, experts' reports and longer trials. For example in *Re Elgindata Ltd*[143] the court hearing lasted over 40 days. Whilst the petitioners were ultimately successful in obtaining an unfair prejudice finding based on breach of duty by the controlling director (who used company assets for his personal benefit and that of friends and family) a significant part of the hearing and related costs were consumed in dealing with ultimately unsuccessful allegations of mismanagement.

In *Fisher v Cadman*[144] one of Mrs Fisher's complaints about her brothers was that, as directors, they had failed to actively manage the company's property portfolio. The judge found that in doing so they had basically 'continued a policy which had originated with their father.' Since they kept this policy under review, a practice of spending little

---

[143] [1991] BCLC 959.
[144] [2005] EWHC 377 (Ch).

and simply relying on property price inflation, 'was within the band of reasonable decisions available for them to take as managers of the company'.[145]

In *Samuel Weller & Sons Ltd*[146] one of grounds of complaint was proposed capital expenditure of £130,000. This was equivalent to over 50 years of dividends at a rate consistent with the historic practice of the company. Of course reinvestment in the business is usually seen as a purely management decision. But every pound spent on investment is a pound not available for distribution to family members. In this case the judge, with some reluctance, refused to strike out this ground of complaint and allowed the issue to proceed to full trial notwithstanding arguments on behalf of the controlling shareholders that if dividends versus capital expenditure arguments could be the basis of unfair prejudice petitions:[147]

> 'managerial decisions of a company could always be the subject of such a petition. I see the force of the latter point and I have no doubt that the court will ordinarily be very reluctant to accept that decisions of this kind could amount to unfairly prejudicial conduct. But because of the link between this allegation and the allegation relating to the payment of dividends, with some hesitation I have concluded that I should not strike it out.'

Re Macro Ipswich Ltd[148] provides a rare example of where the courts have granted unfair prejudice relief based on serious mismanagement. The case is part of a series of long running disputes (also including the *Gippeswyck* case) between Mr Albert Thompson, a successful estate agent and property investor with his sons and nephews. For the time period relevant to this dispute Mr Thompson was controlling director but had effectively retired and moved abroad to live, leaving the management of the company's property portfolio to senior staff in his estate agency business. The case involved detailed evidence of a pattern of mismanagement on their part, including failures to supervise repairs, to let on suitable terms and individual acts of dishonesty with agency staff effectively taking bribes. However Mr Thompson did nothing to prevent or rectify the situation. He allowed matters to continue. Rather than this being a case of where the sons had alternative views as to what constituted good management or even where 'merely the quality of management has turned out to be poor' Mr Thompson had effectively abdicated his management responsibilities. This was a case where 'viewed overall' that consistent failure 'was sufficient and serious to justify' court intervention.[149]

A more recent example can be found in the Scottish case of *Robertson*,[150] where stockpiling of rather than selling large quantities of metal in a reprocessing business, leading to huge write downs, when the market turned was seen to be unfair prejudice. But this was a family closing ranks case, where the court took the inference that the practice, having no commercial justification, had been employed by two brothers as part of strategy to depress the value of the company and drive out the third, non-family shareholder. In the same case the brothers entered into disastrous speculative foreign exchange contracts, without authorisation of the board and outside the usual business practice of the company. This was also seen to be unfair prejudice.

---

[145] At para 104 of the judgment.
[146] [1990] Ch 682.
[147] At p 694 of the judgment.
[148] [1994] BCC 781.
[149] At p 834 of the judgment.
[150] *Robertson v RM Supplies (Inverkeithing) Ltd* [2009] CSOH 23.

20.9.2 Mismanagement and derivative claims

Disagreements between remote family members and the controlling directors on matters of business policy are often capable of being presented as matters of negligence or breach of duty on the part of the board. For example a decision to buy another business may, particularly with the benefit of hindsight appear to be particularly ill judged. Nevertheless the courts have historically been extremely reluctant to support litigation, being pursued by the minority as a derivative claim, which could involve the retrospective judgment of the court being substituted for the contemporaneous view of the board on such business matters.

The distinction between mismanagement and actionable negligence is sometimes a fine one. *Palvides v Jensen*[151] concerned an action after the directors took a decision to sell off the company's main asset, a mine, at what transpired to be a significant undervalue, £182,000 compared with a market value in excess of £1m. However the directors derived no personal benefit from their mismanagement. In the absence of either bad faith on the part of the directors the court explained that the law was such that the minority might have to put up with 'an amiable set of lunatics' running their business.

As will be seen in chapter 8 (Directors' Duties) modern company law requires a much higher standard of competence and performance from directors. In particular there is now a dual test of directors' competence contained in CA, s 174, effectively requiring all directors to exhibit a basic minimum standard of care, skill and diligence in the execution of their duties.

CA, s 260 now simply contemplates derivative claims based on director's negligence without making any distinction between gross or other negligence or between negligence from which the directors personally benefited and those where they did not. It may well be that the distinctions contained in the earlier cases should now be regarded as artificial. A derivative claim may now lie in all circumstances where the company itself could pursue a director for negligence. Whether that claim will be permitted to proceed will be decided under the detailed statutory process described in chapter 23 (Derivative Claims).

The wider question of the vulnerability of directors to actions for negligence brought by the majority or, following the collapse of a family business, its liquidator is considered in Chapter 8 (Directors' Duties).

20.10 CONCLUSION – *SAUL D HARRISON* – GOVERNANCE APPLICATION POINTS?

The *Saul D Harrison* case has been extensively debated in this chapter and, indeed frequently referred to throughout the book. Although the majority insiders ultimately 'won' their case this must have been at some considerable cost, if not in terms of legal fees,[152] then certainly in terms of disruption and damage to wider family relationships.

---

[151] [1956] Ch 565.
[152] The case note suggests that a large part of these should have been recovered from the claimant.

Could the dispute have been avoided by the application of family business governance at various points in the Saul D Harrison story? We will never know. But possible points include:

- The stage at which the three sons joined the founder, Saul, in the business. Was any consideration given to the purpose of the family being in business together at this stage? This is a key component of modern family business best practice. Alternatively was it simply assumed that sons would follow father into the family firm in accordance with the practice then prevailing?
- The 1960 re-organisation. By this time the business had matured into a cousin consortium. How much thought was given to the key questions of employment policies, wider family ownership, dividend policies etc.? Alternatively are the different share classes explained simply at the level of a tax planning exercise.
- In chapter 1 we explain that the deaths of the second-generation family members, Bernard and Lionel in 1985 and 1987 respectively, were closely followed by that of the third generation family director Seymour also in 1987. Even if this was not evident beforehand, should this have telegraphed that any governance philosophy of each family branch having a working director and voting A shareholder was breaking down? Did this represent an opportunity to install more formal governance mechanisms, including family councils and family charters, so that the interests of those in the outsider family branches could be taken into account?
- To what extent were the wider family consulted over the key decision to reinvest the proceeds of sale of the original site in new premises, rather than return capital to, at least, some shareholders? If not would such consultations have forestalled the proceedings eventually brought by Rosemary? On a related point, was the possibility of introducing an exit route for minority shareholders ever considered or discussed, either at the time the premises were sold or previously?
- Last, but by no means least, once the dispute had arisen between the insiders and the outsider claimant, Rosemary, what attempts were made to resolve this using alternative dispute procedures or family business consultancy interventions as outlined in chapter 25?

It is appreciated that these questions are raised with the benefit of hindsight and in the light of modern family business best practice, largely undeveloped at the relevant time. But the points hold good for family businesses in similar situations today. What this chapter is intended to illustrate is that some fundamental uncertainties associated with bringing family business disputes to court places a large premium on investment in family business governance in an attempt to avoid those disputes in the first place.

CHAPTER 21

UNFAIR PREJUDICE AND THE FAMILY COMPANY

21.1 OVERVIEW

21.1.1 Introduction

As mentioned in chapter 20 an unfair prejudice petition is the principle remedy for an aggrieved minority shareholder in any company, including one that is family owned. That chapter included a detailed analysis of the circumstances in which the courts would apply equitable principles in support of the minority shareholder, what we have termed the 'fairness approach', as opposed to taking a less interventionist 'rules based' approach. This is a key concept for any consideration of the unfair prejudice remedy.

We begin with a brief overview of the remedy, before looking at various cases, where the courts have looked at this remedy in the context of family owned companies.

21.1.2 Statutory basis – CA, s 994

In detail CA, s 994(1) provides that a member of a company[1] may petition the court on the grounds:

(a) that the company's affairs are being or have been conducted in a manner that is unfairly prejudicial to the interests of members generally or of some part of its members (including at least himself); or
(b) that an actual or proposed act or omission of the company (including an act or omission on its behalf) is or would be so prejudicial.

It will be seen that the statutory test has two elements. First, that the affairs of the company are being conducted in a manner that is unfair. Secondly, that the petitioner has suffered prejudice as a result. It is clear from various cases, discussed below, that in the absence of unfairness, relief will not be granted simply because a minority shareholder's position has been prejudiced.[2] Equally a remedy will not be granted on the basis of unfairness alone in the absence of prejudice.[3]

---

[1] Members of a limited liability partnership may also able to make applications based on unfair prejudice as the Limited Liability Partnerships (Application of Companies Act) Regulations 2009 (SI 2009/1804) extends the remedy to LLP's. However the members can contract out of the application of the CA, s 994 remedy. In practice courts may also take a similar approach to intervene and wind up conventional unincorporated partnerships.
[2] For example, the leading case of *O'Neill v Phillips* discussed in detail at **21.2**.
[3] See paras 341–347 of the judgment.

Unfair prejudice actions are almost invariably brought by minority shareholders who are seeking relief against the actions of the majority. However majority shareholder petitions where the majority seek to deal with a disruptive minority, whilst being 'an unusual animal' are permitted under CA, s 994.[4]

21.1.3 Case-law

It is important to stress that each case of unfair prejudice will be considered by the court on its own unique facts. The main reason to look at case-law, at least from a legal standpoint, is to understand the underlying legal principles relating to unfair prejudice that have been developed by the courts. The facts of the various family business cases also provide cautionary tales for business families of what can go wrong and are probably the best advertisement for investment in preventative governance. For that reason the factual background of various family business cases is explained in much more detail than would typically be the case in a typical legal textbook.

The unfair prejudice remedy has been in existence, with some minor changes in its current form since its introduction in the Companies Act 1980. Accordingly case-law pre-dating the introduction of the modern form of remedy must be treated with a degree of caution. However earlier cases may nevertheless still be relevant.

First cases decided under the predecessor remedy, that of oppressive conduct, under s 210 of the Companies Act 1948 where it was necessary to show that the conduct complained of was oppressive (itself interpreted under the strict test of being 'burdensome, harsh and wrongful'[5]), rather than merely unfair. Logically conduct which was sufficient to satisfy the stricter test under the old remedy ought to pass the easier test of unfairness.[6]

Secondly, in the past cases, were often brought under the just and equitable winding up regime.[7] This was because of the difficulty of satisfying the oppressive conduct test under s 210 of the Companies Act 1948.[8] On the basis that just and equitable winding up is now seen as the more drastic remedy circumstances, that would previously have justified this should also open up the less dramatic remedy for unfair prejudice under CA, s 996. Just and equitable winding up is considered in detail in chapter 22.

Reported unfair prejudice cases can be seen to fall into two broad categories. First those of final hearings, including the leading case of *O'Neill v Phillips*, discussed in detail below. There the court is providing a final determination of whether or not the conduct complained of is unfairly prejudicial. Secondly, reports relating to earlier stage interlocutory hearings, usually where the respondent is seeking to strike out a petition on the basis either that the claim is an abuse of process, or, as in *Samuel Weller & Sons Ltd*,[9] that the petition discloses no reasonable cause of action. In that case, as discussed below, whilst the majority of the petitioner's claims were allowed to continue there could be no certainty that these will succeed at full trial. Such cases should

---

[4] See in *Re a Company (No 00836 of 1995)* at p 435 and discussed below.
[5] At p 79 following the test of Viscount Simmonds from the House of Lords in the Scottish case of *Meyer v Scottish Co-operative Wholesale Society* (1957) SC 381.
[6] See *Bovey Hotel Ventures (unreported)* 31 July 1981 and approved in *RA Noble & Sons (Clothing) Ltd* [1983] BCLC 273 at p 290 and also in *Samuel Weller and Sons Ltd* (discussed below) at p 292.
[7] Now IA, s 122(1)(g).
[8] See in *Re Harmer* at p 63.
[9] [1983] BCLC 273.

therefore be seen as carrying less positive authority. However successful 'strike out cases', particularly those upheld by the higher courts will have strong negative authority that in equivalent circumstances unfair prejudice proceedings are likely to fail.

21.1.4 Unfairness

Unfairness itself can be broken down into two broad categories.

Expectation cases

First unfairness, in the sense that a legitimate expectation of the petitioning shareholder has been defeated. Here the petitioner will need to establish that equitable considerations or what we have labelled the 'fairness approach should apply. This is explained in detail in chapter 20.

More often than not this expectation will be one of participation in a quasi-partnership. But there are some examples of the courts, either protecting wider expectations or, on another view, stretching the concept of quasi partnership.[10]

Breach of duty cases

Secondly, more fundamental unfairness, arising from breaches of duty. Almost invariably the breaches will be by the majority shareholders abusing their dual capacity of directors of the family owned business. These breaches result in substantial unfairness and prejudice to the minority, which the courts see as sufficient to provide the minority with the remedy of a statutory exit right.

Both of these categories are considered in detail below.

21.1.5 Prejudice

In many family business situations minority family members may feel that they have been very unfairly treated by the majority, for example in terms of provision of information, of not being 'kept in the know' about the situation of their family business.

But the approach of the courts is basically that the unfair prejudice remedy is to redress financial damage not injury to feelings. Partly this is to prevent both the parties incurring significant expense and the courts becoming clogged up with litigants airing family grievances. In *Re Unisoft Group Ltd (No 2)*[11] (a non-family business case concerned with leave to amend a petition in the middle of a trial) Harman J explained that:

> 'The requirement of prejudice means that the conduct must be shown to have done the members harm and I believe harm in a commercial sense, not in a merely emotional sense. The further requirement that the prejudice is "unfair" is a more uncertain but necessary thing to show, but before the fairness or unfairness of the conduct or act is considered "prejudice" – that is harm or damage – must be shown. Those requirements set out the basic rules that the court must in my view be careful to insist upon to restrain this procedure from breaking all reasonable bounds.'

---

[10] See especially *Fisher v Cadman* [2005] EWHC 377 (Ch).
[11] [1994] BCC 766.

In *Irvine (No 1)*,[12] whilst castigating various failures on the part of Ian to follow proper procedures for the production and approval of accounts and for the approval of his own remuneration as 'plainly wrongful', 'deserving of censure' and 'reprehensible' the judge refused to make a finding of unfair prejudice relating to these issues on the basis that these could not 'fairly be said to have caused Patricia to suffer any material prejudice.'[13]

21.1.6 Unfair prejudice and intention

In many family business cases it appears that the majority often act from a misplaced sense of their own entitlement, which affects the interests of the minority, rather than an active intention to prejudice those interests. Again Ian Irvine provides us with a prime example. Following the death of his brother, Malcolm, Ian assumed additional duties and sought to argue, in effect, that as he was doing the work of both directors he should be entitled to keep pretty much all surplus income generated by the family business.

It is pretty clear from the authorities that there is no need to show bad faith on the part of the majority. The test of unfair prejudice is an objective one. In *In re R A Noble & Sons (Clothing) Ltd*[14] Slade J said:

> 'The test of unfairness must, I think, be an objective, not a subjective, one. In other words it is not necessary for the petitioner to show that the persons who have had de facto control of the company have acted as they did in the conscious knowledge that this was unfair to the petitioner or that they were acting in bad faith; the test, I think, is whether a reasonable bystander observing the consequences of their conduct, would regard it as having unfairly prejudiced the petitioner's interests.'

This approach was followed in *Samuel Weller & Sons Ltd*[15] where an alternative view expressed in an earlier case[16] that failing to pay dividends was not unfair prejudice partly on the basis that this 'was not intended to be discriminatory' was disapproved and the judge said that:[17]

> 'To my mind, the wording of the section imports an objective test. One simply looks to see whether the manner in which the affairs of the company have been conducted can be described as "unfairly prejudicial to the interests of some part of the members." That ... requires an objective assessment of the quality of the conduct. Thus, conduct which is "unfairly prejudicial" to the petitioner's interests, even if not intended to be so, may nevertheless come within the section.'

21.1.7 Membership and beneficial interests

Unfair prejudice petitions are basically remedies available to registered shareholders. However CA, s 994(2) extends the availability to those who are entitled to be registered as members by providing that:

---

[12] [2006] EWHC 406 (Ch).
[13] See paras 344–346 of *Irvine (No 1)*, op cit.
[14] [1983] BCLC 273 at p 290.
[15] [1990] Ch 682.
[16] *Re a Company (No 00370 of 1987) ex parte Glossup* [1988] 1 WLR 1068 at pp 1074–1075.
[17] At p 689.

'The provisions of this Part apply to a person who is not a member of a company but to whom shares in the company have been transferred or transmitted by operation of law as they apply to a member of a company.'

Crucially the remedy follows the legal ownership of shares, not the underlying beneficial interest. Similarly the unfair prejudice complained of can relate to a time before the petitioner became a member. So that once a member is registered in their own right they can complain of past unfairly prejudicial conduct pre-dating that registration.[18] But a former shareholder cannot petition.

21.1.8 Family business trusts

Accordingly if a trust owns shares in a family business the beneficiaries would not be entitled to petition in their own right. The right to present an unfair prejudice petition would instead vest in the trustees. The beneficiaries would need to persuade the trustees to take action.

Alternatively, and particularly if the trustees were themselves in a position to control the family company, or were perhaps even responsible for the alleged unfairly prejudicial treatment, the beneficiaries would first need to take separate trust based proceedings to secure the removal of the existing trustees.[19]

A further permutation would be if disgruntled beneficiaries were also minority shareholders in their own right with the trust as majority shareholders. It would then be possible for the minority to take direct action seeking redress in relation to how the majority trustees have used their voting power.

21.1.9 Interests and rights – *Re Sam Weller and Sons Ltd*

It is clear that the expression 'interests' as used in CA, s 994 has a wider interpretation than rights. Accordingly something that may affect members equally so far as their rights as members are concerned may affect the interests of one or more members differently. If that differential impact is both unfair and prejudicial, the unfair prejudice remedy may be available to the adversely affected members.

This is particularly relevant to the later stage family business where, although all family members may well have the same legal rights attached to their shares,[20] the interests of the more remote family members, the 'have-nots' are likely to differ markedly from the interests of the 'haves' in control of the family company.

This is vividly illustrated by the case of *Re Sam Weller and Sons Ltd*,[21] a case involving a third generation textile company. Roughly 60% of the shares were held by the founder's son, also called Samuel Weller. He was the sole director. His two sons also worked in the business. The remaining shares were beneficially owned by the niece and

---

[18] *Bermuda Cablevision Ltd v Colica Trust Co Ltd* [1998] AC 198.
[19] Proceedings against trustees are discussed in more detail in chapter 14.
[20] Of course some family businesses will have introduced different classes of shares each with different rights. For example in *Saul D Harrison plc*. The share structure is described in detail in chapter 11 (Ownership Overview).
[21] [1990] Ch 682.

nephew of the sole director. They had become entitled to most, of their shares on the death of their mother who was the daughter of the founder and the sister of the sole director.

For almost 40 years the company had paid the same dividend on shares (£0.14p). By the time the matter came to court this amounted to less than 7% of the latest net profits. The 'have-nots' therefore received little return on their interest in the family company which had nearly £217,000 in cash and £464,000 in undistributed reserves.

In contrast a seaside holiday home had been bought for the use of the controlling family, using company funds, at a cost of £22,400. This represented almost 10 years' worth of dividend payments at the usual rate. This was one of the allegations of unfair prejudice made by the niece and nephew. It was unclear what salary, bonus and other benefits the 'haves' Samuel Weller and his two sons enjoyed. Indeed refusal to disclose these was a further allegation of unfair prejudice. The other complaints were the refusal to declare a larger dividend, significant suggested capital expenditure of £130,000, and finally, a refusal to register the niece and nephew as holders of their mother's shares.

The 'haves' sought to strike out the petition and argued that the claims (other than in relation to the refusal to register the share transfer) affected all members of the company to an equal extent. In their capacity as members the rights of the 'haves' were equally affected by the capital expenditure and the low dividends. This argument was even extended to the purchase of the seaside flat.[22] Presumably the logic being that whilst the sons of the controlling family received a benefit this was in their capacity as holiday-makers and their rights as members of the company were equally affected alongside their cousins.

In raising these arguments the controlling family relied on a slightly earlier High Court decision of *Re a Company (No 00370 of 1987) ex parte Glossup*,[23] a case on the failure to pay adequate dividends. This petition was dismissed on the basis that no 'section [994] petition could be based on conduct that has an equal effect on all the shareholders and was not intended to be discriminatory between the shareholders'.[24]

The decision in *Glossup* was disapproved by the High Court in *Samuel Weller & Sons*, Mr Justice Peter-Gibson argued that:[25]

> 'The word "interests" is wider than a term such as "rights", and its presence as part of the test of section [994(1)] to my mind suggests that Parliament recognised that members may have different interests, even if their rights as members are the same.'

Accordingly the interests of the 'have-nots' were different from those of the 'haves' and were also capable of being unfairly prejudiced by the low dividends, the purchase of the flat and some of the other matters. The claims of the niece and nephew were allowed to continue.

---

[22] See p 685.
[23] [1988] 1 WLR 1068.
[24] At pp 1074–1075.
[25] At pp 690 of *Samuel Weller and Sons*.

21.1.10 Relevant interests – *JE Cade and Sons Ltd*

The protection of the unfair prejudice remedy is not necessarily strictly confined to the interests of shareholders as members. The courts have recognised that, particularly in smaller private family companies, membership interests are more complex than interests strictly relating to shareholding and that 'the requirement that prejudice must be suffered as a member should not be too narrowly or technically construed'.[26] Accordingly wider interests than pure membership rights may be recognised by s 994. Examples include:

- Employment and participation in the family owned business (*Brownlow v GH Marshall*[27] discussed below).
- Working capital loans, where the loans had been provided as part of joint venture arrangements.[28]

On the other hand some relationship between the rights allegedly unfairly infringed and the position of the petitioner as shareholder is required. For example conduct mainly affecting a member in their capacity as freeholder of property occupied by a company will not be seen sufficiently closely connected to their interests as a member.

JE Cade and Sons Ltd[29] is both a difficult case, in terms of balancing the fairness of competing interests of family members, and a clear illustration of this principle. The case concerned a family farming company, set up following the dissolution of a much larger family partnership with farming and haulage businesses involving seven second generation brothers and various of their children. The dissolution was amicable. The brothers simply concluded that the business set up by their parents had grown too large and too unwieldy to accommodate the second and third generation.

A re-organisation scheme was devised to assist a younger brother, John, who had a smaller entitlement on dissolution, to eventually gain ownership of the farm that he occupied, Marriott Drove Farm. This involved an older brother, Tony, with a larger entitlement, taking the freehold of the farm as part of his share on the dissolution but granting rights of occupation to John's company, JE Cade and Sons Ltd, for a 5-year period. The occupation by the company was to be rent free and crucially intended to be on a licence basis so that 'a tenancy is not created'.[30] John was the major shareholder of the company and Tony took a minority stake, essentially as a security interest. He also received agreed director's fees.

Under a collateral option agreement John was entitled to buy both the freehold of the farm and Tony's shares in the company during the 5 year licence period at the value of Marriott's Farm which had been used for dissolution purposes. Tony was clearly helping John find some breathing space in which to find the money to buy his 'own' farm.

The arrangement was therefore clearly driven by family considerations agreed to by Tony for John's benefit.

---

[26] Lord Hoffmann in *O'Neill v Phillips* [1999] 1 WLR 1092 at p 1105.
[27] [2000] 2 BCLC 655.
[28] *Gamlestaden Fastigheter AB v Baltic Partners Ltd* [2007] UKPC 26 – a non-family business case.
[29] [1991] BCC 360.
[30] See p 363 of the judgment.

Unfortunately it transpired that John could not raise the required funds to carry through the second part of the plan. Although Tony was prepared to accept some reduction in price the brothers could not agree a revised and affordable price. The plan then disintegrated further. At the end of the 5 year licence period, John neither exercised his option, nor caused the company to give vacant possession of Marriotts Drove Farm. Instead, apparently encouraged by his solicitor, he argued that a protected agricultural tenancy had arisen.

Clearly the basis of the family agreement has collapsed. Equally clearly Tony had reason to feel that he had been unfairly prejudiced by the turn of events. He had neither possession of Marriott's Grove nor his cash entitlement from the dissolution of the original partnership.[31] But that prejudice was not in his capacity as a shareholder of JE Cade and Son Ltd. To the contrary his interest in the company was enhanced by the potential of Agricultural Holdings Act protection of its principal asset, its right to occupy Marriott's Drove farm. Tony had suffered prejudice in his capacity as freeholder. This was a 'fatal flaw' in Tony's unfair prejudice application.[32]

21.1.11 Fairness and equity

Unfair prejudice is an equitable remedy in the sense that it provides the court with a wide discretion to be exercised in the event of unfairness. There is clearly a considerable overlap between concepts of fairness and of equity. However the overlap is not complete. Unfairness and inequity are not synonymous terms. Unfair prejudice is a statutory remedy based on looser concepts than those applicable to strict equitable remedies, in particular just and equitable winding up. Equitable principles, which would otherwise defeat claims based on strict equitable remedies, such as just and equitable winding up, will not be so rigidly applied in unfair prejudice cases. For example:

- **Claimant's misconduct.** The petitioners own misconduct, whilst still being relevant, in particular to valuations and the choice of remedy[33] will not operate as an absolute bar to prevent an unfair prejudice petition succeeding.
  In other words there is no strict requirement for an unfair prejudice petitioner to come to the court with clean hands.
  In *McCarthy Surfacing Ltd*[34] (a family closing ranks case) the petitioners had issued an earlier unfair prejudice petition making serious allegations against the McCarthy brothers. They obtained freezing orders over the company's assets and caused a VAT investigation to be launched, based on alleged fraudulent under declarations. All these allegations were ultimately seen to be without foundation[35] but nevertheless had a 'catastrophic effect' on the company's business and of course shareholder relations. Notwithstanding that the petitioners were largely to blame for this state of affairs they were nevertheless still owed duties by the McCarthy family. These interests could be protected by a further unfair prejudice petition.

---

[31] Although honouring the agreement would have required John and his family to give up their home.
[32] Leaving him to rely on proceedings for vacant possession and a negligence action against the advisors concerned with the initial dissolution scheme.
[33] See *Re London School of Electronics Ltd* [1986] Ch 211 – a non-family business case. In extreme circumstances the petitioner's misconduct could justify conduct in response which would otherwise be unfair. For example exclusion from management in circumstances where the petitioner is colluding with a competitor.
[34] [2008] EWHC 2279 (Ch).
[35] Resulting in the striking out of the unfair prejudice petition as an abuse of process along with a fairly rare award that the petitioners must pay costs on an indemnity basis. See chapter 24 for a more general discussion on costs.

A less extreme example can be found in *Brownlow v GH Marshall*[36] where various criticisms over expenses, dealings with company vehicles etc, were raised against the petitioner Mrs Brownlow. Whilst not being entirely answered, these were not seen as sufficiently significant so as to justify denying relief.[37]

- **Delay.** Again while delay may be relevant there are no strict time limits for bringing unfair prejudice actions. Delay will only defeat the remedy if it is gross and inordinate.

In *The Gate of India*[38] a delay of almost 6 years between the petitioner being excluded from his family business and issuing a CA, s 994 petition and 4 ½ years before even formally complaining about this was not enough to trouble the judge considering the case, particularly as the delay had not prejudiced the respondents.[39]

But the position on delay is unclear. There should be no marks, either from the perspective of family relationships, or from that of litigation protocols for family members rushing to court. Hopefully in considering any questions of delay the court will be more forgiving of 'good excuses', such as exhaustive attempts by the family members concerned to explore alternative ways to resolve their dispute, such as mediation, as opposed to simply ignoring those difficulties.

- **Acquiescence.** Prior acquiescence by the petitioner in the conduct complained of will also not be a bar to a successful claim. There will usually be nothing to prevent the petitioner from changing their mind and subsequently asserting their rights.

In *Fisher v Cadman*[40] little regard had been paid to the requirements of the Companies Acts in relation to statutory formalities including accounting requirements and annual general meetings, pretty much since the incorporation of the small family business concerned. The court described the affairs of the family company as being conducted with 'extreme informality'.

This had not seemed to trouble the petitioner, Mrs Fisher, for the first 13 years or so after she became a shareholder. However a combination of an increased shareholding, the death of her parents and an escalating dispute with her brothers, who were the majority shareholders, caused Mrs Fisher to change her mind. Her previous acquiescence did not prevent her insisting that things were done properly from then on or from relying on her brothers' failure to do so as a component in a successful unfair prejudice claim.[41]

21.2 O'NEILL V PHILLIPS

21.2.1 The facts

Moving now to look at some decided cases on unfair prejudice and to consider their application to the situation of family owned companies.

---

[36] [2000] 2 BCLC 655.
[37] See also *Shah v Shah* [2010] EWHC 313 (Ch) and also *Re Gate of India (Tynemouth) Ltd*, also known as *Rahman v Malik* [2008] EWHC 959 (Ch), [2008] 2 BCLC 403. Both discussed below and in chapter 20.
[38] [2008] EWHC 959 (Ch) – discussed in detail below.
[39] See paras 122 and 123 of the judgment. There were extenuating circumstances including the claimant's illness.
[40] [2005] EWHC 377 (Ch).
[41] See paras 90–97 of the judgment. The case is discussed in detail below.

The leading case on unfair prejudice is a House of Lords decision, *O'Neill v Phillips*.[42] Although not concerned with a family owned business the case does touch on and discuss the position of family businesses. It has also been followed in a number of subsequent cases involving family businesses.

The case concerned a small business, Pectel Ltd, which operated as an asbestos removal contractor in the construction industry. Pectel was owned by the defendant, Mr Phillips. The claimant Mr O'Neill joined later, initially simply as an employee and manual worker. After 2 years Mr Phillips gave Mr O'Neill shares representing 25% of the equity and appointed him a director. At this time Mr Phillips expressed the hope that Mr O'Neill would one day take over the running of the company when he would be allowed to draw 50% of the profits. This happened and was followed by further discussions in which Mr Phillips indicated a willingness in principle to increase Mr O'Neill's actual underlying shareholding and voting rights to 50%. This was subject to the business achieving certain targets.

However, 2 years or so later, and following a slump in the construction industry, Mr Phillips who had become concerned about Mr O'Neill's management, decided to take back the running of the company personally. He stopped the profit sharing arrangements. So that instead of Mr O'Neill continuing to receive 50% of the profits he received only his ordinary salary and any dividends paid on the 25% of the shares legally registered in his own name.

Reversing the decision in the Court of Appeal, the House of Lords decided that, in the circumstances of the case, the indication in principle by Mr Phillips, that he would consider increasing Mr O'Neill's stake, was not sufficient to create a legitimate expectation on Mr O'Neill's part that this would unconditionally and definitely happen. Accordingly although Mr O'Neill's position had worsened (and could be seen to have been prejudiced) he had not been unfairly treated.

21.2.2   Rationale – the 'rules based approach'

In coming to their conclusion the House of Lords placed the business concerned in *O'Neill v Phillips* into our first category referred above, namely those where (in the absence of misconduct) the rules based approach was sufficient. It was not appropriate or unfair not to go beyond or behind the strict legal position contained in the constitution of the company.

As Lord Hoffmann explained, the rules based approach:[43]

> '... leads to the conclusion that a member of a company will not ordinarily be entitled to complain of unfairness unless there has been some breach of the terms on which he agreed that the affairs of the company should be conducted.'

Although Pectel was clearly a small company and although Mr O'Neill and Mr Phillips were in effect quasi partners, there was nothing in their situation, and on the facts of that case that would put them into the second category where good faith considerations could be seen to have been breached. Namely:[44]

---

[42] [1999] 1 WLR 1092.
[43] At p 1098.
[44] At p 1098.

'... cases in which equitable considerations make it unfair for those conducting the affairs of the company to rely upon their strict legal powers. Thus unfairness may consist in a breach of the rules or in using the rules in a manner which equity would regard as contrary to good faith.'

In particular, although Mr O'Neill had invested in Pectel (by capitalising undrawn profits) and had provided secured guarantees for the company's borrowings and although he had an expectation to a 50:50 joint ownership (in the sense that this had been discussed) there was nothing in their relationship that made it unfair for Mr Phillips to change his mind in the absence of a formal and unconditional agreement to move to equal ownership. Accordingly there was 'no basis, consistent with established principles of equity, for a court to hold that Mr. Phillips was behaving unfairly in withdrawing from the negotiation'.[45]

21.2.3 Exclusion (... or not)

A key finding in the case was that Mr O'Neill (who had in fact left with two employees to set up in competition with Pectel), whilst clearly upset with Mr Phillips, had not been excluded from the business by him, whether actually or constructively. As Lord Hoffmann explained:[46]

'It follows in my opinion that there was no basis for the Court of Appeal's finding that Mr. O'Neill had been driven out of the company. He may have decided that he had lost confidence in Mr. Phillips and that he could no longer work with him. After Christmas 1992 Mr. Phillips said that he recognised that Mr. O'Neill had come to this conclusion and that there was no way in which he could put their relationship together again. But Mr. O'Neill's decision was not the result of anything wrong or unfair which Mr. Phillips had done.'

It follows that if the House of Lords had thought that Mr O'Neill had been forced out of, or excluded from, the company (as the Court of Appeal concluded was the case) this leading authority would have been decided differently. See, for example Brownlow or Shah (both of which are discussed below).

21.2.4 Legitimate expectations

Another argument often used in the context of unfair prejudice cases is that the 'legitimate expectations' of the minority have been defeated by the conduct of the majority.

Lord Hoffmann acknowledged that he had used the expression himself in the Court of Appeal in the earlier case of *Saul D Harrison plc*.[47] But he was similarly keen to stress that the term should be narrowly interpreted, consistent with equitable principles derived from previous cases, rather than suggesting that the courts should intervene simply because a minority shareholder has reasonable expectations that have not been met.

---

[45] At p 1103.
[46] At p 1104 of the judgment.
[47] [1995] 1 BCLC 14 considered in detail below and in chapter 20.

Mr O'Neill clearly expected that he would end up owning 50% of the Pectel business. There was nothing inherently unreasonable in that expectation. It had been discussed and negotiated. But that expectation, however legitimate, was not capable of creating a right:[48]

> 'The concept of a legitimate expectation should not be allowed to lead a life of its own, capable of giving rise to equitable restraints in circumstances to which the traditional equitable principles have no application. That is what seems to have happened in this case.'

Instead something approaching a clear agreement is likely to be required. However this can be an informal agreement or understanding. Certainly it does not need to be something capable of legal enforcement as a binding contract.

21.2.5 Break down of relationships and (no) non-fault corporate divorce

Wealth, whether arising from initial investment or subsequent effort, might be locked up in a family or other privately owned business. It may be apparent that the relationships between the participators in that business have become unworkable. The only sensible way to resolve matters may appear to be for one party, usually the majority owner, to buy the other party out. The only other alternative would appear to be the winding up of the company. That is not where the law stands.

The position stated above was, in essence, argued on behalf of Mr O'Neill and roundly rejected by Lord Hoffmann who said[49] that: 'I do not think that there is any support in the authorities for such a stark right of unilateral withdrawal' and explained that this was the case even though:[50]

> 'breakdowns often occur (as in this case) without either side having done anything seriously wrong or unfair. It is not fair to the excluded member, who will usually have lost his employment, to keep his assets locked in the company. But that does not mean that a member who has not been dismissed or excluded can demand that his shares be purchased simply because he feels that he has lost trust and confidence in the others.'

Recognising this difficulty, and also the cost, complexity and uncertainty of bringing unfair prejudice proceedings the Law Commission have recommended that if, in a private company a member with over 10% of the share capital, has been removed as a director or has been largely prevented from acting as a director, there should be a (rebuttable) presumption of unfair prejudice.[51] Notwithstanding the major reforms in the Companies Act 2006 this recommendation has not been followed through.

There is therefore no legal mechanism to provide a no fault corporate divorce. Instead an aggrieved minority shareholder in a family owned business must show either exclusion, accompanied by appropriate equitable circumstances (bringing the fairness approach into play) or, alternatively, what amounts to breach of duty on the part of the majority.

---

[48] At p 1102.
[49] At para 8 of the judgment (pp 104–1105).
[50] At p 1104.
[51] Law Commission report on *Shareholder Remedies* (Law Com No 246, cm 3769). The report also included a draft article containing an precedent exit right to apply in two circumstances, namely the removal of a director (other than for serious breach of duty) and the death of a shareholder.

That is of course unless they are able to rely on express exit rights as part of the governance structure of their own family business.

21.2.6 Family business context

In *O'Neill* the House of Lords took the view that in the absence of exclusion, proven misconduct, bad faith, or breach of a clear agreement or understanding on the part of Mr Phillips there was nothing in the relationship between the two shareholders making it unfair for Mr Phillips to change his mind about the proposed equalisation of shareholdings.

Mr Phillips and Mr O'Neill of course had an arm's length relationship, initially as employer and employee and later as co-directors and co-shareholders. But the court acknowledged that 'context and background are very important' and that 'conduct which is perfectly fair between competing businessmen may not be fair between members of a family'.[52]

So how will the courts apply the principles set out in *O'Neill v Phillips* to situations actually involving family owned businesses? We will answer the question by looking at various family business dispute scenarios. It is important to emphasise that this approach is our own. There are no reported examples of the courts applying an analysis based on family business principles and theory to the cases before them.

21.3 UNFAIR PREJUDICE AND SUCCESSION

21.3.1 Letting go

In chapter 7 (Management Succession) we suggest that the succession process has a number of elements. For the purpose of this chapter (at least) ownership succession is the most important element. In fact, as suggested below, ownership disputes may themselves be triggered by problems arising in management succession. Of course succession problems may arise at any stage in the life of a family owned business. But perhaps they are more likely to occur in early stage businesses on the transfer from the founding entrepreneur to the next generation.

Decided legal cases involving disputes in first generation early stage entrepreneurial family owned businesses are comparatively rare, especially when compared with reported disputes involving second-generation sibling partnerships. But those early stage family business cases that do make it to court tend to exhibit a common and familiar characteristic, explored in more detail in chapter 2 (Themes), the unwillingness of the dominant founder to let go of control of the business that they have created.

21.3.2 Protecting ownership expectations

Often there will be unwillingness on the part of the founder or senior generation to let go of ownership. It is most unlikely that the unfair prejudice remedy will help the disappointed next generation family member if that unwillingness consists of the common situation of a refusal to hand over shares. Various assurances and promises

---
[52] At p 1098.

may have created expectations on the part of the second generation that they would soon take over full ownership and control. These may well have little legal value.

The next generation family member may not be a member of the family company. Nor will they be a person to whom shares have been transferred. The alleged unfairness may well consist of broken promises to let the generation have an interest in the family business. It will not often be the case that these promises can be seen to amount an enforceable contract to transfer shares. In which case the only remedy available to the aggrieved next generation may be an action based on estoppel. This remedy is discussed in detail in chapter 19.

Possibly the next generation family member may have been given a minority holding. This will at least give them *locus standi* to get through the doors of the court to present an unfair prejudice petition. However usually expectations of further transfers of ownership will be based on the most vague criteria, such as 'one day all of this will be yours'. It would be extremely difficult in the light of *O'Neill v Phillips* to envisage circumstances where the expectations of the next generation were based on such agreements or assurances would be seen as sufficiently concrete so as to create an enforceable obligation, based on CA, s 994, to complete the transfer of ownership.

Even if the courts were in principle prepared to grant relief the next generation would face two further difficulties. First (as will be explained in more detail in chapter 24) the basic approach of the Court in granting remedies under CA, s 996 is to preserve the operating status quo of the business. Usually this translates into an order for the majority to buy out the minority. Orders requiring the majority to sell are comparatively rare. The next generation would need to convince the court that the tipping point of the succession process had been reached so that de-facto control of the family business now rested in them. In other words more damage would be caused to the business by the departure of the next generation than by that of the founder or senior generation.

Secondly, the expectation of the next generation will usually (but not invariably) be that they will receive the shares of the senior generation as a gift or at less than market value. Or perhaps, at least in the view of the next generation, as a reward for their past commitment to the family business. Mr O'Neill in *O'Neill v Phillips* also appeared to be expecting his holding to increase without payment. Although the court could, in theory order the transfer of shares without payment, we cannot trace any reported case where the court has ever done so. The usual practice is for the outgoing shareholder to receive a fair value for their holding. The next generation would therefore either have to persuade the court that it was appropriate to depart from this practice, or alternatively finance the buy out of the senior generation.

21.3.3 Exclusion of the next generation

A much more likely scenario would be that tensions over the stalled ownership succession would lead to a breakdown in relationships between the generations so that the senior generation effectively exclude the next generation from full participation in the family business. Alternatively, that the founder might retaliate to the extent of breaching the duties they owe to the next generation as minority shareholders.

Whilst either scenario might open up unfair prejudice remedies, the most likely outcome would be that the next generation would gain a capital sum on the sale of their minority stake but lose their career with the family business, their succession expectations and their relationship with their parent. Clearly this could represent a somewhat pyric victory.

The unfair prejudice remedy may be of limited use in policing the primary expectations of the next generation in an early stage family business, still under the control of its founding entrepreneur. But as will be seen below, the remedy may be more relevant in slightly more mature family businesses, under the control of members of the next generation.

21.3.4 Management succession

As discussed in chapter 7, after ownership, the second key element of the succession process is the transfer of power and management control of the family business.

As suggested above, it will often be incredibly difficult for a founding entrepreneur to let go of the business that they have created. We also suggest that succession is a process not an event. In many cases the succession process may begin, perhaps with some ownership or management responsibility being transferred to the next generation, but the process may stall before a complete and effective succession to the next generation can be seen to have taken place. That incomplete succession process will often be a primary source of tension and conflict in a family owned business. The succession difficulties between Henry and Edsel in the Ford family business provide a well-known example of this.[53] But there are reported examples of this phenomenon in more typical cases much closer to home.

In *re HR Harmer Ltd*[54] the Court of Appeal had to consider an extreme example of the founder's reluctance to let go of control of the family business he had founded.

21.3.5 *In re Harmer Ltd*

The case concerned a leading worldwide stamp dealership established by the father, Mr Harmer senior. His three sons joined the business, although one of them had left before the matter came to court. Both of the remaining sons had been appointed directors. The father had also given his sons the majority of the equity in the company. However this may have been driven by a desire to mitigate estate duty rather than a positive intention to start the succession ball rolling.

By the time the matter went to court the sons, together who with their wives, owned something like 90% of the equity or beneficial ownership of the family company. However, under the share structure, the sons and their wives held only 21% of the voting rights. Their father and mother had retained voting control.

Although he was only one of several directors the father nevertheless continued to act as if he was the sole decision maker, effectively ignoring the sons and the remainder of the board. Having made a unilateral decision to set up a branch office in Australia against the wishes of the board he responded by saying that 'unless my judgement is accepted [I]

---

[53] See chapter 2 (Themes).
[54] [1959] 1 WLR 62.

shall exercise my agreed control of the company to compel my views'.[55] He ignored decisions of the board of directors. He interfered with other management decisions. He arbitrarily removed senior employees. He used his voting control to pack the board with his own stooges as nominees.

Matters deteriorated to such an extent that at board meetings it was necessary 'to have solicitors sitting at the elbows of the various parties'.[56] The business had effectively become ungovernable. So much so that all parties agreed that the drastic remedy of an order to wind the company up on just and equitable basis would be available (see chapter 22).

However the proceedings had been brought under s 210 of the Companies Act 1948 the statutory predecessor of s 994, under which it was necessary to show that the conduct complained of was oppressive (itself interpreted under the strict test of being 'burdensome, harsh and wrongful'[57]), rather than merely unfair.

Attributing much of the father's conduct to his age (Mr Harmer senior was then 88) and his deafness, rather than bad faith, the judge in the High Court nevertheless found oppression to exist.

21.3.6 Inherited shares

As noted above, and in common with many, if not most family business situations the Harmer sons had been given their shares rather than paying for them or investing in the business. It was also argued on behalf of the father that this was a factor that ought to disentitle the sons from relief and that 'the sons should not be heard to complain since they had acquired their shares through the generosity of their father'. This argument was rejected by the Court of Appeal.

First it was noted that the sons had actually paid for some preference shares that they also held. Secondly the court noted that the sons had invested a lot of their time working in the family business and that one 'gave up his career' (working in what was then the Colonial Office) to join the family business.

The concept of investment by work, as recognised in *Re Harmer*, was approved by Lord Hoffmann in *O'Neill* where he said that the earlier case:[58]

> '... shows that shareholders who receive shares as a gift but afterward work in the business may become entitled to enforce equitable constraints upon the conduct of the majority shareholder.'

However the fact the sons worked in the business was, according to the Court of Appeal in *Harmer*, a relevant but not necessary factor. In giving the leading judgment in the Court of Appeal Jenkins LJ was quite clear that:[59]

---

[55] At p 66.
[56] At p 91.
[57] At p 79 following the test of Viscount Simmonds from the House of Lords in the Scottish case of *Meyer v Scottish Co-operative Wholesale Society* (1957) SC 381.
[58] *O'Neill v Phillips* op cit at p 1103.
[59] *Harmer* at p 83.

'the question of consideration appears to me to be irrelevant, a matter of prejudice. Suppose the transaction was a mere matter of gift, the gift, if valid ... must surely have conferred the same rights as if the transaction had been for full consideration.'

Harmer was of course decided before the detailed analysis of rights arising from equitable circumstances by the House of Lords in the later case of *Ebrahimi*. It is now clear that in most circumstances (absent a breach of duty on the part of the majority) a petitioner will need to establish that their family business falls into the second category of cases, justifying equitable intervention. However the fact that shares have been given to the next generation, rather than bought by them, does not itself seem to be a bar to a fairness based intervention.

21.3.7 Voting structure and governance expectations

It was also argued on behalf of Mr Harmer senior that the voting structure (where he and his wife) held a sufficient majority of the voting B ordinary shares to enable them to pass both ordinary and special resolutions and thereby control the company for almost all purposes was known and understood by the sons and accepted by them on the incorporation of the company. They knew the score from the outset. The Court of Appeal also rejected this argument. Although it was clear (as will often be the case in first generation family business) that the founding entrepreneur will remain in ultimate control, the sons had a legitimate expectation that such control would be exercised reasonably, wisely and for the benefit of the company as a whole and that the governance mechanisms of the company will function properly:

'Members are entitled to expect that their board shall perform its functions as a board, and that proceedings of the directors shall be carried out in a normal and orthodox manner. They are entitled to the benefit of the collective experience of the directors and to expect that the directors and each of them can freely express their views at board meetings, and that regard shall be had to what they say and to resolutions properly passed.'

Conversely if:[60]

'... the board is browbeaten and either ignored or overruled by one of its number, in this case the father, in reliance of his superior voting power, the proprietary interests of the minority shareholders cannot fail to be affected.'

Minority shareholders in a family company can therefore be seen to have agreed to a level of management control by the majority. This can be contrasted with unreasoning dictatorship.

21.3.8 The order in *re Harmer*

As will be explained in detail in chapter 24, the usual order in a successful unfair prejudice petition will be for the purchase by the majority of the aggrieved minorities holding. On rare occasions the minority will seek to buy out the majority. In *re Harmer* the sons did look to buy out their father.

Rather than make an order for the sale and purchase of the father's shares by the sons the High Court judge exercised his general discretion to make a most unusual order. This

---
[60] At p 97.

in effect provided for the father to be removed from any further management role. In other words a court order that the family business management succession process should be completed. The order in *re Harmer* is discussed in more detail in chapter 24.

21.3.9 Majority petitions: Albert Thompson and the *Gippeswyck* case

The succession tipping point had also been reached in the *Gippeswyck* case,[61] one of a number of cases involving a successful estate agent and property investor, Albert Thompson. As was explained in another reported case involving the Thompson family[62] 'Mr Thompson's evidence shows that in his personal relationships he has not had similar success'. The cases reveal serious disputes with his first wife, her parents, his sister and brother in law, all three of his sons and two nephews. These disputes mostly related to family businesses.

The *Gippeswyck* case concerned a property investment company of that name and originally set up by Mr Thompson. By the time the matter reached court the succession process was well advanced. Mr Thompson had retired to Lanzarote, and, for complicated reasons connected with the dispute, the majority of the shares were held by one of Mr Thompson's sons, Julian.

Mr Thompson had issued proceedings seeking to set aside the transfer of shares by another son, John, which had given Julian this majority. Mr Thompson also claimed that his sons had managed the business to his unfair prejudice. Julian had cross petitioned and issued a 'majority shareholder's petition' essentially based on an argument that his father's continuing presence in the company was unfairly prejudicial to Julian's own interests.

Father and son then issued cross summons, each seeking to strike out the others petition. Julian succeeded. Partly this was based on his having made a reasonable offer to buy out his father. That offer took into account the effect of Julian's own alleged unfair prejudice (see below). The offer had been rejected by the father.

But the key point of the case was that the court recognised that the succession tipping point had been reached. Mr Thompson argued that the court should recognise his position as founding shareholder and that the majority shareholding now vested in Julian had originally been a gift. He, Mr Thompson, had successfully run the company previously and could do so again.

The court refused to turn back the clock confirming that 'cases where a majority shareholder is forced to sell his shareholding to the petitioning minority shareholder must be very rare indeed'.[63] The present circumstances, particularly bearing in mind Mr Thompson's age and that he had been away from the management of the business for 4 years, clearly dictated that the usual rule would apply. The court therefore ordered the completion of the succession process by ordering that the founder sell the remainder of his shares to his son.

---

[61] More usually cited as *Re a Company No 00836 of 1995*.
[62] *Re Macro (Ipswich) Ltd & another* [1994] BCC 781 at para 5 of the judgment.
[63] At p 442 of the judgment.

So whilst majority petitions are rare animals, orders for the purchase of a majority holding are rarer still.

21.4 SIBLING PARTNERSHIPS – EXCLUSION CASES

21.4.1 Introduction

A considerable number of family business cases involve second generation or other sibling family partnerships. Often, following the death of the senior generation founders and perhaps in the absence of the glue and cohesion provided by their presence and influence, relationships between siblings deteriorate to the stage that court proceedings are issued. Frequently such proceedings are based on one or more siblings being excluded from the family business by their more dominant brothers and sisters. Given the close correlation between the family business concept of sibling partnerships and the legal concept of quasi-partnership it will be no surprise that relief will often be granted by the courts in these circumstances.

The relevant concepts are explored in detail in the High Court in *Brownlow v GH Marshall*.[64]

21.4.2 *Brownlow* – The facts

The case concerned a second-generation sibling partnership. The business, that of heating engineers, was initially set up by the father, Mr Marshall senior, in 1951. By the mid 1990's there were three siblings involved as directors and equal shareholders. They were Mrs Brownlow, her brother, Mr Marshall, both of whom worked full time in the business, and a sister Mrs Hall, who lived in California, and whom whilst supportive of Mr Marshall, had appointed an accountant to act as her permanent alternate director.

Another older brother, George, had been ousted form the company some years earlier. At this time George's shares had been bought back by the company, following threats of unfair prejudice proceedings. Relationships between the three remaining siblings had been poor for 10 years or so.

Attempts to resolve matters by introducing basic governance mechanisms resulted in all three directors signing service agreements in 1995. However negotiations broke down over a shareholders' agreement the draft of which contained provisions to entrench the position of all family members. Relationships deteriorated further and Mrs Brownlow was excluded from employment by the company in 1997. She was then removed as a director, by her brother and sister, in 1998.

In addition to launching (what would now be) employment tribunal proceedings (which were settled), Mrs Brownlow petitioned under what is now CA, s 994 and argued that she had a legitimate expectation to participate in the management of the company, or if excluded to have her shares bought out at a fair value. In addition to the buy back of George's shares there was evidence of historic offers to buy out Mrs Brownlow.

---

[64] [2001] BCC 152.

21.4.3 Family expectations

Mr Marshall and Mrs Hall on the other hand sought to argue that the recently signed service agreements, with entire agreement clauses (saying that the terms of those agreements superseded all prior agreements and understandings) over-rode or negated any such expectations. Further that the conduct of Mrs Brownlow in relation to expenses claims and other dealings had undermined the trust and confidence between her and the family company making it appropriate that she should go and without any entitlement to be bought out.

The judge in the case was clear that there was:[65]

> '... a family expectation, growing over the years, that each of the children of Mr and Mrs Marshall Snr would, so far as possible and so far as personal circumstances allowed, be brought into the management of the affairs of the company. Once such status had been achieved (recognised by appointment as directors) it was expected that the relevant person would continue to be involved in that management.'

And further that:[66]

> 'Throughout the various dissensions that I have recounted, it was recognised that if a family shareholder was to be dislodged from management, something would have to be done to realise the value of his or her shares.'

This expectation was not affected by the fact that the family had, with other non-family directors, entered into new service agreements or the express provisions of those agreements.

21.4.4 *Brownlow* – The law and family relationships

Applying the law, as laid down in *O'Neill v Phillips* the judge concluded that the fact that *Brownlow* concerned a family business was a key factor in adopting a fairness approach, where considerations of fairness and equity would apply to over-ride and supplement the formal constitution. The family business concerned:[67]

> '... was indeed a company in which considerations of a personal character arising out of the relationships between these family shareholders, gave rise to the type of conditions in which the equitable considerations, envisaged by Lord Wilberforce in Westbourne Galleries and by Lord Hoffmann in O'Neill, might disentitle the majority to remove a minority shareholder director from office without making a reasonable offer, if asked, for the purchase of the minority member's shares.'

21.4.5 Level of involvement?

The corollary of exclusion is involvement. The principles stated in *Brownlow* have been applied in a number of subsequent sibling partnership family business cases. These also explore the nature and extent of involvement necessary to qualify for equitable treatment and to fall within the s 994 unfair prejudice remedy. It has already been seen

---

[65] At p 163.
[66] At p 165.
[67] At p 166.

in *Harmer* that the *Ebrahimi* principles of over-riding justice will apply in situations where the second generation have been given their shares but work in the family business. What level of work and involvement is required?

21.4.6 *Shah v Shah* – involvement as a director

In *Shah v Shah*[68] a clear distinction emerges between employment and directorship or wider management with exclusion from the latter entitling the petitioner to be bought out. This was the case even though the petitioner had walked away from employment with the family business.

The case concerned three brothers and a cousin (treated as if he were also a brother). They jointly owned and ran a successful fashion business. It was clear that the dominant and driving force behind the business was the oldest brother, known as CJ. The contributions of the remaining family members appeared to be limited to sitting in the basement of the company's head office, dealing with cheques, paying invoices but basically avoiding CJ.

Eventually CJ began to apply pressure to remove the others from the business. In response to this pressure the petitioner, Dinesh, stopped coming into the offices at all, resigned, and presented a claim to the employment tribunal based on constructive dismissal. The employment tribunal dismissed Dinesh's claim on the basis that he had not been constructively dismissed but had simply 'declined to perform his duties as an employee'. In other words there was no exclusion from employment.

The court nevertheless drew a clear distinction between Dinesh's employment and his wider, albeit limited, involvement in the management of the business, finding as a fact that Dinesh's resignation was not intended to extend to his directorship. By purporting to remove Dinesh from the bank mandate, cancel his directorship CJ had 'acted to remove from Dinesh substantially all his functions as a director and to sideline him from overall decision-making regarding the business'.[69] This exclusion was sufficient, to amount to unfair prejudice. In the judge's view:[70]

> 'Dinesh clearly misconducted himself as an employee, but I do not find anything in his attitude to the overall management of the Company that could justify his exclusion.'

This was so notwithstanding that Dinesh's misconduct as an employee and, notwithstanding also, that CJ might have genuinely believed that the best interests of the business would be served by his assuming sole control.

A similar result can be found in the *Harding*[71] case (on just and equitable winding up). But in that case none of the sisters, other than perhaps Elisabeth, had anything other than the remotest participation in management via occasional directors' meetings.

---

[68] [2010] EWHC 313 (Ch).
[69] At para 110 of the judgment.
[70] At para 115 of the judgment.
[71] *Sally Harding, Rosemary Walton v Elizabeth Edwards, Janet Harding, the Executors of BM Harding (deceased), Brandon Harding Limited* [2014] EWHC 247 (Ch).

21.4.7 Family agreements– *Fisher v Cadman*

In *Fisher v Cadman*[72] the court accepted that simply being a shareholder of 'a small family company in which the family relationship would be important alongside the relationship defined in the Articles of Association'.[73] Accordingly reluctance on the part of the two brothers controlling the business to provide information and explanations on financial matters or to convene shareholder meetings laid the foundation for their sister to petition for unfair prejudice based on these and other more substantial breaches of understandings.

What emerges from the report of the case is how strongly the founder and father, Mr Cadman senior, James, had controlled the family business and had dominated the brothers during his lifetime. The court made a finding of fact that the brothers 'had long had a sense that they had been treated harshly by their father, by not being paid remuneration for their day to day running' of the family business.[74] The court looked at the history of the business and noted in particular the reluctance of James Cadman to pay the brothers for work undertaken by them in looking after the company's property portfolio combined with an expectation that they should nevertheless do so.

O'Neill v Phillips talks about the need, when following the fairness approach, to recognise the agreements and understandings between the parties.

In *Fisher v Cadman* the court found that one of those understandings was that the brothers had agreed to manage the portfolio of properties held by the company without remuneration (on the basis that they would receive value through capital appreciation on sale). Accordingly an attempt by the brothers to introduce provisions for their remuneration (which substantially eroded the net asset value of the business) was a further ground for unfair prejudice.[75]

The two brothers also owned a building business, which carried out work for the family company. A provision had been made in the accounts for work carried out some time ago and which had never been paid. An attempt by the brothers to charge retrospective interest on this debt was equally doomed.[76]

21.4.8 Participation expectation as a property right– *The Gate of India*

In *The Gate of India*[77] the court found that an agreement had been reached for the son of one of two quasi partner business founders to take over his father's '... share in the business in the fullest sense, that is as partner with a right and expectation of participation in the running of the business ... and of being consulted about all major decisions'.[78]

---

[72] [2005] EWHC 377 (Ch), discussed above.
[73] Apt para 89 of the judgment.
[74] See para 45 of the judgment.
[75] See para 98 of the judgment.
[76] See paras 101 and 102 of the judgment.
[77] Re Gate of India (Tynemouth) Ltd, also known as: *Rahman v Malik* [2008] EWHC 959 (Ch), [2008] 2 BCLC 403. Discussed in chapter 20.
[78] At para 78 of the judgment.

When the son lost his temper in an argument with another member of staff, his uncle, whilst initially acting reasonably in asking his nephew to take time out of the business to allow tempers to cool, 'used the incident' to justify barring the son from the restaurant permanently. The uncle also failed also to appoint his nephew as a director, in breach of the agreement reached with his brother and co-founder. Again this refusal by the uncle to honour this agreement relating to participation, combined with other breaches of duty on the uncle's part resulted in a successful unfair prejudice petition.

21.5 COUSIN CONSORTIA – UNFAIR PREJUDICE AND THE LATER STAGE FAMILY OWNED BUSINESS

It will be seen that the courts appear to be a willing to regard family sibling partnerships as being within the second category of businesses, those subject to over-riding equitable considerations, particularly in the case of exclusion.

To what extent have the courts applied equitable considerations when dealing with older, more complex family businesses, cousin consortia? The answer is with more reluctance. Most significantly in the case of *Saul D Harrison & Sons plc*,[79] the claimant suggested that fairness demanded a return on investment or an exit route for her as a minority non-management family shareholder. The courts roundly rejected this suggestion.

21.5.1 *Saul D Harrison & Sons plc*

The facts of the case are set out in detail in chapter 1 and the case is discussed extensively in chapter 20.

Briefly the courts refused to support an argument that (what is now) CA, s 994 should be used to provide a non-working outsider cousin, a 'have not' with an exit route at the expense of the insider working family members, the 'haves'. The cousin's claim was based on arguments that the financial position of the company was such that the haves enjoyed whatever financial benefits were available from the company making it unfair that the she received no benefit from her ownership.

On the facts of the case no breach of duty had been established. Those facts included:
- That although there was no profit left for distribution to the have-nots after director's remuneration had been paid the Court of Appeal found that this remuneration was not of itself excessive, based on objective criteria and given the turnover and number of people employed in the operation.
- The directors had plans to turn around the business, including the introduction of new product lines and other diversification. These were combined with recognition that, whereas the business may have stagnated under the leadership of the third generation of the Harrison family, the board was now run by fourth and more recently fifth generation family members who could bring fresh energy to the operations of the moribund family company.
- In particular the possibility of increased efficiency afforded by the move to new premises meant that it was premature to write the company off as never likely to produce a profit.

---

[79] [1994] BCC 475.

- Criticisms about the weight of the evidence and arguments presented by or on behalf of the petitioner (or more precisely the lack of it).
- Recognition that continuing the business, rather than closing it down and distributing the surplus capital to family shareholders, was clearly in the best interests of the 100 or so employees of the family business and accordingly the directors duty to have regard to their interests in accordance with what is now CA, s 172(1)(b) should be recognised.
- Perhaps most importantly timing. The Court of Appeal were clear that if evidence could be produced to show that the business was doomed to continue at a loss or could only produce a paltry return on the assets employed then it would be a breach of duty if the directors continued the business simply to carry on taking their salary. On the facts of the case there was no evidence that this point had been reached.

21.5.2 Clemens v Clemens Brothers Ltd[80]

It is difficult to reconcile the decision in *Saul D Harrison* with the earlier High Court case of *Clemens v Clemens Brothers Ltd*. *Clemens*, which was actually a case where the court was asked to exercise its residual equitable discretion rather than to provide a statutory remedy under CA, s 994 or its statutory predecessors, was not referred to in the later Court of Appeal matter.

Clemens concerned an extremely successful and profitable building and shop fitting business, run by three non-family executive directors, a non-executive non-family chairman with a second generation family member, Miss Clemens also sitting on the board as a director and holding the majority, 55% of the voting shares. The remaining 45% was held by Miss Clemen's niece, also a Miss Clemens, who had previously been a director, and who had resigned (over a dispute with the previous chairman). Miss (niece) Clemens had expressed a wish to return to the board and appeared to be actively seeking information about the company.

The articles also contained pre-emption provisions. These would eventually allow the niece to gain a controlling interest in the business, if she outlived her aunt. It is clear that the niece, who was much younger than her aunt, hoped to rely on those provisions one day.

In many ways *Clemens* can be seen as an attempted appropriation case.[81] The non-family board members had proposed a scheme allowing the directors to acquire 21.5% of the equity with a further 23.5% being held by an employee share trust. The effect of this scheme would be to dilute the family members holdings down to 30.5% (the aunt) and 24.5% (the niece).

Nevertheless these proposals were actively supported by the aunt who wrote to the niece explaining that she believed that 'it would have been my father's wish to always take notice of the interests of the company's long serving employees'.

---

[80] [1976] 2 All ER 268.
[81] The expression 'appropriation sale' was used by Blondell and Klein to describe the situation where lack of control by the family allows non-family management and shareholders to gain de facto control of a family business. Discussed in detail in chapter 12.

The relevant (ordinary) resolutions to put the scheme into place were duly passed at an extra-ordinary general meeting using the aunt's majority control with the niece voting against. The case came before the High Court as an application to set aside these resolutions as 'oppressive'.

That application was duly granted with the court finding as questions of fact:
- that the directors, including the aunt by way of her director's fees were all overpaid already[82] and did not need to hold shares to be further incentivised;
- the employee share scheme could have been established using non-voting shares (which the niece would have supported);
- the aunt genuinely believed that the directors and employees, via the share scheme, holding shares in the company would be in the interests of the company;
- the resolution had nevertheless 'been framed so as to put into the hands of [the aunt] and her fellow directors complete control of the company and to deprive the plaintiff of her existing rights as a shareholder'.[83]

As explained at 20.4.4 the judge in *Clemens* referred to *Ebrahimi* and said that the equitable principles in that case should apply. However he carefully avoided stating any rule or principle why this should be, simply saying that:[84]

> 'it would be unwise to try to produce a principle, since the circumstances of each case are infinitely varied. It would not, I think, assist to say more than that in my judgment Miss Clemens is not entitled as of right to exercise her votes as an ordinary shareholder in any way she pleases.'

The resolutions were therefore set aside and the niece's position in the family business protected.

21.5.3 *Harrison* and *Clemens* compared

The clear message emerging from all of the cases we have looked at so far is that, in deciding whether, or not, to grant unfair prejudice relief each case will be considered on its facts. Clearly this approach, whilst understandable and consistent with the basic approach in equity, creates considerable uncertainty for business owning families in dispute and their advisors.

Both *Harrison* and *Clemens* concerned mature later stage, relatively large (in terms of their turnover and number of employees) family owned businesses. In both cases proceedings were brought by non-management 'have not' family members but were decided differently on their respective facts.

Is it nevertheless worthwhile therefore looking at the factual distinctions between *Harrison* and *Clemens* to see if any circumstances emerge that would point towards or away from equitable intervention?
- **Statutory duty.** At the time *Clemens* was heard considering the interests of employees would have been seen as a legitimate matter to be taken into account by

---

[82] Based on a survey in the case showing that the directors were the best or second best paid in each year of 22 comparable businesses.
[83] At p 282.
[84] Also at p 282.

directors. When *Harrison* was heard in the Court of Appeal nearly 20 years later the directors were under a positive statutory duty to do so.

- **Size of shareholding.** Whereas the plaintiff in *Clemens* was a substantial minority holder with 45% of the equity the claimant in *Harrison* held only 8% or so.
- **Profile of shareholding.** Similarly *Clemens* concerned a small family ownership of two individuals. *Harrison* involved a number of family owners and trusts. It is unclear whether the remaining shareholders in *Harrison* were supportive of the haves, the have-nots, neutral or were simply disinterested outsiders.
- **'Quasi – quasi partnership'.** Although neither then currently an employee nor a director the niece in *Clemens* nevertheless had been a director and appeared to be seeking a return to active involvement in the business. Although we have classified the business as a cousin consortium it also has elements of an inherited sibling partnership (like *The Gate of India* and *Fisher v Cadman*) with the niece inheriting the shares of her father, the previous managing director.
- **Status quo.** The primary mischief complained of in *Harrison* was the failure of the board 'to call it a day' and cease trading the family business. In *Clemens* the majority were seeking to disrupt the status quo, to the detriment of the niece.
- **Relative remuneration.** Dividends were paid to the niece (and her aunt) in *Clemens*. Because of the lack of profit dividends could not be paid in *Harrison*. Nevertheless the findings of fact by the respective courts were that the 'haves' in *Harrison* were reasonably remunerated, whereas in *Clemens* the non-family directors were overpaid. Their pay and the aunt's own remuneration as a family non-executive director had 'increased astonishingly'[85] in the years preceding the court case.
- **Breach of duty.** Although the court did not say so perhaps *Clemens* could be seen as close to a breach of duty case. There is in any event an overlap between cases in which both equitable principles apply and factors indicating a breach of duty are present.
- **Relative authority.** *Saul D Harrison* is a widely quoted and approved judgment of the Court of Appeal. *Clemens v Clemens* has been labelled as 'controversial and much criticised case'.[86]

We will now move on to consider those cases we have categorised as breach of duty matters.

21.6 BREACH OF DUTY

21.6.1 Introduction

Directors' duties are considered in more detail in chapter 8. As a general proposition most serious breaches of duty owed to shareholders will be a ground for unfair prejudice. The exception will be cases where although the directors might be in breach of the duties they owe to the company, no loss, and therefore no prejudice will have been suffered by shareholders. Many cases will involve more than one breach of duty. Often there will be a degree of overlap between breaches of duty, making precise categorisation difficult.

---

[85] *Clemens* at p 279.
[86] Hollington, op cit at para 5.62 – referring to CLRSG's consultation paper and final reports on 'Modern Company Law: Completing the Structure'.

Equally allegations of breach of duty appearing in the decided cases range from, at one end of the scale relatively trivial breaches of statutory administrative requirements, to at the other end of the scale, serious criminal dishonesty. As a further general principle, the more serious the allegation, the more the court will need clear evidence before accepting that the allegation has been proved. So very clear evidence will be required for allegations based on the bad faith of directors and more so on fraud.[87] However the usual civil burden of proof, the balance of probabilities, will still apply.[88]

The remainder of this section examines where courts are likely to intervene and to grant unfair prejudice relief in breach of duty cases and where they are not.

We have separated the breaches of duty into separate sections. This is somewhat artificial. In practice most cases will not involve isolated and individual breaches of duty but rather multiple breaches, which collectively combine to produce a cocktail of unfairness.

21.6.2 Dishonesty

In *The Gate of India* it was alleged that the controlling shareholder, Mr Malik, systematically failed to declare all the takings of the business, thereby depriving HMRC of tax, the company of cash and the petitioner of his entitlement to share in the underlying profits of the family business. Assisted no doubt by the evidence of the petitioner's father that he and his brother had systematically under-declared profits (but shared these to the detriment of HMRC) during his tenure, the court accepted that under-declarations had taken place. The court assessed these at the level that Mr Malik had accepted as a basis to compromise claims made by HMRC. It was ordered that appropriate adjustments should be made to restore the value removed from the company when valuing the nephew's shares.[89]

Of course in many cases the remote minority family members may have a suspicion that dishonesty has occurred but no concrete evidence that this is the case. Given the difficulties of proof and the catastrophic effect that false or unproven allegations could have on family relationships great caution therefore needs to be exercised before raising allegations of dishonesty.

In practice findings of outright dishonesty are quite rare, although perhaps not quite so rare as allegations of dishonesty made by the aggrieved minority. Far more frequent are breaches of duty based on a misplaced sense of entitlement on the part of the insiders. Often this is accompanied by a less than transparent approach to communication and the provision of information by the insider controllers to the more remote minority family members. This of course can create a climate where more serious wrong-doing is suspected.

---

[87] *Re Rica Gold Washing* [1879] 11 ChD 36 approved by the High Court Vinelott J in *Saul D Harrison* at p 492.
[88] See the *Gate of India* at paras 59 and 110.
[89] See paras 110–118 of the judgment.

21.6.3 Excessive remuneration

Overview

Perhaps the main cause of disputes in more widely held family owned businesses are concerns that the directors controlling the business day to day, the 'haves', are taking excessive remuneration out of the business, often leaving little or nothing to be distributed by way of dividends to the more remote family members, the 'have nots'.

Concerns over excessive remuneration in quoted companies are pretty much a daily feature in the financial pages. But a mixture of remuneration committees, shareholder activism and ultimately the exit route provided by a public market prevent such concerns developing into fully-fledged disputes. In most non-family private companies there is a close correlation between ownership and management. Alternatively non-management shareholders are institutions, well able to control remuneration through investment agreements etc. It is therefore likely that the most extreme examples of remuneration disputes will arise as a result of the complexity of the later stage family business situation.

If a controlling shareholder takes excessive remuneration out of the family business, whilst not ensuring a reasonable dividend flow, this can amount to unfair prejudice. What amounts to excessive will be a question of fact.

The general rule – a matter of commercial judgment

In practice it will be by no means easy to establish that remuneration is excessive.

Although theoretically directors have no implied right to be paid, in practice the basic constitution of most companies will allow directors to set their own remuneration.[90] So in the absence of any express restraints contained in the governance documents of the family business concerned, whether in bespoke articles or a shareholders' agreement, the starting point is that the director, 'the haves' can set their own remuneration.

The potential for resentment on the part of the more remote family members, the 'have-nots,' arising from this conflict of interest is clear and obvious. But the starting point is that setting their own remuneration is as much a management decision for the directors as setting the pay of any other employee. The 'have-nots' will need to prove that in setting their remuneration at the level they have done, the directors are acting in breach of duty. No easy task.

The starting point is that deciding the appropriate level of remuneration, even their own, is a matter of commercial judgment for the directors, one with which the courts should be reluctant to interfere.

Disputes can relate to one off substantial payments, for example bonuses or significant pension contributions. Alternatively, concerns might be about excessive remuneration paid as 'routine' regular salary.

---

[90] See Art 19 of the Companies Act 2006 (Model Articles) Regulations, SI 2008/3229. The procedural aspects of directors' remuneration and related issues of breach of directors' duties are considered at 8.9.

Procedural irregularity

The first potential area of challenge for the aggrieved minority is to examine whether the proper procedures under the company's constitution have been followed to approve the relevant remuneration. This is dealt with in chapter 8 (Directors' Duties).

Collateral purpose

In rare cases it may be possible to show that the remuneration is based on irrelevant or aberrant considerations and therefore cannot possibly have been arrived at by a proper exercise of directors' powers. Again this is considered in in chapter 8. Logically if directors have been helping themselves to excessive remuneration in breach of their directors' duties this is likely to be unfairly prejudicial to the have-nots.

Family pay restraint agreements

In rarer cases the family may have reached some private agreement, including an informal agreement, about directors limiting or forgoing pay in the wider interests of the family business. In *Fisher v Cadman* the judge held that the directors were bound by an informal family agreement to work without remuneration and also that, even absent that agreement, the remuneration proposed by the brothers was excessive in the circumstances of the small family business concerned. This should give some encouragement to minority shareholders seeking to rely on understandings set out in a family charter or similar document dealing with employment and other remuneration polices, even if the document is not strictly legally binding.

History

As a related point the factual matrix and the history of remuneration in the family business. Dramatic increases in pay, as in *Clemens*, or changes to the basis of remuneration, such as in *Fisher v Cadman*, or, more spectacularly in *Irvine* can be seen as indicative evidence of unfairness.

Residual unfairness

In many cases it may not be possible to show that the haves are in breach of their duties as directors insofar as their remuneration arrangements are concerned. The have-nots may still harbour residual concerns that the haves are simply overpaid and milking the family company dry.

Here the 'have-nots' will need to show that, on the basis of objective commercial criteria, the remuneration cannot be justified. In practice the minority will need to show that the level of pay is so extreme that, in agreeing to it, the directors have breached their fiduciary duties, including to promote the success of the company. This will be no easy task.

The court may be prepared to consider contributions by or the importance of the director to the business that take the director concerned beyond the normal range of remuneration.[91] The court will also look at the circumstances of the industry concerned, for example the high rewards in the entertainment industry.[92]

In *Saul D Harrison* in the High Court, Vinelott J, was entirely dismissive of allegations that the family directors were excessively remunerated given the size and turnover of the company and partly in the absence of any comparable evidence presented on behalf of the petitioner.[93] Vinelott J was satisfied that there was:[94]

> 'no evidence that the directors are paid in the aggregate (including benefits received by their wives) more than the company would have to pay to secure suitable replacements or that the level of remuneration is out of line with that paid to executive directors of other companies of comparable size and turnover.'

The Court of Appeal agreed.

Irvine v Irvine – the going rate, exceptional contribution and its limits

The facts of *Irvine v Irvine*[95] are referred to in chapter 20. Although the minority succeeded with their arguments of excessive remuneration the case illustrates just how difficult it will be win on this ground.

Briefly the case concerned a successful insurance broking business, run as a sibling partnership and equally owned between two brothers. Malcolm, one of the brothers died leaving his shares to his widow, Pauline. The remaining shares had already been placed in a trust for the benefit of his children.

Crucially the will also provided for the transfer of a single share to the surviving brother, giving that brother a fractional overall majority. Although this share represented only 0.8% of the voting rights, as will be seen in chapter 24, this proved to be significantly more costly for the widow and children in terms of the overall value of the family business.

Following the death the surviving brother Ian used that voting control to determine his own, extremely significant remuneration, in effect taking almost all of the available profits as remuneration so that nothing was left the payment of dividends. In some years this amounted to more than £1m. Generally he appeared to treat the business as his own by survivorship.

As explained above the High Court believed that neither the widow nor the trustees should be regarded as:[96]

> '... having or expecting to have any participation in the running of the company or any other legitimate expectation such as to subject the conduct by Ian of CIHL's affairs to any particular equitable consideration.'

---

[91] As in *Irvine (No 1)*.
[92] *Smith v Croft* [1986] 1 WLR 580.
[93] See discussion at pp 484–486.
[94] At p 735 of the judgment.
[95] [2006] EWHC 406 (Ch).
[96] At para 257.

In considering the relevance of the transfer of the single share the trial judge found that this was not intended to set up any form of family business trust imposing fiduciary obligations, as Pauline contended. Neither was it a signal for Ian to do entirely as he pleased with the company, as Ian argued. Instead it was simply designed to prevent deadlock so as to allow Ian to operate the company on a day-to-day basis.

The judge also found 'that the evidence justifies treating Ian as exceptional with regard to his remuneration'.[97] But even in the absence of equitable constraints and notwithstanding this finding of exceptional contribution, it was held to be unfair of Ian to appropriate the whole of the profit. Although his remuneration should not be limited to a market salary the judge found (after listening to extensive expert evidence from remuneration consultants) that this should be limited to 40% of the net profits (subject to a minimum of £300,000) leaving the remaining 60% to be distributed by way of dividend (of which Ian would of course received fractionally over half). Ian's use of his voting and day-to day control of the family company to help himself to more amounted to unfair prejudice. Accordingly Ian was ordered to buy out the holdings of Pauline and the family trust. The approach taken by the court on valuation is discussed in more detail in chapter 24.

Perhaps one explanation for the decision in *Irvine* was that Ian's remuneration had simply been unilaterally decided by him and not been properly authorised under the company's constitution. The logical extension of this argument is that, if Ian had gone through the proper formalities, using his controlling shareholding, to force through his remuneration package, even if Pauline objected it may not have been treated as unfair.

It is nevertheless clear that a claim based on excessive remuneration will not be easy to establish. The court in *Irvine* was presented with extremely detailed expert evidence from remuneration consultants and accountants. It still came to the conclusion that Ian was entitled to extremely substantial remuneration.

Other excessive remuneration cases

Excessive remuneration (a scheme to take the profits of the business as bonuses) also featured in *Re McCarthy Surfacing Limited* and were found to be excessive both collectively and especially in the individual case of the managing director, Tom McCarthy.[98]

The claimants in *Re Cumana*[99] were also able to show that the remuneration taken by the majority was 'plainly in excess' of anything that the defendant could be seen to have earned and was therefore unfairly prejudicial.

Financial position of the company

The main complaint made in *Saul D Harrison* was that the haves were continuing the business simply to continue taking their remuneration. Whilst labelling that claim as premature and not made out on the facts of the case Vinelott J at first instance said 'that there could be no doubt' that such a claim could succeed if supported by appropriate evidence. He identified two circumstances. First, where a company was trading at a loss.

---

[97] At para 321 of the judgment.
[98] [2008] EWHC 2279 (Ch).
[99] [1986] BCLC 430.

Secondly, where the family company is sufficiently unprofitable so that there was 'no real prospect that that the profits will ever represent a reasonable return on the capital employed'.[100] The claimant's problem was that the directors were able to argue that the company had some prospects of future success.

Similarly in *Re Company ex parte Burr*[101] where the minority also argued that the haves had continued to trade at a loss simply to carry on taking their own, excessive, remuneration was struck out. It was not enough for the have-nots to raise an inference that this was intended. They needed to produce evidence that this was the case.

In *Van Hengel*[102] (a director's disqualification case) the court thought that failure to have regard to the poor financial circumstances of the non-family business concerned was an example of unfitness to act as a director and that:[103]

> 'A director must bear in mind what a company can afford as well as what is the going rate for the job performed by the director if he were an employee elsewhere.'

If that duty is owed to the creditors of an insolvent company or one in financial difficulties should a similar duty be owed to the have-nots in a struggling family owned company?

But there are many other cases where directors have been allowed to take market level remuneration even from struggling companies provided that they had not reached the stage where they had no reasonable prospect of avoiding insolvency under the test in IA, s 214.

21.6.4 Dividends

Starting point – no entitlement

The issues of excessive remuneration and non-payment of dividends are inextricably linked. The higher the remuneration of the working directors, the lower the profits available for distribution by way of dividend.

One of the fundamental 'rights' attached to shareholding is the ability to participate in the surplus profits of the company. However, as a general rule, shareholders have no entitlement to the payment of set dividends. Whether or not dividends are paid is fundamentally a matter of commercial judgment to be made by the directors. This is of course subject to any formal agreement to the contrary, contained in the articles (for example attached to preference shares) or a clear dividend policy in a legally binding shareholders' agreement.

The basic position was confirmed *Irvine (No 1)* where the judge said that:[104]

> '... the petitioners had no legitimate expectation ... that dividends would be paid on their shares ... the petitioners had no expectation of a dividend payment merely because they were

---

[100] At p 482.
[101] [1992] BCLC 724.
[102] *Secretary of State for Trade and Industry v Van Hengel and Another* [1995] BCC 173.
[103] [1995] BCC 173 at p 181.
[104] At para 273.

shareholders and that the reported decisions on the non-payment of dividends (do no more than establish that the non-payment of dividends may, in the particular circumstances of the case, amount to unfairly prejudicial conduct.'

Proper consideration

What shareholders do have is a right for the board to give proper consideration to the payment of dividends. However in practice it may be as hard, if not harder to base an unfair prejudice petition on the non-payment of dividends than on paying excessive remuneration.

If the controlling shareholders take dividends themselves and simply fail to pay appropriate pro-rata dividends to other family members this will of course be an obvious breach of duty and a ground for unfair prejudice, for example as in *The Gate of India*.[105]

As with excessive remuneration, historic practice might be relevant. For example a sudden restriction on dividends, which cannot be explained by the economic performance of the family company, might raise suspicions of unfairness.

In *Re A Company (No 00370 of 1987) ex parte Glossup*[106] it was decided that failure to recommend dividends could be a ground for just and equitable winding up. As Harman J explained:[107]

> 'directors have a duty to see how much they can properly distribute to members. They have a duty, as I see it, to remember that that the members are the owners of the company, that the profits belong to the members, and that subject to the proper needs of the company to ensure that it is not trading in a risky manner and that there are adequate reserves for commercial purposes, by and large the trading profits ought to be distributed by way of dividends.'

Notwithstanding this encouragement minority family shareholders who have been starved of dividends will not have a straightforward claim. There are two inter-related factors at play. First the innate prudence with which many family-owned businesses are operated has been commented on in chapter 1. One feature of this is often the accumulation of significant cash reserves, frequently accompanied by fairly low dividends. Secondly it may be difficult to draw the line between where acceptable business prudence ends and an improper de-facto exclusion from benefit of the minority begins. As explained below, the courts will be extremely reluctant to interfere with management decisions generally. This will apply just as much to dividend practices as any other management decision.

The link to excessive remuneration – Re McCarthy Surfacing Limited and Samuel Weller & Sons

Therefore, in practice most of the successful cases of unfair prejudice based on inadequate dividends have been accompanied by other aggravating factors, usually payment of excessive remuneration.

---

[105] See paras 99–109 of the judgment.
[106] [1988] 1WLR 1068.
[107] At p 1076.

Re McCarthy Surfacing Limited was a case involving a family controlled construction business but with non-family minority shareholders. Two of these fell out with the McCarthy brothers and left the employment of the company. A bonus scheme was put in place whereby the McCarthy family (together with other non family management) were to receive all of the profits of the company, largely derived from a new and lucrative contract.

The company prepared 'paper board minutes' recording that the directors had considered whether to pay dividends but had decided not to. The court rejected these minutes as a sham, deciding that the majority had a fixed intention that the petitioners:[108]

> '… ought not to benefit from the profits of the Company by reason of their past conduct and by reason of the fact that they had played no part in the rebuilding of the Company since their departure.'

The case was not one where the directors had:[109]

> '… bona-fide decided not to declare dividends in the best interests of the Company. It is a case where the board has consistently failed to consider whether or not to declare dividends, and that must be a breach of duty.'

Failure to properly consider whether dividends should be paid was therefore one of the bases on which the court decided that unfair prejudice had been established.

In *Samuel Weller & Sons*[110] the company paid out what the petitioners described as a 'derisory dividend' amounting to less than 7% of annual profits (and less than 2% of available cash reserves). This dividend had remained unchanged for nearly 40 years. The controlling family, had used company funds (representing almost 10 year's worth of dividend payments at the usual rate) to buy a holiday home for their own use.

Nevertheless Mr Justice Peter Gibson[111] (as he then was) clearly did not see the matter as straightforward saying that:

> 'I do not intend to suggest that a shareholder who does not receive an income from the company except by way of dividend is always entitled to complain whenever the company is controlled by persons who do derive an income from the company and when profits are not fully distributed by way of dividend. I have no doubt that the court will view with great caution allegations of unfair prejudice on this ground.'

There was however a clear case of 'haves' and 'have-nots' combined with the payment of inadequate dividends in *Samuel Weller* where:

> '… it is asserted by the petitioners that the sole director is conducting the affairs of the company for the exclusive benefit of himself and his family, and that while he and his sons are taking an income from the company, he is causing the company to pay inadequate

---

[108] At para 82 of the judgment.
[109] At para 83 of the judgment.
[110] [1990] Ch 682.
[111] At p 693.

dividends to the shareholders. The facts are striking because of the absence of any increase in the dividend for so many years and because of the amount of accumulated profits and the amount of cash in hand.'

In those circumstances payment of low dividends might justify the intervention of the courts on behalf of the have-nots. As explained by the judge:

'I ask myself why the payment of low dividends in such circumstances is incapable of amounting to conduct unfairly prejudicial to the interests of those members, like the petitioners, who do not receive directors' fees or remuneration from the company. I am unable to see any sufficient reason. It may be in the interests of Mr. Sam Weller and his sons that larger dividends should not be paid out and that the major part of the profits of the company should be retained in order to enhance the capital value of their holdings. Their interests are not necessarily identical with those of other shareholders. It may well be in the interests of the other shareholders, including the petitioners, that a more immediate benefit should accrue to them in the form of larger dividends. As their only income from the company is by way of dividend, their interests may be not only prejudiced by the policy of low dividend payments, but unfairly prejudiced.'

The issue was therefore allowed to proceed to a full hearing, albeit with less than a ringing endorsement of Peter-Gibson J as to the prospects of success at full trial.

21.6.5 Long term prospects – *Saul D Harrison* revisited

The combination of remuneration (even at reasonable rates) paid to the working family members and low profits, insufficient to justify dividends will inevitably leave the non-working family members, the 'have-nots', with little or no financial benefit from their ownership. Analytically all the benefits from the business may be flowing to the 'haves' through remuneration and other stakeholders such as employees and suppliers. At the same time, as is often the case, the family business may have accumulated substantial cash reserves or be otherwise asset rich. The overall return on those assets may be sub-optimal. In the case of a business making small losses a gradual erosion of shareholder value will occur. At best the risk reward ratio will, so far as the 'have-nots' are concerned, inevitably appear skewed in favour of the 'haves'.

This, in essence was the factual matrix in *Saul D Harrison*.

In the absence of establishing that any equitable considerations applied – as to which see chapter 20 above, the petitioner had to show some form of breach of duty on the part of the directors to have regard to her interests as a 'have-not'. She pointed to the board's decision to keep the business going and, in particular its failure to seize a golden opportunity of calling time on the family business when a considerable cash sum was realised following the compulsory acquisition of the company's trading premises. Instead the compensation was reinvested in new premises. She argued that in doing so the board had acted in bad faith by continuing a moribund business and thereby preferring their own interests as employees to the interests of shareholders.

The court accepted that this could in principle be a valid cause of action.[112] However the evidence presented on behalf of the petitioner was seen to be far too weak. Essentially it was necessary for the petitioner to show that the decision to continue in business was one which no proper board could take.

---
[112] See Vinelott J in the High Court at p 482.

The petitioner pointed to the poor historic performance, fluctuating between significant losses and modest profits. But the respondents pointed to a number of factors providing grounds for optimism, including the energy unleashed by a change of management following a generational succession, diversification of the business and efficiencies provided by the new premises.

On the basis of this evidence Vinelott J concluded that it was:[113]

> 'simply perverse to allege that the board have carried on the business with no or no substantial expectation that they will succeed in making a profit reflecting the value of the assets employed and only with a view to furthering their own interests in preference to the interests of the company and its shareholders.'

By the time the matter came before the Court of Appeal a further set of accounts were available showing that the latest year's trading was, in the words of Hoffmann LJ a 'financial disaster'. Although this might show that the petitioner's expert was 'better at predicting the future than the Board' this did not 'retrospectively cast doubt upon the motives of the board in carrying on the business'.[114]

Vinelott J did offer the thought that the application might have been 'at [best] premature'.[115] So presumably further sustained losses and the absence of objectively realistic turn around plans, combined with the directors continuing to draw or increase their remuneration might make it easier to sustain the inference that they were keeping the business going for their own benefit (or at least to make that suggestion less perverse). But by the time a breach of duty becomes apparent significant shareholder value will have been eroded.

In practice the decision in *Saul D Harrison* can be seen as a graphic example of the reluctance of the courts to interfere in the internal management of a company.

21.6.6 Diversion of business opportunities

Clearly directors have a duty to act in the best interests of the company they serve. Diversion of business by the controlling directors and majority shareholders to another company in which they were interested will almost invariably be seen to be a clear breach of duty by them and unfairly prejudicial to the interests of the minority shareholder. The leading case on this is *Re London School of Electronics Ltd*[116] where, similar to *Ebrahimi* the father and son controllers of the business left the non-family shareholder high and dry. Diversion of business also featured in *Re Cumana Ltd*.[117]

21.6.7 Director's self-dealing and conflicts of interest

The key figure emerging from the report of *McCarthy Surfacing* is the company's managing director Tom McCarthy. He played the lead role in negotiating important contracts and looking after the finances and administration of the business. He appeared to dominate his brothers and the remainder of the board.

---

[113] At p 484.
[114] See p 496.
[115] See p 484.
[116] [1986] Ch 211.
[117] [1986] BCLC 430.

Using his dominant position Tom secured the lion's share of lucrative bonus arrangements for himself. He also caused the company to enter into contracts for his own benefit over letting premises he owned, IT software he had developed and consultancy services. The favourable nature of these contracts and failure to recognise the inherent conflicts of interest represented further breaches on the part of Tom McCarthy (and by implication breaches of duty on the part of the remainder of the board by failing to police the situation). These created further grounds for an unfair prejudice petition.

Similarly in *Fisher v Cadman* the brothers made a significant (and unjustified) provision for interest on an account for work that they had carried out on behalf of the company through another business that they owned. The court decided that during their father's lifetime an understanding had been reached that the principal amount only would be paid. The attempt by the brothers to go beyond this expectation was also unfairly prejudicial to their sister.[118]

21.6.8 Assets transfers

A similar logic applies to the transfer of assets by the controlling directors and minority shareholders at an undervalue. In *Re Little Olympian Each-Ways Ltd (No 3)*[119] the assets of a business were transferred to a newly formed shelf company for £1, which was then resold for £10m. Fairly substantial debts and the petitioning preference shareholder were left behind in the original company. The court made a finding of unfair prejudice and ordered a buy out of the preference shareholder, valued on the basis that the sale proceeds had been received by the original company (as they clearly should have been).

21.6.9 Appropriation

In many family owned businesses there can be gradual progression from the working family members becoming aware of the contribution they are personally making to the success of the family owned business, through resenting the corresponding lack of contribution made by the remaining remote family members to the haves developing a sense of entitlement to the rewards of the business and, finally, taking steps to appropriate that benefit for themselves.

In short the controllers treating the family business as if it belonged exclusively to them and disregarding the interest of the wider family. There are elements of this phenomenon displayed in both *Irvine* by Ian Irvine and the uncle, Mr Malik, in *the Gate of India*. The clearest expression of judicial condemnation can be found in the old case (on just and equitable winding up and discussed in detail in chapter of *Loch v John Blackwood*.[120] In giving judgment in the Privy Council Lord Shaw noted that the leader of the family business, Mr McLaren:[121]

> 'for reasons not unnatural, had come to be of the opinion that the business owed much of its value and prosperity to himself. But he appears to have proceeded to the further stage of feeling that in these circumstances he could manage the business as if it were his own.'

---

[118] At para 101 of the judgment.
[119] [1995] 1 BCLC 636.
[120] [1924] AC 783.
[121] At p 794.

Indications of this were Mr McLaren taking excessive remuneration by way of bonuses whilst at the same time causing only paltry dividends to be paid to the remote family minority shareholders.

The key factor however was an attempt by Mr McLaren (assisted by his own failure to provide proper financial information) to obtain the shares of the minority at a significant and obvious undervalue. An attempted appropriation:[122]

> '... by omitting to hold general meetings, submit accounts and recommend a dividend, their object was to keep the petitioners in ignorance of the truth and acquire their shares at an undervalue.'

In the words of Lord Shaw 'no confidence in the directorate could survive such a proposal'. The application for just and equitable winding up was granted.

21.6.10 Breaches of the Companies Acts

Many failures to strictly observe the requirements of the Companies Acts can be found in the decided cases and are arguably a feature of the family business world generally. The courts usually adopt a realistic and relatively relaxed attitude to this.[123] In *Fisher v Cadman* the court noted that the affairs of the family business concerned were 'run with considerable informality ... This is unsurprising in view of its nature as a small family company'.[124]

Indeed in that case it was suggested that an expectation of informality may be a consequence of accepting that a family business is subject to equitable considerations:[125]

> 'There is no good reason why such equitable considerations should not qualify, as well as add to, the expectations about how the controllers of the company ought to behave to be derived from a simple reading of the articles of association.'

In other words informality may be seen as part of the give and take of family business life. The flipside of the fairness approach.

Often laxity that would pass unremarked at times of family peace becomes a bone of contention when relationships deteriorate. This was the case in *Fisher v Cadman* where for many years Mrs Fisher had not objected to her brothers failing to hold AGM's or provide her with accounts etc.[126] But the court was clear that there was a 'limit to the operation of this principle' so there was nothing to prevent Mrs Fisher from insisting on subsequent proper adherence to statutory requirements and the failure of her brothers to do so amounted to unfair prejudice.[127]

---

[122] At p 794.
[123] At least in unfair prejudice cases. The case is otherwise in proceedings for director's disqualification and other insolvency related proceedings.
[124] At para 21 of the judgment.
[125] At para 90 of the judgment.
[126] It is fairly common in practice for family business members to write to each other in formal terms when relationships break down, castigating each other for breaches of formal requirements of the Companies Acts which have passed unremarked for many years in times of peace.
[127] See para 93–96 of the judgment.

However the High Court took a different approach in *Irvine*. Whilst castigating various failures on the part of Ian to follow proper procedures for the production and approval of accounts and for the approval of his own remuneration as 'plainly wrongful', 'deserving of censure' and 'reprehensible' the judge nevertheless refused to make a finding of unfair prejudice relating to these issues on the basis that these could not 'fairly be said to have caused Patricia to suffer any material prejudice'.[128]

There must therefore be considerable uncertainty as to whether failure to comply with statutory requirements will constitute a stand-alone basis for unfair prejudice as opposed to being an aggravating circumstance where other breaches are present.

21.6.11 Information

One of the key benefits enjoyed by the 'haves' who control a family business and their associates is access to financial and other information. They are in the know. Absent good governance practices, providing for access to an appropriate level of information to foster a sense of belonging for the more remote family members, their legal right to information is extremely limited.[129] The question becomes can the provision of information over and above statutory minimum requirements be capable of forming part of the legitimate expectations of family business members?

Of course directors have a general duty to treat shareholders equally under CA, s 172(10)(f) (the 'need to act fairly as between members of the company'). This would apply just as much to the provision of information as any other matter. Blatant favouritism between family members may therefore give rise to arguments of unfairness. However, in the absence of any other more substantial breaches of duty it may be difficult to show that financial prejudice (rather than the emotional prejudice of feeling left out of family affairs) has occurred.

In many circumstances the 'have-nots' may be the only non-director shareholders. Also, in practice it may be very difficult to establish what additional information the close associates of the directors have received. There might be simply an inference that they know more than the more remote family members. Indeed this might be seen as inevitable.

The attitude of the courts to failure to provide information has been mixed. In the leading case of *Saul D Harrison* the High Court found that the petitioner had already been provided with information which was 'far more detailed than a minority shareholder is entitled to require' so had not been treated unfairly so far as the provision of information was concerned.[130] But failure to provide statutory information has been a factor in courts' decision to allow relief, for example *Loch v John Blackwood*. In *Fisher v Cadman* failure to provide additional information and explanations to supplement the statutory information in the accounts was seen to have been 'deliberately calculated to frustrate ... reasonable attempts to obtain information'.[131] In *Wyatt*[132] the disparity of information between the petitioner and his brother was the main factor in the judge

---

[128] See paras 344–346 of *Irvine (No 1)* op cit.
[129] Basically confined to receiving notices of general meetings with copies of statutory accounts and any supporting paperwork and access to various statutory registers.
[130] At p 485.
[131] At para 63 of the judgment.
[132] *Wyatt v Frank Wyatt and Son Ltd* [2003] EWHC 520 (Ch) at para 44.

allowing the matter to continue to the expensive stage of discovery under which full information on relevant issues would be provided.

Those cases suggest that failure to provide information motivated by a desire to cover up wrong doing on the part of the majority will be a relevant factor in granting relief (or allowing a claim to continue). Perhaps the same would apply if the previous practice had been to provide information on a more liberal basis and this had been discontinued.

However there is little support for a proposition that failure to provide information in the absence of any other breach of duty will be actionable as a stand-alone species of unfair prejudice. The Court of Appeal in *Saul D Harrison* expressly rejected a failure to provide enhanced information as a basis of unfairness. The petitioner had already been provided with a level of information that was 'far more detailed than a minority shareholder is entitled to require'.[133]

21.6.12 Mismanagement

Mismanagement or more precisely the difficulties of bringing an unfair prejudice claim based on this is covered in **20.9**.

21.6.13 'Wrongful rights issues'

In some circumstances shareholders can be affected differently but treated the same. For example rights issues.[134] It may possibly be unfair prejudice for the majority to insist on a rights issue knowing that (perhaps as a result of remuneration historically extracted from the company) they are well able to subscribe, whereas more remote family members are not.

The Court of Appeal decision in the non-family business case of *Re Cumana Ltd*[135] illustrates this. There the majority shareholder used his control of the company to organise a rights issue in the full knowledge that the minority shareholder would not be able to afford to exercise his pre-emption rights. The court accepted that this amounted to one example of unfair prejudice in that case. There were other instances of unfair prejudice in the matter in particular diversion of business (as in *Re London School of Electronics* and payment of excessive bonuses and pension contributions in favour of the majority shareholder as in *Irvine*).

A similar approach was taken *In re A Company (No 007623 of 1986)*[136] another case of a petition based on a rights issue, Hoffmann J said:

> '... I do not think that the bona fides of the decision or the fact that the petitioner was offered shares on the same terms as other shareholders necessarily means that the rights issue could not have been unfairly prejudicial to his interests. If the majority know that the petitioner does not have the money to take up his rights and the offer is made at par when the shares are plainly worth a great deal more than par as part of a majority holding (but

---

[133] At p 485.
[134] Opportunities for shareholders to buy more shares in a company proportionate to their existing shareholdings in accordance with pre-emption rights contained in the company's constitution or under the Companies Acts.
[135] [1986] BCLC 430.
[136] [1986] BCLC 362, at p 367.

very little as a minority holding), it seems to me arguable that carrying through the transaction in that form could, viewed objectively, constitute unfairly prejudicial conduct.'

It may be difficult for a minority to show that a decision to make a rights issue falls outside the scope of a legitimate management decision, as with the payment of dividends (versus capital expenditure or building cash reserves). Something more may need to be shown by the minority arising from the structure of the offer and its impact on them taking it into the sphere of unfair prejudice.

If it can be shown that there are various reasons behind a rights issue it will be necessary to find the substantial purpose of this. If this is to dilute to holding of the minority then the issue may be challenged in its own right[137] or as species of unfair prejudice. But if the substantial purpose was a legitimate commercial one, usually to raise funds needed by the company and dilution of the minority was a collateral consequence, even if this was desired as a subsidiary purpose, then attack will be much harder.

Unfairness can go to both the purpose and price of a rights issue. In *Sunrise Radio*[138] the family members controlling a privately owned Asian radio station closed ranks in support of the majority shareholder family member, Dr Lit against his former girlfriend Ms Kohli. Funds were obviously needed by the company for cash flow reasons. A mixture of her finances and obvious unwillingness to tie herself closer to Dr Lit, clearly made it unlikely that Ms Kohli would take up her entitlement under the rights issue. Having cleared the field of Ms Kohli as a runner and rider in the issue, the allotment, taken up by Dr Lit's company, proceeded at par, when the market value of the shares issued were considerably higher. The failure of the board to consider and obtain the best reasonable price was held to be unfair prejudice.

21.6.14 Changing the constitution

Much of the logic underpinning the 'rules based approach' is that shareholders in a company have signed up to the rules contained in the articles of association and are bound by that agreement. In multi-generational family companies shareholders will often have inherited the agreements and rules made by their parents and grandparents.

Against this, as a matter of procedure, most aspects[139] of the constitution of a company can be changed by shareholders commanding 75% of the voting rights passing a special resolution. The principal relevant exception to this is that an 'entrenchment provision', that is a provision preventing changes to specified articles or imposing more stringent conditions than passing a special resolution must be agreed to by all members at the time of entrenchment or contained in the original articles.[140]

Will the minority, typically the have-nots in a family company, have any form of redress if the haves seek to change the constitution of the family company in a way that damages the interests of the have-nots? Putting the question the other way round to

---

[137] As in *Clemens*.
[138] *Sunrise Radio Limited; Geeta Kohli v Dr Avtar Lit, Ravinder Kumar Jain, Surinderpal Singh Lit, Sunrise Radio Limited* [2009] EWHC 2893 (Ch).
[139] Other exceptions are that the constitution cannot be changed to oblige a member to pay more for their shares or to take more shares (CA, s 25).
[140] Companies Act 2006, s 22.

what extent can the majority make changes to the constitution free of concerns that these might lead to difficulties with other family shareholders?

The starting point is that generally shareholders do not have any obligation to consider the interests of the company or their fellow shareholders in the way that they use their votes. Shareholders are usually free to vote in their own selfish interest.

A key limitation to this in most family owned companies is the overlap between directors and members. In their capacity as directors, owe fiduciary duties to the have-nots. This duty extends to deciding what decisions and resolutions to the members as a whole. The directors cannot escape those duties by simply changing hats and referring matters that would usually be taken by themselves as a board for a decision by themselves in their dual capacity as shareholders. For example they cannot use their votes as shareholders to ratify the terms of a trading agreement that are to the disadvantage the main family company but are to the advantage of a second company in which the haves are interested.

The second limitation on the majority moving the constitutional goal posts to the detriment of the minority arises from the application of equitable principles by the courts. The Court of Appeal examined those principles in the non-family business case of *Arbuthnott v Bonnyman and others*.[141]

Briefly summarised those principles are:

- **Equitable fetter.** The power for the majority to amend the constitution of a company will be subject to equitable restraints.[142] These apply unless the constitution clearly provides that the rights of the majority to amend are unfettered.

- **Good faith.** The power to amend must be exercised in good faith and for the benefit of the company as a whole.[143] This is in itself a complicated area of law and is discussed by the Court of Appeal in *Arbuthnott*. But basically the interests of not only the minority but also potential future members must be taken into account.

- **Mixed test.** The test of whether the power has been exercised for the benefit of the company as a whole is basically a subjective one. If the majority believed that the change would benefit the company it would not usually be for the court to substitute its own view.[144] But the case is otherwise if no reasonable person could come to the conclusion that the company as whole would benefit rather than the majority in their sectional interest.

The burden of showing that the amendment is not made in good faith rests with the minority who are challenging the change.[145] That may not be an easy burden to discharge. An amendment can still be shown to have been for the benefit of the company

---

[141] [2015] EWCA Civ 536 – a case involving amendments to 'drag rights' in the articles of a private equity house.
[142] *Allen v Gold Reefs of West Africa Ltd* [1900] Ch 656.
[143] *Sidebottom v Kershaw Leese and Co Ltd* [1920] 1 Ch 154.
[144] *Shuttleworth v Cox* [1927] 2 KB 9. In this non-family business case the majority were allowed to amend provisions allowing certain directors to remain in office for life (which would now be unenforceable) to remove a director who had seriously neglected his duties to the company. Even though the new provision would clearly damage the interests of the minority it could clearly be shown to be in the interests of the company not to be burdened with such a director for the rest of his life.
[145] *Peters' American Delicacy Co v Heath* [1939] 61 CLR 547.

even if the collateral effect is to damage the interests of the minority. This is so even if that collateral damage was foreseen and even intended by the majority.[146]

Thirdly it might be possible to argue that, although legally valid (in the sense the amendment could not be prevented by stand-alone proceedings taken by the member), an amendment nevertheless has an unfairly prejudicial effect on the minority shareholders. But in practice it may well be difficult to persuade a court to apply over-riding fairness principles.

21.7 UNFAIR PREJUDICE – REMEDIES, REASONABLE OFFERS AND COSTS

We have noted above that the usual and almost invariable remedy following a finding of unfair prejudice in accordance with CA, s 994 is for an order for the minority to be bought out by the majority in accordance with CA, s 996(2)(e).

We have also noted that if a reasonable offer to buy the claimant's shares has been made an unfair prejudice claim will usually be struck out at an early stage. In turn whether or not a suitable offer has been made and refused will be central to the key question of awards of costs.

Equally each of the supporting shareholder remedies, applications for just and equitable winding up under IA, s 122(1)(g) and seeking leave to bring a derivative claim under CA, s 260 may be denied if the claimant has an alternative remedy.[147]

As all of these concepts are inextricably linked a detailed consideration of unfair prejudice remedies is postponed and dealt with alongside these other subjects in chapter 24.

---

[146] *Sidebottom* and *Shuttleworth* cases.
[147] Insolvency Act 1986, s 125(2) in the case of just and equitable winding up and CA, s 263(3)(f) for derivative claims.

CHAPTER 22

JUST AND EQUITABLE WINDING UP

22.1 OVERVIEW

Clearly winding up represents the end of the road for any company. Usually 75% of the voting members will need to be in favour of a voluntary solvent winding up.[1] Winding-up or liquidation typically occurs in the context of insolvency. But asking the court to wind up a company on the basis that it is 'just and equitable' for this to happen provides a possible remedy for aggrieved minority shareholders, including those in a family company.

Just and equitable winding-up is a much more drastic remedy, the nuclear option, when compared with an application for orders under CA, s 996 based on unfair prejudice. It will be readily appreciated that orders for winding up on this ground will be accordingly rare.

There are likely to be other stakeholders involved in a family firm, in addition to the family members in dispute, including employees, customers and suppliers. The court will be aware of the interests of these wider stakeholders before ordering a winding up of a solvent company. An unfair prejudice remedy offers a more practical solution of allowing one party to be bought out, the parties to go their separate ways and for the business to continue.

Of course aggrieved family members who have also made loans or have other debts due from a family business can sometimes use these as leverage under express or implied threats of regular insolvency proceedings to put pressure on the controlling family members to achieve the changes sought by the minority.

Before the introduction of the unfair prejudice remedy in the Companies Act 1980 just and equitable winding up was the weapon of choice for disaffected minority shareholders. So prior to 1980, disputes in a family company were conducted for high stakes, the survival of the family company itself. Nowadays just and equitable winding up must be seen as very much a subsidiary remedy. So this chapter will be correspondingly short. Just and equitable winding up is nevertheless relevant in a narrow range of circumstances. A combination of two factors will usually be present. First asset based family companies, such as hotels, family farming companies or property companies, where a winding-up will unlock the capital value of the underlying assets, without overall value being adversely affected by the cessation of trade and the absence

---

[1] Insolvency Act 1986, s 84(1)(b).

of the majority, as owner managers. Secondly where the circumstances of the dispute are such that it would be unfair to allow the majority to retain ownership of the family company.

22.2 THE LEGISLATION

22.2.1 IA, s 122

IA, s 122(1)(g) simply sets out the ground that:

> 'A company may be wound up by the court if ... the court is of the opinion that it is just and equitable that the company be wound up.'

IA, s 125(2) explains that the court should approach the questions of whether to exercise its discretion through a two stage test:

(1) that the petitioners are entitled to some form of relief, by winding up or otherwise (IA, s 122(2)(a);
(2) that in the absence of another appropriate remedy it would be just and equitable to wind the company up.

22.3 ALTERNATIVE REMEDY

IA, s 122(2) concludes with a warning of significant practical importance to any aggrieved family member contemplating bringing proceedings for just and equitable winding of their family business. This provision states that no winding up order will be made if the court also concludes that:

> '... some other remedy is available to the petitioners and that they are acting unreasonably in seeking to have the company wound up instead of pursuing that remedy.'

22.4 EQUITABLE PRINCIPLES: FAIRNESS AND RULES BASED APPROACH

It will be noted that s 122(1)(g) expressly relies on and refers to justice and equity as the foundation of the remedy in contrast to the unfair prejudice remedy in CA, s 994 which is based on a more general concept of unfairness.

Many cases for just and equitable winding up relief are based on the claimant showing that equitable considerations, what we have termed 'the fairness approach' should apply. In practice this has often come down to showing, or at least arguing, that the family business concerned was run as a 'quasi-partnership'. This key consideration is discussed in detail in chapter 20.

Historically the just and equitable winding up remedy has also been relevant to the second category of cases, what we have termed rules based or breach of duty cases. In these the courts have agreed that the breach or breaches of duty concerned are sufficiently serious to mean that is just and equitable that the family company should be wound up.

22.5 EQUITABLE BARS

22.5.1 Claimant's conduct (sufficiently) clean hands

Similarly the usual bars to equitable relief of equity will apply to restrict the availability of the just and equitable winding up remedy.

As just and equitable winding up is an equitable remedy there is a relationship between the degree of fault of the parties and the availability of the remedy. Relief will therefore be denied if the petitioner's own conduct is to a significant extent responsible for a breakdown in relations between the parties on the basis of the maxim 'he who comes to equity must come with clean hands'.

This may be contrasted with unfair prejudice where misconduct on the part of the petitioner will not necessarily prevent a finding of unfair prejudice although it may, in some circumstances result in the court modifying the form of relief it will offer to take account of misconduct.

As Lord Cross explained in the House of Lords in what is still the leading case of *Ebrahimi*:[2]

> 'A petitioner who relies on the just and equitable clause must come to the court with clean hands, and if the breakdown in confidence between him and the other parties to the dispute appears to have been due to his misconduct he cannot insist on the company being wound up if they wish it to continue.'

In that case Mr Ebrahimi's conduct appeared to consist of little more than being mildly annoying. Certainly nothing to disqualify him from relief. In comparison the conduct of the petitioner in the unfair prejudice case of *Shah*[3] appears to have been of a different order, he walked out of his employment with the family business. But this was still not enough to put an unfair prejudice remedy beyond his reach.

Serious misconduct such as misappropriation of company assets will disqualify a claimant from a just and equitable winding up order. However that does not mean that a petitioner's hands need to be spotless. In most family business disputes it will be rare for all the right or all the wrong to be attributable to any party. The courts have shown a willingness to accept this reality. For example the *Harding*[4] case reveals an unedifying example of the deterioration of family relationships with all three sisters involved in 'hostile correspondence – in unpleasant and confrontational terms'.

The judge in that case, Mrs Justice Rose, adopted a sensible approach to the realities of that extremely bitter family business dispute saying that there is no need for a petitioner to show that they are 'entirely blameless' or to demonstrate saintly forbearance. Instead it was necessary to recognise that parties will usually find themselves before the court after a lengthy dispute during which 'it is rare for any one party to emerge as having

---

[2] *Ebrahimi v Westbourne Galleries Ltd* [1973] AC 360 at p 387. *Ebrahimi* is explained and discussed in detail in chapter 20.
[3] [2010] EWHC 313 (Ch).
[4] Sally Harding, Rosemary Walton v Elizabeth Edwards, Janet Harding, The Executors of BM Harding (deceased), Brand Harding Limited [2014] EWHC 247 (Ch) – discussed in detail in **22.7** below.

behaved with exemplary politeness and reasonable throughout'. Accordingly it was enough in that case that the petitioner's hands were 'sufficiently clean'.[5]

22.5.2 Delay and acquiescence

A second well-known maxim is that 'delay will defeat equity'. Otherwise referred to as the ancient legal concept of laches. A petition for just and equitable winding up should therefore, under general equitable principles, be presented within a relatively short period after the conduct complained of.

It appears that only more extreme delay will bar an unfair prejudice action.[6] But the situation is fairly unclear so far as both remedies are concerned. The moral must be for any aggrieved minority to proceed quickly. If not to court at least to complain and to invoke governance and informal alternative dispute resolution mechanisms.

Similarly acquiescence on the part of the claimant in the conduct complained of might be a bar to obtaining a just and equitable winding up order. Whereas for an unfair prejudice remedy there might be more scope for a claimant who has previously accepted a certain state of affairs in their family company to change their minds and insist on their rights in the future.[7]

It has been suggested that the over riding test to be applied in cases of acquiescence or delay in just and equitable matters is now 'unconscionability'.[8] This might not be that much different from the approach taken in unfair prejudice cases where courts look at a combination of the reason why the claimant has not previously pursued their rights and the harm that would be done to the respondent in allowing later exercise of these.[9]

22.6 DUAL CLAIMS

In the early life of the unfair prejudice remedy it had been the practice to include a claim (or prayer) for just and equitable winding up as an alternative claim to unfair prejudice. Often this was a negotiating tactic to encourage the respondent to settle. However this practice is now discouraged.[10] So a claim for just and equitable winding up should only be included if this is genuinely sought by the petitioner as a viable and reasonable alternative remedy.[11]

The modern unfair prejudice remedy was introduced specifically to provide a more flexible alternative to just and equitable winding up. Accordingly an unfair prejudice petition is more likely to be seen as the primary remedy for an aggrieved member of a family business, with just and equitable winding up orders playing very much a minor role. That is not to say that just and equitable winding up has no place to play in dealing with family business disputes, as illustrated by the *Harding* family business case which has already been briefly discussed in chapter 20 above.

---

[5] At para 20 of the judgment.
[6] See chapter 21.
[7] See *Fisher v Cadman* [2005] EWHC 377 (Ch).
[8] See *Hollington* at p 116.
[9] See, for example the *Gate of India* [2008] EWHC 959 (Ch).
[10] See CPR Practice Direction 49B, para 9(1).
[11] See **22.16.1** for a discussion on unfair prejudice and just and equitable winding up as alternative remedies.

22.7 THE HARDING FAMILY

22.7.1 The facts

The *Harding*[12] case concerned an application for just and equitable winding up and was based on a complete breakdown of working relationships between three sisters in a third generation family farming company.[13] The company was established by their maternal grandfather jointly with their father, Bryan Harding in 1955 and farmed about 250 acres of prime arable land in Cambridgeshire.

Bryan died in 2001 (and the grandfather some time before this). Arrangements were made for a non-family manager to take over the day-to day running of the farm as a contractor. It was clear that Bryan wanted the farm to remain in family ownership and for the sisters to work together in the residual management of the farm. It was not to be.

By the time the matter came to court in 2014 relations between the three sisters were completely dysfunctional. In practice the involvement of the sisters appears to have descended into a wrestling match between two rival camps, each battling for control of the company and each refusing to recognise the legitimacy of the others position in the family business. There were numerous elements to the breakdown in relationships including:

- disputes over the remuneration of the older sister, Elizabeth, as book keeper;
- arguments over whether Elizabeth's husband should continue as accountant for the business or whether a third party, favoured by the other two sisters, should be appointed;
- the two camps of sisters purporting to hold rival directors' meetings;
- the purported suspension of her sisters as directors by Elizabeth;
- arguments about whether the registered office should be moved from Elizabeth's house;
- associated arguments about access to company records;
- conflicting instructions being sent to key suppliers and the Rural Payments Agency about where the head office of the company was based and to where payments should be sent;
- 'hostile correspondence in unpleasant and confrontational terms on both sides'.[14]

22.7.2 A quasi-partnership

Although all three sisters were directors in the company none of them took any part in the day-to-day farming activity. This was undertaken by the non-family manager as a contractor. The sisters took very little part in the administration of the business. The evidence was that the role of the most active of the sisters, Mrs Edwards, (as a book keeper/administrator) occupied only about 3 or 4 hours a week which she fitted in around her full time job as a radiographer.[15] Another sister, Sally Harding had carried

---

[12] *Sally Harding, Rosemary Walton v Elizabeth Edwards, Janet Harding, the Executors of BM Harding (deceased), Brandon Harding Limited* [2014] EWHC 247 (Ch).
[13] It might be that the actual farm had been in family hands before 1955 and was incorporated when their father, joined the business. The case report is unclear.
[14] At para 31 of the judgment.
[15] Paragraph 14 of the judgment.

out book-keeping work in the business previously and her father had expressed a wish in his will that this should continue, but her practical involvement had ceased 10 years or so before the matter came to court. The third sister, Mrs Walton, lived in London but returned to the farm for occasional meetings.

As explained in chapter 20, the court nevertheless seemed to find little difficulty in deciding that the Harding family company was both intended to be run and actually operated as a quasi-partnership, notwithstanding the low level of involvement of all three sisters concerned in the dispute. Accordingly equitable considerations and the fairness approach applied to the matter.

22.7.3 Grounds for intervention

The court found two basic grounds for intervention. First, the complete breakdown of relationships between the sisters. This is explained in more detail at **22.10**. Secondly, the judge thought a deadlock had been created by the share-holding profile of the company as a further reason to order a just and equitable winding up. This aspect is discussed in more detail in **22.11** below.

22.7.4 Alternative remedy

The judge ruled out any alternative remedy, in particular the practicality of arriving at a valuation of the younger sisters' shares that would be acceptable to them and which Elizabeth could afford to pay. It is significant that the court rejected an offer made by Elizabeth to buy out her sisters (or more precisely a request that that they give an irrevocable commitment to surrender their interests to a sale process initiated by Elizabeth) as 'wholly unrealistic'.[16]

22.7.5 The order in *Harding*

Therefore rather than allow Elizabeth and her husband to 'simply expunge' her sisters from the family business the judge made an order to wind up a profitable, cash-rich farming company over 50 years old.

22.8 CIRCUMSTANCES JUSTIFYING JUST AND EQUITABLE WINDING UP

Various features can be identified in the *Harding* case. First the qualifying condition of a quasi-partnership or, put more generally, circumstances justifying the *Ebrahimi* or fairness approach.

One of the key points made by Lord Wilberforce in *Ebrahimi* is that the circumstances in which a court will intervene and agree to a just and equitable winding up are not capable of comprehensive classification. Nevertheless there are a number of cases on similar points allowing for a degree of tentative categorisation. In practice, as a result of the close overlap and evolution between the two remedies, these bear close resemblance to the circumstances where the court will intervene in cases of unfair prejudice.

---

[16] At para 57 of the judgment.

A key and related point is that most of the cases discussed below pre-date the introduction of the unfairness remedy. In many circumstances this may be seen by the courts, if not the parties themselves, as a more suitable alternative remedy. That a just and equitable winding up has been granted in similar circumstances in the past is therefore no precedent that the same remedy will be granted now.

22.9 EXCLUSION

Ebrahimi itself was, of course, a successful case for just and equitable winding up, based on exclusion from a classic quasi-partnership. However if a case based on similar facts were to be heard today, a buy out of Mr Ebrahimi's holding by the father and son controlling the business, based on CA, s 994 (unfair prejudice), would be a more likely alternative remedy.

As referred to above the attempted exclusion by Elizabeth of her sisters from the Harding family business was one of the grounds held to justify a winding up of that business on just and equitable grounds. Exclusion was also a factor in the old Scottish case of *Symington v Symington Quarries Ltd*.[17]

22.10 BREAKDOWN OF TRUST AND CONFIDENCE

One of the grounds justifying the winding up of the family business in *Harding* was the breakdown of trust and confidence between the three sisters. The judge in that case followed the earlier Court of Appeal decision in *Re Yenidje Tobacco Co Ltd*,[18] a non-family business case, where the relationship between the two co-shareholders had reached such a state where there was a 'refusal to meet on matters of business, continued quarrelling, and such a state of animosity as precludes all reasonable hope of reconciliation and friendly co-operation'.

Although usually referred to in the cases as a breakdown of trust and confidence what is usually involved is a breakdown in personal and working relationships. This in turn eliminates trust and confidence between the shareholders concerned.

There is no need for the lack of trust and confidence to be caused by actual or suspected dishonesty. Again in *Harding* the judge noted that:[19]

> 'I am sure that [Elizabeth's] handling of the Company's money has at all times been entirely honest and straight-forward and that the Petitioners know this to be the case.'

Nevertheless the trial judge concluded that:[20]

> '... there has been a complete breakdown in the mutual trust and confidence that should exist between the sisters and the Company is being improperly managed because the personal hostilities between the sisters seriously impede the taking of proper decisions in the interests of the Company.'

---

[17] [1905] 8 F 121.
[18] [1916] 2 Ch 426.
[19] At para 40.
[20] At para 53 of the judgment.

Elizabeth argued that the business itself was in a perfectly healthy condition. It was profitable. She had the support of the non-family full time working manager and of the bank. The problem was the interference of her sisters.

Rejecting these arguments the trial judge found that a combination of the effective exclusion of the younger sisters from participation in management and the breakdown of relationships and trust and confidence between the sisters meant that the younger sisters were entitled to relief.

22.11 DEADLOCK

Here a wider concept of deadlock may exist and the courts may intervene even if there is no deadlock in the strict and absolute mathematical sense. It may be sufficient for a company to have descended into sufficiently entrenched factionalism so as to undermine the proper functioning of the business even though one faction remains numerically superior and always likely to triumph on the basis of strict voting.

Certainly this approach was followed in the *Harding* case. There Elizabeth held 16.75% of the equity in her own right with a further 24.5% of the shares held in a family trust of which Elizabeth's husband was the main trustee. The two younger sisters held 32.75% of the company between them. The balance of the shares, 26%, were held by their mother, who had unfortunately lost capacity and whose Court of Protection Deputy declined to become involved and to actively exercise the voting rights attached to those shares. Leaving questions surrounding the duties of Elizabeth's husband as a trustee to one side, the family company was not therefore deadlocked in the strict sense. Rather the voting block of Elizabeth and her husband ensured mathematical control.

Nevertheless the trial judge said that this situation was a 'a recipe for decisions being taken and challenged and having to be reversed. The company is truly deadlocked'.[21]

Although not referred to in *Harding* this approach is consistent with that of the Privy Council in *Ng Eng Hiam v Ng Kee Wei* where it was at said that 'the question of whether such a deadlock exists ... is a question predominantly of fact in each case'.[22] The case before the Privy Council concerned an entrenched dispute between factions of a Chinese family business. Although winding up was not granted, on the basis that the court thought that, notwithstanding the intensity of the dispute to date, the matter could be resolved and the company could be operated properly if 'ordinary good sense is employed'. Not necessarily qualities readily found in entrenched family business disputes.

Although other cases point to a stricter mathematical test, towards that of true technical deadlock, the Privy Council suggested that winding up on the basis of a wider interpretation of deadlock was more likely in quasi partnership situations.

A similar approach was adopted in *Symington v Symington Quarries Ltd*[23] where a company was formed to take over a quarrying business, following a history of disputes between the two brothers carrying on the business. A third brother was given a nominal

---

[21] At para 52 of the judgment.
[22] [1964] 31 MLJ at p 240.
[23] [1905] 8 F. 121.

holding, as part of governance arrangements so that he could have a casting vote to referee any further disputes between the main shareholders. The disputes did indeed continue. In fact the new arrangements barely got off the ground. One of the brothers, Hugh who, as Managing Director, had day-to-day control over the finances and administration, refused to complete the allotment of shares and relied on the support of the nominees from the incorporation agents to remove his two brothers as directors. He then essentially took over the business and assets.

As matters stood Hugh, with the support of the nominees had effective control. Presumably it would have been possible for the court to make orders giving effect to the governance scheme originally proposed, in effect to place the other main shareholder and the 'referee' in control. Recognising that the situation was hopeless because there were 'a small number of partners equally, or nearly equally divided, so that it is impossible that the business of the Company can be carried out'[24] the Court of Session ordered a just and equitable winding up.

22.12 LOSS OF SUBSTRATUM

In fact the members of the Court of Session in *Symington* gave a number of reasons why just and equitable winding up should be ordered in that case. One of which was that the basic substratum of the company, its underlying foundations, had been destroyed.[25] Hugh's 'coup d'état' had ruined the company as both a governance structure and a trading vehicle.

It has been suggested that this ground is rarely relied on in UK (as opposed to commonwealth) jurisdictions nowadays.[26] Those cases, and the historic English cases, typically concern companies set up as 'single purpose vehicles', for example to exploit intellectual property or to manage funds where the initial purpose has disappeared but leaving the vehicle intact.

In *Saul D Harrison*[27] the petitioner, as an alternative to an unfair prejudice order, also asked for a just and equitable winding up of the family business. However no basis for the intervention of equity was pleaded in the petition.[28]

In chapter 20 we suggest, albeit hugely tentatively, that a possible argument that could have been explored in that case to justify the application of equitable considerations and the fairness approach was the loss of family business sub-stratum.

22.13 OPPRESSION

It has been noted that it was common ground between the parties in the *Harmer* case[29] that the conduct of Mr Harmer senior, who at times ignored decisions of the board, and at other times attempted to pack the board with his own nominees was sufficient to justify a just and equitable winding up.

---

[24] Lord McLaren at p 130.
[25] The Lord President and Lord Adam both at p 129.
[26] See *Hollington on Shareholders' Remedies* (7th edn) at para 10.39.
[27] *Saul D Harrison & Sons plc* [1994] BCC 475.
[28] See Vinelott J in the High Court at p 478.
[29] *Re HR Harmer Ltd* [1959] 1 WLR 62.

22.14 APPROPRIATION

Improper conduct so that those controlling a family owned business treated it effectively as their own in total disregard of the rights of the remaining shareholders, could also justify a just and equitable winding up.

The case of *Loch v John Blackwood Ltd*[30] concerned a dominant in-law, Mr McLaren, who as managing director had taken over day-to-day management and control of a family engineering business originally set up in Barbados by his brother in law. Following the death of the founder a company was established with roughly half the shares owned by the founder's sister, Mr McLaren's wife, and roughly half owned by his niece and nephew. Crucially a small number of shares were held by the managing director so that, when taken with his wife's (the founders sister's holding) gave the couple a bare majority.

Although formed as a public company and with the niece and nephew playing no obvious role in the management the Privy Council saw the company as 'practically a domestic and family concern'.[31]

It is clear from the case that the brother in law worked hard and that the business was successful and, in the view of the Privy Council, 'Mr McLaren for reasons not unnatural had come to be of the opinion that the business owed much of it value and prosperity to himself'.[32] He began to treat the company very much as his own and to ignore the rights and interests of the niece and nephew. Information was withheld, no general meetings were held or accounts provided. Dividends were withheld. Meanwhile Mr McLaren helped himself to significant bonuses. The Privy Council were clear that Mr McLaren 'appears to have proceeded to the further stage of feeling that in these circumstances he could manage the business as if it were his own'.

The final straw was when Mr McLaren attempted to acquire the shares of the niece and nephew at a significant undervalue. In the case of the niece, in the order of 60% from net asset value and, because of an historic grudge a reduction of 95% in the case of the nephew. Inevitably the niece and nephew lost confidence in the managing director.

The Privy Council confirmed that:[33]

> 'whenever the loss of confidence is rested on a lack of probity in the conduct of the company' affairs then the former is justified by the latter and it is, under the statute, just and equitable that the company be wound up.'

Similarly an alternative reason or analysis of the decision in *Symington v Symington Quarries Ltd*[34] was the appropriation of the business by Hugh.

---

[30] [1924] AC 783. The case started in Barbados and found its way to the Privy Council via the West Indies Court of Appeal.
[31] At p 786 of the judgment.
[32] At p 794 of the judgment.
[33] Lord Shaw at p 788.
[34] [1905] 8 F. 121.

22.15 REFUSAL OF JUST AND EQUITABLE WINDING UP

We now turn briefly to look at circumstances where the court will refuse to intervene and grant orders for the winding up of the family business under the just and equitable ground.

22.15.1 Equitable bars

As noted in 22.5 above the usual bars to equitable relief, including the claimant's own conduct and delay will apply to applications for just and equitable winding up.

22.15.2 Mismanagement

As with unfair prejudice the courts will not grant a petition for just and equitable winding up based on mismanagement except in extreme circumstances.[35]

22.15.3 Outvoting

Being routinely outvoted on business issues will not in and of itself justify a winding up petition on just and equitable grounds. That would be a natural consequence of being a minority shareholder. In *Loch v John Blackwood* Lord Shaw explained that 'dissatisfaction at being outvoted on the business affairs or on what is called the domestic policy of the company'.[36]

Something more is required. In that case lack of probity.

22.15.4 Tangible interest

There is a line of historic case-law to say that the petitioner must expect to receive some financial return from the winding up. In other words there must be some material point to the proceedings for the petitioner who must have a 'tangible interest' in the winding up.[37]

For example relief will therefore be denied to a holder of ordinary shares in a family business where there are insufficient assets available to meet the claims of creditors or preference shareholders. A minority family member will therefore need to intervene quickly in cases where assets are being dissipated.

22.16 ALTERNATIVE REMEDY

The main reason why an order for winding up on just and equitable grounds is likely to be refused is, however, the availability of an alternative remedy which, in accordance with the final paragraph of IA, s 125(2), the petitioner is acting unreasonably by failing to pursue.

---

[35] See 20.8.
[36] Op cit at p 788.
[37] This expression was used by Jessel MR in *Re Rica Gold Washing Co* [1879] 11 ChD 36 at p 43.

The two most likely alternative remedies are:

22.16.1 Unfair prejudice

First, an action for unfair prejudice under CA, s 994. As discussed previously there is a high degree of overlap between the circumstances that will justify an unfair prejudice petition and those that will justify a winding up on just and equitable grounds.

An order for winding up is a nuclear option, potentially resulting in loss to the wider stakeholders of a family business including; employees, and, even though they will be paid in a solvent winding up disruption and loss of trade for suppliers and customers. Logically an order for the buy out of one party under CA, s 996 as a remedy for unfair prejudice will usually be less disruptive and therefore a more appropriate remedy.

In this context it is appropriate to repeat the warning about the extent to which the older cases on just and equitable winding up can be fully relied on in this context since the introduction of the unfair prejudice remedy, originally as s 75 of the Companies Act 1980. In many of the older cases brought under the just and equitable winding up jurisdiction it was not possible to satisfy the test of oppressive conduct for the remedy in s 210 of the old Companies Act 1948 where it was necessary to show that the conduct of the controlling majority was 'burdensome, harsh and wrongful'.[38] Accordingly establishing that it was just and equitable to wind up a family company was often an easier test to satisfy. For example in the case of in Re Harmer[39] discussed in detail in chapter 21, whilst the father contested the allegation of oppressive conduct all the way up to the Court of Appeal, all parties had accepted earlier in the High Court proceedings that relationships between the father and sons were such that an order for just and equitable winding up was appropriate.. It may well usually follow that circumstances similar to that found in the line of successful cases decided before the unfair prejudice remedy became available will be sufficient to satisfy the first part of the just and equitable winding up test contained in IA, s 125(2)(a) referred to above, ie that the petitioner is entitled to relief of some description. However given the more flexible remedy now contained in CA, s 994 they might struggle to satisfy the second stage of the test contained in IA, s 125(2)(b) that 'in the absence of any other remedy' it would be just and equitable to wind the company up.

A key issue will be the prospect of discounts being applied to minority shareholdings in unfair prejudice cases.[40] Where the family business has tangible assets or saleable goodwill a winding up order may deliver a better result for the aggrieved minority than an order for the purchase of their shares on a discounted basis. Whether the courts will agree to a winding up as an alternative to ordering a buy-out on a discounted basis under s 994 is another question. *Virdi v Abbey Leisure Ltd*[41] (a case on discounts under the articles) suggests that they just might do so.

---

[38] At p 79 following the test of Viscount Simmonds from the House of Lords in the Scottish case of *Meyer v Scottish Co-operative Wholesale Society* (1957) SC 381.
[39] Re HR Harmer Ltd [1959] 1 WLR 62.
[40] There are some cases where the courts have ordered full pro-rata non discounted valuations in non quasi-partnership cases. See *Sunrise Radio Limited; Geeta Kohli v Dr Avtar Lit, Ravinder Kumar Jain, Surinderpal Singh Lit, Sunrise Radio Limited* [2009] EWHC 2893 (Ch). This case and the approach of the courts to valuations in unfair prejudice cases is discussed in detail in chapter 24.
[41] [1990] BCC 60 – a non-family business case where winding up was ordered. The facts are explained at 20.7.1.

Less scientifically the aggrieved minority may simply think that it is unfair that they should be faced with the choice of having to either put up with unfair treatment or to pass their share in the family business to their oppressor, irrespective of valuation.

The *Harding* case provides a good example. Although unfair prejudice was not expressly discussed in the judgment a proposal by Elizabeth to buy out her sisters (which would have the same effect) was rejected on various grounds including the lack of certainty over the offer,[42] the ability of Elizabeth to pay a fair price and, in particular the fact that the sisters were likely to inherit further shares on the death or their mother. Accordingly the dispute was likely to resurrect itself when this happened.

On the facts it appeared to be reasonable for the sisters not to have pursued an unfair prejudice petition.

If a buy-out had been a practical commercial remedy, would it have been unreasonable for the sisters to pursue winding up simply to prevent the family company falling into Elizabeth's exclusive ownership? Most concepts of family fairness would suggest not. If children cannot play nicely no one should have the toys. It may have been that the judge in Harding had some sympathy for this position in saying that it was not appropriate for Elizabeth and her husband to 'simply expunge the Petitioners from the Company much though they would wish to do so'. But the basic legal principle is that the courts exist to provide practical financial remedies to disputes rather than to solve family quarrels and accordingly that might (in the sense of day to day control coupled with financial resource) is right.[43]

22.16.2 Derivative claims

The second likely alternative remedy to winding up would be for the aggrieved minority shareholders to pursue a derivative claim under CA, s 260. Derivative claims are considered in detail in the next chapter.

Again, as derivative claims are made on behalf of the company against wrongdoing directors, thus preserving both the company and the shareholding structure, at first sight they may be seen as a less extreme remedy than just and equitable winding up.

However in practice a derivative claim provides the least permanent and stable remedy to a family dispute. A derivative claim provides 'one-off' protection so is probably only a reasonable practical alternative in limited circumstances where the wrong to the company (and with it the interests of the minority family shareholder) is unlikely to be repeated. For example a one off instance of diversion of a business opportunity or sale of an asset at an undervalue. In most cases a derivative claim could be seen to provide a remedy only for the most recently presenting symptoms of the family dispute, rather than the underlying cause of that dispute, fundamentally dysfunctional family relationships.

Again the availability of a derivative claim was not analysed in any detail in the *Harding* judgment. It might have been the case that various acts or omissions on the part of Elizabeth could have been categorised as breaches of her duty as a director, theoretically

---

[42] Reasonable offers generally are discussed in chapter 24.
[43] See the discussion on bad faith and family business disputes in chapter 20.

actionable through a derivative claim. But to what end? As the judge observed 'if the relationship between the sisters does not improve, there is a risk that the same problems that now trouble the Company will reappear'.[44] She therefore concluded that 'there is no real alternative to wind up the company'.

22.17 JUST AND EQUITABLE WINDING-UP – CONCLUSION

In many and probably most cases an unfair prejudice remedy will provide a much more viable alternative remedy to winding up a family company under the just and equitable ground contained in IA, s 122(1)(g).

On most occasions unfair prejudice will also be the remedy of choice for the claimant in any event. Based on purely commercial considerations, being bought out of a trading business based on a going concern valuation, is likely to provide a better return than insisting that the family silver be broken up and sold.

There might nevertheless be occasions, in asset-based businesses where the position will be much more marginal. Here the risk of a discount being applied to a minority holding following a successful unfair prejudice claim may mean that a just and equitable winding up of a family company could genuinely be sought by an aggrieved family member as a viable alternative remedy to unfair prejudice.

Quite whether the courts would agree to a winding up as an alternative to ordering a buy-out on a discounted basis under unfair prejudice is another question. *Virdi v Abbey Leisure* suggests that they just might do so.

---

[44] At para 58 of the judgment.

CHAPTER 23

DERIVATIVE CLAIMS AND THE DISGRUNTLED FAMILY MEMBER

23.1 OVERVIEW

The remedies discussed in the preceding chapters, unfair prejudice and applications for a just and equitable winding up, are taken by shareholders in their own name to provide them with personal redress. This section will consider a different type of action, a derivative claim, where individual shareholders take action on behalf of the company. Any damages recovered will go into the bank account of the family company.

The right to bring a derivative claim is now contained in CA, s 260, which will be considered in detail below. This section puts what, in common law, were previously called derivative actions onto a statutory footing.[1]

Shareholders in family owned companies are likely to identify with the company as an entity in its own right to a far greater extent than if they were simply financial investors. They have both a financial and an emotional investment in the family business. As a consequence minority family shareholders are more likely than their non-family counterparts to want to protect the interests of the family business for its own sake. In a well-regulated family business this can be achieved through appropriate participation in governance procedures.

However as we have seen comparatively few family-owned businesses have highly evolved governance processes. Formal exit mechanisms might be few and far between. Moreover, if things have gone wrong, it will usually be the case that those responsible for the problem will also be in control of the family company who will be correspondingly reluctant to allow the company to take action. Equally there is a basic reluctance on the part of the courts stretching back for almost two centuries to allow aggrieved shareholders to step in and to fight a company's battles on its behalf.

When the right to bring statutory derivative claims was introduced by CA 2006 there was concern that this might radically change the legal landscape and that the new provisions might provide a fast route for aggrieved minority shareholders to reach into the heart of family businesses. In particular the new provisions seemed to invite claims from remote family shareholders who were concerned about management decisions taken by those leading the family business. In practice many of the decided cases suggest that, rather than providing a super highway to claims, the new provisions should be seen

---

[1] We will use the terms 'derivative action' and 'derivative claim' interchangeably in this section.

more as a road block, stopping claims, or a diversionary route with potential derivative claimants being signposted to alternative remedies, in particular unfair prejudice proceedings.

Given what we perceive to be the limited practical use of the derivative claim remedy this chapter will be fairly short and will concentrate on the difficulties likely to be encountered by those seeking to bring a derivative claim.

23.2 THE RULE IN *FOSS V HARBOTTLE*

The first obstacle that the aggrieved minority will encounter is the Rule in *Foss v Harbottle*,[2] otherwise known as the 'proper plaintiff rule'. Simply stated the rule says that if the interests of a company have been wronged the proper person to sue is the company itself, rather than any of its shareholders. In other words, as a separate legal personality, a family company can mind its own business and should be left to do so.

Over the years the courts have identified various public policy reasons to justify the rule, including that the courts should show respect for the basic principles of internal governance and majority rule of companies, the previously noted reluctance of the courts to get involved in business management issues and a fear of allowing litigious minority shareholders to swamp the courts with claims.

23.3 FRAUD ON THE MINORITY

Nevertheless various exceptions to the rule have been developed over the years where the courts have allowed minority shareholders to bring claims on behalf of the company. At common law these were originally known as a derivative actions. In their statutory form they are known as derivative claims (or, in Scotland, derivative proceedings).

The principal relevant exception arises in circumstances where the act or omission of the directors concerned is sufficiently serious and damaging to the interests of the company, as a separate entity, and with it the interests of the minority shareholders, that it would be improper to allow those directors to shelter behind their controlling position to prevent action being taken against themselves. In legal terminology the act complained of would be a 'fraud on the minority'.

The rule itself and the various exceptions to the rule form one of the most complex areas of company law. For a comparatively little used remedy derivative claims have generated a large volume of case-law. Although we look briefly at this area in 23.8 below, a detailed consideration of the topic is beyond the scope of this book.[3]

---

[2] (1843) 2 Hare 461.
[3] There are many specialist academic articles on the subject which are referred to in the detailed overview on the Rule contained in *Gore Browne* at Chapter 17[2A]. Instead we intend to outline the basic procedure and to consider its practical application to the situation of the family owned business.

23.4 CA, SS 260–264

23.4.1 Scope

Derivative claims were put onto a statutory footing by the introduction of CA Part 11 with ss 260–264 applying to claims made in most of the United Kingdom and broadly equivalent provisions ss 265–269 applying to derivative proceedings in Scotland.

The scope of a derivative claim is set out in CA, s 260(2). Some wrongdoing on the part of a director is required. The section provides that claims may only be brought in relation to:

> '... an actual or proposed act or omission involving negligence, default, breach of duty or breach of trust by a director ...'

However proceedings can be brought against either the director concerned or another relevant party, for example a family member receiving company property at an undervalue as a result of a director's breach of duty.

The statutory derivative claim has two fairly important differences from its common law counterpart.

First the statutory remedy is now limited to actions arising from the wrongful acts of directors in that capacity. Previously, to the extent that a company had a right of action against a shareholder, this could be pursued by another member as a derivative action.

At first glance one of the most likely causes of action would appear to be aggrieved minority family shareholders complaining about the negligent mismanagement of the directors controlling the family business. Previously, at common law, derivative actions were only possible if a director personally benefited by their own failings.[4] The second difference is that this common law rule has not been transferred into the statutory remedy. In theory derivative claims could be made for mismanagement amounting to a breach of CA, s 174 (the directors' duty to exercise reasonable skill and care). However other elements of the statutory procedure, described below are likely to prevent family owned businesses becoming embroiled in inappropriate claims, centered on mismanagement, at the behest of aggrieved remote family members.

23.4.2 Court consent

To guard against the concern that the introduction of these provisions would cause the litigation floodgates to open the Act contains a detailed procedure for the courts to filter potential derivative claims. Basically a claimant will need permission of the court to bring or continue their claim.

That permission can either be:
- as a result of a successful unfair prejudice claim where the court make an order under CA, s 996(2)(c) authorising the claimant to bring a derivative claim as the most appropriate remedy; or

---

[4] *Palvides v Jensen* [1956] Ch 565.

- under CA, s 261 where anyone who brings a derivative claim (except with permission under the above provision) must apply to the court for permission to continue that claim.

The filtration process under CA, s 261 itself has various stages and tests.

Prima facie case – CA, s 261(2)

First the court has a positive duty under CA, s 261(2) to refuse an application for permission to continue with a derivative claim if the applicant cannot demonstrate (on the basis of the affidavit evidence that they have filed) that there is a basic, prima-facie case made out to support the claim.

Beyond this, at least in theory, the claimant does not have to satisfy any particular test or overcome any burden of proof, for example that the case is likely to succeed at full trial. Nevertheless the strength (or otherwise) of the case actually presented by the derivative claimant is likely to have a significant bearing on the outcome of the leave proceedings.

Mandatory refusal – CA, s 263(2)

Secondly the court must refuse leave to continue in the circumstances listed in CA, s 263(2).

(1) **Independent director test.** Significantly CA, s 263(2)(a) requires the court to refuse leave to continue with the claim if 'a person acting in accordance with section 172', in other words a hypothetical independent director with a general duty to promote the success of the company would not seek to continue the claim. The courts have interpreted this test narrowly as needing to be sure that no independent director would seek to continue the claim.[5] Accordingly evidence from actual directors who can demonstrate, so far as is practicable, independence from the parties to the actual dispute will be crucial.[6]

(2) **Authorisation or ratification.** Before the Companies Act 2006 came into force there were a number of cases which established the principle that derivative actions could not be brought if an act (or omission) had been validly authorised by the company or an otherwise invalid act had been subsequently ratified by the members. This makes sense and is justifiable for two basic reasons. First, the principle of majority rule; that the internal voting and governance procedures of the company should prevail over the views of an aggrieved minority. Secondly, and following on from this, to avoid the courts becoming clogged up with complaints based on procedural irregularity when the aggrieved minority or, more precisely, the company has not suffered any real injustice.

These principles are preserved under CA, Part 11 which requires the court to refuse permission to continue a derivative claim if the act or omission under question has not happened but has been authorised in advance[7] or has already happened and was either actually authorised[8] or has been[9] subsequently properly ratified.[10]

---

[5] *Singh v Singh* – High Court at para 30 of the judgment.
[6] *Kleanthous v Paphitis* [2011] EWHC 2287 (Ch).
[7] CA, s 263(2)(b).
[8] CA, s 263(2)(c)(i).
[9] CA, s 263(2)(c)(ii).
[10] Authorisation and ratification are discussed in a little more detail in chapter 8 (Directors' Duties).

The problem arises that whilst some acts or omissions on the part of directors are sensibly capable of authorisation or ratification other acts are sufficiently beyond the pale that it would be unfair on minority shareholders to allow the company, acting by the remaining majority shareholders to do so. A whole raft of case-law was developed on this point between the hearing of *Foss and Harbottle* right at the birth of the modern company and the 2006 Act. This case-law is expressly preserved by CA, s 239(7).

Discretionary refusal – CA, s 263(3)

Assuming that a potential derivative claim has passed through the *prima-facie* case and mandatory refusal filters referred to above, the court then has an obligation to consider a number of further discretionary factors that it may take into account in deciding whether or not to refuse leave.

Some of these factors involve revisiting, this time with a finer filter, issues considered as part of the mandatory refusal filtration stage.

(1) **Claimant's good faith.** Significantly in the context of many family business disputes CA, s 263(3)(a) obliges the court to consider whether the claimant is acting in good faith. This requirement is considered as part of a more detailed look at the issue of good faith in family business disputes generally in chapter 20.

(2) **Importance attached by an independent director.** It might be that the court was not satisfied that no independent director, taking into account their duties under CA, s 172 would not seek to continue the relevant claim. Leave would not then be refused under the mandatory grounds referred to above. CA, s 263(3)(b) requires the court then to consider the importance that a director would attach to the claim. In marginal cases this is a factor that the courts must then take into account in deciding whether to refuse leave to continue. So if factors such as costs, the amount at stake or other litigation risks are such that an independent director would attach low priority to bringing a claim against the director at fault then the court might exercise its discretion and not grant leave to continue.

(3) **The likelihood of approval or ratification.** Again, even if an act or omission has not actually been validly approved or ratified (so as to make refusal of leave mandatory), if the court believe that such approval or ratification is likely and would be legally valid, this is a factor that the court must take into account.[11]

(4) **Attitude of the company.** CA, s 263(3)(e) requires the court to also consider 'whether the company has decided not to pursue the claim'. It is difficult to see what this requirement adds. A legitimate decision not to pursue proceedings, based on sound commercial reasoning, especially if supported by independent advice and by the more disinterested stakeholders, will be covered by the requirements referred to above. Conversely a decision by a company tightly controlled by wrong-doing family directors will inevitably decide not to take or to properly pursue proceedings.[12]

(5) **Availability of personal remedies.**[13] The court is also asked to consider whether the proposed derivative claimant has a personal right of action they could pursue on

---

[11] CA, s 263(3)(c) – proposed acts or omissions and CA, s 263(3)(d) – past acts or omissions.
[12] CA, s 262 contains a provision allowing proceedings originally taken out by the company to be taken over by an aggrieved member as derivative proceedings. This is to prevent 'spoiler proceedings' being instituted against a wrong doing director by tame co-directors and then either not diligently pursed or artificially compromised.
[13] CA, s 263(3)(f).

their own behalf instead of taking proceedings in the name of the company. This is considered in more detail in **23.5.5** below.

Independent member test – CA, s 263(4)

CA, s 263(4) asks the court to 'have particular regard' to any available evidence of the views of any members 'who have no personal interest direct or indirect' in the dispute. Quite how this requirement will be applied in the context of family business disputes remains to be seen.

Logically all members (other than the potential defendant) director will have an equal commercial interest in the outcome of any claim. In particular the benefit of any damages recovered on behalf of the company. Equally all members should be aware of the business reasons for not pursuing litigation, including the costs and risks of this and the inevitable distraction of the executive management.

But family members closely connected with (and loyal to) the director under attack as a result of the proposed derivative claim will have a personal interest in that claim being stopped in its tracks.

Moreover, can any member of a family company truly be seen to 'have no personal interest' in potential litigation involving family members? To what extent would wider family branch allegiances need to be taken into account by the court? Would an over-riding desire to keep the peace and avoid the family being dragged (further) through the courts, be seen as a legitimate concern of more remote family members and sufficient to override the commercial and legal merits of any proposed litigation?

Earlier case-law suggests that the court will adopt a reasonably pragmatic approach. Even if the wrongdoers do not hold an absolute majority, if some combination of influence over and apathy of the unattached shareholders would be sufficient to provide *de-facto* control and thereby deny the minority a practical remedy that might be sufficient to allow the derivative claim to proceed.[14]

23.4.3 Status of application

An application for leave to continue a derivative claim under CA, s 260 is only a procedural step in that potential claim. If leave is granted the claim itself will need to be fully litigated. Of course if leave is refused the claim ceases there and then. At least as a derivative claim, although the same facts may give rise to alternative causes of action. An application for leave is therefore an extremely significant step and may, in practice decide the eventual outcome of the overall action.

---

[14] See the Court of Appeal decision in *Prudential Assurance v Newman Industries (No 2)* [1982] Ch 204 at p 219.

23.5 A DERIVATIVE CLAIM IN PRACTICE – *SINGH V SINGH*

23.5.1 The facts

The case of *Singh v Singh*[15] offers some helpful insights into how the courts approach the derivative claims procedure.

The claimant and his brother (B) were joint shareholders and directors of a demolition company. Both worked in the business and both were directors. Whilst the claimant had an onsite managerial and operational role, B had management control, including managing the finances and accounts. Their mother, who appears to have been a strong matriarch, played a key role in the early stages of the business in its early years, died in 2010 leaving a will gifting her house to B alone. In an earlier will she had left the house equally to all four of her children. The claimant alleged that the second will had been procured by the undue influence of B. The will dispute was the subject of separate proceedings.

The case before the court concerned an application for leave to continue a derivative claim to reclaim on behalf of the company dividends of £424,000 paid only to B. The rest of the family argued that these had been paid on the basis of dividend waivers allegedly procured by a mixture of misrepresentation towards the claimant and undue influence exerted on their mother by B. There was a second claim for the repayment of £449,000 of excessive remuneration taken by B over a 2 year period some 8 or 9 years before the action, allegedly without the knowledge of the claimant or their mother. The company had stopped trading 2 or 3 years before the proceedings.

The High Court considered various issues before refusing the claimant's application for leave to continue. The claimant then sought leave to appeal from the trial judge and on two separate occasions from the Court of Appeal. All the applications failed but nevertheless provide relevant guidance on the approach of the courts to the tests referred to above.

23.5.2 The independent director tests

Both parties accepted that the correct test was whether it could be shown that no independent director, acting in accordance with CA, s 172 would seek to continue the claim. The claimant argued that this was not the case. The amounts at stake were large. The company had ceased to trade. The claim had the support of the rest of the family. B had control over the finances at all material times.

B's lawyers, whilst accepting that the test was a difficult one to satisfy, argued that the overall merits of the claim was sufficiently weak that no director would seek to pursue it. The courts agreed, particularly in relation to the claims based on historic remuneration.[16]

---

[15] Court of Appeal: *Sukhpaul Singh v Satpaul Singh, Singh Bros Contractors (Northwest) Limited* [2014] EWCA Civ 103.
[16] See para 43 of the High Court judgment and para 26 of the Court of Appeal.

It was also clear that, even if B had not satisfied the onerous test of showing that no independent director would pursue the claims the High Court judge believed that:[17]

> '... the importance a person acting in accordance with section 172 would attach to continuing the present claim should lead the court, in the exercise of its discretion under section 263(3)(b), to refuse to allow the claimant to continue.'

So even if the claimant had jumped the first independent director hurdle, the automatic refusal on the basis that no independent director would seek to bring the claim, he would have fallen at the second, on the basis that the difficulties associated with the claim would have made it a low priority.

23.5.3 Authorisation

The principal difficulty faced by the claimant related to prior authorisation. His case was essentially that his signature to dividend waivers and annual accounts had been procured by misrepresentation. B had looked after the accounts and administration and the claimant had trusted his brother to act properly and fairly rather than helping himself to additional income of almost £900,000.

But the claimant faced a significant difficulty. That so far as the outside world was concerned the company had approved the accounts. Accordingly the company was not in a position, via a derivative action to challenge that approval. The claimant as a director of the company could and certainly should have paid attention to the statutory accounts.[18] These would have revealed (or at least pointed him to) the discrepancies in income. Vos LJ sitting alone in the Court of Appeal had to decide whether or not to grant the claimant leave to appeal to the full court was quite clear on this point:[19]

> 'It is no answer, in my judgment, for the appellant to say that his signature or approval to the dividend waiver documents were procured by misrepresentation or indeed that his mother's approval was procured by undue influence. It is no answer because the purpose of the filing of companies' accounts is to represent to the world the true state of the company's affairs. The company, therefore, cannot at the behest of its directors be heard to say that a different state of affairs prevailed.'

The difficulties over prior authorisation were a major weakness in the claimant's case in turn making it easier to find that no independent director would pursue the claim.

Both the High Court and the Court of Appeal were therefore satisfied that leave to continue with the claim had to be refused on two of the mandatory grounds in CA, s 263(2). The courts nevertheless went on to look at the discretionary grounds for refusal under s 263(3). In the case of the High Court judge this was as a failsafe against being wrong that the mandatory grounds for refusing leave had been made out.

---

[17] At para 41 of the High Court judgment.
[18] See the commentary at paras 39–41 of the High Court judgment.
[19] At para 22 of the Court of Appeal judgment.

23.5.4 Bad faith

Issues of the claimant's bad faith in relation to family business disputes generally including derivative claims are discussed in detail in chapter 20. *Singh v Singh* also contains an interesting discussion on the difficult subject of bad faith in family business disputes and is fully discussed there.

However the conclusion reached on this basis of the cases discussed there is that the bad faith discretionary ground is likely to only be relevant in the clearest of cases of bad faith or as an additional discretionary ground to support refusal of leave where other discretionary grounds are present.

23.5.5 Alternative personal remedies

The courts are obliged to consider the availability of causes of action that a claimant could pursue in their own right rather than on behalf of the company via a derivative claim.

In *Barrett v Duckett*[20] 5 months prior to the issue of proceedings by his mother in law Mr Duckett had presented a petition to wind up the original company contending that it was insolvent or alternatively that it was just and equitable to do so because the management of the company had become deadlocked. Before presenting that petition Mr Duckett had sought to put the family company into a voluntary liquidation. Mrs Barrett had also blocked that proposal. The court took the view that much the best approach was to allow that winding up to continue. A liquidator would be in a much better position to take an objective decision on the merits of pursuing Mr Duckett than a vindictive mother in law.

The most likely alternative remedy would be an action for unfair prejudice under CA, s 994. For most breach of duty cases, for example taking excessive remuneration as in *Irvine*,[21] a buy-out of the aggrieved minority might provide a much more pragmatic long term remedy than pursuing a derivative action. Even if successful, this would result only in the offending director being ordered to refund the excess to the company, inevitably with considerable resentment and in many cases with the risk of repetition of the breach of duty or similar misconduct.

In both *Barrett v Duckett* and *Singh* the relevant businesses had ceased to trade removing the risk of repetition and also the risk of damage to other stakeholders of continuing a derivative claim.

In *Singh* the claimant was quite clear that he was not looking for the usual unfair prejudice remedy, the buy back of his shares. Doubts were expressed over whether a liquidator appointed after successful just and equitable winding up proceedings would pursue the claim. There were additional factors in favour of allowing the derivative claim to proceed, including that restoration of the £900,000 of alleged improper remuneration or so, would allow the company to repay arrears of rent on premises owned by the mother for the benefit of the wider family under her estate. Nevertheless the High Court believed that either a just and equitable winding up, unfair prejudice

---

[20] [1995] BCC 362. The facts are set out at 20.8.2.
[21] Discussed in detail in chapter 21.

proceedings, or direct personal actions by the claimant or the estate against B for breach of duty provided the claimant with suitable alternative remedies.[22]

23.5.6 Views of independent members

CA, s 263(4) obliges the court to 'have particular regard' to the views of any independent members. The evidence in *Singh* suggests that the claimant's stance against his brother was supported by the remainder of the family, their two sisters. This issue is not covered in any detail in the judgment. This might have been because the issue of prior approval was seen as a clear-cut question of law, thus removing any question of discretion. Possibly the sisters were not to be treated as members, for example because they were not executors of their mother's will.[23] Alternatively because the estate had a potential claim against the company they were seen to have an indirect interest in the outcome of the derivative claim and therefore not sufficiently disinterested to be regarded as independent for the purposes of CA, s 263(4).

23.6 SUBSTANTIVE FAILURE

23.6.1 After the filtration process

The application for leave to continue will be a highly significant stage in a derivative claim. Even if permission is given to continue that claim there are many cases where derivative actions have failed on more general common law principles. Under these principles the court will not grant relief via derivative actions in various circumstances.

23.6.2 Mismanagement

Remote family members may believe that how the controlling directors run the family business amounts to negligence on the part of the board. Mismanagement is dealt with as a key theme in chapter 20. It is difficult to conceive of circumstances where a dispute centered on management decisions would survive the filtration process described above. Presumably only examples of gross negligence would be allowed through. Even those that were allowed to proceed would then encounter the basic reluctance of the courts to second-guess management decisions.

23.6.3 Majority rule

Similarly the basic justification of the rule in *Foss v Harbottle* will continue to apply. If the majority of the members of a family owned business are content to approve or even accept the position it will take a special set of circumstances for the court to intervene at the behest of the minority.

Bamford v Bamford[24] concerned the proposed takeover of a publically listed but still family controlled agricultural equipment business by the JCB engineering equipment business, owned by more remote members of the Bamford family. The proposal split the family owners of the agricultural business, with the majority of the board being against

---
[22] See paras 45 and 46 of the High Court judgment and para 30 in the Court of Appeal.
[23] This is not clear from the judgments.
[24] [1970] Ch 212, [1969] 1 All ER.

the takeover. They decided to issue unallocated shares to a key distributor known to oppose the takeover. The minority complained that this amounted to an abuse of authority in that the board were issuing the shares to protect their own position, rather than for the benefit of the business of the company. The Court of Appeal were quite clear, that even though this might have been the case, the fact that the majority (as evidenced by a resolution ratifying the allotment) were content with the situation meant that the minority would have to accept the position (and with it the failure of the JCB takeover).

23.6.4 Procedural irregularity

Bamford concerned real points of legal substance. Were the directors in breach of their duty to act in the best interests of the company and, if so, could the majority ratify that breach? It therefore follows that the courts are even less likely to entertain derivative claims where the breach of duty complained of is simply the failure to follow the correct statutory or corporate procedure where that failure does not affect the substantive rights of the minority.

Historically the courts have adopted a realistic attitude in terms of the likelihood, or otherwise, of family owned or other private companies paying strict adherence to the procedural requirements of articles and the administrative requirements of the Companies Acts. As long ago as 1875 the court accepted that:[25]

> 'Looking to the nature of these companies, looking at the way in which their articles are formed, and that they are not all lawyers who attend these meetings, nothing could be more likely that there should be something more or less irregular done at them.'

Recognising the danger that 'if there happens to be one cantankerous member or one member who loves litigation' a private company could become bogged down in litigation any proceedings that need to be carried on in the name of the company by way of derivative claim in relation to such matters (absent the special circumstances below) will only continue if 'there is a majority that really wish for litigation'.

23.6.5 Infringement of personal rights

If the acts complained of provide a personal cause of action for the aggrieved minority shareholder this would be a bar to that shareholder bringing a derivative action under the previous common law regime. As we have seen the availability of alternative remedies is a factor that the court must consider in deciding whether to give permission to continue a derivative claim under the new statutory regime. It remains to be seen whether, having exercised its discretion under CA, s 260 to allow a derivative claim to proceed notwithstanding the availability of alternative personal actions a court hearing the full trial of a derivative claim would reject that claim on the basis of the old case-law.

---

[25] *MacDougal v Gardiner* (1875) 1 Ch 13 at p 25.

23.7 DERIVATIVE CLAIMS – SUCCESSFUL CATEGORIES

It will be seen from the above commentary that the scope for bringing derivative claims or, put another way, the extent of the exceptions to the rule in *Foss v Harbottle* is, in reality, quite narrow. Possible derivative claims fall into four broad categories:

23.7.1 Ultra vires transactions

If directors cause a company to take action, which is beyond its corporate power, this will potentially allow an aggrieved minority to intervene through a derivative claim. Basically the relevant action will put the aggrieved member outside the boundaries of what they could have agreed to on becoming a member. The ultra vires doctrine, although a key part of company law history, has a much reduced significance in modern company law and no special significance for family owned businesses.

23.7.2 Special majorities

Sometimes the articles of association of a family business will specify that a special majority of members is required to take a decision that ordinarily, as a matter of general company law could be taken by either a simple majority or perhaps by the board alone. For example increasing the share capital and providing the directors with power to allot shares or selling the whole or a material part of the assets of the business.

In other cases the articles might prescribe a particular procedure for taking certain decisions, for example obtaining the approval of specially designated family directors before allotting shares to third parties. Attempting to take or ratify these decisions by a simple majority is likely to be a breach of duty on the part of the directors and will give rise to a potential derivative claim. In *Quin and Axtens Ltd v Salmon*[26] the articles required certain key decisions to be taken only with the consent of both joint managing directors. The House of Lords refused to uphold a decision taken by one of the managing directors but approved by a simple majority of members in general meeting. To do otherwise would be to move the goal posts away from the minority members.[27]

23.7.3 Rights of membership

Some rights attached to membership of a company are directly actionable by aggrieved members against that company. These include most rights relating to dividends, for example the right to enforce a declared dividend against the company as a debt.[28]

However a number of 'shareholder's rights' are not directly enforceable by shareholders. If breached the view is that the damage has been done to the company rather than the individual shareholder. For example the right to have accounts prepared in accordance with the requirements of the Companies Acts[29] or the right to force directors to retire in accordance with compulsory retirement provisions in the articles.[30]

---

[26] [1909] AC 442 HL.
[27] This is however a complicated area of law. A number of decided cases are difficult to reconcile with this House of Lords decision.
[28] *Mosely v Koffyfontein Mines Ltd* [1904] 2 Ch 108, CA.
[29] *Devlin v Slough Estates* [1983] BCLC 497.
[30] *Mozley v Alston* [1847] 1 Ph. 790.

Most importantly a shareholder has no direct right to complain if the actions or breach of duty of directors has damaged the value of their shareholding. The primary loss will be that of the company with the shareholder suffering a consequential loss of shareholding value which will not be directly recoverable under the so called 'reflective loss principle'. That is unless the shareholder has a separate and distinct loss arising from the breach.

In circumstances where the shareholder has no direct personal right of action a derivative claim might lie.

23.8 FRAUD ON THE MINORITY

The most important exception to the rule in *Foss v Harbottle* and the most relevant to minority shareholders in the context of the family owned businesses is where the breach by the directors concerned is said to be 'a fraud on the minority'.

23.8.1 Relevance of old case-law

To add two general words of warning at this stage on the relevance of old case-law on derivative actions. First the old case-law on derivative actions is extremely complicated and at times contradictory. Secondly most of the cases where derivative actions have been allowed by the courts pre-date the introduction of CA, s 260 and also the advent of the unfair prejudice remedy. The combination of these two provisions may well mean that matters, which the courts previously would have allowed to be pursued as derivative claims, will now be dealt with under the unfair prejudice regime of CA, s 994.

23.8.2 Fraud or breach of duty?

As stated above the most relevant circumstances where an aggrieved minority shareholder in a family business would want to consider making a derivative claim, via the company, would be when the actions of some or all of the directors can be said to have been a 'fraud on the minority'.

In practice this phrase, whilst widely used is misleading. Derivative actions under this category included, but were not previously limited to, cases of actual and proven fraud. Claims were allowed involving wider abuse or gross negligence on the part of directors, which, in the absence of a derivative action would otherwise go unchecked by the company. A better description might be serious breach of duty.

This is confirmed in the language of CA, s 260 itself referring as it does to acts or omissions 'involving negligence, default, breach of duty or breach of trust by a director of a company'.

23.8.3 Daniel v Daniels[31]

The facts

The case of *Daniel v Daniels* illustrates the approach taken by the courts to such situations, at least prior to the introduction of CA, s 260. The case concerned a family owned building company the shares of which were held as to approximately 60% by Mr Daniels and his wife, who were also the only directors. Mr Daniel's sister and his two brothers held the remaining 40%. Shortly after the death of their father Mr Daniels and his wife transferred land from the company's land bank into Mrs Daniel's sole name for £4,250. Four years later she sold the land for development for £120,000.

No fraud (in the criminal sense) was alleged. Instead the remaining family members argued that their brother and his wife knew or ought to have known that the current value of the relevant land was considerably above the £4,250 paid (which was apparently based on the values used in the probate of the father's will).

The 'fraud'

Accepting that 'fraud is so hard to plead and difficult to prove' the High Court explained that the principle of allowing a derivative action to proceed was not based on fraud in the technical and narrow sense but was that:[32]

> 'a minority shareholder who has no other remedy may sue where directors use their powers, intentionally or unintentionally, fraudulently or negligently, in a manner which benefits themselves at the expense of the company.'

Unlike the earlier case of *Palvides v Jensen*[33] Mr Daniels and his wife had clearly benefited from their own negligent breach of duty. The two brothers and the sister were therefore allowed to continue their derivative claim against their brother and sister in law.[34]

An alternative remedy?

That case was decided on the cusp of the introduction of the unfair prejudice remedy. A claim could clearly now be brought under CA, s 994. A court is obliged to consider the availability of alternative remedies in deciding whether to allow a derivative claim to proceed. There are arguments both ways.

The principal argument against proceeding as a derivative claim would be that, if successful the action would simply provide restoration for the company, which would remain controlled by the wrongdoers. There would be no means to extract the restored funds for the benefit of the wider family. Conversely there would be no guarantee that

---

[31] [1978] Ch 406, [1978] 2 All ER 89.
[32] At p 414.
[33] [1956] Ch 565 – which concerned an action after the directors took a decision to sell off the company's main asset, a mine, at what transpired to be a significant undervalue, £182,000 compared with a market value in excess of £1m. However the directors derived no personal benefit from their mismanagement. The derivative claim was not allowed to proceed.
[34] This distinction between negligence from which the director derives personal benefit and was actionable via a derivative claim and where no benefit was obtained, which was not, does not appear to have been retained by the wording of CA, s 260(3).

their brother and sister in law would not seek to re-extract the cash through salary or other means. A share purchase order under CA, s 996 provides a clean break.

The remainder of the family may of course have no wish to, in effect, be forced out of the family business by their brother's wrongdoing. Leaving aside this emotional consideration, as well might a court, the principle financial and technical drawbacks to an unfair prejudice action lie in the discretionary nature of the remedy itself. It appears from the case that the claimants did not participate in the management of the company. It would not appear to be quasi partnership. There would therefore be, at least, uncertainty over whether the court would apply *Ebrahami* principles and value the shares without a discount.[35]

There are parallels between *Daniels* and both *Irvine*, where the court ordered a discounted valuation and *Fisher v Cadman*, where it did not. The breach of duty in *Daniels* might as be seen a little more extreme than that of the directors concerned in both of these other cases. It is easier to understand how Ian Irvine and the Cadman brothers felt entitled to additional remuneration than how Mr and Mrs Daniels could have believed that the land transfer value was appropriate.

23.9 CONCLUSION

The introduction of the statutory derivative claim remedy under CA, s 260 was accompanied by concerns that this would lead to a multiplicity of claims by disgruntled minority shareholders. It is relatively easy to see how this concern might in theory apply in the context of, particularly later stage family owned businesses. However, in practice those concerns have not been realised to date.

This might be because, in reality, family members are much less altruistic and more likely to pursue remedies for their own advantage, rather than to protect their family company. It might be that the combination of a relatively restricted approach taken by the courts in granting (or more precisely refusing) permission to continue derivative claims and the availability of, alternative remedies makes it impractical to pursue derivative claims, even if outsiders were inclined to do so.

Therefore, rather than creating a pathway for more proceedings to be brought in the name of a family company by way of derivative claim, more claims are being diverted down the unfair prejudice route, thereby reinforcing the status of this as the primary remedy for disgruntled minority shareholders.

For those seeking to defend derivative claims the possibility of these turning into unfair prejudice actions will therefore be ever present. Accordingly the need to consider, at the early stage, whether to make an offer to buy out the aggrieved minority may also become relevant to actions originally started as derivative claims.

---

[35] Discounts and valuations are discussed in detail in chapter 24.

CHAPTER 24

SHAREHOLDER DISPUTES – REMEDIES, REASONABLE OFFERS AND COSTS

24.1 INTRODUCTION

The preceding chapters have looked at the three main routes to relief potentially available to aggrieved shareholders in a family company, namely unfair prejudice under CA, s 994, just and equitable winding up under IA, s 122(1)(g) and derivative claims pursuant to CA, s 260. Those chapters have largely looked at question of whether those routes may actually be available.

Unfair prejudice is by far the most important of those routes in practice. We have noted that the usual and almost invariable remedy following a finding of unfair prejudice in accordance with CA, s 994 is for an order for the minority to be bought out by the majority in accordance with CA, s 996(2)(e). We have also noted that if a reasonable offer to buy the claimant's shares has been made an unfair prejudice claim will usually be struck out at an early stage.

In turn whether or not a suitable offer has been made and refused will be central to the key question of awards of costs.

Each of the supporting shareholder remedies, applications for just and equitable winding up under IA, s 122(1)(g) and seeking leave to bring a derivative claim under CA, s 260 may be denied if the claimant has an alternative remedy.[1]

So the question of what remedy would be awarded under CA, s 996 further to a finding of unfair prejudice is inextricably linked to the question of what would amount to a reasonable offer to make to the claimant to avoid such a finding in the first place. Similarly a family member would be ill advised to pursue either of the other remedies if a suitable offer had already been made that would give that member all they could hope for by going to court.

The starting point is therefore to look in more detail at how unfair prejudice remedies work in practice.

---

[1] Insolvency Act 1986, s 125(2) in the case of just and equitable winding up and CA, s 263(3)(f) for derivative claims.

24.2 UNFAIR PREJUDICE REMEDIES – OVERVIEW – CA, S 996

24.2.1 General discretion – CA, s 996(1)

Once satisfied that a case for unfair prejudice exists the court has a wide (and in theory unlimited) discretion to remedy the situation as it thinks fit. CA, s 996(1) provides that:

> 'If the court is satisfied that a petition under this Part is well founded, it may make such order as it thinks fit for giving relief in respect of the matters complained of …'

24.2.2 CA, s 996(2)

CA, s 996(2) goes on to provide a non-exhaustive shopping list of the remedies that the court may wish to consider. That list provides for orders to:

(a) regulate the conduct of the company's affairs in the future;
(b) require the company –
 (i) to refrain from doing or continuing an act complained of, or
 (ii) to do an act that the petitioner has complained it has omitted to do;
(c) authorise civil proceedings to be brought in the name and on behalf of the company by such person or persons and on such terms as the court may direct;
(d) require the company not to make any, or any specified, alterations in its articles without the leave of the court;
(e) provide for the purchase of the shares of any members of the company by other members or by the company itself and, in the case of a purchase by the company itself, the reduction of the company's capital accordingly.

Whilst we will briefly consider the other potential remedies below we will concentrate on orders for the sale and purchase of shares. This is overwhelmingly the most usual and practical remedy.

24.3 SHARE PURCHASE ORDERS

24.3.1 Usual remedy

In theory the court should make the minimum order necessary to redress the unfair prejudice in question. But in practice an order for the majority to buy out the minority will, in almost every occasion, be the only sensible and practical remedy. The relationship between the family members concerned will almost certainly have suffered irreparable damage as a result of the dispute. It is most unlikely that they will be able to work together in the future.

Orders to regulate the conduct of the company are tools available to the court within CA, s 996.[2] But in practice it would be almost impossible to formulate orders that are both sufficiently flexible to allow a trading business to operate, whilst at the same time

---

[2] For a rare, modern, example of where the court has used its powers to regulate the affairs of a company see *Hawks v Cuddy* [2008] BCC 390 approved in the Court of Appeal [2009] 2 BCLC 427. The outcome of the case was to impose certain governance requirements into the fraught relationships between the participants in the Neath Swansea Ospreys rugby club.

being sufficiently comprehensive to protect the minority from further unfairness. Further disputes and a return to court would be almost inevitable.

24.3.2 Minority purchase orders

In theory the court can order the majority shareholder to sell their shares to the minority shareholders who have succeeded in their unfair prejudice petition. By definition the majority, will have done something to the unfair prejudice of the minority and to a greater or lesser extent could be seen as the guilty party.

However orders requiring the majority to sell to the minority are sufficiently rare so as to be discounted for most practical purposes. The court in the *Gippeswyck* case[3] confirmed that:[4]

> 'Cases where a majority shareholder is forced to sell his shareholding to the petitioning minority shareholder must be very rare indeed.'

It may seem inappropriate that the prejudiced minority family shareholder will be left with no choice other than to have their interest in the family business bought out. The petitioner will almost certainly believe that they are 'in the right'. They will have succeeded in court or, more likely will have achieved a settlement that implicitly recognises that their interests have been unfairly prejudiced. The business may have been in the family for generations.

However the courts are keen to achieve a practical solution. If the controlling family members hold all of the key relationships in the family business including those with, employees, customers, suppliers and bankers there will be little choice but to preserve the status quo.

The position of the minority seeking to acquire the shares of the majority is not necessarily hopeless.[5] The court should consider all relevant circumstances including relative sizes of shareholding, involvement in management, the confidence of employees and the respective conduct of the parties.[6] There is also a residual fairness factor. This is that it may be inappropriate for the majority to benefit from their wrongdoing by acquiring the shares of the minority where they do not want to sell.

In *Robertson* the shares were held as to 50% equally by two brothers, held to have unfairly prejudiced the petitioner, holding the remaining 50%. Each party wanted control of the company concerned and to buy the other out. Ordering the sale to the petitioner Lord Glennie approached the matter from a mixture of fairness and pragmatism. He looked at a number of factors:[7]

- The conduct of the brothers.
- Their commercial mismanagement.
- That the petitioner was the largest single shareholder.

---

[3] Discussed in chapter 21
[4] *Re a Company (No 00836 of 1995)* [1996] BCC 432 at p 442.
[5] An order for the buy-out of the majority was made in the non-family business case of *Nuneaton Borough AFC Ltd ex parte Shooter and Broadhurst* [1990] BCLC 384.
[6] *Ringtower Holdings plc* [1989] 5 BCC 82 generally and *Re Copeland v Craddock Ltd* [1997] BCC 294 for relevance of past involvement in management.
[7] See para 54.

- That the petitioner had the most involvement in the business.
- Greater prospects of business success under the stewardship of the petitioner.
- Management confidence in the petitioner.

In *Harmer* and the *Gippeswyck* cases the next generation held the majority of equity in the relevant companies, albeit in *Harmer* the senior generation had retained voting control.

Many of the above factors might be present in partial succession cases where the next generation are minority shareholders but in effective control of the business on a day-to-day basis. Maybe just maybe the courts could be convinced that in some of these cases the most appropriate remedy would be to continue the succession process by ordering a buy-out of the senior generation majority.

This would still leave the next generation with the problem of how to finance the purchase of the senior generation's shares in circumstances where perhaps the next generation had expected the shares of the senior generation to be gifted to them.

24.3.3 Sibling partnerships and deadlock cases

A good number of disputes will concern small family businesses owned equally as a sibling partnership or by husband and wife, parent and child or other family combinations. There can obviously be no starting presumption of who would buy out whom. In those cases the above factors, involvement in management, confidence of employees and customers and relative conduct[8] will have special significance.

A key and potentially deciding factor may well be which of the two combatants has made the most reasonable offer to either sell their own shares or acquire those of the other family member.[9]

24.3.4 Company buy-back

In most early stage family businesses there will be a close link between those responsible for the unfair prejudice and share ownership. It will be obvious that, if the petitioner's shares are to be sold, then they should be bought by the controlling shareholders.

In later stage family businesses this may not be at all clear. Although the point was academic (because the claim failed utterly) one of the issues that troubled Vinelott J in the High Court in *Saul D Harrison*[10] was that petition asked for an order that the A Shareholders buy Rosemary's shares. The shares in the company were widely held. Although the A Shares, provided voting control of the company these had no real economic value.

---

[8] *Oak Investment Partners XII Ltd Partnership v Broughtwood* [2010] EWCA Civ 23 (a non-family business case).
[9] *Re Clearsprings (Management) Ltd* [2003] EWHC 2516 (Ch). Offers to purchase are discussed in detail in 24.5 below.
[10] See p 486 of the judgment.

In other circumstances some continuing shareholders might be prepared to buy out the interests of the minority but others will be reluctant to do so but perhaps unwilling to see the willing buyers, usually insiders, to increase their proportionate stake.[11]

Perhaps a better approach, particularly in cases relying on a fairness approach, or where less serious breaches of duty where shareholdings are widely spread would be to ask the court, where practicable, to order a buy-back by the family company of its own shares under CA, s 996(2)(e). In that way the cost of providing an exit to the minority is spread across the remaining shareholders as a whole and without any element of direct punishment for those in control.

An alternative approach was taken in *Sunrise Radio*. There Dr Lit, who was seen to be the primary perpetrator of the unfair prejudice and the principal beneficiary of this, was ordered to be the principal buyer of Ms Kohli's holding. But other shareholders and members of the Lit family who were complicit in the prejudice were ordered to, in effect jointly and severally guarantee, completion of the buy-back.[12]

24.4 VALUATION – BASIC PRINCIPLES

If the almost invariable order is for purchase of the minority holding the basis upon which that holding will be valued is clearly of crucial importance.

The basic principle is to arrive at a 'fair value' for the minority holding[13]). Fair value has a number of separate elements. Many of these were examined when the Irvine family (discussed in chapters 20 and 21) found themselves back before the High Court to resolve a further dispute about the valuation of the minority holding of Pamela (the widow) and the family trust (which we will refer to as *Irvine (No 3)*.[14]

The usual formula contained in pre-emption provisions found in shareholders' agreements or articles is that the relevant shares are to be valued on the basis of a sale and purchase between a willing seller and a willing buyer. The courts will also apply this presumption to the compulsory acquisition under CA, s 996 in a successful unfair prejudice application.[15] Of course the reality will be that either the buyer or the seller or perhaps both will be concluding the sale with the utmost reluctance.

24.5 MINORITY DISCOUNTS?

24.5.1 Overview

The most important question in terms of valuation is whether a minority shareholding should be valued on a full pro-rata basis or discounted for the fact that it is a minority being sold.

---

[11] Nevertheless thresholds of controlling interests, explored in chapter 11 (Ownership Overview).
[12] See para 306 of the *Sunrise Radio* judgment.
[13] Lord Hoffmann in *O'Neill* at p 1107.
[14] *Irvine v Irvine (No 3)* [2006] EWHC 1875 (Ch).
[15] *Irvine v Irvine (No 2)* at para 26 of the judgment.

Under usual valuation principles the sale of a minority holding in a family owned or other private company would almost always attract a significant discount from the price be paid if the company as a whole was being sold by way of trade sale.[16] Against this the usual valuation formula in bespoke governance documents is to provide for valuation of minority shareholdings on a full pro rata basis.

The starting point is again the House of Lords in *O'Neill v Phillips* where Lord Hoffmann's view was that this should 'ordinarily' be without a discount to reflect the fact of a minority holding. He said that:[17]

> 'the fair value of the shares should be determined on a pro rata basis. This too reflects the existing practice.'

Lord Hoffmann was clearly placing emphasis on the need to achieve fairness as the foundation of any remedy. This would seem entirely logical for a remedy based on fairness. He also referred in his judgment to the recommendation of the Law Commission to the effect that valuation should ordinarily be without discount.[18] Of course in that case there was no finding of unfair prejudice, so Lord Hoffmann's comments are strictly obiter dicta, rather part of the decision in the case itself.

By definition any finding of unfair prejudice carries with it an implicit finding of fault. At first sight it may seem difficult to envisage circumstances where it would be a fair to remedy an unfair situation by ordering a discounted valuation. But Lord Hoffmann also left the door at least ajar for the possibility of discounted valuations saying:[19]

> 'This is not to say that there may not be cases in which it will be fair to take a discounted value. But such cases will be based upon special circumstances and it will seldom be possible for the court to say that an offer to buy on a discounted basis is plainly reasonable, so that the petition should be struck out.'

One example had already been given in the earlier case of re *Birds Precision Bellows*.[20] In that case shares had been acquired by an investor at a discount. It was held to be unfair for them to expect to be provided with a statutory exit on an enhanced full pro-rata valuation.

But that door has been pushed open in various subsequent decisions. So in practice it is now necessary to distinguish between two, now familiar situations; those where the fairness approach applies (quasi-partnerships) and others.

24.5.2 Equitable consideration cases (quasi-partnerships)

Here the minority shareholding will almost invariably be valued without a discount on a full pro-rata basis.[21]

---

[16] See for example HMRC Share Valuation Manual. In some cases forensic accountants will apply as much as a 90% discount. See for, example, Roger Issacs writing in the Newsletter of the Network of Independent Forensic Accountants – NIFA News 30.
[17] At p 1107.
[18] Law Commission Report on Shareholder Remedies (1997) (Law Com No 246) at paras 3.57–3.62.
[19] At p 1107.
[20] Re Bird Precision Bellows Ltd [1986] Ch 658.
[21] Re Bird Precision Bellows Ltd.

Pectel Ltd, the non-family company concerned in the *O'Neill* case was a fairly small business owned and managed by the two shareholders, Mr O'Neill and Mr Phillips. The House of Lords decided, on the facts of that case that no equitable constraints had been breached. In particular that Mr O'Neill had not been excluded from the business. Lord Hoffmann could therefore be seen to be explaining that, if exclusion had occurred, from what would clearly then be treated as a quasi partnership, Mr O'Neill's holding would be valued on a full pro-rata basis. It may be that Lord Hoffmann's remarks are limited to such cases falling within the *Ebrahimi* principles.

This was the view of the Court of Appeal in *Strachan v Wilcock*[22] where Arden LJ said that:

> 'Shares are generally ordered to be purchased on the basis of their valuation on a non-discounted basis where the party against whom the order is made has acted in breach of the obligation of good faith applicable to the parties' relationship by analogy with partnership law, that is to say where a 'quasi-partnership' relationship has been found to exist.'

This approach has been followed in a number of family business exclusion cases, including *Brownlow* and *Shah* both of which are discussed above.

In other cases, as explained in chapter 20 the concept of quasi-partnership has been stretched well beyond typical circumstances such as those in Pectel Limited, thus clearing the way for a non-discounted valuation, for example in *Fisher v Cadman*.[23]

In that case the claimant sister had never had any active role in the family business or, until shortly before the dispute arose, any apparent interest in it. In what is perhaps the most liberal interpretation of the concept of quasi partnership, the trial judge thought that this could be applied to the family business concerned notwithstanding that 'it did not share all the features typical of a true partnership-type relationship'.[24] Although the report did not deal fully with valuation and discounts the parties were sent away to agree this against a strong steer from the judge that this should be at full pro-rata value.[25]

24.5.3 Non *Ebrahimi* cases

There is a crucial distinction to be made for cases where equitable considerations based on the principles found in *Ebrahimi* do not arise. In shorthand, non-quasi partnership cases.

In an early, but still influential case, on minority discounts, *Re Bird Precision Bellows Ltd*[26] the trial judge drew distinctions between, on the one hand, quasi partnerships (where shares would usually be valued without discount) and non quasi partnership cases where there was no 'universal or general rule' that non-discounted valuation should apply. The trial judge gave examples such as where shares had been

---

[22] [2006] EWCA Civ 13 at p 17.
[23] [2005] EWHC 377 (Ch).
[24] At para 89 of the judgment.
[25] The judge actually said that Mrs. Fisher should not 'be obliged to sell [her interest] only upon the terms set out in the articles of association' and cited *Re Bird Precision Bellows Ltd* [1984] Ch] 419, a leading non discount case in support.
[26] [1984] Ch 419.

bought by an investor from a former quasi partner on a discounted basis, or where the business had never been a quasi partnership. But the judge, Nourse J, did not say that discounts would automatically be made in such circumstances.

The issue was taken further by Arden LJ in *Strachan v Wilcock* who went on to suggest (by way of obiter dicta) that:

> 'It is difficult to conceive of circumstances in which a non-discounted basis of valuation would be appropriate where there was unfair prejudice for the purposes of the 1985 Act but such a [quasi partnership] relationship did not exist. However, on this appeal I need not express a final view on what those circumstances might be.'

In practice subsequent courts have been prepared to agree to discounts in non-quasi partnership family business cases. Indeed this would now seem to be the most likely outcome. It will be recalled that in the first hearing in *Irvine* and notwithstanding that the business was a family company it was found that equitable considerations did not apply. The family also went back to court over a dispute as to whether the minority interest should be valued on a full pro-rata or, alternatively, as discounted basis.

In that hearing, *Irvine (No 2)*,[27] the petitioners submitted that a pro rata basis of valuation should apply as, although since the death of Malcolm Irvine, the company had not been run as quasi partnership in the strict sense:[28]

> '... the company remained nevertheless a "family company" in that all the shares were held by or for the benefit of members of the Irvine family. The articles contained restrictions on the transfer of shares and there is no open market for their disposal.'

It was also suggested that it was only because of Ian Irvine's behaviour over several years that they had been driven to seek an exit from the company through the unfair prejudice proceedings. His greed in taking excessive remuneration had essentially forced the rest of the family out of the business. The court eventually found in *Irvine (No 3)* that the total gross loss to the company of the excess remuneration, with interest was approximately £5.3m.

It was forcefully argued by counsel for the widow and the trustees of the family trust for Malcolm's children that:[29]

> 'If this was not a case where a pro-rata basis of valuation should apply, it would be difficult to think that any such case would ever arise, and there would be a risk therefore that the court's discretion in fixing the basis of valuation for a minority holding in a company which was not a quasi-partnership would be atrophied.'

Against this counsel for Ian, the majority shareholder, argued that the quasi partnership that had previously existed had been terminated on the death of Ian's brother and the transfer of the single controlling share. There were no exceptional circumstances justifying equitable intervention.

---

[27] Patricia Mary Irvine, Michael Cleobury Thatcher, Patricia Mary Irvine as Trustees of the Accumulation and Maintenance Settlement Dated 6 August 1993 v Ian Charles Irvine, Campbell Irvine (Holdings) Limited (No 2) [2006] EWHC 583 (Ch).
[28] At para 9 of the judgment in *Irvine (No 2)*.
[29] At para 9 of the judgment.

The trial judge did not consider Lord Hoffmann's remarks in *O'Neill v Phillips*. In accepting the arguments of Ian's counsel he said:[30]

> 'A minority shareholding, even one where the extent of the minority is as slight as in this case, is to be valued for what it is, a minority shareholding, unless there is some good reason to attribute to it a pro-rata share of the overall value of the company. Short of a quasi-partnership or some other exceptional circumstance, there is no reason to accord to it a quality which it lacks. CIHL is not a quasi-partnership. There are no exceptional circumstances. The shareholdings must therefore be valued for what they are: less than 50% of CIHL's issued share capital.'

The exact effect of this treatment is vividly illustrated by *Irvine No 3*. Notwithstanding that Ian only held 1 more share than the other shareholders, 50.04% of the company, compared with 49.96% the effect of that additional share was to provide the rest of the family with:[31]

> 'no more control over how Ian, who is in control, can conduct the business –within the tolerances allowed by general company law, than if the [minority] holding had been no more than, say 30%.'

This, together with other factors taken into account by the Court meant that the single share, combined with the absence of equitable considerations resulted in the application of a discount of 30%. This cost the minority holders a little over £1m. Bearing in mind that the case was based on Ian taking out excessive remuneration found by the court to be in the region of £3.8m this would seem to represent something of a windfall to the 'perpetrator' of the unfairness.

Is it appropriate that the significant question of whether a discount is to be allowed is reduced to a simple binary question of is this a quasi partnership or not? Should all the wider circumstances of the case be considered to provide a fair remedy to correct the relevant unfair prejudice?

24.5.4 *Sunrise Radio* – an exception or a better statement of the rule?

This issue of the wrongdoer profiting from their own unfair acts was tackled head on in the non-family business case of *Sunrise Radio*.[32] There unfair prejudice was alleged on a number of grounds, including an improper rights issue at an undervalue which significantly diluted the value of the petitioner's holding.

Although the petitioner argued that she should be treated as a quasi-partner, based on work she had done in the business (whilst retaining a full time job elsewhere), investment of cash and provision of guarantees, the trial judge did not agree. However in a lengthy judgment, which carefully considered relevant authorities, including *Bird Precision Bellows* and *Irvine*, the trial judge, HH Judge Purle QC concluded that the correct position arising from these authorities was that there was no general rule relating to discounts, whether for quasi-partnerships or otherwise. He said:

---

[30] At para 11 of the judgment in *Irvine (No 2)*.
[31] At para 29 of the judgment in *Irvine (No 3)*.
[32] *Sunrise Radio Limited; Geeta Kohli v Dr Avtar Lit, Ravinder Kumar Jain, Surinderpal Singh Lit, Sunrise Radio Limited* [2009] EWHC 2893 (Ch).

'In going on to consider the position relating to quasi-partners generally, Nourse J at first instance [in Bird Precision Bellows] was at pains to make clear that there was no rule of universal application. The converse must be true where there is no quasi-partnership relationship. There can in my judgment be no rule of universal application excluding an undiscounted valuation in such a case either.'[33]

Instead each case needed to be looked at on its merits (whilst attempting to achieve a measure of judicial consistency):

'Clearly, the particular circumstances of any given case must be considered, and previous examples from the decided cases should not be applied mechanistically. On the other hand, regard should also be had, in this context as in others, to the fact that the Court does not sit under a palm tree, and should (without losing sight of the justice of the particular case) seek so far as practicable to achieve a consistency of approach'.[34]

A concern about unjust enrichment, where the majority would benefit from their own misconduct by acquiring shares at a discount applied equally to both quasi-partnerships and non quasi-partnerships:

'Unjust enrichment is not limited to cases of quasi-partnerships. Moreover, the Courts in England do not labour under any difficulty in making the most suitable order to suit the facts of the particular case before it. The Court must do what is fair'.[35]

It will be especially fair to order a non-discounted valuation in cases where:[36]

'... there is reason to suspect or believe that their conduct, or some material part of it, may have been influenced by a desire to buy out or worsen the position (for example, by dilution) of the minority.'

Based on 11 detailed reasons the judge went on to order a buy-out on a full pro-rata basis.

Quite how much impact *Sunrise Radio* will have in family business disputes in the future remains to be seen. Although the case went to the Court of Appeal this was to challenge detailed aspects of the High Court's approach to valuation. There appears to have been no challenge to the basic principle emerging from *Sunrise Radio* that there is no general rule requiring a discounted valuation in a non-quasi partnership case if fairness requires otherwise.

It would probably be going much too far to suggest that we are now back to where Lord Hoffmann started when he suggested that the basic assumption should be that no discount will apply. Certainly that was not suggested by HH Judge Purle QC, the judge in *Sunrise Radio*.

---

[33] At para 297.
[34] At para 299. Purle J mentioned Arden LJ's comments in *Strachan v Wilcock* referred to above that it would be difficult to see circumstances where discounted valuations would not be ordered in a non-quasi partner context but took the view that 'this point was expressly left open' – see para 290 of *Sunrise*. He also considered that the suggestion made in *Irvine* that 'exceptional circumstances' were required to justify a non-discounted valuation in non quasi partner situations 'points to the fact that there is no inflexible rule' about this – see para 292.
[35] At para 305.
[36] At para 305.

It might be that in *Sunrise Radio* will result in non-discounted valuations in certain circumstances such as earlier stage family businesses, which are borderline or previous quasi –partnerships. It may also result in full pro-rata valuations being ordered in cases of more severe misconduct by the respondents, especially appropriation cases where the minority can be seen to have been driven out of the family business by the 'haves'.

There appears to be no suggestion that *Sunrise Radio* should be seen as an outlier or an anomaly.[37] *Sunrise* was cited with approval in a subsequent case where no discount was ordered for a holding of 50% in a deadlocked company.[38] The *Sunrise* approach was taken in a Scottish case[39] where Lord Glennie thought that the 'price fixed by the court … will normally be a fair value without any discount being applied for the fact that the shareholding being purchased is a minority shareholding.' The rationale being '… the party is not a willing seller, putting his shares on the market and accepting the reduction in price, usually associated with a minority shareholding, but is being forced to sell to resolve an impasses which is, at least not wholly, of his making' and that 'this does not depend … on it being established that the Company is a "quasi partnership"'.

There are grounds for cautious optimism that, the previously clear distinction between quasi partnership cases resulting in a full pro-rata valuation and discounted valuations in non-quasi partnerships, found in cases such as *Irvine* and *McCarthy*, will no longer be seen as the prevailing orthodoxy. Instead the courts will be free to return to a more general consideration of fairness in looking at discounts, valuations and remedies generally.

24.6 OTHER VALUATION ISSUES

In addition to the key question of discounts there are a number of other factors relevant to the valuation of a shareholding in a family company for the purpose of shareholder remedies.

24.6.1 Changed circumstances

One of the most difficult issues for family businesses is where circumstances change so that the business moves from classification as a straightforward and traditional quasi partnership into something else.

Again *Irvine* provides a stark example of this. There was no doubt that during his lifetime a quasi-partnership existed between Malcolm and Ian. But in the absence of being able to show that some alternative equitable circumstances had arisen on or after Malcolm's sudden death, to justify the application of the fairness approach, his widow Patricia was condemned to a discounted valuation.

---

[37] Hollington suggests that the case is 'encouraging for minority shareholders' – see *Hollington on Shareholders' Rights* (Sweet and Maxwell, 7th edn, 2013), at para 8.158. But Joffee et al take the *Irvine* approach that the 'starting point' should be a discounted valuation; see *Minority Shareholders: Law Practice and Procedure* (Oxford, 5th edn, 2015).

[38] *Attwood v Maidment* [2011] EWHC 3180 (Ch).

[39] *Robertson v RM Supplies (Inverkeithing) Ltd* [2009] CSOH 23 all at para 35. But Lord Glennie found that he was in fact dealing with a quasi-partnership so his remarks are strictly obiter.

Of course the membership of a family owned business may change in much less tragic circumstances as a result of the natural evolution and succession process. The traditional family business model is for the children of the former 'sibling quasi partners' to evolve into a cousin consortium.

Saul D Harrison presents a prime example. The main hurdle in such cases is to convince the court that, absent some breach of duty on the part of the majority, there are legitimate expectations and circumstances justifying the application of the fairness approach and a finding of unfair prejudice in the first place. This issue is considered in detail in chapter 20. Once that barrier has been crossed the aggrieved minority will then need to rely on *Sunrise Radio* to persuade the court that the circumstances of their particular case make it fair to set aside the usual principles of valuation of a minority holding.

24.6.2 Valuations of gifted shares

The position of gifted shares in a family business may present particular difficulties.

In many cases the minority who are exiting the business will have been gifted their shares. Is it right that they collect a windfall, perhaps from a parent who has built the value of the business, on exit? Alternatively should not those shares, once gifted, carry full economic value? A gift once made cannot be retracted.

The latter approach would be consistent with *Harmer* but perhaps difficult to reconcile with *Re Birds Precision Bellows* where shares were valued on the same discounted basis on which they were acquired.

24.6.3 Adjustments

Having arrived at an appropriate valuation for the claimant's holding, with or without difficulty, it might then be necessary to adjust that basic valuation to reflect the circumstances of the particular case.

Adjustments for prejudice

The unfair prejudice complained of may have adversely affected the value of the company. Usually the courts will seek to make an order to adjust for the effect of this so that the successful minority petitioner is not further prejudiced.

The original *Irvine* judgment made a finding of unfair prejudice based on Ian taking excessive remuneration from the business. In *Irvine No 3*[40] the valuation of the company was increased by a notional cash surplus created by adding back the excessive remuneration unfairly taken by Ian Irvine. With interest this resulted in an increase in value of approximately £3.8m.[41]

---

[40] [2006] EWHC 1875 (Ch).
[41] At para 42 of the judgment in *Irvine v Irvine (No 2)*. The judge nevertheless thought that it provided 'a not unfair result' to apply the 30% minority discount to this notional adjustment.

Similarly in the *Gate of India* the value of the company was adjusted to allow for the judge's findings on undeclared profits,[42] and for unpaid dividends.[43] Also in *McCarthy Surfacing*, whilst the petitioner's shares fell to be valued as ex-quasi partners on a discounted basis, this in turn was to be adjusted for the value of dividends that they should nevertheless have received in their residual ownership capacity.[44] And in *Robertson* losses on future foreign exchange contracts, entered into by the brothers, without authority and outside the usual business of the company were deducted from the value to be paid to them on the compulsory sale of their shares to the remaining shareholder.[45]

Adjustment for petitioner's conduct

The opposite side of the coin is where the petitioner has also behaved badly, perhaps provoking retaliatory unfairly prejudicial conduct on the part of the majority.

This was the case in *Re McCarthy Surfacing Ltd*[46] (discussed in chapter 21). There the judge took the view that whilst a quasi-partnership had previously existed, by bringing an earlier unfounded unfair prejudice claim and by seeking to cause trouble between the company and HMRC, the petitioners had 'destroyed the quasi-partnership by their own wrongful acts'.[47] Accordingly their shares were to be valued on a discounted basis.

24.6.4 Date of valuation

Clearly many years may elapse between the onset of unfairly prejudicial conduct and the time that shares are eventually bought out. The value of the family company may well fluctuate considerably during this period. The usual practice is for the relevant holding to be valued as at the date of the court order requiring the buy-out. However if fairness requires a different date, usually to compensate for the effect of the unfair prejudice, exceptions will be made.

So for example in *Re Cumana Ltd*[48] the Court of Appeal confirmed the trial judge's order that the date of valuation should be the date the petition was presented because otherwise the petitioner would have been further prejudiced by a falling market for technology company shares.

24.6.5 Hardship on the respondent

Similarly *in Re Cumana Ltd* the Court of Appeal refused to intervene to help the majority respondent notwithstanding that it was clear that the effect of ordering a buy-out at a higher price in the falling market would mean that it was unlikely that the respondent could afford to pay the court valuation. Accordingly the respondent would need to sell the overall business (or risk bankruptcy) with the sure and certain knowledge that he would receive proportionately less for his shares than the minority

---

[42] [2008] EWHC 959 (Ch) at paras 110–121.
[43] See paras 99–109.
[44] See paras 99 and 100 of the *McCarthy* judgment [2008] EWHC 2279 (Ch).
[45] See para 64 of the judgment.
[46] [2008] EWHC 2279 (Ch).
[47] See para 97 of the judgment.
[48] [1986] BCLC 430.

shareholder. In effect the timing of the date of valuation provided the prejudiced minority with a premium against the current full pro-rata valuation.

24.6.6 Valuation – conclusion

What is crystal clear is that the difficulties and uncertainties surrounding the final hurdle of valuation, further emphasise the importance of governance processes, and in particular viable exit routes, for the more remote family members.

24.7 OTHER UNFAIR PREJUDICE REMEDIES

As explained above, even though by far the most common order is for buy-out of shares, CA, s 996 gives the court a wide discretion to make order to remedy unfair prejudice. In theory the court should provide the minimum relief necessary to right the unfair prejudice complained of. In practice, in most family businesses the courts will be aware of the risk of further wrongdoing on the part of the majority.[49]

Turning to briefly examine those orders in the context of the family owned business the court also has other powers.

24.7.1 Regulate the conduct of the business in the future – CA, s 996(2)(a)

In rare cases it might be possible to devise bespoke orders which will leave the petitioner's shareholding intact (if that is what they want) but not expose them to the risk of further prejudice. In *Sikorski v Sikorski*[50] the parties had an arrangement (essentially a dissolution agreement of a quasi-partnership) whereby the petitioner was paid an agreed fixed dividend financed by rents received from a hotel managed by the other party. An order was made ordering continued payments of the dividends. In the absence of any need for the petitioner to have any continuing involvement in the business and given the simplicity of the arrangement there was no need to order the buy-out of the petitioner's shares against their wishes.

The facts of in *Re Harmer* are discussed in chapter 21. The court found that the conduct of the father was sufficient to amount to oppression under the stricter test under the previous legislation.[51]

Rather than make an order for the sale and purchase of the father's shares by the sons the High Court judge exercised his general discretion to make a most unusual order. This was to order that the company should engage the services of Mr Harmer senior as a paid philatelic consultant, that he be appointed president of the company for life (but on the basis that this position did not carry with it any duties, rights or powers) and that he should take no part in the decision making of the company from then on. In other words that the father would continue to retain some involvement in and to receive an income from the family business that he had created, but that this role should be largely

---

[49] *Grace v Biagioli* [2005] EWCA Civ 1222.
[50] [2012] EWHC 1613 (Ch).
[51] Section 210 of the Companies Act 1948.

symbolic with the real management and control being exercised by the next generation. The effect of the court order was to ensure that the family business management succession process would be completed.

Clearly there were some extreme factors in *Harmer* including:
- that the sons had the majority of the beneficial interest in the company;
- the age and infirmity (including deafness) of Mr Harmer senior, perhaps verging on incapacity;
- his extreme behaviour;
- that the sons were supported in their action by senior non-family management.

So, whereas in the majority of cases the status quo will dictate that those controlling the business will stay and those in the minority whose rights have been prejudiced will leave, in the extreme and unusual circumstances of *Harmer* it could be argued strongly that the best interests of the business were dictated by the departure of the founder of the family business.

In less extreme circumstances, with the senior generation less advanced in age or perhaps if the management differences appear to be less clear-cut, the next generation family members may have little alternative than to be bought out of the family business in which they have invested a proportion of their career.

It is therefore suggested that *Harmer* should be seen as a relatively rare case, decided on its own, fairly unique facts.[52]

Whereas purchase of shares might be a primary remedy and the key part of a final order, the court may nevertheless use its powers under CA, s 996(2)(a) to regulate the affairs of the company to make supplemental or interim orders, for example limiting remuneration of the majority shareholders until the minority have been bought out.

24.7.2   Restraining orders or positive action – CA, s 996(2)(b)

In circumstances where unfair prejudice consists of specific acts or omissions the court can make orders preventing or requiring acts or omissions 'complained of'. For example preventing wrongful rights issues as in *Clemens v Clemens*.

24.7.3   Authorising derivative proceedings – CA, s 996(2)(c)

In breach of duty cases it might be more appropriate to help the minority shareholders take action in the name of the company against the controlling directors, rather than allow the conduct of the majority to effectively force the minority out of the company. The court has power to authorise a derivative action. These are considered in more detail in chapter 23.

24.7.4   Restrictions on alteration of articles – CA, s 996(2)(d)

The restriction can be either general or specific.

---

[52] In contrast see *Grace v Biagioli* [2005] EWCA Civ 1222 and the comments at para 75.

24.7.5 Interim orders

The court has discretion to make interim or temporary orders, which will be exercised, for example to preserve the status quo in a family business, until a full hearing can be arranged.

24.8 OFFERS TO PURCHASE

24.8.1 Overview

The concept of making a reasonable offer to buy-out an aggrieved minority is central to the management of shareholder disputes. It is directly relevant to both unfair prejudice applications under CA, s 994 and applications for just and equitable winding up under IA, s 122(10)(g). It is also likely to be indirectly relevant to the conduct of derivative claims.

As has been illustrated above unfair prejudice in exclusion cases consists not of exclusion in and of itself but exclusion without an offer to purchase the shares held by the minority.

The logic of this is explained fully in the *Gippeswyck* case, where the judge concluded that a buy-out order of the father's minority holding was, as will usually be the case, the most appropriate order. This was because the father:[53]

> '... has no effective way of stopping that unfair treatment at the moment because he is a minority shareholder and locked into the company. If he is given a fair value for his shares that unfairness then ceases. He ceases to be a shareholder and he gets relief in respect of his complaints.'

The principle is also relevant to breach of duty cases such as *Irvine*. Although a reasonable buy-out offer cannot expunge the original breach of duty, by offering the aggrieved minority what they would receive by going to court, the need for them to do so has evaporated. If the minority still wish to proceed their application will then be struck out as an abuse of process.

It will only be in exceptional cases that a claimant is confident that they will be able to both establish unfair prejudice and, crucially and wholly exceptionally that the court will be persuaded to grant an alternative remedy to buy out of the majority will it be safe for a petitioner to refuse a suitable offer of purchase.

Making a suitable offer to purchase is usually a good defence to an unfair prejudice petition. In practice making such an offer, even in situations where the underlying unfair prejudice is disputed or marginal is likely to be a sensible move on the part of the majority. The costs of continuing and defending minority shareholder litigation are likely to be substantial. An application for striking out can be made at a relatively early stage in the litigation, when costs, whilst still perhaps significant, will be a fraction of those incurred at a full trial.

---

[53] At pp 442–443.

At the very least making a reasonable offer to buy out the minority at an early stage of proceedings should provide a considerable degree of protection to the majority, both in terms of protection against orders to contribute to the costs of the minority and also to recover a proportion of their own costs. Particular issues relating to costs in shareholder disputes are discussed in **24.9** below. However a detailed consideration of litigation procedure and tactics and in particular how to frame Part 36 or other offers during the course of proceedings are beyond the scope of this book.

Under the procedure set out in IA, s 125(2) the court must refuse a winding up order if they come to the view that an alternative remedy exists and the applicant is unreasonably refusing to pursue that remedy. Again the principal alternative remedy is likely to be an unfair prejudice action. Clearly the position of those opposing a just and equitable winding up will be significantly improved if not only can they point to unfair prejudice as an alternative remedy but also a reasonable offer to buy out the aggrieved minority, in effect conceding that the alternative unfair prejudice remedy should be granted.

What is therefore highly relevant is the guidance given by courts as to what will and what will not be seen as a reasonable offer to buy out the minority.

24.8.2 O'Neill v Phillips

The starting point in looking at what is a reasonable offer is the leading case of *O'Neill v Phillips*. Mr O'Neill's claim for unfair prejudice was rejected by the House of Lords. But Lord Hoffmann[54] nevertheless took the opportunity to spell out his views on what a reasonable offer to buy out the majority would look like. Strictly, whilst highly persuasive, Lord Hoffmann's remarks are therefore obiter dicta. He identified various elements, each of which are examined in more detail below. These may be summarised as follows:

- an offer at fair value;
- determined by a competent third party;
- acting as an expert;
- on the basis of proper information;
- with a proper consideration of costs.

Looking at each of these elements in turn.

24.8.3 Offer at fair value

An offer

Clearly something recognisable as an offer needs to be made to the minority shareholder.

In the *Harding* just and equitable winding up case[55] Elizabeth made a proposal that the price for her sisters' shares should be set with reference to what an unidentified third party would pay to buy part of the farm in a deal brokered by her. She sought her sister's

---

[54] [1999] 1 WLR 1092 at p 1107.
[55] [2014] EWHC 247 (Ch).

'definite and irrevocable agreement to this process'. The courts dismissed this approach as 'wholly unrealistic'. The judge in that case thought that the petitioners:[56]

> 'did not act unreasonably in insisting that a definite price for the shares should be put on the table before they are expected to commit to a sale.'

That does not mean to say that all elements of the offer need to be fully fleshed out. Frequently the price of the shares cannot be agreed between the parties. The majority may themselves have no clear idea of the value of the family business. They will not want to overpay. Often the price will need to be established by an independent expert (see below). On other occasions the majority will wish to frame alternative offers eg £X or a value to be determined.[57] But some clear and fair mechanism is required. The primary difficulty in *Harding* was that perception that the process and thereby the price were open to manipulation. Accordingly the winding up order was made.

Discounts

A key question will be whether an offer should be on the basis of a full pro-rata valuation or at a discount to reflect the fact of a minority holding.

The approach of the courts to discounts for minority holdings is discussed in detail in 24.5 above. The position is not at all straightforward. This places both parties and, in particular the petitioning minority in a difficult position in judging what is, or is not a reasonable offer so far as discounts are concerned.

We have highlighted a single authority, *Sunrise Radio*, where a non-discounted basis of valuation has been applied in a non-quasi partnership case. There is also the guidance of Lord Hoffmann in *O'Neill*. Against this there is *Irvine*[58] and the other authorities mentioned in that case. In the absence of further reported authorities following the lead in *Sunrise Radio*, or, even better, approval of that approach in an appellate court or unless they were confident that the courts would accept that a quasi-partnership existed, it would take a brave petitioner to reject an offer for purchase on a discounted basis, notwithstanding the feeling of injustice that may leave.

Equally given the fairly liberal interpretation of the concept of quasi partnership in cases such as *Harding* and *Fisher v Cadman* the majority face the risk that the courts could follow the spirit of *Ebrahimi* a little more closely and accept that equitable considerations apply in a broader range of family business situations. Accordingly the majority may well be advised to consider making an offer on a non-discounted basis, particularly in situations where the conduct of the majority is more open to question.

For example in *Wyatt v Frank Wyatt & Son Ltd*[59] the majority framed their offer expressly on a non-discounted basis notwithstanding that the minority petitioner had never been involved as a director or otherwise and therefore the matter was a clear breach of duty case rather than one involving exclusion from a quasi-partnership.[60]

---

[56] See para 57 of the judgment
[57] For example the *Gippeswyck* case: *Re a Company (No 00836 of 1995)* [1996] BB 432 at pp 439–40.
[58] Where the judge was clear that non-quasi partnership cases should result in a discounted valuation.
[59] [2003] EWHC 520 (Ch).
[60] See para 17 of the judgment.

Adjustments for prejudice

On the other hand, and as discussed in paragraph 6.3 above, it is fairly clear from the authorities that a reasonable offer will require an adjustment or add back to be made to compensate the minority for the effect of the unfair treatment that gave rise to the petition in the first place. To do otherwise would be to allow the majority, in some circumstances to benefit from their own wrongdoing.

Accordingly, in the *Gippeswyck* case, the son framed an offer allowing the valuers to adjust their valuation for any depletion of net assets caused by dealings found (by the expert) to have been unfairly prejudicial.[61]

Proceedable offer

An offer will not be reasonable if it is not proceedable, whether for lack of financial backing or otherwise.

West v Blatchet[62] concerned a 50:50 non-family business quasi partnership. Each of the shareholders cross petitioning and both made offers to buy the other out. One offer was clearly financially sound and backed by that party's own resources. This offer was seen to be reasonable. The other offer relied on uncertain third party backing and was held to be unreasonable.

24.8.4 Expert determination

The second component of a reasonable offer identified by Lord Hoffmann is that, if the parties cannot agree the share value, there should be a mechanism for this to be determined by a competent expert. More often than not this will be a chartered accountant. The usual formula adopted is to appoint an accountant agreed by the parties or in default nominated by the President of the Institute of Chartered Accountants. But on occasions, particularly by agreement between the parties, the formula chosen may be more elaborate, for example by specifying that the expert should have the requisite experience in valuing private businesses in the relevant industry.

It therefore follows that if the valuer suggested by the party making an offer cannot be shown to be independent that offer may not be seen as reasonable. In *Re Boswell and Co (Steels) Ltd*[63] the company's accountants, were seen to be sufficiently close to the majority so as to make it reasonable for the minority to question their independence.

On occasions the role of the expert will need to go beyond pure accounting matters, for example, to include property valuations. In which case an offer will need to include a mechanism to allow surveyors or valuer's advice to be included.

On other occasions legal issues will affect the valuation, in particular relevant adjustments to cater for the effect of unfair prejudice. In the *Gippeswyk* case the sons were not prepared to accept that they had unfairly prejudiced their father but their offer

---

[61] See p 440 of the judgment. The relationship between experts, and the court so far as matters of law are concerned are explored in 24.8.4 below.
[62] [2000] 1 BCLC 795.
[63] [1988] 5 BCC 145.

contemplated that this could be the case. Accordingly the sons' offer allowed the expert to take independent legal advice and then to adjust his valuation for any dealings in assets which 'the independent accountant considers both (i) have been unfairly prejudicial ... and (ii) ... have caused a material reduction in the net asset value'.[64]

Mr Thompson senior objected to this, arguing that this required the expert to make legal findings, which should be left to the courts. According to the judge this amounted to an argument that Mr Thompson senior was 'entitled to his day or week or month in court'.[65] This was firmly rejected by the court.

There are limits to the extent that the courts will find it reasonable to delegate issues of legal substance to a valuation expert. In *Gippeswyk* the adjustments for the alleged unfair prejudice appeared relatively immaterial to the overall value. Where there is a genuine dispute, which goes to the root of the unfair prejudice claim, a buy-out offer which ignores that issue is unlikely to be reasonable. In *Re a Company (No 001363 of 1988)*[66] the petitioner's claim was based on an improper share allotment. An offer based on the existing undisputed holding was plainly unreasonable.

In practice the parties will be expected to accept the risk of some degree of imprecision in valuation. A slightly rough and ready but cost effective valuation achieved outside the court will be seen as preferable to the expense achieved by a valuation by the courts involving detailed reports and expert evidence. As explained by Judge Weeks QC in the *Gippeswyck* case:[67]

> 'Of course, there is always a risk that an expert might reach a different valuation from the valuation achieved by a court hearing experts on both sides, but that is a risk which is inherent in the procedure itself and can never be eliminated. In my judgment the respondents have done their best to minimise any risk which the petitioner might undergo in accepting this offer.'

Lord Hoffmann also suggested that a reasonable offer would include some mechanism to deal with the expert's costs. The treatment of the parties' own costs in relation to framing a reasonable offer is dealt with in **24.8.7** below. In his view:[68]

> 'One would ordinarily expect the costs of the expert to be shared but he should have the power to decide that they should be borne in some different way.'

The formula adopted in the *Gippeswyck* case gave the expert a full discretion as to who should pick up his costs and was as follows:[69]

> 'That the costs of the independent accountant will be borne by either or both of our clients as the independent accountant shall think fit and if both in such proportions as the independent accountant shall think fit.'

---

[64] At p 440 of the judgment.
[65] At p 441.
[66] [1989] BCLC 57.
[67] At p 442.
[68] *O'Neill v Phillips* at p 1107.
[69] At p 441.

The hidden message is that the expert has discretion to penalise a party behaving unreasonably and thereby causing costs to increase. This is sometimes articulated expressly in a settlement offer or agreement.

24.8.5 Basis of expert's appointment

In *O'Neill v Phillips* Lord Hoffmann also gave some thought to the technical basis of the expert's appointment, suggesting that this should be 'to have the value determined by the expert as an expert'. In particular there is no requirement for a reasonable offer to include full arbitration machinery, or for the expert to be obliged to give reasons for his decision, (thereby opening up the potential for challenge and further costs). Emphasising the theme of pragmatism over precision Lord Hoffmann explained that:[70]

> 'The objective should be economy and expedition, even if this carries the possibility of a rough edge for one side or the other (and both parties in this respect take the same risk) compared with a more elaborate procedure.'

Lord Hoffmann also pointed out that his approach is in accordance with the recommendations of the Law Commission.[71]

Interestingly the appointment in the *Gippeswyck* case whilst confirming that the independent accountant would be 'acting as an expert' the offer required him to make a 'reasoned determination'.

24.8.6 Proper information

One of the main difficulties for minority shareholders and their advisors is that the majority shareholders, the insiders, will often have better information about the finances and prospects of the family business concerned, and, at times, something approaching a monopoly of information. Indeed this information asymmetry may have been a factor in the dispute itself. In these circumstances it is difficult for the minority to properly assess any firm offer put forward by the majority or to be satisfied that all relevant information has been made available to the expert to make an independent assessment of value.

Lord Hoffmann recognised this and confirmed that a reasonable offer would provide for what he termed 'equality of arms between the parties'. This has two elements. First access to relevant information and secondly, the right to present relevant information to the expert by making either written or, more unusually, oral submissions.

Again this was recognised in the *Gippeswyck case* with the offer including confirmation that those acting on behalf of Mr Thompson senior:[72]

> 'will be given by the company full access to and right to inspect and take copies of all the books records and documents in the company's possession custody or power for the purpose of making such written representations to the independent accountant.'

---

[70] At p 1107.
[71] See draft Regulation 119: Exit Right recommended by the Law Commission: Appendix C to the report at p 133.
[72] See p 440 of the judgment.

In practice it may be extremely difficult to achieve genuine equality of information for the minority, particularly where they have no recent day-to-day role in the family business. It may be even harder to convince the minority that all relevant information has been disclosed and that the majority are not hiding something. The court will have to find a balance between on the one hand the efficient resolution of disputes and, on the other hand making sure that Lord Hoffmann's 'equality of arms' has been achieved.

Wyatt v Frank Wyatt and Son Ltd[73] concerned a second-generation property development company. Following the death of Mr Wyatt senior, claims were made against the sons involved in the business by those who were not. These claims were based on breaches of duty consisting of payment of improper bonuses and transfers of properties at an undervalue. The case contains a strong suggestion that information had to be prised out of the 'haves' over the course of 3 years of litigation. The offer provided for the expert to have full access to the books and records of the company and also for various adjustments to be made to compensate for the alleged breaches of duty. The court regarded the information that had been provided to date as 'partial and limited'[74] and accordingly refused to strike out the unfair prejudice petition until full discovery and inspection, one of the most expensive stages in litigation had taken place.

Clearly many if not most family business disputes are played out against a backdrop of mistrust created by at least inadequate communication and in some cases deliberate withholding of information. It is therefore incumbent on the majority making a purchase offer to do their utmost to dispel this mistrust if that offer is to be seen as reasonable by both the minority and the courts.

24.8.7 Costs

Lord Hoffmann's analysis of the components of a reasonable offer also dealt with the question of costs. Given that costs are likely to be a key consideration in any family business shareholder litigation this topic is considered separately in **24.9** below.

Of course the usual rule in English litigation is that costs follow the event so accordingly any successful settlement offer would usually need to include a costs component. According to Lord Hoffmann this is not invariably the case in unfair prejudice claims. On the basis that, at least for exclusion cases, unfairness is seen to consist not of exclusion alone but exclusion without making a reasonable offer to buy out the minority.

There will be a period between when the breakdown of relationships has been recognised, the position of the minority fully understood and the majority are in a position to formulate and finance a buy-out offer. A buy-out offer made during this period may nevertheless be reasonable even if it does not include an offer to pay the costs of the minority because:[75]

> 'the majority shareholder should be given a reasonable opportunity to make an offer (which may include time to explore the question of how to raise finance) before he becomes obliged

---

[73] [2003] EWHC 520 (Ch).
[74] At para 44 of the judgment.
[75] *O'Neill v Phillips*.

to pay costs ... The mere fact that the petitioner has presented his petition before the offer does not mean that the respondent must offer to pay the costs if he was not given a reasonable time.'

In practice offers to buy out are often made after many years of protracted litigation accompanied by mutual recriminations and a denial that the minority is entitled to any form of remedy. In *O'Neill v Phillips* the parties had been in dispute for 3 years. In such these circumstances the costs of the minority will need to be paid.

Of course this does not mean that a petitioner can proceed with a weak claim with impunity. The usual costs penalties for losing litigants will apply. The exercise by the court of its case management powers may weed out a weak claim.

O'Neill v Phillips of course dealt with an (unsuccessful) exclusion case. Logically in cases based on breach of duty the unfairness will have set in at the time of breach so a reasonable offer must always include a costs component.

24.8.8 Conclusion

The basic point remains that any majority shareholder facing an unfair prejudice claim (or any other form of minority shareholder action) ought to seriously and critically examine the root cause of that action. If there is any element of exclusion or breach of duty on their part they would be well advised to ignore the almost inevitable family back story and to frame a sensible settlement offer in the form of a buy-out proposal.

From a legal perspective it will only be in the clearest of cases that claims can safely be resisted without a buy-out or other settlement offer or for that offer not to recognise the contentious issues of pro-rata valuations, access to information and costs contributions. From a family perspective the costs of not making such an offer is incalculable.

24.9 COSTS

24.9.1 Overview

The cost to family relationships in pursuing an unfair prejudice application will clearly be severe, even catastrophic. Not just to the actual parties to the litigation, but to the wider family, who will be forced to take sides. The litigation is likely to cast a shadow over the family for years to come.

The legal and other professional costs involved will also be hugely a significant factor for the business family, both because of the sheer scale of the costs in their own right and also because of the impact of the costs as an aggravating factor in deteriorating family relationships.

24.9.2 Costs – the basics

By the time the *Gippeswyck* case got to court the combined costs of the Thompson family in that case and related litigation were as much as £2m. No doubt a considerable part of those costs were attributable to the family animosity identified by the judge.

Recent procedural reforms and especially active case management by the courts have made inroads in the 'mountains of costly nonsense' identified by Dickens in *Bleak House*.

In particular CPR, r 1.1(2)(c)(i) requires the court to adopt an approach to a case that is proportionate to the amount at stake. Nevertheless pursuing litigation between family members is likely to remain a risky and costly exercise, one to be pursued only as a last resort.

The approach taken to costs and the wider tactics and strategy of litigation are well beyond the scope of this book. But in the most general terms a successful party would expect to recover a significant contribution (in the most general terms about 70%) towards, but by no means all of their overall costs.[76] The previous approach to awarding costs tended towards a 'winner takes all' approach so that, except in the rarest of cases, almost all of the costs awarded followed the eventual outcome of the case. Under modern case management it is much more likely that costs awards will be made in stages so that a litigant although ultimately successful but whose approach to a particular stage of the litigation had been poor may be penalised and have to pay the other side's costs relating to that stage.

In rare cases where the court strongly disapprove of the conduct of a party either in relation to a case generally, or a particular aspect of it, costs will be awarded on an indemnity basis. So that instead of making a substantial contribution to costs on a 'party and party basis' the losing party will be ordered to pay all of their opponents costs for the relevant stage of the action. For example in *Saul D Harrison* the petitioner was ordered to pay the costs of the hearing itself on an indemnity basis, but to contribute to the respondents' costs up until trial on a party and party basis. This is of course in addition to paying her own costs.[77]

For indemnity costs to be ordered the court must be satisfied that the conduct of the paying party was out of the norm or unreasonable to a high degree (for example the refusal of a reasonable settlement offer). This may well have been the basis of the order in *Saul D Harrison*. The facts of *Burry & Knight*,[78] referred to in chapter 20, above show that this can be a fairly hard test to satisfy.

Just about the most significant tactical consideration in any litigation is the consideration of whether and when to make or accept settlement offers and if so on what terms. These offers will usually be structured either as CPR Part 36 Offers or 'Calderbank' offers.[79] The basic underlying idea will be that the defendant will be well insulated against adverse costs orders if the claimant fails to beat the offer at trial and should also recover a substantial proportion of the defendant's own costs from the date of the offer. Conversely absent an offer and assuming that the claimant's case does not fail completely at trial their risks of continuing the litigation are substantially reduced.

---

[76] The introduction of active case management and, in particular, active costs budgeting has considerably changed the position. A successful party that has managed to adhere to a court approved costs budget can now expect to be awarded the vast majority or, in some cases, all of their costs.
[77] See note at p 486 of the case report.
[78] [2104] EWCA Civ 604.
[79] *Calderbank v Calderbank* [1976] Fam 93.

As explained above in many cases relating to family business shareholder disputes framing a reasonable settlement offer by the defendants has often led to the claimant's case being struck out by the courts as an abuse of process.

The following sub-paragraphs deal with other particular aspects of costs in relation to the litigation of shareholder disputes.

24.9.3 The family company and costs

Obviously any litigation involving the shareholders of a family company deeply affects that company and its stakeholders. As a matter of legal technicality the company will also be a party to each of three main types of shareholder litigation referred to above, namely unfair prejudice proceedings, just and equitable winding up and derivative claims. However the involvement of the company and the treatment of the costs incurred by the company is likely to be different depending on the chosen remedy.

Company costs in unfair prejudice proceedings

The family company will be a party to any unfair prejudice proceedings. However this is a purely procedural matter as required by the Companies (Unfair Prejudice Applications) Proceedings Rules.[80] Whilst the family company may be the battleground over which the dispute is fought it is not a combatant. If necessary the company should be separately represented by solicitors independent from the family members in dispute. In practice the role of the family company in such proceedings will often be purely nominal.

The exception to this is if extensive disclosure of information held by the company is required, including for valuation purposes, or if there is a dispute about whether information sought by the outsiders is commercially confidential.

The real parties to the dispute are, of course, the family members alleging unfair prejudice and those family members causing or supporting that treatment. It follows that the major costs in any unfair prejudice proceedings are for the account of the real parties to the litigation, not the company.[81]

Of course one of the things that the majority 'haves' will have control over is the company cheque-book. Accordingly one of the first tactical moves on the part of a claimant ought to be to seek written assurances that the company will not be picking up the costs of the majority. If appropriate assurances are not forthcoming the court should grant an injunction preventing the majority from using company funds to defend the claim against them.[82] The court may even order that the company indemnifies the petitioner for the costs incurred in policing the interests of the company in this way.[83]

---

[80] SI 2009/2469.
[81] *Re Kenyon Swansea Ltd* [1987] BCLC 514.
[82] *Re Milgate Developments Ltd* [1993] BCLC 291; *Re a Company (No 004502 of 1988)* [1988] BCLC 701.
[83] *Clark v Cutland* [2003] EWHC 810, [2004] WLR 783.

Costs and just and equitable winding up

The position here is very similar to that in unfair prejudice proceedings. In particular a contested just and equitable winding up petition will usually be seen as a dispute between shareholders. Accordingly it will rarely be appropriate for the company to pay the costs involved.

It might be necessary for the minority shareholder pursuing a just and equitable winding up to guarantee the costs of the liquidator. This will particularly be the case if the liquidator is to take litigation against the directors or others as part of the winding up process.

Company costs in derivative claims

The opposite logic applies to derivative claims. There the theory is that the company is the wronged party. The minority shareholder is simply stepping in to police the interests of the family company in the absence of a proper intention on the part of the board to do so. Logically the company should pick up any costs incurred.

Under the CPR, r 19.9E the court has the discretion to make an order (known as a pre-emptive costs order or a *Wallersteiner* order[84]) requiring the company to pay the derivative claimant's costs. This order can be made irrespective of the outcome of the eventual proceedings.

However pre-emptive costs orders are not made as a matter of course. The court will consider all the relevant circumstances. If the litigation has the look and feel of a dispute between shareholders rather than a legitimate attempt to protect the company it would be unfair for a successful defendant to in effect be required to pay a proportion of the overall costs as a result of their shareholding in the company.

In addition to finding five reasons why permission to continue the proposed derivative claim should be refused in *Singh Contractors* the High Court judge was quite clear that even if permission had been given to continue no costs indemnity would have been forthcoming in favour of the claimant. The judge said that he:[85]

> '... would, in any event, have refused any indemnity out of the company's assets in advance of the final disposal of the derivative claim ... [because] ... it would be quite wrong for any indemnity to be given out of the company's assets in respect of the costs of what is, essentially, a personal dispute between two individual shareholders and directors.'

Cost indemnities for directors– CA, ss 232-234

Any attempt by directors to obtain an indemnity from the company for any costs they incur personally in relation breach of duty proceedings will be void under CA, s 232.

The directors defending a derivative claim would usually look to recover the majority of their costs directly from the company if a pre-emptive costs order had been made, or from the family member initiating those proceedings in the absence of such an order. But

---

[84] Following the decision in *Wallersteiner v Moir (No 2)* [1975] QB 373.
[85] *Sukhpaul Singh v Satpaul Singh, Singh Brothers Contractors (North West) Limited* [2013] EWHC 2138 (Ch) at para 48 of the judgment.

any residual irrecoverable costs, whether to cover the shortfall against any costs ordered by the court or because of difficulties in enforcing against the unsuccessful family member could be indemnified by the company.

In *Branch v Bagley*[86] it was confirmed that indemnities could extend to the costs incurred by a director in their dual capacity as a shareholder in successfully defending unfair prejudice proceedings based on breach of duty.

Directors' and officers' insurance – 'D&O'

However directors' and officers' insurance policies are now expressly permitted under CA, s 233. A suitably broad policy may cover the directors for most breach of duty claims.

An agreement by the company to retrospectively agree to indemnify a director against civil proceedings based on breach of duty and successfully defended by that director should be permissible as within the definition of a 'qualifying third party indemnity provision' within the meaning of CA, s 234(1).

24.10 CONCLUSION

One of the biggest challenges for family business members involved in a dispute is to separate out, so far as is humanly possible the emotional and legal elements of their case. There will inevitably be a huge overlap between these. Questions such as 'can they do this?', 'this must be wrong?' have both a legal and a behavioural or moral context.

But the legal issues go way beyond the narrow question of legal merits. A family member may well have been badly treated both against most moral scales and within the scope of, for example the unfair prejudice remedy. However pursuing such a case against the background of a reasonable offer to buy out the aggrieved minority could have serious repercussion. These could well include significant adverse costs orders. The family member concerned may well approach the dispute professing that in doing so 'they are concerned with the principle of the matter, not the money'. However it is difficult to see what principle is being served by an unfocused pursuit of an illusory concept of justice. Particularly if that pursuit results in a costs award in favour of the 'other side'.

It must be a primary duty for the advisors concerned not to lose sight of these wider elements. There is a corresponding duty on the part of the family business member, owed both to themselves and to the wider business family, to listen carefully to any resulting advice.

---

[86] [2004] EWHC 426 (Ch).

24.11 FURTHER READING FOR PART E

- A Alcock (ed), *Gore Browne on Companies* (Jordan Publishing Looseleaf/Online). A key legal practitioner work. Regularly updated and maintained. Available in hard copy and on-line versions. Thorough explanation of the background to this topic.
- R Hollington QC *Hollington on Shareholders' Remedies* (Sweet and Maxwell, 7th edn, 2013). Leading legal practitioner text-book often referred to in court. Contains a detailed explanation of the underlying legal principles and deals extensively with the case-law of both English and other common law jurisdictions.
- Joffe, Drake Richardson, Lightman and Collingwood *Minority Shareholders: Law Practice and Procedure* (Oxford University Press, 2015). An up to date and comprehensive treatment of the remedies available to minority shareholders as well as the relevant substantive law and practice.
- A Marsden *Shareholder Protection from Unfairly Prejudicial Conduct Case and Statute Citator 2016* (Commercial Chambers, Bristol). An extremely useful source of references to key unfair prejudice cases, compiled and regularly updated by a barrister specialising almost exclusively in shareholder remedy cases involving family owned and other private companies. The citator is available for download at www.commercialchambers.org.

PART F

THE FAMILY BUSINESS ADVISOR

CHAPTER 25

PROCESS CONSULTING AND THE ROLE OF THE FAMILY BUSINESS CONSULTANT

25.1 INTRODUCTION

Much of this book has been devoted to examining why family businesses are a special category of organisation and distinct from their non-family counterparts. In essence this boils down to the complexities stemming from the different family, business and ownership systems in operation in a family business: 'you can't take the family out of the business'.

The final part of this book looks at the implications of this for the professional advisory community and the responses and approaches that have been developed as a result over the last 30 years or so. The reason why this period has been chosen is that it roughly coincides with the birth of, what we have termed, the family business movement, when a group of academics and professionals working in the family business field first began to seriously consider the family owned business in this way.[1] This chapter largely concentrates on the results of that work, the application of process consulting to the family business field and the growth of a new category of professionals, family business consultants.

This chapter also looks in detail at family business consultancy and, in particular how it differs from but relates to other, more traditional and established professional disciplines such as accountancy and the law.

The following and final chapter of the book concentrates on the implications of this body of thinking for those in traditional advisory professions, when advising their family business clients.

25.2 THE THREE-CIRCLE MODEL AND THE FAMILY BUSINESS ADVISOR

The key model for understanding the family owned business, the three-circle model, is explained in detail in chapter 3 (Tools Models and Theories) and is referred to throughout this book. Although the model is primarily intended to show the relative positions of stakeholders within the family business system, Jane Hilburt-Davis and W Gibb Dyer suggest that the model can be borrowed to show the corresponding focus of advisors to the family business.[2]

---

[1] An overview of some of the organisations forming part of the family business movement is included as Appendix 2.
[2] Jane Hilburt-Davis and W Gibb Dyer *Consulting to Family Businesses* (Jossey Bass, 2003) at p 15.

Figure 25.1: Family business advisors and the three-circle model

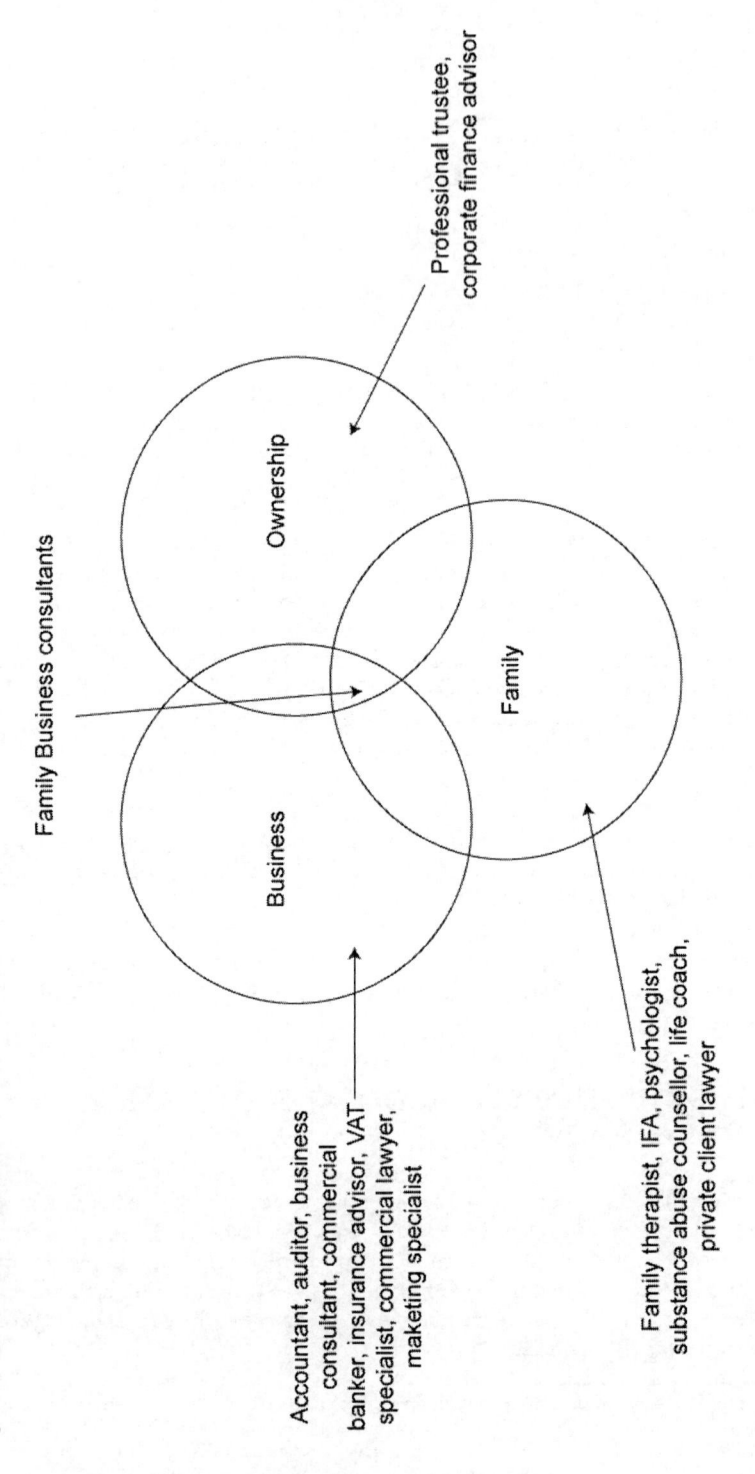

Professional trustee, corporate finance advisor

Family Business consultants

Ownership

Family

Business

Accountant, auditor, business consultant, commercial banker, insurance advisor, VAT specialist, commercial lawyer, maketing specialist

Family therapist, IFA, psychologist, substance abuse counsellor, life coach, private client lawyer

In some cases the positioning on the model is obvious.

The remit of a marketing consultant is clearly within the business arena. The same applies to a commercial lawyer, taking instructions on a distribution agreement. But there is an additional challenge, to be aware of the wider context of the family system and the opportunities or threats that might bring. Similarly a family therapist or life coach working with an individual family member will be primarily concerned with their client's position in the family system, although this might be heavily affected by the other systems.

The position of other professionals is more complex and debatable. For example, a private client lawyer, taking instructions on a will. Their contractual client will be an individual family member. If the assets of the family member concerned include shares in the family firm does this mean that the true position of the lawyer concerned ought more accurately to be shown as in the intersection between the family and ownership systems? The outcome of those instructions will inevitably have implications to the operation of the family business itself. So there is an argument for suggesting that the private client lawyer is acting at the centre of the model. At the very least the lawyer needs to be aware of the implications of their work for the other systems comprised within the family firm.

Ultimately it does not matter over much to determine the precise position any given advisor or piece of family business advice occupies within this adaptation of the three-circle model. In using the model for its primary purpose, to illustrate the possible positions and perspectives of the stakeholders directly involved in the family business system, questions can arise, for example, about the positions of in-laws or remote family members that might have a nominal position on the board. Using the model for this secondary purpose, of analysing the source of and influences on the instructions received by a professional advisor, also helps to illustrate the complexity of the family business situation and allows the advisor to frame their approach accordingly.

It will be noted that Hilburt-Davis and Dyer have positioned the family business consultant as working at the centre of the model, within the area of overlap between all three systems. This must be correct. Whether family business consultants are unique in doing so, as the authors suggest,[3] is perhaps more debatable.

25.3 FAMILY BUSINESS CONSULTANCY

We have used the term 'family business consultant' on various occasions throughout this book and have argued that they have a key role to play in achieving good outcomes for family business clients. So what exactly is a family business consultant?

The Family Firm Institute (FFI) offer a partial and non-exhaustive definition in the glossary to their introductory book on the *Family Enterprise*,[4] suggesting that the term 'consultant':

> 'includes family business consultants and family wealth consultants who tend to have a balanced process/content focus and help integrate the plans and interactions of the family,

---

[3] See p 15.
[4] *Family Enterprise: Understanding Families in Business and Families of Wealth* (The Family Firm Institute, Wiley, 2014) at p 148.

ownership and management groups as well as the individuals within each group; typically they no longer practice in their profession of origin.'

Several points emerge from this.

First the difficulties that stem from using generic umbrella terms like 'consultancy'. Hilburt-Davis and Gibbs use the term widely to embrace all professionals providing advice to family owned businesses. Many general business consultants, operating wholly or mainly within the business domain and acting primarily for family firms, might see themselves as family business consultants.

In practice, although the term 'family business consultant' is meant to be more precise and focused, it is in fact difficult to define precisely. The process of family business consultancy is increasingly called 'facilitation' (and the individual carrying it out, a facilitator). Partly this is to distinguish the specialist family business consultant, skilled and trained in family dynamics and able to understand the complex inter-relationship between, not only the business and family systems, but also between family members themselves.

Partly this is to emphasise that the role of the family business consultant is not to offer a solution based on external expertise. Rather the role is to help or facilitate the business family to develop their own solution, based on a shared common view of what is best for their own unique family business, which emerges through the consultancy process. Although the facilitator or family business consultant will bring in expertise and knowledge of approaches taken by other family businesses, this will be as a background reference point and not as a prescriptive solution to be applied in the subject case.

So the second distinguishing feature is the use of process consulting skills (explained below), as their primary professional tool, as opposed to content or expert skills. Interestingly the FFI definition positions family business consultants alongside family wealth advisors (IFA's) in this regard, as does Figure 25.3 below. Similarly the FFI make a distinction between a family business advisor, operating in their core profession of origin and family enterprise consultants working in the centre of the three-circle model.[5]

The third and perhaps defining feature of a family business consultant is that they will usually have left their profession of origin behind and hold themselves out to the world as practising as family business consultants.

Family business consultants come from a wide variety of relevant professions, each inevitably contributing different perspectives and taking slightly different approaches to family business consultancy assignments. Family business consultants include organisational development specialists, accountants and lawyers. They also include psychologists and family therapists. However it is important to emphasise that there is a distinction between family business consultancy and family therapy, although Gersick *et al* warn that:[6]

> 'defining the boundary between family focused business consulting and family therapy is one of the most difficult and important challenges of this work.'

---

[5] Ibid at p 87.
[6] Gersick, Davis, Hampton & Lansberg *Generation to Generation: Life cycles of a family business* (Harvard Business School Press, 1997) at p 269.

On occasions consultants will work in pairs or teams, drawn from different professions of origin, to provide their family business clients with the most rounded perspective possible.[7]

Figure 25.2: The family business advisor development model

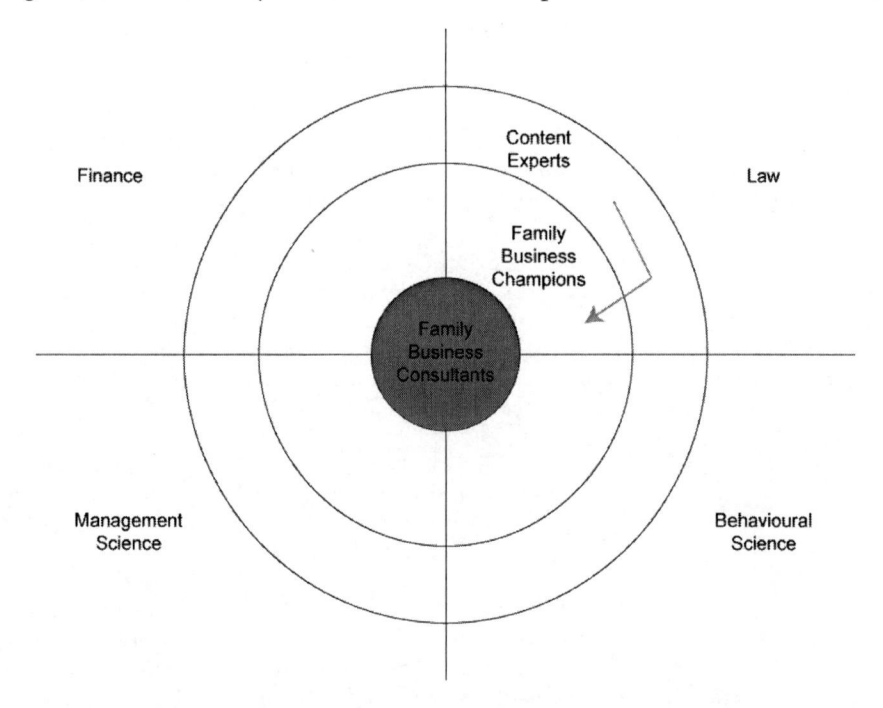

[Figure: concentric circles diagram with four quadrants labelled Finance, Law, Behavioural Science, and Management Science. Inner rings labelled Content Experts, Family Business Champions, with Family Business Consultants at the centre.]

Source: adapted from FFI model

One key difference between family business consultants and other advisors with an interest in family business work, is that the latter will clearly be operating within their own professional dimension, albeit with an increasingly deep understanding of family business issues and at ever-closer proximity to the family business consultancy world. On the other hand, when faced with the cocktail party test of answering the question 'what do you do for a living?' family business consultants will no longer reply that they are accountants, lawyers, financial advisors or whatever the case used to be, but will explain that they are family business consultants.

The process of becoming a family business consultant involves much more than a declaration of intent. Although there are basic entry-level qualifications,[8] these are aimed more at what we have labelled family business champions, still operating within their core profession of origin. Whilst growing rapidly, as a profession, family business consultancy is still very much in its infancy.

---

[7] This is explained in detail in an article by Steve Swartz 'The Challenges of Multidisciplinary Consulting to Family-Owned Businesses' *Family Business Review* (1988) Vol 2(4), 329–339. Swartz recommends, wherever possible assembling a consultancy team based on a different professions of origin and gender.
[8] The most widely recognised being from the FFI – see Appendix 2.

The means by which most family business consultants have moved beyond their profession of origin is by a commitment to a deeper and broader understanding of the theory and practice of core family business work. This is necessary to work with the complexity of the family business system. Gersick also identifies a further quality, the preparedness 'experience and skill to work in highly charged emotional atmospheres'.[9]

25.4 PROCESS AND CONTENT CONSULTING

The key differentiating factor between family business consultants and other, more traditional family business advisors is methodology, in particular the use by family business consultants of process consulting as their core methodology.

Process consulting is based on the work of Edgar Schein[10] and is basically a methodology to understand and work with dynamics of particular 'client systems', be they whole organisations, groups or individuals. The methodology is based on a mixture of psychology, sociology and behavioural sciences. Leading family business consultants Hilburt-Davis and Dyer describe the process consulting or the action research approach used by organisational development professionals like this:[11]

> 'the consultant helps the client generate data about the client's problems which is then fed back to the client. This feedback is then used to develop a plan for change and the consultant's role is then expanded to serve as a change agent to help the client manage the change process.'

The key point is that the role of the process consultant is to observe and question the dynamics of the client system they are working with. It is not to directly offer advice or solutions, although, the client will be encouraged to develop their own answers and solutions by participating in the consultancy process. As Gersick puts it:[12]

> '... the consultant engages the client as an active partner, not just a source, in the data gathering.'

As such the process consultant can be contrasted with those dealing with traditional professional advisory work. The differentiating label applied to the latter is content or expert consulting. There the role is very much to draw from a specialist body of knowledge to provide detailed technical advice and appropriate solutions. The clearest example is a corporate tax advisor.

The process consulting approach has application for organisational development, group development and dispute resolution, so is clearly relevant to family business work. In fact Hilburt-Davis and Dyer argue that the process consulting approach should be the one taken by all professionals working in the family business field. They say that:[13]

> 'regardless of the consultant's profession, we believe that the action research framework from the field of organisational development provides the best approach to help family firms manage the difficult changes they need to make.'

---

[9] Op cit at p 253.
[10] Schein *Process Consultation Revisited* (Addison-Wesley, 1999).
[11] Jane Hilburt-Davis and W Gibb Dyer *Consulting to Family Businesses* (Jossey Bass, 2003) at p 10.
[12] Op cit at p 261.
[13] Ibid at p 11.

Although the terms 'expert' and 'process' consulting are sometimes used as labels for the two approaches, this can be confusing. Process consultants are highly expert in their own professions. Equally there is a large process element to certain transactional advisory work, such as corporate finance, where those involved typically talk about, for example, the 'sale process', which would typically be seen as highly 'expert' within the Hilburt-Davis and Dyer classification.[14]

A better distinction might be between content consultants, who focus more on the delivery of technical content and advice and, on the other hand, process consultants, might be more helpful.

The differences between the content and process consulting models can be summarised as follows:

Feature	Content Consulting Model	Process Consulting Model
Role	Provide answers or advice to client	Provide framework, facilitate process, shape questions
Issue	Client comes with problem for technical (eg legal/tax) solutions provided by others	Client comes with problem and is facilitated to find own solution
Client	One person or organisation	Family business system,
Focus	Mostly transactional	Open-ended, dynamic, systems orientated and relational, dealing with transitions
Primary Resources	Expertise of advisor, specialised body of knowledge	Process management, multi- or inter-disciplinary, subjective, designs and facilitates process for engagement by stakeholders
Mindset	Certainty, structured, advisory/directive, expertise, specialised knowledge, set within framework of rules and best practice, expert mindset	Unstructured, emergent, driven by curiosity, dynamic process of learning by all parties, including family business advisor

Seen as continuum, with expert consultants at one end of the scale and those whose core professions are based on process consulting at the other, the positions might be seen as in Figure 25.3 below.

The precise position of any given professional will vary depending on many factors including the nature of their instructions, the requirements of the client and the skill-set, experience and approach of the professional involved.

---

[14] A possible explanation could be that, on closer analysis, much transactional work is relatively low on technical issues and is much more characterised by relationship and dynamic issues.

Figure 25.3: The family business consulting continuum

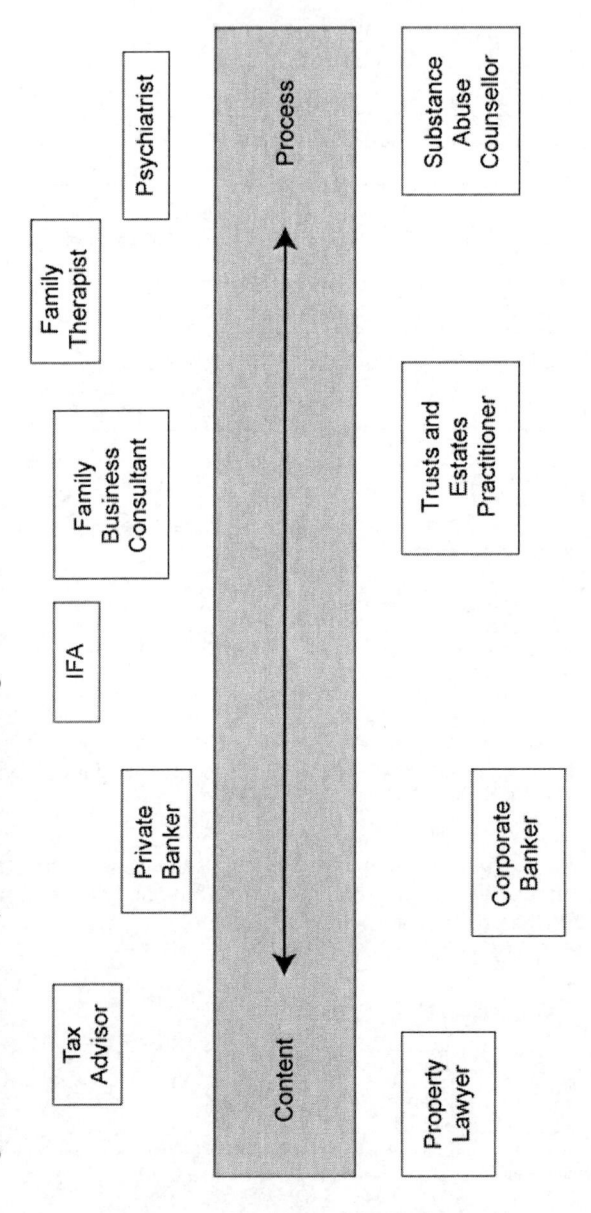

25.5 PROCESS, CONTENT AND CONTEXT

Context is also key. Jane Hilburt-Davies and Peg Senturia[15] point out that 'all consultants, whatever their profession of origin are always operating in two modes'. No-one will advance far in their chosen profession, even the most technical and content laden, without a modicum of client care skills, or 'bedside manner'.

The point cuts both ways. Process consultants must also develop an awareness of when to take control of the process and focus on technical content related issues rather than relationships or dynamics. As the authors put it:

> 'Because process and content exist together, focusing on only one or the other means doing only part of the job.'

Given the complexity and dynamics, there is likely to be a correspondingly greater need for content professionals to deploy process consulting skills and approaches when working in a family business setting. Hilburt-Davies and Senturia offer a number of guidelines to help identify when it is time to move between approaches:

- **Incongruence and timing.** There will be occasions when there is a disconnection between what a business family say they want to happen and what they actually do. Stalled succession planning is a classic example (and one used by the authors). Faced with this situation, rather than concentrate on an ever more elaborate technical analysis, the advisors concerned might need to change their emphasis and focus on process issues.
  This might involve starting with simple things like facilitating meetings that the family never seem to find time to organise, or encouraging input from a reluctant participator.
  It could involve a more fundamental process based intervention, such as a series of detailed 'heart-to heart' discussions with the senior generation business leader to help them identify 'what is really going on' and what the real obstacles to succession are.[16]

- **Self awareness.** The authors suggest that the advisor's 'own baggage' can sometimes mean that they over-identify with issues in a case and lose objectivity. In which case, analytically the advisor can be seen to be neglecting their primary professional task, to provide advice which is in the best overall interests of their client. For example a lawyer who encourages a client to continue litigation, motivated more by a sense that their client has been badly treated or wanting to win for them, rather than focusing on the merits of the case or their clients real interests, which may well be early settlement or even not pursuing the claim in the first place.[17]

- **Address underlying issues.** Hilburt-Davies and Senturia argue that 'relatives rarely fight openly about what they are really fighting about'. Content consulting tackles the problem at a surface level. It focuses on the technical aspects of a family business dispute such as legal merits, forensic accounting, tactics and evidence. Process consulting attempts to help the clients understand what is really going on beneath the surface. Here the focus is on relationships and family dynamics.

---

[15] Jane Hilburt-Davies and Peg Senturia 'Using the Process/Content Framework: Guidelines for the Content Expert' *Family Business Review* (1995) Vol 8(3).
[16] Some possibilities are explored in chapter 7.
[17] The distinction between a lawyer or other content professional advising a client on their options (sometimes forcibly) and dictating how the client should proceed, is sometimes a fine one.

- **Safe environment for new learning.** The authors recognise that for a client to change at a fundamental process level they will need to think about and learn from their situation. The client will need a safe environment to do so. Family meetings and the like will need to be carefully managed. It is the advisor's responsibility to create this safe space, so that all family members can learn and move forward.
- **Respect resistance to change.** The prospect of change can be frightening or overwhelming for clients. The process consultant understands this and by supporting the client, helps them overcome their fears.

Other family business consultants take a more purist approach, arguing that a process consultant should always operate as such and should always maintain a non-directive approach and allow the client to retain control of the process. John Tucker argues:[18]

> 'My view is that it is not a simple case of awareness and then switching in mid-stream. I believe that one is skills based and the other is knowledge based. Just because you are steeped in one discipline does not mean that because you a have a level of awareness in the one that is not your primary discipline that you simply shift from one to the other. Whilst I agree that process and content co-exist, I do not agree that by focusing on only one or the other means doing only half a job I believe that a skilled and knowledgeable process consultant works with their client. As Schein says:
>
>> "Process consulting is a set of activities on the part of the consultant that helps the client to perceive, understand and act upon the process events that occur in the client's environment in order to improve the situation as defined by the client".
>
> I believe that is wholly different from giving technical advice and is a philosophy of working with clients that transcends the giving of technical advice and is most certainly not part of taking control'.

Just looking at the analysis by Hilburt-Davies and Senturia above it will be seen that some of the suggestions made by the authors might fall outside the comfort zone and skill-set of the typical content advisor. This coincides with the comments made by John Tucker about the difficulties for technical advisors to work in process consulting mode.

If so the question becomes how exactly can the content focused advisor best help their client? The answer is likely to involve collaboration between process consultants and the various content professionals engaged in the matter.

Those between the private client and corporate teams of law firms merit particular attention.

25.6 DEFINING THE ISSUES

One of the key features about process consulting is who defines the issue that is the subject of the intervention and the related question of who generates the solution to the problem? In content related or transactional matters this will often be the professional advisor, who when presented with a set of facts will define the issue, for example that on

---

[18] From an exchange of views written during the editing process of this book.

the basis of excessive remuneration taken by a family business insider, their family outsider client has been unfairly prejudiced, together with the possible solution, a petition to court.[19]

The approach of the process consultant is quite different. There the role is much more to act as a catalyst, encouraging the client to identify relevant facts and issues and to generate their own solutions. For example it might emerge that the dispute over the remuneration follows a typical pattern for the family concerned and that there are much deeper underlying issues, stemming from the core of the relationship between the family members concerned,[20] a solution which can only be explored by consultancy or some form of whole family based intervention.

Of course content professionals will often say to do their job properly they need to obtain full details of their client's background, listen carefully to their wishes and generate a range of options for the client to choose from. But this is subtly different from process consulting.

It is also the case that family business clients are sometimes convinced that they need a hired gun as a lawyer and that legal proceedings against their relatives is the only solution. In which case the client may not be too keen to hire a lawyer they perceive is bent on acting as a peacemaker.

25.7 FAMILY BUSINESS CLIENTS AND ROLES

One key difference in the approach between process consultancy and traditional content advisory professionals is, whom the two groups identify as their client, when working with family businesses.

In broad terms, process consultant, including family business consultants will tend to see themselves as acting for the family business system in its entirety. Traditional advisory professionals, such as lawyers and accountants will accept instructions from either the family company, as a corporate entity, or from specific individuals, identified in their engagement terms.

The issue of how to identify the client is explored in detail in chapter 26, as is the related topic of the variety of roles that a professional might be called on to play when advising family business clients.

25.8 THE FAMILY BUSINESS ADVISOR AND CONFLICT RESOLUTION

25.8.1 Overview

The point that the legal process provides a fundamentally unsatisfactory forum to resolve family business disputes has been consistently made throughout this book. In

---

[19] Under CA, s 994 – see chapter 21.
[20] For example that the insider is the oldest sibling, with a long standing resentment of the younger outsider, based on a perception that the insider was the favourite younger child, who received the lion's share of parental attention growing up.

Part E we illustrate that the remedies available, in particular, to remote owners of later stage family companies, are both uncertain and unsatisfactory. The precarious position of next generation family members seeking to assert ownership rights, particularly in farming businesses, is exposed in chapter 19. Even the notional winners of family business court battles will succeed only at the expense of irreparable damage to family relationships. The suggestion that 'the only winners are the lawyers' is no less true because it has become a cliché'.

So the arguments for both prevention, via investment in governance and early cure, through non-legal and alternative dispute resolution mechanisms are incontrovertible.

25.8.2 Conflict, governance and communication

Clearly prevention is better than a cure. In an ideal world a comprehensive family governance system would anticipate and cater for all of the situations and pressure points that are likely to produce disputes within the business family. Indeed it will be seen from chapter 17 that, in covering employment, remuneration, dividend policies, ownership and retirement, this is precisely what governance structures try to do.

We believe that the single most significant common factor in serious family business disputes is a lack of communication. For example it emerges from the case report in *Irvine*[21] that Ian Irvine made no real attempt to communicate the level of his remuneration to his sister in law, Patricia. In fact the implication is that he tried to disguise this. Equally there appears to be little evidence that Patricia could pluck up the courage to broach the subject of her own financial position with Ian, notwithstanding the precariousness of this, following the sudden death of her husband, Malcolm.

Perhaps the single most important function of family business governance is to set up systems to encourage proper, appropriate and timely communication. One of the leading authorities on family business governance, John Ward places communication skills firmly on his list of lessons learned from successful family businesses observing that:[22]

> 'The most successful business families I know invest a great amount of time and effort into learning communication skills, and they find it very, very powerful to learn those skills together.'

Elements of communication skills include listening skills, non-verbal communication, presentation skills, meeting management or facilitation skills and even confrontation skills (discussed below).

Although we are convinced of the potential benefits to the family business of a comprehensive governance system, this will not be a panacea to prevent conflict. A governance system that relies heavily on paper and procedures, without securing the buy in of the hearts and minds of the business family, is most unlikely to succeed in preventing damaging conflict.

Even with the most comprehensive governance system in creation, in the hands of highly empathetic and emotionally aware family members, some level of conflict is inevitable.

---

[21] Discussed in detail in chapter 21.
[22] John L Ward *Perpetuating the Family Business: 50 Lessons Learned from Long Standing Successful Families in Business* (Palgrave, 2004) Lesson 21 (Communication Skills) at p 86.

We know of one family who have recognised this and have adopted a 'family first' policy in dealing with disputes. If a disagreement on a business issue is in danger of crossing the line into a full blown family argument, their policy is to call a 'time out', stop discussions on the point, allow all concerned to reflect on their own and others' positions before and if necessary reconvening to talk further. The family are convinced that family harmony must prevail over business differences.

In chapter 2 we introduce the analysis and categorisation of types of conflict used by Jehn and Mannix,[23] which were task, process and relationship conflicts. In effect this family have recognised the dangers of, what starts out as an example of a task conflict, deteriorating into full-blown relationship conflict. The boundary between dispute avoidance, where prioritising preserving family relationships can ultimately damage the health and growth of the business and dispute resolution may be difficult to judge but is explored further below. John Ward talks of families including training in confrontation skills into family education programmes so that:[24]

> 'It becomes possible for family members to talk about difficult, even explosive issues and to feel safe in doing so because they have developed a methodology that everyone follows and accepts.'

A key component of family charters or other formal family business governance documents will usually be dispute resolution procedures. These can vary in sophistication but the key theme will almost invariably be a stress on informal resolution of disputes and a corresponding discouragement of the use of formal litigation proceedings. More sophisticated procedures often provide for an escalating procedure, including some or all of the following steps:

- as a first step, encouraging the family members themselves to resolve their dispute informally and without involving others;
- using cooling off periods;
- involving family insiders as informal mediators, for example the chair of the family council;
- involving third party facilitators (discussed below);
- formal mediation.

A common feature will usually be a restriction on instituting formal litigation.[25]

---

[23] K A Jehn and E A Mannix 'The dynamic nature of conflict: A longitudinal study of intragroup conflict and group performance' *Academy of Management Journal* (2001) 44(2), 238–251 – reviewed in FFI Practitioner 25 January 2015 by Anthony Devine.

[24] John L Ward *Perpetuating the Family Business: 50 Lessons Learned from Long Standing Successful Families in Business* (Palgrave, 2004) at p 87.

[25] Based on the Fulham Football Club decision this would seem to be enforceable and binding on the family members in most circumstances (*Fulham Football Club v Richards and another* [2011] EWCA Civ 855). This was a non-family business case where a private agreement to submit disputes between shareholders to arbitration was upheld by the Court of Appeal so that an aggrieved shareholder was prevented from pursuing an unfair prejudice claim in the Courts. Logically the decision could apply to wider forms of ADR but this has not been tested. Some family dispute procedures go so far as to include outright bans on instituting court proceedings and provide that all disputes will be settled by internal family mechanisms. As arbitration provides a quasi-judicial remedy it might be that the more alternative the ADR mechanism, the less likely this is to be fully binding, as ousting the jurisdiction of the courts.

25.9 ALTERNATIVE FAMILY DISPUTE RESOLUTION

The role of governance, both in facilitating communication to help minimise conflict and also setting out procedures for dealing with conflicts that actually arise has been noted above. What else can families do to prevent conflict escalating to damaging proportions? The suggestions below are not mutually exclusive. They are cumulative, in the sense that they overlap with each other and can often be used in parallel or sequentially. The first few suggestions are much more about dispute prevention than resolution. As will be seen, the suggestions are also much wider than the approaches (centering on mediation) usually considered in the legal context of alternative dispute resolution (ADR).

25.9.1 Self-help

The shelves of bookshops positively groan under the weight of self-help and lay psychology books. Many of these are focused on providing individuals with basic tools to understand their own personality, behaviour and psychological make-up. Others look at relationships, not only with spouses or life partners, but also between wider family members and work relationships.

Lucia Ceja Barba[26] argues that, that 'we acquire our character and therefore we can change it' and advocates taking positive steps to acquire self-awareness and achieve movement towards, for example, in the case of an entrepreneur, 'balanced narcissism'.[27]

A sensible first step, particularly for family members experiencing milder difficulties, would be to invest some time in understanding themselves better, to build an awareness of the trigger points and issues that cause tension and difficulties for the individual concerned.

25.9.2 'The family business movement'[28]

There are also a considerable number of specialist works, dedicated to those involved with family owned businesses. Many of these are mentioned in this book. There are also various family business membership organisations, aimed at educating family business members and fostering a wider family business community. Again a number of organisations are mentioned in this book.[29] These are supplemented by a number of family business conferences and one-off events, usually featuring case studies presented by members of business owning families, explaining the trials and tribulations as well as the successes that go to make up their own family business story.

Time spent gaining an introduction to family business thinking is likely to be well spent. It may have the added advantage of reassuring the family member concerned that, whilst the circumstances of their family business may be different, the issues that they are facing are not unique.

---

[26] 'Balancing Personality Traits: Capitalizing on the strengths of our "true self"' *FFI Practitioner*, 23 April 2014.
[27] In effect building an awareness of the needs of colleagues and family members, whilst retaining the confidence and drive of a successful entrepreneur.
[28] See also **25.10** below.
[29] See, Appendix 2.

25.9.3 Counselling

Some form of counselling, including psychotherapy, or psychological support might be helpful for family members with more protracted or pronounced difficulties. But there still appears to be stigma attached to the use of such support in the UK. Notwithstanding this it is difficult to see who would not benefit from the greater level of self-awareness that it likely to result from engaging in these processes.

The intervention need not take the form of stereotypical sessions on the psychiatrist's couch. There are a number of highly focused practical approaches available, often based on questionnaires or psychometric testing, which aim to provide the client with an accessible insight into their own psychological fingerprint and behavioural patterns.

Some issues with family relationships might be much deeper and problematic. Detailed group or family counselling is available but is highly specialised. It may well be difficult to achieve radical change in the relationships between family business members through a family therapy intervention. If family business members are reluctant to engage in a form of counselling on a one to one basis, it is correspondingly less likely that the key members of a business family will agree to participate in a collective intervention. Family therapy may therefore often not be considered at all by a business family, or, if considered quickly dismissed as too painful.[30] Sadly, families might prefer to litigate, rather than engage in the painful and challenging soul searching involved.

25.9.4 Coaching

Like counselling, coaching is primarily focused on the individual. Whereas counselling is primarily inwardly focused, coaching is aimed at helping individuals achieve specific identified external goals. These are often business focused, for example, help in building the behaviours needed to become a successful sales director. Coaching can also be more personally focused, for example on developing assertiveness.

If the problem in the family business and the cause of the resulting tension and conflict has been correctly attributed to issues with the development or skill set of a particular individual, then coaching may have a valuable role to play. However the primary issue might really be the relationship between family members, so that any performance difficulties are either a symptom of these or a product of scapegoating.[31] In which case coaching can play only a limited role in resolving conflict in the family business.

25.9.5 Organisational development

Whilst self-knowledge can be a key building block to resolving or preventing conflict the individual family member is but one part of the complex family business system. Effective conflict resolution will need to operate at a systemic level.

---

[30] Steve Swartz suggests that a commitment to engage in family therapy should sometimes be a pre-condition for some business families before they start a family business consultancy process. See 'The Challenges of Multidisciplinary Consulting to Family-Owned Businesses' *Family Business Review* (1988) Vol 2(4), 329–339 at p 337.

[31] The concepts of scapegoating and triangulation are discussed in chapter 3.

Again a huge amount of work has been undertaken on organisational development in recent decades, both at academic and practitioner level. Many management consultants offer management development and team building programmes alongside strategic advice. Some of the tools and techniques referred to in the context of counselling are often used by consultants in group settings or team building exercises, as a gentle way of exploring differences. Clearly there are considerable benefits of a business family or relevant sub-groups, jointly participating in these team building or awareness raising exercises.

Succession is likely to be the biggest change affecting a family owned business, and therefore the event most likely to produce conflict. Change management has become an industry in its own right. It might be argued that a family business is fundamentally a business entity and therefore an organisational approach, delivered by a competent business consultant could help to reduce the likelihood of conflict. However, the danger of concentrating exclusively or predominantly on the business dimension, is that issues stemming from the parallel family system may remain unrecognised and unresolved or, at least, will receive correspondingly less focus.

25.9.6 Trusted third party intervention

Family business disputes are often resolved with the help of a trusted third party. This might be a friend of the family. Sometimes this will be a family insider, for example an uncle or aunt. On other occasions it will be a business insider, perhaps a non-executive director or even a long standing and trusted advisor although (as explained in chapter 26) any advisor will need to think very carefully about the basis of their engagement and their professional position.

This dispute resolution role may be enshrined in the family business governance system. Perhaps the chair of the family council or, in some cases, the chairman of the board, will be designated to act. In some cultures the wider religious or cultural community have a semi-official role to assist in resolving disputes involving their membership.

Made to Last[32] talks about events following the death of Cyrus Clark, the first generation co-founder of the famous shoe business. This was followed by an 'unfortunate 3 years of wrangling' between the surviving brother, James and Cyrus' family over whether Cyrus' son Beaven should succeed to his father's interest and actively participate in, what was then, a partnership, or whether Cyrus' branch of the family should be bought out and, if so at what price. The author refers to the role taken by the wider Quaker community in helping to resolve the matter (in favour of a buy-out).

Unfortunately this resolution was delayed and complicated because the dispute had widened into a clear relationship conflict with, in particular one of Cyrus' daughters, who pursued in parallel a grievance that James had maligned her father's reputation. But there was a happy ending. As a result of the intervention of the Quaker community and strenuous efforts on James' part to build bridges with his brother's family wider family relationships were restored.

---

[32] Mark Palmer *Made to Last – The story of Britain's best known shoe firm* (Profile Books, 2013) at pp 71–78.

Beaven, later recognised the necessity of keeping channels of communication open between family members, notwithstanding and, indeed especially, in the face of family conflict. He eventually wrote to his uncle to acknowledge that:[33]

> 'I consider myself to blame for not speaking to thyself when I first heard of the state complained of as mutual explanations might probably have prevented the unpleasant misunderstanding which has occurred.'

The Gate of India case (discussed in detail in chapter 21) also provides a much more recent example of an attempt by the wider community to resolve a family business dispute. Unfortunately that matter ended in bitter litigation. There the son of and nominated successor of a sibling partnership restaurant business was excluded from participation in the business by his uncle. The local Muslim community leaders took an active role in trying to resolve the dispute between the uncle and nephew. Indeed there was a strong cultural expectation that the nephew would participate in this process, notwithstanding his perception that the community leaders would naturally side with his uncle, as a fellow member of the senior generation.[34]

The emphasis therefore has to be on the word 'trusted'. Such informal third party intervention is most unlikely to succeed if the moderator is perceived to be partial, much less the mouthpiece of any party to the dispute and simply tasked with bringing the other party back on message.

25.9.7 Family business consultancy

Often family business consultants are brought into family businesses to help with succession and transition, to develop governance systems or in response to family conflicts. On occasions more than one of these factors will be present. For example difficulties experienced during the transition period might have highlighted the need for an increased focus on governance and improved communication, to reduce the potential for future conflict within the family firm concerned.

The key point is that, by looking for the support of family business consultant, rather than reaching for their lawyers, the business family are recognising that the presenting issue of conflict should be seen as a symptom and not a cause of the family's difficulties. By working on the underlying systems and dynamics, with the guidance of their family business consultant, the business family would hope to not only put into context and resolve the initial conflict, but also establish the foundations to both minimise and deal with future sources of conflict.

25.9.8 Mediation

The objective of mediation, in contrast, is to resolve an actual and specific conflict. Although mediation may expose underlying rifts and faults in the structure of the family business or highlight issues of family dynamics, this is not its primary aim.

---

[33] *Made to Last* at p 78.
[34] See [2008] EWHC 959 (Ch) at para 123.

Like the collaborative conflict management strategy discussed in Sorenson's research paper[35] the theory of mediation[36] is that, by focusing on the parties true underlying interests, it will unlock a mutually beneficial solution to the issue causing conflict and, at least maintain, if not rebuild and enhance relationships between the erstwhile conflicted family members.

Traditionally, commercial mediation has been organised as a set piece or show case event, with the mediator (and a neutral venue) being hired for a set time, typically one or two days, for the mediation to take place. Part of the logic behind this approach, in addition to limiting the mediator's costs, is that the pressure of time will force the parties to commit to the process and move towards an outcome. Often a mediation of this nature will be used as a last ditch attempt to avoid a full court hearing. This may work well in providing a resolution of the more commercial elements of a family business dispute. It is less likely to be effective and may indeed be seen as a brutally blunt tool to pick apart the complexities of the family dynamics underlying the dispute, especially if the dispute is well advanced.[37] For these issues a more open and fluid process may be more appropriate, allowing the mediator and the family members time to explore and resolve relevant issues and grow towards a resolution with the minimum of added pressure.

This open mediation approach will be more uncertain in terms of cost, timescale and outcome. However it has the advantage that any resolution reached is less likely to be perceived to have been forced or railroaded under pressure and more likely to be seen as careful and consensual and accordingly, longer lasting. The more open the mediation approach, the closer it will be to the process of facilitation by a family business consultant, described above.

A further issue is that mediators tend to specialise in either family or commercial mediation. Of course family business disputes have elements of both.[38]

If mediation fails, the parties are then free to pursue their dispute through the courts. Indeed mediation often occurs in parallel with litigation, usually as a last ditch attempt to resolve matters, before pursuing a particular stage of litigation. This might be issuing proceedings or, at a later stage, the hugely costly step of setting a matter down for trial.

25.9.9 Collaborative law

The collaborative law movement originated in the USA. Whilst it is now gaining traction in the UK, collaborative law is mainly used in the field of matrimonial disputes. Collaborative law can nevertheless be used in a commercial context and has a potentially clear application for family business disputes.

The basic underlying philosophy of the collaborative law approach is that a dispute is a misfortune that needs to be dealt with, rather than an opportunity to apportion blame or

---

[35] See chapter 2.
[36] Indeed the cornerstone mediation text, Fisher and Ury's *Getting to Yes – Negotiating agreement without giving in*, is cited as a source of reference in Sorenson's paper.
[37] See **19.2.8** for a discussion on the outcome of mediation in the case study referred to there.
[38] See the discussion on this in Lisa Parkinson *Family Mediation* (Jordan Publishing, Family Law, 3rd edn, 2014). Although written in the context of inheritance disputes and matrimonial matters the point holds good for family business related mediation.

to be proved right. The parties, supported by their lawyers have a clear and joint interest in resolving the dispute in a manner that provides the best possible solution for each and causes the least damage to their on-going relationship.

Collaborative law is a formal procedure, with the parties signing a written collaborative law agreement agreeing to participate in the approach. Proceedings will be semi-formal, usually centred around meetings in lawyer's offices or at a neutral venue. Sometimes these will be supported by a third party mediator. Experts might also be brought into the process, for example financial, tax or valuation advisors. But their role will not be to advocate the position of either party. Rather it will be to provide neutral advice on the options available to the parties, similar to a single court appointed expert.

If the approach fails, the parties are nevertheless free to take their dispute on to the courts in the traditional way. The clever trick underpinning the collaborative law approach is the requirement for the lawyers concerned to agree that, if the approach fails and the parties choose to issue proceedings, then neither lawyer can act in those proceedings. Accordingly the traditional concern that lawyers have a vested interest in prolonging and exacerbating the dispute is removed.

In the matrimonial context preserving the remnants of a relationship obviously make sense 'for the good of the children'.[39] But the same logic is capable of extending for the good of the wider family and the family business.

25.9.10   Arbitration

In theory family business disputes could be subject to formal arbitration under the Arbitration Acts, either under the terms of a pre-existing legally binding agreement to do so, or by separate agreement between the parties.[40]

There are potential advantages of including arbitration provisions in family shareholders' agreements, as an alternative to court proceedings. Crucially by submitting to arbitration whilst the family members in dispute will have failed to resolve their dispute themselves they will at least have avoided literally seeing each other in court. There is the further advantage that arbitration proceedings are private, so the family would not run the risk of the details of their dispute becoming public knowledge (to the extent that their case might be reported and read).

However arbitration is best suited as machinery for deciding relatively narrow questions of law. It is most unlikely to provide an effective way to identify and resolve underlying issues of family relationships. There are disadvantages to arbitration, in particular the need for the parties to pay the arbitrators costs.[41] Also as, under arbitration, the dispute will be decided by a lawyer in a suit, it may lack the closure that could conceivably follow from a 'full-blown' judicial process. But, as that closure is by no means certain and is likely to come at a considerable cost, this is very much a secondary consideration.

---

[39]   In chapter 2 we point to the suggestion that a family business can sometimes have the status of a surrogate child in any event.
[40]   *Fulham Football Club v Richards and another* [2011] EWCA Civ 855.
[41]   Whereas, notwithstanding recent rises in fees, court costs remain heavily subsidised by central taxes.

25.9.11 Early neutral evaluation

Early neutral evaluation is a recent innovation in dispute resolution. Basically an agreed independent third party, usually a senior barrister or even a judge,[42] is appointed, at an early stage, to evaluate the strengths and weaknesses of the respective cases of the parties to the dispute. This will usually be on the basis of actual or draft pleadings. The evaluator expresses a preliminary and non-binding opinion on the merits and their view (based on what they have seen) of what could happen if the matter went to trial. The objective is to encourage the parties to take a realistic view of their prospects and therefore encourage settlement, before litigation proceeds too far, significant costs have been incurred and (in the context of family business disputes) family relationships have been ruined.

Early neutral evaluation can therefore be seen as a hybrid between mediation and arbitration.

25.9.12 Litigation

Last and definitely least, litigation.

Litigation must be seen as the apotheosis of the competitive strategy[43] for resolving family business conflicts. Sorenson's research indicates that this is the most damaging approach, both for the family business and the business family. When one considers the impact of litigation it is easy to see why. It is pretty much inconceivable that family relationships could survive the brutal process of litigation.

Even preliminary steps, such as letters before action, possibly intended to 'explain my position' or to 'bring the other side to their senses' can have the effect of digging the first trench in a family war. Few family members will react well to being told in writing that they have behaved unfairly, are in breach of duty or whatever the allegation might be, particularly by a lawyer acting for their family accuser. Even the act of consulting a lawyer may be seen as a betrayal of the privacy of the family business system. Almost inevitably a letter before action will concentrate on the lawyer's client's 'strong points', give little or no acknowledgement of points of common interest, much less the difficulties their own client faces in pursuing their claim. Equally inevitably, the response sent on behalf of the other side will take the opposite approach. And on it goes. With each party digging themselves deeper into the mud of family conflict with each salvo of the litigation process. Usually members of the wider family are dragged into the war and forced to enlist on one side or another.

Indeed an FFI founding father (a former lawyer turned family business consultant) has suggested[44] that no lawyer, genuinely committed to helping their client resolve a family business dispute without material damage to family relationships, should contemplate even writing a letter before action, unless or until other forms of intervention have been exhausted.

---

[42] For example Commercial Court judges sitting in Cardiff and Bristol will provide an evaluation of the merits of cases presented in each other's courts.
[43] As identified by Sorenson.
[44] In closed training sessions.

If the dispute was merely over commercial and financial issues, litigation could perhaps be regarded as simply an inefficient method (when compared, for example with mediation) of achieving the desired outcome.

However if there is any truth behind Ian Marsh's observation that it 'it is never just about the money'[45] something else will be involved in family business disputes. The 'something else' might be an apology from the other party to the dispute or even an acknowledgement of the validity of the claimant's position. In theory a litigant might obtain vindication, in the form of a judgment from the courts, that they are in the right and have been badly treated.

Realistically the chance of the litigation process providing the clients with this are slim. Notwithstanding the wealth of family business disputes that find their way to court, some of which are discussed in this book, the vast majority settle before trial. The effect of the litigation process is likely to generate the pressure to force a settlement. But things are likely to get considerably worse before they get better. Positions between the family members will polarise. It is therefore incumbent on lawyers advising on family business disputes, to the greatest extent possible,[46] to adopt the role of counsellor, helping the family business member concerned to identify their true best interests, rather than a hired-gun advising, on the best tactics to achieve a narrow litigation focused outcome.

And of course there are the bills. Litigation is clearly an expensive process. But it is trite to say that only lawyers benefit. Few lawyers set out to provoke or fuel a family business dispute simply to maximise fee income. It is more often the case that family business disputes escalate out of a desire on the lawyer's part to deliver to the client what they have asked for, to be proved right, rather than what they really need, to resolve their dispute.

There are also the risks of litigation. It is widely accepted that there is no such thing as a sure-fire case.[47]

A further reason why the litigation process is unlikely to provide the 'closure' or vindication sought by the family business litigant lies in the so-called 'parallel forces of litigation'.[48] Statistically the vast majority of litigated claims are settled out of court, whether by abandonment, negotiated settlement, formal mediation or the mechanisms of the litigation process.[49] Whilst a negotiated settlement may produce an economically

---

[45] See chapter 2.
[46] Ultimately a lawyer may advise but their duty remains to follow their client's instructions.
[47] Experienced counsel in litigation advised a client that they had a 70% chance of success but explained that he never gave cases a higher rating. A wise colleague noted that still left the client facing a 30% prospect of failure. Although the client eventually 'won', in the sense of collecting damages well into six figures, they received only partial acknowledgement from the courts that those then in charge of the family business he had founded had managed it badly.
[48] The logic is that whilst litigants might start from parallel and opposing positions, the combination of the litigation process which forces each party to examine both the strengths and weaknesses of both their own position and those of the other party, combined with the procedural machinery of the justice system drives the parties to a point where their interests converge, so that neither party has an incentive to continue with the litigation. A settlement emerges. Under the English system these parallel forces are reinforced by severe costs penalties of overestimating the strength and value of a legal case, proceeding further with the litigation, especially to full trial and losing.
[49] Including offers made under Part 36 of the Civil Procedure Rules.

rational outcome, such a settlement is fundamentally incapable of providing the emotional resolution sought by a family business litigant. In short the process will not have given them their day in court.

In many areas the litigation process has itself evolved to deny family business litigants a court appearance. In particular the remedy most commonly sought in family business disputes, relief from unfair prejudice,[50] will be denied and the family litigant's claim will be struck out in most circumstances where the 'guilty party' has made a reasonable offer to buy the shares of the litigant.[51] Accordingly, whilst the aggrieved family member may well be left with a pot of cash, they will not have had any solid recognition of their grievance and will have lost their stake in the family business.

As will be seen from the cases discussed in Part E many family business members nevertheless chose to use the courts to resolve their family business conflicts. Of course they have a right to do so. But given the costs, risks and uncertainties of litigation, combined with the certainty that family relationships will inevitably be irretrievably damaged by the litigation process it must be worth trying the above steps first.

Reading Part E should remove any lingering doubt about this.

25.10 THE FAMILY BUSINESS MOVEMENT

It is suggested in the introduction to this chapter that what we have termed the family business movement can be traced back to, in effect, the mid 1980's.[52] The Family Firm Institute, or FFI was founded in the USA 1984, by a group of academics and family business practitioners. On the basis that family enterprises are not only the most common form of business organisation in the world, but also the oldest, it might seem surprising that it took so long so for the unique characteristics, challenges and complexities of family businesses to be recognised.

One of the founding assumptions of FFI was that no single profession, much less an individual practitioner was likely to able to deal effectively with these issues. Accordingly, cross-disciplinary collaboration[53] would be needed. This collaboration was often based on cross-disciplinary communities of practice, where groups of family business practitioners met together on a regular basis to learn together, to discuss family business theory and to support each other on current family business cases. Their primary purpose was to create a group learning environment. This approach has been tried in the UK, but only to a relatively limited extent.[54]

Over the last 30 years or so, the original group of 'founding fathers' has expanded into a worldwide family business movement, albeit a movement that still has some way to go, before the recognition of family business issues reaches a level commensurate with the importance of family businesses to the overall economy.[55] The family business

---

[50] Under CA, s 996.
[51] This is explained in chapter 25.
[52] Although others trace the interest in family businesses as a distinct organisational structure to the work of Leon Danco, at least 10 years earlier.
[53] Explored further in chapter 25.
[54] For example the STEP Business Families Special Interest Group – see Appendix 2 for further details. There are also a small number of ad-hoc study groups based on the FFI model.
[55] As explained in chapter 1.

movement initially took hold in the USA, where most of the key family business thinkers and writers, including many referred to in this book, are based. However family business organisations are increasingly forming part of the business landscape in Latin America, mainland Europe, Asia and Australasia.

The family business movement has a number of inter-related strands. First academic, with a growing number of individual academics and business schools taking an interest in family business matters. This academic work has led to various education programmes aimed at supporting both those directly involved in family businesses and the professional advisory community, including the establishment of a number of specialist family business centres, often based in universities. Secondly a number of organisations to support family businesses.[56] Thirdly, organisations to support family business advisors, of which the FFI is by far the most prominent worldwide. Finally, specialist family business consultants, as described above. Although now specialist consultants can be found throughout the world, including a number in the UK, they remain a rare breed (but not an endangered species), the majority of whom are still be found in the USA.

Arguably the United Kingdom is comparatively under-represented in the family business movement, especially at an academic level,[57] notwithstanding a number of dedicated family business practitioners and organisations. Details of organisations of particular relevance to family businesses and practitioners in the UK are contained in Appendix 2.

25.11 CONCLUSION

This chapter has focused on the work of the specialist family business consultant and the core tools and methodology used by them, process consulting. Their role and approach has been contrasted with the content or expert advisory professionals, found in more traditional advisory professions. However one of the key messages from the family business movement is that, to provide effective advice and support to family business clients, professionals need to collaborate with and learn from each other.

There are many insights and approaches from the process consulting world and the work of family business consultants that are capable of application by traditional advisory professionals in working with family businesses. These themes are developed in the following and final chapter.

---

[56] The most significant organisation in the UK is the Institute for Family Business or IFB.
[57] See Martin Stepek 'No visible means of support' *Journal of Family Business Management*, Vol 1 Issue 2 at pp 174–180.

CHAPTER 26

ADVISING THE FAMILY BUSINESS CLIENT

26.1 INTRODUCTION

In the previous chapter we suggested that the development of most family business theory and with it the specialist family business advisory profession, in particular family business consultancy, has really come into being in the last 30 years or so. This final chapter looks at the implications of this thinking, together with various technical legal issues explored throughout this book, on the day-to-day practice of more traditional professionals, especially lawyers, when advising their family business clients.

26.2 THE TRUSTED ADVISOR

At the beginning of this 30-year period the trusted advisor was a widely seen breed. They were likely to have spent sufficient time working with their family business clients, so that the advisor would know their clients almost as well as they would know their own family. The advisor would also be sufficiently expert and skilled in his or her own core profession as to be able to look after the business needs of the family firm, albeit in a less complex and challenging commercial environment.

In chapter 25 we look at the application of the key family business systems approach, the three-circle model, to the family business advisory world. The core paradox for most professionals is that, whilst the systemic view of the family firm requires a broad overview of both family and business issues and an ability to understand and work with the complex relationships and emotions that are part of family business life, over this 30 year period professional practice has become increasingly specialised, forcing practitioners to inhabit ever more discreet technical silos and to rely on standardised products, services and approaches. This is unlikely to suit the idiosyncratic needs of family business clients.

The silos are confined to discrete parts of the advisory three-circle model, from which it is difficult to gain an overall perspective of the entire family business system. As a result the old fashioned trusted advisor, to whom the business family would instinctively turn for general advice and support, has become an endangered species. They survive only in isolated pockets, largely looking after the smaller family firm, particularly in rural communities.

The difficulty is that a large proportion of family firms, are faced with a choice, between highly proficient technical advice, that might be delivered in a family business vacuum, or more personal advice, specific to their own family business situation, but potentially lacking in technical finesse.

The answer to this dilemma, at least in our view, is unlikely to be to encourage a new generation of trusted advisor general practitioners back into the wilds of twenty-first century practice.[1] Instead, we believe that the solution lies partly in raising the awareness of family business issues amongst professionals generally. Earlier parts of this book concentrate on this and are revisited here, in the particular context of professional practice. This education can be combined with encouraging collaborative working between the various professions involved in providing advice to family businesses and also, what we have labelled, collegiate practice, intra-firm collaboration between the various specialists within individual professional service firms, to create coherent and effective family business teams.

26.3 COLLABORATIVE PRACTICE

For discreet areas of advice, such as a trade mark or VAT issue, a single professional might be able to deal with the matter in hand, armed only with their content related expertise[2] and the background knowledge that their client is a family owned firm. The client is likely to need a team of advisors to deal with other, more complex instructions from family business clients, such as succession planning.

One of the main messages from the 'family business movement' is that no single profession has a monopoly of family business wisdom, although all have a role to play in supporting family business clients. Exactly how this multi-disciplinary team is selected and how roles are allocated and executed to produce a coherent and comprehensive solution for the family business client is another matter.

As Gersick *et al* explain:[3]

> '... professionals are put in a difficult position by their family business clients because the problems they are asked to help with cut across many fields and require concepts and experience outside their own.'

There are a range of potential approaches:

---

[1] Others take a different view. US lawyers John Dadakis and Michael De Leon Hawthorn argue for the need of a new breed of 'Personal General Counsel 'typically attorneys with a broad knowledge base. They handle all types of business and personal matters while building an ongoing relationship with their clients and getting a clear understanding of business and family dynamics'. They see this new breed of family business lawyer as both an antidote to the over-specialised transactional lawyer and best able to serve the needs of their family business clients. See 'The Role of the Attorney Comes Full Circle' *FFI Practitioner* 29 April 2015.

[2] The key distinction between content or expert advisory work and process consulting is explored in detail in chapter 25.

[3] Gersick, Davis, Hampton & Lansberg *Generation to Generation: Life cycles of a family business* (Harvard Business School Press, 1997) at pp 251–252.

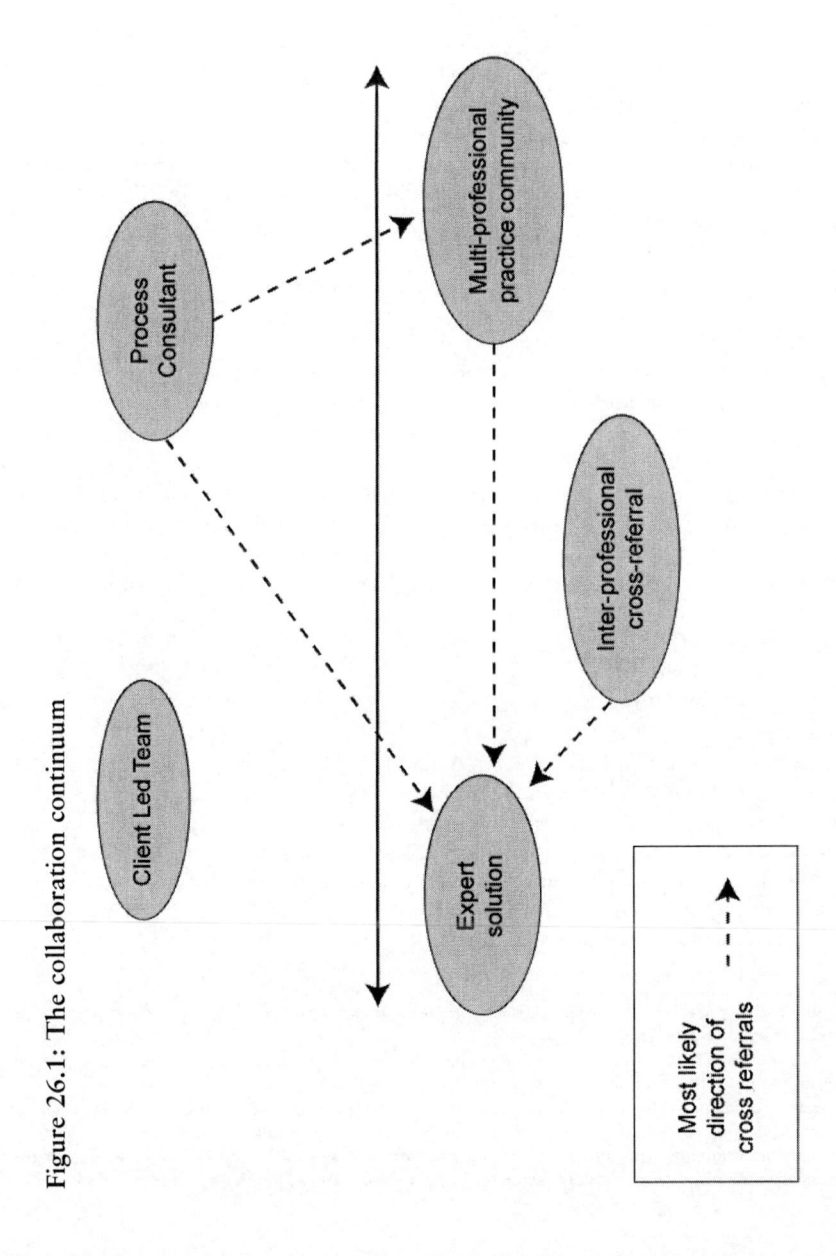

Advising the Family Business Client   923

Figure 26.1: The collaboration continuum

Assuming that more is required to deal with the issue than a single expert solution, the next port of call could well be a random team of advisors assembled by the client, and usually based around a hard core of long standing and trusted advisors, what commentators have called an 'accidental team'.[4] This could work well. Some of the advisors might know the business and the business family well. They might have worked together on behalf of the client and have already established good teamwork and rapport. Happy accidents do occur. But the dangers for the client to guard against may be the innate conservatism of long standing advisors together with a lack of family business specific expertise.

There can often be a finding dividing line between the accidental team and a further category identified by the same authors, the dysfunctional team, where the advisors operate in isolation with little or no co-ordination between themselves, or in the worst cases, outright competition, with different professionals offering conflicting advice and competing solutions, motivated by a mixture of professional pride and a naked desire to grab the largest share of the advisory cake. This dysfuntionality might be avoided if the professionals concerned are involved in assembling the team. Often a lead advisor will choose or recommend to the client appropriate colleagues from other disciplines. If the lead professional has been chosen well it would be hoped that equally good cross referrals will be made.

Problems with cross-disciplinary teams can also be managed, if not avoided completely. Steve Swartz recognises that 'teamwork necessitates the management of differences'[5] and cautions that 'each profession instils in its members a set of lenses through which to interpret reality'.[6] Dialogue to constructively examine and explore perspectives and alternatives can help the professional team to an overall solution that best fits their client's family business reality.

Advising families in circumstances of conflict, crisis or tension will inevitably be demanding for the professionals involved. The natural reaction is to retreat to the comfort zone of what one knows best, our own core profession and knowledge base. What is required to best serve the business family client will often be a willingness to look beyond those boundaries. One of the key benefits of applying the three-circle model to family business professional advisory practice, is to illustrate that the extent of the circles mark boundaries, not barriers to understanding, between the different professional disciplines involved.

A distinction can be made between a traditional 'pass the baton' cross-referral and genuinely collaborative teamwork. In the former, each professional operates in their own discrete professional space, runs their own leg of the engagement relay and then, with a minimum of overlap, hands the project on to the next professional in the chain. The classic example of this would be the family business accountant producing a piece of tax planning or restructuring, which is then simply documented by the lawyer, often without being privy to any initial meetings with the client.

---

[4] See *Family Enterprise: Understanding Families in Business and Families of Wealth* (The Family Firm Institute, Wiley, 2014) at pp 101–102.
[5] See Steve Swartz 'The Challenges of Multidisciplinary Consulting to Family-Owned Businesses' *Family Business Review* (1988) Vol 2(4), 329–339 at p 336.
[6] Op cit at p 333. Swartz was actually describing the workings of an internal team of family business consultants, drawn from various professions of origin. But the argument holds good for collaborative team working of professionals form separate firms and different professions and for that matter what we have labelled collegiate teams from the same firm but different specialisations working together as a team.

Genuinely collaborative teamwork is more like a football team, with the ball being passed between the team members, on the basis of almost constant communication and an understanding of whom, amongst the team, is in the best position to take the engagement forward at any particular time. Just as in a football team, the collaborative advisory team are likely to have a number of briefings, meetings and reviews, throughout the course of the engagement, to make sure that everyone understands the basis of the family business client's issues, has an opportunity to contribute suggestions and solutions and to review progress.

The collaborative advisor team is likely also to have a recognised lead advisor, in effect the manager, responsible for selecting other team members, planning and coordinating the assignment.[7] This could be an advisor with whom the client has an existing relationship. All other things being equal a family business consultant is uniquely suited to this role in the context of major family business projects, such as succession planning or helping a business owning family establish a governance programme.

The question then becomes how are members of the collaborative team selected? This could be on the basis of choosing the most suitable candidate from the lead advisor's general professional contact base. Alternatively selection could lean towards members of a pre-established family business specific professional practice community. The members are likely to know one another. They will share a common understanding of family business issues and will have undergone some level of family business specific training and education.[8] There is also the possibility of bringing in expert consultants on an ad-hoc basis to supplement and complement the team.

The purpose and challenge of collaborative practice is therefore for the professionals involved to actively combine together to achieve the client centred and family business focused outcome for their joint family business client.

There are a number of factors that might conspire against this:

- **Awareness.** The family business client and the advisor team both need to have an awareness of family business issues and also possible solutions for the collaborative approach to even enter into consideration. Take, for example, a family business struggling with insider and outsider factionalism. Absent an understanding of family dynamics and the potential benefits of family councils and other governance mechanisms, advisors might be tempted to give up the possibility of the family remaining in business together as a lost cause and immediately suggest more fundamental solutions, such as employee or family buy-outs or the sale of the company.
- **Resistance to change.** The collaborative teamwork approach requires that those involved embrace the challenge of new ideas and methods of working. Against the background of difficult family relationships, resistance to change can arise, and for the professionals an instinct to revert to the solution and approach dictated by their profession of origin takes over.
- **Cost.** The fully-fledged collaborative teamwork approach described above can undoubtedly be expensive. Even if the number and length of briefings and meetings

---

[7] Upton et al suggest that on occasions the family business client ends up 'quarterbacking' the advisory team. See Upton, Vinton, Seaman and Moore 'Family Business Consultants – Who We Are, What We Do, and How We Do It' *Family Business Review* (1993) Vol 6(3) at p 307. Presumably this is more likely to happen in an accidental team as categorised above.

[8] This is explored in a little more detail later in chapter 25 in the section on the family business movement.

involving the cross disciplinary team are kept to a minimum, the combined hourly charging rate of those involved will no doubt appear frightening to all concerned, especially the family business client.

At first sight the approach may seem to be applicable only in the largest cases and for the wealthiest family business clients, or perhaps those in most pain from their struggles with their family relationship issues.

Against this, the cost of pursuing uncoordinated, even conflicting approaches, as a result of engaging a dysfunctional accidental team are potentially greater, both in terms of the aggregate costs eventually chalked up by the advisors and the damage to family relationship caused, either by the original issue remaining unresolved or problems surfacing later.

This may all seem a little theoretical and abstract. Some real life concrete examples should help to illustrate the points being made. Both matters concerned difficult cases where the succession process has become 'stuck'.[9]

Case 1

In this case the three senior generation family members were approaching retirement age. Two worked in the fifth generation family firm and one did not. The business family was wrestling with their overall ownership approach. There was a broad spectrum of opinion within the family. One view favoured the sale the business and another that ownership should be concentrated in the hands of the next generation insiders working in the business.

A third view championed a wider long-term family ownership approach through the use of trusts. This view was underpinned by a stewardship philosophy, the belief that the family business had been handed down to the current generation and it was their obligation to look after the business and hand it on to the whole of the next generation rather than to sell or claim outright personal ownership of it. Notwithstanding that this approach was not the most tax efficient[10] it gradually gained support from the majority of the family.

Apparently unable to accept that parts of the family had rejected their advice, the tax accountants involved began to 'brief against' the other advisors, issuing conflicting advice notes and acting as allies to those still in favour of the sale or insider ownership solutions.

Of course all three ownership approaches are equally valid.[11] The problem arises when one advisor presents their own preferred solution as the universal truth, rather than one of a number of options for the business owning family to explore.

It took many more months before the family were able to agree on a solution,[12] during which time family relationships remained under strain.

Case 2

The second case involved the succession of a first generation family company from father to son. It was agreed from the outset that the son would to take over management and ownership of the company. The problem was that the son had expected this to be by way of

---

[9] We turn to a more detailed examination of professional conduct issues, in the context of solicitors advising family business clients later in this chapter.
[10] The approach accepted tax leakage by higher marginal rates of tax and a 10 year charge to inheritance tax – see chapter 16.
[11] As explored in chapter 15.
[12] The whole family ownership, trust based approach, eventually prevailed.

gift and believed that this was the basis on which he had agreed to return and take over management of the family business. On the other hand the father wanted to receive full open market value.

Both were strong willed and convinced that their position was justified. The dispute had the potential to split the family and ruin a successful business.

A family business consultant was engaged. He explored the expectations and positions of the son and the father.

In summary the son's position was that he had given up a corporate career to return and rescue the family company and had always expected to be given ownership as a result.

The father, believed that the basis of ownership transfer had never been agreed, that he had worked all his life to build the company, needed to see some value for this and had other children to consider.

The views of the wider family were also canvassed.

The consultant then drew in support from various members of his family business professional practice community, including the following:

- **Accountancy and valuation:** To ascertain a range of open market values for the family company and to look at the potential to generate cash flow to fund a family buy-out.[13]
- **Independent financial advice:** To look at the realistic and likely needs of the senior generation for income and capital in retirement.[14]
- **Tax advisors:** To advise on the tax implications of the various structures and solutions considered.[15]
- **Lawyers:** To document the complex re-organisation structure that was eventually chosen and to ensure that all concerned understood both this and the alternative options that had been foregone.[16]

A compromise was reached which preserved both the business and family relationships. In practice this was achieved in a shorter period of time and at significantly less cost than in the first case. A key factor contributing to this was the involvement and support of a cohesive group of collaborative professionals, able to play their own part properly and fully, whilst also able to appreciate the underlying family dynamics and role of the others involved, so as not to overplay their particular role.

In particular, all concerned understood the role of the specialist family business consultant. This is discussed in detail in chapter 25.

---

[13] See chapter 11. The accountant's role was to provide neutral independent advice on the value (or more precisely range of valuations) of the family business. Analytically this was similar to acting as a single joint expert, but with the family business or the family system as the client.
[14] Although the work and approach of the IFA has been positioned as close to that of a family business process consultant, the detailed work output, of financial reports and investment recommendations had a strong expert or content element and needed to be relied on by the senior generation family member as the contractual client of the advisors concerned.
[15] Again the technical tax advice had a strong expert element requiring an assessment of the individual tax positions of all family members.
[16] Here it will be noted that the lawyer's role was very much to implement a solution arrived at by the family, with the help of family of a business consultancy intervention, rather than to act for any individual family member or to advise on or negotiate that solution.

26.4 COLLEGIATE PRACTICE: INTERNAL FAMILY BUSINESS TEAMS

26.4.1 Family business advice and professional specialisation

We now turn to the subject of family business practice within individual professional firms.

A fair amount of the family advisory literature concerns inter-disciplinary collaborative working between different professions. The working assumption seems to be that, within individual firms, awareness of family business issues is uniformly good and accordingly that family business clients enjoy a consistent level of informed and coherently joined up service. Would that were the case. Intra-firm collaboration and its improvement for the benefit of the family business client, can be a Herculean, if not a Sisyphean, task.

The trend, since the onset of the family business movement, has been for larger professional firms and for individual professionals working within those firms to become increasingly more specialised. What has been the case for the legal and accountancy professions for some while, is becoming increasingly so for banking, financial advisory, insurance and other professionals. So the drift within professional organisations is towards ever larger and more specialised silos of specialist expertise, whereas the wider needs of the family business client are best served by a coordinated and holistic approach.

26.4.2 Two client stories

The facts of two cases brought against law firms for negligence serve to illustrate this point.

Both cases concern the loss of business property relief (BPR) for inheritance tax purposes, rather than issues of family dynamics, so the key family business advisory tools of genograms and the three-circle model can sit in the background.[17] Nevertheless both matters concern the fundamental division that runs through professional firm structures, that between the business system, embodied in corporate and business advisory teams and the family circle in which private client services sit. The fact that one case was decided against the law firm concerned and one against the business owning family is more or less irrelevant to the point we are seeking to make. Both the family and the firm concerned can be seen to have lost on each occasion.

(1) Vinton[18]

The firm in this case were very much the trusted advisors to the business owning family and 'had acted on successive retainers for members of the family,[19] including work on

---

[17] See chapter 3 (Tools, Models and Theories) for a more detailed explanation of these. Both would nevertheless provide useful background information. A genogram and three-circle model for the second, Swain Mason case, would have shown that the founder was then on his fourth marriage, that two of his daughters worked in the family firm, but two did not and that a large percentage of the shares were held in an employee trust.
[18] [2010] EWHC 904 (Ch).
[19] From para 21 of the judgment.

the estate of the deceased senior generation business leader and preparing the will of his widow. They also acted for the family company.

The firm was consulted when, following the death of the founder, it was clear that the company needed more capital. A meeting was arranged and attended by a consultant who was a former partner in the firm and who had acted for the family for many years, together with private client and corporate partners from the firm. They met with two daughters from the next generation who each held several roles in the family business system. They were employees, directors, shareholders, also executors and residuary beneficiaries under both their late father's and their mother's wills.

The outcome of the meeting was a scheme to convert a loan made by the widow to the family company into shares. This was followed by a further subscription of £1m, to be satisfied from the widow's share of her late husband's estate. In total the widow injected about £1.8m into the family firm. The basic idea was to provide much needed capital and to do so by converting loans and free estate, that would otherwise fall within the inheritance tax net into shares, ideally attracting BPR.

Sadly the widow died shortly afterwards and well within the period of 2 years she would usually need to have held shares to qualify for BPR. There is an exception to that rule whereby if new shares can be 'identified' with previously held shares that qualify under the two-year rule, the combined holding then qualifies for BPR. The problem for all concerned was that, whilst the method chosen to capitalise the first tranche of investment, a rights issue, was seen as suitably connected to the widow's initial shareholding, HMRC (and, on appeal, the Special Commissioner) regarded the remainder of the investments, which were structured via a letter of renunciation from other shareholders, as part of the rights issue and a subsequent subscription, as too remote from the original holding. The additional charge to inheritance tax was in region of £360,000.

Much of the case concerns an analysis of the law relating to the duty of care owed by solicitors to the estate of their client and is beyond the scope of this book.

What is directly relevant is the approach taken by the court to trusted advisor retainers. Strictly there is no such thing as a general retainer.[20] But the High Court was extremely reluctant to accept arguments advanced on the part of the firm concerned that its retainer was limited to raising capital for the benefit of the business (which had clearly been satisfactorily achieved). The long standing trusted advisor relationship, and the involvement of the firm's private client team in providing advice to the wider family, alongside the fund raising, all meant that the argument of the family that the retainer extended to achieving the fund raising in a tax efficient way for the benefit of the family and ownership systems, was seen by the High Court as by no means 'fanciful'.[21]

It is easy to feel sympathy for the advisors concerned. They were clearly attempting to look after the business owning family as best they could. Sadly the execution of their instructions appears to have fallen foul of highly technical tax provisions in doing so. Was this just 'one of those things'? The firm had fielded a team that covered the

---

[20] *Midland Bank Trust Co v Hett Stubbs & Kemp* [1979] Ch 384 at 402G–403C referred to at para 30 of the judgment.
[21] Technically the court was hearing an application on the part of the firm to strike out the claim brought on behalf of the family. So the case does not decide that the firm had been negligent. Simply that the firm had been unable to show that the family had been unreasonable to suggest that this was so.

business, ownership and family systems. Did that team include true family business champions?[22] Will there always be more for specialists in one discipline to learn about family business relevant issues within another? This might be private client lawyers obtaining greater awareness of corporate procedures or corporate lawyers understanding more about ownership taxes.

The burden on trusted family business advisors is therefore a heavy one. The closer the relationship, the more they try to help, the greater the expectations of their client and ultimately the courts.

(2) Swain Mason[23]

In contrast the second case concerns one-off instructions to a 'large "full service" law firm',[24] to sell the family company to its management team via a management buy-out (MBO) transaction. The original instructions, were well documented in a formal retainer letter,[25] one of the terms of which expressly excluded tax advice from the retainer, but offered this as an optional extra.

This option was duly exercised by the founder who, by email replied to the corporate finance partner acting for him, saying 'Regarding Tax Advice. Generally, yes please ask [the relevant fee earner] to act for me and the family'.[26] A separate retainer letter was then issued but this was confined to corporate tax advice relating to the structure of the MBO transaction.[27] The tax retainer focused on tax issues relating to the structure of the transaction and did not extend to wider and general tax advice.

The firm proceeded diligently with the MBO transaction, which was duly completed.

Sadly the founder died during a heart operation less than three weeks later. As a result of his death the family lost about £1.2m. £1m of this loss was additional inheritance tax payable on the founder's estate which then had a large lump of cash from the sale of his shares which was subject to IHT, rather than the shares themselves, which would have attracted BPR. The balance was £200,000 of CGT, which would have been wiped out by the uplift in base value on the founder's death.[28] The family sued the firm for this loss.

It was accepted that the firm knew that the founder was in generally poor health and, by an indirect route[29] that they knew about the pending heart operation. But no one, including the founder or his family, had any reason to believe that this was anything other than routine.

---

[22] See below.
[23] [2012] EWCA Civ 498.
[24] From para 6 of the judgment.
[25] The position on retainer letters and scope of the firm's instructions in *Vinton* is unclear. Whilst certain emails, confirming instructions and roles are mentioned in the judgment formal engagement letters are not.
[26] See para 13 of the judgment.
[27] In particular rolling over the capital gain into loan notes.
[28] A brief overview of tax issues on the sale of a family business is provided in chapter 16.
[29] The matter partner was copied into an email trail, dealing with various other matters more relevant to the MBO transaction but headed 'Heart Operation' and, by way of routine small talk, during a lengthy completion meeting the matter partner talked to the founder about the pending operation.

The family argued that the firm should have advised them of the tax risks posed by the possible death of the founder,[30] and should have suggested the possibility of postponing completion of the MBO transaction until the operation had been safely completed.

Both the High Court and the Court of Appeal were quite clear that, just because the firm had by 'pure happenstance' learned about the pending operation, this did not create any duty to provide advice to the founder of the tax consequences of him not surviving that operation. This was advice that the founder was 'not seeking or asking for'.[31]

Nevertheless the High Court judge was critical about the lack of clarity with which the firm disclaimed their duty to provide general, non-transactional tax advice, but thought that it was incumbent on the founder to ask for that advice, rather than for the firm to volunteer it. If exclusion of general private client tax advice had been clearer it was quite likely that the founder would have asked for additional advice to be provided. The judge thought that 'it is likely in those circumstances that [the corporate tax team] would have introduced [the founder] to one of their private client tax colleagues'.[32] That, of course is quite different from saying that the founder would have postponed completion of the MBO, or would have proceeded, but on the basis of putting into place IHT mitigation schemes,[33] as a result of any advice actually given.

26.4.3 Scoping and engagement terms

Can we draw any conclusions or extract any learning points from these two cases?

One possibility is that firms should retreat deeper into their professional silos and, by the careful use of engagement letters, limit the scope of their retainers with family business clients. In effect to try to turn the boundaries between the family and business systems into barriers. Both of these cases concern private client tax advice. From the case reports it appears that this element represented only a modest proportion of the overall fees charged. High risk, low reward what's to like about that?

26.4.4 Full family business service

But if one takes the standpoint that the primary duty of a professional is to help their client[34] to the best of their professional ability, this approach falls short of that ideal.[35] It may also be commercially limiting for the firm concerned.[36] Some family owned business clients prefer to adopt a portfolio approach, selecting one firm for private family matters, such as estate planning) and others for business issues (like employment advice). But we suggest that these family business clients are in a minority.

---

[30] In practice it seems that the founder knew the basic position anyway. The report refers to an email from him to the corporate tax lawyer involved asking her to 'pray for my continued reasonable health – well for at least 7 years' – see para 14 of the judgment.
[31] At para 50 of the judgment.
[32] Quoted at para 39 of the judgment.
[33] Various 'products' are available to 'roll-over' proceeds of sale from the sale of private company shares subject to BPR relief into funds investing in non-quoted shares or other investments that also attract BPR.
[34] The potentially difficult of defining who is the client in family business matters is discussed below.
[35] See, for example the arguments of David Maister in *True Professionalism* (Simon & Schuster, 2001).
[36] See Richard Susskind *The End of Lawyers?* (Oxford University Press, 2010).

Even if private client services generally and tax advice in particular, represent modest fees in relation to corporate and transactional advice, the ability to offer a 'full service' might be a key factor in obtaining those instructions in the first place. How long would the firm in the *Vinton* case have retained their trusted advisor status over the years, if they were not seen as capable of looking after both family and business interests?

So what can professionals do break out of their silos and provide a firm-wide solution to best support their family business client base?

Careful, clear and fair, scoping of assignments has a role to play. By explaining clearly both what is excluded from the brief and, as best as possible, the consequences of this, the firm is providing their family business client with a clear choice. As a result the firm should either maximise its revenue or minimise its exposure.

The most significant benefits for both firm and family business client are likely to be obtained from fully joined up family business thinking amongst all professionals involved, both, within individual firm and as suggested earlier, collaborators in other disciplines.

The smaller or medium sized practice might have natural advantages over their larger counterparts where family business practice is concerned. We are certainly not advocating a return to the 'jack of all trades' general practitioner. Nor are we suggesting it is realistic to swim against the tide of increasing specialisation. Our point is that in a small to medium sized firm over-specialisation is less likely. An individual tax professional in such a firm is likely to deal with income tax, inheritance tax and capital gains, rather than just one of these. On a more practical level a private client lawyer may be more likely to be sitting in an office close to their corporate colleagues rather than on a different floor or in a separate office. Communication between teams becomes so much easier (at least in theory).

Also family firms are likely to represent a greater proportion of the client base for professionals in smaller or medium sized firms. Accordingly some of the issues of family dynamics might be much more second nature to the professionals concerned, who may well have developed an instinctive way of dealing with family business clients in general, or specific key clients in particular. That is not to say that smaller or medium sized firms have nothing new to learn and will not benefit from investment in their family business offering, if only to reinforce what they see as a natural competitive advantage.

26.4.5 Family business teams

The logic stemming from chapter one, where we analyse the demographics of the family business market is that, on closer analysis, family owned firms are likely to be of considerable importance to even the largest of professional firms. So how does the larger practice best serve its family business clients and provide them with a coherent and cohesive service across the boundaries of the three-circle model, whilst taking into account the unique family dynamics of the family business concerned?

There is no universally guaranteed prescription for success. But some ideas and pointers should help.

- **Awareness.** The first and most important step is to develop a firm wide awareness of the simple message that family owned businesses are different, for the reasons of family dynamics and culture, explained in this book. Secondly, and leading on from the first point, capturing an awareness of just which of the firm's clients are family owned. This awareness might be pretty much irrelevant to, for example a junior property lawyer, dealing with a non-family middle manager in the family business client company over a licence to assign. But it might just not be, for example, if there is a family or ownership complication.[37] A more complex aspect of awareness is self-awareness. Therapy based professionals are required to undertake extensive therapy themselves, to help them identify where their own emotional and psychological triggers might influence the approach they take to their clients. No such commitment is required from other professionals working with business families. But there must be a danger, particularly where the professional is seen as a trusted advisor, for their own beliefs and prejudices to influence the advice they give. For example an accountant with a firm belief that everyone should 'stand on their own two feet' may subtly influence a family business owner against gifting their business to the next generation in favour of a family buy-out or even an outright trade sale. Again we are not suggesting that all professionals working with family owned businesses should subject themselves to formal therapy. Merely that sensible steps need to be taken to make sure that advice, with the potential for a major effect on the family business system, should be as free as possible from the 'perceptual filters' arising from the professional's own personal and professional background.[38]

- **Training.** Secondly building awareness through training and otherwise. There are two areas that merit attention: first training in family business theory and family dynamics; and secondly cross-disciplinary technical training, focusing on the boundaries and areas of overlap between the three systems. Tax is as good a place as any to start. That is not to say that the objective is to turn private client lawyers into corporate lawyers, or *vice-versa*. It is just to develop awareness and connections between the various disciplines. The sharper the synapses, the more readily connections can be made between the silos when a family business situation requires this.[39]

- **Family business champions.** Exactly who undergoes family business specific training and at what level is another question. It would be entirely unrealistic to expect every professional within a large firm to be highly trained in family business issues. Leaving aside the question of cost and competing demands for training budgets and fee earner time, there may only be a marginal benefit from detailed family business training for some highly specialised expert or content advisors. Other professionals will simply not have the time, interest or personality to become deeply immersed in family business theory. But if the net is cast wide enough, it should prove possible to trawl up a sufficient number of professionals who have the interest and commitment to become family business champions.

---

[37] For example in the *Harrison Properties* case discussed in chapter 8, where professionals were instructed by the family company to obtain planning permission on land subsequently sold to the family managing director for his own property development projects.

[38] *Family Enterprise: Understanding Families in Business and Families of Wealth* (The Family Firm Institute, Wiley, 2014) at p 95.

[39] It could well have been that the corporate lead partner in the *Swain Mason* case had a good working knowledge of private client tax issues including the inheritance tax consequences of dying with large lumps of cash rather than shares that attracted BPR relief. The alternative possibility could be that if these issues were closer to the front of the partner's mind, or if the intra-firm thinking had been more closely joined up, maybe just maybe things would have turned out better for both the firm and the family concerned (although sadly not the family business founder who died shortly after his operation).

Exactly what that role will encompass will vary from firm to firm, but is likely to involve some combination of learning about family business issues, passing on that knowledge to colleagues, leading on or supporting others where family business technical issues are involved, together with family business focused marketing and business development. In an ideal world these family business champions would be drawn from all relevant practice areas and at various levels of seniority. It is comparatively easier to preach the virtues of developing the next generation of leadership to a family business client if a firm can be seen to be doing this themselves.[40] Ultimately enthusiasm and commitment to the family business field will be the key requisites for family business champions. The object is to create a family business wave effect, the ripples of which will spread throughout the professional firm concerned.

- **The role of the client partners.** It might seem logical for family business champions to fill the role of client partner or liaison partner for the family business clients of a professional firm. Whilst this might be ideal, it may not be either practicable or necessary in every case. First, as a product of family business statistics, there might simply be too many family owned businesses for a firm's acknowledged family business champions to support. Secondly the firm might prefer to organise relationships and practice groups along industry lines. Finally there will be an understandable reluctance to interfere with existing client partner relationships that are seen to work perfectly well in practice. So the role of the family business champion might well be to offer background support for designated client partners and front line assistance on recognised family business specific issues, such as governance or succession planning.

- **Cross disciplinary family business teams.** The ultimate aim is for a professional services firm to develop a cross-disciplinary family business team, comprised of family business champions, who have an understanding of both family business dynamics and the areas of overlap between their own area of specialisation and other disciplines, both inside and outside their firm, which might be relevant to the needs of their family business client. The team will increasingly work together and be seen as the natural port of call for new family business instructions and as a source of support and knowledge for colleagues in the wider firm dealing with other family business clients. As a starting point, firms can look to build a firm bridge between the business and private client offerings of a professional services firm. Those between the private client and corporate teams merit particular attention.

26.5 DEFINING THE FAMILY BUSINESS CLIENT

In chapter 25 we venture into the world of the process consultancy and the family business consultant. We now examine a key difference in approach between process consultancy and the content advisory professional. This is how to identify your client.

For accountants undertaking audit and corporation tax work this will be the family company. Similarly lawyers will be entirely clear that they are acting for the family company, when consulted on business related matters, such as dealing with the

---

[40] Swartz take a different view, at least in the context of family business consultancy (as opposed to family business advice provided in a traditional advisory setting). He argues that a certain level of experience and maturity is required to undertake family business consultancy work and suggests that most consultants will be over 45. See Steve Swartz 'The Challenges of Multidisciplinary Consulting to Family-Owned Businesses' *Family Business Review* (1988) Vol 2(4), at p 334.

mechanics of a new share issue. The client of a private client lawyer will be individual family members, when instructed on matters, such as a divorce or preparing a new will.

As illustrated by the discussion above, on the application of the three-circle model to family business advisory work, the danger of this conventional approach is that the complexity of the family business situation is lost. Instead Hilburt–Davis and Dyer believe that:[41]

> 'the family business is best served by the consultant who defines the family business system as the client.'

In practice it will always be necessary to reconcile an understanding that any advice provided needs to be seen in the context of the wider family business system with compliance with potentially more narrow and restrictive duties to which the content professional is subject as a result of membership of their profession of origin.

An American lawyer, Henry Krasnow, argues powerfully that this wider formulation of the client is dangerous, for some (but not all) professionals concerned and that:[42]

> 'for lawyers, accountants and other professionals exposed to malpractice claims, the client should always be recognised as and **limited** to the person or entity that can sue for malpractice.'

Obviously a concept, the family business system, cannot be a client for contractual and compliance purposes.[43] Great caution needs to be exercised against routinely raising VAT invoices to a VAT registered business client, when the subject matter of the underlying instructions is not directly connected to the trading operation of the family business.[44]

Moving beyond these basic issues of compliance hygiene, we come back full circle to the nub of the point made by Hilburt–Davis and Dyer, the need to have regard to the wider family business system. Take, as an example, instructions to a solicitor, or possibly an accountant to prepare a shareholders' agreement.

As a basic instrument of corporate governance, a shareholders' agreement will usually include provisions to regulate the relationship between the board and the shareholders. We would suggest that, in the vast majority of cases, advisors will recognise that such an agreement has a benefit for the trade. Accordingly it be appropriate to act for and to bill the family company. Alternative views and approaches are possible,[45] and in some cases

---

[41] Jane Hilburt-Davis and W Gibb Dyer *Consulting to Family Businesses* (Jossey Bass, 2003) at p 36.
[42] 'How I know my client … or, Why I Can't Represent a Family' *FFI Practitioner*, July 2012. Mr Krasnow is an FFI Fellow and winner of the FFI award for Interdisciplinary Achievement so is well aware of the family system argument.
[43] Including, in the case of solicitors subject to the conduct rules of the Law Society in England and Wales issuing retainer or engagement letters.
[44] It still might be possible for the family firm to pay the expenses involved in providing advice to the 'system' on an issue that is largely centered in the family or ownership domains, for example a pre-nuptial agreement, by issuing 'Non VAT invoices' making it clear that the client is a one or more family members although the costs are payable by the family company provided that no attempt is made to reclaim VAT input tax.
[45] For example apportioning the costs, including VAT, between the shareholders.

necessary.[46] Similarly, whilst there might be occasions where conflicts of interests mean that some of the family members need separate representation, in most cases only one single professional will be engaged to act. In theory that professional will be acting for the family company.

The family firm itself might be seen as the closest proxy to the family business system.

In practice instructions will often come from a single source. Usually this will be the professional's main point of contact with the family firm. Often this will be the business leader, the managing director or chairman. As such that individual is likely to also be have a key influence in the family and ownership systems. The business leader might be well placed to act as spokesperson for the family business system as a whole. But inevitably the potential for personal prejudice and preference on the part of the spokesperson creeps in.

What steps can the advisor take to ensure that the document produced really is a shareholders' agreement, reflecting the informed wishes of the family members as a whole, rather than a single shareholder's or 'Chairman's agreement', albeit one binding on all the family members?

The following might help:

- **Questionnaires and briefing notes.** Issuing detailed briefing notes and questionnaires, seeking views from the wider family on what should be included in the agreement.
- **Family meetings.** Facilitating wider family meetings to debate any issues of difference and to provide face-to face briefings and explanations on contentious or complex issues. Making sure that those meetings are conducted in such a way that all views are aired and that all family members concerned, not just the most senior, have the opportunity to be heard.
- **Separate advice.** Actively encouraging any outliers to seek separate advice[47] at appropriate times. If the process is working for the benefit of the family business system as a whole, one or more members obtaining separate advice should not create or add to conflict and tension. Rather a separate perspective should provide reassurance and add to the confidence that process is working to produce a fair and balanced agreement. The separate advisor may be able to add fresh perspectives and refinements that improve the overall solution. Having made their contribution the separate advisor is likely then to be able to withdraw into the background, allowing the remainder of the agreement to be completed by the lead advisor, working with the business family as a whole.
There will often be a fear that involving separate advisors will cause conflict within the business owning family. In reality this is unlikely. But there is a risk that latent underlying conflict might sometimes be exposed and brought to the surface as a

---

[46] For example, buy and sell agreements, dealing solely with cross options between individual shareholders other than those connected with business continuity arrangements such as cross insurance arrangements underpinned by key man life cover.

[47] We do not use the term 'independent advice' on the basis that if the professional advisor is truly acting for the family business system as a whole they should be seen to be independent of any individual within that system. In *Kremen v Agrest* [2012] EWHC 45 (Fam), a case concerning the enforceability of a pre-nuptial agreement drawn up by a notary attached to a firm connected to the husband's father, the court drew a distinction between impartial and strictly independent advice of the lawyer concerned (at para 57). The agreement was upheld.

result of separate advice. In another context, John Ham (whose case is discussed in detail in chapter 13) said of the involvement of his parent's separate lawyers:[48]

> 'There was initially no dispute and my exit from the business was being sorted amicably by our accountant and the farm agent, until my parents sought advice from a new solicitor who advised them not to pay me my fair share of the farm, and as a result we have had this very expensive court case.'

Was that really the case? Alternatively did the parents obtaining separate advice simply expose fault lines and tensions in the Ham family business that had been present for some while?

26.6 ONE CLIENT MANY ROLES?

Part of the problem could be that in representing a family business client an advisor might be called on to play a number of roles and to do so interchangeably. Sometimes the role will be fairly straightforward and will be dictated by context and the client's instructions. On other occasions it will be necessary to switch between roles as, following the Hilburt-Davis and Dyer analysis, the advisor switches from content to process mode.[49]

Those roles could include:

- **Hired gun.** The clearest and simplest role would appear to be that of the 'hired-gun', for example the litigation lawyer, retained by one family member or faction, to act on their behalf in connection with a family dispute. Their role is very close to that described by Henry Krasnow of 'developing and then implementing a strategy to accomplish a goal' the object being to 'to get one person or entity what he, she or it wants' rather than to 'work for the overall good'. Even so, to do their job effectively, the hired gun needs to know when to encourage their client to sue for peace, rather than simply carrying on litigation. To do so they will need to deploy process skills in their dealings with their own client.

- **Wise person.** On other occasions family business advisors are asked to move beyond the limited role envisaged by Krasnow and to actively recommend solutions and suggestions to the wider business family. Even if that advice is only given to a single family member, usually the business leader and majority owner, the implications of that advice will be felt throughout the family business system. The advice given might seem to be heavily content laden, for example on the taxation implications of selling the family company or its saleability. The advice sought might be broader, for example the trusted advisor might be drawn into a discussion on the relative merits of siblings as business leader. The challenge for the advisor is to identify their own pre-conceptions and prejudices and, so far as possible prevent these colouring their advice and influence on the family business system. For example a senior partner in an accountancy practice held very strong views about the inefficiency of second-generation family companies and firmly believed that founders should sell their businesses. Other advisors will hold equally strong family succession biases. Even if wider options are presented how do advisors prevent their own beliefs from intruding on the family decision making process?

---

[48] From *Farmer's Weekly* Friday 1 November 2013.
[49] Explained in chapter 25.

- **Peacemaker.** Trusted advisors might be asked to assume a role in helping resolve differences between members of a business owning family in the early stages of a dispute and before the family have actually categorised it as such. Hilburt-Davis and Dyer would see this an example of the family business advisor needing to deploy process-consulting skills for the good of the family business client, the system as a whole. Conversely Krasnow believes that the content professional is treading on dangerously thin ice. Using the analogy of a chess tutor, he argues that whilst a group of students can be taught the rules of the game, it is not possible to simultaneously teach two players engaged in a match how to win. It is one thing to assume a formal mediation role. It is something entirely different and potentially more dangerous to attempt to help family members 'sort things out' in an informal basis, without proper safeguards and explicit terms of reference. Krasnow is particularly scathing about the professional who gets sucked into the vortex of the family system in a misguided attempt to help or to play God:

> '... there is nothing wrong with a professional who hopes that his or her advice will help many constituencies ... But in the long run a great deal of liability, disappointment, frustration and confusion will be experienced by those who naively fail to make a distinction between their "clients" and those they hope to help.'

The role of peacemaker can be rewarding. It can also be thankless. In *Ackerman v Ackerman*,[50] a leading counsel agreed to advise on the division of a large portfolio of companies and over 100 investment properties, that had been built up by two brothers. Following the death of one of the brothers a dispute arose between the remaining brother and on the other side of the dispute, his sister in law and nephew. The surviving brother believed that the proposed division of assets effectively took the family business away from him. He challenged the validity of the leading counsel's approach. The High Court judge thought that the leading counsel had taken on 'an extraordinarily difficult task' and that he might be said to have been 'mad to do so' but he had done so fairly. Despite some procedural irregularities, the Court dismissed the brother's claim of bias and the allocation stood. The key point was that in *Ackerman*, the leading counsel's role was formal and fully documented. Often the professional seeking to 'sort out' differences within a business family will do so on an extremely informal basis, with boundaries between professional trusted advisor and family friend becoming extremely blurred. It is in those circumstances where Krasnow's concerns are most likely to apply.

26.7 THE LAWYERS' ROLE IN *CADMAN DEVELOPMENTS*

Cadman Developments[51] provides some interesting discussion points on the role or potential roles played by family business advisors, and in particular the private client practitioner.

The case report refers to attempts by the three siblings to agree the future ownership of the family company after the death of the father, James, but whilst the mother Edith was still alive. The siblings could not reach agreement. The family lawyers wrote to all three

---

[50] *Estates Gazette* (2012) July 1.
[51] The *Cadman* case is introduced in chapter 1, discussed in detail in chapter 21, but is referred to throughout the book.

siblings 'on Edith's behalf' with a suggestion that the family company should be jointly owned by all three siblings and that each should be a director. The brothers would not agree to this.

A meeting was then arranged between Janis Fisher and her two brothers, at the offices of the family solicitors, to discuss how their mother's estate should be divided. The mother was not present at this meeting. A suggestion was put to Janis that she should take a larger share of the remainder of her mother's assets, in return for the brothers taking full ownership of Cadman Developments, including the shares that Janis had acquired from her father. Janis rejected this proposal, on the basis that she believed that her father had wanted her to stay involved in the family business.

Which of the above roles best describes that assumed by the lawyers concerned? Certainly they were more than mere messengers on Edith Cadman's behalf. Were they attempting to mediate between the siblings? How did they reconcile their role as solicitors to the company with any wider duty to the family business system? In particular, if their historic dealings had been primarily with the brothers, how did they deal even-handedly with Janis, but without overcompensating to the detriment of the brothers? Was their intervention in the 'family system' sufficiently robust? Joint ownership of the family company continued, notwithstanding the clear incompatibility of the siblings as evidenced by the subsequent dispute? And how did the actual role or roles assumed reconcile with their engagement letter?

Probably the most difficult judgment that a family business advisor has to make is when the point has been reached when, notwithstanding the various arguments and factors against this, clients in a position like Janis need to receive separate advice.

26.8 CONFLICTS OF INTEREST

Discussion of family members obtaining separate advice leads on to a wider consideration of the topic of conflicts of interest when acting for family business clients. The issue of conflict of interest will be at the forefront of the professional's mind when dealing with family business matters.

On one analysis the family business system is riddled with actual and potential conflicts. One might attempt to make a distinction between conflicts and conflicts of interest, which will eliminate many cases of sibling rivalry from the latter category, where, typically, brothers may fight, but there is no discernible difference in their economic interests.

This still leaves a whole range of family business situations where the interests of various sections of the family business system are directly opposed. For example between insiders and outsiders over questions of dividend policy, remuneration, access to information, management controls, voting rights or even the fundamental question of ownership rights.[52] Or between current and next generation over the detail of succession arrangements, including such fundamental questions as whether the family business is to be sold to a third party or whether the business should be sold or given to the next generation. If a sale to the next generation is agreed, at what price?

---

[52] Most of these were issues in *Saul D Harrison* case, discussed extensively throughout this book.

How does the professional advisor approach this potential minefield?

As a matter of abstract theory, every stakeholder in the family business system could receive independent and separate advice. But that could be a practical and logistical nightmare, to say nothing of the costs implications. Even if the family could afford to retain an army of professionals would they wish to do so and would this really be in their best interests?

Henry Krasnow holds very clear views. He makes a distinction between process professionals, such as family business consultants 'who have the skill to help [family members] resolve their dispute themselves' and other professionals, in particular lawyers, who, he believes need to choose (or more accurately be chosen by) sides and then help them win.

Of course there will be occasions, such as outright disputes, where separate representation becomes inevitable. On other occasions professionals may choose to act as 'execution only agents', simply documenting their client's instructions without real question or enquiry. Take, as an example, the position of a private client lawyer, sitting in front of the senior generation majority shareholder of a the family company, who asks the lawyer to prepare a will leaving their shares equally to their insider and outsider children.

The Hilburt-Davis and Dyer formula suggests that the all professionals should treat the family business system, including the children (and the business itself) as their client. Realistically this is likely to be going too far in this context. In contractual and engagement terms the client is clearly the individual senior generation family member. But a reformulation of the Hilburt-Davis and Dyer approach is possible, so that the lawyer acts for their individual contractual client, but does so 'having regard to the family system as a whole'. This reformulation allows, requires even, the lawyer concerned to ask questions such as 'have you discussed this with your children?', 'how does the [insider] feel about this?' or 'how do they all get along?'

The resulting answers might provide reassurance that the family have already followed an appropriate process. Alternatively it might highlight the need for a more detailed intervention. Failing to ask those questions could result in a will which, whilst following the client's instructions, is nevertheless not fit for its family business purpose.

This reformulation is also compatible with Henry Krasnow's view that, lawyers in particular have a 'mandate of developing and then implementing a strategy to accomplish a goal'. Whilst the eventual choice of strategy must ultimately be for the client to decide, inevitably the advisor has an influence in its formulation. There is nothing to prevent the advisor from highlighting non-financial goals, such as preservation of family harmony, for possible inclusion in that strategy.

The above example could relate to one-off instructions given to an occasional advisor. The position of a close, trusted advisor is infinitely more complex and potentially more dangerous, both for the advisor and for the family business system. The closer the advisor is to the problem, the greater the risk of them becoming part of it.[53] The advisor

---

[53] This is the rationale behind the supervision system for therapy based professionals who are required to discuss their cases with colleagues not directly involved in the matter at regular intervals. Many family business consultants operate similar systems.

does well not to allow their own views, attitudes, preconceptions, prejudices and loyalties to colour their approach and advice. This might result in over-identification with a particular generation or individual, or an overbearing preference for a particular outcome, such as to save tax, or sell the family business.

A close identification with the client may simply result in a strong wish to help the business owning family and to help resolve any conflict that does arise at any early stage. Historically, trusted advisors, acting as informal mediators, have devised many a workable patch up to a family business dispute. Indeed it will be seem from the quote above that the farm agent and accountant attempted to do just that in the *Ham* case. This may well be the best thing for the family and the business. Such an approach is by no means prevented by modern compliance requirements, although more thought (which is also a good thing) and more paperwork, might be required, than was historically the case. One must always have an eye to a potentially problematic future.

26.9 CONFLICTS AND OUTCOMES FOCUSED REGULATION

For solicitors practising in England and Wales the position on conflicts of interest or potential conflict of interest is now governed by Chapter 3 of the 2011 Solicitors Regulation Authority (SRA) Code of Conduct.[54]

Returning to the example of acting on the preparation of a shareholders' agreement for a family company. It might be possible to argue that the solicitor has only one client, the company itself, and any interactions with individual family members are merely ways of communicating with that inanimate client. But that approach is dangerous. It runs contrary to the Hilburt-Davis/Dyer approach. It also cuts across underlying spirit of the outcomes focused regulation and the underlying rationale of the *Vinton* case.

At least for the purposes of Chapter 3, it is surely safer to regard each signatory to a document that the solicitor is preparing as a separate client or notional client.

On this basis some of the alarm bells set out in O(3.3) might well begin to ring. Such as:

- **Different interests of clients,** for example between insiders and outsiders.
- Fetters on ability to give **independent advice.** The acid test is probably the ability or preparedness to disagree with the business leader who holds the purse strings of future instructions.
- **A need to mediate** between clients, for example to resolve disagreements over which of various options should be included in the agreement over share transfer provisions.
- **Negotiating** on behalf of one client.
- **An imbalance of negotiating power,** for example between the senior generation business leader and the next generation insider who has committed their career to the family firm.

---

[54] The more detailed comments on professional conduct contained in this paragraph are confined to the position of solicitors practicing in England and Wales. Accountants, IFA's and lawyers from other jurisdictions will be subject to their own professional conduct requirements a detailed discussion of which are outside the scope of this book.

If any of these circumstances exist, and it would be difficult to envisage a situation where they did not, the solicitor concerned has a number of choices. They can ignore the situation, on the basis that the alarm bells are only ringing faintly, that such situations are commonplace and unlikely to materialise into real problems. This is not our suggested solution.

The solicitor might retreat to potentially safer ground of acting only for the family business member from whom they take instructions and expressly rejecting any duty of care to the rest of the business family. But this would be both unusual and directly contrary to the Hilburt-Davis/Dyer approach. However it would be consistent with Krasnow's caution.

The lawyer might send for re-enforcements, usually fellow lawyers from a different firm, to provide separate advice to family members. But this may seem expensive and un-necessary, especially to the client.

Alternatively support could be provided by a family business consultant, deploying their process skills to help the family work through any differences and allowing the lawyer to occupy the safer and perhaps more comfortable ground, of providing and documenting technically sound solutions in collaboration with the consultant.

If the solicitor concerned nevertheless decides to press on they might well be able to seek sanctuary in the substantial common interest exemption provided by O(3.6). This allows a solicitor to act for multiple clients, whose interests are in conflict subject to the following safeguards:

- **Explanation and understanding.** The solicitor must explain the relevant issues, giving rise to actual or potential conflict and have a reasonable belief that the client understands these. It therefore follows that, to do this, the lawyer concerned needs a detailed understanding of family business issues and dynamics.
- **Written consent.** The clients have given their informed written consent to the solicitor acting. This could be built into the client engagement letter.
- **Reasonableness.** There is an over-riding test that solicitor must be satisfied that it is reasonable to act for all family members and in their best interests. Logically, the bigger the issue, the less likely this is to be the case. For example an insider might be asked to agree to a document providing for equal distribution of ownership. That insider might also have a reasonable claim to proprietary estoppel[55] that would be waived by the documents. It might be sensible to recommend, or even insist, that the insider concerned takes separate advice on such a key issue.
- **Cost benefit analysis.** Finally, that the lawyer is satisfied that the benefit to the clients of the lawyer in continuing to act for all of them outweigh the risks of doing so. In practice this will often boil down to proportionality. The costs of obtaining independent advice on easily understood, and as yet, potential or hypothetical conflicts of interest might simply be too much for most small or medium sized family businesses to bear.

The analysis required by the OFR regime is supported by lists of indicative behaviours. Of these IB(3.5) jumps out of the page. Here a solicitor may need to demonstrate that

---

[55] Explained and discussed in detail in chapter 19.

they have declined to act where 'the clients cannot be represented even-handedly'. We are back to the hidden dangers inherent in the relationship between the trusted advisor and the family business leader.

At various stages in this book we have asked questions[56] about the role played by advisors in a number of the cases we have discussed. If, as in those cases, the potential conflict of interest between members of a business owning family develops into an actual dispute, the solicitor concerned might expect similar questions to be raised by the Solicitors' Regulation Authority under the OFR regime. It therefore follows that, to answer those questions, solicitors will need to be able to clearly document their thought processes, where they can be seen to have acted for more than one stakeholder within a family business system.

Lawyers need to proceed with extreme caution. The over-riding duty remains to act in accordance with the SRA Principles 2011. Various principles are capable of providing guiding light. These include the core duties to act with integrity, to not allow one's independence to be compromised and to act in the best interests of each client.[57] Key distinctions will be between conflicting views and common interests that simply need to be recorded, actual and potential conflicts of interest, along with materiality and proportionality. They need to have one eye permanently on the future and what can go wrong in terms of client relationships, negligence claims and allegations of professional misconduct.

This is no easy task. It calls for careful and on-going judgment. If the lawyer overreacts the client is lost. Family relationships are likely to be damaged, at least in the short term. But if the lawyer leaves matters such as recommending one of the family take separate advice too late, matters are likely to be much worse. Trust between the lawyer and the client and between the family may have been compromised. Full-blown disputes and irreparable damage to family relationships may be the consequence, to say nothing of the professional consequences for the lawyer and firm concerned.

Ideally, in making and monitoring their judgments, individual lawyers would be able to lean on colleagues and compliance officers from within their own firm.[58] The greatest peril often lies in trying to go it alone. Logically the greatest support should come from the overriding SRA Principles, against which all professional conduct will be judged.

That is not to say that a substantial common interest cannot be identified. Usually this will be based on the core common interests of a family wanting to continue in business together and maintaining family harmony, and that most (if not all) areas of conflict are over relative matters detail. To a large extent this instinctive evaluation can be supported by psychological theory, in particular socio-emotional selectivity theory, which suggests that many business families will prioritise 'non-financial wealth' basically family relationships, over purely financially driven goals.[59] So the insider may actually accept

---

[56] Which we sincerely hope have not been interpreted as express or implied criticisms which would be entirely inappropriate in the absence of detailed knowledge of the matter concerned.
[57] Although the SRA Ethics team will provide guidance on the practical application of the Principles and the Code, they will not provide the lawyer concerned with advice much less a safe harbour clearance of their proposed course of action.
[58] One of benefits of internal family business teams is the ability to share common ethical dilemmas in family business work, including issues of professional ethics.
[59] Socio-emotional selectivity theory or SEST and its application to family owned businesses is explained in more detail in Perry, Ring and Broberg 'Which Type of Advisors Do Family Businesses Trust Most? An Exploratory Application of Socioemotional Selectivity Theory' *Family Business Review* (2014), 1–16.

an equal ownership approach, just as outsiders might agree that fairness dictates that the insiders take ownership of the family firm. Basically this is what we have previously referred to as a 'family first' approach.

26.10 CONFIDENTIALITY

Turning now to the related issue of confidentiality.[60]

There are two basic types of confidential information relevant to family business advisory work. In rough terms they can be labelled as content and process related confidentiality.[61]

Content related confidential information usually relates to financial matters, for example financial performance or the development potential of land owned by the family company.[62] Often the issue will be the relative access to information between those insiders 'in the know' and more remote family outsiders.[63]

It will be second nature for advisors to safeguard content related confidential information from third parties completely outside the family business system. But the position is a little more complex when dealing with stakeholders, within the family business system, but still falling either side of the insider outsider divide.

Take the example of a family business founder, who has resigned from the board as part of their succession planning, but still retains ownership control. Consider then the position of an accountant who (might have a long-standing relationship with the founder) who is then asked to provide certain management information to the founder. Should the advisor refuse to do so, at least without first obtaining the consent of the next generation managing director? From a content related confidentiality stand-point, almost certainly yes. Dig a little deeper and it might be seen that the founder's request is in fact process laden. The founder still regards the family business as his to all intents and purposes. He is seeking to exercise control. Knowledge is power to be reclaimed or used, as the case may be.

Ideally the advisor concerned will be able to use process skills to achieve a sensitive reconciliation of corporate governance theory and family business reality. The accountant could explain that, whilst they understand why the founder wants the relevant information, they just need to 'check in' with the next generation before providing this, or encourage the founder to do so.

Other information can be categorised as pure process confidential information. This is information about the hopes, fears, beliefs, intentions and attitudes of individual family members. It has an enormously high emotional content and a corresponding potential to do lasting damage to family relationships, but no financial value as such.

---

[60] For solicitors practicing in England and Wales the applicable detailed professional conduct provisions are in Chapter 4 of the 2011 SRA Code.
[61] These are labels borrowed from rather than used by Hilburt-Davis and Dyer. See above.
[62] See for example the Harrison Properties case discussed in chapter 8.
[63] The importance of information in family business governance is discussed in more detail in chapter 17.

In family firms with blocked communication systems the advisor will often be privy to, or burdened with, pure process confidential information of this kind. The trusted advisor might be told that the founder doubts the abilities of the anointed next generation successor to take over the family firm.

What does the advisor do with that information? Perhaps nothing, on the basis that all the evidence points to the contrary, and the advisor is sufficiently confident that they are simply on the receiving end of the founders' ambivalence. But a closer examination might suggest that there is a deeper problem, into which the advisor is being drawn into, or in technical psychology jargon, triangulated.[64] The advisor is in a difficult position. Do they simply act as a confidant for the founder? Saying nothing might not be seen as a real option if they believe their duty is to actively assist their family business client. Equally, like Albert Camus, they might be concerned that 'saying things badly increases the unhappiness in the world'.

Do they attempt some process related intervention themselves, with all the timing and tact that they can muster? Or do they seek to involve a pure process professional such as a family business consultant to undertake this highly sensitive task?

There are however times when more abstract considerations of the nature of confidentiality crystalise into a hard professional obligations.

Returning again to the example of the family business founder (who has retained ownership control) and his son who now leads the family business. Imagine that the lawyer has been involved in a succession planning project, which is now in its later stages and which involves the gift of a controlling interest to the son. This decision is based on a clearly known wish from the founder that the business should stay in the family (and for this reason the founder's other children, who do not work in the business are to receive only small minority stakes). However the lawyer concerned discovers that the son is contemplating selling the business. What then?

Much will depend on the basis of the retainer. If this is from the father alone and the information was not imparted in confidence the lawyer could advise the father to take appropriate steps to protect the key succession assumption of continuity.

However if there is a joint retainer and the information was imparted by the son in confidence the requirements of the Chapter 4 of the SRA Code are clear. The lawyer concerned is infected with septic confidential information. The source of infection is immaterial.[65] But the information itself is clearly material to the succession planning exercise, the subject of their instructions.[66] The lawyer is caught between the rock of their duty of disclosure to the founder and the hard place of their duty of confidentiality to the son.

Possibly these duties could be reconciled. With the son's agreement, the possibility of sale could be shared with the founder (and possibly the wider family). This might take some careful management, but if full transparency is achieved, the problem disappears.

---

[64] The process of triangulation is explained in more detail in chapter 3.
[65] Perhaps the son told the lawyer directly as a trusted advisor. Possibly a chance comment from a conversation with the accountant mentioned at the start of this running example revealed that the son was making plans for sale.
[66] It is impossible to dismiss the information as simply a throw away comment or a piece of chance gossip.

However if the son refuses to allow disclosure the solicitor must decline to act further in the succession exercise but cannot say why they are doing so. The duty of disclosure to the father and the wider family is trumped by the duty of confidentiality to the son.

The net result will almost inevitably be a lost client and in all probability a massive family row, when matters unravel. The instinct of the solicitor will be to help avoid both. With tact and extreme care, it might be possible to persuade the son to agree to proper disclosure and to restore transparency.[67] Clearly this would present a difficult and sensitive balancing exercise for the lawyer concerned. The family business advisor and conflict resolution.

26.11 FIT FOR FAMILY BUSINESS PURPOSE?

26.11.1 Overview

One consequence of the silo effect, the increased specialisation of the content professional, is the potential for an ever-increasing remoteness from the dynamics affecting their family business clients. Add a couple of features of the content professional's life into that mix, such as costs pressures and a reliance on standardised or template solutions, a real risk arises that the end content product, whilst 'standard', might not be fit for the purposes of the family business client.

There is a danger of defining the problem of a family business client with reference to the advisor's profession or specialisation. Gersick calls this the 'law of the hammer: when your only tool is a hammer every problem looks like a nail'.[68] Much of this book has been about both adding more family business tools to the advisor' tool-box and being aware of the skills of other craftsmen.

The basic message we are seeking to convey is to advocate a family business fitness for purpose review of documents, advice notes and other work outputs of the content professional when acting in the context of a family business. This should reduce the possibility of a family conflict arising as a result of, for example the provisions of a document not being suitable for the family business situation.

Equally, for the advisor, the possibility of embarrassment, a seriously unhappy client, or worse still a professional negligence claim, is replaced by a positive reinforcement of goodwill in favour of an advisor who has made attempts to understand the family business context in which their advice is being given.

Let us discuss one or two examples to illustrate this proposition.

26.11.2 Articles of Association and early stage family companies

In chapter 17 (Governance), we suggest that full governance systems, including family charters or bespoke shareholders' agreements are in place in only a small minority of family owned businesses in the UK. Yet all incorporated family businesses will

---

[67] Possibly this could result in some form of anti-embarrassment provision being included in agreements to protect the interests of the outsiders if the business was sold.
[68] Op cit at p 272.

technically have a constitution even if this is confined to the Articles of Association supplied by the incorporation agent. These documents will almost invariably be fairly basic.

The Model Articles[69] contain little by way of express provisions relating to the key issue of share transfers. The ability of the directors to refuse to register share transfers under Art 63(5) is limited. There are no compulsory transfer provisions. The limited research we have undertaken has not identified any incorporation agents that differentiate their shelf company offerings between those supplied for intended use in a family business and those intended for use in the context of other companies. It will therefore be pretty much a lottery whether and, if so, how the initial constitutions of most family businesses treat family business specific issues. The key issues are likely to relate to share ownership. There may well be winners in that lottery. A number of incorporation agents include permitted transfers provisions, allowing the free transfer of shares between immediate family members as part of their standard shelf company articles. The starting point in other off the shelf packages may well be a general discretion for the board to refuse to register the transfer of shares.

26.11.3 Second generation family companies: the constitution outgrown?

Shelf companies will be used in the vast majority of start-up or early stage, entrepreneurial family companies. Even if the proprietor already has a fixed intention to involve their children or other family members in the business at the time it is set up, it may be unrealistic to expect them to spend precious time or cash on anything other than the most basic family business specific provisions (such as permitted transfer provisions).

The key will be to keep the core constitutional documents under review so that, at an appropriate stage in the evolution of the family business, the initial off the peg articles are discarded and replaced by a more tailored (if not yet fully bespoke) documents. This tailoring sits alongside the development of a wider ownership philosophy.

To a certain extent failure to undertake this review, whilst giving an inconvenient or untidy starting point, may not necessarily be too problematic in practice. Whilst the family is in harmony, the articles can always be amended, most breaches of the articles, for example failure to follow pre-emption provisions, can be ratified or waived. The situation might be retrieved by relying on the *In Re Duomatic*[70] principle. Where family relationships have broken down the implications of off the peg constitutions are potentially much more problematic.

Example 1

Take, for example, a case of a Stage 2 sibling partnership of C Co where the two brothers concerned have fallen out. As often happens, 30 years after incorporation, C Co still has its shelf company articles, which contain an absolute prohibition on share transfers without the board's consent. One brother, A, who had previously and with the agreement of his brother, transferred shares to his children as part of his own succession planning arrangements, seeks to use a combination of this prohibition and the deadlocked board, to prevent an almost identical transfer by the second brother, B.

---

[69] Schedule 1 to the Companies (Model Articles) Regulations 2008, SI 2008/3229.
[70] The *In Re Duomatic* case is discussed in detail in chapter 8.

B might well argue that the historical precedent set in the case of A's own share transfer makes it impossible for him to say that the discretion of the board is being used in the best interests of the shareholders of the company as a whole rather than for A's own private purposes and the furtherance of the dispute between them. It may ultimately be difficult for A to resist an application to the Court by B on this basis.[71]

But B is faced with uncertainty. He faces litigation risk, costs and delay. These could have been avoided relatively easily by the inclusion of family business specific share transfer provisions in the original articles.

Governance is part of the risk management process of any business. The key equation in risk management is essentially the product of the likelihood of a risk materialising and the likely severity of risk. We would suggest that in a family business context the risk is high (and we have advised on a number of cases with similar facts to the above), as is the severity, in terms of both economic and family consequences. On this basis, the investment of a modest amount of attention and cost, by including even the most basic family business permitted share transfer provisions, seems unarguable.

Example 2

Adding a single fact to the above scenario illustrates the point further. Suppose that A had reached retirement age and that the transfer of shares was to his daughter who now works full time in the business instead of A and alongside B.

B now wishes to retire and to transfer his shares to his own daughter but she does not work in the business. A may argue that his share transfer was based on the fact that his daughter would be working in the business and was based on a working member, insider ownership philosophy. Accordingly that his refusal as a director to sanction B's proposed transfer to a non-working, outsider family member is entirely reasonable and is indeed consistent with the interests of the shareholders as a whole.

Absent some reasonably clear evidence, such as a family charter or minutes of a family meeting, to clarify the point, who is to say that A's argument is wrong and that his refusal is challengeable or, for that matter, even unreasonable?

26.11.4 Later stage family companies and bad family business fit

Even greater difficulties can be caused in situations where, either articles of association have been amended, or shareholders' agreements, have been adopted, without appropriate consideration of the family business factors by the advisors concerned. They might not even have expressly recognised that they were dealing with a family owned business.

On such occasions the result can be that a company adopts a bespoke constitution that simply does not fit their family business circumstances. Again provisions concerning share ownership are likely to be of particular concern. This can occur when, for example, articles are amended to deal with a specific operational issue, such as the removal of a chairman's casting vote. The opportunity is taken to introduce the latest precedent set of articles used by the firm concerned.

---

[71] The issue of refusal to register share transfers is discussed in chapter 11.

On other occasions specialists are instructed on a specific business project and introduce constitutional documents that perfectly meet the narrow objectives of that project. However a lack of focus on the wider family business context means that other provisions are introduced which inadvertently remove some of the wider structural underpinning of their client's family business foundations. The problem would be that the courts would take some convincing to look beyond the express terms of a bespoke constitution, especially a recently amended one, so as to recognise arguments advanced, for example as part of an unfair prejudice claim, that over-riding family business factors should apply.[72]

Example

The most extreme example of this we have encountered is in a fifth generation family business. The family were committed to the company remaining in family ownership. Shares were split between family shareholders working in the business and those not. To encourage non-family employees, a share option scheme was introduced. This included the usual provisions whereby employees could be asked to give up their shares on leaving the company. However the share option scheme formed only a peripheral part of the ownership plans of the family business concerned. The overriding ownership philosophy of the family was that their business should stay in the ownership of the wider business owning family.

New articles were adopted as part of the option scheme. These included provisions, which were no doubt common-place in employee schemes and perhaps represented best practice for specialist employee benefits teams. However certain of the new provisions operated against the family ownership philosophy in the following ways:

Provision 1

That all share transfers would be subject to pre-emption provisions with employees receiving preference to other shareholders.

This could lead to the dilution of non-working family members to the benefit of both working family members and non-family employees. Ownership and control could shift from family towards employee (including family insider) ownership. There were no permitted transfer provisions allowing inter family transfers, even by will. So gradually the wider family control would be diluted.

Provision 2

Allowed employees to transfer shares freely between each other.

This could result in individual employees building their stakes in the company. Also family insiders working for the company were treated the same as all other employees, so the balance of control between insiders and outsiders could also shift in an unplanned and unforeseen manner.

Provision 3

Provided that all employees (including family insiders) must offer to sell all their shares on leaving employment. Again no distinction was made between family and non-family employees.

---

[72] See chapter 2 for more detail. The presence of a bespoke constitution was a factor in dismissing the claim in *Saul D Harrison*.

Strangely this could place family insiders in a worse position than family outsiders, who could retain their shares, at least until their death.

In summary, provisions that made perfect sense for an employee owned business, were entirely inappropriate for a family business.

We do not know how this situation came about. A likely possibility is that professionals specialising in share option schemes put together a set of articles to encourage employee participation. Aspects of family ownership were overlooked in a project focused on the narrow objectives of introducing an employee share ownership scheme. The directors or managers involved in the project from the company could well have failed either to brief the lawyers concerned on the family's ownership philosophy, or to consider the implications of draft documents, or both. In this matter no long-term damage was done. The issue surfaced as part of a subsequent family business governance review exercise. The family was at peace. Replacement articles, focusing on family ownership and removing the above mischiefs, were put in place.

But the cards could have fallen very differently. Take a situation where cracks are beginning to appear in the relationships between working and non-working family shareholders. The working family shareholders might be looking to increase their shareholding in the company. The ability for this group to buy departing employees shares would clearly be to the detriment of the outsider non-working shareholders. A messy dispute could easily arise. It would be correspondingly harder for the non-working shareholders to argue that with a bespoke set of articles, these did not reflect the intentions of parties.

26.11.5 Shareholders' agreements

A similar but stronger argument applies in the case of shareholders' agreements prepared for family owned businesses.[73] Shareholders' agreements seem to be almost as rare in family owned companies as family charters.

On occasions family businesses will have agreed to put a shareholders' agreement in place, perhaps at the request of a bank or a third party investor. Perhaps under cost pressure, the advisor concerned may have reverted to a generic precedent document, without real thought of the suitability of the document for a family business situation (much less after detailed consideration, with the family of the key governance questions raised in chapter 17). For the reasons given above such an 'off the peg' solution may well prove to be a very bad fit for the circumstances of the family business, and, in extreme circumstances worse than not having an agreement in the first place.

A related difficulty is presented by the silo effect. The demands of family business advisory work will usually require professionals to think well beyond the narrow confines of their own practice area and to think of the implications of their advice and work outputs for the circumstances of their business family client.

The case in *F v F*[74] (discussed in chapter 18) provides an interesting example. In that case a couple whose marriage was clearly in difficulty at the time, approached lawyers to prepare a shareholders' agreement. The agreement contained provisions defining a clear role for the wife as a director. It also constrained the ability of the husband to

---

[73] See chapter 17.
[74] *F v F* [2012] EWHC 438 (Fam).

extract cash for his own benefit and for the benefit of the children from his first marriage, in effect requiring him to give preference to the infant children from his current (third) marriage.

The agreement had the look and feel of the product of a negotiation to shore up a crumbling marriage. However the document had no provisions dealing with what would happen in terms of the ownership or management of the business if the parties separated. The agreement was criticised by the courts as 'poorly drafted' in this regard. The possibility of separation must have been a foreseeable event. Instead of being able to follow specific exit provisions included to cater for this eventuality (or at least to use these as a starting point in any matrimonial negotiations) the parties ended up in court for the judge to fill in the blanks.

Of course the reason for the absence of separation related exit provisions is unclear. It is perfectly possible that the inclusion of these was raised with the husband and wife and rejected by them. Perhaps the corporate lawyer drafting the shareholders' agreement did not appreciate the wider family context in which the agreement was being prepared. Alternatively warning signs might have been visible to the lawyer concerned, but a mixture of embarrassment, unfamiliarity and a misplaced sense of delicacy prevented a business system lawyer from pursuing the issue of possible relationship breakdown across the systemic boundary into the family domain.

26.11.6 Family business partnership agreements

Often family business partnerships will be created by operation of law, as partnerships at will under s 1 of the Partnership Act 1890. Even in cases where formal partnership agreements have been prepared these may often fail under the strain of broken family relationships, as was the case in the Ham family.

Lawyers and other advisors wrestling with the complexities of partnership law face the additional difficulty of reconciling this to family business dynamics. Often they will be doing so whilst working to limited instructions, against cost constraints and on behalf of clients who have little grasp of the legal issues involved. It is therefore understandable why uncertainties and disputes can arise. But that will be of little comfort to, for example, a family farming partnership involved in a dispute. They will be faced with a breakdown in family relationships. A huge amount is likely to be at stake on the outcome of the dispute. There will be great uncertainty as to how matters will be resolved.

Accordingly the need for effective governance documents, especially formal partnership agreements, are most at a premium in circumstances where they are least likely to exist.

The provisions most likely to be of fundamental importance are those dealing with the exit of a retiring partner or the winding up or dissolution of the partnership. It is extremely unlikely that provisions taken from a standard precedent partnership agreement will prove fit for family business purpose.

There is therefore a potentially important role, in even the smallest of partnerships, for supporting, non-legally enforceable governance documents, such as family charters etc. This is both to help the partners clarify and record their intentions and thus prevent disputes arising in the first place, but also to provide supporting evidence to assist the speediest resolution of any conflict or disputes that do arise.

Sometimes the court will be able to find evidence of the intentions of the business owning family. Of course this cannot be guaranteed. Neither is the prospect of long drawn litigation likely to do much to preserve either family finances or goodwill.

26.11.7 Wills and family business assets

So far we have been talking about situations where business advice is not fit for family purpose. The mirror image question needs to be asked when private client advisors are dealing with family business assets; 'is this advice fit for business purpose?'.

Of course there is plenty of scope for simple mistakes to be made in the overlap between private client and business affairs. For example in *Brooke v Purton*[75] the business owner clearly intended to place the shares in a family company, worth in the region of £2m in a discretionary trust for the benefit of his spouse and five children, some of whom were quite young. The will draftsman limited the trust to 'business property having an aggregate ... value not exceeding the nil rate sum' clearly defeating the object of the trust. In the circumstances the court interpreted the will in accordance with the business owner's intentions.

But fitness for family business purpose in private client situations goes beyond simple technical competence. In the above example would the trust, even if properly constituted legally, have a reasonable prospect of operating satisfactorily in practice? Who were the trustees and how was their suitability assessed? Was the proposed trust part of wider governance arrangements or was it simply a stand-alone standard arrangement?[76]

The advisors in *Cadman* had been retained by Edith to prepare her will, but were in direct contact with her daughter Janis. How much advice did they provide, either to Edith or directly to Janis about the day-to-day practicalities of her position as a minority shareholder in a small family company, controlled by two brothers, who did not want to be in business with her? How much advice could an advisor reasonably be expected to provide in such circumstances?

We have seen a number of wills which include provisions leaving ownership of a family business to the next generation equally, but include options for the insiders to acquire the shares of the outsiders. In such circumstances the senior generation might be accused of abdicating responsibility to the next generation for deciding their ownership philosophy. To what extent should advisors provide advice on family dynamics or encourage a full discussion of this, involving both generations during the lifetime if the senior generation?

If the ownership approach is not fully resolved during the lifetime of the senior generation, how far do advisors need to go to ensure that will based options can operate effectively, against the back drop of family business realities? If the option to buy out the outsiders is not exercised, what governance measures will be put in place to protect their interests so they do not, like Janis Fisher, find that their inheritance is at the mercy of the

---

[75] [2014] EWHC 547 (Ch).
[76] These issues are considered in detail in chapter 14 (Family Business Trusts).

insiders? If the option for the insiders to acquire outright ownership is to work how does the drafting reconcile the interests of the two camps? Does it deal adequately with issues such as price and timescale to create a workable option and provide a fair balance? The issues will be very similar to for pre-emption provisions included in articles or shareholders' agreements.[77]

26.11.9 Property arrangements

Informal property arrangements between a family business and members of the business owning family are fairly common. Potential difficulties created by this are discussed in detail in chapter 10 (Property).

26.11.10 *Ham v Ham* revisited

The case of *Ham v Ham*[78] was discussed in detail in chapter 13 (Family Business Partnerships). By way of reminder the main issues in the case were first, that the partnership agreement failed to make any distinction between income and capital profits, and secondly that, it was unclear on the face of the agreement whether freehold property and other assets were to be revalued for the purposes of establishing an outgoing partner's share or whether it this was to be calculated on the basis of historical book values used in the partnership accounts.

We will let the Court of Appeal in that case have the final word on the legal drafting and fitness for family business purpose. They said that:[79]

> 'it is unfortunate that a matter of such importance should have to turn on an anxious and difficult consideration of factors pointing in different directions, in a context where it has throughout been common ground between counsel that the answer is by no means clear, and where reasonable minds have reached different conclusions. It is unhappily common for this type of issue not to be clearly dealt with in partnership agreements. It is an obvious problem in relation to farming partnerships, where the land forms an asset of the firm. It is to be hoped that, in future, those preparing such agreements will take note of the anxiety, expense and delay which such unnecessary uncertainty can cause.'

26.12 CONCLUSION

The situation of dynamic complexity created for the members business owning family by the interplay of the three separate business, ownership and family systems present in a family owned business, has corresponding implications for the advisors of that family.

Against a background of increasing technical complexity and specialisation, family business advisors need to be able to work beyond these narrow boundaries, so as to gain not only proficiency in related technical issues that arise from within their own discipline, but outside their particular area of specialist expertise which can be of relevance to family owned business clients. They also need a wider appreciation of family business dynamics.

---

[77] Discussed in detail in chapter 11.
[78] [2013] EWCA Civ 1301.
[79] Briggs LJ at para 58 of the judgment.

Collaboration, not only internally, but also with other professionals, including family business consultants, is likely to be necessary to provide a suitably rounded service for family business clients.

The complexity of the situation makes it impossible to provide a universally applicable prescription or set of rules to apply when acting for family business clients. Instead the main aim of this chapter has been to highlight a number of considerations to be taken into account and questions to be asked by the family advisor when doing so.

26.13 FURTHER READING FOR PART F

- Family Firm Institute *Family Enterprise: Understanding Families in Business and Families of Wealth* (Wiley & Sons, 2014). A detailed, but short (169 pages including index etc.) handbook on family business dynamics and the advisory process, produced by the world's leading organisation for family business advisors. The book includes the full text of a number of key articles taken from the *Family Business Review* (many of which are referred to in this book). It also includes a series of multi choice questions, designed to test the reader's understanding of the contents of each chapter.

- Fisher and Ury *Getting to Yes – Negotiating Agreement Without Giving In* (Penguin, 1981). This is a cornerstone book on 'principled negotiation' arising from the work of the Harvard Negotiation Project and a key reference work for mediators.

- K E Gersick et al *Generation to Generation: Life cycles of a family business* (Harvard Business School Press, 1997). This book has been heavily referred to, both in this chapter and elsewhere. It contains a useful chapter dedicated to the practical aspects of the family business consultancy process.

- J Hilburt-Davis and W Gibb Dyer Jr *Consulting to Family Businesses* (Jossey-Bass, 2003). A practical guide to the family business consulting process written by two leading 'process professionals'. It provides a good and comprehensive introduction for traditional 'content based' professionals seeking to work more closely with family owned business clients.

- I Macdonald, J Sutton *Business Families and Family Businesses – The STEP Handbook for Advisers* (Globe Law and Business, 2009). A handbook aimed at the professional advisor, again providing a detailed overview of key issues and concepts in family business practice, with contributions from various practitioners, including a number of 'founding fathers'.

- L Parkinson *Family Mediation* (Jordan Publishing, Family Law, 3rd edn, 2014). A comprehensive work on mediation. Although aimed at matrimonial mediation, much of the book is relevant to mediation in the context of family businesses, as is the explanation of background theory, for example the chapter on dealing with deadlocks.

APPENDIX 1

GLOSSARY

Part 1 – Family business terminology

Ambivalence: Although this is a fairly common word it has particular significance for those involved in family owned businesses because the conflict arising from individuals having multiple roles within the family business system is a potent source of ambivalence. See chapter 2 (Themes).

Copreneurs: Spouses or life partners who work together in owning or managing a family business. See chapter 18 (The family Business and Marriage).

Content consulting: This expression refers to the approach taken by lawyers, accountants and other traditional advisory professionals, focused on delivering expert or content advice on given technical problems. It is to be contrasted with **process consulting**, see below. See chapter 25 (Process Consulting and the Role of the Family Business Consultant).

Cousin collaboration: A later stage family business, typically third generation or beyond where the business is owned and managed by some combination of cousins drawn from different family branches also called **Cousin Consortiums.** See chapter 3 (Tools, Models and Theories).

Family business: There is no single accepted definition of family business, although the definition proposed by the European Commission (broadly where voting control is in the hands of a single family and at least one family member participates in governance) is gaining traction. The expression **family owned business** is also widely used in the book, usually to denote a later stage family business, where there is a division between insider family members working in the business and those who do not. The expressions **family company family firm** and **family firm** are also used, in the latter case to include family businesses generally rather than simply unincorporated family partnerships. See chapter 1 (Introduction) for a detailed discussion of the definition of a family business.

Family business consultants: Specialist advisors and consultants who work with family businesses, using process consulting methodology and who have usually ceased to practice in their profession of origin. See chapter 25 (Process Consulting and the Role of the Family Business Consultant).

Family assembly: A formal or semi formal gathering of family members to discuss issues relating to their family business. Although many of the attendees will also be owners, some will not be, so the family assembly is a wider meeting, distinct from shareholders' meetings. See chapter 17 (Governance).

Family charter: A document, usually not legally binding and prepared by the business owning family (often with support from family business consultants), setting out the relationship of members of the business owning family between themselves and between the family and their family business. Also known by various other names such as a **family constitution, family creed,** or **family values statement.** See chapter 17 (Governance).

Family council: Usually found in larger or later stage family businesses the family council is a representative body of family members whose primary function is to act as the interface and communication channel between the board of directors of the family company and the family members. See chapter 17 (Governance).

Family director: This expression is usually used in a narrow (and fairly pejorative) sense to refer to a director of a family company who has been appointed to their position wholly or largely by reason of their family status. Family directors can be contrasted with other executive or non-executive directors (who may or may not also be family members) and who have been appointed largely on merit and for business reasons. See chapter 8 (Director's Duties).

Governance: Again there is no single accepted definition of family business governance. The term is widely interpreted in this book to include, but go beyond, formal structures such as the board of directors, family assemblies, family councils and related documents including family charters and shareholders' agreements so as to extend to any formal or informal process whereby a stakeholder exerts influence in the business family or ownership systems of a family business. **Governance application points** are occasions where such influence has been or could have been exercised. See chapter 17 (Governance).

Family business life cycle theory: The basic idea is that a family business will evolve through various stages as it matures. This evolution will take place across all three dimensions in the family business system (see below). Although the classic model of family business life cycle theory envisages an increasingly more complex and larger business in the ownership of many members of an increasingly large business owning family there are many variations and exceptions to this rule. See chapter 3 (Tools, Models and Theories).

Individual life cycle theory: This sits alongside family business life cycle theory and refers to the life stages of individual family business members. Depending on the stage reached individuals will have a greater or lesser propensity to collaborate and work together, which has clear implications for succession planning and family business governance. See chapter 3 (Tools, Models and Theories).

Insiders: Usually used to denote family members working in the business, also referred to as **haves** (in the sense of having access to jobs and related benefits in the family firm) but occasionally the use of the term is extended to include other non-family employees.

Owner managed: Usually used to refer to the early stage, typically first generation, entrepreneurial, start up family business. However, on occasions, the owner managed ownership family business format can be perpetuated for several generations, including in relation to large and sophisticated family enterprises.

Outsiders: This term is usually used to describe family owners (and on occasions wider family members) who do not work in the family business. Also referred to as **have-nots**.

Process consulting: Is the methodology used by family business consultants to work with business owning families to help or facilitate the family to develop their own solutions to the family business challenges they are facing. Process consulting is to be contrasted with **content consulting** (see above). See chapter 25 (Process Consulting and the Role of the Family Business Consultant).

Scapegoating: This refers to the tendency for family members, or other parties with a conflicted relationship, to blame a third party or occasionally an entity, such as the family business itself, for their difficulties. See chapter 3 (Tools, Models and Theories).

Sibling partnership: Under classic family business life cycle theory a sibling partnership typically arises in the second generation of a family firm, when two or more siblings take over management and ownership from the senior, founding generation. However, in practice, sibling partnerships can arise at most stages of evolution of a family business. See chapter 3 (Tools, Models and Theories).

Systems theory: Systems theory provides the key theoretical foundation for understanding family business dynamics and is the basis of the three-circle model.

Three-circle model: The three-circle model is the most important model or tool in family business thinking. The basic idea is that any family business will consist of three separate but inter-related and overlapping systems, namely the family, ownership and business systems. Almost all tension and difficulty in family owned businesses can be traced to conflicts between these systems and often to the fact that individuals often occupy positions in more than one system, in the join or interface between systems, leading to role conflict and **ambivalence**. See chapter 3 (Tools, Models and Theories).

Triangulation: This refers to the tendency of family member or other parties with a conflicted relationship to draw or triangulate third parties into that conflict, either as allies, confidantes or occasionally as **scapegoats**. See chapter 3 (Tools, Models and Theories).

Part 2 – Legal terminology

Articles: The Articles of Association, effectively the rule book and basic constitutional document of a limited company.

Claimant: The party initiating litigation, previously known as the **plaintiff**, but also, depending on the type of proceedings referred to as **petitioner** or **applicant**. The terms are used interchangeably and not in a strict legal sense in this book. The modern terminology is usually preferred but not invariably so, for example older terminology, such as plaintiff has been retained when quoting from or referring to older cases.

Common law: The system of law derived from previously decided cases, also known as **case-law** or **precedents**. Common law is to be contrasted with **statutory law** as laid down by parliament in legislation including delegated legislation contained in **statutory**

instruments. Statutory law will always over-ride common law. However a key function of common law and the courts is to interpret the meaning of statutes, so the two systems sit side by side.

Equity: In its broadest sense equity translates into fairness. Many of the legal remedies relevant to family businesses discussed in this book, for example proprietary estoppel (see chapter 19) or just and equitable winding up of companies (see chapter 22) are **equitable remedies**. More technically equity is a separate system of law, from common law, one based on judicial discretion and historically exercised in separate Chancery Courts. Although the two systems were fused many years ago to form one overall system, equitable remedies remain discretionary although also rooted in historic precedent. On occasions equity is included within the overall umbrella term of common law so as to distinguish this from statutory law.

Obiter dicta: This is a judge's expression of opinion usually in a written judgment which is not central to the decision and is therefore not legally binding as a **precedent**. Also often referred to as statements made *per curiam*. Depending on the seniority of the court, *obiter dictum* can nevertheless be highly persuasive in future cases.

Ratio decidendi: In Latin, literally the reason for deciding. *Ratio decidendi* is therefore the opposite of *obiter dicta*. Broadly, depending on the pecking order of the court concerned the *ratio decidendi* of a case decided in a higher court, be that, in ascending order, the High Court, the Court of Appeal or the Supreme Court (previously the House of Lords) will be binding on the lower courts. However judgments, particularly in complicated cases, tend to be fairly long. So it will often not be easy to isolate the *ratio decidendi* of a particular case and to distinguish this from any statement made *obiter dicta* by the judges concerned. Also it will be rare indeed for any two cases to have identical facts. It is therefore sometimes difficult to work out whether the *ratio decidendi* of a decided case applies to another case on similar, but slightly different facts. Many remedies relevant to family businesses, including equitable remedies and unfair prejudice (see chapter 21) are highly fact specific, so that decided cases will have only persuasive bearing in assessing later cases.

APPENDIX 2

THE FAMILY BUSINESS MOVEMENT

A number of references have been made in the body of the book to the family business movement. As explained in chapter 25 this can be seen to have originated in the USA. The movement has grown, so that specialist family business consultants and other practitioners, academic institutions studying family business issues and family business support organisations can be found throughout the world.

As awareness of the these organisations appears to be fairly low, both within the general advisory community and amongst family business owners, this appendix has been included to provide a brief overview of the main organisations providing support to family businesses and practitioners in the UK.

This appendix is not intended to be an exhaustive list of all organisations dealing with family business matters. With the exception only of the Family Firm Institute (FFI) no attempt has been made to identify organisations active in the family business field outside the UK or to outline the family business research or other work undertaken by academic institutions, whether in the UK or elsewhere. Neither have we mentioned any of the well-known general business organisations, such as the Institute of Directors (IOD) or the Small Business Federation (FSB), which will inevitably have an interest in family business matters as part of their activities. Similarly many industries have significant concentrations of family owned businesses, for example in the food and drink industry, so the relevant trade bodies will, from time to time, deal with family business issues for the relevant part of their membership. Finally no attempt has been made to provide details of family business practitioners including family business consultants operating in the UK or elsewhere.

Part 1 – Organisations supporting professional advisors

The Family Firm Institute or FFI

The FFI can justly lay claim to being the leading worldwide organisation to supporting professionals advising family firms and who are interested in understanding the underlying dynamics, latest thinking and issues facing their family business clients. Incorporated in 1986, the FFI now has over 1800 members drawn from more than 80 countries.

The organisation is fully cross disciplinary, with members not only from the traditional advisory professions including lawyers and accountants, but also family business consultants, psychologists and organisational development specialists, together with academics interested in family business issues.

Most of the founding fathers and thought leaders of the family business movement, many of whom are referred to in the body of the book, have held prominent positions within the organisation.

FFI is very much based around learning and research. Current activities include the publication of *Family Business Review*, a leading academic business journal. Various papers and articles from FBR have been referred in the body of this book. The organisation also sends out a weekly e-zine aimed at family business practitioners, *FFI Practitioner*, typically with a short article or occasionally, podcasts on relevant topics of general interest to family business practitioners.

FFI also promote training and professional development courses for family business practitioners, many of which can be accessed through distance learning programmes, together with an annual 'flagship' worldwide conference.

For further details of FFI see http://www.ffi.org.

STEP and the STEP Business Families Special Interest Group

The general work of STEP, training and development of professionals specialising in tax, trusts and private client work has clear relevance to a large percentage of professionals providing technical content advice (as that term is explained in chapter 25) to family business clients.

STEP's publications, including the STEP Journal, often have feature articles covering family business issues.

STEP also promotes a Business Families Special Interest Group (SIG), which is open to non- STEP members and which operates on a cross- disciplinary basis, with membership that includes corporate lawyers, accountants, family business consultants and bankers, in addition to the private client practitioners forming the core membership of the STEP organisation.

The Business Families SIG provides a global community for practitioners, who work with business families and a platform for education, training, continued professional development and the expansion of field networks and support. The group focuses on what makes business families distinct, their particular challenges, and how best to address these. The group aims to marshal expertise, promote best practice and champion the family business practice area.

STEP also provides training in family business dynamics through its Advanced Certificate in Family Business Advising.

For further details of the STEP's Business Families Special Interest Group see http://wwwwww.step.org/business-families-global-special-interest-group.step.org/business-families-global-special-interest-group.

Part 2 – *Organisations supporting family businesses*

Institute for Family Business (IFB)

The IFB is a not for profit membership organisation set up to support family business, their owners, future owners, and trusted executives. The organisation runs various conferences events and training programmes, both regionally and nationally, including special training programmes aimed at the next generation of family business owners and managers. The IFB provides a family business peer-to-peer support network, where family members can share common concerns and solutions with each other in a trusted and non-solicitous environment.

The IFB is UK chapter of the international Family Business Network (FBN), a network of 3,000 family businesses across 58 countries. IFB is also a member of European Family Businesses (EFB), a pan-European representative body.

The IFB's membership has a combined turnover of £100 billion and employ 500,000 people. IFB has members from all sectors and regions, whilst most members are multi-generational businesses there is a growing group of first generation family businesses within the network.

The wider activities of the IFB reach beyond its membership and are of relevance to the family business and advisory communities in the UK generally. Research, carried out through the related IFB Research Foundation, has consistently highlighted the scale and significance of family businesses to the UK economy. This research has been referred to in the body of the book and probably represents the most helpful collection of family business research of specific relevance to the UK.

The IFB is also the voice of family business in Government, ensuring the unique characteristics and needs of family business are reflected in Government policy. IFB also provides the Secretariat for the All Party Parliamentary Group for Family Business.

For further details of the IFB see: http://www.ifb.org.uk.

Family Business United

Family Business United (**FBU**) is a prominent commercial organisation providing a focal point for the UK family business community, both family owned firms and the advisory community. FBU organise an annual flagship conference, the Great British Family Business, together with the Family Business of the Year Awards, Scottish Family Business Week and various other events throughout the year, across the UK. The FBU website is also highly active and provides a source of articles, news stories, research and other items of interest to family business members and the advisory community.

Visit www.familybusinessunited.com for more information.

INDEX

References are to paragraph numbers.

ACAS Code	5.16.4, 5.16.7
capability procedures	5.17.5
conciliation proceedings	5.21
mediation	5.16.9
Accommodation	
taxable benefit in kind	4.11.2
Accountant	
trustee, as	14.10.4
Accounts	
content	4.8.2
filing	4.8.1
publication of	11.2.5
Advising the family business	25.1, 26.1
collaborative practice	26.3
confidentiality	26.10
conflict resolution, and	25.8.1, 25.8.2
conflicts of interest	26.8, 26.9
consultant, role of	25.3
development model	25.3
engagement terms	26.4.3
identification of client	25.7, 26.5, 26.6
internal business teams	26.4.1, 26.4.4, 26.4.5
lawyer, role of	26.7
method consulting	25.4, 25.5, 25.6
negligence case study	26.4.2
process consulting	25.4, 25.5, 25.6
professional competence	26.11.1, 26.11.2, 26.11.3, 26.11.4, 26.11.5, 26.11.6, 26.11.7, 26.11.9, 26.11.10
professional specialisation	26.4.1
three-circle model	25.2
trusted advisor	26.2
wills	26.11.7
Agricultural holdings	10.9
Agricultural property relief	16.4
Alternative dispute resolution *see also* Mediation	25.9
arbitration	25.9.10
coaching	25.9.4
collaborative law	25.9.9
counselling	25.9.3
family business consultancy	25.9.7
litigation following	25.9.12
mediation	25.9.8
neutral evaluation	25.9.11
organisational development	25.9.5
self-help	25.9.1

Alternative dispute resolution —*continued*	
support, business organisations	
from	25.9.2
third party intervention	25.9.6
Ambivalence	2.3
Arbitration	25.9.10
Articles of Association	17.4
amendments to	17.18.2, 17.18.4
unfair prejudice	21.6.14
availability	17.18.2
drag rights	12.9.1
enforceability	17.18.2
family charter, and	17.18.4
inter-relationship with shareholders' agreement	17.18.4
professional advice	26.11.2, 26.11.3, 26.11.4
shareholder remedies	20.7.1
Assured shorthold tenancies	
landlord, possession rights	10.10.3
term of	10.10.3
Assured tenancies	
rent increases	10.10.2
succession rights	10.10.2
Bad faith	20.2.4, 20.8, 20.8.4
derivative claims	20.8.2, 23.5.4
statutory test	20.8.1
unfair prejudice	20.8.3
Bare trusts	14.22.2
Bartlett v Barclays Bank Trust Company	
duty of care	14.11
Beneficiaries	14.1.2
choice of	14.8, 14.8.1
default	14.3.7
disability, with	14.8.6, 14.22.6
grandchildren	14.8.3
information, provision of	14.19, 14.19.2, 14.19.3
multiple	14.5.1
primary	14.3.6
settlor, as	14.8.2
spouses	14.8.5
whole family	14.8.4
Benefits in kind	
accommodation	4.11.2
cars, fuel and vans	4.11.1
national insurance	4.11.4

Bivalence	2.2.4
attributes	2.3
emotional involvement	2.3
lifelong common history	2.3
meaning of the family company	2.3
mutual awareness and privacy	2.3
private language	2.3
shared identity	2.3
simultaneous roles	2.3
Board of directors	17.4
advisory boards	17.9.3
board committee	17.9.6
chairman, role of	17.10.4
composition	17.10.1
early stage business	17.9.1
'family directors'	17.10.5
functioning boards	17.9.4
holding company board	17.9.6
non-executive directors	17.10.3
non-family executive directors	17.10.2
roles	17.9.7
'rubber stamp board'	17.9.2
two-tier boards	17.9.5
Breach of duty	
appropriation	21.6.9
articles, changes to	21.6.14
assets transfers	21.6.8
CA 2006 duties	21.6.10
civil liability	8.5.2
relief	8.5.3
conflicts of interest	21.6.7
criminal sanctions	8.5.1
dishonesty	21.6.2
diversion of business opportunities	21.6.6
Duomatic principle	8.4.5
excessive remuneration	21.6.3
good faith	21.6.14
information, sharing of	21.6.11
mismanagement	21.6.12
non-payment of dividends	21.6.4
ratification	8.4.1, 8.4.2, 8.4.3, 8.4.4, 8.4.5
binding effect of	8.4.3
limitations	8.4.2
statutory procedure	8.4.4
self-dealing	21.6.7
unfair prejudice, and	21.6.1, 21.6.2, 21.6.3, 21.6.4, 21.6.5, 21.6.6, 21.6.7, 21.6.8, 21.6.9, 21.6.10, 21.6.11, 21.6.12, 21.6.13, 21.6.14
'wrongful rights issues'	21.6.13
Business name	
brand, as	9.1, 9.2, 9.6
'own name'	9.4, 9.4.1, 9.4.2
honesty defence	9.4.3, 9.4.4
protection of	9.3, 9.3.1, 9.3.2
sale of	9.5
use following sale	12.16
Business plan	4.8.3
Business property relief	10.2, 16.2
binding contracts for sale, effect of	16.2.8
business partnerships, and	16.2.10
Business property relief—*continued*	
'control' definition	16.2.7
floatation of company	15.3
investment businesses	16.2.3
loan stock	16.2.6
partnership property	16.10.12
property	16.10.2
qualifying conditions	16.2.2
qualifying period	16.2.9
rates	16.2.1
types of	16.2.1
unquoted shares	16.2.4, 16.2.5
Business strategy plan	7.14
C & J Clark	
governance, case study	17.5.1, 17.5.2, 17.5.3, 17.5.4, 17.5.5
larhe family owned business	1.5.5
Cadman Developments Ltd	
family advisor, example	26.7
family tree	3.2.2
sibling partnership, as	1.5.3
three-circle model	3.3.3
Capability	5.17
appraisals	5.17.2
dismissal for	5.17.7
early identification	5.17.1
fair procedure	5.17.1
formal procedure	5.17.5, 5.17.6
informal procedure	5.17.4
managing under-performance	5.17.3
probationary periods	5.17.2
Capacity	
shareholder, of	12.12
Capital gains tax	16.6
entrepreneur's relief	16.7.1, 16.7.2, 16.7.3, 16.7.5, 16.7.6, 16.7.7, 16.7.8
'trading company'	16.7.5
family business property	10.2
gifted asset, relief on	16.6.1
gifts on which inheritance tax is chargeable	16.6.3
holdover relief	16.6.2
property, and	16.10.3, 16.10.12
reliefs	4.3.1
residence issues	16.6.4
tax planning	16.7.4
Car	
benefit in kind	4.11.1
Close companies	
definition	4.3.4
loans	4.3.5
Co-leadership	
chairman as co-leader	7.7.2
overview	7.7.1
Collaboration	2.5.5
Collaborative law	25.9.9
Commercial lease	
contracting out	10.8.2
security of tenure	10.8.1
Communication	
conflict, and	2.4

Index

Communication—*continued*
  disciplinary/grievance procedure   5.16.3
  lack of   2.4
  theory   3.6
    double bind communication   3.6.2
    scapegoating   3.6.4
    transactional analysis   3.6.1
    triangulation   3.6.3
Company
  accounting requirements   4.8.1
  characteristics   4.2.5
  disincorporation
    tax issues   4.3.1
    income tax deductions   4.3.3
    tax advantages for   4.4
Company share option plan   4.12.8
Competition   2.5.5
Compromise   2.5.5
Conductors
  characteristics   2.2.3
Confidentiality
  family business advisor   26.10
Conflict   2.5.1, 2.5.2, 2.5.3, 2.5.4, 2.5.5, 5.22
  accommodation of   2.5.5
  audience for   2.5.4
  avoidance   2.5.5
  categories   2.5.3
  collaboration   2.5.5
  competition   2.5.5
  compromise   2.5.5
  emotional/personal issues   2.5.2
  presenting issue   2.5.4
  process conflict   2.5.3
  proportionality   2.5.4
  relationship conflict   2.5.3
  resolution strategies   2.5.5, 17.22
  symptoms   2.5.4
  task conflict   2.5.3
  terminology   2.5.4
Conflict of interest   8.1.3, 8.9.1, 8.9.2, 8.9.3, 8.9.4, 8.9.5
  Bhullar Brothers   8.7.12, 8.7.13, 8.7.14
  disclosure, duty of   8.7.3, 8.7.5
  duty to avoid   8.7.3, 8.7.4
    authorisation   8.7.4
  early stage family business   8.7.8
  Harrison Properties   8.7.9, 8.7.10, 8.7.11
  introduction   8.7.1
  no conflict rule   8.7.2
  no profit rule   8.7.2, 8.8.1
  overlapping duties   8.7.6
  professional conduct   26.8, 26.9
  sale of business, and   12.10.2, 12.10.3
  sensitive transactions   8.7.15
  sole directors   8.7.7
  unfair prejudice, and   21.6.7
Constructive trusts   14.21.3
Contract of employment   5.12, 5.12.1, 5.12.2
  section 1 statement   5.12.1
Corporation tax
  payment, timing of   4.3.2

Corporation tax—*continued*
  rates   4.3.1, 4.3.6
  share schemes, and   4.12.13
Cousin consortium/collaboration   3.4.1
  genogram   3.8.2
  ownership transition, to   15.4, 15.5
  Saul D Harrison   1.5.4, 3.8.2, 21.5.1
  succession, and   7.3
  unfair prejudice, and   21.5, 21.5.1, 21.5.2, 21.5.3

Derivative claims   22.16.2, 23.1
  alternative personal remedies   23.5.5
  authorisation of activities   23.5.3
  bad faith   20.8.2, 23.5.4
  failure   23.6.1, 23.6.2, 23.6.3, 23.6.4, 23.6.5
  Foss v Harbottle   23.2
  fraud on the minority   23.3, 23.8, 23.8.1, 23.8.2, 23.8.3
  independent director tests   23.5.2
  mismanagement   20.9.2
  settlement   23.9
  Singh v Singh   23.5.1, 23.5.2, 23.5.3, 23.5.4, 23.5.5, 23.5.6
  statutory provisions   23.4.1, 23.4.2, 23.4.3
    application for leave   23.4.3
    permission of court   23.4.2
    scope   23.4.1
  successful claims   23.7, 23.7.1, 23.7.2, 23.7.3

Directors *see also* Family directors
  appointment   17.19.5
  conflicts of interest *see* Conflicts of interest
  courtesy titles   8.2.7
  de facto directors   8.2.3
  de jure directors   8.2.2, 8.2.6
  definition   8.2.1
  disqualification of   8.5.4
  executive   8.2.5, 8.2.6
  insolvency remedies   8.10.2, 8.10.3
  misapplication of company funds   8.10.4
  national insurance deductions   4.3.3
  non-executive   8.2.5, 8.2.6
  removal   17.19.5
  remuneration   8.1.3, 8.8.1, 8.8.2, 8.8.3, 8.8.4, 8.8.5, 8.8.6, 8.8.7
    declaration of   8.8.2
    derivative claims   8.8.6
    disguised returns on capital   8.8.4
    reasonableness   8.8.2
    unfair prejudice   8.8.7
  retirement by rotation   17.19.6
  shadow directors   8.2.4
  weighted voting rights   11.9
Directors' duties
  act within powers, to   8.3.2
  avoid conflicts of interest, to   8.3.6
  breaches *see* Breach of duty

Directors' duties—*continued*
CA 2006, under 8.1, 8.3.1, 8.3.2,
  8.3.3, 8.3.4, 8.3.5, 8.3.6, 8.3.7,
  8.3.8
 codification   8.1, 8.3.1
 criminal sanctions   8.1.1
 declare interest transactions, to 8.3.8
 exercise independent judgment,
  to   8.3.4
 exercise reasonable care, skill and
  diligence, to   8.3.5
 governance, and   8.1.2
 importance of   8.1.1
 key issues   8.1.3
 no profit rule   8.8.1
 not to accept benefits from third
  parties   8.3.7
 promote success of company, to 8.1.3,
  8.3.3, 8.9.1, 8.9.2, 8.9.3, 8.9.4,
  8.9.5
  remuneration   8.8.5
Disability discrimination
 failure to make reasonable
  adjustments   5.9.8
 test for   5.9.6, 5.9.7
Disciplinary procedures   5.16.1
 ACAS Code   5.16.4
 communication   5.16.3
 conduct   5.16.6
 fairness   5.16.2
 internal systems   5.16.5
 investigations   5.16.7
 mediation   5.16.9
 right to be accompanied   5.16.8
Discretionary trusts
 assets   14.3.3
 beneficial rights   14.3.4
 beneficiaries   14.3.6, 14.3.7
 capital, payment   14.3.9
 dividends, distribution   14.3.8
 income and capital, distribution 14.3.2
 income, acculmulation   14.3.8
 overview   14.3.1
 termination   14.3.10
 trustees' meetings   14.3.5
Discrimination
 behaviour between family
  members   5.19.2
 direct   5.9.1
 disability *see* Disability
  discrimination
 harassment   5.9.3
 indirect   5.9.2
 inducing or knowingly helping
  unlawful acts   5.9.5
 non-family employees 6.9, 6.9.2, 6.9.3
  recruitment   6.9.1
 protected characteristics   5.9
 victimisation   5.9.4
Dismissal
 misconduct, for   5.16.6
 under-performance, for 5.17.3, 5.17.7

Dispute resolution *see* Alternative
 dispute resolution; Mediation
Dividends
 non-payment, unfair prejudice 21.6.4
 payment, trust from   14.3.8
 policy   11.7
  family charter, in   17.15.7
 right to receive   11.2.1
 scrip or cash dividends 11.20.1
Divorce
 effect of business   18.7
 financial provision
  business valuation   18.10
  clean break   18.10
  contribution to business 18.11
  legislation   18.8
  needs of parties   18.9
  yardstick of equality 18.12
 matrimonial property, business
  as   18.13, 18.13.1, 18.13.2,
    18.13.3, 18.13.4, 18.13.5,
    18.13.6, 18.13.7, 18.13.8, 18.14,
    18.15, 18.16, 18.17
 White v White   18.3, 18.12
Drag rights   12.9.1, 17.21

Employees *see also* Family employees;
 Non-family employees
 complaints etc *see* Grievance
  procedure
 contracts   17.23.3
 discipline *see* Disciplinary procedure
 'insiders' and 'outsiders' 2.7
 long-term sickness *see* Ill health
 national insurance deductions 4.3.3
 ownership policy, and   11.6
 performance issues *see* Capability
 shares for *see* Share scheme
 status   5.11.1
 trusts, and   14.18
Employment law *see also* Disability
 discrimination; Disciplinary
 procedures; Discrimination;
 Unfair dismissal
 compliance   5.10
 employment status   5.11, 5.11.1,
        5.11.2, 5.11.3
  self employed   5.11.3
  worker   5.11.2
 Equality Act 2010   5.9
 family employees 5.7, 5.8.1, 5.8.2,
   5.8.3, 5.8.4, 5.8.5, 5.8.6, 5.9,
   5.9.1, 5.9.2, 5.9.3, 5.9.4, 5.9.5,
   5.9.6, 5.9.7, 5.9.8
 hours *see* Working Time Regulations
 remuneration *see also* National
  Living Wage
Enterprise management incentive 4.12.7
Entrepreneur   2.2, 2.2.3
 'balanced'   2.2.5
 'balanced narcissist'   2.2.5
 behaviour, types of   2.2.4

Entrepreneur—*continued*	
charateristics	2.2.5
emotional attachment to business	2.10
psychology of	2.2.4
Entrepreneur's relief	
importance	16.7.1
independently owned assets	16.7.8
partnership property	16.10.12
partnerships	16.7.7
property, and	16.10.5
qualifying conditions	16.7.2
sole trader	16.7.7
spouses, jointly-held shares	16.7.3
surplus cash	16.7.6
'trading company'	16.7.5
Equal pay	6.9.3
Equality	2.6
Equality Act 2010 Code of Practice	5.9.8, 6.9.1
Estate management	10.11
Family	
definition	
CA 2006	1.3.2
EC expert group	1.3.1
in-laws	1.3.4
loyalty issues	1.3.3
modern family units	1.3.6
second children	1.3.5
step children	1.3.5
Family assemblies	17.4
business size, relevance of	17.12.3
charateristics	17.12.1
family council, need for	17.12.3
membership	17.12.1, 17.12.2
in-laws	17.12.2
procedure	17.15.12
Family business	
advantages	1.1.2
advisor *see* Advising the family business	
ambivalence in	2.3
challenges	1.4
attracting/retaining skilled workforce	1.4.4
EC expert group	1.4.1
governance	1.4.3
succession planning	1.4.2
training	1.4.5
closure	15.3
definition	1.2
European Commission	1.2.1
'familiness'	1.2.9
family involvement in management	1.2.7, 1.2.8
family involvement in ownership	1.2.8
large businesses	1.2.2
multi-generational	1.2.5
owner managed	1.2.3
self-definition	1.2.10
succession intention	1.2.6
wider ownership	1.2.4

Family business—*continued*	
emotional attachment	2.10
employment and systemic balance	5.2
examples	1.5
C & J Clark (Clark's Shoes)	1.5.5
Cadman Developments Ltd	1.5.3
Davies family	1.5.2
Dyson	1.2.11
Park House Properties	1.5.1
Saul D Harrison plc	1.5.4
financial strength	1.1.2
floatation	15.3
importance to economy	1.1.1, 1.1.2, 1.1.3, 1.1.4, 1.1.5, 1.1.6
loyalty	1.1.2
market knowledge	1.1.2
married couples *see* Marriage	
models	3.1
myths	2.13
operations and systems *see* Systems theory	
psychological status	2.10
scripts	2.14
size	1.1.3
speed of decision-making	1.1.2
statistics	1.1.3
structure	
tax planning, and	4.1, 4.3.1, 4.3.2, 4.3.3, 4.3.4, 4.3.5, 4.6
types of	4.2
succession planning *see* Management succession; Ownership succession	
survival rate	1.1.4
themes	2.1
third party sale *see* Sale of family business	
transfer of ownership to family members *see* Ownership succession	
typology	3.7
Saul D Harrison	3.8.3
Family business movement	25.9.2, 25.10
Family charter	17.4
characteristics	17.14.1
contents	17.15
conduct, standards of	17.15.2
constitution of family council	17.15.10
core values, statement of	17.15.1
dispute resolution	17.15.13
dividend policies	17.15.7
employment policies	17.15.6
external share ownership	17.15.5
family assembly procedure	17.15.12
family share ownership	17.15.4
information rights	17.15.8
membership of family council	17.15.11
ownership	
future plans for	17.15.3
shareholder responsibilities	17.15.9
drafting process	17.14.4, 17.14.5

Family charter—*continued*
  facilitation by advisor   17.14.6
  format   17.14.3
  no binding effect   17.14.1, 17.14.2
  review of   17.15.14
  shareholder remedies   20.7.2
Family council   17.4
  administrative role   17.13.6
  chair, role of   17.13.4
  constitution   17.15.10
  membership   17.13.3, 17.15.11
    changes to   17.13.5
  need for   17.12.3, 17.13.1
  role of   17.13.2
Family directors *see also* Directors;
    Directors' duties
  categories   8.2.6
  concept of   8.1.3, 8.6.1
  de jure and de facto directorship   8.6.2
  duty of care   8.6.1, 8.6.2, 8.6.3, 8.6.4,
                          8.6.5, 8.6.6, 8.6.7
    Cohen v Selby   8.6.6
    dual test   8.6.3
    Lexi Holdings plc v Luqman   8.6.4
    Re Park House Properties Ltd   8.6.5
Family employees *see also* Non-family
    employees
  behaviour   5.19, 5.19.1, 5.19.2, 5.19.3
  benefits in kind   4.11, 4.11.1, 4.11.2,
                                  4.11.3, 4.11.4
  contract of employment   5.12, 5.12.1,
                                         5.12.2
  employment law issues   5.7, 5.8.1,
              5.8.2, 5.8.4, 5.8.5, 5.8.6,
              5.9, 5.9.1, 5.9.2, 5.9.3, 5.9.4,
              5.9.5, 5.9.6, 5.9.7, 5.9.8
  employment status   5.11, 5.11.1,
                                  5.11.2, 5.11.3
  governance, and   5.4
  informality of employment
    matters   5.10
  overview   5.1
  remuneration *see also* National
    Living Wage   4.11, 4.11.1,
          4.11.2, 4.11.3, 4.11.4, 5.5.1,
          5.5.2, 5.5.3, 5.5.4, 5.5.5
    boundaries for   5.5.3
    early stage of business   5.5.1
    formal procedure   5.5.5
    later stage of business   5.5.2
    market rate   5.5.4
  retirement   5.6
  sale of business, and   12.10, 12.10.1,
                                12.10.2, 12.10.3
    post sale restrictions   12.16
  terms   5.2
  treatment of   5.3
  young person   5.13
Family enterprise continuity plan   7.14
Family leadership
  succession, following   7.9
Family office
  type of   4.9.3

Family provision
  adult children   19.18.2
  capital sum rewards   19.18
  civil partners   19.19
  claims on family business   19.18.3
  cohabitants   19.18.3
  estranged family members   19.18.5
  limitations to award   19.18.4
  practicalities of claims   19.20
  procedure   19.18.6
  reasonable financial provision   19.17,
                                19.18, 19.18.1
  spouses   19.19, 19.19.1, 19.19.2,
                    19.19.3, 19.19.4, 19.19.5
    equality   19.19.2
    Lilleyman v Lilleyman   19.19.1,
            19.19.2, 19.19.3, 19.19.4, 19.19.5
  transfer of assets   19.18
  wishes of deceased   19.18.1
Family tree *see* Genogram
Farming business
  inheritance dispute   19.3
Father–daughter relationships *see also*
    Gender   2.9
Father–son relationships   2.8
  'black spots', in   3.5.4
  life stages of   3.5.4
  'purple patches', in   3.5.4
Financial controls   4.8.4
Ford, Henry   2.2.1
Founder   2.2, 2.2.1, 2.2.2, 2.2.3, 2.2.4,
                                            2.2.5
  characteristics   2.2.3
  difficulty letting go   2.2.2
  types of   2.2.3
Fraud on the minority   8.4.2, 23.4.2,
                      23.8, 23.8.1, 23.8.2, 23.8.3
Fuel
  benefit in kind   4.11.1

Gender   2.9, 2.11.3
  harassment based on   5.9.3
  married coprenuers   18.4.5
  succession issues   7.12.7
Genogram
  cousin consortium   3.8.2
  identifying key members   3.2.1, 3.2.2
  sibling partnership   3.8.1
  trust   14.14.3
  use of   3.2.1, 3.2.2, 3.2.3, 3.2.4
Good faith   8.3.3, 17.15.2, 19.12, 20.2.4,
                 20.4, 20.6.11, 20.8.2, 21.2.1,
                                21.6.14, 23.4.2
Governance
  advantages   17.2
  appropriate corporate governance
    procedures *see* Institute of
    Directors Corporate
    Governance Guidance
  case study   17.5.1, 17.5.2, 17.5.3,
                                   17.5.4, 17.5.5
  chairman, role in   17.6.2
  definition   17.3

Index

Governance—*continued*
  delegation of authority   17.6.2
  directors' duties, and   8.1.2
  dispute resolution, and   17.22
  documents *see also* Articles of
      Association   17.18.1, 17.18.2,
                                  17.18.3, 17.18.4
    connected party agreements   17.23.6
    contents   17.19.1
      appointment/removal of
        directors   17.19.5
      exit arrangements   17.19.4
      family member, definition 17.19.2
      retirement of directors   17.19.6
      share transfer provisions 17.19.3
    employment contracts   17.23.3
    marriage breakdown, covering 18.19,
                                  18.19.1, 18.19.2
    nuptial agreements   17.23.2
    partnership agreements   17.23.5
    trust deeds   17.23.1
  early stage business, in   17.7.2
  evolution of   17.7.1
  family business boards *see* Board of
      directors
  family employment polices   5.4
  grievance/disciplinary
      procedures   5.16.5
  later stage business, in   17.8, 17.9
  married couple, and   18.4, 18.4.1,
                                  18.4.2, 18.4.3, 18.4.4, 18.4.5,
                                  18.5, 18.6
  next generation transition   17.7.3
  non-family managers, and   6.8
  overview   17.1
  philanthropic activity   17.16
  property of   10.11
  remuneration, and   5.5.1, 5.5.2, 5.5.3,
                                  5.5.5
  sale of business, and   17.20, 17.21
  sources of   17.4
  systems *see also* Family assemblies;
      Family charter; Family
      Council   17.11.1, 17.11.2
    terminology   17.11.2
  systems of   17.1
  teamwork, development   17.6.2
  trusts, and   14.17
  ventures outisise core business 17.17
  volatile relationships   19.12
Grandchildren
  beneficiary, as   14.8.3
Grievance procedures   5.16.1
  ACAS Code   5.16.4
  communication   5.16.3
  conduct   5.16.6
  fairness   5.16.2
  internal systems   5.16.5
  mediation   5.16.9
  right to be accompanied   5.16.8

Ham v Ham   13.5.1, 13.5.2, 13.5.3,
                                  13.5.4, 13.5.5, 13.5.6, 13.5.7,
                                  13.5.8, 13.5.9, 13.5.10
  partnership, case study   13.2, 13.3
Harassment
  types of   5.9.3
Ill health   5.18
Income tax
  deductions   4.3.3
  rates   4.3.1
Individual life-cycle theory *see also*
    Life-cycle theory; Systems
    theory   3.5.1, 3.5.2, 3.5.3, 3.5.4,
                                  3.5.5
  differentiation   3.5.3
  eight ages of man   3.5.2
  father–son relationships   3.5.4
  personality   3.5.5
Inheritance
  taboo, as   2.4
Inheritance disputes
  ambiguity   19.4.2
  business themes   19.4, 19.4.1, 19.4.2,
                                  19.4.3, 19.4.4, 19.4.5, 19.4.6,
                                  19.4.7
  case study   19.2, 19.2.1, 19.2.2, 19.2.3,
                                  19.2.4, 19.2.5, 19.2.6, 19.2.7,
                                  19.2.8, 19.2.9
  claims for financial provision *see*
      Family provision
  communication   19.4.3
  complexity of business systems 19.4.6,
                                  19.5
  conflict   19.4.4, 19.4.7
  'cowshed Cinderella' case   19.3
  fairness and equality   19.4.1
  letting go   19.4.5
  overview   19.1
  proprietary estoppel   19.6
    assurance   19.7.1, 19.7.2, 19.7.3,
                                  19.7.4, 19.8
    case management   19.16.3
    claims, practicalities   19.16
    constructive trust   19.14
    detriment   19.9
    equity   19.10
    evidence   19.16.1
    procedure   19.16.2
    remedy for   19.11.1, 19.11.2,
                                  19.11.3
    Shirt v Shirt   19.15.1, 19.15.2
    unreliablility of   19.13, 19.15
Inheritance tax
  business property relief   16.2, 16.2.1,
                                  16.2.2, 16.2.3, 16.2.4, 16.2.5,
                                  16.2.6, 16.2.7, 16.2.8, 16.2.9,
                                  16.2.10, 16.10.2, 16.10.12
  excepted assets   16.3
    investment activity   16.3.2
    surplus cash   16.3.1
  investment properties   16.10.13,
                                  16.10.14

Inheritance tax—continued
  trusts, and   16.5.1, 16.5.2, 16.5.3,
                       16.5.4
    post-2006   16.5.4
    pre-2006   16.5.3
Insider dealing
  directors' duties, and   8.1.1
Insolvency
  directors' duties, and   8.1.1, 8.1.3
  misapplication of company
    funds   8.10.4
  preferences   8.10.6, 8.10.7
  transactions at an undervalue   8.10.5
  wrongful trading   8.10.1, 8.10.2, 8.10.3
    reliefs   8.10.8
Institute of Directors Corporate
  Governance Guidance   17.4
  chairman, role in governance   17.6.2
  delegation of authority   17.6.2
  overview   17.6.1
  principles   17.6.1, 17.6.2
    phases   17.6.2
  procedures proportionate to
    business   17.6.2
  teamwork, development   17.6.2

Just and equitable winding up
  alternative remedy to   22.3, 22.7.4,
                       22.16, 22.16.1, 22.16.2
  appropriation   22.14
  deadlock   22.11
  delay and acquiescence   22.5.2
  dual claims   22.6
  equitable bars   22.5
  equitable principles   22.4
    claimant's conduct   22.5.1
  grounds   22.7.3, 22.9, 22.12, 22.13,
                       22.14
  oppression   22.13
  overview   22.1
  qualifying condition   22.8
  quasi-partnerships   22.7.2, 22.8
  Re Harding Ltd   22.7.1, 22.7.2, 22.7.3,
                       22.7.4, 22.7.5
  refusal
    equitable bars   22.15.1
    mismanagement   22.15.2
    outvoting   22.15.3
    'tangible interest'   22.15.4
  sale of business, and   12.9.3
  statutory basis   20.2.2, 20.2.3
  statutory provision   22.2.1
  substratum, loss of   22.12
  trust, breakdown of   22.10

Land
  access issues   10.5
  registration of title   10.5
  trust of
    beneficial interest   10.13.6, 10.13.7
Landlord
  right of possession   10.10.1

Lawyer
  business advisor, role of   26.7
  trustee, as   14.10.4
Letter of wishes   14.1.2
  limitations   14.15.2
  use of   14.15.1
Life interest trusts   14.22.5
Life-cycle theory see also Individual
  life-cycle theory; Systems
  theory   3.4.1, 3.4.2, 3.4.3, 3.4.4
  characteristics of business   3.4.4
  composition of business   3.4.1
  intergenerational partnerships   3.4.3
  parent-offspring partnerships   3.4.3
  stages of business   3.4.1
  transition periods   3.4.2
Limited company see Company
Limited liability partnership
  accounting requirements   4.8.1
  characteristics   4.2.3, 4.2.4
  company compared   4.5.1
  ownership changes   4.5.3
  tax issues   4.5.3
  tax, payment of   4.3.1
  timing   4.3.2
Liquidation   4.10.1, 4.10.2, 4.10.3
Loans
  tax relief   16.10.8

Management succession see also
  Ownership succession   2.8
  attitude of senior generation   7.5.1,
                       7.5.2, 7.5.3, 7.5.4, 7.5.5
  barriers to   7.4
    financial   7.4.3
    managerial   7.4.1
    ownership issues   7.4.2
    psychological   7.4.4
  career development programmes   7.13.4
  chairman, role in   7.5.4
  co-leadership   7.7.1, 7.7.2
  competence of next generation   7.6,
             7.6.1, 7.6.2, 7.6.3, 7.6.4, 7.6.5,
                       7.6.6, 7.6.7, 7.6.8, 7.6.9
  core elements   7.1
  definitions   7.2
  elements of   7.2
  family leadership   7.9
  first generation, case study   1.5.2
  formal plan for   7.14
  life-cycle theory, and   7.3
  multi-generational business, in   7.3
  non-family leadership   7.8.1, 7.8.2,
                       7.8.3
  overview   7.1
  ownership transfer, and   7.5.5
  process   7.10
    advisor support   7.13.7
    capability of successor
      characteristics 7.13.5
      evaluation of   7.13.3
      competition   7.13.8
      fairness of   7.13.9

Index

Management succession —*continued*
  process—*continued*
    fixed retirement date   7.13.2
    gender dynamics   7.12.7
    genuine occupational choice   7.11.4
    induction   7.12.1
    life-cycles in   7.13.1
    mentoring   7.12.4
    promotion   7.12.3
    recruitment process   7.11.7
    relationship dynamics   7.12.6
    role of replacement   7.11.6
    socialisation   7.11.1
    supervision   7.12.5
    training   7.11.3
    trial period   7.12.2
    work experience   7.11.2
      external   7.11.5
    working group, for   7.13.6
  reluctance for   7.5.1, 7.5.2
  senior generation's continuing
    role   7.5.3, 7.5.4
  transition period   7.15
  unfair prejudice   21.3.4, 21.3.5, 21.3.6, 21.3.7, 21.3.8, 21.3.9

Marriage *see also* Divorce
  ante and post nuptial agreements *see* Nuptial agreements
  'copreneur' model   18.2, 18.3
  governance issues   18.4, 18.4.1, 18.4.2, 18.4.3, 18.4.4, 18.4.5, 18.5, 18.6
    boundaries   18.4.1
    conflict management   18.4.2, 18.5
    documents covering marriage
      breakdown   18.19, 18.19.1, 18.19.2
    gender issues   18.4.5
    leadership   18.4.4
    responsibilities, establishment   18.4.3
  overview   18.1
  White v White   18.3

Matrimonial claims
  trusts, and   14.9.1, 14.9.2, 14.9.3, 14.9.4, 14.9.5

Mediation *see also* Alternative dispute resolution   5.16.9, 25.9.8

Mismanagement   20.2.4, 20.9, 21.6.12
  derivative claims   20.9.2
  unfair prejudice   20.9.1
  winding up, and   22.15.2

Multi-client family office   4.9.3
Multi-family office   4.9.3

National insurance
  benefits in kind   4.11.4
  deductions   4.3.3
  rates   4.3.1

National Living Wage
  accommodation allowance   5.14.2
  enforcement   5.14.4
  exemption   5.14.1
  rate   5.14
  records   5.14.5

National Living Wage—*continued*
  time spent 'on call'   5.14.3

National Minimum Wage *see* National Living Wage

Nepotism   6.9

Non-family employees *see also* Family employees
  difference in attitudes   6.4
  discrimination   6.9, 6.9.1, 6.9.2, 6.9.3
  governance issues   6.8
  motivation   6.5
  overview   6.1
  professionalisation   6.3
  recruitment   6.10, 6.11
    advantages   6.2.3
    limiting factors   6.2.2
  recruitment of   6.2.1
  share ownership   6.6.1, 6.6.2, 6.6.3, 6.6.4, 6.6.5, 6.6.6, 6.6.7, 6.6.8

Non-family leadership
  appointment   7.8.2
  interim leaders   7.8.3
  overview   7.8.1

Nuptial agreements
  cooling off period   18.18.4
  disclosure   18.18.7
  duress   18.18.6
  effect on family dynamics   18.18.10
  fairness   18.18.9
  formalities   18.18.3
  governance, and   17.23.2
  importance of   18.18
  independent advisor   18.18.5
  legal status   18.18.1
  needs of parties   18.18.2
  terms, review of   18.18.8
  validity   18.18.8

O'Neill v Phillips
  unfair prejudice case   21.2.1, 21.2.2, 21.2.3, 21.2.4, 21.2.5, 21.2.6, 24.8.2

Owner management
  succession, and   7.3

Owner-managed business   3.4.1

Ownership
  balance of   11.20.1, 11.20.2
  control, and   11.4
    restricted matters   11.8
  employees, and   11.6
  importance of   11.1
  non-owning family members   2.7
  'outsider'   2.7
  re-organisation of business   11.19, 11.19.1, 11.19.2
  structures   11.5

Ownership succession *see also* Management succession; Sale of family business
  barriers to   15.18
  closure   15.3
  fairness and equality   15.2, 15.8, 15.19

Ownership succession —*continued*	
family buy-out	15.15.1, 15.15.2, 15.15.3, 15.16
payment structure	15.15.3
price	15.15.2
floatation	15.3
gift, as	15.10, 15.11, 15.12
importance	15.21
'insiders', preference for	15.8
management buy-out	15.16
nine types of	15.4, 15.5
options	15.3
overview	15.1
ownership approach	15.8
assets outside business	15.9.3
defining family	15.9.8
emotional issue	15.9.6
factors influencing	15.9
family dynamics	15.9.10
financial position of outsiders	15.9.4
financial resources	15.9.1
financial security	15.9.5
flexibility	15.9.9
governance	15.9.11
insider employment packages	15.9.2
purpose of ownership	15.9.13
tax issues	15.9.12
tradition	15.9.7
ownership structures	
'freezer' and 'growth' shares	15.13.5
op-co / prop-co	15.13.2
overview	15.13.1
voting and non-voting shares	15.13.3
voting trusts	15.13.4
philosophy, establishment	15.8
planning	15.6, 15.20
reinvestment	15.20
residual interest, retention	15.14
shared vision of family	15.7
tax planning	16.11, 16.11.1, 16.11.2, 16.11.3, 16.11.4, 16.11.5
third party sale	15.3, 15.17
unfair prejudice	21.3.1, 21.3.2, 21.3.3
Parental death	2.11.3
Park House Properties	
directors, duty of care	8.6.5
founder led business	1.5.1
Partnership agreements	
governance, and	17.23.5
professional advice	26.11.6
Partnerships	
accounting requirements	4.8.1
capital profits	13.4.5
characteristics	4.2.2
entrepreneur's relief	16.7.7
evidence of terms	13.4.2
exit arrangements	13.4.3
Ham v Ham	13.2, 13.3, 13.5.1, 13.5.2, 13.5.3, 13.5.4, 13.5.5, 13.5.6, 13.5.7, 13.5.8, 13.5.9, 13.5.10

Partnerships—*continued*	
In re White	13.4.6, 13.4.7, 13.4.8, 13.4.9
informal creation	13.4.1
inheritance tax, and	16.2.10
key legal features	13.4, 13.4.1, 13.4.2, 13.4.3, 13.4.4, 13.4.5, 13.4.6, 13.4.7, 13.4.8, 13.4.9
overview	13.1
property owned by	13.4.4
tax relief	16.10.12
tax, payment of	4.3.1
timing	4.3.2
Passing off	9.3, 9.3.2
'own name' defence	9.4.1
Performance *see* **Capability**	
Preferences	
insolvency	8.10.6, 8.10.7
Professionalisation	2.12.1, 2.12.2, 2.12.3, 2.12.4, 2.12.5, 2.12.6, 2.12.7
barriers	2.12.5
best practices	2.12.4
later stage family businesses	2.12.2
owner-managed family businesses	2.12.2
'stakeholder focused family firm'	2.12.6
'stereotypical dichotomies'	2.12.3
Property *see also* **Commercial lease; Land; Residential lease**	
beneficial interest, protection of	10.13.7
capital asset, as	10.1
double-tax charge	16.10.4
enterprise investment scheme deferral relief	16.10.7
interests, types of	10.6
licences	10.7
loans to buy	
tax relief	16.10.8
management of	10.11
occupation	10.12
overview	10.1
ownership	
case study	10.14
corporate	10.13.1
hybrid	10.3
individual, by	10.13.2
inside business	10.2
joint agreements	10.13.5
joint tenants	10.13.4
legal and equitable interests	10.13.3
outside business	10.2
structure	10.2
tenants in common	10.13.4
parallel interests	10.4
planning consent issues	10.5
plant and machinery	
capital allowances	16.10.9
professional advice	26.11.9
registration of title	10.5
removal of	16.10.10
rental income, from	10.1, 10.2

Index

Property —*continued*
rollover relief	16.10.6
sale of business, and	12.11
tax planning	16.10.1, 16.10.2, 16.10.3, 16.10.4, 16.10.5, 16.10.6, 16.10.7, 16.10.8, 16.10.9, 16.10.10, 16.10.11, 16.10.12, 16.10.13, 16.10.14
investment properties	16.10.13, 16.10.14
transfer of	16.10.11
trust of land	10.13.6

Proprietary estoppel
assurance	
acquiescence	19.7.4
detriment	19.9
implied or express	19.7.1
reliance on	19.8
subject matter of	19.7.3
subjective test	19.7.2
case management	19.16.3
change in circumstances	19.13
claims, practicalities	19.16
constructive trust	19.14
equity	19.10
evidence	19.16.1
farming business	19.3, 19.4.3, 19.4.6, 19.5
key elements of	19.6
procedure	19.16.2
remedy for	19.11.1, 19.11.2, 19.11.3
shareholders	20.6.1
unreliablility of	19.13, 19.15, 19.15.1, 19.15.2

Proprietor
characteristics	2.2.3

Protectors
identity	14.12.4
overview	14.12.1
powers	14.12.2, 14.12.3
sales, veto of	14.20.4

Quasi-partnerships 20.2.4, 20.4, 20.4.1, 20.4.2, 20.4.3, 20.4.4, 20.4.5, 20.4.6, 20.4.7, 20.4.8, 20.4.9, 22.7.2, 22.8

Recruitment
non-family employees	6.2.1, 6.2.2, 6.2.3, 6.9.1, 6.10, 6.11

Remedies see Derivative claims; Just and equitable winding up; Proprietary estoppel; Unfair prejudice

Remuneration see also National Living Wage
committees	5.5.5
directors	8.1.3, 8.8.1, 8.8.2, 8.8.3, 8.8.4, 8.8.5, 8.8.6, 8.8.7
declaration of	8.8.2
derivative claims	8.8.6
disguised returns on capital	8.8.4

Remuneration —*continued*
directors—*continued*
reasonableness	8.8.2
unfair prejudice	8.8.7
excessive, unfair prejudice	21.6.3
informality	5.5.1, 5.5.2
market rate	5.5.4
protection by business systems	5.5.3
trusts, and	14.18

Rent Act tenancies
death of tenant	10.10.1
landlord, possession rights	10.10.1
rent controls	10.10.1

Residential lease
assured shorthold tenancies	10.10.3
assured tenancies	10.10.2
eviction, protection from	10.10.5
Rent Act tenancies	10.10.1
repairs and services	10.10.5
rights of occupation	10.10
service occupancies	10.10.4

Resulting trusts 14.22.4

Retirement
compulsory age of	5.6

Sale of family business 12.1
buyer, choice of	12.7
capacity	
elderly shareholders	12.12
minors	12.12
categories of sale	12.2
deferred purchase price	12.6.3
drag rights	12.9.1, 17.21
due diligence	12.14.1, 12.14.2
earn-outs	12.6.2
family buy-out	12.8, 15.15.1, 15.15.2, 15.15.3, 15.16
payment structure	15.15.3
price	15.15.2
family employees, and	12.10, 12.10.1, 12.10.2, 12.10.3
family owned property	12.11
governance, and	17.20
management buy-out	12.8, 15.16
maximising value on sale	12.4
minority shareholders	12.9, 12.9.1, 12.9.2, 12.9.3
consultation	12.9.3
unfair prejudice	12.9.3
phases	12.3
post sale restrictions	12.16
price and transaction structure	12.6
procedure	12.13, 12.13.1, 12.13.2, 12.13.3, 12.13.4
buy-backs	12.13.1
defects, effect	12.13.4
share transfer	12.13.2
process	12.3
reasons against	12.2
reasons for	12.2
security of assets	12.6.3
shareholder approval, without	11.10

Sale of family business—*continued*	
'squeeze out', statutory provisions	12.9.2
trust, effect of	14.20, 14.20.1, 14.20.2, 14.20.3, 14.20.4, 14.20.5
trustees, position on sale	12.17
unique selling points	12.4
valuation	12.5
discounted cashflow	12.5.4
EBITDA	12.5.3
industry standard approach	12.5.5
net assets	12.5.1
price/earnings	12.5.2
warranties	12.15.1, 12.15.2, 12.15.3, 12.15.4
de-minimis claims	12.15.2
joint and several liability	12.15.2
trustees	14.21.8
working capital adjustments	12.6.1
Saul D Harrison plc	
cousin consortium	1.5.4, 3.8.2
sibling partnership	3.8.1
three-circle model	3.8.2
Save as you earn share option plan	4.12.9
Scapegoating	3.6.4
Settlement agreements	5.20
Settlor	14.1.2
beneficiary, as	14.8.2
reserved powers	14.13
trustee, as	14.10.3
Sexual harassment	5.9.3
Sham trusts	14.16
Share incentive plan	4.12.11
Share schemes	4.12.1, 4.12.2, 4.12.3, 4.12.4, 4.12.5, 4.12.6, 4.12.7, 4.12.8, 4.12.9, 4.12.10, 4.12.11, 4.12.12, 4.12.13
company articles, and	4.12.5
company share option plan	4.12.8
corporation tax, and	4.12.13
direct acquisition	4.12.4
employee shareholder shares	4.12.12
enterprise management incentive	4.12.7
equl treatment of employees	6.7
non-family members	6.6.1, 6.6.2, 6.6.3, 6.6.4, 6.6.5, 6.6.6, 6.6.7, 6.6.8
SAYE plan	4.12.9
share incentive plan	4.12.11
shareholder agreements, and	4.12.5
tax benefits	4.12.1
unapproved share options	4.12.10
valuation of shares	4.12.3
Share transfers	11.11
buy-outs	11.14.1
compulsory transfer provisions	11.15, 11.15.1, 11.15.2, 11.15.3
discretion to refuse	11.11.1
divorce	11.15.3
golden shares	11.11.3
non-family employee	11.15.2
non-family transferees	11.15.1

Share transfers—*continued*	
permitted transfers	11.11.4
pre-emption provisions	11.11.5, 11.16, 11.16.2, 11.16.3, 11.16.4, 11.16.5, 11.16.7, 12.13.2
key issues	11.16.1
restrictions	11.11.2
stamp duty	12.13.3
Shareholders	
accounts, right to receive	11.2.5
agreement	
drag rights	12.9.1
agreements	11.8
trustees' powers, effect on	14.21.6
buy-outs	11.14.1
capacity as seller	12.12
capital	11.2.2
control	
removal of board	11.9
control of business	11.3
democracy right	11.2.7
dividends, right of	11.2.1
exit arrangements for	11.17.1, 11.17.2, 11.17.3, 11.17.4, 11.17.5
legislative protection	11.2.8
notices to	11.2.6
reduction in	11.13, 11.14
rights	11.2
sale, proceeds of	11.2.3
voting rights	11.2.4
legal control by	11.3
widespread shareholding	11.12.1
Shareholders' agreements	17.4
amendments	17.18.4
enforceability	17.18.3
family charter, and	17.18.4
inter-relationship with Articles of Association	17.18.4
number of shareholders	17.18.4
professional advice	26.11.5
use of	17.18.3
Shareholders, remedies for *see also* Derivative claims; Just and equitable winding up; Unfair	
prejudice	20.1, 20.2.1, 20.2.2, 20.2.3, 20.2.4, 24.1, 24.2.2
articles	20.7.1
bad faith	20.2.4, 20.8, 20.8.1, 20.8.2, 20.8.3, 20.8.4
buy-out	24.8.1, 24.8.2, 24.8.3, 24.8.4, 24.8.5, 24.8.6, 24.8.7, 24.8.8
costs	24.9.1, 24.9.2, 24.9.3
courts, exclusion of jurisdiction	20.7.3
equitable principles	20.5
fairness approach	20.5
family charters	20.7.2
minority share purchase orders	24.3.1, 24.3.2, 24.3.3, 24.3.4
discounts	24.5.1, 24.5.2, 24.5.3, 24.5.4
valuation	24.4, 24.6, 24.6.1, 24.6.2, 24.6.3, 24.6.4, 24.6.5, 24.6.6

Shareholders, remedies for —*continued*	
mismanagement	20.2.4, 20.9, 20.9.1, 20.9.2
proprietary estoppel	20.6.1
quasi-partnerships	20.2.4, 20.4, 20.4.1, 20.4.2, 20.4.3, 20.4.4, 20.4.5, 20.4.6, 20.4.7, 20.4.8, 20.4.9
reasonable offers, acceptance of	20.3
relevant family business factors	20.6, 20.6.1, 20.6.2, 20.6.3, 20.6.4, 20.6.5, 20.6.6, 20.6.7, 20.6.8, 20.6.9, 20.6.10, 20.6.11, 20.6.12, 20.6.13, 20.6.14
Shares	
alphabet shares	4.6
buy-backs	12.13.1
company buy-backs	11.18.1, 11.18.2, 11.18.3, 11.18.4, 11.18.5, 11.18.6
dividends, waiver of	4.6
'freezer' and 'growth' shares	15.13.5
gift of	4.6
jointly-held	4.6
tax relief	16.7.3
ownership, details in family charter	17.15.4, 17.15.5
preference shares	
tax relief	16.2.5
rights issues	11.20.2
schemes for *see* Share scheme	
unquoted	
tax relief	16.2.4
voting and non-voting, effect of	15.13.3
Sibling partnerships	3.4.1
Cadman Developments Ltd	1.5.3
co-leadership	7.7.1
genogram	3.8.1
minority share purchase orders	24.3.3
ownership transition, from	15.4, 15.5
Saul D Harrison	3.8.1
succession, and	7.3
unfair prejudice, and	21.4.1, 21.4.2, 21.4.3, 21.4.4, 21.4.5, 21.4.6, 21.4.7, 21.4.8
Sibling rivalry	
age spacing	2.11.3
birth order	2.11.3
effect	2.11.1
examples	2.11.2
family size	2.11.3
gender	2.11.3
later stage family businesses	2.11.3
parental death	2.11.3
predictive factors	2.11.3
prodigal children	2.11.3
reasons	2.11.1
Sickness *see* Ill health	
Single family office	4.9.3
Sole trader	4.2.1
accounting requirements	4.8.1
tax, payment of	4.3.1
timing	4.3.2

Spouse *see also* Divorce; Marriage	
beneficiary, as	14.8.5
Stakeholder interests	
protection of	8.1.3, 8.9.1, 8.9.2, 8.9.3, 8.9.4, 8.9.5
long term interests	8.9.3
Stamp duty	
share transfer	12.13.3
Stock Exchange	
floatation of family company	15.3
Succession *see* Management succession; Ownership succession	
Systems theory *see also* Individual life-cycle theory; Life-cycle theory	3.3.1, 3.3.2, 3.3.3, 3.3.4, 3.3.5, 3.3.6, 3.3.7, 3.3.8, 3.3.9
balance	3.3.6
business system	3.3.1
cohesion	3.3.5
conflict in	3.3.4
family system	3.3.1
homeostasis	3.3.9
owernship system	3.3.1
three-circle model	3.3.2, 3.3.3, 3.3.7, 3.3.8
Taboos	
effect	2.4
examples	2.4
Tagiuri & Davis	
three-circle model	3.3.2, 3.3.3, 3.3.7, 3.3.8
Tax planning	
buy-backs	16.9, 16.9.2, 16.9.3, 16.9.4, 16.9.5, 16.9.6
capital gains tax	16.7.4
deductions	4.3.3
dividend	4.6
extraction of profits	4.6
family business structure	4.1, 4.3.1
overview	16.1
ownership succession, and	16.11, 16.11.1, 16.11.2, 16.11.3, 16.11.4, 16.11.5
payment, timing of	4.3.2
property, and	16.10.2, 16.10.3, 16.10.4, 16.10.5, 16.10.6, 16.10.7, 16.10.8, 16.10.9, 16.10.10, 16.10.11, 16.10.12, 16.10.13, 16.10.14
relevance of ownership	16.10.1
remuneration of family employees	4.11, 4.11.1, 4.11.2, 4.11.3, 4.11.4
accommodation	4.11.2
assets	4.11.3
car benefit	4.11.1
share schemes	4.12.1, 4.12.2, 4.12.3, 4.12.4, 4.12.5, 4.12.6, 4.12.7, 4.12.8, 4.12.9, 4.12.10, 4.12.11, 4.12.12, 4.12.13
trusts, and	14.2
valuation of business for	16.8

Index

Technicians
  characteristics   2.2.3
Tenant
  death of   10.10.1
  rights under Rent Act   10.10.1
Third party sale *see* Sale of family business
Three-circle model   3.3.2, 3.3.3, 3.3.7, 3.3.8, 13.3
  business advisors   25.2
  business trusts   14.4
  Cadman Developments Ltd   3.3.3
  joint and several liability   12.15.2
  Saul D Harrison   3.8.2
  trusts   14.14.3
Trade mark registration   9.3, 9.3.1
  infringement
    'own name' defence   9.4.2
Transaction at an undervalue   8.10.5
Trust deed   14.1.2
Trustees   14.1.2
  accountant   14.10.4
  capital, payment   14.3.9
  choice of   14.10.1
  compromises   14.21.7
  dividends, distribution   14.3.8
  duties, modification of   14.21, 14.21.1, 14.21.2, 14.21.3, 14.21.4, 14.21.5, 14.21.6, 14.21.7, 14.21.8
  duty of care   14.11
  family member   14.10.6
  friends/confidants   14.10.5
  income, acculmation   14.3.8
  information, provision of   14.19, 14.19.1, 14.19.3
  insurance   14.21.5
  investment, by   14.21.2
  lawyer   14.10.4
  liability, exoneration of   14.21.4
  meetings   14.3.5
  position on sale   12.17
  powers of   14.3.4
  removal of   14.14, 14.14.1, 14.14.2, 14.14.3, 14.14.4, 14.14.5
    case study   14.14.3
    disengaged trustees   14.14.1
  sale of business, and
    warranties   14.21.8
  self-dealing rule   14.20.5
  settlor, as   14.10.3
  supervision duty   14.21.3
  trust companies   14.10.2
  voting powers   14.21.1, 15.13.4
Trusts *see also* Beneficiaries; Protectors; Settlor; Trustees
  alternatives of   14.23, 14.23.1, 14.23.2
  beneficiaries   14.8, 14.8.1, 14.8.2, 14.8.3, 14.8.4, 14.8.5, 14.8.6
  bivalence, and   14.6
  deed   14.21, 14.21.1, 14.21.2, 14.21.3, 14.21.4, 14.21.5, 14.21.6, 14.21.7, 14.21.8, 17.23.1
  exoneration clauses   14.21.4

Trusts —*continued*
  discretionary   14.3.1, 14.3.2, 14.3.3, 14.3.4, 14.3.5, 14.3.6, 14.3.7, 14.3.8, 14.3.9, 14.3.10
  employee benefit trusts   14.22.9
  employee share trusts   14.22.9
  employment policies   14.18
  governance, and   14.17
  hybrid ownership   14.7
  inherent jurisdiction   14.2.1
  insurance proceed trusts   14.22.8
  matrimonial claims   14.9.1, 14.9.2, 14.9.3, 14.9.4, 14.9.5
  persons with disabilities   14.22.6
  relevance of family business   14.1.1
  remuneration   14.18
  reserved powers   14.13
  sale of business, and   14.20, 14.20.1, 14.20.2, 14.20.3, 14.20.4, 14.20.5
    golden shares   14.20.3
    protections against sale   14.20.2
    protector's veto   14.20.4
  supervision of   14.12.1, 14.12.2, 14.12.3, 14.12.4
  tax, and   14.2
  terminology   14.1.2
  three-circle model   14.4
  trustees, choice of   14.10.1, 14.10.2, 14.10.3, 14.10.4, 14.10.5, 14.10.6
  use of   14.5.1, 14.5.2

Unfair dismissal   5.8.1
  constructive dismissal   5.8.2
  procedure   5.8.5
  reason for dismissal   5.8.3
  reasonableness of dismissal   5.8.4, 5.8.5
  remedies   5.8.6
  'some other substantial reason'   5.19.3
Unfair prejudice   21.1.1, 22.16.1
  appropriation   21.6.9
  articles, changes to   21.6.14
  assets transfers   21.6.8
  bad faith   20.8.3
  beneficial interest in company   21.1.7
  case-law   21.1.3
  conflicts of interest   21.6.7
  costs   24.9.1, 24.9.2, 24.9.3
  cousin consortia, and   21.5, 21.5.1, 21.5.2, 21.5.3
  directors' duties, breach of   21.6.1, 21.6.2, 21.6.3, 21.6.4, 21.6.5, 21.6.6, 21.6.7, 21.6.8, 21.6.9, 21.6.10, 21.6.11, 21.6.12, 21.6.13, 21.6.14
  CA 2006 duties   21.6.10
  dishonesty   21.6.2
  diversion of business opportunities   21.6.6
  excessive remuneration   21.6.3
  fairness and equity   21.1.11
  information, sharing of   21.6.11
  intention   21.1.6
  'interests'   21.1.9, 21.1.10
  'legitimate expectations'   21.2.4

Unfair prejudice—*continued*
  mismanagement   20.9.1, 21.6.12
  non-payment of dividends   21.6.4
  O'Neill v Phillips   21.2.1, 21.2.2, 21.2.3, 21.2.4, 21.2.5, 21.2.6
  remedies   24.2.2, 24.7
    authorising derivative proceedings   24.7.3
    interim orders   24.7.5
    minority share purchase orders   24.3.1, 24.3.2, 24.3.3, 24.3.4, 24.4, 24.5.1, 24.5.2, 24.5.3, 24.5.4, 24.6, 24.6.1, 24.6.2, 24.6.3, 24.6.4, 24.6.5, 24.6.6
    regulating conduct business   24.7.1
    restraining orders   24.7.2
    restrictions on alteration of articles   24.7.4
  remedy, buy-out of minority   21.7
  remuneration, and   8.8.7
  sale of business, and   12.9.3
  self-dealing   21.6.7
  sibling partnerships, and   21.4.1, 21.4.2, 21.4.3, 21.4.4, 21.4.5, 21.4.6, 21.4.7, 21.4.8
  statutory basis   20.2.1, 21.1.2, 24.2
    discretion   24.2.1
  succession, and   21.3.1, 21.3.2, 21.3.3, 21.3.4, 21.3.5, 21.3.6, 21.3.7, 21.3.8, 21.3.9

Unfair prejudice—*continued*
  trust-owned shares   21.1.8
  'unfair'   21.1.5
  'unfairness'   21.1.4
  'wrongful rights issues'   21.6.13

Van
  benefit in kind   4.11.1
Victimisation   5.9.4
Voting
  general meetings, at   11.2.4
  thresholds   11.3
  trusts holding   14.22.7
  weighted voting rights   11.9

Wealth planning   4.9.1, 4.9.2, 4.9.3
Will
  bequest of business property   14.22.1
Without prejudice proceedings   5.20
Worker
  definition   5.11.2
Working Time Regulations   5.15
Wrongful trading   8.10.3
  reliefs   8.10.8

Young person
  definition   5.13
  employment of   5.13